A Reference Guide: When Do I Do What?

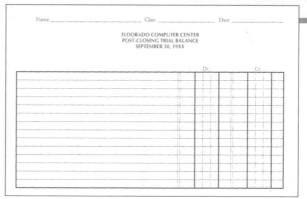

Name _____ Class _____ Date _____

ELDORADO COMPUTER CENTER
POST-CLOSING TRIAL BALANCE
SEPTEMBER 30, 19XX

9. Prepare a post-closing trial balance.

S0-DYE-425

4. Prepare a trial balance.

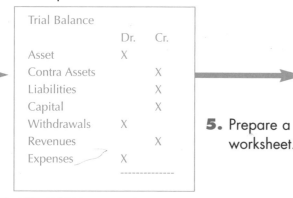

Trial Balance

	Dr.	Cr.
Asset	X	
Contra Assets		X
Liabilities		X
Capital		X
Withdrawals	X	
Revenues		X
Expenses	X	

5. Prepare a worksheet.

WORKSHEET

CLARK'S WORD PROCESSING SERVICES
WORKSHEET
FOR MONTH ENDING MAY 31, 19XX

Account Titles	Trial Balance Dr.	Trial Balance Cr.	Adjustments Dr.	Adjustments Cr.	Adjusted Trial Balance Dr.	Adjusted Trial Balance Cr.	Income Dr.
Cash	6 1 5 5 00						
Accounts Receivable	5 0 0 0 00						
Office Supplies	6 0 0 00						
Prepaid Rent	1 2 0 0 00						
Word Processing Equipment	6 0 0 0 00						
Accounts Payable		3 3 5 0 00					
Brenda Clark, Capital		10 0 0 0 00					
Brenda Clark, Withdrawals	6 2 5 00						
Word Processing Fees		8 0 0 0 00					
Office Salaries Expense	1 3 0 0 00						
Advertising Expense	2 5 0 00						
Telephone Expense	2 2 0 00						
	21 3 5 0 00	21 3 5 0 00					

8. Journalize and post closing entries from worksheet.

6. Prepare the financial statements from worksheet.

Income Statement	Statement of Owners equity	Balance Sheet
Revenues - expenses = net income	Begining Capital + net income - withdrawals = Ending Capital	Assets Liabilities Owner's equity Ending Capital

(7) Adjustments from the worksheet are journalized in the SAME JOURNAL as Step 2 and posted to SAME ledger as Step 3.

(8) All closing entries are recorded in SAME JOURNAL (Step 2) and posted to SAME LEDGER (Step 3).

(9) After closing entries have been journalized and posted, only PERMANENT accounts will have balances left in the ledger to carry over to the next.

ACCOUNT TITLE	NORMAL BALANCE	FINANCIAL REPORT FOUND ON	CATEGORY	PERMANENT OR TEMPORARY
Accounts Payable	Credit	Balance Sheet	Current Liability	Permanent
Accounts Receivable	Debit	Balance Sheet	Current Asset	Permanent
Accumulated Depreciation	Credit	Balance Sheet	Contra Plant & Equipment	Permanent
Advertising Expense	Debit	Income Statement	Operating Expense	Temporary
Allowance for Doubtful Accounts	Credit	Balance Sheet	Contra Current Asset	Permanent
Bad Debts Recovered	Credit	Income Statement	Other Income	Temporary
Bad Debts Expense	Debit	Income Statement	Operating Expense	Temporary
Bond Interest Expense	Debit	Income Statement	Operating Expense	Temporary
Bond Interest Payable	Credit	Balance Sheet	Current Liability	Permanent
Bonds Payable	Credit	Balance Sheet	Long-Term Liability	Permanent
Building	Debit	Balance Sheet	Plant & Equipment	Permanent
Capital	Credit	Statement of Owner's Equity; Balance Sheet	Owner's Equity	Permanent
Cash	Debit	Balance Sheet	Current Asset	Permanent
Cash Short and Over (Assume Short)	Debit	Income Statement	Miscellaneous Expense	Temporary
(Assume Over)	Credit	Income Statement	Other Income	Temporary
Change Fund	Debit	Balance Sheet	Current Asset	Permanent
Commissions Earned	Credit	Income Statement	Revenue	Temporary
Common Stock	Credit	Balance Sheet	Stockholders' Equity	Permanent
Common Stock Subscribed	Credit	Balance Sheet	Stockholders' Equity	Permanent
Common Stock Dividend Distributable	Credit	Balance Sheet	Stockholders' Equity	Permanent
Copyright	Debit	Balance Sheet	Intangible Asset	Permanent
Credit Card Expense	Debit	Income Statement	Other Expense	Temporary
Depletion Expense	Debit	Income Statement	Operating Expense	Temporary
Depreciation Expense	Debit	Income Statement	Operating Expense	Temporary
Discount on Bonds Payable	Debit	Balance Sheet	Contra Long-Term Liability	Permanent
Discount on Notes Payable	Debit	Balance Sheet	Contra Current Liability	Permanent
Dividends Payable	Credit	Balance Sheet	Current Liability	Permanent
Equipment	Debit	Balance Sheet	Plant & Equipment	Permanent
Federal Income Tax Payable	Credit	Balance Sheet	Current Liability	Permanent
FICA Tax Payable	Credit	Balance Sheet	Current Liability	Permanent
Freight-In	Debit	Income Statement	Cost of Goods Sold	Temporary
FUTA Tax Payable	Credit	Balance Sheet	Current Liability	Permanent
Gain on Sale of Asset	Credit	Income Statement	Other Income	Temporary
Goodwill	Debit	Balance Sheet	Intangible Asset	Permanent
Income Summary	—	—	Owner's Equity	Temporary
Insurance Expense	Debit	Income Statement	Operating Expense	Temporary
Interest Earned	Credit	Income Statement	Other Income	Temporary
Interest Expense	Debit	Income Statement	Other Expense	Temporary
Interest Payable	Credit	Balance Sheet	Current Liability	Permanent
Land	Debit	Balance Sheet	Plant & Equipment	Permanent
Land Improvement	Debit	Balance Sheet	Plant & Equipment	Permanent
Loss from Fire	Debit	Income Statement	Other Expense	Temporary
Loss on Sale of (Asset)	Debit	Income Statement	Other Expense	Temporary
Loss or Gain from Realization (Assume Loss)	Debit	Income Statement	Other Expense	Temporary
(Assume Gain)	Credit	Income Statement	Other Income	Temporary
Machinery	Debit	Balance Sheet	Plant & Equipment	Permanent

ACCOUNT TITLE	NORMAL BALANCE	FINANCIAL REPORT FOUND ON	CATEGORY	PERMANENT OR TEMPORARY
Medicare Tax Payable	Credit	Balance Sheet	Liability	Permanent
Merchandise Inventory	Debit	Balance Sheet; Income Statement	Current Asset; Cost of Goods Sold	Permanent
Mortgage Payable	Credit	Balance Sheet	Long-Term Liability	Permanent
Notes Payable	Credit	Balance Sheet	Current Liability	Permanent
Notes Receivable	Debit	Balance Sheet	Current Asset	Permanent
Organization Costs	Debit	Balance Sheet	Intangible Asset	Permanent
Patents	Debit	Balance Sheet	Intangible Asset	Permanent
Paid-In Capital from Treasury Stock	Credit	Balance Sheet	Stockholders' Equity	Permanent
Paid-In Capital in Excess of (. . .)	Credit	Balance Sheet	Stockholder's Equity	Permanent
Payroll Tax Expense	Debit	Income Statement	Operating Expense	Temporary
Petty Cash	Debit	Balance Sheet	Current Asset	Permanent
Premium on Bonds Payable	Credit	Balance Sheet	Long-Term Liability	Permanent
Prepaid Insurance	Debit	Balance Sheet	Current Asset	Permanent
Prepaid Rent	Debit	Balance Sheet	Current Asset	Permanent
Preferred Stock	Credit	Balance Sheet	Stockholders' Equity	Permanent
Purchases	Debit	Income Statement	Cost of Goods Sold	Temporary
Purchases Discount	Credit	Income Statement	Contra Cost of Goods Sold	Temporary
Purchases Returns and Allowances	Credit	Income Statement	Contra Cost of Goods Sold	Temporary
Retained Earnings	Credit	Statement of Retained Earnings; Balance Sheet	Stockholders' Equity	Permanent
Salaries Expense	Debit	Income Statement	Operating Expense	Temporary
Salaries Payable	Credit	Balance Sheet	Current Liability	Permanent
Sales	Credit	Income Statement	Revenue	Temporary
Sales Discount	Debit	Income Statement	Contra Revenue	Temporary
Sales Returns and Allowances	Debit	Income Statement	Contra Revenue	Temporary
Sales Tax Payable	Credit	Balance Sheet	Current Liability	Permanent
Social Security Tax Payable	Credit	Balance Sheet	Liability	Permanent
Stock Dividend Distributable	Credit	Balance Sheet	Stockholders' Equity	Permanent
Stock Subscriptions Receivable	Debit	Balance Sheet	Current Asset	Permanent
Supplies	Debit	Balance Sheet	Current Asset	Permanent
Treasury Stock	Debit	Balance Sheet	Contra Stockholder's Equity	Permanent
Unearned Revenue	Credit	Balance Sheet	Current Liability	Permanent
Vouchers Payable	Credit	Balance Sheet	Current Liability	Permanent
Withdrawals	Debit	Statement of Owner's Equity; Balance Sheet	Owners' Equity	Temporary

KEY TO USE OF COLOR IN TEXT

	Yellow	journals, special journals, combination journals
	Green	general ledgers, trial balance, worksheets, payroll registers
	Blue	subsidiary ledgers, forms, documents
	Orange	financial reports
	Buff	tables
	Magenta	key numbers, emphasis, steps

The debit or credit behavior of accounts for assets, liabilities, owners' equity, revenues, and expenses is summarized in the following illustration:

Account Name	
Debit side	*Credit* side
Normal balance for:	Normal balance for:
+ Assets	+ Liabilities
+ Expenses	+ Owners' equity
	+ Revenues
Debit entries increase:	Credit entries increase:
+ Assets	+ Liabilities
+ Expenses	+ Owners' equity
	+ Revenues
Debit entries decrease:	Credit entries decrease:
− Liabilities	− Assets
− Owners' equity	− Expenses
− Revenues	

Referring to the transactions that were illustrated in Exhibit 4-1, a bookkeeper would say that in transaction (1). which was the investment of $30 in the firm by the owners, Cash was debited—it increased—and Paid-In Capital was credited, each for

owners' equity accounts, the opposite will be true. To illustrate:

Assets		=	Liabilities		+	Owners' Equity	
Debit Increases	*Credit* Decreases		*Debit* Decreases	*Credit* Increases		*Debit* Decreases	*Credit* Increases
+	−		−	+		−	+
Normal balance				Normal balance			Normal balance

It is no coincidence that the debit and credit system of normal balances coincides with the balance sheet presentation illustrated earlier. In fact, most of the balance sheets illustrated so far have been presented in what is known as the *account format*. An alternative approach is to use the *report format*, in which assets are shown above liabilities and owners' equity.

Entries to revenue and expense accounts follow a pattern that is consistent with entries to other owners' equity accounts. Revenues are increases in owners' equity, so revenue accounts normally will have a credit balance and will increase with credit entries. Expenses are decreases in owners' equity, so expense accounts normally will have a debit balance and will increase with debit entries. Gains and losses are recorded like revenues and expenses, respectively.

College Accounting

A Practical Approach

Chapters 1–25
Ninth Edition

College Accounting

A Practical Approach

Chapters 1–25
Ninth Edition

Jeffrey Slater

North Shore Community College
Danvers, Massachusetts

Prentice Hall
Upper Saddle River, New Jersey 07458

Library of Congress Cataloging-in-Publication Data
Slater, Jeffrey, 1947–
    College accounting: a practical approach, chapters 1–25 / Jeffrey
Slater.—9th ed.
        p. cm.
Includes index.
    ISBN 0-13-143961-8
    1. Accounting.   I. Title.

    HF5635.S6315 2003
    657'.044—dc22

                                                        2003064991

Editor-in-Chief: PJ Boardman
Managing Editor (Editorial): Alana Bradley
Assistant Editor: Sam Goffinet
Senior Media Project Manager: Nancy Welcher
Executive Marketing Manager: Beth Toland
Marketing Assistant: Patrick Dansuzo
Managing Editor (Production): Cynthia Regan
Production Editor: Kerri M. Tomasso
Manufacturing Buyer: Diane Peirano
Design Manager: Maria Lang
Interior Designer: Blair Brown
Cover Design: Blair Brown
Cover Illustration/Photo: Courtesy of Rob Casey & Getty Images, Inc.
Photo Researcher: Teri Stratford
Image Permission Coordinator: Tara Gardner
Manager, Multimedia Production: Christy Mahon
Composition/Full-Service Project Management: Progressive Publishing Alternatives
Printer/Binder: Courier–Kendallville

Microsoft® and Windows® are registered trademarks of the Microsoft Corporation in the U.S.A. and other countries. Screen shots and icons reprinted with permission from the Microsoft Corporation. This book is not sponsored or endorsed by or affiliated with the Microsoft Corporation.

Pearson Prentice Hall™ is a trademark of Pearson Education, Inc.
Pearson® is a registered trademark of Pearson plc
Prentice Hall® is a registered trademark of Pearson Education, Inc.

Pearson Education LTD.   Pearson Education Australia PTY, Limited
Pearson Education Singapore, Pte. Ltd   Pearson Education North Asia Ltd
Pearson Education, Canada, Ltd   Pearson Educación de Mexico, S.A. de C.V.
Pearson Education–Japan   Pearson Education Malaysia, Pte. Ltd

10 9 8 7 6 5 4 3 2 1
ISBN 0-13-143961-8

Brief Contents

Contents

5 The Accounting Cycle Completed   162

8 The Employer's Tax Responsibilities   288

Special Journals: Sales and Cash Receipts   338

Special Journals: Purchases and Cash Payments   386

11 Preparing a Worksheet for a Merchandise Company 434

12 Completion of the Accounting Cycle for a Merchandise Company 466

15 Accounting for Merchandise Inventory

568

16 Accounting for Property, Plant, Equipment, and Intangible Assets   608

17 Partnerships   640

18 Corporations: Organizations and Capital Stock

21 Statement of Cash Flows   758

22 Analyzing Financial Statements   780

Subway Case Boxes

Peachtree® Computer Workshops

A Note to Faculty from Jeff Slater . . .

We share common goals. We want to motivate our students to be interested in accounting and to see accounting as the most dynamic tool of business. We want to introduce students to the accounting cycle and to learn double entry accounting. We want our students to see the critical role accounting plays in making business decisions. And, along the way, we want students to develop skills that will enable them to succeed in the workforce.

These are my goals for each edition of **College Accounting.** Nothing has changed and yet everything has changed. Now we have the opportunity to utilize the excitement of a new text design, provide a wealth of pedagogical tools, and exploit the learning mediums and available technologies to enhance your teaching environment and your students' learning experience.

Thank you for your interest in the Ninth Edition of **College Accounting** and, as you peruse the remainder of this preface, I encourage you to *Taste the Slater Difference!*

UNIQUE SLATER LEARNING SYSTEM

Three Text Versions!

Three versions of **College Accounting 9e** are available to enable faculty to customize the text to fit their individual course need.

Learning Units with Immediate Application

A Slater hallmark! Unlike other texts that require students to read 30+ pages before they have a chance to test their understanding, **College Accounting 9e** organizes each chapter into small, bite-sized units. Students are introduced to new concepts in the **Learning Unit** and then immediately have the opportunity to test their understanding in the **Learning Unit Reviews.**

Study Guide and Working Papers

The Study Guide and Working Papers are available for each of the three text versions. All of the forms needed to solve the chapter problems are included in the working papers and are referenced by page to the text.

Unique Presentation of Perpetual and Periodic Inventory

Slater has an appendix to Chapter 9 that provides an introduction to merchandising through general journals for a perpetual inventory system instead of special journals. **College Accounting 9e** completes the merchandise cycle by Chapter 12 and then provides the OPTION to cover perpetual inventory for a merchandise company in the Appendices.

In-Text Practice Set

The in-text Valdez Realty Practice Set (Chapter 5) enables students to complete two cycles of transactions (in your choice of manual or electronic formats). And source documents to complete the practice set are now included.

END-OF-CHAPTER ASSIGNMENT MATERIAL INCLUDES:

Key Terms/Blueprint

This feature is designed to highlight the key terms that students should know for each chapter, and the blueprint highlights important accounting processes they should know.

YOU make the call

These action-oriented exercises encourage students to put themselves in the decision-maker's seat.

Internet Exercises

These exercises provide students with the opportunity to use the Internet to solve specific accounting problems.

Continuing Problem

Throughout the book, students will read about a single company, called El Dorado Computer Company. At the end of each chapter, students will apply concepts you have learned to solve a specific accounting problem. In the next chapter, students will see the next evolution in the organization.

Comprehensive Problem

This problem helps students recall concepts from previous chapters as they pull upon all of their knowledge to solve these problems.

Unique In-Text Computer Workshops

These Workshops (beginning at the end of Chapter 3) enable students to use the latest release of Peachtree Complete Accounting Software in order to solve specific accounting problems. *Note that the full version of this software may be packaged with new copies of the text at a minimal charge.*

NEW FOR THE NINTH EDITION

New Text Versions!

The Slater text is available in three text versions: Chapters 1–8, 1–12, or 1–25. *Note that Working Papers and Study Guides are packaged free with the briefer texts.*

New! Subway Boxes

This unique feature appears at the ends of many chapters (13 boxed inserts) and shows students how this well-known company uses accounting information to make business. A **new** video (on the DVD) takes students inside Subway to review accounting concepts.

New Content Enhancements

The key content enhancements for **College Accounting 9e** include: eliminating Chapter 11 on Combined Journals from the previous edition, updating all payroll chapters, including updated bank statements reflecting current banking trends (Chapter 4), and a new presentation (Chapter 4) to show adjustments one at a time.

New Chapter-Opening Stories

The chapter-opening stories show students how accounting issues touch their lives each day and motivate students with the topics to be covered in each chapter.

Margin Notes

These "coaching tips" appear in the side margins of each chapter to provide extra insights for students.

NEW TECHNOLOGY RESOURCES FOR THE NINTH EDITION

New! Accounting in the Reel World Video Cases

These in-text video cases are designed to show students how accounting is relevant to the things they are interested in and care about: dating, shopping, sports, dining, and so forth. These are linked to the Slater custom-crafted *On Location! Videos* on the DVD.

New DVD Icons

The icon signals faculty and students that there are resources available to use with the **FREE DVD packaged only with New Student Texts!** These include:

Videos

- **New!** Subway *On Location! Video* linked to the new Subway in-text boxes
- **New!** *On Location! Videos!* linked to the new in-text video cases
- **New!** Jeff Slater Learning Unit Review Video for Chapters 1–5
- **New!** 5 Steps in Accounting Cycle Video

Software

- General Ledger Software
- Data files for the latest releases of the Getting Started Series (Peachtree, QuickBooks, Simply Accounting)
- PowerPoint® slides
- Links to the Slater Website and online courses

SUPPLEMENTS:

Technology Resources

INNOVATION! Instructor Resource CD-ROM   This unique tool enables faculty to **save time** and **quickly prepare highly effective and interactive multimedia classroom presentations.** Using a **highly accessible menu,** faculty can easily customize their lectures using an interactive library of video, PowerPoints, and additional resources by simply clicking on a chapter or key word.

Enjoy the freedom to transport the entire package from office, to home, to class-room. The Instructor CD-ROM enables you to customize any of the ancillaries, print only the chapters or materials you wish, or access any item from the package within the classroom!

***INNOVATION!* Getting Started Series**   Upon request, faculty may package your choice of one of these approximately 90-page manuals on the latest professional accounting software packages with **College Accounting 9/e** at no charge. Each manual introduces students to the concepts of Excel, Peachtree, QuickBooks, or Simply Accounting.

***INNOVATION!* Special Offers—Professional Accounting Software Packages** Package your choice of the latest software releases of Peachtree or Simply Accounting at $11.00 net with new text purchase.

General Ledger Software   The General Ledger software enables students to complete homework assignments using a general ledger software package. Students may also enter and solve their own problems. Available on the Student DVD, Instructor CD-ROM, and downloadable from the Companion Website.

***INNOVATION!* Standard Online Courses in WebCT, CourseCompass, and BlackBoard**   Teach a complete online course or a Web-enhanced course. Add your own course materials, take advantage of online testing and Gradebook opportunities, and utilize the bulletin board and discussion board functions. Free upon request. This is an excellent time to build your own course using our CD-ROMs with your choice of platform. (The courses will not be "robust".)

Companion Website at www.prenhall.com/slater   Prentice Hall's Learning on the Internet Partnership offers extensive Internet-based support. Our Website provides a wealth of resources for students and faculty resources, including an Online Study Guide with Quizzes, Internet Exercises, PowerPoint slides, software downloads, complete faculty supplements, and much more.

Instructor Supplements

***INNOVATION!* Instructor CD-ROM**   The **IRCD** contains all print and technology (e.g., videos, data files, PowerPoint slides) supplements on a single CD-ROM.

Instructor's Solutions Manual   Each chapter of this comprehensive resource consists of a list of the student learning objectives and the fully worked-out solutions to the chapter problems.

Test Item File and Achievement Tests   The printed Test Item File consists of hundreds of premade questions, including true/false questions, conceptual and quantitative multiple-choice questions, critical thinking problems, and exercises. Each question identifies the difficulty level and the corresponding learning objective. The Achievement Tests give faculty the flexibility to pop a quiz with little effort. **Prentice Hall TestGenEQ** can create exams and evaluate and track student results.

Solutions and Teaching Transparencies   Every page of the Solutions Manual has been reproduced in acetate form for use on the overhead projector. These acetates have been enhanced for easier viewing.

On Location! Videos   These eight brief videos take students "on location" to real companies where real accounting situations are discussed and explained.

Student Supplements

New! **Computerized Accounting Practice Sets**   The **A-1 Photography and Runners Corporation** practice sets are available complete with data files for Peachtree, QuickBooks, and Simply Accounting. Each practice set also includes business stationary for manual entry work. In addition, the Who-Dun-It Bookstore practice set (for use with Chapters 12–25) has been revised and updated.

INNOVATION! **Student DVD**   The **Student DVD** is free with every new text purchased from Prentice Hall (it can also be purchased separately) and contains the General Ledger software package, PowerPoints, Getting Started data files, On Location! videos, Learning Unit Review videos (for Chapters 1–5), and 5 Steps in the Accounting Cycle videos.

Study Guide with Working Papers   This chapter-by-chapter learning aid systematically and effectively helps students study college accounting and get the maximum benefit from their study time. Each chapter provides a Summary Practice Test with fill-in-the-blanks, multiple choice, and true/false problems AND solutions to all the questions, and the Working Papers contain tailor-made spreadsheets to all end-of-chapter problems.

Who-Dun-It Practice Set   A case study (with solutions available for instructors) that follows a sole proprietorship throughout end-of-year transactions, cash sales, sales tax, payroll, purchases, and other year-end processes. This practice set is most effectively used with Chapters 12–25 of the text.

ACKNOWLEDGMENTS

Reviewers

I wish to thank the following reviewers for their suggestions, many of which made their way into this text, and for their support, without which this text would not be the success that it is today.

Kevin Bess, Florida Metropolitan, Melbourne

Janell Spencer, College of the Sequoias

Susan Davis, Green River Community College

James Mann, Huntington Junior College

Michael Farina, Cerritos College

Thomas Milligan, St. Philip's College

Harry Gray, Ivy Tech State College, Indianapolis

Claire Moore, Heald College, Roseville

Scott Steinhamp, College of Lake County

Richard Williams, Nashville State Technical Community College

Marjorie Ashton, Truckee Meadows Community College

Thea Hosselrode, Allegany College

Julie Dailey, Tidewater Community College

Beverly Bugay, Tyler Junior College

Mark Preising, Florida Metropolitan, Orlando

William Hood, Central Michigan University

Brenda Bindschatel, Spokane Falls Community College

Elaine Anes, Heald College, Fresno

Cornelia Alsheimer, Santa Barbara City College

Michelle Berube, Florida Metropolitan, Clearwater

Dorenda Haynes, Heald College, San Jose

Tom Snavely, Yavapai Community College

Angela Harper, Indiana Business College, Evansville

Wayne Smith, Indiana Business College, Lafayette

Ruth Turner, National College of Business & Technology, Lynchburg

Brennan Randolph, Indiana Business College, Terre Haute

Brenda Jenkins, National College of Business & Technology, Bluefield

Sara Bottomley, Indiana Business College, Terre Haute

John Hudson, National College of Business & Technology, Bluefield

Michael Kulper, Santa Barbara City College

SUPPLEMENT AUTHORS

Test Bank/Achievement Tests—Patti Holmes, Des Moines Area CC

Online Study Guide—Tim Carse

Who-Dun-It Practice Set—Shari DeMarco

PowerPoints—Olga Quintana, University of Miami

Getting Started with Peachtree Complete Accounting 2003—Errol Osteraa, Heald College

Getting Started with Simply Accounting 2003—Jean Insinga, Middlesex Community College

Getting Started with QuickBooks Pro 2003—Janet Horne, Los Angeles Pierce College

Transparency Acetates—Jeff Slater

Instructor Solutions Manual—Jeff Slater

Study Guide w/Working Papers—Jeff Slater

On Location! Videos—Beverly Amer, Northern Arizona University

Subway Case Videos—Beverly Amer, Northern Arizona University

5 Steps in the Accounting Cycle Videos—Beverly Amer, Northern Arizona University

Jeff Slater's One on One Videos—Beverly Amer, Northern Arizona University

Additionally, there are a few people who need to be mentioned for their help with this edition: Nancy Brandwein, for writing the Subway Cases for me; Les Winograd, of Subway World Headquarters, who worked closely with Nancy Brandwein as she created our Subway Cases; and Jim Hatfield, owner of Subway of Upstate South Carolina, who provided real-world examples and first-hand knowledge for the Cases. Tim Carse did a great job as he wrote the chapters on Payroll and worked closely with Errol Osteraa, who once again did an outstanding job writing the Computer Workshops (and the *Getting Started with Peachtree Complete Accounting 2003*). Their effort and expertise are most valuable and much appreciated. Abby Kaminsky did a wonderful job checking proofs, paging the study guide, and coordinating all text reviews. All these people helped me write the text, and I couldn't have done it without them.

The people at Prentice Hall who worked together to make this text a reality also deserve a heartfelt thank you: Kerri Tomasso, for her careful eye on the production of the text; Blair Brown, for his excellent design work both interior and on the cover; Beth Toland; for her non-stop marketing efforts, Sam Goffinet, for all his dedication in getting the supplements out on time AND done right; and to wonderful Jane Avery for keeping us honest at all times. Special thanks to Alana Bradley, my editor, who has shown patience beyond the call of duty. Thanks for always finding a way to resolve my many requests. You are a real jewel.

A Note to Students from Jeff Slater . . .

Welcome! **College Accounting 9e** will introduce you to Accounting, the most dynamic tool of business. This textbook focuses on real-world applications designed to help you see the critical role accounting plays in the business world. Each text chapter opens with a real-life situation where an individual learns how accounting is a part of the everyday world. In every instance, I have tried to think of the most interesting and applicable examples for you . . . including selecting Subway, the largest franchised business in the world as the spotlight business for this edition of the text. I hope you will enjoy learning about this tasty business as you devour new accounting concepts.

Please take a few moments to "walk through" the features of the Ninth Edition to see all of the tools that are available to assist you in this course.

New Chapter-Opening Stories

The chapter-opening stories show how accounting issues touch your life each day and motivate topics to be covered in each chapter.

CHAPTER 4

The Accounting Cycle Continued

Preparing Worksheets and Financial Statements

Your roommate Sam is an art major. Sam is skilled at drawing and always has his sketchpad with him. Sam records all of his ideas for a picture by creating various drawings in his pad. Sam will begin a drawing and then make various changes and adjustments to it. Sam said that after he's completed the drawing he goes on to use it when completing a painting.

Sam and several other artists in the area have opened an art studio to display their works. You recently attended a show that featured several of Sam's paintings. While you were at the show, someone bought one of Sam's paintings. Sam was excited and happy. "Now I can pay my share of the rent and utilities for the studio. Everyone here loves art, but we have to run the studio like a business," Sam told you. Even an art studio needs to use accounting to record sales and expenses like other businesses.

Accounting is very different than art, but it does have its own "sketchpad," which is called a worksheet. In Chapter 3 we learned about the first four steps in the accounting cycle. In Chapter 4 we expand our understanding of the accounting cycle by focusing on the next step—preparing a worksheet. And similar to how Sam changes and revises his drawings, an accountant can use the worksheet to make changes and adjustments to numbers found in the trial balance.

In this chapter we also discuss the sixth step in the accounting cycle—using the worksheet to prepare financial statements. And like a sketchpad, the accounting worksheet is a tool that takes us from a trial balance to financial statements, or as Sam would say, from a sketch to a painting.

Learning Objectives

- Adjustments: prepaid rent, office supplies, depreciation on equipment, and accrued salaries. (p. 121)
- Preparation of adjusted trial balance on the worksheet. (p. 129)
- The income statement and balance sheet sections of the worksheet. (p. 130)
- Preparing financial statements from the worksheet. (p. 135)

Learning Objectives

At the beginning of each chapter you'll see a list of the key points to be covered within the chapter.

Key Content Changes

- Eliminated Chapter 11 on Combined Journals from the previous edition

- Updated all payroll chapters

- Include updated bank statements reflecting trends in banking (Chapter 4)

- Shows adjustments one at a time (Chapter 4). No other book takes this much time to reinforce learning

- In-text Valdez practice set (manual & computerized) now includes source documents

- Slater covers perpetual inventory with general journal entries (along with samples of perpetual inventory for special journals and worksheets)

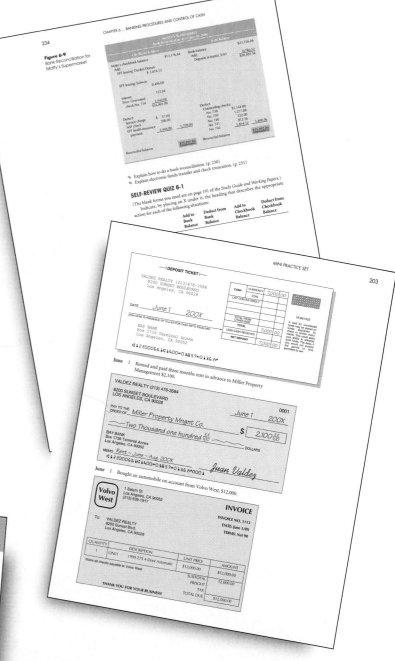

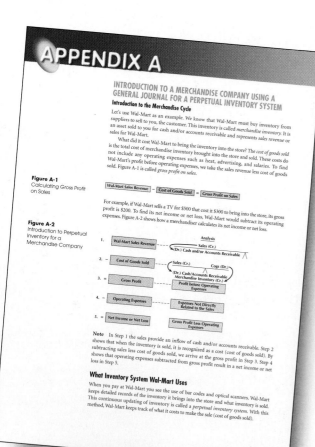

Hallmark Features

Covers both Perpetual and Periodic Inventory

College Accounting 9e has an appendix to Chapter 9 that provides an introduction to merchandizing through general journals for a perpetual inventory system instead of special journals. This edition completes the merchandise cycle by Chapter 12 and then provides the OPTION to cover perpetual inventory for a merchandise company in the Appendices.

Learning Unit

A Slater hallmark! Jeff Slater organizes each chapter into small, bite-sized units. First you are introduced to new concepts and then you have the opportunity to test your understanding in the **Learning Unit Reviews.**

Margin Notes

These "coaching tips" appear in the side margins of each chapter to provide extra insights.

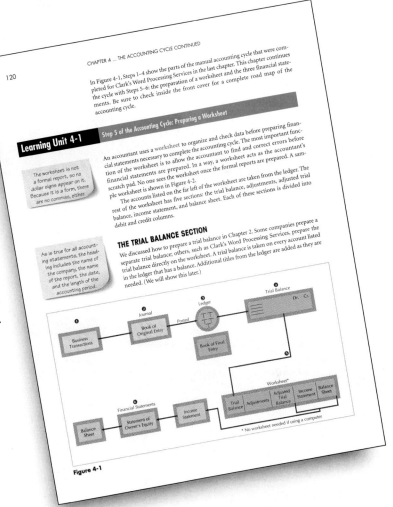

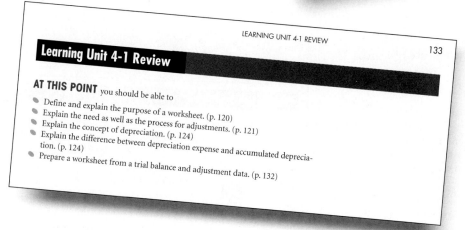

Learning Unit Reviews

A Slater hallmark! Unlike others texts which make you read 30+ pages before you have a chance to test your understanding, Jeff Slater organizes each chapter into small, bite-sized units. After you are introduced to new concepts in the **Learning Unit,** you have the opportunity to test your understanding in the **Learning Unit Reviews.**

Check your understanding by viewing the author's video in which he walks the viewer through the Learning Unit Reviews for the first five chapters.

New! Subway Boxes

This unique feature appears at the end of twelve chapters and shows you how this student-recognizable company uses accounting information to make business decisions. A new video (on the DVD) takes you inside Subway to review accounting concepts.

SUBWAY Case

WHERE THE DOUGH GOES . . .

No matter how harried Stan Hernandez feels as the owner of his own Subway restaurant, the aroma of his fresh-baked gourmet breads *always* perks him up. However, the sales generated by Subway's line of gourmet seasoned breads perks Stan up even more. Subway restaurants introduced freshly baked bread in 1983, a practice that made it stand out from other fast-food chains and helped build its reputation for made-to-order freshness. Since then Subway franchisees have introduced many types of gourmet seasoned breads—such as Hearty Italian or Monterey Cheddar—according to a schedule determined by headquarters.

LEARNING UNIT 4-2   135

Accounting in the Reel World

Dating . . . and Accounting?

Everyone, at one point or another, has probably set up two friends on a blind date or been set up on one. Yet, not everyone sees this matchmaking activity as a business opportunity.

Jilted just five weeks before she was to walk down the aisle, Andrea McGinty turned her personal frustration at finding eligible singles into a lucrative matchmaking business. It's Just Lunch has over $2.5 million in revenues, over 20 locations across the country, and plans to open 1–2 units per month. As you watch the brief It's Just Lunch on-location video on your DVD, think about what it takes to set up a matchmaking business such as It's Just Lunch, and answer the following questions.

1. Can you name some account titles in the assets category? In the Liabilities category? In the Expenses category?
2. How often does It's Just Lunch generate financial statements and why does owner Andrea McGinty need them that often?
3. Is depreciation likely to show up on the It's Just Lunch balance sheet, and if so, for what types of things would Andrea McGinty make a depreciation adjustment?
4. What is the difference between It's Just Lunch's revenues and its income, and what could Andrea McGinty do to increase the company's income?

New! Accounting in the Reel World Video Cases

These in-text video cases are designed to show you how accounting is relevant to the things you care about: dating, shopping, sports, dining, etc. These are linked to our custom-crafted *On Location! Videos* on the DVD.

New DVD Icons

The icon signals to you that there are resources available to use with the *FREE DVD packaged only with New Student Texts*. These include:

Videos

- **New!** Subway *On Location! Videos* linked to the new Subway in-text boxes
- **New!** *On Location! Videos!* linked to the new in-text video cases
- **New!** Jeff Slater Learning Unit Review Video for Chapters 1–5
- **New!** 5 Steps in Accounting Cycle Video

Software

- General Ledger Software
- Data files for the latest releases of the Getting Started Series (Peachtree, QuickBooks, Simply Accounting)
- PowerPoints
- Links to the Slater Website and online courses

Learning Unit 2-3 Review

AT THIS POINT you should be able to

- Explain the role of footings. (p. 51)
- Prepare a trial balance from a set of accounts. (p. 52)
- Prepare financial statements from a trial balance. (p. 53)

SELF-REVIEW QUIZ 2-3

(The blank forms you need are on page 27 of the *Study Guide and Working Papers*. See your DVD for worked out solutions.)

As the bookkeeper of Pam's Hair Salon, you are to prepare from the following accounts below Figure 2-3, p. 53 on June 30, 200X, (1) a trial balance as of June 30, (2) an income statement for the month ended June 30, (3) a statement of owner's equity for the month ended June 30, and (4) a balance sheet as of June 30, 200X.

Continuing Problem

Throughout the book, you will read about Eldorado Computer Center. At the end of each chapter, you will apply concepts you have learned to solve a specific accounting problem. In the next chapter, you will see the next evolution in the organization.

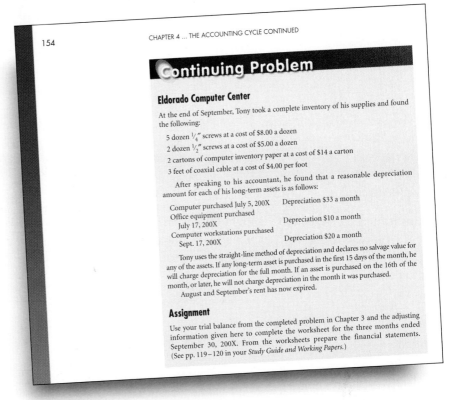

154   CHAPTER 4 ... THE ACCOUNTING CYCLE CONTINUED

Continuing Problem

Eldorado Computer Center

At the end of September, Tony took a complete inventory of his supplies and found the following:

5 dozen $\frac{1}{4}''$ screws at a cost of $8.00 a dozen
2 dozen $\frac{1}{2}''$ screws at a cost of $5.00 a dozen
2 cartons of computer inventory paper at a cost of $14 a carton
3 feet of coaxial cable at a cost of $4.00 per foot

After speaking to his accountant, he found that a reasonable depreciation amount for each of his long-term assets is as follows:

Computer purchased July 5, 200X	Depreciation $33 a month
Office equipment purchased July 17, 200X	Depreciation $10 a month
Computer workstations purchased Sept. 17, 200X	Depreciation $20 a month

Tony uses the straight-line method of depreciation and declares no salvage value for any of the assets. If any long-term asset is purchased in the first 15 days of the month, he will charge depreciation for the full month. If an asset is purchased on the 16th of the month, or later, he will not charge depreciation in the month it was purchased.

August and September's rent has now expired.

Assignment

Use your trial balance from the completed problem in Chapter 3 and the adjusting information given here to complete the worksheet for the three months ended September 30, 200X. From the worksheets prepare the financial statements. (See pp. 119–120 in your *Study Guide and Working Papers*.)

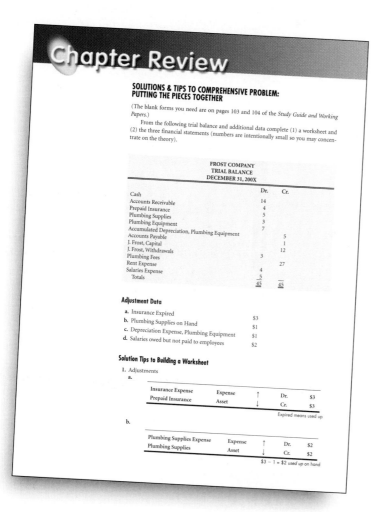

Chapter Review

SOLUTIONS & TIPS TO COMPREHENSIVE PROBLEM: PUTTING THE PIECES TOGETHER

(The blank forms you need are on pages 103 and 104 of the *Study Guide and Working Papers*.)

From the following trial balance and additional data complete (1) a worksheet and (2) the three financial statements (numbers are intentionally small so you may concentrate on the theory).

FROST COMPANY TRIAL BALANCE DECEMBER 31, 200X		
	Dr.	Cr.
Cash	14	
Accounts Receivable	4	
Prepaid Insurance	5	
Plumbing Supplies	3	
Plumbing Equipment	7	
Accumulated Depreciation, Plumbing Equipment		5
Accounts Payable		1
J. Frost, Capital		12
J. Frost, Withdrawals	3	
Plumbing Fees		27
Rent Expense	4	
Salaries Expense	5	
Totals	45	45

Adjustment Data

a. Insurance Expired $3
b. Plumbing Supplies on Hand $1
c. Depreciation Expense, Plumbing Equipment $1
d. Salaries owed but not paid to employees $2

Solution Tips to Building a Worksheet

1. Adjustments
   a.

Insurance Expense	Expense	↑	Dr.	$3
Prepaid Insurance	Asset	↓	Cr.	$3

   Expired means used up

   b.

Plumbing Supplies Expense	Expense	↑	Dr.	$2
Plumbing Supplies	Asset	↓	Cr.	$2

   $3 − 1 = $2 used up on hand

Comprehensive Problem

This problem helps you recall concepts from previous chapters as you pull upon all of your knowledge to solve these problems.

Key Terms/Blueprint

This feature is designed to highlight the key terms you should know for each chapter and the blueprint highlights important accounting processes you should know.

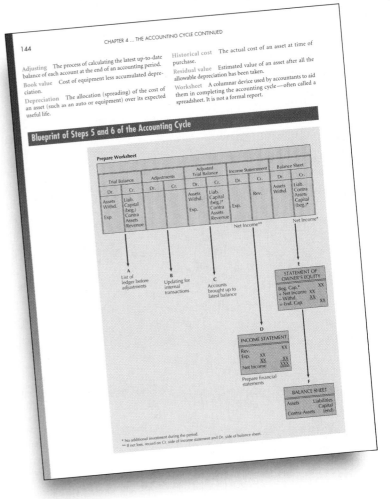

YOU make the call

These action-oriented exercises encourage you to put yourself in the decision-marker's seat.

Cash received for: Rent   2,300

As his best friend, could you help Harry show the amounts that are to be reported on the income statement for (a) Advertising Expense, (b) Interest Expense, and (c) Rent Fees Earned. Please explain in writing why Unearned Rent is considered a liability.

YOU make the call

Critical Thinking/Ethical Case

4R-3. Janet Fox, President of Angel Co., went to a tax seminar. One of the speakers at the seminar advised the audience to put off showing expenses until next year because doing so would allow them to take advantage of a new tax law. When Janet returned to the office, she called in her accountant, Frieda O'Riley. She told Frieda to forget about making any adjustments for salaries in the old year so more expenses could be shown in the new year. Frieda told her that putting off these expenses would not follow generally accepted accounting procedures. Janet said she should do it anyway. You make the call. Write your specific recommendations to Frieda.

Internet Exercises: Office Max

EX-1. [www.officemax.com] On the Web site look for "General Information," then click on "Corporate Information." Under "Investor Information" look up Annual Reports and find the Consolidated Balance Sheet for 2001.

1. Under the caption "other current assets," what accounts do you think could be there that required end-of-period adjustments?
2. If Office Max rented the property where its stores are located and paid the rent in advance for 24 months, how would adjustments have been made in its financial statements?
3. What effect would these adjustments have on (a) Total Assets, and (b) Net Income?
4. Look at "current liabilities" in the balance sheet. Which accounts there seem most susceptible to the adjustment process, and why did you choose these accounts?

EX-2. [www.officemax.com] Click on "CEO Sworn Statement." Why do you think the CEO is required to report this information?

Internet Exercises

These exercises give you the opportunity to use the Internet to solve specific accounting problems.

Unique In-Text Computer Workshops

These Workshops enable the use of the latest release of Peachtree Complete Software in order to solve specific accounting problems. *Note that the full educational version of this software may be packaged with new copies of the text at a minimal charge.*

COMPUTERIZED ACCOUNTING APPLICATION FOR CHAPTER 4

PART A: Compound Journal Entries, Adjusting Entries, and Financial Reports

PART B: Backup Procedures

Before starting on this assignment, read and complete the tasks discussed in Parts A, B, and F of the Computerized Accounting appendix at the back of this book and complete the Computerized Accounting Application assignment at the end of Chapter 3.

PART A: COMPOUND JOURNAL ENTRIES, ADJUSTING ENTRIES, AND FINANCIAL REPORTS

How to Open the Company Data Files

1. Click on the Start button. Point to Programs; point to the Peachtree folder and select Peachtree Complete Accounting. Your desktop may have the Peachtree icon allowing for a quicker entrance into the program.
2. Follow the "Open a File" instructions in Part A of the Computerized Accounting appendix at the back of this book to open **The Zell Company.** You may be initially presented with the Peachtree Today window. If so, simply close it. If you are missing the navigation aids at the bottom of the screen and want them, you can activate them under the **Options** menu. Select **View Navigation Aid.** It will remain on until you turn it off. This feature offers an alternative way to access the different features of Peachtree.

How to Add Your Name to the Company Name

3. Click on the **Maintain** menu option. Then select **Company Information.** The program will respond by bringing up a dialogue box allowing the user to edit/add information about the company.
4. Click in the **Company Name** entry field at the end of **The Zell Company.** If it is already highlighted, press the right arrow key. Add a dash and your name "**-Student Name**" to the end of the company name. Click on the OK button to return to the Menu Window.

How to Record a Compound Journal Entry

5. In the computerized accounting application assignment in Chapter 3 you learned how to record journal entries in the General Journal dialog box. Compound journal entries can also be recorded in the General Journal dialog box. The owner of The Zell Company has made an investment in the business consisting of $5,000 in cash and an automobile valued at $12,000. Select **General Journal Entry** from the **Tasks** menu to open the General Journal dialog box. Enter the date 1/1/04 into the **Date** field; press the TAB key; enter "Memo" into the **Reference** field and press TAB.
6. With the flashing insertion point positioned in the **Account No.** field, click on the pull down menu (magnifying glass icon) and double click on "1110 Cash". The program will enter the account number and name into the **Account No.** field and the flashing insertion point will move to the **Description** field. Enter "Initial investment by owner" into this field and press TAB to move to the **Debit** field. Enter "5000" and press TAB three times to move back to the **Account No.** field.
7. With the flashing insertion point positioned in the **Account No.** field, click on the pull down menu (magnifying glass icon) and double click on "1230 Automobile". Press TAB to move to the **Description** field. This should repeat the information entered in step 6 by default. Press the TAB key again to move to the **Debit** field. Enter "12000". Hit TAB three times to move the cursor back to the **Account No.** field. You should now have two debit entries.

Learning accounting means familiarizing yourself with many new terms and concepts. Don't let the temptation to cut corners and take shortcuts fool you. It is to your advantage to follow the detailed step-by-step directions provided in the text so that you can learn good habits from the start. Once you have learned basic terms and concepts the rest will quickly fall into place. I've enclosed my own **Tips to Success** that I share with my students when I teach the course. I encourage you to read these Tips and apply them in your daily reading and classwork:

TIPS TO SUCCESS . . . FROM JEFF SLATER

1. **Read each chapter by Learning Unit.** Don't try to read a chapter all at once, but instead, focus just on the learning unit, and don't overdo it.

2. **Complete each self-review quiz** given at the end of each learning unit to immediately assess your understanding of the material.

Remember! In **College Accounting 9e,** *each chapter builds on the previous chapter. You need to build a solid foundation before going on to the next chapter. Accounting is one discipline where you can only learn by doing, so follow this advice!*

3. **Utilize the DVD** to review core accounting concepts: the Self Review Quiz videos and the Accounting Cycle videos will give you the best foundation available.

4. **Use the Website** at www.prenhall.com/slater for extra help in drill and practice.

5. **Review the Comprehensive Review Problems** with worked-out solutions that are at the end of the first five chapters in the text. These special problems are great for putting all the learning units together to give you an overview of how accounting works. All the forms are available in your study guide/working papers.

As you can see, I really enjoy teaching accounting and providing my students with every possible resource to maximize their learning experience. I wish you the best of luck in your class and I welcome your input as you use the text. You may feel free to contact me at jeffslater@aol.com.

College Accounting

A Practical Approach

Chapters 1–25
Ninth Edition

CHAPTER 1

Accounting Concepts and Procedures

An Introduction

When you stop to think about accounting, it surrounds you, every day.

You go to the school bookstore and buy your textbooks for the new term. The cashier rings up your purchase by scanning the bar codes on each book. The electronic register keeps track of the sale, adds the tax, and bills you a total of $342.28. You present the cashier with your credit card, sign your name on an electronic touch pad with a special pen, and then take your receipt and your books. While standing in the checkout line you hear one bookstore employee tell another that she's going to be working an extra shift this weekend and that she'll be paid overtime for the extra hours.

It's simple to use your credit card to buy books, but how does the bookstore keep track of book sales, book orders, and paying its employees? What process does a business like a bookstore use to keep it operating efficiently? It's all tracked through accounting, the language of business.

Throughout this text we will be looking at how accounting helps businesses like the bookstore keep track of book orders and sales and paying its employees. In this chapter we discuss the types of business organizations and how accounting differs from bookkeeping. We will look at the basics of recording business events using accounting. We will learn that accounting starts with a basic set of rules that make up the accounting equation. Then we build on the accounting equation to learn how a business records its events and reports them. We conclude this chapter by discussing how to summarize the results of accounting using financial statements such as the balance sheet, income statement, and statement of owner's equity.

The world of business surrounds us, and accounting is the language spoken in the world of business.

Learning Objectives

- Defining and listing the functions of accounting. (p. 4)

- Recording transactions in the basic accounting equation. (p. 4)

- Seeing how revenue, expenses, and withdrawals expand the basic accounting equation.
  (p. 11)

- Preparing an income statement, a statement of owner's equity, and a balance sheet. (p. 17)

Accounting is the language of business; it provides information to managers, owners, investors, governmental agencies, and others inside and outside the organization. Accounting provides answers and insights to questions like these:

- Should I invest in Disney stock?
- Will McDonald's show good returns in the future?
- Can American Airlines pay its debt obligations?
- What percentage of Apple's marketing budget is for e-business? How does that percentage compare with the competition? What is the overall financial condition of Apple?

Smaller businesses also need answers to their financial questions:

- At a local Pizza Hut did business increase enough over the last year to warrant hiring a new assistant?
- Should Eatons Drug-Store spend more money to design, produce, and send out new brochures in an effort to create more business?
- What role should the Internet play in our business?

Accounting is as important to individuals as it is to businesses; it answers questions like these:

- Should I take out a loan to buy a new Volvo SUV or wait until I can afford to pay cash for it?
- Would my money work better in a money market or in the stock market?

Accounting is the process that analyzes, records, classifies, summarizes, reports, and interprets financial information to decision makers—whether individuals, small businesses, large corporations, or governmental agencies—in a timely fashion. It is important that students understand the "whys" of the accounting process. Just knowing the mechanics is not enough.

There are three main categories of business organization: (1) sole proprietorships, (2) partnerships, and (3) corporations. Let's define each of them and look at their advantages and disadvantages. This information also appears in Table 1-1.

Sole Proprietorship

A sole proprietorship, such as Gracie's Nail Care, is a business that has one owner. That person is both the owner and the manager of the business. An advantage of

> The Internet is creating many new opportunities and challenges for all forms of business organizations.

TABLE 1-1 Types of Business Organizations

	Sole Proprietorship (Gracie's Nail Care)	Partnership (Matthew and Jones)	Corporation (Home Depot)
Ownership	Business owned by one person.	Business owned by more than one person.	Business owned by stockholders.
Formation	Easy to form.	Easy to form.	More difficult to form.
Liability	Owner could lose personal assets to meet obligations of business.	Partners could lose personal assets to meet obligations of partnership.	Limited personal risk. Stockholders' loss is limited to their investment in the company.
Closing	Ends with death of owner or closing of business.	Ends with death of partner or exit of a partner.	Can continue indefinitely.

a sole proprietorship is that the owner makes all the decisions for the business. A disadvantage is that if the business cannot pay its obligations, the business owner must pay them, which means that the owner could lose some of his or her personal assets (e.g., house or savings).

Sole proprietorships are easy to form. They end if the business closes or when the owner dies.

Partnership

A **partnership,** such as Matthew and Jones, is a form of business ownership that has at least two owners (partners). Each partner acts as an owner of the company, which is an advantage because the partners can share the decision making and the risks of the business. A disadvantage is that, as in a sole proprietorship, the partners' personal assets could be lost if the partnership cannot meet its obligations.

Partnerships are easy to form. They end when a partner dies or leaves the partnership.

Corporation

A **corporation,** such as Home Depot, is a business owned by stockholders. The corporation may have only a few stockholders, or it may have many stockholders. The stockholders are not personally liable for the corporation's debts, and they usually do not have input into the business decisions.

eBay is an example of a corporation.

Corporations are more difficult to form than sole proprietorships or partnerships. Corporations can exist indefinitely.

CLASSIFYING BUSINESS ORGANIZATIONS

Whether we are looking at a sole proprietorship, a partnership, or a corporation, the business can be classified by what the business does to earn money. Companies are categorized as service, merchandise, or manufacturing businesses.

A limo service is a good example of a **service company** because it provides a service. The first part of this book focuses on service businesses.

Gap and J.C. Penney sell products. They are called merchandise companies. **Merchandise companies** can either make their own products or sell products that are made by another supplier. Companies like Mattel and Ford Motor Company that make their own products are called **manufacturers.** (See Table 1-2.)

TABLE 1-2 Examples of Service, Merchandise, and Manufacturing Business

Service Businesses	Merchandise Businesses	Manufacturing Businesses
Lou's Detailing Co.	L.L. Bean	GE
eBay	J.C. Penney	Ford
Dr. Wheeler, M.D.	Amazon.com	Toro
Accountemps	Home Depot	Levi's
CellularOne Paging Services	Staples	Intel

DEFINITION OF ACCOUNTING

Accounting (also called the accounting process) is a system that measures the activities of a business in financial terms. It provides various reports and financial statements that show how the various transactions the business undertook (e.g., buying and selling goods) affected the business. It does this by performing the following functions:

- **Analyzing:** Looking at what happened and how the business was affected.
- **Recording:** Putting the information into the accounting system.
- **Classifying:** Grouping all the same activities (e.g., all purchases) together.
- **Summarizing:** Explaining the results.
- **Reporting:** Issuing the statements that tell the results of the previous functions.
- **Interpreting:** Examining the statements to determine how the various pieces of information they contain relate to each other.

The system communicates the reports and financial statements to people who are interested in the information, such as the business's decision makers, investors, creditors, and governmental agencies (e.g., the Internal Revenue Service).

As you can see, a lot of people use these reports. A set of procedures and guidelines were developed to make sure that everyone prepares and interprets them the same way. These guidelines are known as generally accepted accounting principles (GAAP).

Now let's look at the difference between bookkeeping and accounting. Keep in mind that we use the terms *accounting* and the *accounting process* interchangeably.

DIFFERENCE BETWEEN BOOKKEEPING AND ACCOUNTING

Confusion often arises concerning the difference between bookkeeping and accounting. Bookkeeping is the recording (recordkeeping) function of the accounting process; a bookkeeper enters accounting information in the company's books. An accountant takes that information and prepares the financial statements that are used to analyze the company's financial position. Accounting involves many complex activities. Often, it includes the preparation of tax and financial reports, budgeting, and analyses of financial information.

Today, computers are used for routine bookkeeping operations that used to take weeks or months to complete. The text takes this into consideration by explaining how the advantages of the computer can be applied to a manual accounting system by using hands-on knowledge of how accounting works. Basic accounting knowledge is needed even though computers can do routine tasks. QuickBooks and Peachtree are two popular software packages in use today.

Learning Unit 1-1   The Accounting Equation

ASSETS, LIABILITIES, AND EQUITIES

Let's begin our study of accounting concepts and procedures by looking at a small business: Cathy Hall's law practice. Cathy decided to open her practice at the end of August. She consulted her accountant before she made her decision. The accountant told her some important things before she made this decision. First, he told her the new business would be considered a separate business entity whose finances had to be kept separate and distinct from Cathy's personal finances. The accountant went on to say that all transactions can be analyzed using the basic accounting equation: Assets = Liabilities + Owner's Equity.

Cathy had never heard of the basic accounting equation. She listened carefully as the accountant explained the terms used in the equation and how the equation works.

Assets

Cash, land, supplies, office equipment, buildings, and other properties of value *owned* by a firm are called assets.

Equities

The rights of financial claim to the assets are called equities. Equities belong to those who supply the assets. If you are the only person to supply assets to the firm, you have the sole rights, for financial claims, to them. For example, if you supply the law firm with $5,000 in cash and $4,000 in office equipment, your equity in the firm is $9,000.

Relationship Between Assets and Equities

The relationship between assets and equities is

Assets   =   **Equities**
(Total value of items *owned* by business)   **(Total claims against the assets)**

The total dollar value of the assets of your law firm will be equal to the total dollar value of the financial claims to those assets, that is, equal to the total dollar value of the equities.

The total dollar value is broken down on the left-hand side of the equation to show the specific items of value owned by the business and on the right-hand side to show the types of claims against the assets owned.

Liabilities

A firm may have to borrow money to buy more assets; when this occurs it means the firm is *buying assets on account* (buy now, pay later). Suppose the law firm purchases a new computer for $2,300 on account from Gateway, and the company is willing to wait 10 days for payment. The law firm has created a liability: an obligation to pay that comes due in the future. Gateway is called the creditor. This liability—the amount owed to Gateway—gives the store the right, or the financial claim, to $2,300 of the law firm's assets. When Gateway is paid, the store's rights to the assets of the law firm will end, because the obligation has been paid off.

Basic Accounting Equation

To best understand the various claims to a business's assets, accountants divide equities into two parts. The claims of creditors—outside persons or businesses—are labeled *liabilities*. The claim of the business's owner are labeled owner's equity. Let's see how the accounting equation looks now.

❦ **Assets** =   **Equities**
                                1. Liabilities: rights of creditors
                                2. Owner's equity: rights of owner

Assets = Liabilities + Owner's Equity

Elements of basic accounting equation

Assets
− Liabilities
= Owner's Equity

The total value of all the assets of a firm equals the combined total value of the financial claims of the creditors (liabilities) and the claims of the owners (owner's equity). This is known as the **basic accounting equation.** The basic accounting equation provides a basis for understanding the conventional accounting system of a business. The equation records business transactions in a logical and orderly way that shows their impact on the company's assets, liabilities, and owner's equity.

Importance of Creditors

Another way of presenting the basic accounting equation is

$$\textbf{Assets} - \textbf{Liabilities} = \textbf{Owner's Equity}$$

In accounting, capital does not mean cash. Capital is the owner's current investment, or equity, in the assets of the business.

This form of the equation stresses the importance of creditors. The owner's rights to the business's assets are determined after the rights of the creditors are subtracted. In other words, creditors have first claim to assets. If a firm has no liabilities—and therefore no creditors—the owner has the total rights to assets. Another term for the owner's current investment, or equity, in the business's assets is capital.

As Cathy Hall's law firm engages in business transactions (paying bills, serving customers, and so on), changes will take place in the assets, liabilities, and owner's equity (capital). Let's analyze some of these transactions.

> **Transaction A   Aug. 28:** Cathy invests $7,000 in cash and $800 of office equipment into the business.

On August 28, Cathy withdraws $7,000 from her personal bank account and deposits the money in the law firm's newly opened bank account. She also invests $800 of office equipment in the business. She plans to be open for business on September 1. With the help of her accountant, Cathy begins to prepare the accounting records for the business. We put this information into the basic accounting equation as follows:

Note:
Capital is part of owner's equity; it is not an asset. In our analyses, assume that any number without a sign in front of it is a +.

	Assets		= Liabilities +	Owner's Equity
Cash	+	Office Equipment	=	Cathy Hall, Capital
$7,000	+	$800	=	$7,800
		$7,800 = $7,800		

Note that the total value of the assets, cash, and office equipment—$7,800—is equal to the combined total value of liabilities (none, so far) and owner's equity ($7,800). Remember, Hall has supplied all the cash and office equipment, so she has the sole financial claim to the assets. Note how the heading "Cathy Hall, Capital" is written under the owner's equity heading. The $7,800 is Cathy's investment, or equity, in the firm's assets.

> **Transaction B   Aug. 29:** Law practice buys office equipment for cash, $900.

From the initial investment of $7,000 cash, the law firm buys $900 worth of office equipment (such as a computer desk), which lasts a long time, whereas **supplies** (such as pens) tend to be used up relatively quickly.

	Assets		=	Liabilities +	Owner's Equity	
Cash	+	Office Equipment	=		Cathy Hall, Capital	
$7,000	+	$800	=		$7,800	BEGINNING BALANCE
−900		+900				TRANSACTION
$6,100	+	$1,700	=		$7,800	ENDING BALANCE

$$\$7,800 = \$7,800$$

Shift in Assets

As a result of the last transaction, the law office has less cash but has increased its amount of office equipment. This is called a shift in assets; the makeup of the assets has changed, but the total of the assets remains the same.

Suppose you go food shopping at Wal-Mart with $90 and spend $60. Now you have two assets, food and money. The composition of the assets has been *shifted*—you have more food and less money than you did—but the *total* of the assets has not increased or decreased. The total value of the food, $60, plus the cash, $30, is still $90. When you borrow money from the bank, on the other hand, you have an increase in cash (an asset) and an increase in liabilities; overall there is an increase in assets, not just a shift.

An accounting equation can remain in balance even if only one side is updated. The key point to remember is that the left-hand-side total of assets must always equal the right-hand-side total of liabilities and owner's equity.

> ### Transaction C   Aug. 30: Buys additional office equipment on account, $400.

The law firm purchases an additional $400 worth of chairs and desks from Wilmington Company. Instead of demanding cash right away, Wilmington agrees to deliver the equipment and to allow up to 60 days for the law practice to pay the invoice (bill).

This liability, or obligation to pay in the future, has some interesting effects on the basic accounting equation. Wilmington Company has accepted as payment a partial claim against the assets of the law practice. This claim exists until the law firm pays off the bill. This unwritten promise to pay the creditor is a liability called accounts payable.

	Assets		=	Liabilities	+	Owner's Equity	
Cash	+	Office Equipment	=	Accounts Payable	+	Cathy Hall, Capital	
$6,100	+	$1,700	=			$7,800	BEGINNING BALANCE
		+400		+$400			TRANSACTION
$6,100	+	$2,100	=	$400	+	$7,800	ENDING BALANCE

$$\$8,200 = \$8,200$$

When this information is analyzed, we can see that the law practice has increased what it owes (accounts payable) as well as what it owns (office equipment) by $400. The law practice gains $400 in an asset but has an obligation to pay Wilmington Company at a future date.

The owner's equity remains unchanged. This transaction results in an increase of total assets from $7,800 to $8,200.

Finally, note that after each transaction the basic accounting equation remains in balance.

Learning Unit 1-1 Review

AT THIS POINT you should be able to

- Define and explain the differences between sole proprietorships, partnerships, and corporations. (p. 2)
- List the functions of accounting. (p. 4)
- Compare and contrast bookkeeping and accounting. (p. 4)
- Explain the role of the computer as an accounting tool. (p. 4)
- State the purpose of the accounting equation. (p. 5)
- Explain the difference between liabilities and owner's equity. (p. 5)
- Define capital. (p. 6)
- Explain the difference between a shift in assets and an increase in assets. (p. 7)

To test your understanding of this material, complete Self-Review Quiz 1-1. The blank forms you need are in the *Study Guide and Working Papers* for Chapter 1. The solution to the quiz immediately follows here in the text. If you have difficulty doing the problems, review Learning Unit 1-1 and the solution to the quiz. The DVD has worked out solutions for Chapters 1–5 for these Quizzes. Be sure to check the Slater Web site for student study aids. Check with your instructor on availability.

Keep in mind that learning accounting is like learning to type: The more you practice, the better you become. You will not be an expert in one day. Be patient. It will all come together.

Quiz Tip:
Note that transaction 2 below is a shift in assets, whereas transaction 3 is an increase in assets. Keep asking yourself, What did the business get and who supplied it to the business? Remember, capital is not cash. Cash is an asset, whereas capital is part of owner's equity.

SELF-REVIEW QUIZ 1-1

(The blank forms you need are on page 1 of the *Study Guide and Working Papers*. See your DVD for worked-out solutions.)

Record the following transactions in the basic accounting equation:

1. Gracie Ryan invests $17,000 to begin a real estate office.
2. The real estate office buys $600 of computer equipment from Wal-Mart for cash.
3. The real estate company buys $800 of additional computer equipment on account from Circuit City.

SOLUTION TO SELF-REVIEW QUIZ 1-1

	Assets		=	Liabilities	+	Owner's Equity
	Cash	+ Computer Equipment	=	Accounts Payable	+	Gracie Ryan, Capital
1.	+$17,000					+$17,000
BALANCE	17,000		=			17,000
2.	−600	+$600				
BALANCE	16,400	+ 600	=			17,000
3.		+800		+$800		
ENDING BALANCE	$16,400	+ $1,400	=	$800	+	$17,000

$$\$17,800 = \$17,800$$

Accounting in the Reel World

Happy Ice Cream Memories = A Cool $3.5 Million

Many people think of ice cream as fleeting pleasure—something you enjoy in the few minutes it takes to lick up a scoop and keep it from dripping onto your lap. Not Amy Miller, the founder of the Austin, Texas-based Amy's Ice Creams of Austin. At her nine stores she not only dishes out super-premium flavors like Mexican Vanilla with crushed strawberries, but she also seeks to create "happy ice cream memories." For instance, her exhuberant, creative employees host theme nights, spoon out samples, and host events for local charities.

While the values Amy's Ice Creams espouses are warm and fuzzy, there's nothing remotely fuzzy about the figures.

Amy Miller's privately held corporation pulls in $3.5 million a year, and she and her fellow investors must wrestle with tough business decisions every day. As you watch the Amy's Ice Creams on-location video on your DVD, think about the formal business structure behind the informal, vibrant atmosphere at Amy's Ice Creams stores.

1. Why do you think that Amy decided to form a corporation instead of a partnership?
2. What are some of the assets and liabilities of Amy's Ice Creams?
3. Do you think corporations can be as creative as sole proprietorships or partnerships? Why or why not?

Learning Unit 1-2   The Balance Sheet

In the first learning unit, the transactions for Cathy Hall's law firm were recorded in the accounting equation. The transactions we recorded occurred before the law firm opened for business. A statement called a **balance sheet** or **statement of financial position** can show the history of a company before it opened. The balance sheet is a formal statement that presents the information from the ending balances of both sides of the accounting equation. Think of the balance sheet as a snapshot of the business's financial position as of a particular date.

> The balance sheet shows the company's financial position as of a particular date. (In our example, that date is at the end of August.)

Let's look at the balance sheet of Cathy Hall's law practice for August 31, 200X, shown in Figure 1-1. The figures in the balance sheet come from the ending balances of the accounting equation for the law practice as shown in Learning Unit 1-1.

Note in Figure 1-1 that the assets owned by the law practice appear on the left-hand side and that the liabilities and owner's equity appear on the right-hand side.

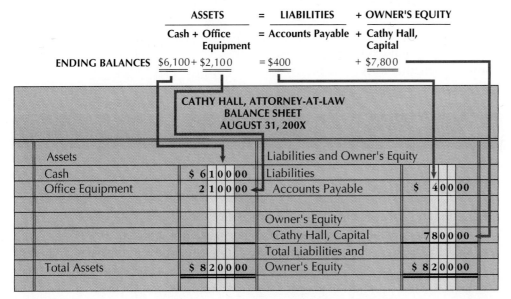

Figure 1-1
The Balance Sheet

> Remember:
> The balance sheet is a formal statement.

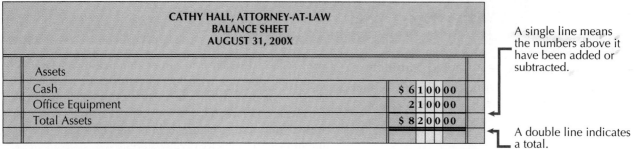

Figure 1-2 Partial Balance Sheet

Both sides equal $8,200. This *balance* between left and right gives the balance sheet its name. In later chapters we look at other ways to set up a balance sheet.

> Do you remember the three elements that make up a balance sheet? Assets, liabilities, and owner's equity.

POINTS TO REMEMBER IN PREPARING A BALANCE SHEET

The Heading

The heading of the balance sheet provides the following information:

- The company name: Cathy Hall, Attorney-at-Law.
- The name of the statement: Balance Sheet.
- The date for which the report is prepared: August 31, 200X.

Use of the Dollar Sign

Note that the dollar sign is not repeated each time a figure appears. As shown in Figure 1-2, the balance sheet for Cathy Hall's law practice, it usually is placed to the left of each column's top figure and to the left of the column's total.

Distinguishing the Total

When adding numbers down a column, use a single line before the total and a double line beneath it. A single line means that the numbers above it have been added or subtracted. A double line indicates a total. It is important to align the numbers in the column; many errors occur because these figures are not lined up. These rules are the same for all accounting reports.

The balance sheet gives Cathy the information she needs to see the law firm's financial position before it opens for business. This information does not tell her, however, whether or not the firm will make a profit.

Learning Unit 1-2 Review

AT THIS POINT you should be able to

- Define and state the purpose of a balance sheet. (p. 9)
- Identify and define the elements making up a balance sheet. (p. 9)
- Show the relationship between the accounting equation and the balance sheet. (p. 9)
- Prepare a balance sheet in proper form from information provided. (p. 9)

SELF-REVIEW QUIZ 1-2

(The blank forms you need are on page 2 of the *Study Guide and Working Papers.* See your DVD for worked-out solutions)

The date is November 30, 200X. Use the following information to prepare in proper form a balance sheet for Janning Company:

Accounts Payable	$40,000
Cash	18,000
A. Janning, Capital	9,000
Office Equipment	31,000

Quiz Tip:
The heading of a balance sheet answers the questions who, what, and when. November 30, 200X is the particular date.

SOLUTION TO SELF-REVIEW QUIZ 1-2

JANNING COMPANY
BALANCE SHEET
NOVEMBER 30, 200X

Assets		Liabilities and Owner's Equity	
Cash	$18 0 0 0 00	Liabilities	
Office Equipment	31 0 0 0 00	Accounts Payable	$ 40 0 0 0 00
		Owner's Equity	
		A. Janning, Capital	9 0 0 0 00
		Total Liabilities and	
Total Assets	$ 4 9 0 0 0 00	Owner's Equity	$ 49 0 0 0 00

Capital does not mean cash. The capital amount is the owner's current investment of assets in the business.

Figure 1-3 Balance Sheet

Learning Unit 1-3 — The Accounting Equation Expanded: Revenue, Expenses, and Withdrawals

As soon as Cathy Hall's office opened, she began performing legal services for her clients and earning revenue for the business. At the same time, as a part of doing business, she incurred various expenses, such as rent.

When Cathy asked her accountant how these transactions fit into the accounting equation, he began by defining some terms.

Revenue   A service company earns revenue when it provides services to its clients. Cathy's law firm earned revenue when she provided legal services to her clients for legal fees. When revenue is earned, owner's equity is increased. In effect, revenue is a subdivision of owner's equity.

Assets are increased. The increase is in the form of cash if the client pays right away. If the client promises to pay in the future, the increase is called accounts receivable. When revenue is earned, the transaction is recorded as an increase in revenue and an increase in assets (either as cash and/or as accounts receivable, depending on whether it was paid right away or will be paid in the future).

Expenses   A business's expenses are the costs the company incurs in carrying on operations in its effort to create revenue. Expenses are also a subdivision of owner's equity; when expenses are incurred, they *decrease* owner's equity. Expenses can be paid for in cash or they can be charged.

Accounts receivable is an asset. The law firm expects to be able to receive amounts owed from customers at a later date.

Remember:
Accounts receivable results from earning revenue even when cash is not yet received.

Record an expense when it is incurred, whether it is paid then or is to be paid later.

Figure 1-4
Owner's Equity

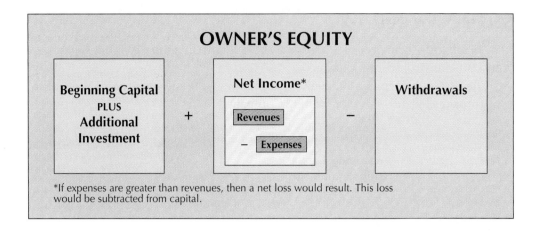

Net Income/Net Loss   When revenue totals more than expenses, net income is the result; when expenses total more than revenue, net loss is the result.

Withdrawals   At some point Cathy Hall may need to withdraw cash or other assets from the business to pay living or other personal expenses that do not relate to the business. We will record these transactions in an account called withdrawals. Sometimes this account is called the *owner's drawing account*. Withdrawals is a subdivision of owner's equity that records personal expenses not related to the business. Withdrawals decrease owner's equity (see Fig. 1-4).

It is important to remember the difference between expenses and withdrawals. Expenses relate to business operations; withdrawals are the result of personal needs outside the normal operations of the business.

Now let's analyze the September transactions for Cathy Hall's law firm using an expanded accounting equation that includes withdrawals, revenues, and expenses.

EXPANDED ACCOUNTING EQUATION

> Transaction D   Sept. 1–30: Provided legal services for cash,
> $3,000.

Transactions A, B, and C were discussed earlier, when the law office was being formed in August. See Learning Unit 1-1.

	Assets			= Liabilities +			Owner's Equity		
	Cash	+ Accts. Rec.	+ Office Equip.	= Accts. Pay.	+ C. Hall, Capital	− C. Hall, Withdr.	+ Revenue	− Expenses
BALANCE FORWARD	$6,100		+ $ 2,100	= $ 400	+ $7,800			
TRANSACTION	+3,000						+$3,000	
ENDING BALANCE	$9,100		+ $ 2,100	= $ 400	+ $7,800		+ $3,000	

$$\$11,200 = \$11,200$$

In the law firm's first month of operation, a total of $3,000 in cash was received for legal services performed. In the accounting equation, the asset Cash is increased by $3,000. Revenue is also increased by $3,000, resulting in an increase in owner's equity.

A revenue column was added to the basic accounting equation. Amounts are recorded in the revenue column when they are earned. They are also recorded in the assets column, either under Cash and/or under Accounts Receivable. Do not think of revenue as an asset. It is part of owner's equity. It is the revenue that creates an inward flow of cash and accounts receivable.

> ### Transaction E   Sept. 1–30: Provided legal services on account, $4,000.

	Assets		= Liabilities +			Owner's Equity			
Cash	+ Accts. Rec.	+ Office Equip.	= Accts. Pay.		+ C. Hall, Capital	− C. Hall, Withdr.	+ Revenue	− Expenses	
$9,100		+ $ 2,100	= $ 400		+ $7,800		+ $3,000		BAL. FOR.
	+4,000						+4,000		TRANS.
$9,100 +	$4,000	+ $ 2,100	= $ 400		+ $7,800		+ $7,000		END. BAL.
		$15,200 = $15,200							

Cathy's law practice performed legal work on account for $4,000. The firm did not receive the cash for these earned legal fees; it accepted an unwritten promise from these clients that payment would be received in the future.

> ### Transaction F   Sept. 1–30: Received $700 cash as partial payment from previous services performed on account.

During September some of Cathy's clients who had received services and promised to pay in the future decided to reduce what they owed the practice by $700 when their bills came due. This is shown as follows on the expanded accounting equation.

	Assets		= Liabilities +			Owner's Equity			
Cash	+ Accts. Rec.	+ Office Equip.	= Accts. Pay.		+ C. Hall, Capital	− C. Hall, Withdr.	+ Revenue	− Expenses	
$9,100 +	$4,000	+ $ 2,100	= $ 400		+ $7,800		+ $7,000		BAL. FOR.
+700	−700								TRANS.
$9,800 +	$3,300	+ $ 2,100	= $ 400		+ $7,800		+ $7,000		END. BAL.
		$15,200 = $15,200							

The law firm increased the asset Cash by $700 and reduced another asset, Accounts Receivable, by $700. The *total* of assets does not change. The right-hand side of the expanded accounting equation has not been touched because the total on the left-hand side of the equation has not changed. The revenue was recorded when it was earned, and the *same revenue cannot be recorded twice.* This transaction analyzes the situation *after* the revenue has been previously earned and recorded. Transaction F shows a shift in assets: more cash and less accounts receivable.

> ### Transaction G   Sept. 1–30: Paid salaries expense, $600.

	Assets			= Liabilities +		Owner's Equity		
	Cash	+ Accts. Rec.	+ Office Equip.	= Accts. Pay.	+ C. Hall, Capital	− C. Hall, Withdr.	+ Revenue	− Expenses
BAL. FOR. TRANS.	$9,800 −600	+ $3,300	+ $ 2,100	= $ 400	+ $7,800		+ $7,000	+$600
END. BAL.	$9,200	+ $3,300	+ $ 2,100	= $ 400	+ $7,800		+ $7,000	− $600
	$14,600 = $14,600							

As expenses increase, they decrease owner's equity. This incurred expense of $600 reduces the cash by $600. Although the expense was paid, the total of our expenses to date has *increased* by $600. Keep in mind that owner's equity decreases as expenses increase, so the accounting equation remains in balance.

Transaction H   Sept. 1–30: Paid rent expense, $700.

	Assets			= Liabilities +		Owner's Equity		
	Cash	+ Accts. Rec.	+ Office Equip.	= Accts. Pay.	+ C. Hall, Capital	− C. Hall, Withdr.	+ Revenue	− Expenses
BAL. FOR. TRANS.	$9,200 −700	+ $3,300	+ $ 2,100	= $ 400	+ $7,800		+ $7,000	− $ 600 +700
END. BAL	$8,500	+ $3,300	+ $ 2,100	= $ 400	+ $7,800		+ $7,000	− $1,300
	$13,900 = $13,900							

During September the practice incurred rent expenses of $700. This rent was not paid in advance; it was paid when it came due. The payment of rent reduces the asset Cash by $700 as well as increases the expenses of the firm, resulting in a decrease in owner's equity. The firm's expenses are now $1,300.

Transaction I   Sept. 1–30: Incurred advertising expenses of $300, to be paid next month.

	Assets			= Liabilities +		Owner's Equity		
	Cash	+ Accts. Rec.	+ Office Equip.	= Accts. Pay.	+ C. Hall, Capital	− C. Hall, Withdr.	+ Revenue	− Expenses
BAL. FOR. TRANS.	$8,500	+ $3,300	+ $ 2,100	= $ 400 +300	+ $7,800		+ $7,000	− $1,300 +300
END. BAL.	$8,500	+ $3,300	+ $ 2,100	= $ 700	+ $7,800		+ $7,000	− $1,600
	$13,900 = $13,900							

Cathy ran an ad in the local newspaper and incurred an expense of $300. This increase in expenses caused a corresponding decrease in owner's equity. Because Cathy has not paid the newspaper for the advertising yet, she owes $300. Thus her liabilities (Accounts Payable) increase by $300. Eventually, when the bill comes in and is paid, both Cash and Accounts Payable will be decreased.

Transaction J   Sept. 1–30: Cathy withdrew $200 for personal use.

Assets			= Liabilities +		Owner's Equity				
Cash	+ Accts. Rec.	+ Office Equip.	= Accts. Pay.	+ C. Hall, Capital	− C. Hall, Withdr.	+ Revenue	− Expenses		
$8,500	+ $3,300	+ $ 2,100	= $ 700	+ $7,800		+ $7,000	− $1,600		**BAL. FOR. TRANS.**
−200					+$200				
$8,300	+ $3,300	+ $ 2,100	= $ 700	+ $7,800	− $200	+ $7,000	− $1,600		**END. BAL**

$$\$13,700 = \$13,700$$

By taking $200 for personal use, Cathy has *increased* her withdrawals from the business by $200 and decreased the asset Cash by $200. Note that as withdrawals increase, the owner's equity *decreases*. Keep in mind that a withdrawal is *not* a business expense. It is a subdivision of owner's equity that records money or other assets an owner withdraws from the business for *personal* use.

Subdivision of Owner's Equity

Take a moment to review the subdivisions of owner's equity:

- As capital increases, owner's equity increases (see transaction A).
- As withdrawals increase, owner's equity decreases (see transaction J).
- As revenue increases, owner's equity increases (see transaction D).
- As expenses increase, owner's equity decreases (see transaction G).

Cathy Hall's Expanded Accounting Equation

The following is a summary of the expanded accounting equation for Cathy Hall's law firm.

Cathy Hall
Attorney-at-Law
Expanded Accounting Equation: A Summary

Assets			= Liabilities +		Owner's Equity				
Cash	+ Accts. Rec.	+ Office Equip.	= Accts. Pay	+ C. Hall, Capital	− C. Hall, Withdr.	+ Revenue	− Expenses		
$7,000		+ $800 =		+ $7,800					**A.**
7,000	+	800 =		7,800					**BALANCE B.**
−900		+ 900							**BALANCE C.**
6,100	+	1,700 =		7,800					
		+ 400	+ $400						**BALANCE C.**
6,100	+	2,100 =	400	+ 7,800					**BALANCE D.**
+3,000						+ $3,000			
9,100	+	2,100 =	400	+ 7,800		+ 3,000			**BALANCE E.**
	+ $4,000					+4,000			
9,100	+ 4,000 +	2,100 =	400	+ 7,800		+ 7,000			**BALANCE F.**
+700	−700								
9,800	+ 3,300 +	2,100 =	400	+ 7,800		+ 7,000			**BALANCE G.**
−600							+ $600		
9,200	+ 3,300 +	2,100 =	400	+ 7,800		+ 7,000	− 600		**BALANCE H.**
−700							+700		
8,500	+ 3,300 +	2,100 =	400	+ 7,800		+ 7,000	− 1,300		**BALANCE I.**
			+ 300				+300		
8,500	+ 3,300 +	2,100 =	700	+ 7,800		+ 7,000	− 1,600		**BALANCE J.**
−200					+ $200				
$8,300	+ $3,300 +	$ 2,100 =	$ 700	+ $7,800	− $200	+ $7,000	− $1,600		**END BALANCE**

$$\$13,700 = \$13,700$$

Learning Unit 1-3 Review

AT THIS POINT you should be able to

- Define and explain the difference between revenue and expenses. (p. 11)
- Define and explain the difference between net income and net loss. (p. 12)
- Explain the subdivisions of owner's equity. (p. 15)
- Explain the effects of withdrawals, revenue, and expenses on owner's equity. (p. 15)
- Record transactions in an expanded accounting equation and balance the basic accounting equation as a means of checking the accuracy of your calculations. (p. 15)

SELF-REVIEW QUIZ 1-3

(The blank forms you need are on page 3 of the *Study Guide and Working Papers*. See your DVD for worked-out solutions.)

Record the following transactions into the expanded accounting equation for the Bing Company. Note that all titles have a beginning balance.

1. Received cash revenue, $4,000.
2. Billed customers for services rendered, $6,000.
3. Received a bill for telephone expenses (to be paid next month), $125.
4. Bob Bing withdrew cash for personal use, $500.
5. Received $1,000 from customers in partial payment for services performed in transaction 2.

Quiz Tip:
Think of expenses and withdrawals as increasing. As they increase, they will reduce the owner's rights. For example, Transaction 4 withdrawals increased by $500, resulting in withdrawals increasing from $800 to $1,300. This represents a $500 decrease to owner's equity.

SOLUTION TO SELF-REVIEW QUIZ 1-3

	Cash	+	Accts. Rec.	+	Cleaning Equip.	=	Accts. Pay.	+	B. Bing, Capital	−	B. Bing, Withdr.	+	Revenue	−	Expenses
							Assets		= Liabilities +				Owner's Equity		
BEG. BALANCE	$10,000	+	$ 2,500	+	$ 6,500	=	$ 1,000	+	$11,800	−	$ 800	+	$ 9,000	−	$2,000
1.	+4,000												+4,000		
BALANCE	14,000	+	2,500	+	6,500	=	1,000	+	11,800	−	800	+	13,000	−	2,000
2.			+6,000										+6,000		
BALANCE	14,000	+	8,500	+	6,500	=	1,000	+	11,800	−	800	+	19,000	−	2,000
3.							+125								+125
BALANCE	14,000	+	8,500	+	6,500	=	1,125	+	11,800	−	800	+	19,000	−	2,125
4.	−500										+500				
BALANCE	13,500	+	8,500	+	6,500	=	1,125	+	11,800	−	1,300	+	19,000	−	2,125
5.	+1,000		−1,000												
END BALANCE	$14,500	+	$ 7,500	+	$ 6,500	=	$ 1,125	+	$11,800	−	$1,300	+	$19,000	−	$2,125

$$\$28,500 = \$28,500$$

Learning Unit 1-4 — Preparing Financial Statements

Cathy Hall would like to be able to find out whether her firm is making a profit, so she asks her accountant whether he can measure the firm's financial performance on a monthly basis. Her accountant replies that there are a number of financial statements that he can prepare, such as the income statement, which shows how well the law firm has performed over a specific period of time. The accountant can use the information in the income statement to prepare other reports.

THE INCOME STATEMENT

An **income statement** is an accounting statement that shows business results in terms of revenue and expenses. If revenues are greater than expenses, the report shows net income. If expenses are greater than revenues, the report shows net loss. An income statement can cover one, three, six, or twelve months. It cannot cover more than one year. The statement shows the result of all revenues and expenses throughout the entire period and not just as of a specific date. The income statement for Cathy Hall's law firm is shown in Figure 1-5.

> The income statement is prepared from data found in the revenue and expense columns of the expanded accounting equation.

Points to Remember in Preparing an Income Statement

Heading The heading of an income statement tells the same three things as all other accounting statements: the company's name, the name of the statement, and the period of time the statement covers.

The Setup As you can see on the income statement, the inside column of numbers ($600, $700, and $300) is used to subtotal all expenses ($1,600) before subtracting them from revenue ($7,000 − $1,600 = $5,400).

Operating expenses may be listed in alphabetical order, in order of largest amounts to smallest, or in a set order established by the accountant.

> The inside column of numbers ($600, $700, $300) is used to subtotal all expenses ($1,600) before subtracting from revenue.

THE STATEMENT OF OWNER'S EQUITY

As we said, the income statement is a business statement that shows business results in terms of revenue and expenses, but how does net income or net loss affect owner's

Figure 1-5
The Income Statement

CATHY HALL, ATTORNEY-AT-LAW INCOME STATEMENT FOR MONTH ENDED SEPTEMBER 30, 200X		
Revenue:		
Legal Fees		$ 7 0 0 0 00
Operating Expenses:		
Salaries Expense	$ 6 0 0 00	
Rent Expense	7 0 0 00	
Advertising Expense	3 0 0 00	
Total Operating Expenses		1 6 0 0 00
Net Income		$ 5 4 0 0 00

CATHY HALL, ATTORNEY-AT-LAW STATEMENT OF OWNER'S EQUITY FOR MONTH ENDED SEPTEMBER 30, 200X		
Cathy Hall, Capital, September 1, 200X		$ 7 80 0 00
Net Income for September	$ 5 40 0 00	
Less Withdrawals for September	2 0 0 00	
Increase in Capital		5 2 0 0 00
Cathy Hall, Capital, September 30, 200X		$ 13 0 0 0 00

Comes from Income Statement

Figure 1-6 Statement of Owner's Equity

> If this statement of owner's equity is omitted, the information will be included in the owner's equity section of the balance sheet.

equity? To find that out we have to look at a second type of statement, the statement of owner's equity.

The statement of owner's equity shows for a certain period of time what changes occurred in Cathy Hall, Capital. The statement of owner's equity is shown in Figure 1-6 above.

The capital of Cathy Hall can be

Increased by:	Owner Investment
	Net Income (Revenue − Expenses)
Decreased by:	Owner Withdrawals
	Net Loss (Expenses Greater than Revenue)

✎ Remember, a withdrawal is *not* a business expense and thus is not involved in the calculation of net income or net loss on the income statement. It appears on the statement of owner's equity. The statement of owner's equity summarizes the effects of all the subdivisions of owner's equity (revenue, expenses, withdrawals) on beginning capital. The ending capital figure ($13,000) will be the beginning figure in the next statement of owner's equity.

Suppose Cathy's law firm had operated at a loss in the month of September. Suppose instead of net income there was a $600 net loss and an additional investment of $800 was made on September 15. Figure 1-7 shows how the statement would look if that had happened.

Figure 1-7

CATHY HALL, ATTORNEY-AT-LAW STATEMENT OF OWNER'S EQUITY FOR MONTH ENDED SEPTEMBER 30, 200X		
Cathy Hall, Capital, September 1, 200X		$ 7 80 0 00
Additional Investment, September 15, 200X		8 0 0 00
Total Investment for September		$ 8 60 0 00
Less: Net Loss for September	$ 6 0 0 00	
Withdrawals for September	2 0 0 00	
Decrease in Capital		8 0 0 00
Cathy Hall, Capital, September 30, 200X		$ 7 80 0 00

THE BALANCE SHEET

Now let's look at how to prepare a balance sheet from the expanded accounting equation (see Fig. 1-8). As you can see, the asset accounts (cash, accounts receivable, and office equipment) appear on the left side of the balance sheet.

Accounts payable and Cathy Hall, Capital appear on the right side. Notice that the $13,000 of capital can be calculated within the accounting equation or can be read from the statement of owner's equity.

MAIN ELEMENTS OF THE INCOME STATEMENT, THE STATEMENT OF OWNER'S EQUITY, AND THE BALANCE SHEET

In this chapter we have discussed three financial statements: the income statement, the statement of owner's equity, and the balance sheet. A fourth statement, called the statement of cash flows, will not be covered at this time. Let us review what elements of the expanded accounting equation go into each statement and the usual order in which the statements are prepared. Figure 1-8 presents a diagram of the accounting equation and the balance sheet. Table 1-3 summarizes the following points:

Test

- The income statement is prepared first; it includes revenues and expenses and shows net income or net loss. This net income or net loss is used to update the next statement, the statement of owner's equity.
- The statement of owner's equity is prepared second; it includes beginning capital and any additional investments, the net income or net loss shown on the income statement, withdrawals, and the total, which is the **ending capital**. The balance in Capital comes from the statement of owner's equity.
- The balance sheet is prepared last; it includes the final balances of each of the elements listed in the accounting equation under Assets and Liabilities. The balance in Capital comes from the statement of owner's equity.

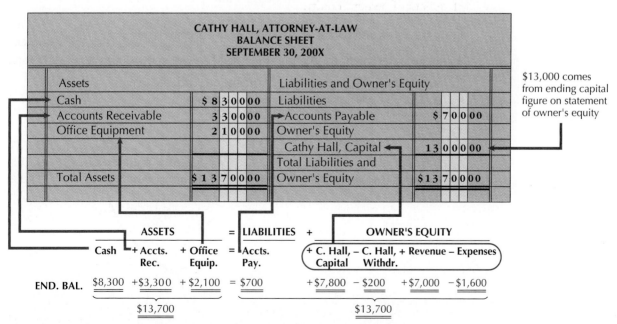

Figure 1-8 The Accounting Equation and the Balance Sheet

TABLE 1-3 **What Goes on Each Financial Statement**

	Income Statement	Statement of Owner's Equity	Balance Sheet
Assets			X
Liabilities			X
Capital* (beg.)		X	
Capital (end) ← Balance Sheet		X	X
Withdrawals		X	
Revenues	X		
Expenses	X		

*Note: Additional Investments go on the Statement of Owner's Equity.

Learning Unit 1-4 Review

AT THIS POINT you should be able to

- Define and state the purpose of the income statement, the statement of owner's equity, and the balance sheet. (p. 17)
- Discuss why the income statement should be prepared first. (p. 17)
- Show what happens on a statement of owner's equity if there is a net loss. (p. 18)
- Compare and contrast these three financial statements. (p. 19)
- Calculate a new figure for capital on the statement of owner's equity and the balance sheet. (p. 19)

SELF-REVIEW QUIZ 1-4

(The blank forms you need are on pages 4 and 5 of the *Study Guide and Working Papers*. See your DVD for worked-out solutions.)

From the following balances for Rusty Realty prepare:

1. Income statement for the month ended November 30, 200X.

2. Statement of owner's equity for the month ended November 30, 200X.

3. Balances as of November 30, 200X.

Cash	$4,000	R. Rusty, Capital	
Accounts Receivable	1,370	November 1, 200X	$5,000
Store Furniture	1,490	R. Rusty, Withdrawals	100
Accounts Payable	900	Commissions Earned	1,500
		Rent Expense	200
		Advertising Expense	150
		Salaries Expense	90

SOLUTION TO SELF-REVIEW QUIZ 1-4

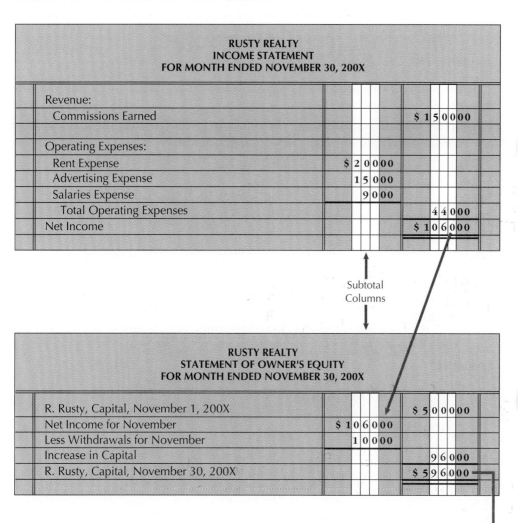

Figure 1-9
Financial Reports

RUSTY REALTY
INCOME STATEMENT
FOR MONTH ENDED NOVEMBER 30, 200X

Revenue:			
Commissions Earned			$ 1 5 0 0 0 0
Operating Expenses:			
Rent Expense	$ 2 0 0 0 0		
Advertising Expense	1 5 0 0 0		
Salaries Expense	9 0 0 0		
Total Operating Expenses		4 4 0 0 0	
Net Income		$ 1 0 6 0 0 0	

Quiz Tip:
Note that the inside column is only used for subtotaling.

Subtotal Columns

RUSTY REALTY
STATEMENT OF OWNER'S EQUITY
FOR MONTH ENDED NOVEMBER 30, 200X

R. Rusty, Capital, November 1, 200X			$ 5 0 0 0 0 0
Net Income for November	$ 1 0 6 0 0 0		
Less Withdrawals for November	1 0 0 0 0		
Increase in Capital		9 6 0 0 0	
R. Rusty, Capital, November 30, 200X		$ 5 9 6 0 0 0	

The net income from the income statement is used to help build the statement of owner's equity.

RUSTY REALTY
BALANCE SHEET
NOVEMBER 30, 200X

Assets		Liabilities and Owner's Equity		
Cash	$ 4 0 0 0 0 0	Liabilities		
Accounts Receivable	1 3 7 0 0 0	Accounts Payable	$ 9 0 0 0 0	
Store Furniture	1 4 9 0 0 0			
		Owner's Equity		
		R. Rusty, Capital	5 9 6 0 0 0	
		Total Liabilities and		
Total Assets	$ 6 8 6 0 0 0	Owner's Equity	$ 6 8 6 0 0 0	

The new figure for capital from the statement of owner's equity is used as the capital figure on the balance sheet.

SOLUTIONS & TIPS TO COMPREHENSIVE PROBLEM: PUTTING THE PIECES TOGETHER

(The blank forms you need are on pages 6 and 7 of the *Study Guide and Working Papers*.)

Michael Brown opened his law office on June 1, 200X. During the first month of operations, Michael conducted the following transactions:

1. Invested $6,000 in cash into the law practice.
2. Paid $600 for office equipment.
3. Purchased additional office equipment on account, $1,000.
4. Received cash for performing legal services for clients, $2,000.
5. Paid salaries, $800.
6. Performed legal services for clients on account, $1,000.
7. Paid rent, $1,200.
8. Withdrew $500 from his law practice for personal use.
9. Received $500 from customers in partial payment for legal services performed, transaction 6.

Assignment

a. Record these transactions in the expanded accounting equation.
b. Prepare the financial statements at June 30 for Michael Brown, Attorney-at-Law.

Solution to Comprehensive Problem

	Assets			= Liabilities +		Owner's Equity			
A.	Cash +	Accts. Rec. +	Office Equip. =	Accounts Payable +	M. Brown, Capital −	M. Brown, Withdr. +	Legal Fees −	Expenses
1.	+$6,000				+$6,000			
BAL.	6,000		=		6,000			
2.	−600		+$600					
BAL.	5,400	+	600 =		6,000			
3.			+1,000	+$1,000				
BAL.	5,400	+	1,600 =	1,000 +	6,000			
4.	+2,000						+$2,000	
BAL.	7,400	+	1,600 =	1,000 +	6,000	+	2,000	
5.	−800							+$800
BAL.	6,600	+	1,600 =	1,000 +	6,000	+	2,000 −	800
6.		+$1,000					+1,000	
BAL.	6,600 +	1,000 +	1,600 =	1,000 +	6,000	+	3,000 −	800
7.	−1,200							+1,200
BAL.	5,400 +	1,000 +	1,600 =	1,000 +	6,000	+	3,000 −	2,000
8.	−500					+$500		
BAL.	4,900 +	1,000 +	1,600 =	1,000 +	6,000 −	500 +	3,000 −	2,000
9.	+500	−500						
END BAL.	$5,400 +	$ 500 +	$1,600 =	$1,000 +	$6,000 −	$500 +	$3,000 −	$2,000

$$\$7,500 = \$7,500$$

Solution Tips to Expanded Accounting Equation

A.

- **Transaction 1:** The business increased its Cash by $6,000. Owner's Equity (capital) increased when Michael supplied the cash to the business.
- **Transaction 2:** There was a shift in assets when the equipment was purchased. The business lowered its Cash by $600, and a new column—Equipment—was increased for the $600 of equipment that was bought. The amount of capital is not touched because the owner did not supply any new funds.
- **Transaction 3:** When creditors supply $1,000 of additional equipment, the business Accounts Payable shows the debt. The business had increased what it *owes* the creditors.
- **Transaction 4:** Legal Fees, a subdivision of Owner's Equity, is increased when the law firm provides a service even if no money is received. The service provides an inward flow of $2,000 Cash, an asset. Remember that Legal Fees are *not* an asset. As Legal Fees increase, Owner's Equity increases.
- **Transaction 5:** The salary paid by Michael shows an $800 increase in Expenses and a corresponding decrease in Owner's Equity.
- **Transaction 6:** Michael did the work and earned the $1,000. That $1,000 is recorded as revenue. This time the Legal Fees create an inward flow of assets called Accounts Receivable for $1,000. Remember that Legal Fees are *not* an asset. They are a subdivision of Owner's Equity.
- **Transaction 7:** The $1,200 rent expense reduces Owner's Equity as well as Cash.
- **Transaction 8:** Withdrawals are for personal use. Here, the business decreases Cash by $500 while Michael withdrawals increase $500. Withdrawals decrease the Owner's Equity.
- **Transaction 9:** This transaction does not reflect new revenue in the form of Legal Fees. It is only a shift in assets: more Cash and less Accounts Receivable.

B-1.

MICHAEL BROWN, ATTORNEY-AT-LAW
INCOME STATEMENT
FOR MONTH ENDED JUNE 30, 200X

Revenue:		
Legal Fees		$3,000
Operating expenses:		
Salaries expense	$ 800	
Rent expense	1,200	
Total operating expenses		2,000
Net income		$1,000

B-2.

MICHAEL BROWN, ATTORNEY-AT-LAW
STATEMENT OF OWNER'S EQUITY
FOR MONTH ENDED JUNE 30, 200X

Michael Brown, Capital, June 1, 200X		$6,000
Net income for June	$1,000	
Less withdrawals for June	500	
Increase in Capital		500
Michael Brown, Capital, June 30, 200X		$6,500

B-3.	MICHAEL BROWN, ATTORNEY-AT-LAW BALANCE SHEET JUNE 30, 200X		
Assets		**Liabilities and Owner's Equity**	
Cash	$5,400	Liabilities	
Accounts Receivable	500	Accounts Payable	$1,000
Office Equipment	1,600	Owner's Equity	
		M. Brown, Capital	6,500
Total Assets	$7,500	Total Liabilities and Owner's Equity	$7,500

Solution Tips to Financial Statements

B-1. The income statement lists only Revenues and Expenses for a period of time. The inside column is for subtotaling. Withdrawals are not listed here.

B-2. The statement of Owner's Equity takes the net income figure of $1,000 and adds it to Beginning Capital less any withdrawals. This new capital figure of $6,500 will go on the balance sheet. This statement shows changes in Capital for a period of time.

B-3. The $5,400, $500, $1,600, and $1,000 came from the totals of the expanded accounting equation. The Capital figure of $6,500 came from the statement of Owner's Equity. This balance sheet reports Assets, Liabilities, and a new figure for Capital at a specific date.

Summary of Key Points

Learning Unit 1-1

1. The functions of accounting involve analyzing, recording, classifying, summarizing, reporting, and interpreting financial information.
2. A sole proprietorship is a business owned by one person. A partnership is a business owned by two or more persons. A corporation is a business owned by stockholders. All forms of business organizations are found in Internet businesses.
3. Bookkeeping is the recording part of accounting.
4. The computer is a tool to use in the accounting process.
5. Assets = Liabilities + Owner's Equity is the basic accounting equation that aids in analyzing business transactions.
6. Liabilities represent amounts owed to creditors, whereas capital represents what is invested by the owner.
7. Capital does not mean cash. Capital is the owner's current investment. The owner could have invested equipment that was purchased before the new business was started.
8. In a shift of assets, the composition of assets changes, but the total of assets does not change. For example, if a bill is paid by a customer, the firm increases Cash (an asset) but decreases Accounts Receivable (an asset), so there is no overall increase in assets; total assets remain the same. When you borrow money from a bank, you have an increase in cash (an asset) and an increase in liabilities; overall there is an increase in assets, not just a shift.

Learning Unit 1-2

1. The balance sheet is a statement written as of a particular date. It lists the assets, liabilities, and owner's equity of a business. The heading of the balance sheet answers the questions *who, what,* and *when* (as of a specific date).
2. The balance sheet is a formal statement of a financial position.

Learning Unit 1-3

1. Revenue generates an inward flow of assets. Expenses generate an outward flow of assets or a potential outward flow. Revenue and expenses are subdivisions of owner's equity. Revenue is not an asset.
2. When revenue totals more than expenses, net income is the result; when expenses total more than revenue, net loss is the result.
3. Owner's equity can be subdivided into four elements: capital, withdrawals, revenue, and expenses.
4. Withdrawals decrease owner's equity, revenue increases owner's equity, and expenses decrease owner's equity. A withdrawal is not a business expense; it is for personal use.

Learning Unit 1-4

1. The income statement is a statement written for a specific period of time that lists earned revenue and expenses incurred to produce the earned revenue. The net income or net loss will be used in the statement of owner's equity.
2. The statement of owner's equity reveals the causes of a change in capital. This statement lists any investments, net income (or net loss), and withdrawals. The ending figure for capital will be used on the balance sheet.
3. The balance sheet uses the ending balances of assets and liabilities from the accounting equation and the capital from the statement of owner's equity.
4. The income statement should be prepared first because the information on it about net income or net loss is used to prepare the statement of owner's equity, which in turn provides information about capital for the balance sheet. In this way one statement builds upon the next, beginning with the income statement.

Key Terms

Accounting A system that measures the business's activities in financial terms, provides written reports and financial statements about those activities, and communicates these reports to decision makers and others.

Accounts payable Amounts owed to creditors that result from the purchase of goods or services on account: a liability.

Accounts receivable An asset that indicates amounts owed by customers.

Assets Properties (resources) of value owned by a business (cash, supplies, equipment, land).

Balance sheet A statement, as of a particular date, that shows the amount of assets owned by a business as well as the amount of claims (liabilities and owner's equity) against these assets.

Basic accounting equation Assets = Liabilities + Owner's Equity.

Bookkeeping The recording function of the accounting process.

Capital The owner's investment of equity in the company.

Corporation A type of business organization that is owned by stockholders. Stockholders usually are not personally liable for the corporation's debts.

Creditor Someone who has a claim to assets.

Ending capital Beginning Capital + Additional Investments + Net Income − Withdrawals = Ending Capital. Or: Beginning Capital + Additional Investments − Net Loss − Withdrawals = Ending Capital.

Equities The interest or financial claim of creditors (liabilities) and owners (owner's equity) who supply the assets to a firm.

Expanded accounting equation Assets = Liabilities + Capital − Withdrawals + Revenue − Expenses.

Expense A cost incurred in running a business by consuming goods or services in producing revenue; a subdivision of owner's equity. When expenses increase, there is a decrease in owner's equity.

Generally accepted accounting principles (GAAP) The procedures and guidelines that must be followed during the accounting process.

Income statement An accounting statement that details the performance of a firm (revenue minus expenses) for a specific period of time.

Liabilities Obligations that come due in the future. Liabilities result in increasing the financial rights or claims of creditors to assets.

Manufacturer   Business that makes a product and sells it to its customers.

Merchandise company   Business that buys a product from a manufacturing company to sell to its customers.

Net income   When revenue totals more than expenses, the result is net income.

Net loss   When expenses total more than revenue, the result is net loss.

Owner's equity   Rights or financial claims to the assets of a business (in the accounting equation, assets minus liabilities).

Partnership   A form of business organization that has at least two owners. The partners usually are personally liable for the partnership's debts.

Revenue   An amount earned by performing services for customers or selling goods to customers; it can be in the form of cash and/or accounts receivable. A subdivision of owner's equity: As revenue increases, owner's equity increases.

Service company   Business that provides a service.

Shift in assets   A shift that occurs when the composition of the assets has changed, but the total of the assets remains the same.

Sole proprietorship   A type of business ownership that has one owner. The owner is personally liable for paying the business's debts.

Statement of financial position   Another name for a balance sheet.

Statement of owner's equity   A financial statement that reveals the change in capital. The ending figure for capital is then placed on the balance sheet.

Supplies   One type of asset acquired by a firm; it has a much shorter life than equipment.

Withdrawals   A subdivision of owner's equity that records money or other assets an owner withdraws from a business for personal use.

Blueprint: Financial Statements

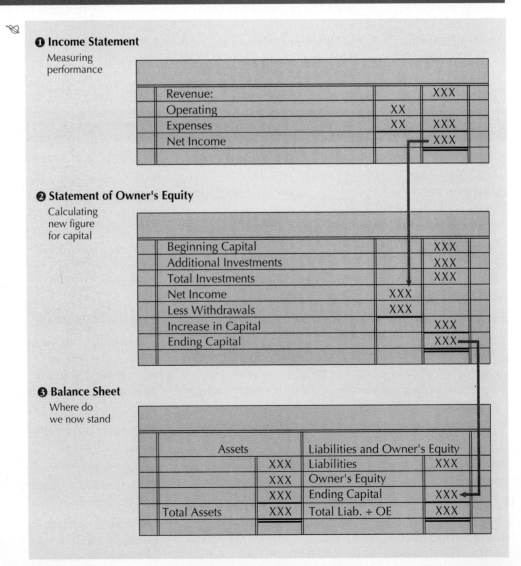

❶ Income Statement

Measuring performance

Revenue:		XXX	
Operating	XX		
Expenses	XX	XXX	
Net Income		XXX	

❷ Statement of Owner's Equity

Calculating new figure for capital

Beginning Capital		XXX
Additional Investments		XXX
Total Investments		XXX
Net Income	XXX	
Less Withdrawals	XXX	
Increase in Capital		XXX
Ending Capital		XXX

❸ Balance Sheet

Where do we now stand

Assets		Liabilities and Owner's Equity	
	XXX	Liabilities	XXX
	XXX	Owner's Equity	
	XXX	Ending Capital	XXX
Total Assets	XXX	Total Liab. + OE	XXX

Questions, Mini Exercises, Exercises, and Problems

Discussion Questions

1. What are the functions of accounting?
2. Define, compare, and contrast sole proprietorships, partnerships, and corporations.
3. How are businesses classified?
4. What is the relationship of bookkeeping to accounting?
5. List the three elements of the basic accounting equation.
6. Define capital.
7. The total of the left-hand side of the accounting equation must equal the total of the right-hand side. True or false? Please explain.
8. A balance sheet tells a company where it is going and how well it will perform. True or false? Please explain.
9. Revenue is an asset. True or false? Please explain.
10. Owner's equity is subdivided into what categories?
11. A withdrawal is a business expense. True or false? Please explain.
12. As expenses increase they cause owner's equity to increase. Defend or reject.
13. What does an income statement show?
14. The statement of owner's equity only calculates ending withdrawals. True or false? Please explain.

Mini Exercises

(The blank forms you need are on page 9 of the *Study Guide and Working Papers*.)

Classifying Accounts

1. Classify each of the following items as an Asset (A), Liability (L), or Part of Owner's Equity (OE).

    a. Panasonic DVD   _____
    b. Accounts Payable   _____
    c. B. Aster, Capital   _____
    d. Office Supplies   _____
    e. Cash   _____
    f. Sony Digital Camera   _____

The Accounting Equation

2. Complete the following statements.

    a. A _____ _____ _____ results when the total of the assets remains the same but the makeup of the assets has changed.
    b. Assets − _____ = Owner's Equity.
    c. Capital does not mean _____.

Shift Versus Increase in Assets

3. Identify which transaction results in a shift in assets (S) and which transaction causes an increase in assets (I).

    a. Office Max bought computer equipment for cash.
    b. The Gap bought office equipment on account.

The Balance Sheet

4. From the following, calculate what would be the total of assets on the balance sheet.

H. Sung, Capital	$11,000
Word Processing Equipment	1,000
Accounts Payable	2,000
Cash	12,000

The Accounting Equation Expanded

5. From the following, which are subdivisions of Owner's Equity?

a. Land _____   e. Accounts Payable _____
b. M. Kaminsky, Capital _____   f. Rent Expense _____
c. Accounts Receivable _____   g. Office Equipment _____
d. M. Kaminsky, Withdrawals _____   h. Hair Salon Fees Earned _____

Identifying Assets

6. Identify which of the following are *not* assets.

a. Fax Machines _____   c. Legal Fees Earned _____
b. Accounts Payable _____   d. Accounts Receivable _____

The Accounting Equation Expanded

7. Which of the following statements are false?

a. _____ Revenue is an asset.
b. _____ Revenue is a subdivision of Owner's Equity.
c. _____ Revenue provides an inward flow of Cash and/or Accounts Receivable.
d. _____ Withdrawals are part of Total Assets.

Preparing Financial Statements

8. Indicate whether the following items would appear on the income statement (IS), statement of owner's equity (OE), or balance sheet (BS).

a. _____ B. Clo, Withdrawals   e. _____ Commission Fees Earned
b. _____ Office Supplies   f. _____ Salaries Expense
c. _____ Accounts Payable   g. _____ B. Clo, Capital (Beg.)
d. _____ Computer Equipment   h. _____ Accounts Receivable

Preparing Financial Statements

9. Indicate next to each statement whether it refers to the income statement (IS), statement of owner's equity (OE), or balance sheet (BS).

a. _____ Calculate new figure for Capital
b. _____ Prepared as of a particular date
c. _____ Statement that is prepared first
d. _____ Statement listing Revenues and Expenses

Exercises

(The forms you need are on pages 10–12 of the *Study Guide and Working Papers*.)

1-1. Complete the following table:

The accounting equation.

	Assets	=	Liabilities	+	Owner's Equity
a.	10,000	=	?	+	$2,000
b.	?	=	$6,000	+	$8,000
c.	$10,000	=	$4,000	+	?

1-2. Record the following transactions in the basic accounting equation. Treat each one separately.

Recoding transactions into the expanded accounting equation.

$$Assets = Liabilities + Owner's\ Equity$$

a. Ron invests $90,000 in company.
b. Bought equipment for cash, $600.
c. Bought equipment on account, $900.

Preparing a balance sheet.

1-3. From the following, prepare a balance sheet for Avon's Cleaners at the end of November 200X: Cash, $40,000; Cleaning Equipment, $8,000; Accounts Payable, $19,000; A. Avon, Capital.

1-4. Record the following transactions into the expanded accounting equation. The running balance may be omitted for simplicity.

Recording transactions into the accounting equation.

Assets	= Liabilities +			Owner's Equity		
Cash + Accounts + Computer	= Accounts +	B. Wong,	− B. Wong,		+ Revenues	− Expenses
Receivable Equipment	Payable	Capital	Withdrawals			

a. Bill invested $60,000 in a computer company.
b. Bought computer equipment on account, $7,000.
c. Bill paid personal telephone bill from company checkbook, $200.
d. Received cash for services rendered, $14,000.
e. Billed customers for services rendered for month, $30,000.
f. Paid current rent expense, $4,000.
g. Paid supplies expense, $1,500.

1-5. From the following account balances, prepare in proper form for June (a) an income statement, (b) a statement of owner's equity, and (c) a balance sheet for French Realty.

Preparing the income statement, statement of owner's equity, and balance sheet.

Cash	$3,310	S. French, Withdrawals	$ 40
Accounts Receivable	1,490	Professional Fees	2,900
Office Equipment	6,700	Salaries Expense	500
Accounts Payable	2,000	Utilities Expense	360
S. French, Capital, June 1, 200X	8,000	Rent Expense	500

Group A Problems

(The forms you need are on pages 13–19 of the *Study Guide and Working Papers*.)

The accounting equation.

1A-1. Lee Stone decided to open Lee's Nail Care Center. Lee completed the following transactions:

a. Invested $18,000 cash from her personal bank account into the business.
b. Bought equipment for cash, $4,000.
c. Bought additional equipment on account, $1,000.
d. Paid $400 cash to partially reduce what was owed from transaction C.

Check Figure:
Total Assets $18,600

Based on this information, record these transactions into the basic accounting equation.

Preparing a balance sheet.

1A-2. Joyce Hill is the accountant for Green's Advertising Service. From the following information, her task is to construct a balance sheet as of September 30, 200X, in proper form. Could you help her?

Check Figure:
Total Assets $59,000

Building	$35,000	Cash	$10,000
Accounts Payable	30,000	Equipment	14,000
Green, Capital	29,000		

Recording transactions in the expanded accounting equation.

1A-3. At the end of November, Rick Fox decided to open his own typing service. Analyze the following transactions he completed by recording their effects into the expanded accounting equation.

    a. Invested $10,000 in his typing service.
    b. Bought new office equipment on account, $4,000.
    c. Received cash for typing services rendered, $500.
    d. Performed typing services on account, $2,100.
    e. Paid secretary's salary, $350.
    f. Paid office supplies expense for the month, $210.
    g. Rent expenses for office due but unpaid, $900.
    h. Withdrew cash for personal use, $400.

Check Figure:
Total Assets $15,640

1A-4. Jane West, owner of West Stenciling Service, has requested that you prepare from the following balances (a) an income statement for June 200X, (b) a statement of owner's equity for June, and (c) a balance sheet as of June 30, 200X.

Preparing the income statement, statement of owner's equity, and balance sheet.

Cash	$2,300	Stenciling Fees	$3,000
Accounts Receivable	400	Advertising Expense	110
Equipment	685	Repair Expense	25
Accounts Payable	310	Travel Expense	250
J. West, Capital, June 1, 200X	1,200	Supplies Expense	190
J. West, Withdrawals	300	Rent Expense	250

Check Figure:
Total Assets $3,385

1A-5. John Tobey, a retired army officer, opened Tobey's Catering Service. As his accountant, analyze the transactions listed next and present them in proper form.

    a. The analysis of the transactions by using the expanded accounting equation.
    b. A balance sheet showing the position of the firm before opening for business on October 31, 200X.
    c. An income statement for the month of November.
    d. A statement of owner's equity for November.
    e. A balance sheet as of November 30, 200X.

Comprehensive problem.

200X
Oct.   25   John Tobey invested $20,000 in the catering business from his personal savings account.
     27   Bought equipment for cash from Munroe Co., $700
     28   Bought additional equipment on account from Ryan Co., $1,000.
     29   Paid $600 to Ryan Co. as partial payment of the October 28 transaction.

(You should now prepare your balance sheet as of October 31, 200X)

Check Figure:
Total Assets,
Nov. 30 $24,060

Nov.   1   Catered a graduation and immediately collected cash, $2,400.
     5   Paid salaries of employees, $690.
     8   Prepared desserts for customers on account, $300.
     10   Received $100 cash as partial payment of November 8 transaction.
     15   Paid telephone bill, $60.
     17   Paid his home electric bill from the company's checkbook, $90.
     20   Catered a wedding and received cash, $1,800.
     25   Bought additional equipment on account, $400.
     28   Rent expense due but unpaid, $600.
     30   Paid supplies expense, $400.

Group B Problems

(The forms you need are on pages 13–19 of the *Study Guide and Working Papers*.)

The accounting equation.

    1B-1. Lee Stone began a new business called Lee's Nail Care Center. The following transactions resulted:

        a. Lee invested $21,000 cash from her personal bank account into the Nail Care Center.

b. Bought equipment on account, $1,800.
c. Paid $800 cash to partially reduce what was owed from transaction B.
d. Purchased additional equipment for cash, $3,000.

Record these transactions into the basic accounting equation.

Check Figure:
Total Assets $22,000

1B-2. Joyce Hill, accountant, has asked you to prepare a balance sheet as of September 30, 200X, for Green's Advertising Service. Could you assist Joyce?

Preparing a balance sheet.

R. Green, Capital	$19,000
Accounts Payable	70,000
Equipment	41,000
Building	16,000
Cash	32,000

Check Figure:
Total Assets $89,000

1B-3. Rick Fox decided to open his own typing service company at the end of November. Analyze the following transactions by recording their effects on the expanded accounting equation:

Recording transactions in the expanded accounting equation.

a. Rick invested $9,000 in the typing service.
b. Purchased new office equipment on account, $3,000.
c. Received cash for typing services rendered, $1,290.
d. Paid secretary's salary, $310.
e. Billed customers for typing services rendered, $2,690.
f. Paid rent expense for the month, $500.
g. Rick withdrew cash for personal use, $350.
h. Advertising expense due but unpaid, $100.

Check Figure:
Total Assets $14,820

1B-4. Jane West, owner of West Stenciling Service, has requested that you prepare from the following balances (a) an income statement for June 200X, (b) a statement of owner's equity for June, and (c) a balance sheet as of June 30, 200X.

Preparing an income statement, statement of owner's equity, and balance sheet.

Cash	$2,043	Stenciling Fees	$1,098
Accounts Receivable	1,140	Advertising Expense	135
Equipment	540	Repair Expense	45
Accounts Payable	45	Travel Expense	90
J. West, Capital, June 1, 200X	3,720	Supplies Expense	270
J. West, Withdrawals	360	Rent Expense	240

Check Figure:
Total Assets $3,723

1B-5. John Tobey, a retired army officer, opened Tobey's Catering Service. As his accountant, analyze the transactions and present the following information in proper form:

a. The analysis of the transactions by using the expanded accounting equation.
b. A balance sheet showing the financial position of the firm before opening on November 1, 200X.
c. An income statement for the month of November.
d. A statement of owner's equity for November.
e. A balance sheet as of November 30, 200X.

Comprehensive problem.

200X
Oct. 25 John Tobey invested $17,500 in the catering business.
27 Bought equipment on account from Munroe Co., $900.
28 Bought equipment for cash from Ryan Co., $1,500.
29 Paid $300 to Munroe Co. as partial payment of the October 27 transaction.

Nov. 1 Catered a business luncheon and immediately collected cash, $2,000.
5 Paid salaries of employees, $350.
8 Provided catering services to Northwest Community College on account, $4,500.

Check Figure:
Total Assets,
Nov. 30 $25,005

10 Received from Northwest Community College $1,000 cash as partial payment of November 8 transaction.

15 Paid telephone bill, $95.

17 John paid his home mortgage from the company's checkbook, $650.

20 Provided catering services and received cash, $1,800.

25 Bought additional equipment on account, $300.

28 Rent expense due but unpaid, $750.

30 Paid supplies expense, $600.

Real-World Applications

1R-1. You have just been hired to prepare, if possible, an income statement for the year ended December 31, 200X, for Roger's Window Washing Company. The problem is that Roger Smith kept only the following records (on the back of a piece of cardboard):

Figure 1-10

Income Statement
Net Income
$5,601

Dollars in:
C My investment $ 1,200
R Window cleaning   11,376
A/P Loan from brother-in-law   4,000

Dollars out:
E Salaries $5,080
W Withdrawals   6,200
E Supplies expense   1,400

What I owe or they owe me
E A. People who work for me but I still owe salaries to $1,800
E B. Owe bank interest of $300
R C. Work done but clients still owe me $2,900
E D. Advertising bill due but not paid $95

Assume that Roger's Window Washing Company records all revenues when earned and all expenses when incurred.

You feel that it is part of your job to tell Roger how to organize his records better. What would you tell him?

monday

1R-2. While Jon Lune was on a business trip, he asked Abby Slowe, the bookkeeper for Lune Co., to try to complete a balance sheet for the year ended December 31, 200X. Abby, who had been on the job only two months, submitted the following:

Figure 1-11

Fix The Balance Sheet
Cash
Build
Land
A/R
Desk

LUNE CO.					
FOR THE YEAR ENDED DECEMBER 31, 200X					
Building	$44 6 0 0 00	Accounts Payable	$127 6 0 4 00		
Land	72 9 3 5 00	Accounts Receivable	104 3 3 7 00		
Notes Payable	75 3 2 8 00	Auto	14 2 6 8 00		
Cash	10 0 1 6 00	Desks	6 8 2 5 00		
J. Lune, Capital	?	Total Equity	$250 0 3 4 00		

1. Could you help Abby fix as well as complete the balance sheet?

2. What written recommendations would you make about the bookkeeper? Should she be retained?

3. Suppose that (a) Jon Lune invested an additional $20,000 in cash as well as additional desks with a value of $8,000 and (b) Lune Co. bought an auto for $6,000 that was originally marked $8,000, paying $2,000 down and issuing a note for the balance. Could you prepare an updated balance sheet?

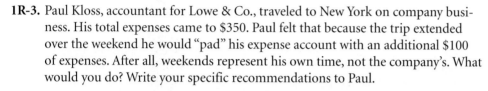

YOU make the call

Critical Thinking/Ethical Case

(The forms you need are on page 8 of the *Study Guide and Working Papers*.)

1R-3. Paul Kloss, accountant for Lowe & Co., traveled to New York on company business. His total expenses came to $350. Paul felt that because the trip extended over the weekend he would "pad" his expense account with an additional $100 of expenses. After all, weekends represent his own time, not the company's. What would you do? Write your specific recommendations to Paul.

Internet Exercises: Microstrategy: Best in Business Intelligence

EX-1. [**www.microstrategy.com**]   In the financial statements for Microstrategy, amounts received from customers for service policies are reported in two dimensions. One dimension is actual revenue, or amounts earned from providing a service or a product to its customers. The other dimension is that of receiving cash, which represents services to be provided in future accounting periods. Suppose that, in 2003, Microstrategy received $200,000 from customers. That $200,000 represented $125,000 that was amounts for products sold or services actually rendered. The remaining $75,000 represents services to be provided later.

1. What is the company's addition to revenue if the full amount is recorded all in one year?

2. How is the revenue number different if the amount for future services is recorded as a liability?

3. What is the justification of reporting these amounts in two separate segments?

4. Explain how reporting the revenue all at one time could mislead the reader of the company's financial statements.

EX-2. [**www.microstrategy.com**]   In this chapter you have been introduced to the basic concepts of assets and liabilities. Go to the Microstrategy Web site and read about the company and its operations. After reading about the company, consider these questions:

1. What are three assets you would expect it to have, other than cash?

2. What are three liabilities you would expect it to have, other than accounts payable?

3. How do liabilities represent equities, or claims?

4. In the accounting equation, why do you think the liabilities (claims of creditors) are listed before the stockholders' equity (claims of owners)?

Continuing Problem

Eldorado Computer Center

The following problem continues from one chapter to the next, carrying the balances of each month forward. Each chapter focuses on the learning experience of the chapter and adds additional information as the business grows. Forms are on page 23 of the *Study Guide and Working Papers*.

Assignment

1. Set up an expanded accounting equation spreadsheet using the following accounts:

Assets	Liabilities	Owner's Equity
Cash	Accounts Payable	Freedman, Capital
Supplies		Freedman, Withdrawal
Computer Shop		Service Revenue
Equipment		Expenses (notate type)
Office Equipment		

2. Analyze and record each transaction in the expanded accounting equation.
3. Prepare the financial statements ending July 31 for Eldorado Computer Center.

On July 1, 200X, Tony Freedman decided to begin his own computer service business. He named the business the Eldorado Computer Center. During the first month Tony conducted the following business transactions:

   a. Invested $4,500 of his savings into the business.
   b. Paid $1,200 (check #8095) for the computer from Multi Systems, Inc.
   c. Paid $600 (check # 8096) for office equipment from Office Furniture, Inc.
   d. Set up a new account with Office Depot and purchased $250 in office supplies on credit.
   e. Paid July rent, $400 (check # 8097).
   f. Repaired a system for a customer; collected $250.
   g. Collected $200 for system upgrade labor charge from a customer.
   h. Electric bill due but unpaid, $85.
   i. Collected $1,200 for services performed on Taylor Golf computers.
   j. Withdrew $100 (check # 8098) to take his wife, Carol, out in celebration of opening the new business.

SUBWAY Case

A FRESH START

"Hey, Stan the man!" a loud voice boomed. "I never thought I'd see you making sandwiches!" Stan Hernandez stopped layering lettuce in a foot-long submarine sandwich and grinned at his old college buddy, Ron.

"Neither did I. But then again," said Stan, "I never thought I'd own a profitable business either."

That night, catching up on their lives over dinner, Stan told Ron how he became the proud owner of a Subway sandwich restaurant.

"After working like crazy at Xellent Media for five years and *finally* making it to marketing manager, then wham . . . I got laid off," said Stan. "That very day I was having my lunch at the local Subway as usual, when. . . ."

"Hmmm, wait a minute! I did notice you've lost quite a bit of weight," Ron interrupted and began to hum the bars of Subway's latest ad featuring Clay Henry, yet another hefty male who lost weight on a diet of Subway sandwiches.

"Right!" Stan quipped, "Not only was I laid off, but I was 'downsizing!' *Anyway*, I was eating a Dijon horseradish melt when I opened up an *Entrepreneur* magazine someone had left on the table—right to the headline 'Subway Named #1 Franchise in All Categories for 11th Time in 15 Years.'"

Well, to make a foot-long submarine sandwich story short, Stan realized his long-time dream of being his own boss by owning a business with a proven product and highly successful business model. When you look at Stan's restaurant, you are really seeing two businesses. While Stan is the sole proprietor of his business, he operates under an agreement with Subway of Milford, Connecticut. Subway supplies the business know-how and support (like training at Subway University, national advertising, and gourmet bread recipes). Stan supplies capital (his $12,500 investment) and his food preparation, management, and elbow grease. Subway and Stan operate interdependent businesses, and both rely on accounting information for their success.

Subway, in business since 1965, has grown dramatically over the years and now has over 18,000 locations in 73 countries. It has even surpassed McDonald's in the number of locations in the United States and Canada. To manage this enormous service business requires very careful control of each of its stores. At a Subway regional office, Mariah Washington, a field consultant for Stan's territory, monitors Stan's restaurant closely. In addition to making monthly visits to check whether Stan is complying with Subway's model in everything from décor to uniforms to food quality and safety, she also looks closely at Stan's weekly sales and inventory reports. When Stan's sales go up, Subway's do too, because each Subway franchisee, like Stan, pays Subway, the franchiser, a percentage of sales in the form of royalties.

Why does headquarters require accounting reports? Accounting reports give the information both Stan and the company need to make business decisions in a number of vital areas. For example:

- Before Stan could buy his Subway restaurant, the company needed to know how much cash Stan had and his assets and liabilities (such as credit card debt). Stan prepared a personal balance sheet to give them this information.
- Stan must have the right amount of supplies on hand. If he has too few, he can't make the sandwiches. If he has too many for the amount he expects to sell, items like sandwich meats and bread dough may spoil. The inventory report tells Mariah what supplies are on hand. In combination with the sales report, it also alerts Mariah to potential red flags: If Stan is reporting that he is using far too much bread dough for the amount of sandwiches he is selling, then there is a problem.
- Although Subway does not require its restaurant owners to report operating costs and profit information, Subway gives them the option and most franchisees take it. Information on profitability helps Mariah and Stan make decisions like whether and when to remodel or buy new equipment.

So that its restaurant owners can make business decisions in a timely manner, Subway requires them to submit the weekly sales and inventory report to headquarters electronically every Thursday by 2:00 P.M. Stan has his latest report in mind as he makes a move to pay the bill for his dinner with Ron. "We had a great week. Let me get this," he says. "Thanks Stan the Man. I'm going to keep in touch because I may just be ready for a business opportunity of my own!"

Discussion Questions

1. What makes Stan a sole proprietor?
2. Why are Stan and Subway interdependent businesses?
3. Why did Stan have to share his personal balance sheet with Subway? Do you think most interdependent businesses do this?
4. What does Subway learn from Stan's weekly sales and inventory reports?

Debits and Credits

Analyzing and Recording Business Transactions

Now that you are enrolled in college, your parents decided they wanted a home that was a little smaller, with less maintenance. They purchased a patio home in a new subdivision a few months ago.

Your parents went to a law office when they sold their home. An attorney who specializes in real estate law prepared the paperwork for your parents and conducted what is called a real estate closing. You remember seeing a thick legal-size file folder your parents brought home after the closing. The folder held numerous sheets of paper with estimate information, bank forms, a house appraisal, and a document called a settlement statement. The settlement statement struck you as pparticularly important because it listed all of the amounts that were part of the sale. The form had two long columns—one column listed amounts for the seller, and the other column listed amounts for the buyer. There were various numbers in each of the two columns, but you saw that the total amount in both columns was the same. In other words, the amounts listed in this document were in balance. The attorney used accounting in completing the sale of your parents' home.

It is important that the settlement statement achieve balance. In accounting, a key goal is keeping transactions in balance. In Chapter 1 we learned how to record business transactions using the accounting equation. In this chapter we will learn how to use the accounting equation to keep business transactions in balance. We will discuss the five steps in analyzing business transactions and a method accountants use to prove that recorded business transactions are in balance.

Your growing knowledge of accounting will make all the difference in your understanding of the world of business.

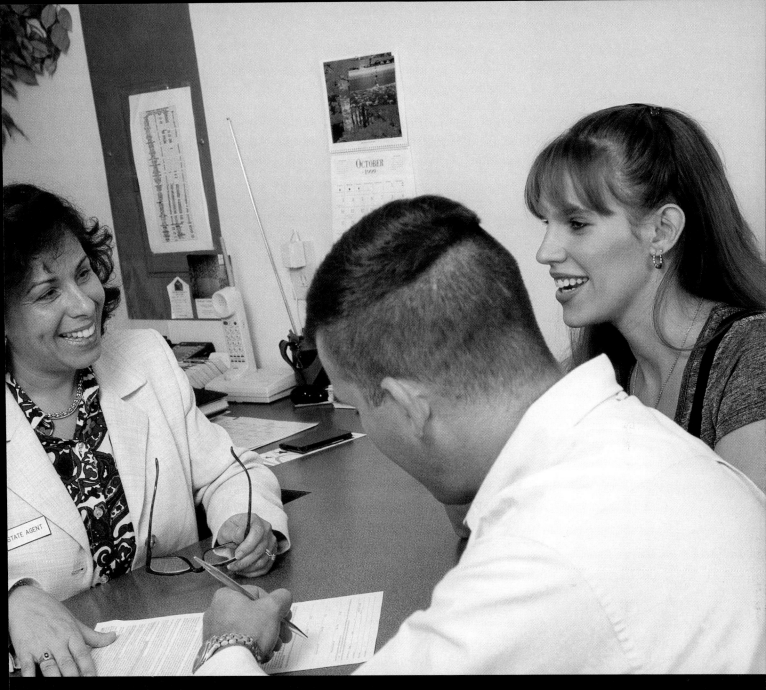

Learning Objectives

In Chapter 1 we used the expanded accounting equation to document the financial transactions performed by Cathy Hall's law firm. Remember how long it was: The cash column had a long list of pluses and minuses, and there was no quick system of recording and summarizing the increases and decreases of cash or other items. Can you imagine the problem Subway or Holiday Inn would have if they used the expanded accounting equation to track the thousands of business transactions they do each day?

Learning Unit 2-1   The T Account

Let's look at the problem a little more closely. Each business transaction is recorded in the accounting equation under a specific **account.** There are different accounts for each of the subdivisions of the accounting equation: asset accounts, liabilities accounts, expense accounts, revenue accounts, and so on. What is needed is a way to record the increases and decreases in specific account *categories* and yet keep them together in one place. The answer is the **standard account** form (see Fig. 2.1). A standard account is a formal account that includes columns for date, explanation, posting reference, debit, and credit. Each account has a separate form, and all transactions affecting that account are recorded on the form. All the business's account forms (which often are referred to as *ledger accounts*) are then placed in a **ledger.** Each page of the ledger contains one account. The ledger may be in the form of a bound or a loose-leaf book. If computers are used, the ledger may be part of a computer printout. For simplicity's sake, we use the **T account** form. This form got its name because it looks like the letter T. Generally, T accounts are used for demonstration purposes. Each T account contains three basic parts:

Title of Account	
Left side	**Right side**

All T accounts have this structure.

In accounting, the left side of any T account is called the **debit** side.

Left side	
Dr. (debit)	

Just as the word *left* has many meanings, the word *debit* for now in accounting means a position, the left side of an account. Do not think of it as good (+) or bad (−).

Debit defined:
1. The left side of any T account.
2. A number entered on the left side of any account is said to be debited to an account.

Figure 2-1 The Standard Account Form Is the Source of the T Account's Shape

Amounts entered on the left side of any account are said to be *debited* to an account. The abbreviation for debit, Dr., is from the Latin *debere*.

The right side of any T account is called the credit side.

	Right side
	Cr. (credit)

Amounts entered on the right side of an account are said to be *credited* to an account. The abbreviation for credit, Cr., is from the Latin *credere*.

At this point do not associate the definition of debit and credit with the words *increase* or *decrease*. Think of debit or credit as only indicating a *position* (left or right side) of a T account.

> **Credit defined:**
> 1. The right side of any T account.
> 2. A number entered on the right side of any account is said to be credited to an account.

BALANCING AN ACCOUNT

No matter which individual account is being balanced, the procedure used to balance it is the same.

	Dr.	**Cr.**
Entries →	4,000	300
	500	400
Footings →	4,500	700
Balance 3,800		

In the "real" world, the T account would also include the date of the transaction. The date would appear to the left of the entry:

		Dr.	**Cr.**
4/2		4,000	300
4/20		500	400
		4,500	700
Bal	3,800		

Note that on the debit (left) side the numbers add up to $4,500. On the credit (right) side the numbers add up to $700. The $4,500 and the $700 written in small type are called **footings.** Footing help in calculating the new (or ending) balance. The ending balance ($3,800) is placed on the debit or left side, because the balance of the debit side is greater than that of the credit side.

Remember that the ending balance does not tell us anything about increase or decrease. It only tells us that we have an ending balance of $3,800 on the debit side.

> Footings aid in balancing an account. The ending balance is the difference between the footings.

> If the balance is greater on the credit side, that is the side the ending balance would be on.

Learning Unit 2-1 Review

AT THIS POINT you should be able to

- Define ledger. (p. 38)
- State the purpose of a T account. (p. 38)
- Identify the three parts of a T account. (p. 38)
- Define debit. (p. 38)
- Define credit. (p. 39)
- Explain footings and calculate the balance of an account. (p. 39)

SELF-REVIEW QUIZ 2-1

(The blank forms you need are on page 25 of the *Study Guide and Working Papers.* See your DVD for worked-out solutions.)

Respond True or False to the following:

Quiz Tip:
Dr. + Dr. → Add to get
    Dr. balance
Cr. + Cr. → Add to get
    Cr. balance
Dr. − Cr. → Subtract to get
    balance for the
    larger side.

1.

Dr.	Cr.
3,000	200
200	600

The balance of the account is $2,400 Cr.

2. A credit always means increase.

3. A debit is the left side of any account.

4. A ledger can be prepared manually or by computer.

5. Footings replace the need for debits and credits.

SOLUTIONS TO SELF-REVIEW QUIZ 2-1

1. False   **2.** False   **3.** True   **4.** True   **5.** False

---

Learning Unit 2-2   Recording Business Transactions: Debits and Credits

Can you get a queen in checkers? In a baseball game does a runner rounding first base skip second base and run over the pitcher's mound to get to third? No; most of us don't do such things because we follow the rules of the game. Usually we learn the rules first and reflect on the reasons for them afterward. The same is true in accounting.

Instead of first trying to understand all the rules of debit and credit and how they were developed in accounting, it is easier to learn the rules by "playing the game."

Accounting in the Reel World

How Much Is That Dog Treat In the Window?

When their business is "going to the dogs" Dan Dye and Mark Beckloff have reason to cheer. The two business partners started Three Dog Bakery in 1989 to sell fresh, all-natural dog treats with names like "snickerpoodles" and "rollovers."

The idea of a bakery for dogs might seem far-fetched, yet people continue to spend ever more money on their pets. Now the partners have 30 stores in the United States, Canada, and Japan, national retail accounts with chains like PetsMart and even a "dogalogue" for direct-to-consumer sales.

As you watch the Three Dog Bakery on-location video on your DVD, pay attention to the relationship between what this company produces and how they sell their goods and the accounting process. After you have watched this brief segment, answer the questions below.

1. Why does Three Dog Bakery's VP of finance need to analyze accounting information to make business decisions?

2. What are at least three types of business decisions that the owners need to make?

3. On which item is the company losing money and why? What would you suggest to make this item more profitable?

T ACCOUNT ENTRIES FOR ACCOUNTING IN THE ACCOUNTING EQUATION

Have patience. Learning the rules of debit and credit is like learning to play any game: the more you play, the easier it becomes. Table 2-1 shows the rules for the side on which you enter an increase or a decrease for each of the separate accounts in the accounting equation. For example, an increase is entered on the debit side in the asset account but on the credit side for a liability account.

It might be easier to visualize these rules of debit and credit if we look at them in the T account form, using + to show increase and − to show decrease.

Assets	=	Liabilities	+			Owner's Equity					
				Capital	− Withdrawals	+ Revenue	− Expenses				
Dr. | Cr.		Dr. | Cr.	+	Dr. | Cr.	Dr. | Cr.	Dr. | Cr.	Dr. | Cr.				
+ | −		− | +		− | +	+ | −	− | +	+ | −				

Rules for Assets Work in the Opposite Direction to Those for Liabilities When you look at the equation you can see that the rules for assets work in the opposite direction to those for liabilities. That is, for assets the increases appear on the debit side and the decreases are shown on the credit side; the opposite is true for liabilities. As for the owner's equity, the rules for withdrawals and expenses, which *decrease* owner's equity, work in the opposite direction to the rules for capital and revenue, which *increase* owner's equity.

Assets	+ Withdrawals	+ Expenses	= Liabilities	+ Capital	+ Revenue
Dr. | Cr.	Dr. | Cr.	Dr. | Cr.	Dr. | Cr.	Dr. | Cr.	Dr. | Cr.
+ | −	+ | −	+ | −	− | +	− | +	− | +

This setup may help you visualize how the rules for withdrawals and expenses are just the opposite of those for capital and revenue.

A **normal balance of an account** is the side that increases by the rules of debit and credit. For example, the balance of cash is a debit balance, because an asset is increased by a debit. We discuss normal balances further in Chapter 3.

Balancing the Equation It is important to remember that any amount(s) entered on the debit side of a T account or accounts also must be on the credit side of another T account or accounts. This ensures that the total amount added to the debit side will equal the total amount added to the credit side, thereby keeping the accounting equation in balance.

Chart of Accounts Our job is to analyze Cathy Hall's business transactions — the transactions we looked at in Chapter 1 — using a system of accounts guided by the

> Normal Balance
>
> | Dr. | Cr. |
> |-----|-----|
> | Assets | Liabilities |
> | Expenses | Capital |
> | Withdrawals | Revenue |

TABLE 2-1 Rules of Debit and Credit

Account Category	Increase (Normal Balance)	Decrease
Assets	Debit	Credit
Liabilities	Credit	Debit
Owner's Equity		
Capital	Credit	Debit
Withdrawals	Debit	Credit
Revenue	Credit	Debit
Expenses	Debit	Credit

> Be sure to follow the rules of debits and credits when recording accounts. They were designed to keep the accounting equation in balance.

TABLE 2-2 Chart of Accounts for Cathy Hall, Attorney-at-Law

Balance Sheet Accounts	
Assets	**Liabilities**
111 Cash	211 Accounts Payable
112 Accounts Receivable	**Owner's Equity**
121 Office Equipment	311 Cathy Hall, Capital
	312 Cathy Hall, Withdrawals

Income Statement Accounts	
Revenue	**Expenses**
411 Legal Fees	511 Salaries Expense
	512 Rent Expense
	513 Advertising Expense

The chart of accounts aids in locating and identifying accounts quickly.

Large companies may have up to four digits assigned to each title.

rules of debits and credits that will summarize increases and decreases of individual accounts in the ledger. The goal is to prepare an income statement, statement of owner's equity, and balance sheet for Cathy Hall. Sound familiar? If this system works, the rules of debits and credits and the use of accounts will give us the same answers as in Chapter 1, but with greater ease.

Cathy's accountant developed what is called a **chart of accounts.** The chart of accounts is a numbered list of all of the business's accounts. It allows accounts to be located quickly. In Cathy's business, for example, 100s are assets, 200s are liabilities, and so on. As you see in Table 2-2, each separate asset and liability has its own number. Note that the chart may be expanded as the business grows.

THE TRANSACTION ANALYSIS: FIVE STEPS

We will analyze the transactions in Cathy Hall's law firm using a teaching device called a *transaction analysis chart* to record these five steps. (Keep in mind that the transaction analysis chart is not a part of any formal accounting system.) There are five steps to analyzing each business transaction:

Steps to analyze and record transactions. Steps 1 and 2 will come from the chart of accounts.

Step 1:   Determine which accounts are affected. Example: Cash, Accounts Payable, Rent Expense. A transaction always affects at least two accounts.

Step 2:   Determine which categories the accounts belong to: assets, liabilities, capital, withdrawals, revenue, or expenses. Example: Cash is an asset.

Normal Bal

Step 3:   Determine whether the accounts increase or decrease. Example: If you receive cash, that account is increasing.

Step 4:   What do the rules of debits and credits say (Table 2-1)?

Step 5:   What does the T account look like? Place amounts into accounts either on the left or right side depending on the rules in Table 2-1.

Remember that the rules of debit and credit only tell us on which side to place information. Whether the debit or credit represents increases or decreases depends on the account category: assets, liabilities, capital, and so on. Think of a business transaction as an exchange: You get something and you give or part with something.

This is how the five-step analysis looks in chart form:

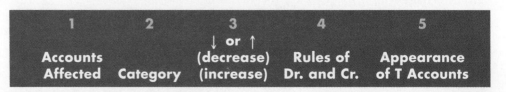

1	2	3	4	5
		↓ or ↑		
		(decrease)	Rules of	Appearance
Accounts		(increase)	Dr. and Cr.	of T Accounts
Affected	Category			

Let us emphasize a major point: *Do not try to debit or credit an account until you have gone through the first three steps of the transaction analysis.*

APPLYING THE TRANSACTION ANALYSIS TO CATHY HALL'S LAW PRACTICE

Transaction A   August 28: Cathy Hall invests $7,000 cash and $800 of office equipment in the business.

1 Accounts Affected	2 Category	3 ↓ ↑	4 Rules of Dr. and Cr.	5 Appearance of T Accounts
Cash	Asset	↑	Dr.	Cash 111 (A) 7,000 |
Office Equipment	Asset	↑	Dr.	Office Equipment 121 (A) 800 |
Cathy Hall, Capital	Capital	↑	Cr.	Cathy Hall, Capital 311 | 7,800 (A)

> Note in column 3 of the chart that it doesn't matter if both arrows go up, as long as the sum of the debits equals the sum of the credits in the T accounts in column 5.

Note again that every transaction affects at least two T accounts and that the total amount added to the debit side(s) must equal the total amount added to the credit side(s) of the T accounts of each transaction.

Analysis of Transaction A

Step 1:   Which accounts are affected? The law firm receives its cash and office equipment, so three accounts are involved: Cash, Office Equipment, and Cathy Hall, Capital. These account titles come from the chart of accounts.

Step 2:   Which categories do these accounts belong to? Cash and Office Equipment are assets. Cathy Hall, Capital, is capital.

Step 3:   Are the accounts increasing or decreasing? The Cash and Office Equipment, both assets, are increasing in the business. The rights or claims of Cathy Hall, Capital, are also increasing, because she invested money and office equipment in the business.

Step 4:   What do the rules say? According to the rules of debit and credit, an increase in assets (Cash and Office Equipment) is a debit. An increase in Capital is a credit. Note that the total dollar amount of debits will equal the total dollar amount of credits when the T accounts are updated in column 5.

Step 5:   What does the T account look like? The amount for Cash and Office Equipment is entered on the debit side. The amount for Cathy Hall, Capital, goes on the credit side.

A transaction that involves more than one credit or more than one debit is called a **compound entry.** This first transaction of Cathy Hall's law firm is a compound entry; it involves a debit of $7,000 to Cash and a debit of $800 to Office Equipment (as well as a credit of $7,800 to Cathy Hall, Capital).

> **Double-entry bookkeeping system:** The total of all debits is equal to the total of all credits.

There is a name for this double-entry analysis of transactions, where two or more accounts are affected and the total of debits and credits is equal. It is called **double-entry bookkeeping.** This double-entry system helps in checking the recording of business transactions.

As we continue, the explanations will be brief, but do not forget to apply the five steps in analyzing and recording each business transaction.

Transaction B   Aug. 29: Law practice bought office equipment for cash, $900.

1 Accounts Affected	2 Category	3 ↓ ↑	4 Rules of Dr. and Cr.	5 T Account Update
Office Equipment	Asset	↑	Dr.	Office Equipment 121 (A) 800 (B) 900
Cash	Asset	↓	Cr.	Cash 111 (A) 7,000 | 900 (B)

Analysis of Transaction B

Step 1: The law firm paid cash for the office equipment it received. The accounts involved in the transaction are Cash and Office Equipment.

Step 2: The accounts belong to these categories: Office Equipment is an asset; Cash is an asset.

Step 3: The asset Office Equipment is increasing. The asset Cash is decreasing; it is being reduced to buy the office equipment.

Step 4: An increase in the asset Office Equipment is a debit; a decrease in the asset Cash is a credit.

Step 5: When the amounts are placed in the T accounts, the amount for Office Equipment goes on the debit side and the amount for Cash on the credit side.

Transaction C   Aug. 30: Bought more office equipment on account, $400.

1 Accounts Affected	2 Category	3 ↓ ↑	4 Rules of Dr. and Cr.	5 T Account Update
Office Equipment	Asset	↑	Dr.	Office Equipment 121 (A) 800 (B) 900 (C) 400
Accounts Payable	Liability	↑	Cr.	Accounts Payable 211 | 400 (C)

Analysis of Transaction C

Step 1: The law firm receives office equipment by promising to pay in the future. An obligation or liability, Accounts Payable, is created.

Step 2: Office Equipment is an asset. Accounts Payable is a liability.

Step 3: The asset Office Equipment is increasing; the liability Accounts Payable is increasing because the law firm is increasing what it owes.

Step 4: An increase in the asset Office Equipment is a debit. An increase in the liability Accounts Payable is a credit.

Step 5: Enter the amount for Office Equipment on the debit side of the T account. The amount for the Accounts Payable goes on the credit side.

Transaction D   Sept. 1–30: Provided legal services for cash, $3,000.

1 Accounts Affected	2 Category ↓ ↑	3	4 Rules of Dr. and Cr.	5 T Account Update
Cash	Asset	↑	Dr.	Cash 111
				(A) 7,000 | 900 (B)
				(D) 3,000 |
Legal Fees	Revenue	↑	Cr.	Legal Fees 411
				| 3,000 (D)

Analysis of Transaction D

Step 1: The firm has earned revenue from legal services and receives $3,000 in cash.

Step 2: Cash is an asset. Legal Fees are revenue.

Step 3: Cash, an asset, is increasing. Legal Fees, or revenue, are also increasing.

Step 4: An increase in Cash, an asset, is debited. An increase in Legal Fees, or revenue, is credited.

Step 5: Enter the amount for Cash on the debit side of the T account. Enter the amount for Legal Fees on the credit side.

Transaction E   Sept. 1–30: Provided legal services on account, $4,000.

1 Accounts Affected	2 Category ↓ ↑	3	4 Rules of Dr. and Cr.	5 T Account Update
Accounts Receivable	Asset	↑	Dr.	Accounts Receivable 112
				(E) 4,000 |
Legal Fees	Revenue	↑	Cr.	Legal Fees 411
				| 3,000 (D)
				| 4,000 (E)

Analysis of Transaction E

Step 1: The law practice has earned revenue but has not yet received payment (cash). The amounts owed by these clients are called Accounts Receivable. Revenue is earned at the time the legal services are provided, whether payment is received then or will be received some time in the future.

Step 2: Accounts Receivable is an asset. Legal Fees are revenue.

Step 3: Accounts Receivable is increasing because the law practice has increased the amount owed to it for legal fees that have been earned but not paid. Legal Fees, or revenue, are increasing.

Step 4: An increase in the asset Accounts Receivable is a debit. An increase in Revenue is a credit.

Step 5: Enter the amount for Accounts Receivable on the debit side of the T account. The amount for Legal Fees goes on the credit side.

> **Transaction F   Sept. 1–30: Received $700 cash from clients for services rendered previously on account.**

1 Accounts Affected	2 Category	3 ↓ ↑	4 Rules of Dr. and Cr.	5 T Account Update
Cash	Asset	↑	Dr.	**Cash 111**
				(A) 7,000 | 900 (B) (D) 3,000 (F) 700
Accounts Receivable	Asset	↓	Cr.	**Accounts Receivable 112**
				(E) 4,000 | 700 (F)

Analysis of Transaction F

Step 1: The law firm collects $700 in cash from previous revenue earned. Because the revenue is recorded at the time it is earned, and not when the payment is made, in this transaction we are concerned only with the payment, which affects the Cash and Accounts Receivable accounts.

Step 2: Cash is an asset. Accounts Receivable is an asset.

Step 3: Because clients are paying what is owed, Cash (asset) is increasing and the amount owed (Accounts Receivable) is decreasing (the total amount owed by clients to Hall is going down). This transaction results in a shift in assets, more Cash for less Accounts Receivable.

Step 4: An increase in Cash, an asset, is a debit. A decrease in Accounts Receivable, an asset, is a credit.

Step 5: Enter the amount for Cash on the debit side of the T account. The amount for Accounts Receivable goes on the credit side.

> **Transaction G   Sept. 1–30: Paid salaries expense, $600.**

1 Accounts Affected	2 Category ↓ ↑	3	4 Rules of Dr. and Cr.	5 T Account Update
Salaries Expense	Expense	↑	Dr.	Salaries Expense 511
				(G) 600
Cash	Asset	↓	Cr.	Cash 111
				(A) 7,000 900 (B)
				(D) 3,000 600 (G)
				(F) 700

Analysis of Transaction G

Step 1: The law firm pays $600 worth of salaries expense by cash.

Step 2: Salaries Expense is an expense. Cash is an asset.

Step 3: The Salaries Expense of the law firm is increasing, which results in a decrease in Cash.

Step 4: An increase in Salaries Expense, an expense, is a debit. A decrease in Cash, an asset, is a credit.

Step 5: Enter the amount for Salaries Expense on the debit side of the T account. The amount for Cash goes on the credit side.

Transaction H   Sept. 1–30: Paid rent expense, $700.

1 Accounts Affected	2 Category ↓ ↑	3	4 Rules of Dr. and Cr.	5 T Account Update
Rent Expense	Expense	↑	Dr.	Rent Expense 512
				(H) 700
Cash	Asset	↓	Cr.	Cash 111
				(A) 7,000 900 (B)
				(D) 3,000 600 (G)
				(F) 700 700 (H)

Analysis of Transaction H

Step 1: The law firm's rent expenses are paid in cash.

Step 2: Rent is an expense. Cash is an asset.

Step 3: The Rent Expense increases the expenses, and the payment for the Rent Expense decreases the cash.

Step 4: An increase in Rent Expense, an expense, is a debit. A decrease in Cash, an asset, is a credit.

Step 5: Enter the amount for Rent Expense on the debit side of the T account. Place the amount for Cash on the credit side.

Transaction I   Sept. 1–30: Received a bill for Advertising Expense (to be paid next month), $300.

1 Accounts Affected	2 Category	3 ↓ ↑	4 Rules of Dr. and Cr.	5 T Account Update
Advertising Expense	Expense	↑	Dr.	Advertising Expense 513
				(I) 300 |
Accounts Payable	Liability	↑	Cr.	Accounts Payable 211
				400 (C) 300 (I)

Analysis of Transaction I

Step 1: The advertising bill has come in and payment is due but has not yet been made. Therefore, the accounts involved here are Advertising Expense and Accounts Payable; the expense has created a liability.

Step 2: Advertising Expense is an expense. Accounts Payable is a liability.

Step 3: Both the expense and the liability are increasing.

Step 4: An increase in an expense is a debit. An increase in a liability is a credit.

Step 5: Enter the amount for Advertising Expense on the debit side of the T Account. Enter the amount for Accounts Payable on the credit side.

> **Transaction J   Sept. 1–30: Hall withdrew cash for personal use, $200.**

1 Accounts Affected	2 Category	3 ↓ ↑	4 Rules of Dr. and Cr.	5 T Account Update
Cathy Hall, Withdrawals	Withdrawals	↑	Dr.	Cathy Hall, Withdrawals, 312
				(J) 200 |
Cash	Asset	↓	Cr.	Cash 111
				(A) 7,000 | 900 (B) (D) 3,000 | 600 (G) (F) 700 | 700 (H) | 200 (J)

Analysis of Transaction J

Step 1: Cathy Hall withdraws cash from business for *personal* use. This withdrawal is not a business expense.

Step 2: This transaction affects the Withdrawals and Cash accounts.

Step 3: Cathy has increased what she has withdrawn from the business for personal use. The business cash has been decreased.

Withdrawals are always increased by debits.

Step 4: An increase in Withdrawals is a debit. A decrease in Cash is a credit. (*Remember:* Withdrawals go on the statement of owner's equity; expenses go on the income statement.)

Step 5: Enter the amount for Cathy Hall, Withdrawals on the debit side of the T account. The amount for Cash goes on the credit side.

Summary of Transactions for Cathy Hall

Assets		=	Liabilities	+				Owner's Equity					
Cash 111		=	**Accounts Payable 211**	+	**Capital**	−	**Withdrawals**	+	**Revenue**	−	**Expenses**		
(A) 7,000	900 (B)			+	Cathy Hall,	−	Cathy Hall,	+	Legal	−	Salaries		
(D) 3,000	600 (G)		400 (C)		Capital 311		Withdrawals 312		Fees 411		Expense 511		
(F) 700	700 (H)		300 (I)		7,800 (A)		(J) 200		3,000 (D)		(G) 600		
	200 (J)								4,000 (E)				

Accounts Receivable 112
(E) 4,000 | 700 (F)

Office Equipment 121
(A) 800
(B) 900
(C) 400

− **Rent Expense 512**
(H) 700

− **Advertising Expense 513**
(I) 300

Learning Unit 2-2 Review

AT THIS POINT you should be able to

- State the rules of debit and credit. (p. 41)
- List the five steps of a transaction analysis. (p. 42)
- Show how to fill out a transaction analysis chart. (p. 43)
- Explain double-entry bookkeeping. (p. 44)

SELF-REVIEW QUIZ 2-2

(The blank forms you need are on pages 25 and 26 of the *Study Guide and Working Papers*. See your DVD for worked-out solutions.)

King Company uses the following accounts from its chart of accounts: Cash (111), Accounts Receivable (112), Equipment (121), Accounts Payable (211), Jamie King, Capital (311), Jamie King, Withdrawals (312), Professional Fees (411), Utilities Expense (511), and Salaries Expense (512).

Record the following transactions into transaction analysis charts.

a. Jamie King invested in the business $1,000 cash and equipment worth $700 from his personal assets.

b. Billed clients for services rendered, $12,000.

c. Utilities bill due but unpaid, $150.

d. Withdrew cash for personal use, $120.

e. Paid salaries expense, $250.

SOLUTION TO SELF-REVIEW QUIZ 2-2

Quiz Tip:
Column 1: Row titles must come from the chart of accounts. The order doesn't matter as long as the total of all debits equals the total of all credits.

a.

1 Accounts Affected	2 Category	3 ↓↑	4 Rules of Dr. and Cr.	5 T Account Update
Cash	Asset	↑	Dr.	Cash 111 (A) 1,000
Equipment	Asset	↑	Dr.	Equipment 121 (A) 700
Jamie King, Capital	Capital	↑	Cr.	Jamie King, Capital 311 1,700 (A)

When a business bills a client, it creates an asset, a claim for payment called an "account receivable."

b.

1 Accounts Affected	2 Category	3 ↓↑	4 Rules of Dr. and Cr.	5 T Account Update
Accounts Receivable	Asset	↑	Dr.	Accounts Receivable 112 (B) 12,000
Professional Fees	Revenue	↑	Cr.	Professional Fees 411 12,000 (B)

Record an expense when it happens, whether it is paid for or not.

c.

1 Accounts Affected	2 Category	3 ↓↑	4 Rules of Dr. and Cr.	5 T Account Update
Utilities Expense	Expense	↑	Dr.	Utilities Expense 511 (C) 150
Accounts Payable	Liability	↑	Cr.	Accounts Payable 211 150 (C)

Think of withdrawals as always increasing.

d.

1 Accounts Affected	2 Category	3 ↓↑	4 Rules of Dr. and Cr.	5 T Account Update
Jamie King, Withdrawls	Withdrawals	↑	Dr.	Jamie King, Withdrawals 312 (D) 120
Cash	Asset	↓	Cr.	Cash 111 (A) 1,000	120 (D)

Think of expenses as always increasing.

e.

1 Accounts Affected	2 Category	3 ↓↑	4 Rules of Dr. and Cr.	5 T Account Update
Salaries Expense	Expense	↑	Dr.	Salaries Expense 512 (E) 250
Cash	Asset	↓	Cr.	Cash 111 (A) 1,000	120 (D) / 250 (E)

Learning Unit 2-3   The Trial Balance and Preparation of Financial Statements

Let us look at all the transactions we have discussed, arranged by T accounts and recorded using the rules of debit and credit. This grouping of accounts is much easier to use than the expanded accounting equation because all the transactions that affect a particular account are in one place.

As we saw in Learning Unit 2-2, when all the transactions are recorded in the accounts, the total of all the debits should be equal to the total of all the credits. (If they are not, the accountant must go back and find the error by checking the numbers and adding every column again.)

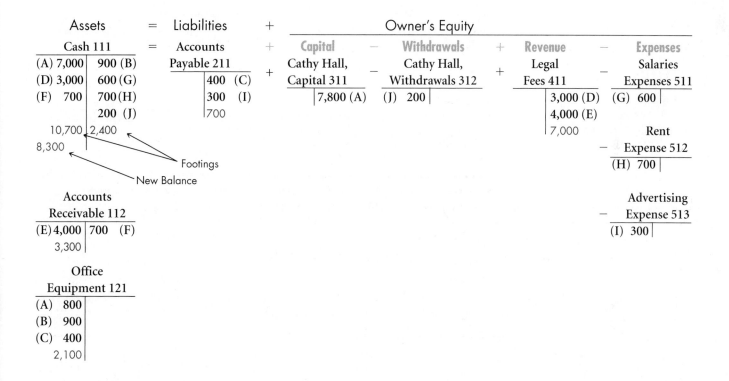

THE TRIAL BALANCE

Footings are used to obtain the balance of each side of every T account that has more than one entry. The footings are used to find the ending balance. The ending balances are used to prepare a **trial balance.** The trial balance is not a financial statement, although it is used to prepare financial statements. The trial balance lists all the accounts with their balances in the same order as they appear in the chart of accounts. It proves the accuracy of the ledger. For example, look at the preceding Cash account. The footing for the debit side is $10,700, and the footing for the credit side is $2,400. Because the debit side is larger, we subtract $2,400 from $10,700 to arrive at an *ending balance* of $8,300. Now look at the Rent Expense account. There is no need for a footing because there is only one entry. The amount itself is the ending balance. When the ending balance has been found for every account, we should be able to show that the total of all debits equals the total of all credits.

In the ideal situation, businesses would take a trial balance every day. The large number of transactions most businesses conduct each day makes this impractical. Instead, trial balances are prepared periodically.

Footings are used to obtain the balance of each side of the T account. They are not needed if there is only one entry in the account.

As mentioned earlier, the ending balance of Cash, $8,300, is a normal balance because it is on the side that increases the asset account.

Figure 2-2
Trial Balance for Cathy
Hall's Law Firm

Because this is not a formal statement, there is no need to use dollar signs; the single and double lines under subtotals and final totals, however, are still used for clarity.

CATHY HALL, ATTORNEY-AT-LAW TRIAL BALANCE SEPTEMBER 30, 200X		
	Dr.	Cr.
Cash	8 3 0 0 00	
Accounts Receivable	3 3 0 0 00	
Office Equipment	2 1 0 0 00	
Accounts Payable		7 0 0 00
Cathy Hall, Capital		7 8 0 0 00
Cathy Hall, Withdrawals	2 0 0 00	
Legal Fees		7 0 0 0 00
Salaries Expense	6 0 0 00	
Rent Expense	7 0 0 00	
Advertising Expense	3 0 0 00	
Totals	15 5 0 0 00	15 5 0 0 00

Only the ending balance of each account is listed.

Keep in mind that the figure for capital might not be the beginning figure if any additional investment has taken place during the period. You can tell this by looking at the capital account in the ledger.

A more detailed discussion of the trial balance is provided in the next chapter. For now, notice the heading, how the accounts are listed, the debits in the left column, the credits in the right, and that the total of debits is equal to the total of credits.

A trial balance of Cathy Hall's accounts is shown in Figure 2-2.

PREPARING FINANCIAL STATEMENTS

The trial balance is used to prepare the financial statements. The diagram in Figure 2-3 on page 53 shows how financial statements can be prepared from a trial balance. Statements do not have debit or credit columns. The left column is used only to subtotal numbers.

Learning Unit 2-3 Review

AT THIS POINT you should be able to

- Explain the role of footings. (p. 51)
- Prepare a trial balance from a set of accounts. (p. 52)
- Prepare financial statements from a trial balance. (p. 53)

SELF-REVIEW QUIZ 2-3

(The blank forms you need are on page 27 of the *Study Guide and Working Papers*. See your DVD for worked-out solutions.)

As the bookkeeper of Pam's Hair Salon, you are to prepare from the following accounts below Figure 2-3, p. 53 on June 30, 200X, (1) a trial balance as of June 30, (2) an income statement for the month ended June 30, (3) a statement of owner's equity for the month ended June 30, and (4) a balance sheet as of June 30, 200X.

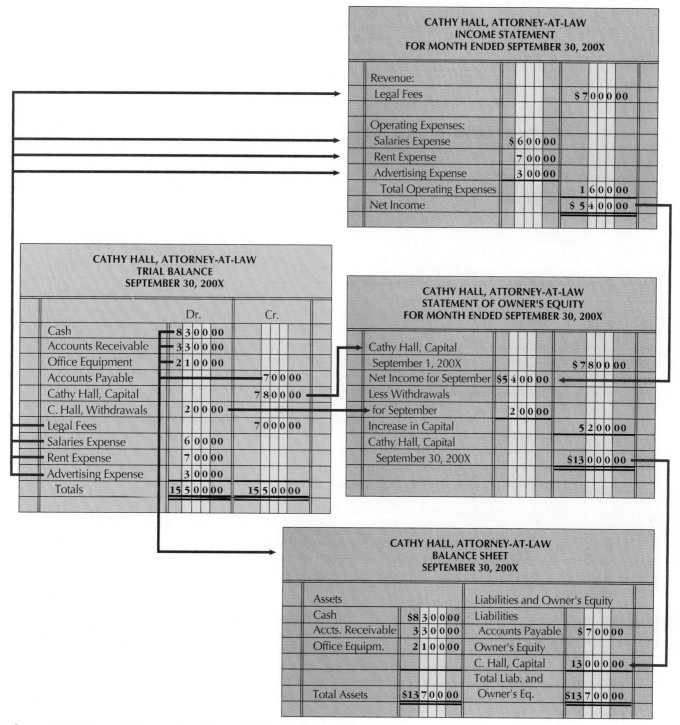

Figure 2-3 Steps in Preparing Financial Statements from a Trial Balance

Cash 111		Accounts Payable 211		Salon Fees 411	
4,500	300	300	700		3,500
2,000	100				1,000
1,000	1,200				
300	1,300				
	2,600				

Accounts Receivable 121		Pam Jay, Capital 311		Rent Expense 511	
1,000	300		4,000*	1,200	

(cont. on p. 54)

Salon Equipment 131	Pam Jay, Withdrawals 321	Salon Supplies Expense 521
700		100		1,300	
			Salaries Expense 531
			2,600	

*No additional investments.

SOLUTION TO SELF-REVIEW QUIZ 2-3

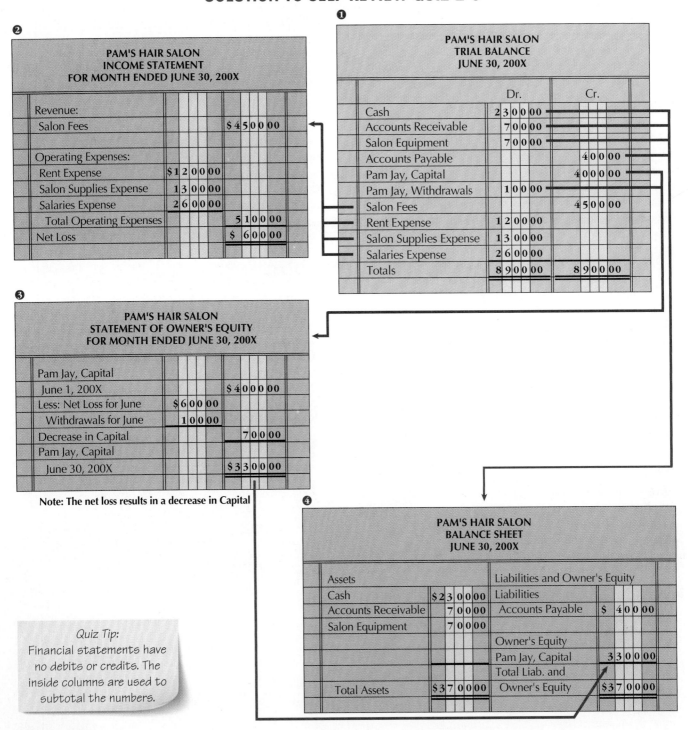

❷

PAM'S HAIR SALON
INCOME STATEMENT
FOR MONTH ENDED JUNE 30, 200X

Revenue:			
Salon Fees		$ 4 5 0 0 00	
Operating Expenses:			
Rent Expense	$ 1 2 0 0 00		
Salon Supplies Expense	1 3 0 0 00		
Salaries Expense	2 6 0 0 00		
Total Operating Expenses		5 1 0 0 00	
Net Loss		$ 6 0 0 00	

❶

PAM'S HAIR SALON
TRIAL BALANCE
JUNE 30, 200X

	Dr.	Cr.
Cash	2 3 0 0 00	
Accounts Receivable	7 0 0 00	
Salon Equipment	7 0 0 00	
Accounts Payable		4 0 0 00
Pam Jay, Capital		4 0 0 0 00
Pam Jay, Withdrawals	1 0 0 00	
Salon Fees		4 5 0 0 00
Rent Expense	1 2 0 0 00	
Salon Supplies Expense	1 3 0 0 00	
Salaries Expense	2 6 0 0 00	
Totals	8 9 0 0 00	8 9 0 0 00

❸

PAM'S HAIR SALON
STATEMENT OF OWNER'S EQUITY
FOR MONTH ENDED JUNE 30, 200X

Pam Jay, Capital			
June 1, 200X		$ 4 0 0 0 00	
Less: Net Loss for June	$ 6 0 0 00		
Withdrawals for June	1 0 0 00		
Decrease in Capital		7 0 0 00	
Pam Jay, Capital			
June 30, 200X		$ 3 3 0 0 00	

Note: The net loss results in a decrease in Capital

❹

PAM'S HAIR SALON
BALANCE SHEET
JUNE 30, 200X

Assets		Liabilities and Owner's Equity	
Cash	$ 2 3 0 0 00	Liabilities	
Accounts Receivable	7 0 0 00	Accounts Payable	$ 4 0 0 00
Salon Equipment	7 0 0 00		
		Owner's Equity	
		Pam Jay, Capital	3 3 0 0 00
		Total Liab. and	
Total Assets	$ 3 7 0 0 00	Owner's Equity	$ 3 7 0 0 00

Quiz Tip:
Financial statements have no debits or credits. The inside columns are used to subtotal the numbers.

Figure 2-4

If there were more than one liability we would have two columns, one to subtotal the liabilities (inside column) and one to total the liabilities (right column).

SOLUTION & TIPS TO COMPREHENSIVE PROBLEM: PUTTING THE PIECES TOGETHER

(The blank forms you need are on pages 30–32 of the *Study Guide and Working Papers.*)

The chart of accounts of Mel's Delivery Service includes the following: Cash, 111; Accounts Receivable, 112; Office Equipment, 121; Delivery Trucks, 122; Accounts Payable, 211; Mel Free, Capital, 311; Mel Free, Withdrawals, 312; Delivery Fees Earned, 411; Advertising Expense, 511; Gas Expense, 512; Salaries Expense, 513; and Telephone Expense, 514. The following transactions resulted for Mel's Delivery Service during the month of July:

Transaction A: Mel invested $10,000 in the business from his personal savings account.
Transaction B: Bought delivery trucks on account, $17,000.
Transaction C: Advertising bill received but unpaid, $700.
Transaction D: Bought office equipment for cash, $1,200.
Transaction E: Received cash for delivery services rendered, $15,000.
Transaction F: Paid salaries expense, $3,000.
Transaction G: Paid gas expense for company trucks, $1,250.
Transaction H: Billed customers for delivery services rendered, $4,000.
Transaction I: Paid telephone bill, $300.
Transaction J: Received $3,000 as partial payment of transaction H.
Transaction K: Mel paid home telephone bill from company checkbook, $150.

Assignment

As Mel's newly employed accountant, you must do the following:

1. Set up T accounts in a ledger.
2. Record transactions in the T accounts. (Place the letter of the transaction next to the entry.)
3. Foot the T accounts where appropriate.
4. Prepare a trial balance at the end of July.
5. Prepare from the trial balance, in proper form, (a) an income statement for the month of July, (b) a statement of owner's equity, and (c) a balance sheet as of July 31, 200X.

Solution to Comprehensive Problem

1,2,3.   **GENERAL LEDGER**

Cash 111			
(A) 10,000	1,200	(D)	
(E) 15,000	3,000	(F)	
(J) 3,000	1,250	(G)	
	300	(I)	
	150	(K)	
28,000	5,900		
22,100			

Acc. Payable 211	
	17,000 (B)
	700 (C)
	17,700

Advertising Expense 511	
(C) 700	

Acc. Receivable 112		
(H) 4,000	3,000	(J)
1,000		

Mel Free, Capital 311	
	10,000 (A)

Gas Expense 512	
(G) 1,250	

Office Equipment 121	
(D) 1,200	

Mel Free, Withdrawals 312	
(K) 150	

Salaries Expense 513	
(F) 3,000	

Delivery Trucks 122	Delivery Fees Earned 411	Telephone Expense 514
(B) 17,000	15,000 (E) 4,000 (H) 19,000	(I) 300

Solution Tips to Recording Transactions

A.	Cash	A	↑	Dr.	G.	Gas Expense	Exp.	↑	Dr.
	Mel Free, Capital	Cap.	↑	Cr.		Cash	A	↓	Cr.
B.	Delivery Trucks	A	↑	Dr.	H.	Acc. Receivable	A	↑	Dr.
	Acc. Payable	L	↑	Cr.		Del. Fees Earned	Rev.	↑	Cr.
C.	Advertising Expense	Exp.	↑	Dr.	I.	Tel. Expense	Exp.	↑	Dr.
	Acc. Payable	L	↑	Cr.		Cash	A	↓	Cr.
D.	Office Equipment	A	↑	Dr.	J.	Cash	A	↑	Dr.
	Cash	A	↓	Cr.		Acc. Receivable	A	↓	Cr.
E.	Cash	A	↑	Dr.	K.	Mel Free, Withd.	Withd.	↑	Dr.
	Del. Fees Earned	Rev.	↑	Cr.		Cash	A	↓	Cr.
F.	Salaries Expense	Exp.	↑	Dr.					
	Cash	A	↓	Cr.					

MEL'S DELIVERY SERVICE
TRIAL BALANCE
JULY 31, 200X

	Dr.	Cr.
Cash	22,100	
Accounts Receivable	1,000	
Office Equipment	1,200	
Delivery Trucks	17,000	
Accounts Payable		17,700
Mel Free, Capital		10,000
Mel Free, Withdrawals	150	
Delivery Fees Earned		19,000
Advertising Expense	700	
Gas Expense	1,250	
Salaries Expense	3,000	
Telephone Expense	300	
TOTALS	46,700	46,700

Solution Tips to Footings and Preparation of a Trial Balance

3. Footings: Cash — Add left side, $28,000.
Add right side, $5,900.
Take difference, $22,100, and stay on side that is larger.

Accounts Payable — Add $17,000 + $700 and stay on same side.
Total is $17,700.

4. Trial balance is a list of the ledger's ending balances. The list is in the same order as the chart of accounts. Each title has only one number listed either as a debit or credit balance.

5a.

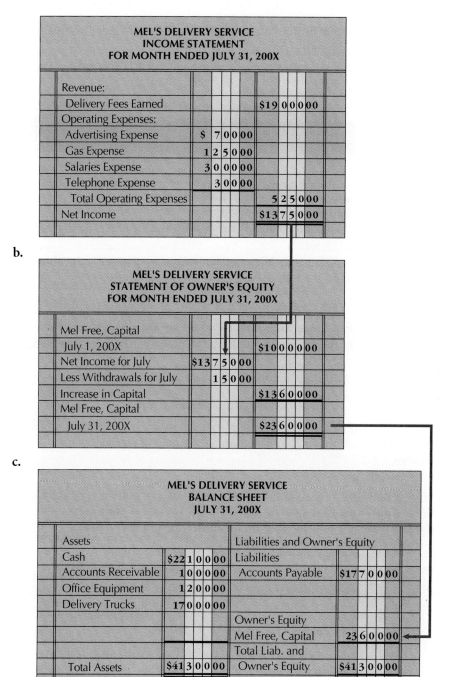

Figure 2-5

MEL'S DELIVERY SERVICE INCOME STATEMENT FOR MONTH ENDED JULY 31, 200X		
Revenue:		
Delivery Fees Earned		$19 00 00
Operating Expenses:		
Advertising Expense	$ 7 00 00	
Gas Expense	1 2 5 0 00	
Salaries Expense	3 0 0 0 00	
Telephone Expense	3 00 00	
Total Operating Expenses		5 2 5 0 00
Net Income		$13 7 5 0 00

b.

MEL'S DELIVERY SERVICE STATEMENT OF OWNER'S EQUITY FOR MONTH ENDED JULY 31, 200X		
Mel Free, Capital		
July 1, 200X		$10 0 0 0 00
Net Income for July	$13 7 5 0 00	
Less Withdrawals for July	1 5 0 00	
Increase in Capital		$13 6 0 0 00
Mel Free, Capital		
July 31, 200X		$23 6 0 0 00

c.

MEL'S DELIVERY SERVICE BALANCE SHEET JULY 31, 200X				
Assets		Liabilities and Owner's Equity		
Cash	$22 1 0 0 00	Liabilities		
Accounts Receivable	1 0 0 0 00	Accounts Payable	$17 7 0 0 00	
Office Equipment	1 2 0 0 00			
Delivery Trucks	17 0 0 0 00			
		Owner's Equity		
		Mel Free, Capital	23 6 0 0 00	
		Total Liab. and		
Total Assets	$41 3 0 0 00	Owner's Equity	$41 3 0 0 00	

Solution Tips to Prepare Financial Statements from a Trial Balance

Trial Balance

		Dr.	Cr.
Balance Sheet	Assets	X	
	Liabilities		X
Statement of Equity	Capital		X
	Withdrawals	X	
Income Statement	Revenues		X
	Expenses	X	
		XX	XX

Net income of $13,750 on the income statement goes on the statement of owner's equity.

Ending capital of $23,600 on the statement of owner's equity goes on the balance sheet as the new figure for capital.

Note: There are no debits or credits on financial statements. The inside column is used for subtotaling.

Summary of Key Points

Learning Unit 2-1

1. A T account is a simplified version of a standard account.
2. A ledger is a group of accounts.
3. A debit is the left-hand position (side) of an account, and a credit is the right-hand position (side) of an account.
4. A footing is the total of one side of an account. The ending balance is the difference between the footings.

Learning Unit 2-2

1. A chart of accounts lists the account titles and their numbers for a company.
2. The transaction analysis chart is a teaching device, not to be confused with standard accounting procedures.
3. A compound entry is a transaction involving more than one debit or credit.

Learning Unit 2-3

1. In double-entry bookkeeping, the recording of each business transaction affects two or more accounts, and the total of debits equals the total of credits.
2. A trial balance is a list of the ending balances of all accounts, listed in the same order as on the chart of accounts.
3. Any additional investments during the period result in the Capital balance on the trial balance not being the beginning figure for the Capital account.
4. There are *no* debit or credit columns on the three financial statements.

Key Terms

Account An accounting device used in bookkeeping to record increases and decreases of business transactions relating to individual assets, liabilities, capital, withdrawals, revenue, expenses, and so on.

Chart of accounts A numbering system of accounts that lists the account titles and account numbers to be used by a company.

Compound entry A transaction involving more than one debit or credit.

Credit The right-hand side of any account. A number entered on the right side of any account is said to be credited to an account.

Debit The left-hand side of any account. A number entered on the left side of any account is said to be debited to an account.

Double-entry bookkeeping An accounting system in which the recording of each transaction affects two or more accounts and the total of the debits is equal to the total of the credits.

Ending balance The difference between footings in a T account.

Footings The totals of each side of a T account.

Ledger A group of accounts that records data from business transactions.

Normal balance of an account The side of an account that increases by the rules of debit and credit.

Standard account A formal account that includes columns for date, explanation, posting reference, debit, and credit.

T account A skeleton version of a standard account, used for demonstration purposes.

Trial balance A list of the ending balances of all the accounts in a ledger. The total of the debits should equal the total of the credits.

Account Balance

Blueprint: Preparing Financial Statements from a Trial Balance

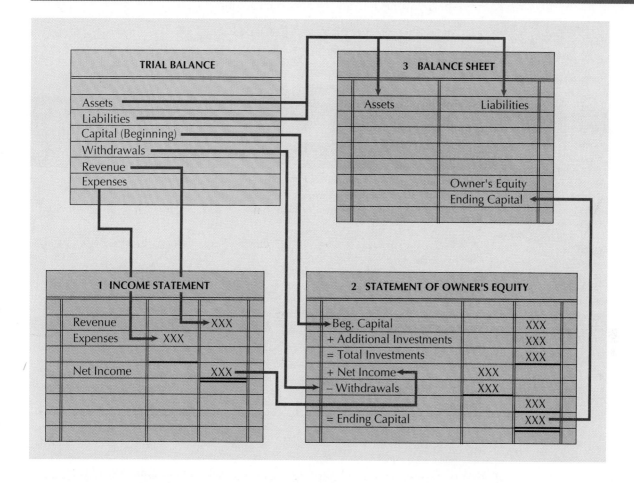

Questions, Mini Exercises, Exercises, and Problems

Discussion Questions

1. Define a ledger.
2. Why is the left-hand side of an account called a debit?
3. Footings are used in balancing all accounts. True or false? Please explain.
4. What is the end product of the accounting process?
5. What do we mean when we say that a transaction analysis chart is a teaching device?
6. What are the five steps of the transaction analysis chart?
7. Explain the concept of double-entry bookkeeping.
8. A trial balance is a formal statement. True or false? Please explain.
9. Why are there no debit or credit columns on financial statements?
10. Compare the financial statements prepared from the expanded accounting equation with those prepared from a trial balance.

Mini Exercises

(The blank forms you need are on page 34 in the *Study Guide and Working Papers*.)

The T Account

1. From the following, foot and balance each account.

Cash 110				C. Clark, Capital 311		
6/9	4,000	4/8	500		3/7	7,000
7/14	8,000				3/9	3,000
					4/12	6,000

Transaction Analysis

2. Complete the following:

Account	Category	↑	↓	Normal Balance
A. Digital Cameras	Asset	↑		DR
B. Prepaid Rent	Asset	↑		DR
C. Accounts Payable	Liability	↑		CR
D. A. Sung, Capital	Capital	↑		CR
E. A. Sung, Withdrawals	Withdrawal	↑		DR
F. Legal Fees	Revenue	↑		CR
G. Salary Expense	Expense	↑		DR

Transaction Analysis

3. Record the following transaction into the transaction analysis chart: Provided legal services for $4,000, receiving $3,000 cash with the remainder to be paid next month.

Accounts Affected	Category	↓	↑	Rules of Dr. and Cr.	T Accounts
Cash	Asset		↑	DR	
A/R	Asset		↑	DR	
Fees Earned	Revenue		↑	CR	

Trial Balance

4. Rearrange the following titles in the order they would appear on a trial balance:

Selling Expense
Accounts Receivable
Accounts Payable
D. Cope, Capital
Computer Equipment
Legal Fees
D. Cope, Withdrawals
Rent Expense
Advertising Expense
Cash

Trial Balance/Financial Statements

5. From the following trial balance, identify which statement each title will appear on:

- Income statement (IS)
- Statement of owner's equity (OE)
- Balance sheet (BS)

HEATH CO.
TRIAL BALANCE
SEPT. 30, 200X

		Dr.	Cr.
A. _____	Cash	390	
B. _____	Supplies	100	
C. _____	Office Equipment	200	
D. _____	Accounts Payable		100
E. _____	D. Heath, Capital		450
F. _____	D. Heath, Withdrawals	160	
G. _____	Fees Earned		290
H. _IS_	Hair Salon Fees		300
I. _IS_	Salaries Expense	130	
J. _IS_	Rent Expense	120	
K. _IS_	Advertising Expense	40	
	TOTALS	1,140	1,140

Exercises

(The blank forms you need are on page 35 in the *Study Guide and Working Papers.*)

2-1. From the following, prepare a chart of accounts, using the same numbering system used in this chapter.

Digital Cameras   Professional Fees
Rent Expense   A. Sting, Capital
Accounts Payable   Cash
Accounts Receivable   Salaries Expense
Repair Expense   A. Sting, Withdrawals

Preparing a chart of accounts.

2-2. Record the following transaction into the transaction analysis chart: Abe Reese bought a new piece of office equipment for $16,000, paying $4,000 down and charging the rest.

Preparing a transaction analysis chart.

2-3. Complete the following table. For each account listed on the left, fill in what category it belongs to, whether increases and decreases in the account are marked on the debit or credit sides, and which financial statement the account appears on. A sample is provided.

Accounts Affected	Category	↑	↓	Appears on which Financial Statements
Computer Supplies	Asset	Dr.	Cr.	Balance Sheet
Legal Fees Earned	Revenue	CR	DR	IS
P. Rey, Withdrawals	WITHDRAWAL	DR.	CR	OE
Accounts Payable	Liability	CR	DR.	BS
Salaries Expense	Expense	DR	CR	IS
Auto	Asset	DR	CR	BS

Accounts categorizing, rules, and on which reports they appear.

2-4. Given the following accounts, complete the table by inserting appropriate numbers next to the individual transaction to indicate which account is debited and which account is credited.

Rules of debits and credits.

1. Cash
2. Accounts Receivable
3. Equipment
4. Accounts Payable
5. B. Baker, Capital
6. B. Baker, Withdrawals
7. Plumbing Fees Earned
8. Salaries Expense
9. Advertising Expense
10. Supplies Expenses

	Transaction	Rules	
		Dr.	Cr.
Example:	A. Paid salaries expense.	8	1
	B. Bob paid personal utilities bill from the company checkbook.		
	C. Advertising bill received but unpaid.		
	D. Received cash from plumbing fees.		
	E. Paid supplies expense.		
	F. Bob invested in additional equipment for the business.		
	G. Billed customers for plumbing services rendered.		
	H. Received one-half the balance from transaction G.		
	I. Bought equipment on account.		

> **Preparing financial statements.**

2-5. From the following trial balance of Hall's Cleaners (Fig. 2-6), prepare the following:

- Income statement
- Statement of owner's equity
- Balance sheet

Figure 2-6

HALL'S CLEANERS
TRIAL BALANCE
JULY 31, 200X

	Dr.	Cr.
Cash	5 5 0 00	
Equipment	6 9 2 00	
Accounts Payable		4 5 5 00
J. Hall, Capital		8 0 0 00
J. Hall, Withdrawals	1 9 8 00	
Cleaning Fees		4 5 8 00
Salaries Expense	1 6 0 00	
Utilities Expense	1 1 3 00	
Totals	1 7 1 3 00	1 7 1 3 00

Group A Problems

> **Use of a transaction analysis chart.**

(The forms you need are on pages 38–45 of the *Study Guide and Working Papers*.)

2A-1. The following transactions occurred in the opening and operation of Melissa's Bookkeeping Service.

- a. Melissa Montgomery opened the bookkeeping service by investing $8,000 from her personal savings account.
- b. Purchased store equipment on account, $3,000.
- c. Rent expense due but unpaid, $600.
- d. Received cash for bookkeeping services rendered, $800.
- e. Billed a client on account, $500.
- f. Melissa withdrew cash for personal use, $200.

> **Check Figure:**
> After F:
>
> | Cash | |
> |---|---|
> | 8,000 | 200 |
> | 800 | |

Complete the transaction analysis chart in the *Study Guide and Working Papers*. The chart of accounts includes Cash; Accounts Receivable; Store Equipment; Accounts Payable; Melissa Montgomery, Capital; Melissa Montgomery, Withdrawals; Bookkeeping Fees Earned; and Rent Expense.

> **Recording transactions into ledger accounts.**

2A-2. Matt Slater opened a travel agency, and the following transactions resulted:

- a. Matt invested $40,000 in the travel agency.
- b. Bought office equipment on account, $4,000.
- c. Agency received cash for travel arrangements that it completed for a client, $3,000.
- d. Matt paid a personal bill from the company checkbook, $50.

  e. Paid advertising expense for the month, $700.
  f. Rent expense for the month due but unpaid, $900.
  g. Paid $800 as partial payment of what was owed from transaction B.

As Matt's accountant, analyze and record the transactions in T account form. Set up the T accounts and label each entry with the letter of the transaction.

Check Figure:
After G:

Cash

(A) 40,000	50 (D)
(C) 3,000	700 (E)
	800 (G)

Chart of Accounts

Assets
Cash   111
Office Equipment   121

Liabilities
Accounts Payable   211

Owner's Equity
M. Slater, Capital   311
M. Slater, Withdrawals   312

Revenue
Travel Fees Earned   411

Expenses
Advertising Expense   511
Rent Expense   512

2A-3. From the following T accounts of Mike's Window Washing Service, (a) record and foot the balances in the *Study Guide and Working Papers* where appropriate, and (b) prepare a trial balance in proper form for May 31, 200X.

Preparing a trial balance from the T accounts.

Cash 111		
5,000 (A)	100	(D)
3,500 (G)	200	(E)
	400	(F)
	200	(H)
	900	(I)

Accounts Payable 211	
100 (D)	1,300 (C)

Fees Earned 411
6,500 (B)

Check Figure:
Trial Balance Total $12,700

Accounts Receivable 112	
6,500 (B)	3,500 (G)

Mike Frank, Capital 311
5,000 (A)

Rent Expense 511
400 (F)

Office Equipment 121
1,300 (C)
200 (H)

Mike Frank, Withdrawals 312
900 (I)

Utilities Expense 512
200 (E)

2A-4. From the trial balance of Gracie Lantz, Attorney-at-Law (Fig. 2-7), prepare (a) an income statement for the month of May, (b) a statement of owner's equity for the month ended May 31, and (c) a balance sheet as of May 31, 200X.

Preparing financial statements from the trial balance.

Figure 2-7

GRACIE LANTZ, ATTORNEY-AT-LAW
TRIAL BALANCE
MAY 31, 200X

	Dr.	Cr.
Cash	5 0 0 0 00	
Accounts Receivable	6 5 0 00	
Office Equipment	7 5 0 00	
Accounts Payable		4 3 0 0 00
Salaries Payable		6 7 5 00
G. Lantz, Capital		1 2 7 5 00
G. Lantz, Withdrawals	3 0 0 00	
Revenue from Legal Fees		1 3 5 0 00
Utilities Expense	3 0 0 00	
Rent Expense	4 5 0 00	
Salaries Expense	1 5 0 00	
Totals	7 6 0 0 00	7 6 0 0 00

Check Figure:
Total Assets $6,400

2A-5. The chart of accounts for Angel's Delivery Service is as follows:

Chart of Accounts

Assets	Revenue
Cash 111	Delivery Fees Earned 411
Accounts Receivable 112	**Expenses**
Office Equipment 121	Advertising Expense 511
Delivery Trucks 122	Gas Expense 512
Liabilities	Salaries Expense 513
Accounts Payable 211	Telephone Expense 514
Owner's Equity	
Alice Angel, Capital 311	
Alice Angel, Withdrawals 312	

Angel's Delivery Service completed the following transactions during the month of March:

Transaction A: Alice Angel invested $16,000 in the delivery service from her personal savings account.
Transaction B: Bought delivery trucks on account, $18,000.
Transaction C: Bought office equipment for cash, $600.
Transaction D: Paid advertising expense, $250.
Transaction E: Collected cash for delivery services rendered, $2,600.
Transaction F: Paid drivers' salaries, $900.
Transaction G: Paid gas expense for trucks, $1,200.
Transaction H: Performed delivery services for a customer on account, $800.
Transaction I: Telephone expense due but unpaid, $700.
Transaction J: Received $300 as partial payment of transaction H.
Transaction K: Alice withdrew cash for personal use, $300.

As Alice's newly employed accountant, you must:

1. Set up T accounts in a ledger.
2. Record transactions in the T accounts. (Place the letter of the transaction next to the entry.)
3. Foot the T accounts where appropriate.
4. Prepare a trial balance at the end of March.
5. Prepare from the trial balance, in proper form, (a) an income statement for the month of March, (b) a statement of owner's equity, and (c) a balance sheet as of March 31, 200X.

Group B Problems

(The forms you need are on pages 38–45 of the *Study Guide and Working Papers.*)

2B-1. Melissa Montgomery decided to open a bookkeeping service. Record the following transactions into the transaction analysis charts:

Transaction A: Melissa invested $2,500 in the bookkeeping service from her personal savings account.
Transaction B: Purchased store equipment on account, $900.
Transaction C: Rent expense due but unpaid, $250.
Transaction D: Performed bookkeeping services for cash, $1,200.
Transaction E: Billed clients for bookkeeping services rendered, $700.
Transaction F: Melissa paid her home heating bill from the company checkbook, $275.

The chart of accounts for the shop includes Cash; Accounts Receivable; Store Equipment; Accounts Payable; Melissa Montgomery, Capital; Melissa Montgomery, Withdrawals; Bookkeeping Fees Earned; and Rent Expense.

2B-2. Matt Slater established a new travel agency. Record the following transactions for Matt in T account form. Label each entry with the letter of the transaction.

Transaction A: Matt invested $20,000 in the travel agency from his personal bank account.

Transaction B: Bought office equipment on account, $6,000.

Transaction C: Travel agency rendered service to Jensen Corp. and received cash, $1,200.

Transaction D: Matt withdrew cash for personal use, $200.

Transaction E: Paid advertising expense, $600.

Transaction F: Rent expense due but unpaid, $500.

Transaction G: Paid $400 in partial payment of transaction B.

Check Figure:
After G:

Cash			
(A) 20,000	200	(D)
(C) 1,200	600	(E)
	400	(G)

The chart of accounts includes Cash, 111; Office Equipment, 121; Accounts Payable, 211; M. Slater, Capital, 311; M. Slater, Withdrawals, 312; Travel Fees Earned, 411; Advertising Expense, 511; and Rent Expense, 512.

2B-3. From the following T accounts of Mike's Window Washing Service, (a) record and foot the balances in the *Study Guide and Working Papers* where appropriate and (b) prepare a trial balance for May 31, 200X.

Preparing a trial balance from the T accounts.

Cash 111				Accounts Receivable 112				Office Equipment 121			
10,000 (A)	4,000	(C)		2,000 (G)				2,000	(B)		
4,000 (F)	310	(D)						4,000	(C)		
2,000 (G)	50	(E)									
16000	600	(H)									
4960	4960										
15040											

Accounts Payable 211				Mike Frank, Capital 311				Mike Frank, Withdrawals 312			
	2,000	(B)			10,000	(A)		600 (H)			

Fees Earned 411				Rent Expense 511				Utilities Expense 512			
	4,000	(F)		310 (D)				50 (E)			
	4,000	(G)									

Check Figure:
Trial Balance Total
$20,000

2B-4. From the trial balance of Gracie Lantz, Attorney-at-Law (Fig. 2-8), prepare (a) an income statement for the month of May, (b) a statement of owner's equity for the month ended May 31, and (c) a balance sheet as of May 31, 200X.

Preparing financial statements from the trial balance.

Figure 2-8

GRACIE LANTZ, ATTORNEY-AT-LAW TRIAL BALANCE MAY 31, 200X	Debit	Credit
Cash	6 0 0 0 00	
Accounts Receivable	2 4 0 0 00	
Office Equipment	2 4 0 0 00	
Accounts Payable		2 0 0 00
Salaries Payable		6 0 0 00
G. Lantz, Capital		4 0 0 0 00
G. Lantz, Withdrawals	2 0 0 0 00	
Revenue from Legal Fees		8 8 0 0 00
Utilities Expense	1 0 0 00	
Rent Expense	3 0 0 00	
Salaries Expense	4 0 0 00	
Totals	13 6 0 0 00	13 6 0 0 00

Check Figure:
Total Assets $10,800

2B-5. The chart of accounts of Angel's Delivery Service includes the following: Cash, 111; Accounts Receivable, 112; Office Equipment, 121; Delivery Trucks, 122; Accounts Payable, 211; Alice Angel, Capital, 311; Alice Angel, Withdrawals, 312; Delivery Fees Earned, 411; Advertising Expense, 511; Gas Expense, 512; Salaries Expense, 513; and Telephone Expense, 514. The following transactions resulted for Angel's Delivery Service during the month of March:

Transaction A: Alice invested $40,000 in the business from her personal savings account.
Transaction B: Bought delivery trucks on account, $25,000.
Transaction C: Advertising bill received but unpaid, $800.
Transaction D: Bought office equipment for cash, $2,500.
Transaction E: Received cash for delivery services rendered, $13,000.
Transaction F: Paid salaries expense, $1,850.
Transaction G: Paid gas expense for company trucks, $750.
Transaction H: Billed customers for delivery services rendered, $5,500.
Transaction I: Paid telephone bill, $400.
Transaction J: Received $1,600 as partial payment of transaction H.
Transaction K: Alice paid her home telephone bill from company checkbook, $88.

As Alice's newly employed accountant, you must

1. Set up T accounts in a ledger.
2. Record transactions in the T accounts. (Place the letter of the transaction next to the entry.)
3. Foot the T accounts where appropriate.
4. Prepare a trial balance at the end of March.
5. Prepare from the trial balance, in proper form, (a) an income statement for the month of March, (b) a statement of owner's equity, and (c) a balance sheet as of March 31, 200X.

Real-World Applications

2R-1. Andy Leaf is a careless bookkeeper. He is having a terrible time getting his trial balance to balance. Andy has asked for your assistance in preparing a correct trial balance. The following is the incorrect trial balance:

Figure 2-9

RANCH COMPANY
TRIAL BALANCE
JUNE 30, 200X

	Dr.	Cr.
Cash	5 1 0 00	
Accounts Receivable		6 3 5 00
Office Equipment	3 6 0 00	
Accounts Payable	1 1 0 00	
Wages Payable	1 0 00	
H. Clo, Capital	6 3 5 00	
H. Clo, Withdrawals	1 4 4 0 00	
Professional Fees		2 2 4 0 00
Rent Expense		2 4 0 00
Advertising Expense	2 5 00	
Totals	3 0 9 0 00	3 1 1 5 00

Facts you have discovered:

● Debits to the Cash account were $2,640; credits to the Cash account were $2,150.

- Amy Hall paid $15 but was not updated in Accounts Receivable.
- A purchase of office equipment for $5 on account was never recorded in the ledger.
- Revenue was understated in the ledger by $180.

Show how these errors affected the ending balances for the accounts involved and explain how the trial balance will indeed balance once they are corrected.

Tell Ranch Company how it can avoid this problem in the future. Write your recommendations.

2R-2. Cookie Mejias, owner of Mejias Company, asked her bookkeeper how each of the following situations will affect the totals of the trial balance and individual ledger accounts:

1. An $850 payment for a desk was recorded as a debit to Office Equipment, $85, and a credit to Cash, $85.

2. A payment of $300 to a creditor was recorded as a debit to Accounts Payable, $300, and a credit to Cash, $100.

3. The collection on an Accounts Receivable for $400 was recorded as a debit to Cash, $400, and a credit to C. Mejias, Capital, $400.

4. The payment of a liability for $400 was recorded as a debit to Accounts Payable, $40, and a credit to Supplies, $40.

5. A purchase of equipment of $800 was recorded as a debit to Supplies, $800, and a credit to Cash, $800.

6. A payment of $95 to a creditor was recorded as a debit to Accounts Payable, $95, and a credit to Cash, $59.

What did the bookkeeper tell her? Which accounts were overstated, and which were understated? Which were correct? Explain in writing how mistakes can be avoided in the future.

YOU make the call

Critical Thinking/Ethical Case

2R-3. Audrey Flet, the bookkeeper of ALN Co., was scheduled to leave on a three-week vacation at 5 o'clock on Friday. She couldn't get the company's trial balance to balance. At 4:30, she decided to put in fictitious figures to make it balance. Audrey told herself she would fix it when she got back from her vacation. Was Audrey right or wrong to do this? Why?

Internet Exercises: Priceline

EX-1. [**www.priceline.com**]   In this chapter you have learned about debits and credits and their place in creating financial statements. Go to the Web site for Priceline, click on Investor Relations, and click on Financial Reports June 30, 2002. Print out the Condensed Financial Balance Sheet. How were debits and credits used to prepare the report?

EX-2. [**www.priceline.com**]   Use your knowledge of debits and credits in this exercise. Look at the solution for exercise and answer these questions:

1. Calculate Total Assets, Total Liabilities, and Total Stockholders' Equity.

2. Use the accounting equation and calculate the balance of Stockholders' Equity (the Owner's Equity equivalent of a corporation), using the totals of Assets and Liabilities.

Continuing Problem

Eldorado Computer Center

The Eldorado Computer Center created its chart of accounts as follows:

Chart of Accounts
as of July 1, 200X

Assets		Revenue	
1000	Cash	4000	Service Revenue
1020	Accounts Receivable	**Expenses**	
1030	Supplies	5010	Advertising Expense
1080	Computer Shop Equipment	5020	Rent Expense
1090	Office Equipment	5030	Utilities Expense
Liabilities		5040	Phone Expense
2000	Accounts Payable	5050	Supplies Expense
Owner's Equity		5060	Insurance Expense
3000 Freedman, Capital		5070	Postage Expense
3010 Freedman, Withdrawals			

You will use this chart of accounts to complete the Continuing Problem.

The following problem continues from Chapter 1. The balances as of July 31 have been brought forward in your *Study Guide and Working Papers* on page 49.

Assignment for K–S

1. Set up T accounts in a ledger.
2. Record transactions k through s in the appropriate T accounts.
3. Foot the T accounts where appropriate.
4. Prepare a trial balance at the end of August.
5. Prepare from the trial balance an income statement, statement of owner's equity, and a balance sheet for the two months ending with August 31, 200X.

k. Received the phone bill for the month of July, $155.
l. Paid $150 (check #8099) for insurance for the month.
m. Paid $200 (check #8100) of the amount due from transaction d in Chapter 1.
n. Paid advertising expense for the month, $1,400 (check #8101).
o. Billed a client (Jeannine Sparks) for services rendered, $850.
p. Collected $900 for services rendered.
q. Paid the electric bill in full for the month of July (check #8102, transaction h, Chapter 1).
r. Paid cash (check #8103) for $50 in stamps.
s. Purchased $200 worth of supplies from Computer Connection on credit.

SUBWAY Case

DEBITS ON THE LEFT . . .

When Stan took the big leap from being an employee to a Subway owner, the thing that terrified him most was *not* the part about managing people—that was one of his strengths as a marketing manager. Why, at Xellent Media, 40 sales reps reported to him! No, Stan was terrified of having to manage the accounts. Subway restaurant owners have so many accounts to deal with—food costs, payroll, rent, utilities, supplies, advertising, promotion, and, biggest of all, cash. It's critical for them to keep debits and credits straight. If not, both they and Subway could lose a lot of money, quickly.

While Stan got some intense training in accounting and bookkeeping at Subway University, he still felt shaky about doing his own books. When he confided his fears to Mariah Washington, his field consultant, she suggested he hire an accountant. "You need to play to your strengths," said Mariah, and she told Stan, "More and more owners are using accountants, and almost all owners of multiple franchises do. In fact, some accountants actually specialize in handling Subway accounts for these multirestaurant owners."

Even though Stan decided to hire his cousin, Lila, to do his accounting, he still needs to feed her the right data so she can calculate his T accounts. Like many small business owners, Stan enters data into an accounting software program such as QuickBooks or Peachtree, which he then uploads to his accountant, who edits it and reviews it for accuracy. Several times in the beginning Stan mistakenly debited both cash and supplies when he paid for orders of paper cups, bread dough, and other supplies.

Lila urged Stan to review the rules for recording debits and credits. She even told him to practice for awhile using a paper ledger. "On the computer debits and credits are not as visible as they are with your paper system. Since you only enter the payables, the computer does the other side of the balance sheet. So you have to bone up on debits and credits to ensure that your Peachtree data is correct."

Discussion Questions

1. Why is the cash account so important in Stan's business?
2. Why do you think that most owners of the larger shops use accountants to do their books instead of doing them themselves?
3. Is the difference between debits and credits important to Subway restaurant owners who don't do their own books?

CHAPTER 3

Beginning the Accounting Cycle

Journalizing, Posting, and the Trial Balance

You stop by Hoffman's, a bagel shop just off campus. The owner, Stuart Hoffman, has been in the business of baking bagels for years. You wonder what makes Hoffman's bagels so good. You ask Mr. Hoffman how he does it. He replies simply, "Baking is nothing more than following several steps in order. You follow the same steps with every batch you bake—you don't change anything. It's just a cycle."

Accounting is also a cycle. You will recall in Chapters 1 and 2 we learned about the accounting equation and how it is used to record business transactions. We also learned about accounts, debits and credits, and how to prepare a trial balance. Now in Chapter 3 we will build upon this information and learn that recording business transactions is a set of steps that occur in a certain order and are then repeated. This series of steps is referred to as "the accounting cycle."

In a sense, the accounting cycle is similar to baking, since both accountants and bakers follow a set of steps in a certain order. In baking, once a batch of bagels has been baked, the baker begins another. And in accounting, once one accounting cycle is complete, the accountant begins another. Knowing about and understanding the accounting cycle won't turn you into a baker, but it will help you to succeed in gaining a better understanding of business and knowing how to speak its language, accounting.

Learning Objectives

- Journalizing: analyzing and recording business transactions into a journal. (p. 72)

The normal accounting procedures that are performed over a period of time are called the accounting cycle. The accounting cycle takes place in a period of time called an accounting period. An accounting period is the period of time covered by the income statement. Although it can be any time period up to one year (e.g., one month or three months), most businesses use a one-year accounting period. The year can be either a calendar year (January 1 through December 31) or a fiscal year.

A fiscal year is an accounting period that runs for any 12 consecutive months, so it can be the same as a calendar year. A business can choose any fiscal year that is convenient. For example, some retailers may decide to end their fiscal year when inventories and business activity are at a low point, such as after the Christmas season. This period is called a natural business year. Using a natural business year allows the business to count its year-end inventory when it is easiest to do so.

Businesses would not be able to operate successfully if they only prepared financial reports at the end of their calendar or fiscal year. That is why most businesses prepare interim reports on a monthly, quarterly, or semiannual basis.

In this chapter, as well as in Chapters 4 and 5, we follow Brenda Clark's new business, Clark's Word Processing Services. We follow the normal accounting procedures that the business performs over a period of time. Clark has chosen to use a fiscal period of January 1 to December 31, which also is the calendar year.

Take a moment to look at the four-color road map of the accounting cycle on the inside front cover. Use this map as a reference for Chapters 3, 4, and 5. It will help you to answer the question, When do I do what?

> This chapter covers Steps 1 to 4 of the accounting cycle. (See the road map on the inside front cover.)

Learning Unit 3-1	Analyzing and Recording Business Transactions into a Journal: Steps 1 and 2 of the Accounting Cycle

THE GENERAL JOURNAL

Chapter 2 taught us how to analyze and record business transactions into T accounts, or ledger accounts. Recording a debit in an account on one page of the ledger and recording the corresponding credit on a different page of the ledger, however, can make it difficult to find errors. It would be much easier if all the business's transactions were located in the same place. That is the function of the journal or general journal. Transactions are entered in the journal in chronological order (January 1, 8, 15, etc.), and then this recorded information is used to update the ledger accounts. In computerized accounting, a journal may be recorded on disk or tape.

> A business uses a journal to record transactions in chronological order. A ledger accumulates information from a journal. The journal and the ledger are in two different books.

We will use a general journal, the simplest form of a journal, to record the transactions of Clark's Word Processing Services. A transaction [debit(s) + credit(s)] that has been analyzed and recorded in a journal is called a journal entry. The process of recording the journal entry into the journal is called journalizing.

The journal is called the book of original entry, because it contains the first formal information about the business transactions. The ledger is known as the book of final entry, because the information the journal contains will be transferred to the ledger. Like the ledger, the journal may be a bound or loose-leaf book. Each of the journal pages looks like the one in Figure 3-1. The pages of the journal are numbered consecutively from page 1. Keep in mind that the journal and the ledger are separate books.

> Journal: book of original entry.

Figure 3-1
The General Journal

CLARK'S WORD PROCESSING SERVICES **GENERAL JOURNAL**						
						Page 1
Date		Account Titles and Description	PR	Dr.	Cr.	

Index to the ledger.

Relationship Between the Journal and the Chart of Accounts

The accountant must refer to the business's chart of accounts for the account name that is to be used in the journal. Every company has its own "unique" chart of accounts.

The chart of accounts for Clark's Word Processing Services appears below. By the end of Chapter 5, we will have discussed each of these accounts.

Note that we will continue to use transaction analysis charts as a teaching aid in the journalizing process.

Clark's Word Processing Services
Chart of Accounts

Assets (100–199)
111   Cash
112   Accounts Receivable
114   Office Supplies
115   Prepaid Rent
121   Word Processing Equipment
122   Accumulated Depreciation, Word Processing Equipment

Liabilities (200–299)
211   Accounts Payable
212   Salaries Payable

Owner's Equity (300–399)
311   Brenda Clark, Capital
312   Brenda Clark, Withdrawals
313   Income Summary

Revenue (400–499)
411   Word Processing Fees

Expenses (500–599)
511   Office Salaries Expense
512   Advertising Expense
513   Telephone Expense
514   Office Supplies Expense
515   Rent Expense
516   Depreciation Expense, Word Processing Equipment

Journalizing the Transactions of Clark's Word Processing Services

Certain formalities must be followed in making journal entries:

- The debit portion of the transaction always is recorded first.
- The credit portion of a transaction is indented $\frac{1}{2}$ inch and placed below the debit portion.
- The explanation of the journal entry follows immediately after the credit and 1 inch from the date column.
- A one-line space follows each transaction and explanation. This makes the journal easier to read, and there is less chance of mixing transactions.
- Finally, as always, the total amount of debits must equal the total amount of credits. The same format is used for each of the entries in the journal.

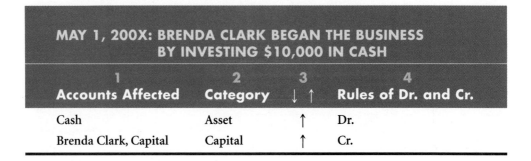

MAY 1, 200X: BRENDA CLARK BEGAN THE BUSINESS BY INVESTING $10,000 IN CASH			
1 Accounts Affected	**2** Category	**3** ↓ ↑	**4** Rules of Dr. and Cr.
Cash	Asset	↑	Dr.
Brenda Clark, Capital	Capital	↑	Cr.

Figure 3-2
Owner Investment

> For now the PR (posting reference) column is blank; we discuss it later.

CLARK'S WORD PROCESSING SERVICES GENERAL JOURNAL					
					Page 1
Date		Account Titles and Description	PR	Dr.	Cr.
200X May	1	Cash		10000 00	
		Brenda Clark, Capital			10000 00
		Initial investment of cash by owner			

Let's now look at the structure of this journal entry (Fig. 3-2). The entry contains the following information:

1. Year of the journal entry   200X
2. Month of the journal entry   May
3. Day of journal entry   1
4. Name(s) of accounts debited   Cash
5. Name(s) of accounts credited   Brenda Clark, Capital
6. Explanation of transaction   Investment of cash
7. Amount of debit(s) $10,000
8. Amount of credit(s) $10,000

MAY 1: PURCHASED WORD PROCESSING EQUIPMENT FROM BEN CO. FOR $6,000, PAYING $1,000 AND PROMISING TO PAY THE BALANCE WITHIN 30 DAYS			
1 Accounts Affected	**2** Category	**3** ↓ ↑	**4** Rules of Dr. and Cr.
Word Processing Equipment	Asset	↑	Dr.
Cash	Asset	↓	Cr.
Accounts Payable	Liability	↑	Cr.

> Note that in this compound entry we have one debit and two credits, but the total amount of debits equals the total amount of credits.

This transaction affects three accounts. When a journal entry has more than two accounts, it is called a compound journal entry.

In this entry, only the day is entered in the date column, because the year and month were entered at the top of the page from the first transaction. There is

	1	Word Processing Equipment		6 0 0 0 00					
		Cash				1 0 0 0 00			
		Accounts Payable				5 0 0 0 00			
		Purchase of equipment from Ben Co.							

Figure 3-3
Purchase of Equipment

> A journal entry that requires three or more accounts is called a compound journal entry.

no need to repeat this information until a new page is needed or a change of months occurs.

MAY 1: RENTED OFFICE SPACE, PAYING $1,200 IN ADVANCE FOR THE FIRST THREE MONTHS			
1 Accounts Affected	**2** Category	**3** ↓ ↑	**4** Rules of Dr. and Cr.
Prepaid Rent	Asset	↑	Dr.
Cash	Asset	↓	Cr.

In this transaction Clark gains an asset called prepaid rent and gives up an asset, cash. The prepaid rent does not become an expense until it expires.

> Rent paid in advance is an asset.

	1	Prepaid Rent		1 2 0 0 00				
		Cash				1 2 0 0 00		
		Rent paid in advance—3 mos.						

Figure 3-4
Rent Paid in Advance

MAY 3: PURCHASED OFFICE SUPPLIES FROM NORRIS CO. ON ACCOUNT, $600			
1 Accounts Affected	**2** Category	**3** ↓ ↑	**4** Rules of Dr. and Cr.
Office Supplies	Asset	↑	Dr.
Accounts Payable	Liability	↑	Cr.

Remember, supplies are an asset when they are purchased. Once they are used up or consumed in the operation of business, they become an expense.

> Supplies become an expense when used up.

	3	Office Supplies		6 0 0 00				
		Accounts Payable				6 0 0 00		
		Purchase of supplies on account						
		from Norris						

Figure 3-5
Purchased Supplies on Account

MAY 7: COMPLETED SALES PROMOTION PIECES FOR A CLIENT AND IMMEDIATELY COLLECTED $3,000			
1 Accounts Affected	2 Category	3 ↓ ↑	4 Rules of Dr. and Cr.
Cash	Asset	↑	Dr.
Word Processing Fees	Revenue	↑	Cr.

Figure 3-6
Services Rendered

		7	Cash		3 0 0 0 00	
			Word Processing Fees			3 0 0 0 00
			Cash received for services rendered			

MAY 13: PAID OFFICE SALARIES, $650			
1 Accounts Affected	2 Category	3 ↓ ↑	4 Rules of Dr. and Cr.
Office Salaries Expense	Expense	↑	Dr.
Cash	Asset	↓	Cr.

Figure 3-7
Paid Salaries

		13	Office Salaries Expense		6 5 0 00	
			Cash			6 5 0 00
			Payment of office salaries			

> Remember, expenses are recorded when they are incurred, no matter when they are paid.

MAY 18: ADVERTISING BILL FROM AL'S NEWS CO. COMES IN BUT IS NOT PAID, $250			
1 Accounts Affected	2 Category	3 ↓ ↑	4 Rules of Dr. and Cr.
Advertising Expense	Expense	↑	Dr.
Accounts Payable	Liability	↑	Cr.

Figure 3-8
Advertising Bill

		18	Advertising Expense		2 5 0 00	
			Accounts Payable			2 5 0 00
			Bill in but not paid from Al's News			

MAY 20: BRENDA CLARK WROTE A CHECK ON THE BANK ACCOUNT OF THE BUSINESS TO PAY HER HOME MORTGAGE PAYMENT OF $625

1 Accounts Affected	2 Category	3 ↓ ↑	4 Rules of Dr. and Cr.
Brenda Clark, Withdrawals	Withdrawals	↑	Dr.
Cash	Asset	↓	Cr.

Keep in mind that as withdrawals increase, owner's equity decreases.

		20	Brenda Clark, Withdrawals			6 2 5 00		
			Cash				6 2 5 00	
			Personal withdrawal of cash					

Figure 3-9
Personal Withdrawal

MAY 22: BILLED MORRIS COMPANY FOR A SOPHISTICATED WORD PROCESSING JOB, $5,000

1 Accounts Affected	2 Category	3 ↓ ↑	4 Rules of Dr. and Cr.
Accounts Receivable	Asset	↑	Dr.
Word Processing Fees	Revenue	↑	Cr.

Reminder:
Revenue is recorded when it is earned, no matter when the cash is actually received.

		22	Accounts Receivable			5 0 0 0 00		
			Word Processing Fees				5 0 0 0 00	
			Billed Morris Co. for fees earned					

Figure 3-10
Fees Earned

MAY 27: PAID OFFICE SALARIES, $650

1 Accounts Affected	2 Category	3 ↓ ↑	4 Rules of Dr. and Cr.
Offices Salaries Expense	Expense	↑	Dr.
Cash	Asset	↓	Cr.

CLARK'S WORD PROCESSING SERVICES
GENERAL JOURNAL

Page 2

Date		Account Titles and Description	PR	Dr.	Cr.
200X May	27	Office Salaries Expense		6 5 0 00	
		Cash			6 5 0 00
		Payment of office salaries			

Figure 3-11
Paid Salaries

Note:
Since we are on page 2 of the journal, the year and month are repeated.

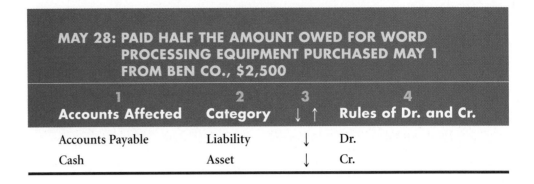

		MAY 28: PAID HALF THE AMOUNT OWED FOR WORD PROCESSING EQUIPMENT PURCHASED MAY 1 FROM BEN CO., $2,500		
	1 Accounts Affected	2 Category	3 ↓ ↑	4 Rules of Dr. and Cr.
	Accounts Payable	Liability	↓	Dr.
	Cash	Asset	↓	Cr.

Figure 3-12
Partial Payment

		28	Accounts Payable		2 5 0 0 00	
			Cash			2 5 0 0 00
			Paid half the amount owed Ben Co.			

		MAY 29: RECEIVED AND PAID TELEPHONE BILL, $220		
	1 Accounts Affected	2 Category	3 ↓ ↑	4 Rules of Dr. and Cr.
	Telephone Expense	Expense	↑	Dr.
	Cash	Asset	↓	Cr.

Figure 3-13
Paid Telephone

		29	Telephone Expense		2 2 0 00	
			Cash			2 2 0 00
			Paid telephone bill			

This concludes the journal transactions of Clark's Word Processing Services. (See page 83 for a summary of all the transactions.)

Learning Unit 3-1 Review

AT THIS POINT you should be able to

- Define an accounting cycle. (p. 72)
- Define and explain the relationship of the accounting period to the income statement. (p. 72)
- Compare and contrast a calendar year to a fiscal year. (p. 72)
- Explain the term *natural business year.* (p. 72)
- Explain the function of interim reports. (p. 72)
- Define and state the purpose of a journal. (p. 72)
- Compare and contrast a book of original entry to a book of final entry. (p. 72)

- Differentiate between a chart of accounts and a journal. (p. 73)
- Explain a compound entry. (p. 74)
- Journalize a business transaction. (p. 74)

SELF-REVIEW QUIZ 3-1

(The blank forms you need are on pages 52–53 of the *Study Guide and Working Papers*. See your DVD for worked-out solutions.)

The following are the transactions of Lowe's Repair Service. Journalize the transactions in proper form. The chart of accounts includes Cash; Accounts Receivable; Prepaid Rent; Repair Supplies; Repair Equipment; Accounts Payable; A. Lowe, Capital; A. Lowe, Withdrawals; Repair Fees Earned; Salaries Expense; Advertising Expense; and Supplies Expense.

200X

June 1 A. Lowe invested $7,000 cash and $5,000 of repair equipment in the business.

1 Paid two months' rent in advance, $1,200.

4 Bought repair supplies from Melvin Co. on account, $600. (These supplies have not yet been consumed or used up.)

15 Performed repair work, received $600 in cash, and had to bill Doe Co. for remaining balance of $300.

18 A. Lowe paid his home telephone bill, $50, with a check from the company.

20 Advertising bill for $400 from Jones Co. received but payment not due yet. (Advertising has already appeared in the newspaper.)

24 Paid salaries, $1,400.

SOLUTION TO SELF-REVIEW QUIZ 3-1

Figure 3-14
Transactions Journalized

LOWE'S REPAIR SERVICE
GENERAL JOURNAL

Page 1

Date			Account Titles and Description	PR	Dr.	Cr.
200X June	1		Cash		7 0 0 0 00	
			Repair Equipment		5 0 0 0 00	
			A. Lowe, Capital			12 0 0 0 00
			Owner investment			
	1		Prepaid Rent		1 2 0 0 00	
			Cash			1 2 0 0 00
			Rent paid in advance—2 mos.			
	4		Repair Supplies		6 0 0 00	
			Accounts Payable			6 0 0 00
			Purchase on account from Melvin Co.			
	15		Cash		6 0 0 00	
			Accounts Receivable		3 0 0 00	
			Repair Fees Earned			9 0 0 00
			Performed repairs for Doe Co.			
	18		A. Lowe, Withdrawals		5 0 00	
			Cash			5 0 00
			Personal withdrawal			
	20		Advertising Expense		4 0 0 00	
			Accounts Payable			4 0 0 00
			Advertising bill from Jones Co.			
	24		Salaries Expense		1 4 0 0 00	
			Cash			1 4 0 0 00
			Paid salaries			

Quiz Tip:
All titles for the debits and credits come from the chart of accounts, debits are entered next to the date column, and credits are indented. The PR column is left blank in the journalizing process.

Learning Unit 3-2   Posting to the Ledger: Step 3 of the Accounting Cycle

The general journal serves a particular purpose: It puts every transaction the business does in one place. There are things it cannot do, though. For example, if you were asked to find the balance of the cash account from the general journal, you would have to go through the entire journal and look for only the cash entries. Then you would have to add up the debits and credits for the Cash account and determine the difference between the two.

What we really need to do to find balances of accounts is to transfer the information from the journal to the ledger. This is called **posting.** In the ledger we will accumulate an ending balance for each account so that we can prepare financial statements.

Accounts Payable								Account No. 211	
			Post. Ref.	Debit	Credit		Balance		
Date		Explanation					Debit	Credit	
200X May	1		GJ1		5 0 0 0 00			5 0 0 0 00	
	3		GJ1		6 0 0 00			5 6 0 0 00	
	18		GJ1		2 5 0 00			5 8 5 0 00	
	28		GJ2	2 5 0 0 00				3 3 5 0 00	

Figure 3-15
Four-Column Account

In Chapter 2 we used the T account form to make our ledger entries. T accounts are very simple, but they are not used in the real business world; they are only used for demonstration purposes. In practice, accountants often use a **four-column account** form that includes a column for the business's running balance. Figure 3-15 shows a standard four-column account. We use that format in the text from now on.

Footings are not needed in four-column accounts.

POSTING

Now let's look at how to post the transactions of Clark's Word Processing Service from its journal. The diagram in Figure 3-16, p. 82 shows how to post the cash line from the journal to the ledger. The steps in the posting process are numbered and illustrated in the figure.

Step 1:   In the Cash account in the ledger, record the date (May 1, 200X) and the amount of the entry ($10,000).

Step 2:   Record the page number of the journal "GJ1" in the posting reference (PR) column of the Cash account.

Step 3:   Calculate the new balance of the account. You keep a running balance in each account as you would in your checkbook. To do so, you take the present balance in the account on the previous line and add or subtract the transaction as necessary to arrive at your new balance.

Step 4:   Record the account number of Cash (111) in the posting reference (PR) column of the journal. This is called **cross-referencing.**

The same sequence of steps occurs for each line in the journal. In a manual system like Clark's, the debits and credits in the journal may be posted in the order they were recorded, or all the debits may be posted first and then all the credits. If Clark used a computer system, the program menu would post at the press of a button.

Using Posting References

The posting references are very helpful. In the journal, the PR column tells us which transactions have or have not been posted and also to which accounts they were posted. In the ledger, the posting reference leads us back to the original transaction in its entirety, so we can see why the debit or credit was recorded and what other accounts were affected. (It leads us back to the original transaction by identifying the journal and the page in the journal from which the information came.)

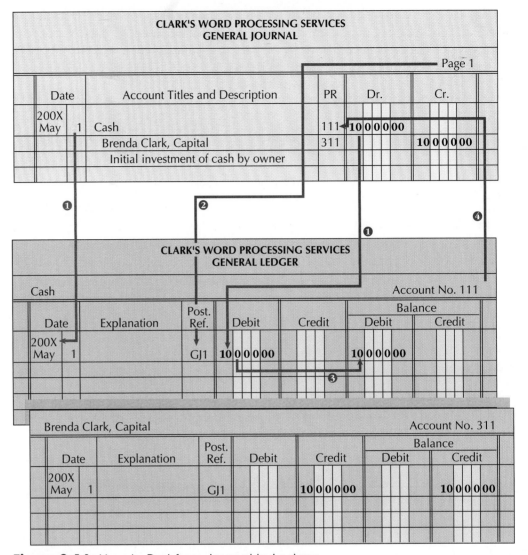

Figure 3-16 How to Post from Journal to Ledger

Learning Unit 3-2 Review

AT THIS POINT you should be able to

- State the purpose of posting. (p. 80)
- Discuss the advantages of the four-column account. (p. 81)
- Identify the elements to be posted. (p. 82)
- From journalized transactions, post to the general ledger. (p. 82)

SELF-REVIEW QUIZ 3-2

(The blank forms you need are on pages 54–59 of the *Study Guide and Working Papers.* See your DVD for worked-out solutions.)

Figure 3-17 shows the journalized transactions of Clark's Word Processing Services. Your task is to post information to the ledger. The ledger in your workbook has all the account titles and numbers that were used from the chart of accounts.

CLARK'S WORD PROCESSING SERVICES
GENERAL JOURNAL

Page 1

Date		Account Titles and Description	PR	Dr.	Cr.
200X May	1	Cash		10 00 00	
		Brenda Clark, Capital			10 00 00
		Initial investment of cash by owner			
	1	Word Processing Equipment		6 00 00	
		Cash			1 00 00
		Accounts Payable			5 00 00
		Purchase of equip. from Ben Co.			
	1	Prepaid Rent		1 20 00	
		Cash			1 20 00
		Rent paid in advance (3 months)			
	3	Office Supplies		6 00 00	
		Accounts Payable			6 00 00
		Purchase of supplies on acct. from Norris			
	7	Cash		3 00 00	
		Word Processing Fees			3 00 00
		Cash received for services rendered			
	13	Office Salaries Expense		6 50 00	
		Cash			6 50 00
		Payment of office salaries			
	18	Advertising Expense		2 50 00	
		Accounts Payable			2 50 00
		Bill received but not paid from Al's News			
	20	Brenda Clark, Withdrawals		6 25 00	
		Cash			6 25 00
		Personal withdrawal of cash			
	22	Accounts Receivable		5 00 00	
		Word Processing Fees			5 00 00
		Billed Morris Co. for fees earned			

Figure 3-17 Journalized Entries

Figure 3-17
(*continued*)

CLARK'S WORD PROCESSING SERVICES
GENERAL JOURNAL

Page 2

Date		Account Titles and Description	PR	Dr.	Cr.
200X May	27	Office Salaries Expense		650 00	
		Cash			650 00
		Payment of office salaries			
	28	Accounts Payable		2500 00	
		Cash			2500 00
		Paid half the amount owed Ben Co.			
	29	Telephone Expense		220 00	
		Cash			220 00
		Paid telephone bill			

SOLUTION TO SELF-REVIEW QUIZ 3-2

> Remember, the PR column remains empty until the entries have been posted.

CLARK'S WORD PROCESSING SERVICES
GENERAL JOURNAL

Page 1

Date		Account Titles and Description	PR	Dr.	Cr.
200X May	1	Cash	111	10000 00	
		Brenda Clark, Capital	311		10000 00
		Initial investment of cash by owner			
	1	Word Processing Equipment	121	6000 00	
		Cash	111		1000 00
		Accounts Payable	211		5000 00
		Purchase of equip. from Ben Co.			
	1	Prepaid Rent	115	1200 00	
		Cash	111		1200 00
		Rent paid in advance (3 months)			
	3	Office Supplies	114	600 00	
		Accounts Payable	211		600 00
		Purchase of supplies on acct. from Norris			
	7	Cash	111	3000 00	
		Word Processing Fees	411		3000 00
		Cash received from services rendered			
	13	Office Salaries Expense	511	650 00	
		Cash	111		650 00
		Payment of office salaries			

Figure 3-18 Postings

	18	Advertising Expense	512	2 5 0 00	
		Accounts Payable	211		2 5 0 00
		Bill received but not paid from Al's News			
	20	Brenda Clark, Withdrawals	312	6 2 5 00	
		Cash	111		6 2 5 00
		Personal withdrawal of cash			
	22	Accounts Receivable	112	5 0 0 0 00	
		Word Processing Fees	411		5 0 0 0 00
		Billed Morris Co. for fees earned			

CLARK'S WORD PROCESSING SERVICES
GENERAL JOURNAL

Page 2

Date		Account Titles and Description	PR	Dr.	Cr.
200X May	27	Office Salaries Expense	511	6 5 0 00	
		Cash	111		6 5 0 00
		Payment of office salaries			
	28	Accounts Payable	211	2 5 0 0 00	
		Cash	111		2 5 0 0 00
		Paid half the amount owed Ben Co.			
	29	Telephone Expense	513	2 2 0 00	
		Cash	111		2 2 0 00
		Paid telephone bill			

Figure 3-18 (continued)

CLARK'S WORD PROCESSING SERVICES
PARTIAL GENERAL LEDGER

Cash   Account No. 111

Date		Explanation	Post. Ref.	Debit	Credit	Balance Debit	Balance Credit
200X May	1		GJ1	10 0 0 0 00		10 0 0 0 00	
	1		GJ1		1 0 0 0 00	9 0 0 0 00	
	1		GJ1		1 2 0 0 00	7 8 0 0 00	
	7		GJ1	3 0 0 0 00		10 8 0 0 00	
	13		GJ1		6 5 0 00	10 1 5 0 00	
	20		GJ1		6 2 5 00	9 5 2 5 00	
	27		GJ2		6 5 0 00	8 8 7 5 00	
	28		GJ2		2 5 0 0 00	6 3 7 5 00	
	29		GJ2		2 2 0 00	6 1 5 5 00	

Figure 3-19 Partial General Ledger

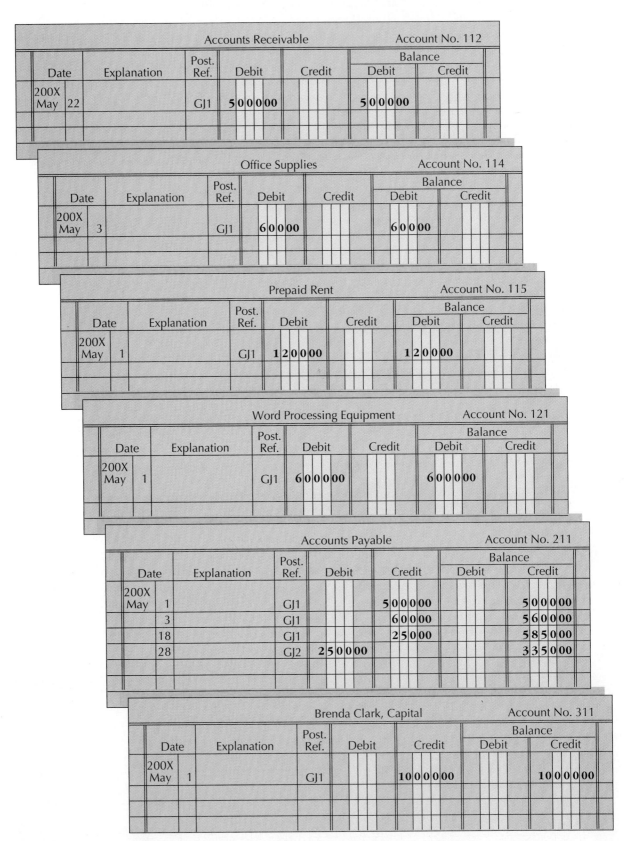

Accounts Receivable — Account No. 112

Date	Explanation	Post. Ref.	Debit	Credit	Balance Debit	Balance Credit
200X May 22		GJ1	5 0 0 0 00		5 0 0 0 00	

Office Supplies — Account No. 114

Date	Explanation	Post. Ref.	Debit	Credit	Balance Debit	Balance Credit
200X May 3		GJ1	6 0 0 00		6 0 0 00	

Prepaid Rent — Account No. 115

Date	Explanation	Post. Ref.	Debit	Credit	Balance Debit	Balance Credit
200X May 1		GJ1	1 2 0 0 00		1 2 0 0 00	

Word Processing Equipment — Account No. 121

Date	Explanation	Post. Ref.	Debit	Credit	Balance Debit	Balance Credit
200X May 1		GJ1	6 0 0 0 00		6 0 0 0 00	

Accounts Payable — Account No. 211

Date	Explanation	Post. Ref.	Debit	Credit	Balance Debit	Balance Credit
200X May 1		GJ1		5 0 0 0 00		5 0 0 0 00
3		GJ1		6 0 0 00		5 6 0 0 00
18		GJ1		2 5 0 00		5 8 5 0 00
28		GJ2	2 5 0 0 00			3 3 5 0 00

Brenda Clark, Capital — Account No. 311

Date	Explanation	Post. Ref.	Debit	Credit	Balance Debit	Balance Credit
200X May 1		GJ1		1 0 0 0 0 00		1 0 0 0 0 00

Figure 3-19 (continued)

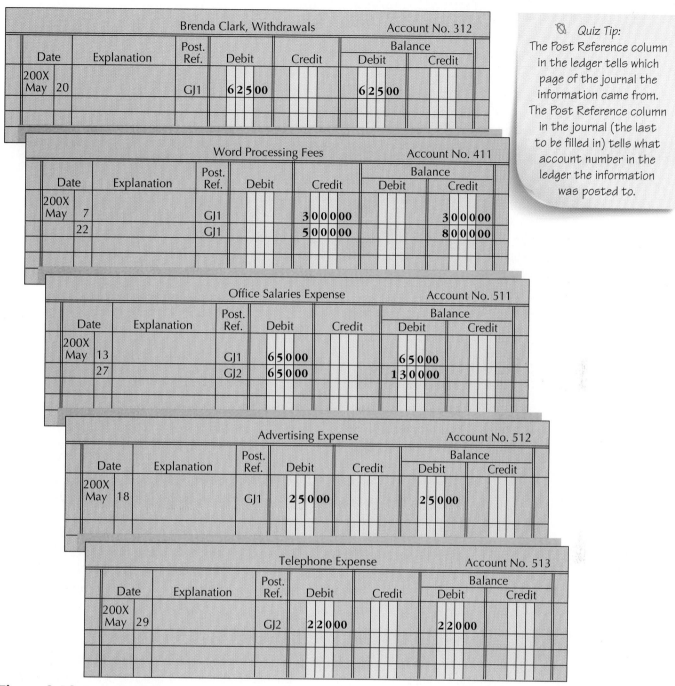

Figure 3-19 (continued)

Learning Unit 3-3 | Preparing the Trial Balance: Step 4 of the Accounting Cycle

Did you note in Quiz 3-2 how each account had a running balance figure? Did you know the normal balance of each account in Clark's ledger? As we discussed in Chapter 2, the list of the individual accounts with their balances taken from the ledger is called a **trial balance.**

The trial balance shown in Figure 3-20, p. 88 was developed from the ledger accounts of Clark's Word Processing Services that were posted and balanced in Quiz 3-2. If the information is journalized or posted incorrectly, the trial balance will not be correct.

CLARK'S WORD PROCESSING SERVICE
TRIAL BALANCE
MAY 31, 200X

	Debit	Credit
Cash	6 1 5 5 00	
Accounts Receivable	5 0 0 0 00	
Office Supplies	6 0 0 00	
Prepaid Rent	1 2 0 0 00	
Word Processing Equipment	6 0 0 0 00	
Accounts Payable		3 3 5 0 00
Brenda Clark, Capital		10 0 0 0 00
Brenda Clark, Withdrawals	6 2 5 00	
Word Processing Fees		8 0 0 0 00
Office Salaries Expense	1 3 0 0 00	
Advertising Expense	2 5 0 00	
Telephone Expense	2 2 0 00	
Totals	21 3 5 0 00	21 3 5 0 00

The trial balance lists the accounts in the same order as in the ledger. The $6,155 figure of cash came from the ledger, p. 85.

Figure 3-20 Trial Balance

There are some things the trial balance will not show:

- The capital figure on the trial balance may not be the beginning capital figure. For instance, if Brenda Clark had made additional investments during the period, the additional investment would have been journalized and posted to the Capital account. The only way to tell if the capital balance on the trial balance is the original balance is to check the ledger Capital account to see whether any additional investments were made. This will be important when we make financial reports.
- There is no guarantee that transactions have been properly recorded. For example, the following errors would remain undetected: (1) a transaction that may have been omitted in the journalizing process, (2) a transaction incorrectly analyzed and recorded in the journal, and (3) a journal entry journalized or posted twice.

> The totals of a trial balance can balance and yet be incorrect.

WHAT TO DO IF A TRIAL BALANCE DOESN'T BALANCE

The trial balance of Clark's Word Processing Services shows that the total of debits is equal to the total of credits. What happens, however, if the trial balance is in balance but the correct amount is not recorded in each ledger account? Accuracy in the journalizing and posting process will help ensure that no errors are made.

Even if there is an error, the first rule is "don't panic." Everyone makes mistakes, and there are accepted ways of correcting them. Once an entry has been made in ink, correcting an error in it must always show that the entry has been changed and who changed it. Sometimes the change has to be explained.

SOME COMMON MISTAKES

If the trial balance does not balance, the cause could be something relatively simple. Here are some common errors and how they can be fixed:

- If the difference (the amount you are off) is 10, 100, 1,000, and so forth, there is probably a mathematical error in addition.

- If the difference is equal to an individual account balance in the ledger, the amount could have been omitted. It is also possible the figure was not posted from the general journal.
- Divide the difference by 2, then check to see if a debit should have been a credit and vice versa in the ledger or trial balance. Example: $150 difference ÷ 2 = $75. This means you may have placed $75 as a debit to an account instead of a credit, or vice versa.
- If the difference is evenly divisible by 9, a slide or transposition may have occurred. A slide is an error resulting from adding or deleting zeros in writing numbers. For example, $4,175.00 may have been copied as $41.75. A transposition is the accidental rearrangement of digits of a number. For example, $4,175 might have been accidentally written as $4,157.
- Compare the balances in the trial balance with the ledger accounts to check for copying errors.
- Recompute balances in each ledger account.
- Trace all postings from journal to ledger.

If you cannot find the error after you have done all this, take a coffee break. Then start all over again.

MAKING A CORRECTION BEFORE POSTING

Before posting, error correction is straightforward. Simply draw a line through the incorrect entry, write the correct information above the line, and write your initials near the change.

Correcting an Error in an Account Title   Figure 3-21 shows an error and its correction in an account title:

	1	Word Processing Equipment		6 0 0 0 00		
		Cash			1 0 0 0 00	
		~~Accounts Payable~~ *amp*				
		~~Accounts Receivable~~			5 0 0 0 00	
		Purchase of equipment from Ben Co.				

Figure 3-21
Account Error

Correcting a Numerical Error   Numbers are handled the same way as account titles, as the next change from 520 to 250 in Figure 3-22 shows:

	18	Advertising Expense		2 5 0 00	
		Accounts Payable			*amp* 2 5 0 00 ~~5 2 0 00~~
		Bill from Al's News			

Figure 3-22
Number Error

Correcting an Entry Error   If a number has been entered in the wrong column, a straight line is drawn through it. The number is then written in the correct column, as shown in Figure 3-23:

	1	Word Processing Equipment		6 0 0 0 00	
		Cash			1 0 0 0 00
		Accounts Payable	*amp* ~~5 0 0 0 00~~		5 0 0 0 00
		Purchase of equip. from Ben Co.			

Figure 3-23
Correcting Entry

MAKING A CORRECTION AFTER POSTING

It is also possible to correct an amount that is correctly entered in the journal but posted incorrectly to the ledger of the proper account. The first step is to draw a line through the error and write the correct figure above it. The next step is changing the running balance to reflect the corrected posting. Here, too, a line is drawn through the balance and the corrected balance is written above it. Both changes must be initialed, as shown in Figure 3-24.

Figure 3-24
Correction After Posting

				Word Processing Fees			Account No. 411	
			Post.				Balance	
Date		Explanation	Ref.	Debit	Credit		Debit	Credit
200X May	7		GJ1		2 5 0 0 00			2 5 0 0 00
	22		GJ1		~~1 0 0 00~~ 4 1 0 0 00 dmp			~~2 6 0 0 00~~ 6 6 0 0 00 dmp

CORRECTING AN ENTRY POSTED TO THE WRONG ACCOUNT

Drawing a line through an error and writing the correction above it is possible when a mistake has occurred within the proper account, but when an error involves a posting to the wrong account, the journal must include a correction accompanied by an explanation. In addition, the correct information must be posted to the appropriate ledgers.

Suppose, for example, as a result of tracing postings from journal entries to ledgers you find that a $180 telephone bill was incorrectly debited as an advertising expense. The following illustration shows how this is done.

Step 1: The journal entry is corrected and the correction is explained (Fig. 3-25):

Figure 3-25
Corrected Entry
for Telephone

		GENERAL JOURNAL				Page 3	
Date		Account Titles and Description	PR	Dr.		Cr.	
200X May	29	Telephone Expense	513	1 8 0 00			
		Advertising Expense	512			1 8 0 00	
		To correct error in which					
		Advertising Exp. was debited					
		for charges to Telephone Exp.					

Step 2: The Advertising Expense ledger account is corrected (Fig. 3-26):

Figure 3-26
Ledger Update
for Advertising

				Advertising Expense			Account No. 512	
			Post.				Balance	
Date		Explanation	Ref.	Debit	Credit		Debit	Credit
200X May	18		GJ1	1 7 5 00			1 7 5 00	
	23		GJ1	1 8 0 00			3 5 5 00	
	29	Correcting entry	GJ3		1 8 0 00		1 7 5 00	

Step 3:   The Telephone Expense ledger is corrected (Fig. 3-27):

			Telephone Expense				Account No. 513	
Date	Explanation	Post. Ref.	Debit	Credit	Balance			
					Debit		Credit	
200X May 29		GJ3	1 8 0 00		1 8 0 00			

Figure 3-27
Ledger Update for Telephone

Learning Unit 3-3 Review

AT THIS POINT you should be able to

- Prepare a trial balance with a ledger, using four-column accounts. (p. 88)
- Analyze and correct a trial balance that doesn't balance. (p. 89)
- Correct journal and posting errors. (p. 90)

SELF-REVIEW QUIZ 3-3

(The blank forms you need are on page 60 of the *Study Guide and Working Papers*. See your DVD for worked-out solutions.)

1.

> **MEMO**
>
> To: Al Vincent
>
> From: Professor Jones
>
> Re: Trial Balance
>
> You have submitted to me an incorrect trial balance (Fig. 3-28). Could you please rework and turn in to me before next Friday?
>
> Note: Individual amounts look OK.

A. RICE
TRIAL BALANCE
OCTOBER 31, 200X

	Dr.	Cr.
Cash		8 0 6 0 00
Operating Expenses		1 7 0 0 00
A. Rice, Withdrawals		4 0 0 00
Service Revenue		5 4 0 0 00
Equipment	5 0 0 0 00	
Accounts Receivable	3 5 4 0 00	
Accounts Payable	2 0 0 0 00	
Supplies	3 0 0 00	
A. Rice, Capital		11 6 0 0 00

Figure 3-28
Incorrect Trial Balance

2. An $8,000 debit to Office Equipment was mistakenly journalized and posted on June 9, 200X to Office Supplies. Prepare the appropriate journal entry to correct this error.

SOLUTION TO SELF-REVIEW QUIZ 3-3

1.

Figure 3-29
Correct Trial Balance

Quiz Tip:
Items in a trial balance are listed in the same order as in the ledger or the chart of accounts. Expect each account to have its normal balance (either debit or credit).

A. RICE TRIAL BALANCE OCTOBER 31, 200X	Dr.	Cr.
Cash	8 0 6 0 00	
Accounts Receivable	3 5 4 0 00	
Supplies	3 0 0 00	
Equipment	5 0 0 0 00	
Accounts Payable		2 0 0 0 00
A. Rice, Capital		11 6 0 0 00
A. Rice, Withdrawals	4 0 0 00	
Service Revenue		5 4 0 0 00
Operating Expenses	1 7 0 0 00	
Totals	19 0 0 0 00	19 0 0 0 00

2.

Figure 3-30
Correcting Entry

	GENERAL JOURNAL				Page 4
Date	Account Titles and Description	PR	Dr.	Cr.	
200X June 9	Office Equipment		8 0 0 0 00		
	Office Supplies			8 0 0 0 00	
	To correct error in which office supplies				
	had been debited for purchase of				
	office equipment				

SOLUTIONS & TIPS TO COMPREHENSIVE PROBLEM: PUTTING THE PIECES TOGETHER

(The blank forms you need are on pages 61–65 in the *Study Guide and Working Papers.*)

In March, Abby's Employment Agency had the following transactions:

200X

Mar. 1 Abby Todd invested $5,000 in the new employment agency.
4 Bought equipment for cash, $200.
5 Earned employment fee commission, $200, but payment from Blue Co. will not be received until June.
6 Paid wages expense, $300.
7 Abby paid her home utility bill from the company checkbook, $75.
9 Placed Rick Wool at VCR Corporation, receiving $1,200 cash.
15 Paid cash for supplies, $200.
28 Telephone bill received but not paid, $180.
29 Advertising bill received but not paid, $400.

The chart of accounts includes Cash, 111; Accounts Receivable, 112; Supplies, 131; Equipment, 141; Accounts Payable, 211; A. Todd, Capital, 311; A. Todd, Withdrawals, 321; Employment Fees Earned, 411; Wage Expense, 511; Telephone Expense, 521; and Advertising Expense, 531.

Your task is to

a. Set up a ledger based on the chart of accounts.
b. Journalize (all page 1) and post transactions.
c. Prepare a trial balance for March 31.

Solution to Comprehensive Demonstration Problem

b.

ABBY'S EMPLOYMENT AGENCY					Page 1	
Date	Account Titles and Description	PR	Dr.		Cr.	
200X Mar. 1	Cash	111	5 0 0 0 00			
	A. Todd, Capital	311			5 0 0 0 00	
	Owner investment					
4	Equipment	141	2 0 0 00			
	Cash	111			2 0 0 00	
	Bought equipment for cash					
5	Accounts Receivable	112	2 0 0 00			
	Employment Fees Earned	411			2 0 0 00	
	Fees on account from Blue Co.					
6	Wage Expense	511	3 0 0 00			
	Cash	111			3 0 0 00	
	Paid wages					

Figure 3-31
Journal Entries and Post References

Figure 3-31
(*continued*)

			PR	Dr.	Cr.
	7	A. Todd, Withdrawals	321	75 00	
		Cash	111		75 00
		Personal withdrawals			
	9	Cash	111	1 20 0 00	
		Employment Fees Earned	411		1 20 0 00
		Cash fees			
	15	Supplies	131	2 00 00	
		Cash	111		2 00 00
		Bought supplies for cash			
	28	Telephone Expense	521	1 80 00	
		Accounts Payable	211		1 80 00
		Telephone bill owed			
	29	Advertising Expense	531	4 00 00	
		Accounts Payable	211		4 00 00
		Advertising bill received			

a.

GENERAL LEDGER

Cash   111

Date		PR	Dr.	Cr.	Balance Dr.	Balance Cr.
200X Mar.	1	GJ1	5,000		5,000	
	4	GJ1		200	4,800	
	6	GJ1		300	4,500	
	7	GJ1		75	4,425	
	9	GJ1	1,200		5,625	
	15	GJ1		200	5,425	

Accounts Receivable   112

Date		PR	Dr.	Cr.	Balance Dr.	Balance Cr.
200X Mar.	5	GJ1	200		200	

Supplies   131

Date		PR	Dr.	Cr.	Balance Dr.	Balance Cr.
200X Mar.	15	GJ1	200		200	

A. Todd, Capital   311

Date		PR	Dr.	Cr.	Balance Dr.	Balance Cr.
200X Mar.	1	GJ1		5,000		5,000

A. Todd, Withdrawals   321

Date		PR	Dr.	Cr.	Balance Dr.	Balance Cr.
200X Mar.	7	GJ1	75		75	

Employment Fees Earned   411

Date		PR	Dr.	Cr.	Balance Dr.	Balance Cr.
200X Mar.	5	GJ1		200		200
	9	GJ1		1,200		1,400

Wage Expense   511

Date		PR	Dr.	Cr.	Balance Dr.	Balance Cr.
200X Mar.	6	GJ1	300		300	

Figure 3-32 General Ledger (cont. on p. 95)

Equipment					141
				Balance	
Date	PR	Dr.	Cr.	Dr.	Cr.
200X Mar. 4	GJ1	200		200	

Telephone Expense					521
				Balance	
Date	PR	Dr.	Cr.	Dr.	Cr.
200X Mar. 28	GJ1	180		180	

Accounts Payable					211
				Balance	
Date	PR	Dr.	Cr.	Dr.	Cr.
200X Mar. 28	GJ1		180		180
29	GJ1		400		580

Advertising Expense					531
				Balance	
Date	PR	Dr.	Cr.	Dr.	Cr.
200X Mar. 29	GJ1	400		400	

Figure 3-32 *(continued)*

Solution Tips to Journalizing

1. When journalizing, the PR column is not filled in.
2. Write the name of the debit against the date column. Indent credits and list them below debits. Be sure total debits for each transaction equal total credits.
3. Skip a line between each transaction.

The Analysis of the Journal Entries

March 1	Cash	A	↑	Dr.	$5,000
	A. Todd, Capital	Capital	↑	Cr.	$5,000

4	Equipment	A	↑	Dr.	$ 200
	Cash	A	↓	Cr.	$ 200

5	Acc. Receivable	A	↑	Dr.	$ 200
	Empl. Fees Earned	Rev.	↑	Cr.	$ 200

6	Wage Expense	Exp.	↑	Dr.	$ 300
	Cash	A	↓	Cr.	$ 300

7	A. Todd, Withdrawals	Withd.	↑	Dr.	$ 75
	Cash	A	↓	Cr.	$ 75

9	Cash	A	↑	Dr.	$1,200
	Empl. Fees Earned	Rev.	↑	Cr.	$1,200

This analysis is what should be going through your head before determining debit or credit.

15	Supplies	A	↑	Dr.	$ 200
	Cash	A	↓	Cr.	$ 200

28	Telephone Expense	Exp.	↑	Dr.	$ 180
	Accounts Payable	L	↑	Cr.	$ 180

28	Advertising Expense	Exp.	↑	Dr.	$ 400
	Accounts Payable	L	↑	Cr.	$ 400

Solution Tips to Posting

The PR column in the ledger cash account tells you from which page journal information came (see page 94). After the ledger cash account is posted, Account Number 111 is put in the PR column of the journal. (This is called cross-referencing.)

Note how we keep a running balance in the cash account. A $5,000 debit balance and a $200 credit entry result in a new debit balance of $4,800 on page 94.

Figure 3-33

ABBY'S EMPLOYMENT AGENCY TRIAL BALANCE MARCH 31, 200X		
	Dr.	Cr.
Cash	5 4 2 5 00	
Accounts Receivable	2 0 0 00	
Supplies	2 0 0 00	
Equipment	2 0 0 00	
Accounts Payable		5 8 0 00
A. Todd, Capital		5 0 0 0 00
A. Todd, Withdrawals	7 5 00	
Employment Fees Earned		1 4 0 0 00
Wage Expense	3 0 0 00	
Telephone Expense	1 8 0 00	
Advertising Expense	4 0 0 00	
Totals	6 9 8 0 00	6 9 8 0 00

Solution Tip to Trial Balance

The trial balance lists the ending balance of each title in the order in which they appear in the ledger. The total of $6,980 on the left equals $6,980 on the right.

Summary of Key Points

Learning Unit 3-1

1. The accounting cycle is a sequence of accounting procedures that are usually performed during an accounting period.
2. An accounting period is the time period for which the income statement is prepared. The time period can be any period up to one year.

3. A calendar year is from January 1 to December 31. The fiscal year is any 12-month period. A fiscal year could be a calendar year but does not have to be.
4. Interim statements are statements that are usually prepared for a portion of the business's calendar or fiscal year (e.g., a month or a quarter).
5. A general journal is a book that records transactions in chronological order. Here debits and credits are shown together on one page. It is the book of original entry.
6. The ledger is a collection of accounts where information is accumulated from the postings of the journal. The ledger is the book of final entry.
7. Journalizing is the process of recording journal entries.
8. The chart of accounts provides the specific titles of accounts to be entered in the journal.
9. When journalizing, the post reference (PR) column is left blank.
10. A compound journal entry occurs when more than two accounts are affected in the journalizing process of a business transaction.

Learning Unit 3-2

1. Posting is the process of transferring information from the journal to the ledger.
2. The journal and ledger contain the same information but in a different form.
3. The four-column account aids in keeping a running balance of an account.
4. The normal balance of an account will be located on the side that increases it according to the rules of debits and credits. For example, the normal balances of liabilities occur on the credit side.
5. The mechanical process of posting requires care in transferring to the appropriate account the dates, post references, and amounts.

Learning Unit 3-3

1. A trial balance can balance but be incorrect. For example, an entire journal entry may not have been posted.
2. If a trial balance doesn't balance, check for errors in addition, omission of postings, slides, transpositions, copying errors, and so on.
3. Specific procedures should be followed in making corrections in journals and ledgers.

Key Terms

Accounting cycle For each accounting period, the process that begins with the recording of business transactions or procedures into a journal and ends with the completion of a post-closing trial balance.

Accounting period The period of time for which an income statement is prepared.

Book of final entry Book that receives information about business transactions from a book of original entry (a journal). Example: a ledger.

Book of original entry Book that records the first formal information about business transactions. Example: a journal.

Calendar year January 1 to December 31.

Compound journal entry A journal entry that affects more than two accounts.

Cross-referencing Adding to the PR column of the journal the account number of the ledger account that was updated from the journal.

Fiscal year The 12-month period a business chooses for its accounting year.

Four-column account A running balance account that records debits and credits and has a column for an ending balance (debit or credit). Replaces the standard two-column account we used earlier.

General journal The simplest form of a journal, which records information from transactions in chronological order as they occur. This journal links the debit and credit parts of transactions together.

Interim reports Financial statements that are prepared for a month, quarter, or some other portion of the fiscal year.

Journal   A listing of business transactions in chronological order. The journal links on one page the debit and credit parts of transactions.

Journal entry   The transaction (debits and credits) that is recorded into a journal once it is analyzed.

Journalizing   The process of recording a transaction entry into the journal.

Natural business year   A business's fiscal year that ends at the same time as a slow seasonal period begins.

Posting   The transferring, copying, or recording of information from a journal to a ledger.

Slide   The error that results in adding or deleting zeros in the writing of a number. Example: $79,200 \rightarrow 7,920$.

Transposition   The accidental rearrangement of digits of a number. Example: $152 \rightarrow 125$.

Trial balance   An informal listing of the ledger accounts and their balances in the ledger that aids in proving the equality of debits and credits.

Blueprint of First Four Steps of Accounting Cycle

See the inside front cover for a road map of entire accounting cycle.

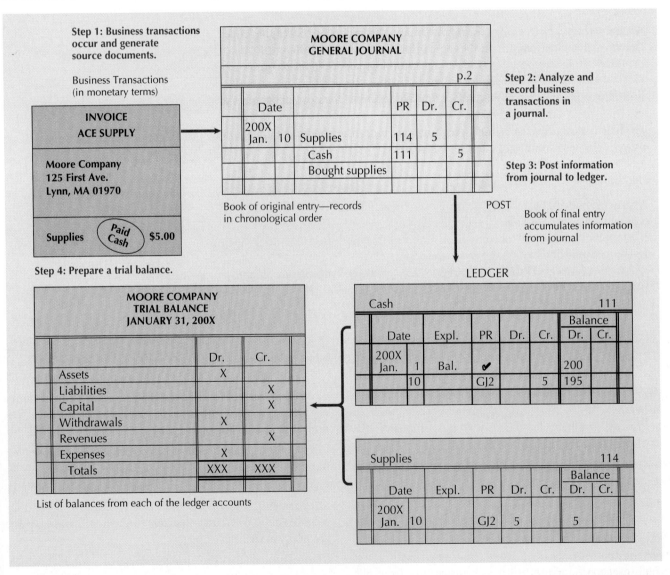

Questions, Mini Exercises, Exercises, and Problems

Discussion Questions

1. Explain the concept of the accounting cycle.
2. An accounting period is based on the balance sheet. Agree or disagree.
3. Compare and contrast a calendar year versus a fiscal year.
4. What are interim statements?
5. Why is the ledger called the book of final entry?
6. How do transactions get "linked" in a general journal?
7. What is the relationship of the chart of accounts to the general journal?
8. What is a compound journal entry?
9. Posting means updating the journal. Agree or disagree. Please comment.
10. The side that decreases an account is the normal balance. True or false?
11. The PR column of a general journal is the last item to be filled in during the posting process. Agree or disagree.
12. Discuss the concept of cross-referencing.
13. What is the difference between a transposition and a slide?

Mini Exercises

(The blank forms you need are on page 67 of the *Study Guide and Working Papers.*)

General Journal

1. Complete the following from the general journal of Ranger Co.:

RANGER COMPANY
GENERAL JOURNAL   Page 1

Date	Account Titles and Descriptions	PR	Dr.	Cr.
200X Oct. 15	Cash		6 0 0 00	
	Equipment		4 0 00	
	L. Swan, Capital			6 4 0 00
	Initial Investment by Owner			

Figure 3-34
General Journal

a. Year of journal entry _____
b. Month of journal entry _____
c. Day of journal entry _____
d. Name(s) of accounts debited _____
e. Name(s) of accounts credited _____
f. Explanation of transaction _____
g. Amount of debit(s) _____
h. Amount of credit(s) _____
i. Page of journal _____

General Journal

2. Provide the explanation for each of the general journal entries in Figure 3-35:

Figure 3-35
Journal Entries

	Date		Account Titles and Descriptions	PR	Debit	Credit
	200X July	9	Cash		8 0 0 0 00	
			Office Equipment		5 0 0 0 00	
			J. Walsh, Capital			13 0 0 0 00
			(A)			
		15	Cash		3 0 00	
			Accounts Receivable		6 0 00	
			Hair Fees Earned			9 0 00
			(B)			
		20	Advertising Expense		4 0 00	
			Accounts Payable			4 0 00
			(C)			

GENERAL JOURNAL — Page 4

Posting and Balancing

3. Balance this four-column account. What function does the PR column serve? When will Account 111 be used in the journalizing and posting process?

Cash — Acct. 111

Date	Explanation	PR	Dr.	Cr.	Balance Dr.	Cr.
200X						
June 4		GJ 1	15			
5		GJ 1	6			
9		GJ 2		4		
10		GJ 3	1			

The Trial Balance

4. The following trial balance (Figure 3-36) was prepared *incorrectly*.

   a. Rearrange the accounts in proper order.

Figure 3-36

LARKIN CO.
TRIAL BALANCE
OCTOBER 31, 200X

	Dr.	Cr.
B. Larkin, Capital	1 7 00	
Equipment	1 2 00	
Rent Expense		4 00
Advertising Expense		3 00
Accounts Payable		8 00
Taxi Fees	1 6 00	
Cash	1 7 00	
B. Larkin, Withdrawals	—	5 00
Totals	6 2 00	2 0 00

b. Calculate the total of the trial balance. (Small numbers are used intentionally so that you can do the calculations in your head.) Assume each account has a normal balance.

Correcting Entry

5. On May 1, 2001, a telephone expense for $180 was debited to Repair Expense. On June 12, 2002, this error was found. Prepare the corrected journal entry. When would a correcting entry *not* be needed?

Exercises

(The forms you need are on pages 68–73 of the *Study Guide and Working Papers.*)

3-1. Prepare journal entries for the following transactions that occurred during October:

Preparing journal entries.

200X
Oct.
1 Walter Lantz invested $40,000 cash and $2,000 of equipment into his new business.
3 Purchased building for $60,000 on account.
12 Purchased a truck from Lange Co. for $18,000 cash.
18 Bought supplies from Green Co. on account, $700.

3-2. Record the following into the general journal of Reggie's Auto Shop.

200X
Jan.
1 Reggie Long invested $16,000 cash in the auto shop.
5 Paid $7,000 for auto equipment.
8 Bought from Lowell Co. auto equipment for $6,000 on account.
14 Received $900 for repair fees earned.
18 Billed Sullivan Co. $900 for services rendered.
20 Reggie withdrew $300 for personal use.

Preparing journal entries.

3-3. Post the transactions in Figure 3-37 to the ledger of King Company. The partial ledger of King Company is Cash, 111; Equipment, 121; Accounts Payable, 211; and A. King, Capital, 311. Please use four-column accounts in the posting process.

Posting.

Figure 3-37
Journal Entries

Date 200X			PR	Dr.	Cr.
					Page 4
April	6	Cash		15 0 0 0 00	
		A. King, Capital			15 0 0 0 00
		Cash investment			
	14	Equipment		9 0 0 0 00	
		Cash			4 0 0 0 00
		Accounts Payable			5 0 0 0 00
		Purchase of equipment			

3-4. From the following transactions for Lowe Company for the month of July, (a) prepare journal entries (assume that it is page 1 of the journal), (b) post to the ledger (use a four-column account), and (c) prepare a trial balance.

Journalizing, posting, and preparing a trial balance.

200X
July

1	Joan Lowe invested $6,000 in the business.
4	Bought from Lax Co. equipment on account, $800.
15	Billed Friend Co. for services rendered, $4,000.
18	Received $5,000 cash for services rendered.
24	Paid salaries expense, $1,800.
28	Joan withdrew $400 for personal use.

A partial chart of accounts includes Cash, 111; Accounts Receivable, 112; Equipment, 121; Accounts Payable, 211; J. Lowe, Capital, 311; J. Lowe, Withdrawals, 312; Fees Earned, 411; and Salaries Expense, 511.

3-5. You have been hired to correct the trial balance in Figure 3-38 that has been recorded improperly from the ledger to the trial balance:

Figure 3-38
Incorrect Trial Balance

Correcting the trial balance.

		Dr.	Cr.
	SUNG CO. **TRIAL BALANCE** **MARCH 31, 200X**		
3	Accounts Payable	2 0 0 0 00	
	A. Sung, Capital		6 5 0 0 00
	A. Sung, Withdrawals		3 0 0 00
	Services Earned		4 7 0 0 00
	Concessions Earned	2 5 0 0 00	
	Rent Expense	4 0 0 00	
	Salaries Expense	2 5 0 0 00	
	Miscellaneous Expense		1 3 0 0 00
1	Cash	10 0 0 0 00	
2	Accounts Receivable		1 2 0 0 00
	Totals	17 4 0 0 00	14 0 0 0 00

3-6. On February 6, 200X, Mike Sullivan made the journal entry in Figure 3-39 to record the purchase on account of office equipment priced at $1,400. This transaction had not yet been posted when the error was discovered. Make the appropriate correction.

Figure 3-39
Recording Error

Correcting an entry.

	GENERAL JOURNAL			
Date	Account Titles and Description	PR	Dr.	Cr.
200X Feb. 6	Office Equipment		9 0 0 00	
	Accounts Payable			9 0 0 00
	Purchase of office equip. on account			

Group A Problems

(The forms you need are on pages 74–85 of the *Working Papers and Study Guide*.)

Journalizing.

3A-1. Al Vincent operates Al's Fitness Center. As the bookkeeper, you have been requested to journalize the following transactions:

200X

Aug. 1 Paid rent for two months in advance, $6,000.

3 Purchased fitness equipment on account from Leek's Supply House, $4,200.

10 Purchased fitness supplies from Angel's Wholesale for $700 cash.

12 Received $1,400 cash from fitness fees earned.

20 Al withdrew $600 for his personal use.

21 Advertising bill received from *Daily Sun* but unpaid, $120.

25 Paid cleaning expense, $90.

28 Paid salaries expense, $500.

29 Performed fitness work for $1,700, but payment will not be received until May.

30 Paid Leek's Supply House half the amount owed from Aug. 3 transaction.

Check Figure:
July 21
Dr. Advertising
expense $120
Cr. Accounts
Payable $120

Your task is to journalize the preceding transactions. The chart of accounts for Al's Fitness Center is as follows:

Chart of Accounts

Assets		Owner's Equity	
111	Cash	311	Al Vincent, Capital
112	Accounts Receivable	312	Al Vincent, Withdrawals
114	Prepaid Rent	**Revenue**	
116	Fitness Supplies	411	Fitness Fees Earned
120	Office Equipment		
121	Fitness Equipment	**Expenses**	
Liabilities		511	Advertising Expense
211	Accounts Payable	512	Salaries Expense
		514	Cleaning Expense

3A-2. On June 1, 200X, Molly Taylor opened Taylor's Dance Studio. The following transactions occurred in June:

Comprehensive problem:
Journalizing, posting, and
preparing a trial balance.

200X

June 1 Molly Taylor invested $9,000 in the dance studio.

1 Paid three months' rent in advance, $1,000.

3 Purchased $700 of equipment from Astor Co. on account.

5 Received $900 cash for fitness-training workshop for dancers.

8 Purchased $300 of supplies for cash.

9 Billed Lester Co. $2,100 for group dance lesson for its employees.

10 Paid salaries of assistants, $400.

15 Molly withdrew $150 from the business for her personal use.

28 Paid electrical bill, $125.

29 Paid telephone bill for June, $190.

Your task is to

a. Set up the ledger based on the following chart of accounts.

b. Journalize (journal is page 1) and post the June transactions.

c. Prepare a trial balance as of June 30, 200X.

Check Figure:
Trial Balance
Total $12,700

The chart of accounts for Taylor's Dance Studio is as follows:

Chart of Accounts

Assets		Owner's Equity	
111	Cash	311	Molly Taylor, Capital
112	Accounts Receivable	312	Molly Taylor, Withdrawals
114	Prepaid Rent	**Revenue**	
121	Supplies	411	Fees Earned
131	Equipment		

Liabilities		Expenses	
211	Accounts Payable	511	Electrical Expense
		521	Salaries Expense
		531	Telephone Expense

Comprehensive problem:
Journalizing, posting, and
preparing a trial balance.

3A-3. The following transactions occurred in June 200X for A. French's Placement Agency:

200X

June 1 A. French invested $9,000 cash in the placement agency.
1 Bought equipment on account from Hook Co., $2,000.
3 Earned placement fees of $1,600, but payment will not be received until July.
5 A. French withdrew $100 for his personal use.
7 Paid wages expense, $300.
9 Placed a client on a local TV show, receiving $600 cash.
15 Bought supplies on account from Lyon Co., $500.
28 Paid telephone bill for June, $160.
29 Advertising bill from Shale Co. received but not paid, $900.

Check Figure:
Trial Balance
    Total $14,600

The chart of accounts for A. French Placement Agency is as follows:

Chart of Accounts

Assets		Owner's Equity	
111	Cash	311	A. French, Capital
112	Accounts Receivable	312	A. French, Withdrawals
131	Supplies	**Revenue**	
141	Equipment	411	Placement Fees Earned
Liabilities		**Expenses**	
211	Accounts Payable	511	Wage Expense
		521	Telephone Expense
		531	Advertising Expense

Your task is to

a. Set up the ledger based on the chart of accounts.
b. Journalize (page 1) and post the June transactions.
c. Prepare a trial balance as of June 30, 200X.

Group B Problems

(The forms you need are on pages 74–85 of the *Study Guide and Working Papers.*)

3B-1. In April Al Vincent opened a new Fitness Center. Please assist him by journalizing the following business transactions:

Journalizing.

200X

Apr. 1 Al Vincent invested $6,000 of fitness equipment as well as $3,000 cash in the new business.
3 Purchased fitness supplies on account from Rex Co., $500.
10 Purchased office equipment on account from Ross Stationery, $400.
12 Al paid his home telephone bill from the company checkbook, $60.
20 Received $600 cash for fitness services performed.
21 Advertising bill received but not paid, $75.
25 Cleaning bill received but not paid, $90.
28 Performed fitness work for $700, but payment will not be received until May.
29 Paid salaries expense, $400.
30 Paid Ross Stationery half the amount owed from April 10 transaction.

Check Figure:
April 21
Dr. Advertising
    expense $75
Cr. Accounts
    payable $75

The chart of accounts for Al's Fitness Center includes Cash, 111; Accounts Receivable, 112; Prepaid Rent, 114; Fitness Supplies, 116; Office Equipment, 120; Fitness Equipment, 121; Accounts Payable, 211; Al Vincent, Capital, 311; Al Vincent, Withdrawals, 312; Fitness Fees Earned, 411; Advertising Expense, 511; Salaries Expense, 512; and Cleaning Expense, 514.

3B-2. In June the following transactions occurred for Taylor's Dance Studio:

Comprehensive problem: Journalizing, posting, and preparing a trial balance.

200X

June 1 Molly Taylor invested $6,000 in the dance studio.
1 Paid four months rent in advance, $1,200.
3 Purchased supplies on account from A.J.K., $700.
5 Purchased equipment on account from Reese Company, $900.
8 Received $1,300 cash for dance-training program provided to Northwest Junior College.
9 Billed Long Co. for dance lessons provided, $600.
10 Molly withdrew $400 from the dance studio to buy a new chain saw for her home.
15 Paid salaries expense, $400.
28 Paid telephone bill, $118.
29 Electric bill received but unpaid, $120.

Check Figure: Total Trial Balance $9,620

Your task is to

a. Set up a ledger.
b. Journalize (all page 1) and post the June transactions.
c. Prepare a trial balance as of June 30, 200X.

The chart of accounts includes Cash, 111; Accounts Receivable, 112; Prepaid Rent, 114; Supplies, 121; Equipment, 131; Accounts Payable, 211; M. Taylor, Capital, 311; M. Taylor, Withdrawals, 321; Fees Earned, 411; Electrical Expense, 511; Salaries Expense, 521; and Telephone Expense, 531.

3B-3. In June A. French's Placement Agency had the following transactions:

Comprehensive problem: Journalizing, posting, and preparing a trial balance.

200X

June 1 A. French invested $6,000 in the new placement agency.
2 Bought equipment for cash, $350.
3 Earned placement fee commission of $2,100, but payment from Avon Co. will not be received until July.
5 Paid wages expense, $400.
7 A. French paid his home utility bill from the company checkbook, $69.
9 Placed Jay Diamond on a national TV show, receiving $900 cash.
15 Paid cash for supplies, $350.
28 Telephone bill received but not paid, $185.
29 Advertising bill received but not paid, $200.

Check Figure: Total Trial Balance $9,385

The chart of accounts includes Cash, 111; Accounts Receivable, 112; Supplies, 131; Equipment, 141; Accounts Payable, 211; A. French, Capital, 311; A. French, Withdrawals, 312; Placement Fees Earned, 411; Wage Expense, 511; Telephone Expense, 521; and Advertising Expense, 531.

Your task is to

a. Set up a ledger based on the chart of accounts.
b. Journalize (all page 1) and post transactions.
c. Prepare a trial balance for June 30, 200X.

Real-World Applications

3R-1. Paul Regan, bookkeeper of Hampton Co., has been up half the night trying to get his trial balance to balance. Figure 3-40 shows his results:

Figure 3-40
Incorrect Trial Balance

	Dr.	Cr.
HAMPTON CO. **TRIAL BALANCE** **JUNE 30, 200X**		
Office Sales		5 7 2 0 00
Cash in Bank	3 2 6 0 00	
Accounts Receivable	5 6 6 0 00	
Office Equipment	8 4 0 0 00	
Accounts Payable		4 1 6 0 00
D. Hole, Capital		11 5 6 0 00
D. Hole, Withdrawals		7 0 0 00
Wage Expense	2 6 0 0 00	
Rent Expense	9 4 0 00	
Utilities Expense	2 6 00	
Office Supplies	1 2 0 00	
Prepaid Rent	1 8 0 00	

Ken Small, the accountant, compared Paul's amounts in the trial balance with those in the ledger, recomputed each account balance, and compared postings. Ken found the following errors:

1. A $200 debit to D. Hole, Withdrawals, was posted as a credit.
2. D. Hole, Withdrawals, was listed on the trial balance as a credit.
3. A Note Payable account with a credit balance of $2,400 was not listed on the trial balance.
4. The pencil footings for Accounts Payable were debits of $5,320 and credits of $8,800.
5. A debit of $180 to Prepaid Rent was not posted.
6. Office Supplies bought for $60 was posted as a credit to Supplies.
7. A debit of $120 to Accounts Receivable was not posted.
8. A cash payment of $420 was credited to Cash for $240.
9. The pencil footing of the credits to Cash was overstated by $400.
10. The Utilities Expense of $260 was listed in the trial balance as $26.

Assist Paul Regan by preparing a correct trial balance. What advice could you give Ken about Paul? Can you explain the situation to Paul? Put your answers in writing.

3R-2. Lauren Oliver, an accountant lab tutor, is having a debate with some of her assistants. They are trying to find out how each of the following five unrelated situations would affect the trial balance:

1. A $5 debit to Cash in the ledger was not posted.
2. A $10 debit to Computer Supplies was debited to Computer Equipment.
3. An $8 debit to Wage Expense was debited twice to the account.
4. A $4 debit to Computer Supplies was debited to Computer Sales.
5. A $35 credit to Accounts Payable was posted as a $53 credit.

Could you indicate to Lauren the effect that each situation will have on the trial balance? If a situation will have no effect, indicate that fact. Put in writing how each of these situations could be avoided in the future.

YOU make the call

Critical Thinking/Ethical Case

3R-3. Jay Simons, the accountant of See Co., would like to buy a new software package for his general ledger. He couldn't do it because all funds were frozen for the rest of the fiscal period. Jay called his friend at Joor Industries and asked whether he could copy their software. Why should or shouldn't Jay have done that?

Internet Exercises: STAtravel — Student Travel, Discount Travel

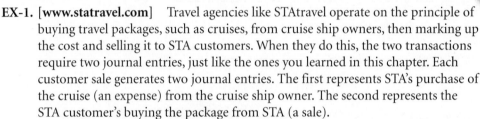

EX-1. **[www.statravel.com]**   Travel agencies like STAtravel operate on the principle of buying travel packages, such as cruises, from cruise ship owners, then marking up the cost and selling it to STA customers. When they do this, the two transactions require two journal entries, just like the ones you learned in this chapter. Each customer sale generates two journal entries. The first represents STA's purchase of the cruise (an expense) from the cruise ship owner. The second represents the STA customer's buying the package from STA (a sale).

Suppose that you purchase a spring break cruise for $1,500 from STA and pay them with a check. They in turn will record the other transaction with the cruise ship owner for $1,200. The $300 difference is STA's profit.

1. Write the journal entry STA would make showing your booking the cruise for $1,500 with STA.

2. Write the journal entry showing, from STA's perspective, STA's purchase of your cruise for $1,200 from the cruise ship owner.

EX-2. **[www.statravel.com]**   Suppose STA has the following accounts in their accounting system:

Accounts Receivable	Cash
Airline Revenue	Cruise Ship Packages Payable
Airline Tickets Payable	Cruise Ship Package Purchase Expense
Airline Ticket Purchase Expense	Cruise Ship Revenue

1. List accounts in proper order with account numbers (you make them up).

2. Draw a table showing account name, account number, category, normal balance, and which financial statement these are found on.

Continuing Problem

Eldorado Computer Center

Tony's computer center is picking up in business, so he has decided to expand his bookkeeping system to a general journal/ledger system. The balances from August have been forwarded to the ledger accounts. (The forms are in the *Study Guide and Working Papers*, pages 89–99.

Assignment

1. Use the chart of accounts provided in Chapter 2 to record the following transactions in Figures 3-41 to 3-51:

Figure 3-41 Prepaid Rent

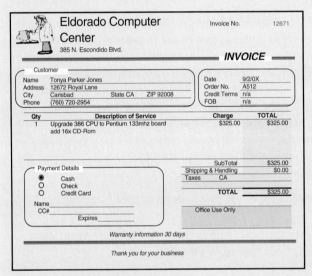

Figure 3-42 Service Revenue

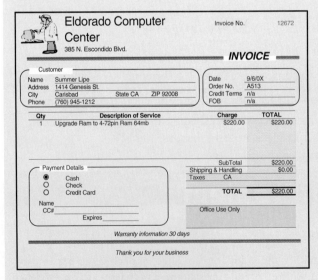

Figure 3-43 Service Revenue

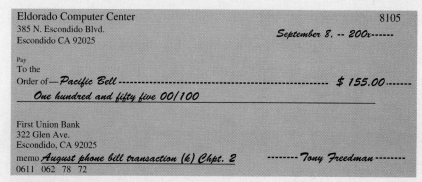

Eldorado Computer Center   8105
385 N. Escondido Blvd.
Escondido CA 92025   *September 8, -- 200x------*

Pay
To the
Order of— *Pacific Bell* -- *$ 155.00*-------
       One hundred and fifty five 00/100

First Union Bank
322 Glen Ave.
Escondido, CA 92025
memo *August phone bill transaction (k) Chpt. 2*   -------- *Tony Freedman* --------
0611 062 78 72

Figure 3-44 Phone Bill

Refer back to Chapter 2, transaction k.

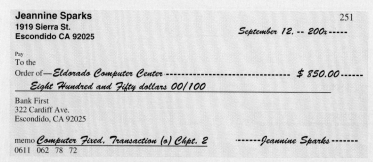

Jeannine Sparks   251
1919 Sierra St.
Escondido CA 92025   *September 12, -- 200x-----*

Pay
To the
Order of— *Eldorado Computer Center* -------------------------- *$ 850.00*------
       Eight Hundred and Fifty dollars 00/100

Bank First
322 Cardiff Ave.
Escondido, CA 92025

memo *Computer Fixed, Transaction (o) Chpt. 2*   -------*Jeannine Sparks*-------
0611 062 78 72

Figure 3-45 Sparks Collection

Refer back to Chapter 2, transaction o.

Eldorado Computer Center   8106
385 N. Escondido Blvd.
Escondido CA 92025   *September 15, -- 200x-----*

Pay
To the
Order of— *Computer Connection* -------------------------------- *$ 200.00*------
       Two hundred dollars and 00/100

First Union Bank
322 Glen Ave.
Escondido, CA 92025
memo *Account due from transaction (s) Chpt. 2*   ------- *Tony Freedman*-------
0611 062 78 72

Figure 3-46 Paid Computer Connection

Refer back to Chapter 2, transaction s.

Eldorado Computer Center   8107
385 N. Escondido Blvd.
Escondido CA 92025   *September 17, -- 200x------*

Pay
To the
Order of— *Multi Systems, Inc* ------------------------------- *$ 1,200.00*-------
       Twelve hundred dollars and 00/100

First Union Bank
322 Glen Ave.
Escondido, CA 92025
           Purchase order 200
memo *Computer Equipment-Bench Workstations*   -------- *Tony Freedman*--------
0611 062 78 72

Figure 3-47 Purchased Computer Equipment

Pacific Bell USA
411 Center St.
Escondido, CA 92025
800-411-4111 fax 760-745-9991

Invoice No. ECC743-7434

INVOICE

Customer

Name: Eldorado Computer Center
Address: 385 N. Escondido Blvd.
City: Escondido State CA ZIP 92025
Phone: (760) 743-7434

Date: 9/20/0X
Order No.: ECC7437434
Credit Terms: net 30
FOB: n/a

Qty	Description of Service	Charge	TOTAL
1	8/1/XX to 8/31/XX Phone Service, Call Waiting, Call Forwarding Business Use	$65.00	$65.00

Payment Details
- O Cash
- ◉ Net 30
- O Credit Card

Name
CC#
Expires

SubTotal	$65.00
Late Charge	$0.00
Amount Due	$65.00

Office Use Only

Customer Service Call Toll Free 800-411-4111

Payment due by 10/19/XX

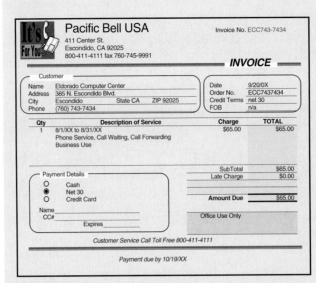

Figure 3-48 Paid Phone Bill

San Diego Electric
1515 Industrial Blvd.
Escondido, CA 92025
760-745-1999 fax 760-745-9991

Invoice No. A60692443

INVOICE

Customer

Name: Eldorado Computer Center
Address: 385 N. Escondido Blvd.
City: Escondido State CA ZIP 92025
Phone: (760) 743-7434

Date: 9/22/0X
Order No.: 385-66725-9045
Credit Terms: net 30
FOB: n/a

Qty	Description of Service	Charge	TOTAL
1	8/1/XX to 8/31/XX Baseline Allowance 241 kWh @ 1270	$95.00	$95.00

Payment Details
- O Cash
- ◉ Net 30
- O Credit Card

Name
CC#
Expires

SubTotal	$95.00
Late Charge	$0.00
Amount Due	$95.00

Office Use Only

Questions? Please Call: 1-800-411-7227

Payment due by 10/22/XX

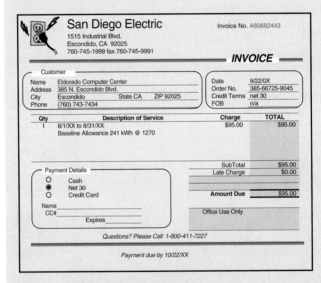

Figure 3-49 Paid Electric Bill

Eldorado Computer Center
385 N. Escondido Blvd.

Invoice No. 12673

INVOICE

Customer

Name: Mike Hammer
Address: 300 Carisbad Dr.
City: Carisbad State CA ZIP 92008
Phone: (760) 720-2199

Date: 9/26/0X
Order No.: A514
Credit Terms: n/a
FOB: n/a

Qty	Description of Service	Charge	TOTAL
1	add video card 2mb dram 64 diamond stealth	$140.00	$140.00

Payment Details
- ◉ Cash
- O Check
- O Credit Card

Name
CC#
Expires

SubTotal	$140.00
Shipping & Handling	$0.00
Taxes CA	
TOTAL	$140.00

Office Use Only

Warranty information 30 days

Thank you for your business

Figure 3-50 Service Revenue

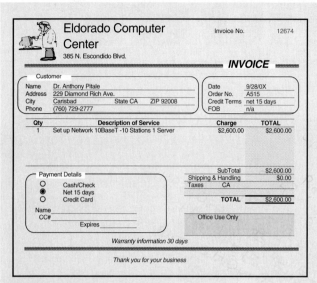

Figure 3-51 Service Revenue

2. Post all transactions to the general ledger accounts (the Prepaid Rent Account #1025 has been added to the chart of accounts).
3. Prepare a trial balance for September 30, 200X.
4. Prepare the financial statements for the three months ended September 30, 200X.

COMPUTERIZED ACCOUNTING APPLICATION FOR CHAPTER 3

JOURNALIZING, POSTING, GENERAL LEDGER, TRIAL BALANCE, AND CHART OF ACCOUNTS

Before starting on this assignment, read and complete the tasks discussed in Parts A, B, and F of the Computerized Accounting appendix at the back of this book.

How to Open the Company Data Files

1. Click on the Start button. Point to Programs; point to the Peachtree folder and select Peachtree Complete Accounting. Your desktop may have the Peachtree icon, allowing for a quicker entrance into the program by double clicking it.

2. Follow the "Open a File" instructions in Part A of the Computerized Accounting appendix at the back of this book to open **The Atlas Company.** You may be initially presented with the Peachtree Today window. If so, simply close it. Your screen should then look something like the screen capture below:

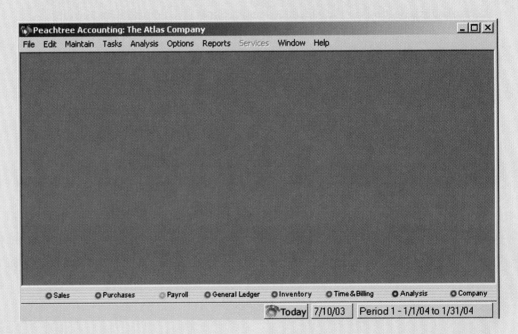

If you are missing the navigation aids at the bottom of the screen, you can activate them under the **Options** menu. Select **View Navigation Aid**. It will remain on until you turn it off. This feature offers an alternative way to access the different features of Peachtree.

3. Click on the **Maintain** menu option. Then select **Company Information**. The program will respond by bringing up a dialogue box allowing the user to edit/add information about the company.

How to Add Your Name to the Company Name

4. It is important for you to be able to identify the specific reports that you print for each assignment as your own, particularly if you are using a computer that shares a printer with other computers. Peachtree Complete Accounting 2003 prints the name of the company you are working with at the top of each report. To personalize your reports so that you can identify both the company and your printed reports, the company name needs to be modified to include your name:

   a. Click in the **Company Name** entry field at the end of **The Atlas Company**. If it is already highlighted, press the right arrow key.

b. Add a dash and your name **"-Student Name"** to the end of the company name. If your name is too long, you may abbreviate or use your initials. Your screen will look similar to the one shown below:

c. Click on the OK button to return to the Menu Window.

5. The owner of The Atlas Company has invested $10,000 in the business. Select **General Journal Entry** from the **Tasks** menu to open the General Journal dialog box. Enter the date 1/1/04 into the **Date** field; press the TAB key; enter "Memo" into the **Reference** field and press TAB. The **Date** text box is used to record the date the transaction occurred. The **Reference** text box can be used for any reference number or notation you wish to associate with a general journal entry and/or the source document that authorizes the entry. Pressing the TAB key will take you to the General Journal's **Account** field. Note that pressing ENTER will also move you from field to field.

6. With the flashing insertion point positioned in the **Account No.** field, click on the pull down menu (magnifying glass icon) and double click on "1110 Cash". Alternatively, you can highlight the account and click OK at the bottom. The program will enter the account number and name into the **Account No.** field and the flashing insertion point will move to the **Description** field. Enter "Initial investment of cash by owner" into this field and press TAB to move to the **Debit** field.

7. Enter "10000" into the **Debit** field. Dollar amounts can be entered in several ways. For example, to enter $10,000.00, type 10000, or 10,000.00 or 10,000. The comma separator is always optional while the decimal point is optional when dealing with whole dollar amounts. To enter an amount containing a decimal point, type the decimal point as part of the amount. For example, enter five dollars and twenty-five cents as 5.25. Press the TAB key three times to move through the **Credit** and **Job** fields.

8. With the flashing insertion point again positioned in the **Account No.** field, click on the pull down menu. Double click on "3110 Owner's Capital". Use the scroll bar if the account is not visible in the pull down menu. Press TAB to move to the **Description** field. This should repeat the information entered in step 6 by default. Although you can change the description for the credit, we will leave it the same.

How to Record a General Journal Entry

9. Press the TAB key twice to move to the **Credit** field. Enter "10000" as you did in step 7. Hit TAB twice to move the cursor back to the **Account No.** field. This completes the data you need to enter into the General Journal dialog box to record the journal entry for the initial investment of cash by the owner. Your screen should look like this:

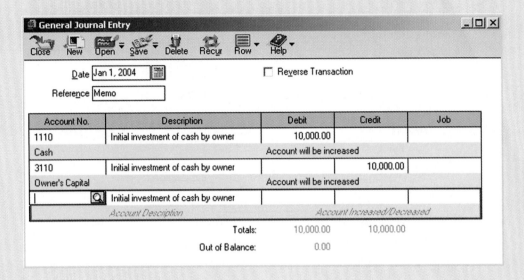

Review the Journal Entry Before Saving

10. Before saving this transaction, you should verify that the transaction data are correct by reviewing the journal entry. Review the journal entry for accuracy, noting any errors.

11. If you have made an error, use the following editing techniques to correct the error.

Editing a General Journal Entry

How to Edit an Entry Prior to Saving

- Using your mouse, click in the field that contains the error. This will highlight the selected text box information so that you can change it.
- Type the correct information; then press the TAB key to enter it. You may then either TAB to other fields needing corrections or again use the mouse to click in the proper field.
- If you have selected an incorrect account number, use the pull down menu to select the correct account. This will replace the incorrect account with the correct account.
- Note that even though the **Save** icon will be available if the entry is out of balance, Peachtree will not allow you to save the transaction until the entry is in balance.
- To discard an entry and start over, click on the **Delete** icon. You will not be given the opportunity to verify this step so be sure you want to delete the transaction before selecting this option.
- Review the journal entry for accuracy after any editing corrections.

How to Save an Entry

12. After verifying that the journal entry is correct, click on the **Save** icon to post this transaction. A blank General Journal dialog box is displayed, ready for additional General Journal transactions to be recorded. Peachtree has added a 1 to our memo in the **Reference** field and will do so as long as we remain in this input box and save as we go. Alternatively, we could have added more entries to the previous screen before saving. To keep the same reference for multiple entries on the same day, do not save between transactions.

Record Additional Transactions

13. Record the following additional journal entries Enter the **Date** listed for each transaction (you may use the "+" key to advance the date or use the calendar icon next to the field to select the date from a calendar). Enter "Memo" into the **Source** text

box for each transaction or accept Peachtree's additional number added to memo by pressing TAB:

2004

Jan.
   1 Paid rent for two months in advance, $400.
   3 Purchased office supplies on account, $100.
   9 Billed a customer for fees earned, $1,500.
  13 Received and paid telephone bill, $180.
  20 Owner withdrew $500 from the business.
  27 Received $450 for fees earned.
  31 Paid salaries expense, $700.

14. After you have saved the additional journal entries, click on the close button to close the General Journal dialog box. This will restore the menu window.

15. Select **General Ledger** from the **Reports** menu to bring up reports associated with the general ledger such as the **General Journal** and the **Trial Balance.** Select **General Journal** from the report selection window to bring up the report. Your screen should display something similar to this:

How to Display and Print a General Journal

The Atlas Company- Student Name
General Journal
For the Period From Jan 1, 2004 to Jan 31, 2004

Filter Criteria includes: Report order is by Date. Report is printed with Accounts having Zero Amounts and with Truncated Transaction Descriptions and in Detail Format.

Date	Account ID	Reference	Trans Description	Debit Amt	Credit Amt
1/1/04	1110	Memo	Initial investment of cash by owner	10,000.00	
	3110		Initial investment of cash by owner		10,000.00
1/1/04	1140	Memo1	Prepaid rent	400.00	
	1110		Prepaid rent		400.00
1/3/04	1150	Memo2	Purchased office supplies on account	100.00	
	2110		Purchased office supplies on account		100.00
1/9/04	1120	Memo3	Performed services on account	1,500.00	
	4110		Performed services on account		1,500.00
1/13/04	5150	Memo4	Paid telephone bill	180.00	
	1110		Paid telephone bill		180.00
1/20/04	3120	Memo5	Owner withdrawal	500.00	
	1110		Owner withdrawal		500.00
1/27/04	1110	Memo6	Performed services for cash	450.00	
	4110		Performed services for cash		450.00
1/31/04	5120	Memo7	Paid salaries expense	700.00	
	1110		Paid salaries expense		700.00
		Total		13,830.00	13,830.00

16. The scroll bars can be used to advance the display to view other portions of the report if they are not visible. Note: You may display the entire General Journal Display window by clicking the maximize icon.

17. Click on the **Print** icon to print the General Journal. If you experience any difficulties with your printer (for example, the type size is too small), refer to Part F of the Computerized Accounting appendix for information on how to adjust the print and display settings.

18. Review your printed General Journal. If you note an error at this point, it can be easily fixed. With the General Journal report on your screen, place your cursor over the incorrect entry (it will resemble a magnifying glass with a "z" in the center). Double click on the entry you wish to correct and you will be taken to the **General Journal Entry** window that contains the entry. You may edit it using the same procedures as editing an unsaved entry in step 11. After making the necessary changes,

What to Do If You Saved an Incorrect Entry

click on the **Save** icon to save your changes. You will be returned to your report where you can view the changes made.

How to Display and Print
a General Ledger Report

19. Click on the **Close** icon to close the General Journal report. You are taken back to the report selection window where you can select (double-click) **General Ledger.** Your screen will look something like this:

The Atlas Company- Student Name
General Ledger
For the Period From Jan 1, 2004 to Jan 31, 2004
Filter Criteria includes: Report order is by ID. Report is printed with Truncated Transaction Descriptions and in Detail Format.

Account ID Account Description	Date	Reference	Jrnl	Trans Description	Debit Amt	Credit Amt	Balance
1110	1/1/04			Beginning Balance			
Cash	1/1/04	Memo	GENJ	Initial investment of cash by	10,000.00		
	1/1/04	Memo1	GENJ	Prepaid rent		400.00	
	1/13/04	Memo4	GENJ	Paid telephone bill		180.00	
	1/20/04	Memo5	GENJ	Owner withdrawal		500.00	
	1/27/04	Memo6	GENJ	Performed services for cash	450.00		
	1/31/04	Memo7	GENJ	Paid salaries expense		700.00	
				Current Period Change	10,450.00	1,780.00	8,670.00
	1/31/04			Ending Balance			8,670.00
1120	1/1/04			Beginning Balance			
Accounts Receivable	1/9/04	Memo3	GENJ	Performed services on accou	1,500.00		
				Current Period Change	1,500.00		1,500.00
	1/31/04			Ending Balance			1,500.00

---

20. You will not see the entire report on the screen. The scroll bars can be used to advance the display to view other portions of the report. You may also double click your mouse on any transaction to bring up the entry window for that transaction.

21. Click on the **Print** icon to print the General Ledger report.

22. Click on the **Close** button to close the General Ledger report and return to the reports selection window. Double-click on the General Ledger Trial Balance option from this window. Your screen will look something like this:

How to Display and Print
a Trial Balance

The Atlas Company- Student Name
General Ledger Trial Balance
As of Jan 31, 2004
Filter Criteria includes: Report order is by ID. Report is printed in Detail Format.

Account ID	Account Description	Debit Amt	Credit Amt
1110	Cash	8,670.00	
1120	Accounts Receivable	1,500.00	
1140	Prepaid Rent	400.00	
1150	Office Supplies	100.00	
2110	Accounts Payable		100.00
3110	Owner's Capital		10,000.00
3120	Owner's Withdrawals	500.00	
4110	Fees Earned		1,950.00
5120	Salaries Expense	700.00	
5150	Telephone Expense	180.00	
	Total:	12,050.00	12,050.00

---

23. The scroll bar can be used to advance the display to view other portions of the report. You may also display zero balance accounts by clicking on the **Options** icon and clicking the box next to **Include Accounts with Zero Amounts.** Clicking on **OK** will return you to the report. Click on the **Print** icon to print the Trial Balance.

24. Again click on the **Close** button to close the Trial Balance report. Select **Chart of Accounts** from the report selection window. Your screen will look something like this:

How to Display and Print a Chart of Accounts

The Atlas Company- Student Name
Chart of Accounts
As of Jan 31, 2004
Filter Criteria includes: Report order is by ID. Report is printed with Accounts having Zero Amounts and in Detail Format.

Account ID	Account Description	Active	Account Type
1110	Cash	Yes	Cash
1120	Accounts Receivable	Yes	Accounts Receivable
1140	Prepaid Rent	Yes	Other Current Assets
1150	Office Supplies	Yes	Other Current Assets
1210	Office Equipment	Yes	Fixed Assets
1221	Accum. Depr- Office Equipment	Yes	Accumulated Depreciation
1230	Automobile	Yes	Fixed Assets
1241	Accum. Depr- Automobile	Yes	Accumulated Depreciation
1250	Store Equipment	Yes	Fixed Assets
1261	Accum Depr- Store Equipment	Yes	Accumulated Depreciation
2110	Accounts Payable	Yes	Accounts Payable
3110	Owner's Capital	Yes	Equity-doesn't close
3120	Owner's Withdrawals	Yes	Equity-gets closed
3130	Retained Earnings	Yes	Equity-Retained Earnings
4110	Fees Earned	Yes	Income
5110	Rent Expense	Yes	Expenses
5120	Salaries Expense	Yes	Expenses
5150	Telephone Expense	Yes	Expenses

25. Click the **Print** icon to print the report. Click on the **Close** button to close the Chart of Accounts window and return to the Menu Window.

26. Click on the Menu Window **File** menu; then click on **Exit** to end the current work session and return to your Windows desktop. Your work will automatically be saved.

How to Exit from the Program

27. You can exit from Peachtree Complete Accounting 2003 at any time during a current work session from any window that offers the **File** menu. You may be asked if you wish to save any unsaved work.

28. Generally speaking, there is no need to save your work in Peachtree. Each time you make a change and click save, your work is automatically saved to your hard drive. You should back up your work after each session. This was discussed in Part A of the Appendix and will be discussed again in Chapter 4.

Saving Your Work During a Current Work Session

The Accounting Cycle Continued

Preparing Worksheets and Financial Statements

Your roommate Sam is an art major. Sam is skilled at drawing and always has his sketchpad with him. Sam records all of his ideas for a picture by creating various drawings in his pad. Sam will begin a drawing and then make various changes and adjustments to it. Sam said that after he's completed the drawing he goes on to use it when completing a painting.

Sam and several other artists in the area have opened an art studio to display their works. You recently attended a show that featured several of Sam's paintings. While you were at the show, someone bought one of Sam's paintings. Sam was excited and happy. "Now I can pay my share of the rent and utilities for the studio. Everyone here loves art, but we have to run the studio like a business," Sam told you. Even an art studio needs to use accounting to record sales and expenses like other businesses.

Accounting is very different than art, but it does have its own "sketchpad," which is called a worksheet. In Chapter 3 we learned about the first four steps in the accounting cycle. In Chapter 4 we expand our understanding of the accounting cycle by focusing on the next step—preparing a worksheet. And similar to how Sam changes and revises his drawings, an accountant can use the worksheet to make changes and adjustments to numbers found in the trial balance.

In this chapter we also discuss the sixth step in the accounting cycle—using the worksheet to prepare financial statements. And like a sketchpad, the accounting worksheet is a tool that takes us from a trial balance to financial statements, or as Sam would say, from a sketch to a painting.

Learning Objectives

- Adjustments: prepaid rent, office supplies, depreciation on equipment, and accrued salaries. (p. 121)

- Preparation of adjusted trial balance on the worksheet. (p. 129)

- The income statement and balance sheet sections of the worksheet. (p. 130)

- Preparing financial statements from the worksheet. (p. 135)

In Figure 4-1, Steps 1–4 show the parts of the manual accounting cycle that were completed for Clark's Word Processing Services in the last chapter. This chapter continues the cycle with Steps 5–6: the preparation of a worksheet and the three financial statements. Be sure to check inside the front cover for a complete road map of the accounting cycle.

Learning Unit 4-1 | Step 5 of the Accounting Cycle: Preparing a Worksheet

> The worksheet is not a formal report, so no dollar signs appear on it. Because it is a form, there are no commas, either.

An accountant uses a **worksheet** to organize and check data before preparing financial statements necessary to complete the accounting cycle. The most important function of the worksheet is to allow the accountant to find and correct errors before financial statements are prepared. In a way, a worksheet acts as the accountant's scratch pad. No one sees the worksheet once the formal reports are prepared. A sample worksheet is shown in Figure 4-2.

The accounts listed on the far left of the worksheet are taken from the ledger. The rest of the worksheet has five sections: the trial balance, adjustments, adjusted trial balance, income statement, and balance sheet. Each of these sections is divided into debit and credit columns.

THE TRIAL BALANCE SECTION

> As is true for all accounting statements, the heading includes the name of the company, the name of the report, the date, and the length of the accounting period.

We discussed how to prepare a trial balance in Chapter 2. Some companies prepare a separate trial balance; others, such as Clark's Word Processing Services, prepare the trial balance directly on the worksheet. A trial balance is taken on every account listed in the ledger that has a balance. Additional titles from the ledger are added as they are needed. (We will show this later.)

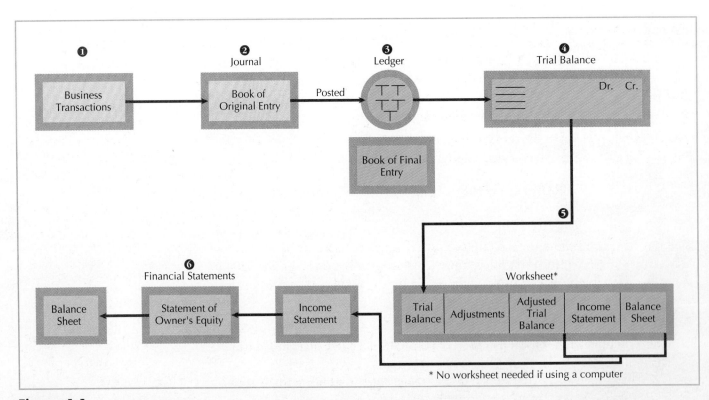

Figure 4-1

CLARK'S WORD PROCESSING SERVICES
WORKSHEET
FOR MONTH ENDING MAY 31, 200X

Account Titles	Trial Balance Dr.	Trial Balance Cr.	Adjustments Dr.	Adjustments Cr.	Adjusted Trial Balance Dr.	Adjusted Trial Balance Cr.	Income Statement Dr.	Income Statement Cr.
Cash	6 1 5 5 00							
Accounts Receivable	5 0 0 0 00							
Office Supplies	6 0 0 00							
Prepaid Rent	1 2 0 0 00							
Word Processing Equipment	6 0 0 0 00							
Accounts Payable		3 3 5 0 00						
Brenda Clark, Capital		10 0 0 0 00						
Brenda Clark, Withdrawals	6 2 5 00							
Word Processing Fees		8 0 0 0 00						
Office Salaries Expense	1 3 0 0 00							
Advertising Expense	2 5 0 00							
Telephone Expense	2 2 0 00							
	21 3 5 0 00	21 3 5 0 00						

Figure 4-2 Sample Worksheet

THE ADJUSTMENTS SECTION

Chapters 1–3 discussed transactions that occurred with outside suppliers and companies. In a real business, though, inside transactions also occur during the accounting cycle. These transactions must be recorded, too. At the end of the worksheet process, the accountant will have all of the business's accounts up-to-date and ready to be used to prepare the formal financial reports. By analyzing each of Clark's accounts on the worksheet, the accountant will be able to identify specific accounts that must be adjusted, to bring them up-to-date. The accountant for Clark's Word Processing Services needs to adjust the following accounts:

A. Office Supplies **C.** Word Processing Equipment
B. Prepaid Rent **D.** Office Salaries Expense

Let's look at how to analyze and adjust each of these accounts.

A. Adjusting the Office Supplies Account

On May 31, the accountant found out that the company had only $100 worth of office supplies on hand. When the company had originally purchased the $600 of office supplies, they were considered an asset. But as the supplies were used up, they became an expense.

- Office supplies available, $600 on trial balance.
- Office supplies left or on hand as of May 31, $100 will end up on adjusted trial balance.
- Office supplies used up in the operation of the business for the month of May, $500 is shown in the adjustments column.

Worksheets can be completed on Excel spreadsheets

Adjusting is like fine-tuning your TV set.

The adjustment for supplies deals with the amount of supplies used up.

Adjustments affect both the income statement and balance sheet.

Office Supplies Exp. 514

500

This is supplies used up.

Office Supplies 114

600 | 500
100
↑

This is supplies on hand.

Note: All accounts listed below the trial balance will be increasing.

The Office Supplies Expense account indicates the amount of supplies used up. It is listed below other trial balance accounts, since it was not on the original trial balance.

As a result, the asset Office Supplies is too high on the trial balance (it should be $100, not $600). At the same time, if we don't show the additional expense of supplies used, the company's *net income* will be too high.

If Clark's accountant does not adjust the trial balance to reflect the change, the company's net income would be too high on the income statement and both sides (Assets and Owner's Equity) of the balance sheet would be too high.

Now let's look at the adjustment for office supplies in terms of the transaction analysis chart.

Will go on income statement

Accounts Affected	Category	↓ ↑	Rules
Office Supplies Expense	Expense	↑	Dr.
Office Supplies	Asset	↓	Cr.

Will go on balance sheet

The Office Supplies Expense account comes from the chart of accounts on page 73. Since it is not listed in the account titles, it must be listed below the trial balance. Let's see how we enter this adjustment on the worksheet on the following page in Figure 4-3.

Place $500 in the debit column of the adjustments section on the same line as Office Supplies Expense. Place $500 in the credit column of the adjustments section on the same line as Office Supplies. The numbers in the adjustment column show what is used, *not* what is on hand.

B. Adjusting the Prepaid Rent Account

Back on May 1, Clark's Word Processing Services paid three months' rent in advance. The accountant realized that the rent expense would be $400 per month ($1,200 ÷ 3 months = $400).

Remember, when rent is paid in advance, it is considered an asset called *prepaid rent*. When the asset, prepaid rent, begins to expire or be used up, it becomes an expense. Now it is May 31, and one month's prepaid rent has become an expense.

How is this handled? Should the account be $1,200, or is there really only $800 of prepaid rent left as of May 31? What do we need to do to bring Prepaid Rent to the "true" balance? The answer is that we must increase Rent Expense by $400 and decrease Prepaid Rent by $400 (see Fig. 4-4).

Without this adjustment, the expenses for Clark's Word Processing Services for May will be too low, and the asset Prepaid Rent will be too high. If unadjusted amounts were used in the formal reports, the net income shown on the income statement would be too high, and both sides (Assets and Owner's Equity) would be too high on the balance sheet. In terms of our transaction analysis chart, the adjustment would look like this:

Adjusting Prepaid Rent: On p. 88 the trial balance showed a figure for Prepaid Rent of $1,200. The amount of rent expired is the adjustment figure used to update Prepaid Rent and Rent Expense.

Rent Expense 515

400

Prepaid Rent 115

1200 | 400 Adj.
800

Will go on income statement

Accounts Affected	Category	↓ ↑	Rules
Rent Expense	Expense	↑	Dr.
Prepaid Rent	Asset	↓	Cr.

Will go on balance sheet

Like the Office Supplies Expense account, the Rent Expense account comes from the chart of accounts on page 73.

Figure 4-4 shows how to enter an adjustment to Prepaid Rent.

Note: Amount "used up" for supplies $500 goes in adjustments column.

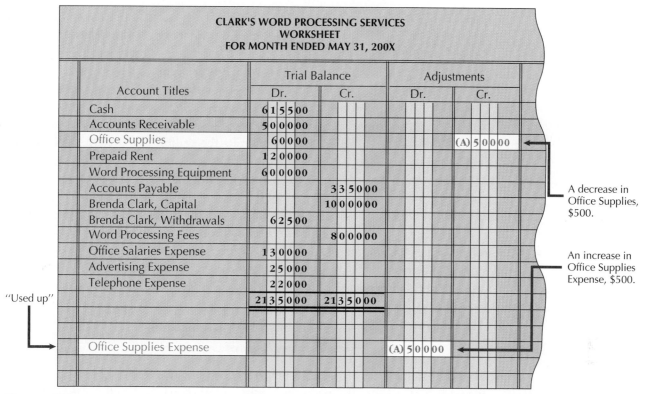

Figure 4-3

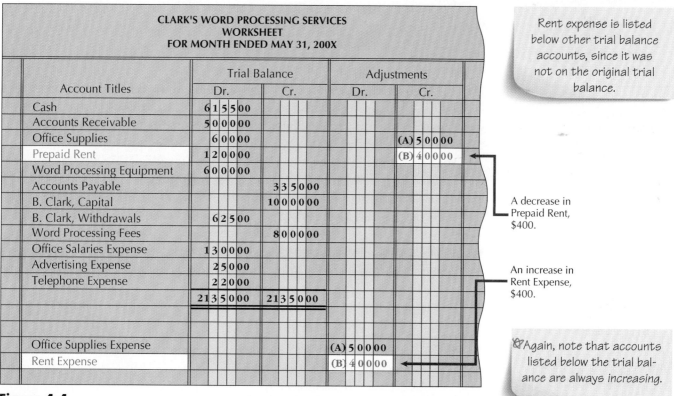

Figure 4-4

C. Adjusting the Word Processing Equipment Account for Depreciation

The life of the asset affects how it is adjusted. The two accounts we just discussed, Office Supplies and Prepaid Rent, involved things that are used up relatively quickly. Equipment—like word processing equipment—is expected to last much longer. Also, it is expected to help produce revenue over a longer period. That is why accountants treat it differently. The balance sheet reports the **historical cost**, or original cost, of the equipment. The original cost also is reflected in the ledger. The adjustment shows how the cost of the equipment is allocated (spread) over its expected useful life. This spreading is called **depreciation**. To depreciate the equipment, we have to figure out how much its cost goes down each month. Then we have to keep a running total of how that depreciation mounts up over time. The Internal Revenue Service (IRS) issues guidelines, tables, and formulas that must be used to estimate the amount of depreciation. Different methods can be used to calculate depreciation (see the Appendix at the end of the text). We will use the simplest method—straight-line depreciation—to calculate the depreciation of Clark's Word Processing Services' equipment. Under the straight-line method, equal amounts are taken over successive periods of time.

The calculation of depreciation for the year for Clark's Word Processing Services is as follows:

$$\frac{\text{Cost of Equipment} - \text{Residual Value}}{\text{Estimated Years of Usefulness}}$$

According to the IRS, word processing equipment has an expected life of five years. At the end of that time, the property's value is called its "residual value." Think of **residual value** as the estimated value of the equipment at the end of the fifth year. For Clark, the equipment has an estimated residual value of $1,200.

$$\frac{\$6{,}000 - \$1{,}200}{5 \text{ Years}} = \frac{\$4{,}800}{5} = \$960 \text{ Depreciation per Year}$$

Our trial balance is for one month, so we must determine the adjustment for that month:

$$\frac{\$960}{12 \text{ Months}} = \$80 \text{ Depreciation per Month}$$

This $80 is known as Depreciation Expense and will be shown on the income statement.

Next, we have to create a new account that can keep a running total of the depreciation amount apart from the original cost of the equipment. That account is called **Accumulated Depreciation**.

The Accumulated Depreciation account shows the relationship between the original cost of the equipment and the amount of depreciation that has been taken or accumulated over a period of time. This is a *contra-asset* account; it has the opposite balance of an asset such as equipment. Accumulated Depreciation will summarize, accumulate, or build up the amount of depreciation that is taken on the word processing equipment over its estimated useful life.

Figure 4-5 shows how this would look on a partial balance sheet of Clark's Word Processing Services.

Let's summarize the key points before going on to mark the adjustment on the worksheet:

1. Depreciation Expense goes on the income statement, which results in
   - An increase in total expenses.
   - A decrease in net income.
   - Therefore, less to be paid in taxes.

Sidebar notes (left margin):

Original cost of $6,000 for word processing equipment remains unchanged after adjustments.

Assume equipment has a five-year life.

Clark will record $960 of depreciation each year.

Depreciation is an expense reported on the income statement.

Accumulated Depreciation

Dr.	Cr.

is a contra-asset account found on the balance sheet.

At the end of June the accumulated depreciation will be $160, but historical cost will stay at $6,000.

Taking depreciation does not result in any new payment of cash. The result of depreciation provides some tax savings.

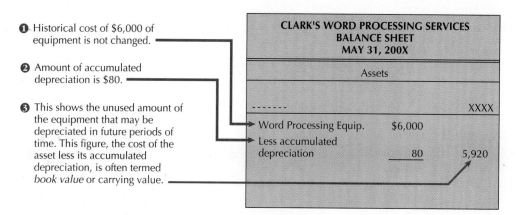

Figure 4-5

❶ Historical cost of $6,000 of equipment is not changed.

❷ Amount of accumulated depreciation is $80.

❸ This shows the unused amount of the equipment that may be depreciated in future periods of time. This figure, the cost of the asset less its accumulated depreciation, is often termed *book value* or carrying value.

CLARK'S WORD PROCESSING SERVICES
BALANCE SHEET
MAY 31, 200X

Assets

- - - - - - -   XXXX

Word Processing Equip. $6,000
Less accumulated
depreciation   80   5,920

2. Accumulated depreciation is a contra-asset account found on the balance sheet next to its related equipment account.

3. The original cost of equipment is not reduced; it stays the same until the equipment is sold or removed.

4. Each month the amount in the Accumulated Depreciation account grows larger, while the cost of the equipment remains the same.

Now, let's analyze the adjustment on the transaction analysis chart:

Will go on income statement

Accounts Affected	Category	↓ ↑	Rules
Depreciation Expense, Word Processing Equipment	Expense	↑	Dr.
Accumulated Depreciation, Word Processing Equipment	Contra Asset	↑	Cr.

Will go on balance sheet

Remember, the original cost of the equipment never changes: (1) The Equipment account is not included among the affected accounts because the original cost of equipment remains the same, and (2) the original cost does not change. Even though the Accumulated Depreciation increases (as a credit), the equipment's book value decreases.

Figure 4-6 (p. 126) shows how we enter the adjustment for depreciation of word processing equipment.

Because this is a new business, neither account had a previous balance. Therefore, neither is listed in the account titles of the trial balance. We need to list both accounts below Rent Expense in the account titles section. On the worksheet, put $80 in the debit column of the adjustments section on the same line as Depreciation Expense, W. P. Equipment, and put $80 in the credit column of the adjustments section on the same line as Accumulated Depreciation, W. P. Equipment.

Next month, on June 30, $80 would be entered under Depreciation Expense, and Accumulated Depreciation would show a balance of $160. Remember, in May, Clark's was a new company, so no previous depreciation was taken.

Now let's look at the last adjustment for Clark's Word Processing Services.

D. Adjusting the Salaries Accrued Account

Clark's Word Processing Services paid $1,300 in Office Salaries Expense (see the trial balance of any previous worksheet in this chapter). The last salary checks for the

---

Remember, book value is not the same as market value.

Dep. Expense, W. P. 516
80 |

Accum. Dep., W. P. 122
| 80

Note that the original cost of the equipment on the worksheet has *not* been changed ($6,000).

Next month (June in our example), accumulated depreciation will appear listed in the original trial balance.

Accumulated Depreciation
| Dr. | Cr.
| | History of amount of depreciation taken to date

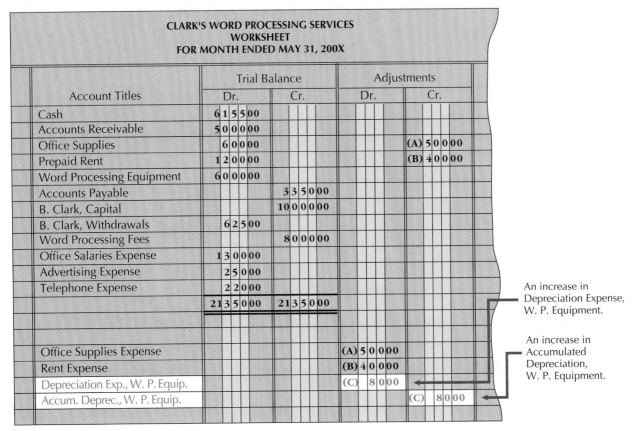

Figure 4-6

(see Fig. 4-7)

Adjusting Salaries

month were paid on May 27. How can we update this account to show the salary expense as of May 31?

John Murray worked for Clark on May 28, 29, 30, and 31 (see Fig. 4-7), but his next paycheck is not due until June 3. John earned $350 for these four days. Is the $350 an expense to Clark in May, when it was earned, or in June when it is due and is paid?

Think back to Chapter 1, when we first discussed revenue and expenses. We noted then that revenue is recorded when it is earned, and expenses are recorded when they are incurred, not when they are actually paid off. This principle will be discussed further in a later chapter; for now it is enough to remember that we record revenue and expenses when they occur, because we want to match earned revenue with the expenses that resulted in earning those revenues. In this case, by working those four days, John Murray created some revenue for Clark in May. Therefore, the office salaries expense must be shown in May—the month the revenue was earned.

✍ An expense can be incurred without being paid as long as it has helped in creating earned revenue for a period of time.

Figure 4-7

May						
Sunday	Monday	Tuesday	Wednesday	Thursday	Friday	Saturday
						1
2	3	4	5	6	7	8
9	10	11	12	13	14	15
16	17	18	19	20	21	22
23	24	25	26	27	28	29
30	31					

The results are:

Office Salaries Expense is increased by $350. This unpaid and unrecorded expense for salaries for which payment is not yet due is called accrued salaries. In effect, we now show the true expense for salaries ($1,650 instead of $1,300):

Office Salaries Expense
| 1,300 | |
| 350 | |

The second result is that Salaries Payable is increased by $350. Clark's has created a liability called Salaries Payable, meaning that the firm owes money for salaries. When the firm pays John Murray, it will reduce its liability, Salaries Payable, as well as decrease its cash.

In terms of the transaction analysis chart, the following would be done:

Accounts Affected	Category	↓ ↑	Rules
Office Salaries Expense,	Expense	↑	Dr.
Salaries Payable	Liability	↑	Cr.

Office Salaries Exp. 511
| 1,300 | |
| 350 | |

Salaries Payable 212
| | 350 |

How the adjustment for accrued salaries is entered is shown in Figure 4-8 below.

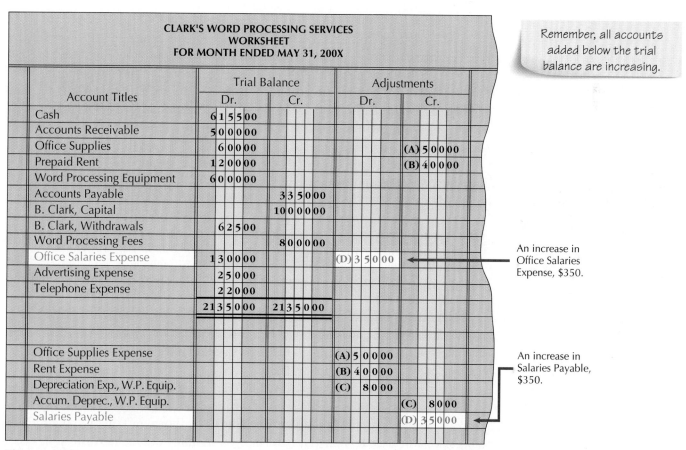

Remember, all accounts added below the trial balance are increasing.

CLARK'S WORD PROCESSING SERVICES
WORKSHEET
FOR MONTH ENDED MAY 31, 200X

Account Titles	Trial Balance Dr.	Trial Balance Cr.	Adjustments Dr.	Adjustments Cr.	
Cash	6 1 5 5 00				
Accounts Receivable	5 0 0 0 00				
Office Supplies	6 0 0 00			(A) 5 0 0 00	
Prepaid Rent	1 2 0 0 00			(B) 4 0 0 00	
Word Processing Equipment	6 0 0 0 00				
Accounts Payable		3 3 5 0 00			
B. Clark, Capital		10 0 0 0 00			
B. Clark, Withdrawals	6 2 5 00				
Word Processing Fees		8 0 0 0 00			
Office Salaries Expense	1 3 0 0 00		(D) 3 5 0 00		An increase in Office Salaries Expense, $350.
Advertising Expense	2 5 0 00				
Telephone Expense	2 2 0 00				
	21 3 5 0 00	21 3 5 0 00			
Office Supplies Expense			(A) 5 0 0 00		
Rent Expense			(B) 4 0 0 00		
Depreciation Exp., W.P. Equip.			(C) 8 0 00		
Accum. Deprec., W.P. Equip.				(C) 8 0 00	
Salaries Payable				(D) 3 5 0 00	An increase in Salaries Payable, $350.

Figure 4-8

Figure 4-9
The Adjustments Section of the Worksheet

Account Titles	Trial Balance Dr.	Trial Balance Cr.	Adjustments Dr.	Adjustments Cr.
	CLARK'S WORD PROCESSING SERVICES WORKSHEET FOR MONTH ENDED MAY 31, 200X			
Cash	6 1 5 5 00			
Accounts Receivable	5 0 0 0 00			
Office Supplies	6 0 0 00			(A) 5 0 0 00
Prepaid Rent	1 2 0 0 00			(B) 4 0 0 00
Word Processing Equipment	6 0 0 0 00			
Accounts Payable		3 3 5 0 00		
B. Clark, Capital		10 0 0 0 00		
B. Clark, Withdrawals	6 2 5 00			
Word Processing Fees		8 0 0 0 00		
Office Salaries Expense	1 3 0 0 00		(D) 3 5 0 00	
Advertising Expense	2 5 0 00			
Telephone Expense	2 2 0 00			
	21 3 5 0 00	21 3 5 0 00		
Office Supplies Expense			(A) 5 0 0 00	
Rent Expense			(B) 4 0 0 00	
Depreciation Exp., W.P. Equip.			(C) 8 0 00	
Accum. Deprec., W.P. Equip.				(C) 8 0 00
Salaries Payable				(D) 3 5 0 00
			1 3 3 0 00	1 3 3 0 00

The account Office Salaries Expense is already listed in the account titles, so $350 is placed in the debit column of the adjustments section on the same line as Office Salaries Expense. However, because the Salaries Payable is not listed in the account titles, it is added below the trial balance after Accumulated Depreciation, W. P. Equipment. Also, $350 is placed in the credit column of the adjustments section on the same line as Salaries Payable.

Now that we have finished all the adjustments that we intended to make, we total the adjustments section, as shown in Figure 4-9.

THE ADJUSTED TRIAL BALANCE SECTION

The adjusted trial balance is the next section on the worksheet. To fill it out, we must summarize the information in the trial balance and adjustments sections, as shown in Figure 4-10 on page 129.

Note that when the numbers are brought across from the trial balance to the adjusted trial balance, two debits will be added together and two credits will be added together. If the numbers include a debit and a credit, take the difference between the two and place it on the side that is larger.

Now that we have completed the adjustments and adjusted trial balance sections of the worksheet, it is time to move on to the income statement and the balance sheet sections. Before we do that though, look at the chart shown in Table 4-1, p. 130. This table should be used as a reference to help you in filling out the next two sections of the worksheet.

CLARK'S WORD PROCESSING SERVICES
WORKSHEET
FOR MONTH ENDED MAY 31, 200X

Account Titles	Trial Balance Dr.	Trial Balance Cr.	Adjustments Dr.	Adjustments Cr.	Adjusted Trial Balance Dr.	Adjusted Trial Balance Cr.
Cash	6155 00				6155 00	
Accounts Receivable	5000 00				5000 00	
Office Supplies	600 00			(A) 500 00	100 00	
Prepaid Rent	1200 00			(B) 400 00	800 00	
Word Processing Equipment	6000 00				6000 00	
Accounts Payable		3350 00				3350 00
Brenda Clark, Capital		10000 00				10000 00
Brenda Clark, Withdrawals	625 00				625 00	
Word Processing Fees		8000 00				8000 00
Office Salaries Expense	1300 00		(D) 350 00		1650 00	
Advertising Expense	250 00				250 00	
Telephone Expense	220 00				220 00	
	21350 00	21350 00				
Office Supplies Expense			(A) 500 00		500 00	
Rent Expense			(B) 400 00		400 00	
Depreciation Exp., W.P. Equip.			(C) 80 00		80 00	
Accum. Deprec., W.P. Equip.				(C) 80 00		80 00
Salaries Payable				(D) 350 00		350 00
			1330 00	1330 00	21780 00	21780 00

Annotations:

If no adjustment is made, just carry over amount from trial balance on same side.

Supplies were $600 but we used up $500, leaving us with a $100 balance (on hand) in Supplies. *Note:* If there are a debit and a credit, take the *difference* between the two and place it on the side that is larger.

Note: Equipment is *not* adjusted here.

Two debits are added together. If there were two credits, they also would have been added together.

Carry these amounts over to adjusted trial balance in the same positions.

Note: The total of the left (debit) must equal the total of the right (credit) ($21,780).

Figure 4-10 The Adjusted Trial Balance Section of the Worksheet

TABLE 4-1 Normal Balances and Account Categories

Account Titles	Category	Normal Balance on Adjusted Trial Balance	Income Statement Dr.	Income Statement Cr.	Balance Sheet Dr.	Balance Sheet Cr.
Cash	Asset	Dr.			X	
Accounts Receivable	Asset	Dr.			X	
Office Supplies	Asset	Dr.			X	
Prepaid Rent	Asset	Dr.			X	
Word Proc. Equip.	Asset	Dr.			X	
Accounts Payable	Liability	Cr.				X
Brenda Clark, Capital	Capital	Cr.				X
Brenda Clark, Withdrawals	Withdrawal	Dr.			X	
Word Proc. Fees	Revenue	Cr.		X		
Office Salaries Exp.	Expense	Dr.	X			
Advertising Expense	Expense	Dr.	X			
Telephone Expense	Expense	Dr.	X			
Office Supplies Exp.	Expense	Dr.	X			
Rent Expense	Expense	Dr.	X			
Dep. Exp., W. P. Equip.	Expense	Dr.	X			
Acc. Dep., W. P. Equip.	Contra Asset	Cr.				X
Salaries Payable	Liability	Cr.				X

In the worksheet, Net Income is placed in the debit column of the income statement. Net loss goes in the credit column.

The difference between $3,100 Dr. and $8,000 Cr. indicates a Net Income of $4,900. Do not think of the Net Income as a Dr. or Cr. The $4,900 is placed in the debit column to balance both columns to $8,000. Actually, the credit side is larger by $4,900.

only to math door

⌈Keep in mind that the numbers from the adjusted trial balance are carried over to one of the last four columns of the worksheet before the bottom section is completed.⌉

THE INCOME STATEMENT SECTION

As shown in Figure 4-11 on page 131, the income statement section lists only revenue and expenses from the adjusted trial balance. Note that Accumulated Depreciation and Salaries Payable do not go on the income statement. Accumulated Depreciation is a contra-asset found on the balance sheet. Salaries Payable is a liability found on the balance sheet.

The revenue ($8,000) and all the individual expenses are listed in the income statement section. The revenue is placed in the credit column of the income statement section because it has a credit balance. The expenses have debit balances, so they are placed in the debit column of the income statement section. The following steps must be taken after the debits and credits are placed in the correct columns:

Step 1: Total the debits and credits.

Step 2: Calculate the balance between the debit and credit columns and place the difference on the smaller side.

Step 3: Total the columns.

The worksheet in Figure 4-11 shows that the label Net Income is added in the account title column on the same line as $4,900. When there is a net income, it will be placed in the debit column of the income statement section of the worksheet. If there is a net loss, it is placed in the credit column. The $8,000 total indicates that the two columns are in balance.

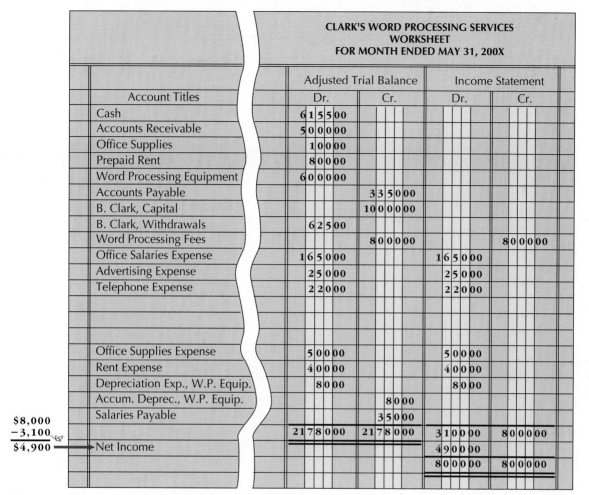

CLARK'S WORD PROCESSING SERVICES
WORKSHEET
FOR MONTH ENDED MAY 31, 200X

Account Titles	Adjusted Trial Balance Dr.	Adjusted Trial Balance Cr.	Income Statement Dr.	Income Statement Cr.
Cash	6 1 5 5 00			
Accounts Receivable	5 0 0 0 00			
Office Supplies	1 0 0 00			
Prepaid Rent	8 0 0 00			
Word Processing Equipment	6 0 0 0 00			
Accounts Payable		3 3 5 0 00		
B. Clark, Capital		1 0 0 0 0 00		
B. Clark, Withdrawals	6 2 5 00			
Word Processing Fees		8 0 0 0 00		8 0 0 0 00
Office Salaries Expense	1 6 5 0 00		1 6 5 0 00	
Advertising Expense	2 5 0 00		2 5 0 00	
Telephone Expense	2 2 0 00		2 2 0 00	
Office Supplies Expense	5 0 0 00		5 0 0 00	
Rent Expense	4 0 0 00		4 0 0 00	
Depreciation Exp., W.P. Equip.	8 0 00		8 0 00	
Accum. Deprec., W.P. Equip.		8 0 00		
Salaries Payable		3 5 0 00		
	2 1 7 8 0 00	2 1 7 8 0 00	3 1 0 0 00	8 0 0 0 00
Net Income			4 9 0 0 00	
			8 0 0 0 00	8 0 0 0 00

$8,000
−3,100
$4,900

Figure 4-11 The Income Statement Section of the Worksheet

THE BALANCE SHEET SECTION

To fill out the balance sheet section of the worksheet, the following are carried over from the adjusted trial balance section: assets, contra-assets, liabilities, capital, and withdrawals. Because the beginning figure for Capital* is used on the worksheet, the Net Income is brought over to the credit column of the balance sheet so both columns balance.

Let's now look at the completed worksheet in Figure 4-12 (p. 132) to see how the balance sheet section is completed. Note how the Net Income of $4,900 is brought over to the Credit column of the worksheet. The figure for Capital is also in the credit column, while the figure for Withdrawals is in the debit column. By placing the net income in the credit column, both sides total $18,680. If a net loss were to occur, it would be placed in the debit column of the balance sheet column.

Now that we have completed the worksheet, we can go on to the three financial reports. But first let's summarize our progress.

> Remember: The ending figure for capital is not on the worksheet.

> To see whether additional investments occurred for the period you must check the Capital account in the ledger.

> The amounts come from the adjusted trial balance, except the $4,900, which was carried over from the income statement section.

*We assume no additional investments during the period.

CLARK'S WORD PROCESSING SERVICES
WORKSHEET
FOR MONTH ENDED MAY 31, 200X

Account Titles	Trial Balance Dr.	Trial Balance Cr.	Adjustments Dr.	Adjustments Cr.	Adjusted Trial Balance Dr.	Adjusted Trial Balance Cr.	Income Statement Dr.	Income Statement Cr.	Balance Sheet Dr.	Balance Sheet Cr.
Cash	6155 00				6155 00				6155 00	
Accounts Receivable	5000 00				5000 00				5000 00	
Office Supplies	600 00			(A) 500 00	100 00				100 00	
Prepaid Rent	1200 00			(B) 400 00	800 00				800 00	
Word Processing Equipment	6000 00				6000 00				6000 00	
Accounts Payable		3350 00				3350 00				3350 00
B. Clark, Capital		10000 00				10000 00				10000 00
B. Clark, Withdrawals	625 00				625 00				625 00	
Word Processing Fees		8000 00				8000 00		8000 00		
Office Salaries Expense	1300 00		(D) 350 00		1650 00		1650 00			
Advertising Expense	250 00				250 00		250 00			
Telephone Expense	220 00				220 00		220 00			
	21350 00	21350 00								
Office Supplies Expense			(A) 500 00		500 00		500 00			
Rent Expense			(B) 400 00		400 00		400 00			
Depreciation Exp., W. P. Equip.			(C) 80 00		80 00		80 00			
Accum. Deprec., W. P. Equip.				(C) 80 00		80 00				80 00
Salaries Payable				(D) 350 00		350 00				350 00
			1330 00	1330 00	21780 00	21780 00	3100 00	8000 00	18680 00	13780 00
Net Income							4900 00			4900 00
							8000 00	8000 00	18680 00	18680 00

Original cost of $6,000 is *not* adjusted

"used up"

"on hand"

contra-asset

Figure 4-12 The Completed Worksheet

Learning Unit 4-1 Review

AT THIS POINT you should be able to

- Define and explain the purpose of a worksheet. (p. 120)
- Explain the need as well as the process for adjustments. (p. 121)
- Explain the concept of depreciation. (p. 124)
- Explain the difference between depreciation expense and accumulated depreciation. (p. 124)
- Prepare a worksheet from a trial balance and adjustment data. (p. 132)

SELF-REVIEW QUIZ 4-1

From the accompanying trial balance and adjustment data in Figure 4-13, complete a worksheet for P. Logan Co. for the month ended Dec. 31, 200X. (You can use the blank fold-out worksheet located at the end of the *Study Guide and Working Papers.* See your DVD for worked-out solutions.)

Note: The numbers used on this quiz may seem impossibly small, but we have done that on purpose, so that at this point you don't have to worry about arithmetic, just about preparing the worksheet correctly.

ADJUSTMENT DATA

a. Depreciation Expense, Store Equipment, $1.

b. Insurance Expired, $2

c. Supplies on hand, $1.

d. Salaries owed but not paid to employees, $3.

Figure 4-13

P. LOGAN
TRIAL BALANCE
DECEMBER 31, 200X

	Dr.	Cr.
Cash	15 00	
Accounts Receivable	3 00	
Prepaid Insurance	3 00	
Store Supplies	5 00	
Store Equipment	6 00	
Accumulated Depreciation, Store Equipment		4 00
Accounts Payable		2 00
P. Logan, Capital		14 00
P. Logan, Withdrawals	3 00	
Revenue from Clients		25 00
Rent Expense	2 00	
Salaries Expense	8 00	
	45 00	45 00

SOLUTION TO SELF-REVIEW QUIZ 4-1

Don't adjust this line! Store Equipment always contains the historical cost.

Amount used up

Note that on hand ends up on the adjusted trial balance

P. LOGAN COMPANY
WORKSHEET
FOR MONTH ENDED DECEMBER 31, 200X

Account Titles	Trial Balance Dr.	Trial Balance Cr.	Adjustments Dr.	Adjustments Cr.	Adjusted Trial Balance Dr.	Adjusted Trial Balance Cr.	Income Statement Dr.	Income Statement Cr.	Balance Sheet Dr.	Balance Sheet Cr.
Cash	1500				1500				1500	
Accounts Receivable	300				300				300	
Prepaid Insurance	300			(B) 200	100				100	
Store Supplies	500			(C) 400	100				100	
Store Equipment	600				600				600	
Accum. Depr., Store Equipment		400		(A) 100		500				500
Accounts Payable		200				200				200
P. Logan, Capital		1400				1400				1400
P. Logan, Withdrawals	300				300				300	
Revenue from Clients		2500				2500		2500		
Rent Expense	200				200		200			
Salaries Expense	800		(D) 300		1100		1100			
	4500	4500								
Depr. Exp., Store Equipment			(A) 100		100		100			
Insurance Expense			(B) 200		200		200			
Supplies Expense			(C) 400		400		400			
Salaries Payable				(D) 300		300				300
			1000	1000	4900	4900	2000	2500	2900	2400
Net Income							500			500
							2500	2500	2900	2900

Note that Accumulated Depreciation is listed in trial balance, since this is not a new company. Store Equipment has already been depreciated $4.00 from an earlier period.

Figure 4-14

Accounting in the Reel World

Dating . . . and Accounting?

Everyone, at one point or another, has probably set up two friends on a blind date or been set up on one. Yet, not everyone sees this matchmaking activity as a business opportunity.

Jilted just five weeks before she was to walk down the aisle, Andrea McGinty turned her personal frustration at finding eligible singles into a lucrative matchmaking business. It's Just Lunch has over $2.5 million in revenues, over 20 locations across the country, and plans to open 1–2 units per month. As you watch the brief It's Just Lunch on-location video on your DVD, think about what it takes to set up a matchmaking business such as It's Just Lunch, and answer the following questions.

1. Can you name some account titles in the assets category? In the Liabilities category? In the Expenses category?
2. How often does It's Just Lunch generate financial statements and why does owner Andrea McGinty need them that often?
3. Is depreciation likely to show up on the It's Just Lunch balance sheet, and if so, for what types of things would Andrea McGinty make a depreciation adjustment?
4. What is the difference between It's Just Lunch's revenues and its income, and what could Andrea McGinty do to increase the company's income?

Learning Unit 4-2   Step 6 of the Accounting Cycle: Preparing the Financial Statements from the Worksheet

The formal financial statements can be prepared from the worksheet completed in Learning Unit 4-1. Before beginning, we must check that the entries on the worksheet are correct and in balance. To do this, we have to be sure that (1) all entries are recorded in the appropriate column, (2) the correct amounts are entered in the proper places, (3) the addition is correct across the columns (i.e., from the trial balance to the adjusted trial balance to the financial statements), and (4) the columns are added correctly.

PREPARING THE INCOME STATEMENT

The first statement to be prepared for Clark's Word Processing Services is the income statement. When preparing the income statement, it is important to remember that

1. Every figure on the formal statement is on the worksheet. Figure 4-15 (p. 136) shows where each of these figures goes on the income statement.
2. There are no debit or credit columns on the formal statement.
3. The inside column on financial statements is used for subtotaling.
4. Withdrawals do not go on the income statement; they go on the statement of owner's equity.

Take a moment to look at the income statement in Figure 4-15. Note where items go from the income statement section of the worksheet onto the formal statement.

PREPARING THE STATEMENT OF OWNER'S EQUITY

Figure 4-16 (p. 136) is the statement of owner's equity for Clark's. The figure shows where the information comes from on the worksheet. It is important to remember that if there were additional investments, the figure on the worksheet for Capital would not be the beginning figure for Capital. Checking the ledger account for Capital will tell you whether the amount is correct. Note how Net Income and Withdrawals aid in calculating the new figure for Capital.

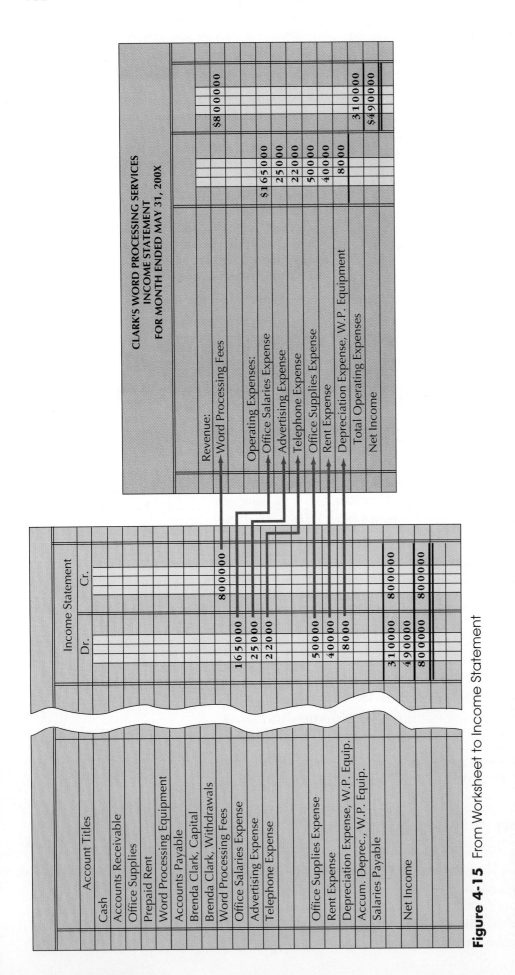

Figure 4-15 From Worksheet to Income Statement

CLARK'S WORD PROCESSING SERVICES INCOME STATEMENT FOR MONTH ENDED MAY 31, 200X		
Revenue:		
Word Processing Fees		$8 0 0 0 00
Operating Expenses:		
Office Salaries Expense	$1 6 5 0 00	
Advertising Expense	2 5 0 00	
Telephone Expense	2 2 0 00	
Office Supplies Expense	5 0 0 00	
Rent Expense	4 0 0 00	
Depreciation Expense, W.P. Equipment	8 0 00	
Total Operating Expenses		3 1 0 0 00
Net Income		$4 9 0 0 00

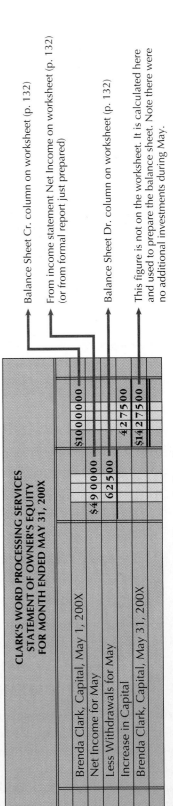

CLARK'S WORD PROCESSING SERVICES STATEMENT OF OWNER'S EQUITY FOR MONTH ENDED MAY 31, 200X		
Brenda Clark, Capital, May 1, 200X		$1 0 0 0 0 00
Net Income for May	$4 9 0 0 00	
Less Withdrawals for May	6 2 5 00	
Increase in Capital		4 2 7 5 00
Brenda Clark, Capital, May 31, 200X		$1 4 2 7 5 00

- Balance Sheet Cr. column on worksheet (p. 132)
- From income statement Net Income on worksheet (p. 132) (or from formal report just prepared)
- Balance Sheet Dr. column on worksheet (p. 132)
- This figure is not on the worksheet. It is calculated here and used to prepare the balance sheet. Note there were no additional investments during May.

Figure 4-16 Completing a Statement of Owner's Equity

PREPARING THE BALANCE SHEET

In preparing the balance sheet (Fig. 4-17) remember that the balance sheet section totals on the worksheet ($18,680) do *not* match the totals on the formal balance sheet ($17,975). This is because information is grouped differently on the formal statement. First, in the formal report Accumulated Depreciation ($80) is subtracted from Word Processing Equipment, reducing the balance. Second, Withdrawals ($625) are subtracted from Owner's Equity, reducing the balance further. These two reductions (−$80 − $625 = −$705) represent the difference between the worksheet and the formal version of the balance sheet ($17,975 − $18,680 = −$705). Figure 4-17 shows how to prepare the balance sheet from the worksheet.

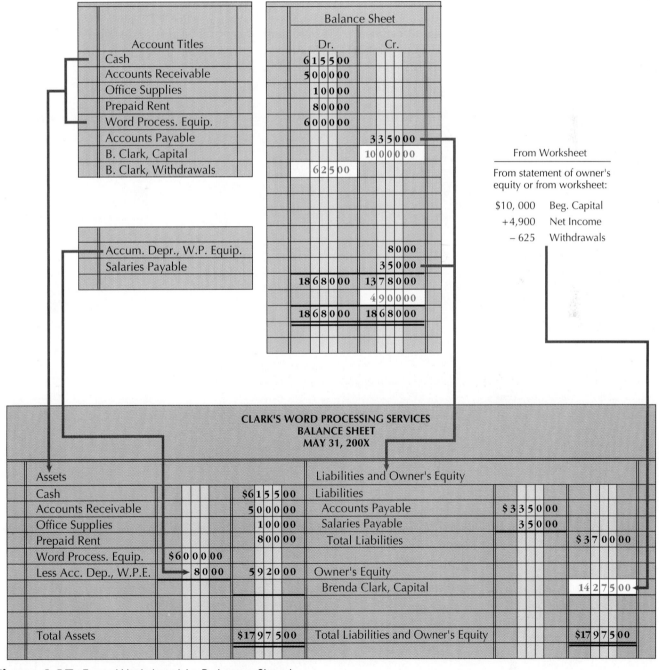

Figure 4-17 From Worksheet to Balance Sheet

Learning Unit 4-2 Review

AT THIS POINT you should be able to

- Prepare the three financial statements from a worksheet. (p. 136)
- Explain why totals of the formal balance sheet don't match totals of balance sheet columns on the worksheet. (p. 137)

SELF-REVIEW QUIZ 4-2

(The forms you need are located on pages 101 and 102 of the *Study Guide and Working Papers.* See your DVD for worked-out solutions.)

From the worksheet on page 134 for P. Logan, please prepare (1) an income statement for December, (2) a statement of owner's equity, and (3) a balance sheet for December 31, 200X. No additional investments took place during the period.

SOLUTION TO SELF-REVIEW QUIZ 4-2

Quiz Tips:
The income statement is made up of revenue and expenses. Use the inside column for subtotaling. The $5 on the income statement is used to update the statement of owner's equity.

P. LOGAN
INCOME STATEMENT
FOR THE MONTH ENDED DECEMBER 31, 200X

Revenue:			
Revenue from clients			$2500
Operating Expenses:			
Rent Expense	$200		
Salaries Expense	1100		
Depreciation Expense, Store Equipment	100		
Insurance Expense	200		
Supplies Expense	400		
Total Operating Expenses		2000	
Net Income		$500	

P. LOGAN
STATEMENT OF OWNER'S EQUITY
FOR THE MONTH ENDED DECEMBER 31, 200X

P. Logan, Capital, December 1, 200X			$1400
Net Income for December	$500		
Less Withdrawals for December	300		
Increase in Capital		200	
P. Logan, Capital, December 31, 200X		$1600	

The ending Capital figure on the statement of owner's equity ($16) is used as the Capital figure on the balance sheet.

P. LOGAN
BALANCE SHEET
DECEMBER 31, 200X

Assets				Liabilities and Owner's Equity			
Cash		$1500		Liabilities			
Accounts Receivable		300		Accounts Payable	$200		
Prepaid Insurance		100		Salaries Payable	300		
Store Supplies		100		Total Liabilities		$500	
Store Equipment	$600			Owner's Equity			
Less Acc. Dep., St. Eq.	500	100		P. Logan, Capital		1600	
				Total Liabilities and			
Total Assets		$2100		Owner's Equity		$2100	

Figure 4-18

SOLUTIONS & TIPS TO COMPREHENSIVE PROBLEM: PUTTING THE PIECES TOGETHER

(The blank forms you need are on pages 103 and 104 of the *Study Guide and Working Papers.*)

From the following trial balance and additional data complete (1) a worksheet and (2) the three financial statements (numbers are intentionally small so you may concentrate on the theory).

FROST COMPANY
TRIAL BALANCE
DECEMBER 31, 200X

	Dr.	Cr.
Cash	14	
Accounts Receivable	4	
Prepaid Insurance	5	
Plumbing Supplies	3	
Plumbing Equipment	7	
Accumulated Depreciation, Plumbing Equipment		5
Accounts Payable		1
J. Frost, Capital		12
J. Frost, Withdrawals	3	
Plumbing Fees		27
Rent Expense	4	
Salaries Expense	5	
Totals	45	45

Adjustment Data

a.	Insurance Expired	$3
b.	Plumbing Supplies on Hand	$1
c.	Depreciation Expense, Plumbing Equipment	$1
d.	Salaries owed but not paid to employees	$2

Solution Tips to Building a Worksheet

1. Adjustments

   a.

Insurance Expense	Expense	↑	Dr.	$3
Prepaid Insurance	Asset	↓	Cr.	$3

   Expired means used up

   b.

Plumbing Supplies Expense	Expense	↑	Dr.	$2
Plumbing Supplies	Asset	↓	Cr.	$2

   $3 − 1 = $2 *used up* on hand

Solution to Worksheet

FROST COMPANY
WORKSHEET
FOR MONTH ENDED DECEMBER 31, 200X

Account Titles	Trial Balance Dr.	Trial Balance Cr.	Adjustments Dr.	Adjustments Cr.	Adjusted Trial Balance Dr.	Adjusted Trial Balance Cr.	Income Statement Dr.	Income Statement Cr.	Balance Sheet Dr.	Balance Sheet Cr.
Cash	1400				1400				1400	
Accounts Receivable	400				400				400	
Prepaid Insurance	500			(A) 300	200				200	
Plumbing Supplies	300			(B) 200	100				100	
Plumbing Equipment	700				700				700	
Accum. Depr., Plumb. Equip.		500		(C) 100		600				600
Accounts Payable		100				100				100
J. Frost, Capital		1200				1200				1200
J. Frost, Withdrawals	300				300				300	
Plumbing Fees		2700				2700		2700		
Rent Expense	400				400		400			
Salaries Expense	500		(D) 200		700		700			
	4500	4500								
Insurance Expense			(A) 300		300		300			
Plumbing Supplies Expense			(B) 200		200		200			
Depr. Exp. Plumb. Equip.			(C) 100		100		100			
Salaries Payable				(D) 200		200				200
			800	800	4800	4800	1700	2700	3100	2100
Net Income							1000			1000
							2700	2700	3100	3100

Original cost not adjusted

"used up"   "on hand"

Figure 4-19

c.

| Depreciation Expense, Plumbing Equipment | Expense | ↑ | Dr. | $1 |
| Contra Asset Accumulated Depreciation, Plumbing Equipment | Contra Asset | ↑ | Cr. | $1 |

The original cost of equipment of $7 is not "touched."

d.

| Salaries Expense, | Expense | ↑ | Dr. | $2 |
| Salaries Payable | Liability | ↑ | Cr. | $2 |

2. Last four columns of worksheet prepared from adjusted trial balance.
3. Capital of $12 is the old figure. Net income of $10 (revenue − expenses) is brought over to same side as capital on the balance sheet Cr. column to balance columns.

FROST COMPANY
INCOME STATEMENT
FOR MONTH ENDED DECEMBER 31, 200X

Revenue:		
Plumbing Fees		$27
Operating Expenses:		
Rent Expense	$4	
Salaries Expense	7	
Insurance Expense	3	
Plumbing Supplies Expense	2	
Depreciation Expense, Plumbing Equipment	1	
Total Operating Expenses		17
Net Income		$10

FROST COMPANY
STATEMENT OF OWNER'S EQUITY
FOR MONTH ENDED DECEMBER 31, 200X

J. Frost Capital, Dec. 1, 200X		$12
Net Income for December	$10	
Less Withdrawals for December	3	
Increase in Capital		7
J. Frost, Capital Dec. 31, 200X		$19

FROST COMPANY
BALANCE SHEET
DECEMBER 31, 200X

Assets			Liabilities and Owner's Equity		
Cash		$14	Liabilities		
Accounts Receivable		4	Accounts Payable	$1	
Prepaid Insurance		2	Salaries Payable	2	
Plumbing Supplies		1	Total Liabilities		$3
Original Cost					
Plumbing Equipment	$7				
Less Accumulated Dep.	6	1	Owner's Equity		
			J. Frost, Capital		19
			Total Liabilities and		
Total Assets		$22	Owner's Equity		$22

Solution Tips for Preparing Financial Statements from a Worksheet

Inside columns of the three financial statements are used for subtotaling. There are no debits or credits on the formal statements.

STATEMENTS

Income Statement	From Income Statement columns of worksheet for revenue and expenses.
Statement of Owner's Equity	From Balance Sheet Cr. column for old figure for Capital. Net Income from Income Statement. From Balance Sheet Dr. Column for Withdrawal figure.
Balance Sheet	From Balance Sheet Dr. column for Assets. From Balance Sheet Cr. Column for Liabilities and Accumulated Depreciation. New figure for Capital from statement of owner's equity.

Note how Plumbing Equipment $7 and Accumulated Depreciation $6 are rearranged on the formal balance sheet. The Total Assets of $22 is not on the worksheet. Remember there are no debits or credits on formal statements.

Summary of Key Points

Learning Unit 4-1

1. The worksheet is not a formal statement.
2. Adjustments update certain accounts so that they will be up to their latest balance before financial statements are prepared. Adjustments are the result of internal transactions.
3. Adjustments will affect both the income statement and the balance sheet.
4. Accounts listed *below* the account titles on the trial balance of the worksheet are *increasing*.
5. The original cost of a piece of equipment is not adjusted; historical cost is not lost.
6. Depreciation is the process of spreading the original cost of the asset over its expected useful life.
7. Accumulated depreciation is a contra-asset on the balance sheet that summarizes, accumulates, or builds up the amount of depreciation that an asset has accumulated.
8. Book value is the original cost less accumulated depreciation.
9. Accrued salaries are unpaid and unrecorded expenses that are accumulating but for which payment is not yet due.
10. Revenue and expenses go on income statement sections of the worksheet. Assets, contra-assets, liabilities, capital, and withdrawals go on balance sheet sections of the worksheet.

Learning Unit 4-2

1. The formal statements prepared from a worksheet do not have debit or credit columns.
2. Revenue and expenses go on the income statement. Beginning capital plus net income less withdrawals (or: beginning capital minus net loss less withdrawals) go on the statement of owner's equity. Be sure to check the capital account in the ledger to see if any additional investments took place. Assets, contra-assets, liabilities, and the new figure for capital go on the balance sheet.

Key Terms

Accrued salaries Salaries that are earned by employees but unpaid and unrecorded during the period (and thus need to be recorded by an adjustment) and will not come due for payment until the next accounting period.

Accumulated depreciation A contra-asset account that summarizes or accumulates the amount of depreciation that has been taken on an asset.

Adjusting The process of calculating the latest up-to-date balance of each account at the end of an accounting period.

Book value Cost of equipment less accumulated depreciation.

Depreciation The allocation (spreading) of the cost of an asset (such as an auto or equipment) over its expected useful life.

Historical cost The actual cost of an asset at time of purchase.

Residual value Estimated value of an asset after all the allowable depreciation has been taken.

Worksheet A columnar device used by accountants to aid them in completing the accounting cycle—often called a spreadsheet. It is not a formal report.

Blueprint of Steps 5 and 6 of the Accounting Cycle

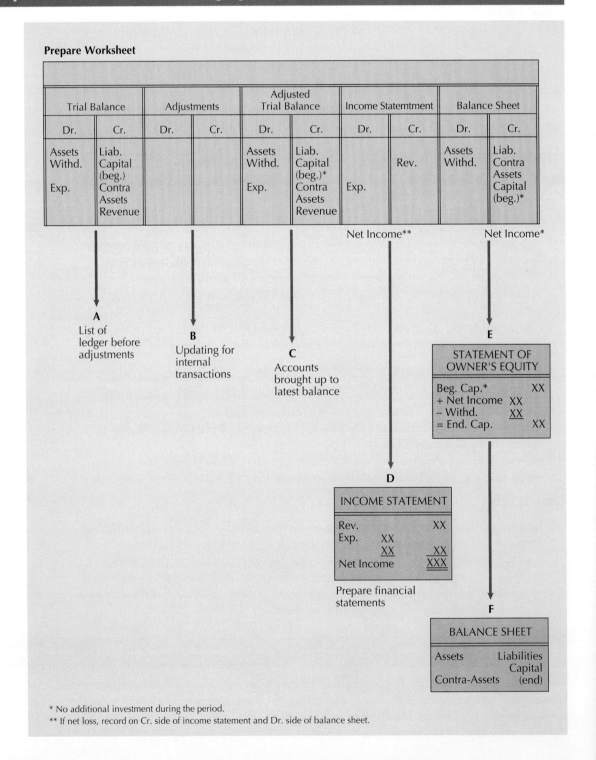

Prepare Worksheet

	Trial Balance		Adjustments		Adjusted Trial Balance		Income Statemtment		Balance Sheet	
	Dr.	Cr.	Dr.	Cr.	Dr.	Cr.	Dr.	Cr.	Dr.	Cr.
	Assets Withd. Exp.	Liab. Capital (beg.) Contra Assets Revenue			Assets Withd. Exp.	Liab. Capital (beg.)* Contra Assets Revenue	Exp.	Rev.	Assets Withd.	Liab. Contra Assets Capital (beg.)*

Net Income**   Net Income*

A
List of ledger before adjustments

B
Updating for internal transactions

C
Accounts brought up to latest balance

E

STATEMENT OF OWNER'S EQUITY	
Beg. Cap.*	XX
+ Net Income	XX
– Withd.	XX
= End. Cap.	XX

D

INCOME STATEMENT		
Rev.		XX
Exp.	XX	
	XX	XX
Net Income		XXX

Prepare financial statements

F

BALANCE SHEET	
Assets	Liabilities
	Capital
Contra-Assets	(end)

* No additional investment during the period.
** If net loss, record on Cr. side of income statement and Dr. side of balance sheet.

Questions, Mini Exercises, Exercises, and Problems

Discussion Questions

1. Worksheets are required in every company's accounting cycle. Please agree or disagree and explain why.
2. What is the purpose of adjusting accounts?
3. What is the relationship of internal transactions to the adjusting process?
4. Explain how an adjustment can affect both the income statement and balance sheet. Please give an example.
5. Why do we need the Accumulated Depreciation account?
6. Depreciation expense goes on the balance sheet. True or false. Why?
7. Each month Accumulated Depreciation grows while Equipment goes up. Agree or disagree. Defend your position.
8. Define the term *accrued salaries.*
9. Why don't the formal financial statements contain debit or credit columns?
10. Explain how the financial statements are prepared from the worksheet.

Mini Exercises

(The blank forms you need are on pages 106–107 of the *Study Guide and Working Papers.*)

Adjustment for Supplies

1. *Before Adjustment*

   Computer Supplies   Computer Supplies Expense
   700

   Given: At year end an inventory of supplies showed $100.

   a. How much is the adjustment for Supplies?
   b. Draw a transaction analysis box for this adjustment.
   c. What will the balance of Supplies be on the adjusted trial balance?

Adjustment for Prepaid Rent

2. *Before Adjustment*

   Prepaid Rent   Rent Expense
   700

   Given: At year end, rent expired is $300.

   a. How much is the adjustment for Prepaid Rent?
   b. Draw a transaction analysis box for this adjustment.
   c. What will be the balance of Prepaid Rent on the adjusted trial balance?

Adjustment for Depreciation

3. *Before Adjustment*

   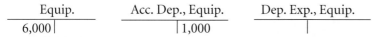

   Equip.   Acc. Dep., Equip.   Dep. Exp., Equip.
   6,000   1,000

   Given: At year end depreciation on Equipment is $1,000.

   a. Which of the three T Accounts above is not affected?
   b. Which account is a contra-asset?

c. Draw a transaction analysis box for this adjustment.

d. What will be the balance of these three accounts on the adjusted trial balance?

Adjustment for Accrued Salaries

4. *Before Adjustment*

Salaries Expense	Salaries Payable
900	200

300

Given: Accrued Salaries, $200.

a. Draw a transaction analysis box for this adjustment.

b. What will be the balance of these two accounts on the adjusted trial balance?

Worksheet

5. From the following adjusted trial balance titles of a worksheet, identify in which column each account will be listed on the last four columns of the worksheet:

(ID) Income Statement Dr. Column

(IC) Income Statement Cr. Column

(BD) Balance Sheet Dr. Column

(BC) Balance Sheet Cr. Column

Income Statement
Revenue
Expenses

Balance Sheet
Assets
Liabilities
Capital

	ATB	IS	BS
A. Ex: Supplies	~~~	~~~	___ BD
B. Acc. Receivable	~~~	~~~	BD
C. Cash	~~~	~~~	BD
D. Prepaid Rent	~~~	~~~	BS
E. Equipment	~~~	~~~	BD
F. Acc. Depreciation	~~~	~~~	BC
G. B., Capital	~~~	~~~	BSC
H. B., Withdrawals	~~~	~~~	BSD
I. Taxi Fees	~~~	~~~	ISC
J. Advertising Expense	~~~	~~~	ISD
K. Off. Supplies Expense	~~~	~~~	''
L. Rent Expense	~~~	~~~	''
M. Depreciation Expense	~~~	~~~	''
N. Salaries Payable	~~~	~~~	) BSC

6. From the following balance sheet (which was made from the worksheet and other financial statements), explain why the lettered numbers were not found on the worksheet. *Hint:* There are no debits or credits on the formal financial statements.

H. WELLS
BALANCE SHEET
DECEMBER 31, 200X

Assets			Liabilities and Owner's Equity		
Cash		$6	Liabilities		
Acc. Receivable		2	Accounts Payable	$2	
Supplies		2	Salaries, Payable	1	
Equipment	$10		Total Liabilities		$ 3 (B)
Less Acc. Dep.	4	6	Owner's Equity		
			H. Wells, Capital		13 (C)
			Total Liability and		
Total Assets		$16 (A)	**Owner's Equity**		$16 (D)

Exercises

(The blank forms you need are on pages 108–110 of the *Study Guide and Working Papers*.)

4-1. Complete the following table.

Categorizing accounts.

Account	Category	Normal Balance	Which Financial Statement(s) Found
Fax Machine	Asset	Debit	BS
Prepaid Insurance	Asset	Debit	BS
Digital Camera	Asset	Debit	BS
Accumulated Depreciation	Contra Asset	Credit	BS
A. Jax, Capital	Capital	Credit	OE
A. Jax, Withdrawals	Withdraw	Debit	OE
Salaries Payable	Liability	Credit	BS
Depreciation Expense	Expense	Debit	IS

4-2. Use transaction analysis charts to analyze the following adjustments:

a. Depreciation on equipment, $500.
b. Rent expired, $200.

Reviewing adjustments and the transaction analysis charts.

4-3. From the following adjustment data, calculate the adjustment amount and record appropriate debits or credits:

a. Supplies purchased, $600.
   Supplies on hand, $200.
b. Store equipment, $10,000.
   Accumulated depreciation before adjustment, $900.
   Depreciation expense, $100.

Recording adjusting entries.

4-4. From the following trial balance (Fig. 4-20) and adjustment data, complete a worksheet for J. Trent as of December 31, 200X:

a. Depreciation expense, equipment $2.00
b. Insurance expired   1.00
c. Store supplies on hand   4.00
d. Wages owed, but not paid for
   (they are an expense in the old year)   5.00

Preparing a worksheet.

Figure 4-20

J. TRENT TRIAL BALANCE DECEMBER 31, 200X	Dr.	Cr.
Cash	9 00	
Accounts Receivable	2 00	
Prepaid Insurance	7 00	
Store Supplies	6 00	
Store Equipment	7 00	
Accumulated Depreciation, Equipment		2 00
Accounts Payable		4 00
J. Trent, Capital		17 00
J. Trent, Withdrawals	6 00	
Revenue from Clients		24 00
Rent Expense	4 00	
Wage Expense	6 00	
	47 00	47 00

Preparing financial statements from a worksheet.

4-5. From the completed worksheet in Exercise 4-4, prepare

   a. An income statement for December.
   b. A statement of owner's equity for December.
   c. A balance sheet as of December 31, 200X.

Group A Problems

(The blank forms you need are on pp. 111–114 of the *Study Guide and Working Papers.*)

4A-1.

   Given the following adjustment data on December 31:

   a. Grooming supplies on hand, $800.
   b. Depreciation taken on grooming equipment, $500.

   complete a partial worksheet (Fig. 4-21) up to the adjusted trial balance.

Figure 4-21

Completing a partial worksheet up to the adjusted trial balance.

Check Figure:
Total of adjusted trial balance $30,150

MATTY'S GROOMING SERVICE TRIAL BALANCE DECEMBER 31, 200X	Debit	Credit
Cash in Bank	7 0 0 0 00	
Accounts Receivable	6 0 0 0 00	
Grooming Supplies	5 4 0 0 00	
Grooming Equipment	7 2 0 0 00	
Accumulated Depreciation, Grooming Equipment		6 0 0 0 00
M. Magee, Capital		1 2 3 5 0 00
M. Magee, Withdrawals	3 0 0 0 00	
Grooming Fees		1 1 3 0 0 00
Rent Expense	9 0 0 00	
Advertising Expense	1 5 0 00	
	29 6 5 0 00	29 6 5 0 00

4A-2. The trial balance for Fred's Plumbing Service (Fig. 4-22) for December 31, 200X.

Figure 4-22

Completing a worksheet.

Check Figure:
Net Income $804

FRED'S PLUMBING SERVICE TRIAL BALANCE DECEMBER 31, 200X	Dr.	Cr.
Cash in Bank	3 6 0 6 00	
Accounts Receivable	7 0 0 0 00	
Prepaid Rent	8 0 0 00	
Plumbing Supplies	7 4 2 00	
Plumbing Equipment	1 4 0 0 00	
Accumulated Depreciation, Plumbing Equipment		1 0 6 0 00
Accounts Payable		4 4 2 00
Fred Jack, Capital		3 2 5 0 00
Plumbing Revenue		4 3 5 6 00
Heat Expense	4 0 0 00	
Advertising Expense	2 0 0 00	
Wage Expense	1 2 6 0 00	
	9 1 0 8 00	9 1 0 8 00

Adjustment Data to Update the Trial Balance

a. Rent expired, $500.
b. Plumbing supplies on hand (remaining), $100.
c. Depreciation expense, plumbing equipment, $200.
d. Wages earned by workers but not paid or due until January, $350.

Your task is to prepare a worksheet for Fred's Plumbing Service for the month of December.

4A-3. The following is the trial balance (Fig. 4-23) for Kevin's Moving Co.

Figure 4-23

KEVIN'S MOVING CO. TRIAL BALANCE OCTOBER 31, 200X	Dr.	Cr.
Cash	5 0 0 0 00	
Prepaid Insurance	2 5 0 0 00	
Moving Supplies	1 2 0 0 00	
Moving Truck	11 0 0 0 00	
Accumulated Depreciation, Moving Truck		9 0 0 00
Accounts Payable		2 7 6 8 00
K. Hoff, Capital		5 4 4 2 00
K. Hoff, Withdrawals	1 4 0 0 00	
Revenue from Moving		9 0 0 0 00
Wage Expense	3 7 1 2 00	
Rent Expense	1 0 8 0 00	
Advertising Expense	3 1 8 00	
	26 2 1 0 00	26 2 1 0 00

Comprehensive Problem

Check Figure:
Net Income $2,140

Adjustment Data to Update Trial Balance

a. Insurance expired, $700.
b. Moving supplies on hand, $900.
c. Depreciation on moving truck, $500.
d. Wages earned but unpaid, $250.

Your task is to

1. Complete a worksheet for Kevin's Moving Co. for the month of October.
2. Prepare an income statement for October, a statement of owner's equity for October, and a balance sheet as of October 31, 200X.

4A-4.

Adjustment Data to Update Trial Balance

a. Insurance expired, $700.
b. Repair supplies on hand, $3,000.
c. Depreciation on repair equipment, $200.
d. Wages earned but unpaid, $400.

Your task is to

1. Complete a worksheet for Dick's Repair Service (Fig. 4-24) for the month of November.
2. Prepare an income statement for November, a statement of owner's equity for November, and a balance sheet as of November 30, 200X.

Comprehensive Problem

Figure 4-24

DICK'S REPAIR SERVICE TRIAL BALANCE NOVEMBER 30, 200X		
	Dr.	Cr.
Cash	3 2 0 0 00	
Prepaid Insurance	4 0 0 0 00	
Repair Supplies	4 6 0 0 00	
Repair Equipment	3 0 0 0 00	
Accumulated Depreciation, Repair Equipment		7 0 0 00
Accounts Payable		5 5 7 0 00
D. Horn, Capital		3 8 0 0 00
Revenue from Repairs		7 0 0 0 00
Wages Expense	1 8 0 0 00	
Rent Expense	3 6 0 00	
Advertising Expense	1 1 0 00	
	17 0 7 0 00	17 0 7 0 00

Check Figure:
Net Income $1,830

Group B Problems

(The blank forms you need are on pages 111–114 of the *Study Guide and Working Papers.*)

4B-1. Please complete a partial worksheet (Fig. 4-25) up to the adjusted trial balance for Matty's Grooming Center using the following adjustment data:

Figure 4-25

MATTY'S GROOMING CENTER TRIAL BALANCE DECEMBER 31, 200X		
	Dr.	Cr.
Cash	6 0 0 0 00	
Accounts Receivable	2 0 0 0 00	
Grooming Supplies	4 2 0 0 00	
Grooming Equipment	8 0 0 0 00	
Accumulated Depreciation, Grooming Equipment		9 7 0 0 00
M. Magee, Capital		11 0 0 0 00
M. Magee, Withdrawals	1 0 0 0 00	
Grooming Fees		1 4 0 0 00
Rent Expense	8 0 0 00	
Advertising Expense	1 0 0 00	
	22 1 0 0 00	22 1 0 0 00

Completing a partial worksheet up to adjusted trial balance.

Check Figure:
Total of Adjusted Trial
Balance $22,600

a. Grooming supplies on hand, $3,000.
b. Depreciation taken on grooming equipment, $500.

4B-2. Given the trial balance in Figure 4-26 and adjustment data of Fred's Plumbing Service, your task is to prepare a worksheet for the month of December.

Adjustment Data

a. Plumbing supplies on hand, $60.
b. Rent expired, $150.
c. Depreciation on plumbing equipment, $200.
d. Wages earned but unpaid, $115.

Figure 4-26

Completing a worksheet.

FRED'S PLUMBING SERVICE TRIAL BALANCE DECEMBER 31, 200X	Dr.	Cr.
Cash in Bank	3 9 6 00	
Accounts Receivable	2 8 4 00	
Prepaid Rent	4 0 0 00	
Plumbing Supplies	3 1 0 00	
Plumbing Equipment	1 0 0 0 00	
Accumulated Depreciation, Plumbing Equipment		2 0 0 00
Accounts Payable		3 4 6 00
Fred Jack, Capital		4 5 6 00
Plumbing Revenue		4 6 8 0 00
Heat Expense	6 3 2 00	
Advertising Expense	1 2 0 0 00	
Wage Expense	1 4 6 0 00	
Total	5 6 8 2 00	5 6 8 2 00

Check Figure:
Net Income $673

4B-3. Using the trial balance in Figure 4-27 and adjustment data of Kevin's Moving Co., prepare

1. A worksheet for the month of October.
2. An income statement for October, a statement of owner's equity for October, and a balance sheet as of October 31, 200X.

Adjustment Data

a. Insurance expired $600
b. Moving supplies on hand $310
c. Depreciation on moving truck $580
d. Wages earned but unpaid $410

Figure 4-27

Comprehensive Problem

KEVIN'S MOVING CO. TRIAL BALANCE OCTOBER 31, 200X	Dr.	Cr.
Cash	3 9 2 0 00	
Prepaid Insurance	3 2 8 8 00	
Moving Supplies	1 4 0 0 00	
Moving Truck	10 6 5 8 00	
Accumulated Depreciation, Moving Truck		3 6 6 0 00
Accounts Payable		1 3 1 2 00
K. Hoff, Capital		17 4 8 2 00
K. Hoff, Withdrawals	4 2 4 0 00	
Revenue from Moving		8 1 6 2 00
Wages Expense	5 7 1 2 00	
Rent Expense	1 0 8 0 00	
Advertising Expense	3 1 8 00	
	30 6 1 6 00	30 6 1 6 00

Check Figure:
Net Loss $1,628

Figure 4-28

Comprehensive Problem

Check Figure:
Net Income $1,012

DICK'S REPAIR SERVICE TRIAL BALANCE NOVEMBER 30, 200X		
	Dr.	Cr.
Cash	3 2 0 4 00	
Prepaid Insurance	4 0 0 0 00	
Repair Supplies	7 7 0 00	
Repair Equipment	3 1 0 6 00	
Accumulated Depreciation, Repair Equipment		6 5 0 00
Accounts Payable		1 9 0 4 00
D. Horn, Capital		6 2 5 8 00
Revenue from Repairs		5 6 3 4 00
Wages Expense	1 6 0 0 00	
Rent Expense	1 5 6 0 00	
Advertising Expense	2 0 6 00	
	14 4 4 6 00	14 4 4 6 00

4B-4. As the bookkeeper of Dick's Repair Service, use the information in Figure 4-28 to prepare

1. A worksheet for the month of November.
2. An income statement for November, a statement of owner's equity for November, and a balance sheet as of November 30, 200X.

Adjustment Data

a.	Insurance expired	$300
b.	Repair supplies on hand	$170
c.	Depreciation on repair equipment	$250
d.	Wages earned but unpaid	$106

Real-World Applications

4R-1

MEMO

To: Hal Hogan, Bookkeeper

From: Pete Tennant, V. P.

Re: Adjustments for year ended December 31, 200X

Hal, here is the information you requested. Please supply me with the adjustments needed ASAP. Also, please put in writing why we need to do these adjustments.

Thanks.

Attached to memo:

a. Insurance data:

Policy No.	Date of Policy Purchase	Policy Length	Cost
100	November 1 of previous year	4 years	$480
200	May 1 of current year	2 years	600
300	September 1 of current year	1 year	240

b. Rent data: Prepaid rent had a $500 balance at the beginning of the year. An additional $400 of rent was paid in advance in June. At year end, $200 of rent had expired.

c. Revenue data: Accrued storage fees of $500 were earned but uncollected and unrecorded at year end.

4R-2.　　　　　　**Hint: Unearned Rent is a liability on the balance sheet.**

On Friday, Harry Swag's boss asks him to prepare a special report, due on Monday at 8:00 A.M. Harry gathers the following material in his briefcase:

		Dec. 31	
		2004	**2005**
Prepaid Advertising		$300	$600
Interest Payable		150	350
Unearned Rent		500	300
Cash paid for: Advertising	$1,900		
Interest	1,500		
Cash received for: Rent	2,300		

As his best friend, could you help Harry show the amounts that are to be reported on the income statement for (a) Advertising Expense, (b) Interest Expense, and (c) Rent Fees Earned. Please explain in writing why Unearned Rent is considered a liability.

YOU make the call

Critical Thinking/Ethical Case

4R-3. Janet Fox, President of Angel Co., went to a tax seminar. One of the speakers at the seminar advised the audience to put off showing expenses until next year because doing so would allow them to take advantage of a new tax law. When Janet returned to the office, she called in her accountant, Frieda O'Riley. She told Frieda to forget about making any adjustments for salaries in the old year so more expenses could be shown in the new year. Frieda told her that putting off these expenses would not follow generally accepted accounting procedures. Janet said she should do it anyway. You make the call. Write your specific recommendations to Frieda.

Internet Exercises: Office Max

EX-1. [www.officemax.com]　　On the Web site look for "General Information," then click on "Corporate Information." Under "Investor Information" look up Annual Reports and find the Consolidated Balance Sheet for 2001.

1. Under the caption "other current assets," what accounts do you think could be there that required end-of-period adjustments?

2. If Office Max rented the property where its stores are located and paid the rent in advance for 24 months, how would adjustments have been made in its financial statements?

3. What effect would these adjustments have on (a) Total Assets, and (b) Net Income?

4. Look at "current liabilities" in the balance sheet. Which accounts there seem most susceptible to the adjustment process, and why did you choose these accounts?

EX-2. [www.officemax.com]　　Click on "CEO Sworn Statement." Why do you think the CEO is required to report this information?

Continuing Problem

Eldorado Computer Center

At the end of September, Tony took a complete inventory of his supplies and found the following:

40   5 dozen ¼″ screws at a cost of $8.00 a dozen

10   2 dozen ½″ screws at a cost of $5.00 a dozen

28   2 cartons of computer inventory paper at a cost of $14 a carton

12   3 feet of coaxial cable at a cost of $4.00 per foot

After speaking to his accountant, he found that a reasonable depreciation amount for each of his long-term assets is as follows:

3 months   99

2 months   30

Computer purchased July 5, 200X	Depreciation $33 a month
Office equipment purchased July 17, 200X	Depreciation $10 a month
Computer workstations purchased Sept. 17, 200X	Depreciation $20 a month

Tony uses the straight-line method of depreciation and declares no salvage value for any of the assets. If any long-term asset is purchased in the first 15 days of the month, he will charge depreciation for the full month. If an asset is purchased on the 16th of the month, or later, he will not charge depreciation in the month it was purchased.

August and September's rent has now expired.

Assignment

Use your trial balance from the completed problem in Chapter 3 and the adjusting information given here to complete the worksheet for the three months ended September 30, 200X. From the worksheets prepare the financial statements. (See pp. 119–120 in your *Study Guide and Working Papers*.)

SUBWAY Case

WHERE THE DOUGH GOES . . .

No matter how harried Stan Hernandez feels as the owner of his own Subway restaurant, the aroma of his fresh-baked gourmet breads *always* perks him up. However, the sales generated by Subway's line of gourmet seasoned breads perks Stan up even more. Subway restaurants introduced freshly baked bread in 1983, a practice that made it stand out from other fast-food chains and helped build its reputation for made-to-order freshness. Since then Subway franchisees have introduced many types of gourmet seasoned breads—such as Hearty Italian or Monterey Cheddar—according to a schedule determined by headquarters.

Stan was one month into the "limited-time promotion" for the chain's new Roasted Garlic seasoned bread when his bake oven started faltering. "The temperature controls just don't seem quite right," said his employee and "sandwich artist," Rashid. "It's taking incrementally longer to bake the bread."

"This couldn't happen at a worse time," moaned Stan. "We're baking enough Roasted Garlic bread to keep a whole town of vampires away, but if we don't get it out of the oven fast enough, we'll keep our customers away!"

That very day Stan called his field consultant, Mariah, to discuss what to do about his bake oven. Mariah reminded Stan that his oven trouble illustrated the flip side of buying an existing store from a retired franchisee—having to repair or replace worn or old equipment. After receiving a rather expensive repair estimate and considering the age of the oven, Stan ultimately decided it would make sense for him to purchase a new one. Mariah concurred, "At the rate your sales are going, Stan, you're going to need that roomier new model."

"Wow, do you realize how much this new bake oven is going to cost me?— $3,000!" Stan exclaimed while meeting with his cousin-turned-Subway-accountant, Lila Hernandez. "Yes, it's a lot to lay out, Stan," said Lila, "but you'll be depreciating the cost over a period of 10 years, which will help you at tax time. Let's do the adjustment on your worksheet, so you can see it."

The two of them were sitting in Stan's small office, behind the Subway kitchen, and they pulled up this month's worksheet on Stan's Peachtree program. Lila laughed, "I'm sure glad you started entering your worksheets on Peachtree again! The figures on those old ones were so doodled over and crossed out that I could barely decipher them! We may need your worksheets at tax time."

"Anything for you, *mi prima*," Stan said, "I may depreciate my bake oven, but my gratitude for your accounting skills only appreciates with time!"

Discussion Questions

1. If you are using a straight-line method of depreciation and Stan's bake oven has a residual value of $1,000, how much depreciation will he account for each year and what would the adjustment be for each month?
2. Where does Lila get the information on the useful life of Stan's bake oven and the estimate for its residual value? Why do you think she gets her information from this particular source?
3. Why is a clear worksheet helpful even after that month's statements have been prepared?

$$\frac{3000 - 1000}{10 \text{ YRS}} = \frac{2000}{10 \text{ YRS}} = 200 \text{ PER YEAR}$$

$$\frac{200}{12 \text{ MONTHS}} = 16.67 \text{ PER MONTH}$$

COMPUTERIZED ACCOUNTING APPLICATION FOR CHAPTER 4

PART A: *Compound Journal Entries, Adjusting Entries, and Financial Reports*

PART B: *Backup Procedures*

Before starting on this assignment, read and complete the tasks discussed in Parts A, B, and F of the Computerized Accounting appendix at the back of this book and complete the Computerized Accounting Application assignment at the end of Chapter 3.

PART A: COMPOUND JOURNAL ENTRIES, ADJUSTING ENTRIES, AND FINANCIAL REPORTS

How to Open the Company Data Files

1. Click on the Start button. Point to Programs; point to the Peachtree folder and select Peachtree Complete Accounting. Your desktop may have the Peachtree icon allowing for a quicker entrance into the program.
2. Follow the "Open a File" instructions in Part A of the Computerized Accounting appendix at the back of this book to open **The Zell Company.** You may be initially presented with the Peachtree Today window. If so, simply close it. If you are missing the navigation aids at the bottom of the screen and want them, you can activate them under the **Options** menu. Select **View Navigation Aid.** It will remain on until you turn it off. This feature offers an alternative way to access the different features of Peachtree.

How to Add Your Name to the Company Name

3. Click on the **Maintain** menu option. Then select **Company Information.** The program will respond by bringing up a dialogue box allowing the user to edit/add information about the company.
4. Click in the **Company Name** entry field at the end of **The Zell Company.** If it is already highlighted, press the right arrow key. Add a dash and your name "**-Student Name**" to the end of the company name. Click on the OK button to return to the Menu Window.

How to Record a Compound Journal Entry

5. In the computerized accounting application assignment in Chapter 3 you learned how to record journal entries in the General Journal dialog box. Compound journal entries can also be recorded in the General Journal dialog box. The owner of The Zell Company has made an investment in the business consisting of $5,000 in cash and an automobile valued at $12,000. Select **General Journal Entry** from the **Tasks** menu to open the General Journal dialog box. Enter the date 1/1/04 into the **Date** field; press the TAB key; enter "Memo" into the **Reference** field and press TAB.
6. With the flashing insertion point positioned in the **Account No.** field, click on the pull down menu (magnifying glass icon) and double click on "1110 Cash". The program will enter the account number and name into the **Account No.** field and the flashing insertion point will move to the **Description** field. Enter "Initial investment by owner" into this field and press TAB to move to the **Debit** field. Enter "5000" and press TAB three times to move back to the **Account No.** field.
7. With the flashing insertion point positioned in the **Account No.** field, click on the pull down menu (magnifying glass icon) and double click on "1230 Automobile". Press TAB to move to the **Description** field. This should repeat the information entered in step 6 by default. Press the TAB key again to move to the **Debit** field. Enter "12000". Hit TAB three times to move the cursor back to the **Account No.** field. You should now have two debit entries.

8. With the flashing insertion point positioned in the **Account No.** field, click on the pull down menu and double click on "3110 Owner's Capital". Press TAB to move to the **Description** field. This should repeat the information entered in step 6 by default. Press the TAB key again twice to move to the **Credit** field. Enter 17000. Hit TAB twice to move the cursor back to the **Account No.** field. This completes the data you need to enter into the General Journal dialog box to record the compound journal entry for the initial investment by the owner. Your screen should look like this:

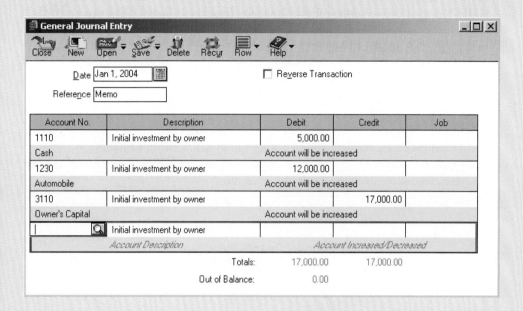

9. Review the compound journal entry for accuracy, noting any errors and making any editing corrections required.

10. After verifying that the compound journal entry is correct, click on the **Save** icon to post this transaction.

11. Record the following additional journal entries: Enter the **Date** listed for each transaction (you may use the "+" key to advance the date or use the calendar icon next to the field to select the date from a calendar). Enter "Memo" into the **Source** text box for each transaction or accept Peachtree's additional number added to memo by pressing TAB:

2004

Jan.
1	Paid rent for two months in advance, $500.
3	Purchased office supplies ($200) and office equipment ($1,100) both on account.
9	Billed a customer for fees earned, $2,000.
13	Received and paid telephone bill, $150.
20	Owner withdrew $475 from the business for personal use.
27	Received $600 for fees earned.
31	Paid salaries expense, $800.

12. After you have saved the additional journal entries, close the General Journal dialogue box and print the following reports accepting all defaults:
   a. General Journal (Totals = $22,825.00)
   b. General Ledger Trial Balance (Totals = $20,900)

Review the Compound Journal Entry

Save the Entry

Record Additional Transactions

Display and Print a General Journal and Trial Balance

How to Record Adjusting
Journal Entries

13. Review your printed reports. If you have made an error in a saved journal entry, see step 18 from the Chapter 3 assignment on page 115.

14. Open the General Journal dialogue box; then record adjusting journal entries based on the following adjustment data (*Date:* 1/31/04; *Reference:* Adjusting). You may enter all of the adjustments on the same page before saving:
    a. One month's rent has expired.
    b. An inventory shows $25 of office supplies remaining.
    c. Depreciation on office equipment, $50.
    d. Depreciation on automobile, $150.

Display and Print a
General Journal, General
Ledger, and Trial Balance

15. After you have saved the adjusting journal entries, close the General Journal dialogue box and print the following reports from the **General Ledger** option of the **Reports** menu:
    a. General Journal (Totals = $23,450)
    b. General Ledger Report (Cash Ending Balance = $3,675)
    c. General Ledger Trial Balance (Totals = $21,100)

16. Review your printed reports. If you have made an error in a saved journal entry, see step 18 from the Chapter 3 assignment.

How to Display and Print
an Income Statement

17. Select the **Financial Statements** option of the **Reports** menu. Select Income Stmnt. An Options dialog box will appear asking you to define the information you want displayed. Press the **OK** button to accept the defaults and display the report on your screen. Your screen will look something like this:

The Zell Company- Student Name
Income Statement
For the One Month Ending January 31, 2004

	Current Month		Year to Date	
Revenues				
Fees Earned	$ 2,600.00	100.00	$ 2,600.00	100.00
Total Revenues	2,600.00	100.00	2,600.00	100.00
Cost of Sales				
Total Cost of Sales	0.00	0.00	0.00	0.00
Gross Profit	2,600.00	100.00	2,600.00	100.00
Expenses				
Rent Expense	250.00	9.62	250.00	9.62
Salaries Expense	800.00	30.77	800.00	30.77
Telephone Expense	150.00	5.77	150.00	5.77
Supplies Expense	175.00	6.73	175.00	6.73
Depr Expense- Office Equipment	50.00	1.92	50.00	1.92
Depr Expense- Automobile	150.00	5.77	150.00	5.77
Total Expenses	1,575.00	60.58	1,575.00	60.58
Net Income	$ 1,025.00	39.42	$ 1,025.00	39.42

18. The scroll bars can be used to advance the display to view other portions of the report as needed.

19. Click on the **Print** icon to print the Income Statement.

20. Close the Income Statement window. This should return you to the Select a Report dialogue box. Select Balance Sheet. An Options dialog box will appear asking you to define the information you want displayed. Press the **OK** button

How to Display and Print a
Balance Sheet

to accept the defaults and display the report on your screen. Your screen will look something like this:

```
                        The Zell Company- Student Name
                              Balance Sheet
                             January 31, 2004

                                  ASSETS

Current Assets
 Cash                          $           3,675.00
 Accounts Receivable                       2,000.00
 Prepaid Rent                                250.00
 Office Supplies                              25.00
                                   _____

 Total Current Assets                                      5,950.00

Property and Equipment
 Office Equipment                          1,100.00
 Accum. Depr- Office Equipment               <50.00>
 Automobile                               12,000.00
 Accum. Depr- Automobile                    <150.00>
                                   _____

 Total Property and Equipment                            12,900.00

Other Assets
                                   _____

 Total Other Assets                                           0.00
                                                     _____

 Total Assets                  $                         18,850.00
                                                     =============
```

21. Use the scroll bars to advance the display to the Owner's Equity section of the Balance Sheet. Note that the program has included the Statement of Owner's Equity information directly in the Capital section of the Balance Sheet.
22. Click on **Print** to print the Balance Sheet and then close the Balance Sheet window.
23. Click on the Menu Window **File** menu; then click on **Exit** to end the current work session and return to your Windows desktop. Your work will automatically be saved.

Exit from the Program

PART B: BACKUP PROCEDURES

Companies that use computerized accounting systems make frequent backup copies of their accounting data for two major reasons:

1. To ensure that they have a copy of the accounting data in case the current data becomes damaged.
2. To permit the printing of historical reports after the period has been advanced to a new period.
3. In the event gross errors require restoring to an earlier time and the re-entering of data.

The methods used to make backup copies of company data files vary greatly. Large companies may backup daily using sophisticated high-speed tape backup devices while small companies may backup weekly on floppy disk using the backup program supplied with their operating system or applications software.

Normally all backup copies of a company's data files are stored on a secondary storage medium separate from the original data files in case the original storage medium becomes damaged. Your instructor will provide specific instructions on where you will store your backup files.

How to Make a Backup Copy of a Company's Data Files

1. If you are not still in Peachtree Complete Accounting 2003, start the program again and open The Zell Company.
2. While in the Menu Window, select **Back Up** from the **File** menu option. This will bring up the Back Up Company dialogue box as follows:

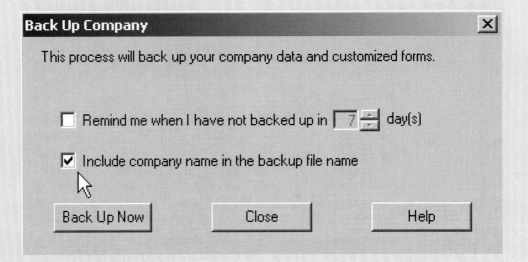

3. Click in the box next to **Include company name in the backup file name**. This will make Peachtree use Zell in the filename it selects for the backup. You could also use this dialogue box to have Peachtree provide a reminder at periodic intervals but we will leave this option alone for now. Press **Back Up Now** to continue.
4. You are now presented with a Save Backup for the Zell Company Student Name as: dialogue box as follows:

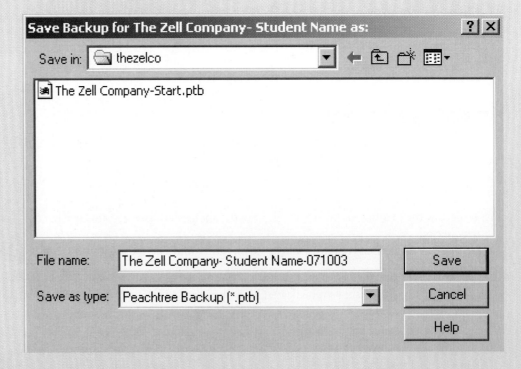

5. Peachtree will save your data files into one compressed .ptb file to any drive or path you specify. It defaults to the location where the program files are stored. Use the **Save in** pull down menu to save the files to a location specified by your instructor. Click **Save** and then **OK** to complete the process. You now have a back up of your data.

6. For more information on making and using backup copies of a company's data files, see Parts D & E of the Computerized Accounting appendix in the back of this book.

The Accounting Cycle Completed

Adjusting, Closing, and Post-Closing Trial Balance

You are planning your school schedule for next term. Your goal is to take a full course load and find a part-time job to help pay your school expenses. You hear through your academic advisor that the school needs to hire someone to help process invoices in the business office a couple of afternoons each week.

You speak with Diane Lemke, the business office manager, about the job. Diane tells you that your work will consist of matching purchase orders with paid invoices and the checks issued for payment. Diane tells you that these last few steps in the process of paying bills is important for the proper operation of the school's business office. "It's essential that this work is done before we can close our books each month," Diane tells you. You believe you'll like the work, and you're happy you can work your school schedule around the hours you're needed at the business office.

In Chapter 4 we learned about using the worksheet as a tool in the accounting cycle to adjust various balances and prepare the financial statements. In this chapter we focus on journalizing and posting adjusting and closing entries. We will also discuss preparing a post-closing trial balance, which is the last step in the accounting cycle.

Like working in your school's business office, the last three steps in the accounting cycle are essential and must be done to prepare a company's books for the next accounting cycle. It's the only way an accountant can begin a new accounting cycle or the business office can prepare itself for a new month of expenses.

Learning Objectives

Remember, for ease of presentation we are using a month as the accounting cycle for Clark. In the "real" world, the cycle can be any time period that does not exceed one year.

In Chapters 3 and 4 we completed these steps of the manual accounting cycle for Clark's Word Processing Services:

Step 1:   Business transactions occurred and generated source documents.

Step 2:   Business transactions were analyzed and recorded into a journal.

Step 3:   Information was posted or transferred from journal to ledger. *Plus footed*

Step 4:   A trial balance was prepared.

Step 5:   A worksheet was completed.

Step 6:   Financial statements were prepared.

This chapter covers the following steps. This will complete Clark's accounting cycle for the month of May:

Step 7:   Journalizing and posting adjusting entries.

Step 8:   Journalizing and posting closing entries.

Step 9:   Preparing a post-closing trial balance.

Be sure to check the inside front cover of the text for the road map to the accounting cycle.

Learning Unit 5-1 — Journalizing and Posting Adjusting Entries: Step 7 of the Accounting Cycle

RECORDING JOURNAL ENTRIES FROM THE WORKSHEET

At this point, many ledger accounts are not up-to-date.

The information in the worksheet is up-to-date. The financial reports prepared from that information can give the business's management and other interested parties a good idea of where the business stands as of a particular date. The problem is that the worksheet is an informal report. The information concerning the adjustments has not been placed into the journal or posted to the ledger accounts. This means that the books are not up-to-date and ready for the next accounting cycle to begin. For example, the ledger shows $1,200 of Prepaid Rent (p. 86), but the balance sheet we prepared in Chapter 4 shows an $800 balance. Essentially, the worksheet is a tool for preparing financial statements. Now we must use the adjustment columns of the worksheet as a basis for bringing the ledger up-to-date. We do this by adjusting journal entries (see Figs. 5-1, 5-2). Again, the updating must be done before the next accounting period starts. For Clark's Word Processing Services, the next period begins on June 1.

Purpose of adjusting entries.

Figure 5-2 shows the adjusting journal entries for Clark taken from the adjustments section of the worksheet. Once the adjusting journal entries are posted to the ledger, the accounts making up the financial statements that were prepared from the worksheet will equal the updated ledger. (Keep in mind that this is the same journal we have been using.) Let's look at some simplified T accounts to show how Clark's ledger looked before and after the adjustments were posted (see Adjustments A–D on pp. 164–166).

Adjustment (A)

Before Posting:	Office Supplies 114		Office Supplies Expense 514	
		600		
After Posting:	Office Supplies 114		Office Supplies Expense 514	
	600	500	500	

Figure 5-1
Journalizing and Posting
Adjustments from the
Adjustments Section
of the Worksheet

Account Titles	Trial Balance Dr.	Trial Balance Cr.	Adjustments Dr.	Adjustments Cr.
Cash	6 1 5 5 00			
Accounts Receivable	5 0 0 0 00			
Office Supplies	6 0 0 00			(A) 5 0 0 00
Prepaid Rent	1 2 0 0 00			(B) 4 0 0 00
Word Processing Equipment	6 0 0 0 00			
Accounts Payable		3 3 5 0 00		
Brenda Clark, Capital		10 0 0 0 00		
Brenda Clark, Withdrawals	6 2 5 00			
Word Processing Fees		8 0 0 0 00		
Office Salaries Expense	1 3 0 0 00		(D) 3 5 0 00	
Advertising Expense	2 5 0 00			
Telephone Expense	2 2 0 00			
	21 3 5 0 00	21 3 5 0 00		
Office Supplies Expense			(A) 5 0 0 00	
Rent Expense			(B) 4 0 0 00	
Depreciation Exp., W.P. Equip.			(C) 8 0 00	
Accum. Deprec., W.P. Equip.				(C) 8 0 00
Salaries Payable				(D) 3 5 0 00
			1 3 3 0 00	1 3 3 0 00

Figure 5-2
Adjustments A–D in the
Adjustments Section of
the Worksheet Must Be
Recorded in the Journal
and Posted to the Ledger

CLARK'S WORD PROCESSING SERVICES
GENERAL JOURNAL

Page 2

Date	Account Titles and Description	PR	Dr.	Cr.
	Adjusting Entries			
May 31	Office Supplies Expense	514	5 0 0 00	
	Office Supplies	114		5 0 0 00
31	Rent Expense	515	4 0 0 00	
	Prepaid Rent	115		4 0 0 00
31	Depreciation Expense, W.P. Equip.	516	8 0 00	
	Accumulated Depreciation, W.P. Equip.	122		8 0 00
31	Office Salaries Expense	511	3 5 0 00	
	Salaries Payable	212		3 5 0 00

Adjustment (B)

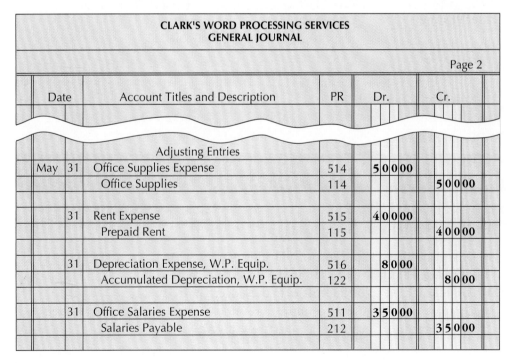

Before Posting:	Prepaid Rent 115	Rent Expense 515
	1,200	

After Posting:	Prepaid Rent 115	Rent Expense 515
	1,200 | 400	400 |

Adjustment (C)

Before Posting:

Word Processing Equipment 121	Depreciation Expense, W. P. Equipment 516	Accumulated Depreciation, W. P. Equipment 122
6,000		

After Posting:

Word Processing Equipment 121	Depreciation Expense, W. P. Equipment 516	Accumulated Depreciation, W. P. Equipment 122
6,000	80	80

The first adjustment in (C) shows the same balances for Depreciation Expense and Accumulated Depreciation. However, in subsequent adjustments the Accumulated Depreciation balance will keep getting larger, but the debit to Depreciation Expense and the credit to Accumulated Depreciation will be the same. We will see why in a moment.

Adjustment (D)

Before Posting:

Office Salaries Expense 511	Salaries Payable 212
650 650	

After Posting:

Office Salaries Expense 511	Salaries Payable 212
650 650 350	350

Learning Unit 5-1 Review

AT THIS POINT you should be able to

- Define and state the purpose of adjusting entries. (p. 164)
- Journalize adjusting entries from the worksheet. (p. 165)
- Post journalized adjusting entries to the ledger. (p. 165)
- Compare specific ledger accounts before and after posting of the journalized adjusting entries. (p. 166)

SELF-REVIEW QUIZ 5-1

(The blank forms you need are on pages 121–122 of the *Study Guide and Working Papers*. See your DVD for worked-out solutions.)

Turn to the worksheet of P. Logan (p. 134) and (1) journalize and post the adjusting entries and (2) compare the adjusted ledger accounts before and after the adjustments are posted. T accounts are provided in your study guide with beginning balances.

SOLUTION TO SELF-REVIEW QUIZ 5-1

Figure 5-3
Journalized Adjusting Entries

	Date		Account Titles and Description	PR	Dr.	Cr.
			Adjusting Entries			
Dec.	31		Depreciation Expense, Store Equip.	511	1 00	
			Accumulated Depreciation, Store Equip.	122		1 00
	31		Insurance Expense	516	2 00	
			Prepaid Insurance	116		2 00
	31		Supplies Expense	514	4 00	
			Store Supplies	114		4 00
	31		Salaries Expense	512	3 00	
			Salaries Payable	212		3 00

Page 2

Quiz Tip:
These journalized entries come from the adjustments column of the worksheet.

Partial Ledger

Before Posting

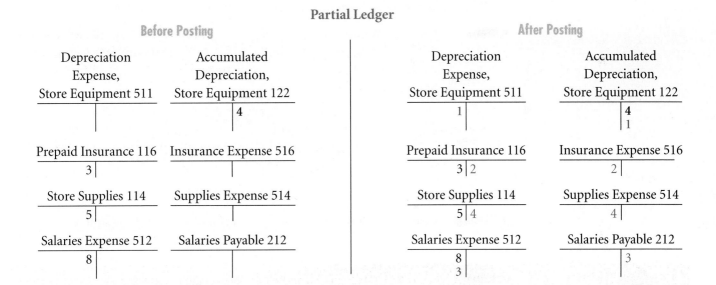

After Posting

Learning Unit 5-2   Journalizing and Posting Closing Entries: Step 8 of the Accounting Cycle

To make recording of the next period's transactions easier, a mechanical step, called *closing*, is taken by Clark's accountant. Closing is intended to end—or close off—the revenue, expense, and withdrawal accounts at the end of the accounting period. The information needed to complete closing entries will be found in the income statement and balance sheet sections of the worksheet.

To make it easier to understand this process, we will first look at the difference between temporary (nominal) accounts and permanent (real) accounts.

Here is the expanded accounting equation we used in an earlier chapter:

Assets = Liabilities + Capital − Withdrawals + Revenues − Expenses

Three of the items in that equation—Assets, Liabilities, and Capital—are known as real or permanent accounts because their balances are carried over from one accounting period to another. The other three items—Withdrawals, Revenues, and

Permanent accounts are found on the balance sheet.

Expenses—are called nominal or temporary accounts, because their balances are not carried over from one accounting period to another. Instead, their "balances" are set at zero at the beginning of each accounting period. This allows us to accumulate new data about revenue, expenses, and withdrawals in the new accounting period. The process of closing summarizes the effects of the temporary accounts on Capital for that period using closing journal entries. When the closing process is complete, the accounting equation will be reduced to

> After all closing entries are journalized and posted to the ledger, all temporary accounts have a zero balance in the ledger. Closing is a step-by-step process.

Assets = Liabilities + Ending Capital

If you look back to page 137 in Chapter 4, you will see that we already calculated the new capital on the balance sheet to be $14,275 for Clark's Word Processing Services. But before the mechanical closing procedures are journalized and posted, the Capital account of Clark in the ledger is only $10,000 (Chapter 3, p. 86). Let's look now at how to journalize and post closing entries.

HOW TO JOURNALIZE CLOSING ENTRIES

There are four steps to be performed in journalizing closing entries:

> An Income Summary is a temporary account located in the chart of accounts under Owner's Equity. It does not have a normal balance of a debit or a credit.

Step 1: Clear the revenue balance and transfer it to Income Summary. Income Summary is a temporary account in the ledger needed for closing. At the end of the closing process there will be no balance in Income Summary.

Revenue ⟶ Income Summary

Step 2: Clear the individual expense balances and transfer them to Income Summary.

Expenses ⟶ Income Summary

Step 3: Clear the balance in Income Summary and transfer it to Capital.

Income Summary ⟶ Capital

> Sometimes, closing the accounts is referred to as "clearing the accounts."

Step 4: Clear the balance in Withdrawals and transfer it to Capital.

Withdrawals ⟶ Capital

Figure 5-4 is a visual representation of these four steps. Keep in mind that this information must first be journalized and then posted to the appropriate ledger accounts. The worksheet presented in Figure 5-5 on page 169 contains all the figures we will need for the closing process.

Step 1: Clear Revenue Balance and Transfer to Income Summary

Here is what is in the ledger before closing entries are journalized and posted:

Word Processing Fees 411	Income Summary 313
| 8,000	|

The income statement section on the worksheet in Figure 5-4 shows that Word Processing Fees has a credit balance of $8,000. To close or clear this to zero, a debit of $8,000 is needed. But if we add an amount to the debit side, we must also add a credit—so we add $8,000 on the credit side of the Income Summary.

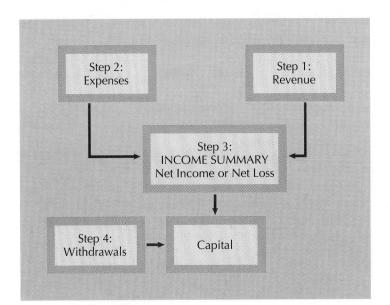

Figure 5-4
Four Steps in Journalizing Closing Entries. All numbers can be found on the worksheet in Figure 5-5.

Don't forget two goals of closing:
1. Clear all temporary accounts in ledger.
2. Update Capital to a new balance that reflects a summary of all the temporary accounts.

All numbers used in the closing process can be found on the worksheet. Note that the account Income Summary is not on the worksheet.

Account Titles	Income Statement Dr.	Income Statement Cr.	Balance Sheet Dr.	Balance Sheet Cr.
Cash			6 1 5 5 00	
Accounts Receivable			5 0 0 0 00	
Office Supplies			1 0 0 00	
Prepaid Rent			8 0 0 00	
Word Processing Equipment			6 0 0 0 00	
Accounts Payable				3 3 5 0 00
B. Clark, Capital		For Step 1		10 0 0 0 00
B. Clark, Withdrawals	For Step 2		6 2 5 00	
Word Processing Fees		8 0 0 0 00	For Step 4	
Office Salaries Expense	1 6 5 0 00			
Advertising Expense	2 5 0 00			
Telephone Expense	2 2 0 00			
Office Supplies Expense	5 0 0 00			
Rent Expense	4 0 0 00			
Depreciation Exp., W.P. Equip.	8 0 00			
Acc. Depreciation, W.P. Equip.	For Step 3			8 0 00
Salaries Payable				3 5 0 00
	3 1 0 0 00	8 0 0 0 00	18 6 8 0 00	13 7 8 0 00
Net Income	4 9 0 0 00 ←			4 9 0 0 00
	8 0 0 0 00	8 0 0 0 00	18 6 8 0 00	18 6 8 0 00

Figure 5-5 Closing Figures on the Worksheet

Figure 5-6 is the journalized closing entry for Step 1:

May	31	Word Processing Fees	411	8 0 0 0 00	
		Income Summary	313		8 0 0 0 00

Figure 5-6 Closing Revenue to Income Summary

This is what Word Processing Fees and Income Summary should look like in the ledger after the first step of closing entries is journalized and posted:

Word Processing Fees 411		Income Summary 313	
8,000 Closing	8,000 Revenue		8,000 Revenue

Note that the revenue balance is cleared to zero and transferred to Income Summary, a temporary account also located in the ledger.

Step 2: Clear Individual Expense Balances and Transfer the Total to Income Summary

Here is what is in the ledger for each expense before Step 2 of closing entries is journalized and posted. Each expense is listed on the worksheet in the debit column of the income statement section on page 169.

Office Salaries Expense 511		Advertising Expense 512	
650		250	
650			
350			

Telephone Expense 513		Office Supplies Expense 514	
220		500	

		Depreciation Expense, W. P. Equipment 516	
Rent Expense 515			
400		80	

> Remember, the worksheet is a tool. The accountant realizes that the information about the total of the expenses will be transferred to the income Summary.

The income statement section of the worksheet lists all the expenses as debits. If we want to reduce each expense to zero, each one must be credited.

Figure 5-7 is the journalized closing entry for Step 2:

Figure 5-7
Closing Each Expense to Income Summary

	31	Income Summary	313	3 1 0 0 00	
		Office Salaries Expense	511		1 6 5 0 00
		Advertising Expense	512		2 5 0 00
		Telephone Expense	513		2 2 0 00
		Office Supplies Expense	514		5 0 0 00
		Rent Expense	515		4 0 0 00
		Depreciation Expense, W.P.Equip.	516		8 0 00

> The $3,100 is the total of the expenses on the worksheet.

The following is what individual expenses and Income Summary should look like in the ledger after Step 2 of closing entries is journalized and posted:

Office Salaries Expense 511			Advertising Expense 512		
650	Closing	1,650	250	Closing	250
650					
350					

Telephone Expense 513			Office Supplies Expense 514		
220	Closing	220	500	Closing	500

Rent Expense 515			Depreciation Expense, W. P. Equipment 516		
400	Closing	400	80	Closing	80

	Income Summary 313		
	Expenses	Revenue	
Step 2	3,100	8,000	Step 1

Step 3: Clear Balance in Income Summary (Net Income) and Transfer It to Capital

This is how the Income Summary and B. Clark, Capital, accounts look before Step 3:

```
      Income Summary 313              B. Clark, Capital 311
         3,100 | 8,000                          | 10,000
               | 4,900
```

Note that the balance of Income Summary (Revenues minus Expenses, or $8,000 − $3,100) is $4,900. That is the amount we must clear from the Income Summary account and transfer to the B. Clark, Capital, account.

In order to transfer the balance of $4,900 from Income Summary (check the bottom debit column of the income statement section on the worksheet in Fig. 5-5) to Capital, it will be necessary to debit Income Summary for $4,900 (the difference between the revenue and expenses) and credit or increase Capital of B. Clark for $4,900.

Figure 5-8 is the journalized closing entry for Step 3:

31	Income Summary	313	4 9 0 0 00	
	B. Clark, Capital	311		4 9 0 0 00

Figure 5-8
Closing Net Income to B. Clark, Capital

This is what the Income Summary and B. Clark, Capital, accounts will look like in the ledger after Step 3 of closing entries is journalized and posted:

```
                Income Summary 313                  B. Clark, Capital 311
Total of
Expenses →      3,100 | 8,000 ← Revenue                      | 10,000
Debit to close →4,900 | 4,900 ← Net                          | 4,900 ← Net Income
account               |         Income
```

The opposite would take place if the business had a net loss.

Step 4: Clear the Withdrawals Balance and Transfer It to Capital

Next, we must close the Withdrawals account. The B. Clark, Withdrawals, and B. Clark, Capital, accounts now look like this:

```
   B. Clark, Withdrawals 312           B. Clark, Capital 311
        625 |                                   | 10,000
                                               | 4,900
```

To bring the Withdrawals account to a zero balance and summarize its effect on Capital, we must credit Withdrawals and debit Capital.

Remember, withdrawals are a nonbusiness expense and thus not transferred to Income Summary. The closing entry is journalized as shown in Figure 5-9.

At the end of these three steps, the Income Summary has a zero balance. If we had a net loss, the end result would be to decrease Capital. The entry would be debit Capital and credit Income Summary for the loss.

31	B. Clark, Capital	311	6 2 5 00	
	B. Clark, Withdrawals	312		6 2 5 00

Figure 5-9
Close Withdrawal to B. Clark, Capital

At this point the B. Clark, Withdrawals, and B. Clark, Capital, accounts would look like this in the ledger.

```
   B. Clark, Withdrawals 312              B. Clark, Capital 311
        625 | Closing 625          → 625 | 10,000 ←
                                Withdrawals | Beg. Balance
                                            | 4,900 ←
                                              Net Income
```

Note that the $10,000 is a beginning balance since no additional investments were made during the period.

Now let's look at a summary of the closing entries in Figure 5-10.

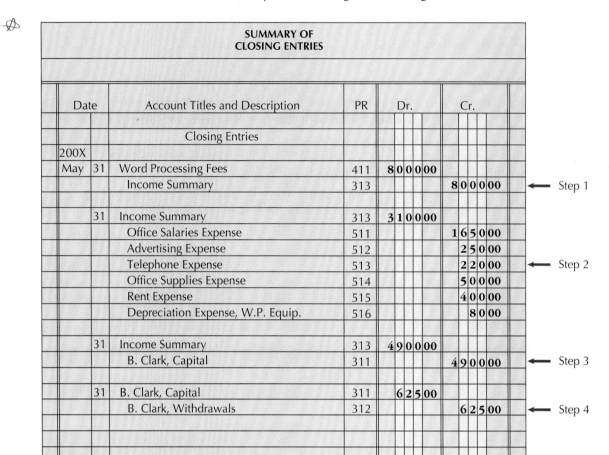

SUMMARY OF CLOSING ENTRIES

Date		Account Titles and Description	PR	Dr.	Cr.	
		Closing Entries				
200X						
May	31	Word Processing Fees	411	8 0 0 0 00		
		Income Summary	313		8 0 0 0 00	← Step 1
	31	Income Summary	313	3 1 0 0 00		
		Office Salaries Expense	511		1 6 5 0 00	
		Advertising Expense	512		2 5 0 00	
		Telephone Expense	513		2 2 0 00	← Step 2
		Office Supplies Expense	514		5 0 0 00	
		Rent Expense	515		4 0 0 00	
		Depreciation Expense, W.P. Equip.	516		8 0 00	
	31	Income Summary	313	4 9 0 0 00		
		B. Clark, Capital	311		4 9 0 0 00	← Step 3
	31	B. Clark, Capital	311	6 2 5 00		
		B. Clark, Withdrawals	312		6 2 5 00	← Step 4

Figure 5-10 Four Closing Entries

The following is the complete ledger for Clark's Word Processing Services (see Fig. 5-11). Note how "adjusting" or "closing" is written in the explanation column of individual ledgers, as for example in the one for Office Supplies. If the goals of closing have been achieved, only permanent accounts will have balances carried to the next accounting period. All temporary accounts should have zero balances.

CLARK'S WORD PROCESSING SERVICES
GENERAL LEDGER

Cash   Account No. 111

Date	Explanation	Post. Ref.	Debit	Credit	Balance Debit	Balance Credit
200X May 1		GJ1	10000 00		10000 00	
1		GJ1		1000 00	9000 00	
1		GJ1		1200 00	7800 00	
7		GJ1	3000 00		10800 00	
15		GJ1		650 00	10150 00	
20		GJ1		625 00	9525 00	
27		GJ2		650 00	8875 00	
28		GJ2		2500 00	6375 00	
29		GJ2		220 00	6155 00	

Accounts Receivable   Account No. 112

Date	Explanation	Post. Ref.	Debit	Credit	Balance Debit	Balance Credit
200X May 22		GJ1	5000 00		5000 00	

Office Supplies   Account No. 114

Date	Explanation	Post. Ref.	Debit	Credit	Balance Debit	Balance Credit
200X May 3		GJ1	600 00		600 00	
31	Adjusting	GJ2		500 00	100 00	

Figure 5-11 Complete Ledger

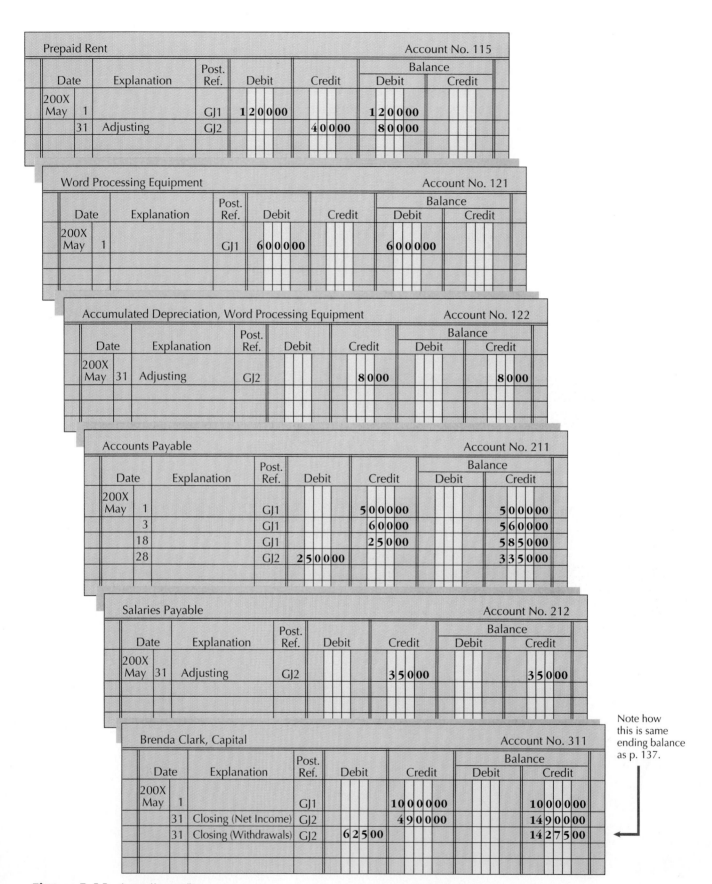

Prepaid Rent   Account No. 115

Date		Explanation	Post. Ref.	Debit	Credit	Balance Debit	Balance Credit
200X May	1		GJ1	1 2 0 0 00		1 2 0 0 00	
	31	Adjusting	GJ2		4 0 0 00	8 0 0 00	

Word Processing Equipment   Account No. 121

Date		Explanation	Post. Ref.	Debit	Credit	Balance Debit	Balance Credit
200X May	1		GJ1	6 0 0 0 00		6 0 0 0 00	

Accumulated Depreciation, Word Processing Equipment   Account No. 122

Date		Explanation	Post. Ref.	Debit	Credit	Balance Debit	Balance Credit
200X May	31	Adjusting	GJ2		8 0 00		8 0 00

Accounts Payable   Account No. 211

Date		Explanation	Post. Ref.	Debit	Credit	Balance Debit	Balance Credit
200X May	1		GJ1		5 0 0 0 00		5 0 0 0 00
	3		GJ1		6 0 0 00		5 6 0 0 00
	18		GJ1		2 5 0 00		5 8 5 0 00
	28		GJ2	2 5 0 0 00			3 3 5 0 00

Salaries Payable   Account No. 212

Date		Explanation	Post. Ref.	Debit	Credit	Balance Debit	Balance Credit
200X May	31	Adjusting	GJ2		3 5 0 00		3 5 0 00

Brenda Clark, Capital   Account No. 311

Note how this is same ending balance as p. 137.

Date		Explanation	Post. Ref.	Debit	Credit	Balance Debit	Balance Credit
200X May	1		GJ1		1 0 0 0 0 00		1 0 0 0 0 00
	31	Closing (Net Income)	GJ2		4 9 0 0 00		1 4 9 0 0 00
	31	Closing (Withdrawals)	GJ2	6 2 5 00			1 4 2 7 5 00

Figure 5-11 (continued)

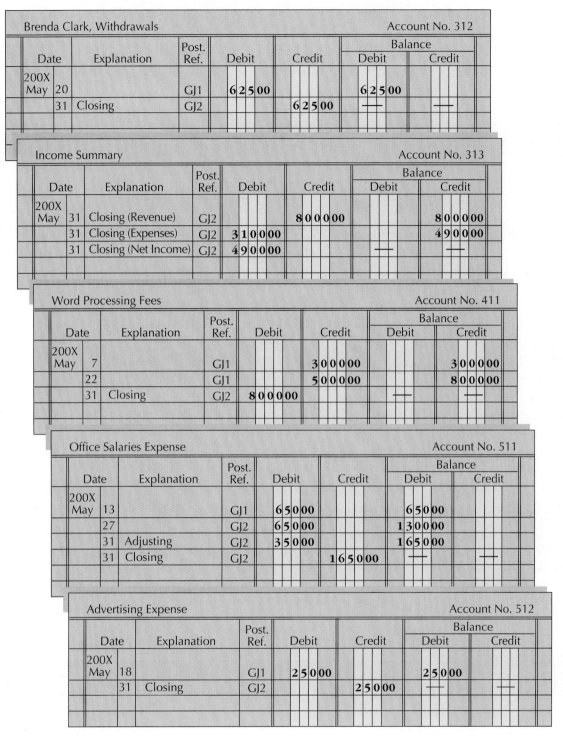

Brenda Clark, Withdrawals — Account No. 312

Date	Explanation	Post. Ref.	Debit	Credit	Balance Debit	Balance Credit
200X May 20		GJ1	6 2 5 00		6 2 5 00	
31	Closing	GJ2		6 2 5 00	—	—

Income Summary — Account No. 313

Date	Explanation	Post. Ref.	Debit	Credit	Balance Debit	Balance Credit
200X May 31	Closing (Revenue)	GJ2		8 0 0 0 00		8 0 0 0 00
31	Closing (Expenses)	GJ2	3 1 0 0 00			4 9 0 0 00
31	Closing (Net Income)	GJ2	4 9 0 0 00		—	—

Word Processing Fees — Account No. 411

Date	Explanation	Post. Ref.	Debit	Credit	Balance Debit	Balance Credit
200X May 7		GJ1		3 0 0 0 00		3 0 0 0 00
22		GJ1		5 0 0 0 00		8 0 0 0 00
31	Closing	GJ2	8 0 0 0 00		—	—

Office Salaries Expense — Account No. 511

Date	Explanation	Post. Ref.	Debit	Credit	Balance Debit	Balance Credit
200X May 13		GJ1	6 5 0 00		6 5 0 00	
27		GJ2	6 5 0 00		1 3 0 0 00	
31	Adjusting	GJ2	3 5 0 00		1 6 5 0 00	
31	Closing	GJ2		1 6 5 0 00	—	—

Advertising Expense — Account No. 512

Date	Explanation	Post. Ref.	Debit	Credit	Balance Debit	Balance Credit
200X May 18		GJ1	2 5 0 00		2 5 0 00	
31	Closing	GJ2		2 5 0 00	—	—

Figure 5-11 (*continued*)

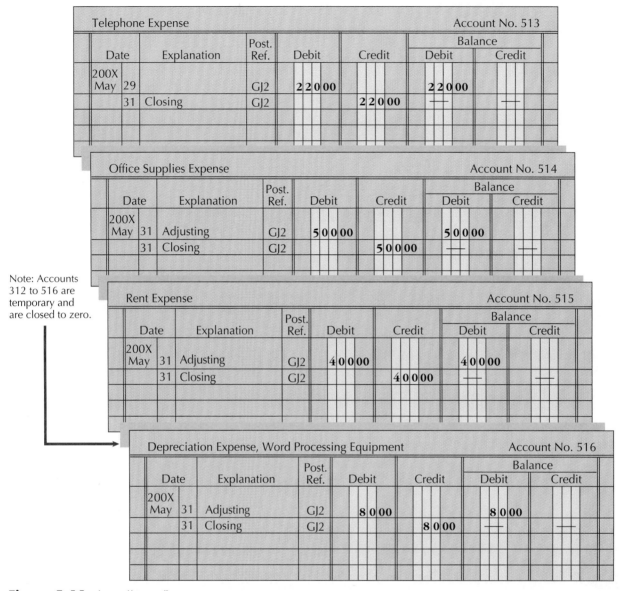

Note: Accounts 312 to 516 are temporary and are closed to zero.

Figure 5-11 (*continued*)

Learning Unit 5-2 Review

AT THIS POINT you should be able to

- Define closing. (p. 168)
- Differentiate between temporary (nominal) and permanent (real) accounts. (p. 168)
- List the four mechanical steps of closing. (p. 168)
- Explain the role of the Income Summary account. (p. 168)
- Explain the role of the worksheet in the closing process. (p. 169)

SELF-REVIEW QUIZ 5-2

(The blank forms you need are on pages 123–124 of the *Study Guide and Working Papers*. See your DVD for worked-out solutions.)

Go to the worksheet for P. Logan on p. 134. Then (1) journalize and post the closing entries and (2) calculate the new balance for P. Logan, Capital.

SOLUTION TO SELF-REVIEW QUIZ 5-2

		Closing Entries			
Dec.	31	Revenue from Clients	410	25 00	
		Income Summary	312		25 00
	31	Income Summary	312	20 00	
		Rent Expense	518		2 00
		Salaries Expense	512		11 00
		Depreciation Expense, Store Equip.	510		1 00
		Insurance Expense	516		2 00
		Supplies Expense	514		4 00
	31	Income Summary	312	5 00	
		P. Logan, Capital	310		5 00
	31	P. Logan, Capital	310	3 00	
		P. Logan, Withdrawals	311		3 00

Figure 5-12 Closing Entries for Logan

Quiz Tip:
Revenue closed to Income Summary

Each expense closed to Income Summary

Net Income closed to Capital

Withdrawals closed to Capital

Partial Ledger

P. Logan, Capital 310	Revenue from Clients 410	Supplies Expense 514
3 | 14	25 | 25	4 | 4
5		
| 16		

P. Logan, Withdrawals 311	Dep. Exp., Store Equip. 510	Insurance Expense 516
3 | 3	1 | 1	2 | 2

Income Summary 312	Salaries Expense 512	Rent Expense 518
20 | 25	11 | 11	2 | 2
5 | 5		

P. Logan, Capital		$14
Net Income	$5	
Less Withdrawals	3	
Increase in Capital		2
P. Logan, Capital (ending)		$16

Quiz Tip:
No calculations are needed in the closing process. ALL numbers come from the worksheet. Income Summary is a temporary account in the ledger.

Learning Unit 5-3

The Post-Closing Trial Balance: Step 9 of the Accounting Cycle and the Cycle Reviewed

> The post-closing trial balance helps prove the accuracy of the adjusting and closing process. It contains the true ending figure for Capital.

PREPARING A POST-CLOSING TRIAL BALANCE

The last step in the accounting cycle is the preparation of a **post-closing trial balance**, which lists only permanent accounts in the ledger and their balances after adjusting and closing entries have been posted. This post-closing trial balance aids in checking whether the ledger is in balance. This checking is important to do because so many new postings go to the ledger from the adjusting and closing process.

The procedure for taking a post-closing trial balance is the same as for a trial balance, except that, since closing entries have closed all temporary accounts, the post-closing trial balance will contain only permanent accounts (balance sheet). Keep in mind, however, that adjustments have occurred.

> Remember no worksheet is needed in a computerized cycle.

TABLE 5-1 Steps of the Manual Accounting Cycle

Steps	Explanation
1. Business transactions occur and generate source documents.	Cash register tape, sales tickets, bills, checks, payroll cards.
↓	↓
2. Analyze and record business transactions into a journal.	Called journalizing.
↓	↓
3. Post or transfer information from journal to ledger.	Copying the debits and credits of the journal entries into the ledger accounts.
↓	↓
4. Prepare a trial balance.	Summarizing each individual ledger account and listing those accounts to test for mathematical accuracy in recording transactions.
↓	↓
5. Prepare a worksheet.	A multicolumn form that summarizes accounting information to complete the accounting cycle.
↓	↓
6. Prepare financial statements.	Income statement, statement of owner's equity, and balance sheet.
↓	↓
7. Journalize and post adjusting entries.	Use figures in the Adjustment columns of worksheet.
↓	↓
8. Journalize and post closing entries.	Use figures in the income statement and balance sheet sections of worksheet.
↓	↓
9. Prepare a post-closing trial balance.	Prove the mathematical accuracy of the adjusting and closing process of the accounting cycle.

must know

THE ACCOUNTING CYCLE REVIEWED

Table 5-1 lists the steps we completed in the manual accounting cycle for Clark's Word Processing Services for the month of May:

Insight   Most companies journalize and post adjusting and closing entries only at the end of their fiscal year. A company that prepares interim statements may complete only the first six steps of the cycle. Worksheets allow the preparation of interim reports without the formal adjusting and closing of the books. If this happens, footnotes on the interim report will indicate the extent to which adjusting and closing were completed.

Insight   To prepare a financial statement for April, the data needed can be obtained by subtracting the worksheet accumulated totals from the end of March from the worksheet prepared at the end of April. In this chapter we chose a month that would show the completion of an entire cycle for Clark's Word Processing Services.

Learning Unit 5-3 Review

AT THIS POINT you should be able to

- Prepare a post-closing trial balance. (p. 178)
- Explain the relationship of interim statements to the accounting cycle. (p. 179)

SELF-REVIEW QUIZ 5-3

(The blank forms you need are on page 124 of the *Study Guide and Working Papers.* See your DVD for worked-out solutions.)
From the ledger on page 173, prepare a post-closing trial balance.

SOLUTION TO SELF-REVIEW QUIZ 5-3

CLARK'S WORD PROCESSING SERVICES POST-CLOSING TRIAL BALANCE MAY 31, 200X	Dr.	Cr.
Cash	6 1 5 5 00	
Accounts Receivable	5 0 0 0 00	
Office Supplies	1 0 0 00	
Prepaid Rent	8 0 0 00	
Word Processing Equipment	6 0 0 0 00	
Accumulated Depreciation, Word Processing Equip.		8 0 0 00
Accounts Payable		3 3 5 0 00
Salaries Payable		3 5 0 00
Brenda Clark, Capital		14 2 7 5 00
Totals	18 0 5 5 00	18 0 5 5 00

Figure 5-13
Post-Closing Trial Balance for Clark's Word Processing Services

Quiz Tip:
The post-closing trial balance contains only permanent accounts because all temporary accounts have been closed. All temporary accounts are summarized in the Capital account.

SOLUTIONS & TIPS TO COMPREHENSIVE PROBLEMS: PUTTING THE PIECES TOGETHER

(The blank forms you need are on pages 125–133 of the *Study Guide and Working Papers*.)

From the following transactions for Rolo Co. complete the entire accounting cycle. The chart of accounts includes:

Assets
111   Cash
112   Accounts Receivable
114   Prepaid Rent
115   Office Supplies
121   Office Equipment
122   Accumulated Depreciation, Office Equipment

Liabilities
211   Accounts Payable
212   Salaries Payable

Owner's Equity
311   Rolo Kern, Capital
312   Rolo Kern, Withdrawals
313   Income Summary

Revenue
411   Fees Earned

Expenses
511   Salaries Expense
512   Advertising Expense
513   Rent Expense
514   Office Supplies Expense
515   Depreciation Expense, Office Equipment

Note: Accounts 312 to 515 are temporary accounts.

We will use unusually small numbers to simplify calculation and emphasize the theory.

200X

Jan.
1   Rolo Kern invested $1,200 cash and $100 of office equipment to open Rolo Co.
1   Paid rent for three months in advance, $300
4   Purchased office equipment on account, $50
6   Bought office supplies for cash, $40
8   Collected $400 for services rendered
12   Rolo paid his home electric bill from the company checkbook, $20
14   Provided $100 worth of services to clients who will not pay till next month
16   Paid salaries, $60
18   Advertising bill received for $70 but will not be paid until next month

Adjustment Data on January 31

a. Supplies on hand	$6
b. Rent Expired	$100
c. Depreciation, Office Equipment	$20
d. Salaries Accrued	$50

Solutions to Comprehensive Problem

Journalizing Transactions and Posting to Ledger, Rolo Company

Figure 5-14
Journal Entries for
Rolo Company

General Journal					Page 1	
Date		Account Titles and Description	PR	Dr.	Cr.	
200X Jan	1	Cash	111	1 2 0 0 00		
		Office Equipment	121	1 0 0 00		
		R. Kern, Capital	311		1 3 0 0 00	
		Initial Investment				
	1	Prepaid Rent	114	3 0 0 00		
		Cash	111		3 0 0 00	
		Rent Paid in Advance—3 mos.				
	4	Office Equipment	121	5 0 00		
		Accounts Payable	211		5 0 00	
		Purchased Equipment on Account				
	6	Office Supplies	115	4 0 00		
		Cash	111		4 0 00	
		Supplies purchased for cash				
	8	Cash	111	4 0 0 00		
		Fees Earned	411		4 0 0 00	
		Services rendered				
	12	R. Kern, Withdrawals	312	2 0 00		
		Cash	111		2 0 00	
		Personal payment of a bill				
	14	Accounts Receivable	112	1 0 0 00		
		Fees Earned	411		1 0 0 00	
		Services rendered on account				
	16	Salaries Expense	511	6 0 00		
		Cash	111		6 0 00	
		Paid salaries				
	18	Advertising Expense	512	7 0 00		
		Accounts Payable	211		7 0 00	
		Advertising bill, but not paid				

Solution Tips to Journalizing and Posting Transactions

Jan 1	Cash	Asset	↑	Dr.	$1,200
	Office Equipment	Asset	↑	Dr.	$ 100
	R. Kern, Capital	Capital	↑	Cr.	$1,300

2	Prepaid Rent	Asset	↑	Dr.	$ 300
	Cash	Asset	↓	Cr.	$ 300

| 4 | Office Equipment | Asset | ↑ | Dr. | $ 50 |
| | Accounts Payable | Liability | ↑ | Cr. | $ 50 |

| 6 | Office Supplies | Asset | ↑ | Dr. | $ 40 |
| | Cash | Asset | ↓ | Cr. | $ 40 |

| 8 | Cash | Asset | ↑ | Dr. | $ 400 |
| | Fees Earned | Revenue | ↑ | Cr. | $ 400 |

| 12 | R. Kern, Withdrawals | Withdrawals | ↑ | Dr. | $ 20 |
| | Cash | Asset | ↓ | Cr. | $ 20 |

| 14 | Accounts Receivable | Asset | ↑ | Dr. | $ 100 |
| | Fees Earned | Revenue | ↑ | Cr. | $ 100 |

| 16 | Salaries Expense | Expense | ↑ | Dr. | $ 60 |
| | Cash | Asset | ↓ | Cr. | $ 60 |

| 18 | Advertising Expense | Expense | ↑ | Dr. | $ 70 |
| | Accounts Payable | Liability | ↑ | Cr. | $ 70 |

Note   All account titles come from the chart of accounts. When journalizing, the PR column of the general journal is blank. It is in the posting process that we update the ledger. The PR column in the ledger accounts tells us from what journal page the information came. After the title in the ledger is posted to, we fill in the PR column of the journal, telling us to what account number the information was transferred.

Completing the Worksheet

See worksheet on page 183.

Solution Tips to the Trial Balance and Completion of the Worksheet

After the posting process is complete from the journal to the ledger, we take the ending balance in each account and prepare a trial balance on the worksheet (see Fig. 5-15). If a title has no balance, it is not listed on the trial balance. New titles on the worksheet will be added below as needed.

Adjustments

> On hand of $6 is not the adjustment. Need to calculate amount used up.

| Office Supplies Expense | Expense | ↑ | Dr. | $ 34 | ($40 – $6) |
| Office Supplies | Asset | ↓ | Cr. | $ 34 | |

> Expired.

| Rent Expense | Expense | ↑ | Dr. | $100 |
| Prepaid Rent | Asset | ↓ | Cr. | $100 |

> Do not touch original cost of equipment.

| Depr. Exp., Office Equip. | Expense | ↑ | Dr. | $ 20 |
| Accum. Dep., Office Equip. | Contra-Asset | ↑ | Cr. | $ 20 |

> Owed but not paid.

| Salaries Expense | Expense | ↑ | Dr. | $ 50 |
| Salaries Payable | Liability | ↑ | Cr. | $ 50 |

ROLO CO
WORKSHEET
FOR MONTH ENDED JANUARY 31, 200X

Supplies used up

Supplies on hand

Account Titles	Trial Balance Dr.	Trial Balance Cr.	Adjustments Dr.	Adjustments Cr.	Adjusted Trial Balance Dr.	Adjusted Trial Balance Cr.	Income Statement Dr.	Income Statement Cr.	Balance Sheet Dr.	Balance Sheet Cr.
Cash	118000				118000				118000	
Accounts Receivable	10000				10000				10000	
Prepaid Rent	30000			(B) 10000	20000				20000	
Office Supplies	4000			(A) 3400	600				600	
Office Equipment	15000				15000				15000	
Accounts Payable		120000				120000				120000
R. Kern, Capital		130000				130000				130000
R. Kern, Withdrawals	2000				2000				2000	
Fees Earned		50000				50000		50000		
Salaries Expense	6000		(D) 5000		11000		11000			
Advertising Expense	7000				7000		7000			
	192000	192000								
Office Supplies Expense			(A) 3400		3400		3400			
Rent Expense			(B) 10000		10000		10000			
Depr. Exp., Office Equip.			(C) 2000		2000		2000			
Acc. Dep., Office Equip.				(C) 2000		2000				2000
Salaries Payable				(D) 5000		5000				5000
			20400	20400	199000	199000	33400	50000	165600	149000
Net Income							16600			16600
							50000	50000	165600	165600

Figure 5-15 Completed Worksheet for Rolo Company

Note   This information is on the worksheet but has *not* been updated in the ledger. (This will happen when we journalize and post adjustments at the end of the cycle.)

Note that the last four columns of the worksheet come from numbers on the adjusted trial balance.

We move the Net Income of $166 to the Balance Sheet credit column since the Capital figure is the old one on the worksheet.

PREPARING THE FORMAL FINANCIAL STATEMENTS

Figure 5-16
Income Statement
for Rolo Company

ROLO CO. INCOME STATEMENT FOR MONTH ENDED JANUARY 31, 200X		
Revenue:		
Fees Earned		$500 00
Operating Expenses		
Salaries Expense	$110 00	
Advertising Expense	70 00	
Office Supplies Expense	34 00	
Rent Expense	100 00	
Depreciation Expense, Office Equipment	20 00	
Total Operating Expenses		334 00
Net Income		$166 00

Figure 5-17
Statement of Owner's
Equity for Rolo Company

ROLO CO. STATEMENT OF OWNER'S EQUITY FOR MONTH ENDED JANUARY 31, 200X		
R. Kern, Capital, January 1, 200X		$1300 00
Net Income for January	$166 00	
Less Withdrawals for January	20 00	
Increase in Capital		146 00
R. Kern, Capital, January 31, 200X		$1446 00

ROLO CO. BALANCE SHEET JANUARY 31, 200X					
Assets			Liabilities & Owner's Equity		
Cash		$1180 00	Liabilities		
Accounts Receivable		100 00	Accounts Payable	$120 00	
Prepaid Rent		200 00	Salaries Payable	50 00	
Office Supplies		6 00	Total Liabilities		$170 00
Office Equipment	$150 00		Owner's Equity		
Less Accum. Depr.	20 00	130 00	R. Kern, Capital		1446 00
			Total Liabilities &		
Total Assets		$1616 00	Owner's Equity		$1616 00

Figure 5-18 Balance Sheet for Rolo Company

Solution Tips to Preparing the Financial Statements

The statements are prepared from the worksheet. (Many of the ledger accounts are not up-to-date.) The income statement (Fig. 5-16) lists revenue and expenses. The Net Income figure of $166 is used to update the statement of owner's equity. The statement of owner's equity (Fig. 5-17) calculates a new figure for Capital, $1,446 (Beginning Capital + Net Income − Withdrawals). This new figure is then listed on the balance sheet (Fig. 5-18) (Assets, Liabilities, and a new figure for Capital).

Journalizing and Posting Adjusting and Closing Entries

See journal in Figure 5-19.

Solution Tips to Journalizing and Posting Adjusting and Closing Entries

Adjustments

The adjustments from the worksheet are journalized (same journal) and posted to the ledger. Now ledger accounts will be brought up-to-date. Remember, we have already prepared the financial statements from the worksheet. Our goal now is to get the ledger up-to-date.

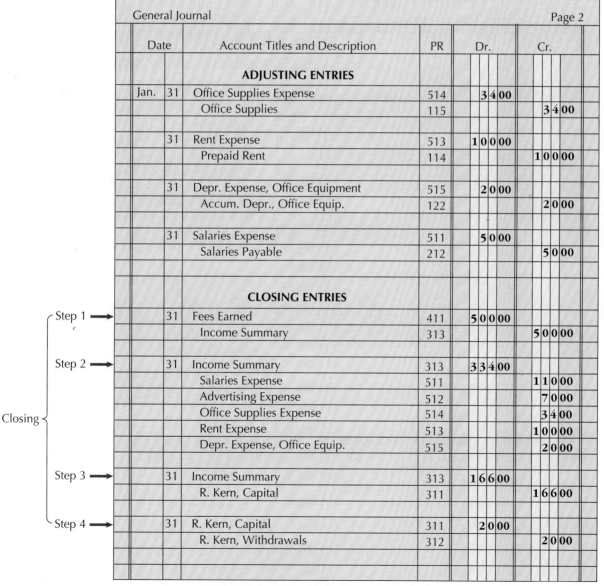

	Date		Account Titles and Description	PR	Dr.	Cr.
			General Journal			Page 2
			ADJUSTING ENTRIES			
	Jan.	31	Office Supplies Expense	514	3400	
			Office Supplies	115		3400
		31	Rent Expense	513	10000	
			Prepaid Rent	114		10000
		31	Depr. Expense, Office Equipment	515	2000	
			Accum. Depr., Office Equip.	122		2000
		31	Salaries Expense	511	5000	
			Salaries Payable	212		5000
			CLOSING ENTRIES			
Step 1 →		31	Fees Earned	411	50000	
			Income Summary	313		50000
Step 2 →		31	Income Summary	313	33400	
			Salaries Expense	511		11000
			Advertising Expense	512		7000
			Office Supplies Expense	514		3400
			Rent Expense	513		10000
			Depr. Expense, Office Equip.	515		2000
Step 3 →		31	Income Summary	313	16600	
			R. Kern, Capital	311		16600
Step 4 →		31	R. Kern, Capital	311	2000	
			R. Kern, Withdrawals	312		2000

Figure 5-19 Adjusting and Closing Entries Journalized and Posted

GENERAL LEDGER

Cash 111

Date	PR	Dr.	Cr.	Balance Dr.	Balance Cr.
1/1	GJ1	1,200		1,200	
1/1	GJ1		300	900	
1/6	GJ1		40	860	
1/8	GJ1	400		1,260	
1/12	GJ1		20	1,240	
1/16	GJ1		60	1,180	

Accounts Receivable 112

Date	PR	Dr.	Cr.	Balance Dr.	Balance Cr.
1/14	GJ1	100		100	

Prepaid Rent 114

Date	PR	Dr.	Cr.	Balance Dr.	Balance Cr.
1/1	GJ1	300		300	
1/31 Adj.	GJ2		100	200	

Office Supplies 115

Date	PR	Dr.	Cr.	Balance Dr.	Balance Cr.
1/6	GJ1	40		40	
1/31 Adj	GJ2		34	6	

Office Equipment 121

Date	PR	Dr.	Cr.	Balance Dr.	Balance Cr.
1/1	GJ1	100		100	
1/4	GJ1	50		150	

Accumulated Depreciation, Equipment 122

Date	PR	Dr.	Cr.	Balance Dr.	Balance Cr.
1/31 Adj.	GJ2		20		20

Accounts Payable 211

Date	PR	Dr.	Cr.	Balance Dr.	Balance Cr.
1/4	GJ1		50		50
1/18	GJ1		70		120

Salaries Payable 212

Date	PR	Dr.	Cr.	Balance Dr.	Balance Cr.
1/31 Adj.	GJ2		50		50

Rolo Kern, Capital 311

Date	PR	Dr.	Cr.	Balance Dr.	Balance Cr.
1/1	GJ1		1,300		1,300
1/31 Clos.	GJ2		166		1,466
1/31 Clos.	GJ2	20			1,446

Rolo Kern, Withdrawals 312

Date	PR	Dr.	Cr.	Balance Dr.	Balance Cr.
1/12	GJ1	20		20	
1/31 Clos.	GJ2		20	—	

Income Summary 313

Date	PR	Dr.	Cr.	Balance Dr.	Balance Cr.
1/31 Clos.	GJ2		500		500
1/31 Clos.	GJ2	334			166
1/31 Clos.	GJ2	166		—	

Figure 5-20 General Ledger for Rolo Company

Fees Earned					411
				Balance	
Date	PR	Dr.	Cr.	Dr.	Cr.
1/8	GJ1		400		400
1/14	GJ1		100		500
1/31 Clos.	GJ2	500		———	

Rent Expense					513
				Balance	
Date	PR	Dr.	Cr.	Dr.	Cr.
1/31 Adj.	GJ2	100		100	
1/31 Clos.	GJ2		100	———	———

Salaries Expense					511
				Balance	
Date	PR	Dr.	Cr.	Dr.	Cr.
1/16	GJ1	60		60	
1/31 Adj.	GJ2	50		110	
1/31 Clos.	GJ2		110	———	———

Office Supplies Expense					514
				Balance	
Date	PR	Dr.	Cr.	Dr.	Cr.
1/31 Adj.	GJ2	34		34	
1/31 Clos.	GJ2		34	———	———

Advertising Expense					512
				Balance	
Date	PR	Dr.	Cr.	Dr.	Cr.
1/18	GJ1	70		70	
1/31 Clos.	GJ2		70	———	———

Depreciation Expenses Office Equipment 515					
				Balance	
Date	PR	Dr.	Cr.	Dr.	Cr.
1/31 Adj.	GJ2	20		20	
1/31 Clos.	GJ2		20	———	———

Figure 5-20 *(continued)*

Closing

Note that Income Summary is a temporary account located in the ledger.

Goals:

1. Wipe out all temporary accounts in the ledger to zero balances.
2. Get a new figure for Capital in the ledger.

Steps in the Closing Process

Step 1: Close revenue to Income Summary.

Step 2: Close individual expenses to Income Summary.

Step 3: Close balance of Income Summary to Capital. (This really is the Net Income figure on the Worksheet.)

Step 4: Close balance of Withdrawals to Capital.

> Where do I get my information for closing?

All the journal closing entries (no new calculations are needed since all figures are on the worksheet) are posted. The result in the ledger is that all temporary accounts have a zero balance (Fig. 5-20).

Solution Tips for the Post-Closing Trial Balance

The post-closing trial balance is a list of the ledger *after* adjusting and closing entries have been completed. Note the figure for Capital, $1,446, is the new figure.

Figure 5-21
Post-Closing Trial Balance for Rolo Company

These are all permanent accounts.

ROLO CO. POST-CLOSING TRIAL BALANCE JANUARY 31, 200X	Dr.	Cr.
Cash	1 1 8 0 00	
Accounts Receivable	1 0 0 00	
Prepaid Rent	2 0 0 00	
Office Supplies	6 00	
Office Equipment	1 5 0 00	
Accum. Dep., Office Equipment		2 0 00
Accounts Payable		1 2 0 00
Salaries Payable		5 0 00
R. Kern, Capital		1 4 4 6 00
TOTAL	1 6 3 6 00	1 6 3 6 00

Beginning Capital	$1,300
+ Net Income	166
− Withdrawals	20
= Ending Capital	$1,446

Next accounting period we will enter new amounts in the Revenues, Expenses, and Withdrawal accounts. For now, the post-closing trial balance is only made up of permanent accounts.

Summary of Key Points

Learning Unit 5-1

1. After formal financial statements have been prepared, the ledger has still not been brought up-to-date.
2. Information for journalizing adjusting entries comes from the Adjustments section of the worksheet.

Learning Unit 5-2

1. Closing is a mechanical process that aids the accountant in recording transactions for the next period.
2. Assets, Liabilities, and Capital are permanent (real) accounts; their balances are carried over from one accounting period to another. Withdrawals, Revenue, and Expenses are temporary (nominal) accounts; their balances are *not* carried over from one accounting period to another.
3. Income Summary is a temporary account in the general ledger and does not have a normal balance. It will summarize revenue and expenses and transfer the balance to Capital. Withdrawals do not go into Income Summary because they are *not* business expenses.
4. All information for closing can be obtained from the worksheet or ledger.
5. When closing is complete, all temporary accounts in the ledger will have a zero balance, and all this information will be updated in the Capital account.
6. Closing entries are usually done only at year end. Interim reports can be prepared from worksheets that are prepared monthly, quarterly, etc.

Learning Unit 5-3

1. The post-closing trial balance is prepared from the ledger accounts after the adjusting and closing entries have been posted.
2. The accounts on the post-closing trial balance are all permanent titles.

Key Terms

Adjusting journal entries Journal entries that are needed in order to update specific ledger accounts to reflect correct balances at the end of an accounting period.

Closing journal entries Journal entries that are prepared to (a) reduce or clear all temporary accounts to a zero balance or (b) update Capital to a new balance.

Income Summary A temporary account in the ledger that summarizes revenue and expenses and transfers the balance (Net Income or Net Loss) to Capital. Does not have a normal balance.

Permanent accounts (real) Accounts whose balances are carried over to the next accounting period. Examples: Assets, Liabilities, Capital.

Post-closing trial balance The final step in the accounting cycle that lists only permanent accounts in the ledger and their balances after adjusting and closing entries have been posted.

Temporary accounts (nominal) Accounts whose balances at the end of an accounting period are not carried over to the next accounting period. These accounts— Revenue, Expenses, Withdrawals—help summarize a new or ending figure for Capital to begin the next accounting period. Keep in mind that Income Summary is also a temporary account.

Blueprint of Closing Process from the Worksheet

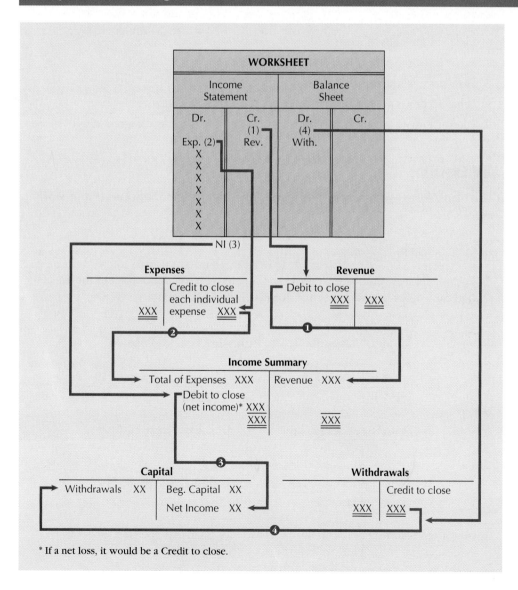

* If a net loss, it would be a Credit to close.

The Closing Steps

1. Close revenue balance to Income Summary.
2. Close each *individual* expense and transfer *total* of all expenses to Income Summary.
3. Transfer balance in Income Summary (Net Income or Net Loss) to Capital.
4. Close Withdrawals to Capital.

Questions, Mini Exercises, Exercises, and Problems

Discussion Questions

1. When a worksheet is completed, what balances are found in the general ledger?
2. Why must adjusting entries be journalized even though the formal statements have already been prepared?
3. "Closing slows down the recording of next year's transactions." Defend or reject this statement with supporting evidence.
4. What is the difference between temporary and permanent accounts?
5. What are the two major goals of the closing process?
6. List the four steps of closing.
7. What is the purpose of Income Summary and where is it located?
8. How can a worksheet aid the closing process?
9. What accounts are usually listed on a post-closing trial balance?
10. Closing entries are always prepared once a month. Agree or disagree. Why?

Mini Exercises

(The blank forms you need are on pages 135–136 of the *Study Guide and Working Papers*.)

Journalizing and Posting Adjusting Entries

1. Post the following adjusting entries (be sure to cross-reference back to the journal) that came from the Adjustment columns of the worksheet:

Ledger Accounts Before Adjusting Entries Posted

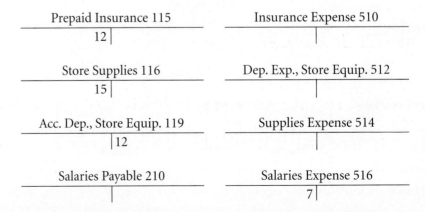

Prepaid Insurance 115		Insurance Expense 510	
12			

Store Supplies 116		Dep. Exp., Store Equip. 512	
15			

Acc. Dep., Store Equip. 119		Supplies Expense 514	
	12		

Salaries Payable 210		Salaries Expense 516	
		7	

General Journal					Page 3	
Date	Account Titles and Description	PR	Dr.		Cr.	
Dec. 31	Insurance Expense		4 00			
	Prepaid Insurance				4 00	
31	Supplies Expense		3 00			
	Store Supplies				3 00	
31	Depr. Exp., Store Equipment		7 00			
	Accum. Depr., Store Equipment				7 00	
31	Salaries Expense		4 00			
	Salaries Payable				4 00	

Figure 5-22
Journalized Adjusting Entries

Steps of Closing and Journalizing Closing Entries

2.

```
              Worksheet

        IS                    BS

 Dr.     Cr.          Dr.      Cr.
 (2)     Rev. (1)     Withd.   (4)
 E
 X
 P
 E
 N
 S
 E
 S
 ____   ____

 NI (3)
```

Figure 5-23

Goals of Closing

1. Temporary accounts in the ledger should have a zero balance.
2. New figure for Capital in closing.

Note All closing can be done from the worksheet. Income Summary is a temporary account in the ledger.

From the preceding worksheet, Fig. 5-23, explain the four steps of closing. Keep in mind that each *individual* expense normally would be listed in the closing process.

Journalizing Closing Entries

3. From the following accounts, journalize the closing entries (assume December 31).

Mel Blanc, Capital 310	Gas Expense 510
30	5

Mel Blanc, Withdr. 312	Advertising Exp. 512
6	4

Income Summary 314		Dep. Exp., Taxi 516	
		6	

Taxi Fees 410	
	18

Posting to Income Summary

4. Draw a T Account of Income Summary and post to it all entries from Question 3 that affect it. Is Income Summary a temporary or permanent account?

Posting to Capital

5. Draw a T Account for Mel Blanc, Capital, and post to it all entries from Question 3 that affect it. What is the final balance of the Capital account?

Exercises

(The blank forms you need are on pages 137–139 of the *Study Guide and Working Papers.*)

5-1. From the adjustments section of a worksheet presented in Figure 5-24, prepare adjusting journal entries for the end of December.

Figure 5-24
Adjustments on Worksheet

> Journalize adjusting entries.

		Adjustments	
		Dr.	Cr.
Prepaid Insurance			(A) 7 0 0 00
Office Supplies			(B) 1 0 0 00
Accumulated Depreciation, Equipment			(C) 4 0 0 00
Salaries Payable			(D) 1 0 0 00
Insurance Expense		(A) 7 0 0 00	
Office Supplies Expense		(B) 1 0 0 00	
Depreciation Expense, Equipment		(C) 4 0 0 00	
Salaries Expense		(D) 1 0 0 00	
		1 5 0 0 00	1 5 0 0 00

5-2. Complete the following table by placing an X in the correct column.

> Temporary vs. permanent accounts.

		Temporary	Permanent	Will Be Closed
Ex.	Accounts Receivable		X	
1.	Income Summary	X		X
2.	Melissa Bryant, Capital		X	
3.	Salary Expense	X		X
4.	Melissa Bryant, Withdrawals	X		X
5.	Fees Earned	X		X
6.	Accounts Payable		X	
7.	Cash		X	

> Closing entries.

5-3. From the following T accounts, journalize the four closing entries on December 31, 200X.

J. King, Capital		Rent Expense	
	14,000	5,000	

J. King, Withdrawals		Wage Expense	
4,000		7,000	

Income Summary		Insurance Expense	
		1,200	

Fees Earned		Dep. Expense, Office Equipment	
	33,000	900	

5-4. From the following posted T accounts, reconstruct the closing journal entries for December 31, 200X.

Reconstructing closing entries.

M. Foster, Capital		Insurance Expense	
Withdrawals 100	2,000 (Dec. 1)	50	Closing 50
	700 Net income		

M. Foster, Withdrawals		Wage Expense	
100	Closing 100	100	Closing 100

Income Summary		Rent Expense	
Expenses 600	Revenue 1,300	200	Closing 200
700	Net Income 700		

Salon Fees		Depreciation Expense, Equipment	
Closing 1,300	1,300	250	Closing 250

5-5. From the following accounts (not in order), prepare a post-closing trial balance for Wey Co. on December 31, 200X. **Note:** These balances are **before** closing.

Post-closing trial balance.

Accounts Receivable	$18,875	Salaries Expense	1,275
Legal Supplies	14,250	P. Wey, Capital	63,450
Office Equipment	59,700	P. Wey, Withdrawals	1,500
Repair Expense	2,850	Legal Fees Earned	12,000
		Accounts Payable	45,000
		Cash	22,000

Group A Problems

(The blank forms you need are on pages 140–157 of the *Study Guide and Working Papers*.)

5A-1. Given the data in Figure 5-25 for Lou's Consulting Service:

LOU'S CONSULTING SERVICE TRIAL BALANCE JUNE 30, 200X		
	Dr.	Cr.
Cash	20 0 0 00	
Accounts Receivable	6 5 0 0 00	
Prepaid Insurance	4 0 0 00	
Supplies	1 5 0 0 00	
Equipment	3 0 0 0 00	
Accumulated Depreciation, Equipment		1 9 0 0 00
Accounts Payable		11 0 0 0 00
Lou Dobbs, Capital		12 8 0 0 00
Lou Dobbs, Withdrawals	3 0 0 00	
Consulting Fees Earned		9 0 0 0 00
Salaries Expense	1 4 0 0 00	
Telephone Expense	1 0 0 0 00	
Advertising Expense	6 0 0 00	
	34 7 0 0 00	34 7 0 0 00

Figure 5-25
Trial Balance for Lou's Consulting Service

Review in preparing a worksheet and journalizing adjusting and closing entries.

Check Figure: Net Income $4,600

Adjustment Data

a. Insurance expired	$300.
b. Supplies on hand	$700.
c. Depreciation on equipment	$100.
d. Salaries earned by employees but not to be paid until July	$200.

Your task is to

1. Prepare a worksheet.
2. Journalize adjusting and closing entries.

Journalizing and posting adjusting and closing entries. Preparing a post-closing trial balance.

5A-2. Enter the beginning balance in each account in your working papers from the Trial Balance columns of the worksheet (Fig. 5-26, p. 195). From the worksheet on page 195, (1) journalize and post adjusting and closing entries after entering the beginning balance in each account in the ledger, and (2) prepare from the ledger a post-closing trial balance for the month of March.

Check Figure:
Post-closing trial balance $3,504

5A-3. As the bookkeeper of Pete's Plowing, you have been asked to complete the entire accounting cycle for Pete from the following information:

Comprehensive review of the entire accounting cycle, Chapters 1–5.

200X

Jan.

	1	Pete invested $7,000 cash and $6,000 worth of snow equipment into the plowing company.
	1	Paid rent for three months in advance for garage space, $2,000.
	4	Purchased office equipment on account from Ling Corp., $7,200.
	6	Purchased snow supplies for $700 cash.
	8	Collected $15,000 from plowing local shopping centers.
	12	Pete Mack withdrew $1,000 from the business for his own personal use.
	20	Plowed North East Co. parking lots, payment not to be received until March, $5,000.
	26	Paid salaries to employees, $1,800.
	28	Paid Ling Corp. one-half amount owed for office equipment.
	29	Advertising bill received from Bush Co. but will not be paid until March, $900.
	30	Paid telephone bill, $210.

Check Figure:
Net income $15,780

Adjustment Data

    a. Snow supplies on hand $400.
    b. Rent expired $600.
    c. Depreciation on office equipment $120. ($7,200 ÷ 5 yr. = $1,440/12 mo. = $120)
    d. Depreciation on snow equipment $100. ($6,000 ÷ 5 yr. = $1,200/12 mo. = $100)
    e. Accrued salaries $190.

POTTER CLEANING SERVICE
WORKSHEET
FOR MONTH ENDED MARCH 31, 200X

Account Titles	Trial Balance Dr.	Trial Balance Cr.	Adjustments Dr.	Adjustments Cr.	Adjusted Trial Balance Dr.	Adjusted Trial Balance Cr.	Income Statement Dr.	Income Statement Cr.	Balance Sheet Dr.	Balance Sheet Cr.
Cash	40000				40000				40000	
Prepaid Insurance	52000			(A) 18000	34000				34000	
Cleaning Supplies	14400			(B) 10000	4400				4400	
Auto	272000				272000				272000	
Accum. Depr. Auto		86000		(C) 15000		101000				101000
Accounts Payable		22400				22400				22400
B. Potter, Capital		54000				54000				54000
B. Potter, Withdrawals	46000				46000				46000	
Cleaning Fees		468000				468000		468000		
Salaries Expense	144000		(D) 16000		160000		160000			
Telephone Expense	26400				26400		26400			
Advertising Expense	19600				19600		19600			
Gas Expense	16000				16000		16000			
	630400	630400								
Insurance Expense			(A) 18000		18000		18000			
Cleaning Supplies Expense			(B) 10000		10000		10000			
Depr. Expense Auto			(C) 15000		15000		15000			
Salaries Payable				(D) 16000		16000				16000
			59000	59000	661400	661400	265000	468000	396400	193400
Net Income							203000			203000
							468000	468000	396400	396400

Figure 5-26 Worksheet for Potter Cleaning Service

Chart of Accounts

Assets
111 Cash
112 Accounts Receivable
114 Prepaid Rent
115 Snow Supplies
121 Office Equipment
122 Accumulated Depreciation, Office Equipment
123 Snow Equipment
124 Accumulated Depreciation Snow Equipment

Liabilities
211 Accounts Payable
212 Salaries Payable

Owner's Equity
311 Pete Mack, Capital
312 Pete Mack, Withdrawals
313 Income Summary

Revenue
411 Plowing Fees

Expenses
511 Salaries Expense
512 Advertising Expense
513 Telephone Expense
514 Rent Expense
515 Snow Supplies Expense
516 Depreciation Expense, Office Equipment
517 Depreciation Expense, Snow Equipment

Group B Problems

(The blank forms you need are on pages 140–157 of the *Study Guide and Working Papers.*)

5B-1.

> Review in preparing a worksheet and journalizing and closing entries.

Figure 5-27
Trial Balance for Lou's Consulting Service

> Check Figure:
> Net income $3,530

MEMO

To: Matt Kaminsky

From: Abby Ellen

Re: Accounting Needs

Please prepare ASAP from the following information (attached) (1) a worksheet along with (2) journalized adjusting and closing entries.

LOU'S CONSULTING SERVICE TRIAL BALANCE JUNE 30, 200X	Dr.	Cr.
Cash	10 1 5 0 00	
Accounts Receivable	5 0 0 0 00	
Prepaid Insurance	7 0 0 00	
Supplies	3 0 0 00	
Equipment	12 9 5 0 00	
Accumulated Depreciation, Equipment		4 0 0 0 00
Accounts Payable		5 7 5 0 00
L. Dobbs, Capital		15 1 5 0 00
L. Dobbs, Withdrawals	4 0 0 00	
Consulting Fees Earned		5 2 0 0 00
Salaries Expense	4 5 0 00	
Telephone Expense	7 0 00	
Advertising Expense	8 0 00	
	30 1 0 0 00	30 1 0 0 00

Adjustment Data

a. Insurance expired $100.
b. Supplies on hand $20.
c. Depreciation on equipment $200.
d. Salaries earned by employees but not due to be paid until July $490.

5B-2. Enter the beginning balance in each account in your working papers from the Trial Balance columns of the worksheet (Fig. 5-28, p. 198). From the worksheet on page 198, (1) journalize and post adjusting and closing entries after entering beginning balances in each account in the ledger, and (2) prepare from the ledger a post-closing trial balance at the end of March.

> Journalizing and posting adjusting and closing entries. Preparing a post-closing trial balance.

5B-3. From the following transactions as well as additional data, please complete the entire accounting cycle for Pete's Plowing (use the chart of accounts on page 196).

> Check Figure:
> Post-closing Trial Balance
> $3,294

200X

Jan.

1	To open the business, Pete invested $8,000 cash and $9,600 worth of snow equipment.
1	Paid rent for five months in advance, $3,000.
4	Purchased office equipment on account from Russell Co., $6,000.
6	Bought snow supplies, $350.
8	Collected $7,000 for plowing during winter storm emergency.
12	Pete paid his home telephone bill from the company checkbook, $70.
20	Billed Eastern Freight Co. for plowing fees earned but not to be received until March, $6,500.
24	Advertising bill received from Jones Co. but will not be paid until next month, $350.
26	Paid salaries to employees, $1,800.
28	Paid Russell Co. one-half of amount owed for office equipment.
29	Paid telephone bill of company, $165.

> Comprehensive review of entire accounting cycle. Review of Chapters 1–5.

> Check Figure:
> Net Income $9,610

Adjustment Data

a. Snow supplies on hand $200.
b. Rent expired $600.
c. Depreciation on office equipment $125.
  ($6,000/4 yr = $1,500 ÷ 12 = $125)
d. Depreciation on snow equipment $400.
  ($9,600 ÷ 2 = $4,800 ÷ 12 = $400)
e. Salaries accrued $300.

Real-World Applications

5R-1. Carol Miller needs a loan from the Charles Bank to help finance her business. She has submitted to the Charles Bank the following unadjusted trial balance. As the loan officer, you will be meeting with Carol tomorrow. Could you make some specific written suggestions to Carol regarding her loan report?

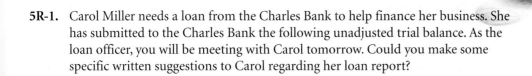

POTTER CLEANING SERVICE
WORKSHEET
FOR MONTH ENDED MARCH 31, 200X

Account Titles	Trial Balance Dr.	Trial Balance Cr.	Adjustments Dr.	Adjustments Cr.	Adjusted Trial Balance Dr.	Adjusted Trial Balance Cr.	Income Statement Dr.	Income Statement Cr.	Balance Sheet Dr.	Balance Sheet Cr.
Cash	172400				172400				172400	
Prepaid Insurance	35000			(A) 20000	15000				15000	
Cleaning Supplies	80000			(B) 60000	20000				20000	
Auto	122000				122000				122000	
Accumulated Depreciation, Auto		66000		(C) 15000		81000				81000
Accounts Payable		67400				67400				67400
B. Potter, Capital		248000				248000				248000
B. Potter, Withdrawals	60000				60000				60000	
Cleaning Fees		370000				370000		370000		
Salaries Expense	200000		(D) 17500		217500		217500			
Telephone Expense	28400				28400		28400			
Advertising Expense	27600				27600		27600			
Gas Expense	26000				26000		26000			
	751400	751400								
Insurance Expense			(A) 20000		20000		20000			
Cleaning Supplies Expense			(B) 60000		60000		60000			
Depreciation Expense, Auto			(C) 15000		15000		15000			
Salaries Payable				(D) 17500		17500				17500
			112500	112500	783900	783900	394500	370000	389400	413900
Net Loss								24500	24500	
							394500	394500	413900	413900

Figure 5-28 Worksheet for Potter Cleaning Service

Cash in Bank	770	
Accounts Receivable	1,480	
Office Supplies	3,310	
Equipment	7,606	
Accounts Payable		684
A. Humphrey, Capital		8,000
Service Fees		17,350
Salaries	11,240	
Utilities Expense	842	
Rent Expense	360	
Insurance Expense	280	
Advertising Expense	146	
Totals	26,034	26,034

5R-2 Janet Smother is the new bookkeeper who replaced Dick Burns, owing to his sudden illness. Janet finds on her desk a note requesting that she close the books and supply the ending Capital figure. Janet is upset, since she can only find the following:

a. Revenue and expense accounts all were zero balance.

b.

Income Summary	
14,360	19,300

c. Owner withdrew $8,000.

d. Owner beginning Capital was $34,400.

Could you help Janet accomplish her assignment? What written suggestions should Janet make to her supervisor so that this situation will not happen again?

YOU make the call

Critical Thinking/Ethical Case

5R-3. Todd Silver is the purchasing agent for Moore Co. One of his suppliers, Gem Co., offers Todd a free vacation to France if he buys at least 75% of Moore's supplies from Gem Co. Todd, who is angry because Moore Co. has not given him a raise in over a year, is considering the offer. Write your recommendation to Todd.

Internet Exercises: TADOnline; Peachtree; QuickBooks

EX-1. [**www.tadonline.com**]   At the beginning of your accounting education is a good time to begin formulating your philosophy of how to do accounting work. By studying and learning you are also learning good work habits. The TADOnline Web site presents a section on "Why Outsource Your Accounting." The discussion presents some good suggestions and may also cause you to reflect on how people choose an accounting or bookkeeping firm.

Use that discussion as a springboard and discuss what factors you believe affect a client's choice of someone to help with vital accounting records. TADOnline is not "just around the corner." Is location an important factor in deciding who will do a business's accounting?

EX-2. [**www.peachtree.com**]; [**www.quickbookscom**]   Most businesses today are employing some type of computerized accounting system. Some businesses' requirements are simple, and they use only a general ledger program. Others are much more complex and employ inventory modules and payroll modules, in addition to accounts receivable and accounts payable modules for tracking customer and vendor information.

1. Browse the two Web sites in this exercise. Compare and contrast the products by looking at information with these questions in mind:

   a. What kind of output is available?
   b. How are the input systems similar?
   c. Does the program have an inventory module?
   d. At each site are there different products for different complexities in accounting systems?
   e. What online help is available?

2. Set up a visit to a local accounting firm. Ask what programs are used in addition to the two sample programs in this exercise.

Continuing Problem

Eldorado Computer Center

Tony has decided to end the Eldorado Computer Center's first year as of September 30, 200X. Following is an updated chart of accounts.

Assets

1000	Cash
1020	Accounts Receivable
1025	Prepaid Rent
1030	Supplies
1080	Computer Shop Equip.
1081	Accum. Depr. CS Equip.
1090	Office Equipment
1091	Accum. Depr. Office Equip.

Liabilities

2000	Accounts Payable

Owner's Equity

3000	T. Freedman, Capital
3010	T. Freedman, Withdrawals
3020	Income Summary

Revenue

4000	Service Revenue

Expenses

5010	Advertising Expense
5030	Utilities Expense
5050	Supplies Expense
5070	Postage Expense
5090	Depr. Exp. Office Equip.
5020	Rent Expense
5040	Phone Expense
5060	Insurance Expense
5080	Depr. Exp. C.S. Equip.

Note: Accounts 3010 to 5080 are temporary accounts.

Assignment

(See pp. 162–169 in your *Study Guide and Working Papers.*)

1. Journalize the adjusting entries from Chapter 4.
2. Post the adjusting entries to the ledger.
3. Journalize the closing entries.
4. Post the closing entries to the ledger.
5. Prepare a post-closing trial balance.

SUBWAY Case

CLOSING TIME

"You wait and see," Stan told his new sandwich artist Wanda Kurtz, "everything will fall into place soon." Wanda had a tough time serving customers quickly enough, and Stan was in the middle of giving her a pep talk when the phone rang.

"I'll let the machine pick up," Stan reassured Wanda, as he proceeded to train her in some crucial POS touch-screen maneuvers.

"Stan!" an urgent voice came over the message machine, "I think you've forgotten something!" Stan picked up the phone and said, "Lila, can I get back to you tomorrow? I'm in the middle of an important talk with Wanda." One of Stan's strong points as an employer was his ability to focus 100% on his employees' concerns. Yet, Lila simply would not wait.

"Stan," Lila said impatiently, "you absolutely must get me your worksheet by 12 noon tomorrow so I can close your books," she insisted. "Tomorrow's the 31st of March and we close on the last day of the month!"

"*Ay caramba!*" Stan sighed, "Looks like I'm going to be up till the wee hours," he confided to Wanda when he put down the phone.

Although Subway company policy doesn't require a closing every month, closing the books is a key part of their accounting training for all new franchisees. By closing their books, business owners can clearly measure their net profit and loss for each period separate from all other periods. This makes activities like budgeting and comparing performance with similar businesses (or performance over time) possible.

At 9:00 A.M. the next morning, an exhausted Stan opened up the restaurant and e-mailed his worksheet to Lila. He was feeling quite pleased with himself—that is, until he heard Lila's urgent-sounding voice coming over the message machine 10 minutes later.

"I've been over and over this," said Lila after Stan picked up, "and I can't get it to balance. I know it's hard for you to do this during working hours, but I need you to go back over the figures."

Stan opened up Peachtree and pored over his worksheets. Errors are hard to find when closing the books and, unfortunately, there is no set way to detect errors and even no set place to start. Stan chose payroll because it is one of the largest expenses and because of the new hire.

At 11:45 he called Lila, who sounded both exasperated and relieved to hear from him. "I think I've got it! It looks like I messed up on adjusting the Salaries Expense account. I looked at the Payroll Register and compared the total to the Salaries Payable account. It didn't match! When I hired Wanda Kurtz on the 26th, I should have increased both the Salaries Expense and the Salaries Payable lines, because she has accrued wages."

"Yes," said Lila, "Salaries Expense is a debit and Salaries Payable is a credit, and you skipped the payable. Great! With this adjusting entry in the general journal, the worksheet will balance."

Stan's sigh of relief turned into a big yawn, and they both laughed. "I guess I just find it easier to hire people and train them than to account for them," said Stan.

Discussion Questions

1. How would the adjustment be made if Wanda Kurtz received $7.00 per hour and worked 25 additional hours? Where do you place her accrued wages?
2. Stan bought three new Subway aprons and hats for Wanda Smith for $20 each but forgot to post it to the Uniforms account. How much will the closing balance be off? In what way will it be off?
3. Put yourself in Stan's shoes: What is the value of doing a monthly closing, no matter how much—or little—business you do?

Due March 29
Grade as a Test

VALDEZ REALTY

Reviewing the Accounting Cycle TWICE

This comprehensive review problem requires you to complete the accounting cycle for Valdez Realty twice. This will allow you to review Chapters 1–5 while reinforcing the relationships between all parts of the accounting cycle. By completing two cycles, you will see how the ending June balances in the ledger are used to accumulate data in July. (The blank forms you need are on pages 170–190 of the *Study Guide and Working Papers.*)

Take a moment to review the road map of the accounting cycle on the inside front cover of the text.

First, look at the chart of accounts for Valdez Realty.

On June 1, 200X, Juan Valdez opened a real estate office called Valdez Realty. The following transactions were completed for the month of June:

Valdez Realty
Chart of Accounts

Assets
111 Cash
112 Accounts Receivable
114 Prepaid Rent
115 Office Supplies
121 Office Equipment
122 Accumulated Depreciation, Office Equipment
123 Automobile
124 Accumulated Depreciation, Automobile

Liabilities
211 Accounts Payable
212 Salaries Payable

Owner's Equity
311 Juan Valdez, Capital
312 Juan Valdez, Withdrawals
313 Income Summary

Revenue
411 Commissions Earned

Expenses
511 Rent Expense
512 Salaries Expense
513 Gas Expense
514 Repairs Expense
515 Telephone Expense
516 Advertising Expense
517 Office Supplies Expense
518 Depreciation Expense, Office Equipment
519 Depreciation Expense, Automobile
524 Miscellaneous Expense

200X
June 1 Juan Valdez invested $7,000 cash in the real estate agency along with $3,000 of office equipment.

⊣ DEPOSIT TICKET ⊢

VALDEZ REALTY (213)478-3584
8200 SUNSET BOULEVARD
Los Angeles, CA 90028

DATE _____ June 1 _____ 200X _____

SIGN HERE IN PRESENCE OF TELLER FOR CASH RET'D FROM DEP.

BAY BANK
Box 1739 Terminal Annex
Los Angeles, CA 90052

⑆122000661⑆1400‴03857‴0136 2⑆

CASH	CURRENCY	7,000	00
	COIN		
LIST CHECKS SINGLY			
TOTAL FROM OTHER SIDE			
TOTAL		7,000	00
LESS CASH RECEIVED			
NET DEPOSIT		7,000	00

16-66/1220

A hold for uncollected funds may be placed on funds deposited by check or similar instruments. This could delay your ability to withdraw such funds. The delay if any would not exceed the period of time permitted by law.

June ⌐1 Rented and paid three months rent in advance to Miller Property Management $2,100.

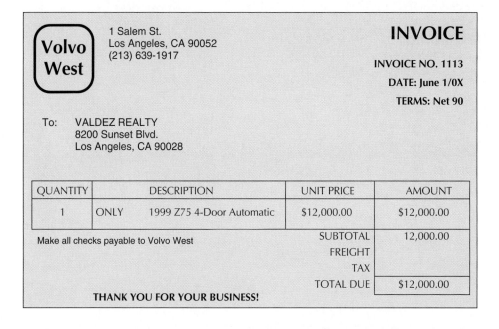

VALDEZ REALTY (213) 478-3584   0001

8200 SUNSET BOULEVARD
LOS ANGELES, CA 90028   June 1   200X

PAY TO THE
ORDER OF _Miller Property Mngnt Co._ $ | 2,100 XX/100 |

~ _Two Thousand one hundred XX/100_ ~ DOLLARS

BAY BANK
Box 1739 Terminal Annex
Los Angeles, CA 90052

MEMO _Rent – June – Aug. 200X_   _Juan Valdez_

⑆122000661⑆1400‴03857‴0136 2⑆0001

June 1 Bought an automobile on __account__ from Volvo West, $12,000.

Volvo West

1 Salem St.
Los Angeles, CA 90052
(213) 639-1917

INVOICE

INVOICE NO. 1113
DATE: June 1/0X
TERMS: Net 90

To: VALDEZ REALTY
      8200 Sunset Blvd.
      Los Angeles, CA 90028

QUANTITY	DESCRIPTION		UNIT PRICE	AMOUNT
1	ONLY	1999 Z75 4-Door Automatic	$12,000.00	$12,000.00
Make all checks payable to Volvo West		SUBTOTAL		12,000.00
		FREIGHT		
		TAX		
		TOTAL DUE		$12,000.00

THANK YOU FOR YOUR BUSINESS!

June 4 Purchased office supplies from Office Depot for cash, $300.

Office Depot   INVOICE

1 Ferncroft Rd.
Los Angeles, CA 90052
Phone (213) 631-0288

DATE: June 4/0X
NUMBER: D198795
TERMS: Cash

SOLD TO:	SHIPPED TO:
Valdez Realty 8200 Sunset Blvd. Los Angeles, CA 90028	Valdez Realty 8200 Sunset Blvd. Los Angeles, CA 90028

DATE	DESCRIPTION	UNIT PRICE	AMOUNT
Jun 4/0X	Office supplies PAYMENT RECEIVED - - CHK #0002 - THANK YOU		$300.00
		Subtotal	300.00
		Total	$300.00

Business Number: 115555559

THANK YOU FOR YOUR BUSINESS

PLEASE PAY
THE ABOVE

VALDEZ REALTY (213) 478-3584		0002

8200 SUNSET BOULEVARD
LOS ANGELES, CA 90028

June 4 *200X*

PAY TO THE
ORDER OF *Office Depot* $ | *300 $\frac{XX}{100}$* |

Three Hundred and $\frac{XX}{100}$ DOLLARS

BAY BANK
Box 1739 Terminal Annex
Los Angeles, CA 90052

MEMO *Office supplies*   *Juan Valdez*

⑆122000⑈66 ⑈⑆1400⑉0 3857⑉0 13 6 2⑉000 2

June 5 Purchased additional office supplies from Office Depot on account, $150.

Office Depot

INVOICE

1 Ferncroft Rd.
Los Angeles, CA 90052
Phone (213) 631-0288

DATE: June 5/0X
NUMBER: D198825
TERMS: net 60

SOLD TO:	SHIPPED TO:
Valdez Realty 8200 Sunset Blvd. Los Angeles, CA 90028	Valdez Realty 8200 Sunset Blvd. Los Angeles, CA 90028

DATE	DESCRIPTION	UNIT PRICE	AMOUNT
Jun 5/0X	Office supplies		$150.00
		Subtotal	150.00
		Total	$150.00

Business Number: 115555559

THANK YOU FOR YOUR BUSINESS

PLEASE PAY THE ABOVE

June 6 Sold a house to Bill Barnes and collected a $6,000 commission.

⊢ **DEPOSIT TICKET** ⊣

VALDEZ REALTY (213)478-3584
8200 SUNSET BOULEVARD
Los Angeles, CA 90028

DATE _____ June 6 _____ 200X _____

SIGN HERE IN PRESENCE OF TELLER FOR CASH RET'D FROM DEP.

BAY BANK
Box 1739 Terminal Annex
Los Angeles, CA 90052

CASH	CURRENCY		
	COIN		
LIST CHECKS SINGLY 250-99		6,000	00
TOTAL FROM OTHER SIDE			
TOTAL			
LESS CASH RECEIVED			
NET DEPOSIT		6,000	00

16-66/1220

A hold for uncollected funds may be placed on funds deposited by check or similar instruments. This could delay your ability to withdraw such funds. The delay if any would not exceed the period of time permitted by law.

⑆122000661⑆1400⑈03857⑈013621⑈

VALDEZ REALTY COMMISSION REPORT				Date: June 6, 200X	
Name: Bill Barnes					
Date:	**Sales Description**	**Sales No.**	**Commission Amount**		
Jun 6/0X	Home at 66 Sullivan St.	A1001	$6,000.00	Paid in full.	
C001		**Remarks:**			

June   8   Paid gas bill to Petro Petroleum, $22.

VALDEZ REALTY (213) 478-3584		0003
8200 SUNSET BOULEVARD LOS ANGELES, CA 90028		June 8 200X

PAY TO THE ORDER OF _Petro Petroleum_ $ | 22 XX/100

Twenty-two and XX/100 ———————————————— DOLLARS

BAY BANK
Box 1739 Terminal Annex
Los Angeles, CA 90052

MEMO _Gas Bill – June 6_   _Juan Valdez_

⑆122000066⑈1400⑊03857⑉0136 2⑈0003

June   15   Paid Betty Long, office secretary, $350.

VALDEZ REALTY (213) 478-3584		0004
8200 SUNSET BOULEVARD LOS ANGELES, CA 90028		June 15 200X

PAY TO THE ORDER OF _Betty Long_ $ | 350 XX/100

Three Hundred fifty and XX/100 ———————————————— DOLLARS

BAY BANK
Box 1739 Terminal Annex
Los Angeles, CA 90052

MEMO _Salary – June 1–15_   _Juan Valdez_

⑆122000066⑈1400⑊03857⑉0136 2⑈0004

June   17   Sold a building lot to West Land Developers and earned a commission, $6,500 payment to be received on July 8.

VALDEZ REALTY COMMISSION REPORT			**Date:**	June 17, 200X
Name:	West Land Developers			
Date:	**Sales Description**	**Sales No.**	**Commission Amount**	
Jun 17/0X	Lot at 8 Ridge Rd.	A1002	$6,500.00	
C002		**Remarks:** Payment due July 8, 200X		

June 20   Juan Valdez withdrew $1,000 from the business to pay personal expenses.

VALDEZ REALTY (213) 478-3584		0005

VALDEZ REALTY (213) 478-3584   0005

8200 SUNSET BOULEVARD
LOS ANGELES, CA 90028   _June 20_   _200X_

PAY TO THE
ORDER OF _Juan Valdez_ $ | _1,000 XX/100_ |

One Thousand and XX/100 ~~~~~~~~~~~~~~~~~~ DOLLARS

BAY BANK
Box 1739 Terminal Annex
Los Angeles, CA 90052

MEMO _Withdrawal_   _Juan Valdez_

⑆1 2 2000 66 1⑆1400⑈03857⑈0136 2⑈0005

June 21   Sold a house to Ms. Laura Harrison and collected a $3,500 commission.

—| DEPOSIT TICKET |—

VALDEZ REALTY (213)478-3584
8200 SUNSET BOULEVARD
Los Angeles, CA 90028

DATE ____ _June 21_   _200X_ ____

SIGN HERE IN PRESENCE OF TELLER FOR CASH RET'D FROM DEP.

BAY BANK
Box 1739 Terminal Annex
Los Angeles, CA 90052

⑆1 2 2000 66 1⑆1400⑈03857⑈0136 2⑈

CASH	CURRENCY		
	COIN		
LIST CHECKS SINGLY 270-88		3,500	00
TOTAL FROM OTHER SIDE			
TOTAL			
LESS CASH RECEIVED			
NET DEPOSIT		3,500	00

16-66/1220

A hold for uncollected funds may be placed on funds deposited by check or similar instruments. This could delay your ability to withdraw such funds. The delay if any would not exceed the period of time permitted by law.

VALDEZ REALTY COMMISSION REPORT			_Date:_	June 21, 200X	
Name:	Ms. Laura Harrison				
Date:	**Sales Description**	**Sales No.**	**Commission Amount**		
Jun 21/0X	_Home at 666 Jersey St._	_A1003_	_$3,500.00_	_Paid in full._	
C003		**Remarks:**			

June 22   Paid gas bill, $25, to Petro Petroleum.

VALDEZ REALTY (213) 478-3584   0006

8200 SUNSET BOULEVARD
LOS ANGELES, CA 90028   *June 22   200X*

PAY TO THE
ORDER OF *Petro Petroleum* $ 25 XX/100

Twenty-five and XX/100 ————————————————— DOLLARS

BAY BANK
Box 1739 Terminal Annex
Los Angeles, CA 90052

MEMO *Gas Bill—June 22*   *Juan Valdez*

⑈⑈⑈⑈⑈ 1 2 2000 6 6 ⑈⑈ 1 4 0 0 ⑈ 0 3 8 5 7 ⑈ 0 1 3 6 2 ⑈ 0006

June 24   Paid Volvo West $600 to repair automobile.

Volvo West	1 Salem St. Los Angeles, CA 90052 (213) 639-1917	**INVOICE**

INVOICE NO. 1184

DATE: June 24/0X

TERMS: Cash

To: VALDEZ REALTY   Ship To:
     8200 Sunset Blvd.   Pickup
     Los Angeles, CA 90028

QUANTITY	DESCRIPTION	UNIT PRICE	AMOUNT
1	ONLY Z75 Air conditioning repair		$ 600.00
Make all checks payable to Volvo West		SUBTOTAL	600.00
		FREIGHT	
PAYMENT RECEIVED - Check #0007		TAX	
		TOTAL DUE	$ 600.00

THANK YOU FOR YOUR BUSINESS!

VALDEZ REALTY (213) 478-3584   0007

8200 SUNSET BOULEVARD
LOS ANGELES, CA 90028   *June 24   200X*

PAY TO THE
ORDER OF *Volvo West* $ 600 XX/100

Six Hundred and XX/100 ————————————————— DOLLARS

BAY BANK
Box 1739 Terminal Annex
Los Angeles, CA 90052

MEMO *Auto Repairs — Inv. 1184*   *Juan Valdez*

⑈⑈⑈⑈⑈ 1 2 2000 6 6 ⑈⑈ 1 4 0 0 ⑈ 0 3 8 5 7 ⑈ 0 1 3 6 2 ⑈ 000 7

June 30   Paid Betty Long, office secretary, $350.

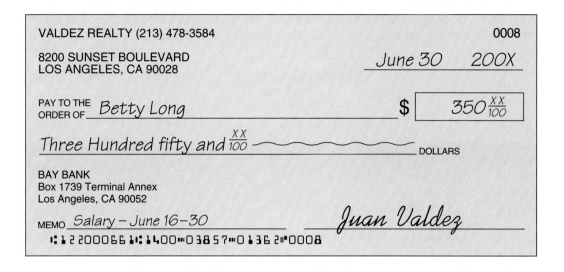

June 30   Paid Verizon June telephone bill, $510.

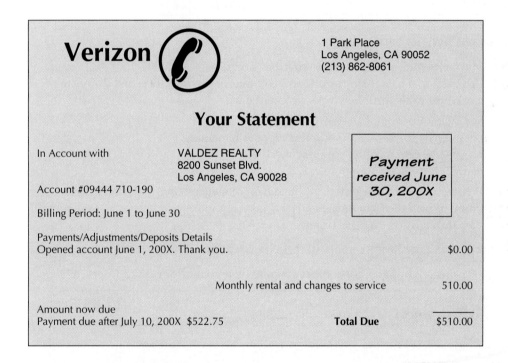

June 30   Received advertising bill for June, $1,200, from *Salem News*. The bill is to be paid on July 2.

Salem News
1 Main St., Los Angeles, CA 90052
(213) 744-1000

I N V O I C E

SOLD TO: Valdez Realty
8200 Sunset Blvd.
Los Angeles, CA 90028

Invoice No.:   4879
Date: June 30, 200X
Due Date: July 2, 200X

DATE	DESCRIPTION		AMOUNT
June 26/0X	Advertising in Salem News during June 200X		$1,200.00
		SUBTOTAL	1,200.00
Business Number 944122338		TOTAL	$1,200.00

MAKE ALL CHECKS PAYABLE TO SALEM NEWS

Required Work for June

1. Journalize transactions and post to ledger accounts.
2. Prepare a trial balance in the first two columns of the worksheet and complete the worksheet using the following adjustment data:

   a. One month's rent had expired.
   b. An inventory shows $50 of office supplies remaining.
   c. Depreciation on office equipment, $100.
   d. Depreciation on automobile, $200.

3. Prepare a June income statement, statement of owner's equity, and balance sheet.
4. From the worksheet, journalize and post adjusting and closing entries (p. 3 of journal).
5. Prepare a post-closing trial balance.

During July, Valdez Realty completed these transactions:

July 1   Purchased additional office supplies on account from Office Depot, $700.

Office Depot   # INVOICE

1 Ferncroft Rd.
Los Angeles, CA 90052
Phone (213) 631-0288

DATE: Jul 1/0X
NUMBER: D1996035
TERMS: Net 60

SOLD TO:
Valdez Realty
8200 Sunset Blvd.
Los Angeles, CA 90028

SHIPPED TO:
Valdez Realty
8200 Sunset Blvd.
Los Angeles, CA 90028

DATE	DESCRIPTION	UNIT PRICE	AMOUNT
Jul 2/0X	Office supplies		$700.00
		Subtotal	700.00
		Total	$700.00

Business Number: 115555559

THANK YOU FOR YOUR BUSINESS

PLEASE PAY
THE ABOVE

July 2 Paid *Salem News* advertising bill for June.

VALDEZ REALTY (213) 478-3584	0010
8200 SUNSET BOULEVARD LOS ANGELES, CA 90028	July 2 200X

PAY TO THE
ORDER OF *Salem News* $ $1,200\frac{XX}{100}$

One Thousand Two Hundred and $\frac{XX}{100}$ ———————— DOLLARS

BAY BANK
Box 1739 Terminal Annex
Los Angeles, CA 90052

MEMO *Invoice # 4879*   *Juan Valdez*

⑈⑈ 1 2 2 0 0 0 6 6 ⑈⑈ 1 4 0 0 ⑊⑊ 0 3 8 5 7 ⑊ 0 1 3 6 2 ⑈⑈ 0 0 1 0

July 3 Sold a house to Melissa King and collected a commission of $6,600.

VALDEZ REALTY **COMMISSION REPORT**			*Date:*	July 3, 200X	
Name:	Melissa King				
Date:	*Sales Description*	*Sales No.*	*Commission Amount*		
July 3/0X	*Home at 800 Rose Ave.*	*A1004*	*$6,600.00*	*Paid in full.*	
C004		*Remarks:*			

⊢ **DEPOSIT TICKET** ⊢					
VALDEZ REALTY (213)478-3584 8200 SUNSET BOULEVARD Los Angeles, CA 90028	**CASH**	CURRENCY			
		COIN			
	LIST CHECKS SINGLY *278-92*		*6,600*	*00*	
					16-66/1220
DATE July 3 200X	TOTAL FROM OTHER SIDE				A hold for uncollected funds may be placed on funds deposited by check or similar instruments. This could delay your ability to withdraw such funds. The delay if any would not exceed the period of time permitted by law.
	TOTAL				
SIGN HERE IN PRESENCE OF TELLER FOR CASH RET'D FROM DEP. →	LESS CASH RECEIVED				
BAY BANK Box 1739 Terminal Annex Los Angeles, CA 90052	**NET DEPOSIT**		*6,600*	*00*	

⑈⑈ 1 2 2 0 0 0 6 6 ⑈⑈ 1 4 0 0 ⑊⑊ 0 3 8 5 7 ⑊ 0 1 3 6 2 ⑈⑈

July 6 Paid gas bill to Petro Petroleum, $29.

VALDEZ REALTY (213) 478-3584   0011

8200 SUNSET BOULEVARD   *July 6   200X*
LOS ANGELES, CA 90028

PAY TO THE *Petro Petroleum* $ 29 XX/100
ORDER OF

Twenty-nine and XX/100 ———————————————— DOLLARS

BAY BANK
Box 1739 Terminal Annex
Los Angeles, CA 90052

MEMO *Gas Bill – July 6*   *Juan Valdez*

⑆122000661⑆1400 03857 0136 2 0011

July 8 Collected commission from West Land Developers for sale of building lot on June 17.

—| DEPOSIT TICKET |—

VALDEZ REALTY (213)478-3584
8200 SUNSET BOULEVARD
Los Angeles, CA 90028

CASH	CURRENCY		
	COIN		
LIST CHECKS SINGLY *228-114*		6,500	00
TOTAL FROM OTHER SIDE			
TOTAL			
LESS CASH RECEIVED			
NET DEPOSIT		6,500	00

DATE *July 8   200X*

SIGN HERE IN PRESENCE OF TELLER FOR CASH RET'D FROM DEP.

16-66/1220

A hold for uncollected funds may be placed on funds deposited by check or similar instruments. This could delay your ability to withdraw such funds. The delay if any would not exceed the period of time permitted by law.

BAY BANK
Box 1739 Terminal Annex
Los Angeles, CA 90052

⑆122000661⑆1400 03857 0136 2

July 12 Paid $300 to Regan Realtors Assoc. to send employees to realtors' workshop.

VALDEZ REALTY (213) 478-3584   0012

8200 SUNSET BOULEVARD   *July 12   200X*
LOS ANGELES, CA 90028

PAY TO THE *Regan Realtors Assoc.* $ 300 XX/100
ORDER OF

Three Hundred and XX/100 ———————————————— DOLLARS

BAY BANK
Box 1739 Terminal Annex
Los Angeles, CA 90052

MEMO *Workshop Registration*   *Juan Valdez*

⑆122000661⑆1400 03857 0136 2 0012

July 15 Paid Betty Long, office secretary, $350.

VALDEZ REALTY (213) 478-3584	0013
8200 SUNSET BOULEVARD LOS ANGELES, CA 90028	July 15 200X

PAY TO THE ORDER OF _Betty Long_ $ | 350 $\frac{XX}{100}$

Three Hundred fifty and $\frac{XX}{100}$ —————————— DOLLARS

BAY BANK
Box 1739 Terminal Annex
Los Angeles, CA 90052

MEMO _Salary July 1–15_   _Juan Valdez_

⑊1 2 2000 66 ⑊ 1400 ⑊ 03 85 7 ⑊ 0 1 36 2⑊ 00 13

July 17 Sold a house to Matt Karminsky and earned a commission of $2,400. Commission to be received on August 10.

VALDEZ REALTY
COMMISSION REPORT   **Date:** July 17, 200X

Name: Matt Karminsky

Date:	Sales Description	Sales No.	Commission Amount	
July 17/0X	Home at RR2, Site 3	A1010	$2,400.00	
C005		**Remarks:** Payment due August 10, 200X		

July 18 Sold a building lot to DiBiasi Builders and collected a commission of $7,000.

⊢ DEPOSIT TICKET ⊢				
VALDEZ REALTY (213)478-3584 8200 SUNSET BOULEVARD Los Angeles, CA 90028	CASH	CURRENCY		
		COIN		
	LIST CHECKS SINGLY 269-10	7,000	00	
DATE ___July 18___ ___200X___	TOTAL FROM OTHER SIDE			
	TOTAL			
SIGN HERE IN PRESENCE OF TELLER FOR CASH RET'D FROM DEP. →	LESS CASH RECEIVED			
	NET DEPOSIT	7,000	00	

16-66/1220

A hold for uncollected funds may be placed on funds deposited by check or similar instruments. This could delay your ability to withdraw such funds. The delay if any would not exceed the period of time permitted by law.

BAY BANK
Box 1739 Terminal Annex
Los Angeles, CA 90052

⑊1 2 2000 66 ⑊ 1400 ⑊ 03 85 7 ⑊ 0 1 36 2⑊

VALDEZ REALTY COMMISSION REPORT					*Date:* July 18, 200X
Name:	DiBiasi Builders				
Date:	*Sales Description*	*Sales No.*	*Commission Amount*		
July 18/0X	*Building lot at 5004 King St. E*	*A1005*	*$7,000.00*	*Paid in full.*	
C006		*Remarks:*			

July   22   Sent a check to Catholic Charities for $40 to help sponsor a local road race to aid the poor. (This is not to be considered an advertising expense, but it is a business expense.)

VALDEZ REALTY (213) 478-3584   0014

8200 SUNSET BOULEVARD
LOS ANGELES, CA 90028   *July 22*   *200X*

PAY TO THE
ORDER OF   *Catholic Charities* $ *40 $\frac{XX}{100}$*

Forty and $\frac{XX}{100}$ ~~~~~~~~~~~~~~~~~~~~~~~ DOLLARS

BAY BANK
Box 1739 Terminal Annex
Los Angeles, CA 90052

MEMO *Aid to Poor*   *Juan Valdez*

⑈ ⑆2200066 ⑆ 1400 ⑈ 03857 ⑈ 0136 2 ⑈ 0014

July   24   Paid Volvo West $590 for repairs to automobile.

Volvo West   1 Salem St.
Los Angeles, CA 90052
(213) 639-1917

INVOICE

INVOICE NO. 2119
DATE: July 24/0X
TERMS: Cash

To: VALDEZ REALTY
8200 Sunset Blvd.
Los Angeles, CA 90028

QUANTITY	DESCRIPTION	UNIT PRICE	AMOUNT
	75,000 maintenance		$ 590.00

Make all checks payable to Volvo West

PAYMENT RECEIVED - Check #0015

SUBTOTAL	590.00
FREIGHT	
TAX	
TOTAL DUE	$ 590.00

THANK YOU FOR YOUR BUSINESS!

VALDEZ REALTY (213) 478-3584   0015

8200 SUNSET BOULEVARD
LOS ANGELES, CA 90028   July 24   200X

PAY TO THE
ORDER OF *Volvo West* $ 590 XX/100

Five Hundred Ninety and XX/100 —————————— DOLLARS

BAY BANK
Box 1739 Terminal Annex
Los Angeles, CA 90052

MEMO *Auto Repairs – Inv. 2119*   *Juan Valdez*

⑆122000066⑆ ⑈1400⑈03857⑈01362⑈0015

July 28   Juan Valdez withdrew $1,800 from the business to pay personal expenses.

VALDEZ REALTY (213) 478-3584   0016

8200 SUNSET BOULEVARD
LOS ANGELES, CA 90028   July 28   200X

PAY TO THE
ORDER OF *Juan Valdez* $ 1,800 XX/100

One Thousand Eight hundred and XX/100 ——————— DOLLARS

BAY BANK
Box 1739 Terminal Annex
Los Angeles, CA 90052

MEMO *Withdrawal*   *Juan Valdez*

⑆122000066⑆ ⑈1400⑈03857⑈01362⑈0016

July 30   Paid Betty Long, office secretary, $350.

VALDEZ REALTY (213) 478-3584   0017

8200 SUNSET BOULEVARD
LOS ANGELES, CA 90028   July 30   200X

PAY TO THE
ORDER OF *Betty Long* $ 350 XX/100

Three Hundred fifty and XX/100 —————————— DOLLARS

BAY BANK
Box 1739 Terminal Annex
Los Angeles, CA 90052

MEMO *Salary – July 16–31*   *Juan Valdez*

⑆122000066⑆ ⑈1400⑈03857⑈01362⑈0017

July   30   Paid Verizon telephone bill, $590.

Verizon   1 Park Place
                                               Los Angeles, CA 90052
                                               (213) 862-8061

Your Statement

In Account with   **VALDEZ REALTY** | Payment
                             8200 Sunset Blvd. | received July
                             Los Angeles, CA 90028 | 30, 200X

Account #09444 710-190

Billing Period: July 1 to July 31

Payments/Adjustments/Deposits Details
Payment Received July 2. Thank you.

                                                            $590.00
                                                           −590.00
                             Monthly rental and changes to service   590.00

Amount now due   _____
Payment due after August 10, 200X $610.75   **Total Due** $590.00

VALDEZ REALTY (213) 478-3584   0018

8200 SUNSET BOULEVARD
LOS ANGELES, CA 90028   *July 30   200X*

PAY TO THE   *Verizon* $ | 590 XX/100
ORDER OF

Five Hundred Ninety and XX/100 ~~~~~~~~~~~~~~~~~~ DOLLARS

BAY BANK
Box 1739 Terminal Annex
Los Angeles, CA 90052

MEMO *July Phone Bill*   *Juan Valdez*

⑈1220006⑈1⑈1400⑈03857⑈0136 2⑈0018

July   30   Advertising bill from *Salem News* for July, $1,400. The bill is to be paid on
                August 2.

Salem News
1 Main St., Los Angeles, CA 90052
(213) 744-1000

INVOICE

SOLD TO: Valdez Realty   **Invoice No.:**   5400
               8200 Sunset Blvd.   **Date:**   July 30, 200X
               Los Angeles, CA 90028   **Due Date:**   August 2, 200X

DATE	DESCRIPTION	AMOUNT
July 30/0X	Advertising in Salem News during July 200X	$1,400.00
		SUBTOTAL 1,400.00
Business Number 944122338		TOTAL $1,400.00

MAKE ALL CHECKS PAYABLE TO SALEM NEWS

Required Work for July

1. Journalize transactions in a general journal (p. 4) and post to ledger accounts.
2. Prepare a trial balance in the first two columns of the worksheet and complete the worksheet using the following adjustment data:

   a. One month's rent had expired.
   b. An inventory shows $90 of office supplies remaining.
   c. Depreciation on office equipment, $100.
   d. Depreciation on automobile, $200.

3. Prepare a July income statement, statement of owner's equity, and balance sheet.
4. From the worksheet, journalize and post adjusting and closing entries (p. 6 of journal).
5. Prepare a post-closing trial balance.

COMPUTERIZED ACCOUNTING APPLICATION FOR VALDEZ REALTY MINI PRACTICE SET (CHAPTER 5)

Closing Process and Post-Closing Trial Balance

Before starting on this assignment, read and complete the tasks discussed in Parts A, B, and F of the Computerized Accounting appendix at the back of this book and complete the Computerized Accounting Application assignments for Chapters 3 and 4.

   This comprehensive review problem requires you to complete the accounting cycle for Valdez Realty twice. This will allow you to review Chapters 1–5 while reinforcing the relationships between all parts of the accounting cycle. By completing two cycles, you will see how the ending June balances in the ledger are used when we accumulate data in July.

PART A: THE JUNE ACCOUNTING CYCLE

On June 1, 2004 Juan Valdez opened a real estate office called Valdez Realty.

Open the Company Data Files

1. Click on the Start button. Point to Programs; point to the Peachtree folder and select Peachtree Complete Accounting. Your desktop may have the Peachtree icon allowing for a quicker entrance into the program.
2. Follow the "Open a File" instructions in Part A of the Computerized Accounting appendix at the back of this book to open **Valdez Realty.**
3. Click on the **Maintain** menu option. Then select **Company Information.** The program will respond by bringing up a dialogue box allowing the user to edit/add information about the company.

How to Add Your Name to the Company Name

4. Click in the **Company Name** entry field at the end of **Valdez Realty.** If it is already highlighted, press the right arrow key. Add a dash and your name "-**Student Name**" to the end of the company name. Click on the **OK** button to return to the Menu Window.

Record June Transactions

5. Record the following journal entries. Enter the **Date** listed for each transaction (you may use the "+" key to advance the date or use the calendar icon next to the field to select the date from a calendar). Enter "Memo" into the **Source** text box for each transaction or accept Peachtree's additional number added to memo by pressing TAB:

2004

Jun.	1	Juan Valdez invested $7,000 cash in the real estate agency along with $3,000 in office equipment.
	1	Rented office space and paid three months' rent in advance, $2,100.
	1	Bought an automobile on account, $12,000.
	4	Purchased office supplies for cash, $300.
	5	Purchased office supplies on account, $150.
	6	Sold a house and collected a $6,000 commission.
	8	Received and paid gas bill, $22.
	15	Paid the salary of the office secretary, $350.
	17	Sold a building lot and earned a commission, $6,500. Expected receipt 7/8/04.
	20	Juan Valdez withdrew $1,000 from the business to pay personal expenses.
	21	Sold a house and collected a $3,500 commission.
	22	Received and paid gas bill, $25.
	24	Paid $600 to repair automobile.
	30	Paid the salary of the office secretary, $350.

30   Received and paid the June telephone bill, $510.

30   Received advertising bill for June, $1,200. The bill is to be paid on 7/2/04.

6. After you have saved the journal entries, close the General Journal; then print the following reports:

    a. General Journal (check figure debit = $44,607)
    b. Trial Balance (check figure debit = $39,350)

    Review your printed reports. If you have made an error in a saved journal entry, correct the error before proceeding.

7. Open the General Journal; then record adjusting journal entries based on the following adjustment data using "Adjusting" in the reference field:

    a. One month's rent has expired
    b. An inventory shows $50 of office supplies remaining.
    c. Depreciation on office equipment, $100
    d. Depreciation on automobile, $200

8. After you have saved the adjusting journal entries, close the General Journal then print the following reports accepting all defaults offered by Peachtree:

    a. General Journal (check figure debit = $46,007)
    b. Trial Balance (check figure debit = $39,650)
    c. General Ledger Report (check figure cash = $11,243)
    d. Income Statement (Net Income = $11,543)
    e. Balance Sheet (Total Capital = $20,543)

    Review your printed reports. If you have made an error in a saved journal entry, use the procedures detailed in step 18 from Chapter 3 to make any necessary corrections. Reprint all reports if corrections are made.

9. Computerized Accounting systems maintain all of it's input in compartments called periods. Some systems identify these periods with the name of the month or with a simple numeric designation such as 1, 2, 3, et al. Peachtree currently has Valdez Realty in Period 6, the June period. You can see this in the status bar at the bottom of the screen. This is because Valdez has elected to use the calendar year for his Fiscal year. We will need to change the current period to the July period prior to inputting the July transactions in part B of this workshop. You must always tell Peachtree to move to the next accounting period when starting on the transactions for a new month. This process is the equivalent of "Closing" in a manual accounting system although the temporary accounts are not really closed until the end of the year.

10. It is always wise to backup accounting data at the end of each month, saving it into a file that will be saved until the end of the year. We will use Peachtree's Backup feature to do this. Click on the Company Window **File** menu; select **Backup,** use a filename such as "ValdezJune" to make sure you can recognize what the backup represents. Click on **OK.**

11. We must now advance the period to prepare Peachtree for the July transactions.

    - Using your mouse, click on **System** from the **Tasks** menu. Select **Change Accounting Periods.** You are presented with the screen on p. 220.
    - Using the menu, select period 7 - Jul 1, 2004 to Jul 31, 2004 and click on **OK.**
    - You will be asked whether you wish to print reports before continuing. Since we have already printed our reports, we can answer "No".
    - Note that the status bar at the bottom of the screen now reflects that you are in period 7.

    ### Period 7 - 7/1/04 to 7/31/04

12. Click on the Company Window **File** menu; then click on Exit to end the current work session and return to your Windows desktop or continue with step 3 below.

Sidebar labels:

Print Working Reports

Record June Adjusting Entries

Print Final Statements

Closing the Accounting Records

Make a Backup Copy of June Accounting Records

Advancing the Period

Exit the Program

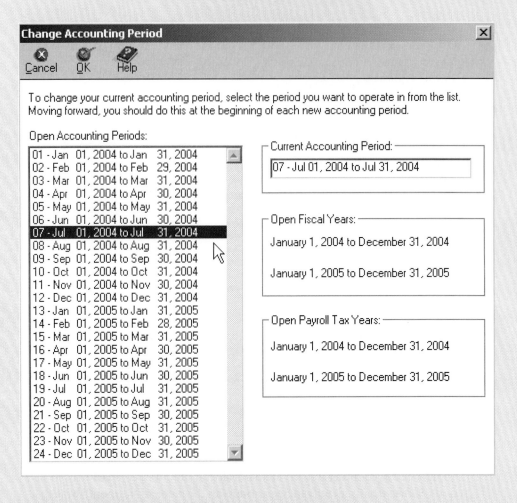

PART B: THE JULY ACCOUNTING CYCLE

1. Start Peachtree Complete Accounting.
2. Open **Valdez Realty.**

Open the Company Data Files

3. Record the following journal entries. Enter the **Date** listed for each transaction (you may use the "+" key to advance the date or use the calendar icon next to the field to select the date from a calendar). Enter "Memo" into the **Source** text box for each transaction or accept Peachtree's additional number added to memo by pressing TAB:

Record July Transactions

2004

Jul. 1 Purchased additional office supplies on account, $700.

2 Paid advertising bill for June, $1,200.

3 Sold a house and collected a commission, $6,600.

6 Received and paid gas bill, $29.

8 Collected commission from sale of building lot on 6/17/04 (collected our accounts receivable).

12 Paid $300 to send employees to realtor's workshop.

15 Paid the salary of the office secretary, $350.

17 Sold a house and earned a commission of $2,400. Expected receipt on 8/10/04.

18 Sold a building lot and collected a commission of $7,000.

22 Sent a check for $40 to help sponsor a local road race to aid the public. (This is not to be considered an advertising expense, but it is a business expense.)

24 Paid for repairs to automobile, $590.

28 Juan Valdez withdrew $1,800 from the business to pay personal expenses.

30 Paid the salary of the office secretary, $350.

30 Received and paid the July telephone bill, $590.

30 Received advertising bill for July, $1,400. The bill is to be paid on 8/2/04.

4. After you have saved the journal entries, close the General Journal; then print the following reports:

Print Working Reports

  a. General Journal (check figure debit = $29,849)
  b. Trial Balance (check figure debit = $56,550)

Review your printed reports. If you have made an error in a saved journal entry, correct the error before proceeding.

5. Open the General Journal; then record adjusting journal entries based on the following adjustment data using "Adjusting" in the reference field:

Record July Adjusting Entries

  a. One month's rent has expired.
  b. An inventory shows $90 of office supplies remaining.
  c. Depreciation on office equipment, $100.
  d. Depreciation on automobile, $200.

6. After you have saved the adjusting journal entries, close the General Journal then print the following reports accepting all defaults offered by Peachtree:

Print Final Statements

  a. General Journal (check figure debit = $31,509)
  b. Trial Balance (check figure debit = $56,850)
  c. General Ledger Report (check figure cash = $26,094)
  d. Income Statement (Net Income = $10,691)
  e. Balance Sheet (Total Capital = $29,434)

Review your printed reports. If you have made an error in a saved journal entry, use the procedures detailed in step 18 from Chapter 3 to make any necessary corrections. Reprint all reports if corrections are made. Note how the income statement shows both current month and year-to-date totals.

7. Computerized Accounting systems maintain all of it's input in compartments called periods. Some systems identify these periods with the name of the month or with a simple numeric designation such as 1, 2, 3, et al. Peachtree currently has Valdez Realty in Period 7, the July period. You can see this in the status bar at the bottom of the screen. This is because Valdez has elected to use the calendar year for his Fiscal year. We will need to change the current period to the August period prior to inputting the next month's transactions. You must always tell Peachtree to move to the next accounting period when starting on the transactions for a new month. This process is the equivalent of "Closing" in a manual accounting system although the temporary accounts are not really closed until the end of the year.

Closing the Accounting Records

8. It is always wise to backup accounting data at the end of each month, saving it into a file that will be saved until the end of the year. We will use Peachtree's Backup feature to do this. Click on the Company Window **File** menu; select **Backup**, use a filename such as "ValdezJuly" to make sure you can recognize what the backup represents.

Make a Backup Copy of July Accounting Records

9. We must now advance the period to prepare Peachtree for the August transactions.

Advancing the Period

  - Using your mouse, click on **System** from the **Tasks** menu. Select **Change Accounting Periods.**
  - Using the pull down menu, select period 8 - Aug 1, 2001 to Aug 31, 2001 and click on **OK.**
  - You will be asked whether you wish to print reports before continuing. Since we have already printed our reports, we can answer "No".
  - Note that the status bar at the bottom of the screen now reflects that you are in period 8.

10. Click on the Company Window **File** menu; then click on **Exit** to end the current work session and return to your Windows desktop.

Exit the Program

CHAPTER 6

Banking Procedures and Control of Cash

Last week you opened your first checking account at a local bank by depositing your first check from working at your school's sports arena. It feels good to be working and making money to help with school expenses. Today you received your first credit card bill in the mail, along with a check from your parents for monthly school expenses. You plan to deposit the check from your parents and then write a check to pay your credit card bill. You know that you will deposit more into your checking account than you will withdraw by writing the check, but exactly how much do you have left to spend? You won't know the answer until you have reconciled your checking account.

You share something in common with virtually every company in business today. Every company needs to know how much cash it has to spend at any point in time. The only way a company can answer this question is to reconcile its accounts.

In the last five chapters we have discussed the accounting equation and the nine steps in the accounting cycle. In this chapter we turn our attention to banking procedures and the control of cash. We will learn about bank statements and how to reconcile a bank account. We will also discuss how a company pays for small amounts such as postage and small supplies by using a petty cash fund. Knowing the basics of how a bank functions and a company maintains control over cash is important to your understanding of the world of business and the role accounting plays in it.

Learning Objectives

- Depositing, writing, and endorsing checks for a checking account. (p. 224)

- Reconciling a bank statement. (p. 230)

- Establishing and replenishing a petty cash fund; setting up an auxiliary petty cash record. (p. 235)

- Establishing and replenishing a change fund. (p. 239)

- Handling transactions involving cash short and over. (p. 240)

> The internal control policies of a company will depend on things such as number of employees, company size, sources of cash, and usage of the Internet.

In the first five chapters of this book, we analyzed the accounting cycle for businesses that perform personal services (for example, word processing or legal services). In this chapter, we turn our attention to Debbie's Wholesale Stationery Company, a merchandising company that earns revenue by selling goods (or merchandise) to customers. When Debbie found that her business was increasing, she became concerned that she was not monitoring the business's cash closely enough. To remedy the situation, Debbie and her accountant decided to develop a system of **internal controls.**

After studying the situation carefully, Debbie began a series of procedures that were to be followed by all company employees. The new company policies that Debbie's Wholesale Stationery Company put into place are as follows:

1. Responsibilities and duties of employees will be divided. For example, the person receiving the cash, whether at the register or by opening the mail, will not record this information into the accounting records. The accountant will not be handling the cash receipts.

2. All cash receipts of Debbie's Wholesale will be deposited into the bank the same day they arrive.

3. All cash payments will be made by check (except petty cash, which is discussed later in this chapter).

4. Employees will be rotated. This change allows workers to become acquainted with the work of others as well as to prepare for a possible changeover of jobs.

5. Debbie Lawrence will sign all checks after receiving authorization to pay from the departments concerned.

6. At time of payment, all supporting invoices or documents will be stamped paid. The stamp will show when the invoice or document is paid as well as the number of the check used.

7. All checks will be prenumbered. This change will control the use of checks and make it difficult to use a check fraudulently without its being revealed at some point.

8. Use of Internet online banking will be continually evaluated.

Now let's look at how Debbie's Wholesale implemented these policies.

Learning Unit 6-1   Bank Procedures, Checking Accounts, and Bank Reconciliations

Before Debbie's Wholesale opened on April 1, 200X, Debbie had a meeting at Security National Bank to discuss the steps in opening up and using a checking account for the company.

OPENING A CHECKING ACCOUNT

> Purpose of a signature card.

The bank manager gave Debbie a signature card to fill out. The signature card included space for signature(s), business and home addresses, references, type of account, and so forth. Because Debbie would be signing all the checks for her company, she was the only employee who had to sign the card. The bank keeps the signature card in its files. When checks are presented for payment, the bank checks it to validate Debbie's signature. Such checking helps avoid possible forgeries.

Once the account was opened, Debbie received a set of checks and deposit tickets that were preprinted with the business's name, address, and account number (see Fig. 6-1). Debbie's Wholesale was to use the deposit tickets when it received cash or checks from any source and deposited them into the checking account.

On a deposit ticket, check amounts are listed separately along with the code number of city and bank on which they are drawn. The code can be found in the upper right corner of a check (see Fig. 6-3 on p. 228). The top part of the fraction (53-393) is known as the *American Bankers' Association Transit Number:* 53 identifies the large city or state the bank is located in; 393 identifies the bank above the amount of the check.

The lower part of the fraction (113) is split in two: 1 represents the First Federal Reserve District; 13 is a routing number used by the Federal Reserve bank. This is the way the code number appears on a check.

Deposit tickets usually come in duplicate. The bank keeps one copy and the company keeps the other so it can verify that the items making up the deposit have

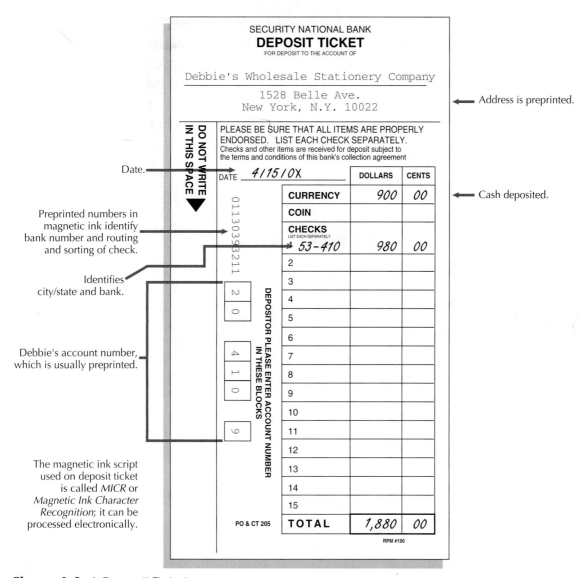

Figure 6-1 A Deposit Ticket

actually been deposited correctly. The bank manager told Debbie that she could give the deposits to a bank teller or she could use an automated teller machine (ATM). The ATM could also be used for withdrawing cash, transferring funds, or paying bills.

Often, Debbie makes her deposits after business hours, when the bank is closed. At those times, she puts the deposit into a locked bag (provided by the bank) and places the bag in the night depository. The bank will credit Debbie's account in the morning, when the deposit is processed. All payments of money are by written check (except petty cash), and all money (checks) received is deposited in the bank account.

Many checking accounts earn interest. For our purposes, however, we assume that the checking account for Debbie's Wholesale does not pay interest. Also assume that the checking account has a monthly service charge and that there is no individual charge for each check written.

> When a bank credits your account, it is increasing the balance.

CHECK ENDORSEMENT

Checks have to be *endorsed* (signed) by the person to whom the check is made out before they can be deposited or cashed. **Endorsement** is the signing or stamping of one's name on the back left-hand side of the check. This signature means that the payee has transferred the right to deposit or cash the check to someone else (the bank). The bank can then collect the money from the person or company that issued the check.

> Endorsements can be made by using a rubber stamp instead of a hand-written signature.

Three different types of endorsement can be used (see Fig. 6-2). The first is a *blank endorsement*. A blank endorsement does not specify that a particular person or firm must endorse it. It can be further endorsed by someone else. The bank will pay

Figure 6-2
Types of Check Endorsement

Types of Check Endorsement

Debbie Lawrence
204109

Blank Endorsement

A signature on the back left side of a check of the person or firm the check is payable to. This check can be *further* endorsed by someone else; the bank will give the money to the last person who signs the check. This type of endorsement is not very safe. If the check is lost, anyone who picks it up can sign it and get the money.

Pay to the order of
Security National Bank.

Debbie's Wholesale Stationery Co.
204109

Full Endorsement

This type of endorsement is safer than a simple signature, because the person or company signing (or stamping) the back of the check indicates the name of the company or person to whom the check is to be paid. Only the person or company named in the endorsement can transfer the check to someone else.

Payable to the order of
Security National Bank
for deposit only.

Debbie's Wholesale Stationery Co.
204109

Restrictive Endorsement

This endorsement is the safest for businesses. Debbie's Wholesale stamps the back of the check so that it must be deposited in the firm's account. This endorsement limits any further use of the check (it can only be deposited in the specified account).

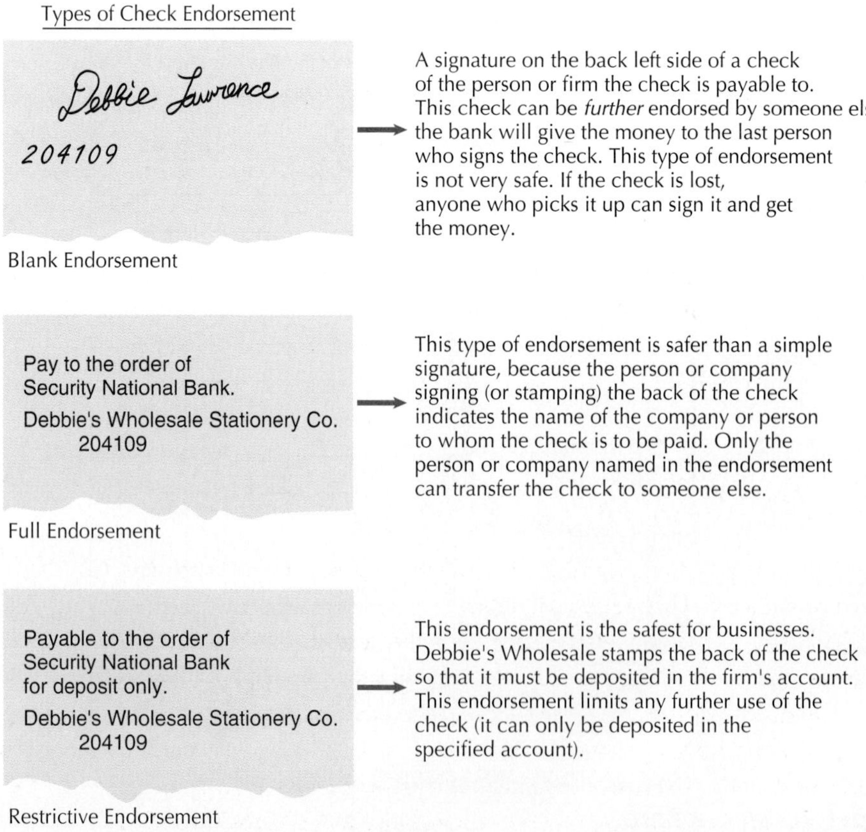

the last person who signs the check. This type of endorsement is not very safe. If the check is lost, the person who finds it can sign it and get the money.

The second type of endorsement is a *full endorsement.* The person or company signing (or stamping) the back of the check indicates the name of the company or the person to whom the check is to be paid. Only the person or company named in the endorsement can transfer the check to someone else.

Restrictive endorsements are the third type of endorsement. This endorsement is the safest one for businesses. Debbie's Wholesale stamps the back of the check so that it must be deposited in the firm's account. This stamp limits any further use of the check.

> The regulations require the endorsement to be within the top 1½ inches to speed up the check clearing process.

THE CHECKBOOK

When Debbie opened her business's checking account, she received checks. These checks could be used to buy things for the business or to pay bills or salaries.

A **check** is a written order signed by a **drawer** (the person who writes the check) instructing a **drawee** (the person who pays the check) to pay a specific sum of money to the **payee** (the person to whom the check is payable). Figure 6-3 shows a check issued by Debbie's Wholesale Stationery Company. Debbie Lawrence is the drawer, Security National Bank is the drawee, and Joe Francis Company is the payee.

> Drawer:
> One who writes the check.

> Drawee:
> One who pays money to payee.

> Payee:
> One to whom the check is payable.

Look at the check in Figure 6-3. Notice that certain things, such as the company's name and address and the check number, are preprinted. Other things you should notice are (1) the line drawn after $\frac{XX}{100}$ which is to fill up the empty space and ensure that the amount cannot be changed, and (2) the word *and,* which should be used only to differentiate between dollars and cents.

Figure 6-3 includes a check stub. The check stub is used to record transactions, and it is kept for future reference. The information found on the stub includes the beginning balance ($7,100), the amount of any deposits ($784), the total amount in the account ($7,884), the amount of the check being written ($4,000), and the ending balance ($3,884). The check stub should be filled out before the check is written.

If the written amount on the check does not match the amount expressed in figures, Security National Bank may pay the amount written in words, return the check unpaid, or contact the drawer to see what was meant.

Many companies use checkwriting machines to type out the information on the check. These machines prevent people from making fraudulent changes on handwritten checks.

> Banking on the Internet is expanding rapidly.

During the same time period, in-company records must be kept for all transactions affecting Debbie's Wholesale Stationery Company's checkbook balance. Figure 6-4 (p. 229) shows these records. Note that the bank deposits ($14,324) minus the checks written ($6,994) give an ending checkbook balance of $7,330.

MONTHLY RECORDKEEPING: THE BANK'S STATEMENT OF ACCOUNT AND IN-COMPANY RECORDS

Each month, Security National Bank will send Debbie's Wholesale Stationery Company a Statement of Account. This statement reflects all the activity in the account during that period. It begins with the beginning balance of the account at the start of the month, along with the checks the bank has paid and any deposits received (see Fig. 6-5, p. 229). Any other charges or additions to the bank balance are indicated by codes found on the statement. All checks that have been paid by the bank are sent back to Debbie's Wholesale. These are called **cancelled checks** because they have been processed by the bank and are no longer negotiable. The ending balance in Figure 6-5 is $6,919.

> Figure 6.5 shows one format for a bank statement. Different banks use different formats.

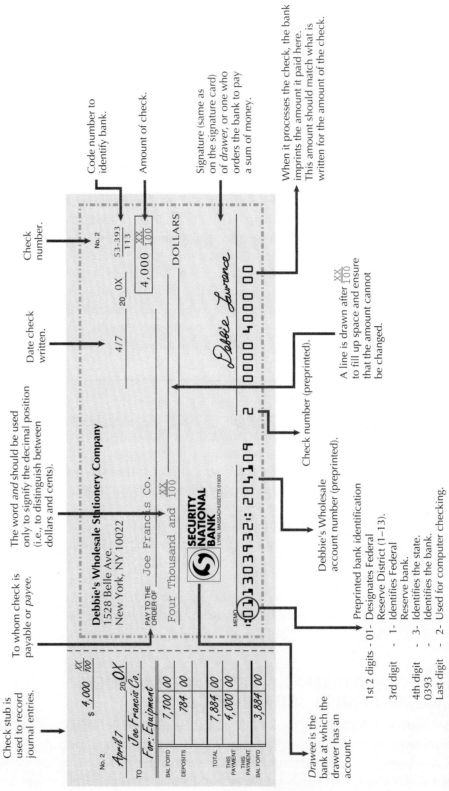

Figure 6-3 A Company Check

Figure 6-4
Transactions Affecting
Checkbook Balance

Bank Deposits Made for April

Date of Deposit	Amount	Received From
Apr. 1	$ 8,000	Debbie Lawrence, Capital
4	784	Check—Hal's Clothing
16	1,880	Cash sales/Check—Bevans Company
22	1,960	Check—Roe Company
27	500	Sale of equipment
30	1,200	Cash sales
Total deposits for month:	$14,324	

Checks Written for Month of April

Date	Check No.	Payment To	Amount	Description
Apr. 2	1	Peter Blum	$ 900	Insurance paid in advance
7	2	Joe Francis Co.	4,000	Paid equipment
9	3	Rick Flo Co.	800	Cash purchases
12	4	Thorpe Co.	594	Paid purchases
28	5	Payroll	700	Salaries
		Total amount of checks written:	$ 6,994	

Cash/checks deposited	$14,324
Checks paid	−6,994
Balance in company checkbook	$ 7,330

> In the next section we will show a more comprehensive bank statement.

SECURITY NATIONAL BANK

```
Debbie's Wholesale Stationery Company      ACCOUNT
1528 Belle Ave.                            NUMBER    20   410   9
New York, New York  10022

                                           CLOSING
                                           PERIOD    4/30/0X

                                                      AMOUNT
                                                      ENCLOSED $_____

RETURN THIS PORTION WITH YOUR PAYMENT IF YOU ARE NOT USING OUR AUTOMATIC PAYMENT PLAN    Address Correction on Reverse Side ☐
```

CHECKING ACCOUNT

ON	YOUR BALANCE WAS	NO.	WE SUBTRACTED CHECKS TOTALING	LESS SERVICE CHARGE	NO.	WE ADDED DEPOSITS OF	MAKING YOUR PRESENT BALANCE
	0	3	5,700.00	5.00	5	12,624.00	6,919.00

DATE	CHECKS • WITHDRAWALS • PAYMENTS			DEPOSITS • INTEREST • ADVANCES	BALANCE
4/1				8,000.00	8,000.00
4/2	900				7,100.00
4/4				784.00	7,884.00
4/7	4,000				3,884.00
4/9	800				3,084.00
4/16				1,880.00	4,964.00
4/22				1,960.00	6,924.00
4/25	5.00 SC				6,919.00

Figure 6-5 A Bank Statement

THE BANK RECONCILIATION PROCESS

The problem is that the ending bank balance of $6,919 does not agree with the amount in Debbie's checkbook, $7,330, or the balance in the cash amount in the ledger, $7,330. Such differences are caused partly by the time a bank takes to process a company's transactions. A company records a transaction when it occurs. A bank cannot record a deposit until it receives the funds, and it cannot pay a check until the check is presented by the payee. In addition, the bank statement will report fees and transactions that the company did not know about.

Debbie's accountant has to find out why there is a $411 difference between the balances and how the records can be brought into balance. The process of reconciling the bank balance on the bank statement versus the company's checkbook balance is called a **bank reconciliation.** Bank reconciliations involve several steps, including calculating the deposits in transit and the outstanding checks. The bank reconciliation usually is done on the back of the **bank statement** (see Fig. 6-6). It can also be done by computer software, however.

> Online banking and computer software has made the reconciliation process even easier.

Deposits in Transit

In comparing the list of deposits received by the bank with the checkbook, the accountant notices that the two deposits made on April 27 and 30 for $500 and $1,200 were not on the bank's statement. The accountant realizes that to prepare this statement, the bank only included information about Debbie's Wholesale Stationery up to April 25. These two deposits made by Debbie were not shown on the monthly bank statement because they arrived at the bank after the statement was printed. Thus, timing becomes a consideration in the reconciliation process. The deposits not yet added to the bank balance are called **deposits in transit**. These two deposits need to be added to the bank balance shown on the bank statement.

Figure 6-6

Bank Reconciliation Using the Back of the Bank Statement

> Keep in mind that both the bank and the depositor can make mistakes that will not be discovered until the reconciliation process.

CHECKS OUTSTANDING				
NUMBER	AMOUNT		1. Enter balance shown on this statement	6,919 00
4	594 00		2. If you have made deposits since the date of this statement add them to the above balance.	
5	700 00			
				1,700 00
			3. SUBTOTAL	8,619 00
			4. Deduct total of checks outstanding	1,294 00
			5. ADJUSTED BALANCE This should agree with your checkbook.	
TOTAL OF CHECKS OUTSTANDING	1,294 00			7,325 00

TO VERIFY YOUR CHECKING BALANCE
1. Sort checks by number or by date issued and compare with your check stubs and prior outstanding list. Make certain all checks paid have been recorded in your checkbook. If any of your checks were not included with this statement, list the numbers and amounts under "CHECKS OUTSTANDING."
2. Deduct the Service Charge as shown on the statement from your checkbook balance.
3. Review copies of charge advices included with this statement and check for proper entry in your checkbook.

IF THE ADJUSTED BALANCE DOES NOT AGREE WITH YOUR CHECKBOOK BALANCE, THE FOLLOWING SUGGESTIONS ARE OFFERED FOR YOUR ASSISTANCE.
- Recheck additions and subtractions in your checkbook and figures to the left.
- Make certain checkbook balances have been carried forward properly.
- Verify deposits recorded on statement against deposits entered in checkbook.
- Compare amount on each checkbook stub.

Debbie's checkbook is not affected, because the two deposits have already been added to its balance. The bank has no way of knowing that the deposits are coming until they are received.

Outstanding Checks

The first thing the accountant does when the bank statement is received is put the checks in numerical order (1, 2, 3, etc.). In doing so, the accountant notices that two payments were not made by the bank and two checks, no. 4 and no. 5, were not returned by the bank.

Debbie's books showed that these two checks had been deducted from the checkbook balance. These **outstanding checks,** however, had not yet been presented to the bank for payment or deducted from the bank balance. When these checks do reach the bank, the bank will reduce the amount of the balance.

Service Charges

Debbie's accountant also notices a bank service charge of $5. Thus, Debbie's checkbook balance should be lowered by $5.

Nonsufficient Funds

An **NSF (nonsufficient funds)** check is a check that has been returned because the drawer did not have enough money in its account to pay the check. Accountants are continually on the lookout for NSF (nonsufficient funds) checks. If there is an NSF check, it means that there is less money in the checking account than was thought. Debbie's Wholesale will have to (1) lower the checkbook balance and (2) try to collect the amount from the customer. The bank would notify Debbie's Wholesale of an NSF (or other deductions) check by a **debit memorandum.** Think of a debit memorandum as a deduction from the depositor's balance.

If the bank acts as a collecting agent for Debbie's Wholesale, say in collecting notes, it will charge Debbie a small fee and the net amount collected will be added to Debbie's bank balance. The bank will send to Debbie a **credit memorandum** verifying the increase in the depositor's balance.

A journal entry is also needed to bring the ledger accounts of Cash and Service Charge expense up-to-date. Any adjustment to the checkbook balance results in a journal entry. The entry in Figure 6-7 was made to accomplish this step:

Apr.	30	Service Charge Expense			5	00			
		Cash					5	00	
		Bank service charge for April							

Figure 6-7
Service Charge
Journalized

Before we look at a more comprehensive bank statement, let's look at trends in banking.

TRENDS IN BANKING

Electronic Funds Transfer

Many financial institutions have developed or are developing ways to transfer funds electronically, without the use of paper checks. Such systems are called **electronic funds transfers (EFT).** Most EFTs are established to save money and avoid theft.

Deposits in transit: These unrecorded deposits could result if a deposit were placed in a night depository on the last day of the month.

Checks #4 and #5 are outstanding.

Checks outstanding are checks drawn by the depositor but not yet presented to the bank for payment by the payee.

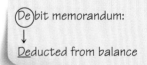

*Debit memorandum:
↓
Deducted from balance*

Credit memorandum: Addition to balance.

Adjustments to the checkbook balance must be journalized and posted. These steps keep the depositor's ledger accounts (especially Cash) up-to-date. This charge could be recorded as a miscellaneous expense.

An automatic payroll deposit is an example of an EFT. It works as follows: The company asks its employees if they would like their paychecks deposited automatically into their checking accounts. Employees who agree to do so are asked to sign an authorization form. The bank, upon receiving computer-coded payroll data, adds each worker's payroll amount to his or her checking account. Employees who do not sign the authorization continue to get paper checks that they must cash themselves.

Another good example is the automatic teller machine (ATM). In some states, ATMs now issue postage stamps, railroad tickets, and grocery coupons. Debit cards are still another example of an EFT. If a customer buys a service or a product with a debit card, the amount of the purchase is deducted directly from the customer's bank account. The Internet continues to expand online banking.

Check Truncation (Safekeeping)

Some banks do not return cancelled checks to the depositor but use a procedure called check truncation or safekeeping. The bank holds a cancelled check for a specific period of time (usually 90 days) and then keeps a microfilm copy handy and destroys the original check. In Texas, for example, some credit unions and savings and loan institutions do not send back checks. Instead, the check date, number, and amount are listed on the bank statement. If the customer needs a copy of a check, the bank will provide the check or a photocopy for a small fee. (Photocopies are accepted as evidence in Internal Revenue Service tax returns and audits.)

Truncation cuts down on the amount of "paper" that is returned to customers and thus provides substantial cost savings. It is estimated that over 80 million checks are written each day in the United States.

Example of a More Comprehensive Bank Statement

The bank reconciliation of Debbie's Stationery was not as complicated as it is for many companies, even using today's computer technology. Let's look at a reconciliation for Matty's Supermarket (Figs. 6-8, 6-9), which is based on the following:

Matty's checkbook balance	$13,176.84
Bank balance	23,726.04
Leased space to Subway	8,456.00
Leased space to Dunkin Donuts	3,616.12
The rental payment is transferred by electronic transfer	
Matty pays a health insurance payment each month by electronic transfer	1,444.00
Deposits in transit 5/30	6,766.52
Checks outstanding	
ck # 738 $1,144.00	
739 1,277.88	
740 332.00	
741 812.56	
742 1,834.12	
Check # 734 was overstated	1,440.00

Note in Figure 6-9 (p. 234) that each adjustment to Matty's checkbook is the reconciliation process that would result in general journal entries.

Figure 6-8
Bank Statement for
Matty's Supermarket

Ranger Bank
1 Left St.
Marblehead, MA 01945

ACCOUNT STATEMENT

Matty's Supermarket
20 Sullivan St.
Lynn, MA 01917

Checking Account: 775800061

Checking Account Summary as of 6/30/0X

Beginning Balance	Total Deposits	Total Withdrawals	Service Charge	Ending Balance
$26,224.48	$17,410.56	$19,852.00	$57.00	$23,726.04

Checking Accounts Transactions

Deposits	Date	Amount
Deposit	6/05	4,000.00
Deposit	6/05	448.00
Deposit	6/09	778.40
EFT leasing: Dunkin Donuts	6/18	3,616.12
EFT leasing: Subway	6/27	8,456.00
Interest	6/30	112.04

Charges	Date	Amount
Service charge: Check printing	6/30	57.00
EFT: Blue Cross/Blue Shield	6/21	1,444.00
NSF	6/21	208.00

Checks

Daily Balance

Number	Date	Amount		Date	Balance		Date	Balance
401	6/07	400.00		5/28	26,224.48		6/18	21,059.00
733	6/13	12,000.00		6/05	30,464.48		6/21	19,615.00
734	6/13	600.00		6/07	29,664.48		6/28	28,071.00
735	6/11	400.00		6/09	30,442.88		6/30	23,726.04
736	6/18	400.00		6/11	30,042.88			
737	6/30	4,400.00		6/13	17,442.88			

Learning Unit 6-1 Review

AT THIS POINT you should be able to

- Define and explain the need for deposit tickets. (p. 225)
- Explain where the American Bankers' Association transit number is located on the check and what its purpose is. (p. 225)
- List as well as compare and contrast the three common types of check endorsement. (p. 226)
- Explain the structure of a check. (p. 228)
- Define and state the purpose of a bank statement. (p. 230)
- Explain deposits in transit, checks outstanding, service charge, and NSF. (p. 231)
- Explain the difference between a debit memorandum and a credit memorandum. (p. 232)

Figure 6-9
Bank Reconciliation for
Matty's Supermarket

MATTY'S SUPERMARKET Bank Reconciliation as of June 30, 2004			
Checkbook balance		**Bank balance**	
Matty's checkbook balance	$13,176.84	Bank balance	$23,726.04
Add:		Add:	
EFT leasing: Dunkin Donuts		Deposits in transit, 5/30	6,766.52
$ 3,616.12			$30,492.56
EFT leasing: Subway			
8,456.00			
Interest	112.04		
Error: Overstated			
check No. 734	1,440.00		
	$26,801.00		
Deduct:		Deduct:	
Service charge	$ 57.00	Outstanding checks:	
NSF check	208.00	No. 738 $1,144.00	
EFT health insurance		No. 739 1,277.88	
payment	1,444.00	1,709.00	No. 740 332.00
		No. 741 812.56	
		No. 742 1,834.12	5,400.56
Reconciled balance	$25,092.00	Reconciled balance	$25,092.00

🔹 Explain how to do a bank reconciliation. (p. 230)
🔹 Explain electronic funds transfer and check truncation. (p. 231)

SELF-REVIEW QUIZ 6-1

(The blank forms you need are on page 191 of the *Study Guide and Working Papers.*)

Indicate, by placing an X under it, the heading that describes the appropriate action for each of the following situations:

Situation	Add to Bank Balance	Deduct from Bank Balance	Add to Checkbook Balance	Deduct from Checkbook Balance
1. Check printing charge			x	
2. Deposits in transit	x			
3. NSF check				
4. A $75 check was written and recorded by the company as $85				
5. Proceeds of a note collected by the bank				
6. Check outstanding				
7. Forgot to record ATM withdrawal				
8. Forgot to record direct depossit of a payroll check				

SOLUTION TO SELF-REVIEW QUIZ 6-1

Situation	Add to Bank Balance	Deduct from Bank Balance	Add to Checkbook Balance	Deduct from Checkbook Balance
1				X
2	X			
3				X
4			X	
5			X	
6		X		
7				X
8			X	

> *Quiz Tip:*
> Deposits in transit are added to the bank balance, whereas checks outstanding are subtracted from the bank balance.

Learning Unit 6-2　The Establishment of Petty Cash and Change Funds

Debbie realized how time-consuming and expensive it would be to write checks for small amounts to pay for postage, small supplies, and so forth, so she set up a **petty cash fund**. Similarly, she established a *change fund* to make cash transactions more convenient. This unit explains how to manage petty cash and change funds.

> Petty Cash is an asset on the balance sheet.

SETTING UP THE PETTY CASH FUND

The *petty cash fund* is an account dedicated to paying small day-to-day expenses. These petty cash expenses are recorded in an auxiliary record and later summarized, journalized, and posted. Debbie estimated that the company would need a fund of $60 to cover small expenditures during the month of May. This petty cash was not expected to last longer than one month. She gave one of her employees responsibility for overseeing the fund. This person is called the *custodian*.

Debbie named her office manager, John Sullivan, as custodian. In other companies, the cashier or secretary may be in charge of petty cash. Check no. 6 was drawn to the order of the custodian and cashed to establish the fund. John keeps the petty cash fund in a small tin box in the office safe.

Shown here is the transaction analysis chart for the establishment of a $60 petty cash fund, which would be journalized on May 1, 200X, as shown in Figure 6-10.

> The check for $60 is drawn to the order of the custodian and is cashed, and the proceeds are turned over to John Sullivan, the custodian.

> Petty Cash is an asset, which is established by writing a new check. The Petty Cash account is debited only once unless a greater or lesser amount of petty cash is needed on a regular basis.

Accounts Affected	Category	↑ ↓	Rules
Petty Cash	Asset	↑	Dr.
Cash (checks)	Asset	↓	Cr.

Note that the new asset called Petty Cash, which was created by writing check no. 6, reduced the asset Cash. In reality, the total assets stay the same; what has occurred is a shift from the asset Cash (check no. 6) to a new asset account called Petty Cash.

GENERAL JOURNAL					Page 1
Date	Account Title and Description	PR	Dr.	Cr.	
200X May 1	Petty Cash		60 00		
	Cash			60 00	
	Establishment				

Figure 6-10 Establishing Petty Cash

The Petty Cash account is not debited or credited again if the size of the fund is not changed. If the $60 fund is used up quickly, the fund should be increased. If the fund is too large, the Petty Cash account should be reduced. We take a closer look at this when we discuss replenishment of petty cash.

MAKING PAYMENTS FROM THE PETTY CASH FUND

John Sullivan has the responsibility for filling out a petty cash voucher for each cash payment made from the petty cash fund. The petty cash vouchers are numbered in sequence.

Note that when the voucher (shown in Fig. 6-11) is completed, it will include

- The voucher number (which will be in sequence).
- The date.
- The person or organization to whom the payment was made.
- The amount of payment.
- The reason for payment: in this case, cleaning.
- The signature of the person who approved the payment.
- The signature of the person who received the payment from petty cash.
- The account to which the expense will be charged.

The completed vouchers are placed in the petty cash box. No matter how many vouchers John Sullivan fills out, *the total of (1) the vouchers in the box and (2) the cash on hand should equal the original amount of petty cash with which the fund was established ($60).*

Figure 6-11
Petty Cash Voucher

Petty Cash Voucher No. 1

Date: May 2, 200X   Amount: $3.00
Paid To: Al's Cleaning
For: Cleaning

Approved By: *John Sullivan*

Payment Received By: *Debbie Lawrence*

Debit Account No.: 619

Date	Voucher No.	Description	Receipts	Payments	Category of Payments				
					Postage Expense	Delivery Expense	Sundry		
							Account	Amount	
200X May 1		Establishment	60 00						
2	1	Cleaning		3 00			Cleaning	3 00	
5	2	Postage		9 00	9 00				
8	3	First Aid		15 00			Misc.	15 00	
9	4	Delivery		6 00		6 00			
14	5	Delivery		15 00		15 00			
27	6	Postage		6 00	6 00				
		Total	60 00	54 00	15 00	21 00		18 00	

Figure 6-12 Auxiliary Petty Cash Record

Assume that at the end of May the following items are documented by petty cash vouchers in the petty cash box as having been paid by John Sullivan:

200X
May 2   Cleaning package, $3.00.
        5   Postage stamps, $9.00.
        8   First-aid supplies, $15.00.
        9   Delivery expense, $6.00.
        14 Delivery expense, $15.00.
        27 Postage stamps, $6.00.

John records this information in the **auxiliary petty cash record** shown in Figure 6-12. It is not a required record but an aid to John, an auxiliary record that is not essential but is quite helpful as part of the petty cash system. You may want to think of the auxiliary petty cash record as an optional worksheet. Let's look at how to replenish the petty cash fund.

HOW TO REPLENISH THE PETTY CASH FUND

No postings are done from the auxiliary book because it is not a journal. At some point the summarized information found in the auxiliary petty cash record is used as a basis for a journal entry in the general journal and eventually posted to appropriate ledger accounts to reflect up-to-date balances.

This $54 of expenses (see Fig. 6-12) is recorded in the general journal (Fig. 6-13 on p. 238) and a new check, no. 17, for $54 is cashed and returned to John Sullivan. In replenishment, old expenses are updated in the journal and ledger to show where money has gone. The order is auxiliary before replenishment. The petty cash box now once again reflects $60 cash. The old vouchers that were used are stamped to indicate that they have been processed and the fund replenished.

Note that in the replenishment process the debits are a summary of the totals (except sundry, because individual items are different) of expenses or other items from the auxiliary petty cash record. Posting these specific expenses will ensure that the expenses will not be understated on the income statement. The credit to Cash allows us to draw a check for $54 to put money back in the petty cash box. The $60 in

A new check is written in the replenishment process, which is payable to the custodian, and is cashed by John, and the cash is placed in the petty cash box.

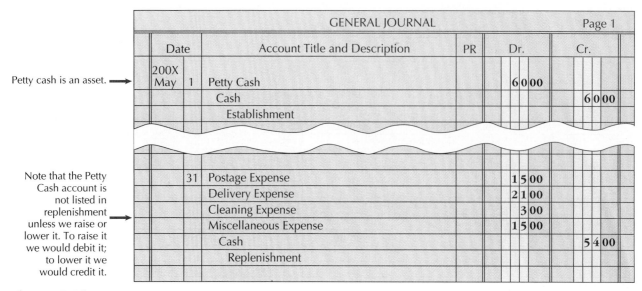

Petty cash is an asset. →

Note that the Petty Cash account is not listed in replenishment unless we raise or lower it. To raise it we would debit it; to lower it we would credit it. →

Figure 6-13 Establishment and Replenishment of Petty Cash Fund

the box now agrees with the Petty Cash account balance. The end result is that our petty cash box is filled, and we have justified for which accounts the petty cash money was spent. Think of replenishment as a single, summarizing entry.

Remember that if at some point the petty cash fund is to be greater than $60, a check can be written that will increase Petty Cash and decrease Cash. If the Petty Cash account balance is to be reduced, we can credit or reduce Petty Cash. For our present purpose, however, Petty Cash will remain at $60.

The auxiliary petty cash record after replenishment would look as shown in Figure 6-14 (keep in mind no postings are made from the auxiliary). Figure 6-15 may help you put the sequence together.

Before concluding this unit, let's look at how Debbie will handle setting up a change fund and problems with cash shortages and overages.

AUXILIARY PETTY CASH RECORD

Date	Voucher No.	Description	Receipts	Payments	Postage Expense	Delivery Expense	Sundry Account	Sundry Amount
200X May 1		Establishment	60 00					
2	1	Cleaning		3 00			Cleaning	3 00
5	2	Postage		9 00	9 00			
8	3	First Aid		15 00			Misc.	15 00
9	4	Delivery		6 00		6 00		
14	5	Delivery		15 00		15 00		
27	6	Postage		6 00	6 00			
		Total	60 00	54 00	15 00	21 00		18 00
		Ending Balance		6 00				
			60 00	60 00				
		Ending Balance	6 00					
31		Replenishment	54 00					
31		Balance (New)	60 00					

Figure 6-14 Auxiliary Petty Cash Record with Replenishment

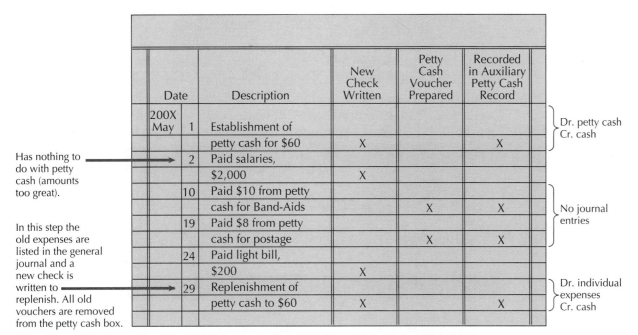

Figure 6-15 Which Transactions Involve Petty Cash and How to Record Them

Has nothing to do with petty cash (amounts too great).

In this step the old expenses are listed in the general journal and a new check is written to replenish. All old vouchers are removed from the petty cash box.

SETTING UP A CHANGE FUND AND INSIGHT INTO CASH SHORT AND OVER

If a company like Debbie's Stationery expects to have many cash transactions occurring, it may be a good idea to establish a change fund. This fund is placed in the cash register drawer and used to make change for customers who pay cash. Debbie decides to put $120 in the change fund, made up of various denominations of bills and coins. Let's look at a transaction analysis chart and the journal entry (Fig. 6-16) for this sort of procedure.

Accounts Affected	Category	↑↓	Dr./Cr.
Change Fund	Asset	↑	Dr.
Cash	Asset	↓	Cr.

Apr.	1	Change Fund		1 2 0 00	
		Cash			1 2 0 00
		Establish change fund			

Figure 6-16
Change Fund Established

At the close of the business day, Debbie will place the amount of the change fund back in the safe in the office. She will set up the change fund (the same $120) in the appropriate denominations for the next business day. She will deposit in the bank the *remainder* of the cash taken in for the day.

In the next section, we look at how to record errors that are made in making change, called cash short and over.

Cash Short and Over

In a local pizza shop the total sales for the day did not match the amount of cash on hand. Errors often happen in making change. To record and summarize the differences in cash, an account called *Cash Short and Over* is used. This account will record both overages (too much money) and shortages (not enough money). Lets first look at the account (in T account form).

Beg change fund
+ Cash register total
= Cash should have on hand
− Counted cash
= Shortage or overage of cash

Cash Short and Over

Dr.	Cr.
shortage	overage

All shortages will be recorded as debits and all overages will be recorded as credits. This account is temporary. If the ending balance of the account is a debit (a shortage), it is considered a miscellaneous expense that would be reported on the income statement. If the balance of the account is a credit (an overage), it is considered as other income reported on the income statement. Let's look at how the Cash Short and Over account could be used to record shortages or overages in sales as well as in the petty cash process.

Example 1: Shortages and Overages in Sales

On December 5 a pizza shop rang up sales of $560 for the day but only had $530 in cash.

Accounts Affected	Category	↑ ↓	Dr./Cr.
Cash	Asset	↑	Debit $530
Cash Short and Over	Misc. Exp.	↑	Debit $30
Sales	Revenue	↑	Credit $560

The journal entry would be as shown in Figure 6-17.

Figure 6-17
Cash Shortage

Dec.	5	Cash			5 3 0 00			
		Cash Short and Over			3 0 00			
		Sales					5 6 0 00	
		Cash shortage						

Note that the shortage of $30 is a debit and would be recorded on the income statement as a miscellaneous expense.

What would the entry look like if the pizza shop showed a $50 overage?

Accounts Affected	Category	↑ ↓	Dr./Cr.
Cash	Asset	↑	Debit $610
Cash Short and Over	Other Income	↑	Credit $50
Sales	Revenue	↑	Credit $560

The journal entry would be as shown in Figure 6-18.

Figure 6-18
Cash Overage

Dec.	5	Cash			6 1 0 00			
		Cash Short and Over					5 0 00	
		Sales					5 6 0 00	
		Cash overage						

Note that the Cash Short and Over account would be reported as other income on the income statement. Now let's look at how to use this Cash Short and Over account to record petty cash transactions.

Example 2: Cash Short and Over in Petty Cash

A local computer company had established petty cash for $200. Today, November 30, the petty cash box had $160 in vouchers as well as $32 in coin and currency. What would be the journal entry to replenish petty cash? Assume the vouchers were made up of $90 for postage and $70 for supplies expense.

If you add up the vouchers and cash in the box, cash is short by $8.

Accounts Affected	Category	↑↓	Dr./Cr.
Postage Expense	Expense	↑	Debit $90
Supplies Expense	Expense	↑	Debit $70
Cash Short and Over	Misc. Expense	↑	Debit $8
Cash	Asset	↓	Credit $168

Note: The account Petty Cash is not used since the level in petty cash is not raised or lowered.

The journal entry is shown in Figure 6-19.

Nov.	8	Postage Expense		9 0 00		
		Supplies Expense		7 0 00		
		Cash Short and Over		8 00		
		Cash			1 6 8 00	

Figure 6-19
Petty Cash Replenished with Shortage

If there had been an overage, the Cash Short and Over would be a credit as other income. The solution to Self-Review Quiz 6-2 shows how a fund shortage would be recorded in the auxiliary record.

Learning Unit 6-2 Review

AT THIS POINT you should be able to

- State the purpose of a petty cash fund. (p. 235)
- Prepare a journal entry to establish a petty cash fund. (p. 235)
- Prepare a petty cash voucher. (p. 236)
- Explain the relationship of the auxiliary petty cash record to the petty cash process. (p. 237)
- Prepare a journal entry to replenish Petty Cash to its original amount. (p. 237)
- Explain why individual expenses are debited in the replenishment process. (p. 238)
- Explain how a change fund is established. (p. 239)
- Explain how Cash Short and Over could be a miscellaneous expense. (p. 239)

SELF-REVIEW QUIZ 6-2

(The blank forms you need are on pages 191–192 of the *Study Guide and Working Papers.*)

As the custodian of the petty cash fund, it is your task to prepare entries to establish the fund on October 1 as well as to replenish the fund on October 31. Please keep an auxiliary petty cash record.

200X

Oct. 1 Establish petty cash fund for $90, check no. 8.
5 Voucher 11, delivery expense, $21.
9 Voucher 12, delivery expense, $15.
10 Voucher 13, office repair expense, $24.
17 Voucher 14, general expense, $12.
30 Replenishment of petty cash fund, $78, check no. 108. (Check would be payable to the custodian.)

SOLUTION TO SELF-REVIEW QUIZ 6-2

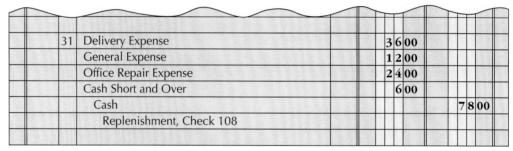

		GENERAL JOURNAL			Page 6	
Date		Account Title and Description	PR	Dr.	Cr.	
200X Oct.	1	Petty Cash		90 00		
		Cash			90 00	
		Establishment, Check 8				

	31	Delivery Expense		36 00		
		General Expense		12 00		
		Office Repair Expense		24 00		
		Cash Short and Over		6 00		
		Cash			78 00	
		Replenishment, Check 108				

Figure 6-20 Establishment and Replenishment of Petty Cash

						Catagory of Payments			
						Delivery Expense	General Expense	Sundry	
Date	Voucher No.	Description	Receipts	Payments				Account	Amount
200X Oct. 1		Establishment	90 00						
5	11	Delivery		21 00		21 00			
9	12	Delivery		15 00		15 00			
10	13	Repairs		24 00				Office Repair	24 00
17	14	General		12 00			12 00		
25		Fund Shortage		6 00				Cash Short and Over	6 00
		Totals	90 00	78 00		36 00	12 00		30 00
		Ending Balance		12 00					
				90 00					
30		Ending Balance	12 00						
31		Replenishment	78 00						
Nov. 1		New Balance	90 00						

AUXILIARY PETTY CASH RECORD

Figure 6-21 Auxiliary Petty Cash Record

Chapter Review

Learning Unit 6-1

1. Restrictive endorsement limits any further negotiation of a check.
2. Check stubs are filled out before a check is written.
3. The payee is the person to whom the check is payable. The drawer is the one who orders the bank to pay a sum of money. The drawee is the bank with which the drawer has an account.
4. The process of reconciling the bank balance with the company's balance is called the bank reconciliation. The timing of deposits, when the bank statement was issued, and so forth, often result in differences between the bank balance and the checkbook balance.
5. Deposits in transit are added to the bank balance.
6. Checks outstanding are subtracted from the bank balance.
7. NSF means that a check has nonsufficient funds to be credited (deposited) to a checking account; therefore, the amount is not included in the bank balance and thus the checking account balance is lowered.
8. When a bank debits your account it is deducting an amount from your balance. A credit to the account is an increase to your balance.
9. All adjustments to the checkbook balance require journal entries.
10. The Internet has expanded online banking options.

Learning Unit 6-2

1. Petty Cash is an asset found on the balance sheet.
2. The auxiliary petty cash record is an auxiliary book; thus no postings are done from this book. Think of it as an optional worksheet.
3. When a petty cash fund is established, the amount is entered as a debit to Petty Cash and a credit to Cash.
4. At the time of replenishment of the petty cash fund, all expenses are debited (by category) and a credit to Cash (a new check) results. This replenishment, when journalized and posted, updates the ledger from the journal.
5. The only time the Petty Cash account is used is to establish the fund initially or to bring the fund to a higher or lower level. If the petty cash level is deemed sufficient, all replenishments will debit specific expenses and credit Cash (new check written). The asset Petty Cash account balance will remain unchanged.
6. A change fund is an asset that is used to make change for customers.
7. Cash Short and Over is an account that is either a miscellaneous expense or miscellaneous income, depending on whether the ending balance is a shortage or overage.

Key Terms

ATM   Automatic teller machine.

Auxiliary petty cash record   A supplementary record for summarizing petty cash information.

Bank reconciliation   The process of reconciling the checkbook balance with the bank balance given on the bank statement.

Bank statement   A report sent by a bank to a customer indicating the previous balance, individual checks processed, individual deposits received, service charges, and ending bank balance.

Cancelled check   A check that has been processed by a bank and is no longer negotiable.

Cash Short and Over   The account that records cash shortages and overages. If the ending balance is a debit, it is recorded on the income statement as a miscellaneous expense; if it is a credit, it is recorded as miscellaneous income.

Change fund   Fund made up of various denominations that are used to make change for customers.

Check   A form used to indicate a specific amount of money that is to be paid by the bank to a named person or company.

Check truncation (safekeeping)   Procedure whereby checks are not returned to the drawer with the bank statement but are instead kept at the bank for a certain amount of time before being first transferred to microfilm and then destroyed.

Credit memorandum   Increase in depositor's balance.

Debit card   A card similar to a credit card except that the amount of a purchase is deducted directly from the customer's bank account.

Debit memorandum   Decrease in depositor's balance.

Deposits in transit   Deposits that were made by customers of a bank but did not reach, or were not processed by, the bank before the preparation of the bank statement.

Deposit ticket   A form provided by a bank for use in depositing money or checks into a checking account.

Drawee   Bank that drawer has an account with.

Drawer   Person who writes a check.

Electronic funds transfer (EFT)   An electronic system that transfers funds without the use of paper checks.

Endorsement   *Blank:* Could be further endorsed. *Full:* Restricts further endorsement to only the person or company named. *Restrictive:* Restricts any further endorsement.

Internal control   A system of procedures and methods to control a firm's assets as well as monitor its operations.

NSF (nonsufficient funds)   Notation indicating that a check has been written on an account that lacks sufficient funds to back it up.

Outstanding checks   Checks written by a company or person that were not received or not processed by the bank before the preparation of the bank statement.

Payee   The person or company to whom the check is payable.

Petty cash fund   Fund (source) that allows payment of small amounts without the writing of checks.

Petty cash voucher   A petty cash form to be completed when money is taken out of petty cash.

Blueprint: A Bank Reconciliation

Checkbook Balance	Bank Balance
+ EFT (electronic funds transfer)	+ Deposits in transit
+ Interest earned	− Outstanding checks
+ Notes collected	± Bank errors
+ Direct deposits	
− ATM withdrawals	
− Check redeposits	
− NSF check	
− Online fees	
− Automatic withdrawals	
− Overdrafts	
− Service charges	
− Stop payments	
± Book errors*	
CM—adds to balance	
DM—deducts from balance	

*If a $60 check is recorded as $50, we must decrease checkbook balance by $10.

Questions, Mini Exercises, Exercises, and Problems

Discussion Questions

1. What is the purpose of internal control?
2. What is the advantage of having preprinted deposit tickets?
3. Explain the difference between a blank endorsement and a restrictive endorsement.
4. Explain the difference between payee, drawer, and drawee.

5. Why should check stubs be filled out first, before the check itself is written?

6. A bank statement is sent twice a month. True or false? Please explain.

7. Explain the end product of a bank reconciliation.

8. Why are checks outstanding subtracted from the bank balance?

9. An NSF check results in a bank issuing the depositor a credit memorandum. Agree or disagree. Please support your response.

10. Why do adjustments to the checkbook balance in the reconciliation process need to be journalized?

11. What is EFT?

12. What is meant by check truncation or safekeeping?

13. Petty cash is a liability. Accept or reject. Explain.

14. Explain the relationship of the auxiliary petty cash record to the recording of the cash payment.

15. At the time of replenishment, why are the totals of individual expenses debited?

16. Explain the purpose of a change fund.

17. Explain how Cash Short and Over can be a miscellaneous expense.

Mini Exercises

(The blank forms you need are on page 194 in the *Study Guide and Working Papers*.)

Bank Reconciliation

1. Indicate what effect each situation will have on the bank reconciliation process:

   1. Add to bank balance.
   2. Deduct from bank balance.
   3. Add to checkbook balance.
   4. Deduct from checkbook balance.

   _3_   a. $12 bank service charge.
   _1_   b. $300 deposit in transit.
   _4_   c. $162 NSF check.
   _3_   d. A $15 check was written and recorded as $25.
   _x_   e. Bank collected a $1,000 note less $50 collection fee.
   _2_   f. Check no. 111 was outstanding for $88.

Journal Entries in Reconciliation Process

2. Which of the transactions in Mini Exercise 1 would require a journal entry?

Bank Reconciliation

3. From the following, construct a bank reconciliation for June Co. as of May 31, 200X.

Checkbook balance	$20
Bank statement balance	30
Deposits in transit	10
Outstanding checks	30
Bank service charge	10

Petty Cash

4. Indicate what effect each situation will have:

   1. New check written.
   2. Recorded in general journal.
   3. Petty cash voucher prepared.
   4. Recorded in auxiliary petty cash record.

_____ **a.** Established petty cash.
_____ **b.** Paid $1,000 bill.
_____ **c.** Paid $2 for Band-Aids from petty cash.
_____ **d.** Paid $3.00 for stamps from petty cash.
_____ **e.** Paid electric bill, $250.
_____ **f.** Replenished petty cash.

Replenishment of Petty Cash

5. Petty cash was originally established for $20. During the month, $5 was paid out for Band-Aids and $6 for stamps. During replenishment, the custodian discovered that the balance in petty cash was $8. Record, using a general journal entry, the replenishment of petty cash back to $20.

Increasing Petty Cash

6. In Mini Exercise 5, if the custodian decided to raise the level of petty cash to $30, what would be the journal entry to replenish (use a general journal entry)?

Exercises

(The blank forms you need are on pages 195–196 of the *Study Guide and Working Papers.*)

6-1. From the following information, construct a bank reconciliation for Lang Co. as of July 31, 200X. Then prepare journal entries if needed.

Checkbook balance	$1,260	Outstanding checks	285
Bank statement balance	900	Bank service charge	45
Deposits (in transit)	600	(debit memo)	

6-2. In general journal form, prepare journal entries to establish a petty cash fund on July 1 and replenish it on July 31.

200X
July 1 A $40 petty cash fund is established.
        31 At end of month $12 cash plus the following paid vouchers exist: donations expense, $10; postage expense, $7; office supplies expense, $7; miscellaneous expense, $4.

6-3. If in Exercise 6-2 cash on hand is $11, prepare the entry to replenish the petty cash on July 31.

6-4. If in Exercise 6-2 cash on hand is $13, prepare the entry to replenish the petty cash on July 31.

6-5. At the end of the day the clerk for Pete's Variety Shop noticed an error in the amount of cash he should have. Total cash sales from the sales tape were $1,100, whereas the total cash in the register was $1,056. Pete keeps a $30 change fund in his shop. Prepare an appropriate general journal entry to record the cash sale as well as reveal the cash shortage.

Group A Problems

(The blank forms you need are on pages 197–204 of the *Study Guide and Working Papers.*)

6A-1. Able.com received a bank statement from Lee Bank indicating a bank balance of $8,000. Based on Able.com's check stubs, the ending checkbook balance was $6,600. Your task is to prepare a bank reconciliation for Able.com as of July 31, 200X, from the following information (journalize entries as needed):

  a. Checks outstanding: no. 122, $1,000; no. 130, $690.
  b. Deposits in transit $1,110.

Margin notes:

Bank reconciliation.

Establishing and replenishing petty cash.

$$\begin{array}{ll} 900 & 1260 \\ 600 & 45 \\ \hline 1500 & 1215 \\ 285 & \\ \hline 1215 & \end{array}$$

Cash shortage in replenishment.

Cash overage in replenishment.

Calculate cash shortage with change fund.

Preparing a bank reconciliation including collection of a note.

Check Figure:
Reconciled
Balance $7,420

c. Bank service charges $83.

d. Lee Bank collected a note for Able.com, $910, less a $7 collection fee.

6A-2. From the following bank statement, please (1) complete the bank reconciliation for Rick's Deli found on the reverse of the bank statement and (2) journalize the appropriate entries as needed.

a. A deposit of $3,000 is in transit.

b. Rick's Deli has an ending checkbook balance of $6,600.

c. Checks outstanding: no. 111, $600; no. 119, $1,200; no. 121, $330.

d. Jim Rice's check for $300 bounced due to lack of sufficient funds.

Lowell National Bank
Rio Mean Brand
Bugna, Texas

Rick's Deli
8811 2nd St,
Bugna, Texas

Old Balance	Checks in Order of Payment		Deposits	Date	New Balance
6,000				2/2	6,000
	90.00	210.00		2/3	5,700
	150.00		300.00	2/10	5,850
	600.00		600.00	2/15	5,850
	300.00	NSF	300.00	2/20	5,850
	1,200.00		1,200.00	2/24	5,850
	600.00	30.00 SC	180.00	2/28	5,400

6A-3. The following transactions occurred in April for Merry Co.:

200X

April 1 Issued check no. 14 for $80 to establish a petty cash fund.

5 Paid $5 from petty cash for postage, voucher no. 1.

8 Paid $10 from petty cash for office supplies, voucher no. 2.

15 Issued check no. 15 to Reliable Corp. for $200 from past purchases on account.

17 Paid $8 from petty cash for office supplies, voucher no. 3.

20 Issued check no. 16 to Roger Corp., $600 for past purchases on account.

24 Paid $4 from petty cash for postage, voucher no. 4.

26 Paid $9 from petty cash for local church donation, voucher no. 5 (a miscellaneous payment).

28 Issued check no. 17 to Roy Kloon to pay for office equipment, $700.

30 Replenish petty cash, check no. 18.

Your tasks are to

1. Record the appropriate entries in the general journal as well as the auxiliary petty cash record as needed.

2. Be sure to replenish the petty cash fund on April 30 (check no. 18).

6A-4. From the following, record the transactions into Logan's auxiliary petty cash record and general journal (p. 2) as needed:

200X

Oct. 1 A check was drawn (no. 444) payable to Roberta Floss, petty cashier, to establish a $100 petty cash fund.

5 Paid $14 for postage stamps, voucher no. 1.

Preparing a bank reconciliation with NSF using the back side of a bank statement.

Check Figure:
Reconciled
Balance $6,270

Establishment and replenishment of petty cash.

Check Figure:
Cash Replenishment $36

Establishing and replenishing petty cash including a cash shortage.

Check Figure:
Cash Replenishment $66

9   Paid $12 for delivery charges on goods for resale, voucher no. 2.
12   Paid $8 for donation to a church (miscellaneous expense), voucher no. 3.
14   Paid $9 for postage stamps, voucher no. 4.
17   Paid $8 for delivery charges on goods for resale, voucher no. 5.
27   Purchased computer supplies from petty cash for $8, voucher no. 6.
28   Paid $4 for postage, voucher no. 7.
29   Drew check no. 618 to replenish petty cash and a $3 shortage.

Group B Problems

(The blank forms you need are on pages 197–204 of the *Study Guide and Working Papers*.)

Preparing a bank reconciliation including collection of a note.

6B-1. As the bookkeeper of Able.com, you received the bank statement from Lee Bank indicating a balance of $9,185. The ending checkbook balance was $8,215. Prepare the bank reconciliation for Able.com as of July 31, 200X, and prepare journal entries as needed based on the following:

Check Figure:
Reconciled Balance
$10,940

    a. Deposits in transit, $3,600.
    b. Bank service charges, $29.
    c. Checks outstanding: no. 111, $590; no. 115, $1,255.
    d. Lee Bank collected a note for Able.com, $2,760, less a $6 collection fee.

Preparing a bank reconciliation with NSF using the back side of a bank statement.

6B-2. Based on the following, please (1) complete the bank reconciliation for Rick's Deli found on the reverse of the bank statement and (2) journalize the appropriate entries as needed.

    a. Checks outstanding: no. 110, $80; no. 116, $160; no. 118, $52.
    b. A deposit of $416 is in transit.
    c. The checkbook balance of Rick's Deli shows an ending balance of $798.
    d. Jim Rice's check for $40 bounced due to lack of sufficient funds.

Check Figure:
Reconciled Balance $756

Lowell National Bank
Rio Mean Brand
Bugna, Texas

Rick's Deli
8811 2nd St,
Bugna, Texas

Old Balance	Checks in Order of Payment		Deposits	Date	New Balance
718.00				4/2	718.00
	12.00	36.00		4/3	670.00
	20.00		40.00	4/10	690.00
	80.00		80.00	4/15	690.00
	40.00	NSF	40.00	4/20	690.00
	160.00		160.00	4/24	690.00
	80.00	2.00 SC	24.00	4/28	632.00

Establishment and replenishment of petty cash.

6B-3. From the following transactions, (1) record the entries as needed in the general journal of Merry Co. as well as the auxiliary petty cash record and (2) replenish the petty cash fund on April 30 (check no. 8).

200X
Apr.
  1   Issued check no. 4 for $60 to establish a petty cash fund.
  5   Paid $9 from petty cash for postage, voucher no. 1.
  8   Paid $12 from petty cash for office supplies, voucher no. 2.
15   Issued check no. 5 to Reliable Corp. for $400 for past purchases on account.
17   Paid $7 from petty cash for office supplies, voucher no. 3.

20   Issued check no. 6 to Roger Corp. $300 for past purchases on account.

24   Paid $6 from petty cash for postage, voucher no. 4.

26   Paid $12 from petty cash for local church donation, voucher no. 5 (a miscellaneous payment).

28   Issued check no. 7 to Roy Kloon to pay for office equipment, $800.

30   Replenish petty cash, check no. 8.

> **Check Figure:**
> Cash Replenishment $46

6B-4. From the following, record the transactions into Logan's auxiliary petty cash record and general journal (p. 2) as needed:

200X

> **Establishing and replenishing petty cash including a cash shortage.**

Oct.   1   Roberta Floss, the petty cashier, cashed a check, no. 444, to establish a $90 petty cash fund.

5   Paid $16 for postage stamps, voucher no. 1.

9   Paid $14 for delivery charges on goods for resale, voucher no. 2.

12   Paid $6 for donation to a church (miscellaneous expense), voucher no. 3.

14   Paid $10 for postage stamps, voucher no. 4.

17   Paid $7 for delivery charges on goods for resale, voucher no. 5.

> **Check Figure:**
> Cash Replenishment $69

27   Purchased computer supplies from petty cash for $9, voucher no. 6.

28   Paid $3 for postage, voucher no. 7.

29   Drew check no. 618 to replenish petty cash and a $4 shortage.

Real-World Applications

6R-1. Claire Montgomery, the bookkeeper of Angel Co., has appointed Mike Kaminsky as the petty cash custodian. The following transactions occurred in November:

200X

Nov.   25   Check no. 441 was written and cashed to establish a $50 petty cash fund.

27   Paid $8.50 delivery charge for goods purchased for resale.

29   Purchased office supplies for $12 from petty cash.

30   Purchased postage stamps for $15 from petty cash.

On December 3, Mike received the following internal memo:

MEMO

To: Mike Kaminsky

From: Claire Montgomery

Re: Petty Cash

Mike, I'll need $5 for postage stamps. By the way, I noticed that our petty cash account seems to be too low. Let's increase its size to $100.

Could you help Mike replenish petty cash on December 3 by providing him with a general journal entry? Support your answer and indicate in writing whether Claire was correct.

6R-2. Lee Company has the policy of depositing all receipts and making all payments by check. On receiving the bank statement, Bill Free, a new bookkeeper, is quite upset that the balance in Cash in the ledger is $4,209.50, whereas the ending bank balance is $4,440.50. Bill is convinced the bank has made an error. Based on the following facts, is Bill's concern warranted? What other written suggestions could you offer Bill in the bank reconciliation process?

a. The November 30 cash receipts, $611, had been placed in the bank's night depository after banking hours and consequently did not appear on the bank statement as a deposit.

b. Two debit memorandums and a credit memorandum were included with the returned check. None of the memorandums had been recorded at the time of the reconciliation. The first debit memorandum had a $130 NSF check written by Abby Ellen. The second was a $6.50 debit memorandum for service charges. The credit memorandum was for $494 and represented the proceeds less a $6 collection fee from a $500 non-interest-bearing note collected for Lee Company by the bank.

c. It was also found that checks no. 942 for $71.50 and no. 947 for $206.50, both written and recorded on November 28, were not among the cancelled checks returned.

d. Bill found that check no. 899 was correctly drawn for $1,094, in payment for a new cash register. This check, however, had been recorded as though it were for $1,148.

e. The October bank reconciliation showed two checks outstanding on September 30, no. 621 for $152.50 and no. 630 for $179.30. Check no. 630 was returned with the November bank statement, but check no. 621 was not.

YOU make the call

Critical Thinking/Ethical Case

6R-3. Sean Nah, the bookkeeper of Revell Co., received a bank statement from Lone Bank. Sean noticed a $250 mistake made by the bank in the company's favor. Sean called his supervisor, who said that as long as it benefits the company, he should not tell the bank about the error. You make the call. Write your specific recommendations to Sean.

Internet Exercises: Federal Reserve Bank of Dallas; Analytics.com

EX-1. [www.dallasfed.org]   This site will provide you details of the operation of the Federal Reserve Bank of Dallas, Texas. The Federal Reserve System, nicknamed "the Fed," has member banks in 13 cities. Each provides a wealth of economic information on the region it serves. The Dallas Fed Web site contains an article on "dot-com" banking.

1. Read that article and answer these questions:

   a. Do dot-com banks present a challenge to local banks in your city?

   b. What do you believe is the future of dot-com banks? Will they be scrutinized more closely than traditional banking institutions?

2. With a group of your fellow students compare paper money. Use the money you have to determine the location of other Federal Reserve banks. Look at the circular seal on the left side of the bills to determine these locations.

3. What services does the Fed offer to member banks?

EX-2. [www.e-analytics.com/bonds/fed20.htm]   Checks that you write on your bank eventually return to your bank and the amount of the check is deducted from your account. In between the time you write the check and it comes back, you have use of the funds because of a phenomenon called *float.* Individual checking accounts are handled much the same way the paragraph at this site describes. Float is the period of time that two banks have the funds on their books. Suppose you pay your bill for a magazine subscription. You write the check on your bank and mail it to the magazine company. When the company deposits it, it is then "float" because your bank has not yet paid the check.

The Federal Reserve System handles float for large commercial accounts in a method detailed in this article.

1. How does the Federal Reserve System handle checks from its member banks?
2. What is the impact of float on the monetary policy of the United States?

Continuing Problem

Eldorado Computer Center

The books have been closed for the first year of business for Eldorado Computer Center. The company ended up with a marginal profit for the first three months in operation. Tony expects faster growth as he enters into a busy season.

Following is a list of transactions for the month of October. Petty Cash account #1010 and Miscellaneous Expense account #5100 have been added to the chart of accounts.

Assignment

(See pages 208–218 in the *Study Guide and Working Papers.*)

1. Record the transactions in general journal or petty cash format.
2. Post the transactions to the general ledger accounts.
3. Prepare a trial balance.

Oct. 1 Paid rent for November, December, and January, $1,200 (check no. 8108).
2 Established a petty cash fund for $100.
4 Collected $3,600 from a cash customer for building five systems.
5 Collected $2,600, the amount due from A. Pitale's invoice no. 12674, customer on account.
6 Purchased $25 worth of stamps, using petty cash voucher no. 101.
7 Withdrew $2,000 (check no. 8109) for personal use.
8 Purchased $22 worth of supplies, using petty cash voucher no. 102.
12 Paid the newspaper carrier $10, using petty cash voucher no. 103.
16 Paid the amount due on the September phone bill, $65 (check no. 8110).
17 Paid the amount due on the September electric bill, $95 (check no. 8111).
22 Performed computer services for Taylor Golf; billed the client $4,200 (invoice no. 12675).
23 Paid $20 for computer paper, using petty cash voucher no. 104.
30 Took $15 out of petty cash for lunch, voucher no. 105.
31 Replenished the petty cash. Coin and currency in drawer total $8.00.

Because Tony was so busy trying to close his books, he forgot to reconcile his last three months of bank statements. What follows on pages 252 and 253 is a list of all deposits and checks written for the past three months (each entry is identified by chapter, transaction date, or transaction letter) and bank statements for July through September. The statement for October won't arrive until the first week of November.

Eldorado Computer Center Summary of Deposits and Checks

Chapter	Transaction	Payor/Payee	Amount
		Deposits	
1	a	Tony Freedman	$4,500
1	f	Cash customer	250
1	i	Taylor Golf	1,200
1	g	Cash customer	200
2	p	Cash customer	900
3	Sept. 2	Tonya Parker Jones	325
3	Sept. 6	Summer Lipe	220
3	Sept. 12	Jeannine Sparks	850
3	Sept. 26	Mike Hammer	140

Chapter	Transaction	Check #	Payor/Payee	Amount
			Checks	
1	b	8095	Multi Systems, Inc.	$1,200
1	c	8096	Office Furniture, Inc.	600
1	e	8097	Capital Management	400
1	j	8098	Tony Freedman	100
2	l	8099	Insurance Protection, Inc.	150
2	m	8100	Office Depot	200
2	n	8101	Computer Edge Magazine	1,400
2	q	8102	San Diego Electric	85
2	r	8103	U.S. Postmaster	50
3	Sept. 1	8104	Capital Management	1,200
3	Sept. 8	8105	Pacific Bell USA	155
3	Sept. 15	8106	Computer Connection	200
3	Sept. 16	8107	Multi Systems, Inc.	1,200

Bank Statement

First Union Bank 322 Glen Ave. Escondido, CA 92025

Eldorado Computer Center   Statement Date: July 22, 200X

Checks Paid:			Deposits and Credits:	
Date paid	Number	Amount	Date received	Amount
7–4	~~8085~~ 8095	1,200.00	7–1	4,500.00
7–7	8096	600.00	7–10	250.00
7–15	8097	400.00	7–20	1,200.00
			7–21	200.00
Total 3 checks paid for $2,200.00			Total Deposits	$6,150.00

Ending balance on July 22 $3,950.00

Received statement July 29, 200X.

Bank Statement

First Union Bank 322 Glen Ave. Escondido, CA 92025

Eldorado Computer Center   Statement Date: August 21, 200X

Checks Paid:			Deposits and Credits:	
Date paid	Number	Amount	Date received	Amount
8-2	8098	100.00	8-12	900.00
8-3	8099	150.00		
8-10	8100	200.00		
8-15	8101	1,400.00		
8-20	8102	85.00		

Total 5 checks paid for $1,935.00   Total Deposits $900.00
Beginning balance on July 22—   Ending balance on August 21—
$3,950.00 $2,915.00

Received statement August 27, 200X.

Bank Statement

First Union Bank 322 Glen Ave. Escondido, CA 92025

Eldorado Computer Center   Statement Date: September 20, 200X

Checks Paid:			Deposits and Credits:	
Date paid	Number	Amount	Date received	Amount
9-2	8103	50.00	9-4	325.00
9-6	8104	1,200.00	9-7	220.00
9-12	8105	155.00	9-14	850.00

Total 3 checks paid for $1,405.00   Total Deposits $1,395.00
Beginning balance on August 21   Ending balance on September 20
$2,915.0 $2,905.00

Received statement September 29, 200X.

Assignment

1. Compare the Computer Center's deposits and checks with the bank statements and complete a bank reconciliation as of September 30, 200X.

SUBWAY Case

COUNTING DOWN THE CASH

Subway now requires all of its franchisees to submit their weekly sales and inventory reports electronically using new point-of-sale (POS) touch-screen cash registers. With the new POS registers, clerks use a touch screen to punch in the number and type of items bought. Franchisees can quickly reconfigure prices and products to match new promotions. Not only is this POS method faster than using the old cash registers but it also allows franchisees to view every transaction as it occurs—from their own back office computers or even from home. Also, individual POS terminals within the restaurant are linked, so franchisees are able to see consolidated data quickly.

The transition to electronic reporting and networked POS terminals, however, has not been without bumps, as Stan can testify. About six months before the deadline for all Subway franchisees to "go electronic," Stan attended a heated meeting on the topic at his local chapter of the North American Association of Subway Franchisees (NAASF). The NAASF is an independent organization of franchisees that serves as an advisory council on Subway policies and issues of common concern. Everyone seemed to be talking at once.

"I just don't trust these machines. What am I supposed to do when the system crashes?" complained one man.

"Yeah, and I don't like the idea of a bunch of kids knowing more about how to run the software than I do," said one older franchisee.

"Don't be so quick to assume that our sandwich artists will love POS," said one woman. "I overheard one of my employees say to another, 'POS means **P**eeking **O**ver **S**houlders.' These young kids we hire have more reason to be resistant than we do!"

"I'll say they do!" rejoined Jay Harden, the president of Stan's local NAASF. "Employee theft is one of the largest problems we face as franchisees. I, for one, really welcome the cash control we get with POS."

Stan had to agree with Jay. Training staff to record every sale and record it correctly is a critical component of a cash business like Subway. In Stan's view, the POS machines would only make that training easier. Cash control is built into the new system, which also provides the owners with information that will help them spot problems—such as employee theft—and track trends. Of course, thought Stan, the chore of counting down the cash at the end of a shift remained. No matter what type of computer program you install, cash still must be counted down and rectified with the register tape at the end of each shift.

As the voices rung louder around him, Stan thought about what had happened that day, when Ellen closed out her cash register drawer. He had spent hours figuring out a discrepancy between the cash in the drawer and the register tape. Ellen had forgotten to void a mistaken entry for $99.99. Stan had first suspected that she had made a huge error in counting change.

Thinking of errors in counting brought him back to the topic of the meeting. Stan raised his hand to speak.

"One thing that concerns me is the potential for accounting errors. I still have to key in data from the POS into my Peachtree accounting software. Every time I have to re-enter data, the potential for error multiplies."

"That shows some foresight, Stan," said Jay Harden. "We're actually exploring computer programs that will feed the data directly from the POS into our accounting programs." Even some of the technophobes and POS skeptics in the group had to agree that would be a great idea.

Discussion Questions

1. What is an advisory council? Why do you think franchisees need one?
2. Why do you think some small business owners fear computerization?
3. How would Stan catch a discrepancy in the Cash account? How would he record a loss?
4. Why does Subway invest time, money, and effort in investigating new cash handling systems like its new POS terminals?

CHAPTER 7

Payroll Concepts and Procedures

You were happy when you received your first check from working at your school's business office. It feels good to be making money to help with school expenses and to save toward your spring break vacation. You had a good idea of how much you earned after working for two weeks at the business office. However, you were a little disappointed when you opened the envelope containing your check. The amount of your check wasn't nearly as much as you thought you would receive. You forgot about the taxes that were withheld from your paycheck. Perhaps you forgot about the taxes, but the payroll accountant at school remembered to withhold them from your check.

Any business that has employees must pay them for their time and services. An important part of preparing a payroll for a company is accurately calculating employee earnings and the proper amounts to withhold in Social Security, Medicare, as well as federal and state income taxes.

In this chapter we will discuss the steps necessary in calculating regular earnings, overtime earnings, and various withholding taxes. We will learn how to calculate federal, Social Security, and Medicare taxes on employee earnings. We will also introduce you to the payroll register and employee earnings records, which are used in recording a payroll for a business. After completing this chapter, you will know the difference between an employee's gross earnings and employee's net pay and the role taxes play when paying employees.

Learning Objectives

- Calculating overtime pay, FICA deductions for Social Security and Medicare, and federal income tax withholding. (p. 258)

- Preparing a payroll register. (p. 265)

- Journalizing and posting the payroll entry from the payroll register. (p. 266)

- Maintaining an individual employee earnings record. (p. 274)

An essential part of running a business is hiring and paying employees. Whether a business is a small mom-and-pop grocery store in your own town or a huge nation-wide corporation, the rules for payroll are really the same. That's why it's important to know how to calculate and record a payroll.

In this chapter we take a close look at the employees of Gradesoft.com, a company that programs and sells teacher grading software, to see how a payroll is figured and recorded. We look at how a payroll is affected by federal, state, and local taxes and how the accountant at Gradesoft.com handles a payroll for the company.

Learning Unit 7-1	Introduction to Payroll Accounting

Ernie Goldman is the accountant for Gradesoft.com. This new company creates software that allows teachers to track and calculate students' grades electronically using a personal computer. Ernie has the responsibility of calculating and recording each payroll for the company. Several key parts of Ernie's job in working with payroll need mention here. First, Ernie *must be accurate* in everything he does, because any mistake he makes in working with the payroll may affect both the employee and the company. Second, Ernie needs to be *on time* when working on the company's payroll so that the employees get their paychecks when they are due. Third, Ernie must at all times *comply with the appropriate federal, state, and local laws governing payroll matters.* Fourth, Ernie always needs to keep everything *confidential* when working on the payroll.

Ernie must first calculate the earnings for Gradesoft.com employees. For Ernie to make the correct calculations, he must know how each employee has been classified for payroll purposes. As a rule, a company will classify each employee as either "hourly" or "salaried" when it comes to paying earnings. If an employee is an *hourly employee,* that employee will only be paid for the hours he or she worked. If an employee is classified as a *salaried employee,* he or she will receive a set dollar amount for the hours worked.

Gradesoft.com has classified three of its six employees as hourly. For these employees, Ernie must compute the hours they have worked during a specific period of time known as a *pay period.* A pay period is important because Ernie uses it to determine how much each hourly employee has earned. For payroll purposes, **pay periods** are defined as daily, weekly, biweekly (every two weeks), semimonthly (twice each month), monthly, quarterly, or annual. A pay period can start on any day of the week and must end after the specified period of time has passed. Most companies use weekly, biweekly, semimonthly, or monthly pay periods when calculating their payrolls.

Gradesoft.com uses a biweekly pay period for its hourly employees and a monthly pay period for its three salaried employees. The biweekly pay period starts on Monday and ends 14 days (two weeks) later on a Sunday. The monthly pay period starts on the first day of the calendar month and ends on the last day.

Now that Ernie knows the pay period for Gradesoft.com's hourly employees, he must calculate their total or *gross earnings.* The **gross earnings** amount for an employee is composed of two amounts; regular earnings and overtime earnings (if any).

Overtime earnings must be figured according to federal (and in some cases, state) law. This federal law is known as the **Fair Labor Standards Act** (also known as Federal Wage and Hour Law). For most employers, the law states that an hourly employee must be paid more per hour for any hours worked over 40 during a period of time called a *workweek.* A **workweek** is a time period that can start at any time on any given day, but it must end 168 hours later (or seven calendar days of 24 hours each). One workweek follows another, and the starting time must be the same time each week.

For rules of the Fair Labor Standards Act to apply to an employer, the employer must be involved in interstate commerce.

For the hourly employees of Gradesoft.com, there are two workweeks in each biweekly pay period. Gradesoft.com's workweek starts on Monday morning at 12:01 A.M. and ends the following Sunday evening at 12:00 midnight (168 hours later). Thus, Ernie must figure any overtime pay if any employee has worked more than 40 hours during each week of the two-week (that is, biweekly) pay period.

The federal law also set the minimum standard for overtime pay. It is one and a half times the regular hourly rate of pay for an employee. Let's look at Lee Jackson, one of the hourly employees of Gradesoft.com who worked overtime hours during the biweekly pay period starting on August 7 and ending on August 20 (remember that there are 14 days in the biweekly pay period and two workweeks in the same pay period for figuring overtime earnings).

Lee worked 45 hours for the week of August 7 to August 13 and 39 for the week of August 14 to August 20. How many regular and overtime hours did Lee work for this biweekly pay period? First, Ernie must look at each workweek separately from the next. Thus, Lee worked 40 regular and 5 overtime hours for the first workweek and 39 regular and 0 overtime hours for the second workweek. Note that Ernie did not take any overtime hours from the first workweek and apply them to the second workweek to pay Lee for 40 hours. Remember that each workweek stands independently of another, even if during another workweek the employee worked fewer than 40 hours.

There are two ways of figuring the regular and overtime hours for Lee during this pay period. Ernie notes here that Lee makes $10.80 per hour. Now let's look at each way to figure the total hours Lee must be paid.

Method One

$$
\begin{aligned}
&\text{Total Hours} \times \text{Regular Rate} = 84 \text{ hours} \times \$10.80 \text{ / hour} = \$907.20 \\
&\quad \text{Worked} \qquad\quad \text{of pay} \\
&+ \text{Overtime} \times \tfrac{1}{2}\text{Regular Rate} = 5 \text{ hours} \times \$5.40 \text{ / hour} = \$\;27.00 \\
&\quad \text{Hours} \qquad\qquad \text{of pay}
\end{aligned}
$$

Total Pay for Lee Jackson	**$934.20**

Method Two

$$
\begin{aligned}
&\text{Regular Hours} \times \text{Regular Rate of Pay} = 79 \text{ hours} \times \$10.80 \text{ / hour} = \$853.20 \\
&+ \text{Overtime Hours} \times 1\tfrac{1}{2} \text{ Regular Rate of Pay} = 5 \text{ hours} \times \$16.20 = \$\;81.00
\end{aligned}
$$

Total Pay for Lee Jackson	**$934.20**

As you can see, Ernie can use either way to arrive at the total or gross earnings for Lee Jackson for the pay period. Method One clearly shows Ernie how much Lee is being paid in overtime. Because Method Two is more commonly used to figure gross earnings, we use it to figure gross earnings for Gradesoft.com employees in this chapter.

EMPLOYEE FEDERAL AND STATE INCOME TAX WITHHOLDING

After Ernie has figured Lee Jackson's gross earnings, he must now start figuring out how much Lee will receive in pay after several different taxes have been withheld. These taxes, known as payroll taxes or income tax withholding, must be paid by each employee based on how much was earned each pay period. Gradesoft.com is required to withhold payroll taxes for each employee and pay them to the government according to a special timetable. The amount paid by Gradesoft.com for payroll taxes is known as a **payroll tax deposit.** We discuss how payroll tax deposits work in Chapter 8.

For Ernie to determine how much to withhold from Lee's check in payroll taxes, Lee must complete a form known as a **Form W-4, Employee's Withholding Allowance Certificate.** This form contains information Ernie needs to calculate Lee's **federal income tax (FIT) withholding** for the pay period. Ernie will use the information from Form W-4, along with special tax withholding tables supplied by the Internal Revenue Service (IRS), to determine how much to withhold in FIT from Lee's check. Lee Jackson is actually paying the government the amount that he would owe in federal income taxes by having Gradesoft.com take it at the time he is paid. In this way Lee pays his taxes on a "pay-as-you-go" basis, which is based on how much he earns each pay period.

Notice in Figure 7-1 below that Lee's Form W-4 shows his marital status and total number of allowances he is claiming for federal income tax purposes. In general, an employee is granted one **allowance** (also known as an **exemption**) for himself or herself, one for a spouse (unless the spouse works and claims his or her own allowance), and one for each of his or her dependents (e.g., children) for whom the employee provides more than one-half support during a year. Employees who wish to have more withheld from their paychecks can elect to claim fewer allowances on Form W-4 than they actually have.

Ernie will use Lee's marital status and number of allowances claimed from his Form W-4 along with Lee's gross earnings for the pay period to look up the amount of federal tax to withhold using an IRS **wage bracket table** (see Fig. 7-2). These tables can be found in an IRS publication known as *Circular E, Employer's Tax Guide,* also known as Publication 15. Note in Figure 7-2 that the wage bracket table has been grouped according to pay period and marital status. *Circular E* contains tables for daily, weekly, biweekly, semimonthly, monthly, quarterly, and annual pay periods. For each pay period

---

Cut here and give Form W-4 to your employer. Keep the top part for your records.

Form **W-4**	**Employee's Withholding Allowance Certificate**	OMB No. 1545-0010
Department of the Treasury Internal Revenue Service	For Privacy Act and Paperwork Reduction Act Notice, see page 2.	20**0X**

1 Type or print your first name and middle initial	Last name	2 Your social security number
LEE	JACKSON	923 85 1316

Home address (number and street or rural route)	3 [X] Single [ ] Married [ ] Married, but withhold at higher Single rate.
1225 HIGHTOWN STREET	**Note:** *If married, but legally separated, or spouse is a nonresident alien, check the Single box.*
City or town, state, and ZIP code	4 If your last name differs from that on your social security card, check
SOUTHSIDE, MA 01945	here. **You must call 1-800-772-1213 for a new card** . . . [ ]

5	Total number of allowances you are claiming (from line **H** above **OR** from the applicable worksheet on page 2)	**5**	1
6	Additional amount, if any, you want withheld from each paycheck	**6** $	
7	I claim exemption from withholding for 200X, and I certify that I meet **BOTH** of the following conditions for exemption:		
	Last year I had a right to a refund of **ALL** Federal income tax withheld because I had **NO** tax liability **AND**		
	This year I expect a refund of **ALL** Federal income tax withheld because I expect to have **NO** tax liability.		
	If you meet both conditions, write "EXEMPT" here	**7**	

Under penalties of perjury, I certify that I am entitled to the number of withholding allowances claimed on this certificate, or I am entitled to claim exempt status.

Employee's signature
(Form is not valid
unless you sign it) ▶ *Lee Jackson*   **Date** ▶ JANUARY 3, 200X

8 Employer's name and address (Employer: Complete lines 8 and 10 only if sending to the IRS.)	9 Office code (optional)	10 Employer identification number

Cat. No. 10220Q

Figure 7-1 Form W-4, Employee's Withholding Allowance Certificate

SINGLE Persons—BIWEEKLY Payroll Period
(For Wages Paid in 200X)

If the wages are—		And the number of withholding allowances claimed is—										
At least	But less than	0	1	2	3	4	5	6	7	8	9	10
		The amount of income tax to be withheld is—										
$800	$820	$95	$77	$60	$42	$24	$12	$0	$0	$0	$0	$0
820	840	98	80	63	45	27	14	2	0	0	0	0
840	860	101	83	66	48	30	16	4	0	0	0	0
860	880	104	86	69	51	33	18	6	0	0	0	0
880	900	107	89	72	54	36	20	8	0	0	0	0
900	920	110	92	75	57	39	22	10	0	0	0	0
920	940	113	95	78	60	42	25	12	1	0	0	0
940	960	116	98	81	63	45	28	14	3	0	0	0
960	980	119	101	84	66	48	31	16	5	0	0	0
980	1,000	122	104	87	69	51	34	18	7	0	0	0
1,000	1,020	125	107	90	72	54	37	20	9	0	0	0
1,020	1,040	128	110	93	75	57	40	22	11	0	0	0
1,040	1,060	131	113	96	78	60	43	25	13	1	0	0
1,060	1,080	134	116	99	81	63	46	28	15	3	0	0
1,080	1,100	137	119	102	84	66	49	31	17	5	0	0
1,100	1,120	140	122	105	87	69	52	34	19	7	0	0
1,120	1,140	143	125	108	90	72	55	37	21	9	0	0
1,140	1,160	146	128	111	93	75	58	40	23	11	0	0
1,160	1,180	150	131	114	96	78	61	43	26	13	1	0
1,180	1,200	156	134	117	99	81	64	46	29	15	3	0
1,200	1,220	161	137	120	102	84	67	49	32	17	5	0
1,220	1,240	167	140	123	105	87	70	52	35	19	7	0
1,240	1,260	172	143	126	108	90	73	55	38	21	9	0
1,260	1,280	177	146	129	111	93	76	58	41	23	11	0
1,280	1,300	183	151	132	114	96	79	61	44	26	13	2
1,300	1,320	188	156	135	117	99	82	64	47	29	15	4
1,320	1,340	194	162	138	120	102	85	67	50	32	17	6
1,340	1,360	199	167	141	123	105	88	70	53	35	19	8
1,360	1,380	204	173	144	126	108	91	73	56	38	21	10
1,380	1,400	210	178	147	129	111	94	76	59	41	24	12
1,400	1,420	215	183	152	132	114	97	79	62	44	27	14
1,420	1,440	221	189	157	135	117	100	82	65	47	30	16
1,440	1,460	226	194	163	138	120	103	85	68	50	33	18
1,460	1,480	231	200	168	141	123	106	88	71	53	36	20
1,480	1,500	237	205	173	144	126	109	91	74	56	39	22
1,500	1,520	242	210	179	147	129	112	94	77	59	42	24
1,520	1,540	248	216	184	153	132	115	97	80	62	45	27
1,540	1,560	253	221	190	158	135	118	100	83	65	48	30
1,560	1,580	258	227	195	163	138	121	103	86	68	51	33
1,580	1,600	264	232	200	169	141	124	106	89	71	54	36
1,600	1,620	269	237	206	174	144	127	109	92	74	57	39
1,620	1,640	275	243	211	180	148	130	112	95	77	60	42
1,640	1,660	280	248	217	185	153	133	115	98	80	63	45
1,660	1,680	285	254	222	190	159	136	118	101	83	66	48
1,680	1,700	291	259	227	196	164	139	121	104	86	69	51
1,700	1,720	296	264	233	201	169	142	124	107	89	72	54
1,720	1,740	302	270	238	207	175	145	127	110	92	75	57
1,740	1,760	307	275	244	212	180	149	130	113	95	78	60
1,760	1,780	312	281	249	217	186	154	133	116	98	81	63
1,780	1,800	318	286	254	223	191	159	136	119	101	84	66
1,800	1,820	323	291	260	228	196	165	139	122	104	87	69
1,820	1,840	329	297	265	234	202	170	142	125	107	90	72
1,840	1,860	334	302	271	239	207	176	145	128	110	93	75
1,860	1,880	339	308	276	244	213	181	149	131	113	96	78
1,880	1,900	345	313	281	250	218	186	155	134	116	99	81
1,900	1,920	350	318	287	255	223	192	160	137	119	102	84
1,920	1,940	356	324	292	261	229	197	166	140	122	105	87
1,940	1,960	361	329	298	266	234	203	171	143	125	108	90
1,960	1,980	366	335	303	271	240	208	176	146	128	111	93
1,980	2,000	372	340	308	277	245	213	182	150	131	114	96
2,000	2,020	377	345	314	282	250	219	187	155	134	117	99
2,020	2,040	383	351	319	288	256	224	193	161	137	120	102
2,040	2,060	388	356	325	293	261	230	198	166	140	123	105
2,060	2,080	393	362	330	298	267	235	203	172	143	126	108
2,080	2,100	399	367	335	304	272	240	209	177	146	129	111

$2,100 and over   Use Table 2(a) for a **SINGLE person** on page 34. Also see the instructions on page 32.

Figure 7-2 Wage Bracket Table—Single Persons

there are separate "single" and "married" tables. Finally, each individual table is organized according to the gross earnings of the employee for the pay period.

Let's look at how Ernie will use the Single Biweekly Payroll Period table in *Circular E* to see how he arrived at the amount of FIT to be withheld from Lee Jackson's check. First, Ernie knows that Lee is paid biweekly (once every two weeks). Ernie has also figured Lee's gross earnings for the last biweekly pay period Lee worked ($934.20). Ernie can then look at Lee's Form W-4 and see that Lee has claimed one allowance (for himself) and has indicated that he is single (look at Fig. 7-1 again). It is now easy for Ernie to look up the FIT amount from the table by going down the left-hand column labeled "If the wages are." Ernie will stop at the line "At least $920 But less than $940." Ernie stops at this line because Lee's earnings are $934.20, which is an amount within that range of earnings. Now Ernie will move to the right until he finds the amount in the column labeled "1," which indicates the number of withholding allowances per Lee's Form W-4. Where the row and the column meet, Ernie finds an amount of $95, the amount of FIT that Ernie will withhold from Lee's paycheck.

Now what would happen if Lee actually earned $940 for the pay period? Ernie would go to the next line below in the table because the first column reads "At least $940." The amount Lee would owe in FIT withholding would be $98; Lee would owe a little more in tax because he made a little more in gross earnings. Had Lee earned $939 instead of $940, his earnings would have still been "Less than $940." Ernie would use the same line of the table and would find that Lee would owe $95 in FIT.

Lee will probably owe state income tax (or SIT) as well as FIT. Many states allow payroll people to use the federal Form W-4 for **state income tax withholding** as well. Other states have their own versions of Form W-4 that employees must fill out. Many states have their own version of the IRS *Circular E* that can be used to look up SIT withholding. These states also require an employer to withhold and collect the state income taxes and then make state payroll tax deposits according to state rules. The majority of states currently tax an employee's gross earnings; several do not and do not require SIT withholding.

EMPLOYEE WITHHOLDING FOR SOCIAL SECURITY TAXES

Another tax that Ernie must compute and withhold from employee checks is known as Social Security Tax or **FICA** (FICA stands for **Federal Insurance Contributions Act,** a 1935 federal law that has required workers to pay this tax since 1937). The proceeds of this tax support federal payments for (1) monthly retirement benefits for those over 62 years old, (2) medical benefits for those over 65 years old, (3) benefits for workers who have become disabled, and (4) benefits for families of deceased workers who were covered by this law. Both employees of companies as well as self-employed individuals must pay FICA taxes.

There are two special things to know about Social Security (or FICA) tax. First, Social Security tax is really two taxes. One of these taxes is called Social Security (or OASDI, which stands for old age, survivors, and disability insurance), and the other is known as Medicare (or HI, which stands for health insurance). Usually, people group both taxes together and call them Social Security (or FICA) tax. Second, the rate of Social Security tax and the maximum dollar amount of earnings upon which the tax can be computed may change each year. The maximum dollar amount of earnings upon which the tax is computed is known as an earnings, or wage-base limit. Note that the wage-base limit applies only to the Social Security (or OASDI) part of the tax because there is no limit for Medicare (or HI) tax.

Let's look at how Ernie computes the Social Security tax on Lee's earnings to give you a better idea of how this tax is calculated. First, Ernie knows both the current year's tax rate and the wage-base limit for the Social Security portion of the tax. Here are the rates and limit he will use:

Current year's rate for Social Security (OASDI) tax = 6.20%

Current year's rate for Medicare (HI) tax = 1.45%

Current year's wage-base limit for Social Security (OASDI) tax = $87,000

Note again that these rates and the wage-base limit may change each year. In general, the wage-base limit will increase from year to year, as may the rate of taxes. Therefore, we use the term *current* when referring to these tax rates and the wage-base limit.

Once Ernie knows the rates and limit he is ready to begin making calculations. First, Ernie needs to look at how much Lee has earned for the year *prior* to his current pay-period earnings. He will use this information to determine whether Lee's earnings are under or over the current wage-base limit for Social Security tax. Ernie finds that Lee's year-to-date (abbreviated YTD) gross earnings before this pay period equal $20,872.65. This dollar amount is below the wage-base limit of $87,000 for the year, so Lee's total gross earnings of $934.20 will be taxed at a rate of 6.20% for Social Security purposes. Ernie will withhold $57.92 in Social Security taxes (or $934.20 × .062 = $57.92).

What if Lee had made close to or more than $87,000 for the year before his current pay-period earnings? Let's suppose that Lee's prior year-to-date earnings are $86,618.95. If we add $934.20 to this amount, Lee's new year-to-date earnings will be $87,553.15 ($86,618.95 + $934.20), which is more than the current $87,000 wage-base limit. In this situation Ernie must withhold Social Security tax *on only the portion of Lee's current gross earnings that will not exceed the* $87,000 *wage-base limit.* Ernie must make the following calculation to determine this amount by subtracting Lee's prior year-to-date earnings from the wage base-limit: $87,000 − $86,618.95 = $381.05. Thus, only $381.05 of Lee's $934.20 in current gross earnings will be subject to Social Security tax at a rate of 6.20%. The remaining $553.15 of Lee's current pay (or $934.20 − $381.05) will not be taxed for Social Security (OASDI) purposes. Therefore, whatever Lee earns for the rest of the current calendar year will not be subject to this tax because Lee has exceeded the wage-base limit for the year.

It is important to know that all these calculations apply only to each current **calendar year.** An employee's year-to-date earnings in one year will never be carried over and used in the next year for the purpose of looking at the Social Security wage-base limit. Every employee starts the new year on January 1 with $0.00 in year-to-date earnings for wage-base limit analysis.

It is easier to figure Medicare (or HI) tax because there is no wage-base limit connected with this tax. Ernie will simply figure Medicare tax at a rate of 1.45% of Lee's earnings no matter how much he earns during the year. Ernie will withhold $13.55 in Medicare (or HI) tax on Lee's gross earnings for the pay period ($934.20 × .0145 = $13.55).

Another important fact about Social Security tax is that the amount withheld and paid by each employee must be matched and paid by the employer, using the same rules we have discussed. In Chapter 8 we look at the employer's side of Social Security and Medicare taxes.

OTHER INCOME TAX WITHHOLDING

We pointed out previously that employees will have state income taxes withheld from their paychecks if they live in one of the states that tax income. In addition, many cities and counties tax employee earnings. Sometimes the tax will be a certain percentage of gross earnings, or it may be a flat dollar amount withheld every pay period. Such cities and counties will have their own rules regarding payroll tax deposits and tax reports for this type of withholding.

WORKERS' COMPENSATION INSURANCE

Workers' compensation insurance provides protection for employees from any loss they may incur due to injury or death while on the job. Each employer (working with an insurance agent or a state agency) must estimate the cost of this insurance. The premium must be paid in advance. In the majority of states, this tax is paid by the employer, not the employee. In Chapter 8 we look at how the premium is figured and what responsibility the employer has in paying this tax.

Learning Unit 7-1 Review

AT THIS POINT you should be able to

- Explain the purpose of the Federal Wage and Hour Law. (p. 258)
- Calculate overtime pay. (p. 259)
- Complete a W-4 form. (p. 260)
- Discuss the term *claiming an allowance.* (p. 260)
- Use a wage-bracket tax table to arrive at the withholding amount for federal income tax. (p. 262)
- Define the purposes of Social Security (FICA) tax. (p. 262)
- Calculate the deductions for Social Security and Medicare taxes. (p. 263)
- Understand the purpose of workers' compensation insurance. (p. 264)

SELF-REVIEW QUIZ 7-1

(The forms you need are found on page 219 of the *Study Guide and Working Papers.*)

John Small is a software engineer who is paid biweekly. He earned $2,064 in the current biweekly pay period. To date this year, *before* the current payroll, John has earned a total $85,800 in salary. Please calculate the amount of tax for Social Security and Medicare, federal income tax, and state income tax deducted for the pay period.

- Social security tax is 6.20% with a wage-base limit of $87,000 for the year.
- Medicare tax is 1.45% with no wage-base limit.
- John is single and claims two withholding allowances.
- The state income tax rate is 8%.
- No other deductions are taken out of John's paycheck by his employer.

SOLUTION TO SELF-REVIEW QUIZ 7-1

- Social Security tax: $74.40 ($1,200 × .062). The $1,200 was found by taking $87,000 − $85,800.
- Medicare tax: $29.93 ($2,064 × .0145). Remember that there is no wage-base limit for this tax.
- State income tax: $165.12 ($2,064 × .08).
- Federal income tax: $330, found by looking at where the "At least $2,060" line meets the "Two withholding allowance" column.

Learning Unit 7-2   The Payroll Process

Ernie Goldman will now enter the payroll information for the three hourly employees of Gradesoft.com into a worksheet known as a **payroll register.** Figure 7-3 (p. 266) shows a completed payroll register for the biweekly pay period from August 7 through August 20. We refer to this figure in both Chapters 7 and 8.

This multicolumn form is used specifically for the purpose of tracking the earnings of employees for any given pay period. Note that Gradesoft.com will have both biweekly and monthly payroll registers because it tracks its hourly employees on a biweekly basis and its salaried employees on a monthly basis. (We only show the biweekly register here.) Let's look closely at each column in the register to see how the numbers were generated.

(A) ALLOWANCES AND MARITAL STATUS

The information in column A comes from the Form W-4 that each employee has completed. You will recall that this form (see Fig. 7-1) indicates the employee's marital status and number of withholding allowances (or exemptions) that is used to arrive at the correct amount of federal income tax (column M) to be withheld for the pay period.

> **Example:** Sheila Stowe is single and provides total support for her 9-year-old daughter. Even though she can claim two withholding allowances, she claims zero allowances because she wants to have more taken out of her paycheck each pay period. If she has paid too much in FIT, she can claim a refund after the end of the year when filing her individual income tax return.

(B) CUMULATIVE (YTD) EARNINGS

Column B shows the employee's year-to-date (or cumulative) earnings for the year *before* the current pay period earnings have been added to it. Ernie will look at the amount in this column to determine if the employee is over or under the Social Security wage-base limit.

> **Example:** Lee Jackson has earned $20,872.65 before the current biweekly pay period.

(C) SALARY FOR PAY PERIOD, NUMBER OF HOURS WORKED, AND WAGES PER HOUR

Specific columns are used to record the amount any salaried employees have earned for the pay period, the hours worked by hourly employees, and the hourly rate of pay for nonsalaried employees.

GRADESOFT.COM INC.
PAYROLL REGISTER
AUGUST 7–20, 200X

Employee Name	Allowances and Marital Status	Cumulative Earnings (YTD)	Salary for Pay Period	No. of Hours Worked	Wages per Hour	Earnings			Cumulative Earnings (YTD)	Taxable Earnings		
						Regular	Overtime	Gross		Federal Unemploy-ment	Soc. Sec.	Medicare
Jackson, L.	S-1	2087265	—	8400	1080	85320	8100	93420	2180685	—	93420	93420
Stowe, S.	S-0	485025	—	8000	2450	196000	—	196000	681025	196000	196000	196000
Regan, P.	S-2	4658705	—	8150	2175	174000	4894	178894	4837599	—	178894	178894
TOTALS		7230995	—			455320	12994	468314	7699309	196000	468314	468314
Discussions in this chapter are keyed to these letters	(A)	(B)	(C)	(C)	(C)	(D)	(E)	(F)	(G)	(H)	(I)	(J)

Figure 7-3 Payroll Register for Gradesoft.com

GRADESOFT.COM INC.
PAYROLL REGISTER
AUGUST 7–20, 200X

	FICA			Deductions						Distribution of Expense Accounts	
	Soc. Sec.	Medicare	Federal Income Tax	State Income Tax	Medical Insurance	Net Pay	Check No.		Business Analyst Expense	Program. Develop. Expense
	5792	1355	9500	7474	4400	67099	506		93420	
	121152	28842	36600	15680	2200	126526	507			196000
	111091	25940	25400	14312	2200	121097	508			178894
	29035	6791	71500	37466	8800	314722			93420	374894
	(K)	(L)	(M)	(N)	(O)	(P)	(Q)		(R)	(S)

Discussions in this chapter are keyed to these letters

Note: Sheila Stowe's medical insurance is $44.00 because she pays to cover both herself and her daughter.

Figure 7-3 (*continued*)

> **Example:** Because this payroll register is used only for hourly employees, no amounts are entered in the salary for pay period column. Please note that Lee Jackson is paid $10.80 per hour, and he worked 84 total hours for the pay period.

(D) "REGULAR" EARNINGS

To get an amount for column D, Ernie must multiply the total regular hours by the hourly rate of pay for each employee.

> **Example:** Sheila Stowe has earned $1,960.00 for the pay period.
>
> | Hours Worked | | Rate of Pay per Hour | | Regular Earnings |
> |---|---|---|---|---|
> | 80 | × | $24.50 | = | $1,960.00 |

(E) OVERTIME EARNINGS

After 40 hours each workweek, hourly employees are entitled to receive overtime pay at a rate of one and one-half times their regular hourly rate of pay.

> **Example:** Pat Regan worked 81.5 hours, of which 80 were regular and 1.5 hours were classified as overtime. Pat is paid overtime at a rate of $32.625 per hour.
>
> | Hourly Rate | | Time and a Half | | Overtime Rate of Pay |
> |---|---|---|---|---|
> | $21.75 | × | 1.5 | = | $32.625 |
> | Overtime Hours Worked | | Overtime Rate | | Overtime Earnings |
> | 1.5 | × | $32.625 | = | $48.94 |

(F) GROSS EARNINGS

Gross earnings is the total amount that an employee has earned (regular earnings plus any overtime earnings). These amounts will be used to fill in columns R and S.

> **Example:** Pat Regan's gross earnings are $1,788.94.
>
> | Regular Earnings | | Overtime Earnings | | Gross Earnings |
> |---|---|---|---|---|
> | $1,740.00 | + | $48.94 | = | $1,788.94 |

(G) CUMULATIVE EARNINGS (YTD)

Column G shows the employee's year-to-date earnings after the current pay period earnings have been computed. This amount will be "carried over" to the next payroll register column B for the next pay period.

Example: Sheila Stowe has earned $6,810.25 as of August 20.

Cumulative Earnings Before the Pay Period		Gross Earnings for the Pay Period		Cumulative Earnings YTD as of August 20
$4,850.25	+	$1,960.00	=	$6,810.25

(H) TAXABLE EARNINGS: UNEMPLOYMENT INSURANCE

In Chapter 8 we talk about certain payroll taxes that are only paid by employers. Federal unemployment taxes (per the Federal Unemployment Tax Act, or FUTA) are paid according to a wage-base limit (like Social Security tax). The current wage-base limit for FUTA tax is the first $7,000 that each employee earns during a calendar year. Note that this column shows the FUTA wage-base limit for each employee, not the amount of FUTA tax that Gradesoft.com has paid.

Example: Before this pay period, Sheila Stowe's cumulative year-to-date earnings are $4,850.25. For the pay period ending on August 20, Sheila earned $1,960. Her new cumulative year-to-date earnings now amount to $6,810.25, which is under the $7,000 FUTA wage-base limit. Gradesoft.com will pay FUTA tax on the $1,960.00 that Sheila earned for the pay period.

During the next pay period, Gradesoft.com will pay FUTA tax only on $189.75 of Sheila's earnings (assuming Sheila earns at least this much during the next pay period) because Sheila's earnings will meet the FUTA wage-base limit of $7,000 in this pay period.

Example:

Total taxable earnings for FUTA tax	$7,000.00
Cumulative earnings for Sheila Stowe	
before the new pay period	6,810.25
Taxable earnings for FUTA tax	$ 189.75

(I) TAXABLE EARNINGS FOR SOCIAL SECURITY (OASDI) TAX

All employees pay Social Security tax until they reach each current year's wage-base limit. Our current limit for this example is $87,000. Column I shows the amount of earnings that will be taxed. It does not show that amount of Social Security tax the employee or employer pays. None of the three hourly employees has reached the wage-base limit as of the August 20 pay period. Keep in mind this column is *not* the tax, it is the amount subject to the tax.

(J) TAXABLE EARNINGS FOR MEDICARE TAX

Column J shows the amount of earnings subject to Medicare tax. Remember that there is no wage-base limit for Medicare tax, so this column will match the amount found in column F, cumulative year-to-date earnings. Keep in mind this column is *not* the tax, it is the amount subject to the tax.

(K) FICA DEDUCTION—SOCIAL SECURITY TAX

The current rate for Social Security tax is 6.20% up to $87,000. The amount in column I is multiplied by the 6.20% rate to arrive at the tax for each employee in this column.

Example: Lee Jackson's Social Security tax for the pay period is $57.92.

Column I Amount		Current Social Security Rate		Column K Social Security Tax
$934.20	×	.062	=	$57.92

(L) FICA DEDUCTION—MEDICARE TAX

The current rate for Medicare tax is 1.45% on all employee earnings with no wage-base limit.

Example: Sheila Stowe's gross earnings of $1,960.00 is multiplied by 1.45% to arrive at $28.42 in Medicare tax.

Gross Earnings		Medicare Tax Rate		Medicare Tax
$1,960.00	×	.0145	=	$28.42

(M) FEDERAL INCOME TAX (FIT)

Recall that federal income tax does not have any wage-base limit. Employees pay FIT on their gross earnings each pay period throughout the year. The amount of tax withheld depends on the employee's (1) income for the pay period, (2) marital status, and (3) number of withholding allowances claimed on Form W-4 (Fig. 7-1).

Ernie has used the IRS table found in *Circular E* (see Fig. 7-2) to find the amount of FIT to withhold from the three employees for the August 20 pay period. Look at Figure 7-2 again and use the information found in column A to verify the amounts Ernie has listed in column M of the payroll register.

(N) STATE INCOME TAX (SIT)

Ernie uses a rate of 8% to calculate and withhold state income tax for the August 20 pay period. Like federal income tax, there is no wage-base limit for state income tax, so all employee gross earnings for the pay period will be taxed.

Example: Pat Regan's state income tax is $143.12.

Gross Earnings		Tax Rate		State Income Tax
$1,788.94	×	.08	=	$143.12

(O) MEDICAL INSURANCE

Gradesoft.com deducts an amount to pay for medical insurance coverage for its employees. The rate is $22.00 per pay period for coverage for an employee only and $44.00 per pay period for coverage of an employee and his or her dependents.

(P) NET PAY

Net pay, or take-home pay, is the employee's gross earnings minus taxes withheld and any other deductions, such as medical insurance. Gross pay is what all employees wish they had; net pay is what employees are left with.

Ernie will subtract all withholding taxes and medical insurance premiums from all employees' gross earnings to arrive at their net pay.

Example: Lee Jackson's net pay is $670.99, computed as follows:

Gross earnings		$934.20
Less: FICA—Social Security tax	$57.92	
FICA—Medicare tax	13.55	
Federal income tax	95.00	
State income tax	74.74	
Medical insurance	22.00	
Net pay		$670.99

(Q) CHECK NUMBER

When Ernie prepares the paychecks, he records each check number in column Q of the payroll register.

(R AND S) DISTRIBUTION OF EXPENSE ACCOUNTS

The gross earnings for each employee is an expense of Gradesoft.com. Ernie uses columns R and S to identify the specific expense account to which each employee's earnings will be posted. This identification will help him make the journal entry to record the August 20 payroll. Note that Lee Jackson's earnings will be posted to the Business Analyst Expense account, whereas Sheila's and Pat's earnings will be posted to the Programming Development Expense account.

Learning Unit 7-2 Review

AT THIS POINT you should be able to

- Explain and prepare a payroll register. (p. 265)
- Explain the purpose of the taxable earnings columns and how they relate to the cumulative earnings columns. (p. 269)

SELF-REVIEW QUIZ 7-2

(The forms you need are on page 219 of the *Study Guide and Working Papers.*)

Mike Chen is an hourly employee who is paid biweekly. He is paid overtime at a rate of 1.5 times his hourly rate of pay for any hours he works over 40 in a workweek. Mike has worked many overtime hours this year to develop a new software program, and as of December 10 he has cumulative earnings of $85,778.06. For the pay period ending on December 24, Mike's gross earnings are $1,940.85. Calculate Mike's net pay based on the following facts:

- The Social Security tax rate is 6.2% with a wage-base limit of $87,000 for the year; the Medicare rate is 1.45% with no wage-base limit.
- Mike is single and claims three withholding allowances per his Form W-4. Use the tax table in Figure 7-2 to find Mike's federal income tax withholding amount.
- The state income tax rate is 8% with no wage-base limit.
- Mike pays $44.00 for medical insurance for the pay period.

SOLUTION TO SELF-REVIEW QUIZ 7-2

Quiz Tip:
Only the first $1,221.94 of Mike's wages is subject to social security tax ($87,000 − $85,778.06).

1. FICA—Social Security tax is $75.76 ($1,221.94 × .062). Remember to subtract the cumulative year-to-date earnings from the wage-base limit when the employee's earnings approach the limit ($87,000 − $85,778.06). FICA—Medicare tax is $28.14 ($1,940.85 × .0145).
2. Federal income tax is $266 by the table (see Fig. 7-2).
3. State income tax is $155.27 ($1,940.85 × .08).

Mike Chen's net pay is $1,371.68 ($1,940.85 − $75.76 − $28.14 − $266.00 − $155.27 − $44.00).

Learning Unit 7-3   Recording and Paying the Payroll

JOURNALIZE THEN POST

After Ernie Goldman has completed the payroll register for the August 20 pay period, he must next take the summary total amounts (found at the bottom of the columns of the payroll register) and post them to specific accounts in the general ledger. Refer back to the payroll register in Figure 7-3.

For Gradesoft.com, the payroll for the biweekly pay period ending on August 20 is recorded in the general journal as shown in Figure 7-4.

Figure 7-4
Journalized Payroll Entry

General Journal							
200X							
Aug.	20	Business Analyst expense	9 3 4 20				
		Programming Development expense	3 7 4 8 94				
		FICA—Social Security tax payable			2 9 0 35		
		FICA—Medicare tax payable			6 7 91		
		Federal income tax payable			7 1 5 00		
		State income tax payable			3 7 4 66		
		Medical insurance payable			8 8 00		
		Wages and salaries payable			3 1 4 7 22		
		To record payroll for August 20, 200X					

Note that the amounts recorded in the Gradesoft.com general journal come from the August 20 payroll register. Look back at Figure 7-3 and note that the two expense account amounts (Business Analyst and Programming Development Expense) are the same figures found in columns R and S. The credit amounts to the various tax payable and medical insurance accounts come from the totals found in columns K through O. The amount of the net pay comes from column P. The ledger (Figure 7-5) of Gradesoft.com will look as follows *after* the posting process has been completed.

Wages and Salaries Payable 202	FICA—Social Security Payable 203	FICA—Medicare Payable 204
	3,147.22		290.35		67.91
Liability on the balance sheet	Liability on the balance sheet	Liability on the balance sheet

Federal Income Tax Payable 205	State Income Tax Payable 206	Medical Insurance Payable 207
	715.00		374.66		88.00
Liability on the balance sheet	Liability on the balance sheet	Liability on the balance sheet

Business Analyst Expense 601	Programming Development Expense 602
934.20		3,748.94	
Expense on the income statement	Expense on the income statement

Figure 7-5 summarizes this process.

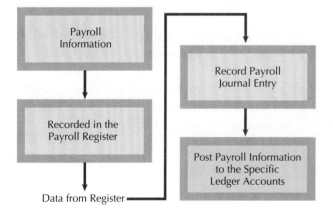

Figure 7-5
The Payroll Recording and Posting Process

PAYROLL CHECKING ACCOUNTS: PAYING THE PAYROLL

Gradesoft.com, like the vast majority of companies, uses a special checking account for paychecks. This account is called Payroll Checking Cash. A company with a medium to a large payroll will use this account to clear paychecks because (1) the company has much better internal control over the funds deposited to pay employees and (2) it is easier for the payroll person to reconcile the account each month and determine if someone has not cashed his or her paycheck for some reason.

A deposit for the total net amount of the payroll is placed in this separate checking account. When all the checks are written, the payroll checking account balance should be zero. The following journal entries would result in paying the payroll.

Figure 7-6
Check from
Gradesoft.com

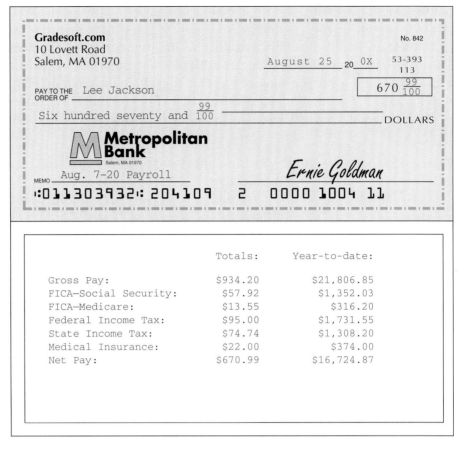

The checks that Gradesoft.com uses for payroll purposes provide a detailed accounting of an employee's gross earnings as well as all deductions withheld, as shown in Figure 7-6.

Remember that if a payroll checking account is not used by a business, its payroll can be paid by debiting Wages and Salaries Payable and crediting Cash. In this instance the company's regular checking account would be used to pay employees.

THE INDIVIDUAL EMPLOYEE EARNINGS RECORD

Ernie has yet another task to attend to when it comes to payroll recordkeeping. Individual employee earnings records must be maintained by Gradesoft.com to meet federal and state employment laws and regulations.

The employee earnings record (see Fig. 7-7) provides a summary of each employee's earnings, deductions, net pay, and cumulative earnings during each calendar year. The information summarized in this record will be used by Ernie to prepare quarterly and annual payroll tax reports (which we discuss in Chapter 8). Thus, the employee earnings record is broken into calendar quarters (each calendar quarter is 13 weeks in length).

Figure 7-8 on p. 276 shows the payroll function for Gradesoft.com. Note that the payroll function begins with recording the hours worked by employees each biweekly and monthly pay period. The flow of information is the same for each pay period during the calendar year.

INDIVIDUAL EMPLOYEE EARNINGS RECORD
FOR PAT REGAN
FOURTH QUARTER, 200X

Pay Period No. and Pay Dates	Hours Worked			Total Earnings	Deductions					Net Pay	Check No.	Cumulative Earnings
	Week #	Regular	Overtime		Soc. Sec.	Medicare	Fed. Inc. Tax	State Inc. Tax	Med. Ins.‡			
10/02–10/15	20	80	4.5	188681	11698	2736	31400	15094	2200	125553	511	5599457
10/16–10/29	21	80	3.75	186234	11546	2700	30900	14899	2200	123989	525	5785691
10/30–11/12	22	80	5.25	191128	11850	2771	32000	15290	2200	127017	530	5976819
11/13–11/26	23	80	6	193575	12002	2808	32600	15486	2200	128479	544	6170394
11/27–12/10	24	80	8.75	202547	12558	2937	35400	16204	2200	133248	565	6372941
12/11–12/24	25	77	0	167475	10383	2428	25300	13398	2200	113766	574	6540416
12/25–12/31	26*	48	0	104400	6473	1514	11000	8352	2200	74861	590	6644816
Total 4th Quarter				1234040	76510	17894	198600	98723	15400	826913		
YTD Total				6644816	411979	96350	826500	531585	57200	4721202		

*Note the last biweekly pay period will end in the next calendar year (January 8); Ernie will only use Pat's hours worked this year to complete her employee earnings record for this year.
‡Note P. Regan decreased medical insurance to $22 from 44 in Fig. 7.3.

Figure 7-7 Individual Employee Earnings Record

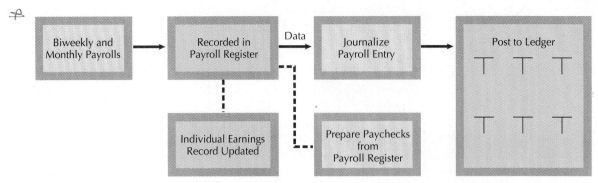

Figure 7-8 Payroll Function for Gradesoft.com

Learning Unit 7-3 Review

AT THIS POINT you should be able to

- Explain how to enter payroll information into the general journal from the payroll register. (p. 272)
- Journalize entries to pay a payroll. (p. 272)
- Update an individual employee earnings record. (p. 274)

SELF-REVIEW QUIZ 7-3

(The forms you need are on page 220 of the *Study Guide and Working Papers.*)
Indicate which of the following statements are false.

1. The use of a payroll register to record a company's payroll is optional.
2. FICA—Social Security Payable is a liability on the income statement.
3. Wages and Salaries Expense has a normal credit balance.
4. Individual employee earnings records are used by employees to keep track of their wages.
5. Every calendar quarter has 13 weeks.

Quiz Tip:
There are four quarters in a year.

SOLUTION TO SELF-REVIEW QUIZ 7-3

1. False   **2.** False   **3.** False   **4.** False   **5.** True

Chapter Review

Summary of Key Points

Learning Unit 7-1

1. The Fair Labor Standards Act states that a worker (1) will receive a minimum hourly rate of pay and (2) will work a maximum of 40 hours during a workweek at the regular rate of pay with time and a half after 40 hours.
2. For the rules of the Fair Labor Standards Act to apply to an employer, the employer must be involved in interstate commerce. Most companies today are involved in interstate commerce.
3. The employee and employer equally contribute to Social Security tax an amount that is based on a given yearly rate and wage base for a calendar year. Only Social Security tax has a wage-base limit of $87,000 as of this writing. Medicare has no wage-base limit, so an employee and employer will pay this tax on all the employee's earnings during the calendar year.
4. Tax tables for federal income tax withholding can be found in IRS *Circular E, Employer's Tax Guide* (also known as Publication 15).

Learning Unit 7-2

1. Gross pay less deductions equals net pay.
2. The taxable earnings columns do not show the tax. They show amount of earnings to be taxed for unemployment taxes, Social Security, and Medicare. Note that FICA is made up of two taxes, Social Security and Medicare.

Learning Unit 7-3

1. A payroll register provides the data for journalizing the payroll entry in the general journal.
2. Deductions for payroll represent liabilities for the employer until paid.
3. The account distribution columns of the payroll register indicate which accounts will be debited to record the total payroll wages and salaries expense when a journal entry is prepared.
4. The accounts FICA—Social Security Payable and FICA—Medicare Payable accumulate the tax liabilities of both the employer and the employee for Medicare and Social Security.
5. Paying a payroll results in debiting Wages and Salaries Payable and crediting Cash (or Payroll Checking Cash).
6. The individual employee earnings records are updated soon after the payroll register is prepared.

Key Terms

Allowance (also called exemption) A certain dollar amount of a person's income that will be considered nontaxable for income tax withholding purposes.

Calendar year A one-year period beginning on January 1 and ending on December 31. Employers must use a calendar year for payroll purposes, even if the employer uses a fiscal year for financial statements and for any other reasons.

Circular E An IRS tax publication of tax tables.

Fair Labor Standards Act (Federal Wage and Hour Law) A law the majority of employers must follow that contains rules stating the minimum hourly rate of pay and the maximum number of hours a worker will work before being paid time and a half for overtime hours worked. This law also has other rules and regulations that employers must follow for payroll purposes.

Federal income tax withholding   Amount of federal income tax withheld by the employer from the employee's gross pay; the amount withheld is determined by the employee's gross pay, the pay period, the number of allowances claimed by the employee on the W-4 form, and the marital status indicated on the W-4 form.

FICA (Federal Insurance Contributions Act)   Part of the Social Security Act of 1935, this law requires that a tax be levied on both the employer and employee up to a certain maximum rate and wage base for Social Security tax purposes. Furthermore, there is a tax for Medicare purposes with no employer or employee wage-base maximum.

FICA—Medicare Payable   A liability account that accumulates tax for Medicare.

FICA—Social Security Payable   A liability account that accumulates tax for Social Security.

Gross earnings   Amount of pay received before any deductions.

Individual employee earnings record   An accounting document that summarizes the total amount of wages paid and the deductions for the calendar year. It aids in preparing governmental reports. A new record is prepared for each employee each year.

Interstate commerce   A test that is applied to determine whether an employer must follow the rules of the Fair Labor Standards Act. If an employer communicates or does business with another business in some other state, it is usually considered to be involved in interstate commerce.

Market Wages Expense   An account that records from the payroll register gross wages earned by employees of a market (grocery) outlet.

Medical insurance   A deduction from employee's paycheck for health insurance.

Net pay   Gross pay less deductions. Net pay (or *take-home pay*) is what the worker actually takes home.

Office Salaries Expense   An account that records from the payroll gross salaries earned by employees of an office.

Pay (or payroll) period   A length of time used by an employer to calculate the amount of an employee's earnings. Pay periods can be weekly, biweekly (once every two weeks), semimonthly (twice each month), monthly, quarterly or annual.

Payroll register   A multicolumn form that can be used to record payroll data. The data in the payroll register are then used to prepare the general journal entry to record the paying of employees for a pay period.

Payroll tax   Amount of federal tax withheld from each employee's gross pay.

Payroll tax deposits   Amounts an employer pays to the government for payroll taxes. We discuss these deposits in more detail in Chapter 8.

State income tax withholding   Amount of state income tax withheld by the employer from the employee's gross pay.

Taxable earnings   Shows amount of earnings subject to a tax. The tax itself is not shown.

W-4 (Employee's Withholding Allowance Certificate)   A form filled out by employees and used by employers to supply needed information about the number of allowances claimed, marital status, and so forth. The form is used for payroll purposes to determine federal income tax withholding from an employee's paycheck.

Wage bracket tables   Various charts in IRS *Circular E* providing information about deductions for federal income tax based on earnings and data supplied on the W-4 form.

Wages and Salaries Payable   A liability account that shows net pay for payroll before employees are paid. Account zeros out after employees are paid.

Workers' compensation insurance   Insurance required by employers to protect their employees against losses due to injury or death incurred while on the job.

Workweek   A seven-day (168-hour) period used to determine overtime hours for employees. A workweek can begin on any given day, but must end seven days later.

Questions, Mini Exercises, Exercises, and Problems

Discussion Questions

1. What is the purpose of the Fair Labor Standards Act (also called the Federal Wage and Hour Law)?

2. Explain how to calculate overtime.

3. Define and state the purpose of completing a W-4 form (called the Employee's Withholding Allowance Certificate).

4. The more allowances an employee claims on a W-4 form, the more take-home pay the employee gets with each paycheck. True or false.

Blueprint: Recording, Posting, and Paying the Payroll

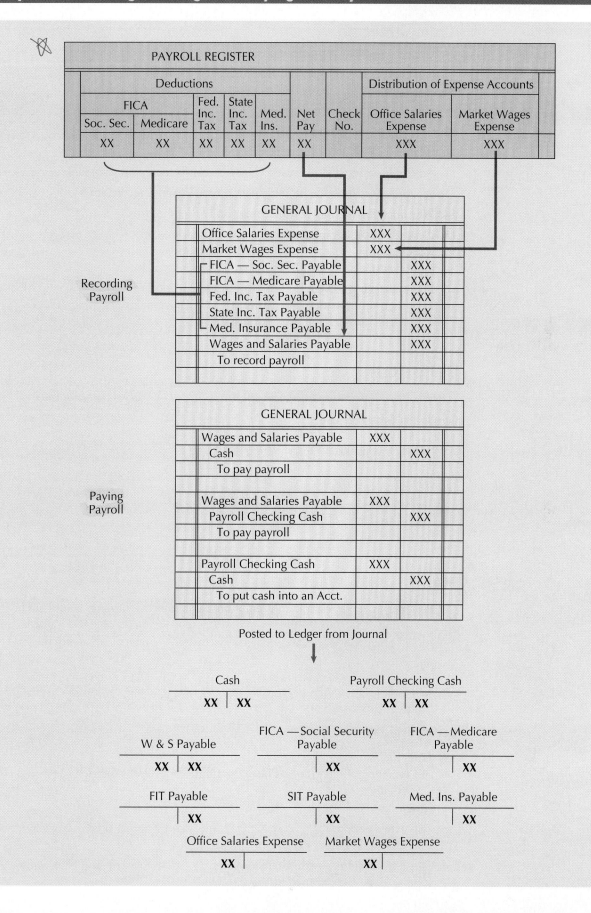

5. Why should a business prepare a payroll register before employees are paid? Please explain.

6. The taxable earnings column of a payroll register records the amount of tax due. True or false?

7. Define and state the purpose of FICA taxes.

8. Explain how to calculate Social Security and Medicare taxes.

9. The employer doesn't have to contribute to Social Security. Agree or disagree. Please explain.

10. Explain how federal and state income tax withholdings are determined.

11. What is a calendar year?

12. An employer must always use a calendar year for payroll purposes. True or false?

13. What purpose does the individual employee earnings record serve?

14. Why does payroll information center on 13-week quarters?

15. Please draw a diagram showing how the following items relate to each other: (a) a weekly payroll, (b) a payroll register, (c) individual employees' earnings, (d) general journal entries for payroll, (e) a payroll checking account.

16. If you earned $130,000 this year, you would pay more Social Security and Medicare taxes than your partner who earned $75,000. Do you agree or disagree? Please provide calculations to support your answer.

Mini Exercises

(The forms you need are on page 222 of the *Study Guide and Working Papers.*)

Calculating Gross Earnings

1. Calculate the total wages earned (assume an overtime rate of time and a half over 40 hours).

Employee	Hourly Rate	No. of Hours Worked
A. Dawn Slow	$10	39
B. Jill Jacobi	12	50

FICA

2. Pete Martin, single, claiming 1 exemption, has cumulative earnings before this biweekly pay period of $86,000. Assuming he is paid $2,000 this week, what will his deduction be for FIT and FICA (Medicare and Social Security)? Use tables and rates in the text.

Net Pay

3. Calculate Pete's net pay from Mini Exercise 2 above. State income tax is 5% and health insurance is $40.

Payroll Register

4. From the following identify
   1. Total of gross pay (comes from distribution of expense accounts).
   2. A deduction.
   3. Net pay.

   _____ **a.** Office Salaries Expense and Wages Expense
   _____ **b.** FICA—Social Security Payable
   _____ **c.** FICA—Medicare Payable
   _____ **d.** Federal Income Tax Payable

_____ **e.** Medical Insurance Payable
_____ **f.** Wages and Salaries Payable

Payroll Account

5. From the following, indicate if the title is

1. An asset.	**4.** Appears on the income statement.
2. A liability.	**5.** Appears on the balance sheet.
3. An expense.	

_____ **a.** FICA—Social Security Payable
_____ **b.** Office Salaries Expense
_____ **c.** Federal Income Tax Payable
_____ **d.** FICA—Medicare Payable
_____ **e.** Wages and Salaries Payable

Exercises

(The forms you need are on pages 223–224 of the *Study Guide and Working Papers*.)

7-1. Calculate the total wages earned for each employee (assume an overtime rate of time and a half over 40 hours).

Calculating wages with overtime.

Employee	Hourly Rate	No. of Hours Worked
Joss Amando	$ 8	39
Jill West	12	44
Dale Aster	11	46

7-2. Compute the net pay for each employee using the federal income tax withholding tables in Figure 7-2. (Assume the following for FICA: Social Security tax is 6.2% on a wage-base limit of $87,000; Medicare is 1.45% on all earnings; the payroll is paid biweekly; there is no state income tax.)

Tax table.

Employee	Status	Claiming	Cumulative Pay	This Week's Pay
Alvin Cell	Single	1	$50,000	$1,190
Angel Lowe	Single	0	$64,300	$1,200

7-3. Complete the table.

Categorizing accounts.

	Category ↑	Normal Balance	Account Appears on Which Financial Statements
Medical Insurance Payable			
Wages and Salaries Payable			
Office Salaries Expense			
Market Wages Expense			
FICA—Social Security Payable			
Federal Income Tax Payable			
State Income Tax Payable			

7-4. The weekly payroll journal entry in Figure 7-9 was prepared by Landcaster Company from its payroll register. Which columns of the payroll register have the data come from? How does the *taxable earnings* column of the payroll register relate to this entry?

Figure 7-9
Payroll Journal Entry

	Oct.	7	Shop Salaries Expense		4 0 0 0 00				
			Factory Wages Expense		2 0 0 0 00				
			FICA—Social Security Payable				3 7 2 00	
			FICA—Medicare Payable				8 7 00	
			Federal Income Tax Payable				1 2 0 0 00	
			State Income Tax Payable				1 2 5 6 00	
			Union Dues Payable				1 1 0 00	
			Wages and Salaries Payable				2 9 7 5 00	

Payroll register and the journal entry.

7-5. The following amounts have been taken from the weekly payroll register for the Wu Lee Company on October 9, 200X. Using the same account title headings that we have used in this chapter, please prepare the general journal entry to record the payroll for Wu Lee Company for October 9.

Recording payroll by journal entry.

Factory Wages Expense	$3,579.00
Office Salaries Expense	1,597.00
Deduction for FICA—Social Security	296.15
Deduction for FICA—Medicare	75.05
Deduction for federal income tax	1,112.84
Deduction for state income tax	258.80
Deduction for union dues	480.00

Group A Problems

(The forms you need are on pages 225–229 of the *Study Guide and Working Papers.*)

7A-1. From the following information, please complete the chart for gross earnings for the week. (Assume an overtime rate of time and one-half over 40 hours.)

Calculating gross earnings with overtime.

	Hourly Rate	No. of Hours Worked	Gross Earnings
a. Joe Vasquez	$ 9	40	
b. Edna Kane	8	47	
c. Dick Wall	10	42	
d. Pat Green	13	50	

Check Figure:
d. $715   Gross Earnings

7A-2. March Company has five salaried employees. Your task is to record the following information into a payroll register:

Completing a payroll register.

Employee	Allowance and Marital Status	Cumulative Earnings Before This Payroll	Biweekly Salary	Department
Kool, Alice	S-1	$42,000	$1,200	Sales
Lose, Bob	S-1	30,000	800	Office
Moore, Linda	S-2	59,200	1,240	Office
Relt, Rusty	S-3	85,830	1,270	Sales
Veel, Larry	S-0	29,000	820	Sales

Assume the following:

1. FICA—Social Security: 6.2% on $87,000; FICA—Medicare: 1.45% on all earnings.
2. Each employee contributes $25 biweekly for union dues.
3. State income tax is 6% of gross pay.
4. FIT is calculated from Figure 7-2.

Check Figure:
Net Pay $3,938.99

7A-3. The bookkeeper of Pearl Co. gathered the following data from individual employee's earnings records and daily time cards. Your tasks are to (1) complete a payroll register on December 12 and (2) journalize the appropriate entry to record the payroll.

Completing a payroll register and journalizing the payroll entry.

Employee	Allowance and Marital Status	Cumulative Earnings Before This Payroll	M	T	W	T	F	Hourly Rate of Pay	FIT	Department
Boy, Pete	M-1	$64,100	5	11	9	8	8	$18	73	Sales
Heat, Donna	S-0	15,000	8	10	9	9	4	16	91	Office
Pyle, Ray	M-3	66,000	8	10	10	10	10	16	69	Sales
Vent, Joan	S-1	19,000	8	8	8	8	8	20	119	Office

Assume the following:

1. FICA—Social Security: 6.2% on $87,000; FICA—Medicare: 1.45% on all earnings.
2. Federal income tax has been calculated from a weekly table for you.
3. Each employee contributes $25 weekly for health insurance.
4. Overtime is paid at a rate of time and a half over 40 hours.

Check Figure:
Net pay $2,336.06

7A-4. Gary Nelson, Accountant, has gathered the following data from the time cards and individual employee earnings records. Your tasks are as follows:

Payroll register completed; journalizing and posting.

1. On December 5, 200X, prepare a payroll register for this biweekly payroll.
2. Journalize (p. 4) in the general journal and post to the general ledger accounts.

Check Figure:
Net Pay $3,450.67

Employee	Allowance and Marital Status	Cumulative Earnings Before This Payroll	Biweekly Salary	Check No.	Department
Aulson, Andy	S-3	$30,000	$ 950	30	Factory
Flynn, Jacki	S-1	50,000	1,000	31	Office
Moore, Jeff	S-2	60,000	1,200	32	Factory
Sullivan, Alison	S-1	65,000	1,300	33	Office

Assume the following:

1. FICA—Social Security: 6.2% on $87,000; FICA—Medicare: 1.45% on all earnings.
2. Federal income tax is calculated from Figure 7-2.
3. State income tax is 5% of gross pay.
4. Union dues are $10 biweekly.

Group B Problems

(The forms you need are on pages 225–229 in the *Study Guide and Working Papers*.)

7B-1. From the following information, please complete the chart for gross earnings for the week. (Assume an overtime rate of time and one-half over 40 hours.)

Calculating gross earnings with overtime.

	Hourly Rate	No. of Hours Worked	Gross Earnings
a. Joe Vasquez	$ 5	40	
b. Edna Kane	10	47	
c. Dick Wall	12	36	
d. Pat Green	14	55	

Check Figure:
d.   Gross Pay. $875

Completing a payroll register.

7B-2. March Company has five salaried employees. Your task is to record the following information into a payroll register.

Employee	Allowance and Marital Status	Cumulative Earnings Before This Payroll	Biweekly Salary	Department
Kool, Alice	S-1	$45,150	$1,290	Sales
Lose, Bob	S-1	22,575	800	Office
Moore, Linda	S-2	59,300	1,240	Office
Relt, Rusty	S-3	86,100	1,300	Sales
Veel, Larry	S-0	21,875	860	Sales

Check Figure:
Net Pay $4,065.41

Assume the following:

1. FICA—Social Security: 6.2% up to $87,000: FICA—Medicare: 1.45% on all earnings.
2. Each employee contributes $25 biweekly for union dues.
3. State income tax is 6% of gross pay.
4. FIT is calculated from Figure 7-2.

Completing a payroll entry and journalizing the payroll entry.

7B-3. The bookkeeper of Pearl Co. gathered the following data from individual employees' earnings records and daily time cards. Your tasks are to (1) complete a payroll register on December 12 and (2) journalize the appropriate entry to record the payroll.

Employee	Allowance and Marital Status	Cumulative Earnings Before This Payroll	M	T	W	T	F	Hourly Rate of Pay	FIT	Department
Boy, Pete	S-1	$64,900	12	11	7	7	7	$16	100	Sales
Heat, Donna	S-0	19,000	8	9	9	9	5	16	91	Office
Pyle, Ray	M-3	87,550	10	10	10	10	5	20	87	Sales
Vent, Joan	S-1	13,500	6	8	8	8	8	19	97	Office

Check Figure:
Net Pay $2,398.73

Assume the following:

1. FICA—Social Security: 6.2% on $87,000; FICA—Medicare: 1.45% on all earnings.
2. Federal income tax has been calculated from a weekly table for you.
3. Each employee contributes $25 weekly for health insurance.
4. Overtime is paid at a rate of time and a half over 40 hours.

Payroll entry completed; journalizing and posting.

7B-4. Gary Nelson, accountant, has gathered the following data from the time cards and individual employee earnings records. Your task is to

1. On December 5, 200X, prepare a payroll register for this biweekly payroll.
2. Journalize (p. 4) in the general journal and post to the general ledger accounts.

Employee	Allowance and Marital Status	Cumulative Earnings Before This Payroll	Biweekly Salary	Check No.	Department
Aulson, Andy	S-3	$30,000	$ 800	30	Factory
Flynn, Jacki	S-1	50,000	1,100	31	Office
Moore, Jeff	S-2	60,000	1,050	32	Factory
Sullivan, Alison	S-1	65,000	1,200	33	Office

Check Figure:
Net Pay $3,126.52

Assume the following:

1. FICA—Social Security: 6.2% on $87,000; FICA—Medicare: 1.45% on all earnings.
2. Federal income tax is calculated from Figure 7-2.
3. State income tax is 6% of gross pay.
4. Union dues are $15 biweekly.

Real-World Applications

7R-1. Small Company, a sole proprietorship, has two employees, Jim Roy and Janice Alter. The owner of Small Co. is Bert Ryan. During the current pay period, Jim worked 48 hours and Janice 56. The reason for these extra hours is that both Jim and Janice worked their regular 40-hour workweek, plus Jim worked 8 extra hours on Sunday and Janice worked 8 extra hours on Saturday and Sunday. Their contract with Small Co. is that they are each paid an hourly rate of $8 per hour with all hours over 40 to be time and a half and double time on Sunday. Bert, the owner, feels he is also entitled to a salary, because he works as many hours. He plans to pay himself $425.

As the accountant for Small Co., (1) calculate the gross pay for Jim and Janice and (2) write a letter to Bert Ryan with your recommendations regarding his salary.

7R-2. Marcy Moore works for Moose Company during the day and GTA Company at night. Both her employers have deducted FICA taxes for Social Security and Medicare. At year end Marcy has earned $78,800 at her job at Moose Company and $12,000 at GTA.

At a party she tells Bill Barnes, an accountant, who tells her she has paid too much Social Security tax and that she is entitled to a refund or credit on her tax return she files for the year. Bill suggests that she call the Internal Revenue Service's toll-free number and ask for taxpayer assistance. Assume Social Security of 6.2% on $87,000 and Medicare of 1.45% on all Marcy's earnings during the year.

As Marcy's friend, (1) check to see if indeed she has overpaid any FICA tax and (2) write a brief note to her and show her your calculations to support your answer.

YOU make the call

Critical Thinking/Ethical Case

7R-3. Russ Todd works for a delicatessen. As the bookkeeper, Russ has been asked by the owner to keep two separate books for meals tax. The owner has asked Todd to hire someone on the weekends to punch in false tapes that can be submitted to the state. These tapes would show low sales and thus less liability for meals tax payments. You make the call. Write down your specific recommendations to Russ.

Internet Exercises: Starbucks; American Payroll Association

EX-1. [www.tei-employment.com]   Suppose that Starbucks decided to follow one of the great trends in American employment, that of "leasing" employees from a temporary agency. One such agency is Temporary Employees, Inc. in Houston, Texas. When a business employs temporary workers, they supervise the temps just like they do their own employees. What they do not have to do is the everyday administrative work that accompanies having employees.

1. Visit the Web site and describe how Starbucks, or any other employer, could save money by hiring temporary employees.
2. While there are advantages to hiring temporary workers, there are also disadvantages. List some of the disadvantages.

EX-2. [www.americanpayroll.org/mission.html]   The American Payroll Association (APA) is an organization of payroll professionals, and it provides a semiannual certification examination. APA provides an avenue for payroll professionals to support others and to assist in meeting common problems encountered in this important profession.

1. From your viewing of their Web site, discuss how this organization fills a niche in the field of human resources and payroll administration.
2. What would be the organization's advantage to you if you were to pursue a career in payroll administration?

Continuing Problem

In preparing for next year, Tony Freedman has hired two employees to work hourly, assisting with some troubleshooting and repair work.

Assignment

(See pages 232–241 in the *Study Guide and Working Papers*.)

1. Record the following transactions in general journal format and post to the general ledger.
2. Prepare a payroll register.
3. Prepare a trial balance as of November 30, 200X.

Assume the following transactions:

a. The following accounts have been added to the chart of accounts: Wage Expense #5110, FICA—Social Security Payable #2020, FICA—Medicare Payable #2030, FIT Payable #2040, State Income Tax Payable #2050, and Wages Payable #2010.
b. FICA—Social Security is taxed at 6.2% up to $76,200* in earnings, and Medicare at 1.45% on all earnings. Note that this is not the current wage-base limit for Social Security.
c. State income tax is 2% of gross pay.
d. Both employees have no federal income tax taken out of their pay.
e. Each employee earns $10 an hour and is paid $1\frac{1}{2}$ times salary for hours worked in excess of 40 weekly.

Nov. 1   Billed Vita Needle Company $6,800; invoice #12675 for services rendered.
      3   Billed Accu Pac, Inc. $3,900; invoice #12676 for services rendered.
      5   Purchased new shop benches, $1,400, on account from System Design Furniture.
      7   Paid the two employee wages: Lance Kumm, 38 hours, and Anthony Hall, 42 hours.
      9   Received the phone bill, $150.
     12   Collected $500 of the amount due from Taylor Golf.
     14   Paid the two employee wages: Lance Kumm, 25 hours, and Anthony Hall, 36 hours.
     18   Collected $800 of the amount due from Taylor Golf.

*Note that this is not the current wage-base limit for Social Security.

20 Purchased a fax machine for the office from Multi Systems, Inc. on credit, $450.

21 Paid the two employee wages: Lance Kumm, 26 hours, and Anthony Hall, 35 hours.

SUBWAY Case

PAYROLL RECORDS: A FULL-TIME JOB

Like every Subway restaurant owner, Stan needs to keep a master file of important employee information. This file contains every employee's name, address, phone number, Social Security number, rate of pay, hours worked per week, and W-4 form.

Stan employs two part-time "sandwich artists" and no full-time managers—yet. If his sales continue to be high, he'll need to hire someone to manage operations so that he can spend more time analyzing the financials—with Lila's help—and growing his business. Most restaurants hire mostly part-timers with a core of full-time employees, but the numbers vary from restaurant to restaurant. Benefits vary too. Stan, for instance, plans to offer health and dental benefits when he hires a manager. He knows what a great incentive these benefits are, with health costs so high. He pays his sandwich artists, Rashid and Ellen, the minimum wage since they both have less than a year's experience. However, he's talking to Mariah Washington about creating some incentives to keep them motivated. If Rashid and Ellen are with him for a full year, they'll see a nice raise in their biweekly paychecks. The frequency of pay varies by state and sometimes by city or county. So, of course, do tax rates.

Stan must record all this vital information and report it to the various state, local, and federal authorities. In addition, Stan includes total payroll expenses on the weekly sales and inventory report, which he submits electronically to headquarters from his POS screen.

Scheduling workers and keeping payroll records are the bane of Stan's existence. These tasks are so incredibly time-consuming. He was pleased to hear, then, at the last meeting of his local North American Association of Subway Franchisees (NAASF) that the new point of sale (POS) terminals will soon offer an electronic scheduling package.

"Wow! That will really help," said Stan cheerfully to another franchisee. "No more different colors of ink just to keep track of who will work when! Now I can plan around Rashid and Ellen's exam schedules without a hassle. Scheduling might just become my favorite module in the new system."

"Sure," said Javier Gonzalez, another owner. "Now you can concentrate on payroll records. What fun!"

"Ay. Que lata," Stan groaned. *What a drag!*

Discussion Questions

1. What payroll records does Stan need to keep for his Subway restaurant?
2. What other information might Stan want so as to schedule working hours for each employee?
3. How does the payroll register help Stan prepare the payroll? Consult the process outlined on page 258.

CHAPTER 8

The Employer's Tax Responsibilities

Principles and Procedures

A favorite place for students to go after classes is the Green Earth Grocery and Coffee Shop. Students stop in and buy coffee, study, and socialize. Many students at school like the offbeat and off-campus atmosphere of the store, which specializes in organic groceries, coffees, teas, and a variety of gifts.

You stop in after school and see Martha Simpson, the owner of Green Earth Grocery, sitting in the corner of the coffee shop area. She appears to be wrestling with some paperwork. When you ask her how she's doing, she looks at you and snarls, "Reports, reports! It isn't enough that I pay everyone here each week and pay their withholding taxes on time, now I have to tell the government how much I paid my employees and how much tax I've paid to the government."

As we discussed in Chapter 7, businesses that employ workers must withhold certain payroll taxes on their earnings. In this chapter, we continue our discussion of payroll for businesses. We will learn that a business that employs workers must not only withhold taxes on earnings but also must summarize and report both the amount employees earn as well as the taxes withheld on those earnings. We will learn about several important federal payroll reports known as the Form 940-EZ, Form 941, and Forms W-2 and W-3. We will also discuss when and how a business must make payroll tax deposits.

Payroll taxes and reports seem to be inseparable when working with a company's payroll. After you finish studying this chapter and working through the problems and exercises, you will be able to help someone like Martha with the various federal payroll reports that must be prepared along with paying employees.

Learning Objectives

- Calculating and journalizing employer payroll tax expenses. (p. 290)

- Completing the Employer's Quarterly Federal Tax Return and Deposit Coupon (Forms 941 and 8109) and paying tax obligations for FICA tax (Social Security and Medicare) and federal income tax. (p. 295)

- Preparing Forms W-2, W-3, and 940-EZ and estimates of workers' compensation insurance premiums. (p. 303)

In Chapter 7 we looked at how Gradesoft.com computed and recorded payroll data about its employees. This chapter focuses on specific tax responsibilities of the employer.

Learning Unit 8-1   The Employer's Payroll Tax Expense

When opening a business, every employer must get a federal **employer identification number** (also known as an **EIN**) for purposes of reporting earnings, taxes, and so forth. When Gradesoft.com began, Ernie Goldman filled out **Form SS-4** to obtain the company's EIN. The SS-4 form asks for the following information:

1. Name of applicant.
2. Trade name of business.
3. Address or place of business.
4. County in which business is located.
5. Name of the principal officer or owner of the business.
6. Type of business (sole proprietor, partnership, etc.).
7. The reason for applying for an EIN.
8. The date the business began.
9. The closing month of the accounting year.
10. First date that the business will pay its employees.
11. The potential number of employees in the coming year.
12. Main activity or nature of the business.

Gradesoft.com's payroll tax obligations are recorded in the general journal when the payroll is recorded. Gradesoft.com is responsible for (1) Social Security and Medicare tax (or FICA), (2) federal unemployment tax, and (3) state unemployment tax. The total of these taxes is recorded in the **Payroll Tax Expense** account in the general ledger.

Let's look at how Ernie calculates the amount of each tax.

CALCULATING THE EMPLOYER'S PAYROLL TAXES

FICA (Federal Insurance Contributions Act)

It is the responsibility of Gradesoft.com to match whatever its employees pay into the **Federal Insurance Contributions Act (FICA)** on a dollar-for-dollar basis each pay period. The accounts in the ledger, FICA—Social Security Payable and FICA—Medicare Payable, record the tax for *both* the employee and the employer. To determine the amount of FICA Gradesoft.com owes, we must use the FICA taxable earnings columns for Social Security and Medicare from the payroll register discussed in Chapter 7 and reproduced here for your convenience as Figure 8-1.

The payroll register shows that $4,683.14 (column I) of wages is subject to Social Security tax, and in column J we also see $4,683.14 of wages is subject to tax for Medicare.

$$\text{Social Security} \quad \$4{,}683.14 \times .062 \quad = \$290.36$$
$$\text{Medicare} \quad \$4{,}683.14 \times .0145 = \$\ 67.91$$

The employer must match the FICA contribution of the employee for Social Security *and* Medicare taxes.

GRADESOFT.COM INC.
PAYROLL REGISTER
AUGUST 7–20, 200X

Employee Name	Allowances and Marital Status	Cumulative Earnings (YTD)	Salary for Pay Period	No. of Hours Worked	Wages per Hour	Earnings Regular	Earnings Overtime	Earnings Gross	Cumulative Earnings (YTD)	Taxable Earnings Unemployment	Taxable Earnings Soc. Sec.	Taxable Earnings Medicare
Jackson, L.	S-1	20 87 2 65	—	84.00	10 80	85 35 20	81 00	9 34 20	21 80 6 85		9 34 20	9 34 20
Stowe, S.	S-0	48 50 25	—	80.00	24 50	19 60 00	—	19 60 00	6 81 0 25	19 60 00	19 60 00	19 60 00
Regan, P.	S-2	46 58 7 05	—	81.50	21 75	17 40 00	48 94	17 88 94	48 37 5 99	—	17 88 94	17 88 94
TOTALS		72 30 9 95	—			4 55 35 20	1 29 94	4 68 33 14	76 99 3 09	19 60 00	4 68 33 14	4 68 33 14
Discussions in this chapter are keyed to these letters	(A)	(B)	(C)			(D)	(E)	(F)	(G)	(H)	(I)	(J)

Figure 8-1 Partial Payroll for Gradesoft.com

FICA—Social Security Payable 203	FICA—Medicare Payable 204
290.36 (employee)	67.91 (employee)
290.36 (employer)	67.91 (employer)

FUTA (Federal Unemployment Tax Act)

Unemployment insurance is a joint effort on the part of the federal government, all 50 states, the District of Columbia, and U.S. territories. Each state is required to run its own unemployment program for its unemployed workers. The state programs are approved and monitored by the federal government.

To raise money for these unemployment programs, the federal government levies taxes on employers under a law called the **Federal Unemployment Tax Act (FUTA).** This law (1) induces states to create their own unemployment programs and (2) allows the federal government to monitor state programs. As mentioned in Chapter 7, the FUTA tax currently is 6.2% of wages paid during the year, and the wage-base limit is $7,000.

Usually, the federal government allows employers a credit against FUTA tax as long as the employer has paid all monies due to the state unemployment fund on time. This credit, called the **normal FUTA tax credit,** cannot exceed 5.4%. So, an employer who is entitled to the normal FUTA credit will pay a net amount of eight-tenths of 1%, as shown below:

6.2%	**FUTA tax**
−5.4%	**normal FUTA tax credit**
.8%	**net FUTA tax for federal purposes**

In effect, the federal law says to employers, "Comply with your state's unemployment tax laws and your total tax will not exceed a maximum of 6.2%: 0.8% to the federal government and a state rate that will vary up to a maximum of 5.4%." Remember that employers alone are responsible for paying FUTA tax; it is never deducted from employees' wages.

In Learning Unit 8-3, we look at how to complete the federal report and the deposit requirements for FUTA tax. For now, let's calculate the amount of accumulated federal unemployment tax for Gradesoft.com based on the unemployment column under taxable earnings in the payroll register. Remember that the $1,960.00 in column H represents the amount of earnings taxable for federal unemployment.

To calculate the FUTA tax, we multiply the FUTA taxable earnings times the net FUTA tax rate.

Taxable FUTA Earnings		**FUTA Rate**		**FUTA Tax**	FUTA Tax Payable 209
$1,960.00	×	**.008**	=	**$15.68**	15.68

FUTA tax is paid after the end of a calendar year if the total tax owed is less than $100 for the year. If the amount owed is more than $100, the tax is paid on a quarterly basis, no later than the end of the month following the end of the quarter.

SUTA (State Unemployment Tax Acts)

To support state unemployment programs, all states charge employers a certain percent in taxes under the **State Unemployment Tax Act (SUTA).** Usually, employers pay more in SUTA tax than FUTA tax.

Each state has its own state unemployment wage-base limit. Currently, these limits range from a low of $7,000 to a high of $28,400. The limits vary according to the needs of each state unemployment fund and are subject to change. For the current rate in your state, check with the state department of labor and employment.

The states vary the percentage rates charged to employers. The differences are based on the total amount of contributions the employer makes into the state fund and the dollar amount of unemployment claim money paid out of the fund to former employees of the employer. For example, employers who do not lay off employees during slack seasons (such as after the Christmas season or at the end of a ski resort season) owe a smaller percentage for state unemployment tax purposes. The variance, which is called an **experience** or **merit rating,** motivates employers to stabilize their workforce.

Gradesoft.com's current state unemployment tax rate is 5.4% of the first $7,000 paid to each of Fred's employees during the calendar year. From the taxable earnings column (column H) of the payroll register in Figure 8-1, we multiply $1,960.00 by the SUTA tax rate of 5.4%.

Taxable Earnings	×	SUTA Rate	=	SUTA Tax		SUTA Tax Payable 208
$1,960.00		.054		$105.84		105.84

SUTA taxes are paid after the end of each **calendar quarter.** Employers are required to complete a state unemployment tax report and pay any SUTA tax due at this time.

JOURNALIZING PAYROLL TAX EXPENSE

Before showing the general journal entry to record Gradesoft.com's payroll tax expense, let's review the categories and rules that affect the specific payroll ledger accounts used to record this expense.

Accounts Affected	Category	↑ ↓	Rules
Payroll Tax Expense	Expense	↑	Dr.
FICA — Social Security Payable	Liability	↑	Cr.
FICA — Medicare Payable	Liability	↑	Cr.
State Unemployment Tax Payable (SUTA)	Liability	↑	Cr.
Federal Unemployment Tax Payable (FUTA)	Liability	↑	Cr.

The total of the employer's portion of FICA for Social Security and Medicare tax, FUTA tax, and SUTA tax equals the total of Gradesoft.com's payroll tax expense.

The Journal Entry

Figure 8-2 is the general journal entry recording Gradesoft.com's payroll tax expense for the biweekly payroll ending August 20. (We look carefully at the general ledger entries in Learning Unit 8-2.)

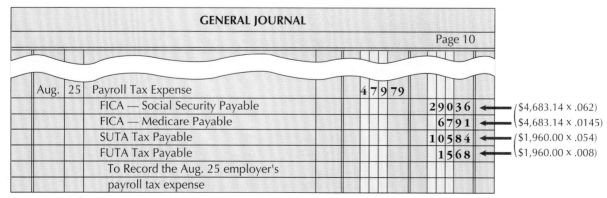

		GENERAL JOURNAL				
					Page 10	
Aug.	25	Payroll Tax Expense	4 7 9 79			
		FICA — Social Security Payable		2 9 0 36		($4,683.14 × .062)
		FICA — Medicare Payable		6 7 9 1		($4,683.14 × .0145)
		SUTA Tax Payable		1 0 5 84		($1,960.00 × .054)
		FUTA Tax Payable		1 5 68		($1,960.00 × .008)
		To Record the Aug. 25 employer's				
		payroll tax expense				

Figure 8-2 Journal Entry for Employer's Payroll Tax Expense

In Learning Unit 8-2 we see how to complete the form that goes with the payment of FICA tax (Social Security and Medicare) of the employee *and* the employer along with the amounts of federal income tax deducted from employees' paychecks. It is important to keep in mind that FUTA and SUTA taxes also have separate report forms to be completed, which we look at in Learning Unit 8-3.

Learning Unit 8-1 Review

AT THIS POINT you should be able to

- Explain the purpose of Form SS-4. (p. 290)
- Explain the use of the taxable earnings column in calculating the employer's payroll tax expense. (p. 290)
- Calculate the employer's payroll taxes. (p. 290)
- Explain the difference between FUTA and SUTA taxes. (p. 292)
- Explain when FUTA and SUTA taxes are paid. (p. 292)
- Journalize the employer's payroll tax expense. (p. 293)

SELF-REVIEW QUIZ 8-1

(The forms you need are on page 242 of the *Study Guide and Working Papers*.)

Given the following, prepare the general journal entry to record the payroll tax expense for Bill Co. for the weekly payroll of July 8. Assume the following: (a) SUTA tax is paid at a rate of 5.6% on the first $7,000 of earnings; (b) FUTA tax is paid at the net rate of .8% on the first $7,000 of earnings; (c) FICA tax rate for Social Security is 6.2% on $87,000, and Medicare is 1.45% on all earnings.

Employee	Cumulative Pay Before This Week's Payroll	Gross Pay for Week
Bill Jones	$6,000	$800
Julie Warner	6,600	400
Al Brooks	7,900	700

SOLUTION TO SELF-REVIEW QUIZ 8-1

Figure 8-3
Employer's Payroll Tax Journal Entry

	July	8	Payroll Tax Expense		2 2 2 15					
			FICA — Social Security Payable				1 1 7 80			
			FICA — Medicare Payable				2 7 55			
			SUTA Tax Payable				6 7 20			
			FUTA Tax Payable				9 60			
			Record employer's payroll tax							

FICA:
SS:	$1,900 × .062	=	$117.80
Med:	1,900 × .0145	=	27.55
SUTA:	1,200 × .056	=	67.20
FUTA:	1,200 × .008	=	9.60
			$222.15

Quiz Tip:
Al Brooks earned more than $7,000; thus his employer takes no SUTA or FUTA tax on the $700 of Al's gross pay.

Learning Unit 8-2 — Form 941: Completing the Employer's Quarterly Federal Tax Return and Paying Tax Obligations for FICA Tax and Federal Income Tax

In this unit we look at Gradesoft.com's last calendar quarter (October, November, and December). Our goals are (1) determining the timing for paying FICA (for both the employees and the employer) and federal income tax (or FIT) and (2) completing **Form 941,** the **Employer's Quarterly Federal Tax Return.**

Before getting into specific deposit rules and form completions, let's look at Figure 8-4, a worksheet that Ernie prepared to monitor Gradesoft.com's deposit requirements for the taxes reported on Form 941: Social Security, Medicare, and federal income taxes. These so-called **Form 941 taxes** are discussed later in this Learning Unit. (The worksheet in Figure 8-2 has nothing to do with unemployment taxes, which follow different rules.)

Do note on the worksheet that the quarter is 13 weeks. Because Form 941 requires FICA information to be separated into Social Security and Medicare, you can see how helpful the worksheet can be. Note that for the December 31 monthly payroll some wages are not taxable for Social Security because the $87,000 wage-base limit was met. *All* wages are taxable for Medicare, however, because there is no wage-base limit for this tax. This worksheet can be built from the information in each individual's employee's earnings record and the weekly payroll registers.

Now let's look at the deposit rules Gradesoft.com must follow regarding Form 941 taxes (which are FICA and FIT).

DEPOSITING FORM 941 TAXES

The amount of tax due must be deposited in what is called an authorized depository in Gradesoft's area or a Federal Reserve bank. Authorized depositories are banks that have been authorized by the Federal Reserve System to accept payroll tax deposits

Payroll Period		Pay Check Date	Earnings	FIT	Taxable FICA Wages for		FICA		Total Tax	Cumulative Tax
					Soc. Sec.	Medicare	Soc. Sec. EE + ER	Medicare EE + ER		
October	2–15	Oct. 20	4,892 75	778 00	4,892 75	4,892 75	606 70	141 89	1,526 59	1,526 59
October	16–29	Nov. 3	5,013 25	810 00	5,013 25	5,013 25	621 64	145 38	1,577 03	3,103 62
October	31	Oct. 31	16,231 84	3,895 00	16,231 84	16,231 84	2,012 75	470 72	6,378 47	9,482 09
Oct./Nov.	30–12	Nov. 17	5,007 15	809 00	5,007 15	5,007 15	620 89	145 21	1,575 09	11,057 18
November	13–26	Dec. 1	5,152 50	832 00	5,152 50	5,152 50	638 91	149 42	1,620 33	12,677 52
November	30	Nov. 30	16,231 84	3,895 00	16,231 84	16,231 84	2,012 75	470 72	6,378 47	19,055 99
Nov./Dec.	27–10	Dec. 15	5,629 00	909 00	5,629 00	5,629 00	698 00	163 24	1,770 24	20,826 22
December	11–24	Dec. 29	5,700 75	921 00	5,700 75	5,700 75	706 89	165 32	1,793 21	22,619 44
December	25–31	Dec. 29	2,105 68	367 00	2,105 68	2,105 68	261 10	61 06	689 17	23,308 61
December	31	Dec. 29	16,231 83	3,895 00	11,354 75	16,231 83	1,407 99	470 72	5,773 71	29,082 32
Totals for the Quarter			82,196 59	17,111 00	77,319 51	82,196 59	9,587 62	2,383 70	29,082 32	29,082 32
			(A)	(B)	(C)	(D)	(E)	(F)	(G)	(H)

Figure 8-4 Worksheet to Monitor Deposit Requirements

from their own checking account customers. A Federal Reserve bank can accept payroll tax deposits from any business, no matter where the business maintains its checking account.

Types of Payroll Tax Depositors

For payroll tax deposit purposes, employers are classified as either **monthly** or **semiweekly depositors.** A monthly depositor is an employer who only has to deposit Form 941 taxes on the fifteenth day of every month. Semiweekly depositors must deposit their Form 941 taxes once or twice each week.

The employer's classification depends on the dollar amount of the Form 941 taxes it has paid in the past. The IRS has developed a rule known as the **look-back period** rule to determine how to classify an employer for payroll tax deposits. Under this rule, the IRS will *look back* to a one-year time period that begins on July 1 and ends the following June 30. (For example, to determine the employer's status for 2004, the IRS will look at the period between July 1, 2002, and June 30, 2003.) If, during this look-back period, the employer has paid under $50,000 of Form 941 taxes, the IRS considers the employer to be a *monthly depositor*. If the employer has paid $50,000 or more during this period, it is considered to be a *semiweekly depositor.* Figure 8-5 shows how the look-back period works for payroll purposes.

Gradesoft.com is a semiweekly depositor because it made in excess of $50,000 in FICA and FIT deposits during the look-back period. If Gradesoft.com had made less than $50,000 in payroll tax deposits during the look-back period, it would have been classified as a monthly depositor.

New employers are automatically classified as monthly depositors until they have been in business long enough to have a look-back period for evaluation purposes. The employer's status is reevaluated every year.

Rules for Monthly Depositors   The rules for monthly depositors are fairly simple. They are

1. The employee and employer Social Security and Medicare taxes and the employees' FIT accumulated during any month must be deposited by the fifteenth of the next month.

2. If the fifteenth of the month is a Saturday, Sunday, or bank holiday, the employer must make the payroll tax deposit on the next **banking day.**

Rules for Semiweekly Depositors   Semiweekly depositors like Gradesoft.com may have to make up to two payroll tax deposits every week, depending on when employees are paid. For this purpose, each seven-day week begins on Wednesday and ends on the following Tuesday. The seven-day week is broken into two payday time periods:

> The IRS examines the amount of Form 941 taxes paid during the period beginning July 1 and ending June 30 of the following year to determine whether the employer is a monthly depositor or a semiweekly depositor. This examination is called the look-back period rule.

Figure 8-5
The Level of Payroll Taxes Paid During the Look-Back Period Determines How Often the Employer Deposits Payroll Taxes

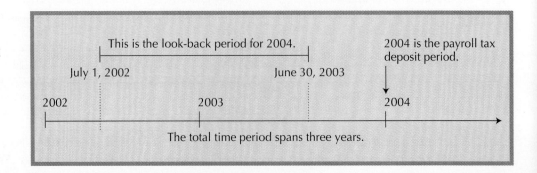

	Monday	Tuesday	Wednesday	Thursday	Friday	Saturday	Sunday
The payday occurs this week ⟶			■ If the payday occurs on one of these days, the deposit will be due Wednesday of the next week.			★ If the payday occurs on Saturday or Sunday, or...	
	★...Monday or Tuesday, then payroll tax deposit will be due and payable on Friday of this week.		■ Deposit day for Wednesday–Friday payday		★ Deposit day for Saturday–Tuesday payday		

Figure 8-6 The Payday Determines When the Tax Deposit Is Due

Wednesday through Friday and Saturday through Tuesday. In addition, the following rules apply:

1. If the company's payday occurs on Wednesday, Thursday, or Friday, the payroll tax deposit is due on the following Wednesday. If the company's payday occurs on Saturday, Sunday, Monday, or Tuesday, the payroll tax deposit is due on the following Friday. Thus, if an employer pays its employees on a Thursday and a Monday, it must make two payroll tax deposits—one on Wednesday for the Thursday payday, and one on Friday for the Monday payday.

2. If a bank holiday occurs after the end of the payday time period but before the day the payroll tax deposit is due, the employer gets one extra day in which to make the deposit. So, a deposit due on a Wednesday will be due on Thursday, and a Friday deposit will be due on the following Monday.

As a general rule, the depositor always has three banking days in which to make the payroll tax deposit. The diagram in Figure 8-6 shows how these rules are applied.

Here is how the rules apply to Gradesoft.com. First, look back at Figure 8-4 (p. 295) to locate the dates of each weekly payday. Next, look at Figure 8-7, which shows a calendar for the last quarter of the year.

Note that each payday falls on a Friday. Because Gradesoft.com is a semiweekly payroll tax depositor, its Form 941 payroll tax deposits are due on the following Wednesday. Gradesoft's first payday in October falls on October 6. Its first payroll tax deposit will be due on October 11. Another deposit will be due every Wednesday from that date until the end of the year. However, if we look at week 52 in Figure 8-7 (beginning Sunday, December 24), the payday for this week is Friday, December 29,

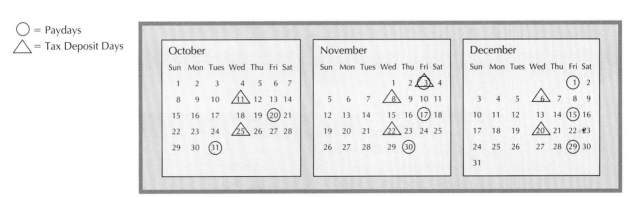

Figure 8-7 Last Calendar Quarter for Gradesoft.com Shows Paydays Falling on Fridays

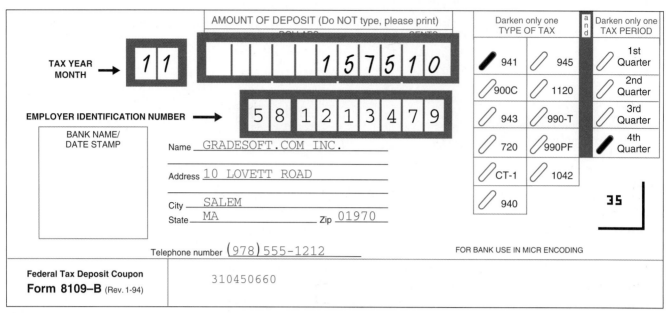

Figure 8-8 Form 8109

which is two days before New Year's Day. Under the law, January 1 is a federal holiday, so Ernie must apply the rule regarding a holiday that falls between a payday and a tax deposit day and will make the Form 941 tax deposit on Thursday, January 4, of the next year, rather than on Wednesday, January 3.

Completion of Form 8109 to Accompany Deposits

To make Gradesoft.com's payroll tax deposits properly, Ernie must write a check for the total amount of the Form 941 tax deposit after each pay period. The deposits must also be accompanied by IRS Form 8109, Federal Tax Deposit Coupon, as shown in Figure 8-8.

Ernie received a book of coupons when he got the EIN for Gradesoft.com. Figure 8-8 shows Form 8109 completed for the October 30/November 12 pay period Form 941 payroll tax deposit. Note that the dollar amount found at the top of the form ($1,575.10) is the same as the amount found in the total tax column for the pay period in Figure 8-2.

In Figure 8-8, in the upper-right-hand corner the "Type of Tax" and "Tax Period" must be indicated by darkening the appropriate oval using a No. 2 pencil. Ernie has darkened the "941" and "4th Quarter" ovals for the October 30/November 12 payday.

Journalizing and Posting Payroll Tax Deposits

Payment of the payroll tax deposit for October 30/November 12 is made in the general journal as shown in Figure 8-9.

Accounts Affected	Category	↑ ↓	Rules
FICA—Social Security Payable	Liability	↓	Dr.
FICA—Medicare Payable	Liability	↓	Dr.
Federal Income Tax Payable	Liability	↓	Dr.
Cash	Asset	↓	Cr.

GRADESOFT.COM GENERAL JOURNAL						
Nov	22	FICA — Social Security Payable	203	6 2 0 89		
		FICA — Medicare Payable	204	1 4 5 21		
		Federal Income Tax Payable	205	8 0 9 00		
		Cash	111		1 5 7 5 10	
		To record the Form 941 tax deposit for the				
		biweekly payroll on November 17, 200X				

Figure 8-9
Journal Entry to Record
Payroll Tax Deposit

Now let's look at the partial general ledger of Gradesoft.com to get a better understanding of how specific payroll accounts in the ledger are updated regarding FICA (Social Security and Medicare) and FIT. Note in the FICA — Social Security and Medicare Payable accounts how the posting came from the general journal for the employees' and employer's share of FICA tax. The general journal is also used when the payroll tax deposit is made, recording a debit to the FICA — Social Security and Medicare Payable accounts as well as the Federal Income Tax Payable account.

Under the Form 941 payroll tax deposit rules, the general journal entries to record the payroll are made biweekly on Friday, whereas the entries to record the payment of the payroll taxes are made the Wednesday after each biweekly payday. Check Figure 8-2 below to see how the Form 941 tax liability has been recorded and then paid in the partial general ledger accounts shown in Figure 8-10.

FORM 941: EMPLOYER'S QUARTERLY FEDERAL TAX RETURN

Ernie Goldman, the controller for Gradesoft.com, used the worksheet in Figure 8-2 in preparing Form 941 for the last quarter of the year (see Fig. 8-11). The top section of the form identifies the taxpayer (Gradesoft.com), its address, the date the quarter ended, and Gradesoft's EIN.

Ernie filled out Form 941 using the dollar amounts from Figure 8-2 as follows. Please refer back to the particular column identified by letter (A, B, C, etc.) to see where Ernie obtained the amounts used in preparing the form:

Line 1a: This line is only filled in for the first quarter of the year. It is left blank for the last quarter.
   2: Total gross pay: $82,196.59 (the total for the quarter). See column A.

FICA—Social Security Payable					203
Date	PR	Dr.	Cr.	Cr. Bal.	
200X					
Nov. 17	GJ28		6 2 0 89	6 2 0 89	
22	GJ28	6 2 0 89		0	
30	GJ28		2 0 1 2 75	2 0 1 2 75	
Dec. 1	GJ29		6 3 8 91	2 6 5 1 66	
6	GJ29	2 6 5 1 66		0	
15	GJ29		6 9 8 00	6 9 8 00	
20	GJ29	6 9 8 00		0	

FICA—Medicare Payable					204
Date	PR	Dr.	Cr.	Cr. Bal.	
200X					
Nov. 17	GJ28		1 4 5 21	1 4 5 21	
22	GJ28	1 4 5 21		0	
30	GJ28		4 7 0 42	4 7 0 42	
1	GJ29		1 4 9 42	6 1 9 84	
6	GJ29	6 1 9 84		0	
15	GJ29		1 6 3 24	1 6 3 24	
20	GJ29	1 6 3 24		0	

Figure 8-10 FICA for Social Security and Medicare

*Note: Each credit would actually be 2 credits: one from the employee and one from the employer.

Form 941

Department of the Treasury
Internal Revenue Service (99)

Employer's Quarterly Federal Tax Return

▶ **See separate instructions** for information on completing this return.

Please type or print.

Enter state code for state in which deposits were made **only** if different from state in address to the right ▶ [:   ]
(see page 2 of separate instructions).

Name (as distinguished from trade name)	Date quarter ended
Gradesoft.com	**Dec. 31, 200X**
Trade name, if any	Employer identification number
Address (number and street)	City, state, and ZIP code
10 Lovett Road	**Salem, MA 01970**

OMB No. 1545-0029

T
FF
FD
FP
I
T

If address is different from prior return, check here ▶ [ ]

IRS Use

1 1 1 1 1 1 1 1 1 1   2   3 3 3 3 3 3 3   4 4 4   5 5 5

6   7   8 8 8 8 8 8 8   9 9 9 9   10 10 10 10 10 10 10 10 10

A If you **do not have to file** returns in the future, check here ▶ [ ] and enter date final wages paid ▶

B If you are a seasonal employer, see **Seasonal employers** on page 1 of the instructions and check here ▶ [ ]

1	Number of employees in the pay period that includes March 12th ▶ [1]	**1**	
2	Total wages and tips, plus other compensation	**2**	82,196 59
3	Total income tax withheld from wages, tips, and sick pay	**3**	17,111 00
4	Adjustment of withheld income tax for preceding quarters of **this calendar year**	**4**	
5	Adjusted total of income tax withheld (line 3 as adjusted by line 4)	**5**	17,111 00

6	Taxable social security wages	**6a**	77,319 51	× 12.4% (.124) =	**6b**	9,587 62
	Taxable social security tips	**6c**		× 12.4% (.124) =	**6d**	
7	Taxable Medicare wages and tips . . .	**7a**	82,196 59	× 2.9% (.029) =	**7b**	2,383 70

8	Total social security and Medicare taxes (add lines 6b, 6d, and 7b). **Check here if wages are not subject to social security and/or Medicare tax** . . . . ▶ [ ]	**8**	11,971 32
9	Adjustment of social security and Medicare taxes (see instructions for required explanation) Sick Pay $ _____ ± Fractions of Cents $ _____ ± Other $ _____ =	**9**	
10	Adjusted total of social security and Medicare taxes (line 8 as adjusted by line 9)	**10**	11,971 32
11	**Total taxes** (add lines 5 and 10)	**11**	29,082 32
12	Advance earned income credit (EIC) payments made to employees (see instructions) . . .	**12**	
13	Net taxes (subtract line 12 from line 11). **If $2,500 or more, this must equal line 17, column (d) below (or line D of Schedule B (Form 941))**	**13**	29,082 32
14	Total deposits for quarter, including overpayment applied from a prior quarter	**14**	29,082 32
15	**Balance due** (subtract line 14 from line 13). See instructions	**15**	

16 **Overpayment.** If line 14 is more than line 13, enter excess here ▶ $ _____

and check if to be: [ ] Applied to next return **or** [ ] Refunded.

- **All filers:** If line 13 is less than $2,500, **do not** complete line 17 **or** Schedule B (Form 941).
- **Semiweekly schedule depositors:** Complete Schedule B (Form 941) and check here . . . . ▶ [X]
- **Monthly schedule depositors:** Complete line 17, columns (a) through (d), and check here. . . . . ▶ [ ]

17 Monthly Summary of Federal Tax Liability. (Complete **Schedule B (Form 941)** instead, if you were a semiweekly schedule depositor.)			
(a) First month liability	**(b)** Second month liability	**(c)** Third month liability	**(d)** Total liability for quarter

Third Party Designee Do you want to allow another person to discuss this return with the IRS (see separate instructions)? [ ] Yes. Complete the following. [X] No

Designee's name ▶   Phone no. ▶ (   )   Personal identification number (PIN) ▶ [ ][ ][ ][ ][ ]

Sign Here Under penalties of perjury, I declare that I have examined this return, including accompanying schedules and statements, and to the best of my knowledge and belief, it is true, correct, and complete.

Signature ▶ *Ernie Goldman*   Print Your Name and Title ▶ Ernie Goldman, Controller   Date ▶ 1-31-200X

For Privacy Act and Paperwork Reduction Act Notice, see back of Payment Voucher.   Cat. No. 17001Z   Form **941**

Figure 8-11 Employer's Quarterly Federal Tax Return

3: Total income tax: $17,111.00. See column B.

4: No adjustment needed here: This line is used only for special situations.

5: Because there was no adjustment amount on line 4, this amount is the same as found on line 3: $17,111.00.

6a: The wages subject to Social Security tax are multiplied by 12.4% (6.2% for the employee and 6.2% for the employer). Total taxable wages are $77,319.51. Note that this line is different from line 2 because of the Social Security wage-base limit of $87,000 for the year. The tax is $9,587.62. See column E.

6b: Ernie multiplies the amount found on line 6a by 12.4% to arrive at the amount entered on line 6b.

6c: If Gradesoft.com had taxable tips for the quarter, the amount would be entered on line 6c.

6d: Since Gradesoft.com had no taxable tips for the quarter, this line is left blank on Form 941.

7a: The taxable wages for Medicare tax are $82,196.59 (see column D). Please note that this line will be the same as line 2 because there is no wage-base limit for Medicare tax. The tax amount is $2,383.70 (1.45% for the employee and 1.45% for the employer). See column F.

7b: Ernie multiplies the amount found on line 7a by 2.9% to arrive at the amount entered on line 7b.

8: The total of Social Security and Medicare taxes is $11,971.32 ($9,587.62 + $2,383.70).

9: Due to the rounding of individual FICA amounts calculated and pay period total FICA amounts paid, there may be a difference between the total taxes shown in a general ledger and the actual payroll tax deposits. Line 9 can be used to reconcile these differences (called *fractions of cents*) to account for rounding. Ernie's amounts do not need adjustment, so no amount is entered on line 9.

10: This line is the sum of lines 8 and 9.

11: This line is the sum of lines 5 and 10. See columns G and H.

12: If Gradesoft.com advanced any earned income credit to its employees, it would deduct the amount on this line.

13: This line is the net of line 11 as adjusted by any amount found on line 12. See columns G and H.

14: The total of the deposits made by Ernie for Gradesoft.com for the last quarter is $29,082.32. Remember that Gradesoft.com uses the semiweekly deposit rules. Note that the last Form 941 deposit is made after the year ends but is allowed to be taken as a last quarter deposit because it applies to the December 31 biweekly and monthly payrolls.

15: There is no balance due to Gradesoft.com.

16: There is no overpayment for Gradesoft.com. Note that directly below line 16 are two boxes that are checked only under certain circumstances. Ernie will check the box for semiweekly depositors and prepare Form 941 Schedule B. This schedule is an itemized listing of the semiweekly deposits made for the last quarter. It is not shown here.

17: This line is filled in only if the employer has been classified as a monthly depositor of employment taxes. Please note that the line is broken into four sections. The first three sections—(a), (b), and (c)—are the monthly Form 941 tax liabilities. The sum of sections (a), (b), (c) must equal the section (d) amount. Likewise, the section (d) amount on line 17 must equal the amount found on line 13 of the return. Ernie does not complete this line because Gradesoft.com has been classified as a semiweekly depositor.

Fraction of cents: If there is a difference between the total tax on line 8 and the total deducted from your employees' wages or tips because of fractions of cents added or dropped in collecting the tax, report the difference on line 9. Use the center column on line 9 with a + or − sign to show the amount of the adjustment.

Learning Unit 8-2 Review

AT THIS POINT you should be able to

- Explain which taxes are reported on Form 941. (p. 295)
- Understand how employers are classified as payroll tax depositors. (p. 296)
- Explain the summary of Form 941 payroll tax deposit rules for monthly depositors. (p. 296)
- Explain the summary of Form 941 payroll tax deposit rules for semiweekly depositors. (p. 296)
- Prepare and explain the purpose of Form 8109. (p. 298)
- Record the general journal entry to pay FICA (Social Security and Medicare) and federal income taxes when a payroll tax deposit is made. (p. 299)
- Review how the general journal entries are posted into the general ledger to record the paying of employees and the paying of payroll taxes. (p. 299)
- Complete an Employer's Quarterly Federal Tax Return from a worksheet. (p. 300)

SELF-REVIEW QUIZ 8-2

(The blank forms you need are on page 243 of the *Study Guide and Working Papers*.)

Carol Ann's Import Chalet is a business that employs five full-time employees and four part-time employees. The accountant for Carol Ann's has determined that the business is a monthly depositor. The accountant prepared a worksheet showing the following payroll tax liabilities for the month of October:

Date	Social Security (EE + ER)	Medicare (EE + ER)	FIT
10/7	$ 486.56	$169.05	$ 829.00
10/14	632.15	165.01	901.00
10/21	579.43	131.05	734.00
10/28	389.99	142.24	765.00
Totals	$2,088.13	$607.35	$3,229.00

1. What is the dollar amount of the Form 941 tax deposit and when must it be made under the monthly deposit rule? Use Figure 8-7 (p. 297) for the date.

2. Assume that Carol Ann's is classified as a semiweekly depositor. Please calculate the amount of each Form 941 tax deposit and when it would be made by completing the table on the next page (use Fig. 8-7 for the dates):

Payday Date	Date of Deposit	Amount of Deposit
10/7	?	?
10/14	?	?
10/21	?	?
10/28	?	?

SOLUTIONS TO SELF-REVIEW QUIZ 8-2

1. As a monthly depositor, Carol Ann's deposit date is Wednesday, November 14. The total amount of the deposit is $5,924.48 ($2,088.13 + $607.35 + $3,229.00).

2. As a semiweekly depositor, Carol Ann's deposit schedule is completed as follows:

Payday Date	Date of Deposit	Amount of Deposit
10/7	10/12	$1,484.61
10/14	10/19	1,698.16
10/21	10/26	1,444.48
10/28	11/2*	1,297.23*

Learning Unit 8-3   W-2, W-3, Form 940-EZ, and Workers' Compensation

W-2: WAGE AND TAX STATEMENT

Form W-2, Wage and Tax Statement is a multipart form that is prepared by the employer each year. Gradesoft.com is required to give (or mail) copies of Form W-2 to each person who was employed in the past year. These forms must be distributed by January 31 of the following year. Employees use the figures on Form W-2 to compute the amount of income tax they must pay. One copy of the form must be attached to the federal income tax return; other copies must be attached to state and local tax returns.

Anyone who stopped working for Gradesoft.com before the end of that year may be given a Form W-2 at any time after the employment ends. If the former employee asks for it, the employer must supply completed copies within 30 days of the request or the final wage payment, whichever is later.

Additional copies of Form W-2 are sent to the Social Security Administration and state and local governments. The employer retains a copy of the W-2 form for each employee for its records.

Figure 8-12 on page 304 shows the W-2 that James T. Zott received from Gradesoft.com. The information was obtained from his individual employee earnings record. Note that Social Security wages and taxes are shown separately from the amounts reported for Medicare wages and taxes because there is a wage-base limit for the Social Security tax, but not for the Medicare tax.

W-3: TRANSMITTAL OF INCOME AND TAX STATEMENTS

Form W-3, Transmittal of Income and Tax Statements, is prepared and sent by the employer to the Social Security Administration along with copies of each employees' Form W-2. Form W-3 reports the total amounts of wages, tips, and compensation paid to employees; the total federal income tax withheld; the total Social Security and Medicare taxes withheld; and some other information.

Employers are required to send Form W-3 and Form W-2 to the Social Security Administration for FICA tax purposes. The Social Security Administration, under

---

*Note that this deposit will be made in November given the calendar dates found in Figure 8-5.

a Control number	22222	Void ☐	For Official Use Only ▶ OMB No. 1545-0008	

b Employer identification number 58-12134791		1 Wages, tips, other compensation $ 77,587.00	2 Federal income tax withheld $ 19,818.00

c Employer's name, address, and ZIP code Gradesoft.com 10 Lovett Road Salem, MA 01970	3 Social security wages $ 77,587.00	4 Social security tax withheld $ 4,810.39
	5 Medicare wages and tips $ 77,587.00	6 Medicare tax withheld $ 1,125.01
	7 Social security tips $	8 Allocated tips $

d Employee's social security number 922-80-1250	9 Advance EIC payment $	10 Dependent care benefits $

e Employee's first name and initial James T.	Last name Zott	11 Nonqualified plans $	12a See instructions for box 12 $

80 Garfield Street
Marblehead, MA 01945

13 Statutory employee ☐   Retirement plan ☐   Third-party sick pay ☐   12b $

14 Other   12c $

12d $

f Employee's address and ZIP code

15 State MA	Employer's state ID number 621-8966-4	16 State wages, tips, etc. $ 77,587.00	17 State income tax $ 6,206.96	18 Local wages, tips, etc. $	19 Local income tax $	20 Locality name
		$	$	$	$	

Form W-2 **Wage and Tax Statement** (99)   **200X**   Department of the Treasury—Internal Revenue Service

Copy A For Social Security Administration—Send this entire page with Form W-3 to the Social Security Administration; photocopies are **not** acceptable.   Cat. No. 10134D   **For Privacy Act and Paperwork Reduction Act Notice, see separate instructions.**

Do Not Cut, Fold, or Staple Forms on This Page — Do Not Cut, Fold, or Staple Forms on This Page

Figure 8-12 Completed Form W-2

a special agreement with the IRS, makes all information found on individual W-2 forms electronically available to the IRS so that it can check to verify the accuracy of the employer's 941 forms and individual employees' federal income tax returns.

The information used to complete Form W-3 in Figure 8-13 came from a summary of the individual employee earnings records that Ernie prepared after the end of the year (see Fig. 8-14 on p. 305).

FORM 940-EZ: EMPLOYER'S ANNUAL FEDERAL UNEMPLOYMENT TAX RETURN

There are two types of federal unemployment tax returns. Form 940-EZ, Employer's Annual Federal Unemployment Tax Return, is used by a business that only employs workers in one state. Businesses that employ workers in several states (multistate employers) must file a Form 940, Employer's Annual Federal Unemployment Tax Return. Form 940 asks for additional information that is not required on Form 940-EZ.

Gradesoft.com must file Form 940-EZ. After the first year it files this form, the IRS will send Ernie a preaddressed Form 940-EZ near the close of each calendar year. Form 940-EZ must be filed no later than January 31 unless all required FUTA deposits have been made during the year, in which case the return can be filed by February 10. The completed form is shown in Figure 8-15.

DO NOT STAPLE OR FOLD

a Control number	33333	For Official Use Only ▶ OMB No. 1545-0008		

b **Kind of Payer** ▶	941 ☒ Military 943 ☐ CT-1 ☐ Hshld. emp. ☐ Medicare govt. emp. ☐ Third-party sick pay ☐	1 Wages, tips, other compensation $ 316,994.82	2 Federal income tax withheld $ 61,996.00

		3 Social security wages $ 316,994.82	4 Social security tax withheld $ 19,653.68

c Total number of Forms W-2 6	d Establishment number	5 Medicare wages and tips $ 316,994.82	6 Medicare tax withheld $ 4,596.43

e Employer identification number 58-12134791	7 Social security tips $	8 Allocated tips $

f Employer's name Gradesoft.com Inc.	9 Advance EIC payments $	10 Dependent care benefits $

	11 Nonqualified plans $	12 Deferred compensation $

10 Lovett Road Salem, MA 01970	13 For third-party sick pay use only

	14 Income tax withheld by payer of third-party sick pay $

g Employer's address and ZIP code	

h Other EIN used this year	

15 State Employer's state ID number MA 621-8966-4	16 State wages, tips, etc. $ 316,994.82	17 State income tax $ 25,359.59

	18 Local wages, tips, etc. $	19 Local income tax $

Contact person E. Goldman	Telephone number (617) 555-1212	For Official Use Only

E-mail address egoldman@gradesoft.com	Fax number (617) 555-1213	

Under penalties of perjury, I declare that I have examined this return and accompanying documents, and, to the best of my knowledge and belief, they are true, correct, and complete.

Signature ▶ *Ernie Goldman*   Title ▶ Controller   Date ▶ 1-31-200X

Form **W-3** Transmittal of Wage and Tax Statements   **200X**   Department of the Treasury
Internal Revenue Service

Send this entire page with the entire Copy A page of Form(s) W-2 to the Social Security Administration. Photocopies are not acceptable.

Do not send any payment (cash, checks, money orders, etc.) with Forms W-2 and W-3.

Figure 8-13 Completed Form W-3

Employee	Total Earnings	FICA Taxable Earnings Soc. Sec.	FICA Taxable Earnings Medicare	FICA Tax Soc. Sec.	FICA Tax Medicare	FIT
Jackson, Lee	34 812 55	34 812 55	34 812 55	2 158 38	504 78	3 984 00
Sheila Stowe	19 872 11	19 872 11	19 872 11	1 232 07	288 15	2 290 00
Regan, Pat	66 448 16	66 448 16	66 448 16	4 119 79	963 50	8 265 00
Goldman, Ernie	38 500 00	38 500 00	38 500 00	2 387 00	558 25	5 989 00
Zott, Jim	77 587 00	77 587 00	77 587 00	4 810 39	1 125 01	19 818 00
Nguyen, Vince	79 775 00	79 775 00	79 775 00	4 946 05	1 156 74	21 650 00
	316 994 82	316 994 82	316 994 82	19 653 68	4 596 43	61 996 00

Figure 8-14 Employee Earnings Record Summary

Form 940-EZ

Department of the Treasury
Internal Revenue Service   (99)

**Employer's Annual Federal
Unemployment (FUTA) Tax Return**

► **See separate Instructions for Form 940-EZ for information on completing this form.**

OMB No. 1545-1110

200X

T	
FF	
FD	
FP	
I	
T	

You must complete this section. ►

Name (as distinguished from trade name)
Gradesoft.com Inc.

Trade name, if any

Address and ZIP code
10 Lovett Road, Salem, MA 01970

Calendar year
200X

Employer identification number
58:12134791

Answer the questions under **Who May Use Form 940-EZ** *on page 2. If you cannot use Form 940-EZ, you must use Form 940.*

A   Enter the amount of contributions paid to your state unemployment fund. (see separate instructions) . . . ► $ 1,890 00

B   (1) Enter the name of the state where you have to pay contributions . . . . ►   .... Massachusetts ....

(2) Enter your state reporting number as shown on your state unemployment tax return ► 281-615

If you will not have to file returns in the future, check here (see **Who Must File** in separate instructions) **and complete and sign the return.** ► ☐

If this is an Amended Return, check here (see **Amended Returns** on page 2 of the separate instructions) . . . . ► ☐

Part I   Taxable Wages and FUTA Tax

1	Total payments (including payments shown on lines 2 and 3) during the calendar year for services of employees	**1**	316,994	82
2	Exempt payments. (Explain all exempt payments, attaching additional sheets if necessary.) ►	**2**		
3	Payments of more than $7,000 for services. Enter only amounts over the first $7,000 paid to each employee. **(see separate instructions)**	**3** 274,994 82		
4	Add lines 2 and 3	**4**	274,994	82
5	**Total taxable wages** (subtract line 4 from line 1) . . . . ►	**5**	42,000	00
6	**FUTA tax.** Multiply the wages on line 5 by .008 and enter here. **(If the result is over $100, also complete Part II.)**	**6**	336	00
7	Total FUTA tax deposited for the year, including any overpayment applied from a prior year	**7**	336	00
8	**Balance due** (subtract line 7 from line 6). Pay to the "United States Treasury." . . . . ►	**8**	–0–	
	If you owe more than $100, see **Depositing FUTA tax** in separate instructions.			
9	**Overpayment** (subtract line 6 from line 7). Check if it is to be: ☐ **Applied to next return** or ☐ **Refunded** ►	**9**		

Part II   Record of Quarterly Federal Unemployment Tax Liability (Do not include state liability.) **Complete only if line 6 is over $100.**

Quarter	First (Jan. 1 – Mar. 31)	Second (Apr. 1 – June 30)	Third (July 1 – Sept. 30)	Fourth (Oct. 1 – Dec. 31)	Total for year
Liability for quarter	198.00	–0–	114.00	24.00	336.00

Third Party Designee

Do you want to allow another person to discuss this return with the IRS (see instructions page 5)? ☐ **Yes.** Complete the following.   ☐ **No**

Designee's name ►

Phone no. ► (   )

Personal identification number (PIN) ►

Under penalties of perjury, I declare that I have examined this return, including accompanying schedules and statements, and, to the best of my knowledge and belief, it is true, correct, and complete, and that no part of any payment made to a state unemployment fund claimed as a credit was, or is to be, deducted from the payments to employees.

Signature ► *Ernie Goldman*   Title (Owner, etc.) ► Controller   Date ► 2-10-200X

For Privacy Act and Paperwork Reduction Act Notice, see separate instructions.   ▼ **DETACH HERE** ▼   Cat. No. 10983G   Form **940-EZ**

Figure 8-15 Completed Form 940-EZ

FUTA As we saw earlier, the FUTA tax rate is .8% (or eight tenths of 1%) on the first $7,000 of each employee's gross pay. If Gradesoft.com's accumulated FUTA tax liability is $100 or more during the calendar year, Ernie must make a FUTA tax deposit with a Federal Reserve bank or a bank authorized to take payroll tax deposits. The FUTA tax deposit rule is quite simple: If the amount of FUTA tax owed is $100 or more during any calendar quarter, the employer must deposit the amount due no later than one month after the quarter ends.

At the end of the first quarter Gradesoft.com owes $198 for FUTA taxes. Ernie has prepared a schedule showing how the tax was computed. (See Table 8-1 for the calculations.) If an employee earned over the $7,000 FUTA wage-base limit, only the first $7,000 will be taxable for FUTA purposes. Note that only one of Gradesoft.com's

TABLE 8-1 Computation of FUTA Tax for the First Quarter of 200X

Employee	Amount Earned in First Quarter	Amount Taxable for FUTA
Lee, Jackson	$ 4,703.56	$ 4,703.56
Stowe, Sheila*	0	0
Regan, Pat	$ 4,512.14	$ 4,512.14
Goldman, Ernie†	$ 3,208.33	$ 3,208.33
Zott, James T.†	$ 5,325.59	$ 5,325.59
Nguyen, Vince	$19,943.75	$ 7,000.00
		$24,749.62 × .008 = $198.00

*Sheila Stowe was not hired until the third quarter of the year.

†Ernie Goldman and James T. Zott were hired in March of the year (one month's earnings for quarter).

employees earned over the $7,000 FUTA limit during the first quarter of the year. Please see Part II of Form 940-EZ in Figure 8-15.

Because Gradesoft.com owes $198 in FUTA taxes, Ernie will make the FUTA tax deposit on April 30 to comply with the FUTA deposit rule. The general journal entry is prepared as shown in Figure 8-16.

SUTA Gradesoft.com must also pay state unemployment tax to Massachusetts. The SUTA tax is also due one month after the quarter ends, on April 30. Ernie will pay out $1,336.48 in tax, based on a SUTA percentage rate of 5.4% on the first $7,000 that each of the employees has earned ($24,749.62 × .054 = $1,336.48). The amount of SUTA Ernie pays is shown on lines A and B of Form 940-EZ.

WORKERS' COMPENSATION INSURANCE

Gradesoft.com is required to have workers' compensation insurance to insure its employees against losses due to accidental injury or death incurred while on the job. Ernie is required to estimate the cost of this insurance and pay the premium in advance.

The premium for workers' compensation insurance is based on the total estimated gross payroll, and the rate is calculated per $100 of weekly payroll. At year end, the actual payroll is compared with the estimated payroll, and Fred will either receive credit for overpayment or be responsible for paying additional premiums.

These are the facts on which Gradesoft.com's insurance cost was calculated:

1. Estimated payroll: $320,000.

2. Two grades of workers: Developers and Managers.

			GRADESOFT.COM GENERAL JOURNAL											
*	April	30	FUTA Payable	212		1	9	8	00					
			SUTA Payable	213	1	3	3	6	48					
			Cash	111						1	5	3	4	48
			To record the FUTA and SUTA tax											
			deposits for the first quarter of the year.											

*Note: This entry could be two separate entries.

Figure 8-16 Recording FUTA and SUTA Deposit

3. Rate per $100 of payroll: Developers, $1.90; Managers $.14.

4. Estimated payroll: Developers, $120,000; Managers, $200,000.

The estimated premium was calculated as follows:

$$\begin{array}{lll}
\text{Developers:} & \$120,000\,/\,\$100 = 1,200 \times \$1.90 = & \$2,280 \\
\text{Managers:} & \$200,000\,/\,\$100 = 2,000 \times \$.14 \;\; = & \underline{280} \\
& \textit{Total Estimated Premium:} & \underline{\underline{\$2,560}}
\end{array}$$

Accounts Affected	Category	↑ ↓	Dr./Cr.
Prepaid Insurance, Worker's Compensation	Asset	↑	Dr.
Cash	Asset	↓	Cr.

Gradesoft.com would have to pay $2,560 in advance. At the end of the year, records show that the Developer payroll was $121,114 and the Manager payroll was $195,881.

Given those amounts, Gradesoft.com's actual premium should be $2,575.16, calculated as follows:

$$\begin{array}{lll}
\text{Developers:} & \$121,114\,/\,\$100 = 1,211 \times \$1.90 = & \$2,300.90 \\
\text{Managers:} & \$195,881\,/\,\$100 = 1,959 \times \$.14 \;\; = & \underline{274.26} \\
& \textit{Total Estimated Premium:} & \underline{\underline{\$2,575.16}}
\end{array}$$

Because the actual premium is $15.16 higher than the estimate, Ernie must pay this amount in January together with the estimated premium for the next year.

The $15.16 adjustment takes place on December 31 by debiting Workers' Compensation Insurance Expense and crediting Workers' Compensation Insurance Payable.

Accounts Affected	Category	↑ ↓	Dr./Cr.
Workers' Compensation Insurance Expense	Expense	↑	Dr.
Workers' Compensation Insurance Payable	Liability	↑	Cr.

Learning Unit 8-3 Review

AT THIS POINT you should be able to

- Prepare a W-2 form. (p. 303)
- Explain the difference between a W-2 form and a W-3 form. (p. 303)
- Prepare a 940-EZ form. (p. 306)
- Explain the difference between a Form 940-EZ and a Form 940. (p. 306)
- Calculate estimated premium for workers' compensation insurance. (p. 307)
- Prepare journal entries to record as well as adjust the premiums for workers' compensation insurance. (p. 307)

SELF-REVIEW QUIZ 8-3

(The forms you need are on page 243 of the *Study Guide and Working Papers*.)
Are the following questions true or false?

1. W-4s must be received by employees by January 31 of the following year.
2. Form W-3 is sent to the Social Security Administration yearly.
3. A Form 940 is prepared by a business that employs workers in only one state.
4. The Employer's Annual Federal Unemployment Tax Return records the employer's FICA and FIT tax liabilities.
5. A FUTA tax liability of $100 must be paid 10 days after the quarter ends.
6. Premiums for workers' compensation insurance may be adjusted based on actual payroll figures.

SOLUTIONS TO SELF-REVIEW QUIZ 8-3

1. False. W-2 forms must be sent to each employee by January 31 of the next year. The W-4 form is filled out by a new employee and is used for calculating federal and state income taxes.
2. True.
3. False. Form 940 will be prepared by a business that employs workers in more than one state. Form 940-EZ will be prepared by an employer with workers in only one state.
4. False. The Employer's Annual Federal Unemployment Tax Return records and reports the FUTA tax liability. Form 941 records and reports the FICA and FIT tax liabilities.
5. False. A FUTA tax liability of $100 must be paid one month after the quarter ends.
6. True.

Quiz Tip:
If you are getting refunds for FIT, you may want to change your withholding.

Chapter Review

Summary of Key Points

Learning Unit 8-1

1. The Payroll Tax Expense for the employer is made up of FICA tax (Social Security and Medicare) and the state and federal unemployment insurance taxes.
2. The maximum amount of credit given for state unemployment taxes paid against the FUTA tax is 5.4%. This figure is known as the normal FUTA tax credit.
3. The Payroll Tax Expense is recorded at the time the payroll is recorded.

Learning Unit 8-2

1. Federal Form 941 is prepared and filed no later than one month after the calendar quarter ends. It reports the amount of Social Security, Medicare, and federal income taxes withheld from employees and the Social Security and Medicare taxes due from the employer during the quarter.
2. Social Security, Medicare, and federal income taxes are known as Form 941 taxes.
3. The total amount of Form 941 taxes paid by a business during a specific period of time determines how often the business will have to make its payroll tax deposits. This time period is called a look-back period.
4. Businesses will make their payroll tax deposits either monthly or semiweekly when paying Form 941 taxes.
5. Different deposit rules apply to monthly and semiweekly depositors.
6. Form 941 payroll tax deposits must be made using Form 8109, known as the Federal Tax Deposit Coupon.

Learning Unit 8-3

1. Information to prepare W-2 forms can be obtained from the individual employee earnings records.
2. Form W-3 is used by the Social Security Administration in verifying that taxes have been withheld as reported on individual employee W-2 forms.
3. 940-EZ is prepared by January 31, after the end of the previous calendar year. This form can be filed by February 10 if all required deposits have been made by January 31.
4. If the amount of FUTA taxes is equal to or more than $100 during any calendar quarter, the deposit must be made no later than one month after the quarter ends. If the amount is less than $100, no deposit is required until the liability reaches the $100 point.
5. Workers' compensation insurance (the estimated premium) is paid at the beginning of the year by the employer to protect against potential losses to its employees due to accidental death or injury incurred while on the job.

Key Terms

Banking day   A banking day is an established time each business day before which bank transactions are considered to be completed on that day. Generally, a banking day will end a 2 or 3 P.M. local time. Banking business transacted after this time is usually considered to be the next day's business. Saturdays, Sundays, and federal holidays are usually not considered banking days.

Calendar quarter   A three-month time period. There are four calendar quarters in a calendar year (January 1 through December 31). The first quarter is January through March, the second is April through June, the third is July through September, and the fourth is October through December.

Employer identification number (EIN)   This number assigned by the IRS is used by an employer when recording and paying payroll and income taxes.

Experience/merit rating   A percentage rate that is assigned to a business by the state in calculating state unemployment taxes. The rate is based on the employment record and amount of contributions paid into the state unemployment fund. The lower the rating, the less tax that must be paid.

Federal Insurance Contributions Act (FICA)   Part of the Social Security law that requires employees and employers to pay Social Security taxes and Medicare taxes.

Federal Unemployment Tax Act (FUTA)   A tax paid by employers to the federal government. The current rate is .8% after applying the normal FUTA tax credit on the first $7,000 of earnings of each employee.

Form 940, Employer's Annual Federal Unemployment Tax Return   One version of the form used by employers at the end of the year to report the amount of unemployment tax due for the calendar year. This version of the form is used by an employer with workers in more than one state. If more than $100 is cumulatively owed in a quarter, it should be paid quarterly, one month after the end of the quarter. Normally, payment is due January 31 after the calendar year, or February 10 if deposits have already been made by an employer.

Form 940-EZ, Employer's Annual Federal Unemployment Tax Return   The other version of the form used by employers at the end of the year to report the amount of unemployment tax due for the calendar year. The "EZ" version of this form is used by an employer with workers in only one state.

Form 941, Employer's Quarterly Federal Tax Return   A tax report that a business will complete after the end of each calendar quarter indicating the total FICA (Social Security and Medicare) owed plus the amount of federal income tax withheld from employees' pay for the quarter. If federal tax deposits have been made on time, the total amount deposited should equal the amount due on Form 941. If there is a difference, a payment may be due.

Form 941 taxes   Another term used to describe Social Security, Medicare, and federal income taxes. This name comes from the form used to report these taxes.

Form 8109, Federal Tax Deposit Coupon   A coupon that is completed and sent along with payments of tax deposits relating to either Forms 940-EZ or 941. This form can also be used to deposit other types of taxes a business may owe the federal government.

Form SS-4   The form filled out by an employer to get an employer identification number. The form is sent to the IRS, which assigns the number to the business.

Form W-2, Wage and Tax Statement   A form completed by the employer at the end of the calendar year to provide a summary of gross earnings and deductions to each employee. At least two copies go to the employee, one copy to the IRS, one copy to any state where employees' income taxes have been withheld, one copy to the Social Security Administration, and one copy into the records of the business.

Form W-3, Transmittal of Income and Tax Statements   A form completed by the employer to verify the number of W-2s and amounts withheld as shown on them. This form is sent to a Social Security Administration data processing center along with copies of each employee's W-2 forms.

Look-back period   A period of time used to determine if a business will make its Form 941 tax deposits on a monthly or semiweekly basis. The IRS has defined this period as July 1 through June 30 of the year prior to the year in which Form 941 tax deposits will be made.

Monthly depositor   A business classified as a monthly depositor will make its payroll tax deposits only once each month for the amount of Form 941 due from the prior month.

Normal FUTA Tax Credit   A credit given to employers who pay their state unemployment taxes on time. The credit is usually 5.4%, which is applied against a 6.2% rate. The result is a net FUTA tax of .8%.

Payroll Tax Expense   The general ledger account that records the total of the employer's FICA (Social Security and Medicare), SUTA, and FUTA tax responsibilities.

Semiweekly depositor   A business classified as a semiweekly depositor may make its payroll tax deposits up to twice in one week. Semiweekly depositors will make a minimum of one Form 941 payroll tax deposit each week.

State Unemployment Tax Act (SUTA)   A tax usually paid only by employers to the state for employee unemployment insurance.

Workers' compensation insurance   Insurance paid for, in advance, by an employer to protect its employees against loss due to injury or death incurred during employment.

Blueprint: Form 941 Tax Deposit Rules

10 Frequently Asked Questions and Answers About Depositing Social Security, Medicare, and Federal Income Taxes to the Government

Here is a summary of questions and answers to help you understand the payroll tax deposit rules for Form 941 taxes.

1. **What are Form 941 taxes?** The term *Form 941 taxes* is used to describe the amount of Social Security, Medicare, and federal income tax paid by employees and the amount of Social Security and Medicare taxes that are

matched and paid by an employer. The total of these taxes are known as Form 941 taxes because they are reported on Form 941 each quarter.

2. **When does an employer deposit Form 941 taxes?** How often an employer deposits Form 941 taxes depends on how the employer is classified for this purpose. The IRS classifies an employer as either a *monthly* or *semiweekly depositor* based on the amount of Form 941 taxes paid during a time period known as a *look-back period*.

3. **When is a look-back period?** A look-back period is a fiscal year that begins on July 1 and ends on June 30 of the year before the calendar year when the deposits will be made. For example, for the 2004 calendar year, an employer's look-back period will begin on July 1, 2002, and end June 30, 2003.

4. **What is the dollar amount used to classify an employer for Form 941 tax deposits?** The key dollar amount used to determine if an employer is a monthly or semiweekly depositor is $50,000 in Form 941 taxes. Two rules apply here:

    a. If the total amount deposited in Form 941 taxes is less than $50,000 during the look-back period, the employer is considered a *monthly tax depositor.*

    b. If the total amount deposited in Form 941 taxes is $50,000 or more during the look-back period, the employer is considered a *semiweekly tax depositor.*

5. **How do employers deposit Form 941 taxes?** An employer fills out a Form 8109 (Federal Tax Deposit Coupon) and gives this form with a check to a bank authorized to receive payroll tax deposits or to a Federal Reserve bank. Usually, authorized banks will only take checks written from an account maintained at that same bank. Therefore, an employer usually cannot make a Form 941 deposit at Bank A using a check written from an account maintained at Bank B. A Federal Reserve bank will accept a check from any U.S. bank for payroll tax deposit purposes.

6. **When do monthly depositors make their deposits?** A monthly depositor will figure the total amount of Form 941 taxes owed in a calendar month and then pay this amount by the fifteenth of the next month. If an employer owes $3,125 in Form 941 taxes for the month of June, it will deposit this same amount no later than July 15 of the same year.

7. **When do semiweekly depositors make their deposits?** The rules for making deposits are a little more complicated for a semiweekly depositor. The depositor may have to make up to two Form 941 deposits each week. When a tax deposit is due depends on when the employees are paid. To keep the rules consistent, the IRS has taken a calendar week and divided it into two payday time periods. It is easiest to think of a two-week period of time when discussing these time periods: *Wednesday, Thursday*, and *Friday* of week one, *Saturday* of week one, and *Sunday, Monday*, and *Tuesday* of week two.

    Two deposit rules apply to these two time periods. We can call these rules the Wednesday and Friday rules.

    a. **Wednesday rule:** If employees are paid during the week one Wednesday–Friday period, the tax deposit will be due on Wednesday of week two.

    b. **Friday rule:** If employees are paid anytime from Saturday of week one or Sunday, Monday, or Tuesday of week two, the tax deposit will be due on Friday of week two.

These rules mean that the payroll tax deposit will be due three banking days after the payday time period ends. For the Wednesday rule, the deposit is due three banking days after Friday of week one, on the following Wednesday (in week two). For the Friday rule, the deposit is due three banking days after Tuesday of week two, on Friday of week two.

8. **What is a banking day?** The term *banking day* refers to any day that a bank is open to the public for business. Saturdays, Sundays, and legal holidays are not banking days.

9. **How do legal holidays affect payroll tax deposits?** If a legal holiday occurs after the last day of a payday time period, the employer will get one extra day to make its Form 941 tax deposit as follows:

   a. **For monthly depositors:** If the fifteenth of the month is a Saturday, Sunday, or legal holiday, the deposit will be due and payable on the next banking day.

   b. **For semiweekly depositors:** A deposit due on Wednesday will be due on Thursday of the same week, and a Friday deposit will be due on Monday of the following week. Remember that the employer will always have three banking days after the last day of either payday time period to make its payroll tax deposit.

10. **What happens if an employer is late with its Form 941 tax deposit?** If a Form 941 tax deposit is not made the day it should be deposited, the employer may be assessed a fine for lateness and may even be charged interest, depending on how late the deposit is.

Questions, Mini Exercises, Exercises, and Problems

Discussion Questions

1. What taxes make up Payroll Tax Expense?
2. Explain how an employer can receive a credit against the FUTA tax due.
3. Explain what an experience or merit rating is and how it affects the amount paid by an employer for state unemployment insurance.
4. How is an employer classified as a monthly or semiweekly depositor for Form 941 tax purposes?
5. What is the purpose of Form 8109?
6. How often is Form 941 completed?
7. Please comment on the following statement: The amount found on line 17(d) of Form 941 must always be the same amount found on line 13 of the form.
8. Bill Smith leaves his job on July 9. He requests a copy of his W-2 form when he leaves. His boss tells him to wait until January of next year. Please discuss whether Bill's boss is correct in making this statement.
9. Why would one employer prepare a Form 940 but another would prepare a 940-EZ?
10. Employer A has a FUTA tax liability of $67.49 on March 31 of the current year. When does the employer have to make the deposit for this liability?
11. Employer B has a FUTA tax liability of $553.24 on January 31 of the current year. When does the employer have to make the deposit for this liability?
12. Why is the year-end adjusting entry needed for workers' compensation insurance?

Mini Exercises

(The forms you need are on page 245 of the *Study Guide and Working Papers*.)

Account Classifications

1. Complete the following table:

Accounts Affected	Category	↑	Rules
a. Payroll Tax Expense			
b. FICA—Social Security Payable			
c. FICA—Medicare Payable			
d. State Unemployment Tax Payable			
e. Federal Unemployment Tax Payable			

Exempt Wages

2. Pete Bole's cumulative earnings before this pay period were $6,800; his gross pay for this week is $500. How much of *this* week's pay will be subject to taxes for: FICA—Medicare, FICA—Social Security, and FUTA. Assume the wage base and rates in the text.

Look-Back Periods

3. Label the following look-back periods for 200C by months.

A	B	C	D
200A		200B	

Monthly Versus Semiweekly Depositor

4. In November 200B, Pete is trying to find out if he is a monthly or semiweekly depositor for FICA (Social Security and Medicare) and federal income tax for 200C. Please advise based on the following taxes owed:

200A	Quarter 3	$28,000
	Quarter 4	12,000
200B	Quarter 1	3,000
	Quarter 2	10,000

Paying the Tax

5. Complete the following table:

Depositor	Four-Quarter Look-Back Period Tax Liability	Payroll Paid	Tax Paid by
Monthly	$28,000	Nov.	A
Semiweekly	$66,000	On Wednesday	B
		On Thursday	C
		On Friday	D
		On Saturday	E
		On Sunday	F
		On Monday	G

Exercises

(The forms you need are on pages 246–248 of the *Study Guide and Working Papers*.)

8-1. From the following information, prepare a general journal entry to record the payroll tax expense for Baker Company for the payroll of August 9:

EMPLOYEE	CUMULATIVE EARNINGS BEFORE WEEKLY PAYROLL	GROSS PAY FOR WEEK
J. Kline	$3,500	$900
A. Met	6,600	750
D. Ring	7,900	300

The FICA tax rate for Social Security is 6.2% on $87,000, and Medicare is 1.45% on all earnings. Federal unemployment tax is .8% (.008 when expressed as a decimal) on the first $7,000 earned by each employee. The experience or merit rating for Baker is 5.6% on the first $7,000 of employee earnings for state unemployment purposes.

Journalizing the payroll tax.

8-2. Using Exercise 8-1, the state changed Baker's experience/merit rating to 4.9%. What effect would this change have on the total payroll tax expense?

Change in merit rating.

8-3. Using Exercise 8-1, if D. Ring earned $2,000 for the week instead of $300, what effect would this change have on the total payroll tax expense?

Change in payroll tax expense.

8-4. At the end of January 200X, the total amount of Social Security, $610, and Medicare, $200, was withheld as tax deductions from the employees of Wheat Fields Inc. Federal income tax of $3,000 was also deducted from their paychecks. Wheat Fields has been classified as a monthly depositor of Form 941 taxes. Indicate when this payroll tax deposit is due and provide a general journal entry to record the payment.

Journalizing payment of deposit.

8-5. The total wage expense for Howell Co. was $160,000. Of this total, $30,000 was beyond the Social Security wage-base limit and not subject to this tax. All earnings are subject to Medicare tax, and $60,000 was beyond the federal and state unemployment wage-base limits and not subject to unemployment taxes. Please calculate the total payroll tax expense for Howell Co. given the following rates and wage-base limits:

Calculating total payroll tax expense.

  a. FICA tax rate: Social Security, 6.2%; Medicare, 1.45%.
  b. State unemployment tax rate: 5.9%.
  c. Federal unemployment tax rate (after credit): .8%.

8-6. Carol's Grocery Store made the following Form 941 payroll tax deposits during the look-back period of July 1, 200A, through June 30, 200B:

Determining when tax deposits are due.

QUARTER ENDED	AMOUNT PAID IN 941 TAXES
September 30, 200A	$13,783.26
December 31, 200A	14,893.22
March 31, 200B	14,601.94
June 30, 200B	15,021.01

Should Carol's Grocery Store make Form 941 tax deposits monthly or semiweekly for 200C?

8-7. If Carol's Grocery Store downsized its operation during the second quarter of 200B and as a result paid only $6,121.93 in Form 941 taxes for the quarter that ended on June 30, 200B, should Carol's Grocery make its Form 941 payroll tax deposits monthly or semiweekly for 200C?

Determining when tax deposits are due.

8-8. From the following accounts, record the payment of (a) the July 3 payment for FICA (Social Security and Medicare) and federal income taxes, (b) the July 30 payment of state unemployment tax, and (c) the July 30 deposit of FUTA tax that may be required. Please prepare general journal entries from the following T accounts:

Journal entry to record payment of taxes.

FICA — Social Security Payable 203			FICA — Medicare Payable 204	
	June 30	400 (EE)		June 30	100 (EE)
		400 (ER)			100 (ER)

FIT Payable 205			FUTA Tax Payable 206	
	June 30	3,005		June 30	143

SUTA Tax Payable 207	
	June 30	612

FUTA.
Recall there are 13 weeks in a calender quarter.

8-9. At the end of the first quarter of 200X, you have been asked to determine the FUTA tax liability for Oscar Company as well as to record any payment of tax liability. The following information has been supplied to you; the FUTA tax rate is .8% on the first $7,000 each employee earns during the year.

EMPLOYEE	GROSS PAY PER WEEK
J. King	$500
A. Lane	500
B. Move	600
C. Slade	900

Workers' compensation.

8-10. From the following data, estimate the annual premium and record it by preparing a general journal entry:

TYPE OF WORK	ESTIMATED PAYROLL	RATE PER $100
Office	$15,000	$ .21
Sales	42,000	1.90

Group A Problems

(The forms you need are on pages 249–255 of the *Study Guide and Working Papers*.)

8A-1. For the biweekly pay period ending on April 8 at Kane's Hardware, the partial payroll summary shown below is taken from the individual employee earnings records.

Your tasks are to

Journal entry to record payroll tax expense.

1. Complete the table. Use the federal income tax withholding table in Figure 7-2 (p. 261) to figure the amount of income tax withheld.
2. Prepare a journal entry to record the payroll tax expense for Kane's. Please show the calculations for FICA taxes.

Check Figure:
Payroll Tax Expense
$593.58

EMPLOYEE	ALLOWANCE AND MARITAL STATUS	GROSS	FICA SOCIAL SECURITY	MEDICARE	FEDERAL INCOME TAX
Al Jones	S-1	$ 850			
Janice King	S-0	900			
Alice Long	S-2	800			
Jill Reese	S-0	1,060			
Jeff Vatack	S-2	1,365			

Assume the FICA tax rate for Social Security is 6.2% up to $87,000 in earnings (no one has earned this much as of April 8) and Medicare is 1.45% on all earnings. The state unemployment tax rate is 5.1% on the first $7,000 of earnings, and the federal unemployment tax rate is .8% of the first $7,000 of earnings. (Only Jeff Vatack has earned more than $7,000 as of April 8.) In cases where the amount of FICA tax calculates to one-half cent, round up to the next cent.

8A-2. The following is the monthly payroll of Hogan Company, owned by Dean Hogan. Employees are paid on the last day of each month.

Employer's tax responsibilities.

January

EMPLOYEE	MONTHLY EARNINGS	YEAR-TO-DATE EARNINGS	FICA SOCIAL SECURITY	MEDICARE	FEDERAL INCOME TAX
Sam Koy	$1,900	$1,900	$117.80	$ 27.55	$ 258
Joy Lane	3,150	3,150	195.30	45.68	361
Amy Hess	4,100	4,100	254.20	59.45	500
	$9,150	$9,150	$567.30	$132.68	$1,119

February

EMPLOYEE	MONTHLY EARNINGS	YEAR-TO-DATE EARNINGS	FICA SOCIAL SECURITY	MEDICARE	FEDERAL INCOME TAX
Sam Koy	$2,100	$ 4,000	$130.20	$ 30.45	$ 302
Joy Lane	2,900	6,050	179.80	42.05	325
Amy Hess	3,775	7,875	234.05	54.74	426
	$8,775	$17,925	$544.05	$127.24	$1,053

March

EMPLOYEE	MONTHLY EARNINGS	YEAR-TO-DATE EARNINGS	FICA SOCIAL SECURITY	MEDICARE	FEDERAL INCOME TAX
Sam Koy	$ 2,975	$ 6,975	$184.45	$ 43.14	$ 586
Joy Lane	4,080	10,130	252.96	59.16	558
Amy Hess	4,250	12,125	263.50	61.63	545
	$11,305	$29,230	$700.91	$163.93	$1,689

Check Figure: Deposit of SUTA Tax $ 1,195.58

Hogan Company is located at 2 Roundy Road, Marblehead, MA 01945. Its employer identification number is 29-3458821. The FICA tax rate for Social Security is 6.2% up to $87,000 in earnings during the year and Medicare is 1.45% on all earnings. The SUTA tax rate is 5.7% on the first $7,000. The FUTA tax rate is .8% on the first $7,000 of earnings. Hogan Company is classified as a monthly depositor for Form 941 taxes.

Your tasks are to

1. Journalize entries to record the employer's payroll tax expense for each pay period in the general journal.
2. Journalize entries for the payment of each tax liability including SUTA tax in the general journal.

8A-3. Ed Ward, accountant of Hogan Company, has been requested to complete Form 941 for the first quarter of the current year. Using Problem 8A-2, Ed gathers the needed data. Ed has suddenly been called away to an urgent budget meeting and has requested you to assist him by preparing the Form 941 for the first quarter. Please note that the difference in the tax liability, a few cents, should be adjusted in the middle column of line 9; this difference is due to the rounding of FICA tax amounts.

Journal entries and Form 941.

Check Figure: Total Liability for Quarter $ 8,333.22

8A-4. The following is the monthly payroll for the last three months of the year for Henson's Sporting Goods Shop, 1 Roe Road, Lynn, MA 01945. The shop is a sole proprietorship owned and operated by Bill Henson. The employer ID number for Henson's Sporting Goods is 28-93118921.

Journal entries and Form 941.

The employees at Henson's are paid once each month on the last day of the month. Pete Avery is the only employee who has contributed the maximum into Social Security. None of the other employees will reach the Social Security wage-base limit by the end of the year. Assume the rate for Social Security to be 6.2% with a wage-base maximum of $87,000, and the rate for Medicare to be 1.45% on all earnings. Henson's is classified as a monthly depositor for Form 941 payroll tax deposit purposes.

October

EMPLOYEE	MONTHLY EARNINGS	YEAR-TO-DATE EARNINGS	FICA SOCIAL SECURITY	MEDICARE	FEDERAL INCOME TAX
Pete Avery	$ 2,950	$ 83,050	$182.90	$ 42.78	$ 530
Janet Lee	3,590	40,150	222.58	52.06	427
Sue Lyons	3,800	43,900	235.60	55.10	536
	$10,340	$167,100	$641.08	$149.94	$1,493

November

EMPLOYEE	MONTHLY EARNINGS	YEAR-TO-DATE EARNINGS	FICA SOCIAL SECURITY	MEDICARE	FEDERAL INCOME TAX
Pete Avery	$ 3,180	$ 86,230	$197.16	$ 46.11	$ 597
Janet Lee	3,772	43,922	233.86	54.69	468
Sue Lyons	3,891	47,791	241.24	56.42	559
	$10,843	$177,943	$672.26	$157.22	$1,624

December

EMPLOYEE	MONTHLY EARNINGS	YEAR-TO-DATE EARNINGS	FICA SOCIAL SECURITY	MEDICARE	FEDERAL INCOME TAX
Pete Avery	$ 4,250	$ 90,480	$ 47.74	$ 61.63	$ 867
Janet Lee	3,800	47,722	235.60	55.10	479
Sue Lyons	4,400	52,191	272.80	63.80	704
	$12,450	$190,393	$556.14	$180.53	$2,050

Your tasks are to

1. Journalize entries to record the employer's payroll tax expense for each pay period in the general journal.
2. Journalize entries for the payment of each tax for FICA tax (Social Security and Medicare) and federal income tax, given that Henson's is a monthly Form 941 tax depositor.
3. Complete Form 941 for the fourth quarter of the current year.

8A-5. Using the information from Problem 8A-4, please complete a Form 940-EZ for Henson's Sporting Goods for the current year. Additional information needed to complete the form is as follows:

  a. FUTA tax deposit for first quarter: $168.00.
  b. SUTA rate: 5.7%.
  c. State reporting number: 025-319-2.

Please note that there were no FUTA tax deposits for the second, third, or fourth quarters of the year. Henson's had three employees for the year who all earned over $7,000.

Group B Problems

(The forms you need are on pages 249–255 of the *Study Guide and Working Papers*.)

8B-1. For the biweekly pay period ending on April 8 at Kane's Hardware, the following partial payroll summary is taken from the individual employee earnings records. Both Jill Reese and Jeff Vatack have earned more than $7,000 before this payroll.

Your tasks are to

1. Complete the table.
2. Prepare a journal entry to record the payroll tax expense for Kane's. Use the federal income tax withholding tables in Figures 7-2 and 7-3 to figure the amount of income tax withheld. Please show the calculations for FICA taxes.

Journal entry to record payroll tax expense.

Check Figure:
Payroll Tax Expense
$536.11

EMPLOYEE	ALLOWANCE AND MARITAL STATUS	GROSS	FICA SOCIAL SECURITY	MEDICARE	FEDERAL INCOME TAX
Al Jones	S-1	$ 820			
Janice King	S-2	890			
Alice Long	S-0	850			
Jill Reese	S-1	1,100			
Jeff Vatack	S-2	1,340			

Assume the FICA tax rate for Social Security is 6.2% up to $87,000 in earnings (no one has earned this much as of April 8) and Medicare is 1.45% on all earnings. The state unemployment tax rate is 5.2% on the first $7,000 of earnings, and the federal unemployment tax rate is .8% of the first $7,000 of earnings. In cases where the FICA tax calculates to one-half cent, round up to the next cent.

8B-2. The following is the monthly payroll of Hogan Company owned by Dean Hogan. Employees are paid on the last day of each month.

Employer's tax responsibilities.

January

EMPLOYEE	MONTHLY EARNINGS	YEAR-TO-DATE EARNINGS	FICA SOCIAL SECURITY	MEDICARE	FEDERAL INCOME TAX
Sam Koy	$1,850	$1,850	$114.70	$ 26.83	$222
Joy Lane	3,000	3,000	186.00	43.50	343
Amy Hess	3,590	3,590	222.58	52.06	396
	$8,440	$8,440	$523.28	$122.39	$961

February

EMPLOYEE	MONTHLY EARNINGS	YEAR-TO-DATE EARNINGS	FICA SOCIAL SECURITY	MEDICARE	FEDERAL INCOME TAX
Sam Koy	$2,200	$ 4,050	$136.40	$ 31.90	$ 293
Joy Lane	2,900	5,900	179.80	42.05	325
Amy Hess	3,775	7,365	234.05	54.74	426
	$8,875	$17,315	$550.25	$128.69	$1,044

March

EMPLOYEE	MONTHLY EARNINGS	YEAR-TO-DATE EARNINGS	FICA SOCIAL SECURITY	MEDICARE	FEDERAL INCOME TAX
Sam Koy	$ 2,820	$ 6,870	$174.84	$ 40.89	$ 405
Joy Lane	4,000	9,900	248.00	58.00	535
Amy Hess	4,300	11,665	266.60	62.35	556
	$11,120	$28,435	$689.44	$161.24	$1,496

Hogan Company is located at 2 Roundy Road, Marblehead, MA 01945. Its employer identification number is 29-3458821. The FICA tax rate for Social Security is 6.2% up to $87,000 in earnings during the year, and Medicare is 1.45% on all earnings. The SUTA tax rate is 5.7% on the first $7,000. The FUTA tax rate is .8% on the first $7,000 of earnings. Hogan Company is classified as a monthly depositor for Form 941 taxes.

Your tasks are to

1. Journalize entries to record the employer's payroll tax expense for each pay period in the general journal.
2. Journalize entries for the payment of each tax liability, including SUTA tax, in the general journal.

> Journal entries and Form 941.

8B-3. Ed Ward, accountant of Hogan Company, has been requested to complete Form 941 for the first quarter of the current year. Using Problem 8B-2, Ed gathers the needed data. Ed has suddenly been called away to an urgent budget meeting and has requested you to assist him by preparing the Form 941 for the first quarter. Please note that the difference in the tax liability, a few cents, should be adjusted in the middle column of line 9; this difference is due to the rounding of FICA tax amounts.

> Check Figure:
> Liability for Quarter
> $7,851.58

> Journal entries and Form 941.

8B-4. The following is the monthly payroll for the last three months of the year for Henson's Sporting Goods Shop, 1 Roe Road, Lynn, MA 01945. The shop is a sole proprietorship owned and operated by Bill Henson. The employer ID number for Henson's Sporting Goods is 28-93118921.

The employees at Henson's are paid once each month on the last day of the month. Pete Avery is the only employee who has contributed the maximum into Social Security. None of the other employees will reach the Social Security wage-base limit by the end of the year. Assume the rate for Social Security to be 6.2% with a wage-base maximum of $87,000 and the rate for Medicare to be 1.45% on all earnings. Henson's is classified as a monthly depositor for Form 941 payroll taxes.

October

EMPLOYEE	MONTHLY EARNINGS	YEAR-TO-DATE EARNINGS	FICA SOCIAL SECURITY	MEDICARE	FEDERAL INCOME TAX
Pete Avery	$ 2,950	$ 84,200	$182.90	$ 42.78	$ 530
Janet Lee	3,590	41,075	222.58	52.06	427
Sue Lyons	3,800	44,000	235.60	55.10	536
	$10,340	$169,275	$641.08	$149.94	$1,493

November

EMPLOYEE	MONTHLY EARNINGS	YEAR-TO-DATE EARNINGS	FICA SOCIAL SECURITY	MEDICARE	FEDERAL INCOME TAX
Pete Avery	$ 3,000	$ 87,200	$173.60	$ 43.50	$ 552
Janet Lee	3,650	44,725	226.30	52.93	439
Sue Lyons	3,710	47,710	230.02	53.80	503
	$10,360	$179,635	$629.92	$150.23	$1,494

Check Figure:
Dec 31 Payroll Tax
Expense $654.51

December

EMPLOYEE	MONTHLY EARNINGS	YEAR-TO-DATE EARNINGS	FICA SOCIAL SECURITY	MEDICARE	FEDERAL INCOME TAX
Pete Avery	$ 4,250	$ 91,450	—	$ 61.63	$ 857
Janet Lee	3,850	48,575	$238.70	55.83	490
Sue Lyons	3,900	51,610	241.80	56.55	559
	$12,000	$191,635	$480.50	$174.01	$1,906

Your tasks are to

1. Journalize entries to record the employer's payroll tax expense for each pay period in the general journal.
2. Journalize entries for the payment of each tax for FICA tax (Social Security and Medicare) and federal income tax.
3. Complete Form 941 for the fourth quarter of the current year.

8B-5. Using the information from Problem 8B-4, please complete a form 940-EZ for Henson's Sporting Goods for the current year. Additional information needed to complete the form is as follows:

   a. FUTA tax deposit for first quarter: $168.
   b. SUTA tax rate: 5.7%.
   c. State reporting number: 025-319-2.

Please note that there were no FUTA tax deposits for the third or fourth quarters of the year. Henson's had three employees for the year who all earned over $7,000.

Form 940-EZ.

Check Figure:
Line 4 Total Exempt
Payments $170,635.00

Real-World Applications

8R-1. Sunshine School Supplies is a leading manufacturer of back-to-school kits and other items used by students in elementary and middle schools. Each summer Sunshine needs additional help to assemble, pack, and ship school items sold in stores around the country. Sunshine's company policy has been to hire 30 additional workers for 12 weeks during the summer. Each employee works 40 hours per week and earns $6.50 per hour. At the end of August these additional workers are laid off.

Sunshine's state unemployment rate has risen to 5.4% with no experience/ merit rating allowed due to these layoffs in the last few years.

Miriam Holtz, who is the president of Sunshine, asks for your help to find a way to reduce Sunshine's 5.4 state unemployment rate. When Miriam called the state department of labor and employment, she was told that Sunshine's employment rate could drop to 4.1% if it stopped laying off workers.

Miriam has thought about using temporary employment agency workers during the summer months as a way to obtain the help the company needs and at the same time stop the seasonal layoffs.

Miriam asks you if this is a good idea. She gives you the following facts to use in analyzing this idea:

1. Five hundred workers who are permanent employees of Sunshine earn in excess of $7,000 each by September of each year.
2. A temporary employment agency told Miriam it would charge Sunshine $7.00 per hour for each worker it supplied during the summer.
3. The current federal unemployment tax rate is .8% up to the first $7,000 each employee earns during a year.
4. The current SUTA wage-base limit is the first $7,000 each employee earns during a year.
5. Sunshine pays a FICA tax rate of 6.2% for Social Security and 1.45% for Medicare. The Social Security wage-base limit is $87,000; there is no wage-base limit for Medicare.

Please write a short memo to Miriam Holtz that shows your analysis of two options: (1) continue to hire 30 additional workers for the summer and then lay them off or (2) have the temporary employment agency provide 30 additional workers for the summer.

In your memo be sure to show the financial effect of both options in terms of the tax calculations on employee earnings for SUTA, FUTA, and FICA. For option 1 be sure to include the SUTA and FUTA tax effects for *both* the permanent and temporary workers. At the end of your memo please provide Miriam with your conclusion so she can make a good decision for her company.

8R-2. Cathy Johnson has just been hired as a bookkeeper for The Pet World Dog Toy Company. She recently graduated from the local community college with an associate degree in business. She took several accounting courses at school but was unable to take the school's payroll accounting course.

Cathy is confused about payroll tax forms and their purpose. She wants to learn more about the forms the business must prepare and send in to the government.

You are the accountant for Pet World. Your boss has asked you to help teach Cathy about the forms and why they are used. The boss feels it is best to give Cathy a brief written summary about the following forms:

1. Form 941.
2. Form 940-EZ.
3. Form 8109.
4. Form W-2.
5. Form W-3.

Please write a brief report to Cathy to help her to understand the following points about these payroll tax forms:

a. The purpose of each form.
b. What is reported on each form.
c. When each form is sent to the government.
d. Where the amounts found on each form come from in the accounting system.

YOU make the call

Critical Thinking/Ethical Case

8R-3. Abby Ross works in the Payroll Department for Lange Co. as a junior accountant. Abby is also going to school for an advanced degree in accounting. After work each day she uses the company's photocopy machine to make extra copies of her assignments. Should she be photocopying personal material on a company machine? You make the call. Write down your specific recommendations to Abby.

Internet Exercises: Microsoft; Automatic Data Processing

EX-1. [**www.microsoft.com**] Microsoft is one of the growing number of American companies who hires temporary workers who are independent contractors to fill permanent spots in its labor force. These "permatemps" do not have the status of employees who enjoy full benefits with Microsoft.

In this exercise, let us say that Microsoft hires a temporary worker and pays her $20 per hour. Assuming this employee does not go over the statutory FICA limits described by the chapter, nor goes over the FUTA $7,000 ceiling, how much does the company save by having an "independent contractor" perform the work over the cost of having an "employee" do the same work?

EX-2. [**http://ebs.adp.com/prod/index.html**] Automatic Data Processing, Inc. (ADP) is a long-recognized leader in payroll preparation for businesses of all sizes. ADP does provide other services to businesses, but much of its professional reputation stems from being one of the early "outsourcing" companies for payroll.

Services it provides in addition to strictly payroll calculation include benefits administration, staffing, time and attendance reporting, and assisting businesses in retaining high-quality employees.

1. From information you obtain from this Web site, explain why ADP has an important niche in human relations and payroll preparation.
2. What advantage can a company of any size obtain by outsourcing its payroll preparation and tax reporting activities?

Continuing Problem

Eldorado Computer Center

As December comes to an end, Tony Freedman wants to take care of his payroll obligations. He will complete Form 941 for the first quarter of the current year and Form 940-EZ for federal unemployment taxes. Tony will make the necessary deposits and payments associated with his payroll.

Assignment

(See pages 260–262 in your *Study Guide and Working Papers*.)

1. Record the payroll tax expense entry in general journal format for the quarter, using the information in the Chapter 7 problem.

2. Journalize entries for the payment of each tax liability, including SUTA tax, in the general journal. Eldorado Computer Center is classified as a quarterly depositor.

3. Prepare Form 941 for the first quarter. Eldorado Computer Center's employer identification number is 35-41325881.

4. Complete Form 940 for Eldorado Computer Center. The FUTA tax ceiling is $7,000, and the SUTA tax ceiling is $10,000 in cumulative wages for each employee. The Eldorado Computer Center's FUTA rate is .8%, and the SUTA rate is 2.7%. No deposits have been made.

Hint: Sometimes the amount of Social Security taxes paid by the employee for the quarter will not equal the employee's tax liability because of rounding. Any overage or difference should be reported on line 9 of Form 941.

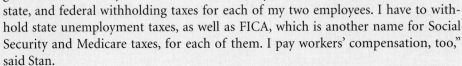

SUBWAY Case

HOLD THE LETTUCE, WITHHOLD THE TAXES

"As an employer, Stan, what are your tax responsibilities?" asked Angel Tavarez, president of the Los Palmos Kiwanis club. They were at one of the luncheons sponsored by the club every month, and Stan had been asked to join a discussion on the Role of Small Business in Our Local Economy. Fortunately, Angel had told the panelists the questions in advance, so Stan had his answers ready.

"Well, of course, I pay city, state, and U.S. government taxes myself. I also have to file city, state, and federal withholding taxes for each of my two employees. I have to withhold state unemployment taxes, as well as FICA, which is another name for Social Security and Medicare taxes, for each of them. I pay workers' compensation, too," said Stan.

"That's strange," said a voice from the audience. "My brother-in-law has a Subway restaurant in the southern part of the state, and he doesn't pay any city taxes. What's going on here?"

"Naturally, the situation is slightly different for Subway owners in different cities in our state—and across the country," said Stan confidently. "Not all cities have city income taxes. Different states have different regulations about worker's comp, as well."

"Oh, right," said the voice, sounding embarrassed.

"So, Stan, how often do you have to pay taxes," asked Angel Tavarez, shifting the topic diplomatically.

Stan picked up a piece of chalk and drew four large circles on the blackboard. Then he wrote the word "ASPIRIN" in each of the circles. A murmur of "Huhs" and "Whats" went around the room.

"The average employee working for a company pays tax once a year on April 15 and has one big tax headache. As an employer," Stan said, "I file tax returns on a quarterly basis, so I have four big tax headaches a year! Rather than filling out the 1040-EZ, I complete Form 941, the Employers Quarterly Federal Return to report and pay payroll taxes to the IRS. Yet, while the form is due quarterly, I need to actually deposit the tax money into a Federal Reserve Bank once a month. In addition, I have to file the 940-EZ at the end of each year to pay my federal and state unemployment taxes. Then, for each employee . . ."

"Stan," Angel interrupted, "I'm afraid time is running out for your segment of the panel discussion. We'll move on to Pamela Pudelle, who is going to tell us about advertising her new pet-grooming parlor." Stan suppressed a chuckle as a woman who looked amazingly like a poodle took the microphone from Stan.

Later, during the reception, Stan tapped Angel on the shoulder, "Sorry I went over my time limit," he said. "You didn't really go over," said Angel, "but you were getting a little too technical for the audience." While Stan was sorry to have let the discussion veer off course, he felt a little burst of pride: who would have thought a year ago that he would be willing—and able—to expound about the tax burden of a small business owner!

Discussion Questions

1. What are the taxes called "Form 941 taxes"?
2. Why is Stan classified as a monthly depositor of Form 941 taxes?
3. Assume Stan owed $2,069.90 in Form 941 taxes for March. When would it be due? What would happen if that day were Sunday?

MINI PRACTICE SET

PETE'S MARKET

Completing Payroll Requirements for First Quarter and Preparing Form 941

This Mini Practice Set aids in putting the pieces of payroll together. In this project you are the bookkeeper and have the responsibility of recording payroll in the payroll register, paying the payroll, recording the employer's tax responsibilities, and paying tax deposits as well as completing the quarterly report. (The forms you need are on pages 263–268 of the *Study Guide and Working Papers*.)

Pete's Market, owned by Pete Reel, is located at 4 Sun Avenue, Swampscott, MA 01970. His employer identification number is 42-4583312. Please assume the following:

1. FICA: Social Security, 6.2% on $87,000; Medicare, 1.45% on all earnings.
2. SUTA: 4.9% (due to favorable merit rating) on $7,000.
3. FUTA: .8% on first $7,000.
4. Employees are paid monthly. The payroll is recorded the last day of each month and is paid on the first day of the next month.
5. FIT table from IRS Circular E, *Employer's Tax Guide* (see p. 328).
6. State income tax is 8%.

The following are the employees of Pete's Market along with their monthly salary exemptions and other information:

SALARY PER MONTH

		January	February	March	
FIT 317 Fred Flynn	S-0	$2,500	$2,590	$2,575	(Sales Salaries)
319 Mary Jones	S-2	3,000	3,000	4,000	(Market Salaries)
388 Lilly Vron	S-1	3,000	3,000	4,260	(Sales Salaries)

Partial Ledger Accounts
as of December 31, 200X

FICA—Social Security Payable 210	
	410.90 (EE)
	410.90 (ER)

FICA—Medicare Payable 212	
	100 (EE)
	100 (ER)

FIT Payable 220	
	600

SIT Payable 225	
	150

FUTA Payable 230	
	88

SUTA Payable 240	
	155

Using the general journal and payroll register provided, please complete the following:

200X

Jan. 15 Record the entry for the deposit of Social Security, Medicare, and FIT from last month's payroll. (For simplicity, we will not record the payment of state income tax in this problem.)

31 Pay state unemployment tax due from last quarter.

31 Pay federal unemployment tax owed.

31 Complete payroll register for January payroll, journalize payroll entry, and journalize entry for employer's payroll tax expense.

Feb. 1 Transfer cash for the January Net Pay from Cash to Payroll Checking Cash.

     1 Pay payroll.

   15 Pay taxes due for Social Security, Medicare, and FIT.

   28 Complete payroll register for February payroll. Journalize payroll entry as well as journalize entry for employer's payroll tax expense.

Mar. 1 Transfer cash for the February Net Pay from Cash to Payroll Checking Cash.

     1 Pay payroll.

   15 Pay taxes due for Social Security, Medicare, and FIT.

   31 Complete payroll register for March payroll. Journalize payroll entry as well as journalize entry for employer's payroll tax expense.

Apr. 1 Transfer cash for the March Net Pay from Cash to Payroll Checking Cash.

     1 Pay payroll.

   15 Pay taxes due for Social Security, Medicare, and FIT.

   30 Pay federal unemployment tax due for quarter 1.

   30 Pay state unemployment tax due for quarter 1.

   30 Complete Form 941 for the first quarter.

SINGLE Persons—MONTHLY Payroll Period

(For Wages Paid in 200X)

If the wages are—		And the number of withholding allowances claimed is—										
At least	But less than	0	1	2	3	4	5	6	7	8	9	10
		The amount of income tax to be withheld is—										
$2,480	$2,520	$317	$279	$241	$203	$165	$127	$89	$50	$25	$0	$0
2,520	2,560	327	285	247	209	171	133	95	56	29	3	0
2,560	2,600	338	291	253	215	177	139	101	62	33	7	0
2,600	2,640	349	297	259	221	183	145	107	68	37	11	0
2,640	2,680	359	303	265	227	189	151	113	74	41	15	0
2,680	2,720	370	309	271	233	195	157	119	80	45	19	0
2,720	2,760	381	315	277	239	201	163	125	86	49	23	0
2,760	2,800	392	323	283	245	207	169	131	92	54	27	2
2,800	2,840	403	334	289	251	213	175	137	98	60	31	6
2,840	2,880	413	345	295	257	219	181	143	104	66	35	10
2,880	2,920	424	356	301	263	225	187	149	110	72	39	14
2,920	2,960	435	366	307	269	231	193	155	116	78	43	18
2,960	3,000	446	377	313	275	237	199	161	122	84	47	22
3,000	3,040	457	388	319	281	243	205	167	128	90	52	26
3,040	3,080	467	399	330	287	249	211	173	134	96	58	30
3,080	3,120	478	410	341	293	255	217	179	140	102	64	34
3,120	3,160	489	420	352	299	261	223	185	146	108	70	38
3,160	3,200	500	431	363	305	267	229	191	152	114	76	42
3,200	3,240	511	442	373	311	273	235	197	158	120	82	46
3,240	3,280	521	453	384	317	279	241	203	164	126	88	50
3,280	3,320	532	464	395	326	285	247	209	170	132	94	56
3,320	3,360	543	474	406	337	291	253	215	176	138	100	62
3,360	3,400	554	485	417	348	297	259	221	182	144	106	68
3,400	3,440	565	496	427	359	303	265	227	188	150	112	74
3,440	3,480	575	507	438	370	309	271	233	194	156	118	80
3,480	3,520	586	518	449	380	315	277	239	200	162	124	86
3,520	3,560	597	528	460	391	323	283	245	206	168	130	92
3,560	3,600	608	539	471	402	333	289	251	212	174	136	98
3,600	3,640	619	550	481	413	344	295	257	218	180	142	104
3,640	3,680	629	561	492	424	355	301	263	224	186	148	110
3,680	3,720	640	572	503	434	366	307	269	230	192	154	116
3,720	3,760	651	582	514	445	377	313	275	236	198	160	122
3,760	3,800	662	593	525	456	387	319	281	242	204	166	128
3,800	3,840	673	604	535	467	398	330	287	248	210	172	134
3,840	3,880	683	615	546	478	409	340	293	254	216	178	140
3,880	3,920	694	626	557	488	420	351	299	260	222	184	146
3,920	3,960	705	636	568	499	431	362	305	266	228	190	152
3,960	4,000	716	647	579	510	441	373	311	272	234	196	158
4,000	4,040	727	658	589	521	452	384	317	278	240	202	164
4,040	4,080	737	669	600	532	463	394	326	284	246	208	170
4,080	4,120	748	680	611	542	474	405	337	290	252	214	176
4,120	4,160	759	690	622	553	485	416	347	296	258	220	182
4,160	4,200	770	701	633	564	495	427	358	302	264	226	188
4,200	4,240	781	712	643	575	506	438	369	308	270	232	194
4,240	4,280	791	723	654	586	517	448	380	314	276	238	200
4,280	4,320	802	734	665	596	528	459	391	322	282	244	206
4,320	4,360	813	744	676	607	539	470	401	333	288	250	212
4,360	4,400	824	755	687	618	549	481	412	344	294	256	218
4,400	4,440	835	766	697	629	560	492	423	354	300	262	224
4,440	4,480	845	777	708	640	571	502	434	365	306	268	230
4,480	4,520	856	788	719	650	582	513	445	376	312	274	236
4,520	4,560	867	798	730	661	593	524	455	387	318	280	242
4,560	4,600	878	809	741	672	603	535	466	398	329	286	248
4,600	4,640	889	820	751	683	614	546	477	408	340	292	254
4,640	4,680	899	831	762	694	625	556	488	419	350	298	260
4,680	4,720	910	842	773	704	636	567	499	430	361	304	266
4,720	4,760	921	852	784	715	647	578	509	441	372	310	272
4,760	4,800	932	863	795	726	657	589	520	452	383	316	278
4,800	4,840	943	874	805	737	668	600	531	462	394	325	284
4,840	4,880	953	885	816	748	679	610	542	473	404	336	290
4,880	4,920	964	896	827	758	690	621	553	484	415	347	296
4,920	4,960	975	906	838	769	701	632	563	495	426	357	302
4,960	5,000	986	917	849	780	711	643	574	506	437	368	308
5,000	5,040	997	928	859	791	722	654	585	516	448	379	314
5,040	5,080	1,007	939	870	802	733	664	596	527	458	390	321

$5,080 and over   Use Table 4(a) for a **SINGLE person** on page 34. Also see the instructions on page 32.

COMPUTERIZED ACCOUNTING APPLICATION FOR PETE'S MARKET MINI PRACTICE SET FOR CHAPTER 8

Completing Payroll Requirements for First Quarter and Preparing Form 941

Before starting on this assignment, read and complete the tasks discussed in Parts A, B, and F of the Computerized Accounting appendix at the back of this book and complete the Computerized Accounting Application assignments for Chapter 3, Chapter 4, and the Valdez Realty Mini Practice Set (Chapter 5).

Pete's Market, owned by Pete Reel, is located at 4 Sun Avenue, Swampscott, Massachusetts, 01970. His employer identification number is 42-4583312. The version of Peachtree Complete Accounting used with this text (2003) uses the state and federal tax laws in effect for calendar year 2003. Federal Income Tax (FIT), State Income Tax (SIT), Social Security, Medicare, FUTA, and SUTA are all calculated automatically by the program based on the following assumptions and built-in tax rates:

1. FICA: Social Security, 6.2 percent on $84,900; Medicare, 1.45 percent on all earnings.
2. SUTA: 4.9 percent on the first $10,800 in earnings.
3. FUTA: .8 percent on the first $7,000 in earnings.
4. Employees are paid monthly. The payroll is recorded and paid on the last day of each month. The company uses a payroll checking account and the net pay must be transferred to that account as part of the payroll process.
5. FIT is calculated automatically by the program based on the marital status and number of exemptions claimed by each employee. These have been set up already.
6. SIT for Massachusetts is calculated automatically by the program based on the marital status and number of exemptions claimed by each employee.

The Payroll module in Peachtree Complete Accounting is designed to work with the General Ledger module in an integrated fashion. When transactions are recorded in the Payroll Journal, the program automatically updates the employee records, records the journal entry, and posts all accounts affected in the general ledger.

The following are the employees of Pete's Market and their monthly wages (note the changes) they will earn for the first payroll quarter:

	JANUARY	FEBRUARY	MARCH
Fred Flynn	$2,500	$2,590	$2,475
Mary Jones	3,000	3,000	4,000
Lilly Vron	3,000	3,000	4,260

The trial balance for Pete's Market as of 1/1/04 appears below:

		Debits	Credits
1010	Cash	$84,964.04	$ —
1020	Payroll Checking Cash	—	—
2310	FIT Payable	—	1,415.94
2320	SIT Payable	—	535.50
2330	Social Security Tax Payable	—	1,116.00
2335	Medicare Tax Payable	—	261.00
2340	FUTA Payable	—	48.00
2350	SUTA Payable	—	1,587.60
3560	Pete Reel, Capital	$ —	$80,000.00
		$84,964.04	$84,964.04

Open the Company Data Files

1. Click on the Start button. Point to Programs; point to the Peachtree folder and select Peachtree Complete Accounting. Your desktop may have the Peachtree icon allowing for a quicker entrance into the program.
2. Follow the "Open a File" instructions in Part A of the Computerized Accounting appendix at the back of this book to open **Pete's Market.**
3. Click on the **Maintain** menu option. Then select **Company Information.** The program will respond by bringing up a dialogue box allowing the user to edit/add information about the company.

Add Your Name to the Company Name

4. Click in the **Company Name** entry field at the end of **Pete's Market.** If it is already highlighted, press the right arrow key. Add a dash and your name "**-Student Name**" to the end of the company name. Click on the **OK** button to return to the Menu Window.

Record Payment of December Payroll Liabilities and Taxes

5. Record the payment of last month's payroll liabilities using the General Journal Entry window. Enter the **Date** listed for each transaction (you may use the "+" key to advance the date or use the calendar icon next to the field to select the date from a calendar). Enter "Memo" into the **Source** text box for each transaction or accept Peachtree's additional number added to memo by pressing TAB:

2004

Jan. 15 Record the compound journal entry for the deposit of Social Security, Medicare, and FIT from last month's payroll. (We will not record the payment of state income tax.) This is a 941 Deposit

31 Record the payment of SUTA taxes owed from last quarter.

31 Record the payment of FUTA tax owed from last quarter. This is a 940 Deposit

How to Record the Payroll

6. Close the General Journal. Peachtree has two options for paying your employees. Both are available under the **Tasks** menu. The first option is **Select for Payroll Entry** that selects all employees who meet a selected criteria while the second, **Payroll Entry,** allows you to select the employees one by one. Since we wish to pay all of our salaried employees, we will select the first option, **Select for Payroll Entry.** This will bring up a dialogue box from which we can filter which employees to pay this period:

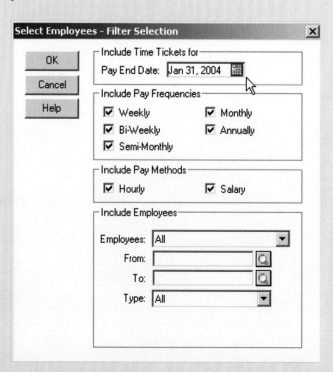

7. Since ours is a monthly payroll paid on the last day of the month, we will change the **Pay End Date:** to reflect January 31 using the small calendar to the right of the field. Click on the small calendar and then select the 31st from the calendar presented. The other filters allow us to pay only a certain frequency type employee, hourly and/or salary, or a range of employees by employee number. You can explore these options but leave them set at the default values shown in the illustration on page 330.

8. Click on the **OK** button when you are ready to continue. This will bring up a Select Employees to Pay dialogue box:

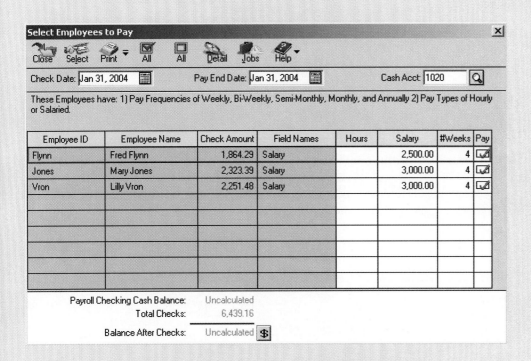

9. Notice how Peachtree has selected all three of our employees and has automatically flagged them for payment with a red check mark. It has also calculated all of the required withholdings and payroll taxes for each employee. Since we are paying the employees on the last day of the month, we should change the **Check Date** to reflect January 31, 2004. Also, verify and/or change the **Cash Acct** to 1020 Payroll Checking Cash using the pull down menu. Any employee can be deselected by clicking in the Pay column.

10. If you want to see the detail on any of the employees, simply double click on that employee's entry to bring up a Detail dialogue box. Try selecting Fred Flynn. If necessary, you can change any of the numbers presented in the white fields of this dialogue box by double clicking on the number you wish to change. We will accept all the information as shown. Leave this dialogue box by clicking on **OK** or **Cancel** since we made no changes:

Review the Payroll

How to Edit a Payroll Journal Entry Prior to Posting

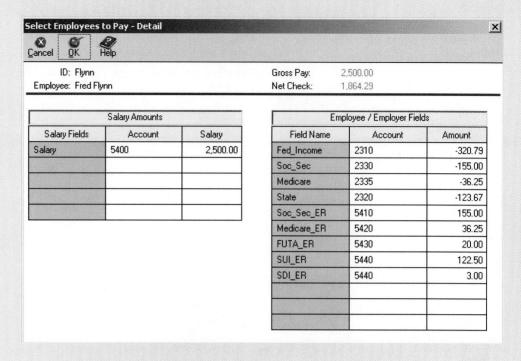

How to Post a Payroll
Entry

11. After verifying that the payroll entries are correct, click on the **Print** icon to print checks and post this transaction. A Print Forms: Payroll Checks dialogue box is presented for the user to select the proper check format and the starting check number. Accept the default form and use check #100 for the starting check number. Your screen should appear as shown below:

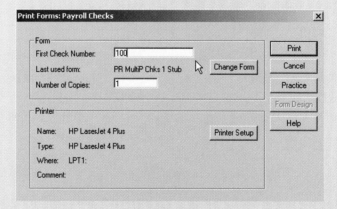

12. You are now presented with a dialogue box to select **Print** or **Practice**. Practice would be used to make sure the checks are aligned in the printer. This is particularly important with dot matrix type printers. Select **Print** since we are not printing on real forms and do not have to worry about alignment. You would normally load blank checks into your printer at this time so it may prompt you to do so. Just tell it to Continue.

13. When the checks have finished, you will be asked to confirm the printing process. This feature allows you to print them a second time if something interfered with the printing process the first time through. Upon confirming a successful run, you will be taken back to the Menu Screen of Peachtree and Peachtree will create and post all the necessary journal entries internally.

14. From the **Reports** menu, select **Payroll**. This will bring up a Select a Report dialogue box containing a list of several payroll reports available to us. Select **Payroll Register** to bring up a payroll register for the checks we just issued. We will use this report to determine the net pay for the payroll period. This amount must be transferred to our Payroll Checking account since our paychecks are drawn on that account. It must be funded prior to issuing the checks to our employees. Accept all defaults provided by Peachtree and we are presented with:

How to Display and Print
a Payroll Register

Pete's Market- Student Name
Payroll Register
For the Period From Jan 1, 2004 to Jan 31, 2004
Filter Criteria includes: Report order is by Check Date. Report is printed in Detail Format.

Employee ID Employee SS No Reference Date	Pay Type	Pay Hrs	Pay Amt	Amount	Gross State SUI_ER	Fed_Income Soc_Sec_ER SDI_ER	Soc_Sec Medicare_ER	Medicare FUTA_ER
Flynn Fred Flynn 100 1/1/04	Salary		2,500.00	1,864.29	2,500.00 -123.67 -122.50	-320.79 -155.00	-155.00 -36.25	-36.25 -20.00
Jones Mary Jones 101 1/1/04	Salary		3,000.00	2,323.39	3,000.00 -126.32 -147.00	-320.79 -186.00	-186.00 -43.50	-43.50 -24.00
Vron Lilly Vron 102 1/1/04	Salary		3,000.00	2,251.48	3,000.00 -130.73 -147.00	-388.29 -186.00	-186.00 -43.50	-43.50 -24.00
Summary Total 1/1/04 thru 1/31/04	Salary		8,500.00	6,439.16	8,500.00 -380.72 -416.50	-1,029.87 -527.00	-527.00 -123.25	-123.25 -68.00
Report Date Final Total 1/1/04 thru 1/31/04	Salary		8,500.00	(6,439.16)	8,500.00 -380.72 -416.50	-1,029.87 -527.00	-527.00 -123.25	-123.25 -68.00

15. We will now transfer cash from our regular Cash account into our Payroll Checking account in order to cover the checks we have just written. Note from the register totals, we have a total of $ 6,439.16 in net pay.

- Select **General Journal Entry** from the **Tasks** menu to open the General Journal dialog box. Enter the date 1/31/04 into the **Date** field; press the TAB key; enter "Memo" into the **Reference** field and press TAB.
- Select account number "1020 Payroll Checking Cash".
- Enter "Transfer net payroll" in the **Description** field.
- Enter "6439.16" in the **Debit** field.
- Tab to **Account No.** and select "1010 Cash".
- Tab to the **Credit** field and enter "6439.16" again.
- Click **Save** to complete the transfer.

Print Reports

16. After you have posted the journal entry, close the General Journal Entry window and print the following reports accepting all defaults offered by Peachtree:

a. General Journal (check figure debit = $10,867.70)
b. Trial Balance (check figure debit = $83,731.09)

Review your printed reports. If you have made an error in a posted journal entry, use the procedures detailed in step 18 from Chapter 3 to make any necessary corrections. Reprint all reports if corrections are made.

Make a January Backup Copy

17. It is always wise to backup accounting data at the end of each month, saving it into a file that will be saved until the end of the year. We will use Peachtree's Backup feature to do this. Click on the Company Window **File** menu; select **Backup,** use a filename such as "PeteJan" to make sure you can recognize what the backup represents. Click on **OK.**

Advancing the Period

18. We must now advance the period to prepare Peachtree for the February transactions.

- Using your mouse, click on **System** from the **Tasks** menu. Select **Change Accounting Periods.**
- Using the pull down menu, select period 2—Feb 1, 2004 to Feb 29, 2004 and click on **OK.**
- You will be asked whether you wish to print reports before continuing. Since we have already printed our reports, we can answer **No.**
- Note that the status bar at the bottom of the screen now reflects that you are in period 2.

Record Payment of January Payroll Liabilities and Taxes

19. Record the following general journal entry:

2004
Feb.   15   Record the compound journal entry for the deposit of Social Security, Medicare, and FIT from last month's payroll. Use the trial balance created in #16 above to determine the amounts owed.

Record February Payroll

20. Record the February payroll journal entries for Fred Flynn, Mary Jones, and Lilly Vron. Remember that Fred Flynn is making more than his usual amount this month. He will earn $2,590 instead of his usual $2,500. After selecting employees to pay (See "How to Record the Payroll" above except use February 29), double click on Fred's Salary field and change his salary to the new amount. Everything will automatically recalculate using the new gross. Follow the same procedure for printing checks as you used in January except use the date February 29. Peachtree should select check #103 as the starting check number automatically. Change this if necessary. Be sure to transfer the net pay into the Payroll Checking Cash account.

Print Reports

21. Print the following reports accepting all defaults:

a. Payroll Register (check figure net = $6,493.20)
b. General Journal (check figure debit = $8,823.57)
c. Trial Balance (check figure debit = $84,644.29)

Make a February Backup Copy

22. Click on the Company Window **File** menu; select **Backup**, use a filename such as "PeteFeb" to make sure you can recognize what the backup represents. Click on **OK.**

Advance Dates

23. We must now advance the period to prepare Peachtree for the March transactions.

- Using your mouse, click on **System** from the **Tasks** menu. Select **Change Accounting Periods.**

- Using the pull down menu, select period 3—Mar 1, 2004 to Mar 31, 2004 and click on **OK**.
- You will be asked whether you wish to print reports before continuing. Since we have already printed our reports, we can answer **No**.
- Note that the status bar at the bottom of the screen now reflects that you are in period 3.

24. Record the following general journal entry:

Record Payment of February Payroll Liabilities and Taxes

2004

Mar.   15   Record the compound journal entry for the deposit of Social Security, Medicare, and FIT from last month's payroll. (941 Deposit)

25. Record the March payroll journal entries for Fred Flynn, Mary Jones, and Lilly Vron. Note from the table at the start of the workshop that all three will receive other than their normal salary for this pay period. Be sure to transfer the net pay into the Payroll Checking Cash account after generating the paychecks. Check numbers should begin with #106.

Record March Payroll

26. Print the following reports accepting all defaults:

Print Reports

   a. Payroll Register (check figure net = $7,781.28)
   b. General Journal (check figure debit = $10,149.73)
   c. Trial Balance (check figure debit = $86,608.09)

27. From the **Reports** menu, select **Payroll**. This will bring up a Select a Report dialogue box containing a list of several payroll reports available to us. Select the **941** folder near the bottom to open up our 941 options. Peachtree will print both pages needed for a semi-weekly depositor (941 and 941B). If you have access to the blank 941 forms, you may print the report directly on the form. If not, you can still print the report on plain paper. You could also select the worksheet option if you wish to fill out the 941 manually using Peachtree's data. With the **941** folder open, select **FedForm 941 2002**. Accept all defaults by clicking on **OK**. Peachtree will automatically print the report. Note that in a real working situation, you would subscribe to Peachtree's Payroll Tax Service which would bring not only the tax tables up to date, but also the forms.

How to Print 941 Summary Reports

28. Peachtree has placed the numbers where they would go on a blank 941. Close the Select a Report Window when you are finished.

29. Click on the Company Window **File** menu; select **Backup,** use a filename such as "PeteMar" to make sure you can recognize what the backup represents. Click on **OK**.

Make a March Backup Copy

30. We must now advance the period to prepare Peachtree for the April transactions.

Advance Dates

- Using your mouse, click on **System** from the **Tasks** menu. Select **Change Accounting Periods**.
- Using the pull down menu, select period 4—Apr 1, 2000 to Apr 30, 2000 and click on **OK**.
- You will be asked whether you wish to print reports before continuing. Since we have already printed our reports, we can answer **No**.
- Note that the status bar at the bottom of the screen now reflects that you are in period 4.

31. Record the following general journal entries using your last trial balance to obtain the amounts owed:

Record Payment of March Payroll Liabilities and Taxes

2004

Apr.   15   Record the compound journal entry for the deposit of Social Security, Medicare, and FIT from last month's payroll. (941 Deposit)

        30   Record the payment of SUTA from last quarter.

        30   Record the payment of FUTA tax owed. (940 Deposit)

Print Reports

32. Print the following reports accepting all defaults:

  a. General Journal (check figure debit = $4,807.21)

  b. Trial Balance (check figure debit = $81,800.88)

Special Journals

With Special Appendix for Merchandise Company Using a General Journal for a Perpetual Inventory System

You need some bookshelf space in your dorm room and decide to buy a couple of wood boards and concrete blocks to make a temporary bookshelf. You drive over to the James Hardware and Lumber Company to buy the materials you'll need. You have heard that Mr. and Mrs. James have owned the business for 35 years and they tend to go about running it in "the old-fashioned way."

Mr. James cuts the boards you need to length and gets the blocks from another section of the lumberyard. He writes down what you are buying on a sales slip and asks you to go into the store and pay for your purchase. Once inside, you see Mrs. James helping a contractor who is making a large purchase. After totaling the invoice, the contractor signs for the building materials. Mrs. James then pulls out a folder from a file cabinet with the contractor's name on it. She files the signed invoice and then makes a notation in a book labeled "Sales Journal."

When you hand Mrs. James your sales slip, she adds the amounts, which total $18.21. After you've paid for your purchase, you notice on your way out that Mrs. James writes the amount of your purchase down in a book labeled "Cash Receipts."

Whether the business is a mom-and-pop hardware store and lumberyard or a gigantic multinational corporation, special journals are used to group and accurately account for specific recurring transactions. In this chapter we discuss two special journals — the sales and cash receipts journals. We will learn that these two special journals are designed to quickly and accurately track sales and cash receipts transactions. After studying this chapter, you will realize that James Lumber and Hardware Company and General Motors, although very different in many ways, still speak the same language of business — accounting.

Learning Objectives

- Journalizing sales on account in a sales journal. (p. 346)

- Posting from a sales journal to the general ledger. (p. 347)

- Recording to the accounts receivable subsidiary ledger from a sales journal. (p. 347)

- Preparing, journalizing, recording, and posting a credit memorandum. (p. 350)

- Journalizing and posting transactions using a cash receipts journal as well as recording to the accounts receivable subsidiary ledger. (p. 355)

In Chapters 9 and 10 we look at how merchandise companies operate. Chapter 9 focuses on sellers of goods; Chapter 10 discusses buyers. In both chapters companies do not keep continual track of their inventory. This is called a periodic inventory system. A company simply takes an inventory at the end of its accounting period of what is left. In this edition is appendix material at the end of Chapters 9 and 10 that looks at how a company keeps continual track of its inventory. This system is called a perpetual inventory system.

Let's first look at Chou's Toy Shop to get an overview of merchandise terms and journal entries. After that, we take an in-depth look at how Art's Wholesale Clothing Company keeps its books. Remember that we will first look at the periodic system (no continual track of inventory).

Learning Unit 9-1	Chou's Toy Shop: Seller's View of a Merchandise Company

Chou's Toy Shop, owned by Chou Li, is a retailer. It buys toys, games, bikes, and so forth from manufacturers and wholesalers and resells these goods (or merchandise) to its customers. The shelving, display cases, and so forth are called "fixtures" or "equipment." These items are not for resale.

GROSS SALES

Gross sales: Revenue earned from sale of merchandise to customers.

Each cash or charge sale made at Chou's Toy Shop is rung up at the register. Suppose the shop had $3,000 in sales on July 18. Of that amount, $1,800 was cash sales and $1,200 was charges. The account that recorded those sales would be

Sales (Gross)

Dr.	Cr.
	3,000	◄——— Revenue account with a credit balance

This account is a revenue account with a credit balance and will be found on the income statement. Figure 9-1 shows the journal entry for the day. *Note:* We talk about sales tax later.

Accounts Affected	Category	↑ ↓	Rules	T Account Update
Cash	Asset	↑	Dr.	Cash
				1,800	
Accounts Receivable	Asset	↑	Dr.	Accounts Receivable
				1,200	
Sales	Revenue	↑	Cr.	Sales
					3,000

Figure 9-1
Recording Cash and Charge Sales for the Day

	July	18	Cash		1 8 0 0 00			
			Accounts Receivable		1 2 0 0 00			
			Sales				3 0 0 0 00	
			Sales for July 18					

SALES RETURNS AND ALLOWANCES

It would be great for Chou if all the customers were completely satisfied, but that rarely is the case. On July 19, Michelle Reese brought back a doll she bought on account for $50. She told Chou that the doll was defective and that she wanted either a price reduction or a new doll. They agreed on a $10 price reduction. Michelle now owes Chou $40. The account called Sales Returns and Allowances (SRA) would record this information.

```
                     Sales Returns and Allowances
                     ──────────────────────────────
Contra-revenue  ──────►   Dr. │ Cr.
account with a            10   │
debit balance
```

This account is a contra-revenue account with a debit balance. It will be recorded on the income statement. Figure 9-2 shows how the journal entry would look:

Accounts Affected	Category	↑ ↓	Rules	T Account Update
Sales Returns and Allowances	Contra-revenue	↑	Dr.	Sales Ret. & Allow Dr. │ Cr. 10 │
Accounts Receivable, Michelle Reese	Asset	↓	Cr.	Accounts Receivable Dr. │ Cr. 1,200 │ 10

Look at how the sales returns and allowances increase.

July	19	Sales Returns and Allowances			1 0 00			
		Accounts Receivable, Michelle Reese					1 0 00	
		Issued credit memorandum						

Figure 9-2
Issuing a Credit Memorandum in the General Journal

SALES DISCOUNT

Chou gives a 2% sales discount to customers who pay their bills early. He wants his customers to know about this policy, so he posted the following sign at the cash register:

Sales Discount Policy

2/10, n/30	2% discount is allowed off price of bill if paid within the first 10 days or full amount is due within 30 days
n/10, EOM	No discount. Full amount of bill is due within 10 days after the end of the month.

Note that the discount period is the time when a discount is granted. The discount period is less time than the credit period, which is the length of time allowed to pay back the amount owed on the bill.

If Michelle pays her $40 bill early, she will get an $.80 discount. This information is recorded as follows:

```
                     Sales Discount
                     ──────────────────────────────
Contra-revenue  ──────►   Dr. │ Cr.
account with a            .80  │
debit balance
```

Michelle's discount is calculated as follows:

$$.02 \times \$40 = \$.80$$

Michelle pays her bill on July 24. She is entitled to the discount because she paid her bill within 10 days. Figure 9-3 shows how Chou would record this payment on his books.

Gross Sales
− Sales discount
− SRA
= Net sales

Accounts Affected	Category	↑ ↓	Rules	T Account Update	
Cash	Asset	↑	Dr.	**Cash**	
				Dr.	Cr.
				39.20	
Sales Discount	Contra-revenue	↑	Dr.	**Sales Discount**	
				Dr.	Cr.
				.80	
Accounts Receivable	Asset	↓	Cr.	**Accounts Receivable**	
				Dr.	Cr.
				1,200	40

Figure 9-3
Recording Sales Discount

July	24	Cash			39 20		
		Sales Discount			80		
		Accounts Receivable, Michelle Reese				40 00	
		Payment from Sale on Account					

Although Michelle pays $39.20, her Accounts Receivable is credited for the full amount, $40.

In the examples so far we have not shown any transactions with sales tax. Note that the actual or net sales for Chou would be gross sales less sales returns and allowances less any sales discounts. Let's look at how Chou would record his monthly sales if sales tax were charged.

SALES TAX PAYABLE

None of the preceding examples shows state sales tax. Still, like it or not, Chou must collect that tax from his customers and send it to the state. Sales tax represents a liability to Chou.

Assume the state Chou's is located in charges a 5% sales tax. Remember that Chou's sales on July 18 were $3,000. Chou must figure out the sales tax on the purchases. For this purpose, let's assume there were only two sales on that date: the cash sale ($1,800) and the charge sale ($1,200).

The sales tax on the cash purchase is calculated as follows:

$$\$1,800 \times .05 = \$90 \text{ Tax}$$
$$\$1,800 + \$90 \text{ tax} = \$1,890 \text{ Cash}$$

Here is how the sales tax on the charge sale is computed:

$$\$1,200 \times .05 = \$60 \text{ Tax} + \$1,200 \text{ Charge} = \$1,260 \text{ Accounts Receivable}$$

It would be recorded as shown in Figure 9-4.

Accounts Affected	Category	↑ ↓	Rules	T Account Update
Cash	Asset	↑	Dr.	Cash Dr. 1,890 | Cr.
Accounts Receivable	Asset	↑	Dr.	Accounts Receivable Dr. 1,260 | Cr.
Sales Tax Payable	Liability	↑	Cr.	Sales Tax Payable Dr. | Cr. 90 | 60
Sales	Revenue	↑	Cr.	Sales Dr. | Cr. 3,000

July	18	Cash	1 8 9 0 00			
		Accounts Receivable	1 2 6 0 00			
		Sales Tax Payable		1 5 0 00		
		Sales		3 0 0 0 00		
		July 18 Sales				

Figure 9-4
Credit Memorandum
with Sales Tax

In Learning Unit 9-3 we show you how to record a credit memorandum with sales tax.

Accounting in the Reel World

Show me the Merchandise!

Have you ever shopped in Express? Lord and Taylor's? Robinson May? Hecht's or Kaufmann's? These are just five of the 300 stores owned by St. Louis department store giant, The May Department Stores Company. While Express may cater to younger shoppers than Hecht's and Lord & Taylor's may have a different market than Kaufmann's, all May's stores need to earn income for the owner.

In the May Department Stores on-location video segment on your DVD, you'll learn about the different types of earnings that appear on May Department Stores' income statement.

1. How is The May Department Stores Company's "gross sales" different than its "earnings from continuous operations."
2. Suppose you buy a tank top for your cousin at an Express store and find a small hole in the side seam. Into what account would Express record the information about the return and where would it be recorded?
3. Any one of the stores owned and operated by May Department Stores has hundreds of thousands of customers. Can each store keep its books in a general ledger and, if not, what type of journals might they need to record account receivables?

Learning Unit 9-1 Review

AT THIS POINT you should be able to

- Explain the purpose of a contra-revenue account. (p. 340)
- Explain how to calculate net sales. (p. 340)

🌑 Define, journalize, and explain gross sales, sales returns and allowances, and sales discounts. (p. 341)

🌑 Journalize an entry for sales tax payable. (p. 343)

SELF-REVIEW QUIZ 9-1

(The forms you need can be found on page 269 of the *Study Guide and Working Papers*.)

Respond true or false to the following:

1. Sales Returns and Allowances is a contra-asset account.

2. Sales Discount has a normal balance of a debit.

3. Sales Tax Payable is a liability.

4. Sales Discount is a contra-asset.

5. A periodic system of inventory keeps continual track of the merchandise.

Quiz Tip:
Sales: Revenue   ↑ Cr.
SRA: Contra-revenue ↑ Dr.
SD: Contra-revenue ↑ Dr.

SOLUTIONS TO SELF-REVIEW QUIZ 9-1

1. False   **2.** True   **3.** True   **4.** False   **5.** False

---

Learning Unit 9-2   The Sales Journal and Accounts Receivable Subsidiary Ledger

SPECIAL JOURNALS*

Now let's examine how Art's Wholesale Clothing Company keeps its books. Art's business conducts many transactions. The partial general journal in Figure 9-5 shows the journal entries Art's must make for these sales on account transactions.

Figure 9-5
Recording Sales on Account in General Journal

			ART'S WHOLESALE CLOTHING COMPANY GENERAL JOURNAL				
Apr.	3	Accounts Receivable, Hal's			8 0 0 00		
		Sales				8 0 0 00
		Sales on Account				
	6	Accounts Receivable, Bevans			1 6 0 0 00		
		Sales				1 6 0 0 00
		Sales on Account				
	18	Accounts Receivable, Roe			2 0 0 0 00		
		Sales				2 0 0 0 00
		Sales on Account				

---

*Special journals for a perpetual system are shown at the end of Chapter 10.

This method is not very efficient. If Art's Wholesale Clothing Company kept a **special journal** for each type of transaction he conducts, however, the number of postings and recordings required for each transaction would be reduced. After carefully looking at the situation with his accountant, Art Newner, the owner, decided to use the following special journals:

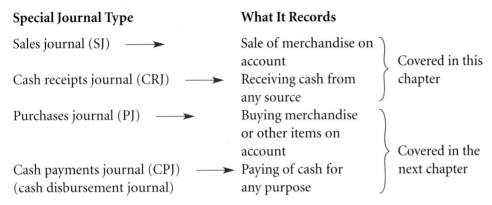

Special Journal Type	What It Records	
Sales journal (SJ) →	Sale of merchandise on account	Covered in this chapter
Cash receipts journal (CRJ) →	Receiving cash from any source	
Purchases journal (PJ) →	Buying merchandise or other items on account	Covered in the next chapter
Cash payments journal (CPJ) (cash disbursement journal) →	Paying of cash for any purpose	

SUBSIDIARY LEDGERS

In the same way Art's Wholesale Clothing Company needs more than just a general journal, the business needs more than just a general ledger. For example, so far in this text, the only title we have used for recording amounts owed to the seller has been Accounts Receivable. Art could have replaced the Accounts Receivable title in the general ledger with the following list of customers who owe him money:

- Accounts Receivable, Bevans Company.
- Accounts Receivable, Hal's Clothing.
- Accounts Receivable, Mel's Department Store.
- Accounts Receivable, Roe Company.

As you can see, this system would not be manageable if Art had 1,000 credit customers. To solve this problem, Art sets up a separate **accounts receivable subsidiary ledger.** Such a special ledger, often simply called a **subsidiary ledger,** contains a single type of account, such as credit customers. An account is opened for each customer, and the accounts are arranged alphabetically.

The diagram in Figure 9-6 on p. 346 shows how the accounts receivable subsidiary ledger fits in with the general ledger. To clarify the difference in updating the general ledger versus the subsidiary ledger, we will *post* to the general ledger and *record* to the subsidiary ledger. The word *post* refers to information that is moved from the journal to the general ledger; the word *record* refers to information that is transferred from the journal into the individual customer's account in the subsidiary ledger.

The accounts receivable subsidiary ledger, or any other subsidiary ledger, can be in the form of a card file, a binder notebook, or computer tapes or disks. It will not have page numbers. The accounts receivable subsidiary ledger is organized alphabetically based on customers' names and addresses; new customers can be added and inactive customers deleted.

When using an accounts receivable subsidiary ledger, the title Accounts Receivable in the general ledger is called the **controlling account**—Accounts Receivable because it summarizes or controls the accounts receivable subsidiary ledger. At the end of the month the total of the individual accounts in the accounts receivable ledger will equal the ending balance in Accounts Receivable in the general ledger.

> The general ledger is not in the same book as the accounts receivable subsidiary ledger.

Figure 9-6
Partial General Ledger of Art's Wholesale Clothing Company and Accounts Receivable Subsidiary Ledger

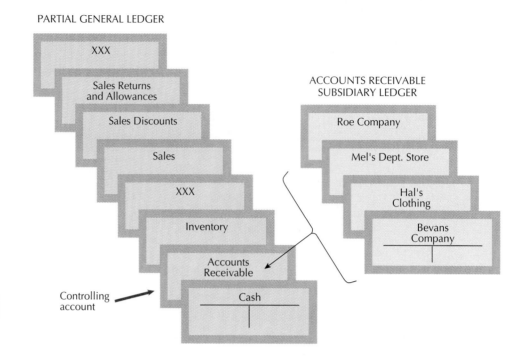

PARTIAL GENERAL LEDGER

ACCOUNTS RECEIVABLE SUBSIDIARY LEDGER

Controlling account

Proving:
At the end of the month, the sum of the accounts receivable subsidiary ledger will equal the ending balance in accounts receivable, the controlling account in the general ledger.

Art's Wholesale Clothing Company will use the following subsidiary ledgers:

Accounts receivable subsidiary ledger (debit balance)	Records money owed by credit customers	Covered in this chapter
Accounts payable subsidiary ledger (credit balance)	Records money owed by Art to creditors	Covered in next chapter

Let's now look closer at the sales journal, general ledger, and subsidiary ledger for Art's to see how transactions are updated in the special journal as well as posted and recorded to specific titles.

THE SALES JOURNAL

The **sales journal** for Art's Wholesale Clothing Company records all sales made on account to customers. Figure 9-7 shows the sales journal at the end of the first month in operation along with the recordings to the accounts receivable ledger and posting to the general ledger. Keep in mind that the reason the balances in the accounts receivable subsidiary ledger are *debit* balances is that the customers listed *owe* Art's Wholesale money. For some other companies, a sales journal might have multiple revenue account columns.

Look at the first transaction listed in the sales journal. It shows that on April 3, Art's Wholesale Clothing Company sold merchandise on account to Hal's Clothing for $800. The bill or **sales invoice** for this sale is shown in Figure 9-8 on p. 348.

Recording to the accounts receivable subsidiary ledger occurs daily.

Hal's Clothing

Dr.	Cr.
4/3 SJ1	
800	

A ✓ means that the accounts receivable ledger has been updated.

Recording from the Sales Journal to the Accounts Receivable Subsidiary Ledger

As shown on the first line of the sales journal in Figure 9-2, the information on the invoice is recorded in the sales journal. The *PR column is left blank,* however. As soon as possible we now update the accounts receivable subsidiary ledger. To do so, we pull out the Hal's Clothing file card and update it: The debit side must show the

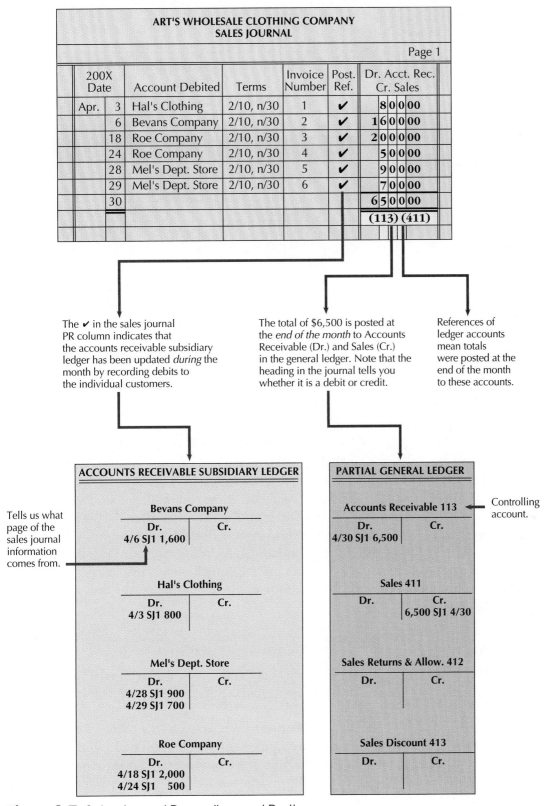

Figure 9-7 Sales Journal Recording and Postings

$800 he owes Art along with the date (April 3) and page of the sales journal (p. 1). Once that is done, place a ✓ in the post-reference column of the sales journal. The accounts receivable subsidiary ledger shows us Hal's outstanding balance at any moment in time. We do not have to go through all the invoices. Note how the sales

Figure 9-8
Sales Invoice

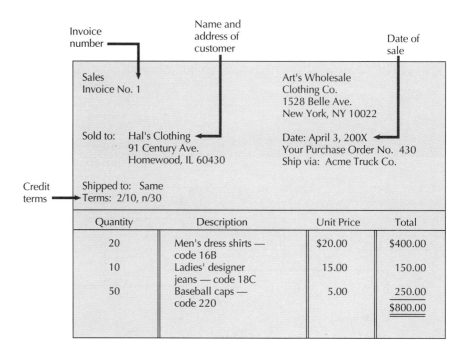

journal only needs one line instead of the three lines that would have been required in a general journal.

Posting at End of Month from the Sales Journal to the General Ledger

The sales journal is totaled ($6,500) at the end of the month. Looking back at page 347, you can see that the heading of Art's sales journal is a debit to Accounts Receivable and a credit to Sales. Therefore, at the end of the month the $6,500 total is posted to Accounts Receivable (debit) *and* to Sales (credit) in the general ledger. In the general ledger we record the date (4/30), the initials of the journal (SJ), the page of the sales journal (1), and appropriate debit or credit ($6,500). Once the account in the general ledger is updated, we place below the totals in the sales journal the account numbers to which the information was posted (in this case, accounts 113 and 411).

Sales Tax

Art's Wholesale Clothing Company does not have to deal with sales tax because it sells goods wholesale. If Art's were a retail company, however, it would have to pay sales tax.

Let's look at how Munroe Menswear Company, a retailer, handles sales tax on a purchase made by Jones Company. Figure 9-9 shows Munroe's sales journal.

A new account, **Sales Tax Payable,** must be created. That account is a liability account in the general ledger with a credit balance. The customer owes Munroe the sale amount plus the tax.

Keep in mind that if sales discounts are available, they are not calculated on the sales tax. The discount is on the selling price less any returns before the tax. For example, if Jones receives a 2% discount, he pays the following:

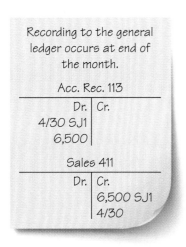

Recording to the general ledger occurs at end of the month.

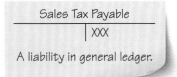

Sales Tax Payable

| | XXX |

A liability in general ledger.

$5,000 × .02 = $100 savings ⟶

$5,250	Total owed (tax is $250)
−100	Savings (discount)
$5,150	Amount paid

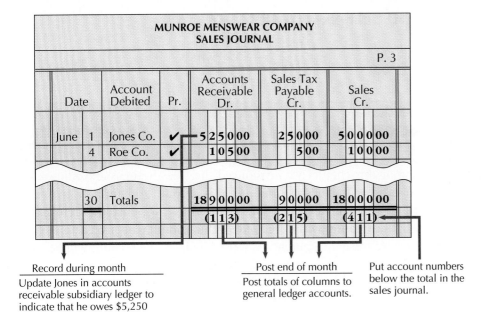

Figure 9-9
Munroe Sales Journal

			Accounts Receivable Dr.	Sales Tax Payable Cr.	Sales Cr.
Date	Account Debited	Pr.			
June 1	Jones Co.	✔	5 2 5 0 00	2 5 0 00	5 0 0 0 00
4	Roe Co.	✔	1 0 5 00	5 00	1 0 0 00
30	Totals		18 9 0 0 00	9 0 0 00	18 0 0 0 00
			(1 1 3)	(2 1 5)	(4 1 1)

MUNROE MENSWEAR COMPANY
SALES JOURNAL
P. 3

Record during month
Update Jones in accounts receivable subsidiary ledger to indicate that he owes $5,250 to Munroe.

Post end of month
Post totals of columns to general ledger accounts.

Put account numbers below the total in the sales journal.

Learning Unit 9-2 Review

AT THIS POINT you should be able to

- Define and state the purposes of special journals. (p. 345)
- Define and state the purposes of the accounts receivable subsidiary ledger. (p. 345)
- Define and state the purpose of the controlling account, Accounts Receivable. (p. 346)
- Journalize, record, or post sales on account to a sales journal and its related accounts receivable and general ledgers. (p. 347)

SELF-REVIEW QUIZ 9-2

(The forms you need are on page 269 of the *Study Guide and Working Papers*.)
Respond true or false to the following:

1. Special journals completely replace the general journal.
2. Special journals aid the division of labor.
3. The subsidiary ledger makes the general ledger less manageable.
4. The subsidiary ledger is separate from the general ledger.
5. The controlling account is located in the accounts receivable subsidiary ledger.
6. The totals of a sales journal are posted to the general ledger at the end of the month.
7. The accounts receivable subsidiary ledger is arranged in alphabetical order.
8. Transactions recorded into a sales journal are recorded only weekly to the accounts receivable subsidiary ledger.

Quiz Tip:
The normal balance of the accounts receivable subsidiary ledger is a debit.

SOLUTIONS TO SELF-REVIEW QUIZ 9-2

1. False **2.** True **3.** False **4.** True
5. False **6.** True **7.** True **8.** False

Learning Unit 9-3	The Credit Memorandum

> A credit memorandum reduces accounts receivable.

> Remember:
> No sales tax was involved because Art's is a wholesale company.

Sales Returns and Allowances

Dr.	Cr.
+	–

A contra-revenue account.

> Note that the Sales Returns and Allowances account is increasing, which in turn reduces sales revenue and reduces the amount owed by the customer (Accounts Receivable).

At the beginning of this chapter we introduced the Sales Returns and Allowances account. Merchandising businesses often use this account to handle transactions involving goods that have already been sold. For example, if a customer returns the goods purchased, the account will be credited for the amount paid; if a customer gets an allowance because the goods purchased were damaged, the account will be credited for the amount of the allowance. In both these examples, the company's sales revenue decreases. Hence, the account is called a contra-revenue account: The sales revenue decreases and the normal balance is a debit.

Companies usually handle sales returns and allowances by means of a **credit memorandum.** Credit memoranda inform customers that the amount of the goods returned or the amount allowed for damaged goods has been subtracted (credited) from the customer's ongoing account with the company.

A sample credit memorandum from Art's Wholesale Clothing Company appears in Figure 9-10. It shows that on April 12 credit memo no. 1 was issued to Bevans Company for defective merchandise that had been returned. (Figure 9-7 shows that Art's Wholesale Clothing Company sold Bevans Company $1,600 of merchandise on April 6.)

Let's assume that Art's Clothing has high-quality goods and does not expect many sales returns and allowances. Based on this assumption, no special journal for sales returns and allowances will be needed. Instead, any returns and allowances will be recorded in the general journal, and all postings and recordings will be done when journalized. Let's look at a transaction analysis chart before we journalize, record, and post this transaction.

Accounts Affected	**Category**	↑ ↓	**Rules**
Sales Returns and Allowances	Contra-revenue account	↑	Dr.
Accounts Receivable, Bevans Co.	Asset	↓	Cr.

Figure 9-10
Credit Memorandum

> The end result is that Bevan owes Art's Wholesale less money.

Art's Wholesale
Clothing Co.
1528 Belle Ave.
New York, NY 10022

Credit
Memorandum No. 1
Date: April 12, 200X
Credit to Bevans Company
          110 Aster Rd.
          Cincinnati, Ohio 45227
We credit your account as follows:
Merchandise returned 60 model 8 B men's dress gloves—$600

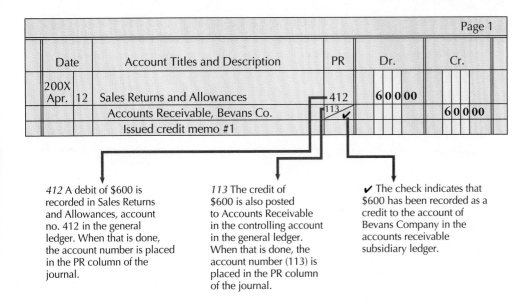

Figure 9-11
Postings and Recordings for the Credit Memorandum into the Subsidiary and General Ledger

412 A debit of $600 is recorded in Sales Returns and Allowances, account no. 412 in the general ledger. When that is done, the account number is placed in the PR column of the journal.

113 The credit of $600 is also posted to Accounts Receivable in the controlling account in the general ledger. When that is done, the account number (113) is placed in the PR column of the journal.

✔ The check indicates that $600 has been recorded as a credit to the account of Bevans Company in the accounts receivable subsidiary ledger.

JOURNALIZING, RECORDING, AND POSTING THE CREDIT MEMORANDUM

The credit memorandum results in two postings to the general ledger and one recording to the accounts receivable subsidiary ledger (see Fig. 9-11).

Note in the PR column next to Accounts Receivable, Bevans Co., that there is a diagonal line with the account number 113 above and a ✔ below. This notation is to show that the amount of $600 has been credited to Accounts Receivable in the controlling account in the general ledger *and* credited to the account of Bevans Company in the accounts receivable subsidiary ledger.

If the accountant for Art's Wholesale Clothing Company decided to develop a special journal for Sales Returns and Allowances, the entry for a credit memorandum such as the one we've been discussing would be as shown in Figure 9-12.

Remember:
Sales discounts are not taken on returns.

THE CREDIT MEMORANDUM WITH SALES TAX

Figure 9-9 (p. 349) shows the sales journal for Munroe Menswear Company. Remember that because Munroe is a retail company, its customers must pay sales tax. Let's assume that on June 8 Roe returns $50 worth of the $100 of merchandise he bought earlier in the month. Let's analyze and journalize the credit memo that Munroe issued. Keep in mind that the customer is no longer responsible for paying for either the returned merchandise or the tax on it.

SALES RETURNS AND ALLOWANCES JOURNAL				
Date	Credit Memo No.	Account Credited	PR	Sales Ret. and Allow. – Dr. Accts. Rec. – Cr.
200X April 12	1	Bevans Company	✔	6 0 0 00

During the month the subsidiary ledger is updated

Figure 9-12
Special Journal for Recording Sales Returns and Allowances

Accounts Affected	Category	↑ ↓	Rules	T Account Update			
Sales Returns and Allowances	Contra-revenue	↑	Dr.	Sales Ret. & Allow.			
				Dr.	Cr.		
				50			
Sales Tax Payable ($5 tax on $100) ($2.50 tax on $50)	Liability	↓	Dr.	Sales Tax Payable			
				Dr.	Cr.		
				2.50			
Accounts Receivable, Roe	Asset	↓	Cr.	Acc. Rec.		Roe Co.	
				Dr.	Cr.	Dr.	Cr.
					52.50	105	52.50

Figure 9-13
Credit Memorandum
with Sales Tax

	June	8	Sales Returns and Allowances			5 0 00		
			Sales Tax Payable			2 50		
			Accounts Receivable, Roe Co.					5 2 50
			Received credit memo					

The journal entry in Figure 9-13 requires three postings to the general ledger and one recording to Roe in the accounts receivable subsidiary ledger. Note that because Roe returned half of his merchandise he was able to reduce what he pays for sales tax by half (from $5 to $2.50).

Learning Unit 9-3 Review

AT THIS POINT you should be able to

- Explain Sales Tax Payable in relation to Sales Discount. (p. 351)
- Explain, journalize, post, and record a credit memorandum with or without sales tax. (p. 351)

SELF-REVIEW QUIZ 9-3

(The forms you need are on pages 269–271 of the *Study Guide and Working Papers.*)

Journalize the following transactions into the sales journal or general journal for Shoes.com. Record to the accounts receivable subsidiary ledger and post to general ledger accounts as appropriate. Use the same journal headings that we used for Art's Wholesale Clothing Company. (All sales carry credit terms of 2/10, n/30.) There is no tax.

200X
May 1   Sold merchandise on account to Jane Company, invoice no. 1, $600.
     5   Sold merchandise on account to Ralph Company, invoice no. 2, $2,500.
   20   Issued credit memo no. 1 to Jane Company for $200 due to defective merchandise returned.

SOLUTION TO SELF-REVIEW QUIZ 9-3

SHOES.COM
SALES JOURNAL

Page 1

Date		Account Debited	Terms	Invoice No.	Post Ref.	Dr. Acct. Rec. Cr. Sales
200X May	1	Jane Company	2/10, n/30	1	✔	600 00
	5	Ralph Company	2/10, n/30	2	✔	2500 00
	31					3100 00
						(112) (411)

Figure 9-14
Sales on Account

Quiz Tip:
The total of accounts receivable subsidiary ledger $400 + $2,500 does indeed equal the balance in the controlling account, Accounts Receivable $2,900 at end of month, in the general ledger.

SHOES.COM
GENERAL JOURNAL

Page 1

Date		Account Titles and Description	PR	Dr.	Cr.
200X May	20	Sales Ret. and Allowances	412	200 00	
		Acct. Rec., Jane Company	112 ✔		200 00
		Issued credit memo #1			

Figure 9-15
Credit Memo Issued

Controlling Account

PARTIAL GENERAL LEDGER

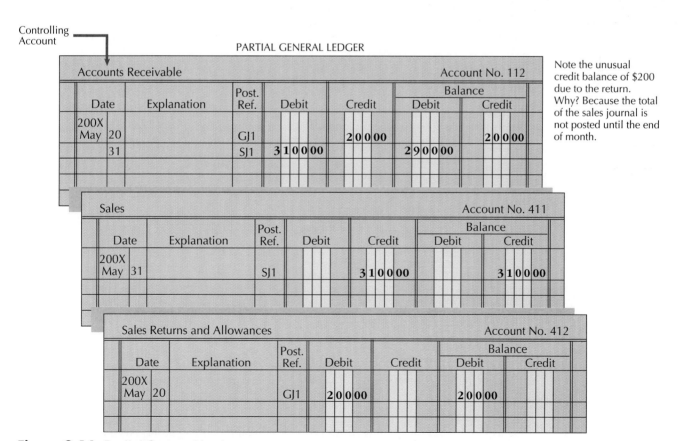

Note the unusual credit balance of $200 due to the return. Why? Because the total of the sales journal is not posted until the end of month.

Accounts Receivable   Account No. 112

Date		Explanation	Post. Ref.	Debit	Credit	Balance Debit	Balance Credit
200X May	20		GJ1		200 00		200 00
	31		SJ1	3100 00		2900 00	

Sales   Account No. 411

Date		Explanation	Post. Ref.	Debit	Credit	Balance Debit	Balance Credit
200X May	31		SJ1		3100 00		3100 00

Sales Returns and Allowances   Account No. 412

Date		Explanation	Post. Ref.	Debit	Credit	Balance Debit	Balance Credit
200X May	20		GJ1	200 00		200 00	

Figure 9-16 Partial General Ledger

ACCOUNTS RECEIVABLE SUBSIDIARY LEDGER

NAME Jane Company
ADDRESS 118 Morris Rd., Boston, MA 01935

Date		Explanation	Post. Ref.	Debit	Credit	Dr. Balance
200X May	1		SJ1	600 00		600 00
	20		GJ1		200 00	400 00

Customers owe Shoes.com money and thus have a debit balance.

NAME Ralph Company
ADDRESS 31 Norris Rd., Boston, MA 01935

Date		Explanation	Post. Ref.	Debit	Credit	Dr. Balance
200X May	5		SJ1	2500 00		2500 00

Figure 9-17 Accounts Receivable Subsidiary Ledger

Learning Unit 9-4   Cash Receipts Journal and Schedule of Accounts Receivable

A **cash receipts journal** is another special journal often used in a merchandising operation. The cash receipts journal records the receipt of cash (or checks) from any source. The number of columns in the cash receipts journal depends on how frequently certain types of transactions occur. Figure 9-18 shows the headings in the cash receipts journal for Art's Wholesale, describes the purpose of each column, and tells when to update the accounts receivable ledger as well as the general ledger.

The following transactions occurred and affected the cash receipts journal for Art's Clothing in April:

200X
Apr.   1   Art Newner invested $8,000 in the business.
           4   Received check from Hal's Clothing for payment of invoice no. 1 less discount.
          15   Cash sales for first half of April, $900.
          16   Received check from Bevans Company in settlement of invoice no. 2 less returns and discount.
          22   Received check from Roe Company for payment of invoice no. 3 less discount.
          27   Sold store equipment, $500.
          30   Cash sales for second half of April, $1,200.

Benefits of a Cash Receipts Journal

Before we look at how these transactions will look in the cash receipts journal, let's see how the April 4 transaction would look if it were put into a general journal (Fig. 9-19). This step illustrates the benefits of using a cash receipts journal.

200X
Apr.   4   Received check from Hal's Clothing for payment of invoice no. 1 less discount. (Keep in mind the sales journal showed the invoice at $800 on April 3.)

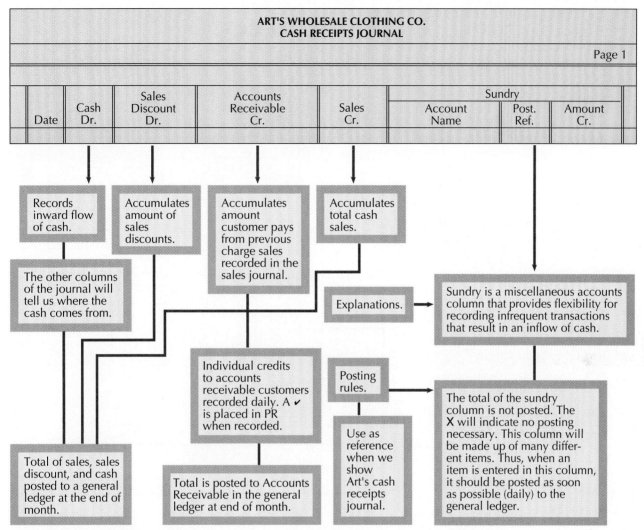

Figure 9-18 Cash Receipts Journal

Accounts Affected	Category	↓ ↑	Rules	T Account Update
Cash	Asset	↑	Dr.	Cash Dr. | Cr. 784 |
Sales Discount	Contra-revenue	↑	Dr.	Sales Discount Dr. | Cr. 16 |
Accounts Receivable, Hal's Clothing	Asset	↓	Cr.	Acc. Rec. Hal's Clothing Dr. | Cr. Dr. | Cr. 800 | 800 800 | 800

Hal's Clothing is located in the accounts receivable subsidiary ledger.

Apr.	4	Cash			7	8	4	00				
		Sales Discount				1	6	00				
		Accounts Receivable, Hal's Clothing							8	0	0	00

Figure 9-19
Recording Sales Discount in General Journal

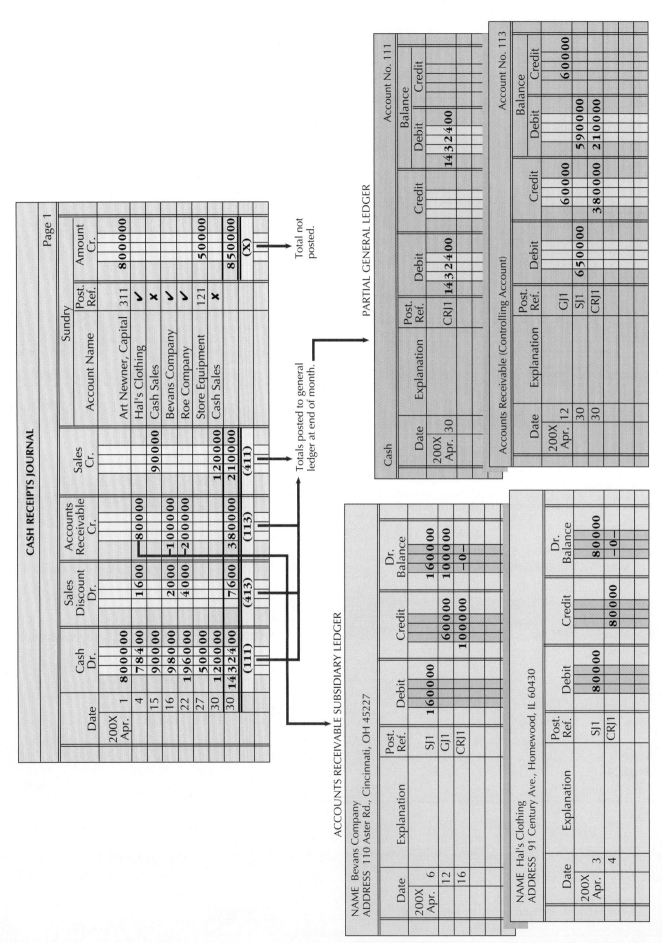

Figure 9-20 Cash Receipts Journal and Posting

PARTIAL GENERAL LEDGER

Store Equipment   Account No. 121

Date	Explanation	Post. Ref.	Debit	Credit	Balance Debit	Balance Credit
200X Apr. 1	Balance	✔			400000 0	
27		CRJ1		50000	350000 0	

Art Newner, Capital   Account No. 311

Date	Explanation	Post. Ref.	Debit	Credit	Balance Debit	Balance Credit
200X Apr. 1		CRJ1		800000		800000

Sales   Account No. 411

Date	Explanation	Post. Ref.	Debit	Credit	Balance Debit	Balance Credit
200X Apr. 30		SJ1		650000		650000
30		CRJ1		210000		860000

Sales Discount   Account No. 413

Date	Explanation	Post. Ref.	Debit	Credit	Balance Debit	Balance Credit
200X Apr. 30		CRJ1	7600		7600	

ACCOUNTS RECEIVABLE SUBSIDIARY LEDGER

NAME Mel's Dept. Store
ADDRESS 181 Foss Rd., Swampscott, MA 01907

Date	Explanation	Post. Ref.	Debit	Credit	Dr. Balance
200X Apr. 28		SJ1	90000 0		90000 0
29		SJ1	70000 0		160000 0

NAME Roe Company
ADDRESS 18 Rantool St., Beverly, MA 01915

Date	Explanation	Post. Ref.	Debit	Credit	Dr. Balance
200X Apr. 18		SJ1	2000000		2000000
22		CRJ1		2000000	-0-
24		SJ1	50000 0		50000 0

Figure 9-20 (continued)

If a general journal had been used, there would have been three postings and one recording. Using a cash receipts journal (see Fig. 9-18 on p. 355), the totals of cash sales discount and accounts receivable are not posted till the end of the month.

The diagram in Figure 9-20 shows the cash receipts journal for the end of April along with the recordings in the accounts receivable subsidiary ledger and posting to the general ledger.

JOURNALIZING, RECORDING, AND POSTING FROM THE CASH RECEIPTS JOURNAL

Now let's look at how the April 4 transaction is recorded in the cash receipts journal.

When payment is received, Art's Wholesale updates the cash receipts journal (see Fig. 9-20 on p. 356) by entering the date (April 4), Cash debit of $784, Sales Discount debit of $16, credit to Accounts Receivable of $800, and which account name (Hal's Clothing) is to be credited. The terms of sale indicate that Hal's Clothing is entitled to the discount and no longer owes Art's Wholesale the $800 balance. As soon as this line is entered into the cash receipts journal, Art's Wholesale will update the card file of Hal's Clothing. Note in the accounts receivable subsidiary ledger of Hal's Clothing how the date (April 4), post reference (CRJ1), and credit amount ($800) are recorded. The balance in the accounts receivable ledger is zero. The last step of this transaction is to go back to the cash receipts journal and put a ✓ in the post-reference column.

In looking back at this cash receipts journal, note the following:

- All totals of the cash receipts journal *except* sundry were posted to the general ledger at the end of the month.
- Art Newner, Capital, and Store Equipment were posted to the general ledger when entered in the sundry column. For now in the general ledger it was assumed that the equipment account had a beginning balance of $4,000.
- The cash sales were not posted when entered (thus the X to show no posting is needed). The Sales and Cash totals are posted at the *end* of the month.
- A ✓ means information was recorded daily to the accounts receivable subsidiary ledger.
- The Account Name column was used to describe each transaction.

We can prove the accuracy of recording transactions of the cash receipts journal by totaling the columns with debit balances and credit balances. This process, called **crossfooting,** is done before the totals are posted.

If a bookkeeper were using more than one page for the cash receipts journal, the balances on the bottom of one page would be brought forward to the next page. Let's crossfoot the cash receipts journal of Art's Wholesale (Fig. 9-20, p. 356).

Debit Columns		Credit Columns		
Cash	+ Sales Discount	= Accounts Receivable	+ Sales	+ Sundry
$14,324	+ $76	= $3,800	+ $2,100	+ $8,500
		$14,400 = $14,400		

Recording Sales Tax

Consider the following situation. It involves Ryan Stationery, a retail stationer that must charge 5% sales tax to its customers. On July 1 Hope Co. bought $600 of equipment for cash from Ryan.

Remember: Subsidiary ledgers can be in the form of a card file, a binder note-book, or computer tapes or disks.

Sundry: Miscellaneous accounts column(s) in a special journal that record transactions that seldom occur.

The last step is to put a ✓ back in the PR of the cash receipts journal to show the accounts receivable ledger is up-to-date.

Crossfooting special journals makes it easier to look for journalizing or posting errors.

The total of Sales Tax Payable would be posted to Sales Tax Payable in the general ledger at the end of the month.

Figure 9-21 shows how the transaction would be recorded in the general journal:

Accounts Affected	Category	↑ ↓	Rules	T Account Update
Cash	Asset	↑	Dr.	Cash 630 |
Sales Tax Payable	Liability	↑	Cr.	Sales Tax Payable | 30
Sales	Revenue	↑	Cr.	Sales | 600

July	1	Cash		6 3 0 00					
		Sales Tax Payable				3 0 00			
		Sales				6 0 0 00			
		Cash Sale							

Figure 9-21
Recording Receipt of Sales Tax in General Journal

The transaction would be recorded in a cash receipts journal as shown in Figure 9-22.

CASH RECEIPTS JOURNAL										
Date	Cash Dr.	Sales Discount Dr.	Accounts Receivable Cr.	Sales Tax Payable Cr.	Sales Cr.	Sundry				
						Acct.	Post Ref.	Amt.		
July 1	6 3 0 00			3 0 00	6 0 0 00		✗			

Figure 9-22 Sales Tax in Cash Receipts Journal

The total of the sales tax as a result of cash sales would be posted to Sales Tax Payable in the general ledger at the end of the month. It represents a liability of the merchant to forward the tax to the government. Remember that no cash discounts are taken on the sales tax.

Now let's prove the accounts receivable subsidiary ledger to the controlling account—Accounts Receivable—at the end of April for Art's Wholesale Clothing Company.

SCHEDULE OF ACCOUNTS RECEIVABLE

The schedule of accounts receivable is an alphabetical list of the companies that have an outstanding balance in the accounts receivable subsidiary ledger. This total should be equal to the balance of the Accounts Receivable controlling account in the general ledger at the end of the month.

Let's examine the schedule of accounts receivable for Art's Wholesale Clothing Company in Figure 9-23.

ART'S WHOLESALE CLOTHING COMPANY SCHEDULE OF ACCOUNTS RECEIVABLE APRIL 30, 200X		
Mel's Dept. Store	$1 6 0 0 00	
Roe Company	5 0 0 00	
Total Accounts Receivable	$ 2 1 0 0 00	

Figure 9-23
Schedule of Accounts Receivable

Schedule is listed in alphabetical order.

The balance of the controlling account, Accounts Receivable ($2,100), in the general ledger (p. 356) does indeed equal the sum of the individual customer balances in the accounts receivable ledger ($2,100) as shown in the schedule of accounts receivable. The schedule of accounts receivable can help forecast potential cash inflows as well as possible credit and collection decisions.

Learning Unit 9-4 Review

AT THIS POINT you should be able to

- Journalize, record, and post transactions using a cash receipts journal with or without sales tax. (p. 354)
- Prepare a schedule of accounts receivable. (p. 359)

SELF-REVIEW QUIZ 9-4

(The forms you need are on pages 272–274 of the *Study Guide and Working Papers*.)

Journalize, crossfoot, record, and post when appropriate the following transactions into the cash receipts journal of Moore Co. Use the same headings as for Art's Wholesale Clothing.

ACCOUNTS RECEIVABLE SUBSIDIARY LEDGER

Name	Balance	Invoice No.
Irene Welch	$500	1
Janis Fross	200	2

Partial General Ledger

	Acct. No.	Balance
Cash	110	$600
Accounts Receivable	120	700
Store Equipment	130	600
Sales	410	700
Sales Discount	420	

200X

May 1 Received check from Irene Welch for invoice no. 1 less 2% discount.
8 Cash sales collected, $200.
15 Received check from Janis Fross for invoice no. 2 less 2% discount.
19 Sold store equipment at cost, $300.

SOLUTION TO SELF-REVIEW QUIZ 9-4

	**MOORE COMPANY** **CASH RECEIPTS JOURNAL**								

MOORE COMPANY
CASH RECEIPTS JOURNAL

Page 2

Date	Cash Dr.	Sales Discount Dr.	Accounts Receivable Cr.	Sales Cr.	Sundry — Account Name	Post. Ref.	Amount Cr.
200X May 1	490 00	10 00	500 00		Irene Welch	✔	
8	200 00			200 00	Cash Sales	✗	
15	196 00	4 00	200 00		Janis Fross	✔	
19	300 00				Store Equipment	130	300 00
31	1186 00	14 00	700 00	200 00			300 00
	(110)	(420)	(120)	(410)			(X)

Crossfooting: $1,200 = $1,200

Figure 9-24 Cash Receipts Journal

PARTIAL GENERAL LEDGER

Cash   Account No. 110

Date	Explanation	Post. Ref.	Debit	Credit	Balance Debit	Balance Credit
200X May 1	Balance	✔			600 00	
31		CRJ2	1186 00		1786 00	

Accounts Receivable   Account No. 120

Date	Explanation	Post. Ref.	Debit	Credit	Balance Debit	Balance Credit
200X May 1	Balance	✔			700 00	
31		CRJ2		700 00	—	—

Store Equipment   Account No. 130

Date	Explanation	Post. Ref.	Debit	Credit	Balance Debit	Balance Credit
200X May 1	Balance	✔			600 00	
19		CRJ2		300 00	300 00	

Sales   Account No. 410

Date	Explanation	Post. Ref.	Debit	Credit	Balance Debit	Balance Credit
200X May 1	Balance	✔				700 00
31		CRJ2		200 00		900 00

Sales Discount   Account No. 420

Date	Explanation	Post. Ref.	Debit	Credit	Balance Debit	Balance Credit
200X May 31		CRJ2	14 00		14 00	

Figure 9-25 Partial General Ledger

Quiz Tip:
Sum of all debits equals sum of all credits.

Quiz Tip:
The total of the sundry column, $300, is not posted. Only individual amounts are posted to the general ledger during the month.

Figure 9-26
Accounts Receivable
Subsidiary Ledger

ACCOUNTS RECEIVABLE SUBSIDIARY LEDGER

NAME Irene Welch
ADDRESS 10 Rong Rd., Beverly, MA 01915

Date		Explanation	Post. Ref.	Debit	Credit	Dr. Balance
200X May	1	Balance	✔			5 0 0 00
	1		CRJ2		5 0 0 00	—

NAME Janis Fross
ADDRESS 81 Foster Rd., Beverly, MA 01915

Date		Explanation	Post. Ref.	Debit	Credit	Dr. Balance
200X May	1	Balance	✔			2 0 0 00
	15		CRJ2		2 0 0 00	—

SOLUTION & TIPS TO COMPREHENSIVE PROBLEM: PUTTING THE PIECES TOGETHER

(The forms you need are on pages 275–278 of the *Study Guide and Working Papers*.)

a. Journalize, record, and post, as needed, the following transactions to the sales, cash receipts, and general journal. All terms are 2/10, n/30.

b. Prepare a schedule of accounts receivable.

Solution Tips to Journalizing

200X

CRJ July	1	Walter Lantze invested $2,000 into the business.
SJ	1	Sold merchandise on account to Panda Co., invoice no. 1 for $300.
SJ	2	Sold merchandise on account to Buzzard Co., invoice no. 2 for $600.
CRJ	3	Cash sale, $400.
GJ	9	Issued credit memorandum no. 1 to Panda Co. for defective merchandise, $100.
CRJ	10	Received check from Panda Co. for invoice no. 1 less returns and discount.
CRJ	16	Cash sale, $500.
SJ	19	Sold merchandise on account to Panda Co., $550, invoice no. 3.

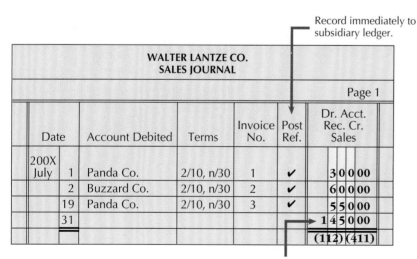

Record immediately to subsidiary ledger.

WALTER LANTZE CO.
SALES JOURNAL

Page 1

Date		Account Debited	Terms	Invoice No.	Post Ref.	Dr. Acct. Rec. Cr. Sales
200X July	1	Panda Co.	2/10, n/30	1	✔	3 0 0 00
	2	Buzzard Co.	2/10, n/30	2	✔	6 0 0 00
	19	Panda Co.	2/10, n/30	3	✔	5 5 0 00
	31					1 4 5 0 00
						(112) (411)

Total posted at end of month to general ledger accounts.

Figure 9-27 Sales on Account

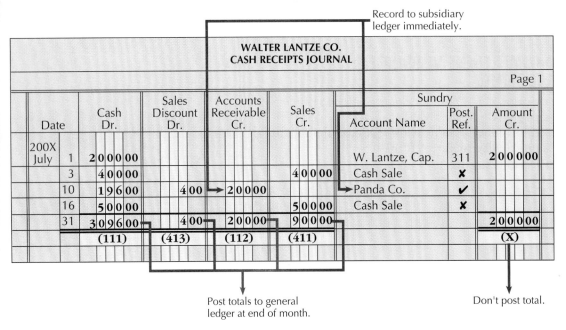

Figure 9-28 Cash Received—Cash Receipts Journal

Accounts receivable subsidiary ledger is usually a debit balance.

Accounts Receivable Subsidiary Ledger

Buzzard Co.

Date	PR	Debit	Credit	Dr. Balance
200X July 2	SJ1	600 00		600 00

Panda Co.

Date	PR	Debit	Credit	Dr. Balance
200X July 1	SJ1	300 00		300 00
9	GJ1		100 00	200 00
10	CRJ1		200 00	—
19	SJ1	550 00		550 00

Figure 9-29 Accounts Receivable Subsidiary Ledger

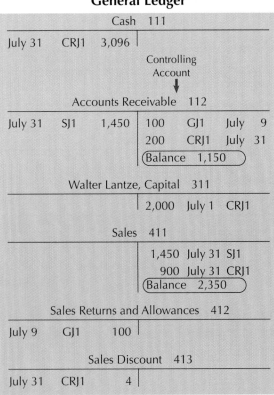

Figure 9-30 General Ledger

The controlling account at end of the month (Fig. 9-31) equals the sum of the accounts receivable subsidiary ledger.

WALTER LANTZE CO. SCHEDULE OF ACCOUNTS RECEIVABLE JULY 31, 200X		
Buzzard Co.	$	6 0 0 00
Panda Co.		5 5 0 00
Total Accounts Receivable	$1	1 5 0 00

Figure 9-31 Schedule of Accounts Receivable

Summary of Key Points

Learning Unit 9-1

1. A periodic inventory system records the cost of ending inventory at the end of each accounting period.
2. A perpetual inventory system keeps a continual update of inventory.
3. Sales Returns and Allowances and Sales Discount are contra-revenue accounts.
4. Net Sales = Gross Sales − Sales Returns and Allowances − Sales Discounts.
5. Discounts are not taken on sales tax, freight, or goods returned. The discount period is shorter than the credit period.

Learning Unit 9-2

1. A general journal is still used with special journals.
2. A sales journal records sales on account.
3. The accounts receivable subsidiary ledger, organized in alphabetical order, is not in the same book as Accounts Receivable, the controlling account in the general ledger.
4. At the end of the month the total of all customers' ending balances in the accounts receivable subsidiary ledger should be equal to the ending balance in Accounts Receivable, the controlling account in the general ledger.

Learning Unit 9-3

1. The ✓ in the PR column of the sales journal means a customer's account in the accounts receivable ledger (or the accounts receivable subsidiary ledger) (on the debit side) has been updated (or recorded) during the month.
2. At the end of the month the totals of the sales journal are posted to general ledger accounts.
3. Sales Tax Payable is a liability found in the general ledger.
4. When a credit memorandum is issued, the result is that Sales Returns and Allowances is increasing and Accounts Receivable is decreasing. When we record this entry into a general journal, we assume all parts of the transaction will be posted to the general ledger and recorded in the subsidiary ledger when the entry is journalized.

Learning Unit 9-4

1. The cash receipts journal records receipt of cash from any source.
2. The sundry column records the credit part of a transaction that does not occur frequently. Never post the *total* of sundry. Post items in the sundry column to the general ledger when entered.

3. A ✓ in the PR column of the cash receipts journal means that the accounts receivable ledger (or the accounts receivable subsidiary ledger) has been updated (recorded) with a credit.

4. An X in the cash receipts journal PR column means no posting was necessary, because the totals of these columns will be posted at the end of the month.

5. Crossfooting means proving that the total of debits and the total of credits are equal in the special journal, thus verifying the accuracy of recording.

6. A schedule of accounts receivable is a listing of the ending balances of customers in the accounts receivable subsidiary ledger. This total should be the same balance as found in the controlling account, Accounts Receivable, in the general ledger.

Key Terms

Accounts receivable subsidiary ledger   A book or file that contains, in alphabetical order, the individual records of amounts owed by various credit customers.

Cash receipts journal   A special journal that records all transactions involving the receipt of cash from any source.

Controlling account—Accounts Receivable   The Accounts Receivable account in the general ledger, after postings are complete, shows a firm the total amount of money owed to it. This figure is broken down in the accounts receivable ledger, where it indicates specifically who owes the money.

Credit memorandum   A piece of paper sent by the seller to a customer who has returned merchandise previously purchased on credit. The credit memorandum indicates to the customer that the seller is reducing the amount owed by the customer.

Credit period   Length of time allowed for payment of goods sold on account.

Crossfooting   The process of proving that the total debit columns of a special journal are equal to the total credit columns of a special journal.

Discount period   A period shorter than the credit period when a discount is available to encourage early payment of bills.

Gross sales   The revenue earned from sale of merchandise to customers.

Merchandise   Goods brought into a store for resale to customers.

Net sales   Gross sales less sales returns and allowances less sales discounts.

Periodic inventory system   An inventory system that, at the *end* of each accounting period, calculates the cost of the unsold goods on hand by taking the cost of each unit times the number of units of each product on hand.

Perpetual inventory system   An inventory system that keeps *continual track* of each type of inventory by recording units on hand at beginning, units sold, and the current balance after each sale or purchase.

Retailers   Merchants who buy goods from wholesalers for resale to customers.

Sales Discount account   A contra-revenue account that records cash discounts granted to customers for payments made within a specific period of time.

Sales invoice   A bill sent to customer(s) reflecting a sale on credit.

Sales journal   A special journal used to record only sales made on account.

Sales Returns and Allowances (SRA) account   A contra-revenue account that records price adjustments and allowances granted on merchandise that is defective and has been returned.

Sales Tax Payable account   An account in the general ledger that accumulates the amount of sales tax owed. It has a credit balance.

Schedule of accounts receivable   A list of the customers, in alphabetical order, that have an outstanding balance in the accounts receivable ledger (or the accounts receivable subsidiary ledger). This total should be equal to the balance of the Accounts Receivable controlling account in the general ledger at the end of the month.

Special journal   A journal used to record similar groups of transactions. Example: The sales journal records all sales on account.

Subsidiary ledger   A ledger that contains accounts of a single type. Example: The accounts receivable subsidiary ledger records all credit customers.

Sundry   Miscellaneous accounts column(s) in a special journal, which records part of transactions that do not occur too often.

Wholesalers   Merchants who buy goods from suppliers and manufacturers for sale to retailers.

Questions, Mini Exercises, Exercises, and Problems

Discussion Questions

1. What is the difference between a perpetual inventory system and a periodic inventory system?
2. Explain the purpose of a contra-revenue account.
3. What is the normal balance of sales discount?
4. Give two examples of contra-revenue accounts.
5. What is the difference between a discount period and a credit period?
6. Explain the terms:
   a. 2/10, n/30.
   b. n/10, EOM.
7. If special journals are used, what purpose will a general journal serve?
8. Compare and contrast the controlling account Accounts Receivable to the accounts receivable subsidiary ledger.
9. Why is the accounts receivable subsidiary ledger organized in alphabetical order?
10. When is a sales journal used?
11. What is an invoice? What purpose does it serve?
12. Why is sales tax a liability to the business?
13. Sales discounts are taken on sales tax. Agree or disagree and tell why.
14. When a seller issues a credit memorandum (assume no sales tax), what accounts will be affected?
15. Explain the function of a cash receipts journal.
16. When is the sundry column of the cash receipts journal posted?
17. Explain the purpose of a schedule of accounts receivable.

Mini Exercises

(The forms you need are on pages 280–281 of the *Study Guide and Working Papers.*)

Overview

1. Complete the table below for Sales, Sales Returns and Allowances, and Sales Discounts.

Accounts Affected	Category	↓ ↑	Temporary or Permanent

Calculating Net Sales

2. Given the following, calculate net sales:

Gross sales	$30
Sales Returns and Allowances	8
Sales Discounts	2

Sales Journal and General Journal

3. Match the following to the three journal entries (more than one number can be used).

   1. Journalized into sales journal.
   2. Record immediately to subsidiary ledger.

3. Post totals from sales journal at end of month to general ledger.
4. Journalized in general journal.
5. Record and post immediately to subsidiary and general ledgers.

  a. _____ Sold merchandise on account to Ree Co., invoice no. 1, $50.
  b. _____ Sold merchandise on account to Flynn Co., invoice no. 2, $100.
  c. _____ Issued credit memorandum no. 1 to Flynn Co. for defective merchandise, $25.

Credit Memorandum

4. Draw a transactional analysis box for the following credit memorandum: Issued credit memorandum to Met.com for defective merchandise, $200.

Sales and Cash Receipts Journal

5. Match the following to the four journal entries (a number can be used more than once).

  1. Journalized into sales journal.
  2. Journalized into cash receipts journal.
  3. Record immediately to subsidiary ledger.
  4. Totals of special journals will be posted at end of month (except sundry column).
  5. Post to general ledger immediately.
  6. Journalize into general journal.

  a. _____ Sold merchandise on account to Ally Co., invoice no. 10, $40.
  b. _____ Received check from Moore Co., $100 less 2% discount.
  c. _____ Cash Sales, $100.
  d. _____ Issued credit memorandum no. 2 to Ally Co. for defective merchandise, $20.

6. From the following, prepare a schedule of accounts receivable for Blue Co. for May 31, 200X.

Accounts Receivable Subsidiary Ledger

Bon Co.
5/6 SJ1   100 |

Peke Co.
5/20 SJ1   30 | 5/27 CRJ1   10

Green Co.
5/9 SJ1   10 |

General Ledger

Accounts Receivable
5/31 SJ1   140 | 5/31 CRJ1   10

Blueprint: Sales and Cash Receipts Journals

SUMMARY OF HOW TO POST AND RECORD
Single-Column Sales Journal

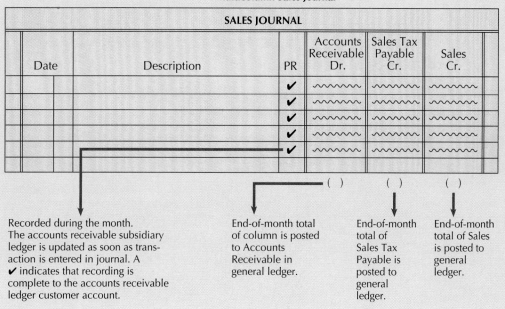

		SALES JOURNAL			
	Date	Description	PR	Accounts Rec.: Dr. Sales: Cr.	
			✔	. . .	
			✔	. . .	
			✔	. . .	
			✔	. . .	
			✔	. . .	

Posted End of Month

Total of column is posted to general ledger accounts Accounts Receivable and Sales.

Recorded During the Month

Accounts receivable subsidiary ledger is updated as soon as transaction is entered in sales journal.
A ✔ indicates that recording is complete to the accounts receivable ledger customer account.

( ) ( )

Multicolumn Sales Journal

		SALES JOURNAL				
	Date	Description	PR	Accounts Receivable Dr.	Sales Tax Payable Cr.	Sales Cr.
			✔	~~~	~~~	~~~
			✔	~~~	~~~	~~~
			✔	~~~	~~~	~~~
			✔	~~~	~~~	~~~
			✔	~~~	~~~	~~~

( )   ( )   ( )

Recorded during the month. The accounts receivable subsidiary ledger is updated as soon as transaction is entered in journal. A ✔ indicates that recording is complete to the accounts receivable ledger customer account.

End-of-month total of column is posted to Accounts Receivable in general ledger.

End-of-month total of Sales Tax Payable is posted to general ledger.

End-of-month total of Sales is posted to general ledger.

Issuing a Credit Memo without Sales Tax Recorded in a General Journal

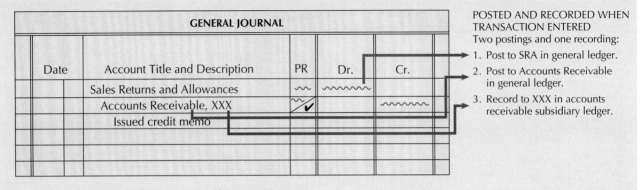

GENERAL JOURNAL

Date	Account Title and Description	PR	Dr.	Cr.
	Sales Returns and Allowances			
	Accounts Receivable, XXX	✓		
	Issued credit memo			

POSTED AND RECORDED WHEN TRANSACTION ENTERED
Two postings and one recording:
1. Post to SRA in general ledger.
2. Post to Accounts Receivable in general ledger.
3. Record to XXX in accounts receivable subsidiary ledger.

Issuing a Credit Memo with Sales Tax Recorded in a General Journal

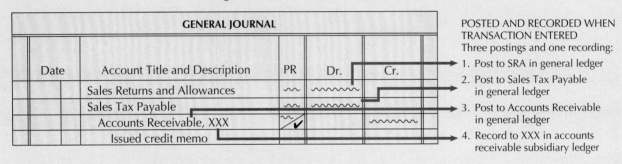

GENERAL JOURNAL

Date	Account Title and Description	PR	Dr.	Cr.
	Sales Returns and Allowances			
	Sales Tax Payable			
	Accounts Receivable, XXX	✓		
	Issued credit memo			

POSTED AND RECORDED WHEN TRANSACTION ENTERED
Three postings and one recording:
1. Post to SRA in general ledger
2. Post to Sales Tax Payable in general ledger
3. Post to Accounts Receivable in general ledger
4. Record to XXX in accounts receivable subsidiary ledger

The Cash Receipts Journal

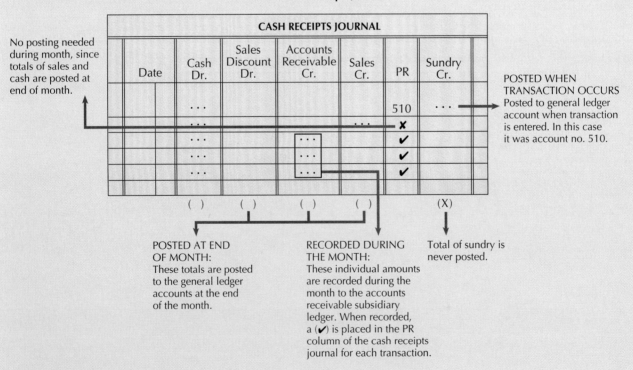

CASH RECEIPTS JOURNAL

Date	Cash Dr.	Sales Discount Dr.	Accounts Receivable Cr.	Sales Cr.	PR	Sundry Cr.
	. . .				510	. . .
	. . .			. . .	✗	
	. . .		. . .		✓	
	. . .		. . .		✓	
	. . .		. . .		✓	
	( )	( )	( )	( )		(X)

No posting needed during month, since totals of sales and cash are posted at end of month.

POSTED WHEN TRANSACTION OCCURS
Posted to general ledger account when transaction is entered. In this case it was account no. 510.

POSTED AT END OF MONTH:
These totals are posted to the general ledger accounts at the end of the month.

RECORDED DURING THE MONTH:
These individual amounts are recorded during the month to the accounts receivable subsidiary ledger. When recorded, a (✓) is placed in the PR column of the cash receipts journal for each transaction.

Total of sundry is never posted.

Note: If a Sales Tax Payable column were added, total of column would be posted at end of month.

Exercises

(The forms you need are on pages 282–284 of the *Study Guide and Working Papers*.)

9-1. From the sales journal in Figure 9-32 record to the accounts receivable subsidiary ledger and post to the general ledger accounts as appropriate.

9-2. Journalize, record, and post when appropriate the following transactions into the sales journal (same heading as Exercise 9-1) and general journal (p. 1) (all sales carry terms of 2/10, n/30):

200X
May 16 Sold merchandise on account to Ronald Co., invoice no. 1, $1,000.
   18 Sold merchandise on account to Bass Co., invoice no. 2, $1,700.
   20 Issued credit memorandum no. 1 to Bass Co. for defective merchandise, $700.

Use the following account numbers: Accounts Receivable, 112; Sales, 411; Sales Returns and Allowances, 412.

9-3. From Exercise 9-2, journalize in the cash receipts journal the receipt of a check from Ronald Co. for payment of invoice no. 1 on May 24. Use the same headings as for Art's Wholesale Clothing (on p. 356).

9-4. From the following transactions for Edna Co., journalize, record, post, and prepare a schedule of accounts receivable when appropriate. Use the same journal headings (all p. 1) and chart of accounts (use Edna Cares, Capital) that Art's Wholesale Clothing used in the text. You will have to set up your own accounts receivable subsidiary ledger and partial general ledger as needed. All sales terms are 2/10, n/30.

200X
June 1 Edna Cares invested $3,000 in the business.
   1 Sold merchandise on account to Boston Co., invoice no. 1, $700.
   2 Sold merchandise on account to Gary Co., invoice no. 2, $900.
   3 Cash sale, $200.
   8 Issued credit memorandum no. 1 to Boston for defective merchandise, $200.
   10 Received check from Boston for invoice no. 1 less returns and discount.
   15 Cash sale, $400.
   18 Sold merchandise on account to Boston Co., invoice no. 3, $600.

Marginal notes:

Recording to accounts receivable ledger and posting to general ledger.

Journalizing, recording, and posting that includes credit memorandum.

Journalizing transaction into cash receipts journal.

Journalizing, recording, and posting sales and cash receipts journal schedule of accounts receivable.

SALES JOURNAL

P. 1

Date		Account Debited	Invoice No.	PR	Dr. Accts. Receivable Cr. Sales
200X Apr.	18	Amazon.com	1		5 0 0 00
	19	Bill Valley Co.	2		6 0 0 00

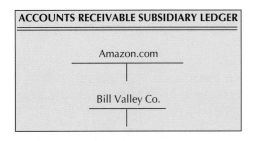

ACCOUNTS RECEIVABLE SUBSIDIARY LEDGER
Amazon.com
Bill Valley Co.

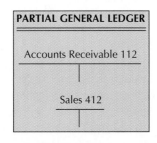

PARTIAL GENERAL LEDGER
Accounts Receivable 112
Sales 412

Figure 9-32
Sales Journal, Subsidiary Ledger; Partial General Ledger

Sales tax and cash discount calculation.

9-5. From the following facts calculate what Ann Frost paid Blue Co. for the purchase of a dining room set. Sale terms are 2/10, n/30.

    a. Sales ticket price before tax, $4,000, dated April 5.
    b. Sales tax, 7%.
    c. Returned one defective chair for credit of $400 on April 8.
    d. Paid bill on April 13.

Group A Problems

(The forms you need are on pages 285–304 of the *Study Guide and Working Papers.*)

9A-1. Jill Blue has opened Food.com, a wholesale grocery and pizza company. The following transactions occurred in June:

Multicolumn journal: Journalizing and posting to general ledger, recording to accounts receivable subsidiary ledger, and preparing a schedule of accounts receivable.

200X

June	1	Sold grocery merchandise to Duncan Co. on account, $500, invoice no. 1.
	4	Sold pizza merchandise to Sue Moore Co. on account, $600, invoice no. 2.
	8	Sold grocery merchandise to Long Co. on account, $700, invoice no. 3.
	10	Issued credit memorandum no. 1 to Duncan Co. for $150 of grocery merchandise returned due to spoilage.
	15	Sold pizza merchandise to Sue Moore Co. on account, $160, invoice no. 4.
	19	Sold grocery merchandise to Long Co. on account, $300, invoice no. 5.
	25	Sold pizza merchandise to Duncan Co. on account, $1,200, invoice no. 6.

Check Figure:
Schedule of accounts receivable $3,310

Required

1. Journalize the transactions in the appropriate journals.
2. Record to the accounts receivable subsidiary ledger and post to the general ledger as appropriate.
3. Prepare a schedule of accounts receivable.

9A-2. The following transactions of Ted's Auto Supply occurred in November (your working papers have balances as of November 1 for certain general ledger and accounts receivable ledger accounts):

Multicolumn sales journal: Use of sales tax, journalizing and posting to general ledger and recording to accounts receivable ledger, and preparing a schedule of accounts receivable.

200X

Nov.	1	Sold auto parts merchandise to R. Volan on account, $1,000, invoice no. 60, plus 5% sales tax.
	5	Sold auto parts merchandise to J. Seth on account, $800, invoice no. 61, plus 5% sales tax.
	8	Sold auto parts merchandise to Lance Corner on account, $9,000, invoice no. 62, plus 5% sales tax.
	10	Issued credit memorandum no. 12 to R. Volan for $500 for defective auto parts merchandise returned from Nov. 1 transaction. (Be careful to record the reduction in Sales Tax Payable as well.)
	12	Sold auto parts merchandise to J. Seth on account, $600, invoice no. 63, plus 5% sales tax.

Check Figure:
Schedule of accounts receivable $13,045

Required

1. Journalize the transactions in the appropriate journals.
2. Record to the accounts receivable subsidiary ledger and post to the general ledger as appropriate.
3. Prepare a schedule of accounts receivable.

9A-3. Mark Peaker owns Peaker's Sneaker Shop. (In your working papers balances as of May 1 are provided for the accounts receivable and general ledger accounts.) The following transactions occurred in May:

200X

May

1 Mark Peaker invested an additional $12,000 in the sneaker store.

3 Sold $700 of merchandise on account to B. Dale, sales ticket no. 60, terms 1/10, n/30.

4 Sold $500 of merchandise on account to Ron Lester, sales ticket no. 61, terms 1/10, n/30.

9 Sold $200 of merchandise on account to Jim Zon, sales ticket no. 62, terms 1/10, n/30.

10 Received cash from B. Dale in payment of May 3 transaction, sales ticket no. 60, less discount.

20 Sold $3,000 of merchandise on account to Pam Pry, sales ticket no. 63, terms 1/10, n/30.

22 Received cash payment from Ron Lester in payment of May 4 transaction, sales ticket no. 61.

23 Collected cash sales, $3,000.

24 Issued credit memorandum no. 1 to Pam Pry for $2,000 of merchandise returned from May 20 sales on account.

26 Received cash from Pam Pry in payment of May 20, sales ticket no. 63. (Don't forget about the credit memo and discount.)

28 Collected cash sales, $7,000.

30 Sold sneaker rack equipment for $300 cash. (Beware.)

30 Sold merchandise priced at $4,000, on account to Ron Lester, sales ticket no. 64, terms 1/10, n/30.

31 Issued credit memorandum no. 2 to Ron Lester for $700 of merchandise returned from May 30 transaction, sales ticket no. 64.

> *Comprehensive Problem: Recording transactions into sales, cash receipts, and general journals. Recording to accounts receivable subsidiary ledger and posting to general ledger. Preparing a schedule of accounts receivable.*

> *Check Figure: Schedule of Accounts Receivable $5,700*

Required

1. Journalize the transactions.
2. Record to the accounts receivable subsidiary ledger and post to the general ledger as needed.
3. Prepare a schedule of accounts receivable.

9A-4. Bill Murray opened Bill's Cosmetic Market on April 1. There is a 6% sales tax on all cosmetic sales. Bill offers no sales discounts. The following transactions occurred in April:

200X

Apr.

1 Bill Murray invested $8,000 in the Cosmetic Market from his personal savings account.

5 From the cash register tapes, lipstick cash sales were $5,000 plus sales tax.

5 From the cash register tapes, eye shadow cash sales were $2,000 plus sales tax.

8 Sold lipstick on account to Alice Koy Co., $300, sales ticket no. 1, plus sales tax.

9 Sold eye shadow on account to Marika Sanchez Co., $1,000, sales ticket no. 2, plus sales tax.

15 Issued credit memorandum no. 1 to Alice Koy Co. for $150 for lipstick returned. (Be sure to reduce Sales Tax Payable for Bill.)

19 Marika Sanchez Co. paid half the amount owed from sales ticket no. 2, dated April 9.

21 Sold lipstick on account to Jeff Tong Co., $300, sales ticket no. 3, plus sales tax.

> *Comprehensive Problem: Using sales tax in recording transactions into sales, cash receipts, and general journals. Recording to accounts receivable subsidiary ledger and posting to general ledger. Crossfooting and preparing a schedule of accounts receivable.*

24   Sold eye shadow on account to Rusty Neal Co., $800, sales ticket no. 4, plus sales tax.
25   Issued credit memorandum no. 2 to Jeff Tong Co. for $200 for lipstick returned from sales ticket no. 3, dated April 21.
29   Cash sales taken from the cash register tape showed:
  1. Lipstick: $1,000 + $60 sales tax collected.
  2. Eye shadow: $3,000 + $180 sales tax collected.
29   Sold lipstick on account to Marika Sanchez Co., $400, sales ticket no. 5, plus sales tax.
30   Received payment from Marika Sanchez Co. of sales ticket no. 5, dated April 29.

Required

1. Journalize the preceeding in the sales journal, cash receipts journal, or general journal.
2. Record to the accounts receivable subsidiary ledger and post to the general ledger when appropriate.
3. Prepare a schedule of accounts receivable for the end of April.

Group B Problems

(The forms you need are on pages 285–304 of the *Study Guide and Working Papers.*)

9B-1. The following transactions occurred for Food.com for the month of June:

200X
June   1   Sold grocery merchandise to Duncan Co. on account, $800, invoice no. 1.
  4   Sold pizza merchandise to Sue Moore Co. on account, $550, invoice no. 2.
  8   Sold grocery merchandise to Long Co. on account, $900, invoice no. 3.
  10   Issued credit memorandum no. 1 to Duncan Co. for $160 of grocery merchandise returned due to spoilage.
  15   Sold pizza merchandise to Sue Moore Co. on account, $700, invoice no. 4.
  19   Sold grocery merchandise to Long Co. on account, $250, invoice no. 5.

Required

1. Journalize the transactions in the appropriate journals.
2. Record to the accounts receivable subsidiary ledger and post to the general ledger as appropriate.
3. Prepare a schedule of accounts receivable.

9B-2. In November the following transactions occurred for Ted's Auto Supply (your working papers have balances as of November 1 for certain general ledger and accounts receivable ledger accounts):

200X
Nov.   1   Sold merchandise to R. Volan on account, $4,000, invoice no. 70, plus 5% sales tax.
  5   Sold merchandise to J. Seth on account, $1,600, invoice no. 71, plus 5% sales tax.
  8   Sold merchandise to Lance Corner on account, $15,000, invoice no. 72, plus 5% sales tax.
  10   Issued credit memorandum no. 14 to R. Volan for $2,000 for defective merchandise returned from Nov. 1 transaction. (Be sure to record the reduction in Sales Tax Payable as well.)
  12   Sold merchandise to J. Seth on account, $1,400, invoice no. 73, plus 5% sales tax.

Required

1. Journalize the transactions in the appropriate journals.
2. Record to the accounts receivable subsidiary ledger and post to the general ledger as appropriate.
3. Prepare a schedule of accounts receivable.

Check Figure:
Schedule of accounts
receivable $22,600

9B-3. (In your working papers all the beginning balances needed are provided for the accounts receivable subsidiary and general ledgers.) The following transactions occurred for Peaker's Sneaker Shop:

Check Figure:
Schedule of accounts
receivable $8,000

Comprehensive Problem:
Recording transactions
into sales, cash receipts,
and general journals.
Recording to accounts
receivable subsidiary ledger
and posting to general
ledger. Preparing a schedule
of accounts receivable.

200X

May 1 Mark Peaker invested an additional $14,000 in the sneaker store.

3 Sold $2,000 of merchandise on account to B. Dale, sales ticket no. 60, terms 1/10, n/30.

4 Sold $900 of merchandise on account to Ron Lester, sales ticket no. 61, terms 1/10, n/30.

9 Sold $600 of merchandise on account to Jim Zon, sales ticket no. 62, terms 1/10, n/30.

10 Received cash from B. Dale in payment of May 3 transaction, sales ticket no. 60, less discount.

20 Sold $4,000 of merchandise on account to Pam Pry, sales ticket no. 63, terms 1/10, n/30.

22 Received cash payment from Ron Lester in payment of May 4 transaction, sales ticket no. 61.

23 Collected cash sales, $6,000.

24 Issued credit memorandum no. 1 to Pam Pry for $500 of merchandise returned from May 20 sales on account.

26 Received cash from Pam Pry in payment of May 20 sales ticket no. 63. (Don't forget about the credit memo and discount.)

28 Collected cash sales, $12,000.

30 Sold sneaker rack equipment for $200 cash.

30 Sold $6,000 of merchandise on account to Ron Lester, sales ticket no. 64, terms 1/10, n/30.

31 Issued credit memorandum no. 2 to Ron Lester for $800 of merchandise returned from May 30 transaction, sales ticket no. 64.

Required

1. Journalize the transactions in the appropriate journals.
2. Record and post as appropriate.
3. Prepare a schedule of accounts receivable.

9B-4. Bill's Cosmetic Market began operating in April. There is a 6% sales tax on all cosmetic sales. Bill offers no discounts. The following transactions occurred in April:

200X

Apr. 1 Bill Murray invested $10,000 in the Cosmetic Market from his personal account.

5 From the cash register tapes, lipstick cash sales were $5,000 plus sales tax.

5 From the cash register tapes, eye shadow cash sales were $3,000 plus sales tax.

8 Sold lipstick on account to Alice Koy Co., $400, sales ticket no. 1, plus sales tax.

9 Sold eye shadow on account to Marika Sanchez Co., $900, sales ticket no. 2, plus sales tax.

Comprehensive Problem:
Using sales tax in recording transactions into
sales, cash receipts, and
general journals. Recording
to accounts receivable
subsidiary ledger and
posting to general ledger,
and preparing a schedule
of accounts receivable.

Check Figure:
Schedule of Accounts
Receivable $2,067

15   Issued credit memorandum no. 1 to Alice Koy Co. for lipstick returned, $200. (Be sure to reduce Sales Tax Payable for Bill.)

19   Marika Sanchez Co. paid half the amount owed from sales ticket no. 2, dated April 9.

21   Sold lipstick on account to Jeff Tong Co., $600, sales ticket no. 3, plus sales tax.

24   Sold eye shadow on account to Rusty Neal Co., $1,000, sales ticket no. 4, plus sales tax.

25   Issued credit memorandum no. 2 to Jeff Tong Co. for $300, for lipstick returned from sales ticket no. 3, dated April 21.

29   Cash sales taken from the cash register tape showed:
  1. Lipstick: $4,000 + $240 sales tax collected.
  2. Eye shadow: $2,000 + $120 sales tax collected.

29   Sold lipstick on account to Marika Sanchez Co., $700, sales ticket no. 5 plus sales tax.

30   Received payment from Marika Sanchez Co. of sales ticket no. 5, dated April 29.

Required

1. Journalize, record, and post as appropriate.
2. Prepare a schedule of accounts receivable for the end of April.

Real-World Applications

9R-1.   Ronald Howard has been hired by Green Company to help reconstruct the sales journal, general journal, and cash receipts journal, which were recently destroyed in a fire. The owner of Green Company has supplied him with the following data. Please ignore dates, invoice numbers, and so forth and enter the entries into the reconstructed sales journal, general journal, and cash receipts journal. What written recommendation should Ron make so reconstruction will not be needed in the future?

Accounts Receivable Subsidiary Ledger

P. Bond			
Bal.	100	150	CRJ
SJ	150	Entitled to 2% discount	

M. Raff		
Bal.	200	
SJ	100	

J. Smooth			
Bal.	300	1,000	GJ
SJ	2,000	1,000	CRJ
SJ	1,000	500	GJ
		Entitled to 1% discount	

R. Venner			
Bal.	200	400	CRJ
SJ	400		

Partial General Ledger

Cash	
Bal. 12,737	

Accounts Receivable			
Bal.	800	1,000	GJ
SJ	3,650	500	GJ
		1,550	CRJ

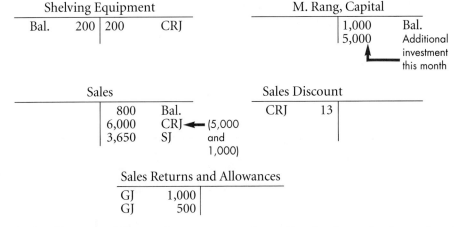

Shelving Equipment

Bal.	200	200	CRJ

M. Rang, Capital

1,000	Bal.
5,000	Additional investment this month

Sales

800	Bal.
6,000	CRJ ← (5,000
3,650	SJ and
	1,000)

Sales Discount

CRJ	13

Sales Returns and Allowances

GJ	1,000
GJ	500

9R-2. The bookkeeper of Floore Company records credit sales in a sales journal and returns in a general journal. The bookkeeper did the following:

1. Recorded an $18 credit sale as $180 in the sales journal.
2. Correctly recorded a $40 sale in the sales journal but posted it to B. Blue's account as $400 in the accounts receivable ledger.
3. Made an additional error in determining the balance of J. B. Window Co. in the accounts receivable ledger.
4. Posted a sales return that was recorded in the general journal to the Sales Returns and Allowance account and the Accounts Receivable account but forgot to record it to the B. Katz Co.
5. Added the total of the sales column incorrectly.
6. Posted a sales return to the Accounts Receivable account but not to the Sales Returns and Allowances account. The Accounts Receivable ledger was recorded correctly.

Could you inform the bookkeeper in writing as to when each error will be discovered?

YOU make the call

Critical Thinking/Ethical Case

9R-3. Amy Jak is the National Sales Manager of Land.com. To get sales up to the projection for the old year, Amy asked the accountant to put the first two weeks of sales in January back into December. Amy told the accountant that this secret would only be between them. Should Amy move the new sales into the old sales year? You make the call. Write down your specific recommendations to Amy.

Internet Exercises: Dillard's

EX-1. [**www.dillards.com**]   Special journals are designed to be excellent labor savers. Now that you have been shown the basics of the sales journal and the cash receipts journal, you will recognize them next time you visit any large retailer. The labor saved by these journals is that transactions in them are posted monthly, rather than as they occur. Briefly explain the advantages of using them instead of merely posting transactions in a general journal. In your explanation discuss posting differences between special journals and the general journal.

EX-2. [www.dillards.com]   Compare the process of entering transactions from source documents into a manual sales journal or cash receipts journal with the "automatic" creation of the entries from a "point-of-sale terminal" you would see in a department store. Mention in your answer what different types of accounting records would be posted at the "point of sale."

Continuing Problem

Eldorado Computer Center

Tony will use two specialized journals for recording business transactions in the month of January. To assist you in recording the transactions, at the end of this problem is the schedule of accounts receivable as of December 31 and an updated chart of accounts with the current balance listed for each account.

Assignment

(See p. 309 in the *Study Guide and Working Papers.*)

1. Journalize the transactions in the appropriate journals (cash receipts, sales journal, or general journal).
2. Record in the accounts receivable subsidiary ledger and post to the general ledger as appropriate. A partial general ledger is included in the *Working Papers.*
3. Prepare a schedule of accounts receivable as of January 31, 200X.

The January transactions are as follows:

Jan.
- 1   Sold $700 worth of merchandise to Taylor Golf on credit, sales invoice no. 5000; terms are 2/10, n/30.
- 10   Sold $3,000 worth of merchandise on account to Anthony Pitale, sales invoice no. 5001; terms are 2/10, n/30.
- 11   Received $3,000 from Accu Pac, Inc. toward payment of its balance; no discount allowed.
- 12   Collected $2,000 cash sales.
- 19   Sold $4,000 worth of merchandise on account to Vita Needle, sales invoice no. 5002; terms are 4/10, n/30.
- 20   Collected balance in full from invoice no. 5001, Anthony Pitale.
- 29   Issued credit memorandum to Taylor Golf for $400 worth of merchandise returned, invoice no. 5000.
- 29   Collected full payment from Vita Needle, invoice no. 5002.

Schedule of Accounts Receivable
Eldorado Computer Center
December 31, 200X

Taylor Golf	$ 2,900.00
Vita Needle	6,800.00
Accu Pac	$ 3,900.00
Total Amount Due	$13,600.00

Chart of Accounts and Current Balances as of 12/31/0X

Account #	Account Name	Debit Balance	Credit Balance
1000	Cash	$ 3,336.65	
1010	Petty Cash	100	
1020	Accounts Receivable	13,600	
1025	Prepaid Rent	1,600	
1030	Supplies	132	
1040	Merchandise Inventory	0	
1080	Computer Shop Equipment	3,800	
1081	Accumulated Dep., CS Equip.		$ 99
1090	Office Equipment	1,050	
1091	Accumulated Dep., Office Equip.		20
2000	Accounts Payable		2,050
2010	Wages Payable		0
2020	FICA—Social Security Payable		0
2030	FICA—Medicare Payable		0
2040	FIT Payable		0
2050	SIT Payable		0
2060	FUTA Payable		0
2070	SUTA Payable		0
3000	Freedman Capital		7,406
3010	Freedman Withdrawals	2,015	
3020	Income Summary		0
4000	Service Revenue		18,500
4010	Sales		0
4020	Sales Returns and Allowances	0	
4030	Sales Discounts	0	
5010	Advertising Expense	0	
5020	Rent Expense	0	
5030	Utilities Expense	0	
5040	Phone Expense	150	
5050	Supplies Expense	0	
5060	Insurance Expense	0	
5070	Postage Expense	25	
5080	Dep. Exp., C.S. Equipment	0	
5090	Dep. Exp., Office Equipment	0	
5100	Miscellaneous Expense	10	
5110	Wage Expense	2,030	
5120	Payroll Tax Expense	226.35	
5130	Interest Expense	0	
5140	Bad Debt Expense	0	
6000	Purchases	0	
6010	Purchases Returns and Allowances		0
6020	Purchases Discounts		0
6030	Freight In	0	

APPENDIX

INTRODUCTION TO A MERCHANDISE COMPANY USING A GENERAL JOURNAL FOR A PERPETUAL INVENTORY SYSTEM

Introduction to the Merchandise Cycle

Let's use Wal-Mart as an example. We know that Wal-Mart must buy inventory from suppliers to sell to you, the customer. This inventory is called *merchandise inventory*. It is an asset sold to you for cash and/or accounts receivable and represents *sales revenue* or sales for Wal-Mart.

What did it cost Wal-Mart to bring the inventory into the store? The *cost of goods sold* is the total cost of merchandise inventory brought into the store and sold. These costs do not include any operating expenses such as heat, advertising, and salaries. To find Wal-Mart's profit before operating expenses, we take the sales revenue less cost of goods sold. Figure A-1 is called *gross profit on sales*.

Figure A-1
Calculating Gross Profit on Sales

| Wal-Mart Sales Revenue | − | Cost of Goods Sold | = | Gross Profit on Sales |

For example, if Wal-Mart sells a TV for $500 that cost it $300 to bring into the store, its gross profit is $200. To find its net income or net loss, Wal-Mart would subtract its operating expenses. Figure A-2 shows how a merchandiser calculates its net income or net loss.

Figure A-2
Introduction to Perpetual Inventory for a Merchandise Company

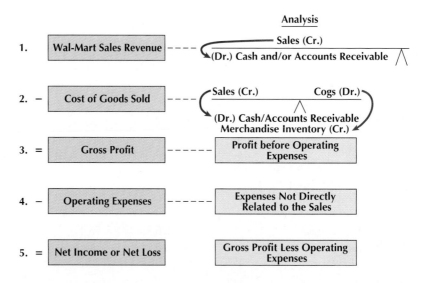

Note In Step 1 the sales provide an inflow of cash and/or accounts receivable. Step 2 shows that when the inventory is sold, it is recognized as a cost (cost of goods sold). By subtracting sales less cost of goods sold, we arrive at the gross profit in Step 3. Step 4 shows that operating expenses subtracted from gross profit result in a net income or net loss in Step 5.

What Inventory System Wal-Mart Uses

When you pay at Wal-Mart you see the use of bar codes and optical scanners. Wal-Mart keeps detailed records of the inventory it brings into the store and what inventory is sold. This continuous updating of inventory is called a *perpetual inventory system*. With this method, Wal-Mart keeps track of what it costs to make the sale (cost of goods sold).

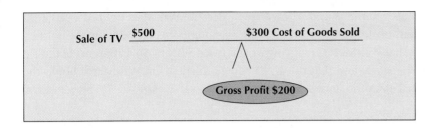

Figure A-3
Matchings Revenues
and Costs

More and more companies large or small are using the perpetual inventory system due to increasing computerization. Wal-Mart knows that using the perpetual inventory system will help control stocks of inventory as well as lost or stolen goods.

Recording Merchandise Transactions

Now let's look at Wal-Mart as both a buyer and seller. Let's first focus on Wal-Mart the buyer.

Wal-Mart: The Buyer

When Wal-Mart brings merchandise inventory into the stores from suppliers it is recorded in the *Merchandise Inventory account*. Think of this account as purchases of merchandise for cash or on account that is for resale to customers. Each order is documented by an invoice for Wal-Mart. Keep in mind Merchandise Inventory is the cost of bringing the merchandise into the store, not the price at which the merchandise will be sold to customers. Let's assume on *July 9 that Wal-Mart bought flat-screen TVs from Sony Corp. for $7,000 with terms 2/10, n/30*. Wal-Mart would record the purchase as shown in Figure A-4.

Analysis:

Merchandise Inventory	A	↑	Dr.	$7,000
Accounts Payable	L	↑	Cr.	$7,000

Journal Entry:

	July	9	Merchandise Inventory	7 0 0 0 00	
			Accounts Payable		7 0 0 0 00
			Purchased Inventory on account		
			from Sony 2/10, n/30		

Figure A-4
Purchase Inventory
on Account

Keep in mind not all purchases will go to Merchandise Inventory. Wal-Mart will buy supplies, equipment and so forth that are not for resale to customers. These amounts will be debited to the specific account. For example, if Wal-Mart bought $5,000 of shelving equipment on account for its store on November 9, the transaction would be recorded as in Figure A-5.

Analysis:

Shelving Equipment	A	↑	Dr.	$5,000
Accounts Payable	L	↑	Cr.	$5,000

Journal Entry:

	Nov.	9	Shelving Equipment	5 0 0 0 00	
			Accounts Payable		5 0 0 0 00
			Bought equipment on account		

Figure A-5
Purchasing of Equipment
on Account

What happens if Wal-Mart finds a TV to be defective from its purchase from Sony?

Recording Purchases Returns and Allowances   Because Wal-Mart noticed a damaged TV in the shipment on July 14, it issues a *debit memorandum.* This document notified Sony, the supplier, that Wal-Mart is reducing what is owed Sony by $600, the cost of the TV (to bring it into the store) and that the TV is being returned. On Wal-Mart's books the analysis and journal entry in Figure A-6 resulted.

Figure A-6
Recording a Debit Memorandum

Analysis:	Accounts Payable	L	↓	Dr.	$600
	Merchandise Inventory	A	↓	Cr.	$600

Journal Entry:	July	14	Accounts Payable	6 0 0 00	
			Merchandise Inventory		6 0 0 00
			To record Debit Memo #10		

Note that the cost of Merchandise Inventory has been reduced by $600 due to the return. In the perpetual inventory system there is no purchases, returns, and allowances title. The savings from the return are recorded *directly* into the Merchandise Inventory account. Let's now look at how Wal-Mart would record any cash discounts it would receive due to payment of the Sony bill within the discount period.

Recording Purchase Discounts   Let's assume Wal-Mart pays Sony within the first 10 days. Keep in mind that we take no discounts on returned goods (the $600 return). The amount of purchase discount will be recorded as a reduction to the cost of Merchandise Inventory. Figure A-7 shows the analysis and journal entry on July 16. A discount lowers the cost of inventory.

Figure A-7
Recording a Purchase Discount

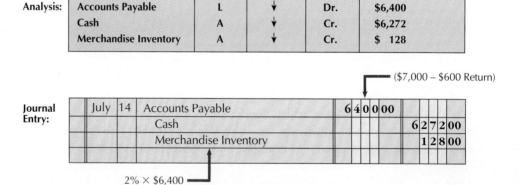

Keep in mind that had Wal-Mart missed the discount period it would have debited Accounts Payable $6,400 and credited Cash for $6,400. Merchandise Inventory would not be reduced.

Recording Cost of Freight   The cost of freight ($300) is to be paid by Wal-Mart. When the purchaser is responsible for cost of freight, it is added to the cost of Merchandise Inventory. If the cost of freight is paid by the seller, it could be recorded in an operating expense account called Freight-out. Figure A-8 is the analysis and journal entry for freight on July 10.

Wal-Mart: The Seller

Now let's look at Wal-Mart as the *seller* of merchandise.

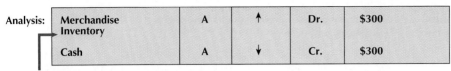

Analysis:	Merchandise Inventory	A	↑	Dr.	$300
	Cash	A	↓	Cr.	$300

Freight Cost added to Merchandise Inventory

Journal Entry:		July	10	Merchandise Inventory	3 0 0 00	
				Cash		3 0 0 00
				Payment of Freight		

Figure A-8
Recording Cost of Freight

Recording Sales at Wal-Mart   Sales revenues are earned at Wal-Mart when the goods are transferred to the buyer. The earned revenue can be for cash and or credit. Let's look at the following example of the sale of a TV at Wal-Mart for $950 on credit on August 10 that cost Wal-Mart $600. Keep in mind when using the perpetual inventory system that at the time of the earned sale Wal-Mart will:

At selling price → 1. **Record the sales (cash and/or credit).**

At cost → 2. **Record the cost of the inventory sold and the reduction in inventory.**

First, let's analyze the transaction in Figure A-9. Note that we will have two entries, one to record the sale and one to show a new cost and less inventory on hand.

Be sure to go back to Steps 1 and 2 of Figure A-2. These two steps reinforce the preceding journal entries. Remember that if the sale were a cash sale, we would have debited Cash instead of Accounts Receivable. Note also that the Sales account only records sales of goods held for resale.

Selling < Price	Accounts Receivable	Asset	↑	Dr.	$950
	Sales	Revenue	↑	Cr.	$950
Cost to < Make sale	Cost of Goods Sold	Cost	↑	Dr.	$600
	Merchandise Inventory	Asset	↓	Cr.	$600

Figure A-9
Recording Sales and Cost of Goods Sold

Journal Entries:		Aug.	10	Accounts Receivable	9 5 0 00	
				Sales		9 5 0 00
				Charge sales		
			10	Cost of Goods Sold	6 0 0 00	
				Merchandise Inventory		6 0 0 00
				To record cost of		
				merchandise sold on account		

How Wal-Mart Records Sales Returns Allowances and Sales Discounts   Keep in mind that we are now looking at how the *seller* of merchandise records a transaction giving the customer a credit due to an allowance or a return of goods from a previous sale. Usually, the seller will issue a *credit memorandum*, a document informing the customer of the adjustment due to the return or allowance. For example, on August 15, let's look at a customer who returned a $950 TV that had been purchased at Wal-Mart. On Wal-Mart's books, the analysis and journal entry in Figure A-10 resulted.

The first entry records the return at the original selling price using the contra-revenue account Sales Returns and Allowances. The second entry records putting the inventory back in Wal-Mart's books at cost and reducing its Cost of Goods Sold because the inventory was

Figure A-10
Return of Goods

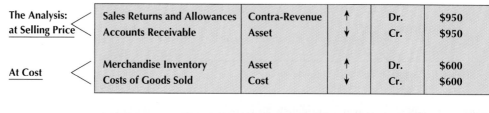

			The Analysis: at Selling Price			
Sales Returns and Allowances	Contra-Revenue	↑	Dr.	$950
Accounts Receivable	Asset	↓	Cr.	$950

At Cost

Merchandise Inventory	Asset	↑	Dr.	$600
Costs of Goods Sold	Cost	↓	Cr.	$600

Journal Entries:

	Aug.	15	Sales Returns and Allowances		9 5 0 00			
			Accounts Receivable				9 5 0 00	
			Returned Goods					
		15	Merchandise Inventory		6 0 0 00			
			Cost of Goods Sold				6 0 0 00	

not sold. Remember that we only record the Cost of Goods Sold when the sale has been earned. Keep in mind that if the customer kept the TV but at a reduced price, no entry affecting Merchandise Inventory and Cost of Goods Sold would be needed. Let's assume a customer on August 25 gets a 2% discount for paying for a $950 TV early. The analysis and entry in Figure A-11 would result on the seller's book:

Figure A-11
Recording Sales Discount

The Analysis:

Cash	Asset	↑	Dr.	$931
Sales Discount	Contra-Revenue	↑	Dr.	$ 19
Accounts Receivable	Asset	↓	Cr.	$950

Journal Entry:

	Aug.	25	Cash		9 3 1 00			
			Sales Discount		1 9 00			
			Accounts Receivable				9 5 0 00	

Now let's summarize (Fig. A-12) all the entries for both the buyer and the seller (in this case, Wal-Mart).

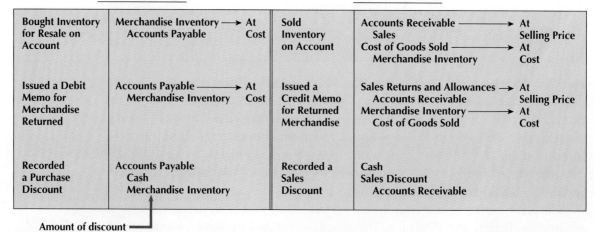

Amount of discount

Figure A-12

PROBLEM FOR APPENDIX

(The blank forms you need are on page 314 of the *Study Guide and Working Papers.*)

Pete's Clock Shops completed the following merchandise transactions in the month of June:

200X

June
1   Purchased merchandise on account from Clock Suppliers, $4,000; terms 2/10, n/30.
3   Sold merchandise on account, $2,000; terms 2/10, n/30. The cost of the merchandise sold was $1,200.
4   Received credit from Clock Suppliers for merchandise returned, $400.
10   Received collections in full, less discounts, from June 3 sales.
11   Paid Clock Suppliers in full, less discount.
14   Purchased office equipment for cash, $500.
15   Purchased $2,800 of merchandise from Abe's Distribution for cash.
16   Received a refund due to defective merchandise from supplier on cash puchase of $400.
17   Purchased merchandise from Rose Corp., $6,000 free on board shipping point (buyer pays freight); terms 2/10, n/30. Freight to be paid on June 20.
18   Sold merchandise for $3,000 cash; the cost of the merchandise sold was $1,600.
20   Paid freight on June 17 purchase, $180.
25   Purchased merchandise from Lee Co., $1,400, free on board destination (seller pays freight); terms 2/10, n/30.
26   Paid Rose Corp. in full, less discount.
27   Made refunds to cash customers for defective clocks, $300. The cost of the defective clocks was $120.

Pete's Clock Shop accounts included the following:

No. 101 Cash, No. 112 Accounts Receivable

No. 120 Merchandise Inventory, No. 124 Office Equipment, No. 201 Accounts Payable

No. 301 P. Rings Capital, No. 401 Sales

No. 412 Sales Discounts, No. 501 Cost of Goods Sold

Assignment

Journalize the transactions using a perpetual inventory system.

Special Journals

With Appendix on What Special Journals Would Look Like in a Perpetual Inventory System

Purchases and Cash Payments

One sport that you love is golf. Now that you're in school you don't have much time to play, but you do your best to keep up with your hero, Tiger Woods, and pro circuit tournaments. On Saturday afternoon, you decide to take a break from your studies and go to the town's municipal golf course and pro shop.

After getting a slot and shooting nine holes, you go into the pro shop to look at all the clubs you wish you owned. Frank Smith, who is the manager of the shop, tells you that he just made a terrific purchase on selected irons, drivers, and putters. Frank told you that he had to really deal to get these prices; in fact, he said he was lucky enough to take advantage of a large cash discount by paying cash to the distributor. After looking at the prices, you definitely agree that Mr. Smith made an excellent purchase on some fine golf clubs.

Driving back to the campus you think about what Frank Smith told you. The pro shop got a special purchase price for the clubs because it took advantage of a cash discount by paying cash. It makes sense and it sounds like a good business practice. You never thought about the purchase side of running a retail business—it's both a buyer as well as a seller.

In Chapter 9 we learned about the use of special journals such as the sales and cash receipts journal and their role in the sales cycle of a merchandising business. In this chapter we discuss two other special journals—the purchases and cash payment journals. The purchases and cash payments journals are essential in the purchasing cycle for a merchandising business. After completing Chapter 10, you'll know about the accounting behind the purchasing side of a merchandising business and have a complete picture of the business as both buyer and seller.

Learning Objectives

- Calculating net purchases. (p. 390)
- Journalizing transactions in a purchases journal. (p. 393)
- Posting from a purchases journal to the accounts payable subsidiary ledger and the general ledger. (p. 393)
- Preparing, journalizing, recording, and posting a debit memorandum. (p. 395)
- Journalizing and posting from a cash payments journal. (p. 398)
- Preparing a schedule of accounts payable. (p. 400)

Chapter 9 focused on the sellers in merchandise companies. This chapter looks at the buyers. Many of the concepts and rules related to special journals carry over to this chapter. At the end of this chapter is an appendix showing how all the special journals in Chapters 9 and 10 would look like in a perpetual inventory system.

Learning Unit 10-1   Chou's Toy Shop: Buyer's View of a Merchandise Company

PURCHASES

Chou brings merchandise into his toy store for resale to customers. The account that records the cost of this merchandise is called Purchases. Suppose Chou buys $4,000 worth of Barbie dolls on account from Mattel Manufacturing on July 6. The Purchases account records all merchandise bought for resale. Here's how this purchase would be recorded if special journals were not used.

	Purchases	
Purchases is a cost.	Dr.	Cr.
The rules work just like they were an expense.	4,000	

This account has a debit balance and is classified as a cost. Purchases represent costs that are directly related to bringing merchandise into the store for resale to customers. The July 6 entry would be analyzed and journalized as in Figure 10-1.

> If Chou's purchased a new display case for the store, it would not show up in the Purchases account. The case is considered equipment that is not for resale to customers.

Accounts Affected	Category	↑ ↓	Rules	T Account Update			
Purchases	Cost	↑	Dr.	Purchases			
					Dr.	Cr.	
					4,000		
Accounts Payable, Mattel	Liability	↑	Cr.	Acc. Payable		Mattel	
				Dr.	Cr.		4,000
				4,000			

Figure 10-1
Purchased Merchandise on Account

	July	6	Purchases		4 0 0 0 00					
			Accounts Payable, Mattel					4 0 0 0 00		
			Purchases on account							

Keep in mind we would have to record to Mattel in the accounts payable subsidiary ledger. We talk about the subsidiary ledger in Learning Unit 10-2.

PURCHASES RETURNS AND ALLOWANCES

Chou noticed that some of the dolls he received were defective, and he notified the manufacturer of the defects. On July 9, Mattel issued a debit memorandum indicating that Chou would get a $500 reduction from the original selling price. Chou then agreed to keep the dolls. The account that records a decrease to a buyer's cost is a contra-cost account called Purchases Returns and Allowances. The account lowers the cost of purchases.

Purchases Returns and Allowances

Dr.	Cr.
	500

← Normal balance is a credit.

Let's analyze this reduction to cost and prepare a general journal entry (Fig 10-2).

Accounts Affected	Category	↑ ↓	Rules	T Account Update	
Accounts Payable Mattel	Liability	↓	Dr.	Acc. Payable Dr. | Cr. 500 | 4,000	Mattel 500 | 4,000
Purchases Returns and Allowances	Contra-cost	↑	Cr.	Purchases Ret. & Allow. Dr. | Cr. | 500	

July	9	Accounts Payable, Mattel		5 0 0 00		
		Purchases Returns and Allowances			5 0 0 00	
		Received debit memorandum				

Figure 10-2
Debit Memorandum Received

When posted to general ledger accounts as well as recorded to Mattel in the accounts payable subsidiary ledger, Chou owes $500 less.

Purchases Discount

Now let's look at the analysis and journal entry when Chou pays Mattel. Mattel offers a 2% cash discount if the invoice is paid within 10 days. To take advantage of this cash discount, Chou sent a check to Mattel on July 15. The discount is taken after the allowance.

$$\begin{array}{l} \$4,000 \\ -\ \ 500\ \ \text{allowance} \\ \hline \$3,500 \times .02 = \$70\ \text{purchases discount} \end{array}$$

The account that records this discount is called **Purchases Discount**. It, too, is a contra-cost account because it lowers the cost of purchases.

Purchases Discount

Dr.	Cr.
	70

← Normal balance is a credit

Remember:
For Mattel, it is a sales discount, whereas for Chou it is a purchases discount.

Remember:
Purchases were a debit; purchases discounts are credits.

Let's analyze and prepare a general journal entry (Fig. 10-3).

Accounts Affected	Category	↑ ↓	Rules	T Account Update	
Accounts Payable Mattel	Liability	↓	Dr.	Acc. Payable Dr. | Cr. 500 | 4,000 3,500 |	Mattel 500 | 4,000 3,500 |
Purchases Discount	Contra-cost	↑	Cr.	Purchases Discount Dr. | Cr. | 70	
Cash	Asset	↓	Cr.	Cash Dr. | Cr. | 3,430	

Figure 10-3
Purchase Discount
Journalized

	July	15	Accounts Payable, Mattel		3 5 0 0 00				
			Purchases Discount				7 0 00		
			Cash				3 4 3 0 00		
			Paid Mattel balance owed						

After the journal entry is posted and recorded to Mattel, the result will show that Chou saved $70 and totally reduced what he owed to Mattel. The actual — or net — cost of his purchase is $3,430, calculated as follows:

Purchases	**$4,000**
− Purchases Returns and Allowances	**500**
− Purchases Discounts	**70**
= Net Purchases	**$3,430**

Freight charges are not taken into consideration in calculating net purchases. Still, they are very important. If the seller is responsible for paying the shipping cost until the goods reach their destination, the freight charges are F.O.B. destination. (F.O.B. stands for "free on board" the carrier.) For example, if a seller located in Boston sold goods F.O.B. destination to a buyer in New York, the seller would have to pay the cost of shipping the goods to the buyer.

If the buyer is responsible for paying the shipping costs, the freight charges are F.O.B. shipping point. In this situation, the seller will sometimes prepay the freight charges as a matter of convenience and will add it to the invoice of the purchaser.

Example:

Bill amount ($800 + $80 prepaid freight)	**$880**
Less 5% cash discount (.05 × $800)	**40**
Amount to be paid by buyer	**$840**

Purchases discounts are not taken on freight. The discount is based on the purchase price.

If the seller ships goods F.O.B. shipping point, legal ownership (title) passes to the buyer *when the goods are shipped*. If goods are shipped by the seller F.O.B. destination, title will change *when goods have reached their destination*.

> F.O.B. Destination:
> Seller pays freight to point of destination.

> F.O.B. Shipping Point:
> Buyer pays freight from seller's shipping point.

> When does title change to goods shipped?

Learning Unit 10-1 Review

AT THIS POINT you should be able to

- Explain and calculate purchases, purchases returns and allowances, and purchases discounts. (p. 388)
- Calculate net purchases. (p. 390)
- Explain why purchase discounts are not taken on freight. (p. 390)
- Compare and contrast F.O.B. destination with F.O.B. shipping point. (p. 390)

SELF-REVIEW QUIZ 10-1

(The forms you need can be found on page 316 of the *Study Guide and Working Papers*.)
Respond true or false to the following:

1. Net purchases = Purchases − Purchases Returns and Allowances − Purchases Discount.

2. Purchases is a contra-cost.

3. F.O.B. destination means the seller covers shipping cost and retains title till goods reach their destination.

4. Purchases discounts are not taken on freight.

5. Purchases Discount is a contra-cost account.

SOLUTIONS TO SELF-REVIEW QUIZ 10-1

1. True **2.** False **3.** True **4.** True **5.** True

Quiz Tip:

	Buyer			Seller	
Purchase	Dr.	Cost	Sale	Cr	Revenue
PRA	Cr.	Contra-cost	SRA	Dr.	Contra-revenue
PD	Cr.	Contra-cost	SD	Dr.	Contra-revenue

Learning Unit 10-2   Steps Taken in Purchasing Merchandise and Recording Purchases

Merchandising companies must take specific steps when they purchase goods for resale. Let's look at the steps Art's Wholesale Clothing Company took when it ordered goods from Abby Blake Company on April 3.

Step 1: Prepare a Purchase Requisition at Art's Wholesale Clothing Company

The inventory clerk notes a low inventory level of ladies' jackets for resale, so the clerk sends a **purchase requisition** to the purchasing department. A duplicate copy is sent to the accounting department. A third copy remains with the department that initiated the request, to be used as a check on the purchasing department.

> Authorized personnel initiate purchase requisition.

Step 2: Purchasing Department of Art's Wholesale Clothing Company Prepares a Purchase Order

After checking various price lists and suppliers' catalogs, the purchasing department fills out a form called a **purchase order**. This form gives Abby Blake Company the authority to ship the ladies' jackets ordered by Art's Wholesale Clothing Company (see Fig. 10-4).

> Four copies of purchase order: (1) (original) to supplier, (2) to accounting department, (3) to department that initiated purchase requisition, and (4) to file of purchasing department.

Step 3: Sales Invoice Prepared by Abby Blake Company

Abby Blake Company receives the purchase order and prepares a sales invoice. The sales invoice for the seller is the **purchase invoice** for the buyer. A sales invoice is shown in Figure 10-5.

The invoice shows that the goods will be shipped F.O.B. Englewood Cliffs. Thus, Art's Wholesale Clothing Company is responsible for paying the shipping costs.

The sales invoice also shows a freight charge. Thus, Abby Blake prepaid the shipping costs as a matter of convenience. Art's will repay the freight charges when it pays the invoice.

Figure 10-4
Purchase Order

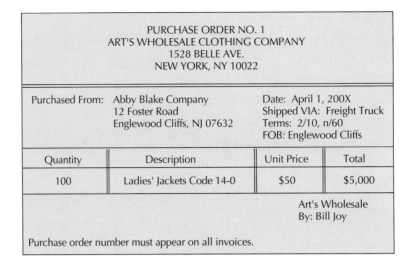

```
                    PURCHASE ORDER NO. 1
              ART'S WHOLESALE CLOTHING COMPANY
                      1528 BELLE AVE.
                     NEW YORK, NY 10022
```

| Purchased From: | Abby Blake Company 12 Foster Road Englewood Cliffs, NJ 07632 | Date: April 1, 200X Shipped VIA: Freight Truck Terms: 2/10, n/60 FOB: Englewood Cliffs |

Quantity	Description	Unit Price	Total
100	Ladies' Jackets Code 14-0	$50	$5,000

Art's Wholesale
By: Bill Joy

Purchase order number must appear on all invoices.

Figure 10-5
Sales Invoice

```
                    SALES INVOICE NO. 228
                     ABBY BLAKE COMPANY
                      12 FOSTER ROAD
                 ENGLEWOOD, CLIFFS, NJ 07632
```

| Sold To: | Art's Wholesale Clothing Co. 1528 Belle Ave. New York, NY 10022 | Date: April 3, 200X Shipped VIA: Freight Truck Terms: 2/10, n/60 Your Order No: 1 FOB: Englewood Cliffs |

Quantity	Description	Unit Price	Total
100	Ladies' Jackets Code 14-0 Freight	$50	$5,000 50 $5,050

Step 4: Receiving the Goods

When goods are received, Art's Wholesale inspects the shipment and completes a **receiving report.** The receiving report verifies that the exact merchandise that was ordered was received in good condition.

Step 5: Verifying the Numbers

Before the invoice is approved for recording and payment, the accounting department must check the purchase order, invoice, and receiving report to make sure that all are in agreement and that no steps have been omitted. The form used for checking and approval is an **invoice approval form** (see Fig. 10-6).

Figure 10-6
Invoice Approval Form

```
                    INVOICE APPROVAL FORM
                   Art's Wholesale Clothing Co.

  Purchase Order #              _____
  Requisition check            _____
  Purchase Order check         _____
  Receiving Report check       _____
  Invoice check                _____
  Approved for Payment         _____
```

Keep in mind that Art's Wholesale Clothing Company does not record this purchase until the *invoice is approved for recording and payment.* Abby Blake Company records this transaction in its records when the sales invoice is prepared, however.

THE PURCHASES JOURNAL AND ACCOUNTS PAYABLE SUBSIDIARY LEDGER

Let's look at how Art's Wholesale Clothing Company journalizes, posts, and records to the accounts payable subsidiary ledger (Fig. 10-7). We also look at the purchases

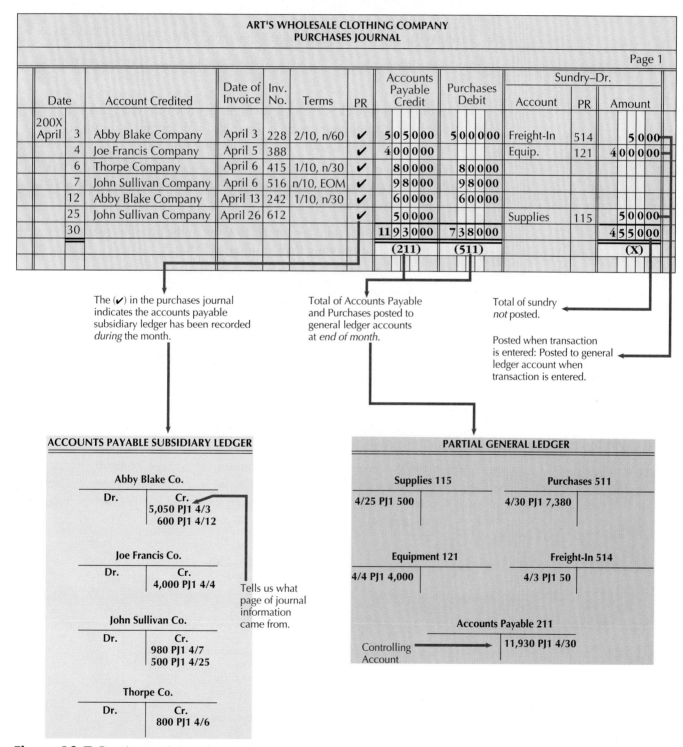

Figure 10-7 Purchases Journal

journal, a multicolumn special journal Art's uses to record the buying of merchandise or other items on account, and the accounts payable subsidiary ledger, an alphabetical list of the amounts owed to creditors from purchases on account.

For example, on April 3 Art's Wholesale Clothing Company records in its purchases journal the following:

- Date: April 3, 200X.
- Account Credited: Abby Blake Company.
- Date of Invoice: April 3.
- Invoice Number: 228.
- Terms: 2/10, n/60.
- Accounts Payable: $5,050; Purchases: $5,000; Freight-In, $50.

As soon as the information is journalized in the purchases journal (see Fig. 10-7), you should:

1. Record to Abby Blake Co. in the accounts payable subsidiary ledger to indicate that the amount owed is now $5,050. When this is complete, place a "✓" in the PR column of the purchases journal.

2. Post to Freight-In, account no. 514, in the general ledger right away. When this posting is complete, record the 514 in the PR column under Sundry in the purchases journal.

The posting and recording rules are similar to those in the previous chapter, but here we are looking at the buyer rather than at the seller.

THE DEBIT MEMORANDUM

In Chapter 9, Art's Wholesale Clothing Company had to handle returned goods as a seller. It did so by issuing credit memoranda to customers who returned or received an allowance on the price. In this chapter, Art's must handle returns as a buyer. It does so by using debit memoranda. A debit memorandum is a piece of paper issued by a customer to a seller. It indicates that a return or allowance has occurred.

Suppose Art's Wholesale had purchased men's hats for $800 from Thorpe Company on April 6 (p. 393). On April 9, 20 hats valued at $200 were found to have defective brims. Art's issued a debit memorandum to Thorpe Company, as shown in Figure 10-8. At some point in the future, Thorpe will issue Art's a credit memorandum. Let's look at how Art's Wholesale Clothing Company handles such a transaction in its accounting records.

> See Figure 10-7 for a complete purchases journal.

> Note that the normal balance in the accounts payable subsidiary ledger is a credit.

Figure 10-8
Debit Memorandum

> A debit memo shows that Art's does not owe as much money as was indicated in the company's purchases journal.

DEBIT MEMORANDUM		No. 1
Art's Wholesale Clothing Company 1528 Belle Ave. New York, NY 10022		
TO: Thorpe Company 3 Access Road Beverly, MA 01915		April 9, 200X
WE DEBIT your account as follows:		

Quantity		Unit Cost	Total
20	Men's Hats Code 827 – defective brims	$10	$200

Journalizing and Posting the Debit Memo

First, let's look at a transactional analysis chart.

Accounts Affected	Category	↑ ↓	Rules
Accounts Payable	Liability	↓	Dr.
Purchases Returns and Allowances	Contra-cost	↑	Cr.

Next, let's examine the journal entry for the debit memorandum (Fig. 10-9).

GENERAL JOURNAL

Page 1

Date		Account Titles and Description	PR	Dr.	Cr.
April	9	Accounts Payable, Thorpe Company	211 ✓	2 0 0 00	
		Purchases Returns and Allowances	513		2 0 0 00
		Debit memo #1			

> Result of debit memo: debits or reduces Accounts Payable. On seller's books, accounts affected would include Sales Returns and Allowances and Accounts Receivable.

Figure 10-9
Debit Memorandum Journalized and Posted

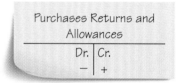

> A contra-cost-of-goods-sold account.

The two postings and one recording are

1. **211:** Post to Accounts Payable as a debit in the general ledger account no. 211. When done, place in the PR column the account number, 211, above the diagonal on the same line as Accounts Payable in the journal.

2. **✓:** Record to Thorpe Co. in the accounts payable subsidiary ledger to show that Art's doesn't owe Thorpe as much money. When done, place a ✓ in the journal in the PR column below the diagonal line on the same line as Accounts Payable in the journal.

3. **513:** Post to Purchases Returns and Allowances as a credit in the general ledger (account no. 513). When done, place the account number, 513, in the PR column of the journal on the same line as Purchases Returns and Allowances. (If equipment was returned that was not merchandise for resale, we would credit Equipment and not Purchases Returns and Allowances.)

Learning Unit 10-2 Review

AT THIS POINT you should be able to

- Explain the relationship between a purchase requisition, a purchase order, and a purchase invoice. (p. 391)
- Explain why a typical invoice approval form may be used. (p. 392)
- Journalize transactions into a purchases journal. (p. 393)
- Explain how to record the accounts payable subsidiary ledger and post to the general ledger from a purchases journal. (p. 393)
- Explain a debit memorandum and be able to journalize an entry resulting from its issuance. (p. 394)

SELF-REVIEW QUIZ 10-2

(The forms you need are on pages 317 of the *Study Guide and Working Papers*.)
   Journalize the following transactions into the purchases journal or general journal for Munroe Co. Record accounts as appropriate to the accounts payable subsidiary ledger and post to the general ledger. Use the same journal headings we used for Art's Wholesale Clothing Company.

200X

May 5   Bought merchandise on account from Flynn Co., invoice no. 512, dated May 6, $900, terms 1/10, n/30.

   7   Bought merchandise from John Butler Company, invoice no. 403, dated May 7, $1,000, terms n/10 EOM.

   13   Issued debit memo no. 1 to Flynn Co. for merchandise returned, $300, from invoice no. 512.

   17   Purchased $400 of equipment on account from John Butler Company, invoice no. 413, dated May 18.

SOLUTION TO SELF-REVIEW QUIZ 10-2

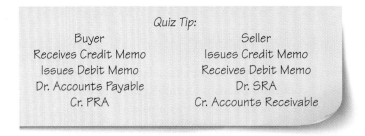

Quiz Tip:

Buyer	Seller
Receives Credit Memo	Issues Credit Memo
Issues Debit Memo	Receives Debit Memo
Dr. Accounts Payable	Dr. SRA
Cr. PRA	Cr. Accounts Receivable

			Date of Invoice	Inv. No.	Terms	PR	Accounts Payable Credit	Purchases Debit	Sundry–Dr. Account	PR	Amount
Date		Account Credited									
200X May	5	Flynn Co.	May 6	512	1/10, n/30	✔	9 0 0 00	9 0 0 00			
	7	John Butler	May 7	403	n/10, EOM	✔	1 0 0 0 00	1 0 0 0 00			
	17	John Butler	May 18	413		✔	4 0 0 00		Equip.	121	4 0 0 00
	31						2 3 0 0 00	1 9 0 0 00			4 0 0 00
							(212)	(512)			(X)

Page 2

Figure 10-10 Purchases Journal

Figure 10-11
General Journal

MUNROE CO.
GENERAL JOURNAL

Page 1

Date		Account Titles and Description	PR	Dr.	Cr.
200X May	13	Accounts Payable, Flynn Co.	212 ✔	3 0 0 00	
		Purchases Returns and Allowances	513		3 0 0 00
		Issued Debit Memo			

Figure 10-12
Accounts Payable
Subsidiary Ledger

ACCOUNTS PAYABLE SUBSIDIARY LEDGER

JOHN BUTLER COMPANY
18 REED RD.
HOMEWOOD, ILLINOIS 60430

Date		Explanation	Post. Ref.	Debit	Credit	Cr. Balance
200X May	7		PJ2		1 0 0 0 00	1 0 0 0 00
	17		PJ2		4 0 0 00	1 4 0 0 00

FLYNN COMPANY
15 FOSS AVE.
ENGLEWOOD CLIFFS, NEW JERSEY 07632

Date		Explanation	Post. Ref.	Debit	Credit	Cr. Balance
200X May	5		PJ2		9 0 0 00	9 0 0 00
	13		GJ1	3 0 0 00		6 0 0 00

PARTIAL GENERAL LEDGER

Equipment   Account No. 121

Date		Explanation	Post. Ref.	Debit	Credit	Balance Debit	Balance Credit
200X May	17		PJ2	4 0 0 00		4 0 0 00	

Accounts Payable   Account No. 212

Date		Explanation	Post. Ref.	Debit	Credit	Balance Debit	Balance Credit
200X May	13		GJ1	3 0 0 00		3 0 0 00	
	31		PJ2		2 3 0 0 00		2 0 0 0 00

Purchases   Account No. 512

Date		Explanation	Post. Ref.	Debit	Credit	Balance Debit	Balance Credit
200X May	31		PJ2	1 9 0 0 00		1 9 0 0 00	

Purchases, Returns, and Allowances   Account No. 513

Date		Explanation	Post. Ref.	Debit	Credit	Balance Debit	Balance Credit
200X May	13		GJ1		3 0 0 00		3 0 0 00

Figure 10-13 Partial General Ledger

Learning Unit 10-3   The Cash Payments Journal and Schedule of Accounts Payable

Art's Wholesale Clothing Company will record all payments made in cash (or by check) in a cash payments journal (also called a cash disbursements journal). In many ways the structure of this journal resembles that of the cash receipts journal discussed in Chapter 9. Now, however, we are looking at the outward flow of cash instead of the inward flow.

Art's conducted the following cash transactions in April:

200X

Apr.	2	Issued check no. 1 to Pete Blum for insurance paid in advance, $900.
	7	Issued check no. 2 to Joe Francis Company in payment of its April 5 invoice no. 388.
	9	Issued check no. 3 to Rick Flo Co. for merchandise purchased for cash, $800.
	12	Issued check no. 4 to Thorpe Company in payment of its April 6 invoice no. 414 less the return and discount.
	28	Issued check no. 5, $700, for salaries paid.

Figure 10-14 on pages 399–400 shows the cash payments journal for the end of April along with the recordings to the accounts payable subsidiary ledger and postings to the general ledger. Study the diagram; we review it in a moment.

> Posting and recording rules for this journal are similar to those for the cash receipts journal in Chapter 9.

JOURNALIZING, POSTING, AND RECORDING FROM THE CASH PAYMENTS JOURNAL TO THE ACCOUNTS PAYABLE SUBSIDIARY LEDGER AND THE GENERAL LEDGER

Figure 10-14 shows how Art's Wholesale Clothing Company recorded the payment of cash on April 12 to Thorpe Company. The purchases journal shows that Art's purchased $800 of merchandise from Thorpe on account on April 6. The amount Art's owes is discounted 1%. The amount owed ($800–$200 returns) is recorded in the accounts payable subsidiary ledger as soon as the entry is made in the cash payments journal. The payment reduces the balance to Thorpe to zero. Art's Wholesale Clothing Company receives a $6 purchases discount.

At the end of the month, the totals of the Cash, Purchases Discount, and Accounts Payable accounts are posted to the general ledger. The total of Sundry is *not* posted. The accounts Prepaid Insurance, Purchases, and Salaries Expense are posted to the general ledger at the time the entry is put in the journal.

> As explained in Chapter 9, Sundry is a miscellaneous accounts column that provides flexibility for reporting infrequent transactions that result in an inflow of cash.

The cash payments journal of Art's Wholesale Clothing Company can be cross-footed as follows:

$$\textbf{Debit} = \textbf{Credit Columns}$$
$$\textbf{Sundry} + \textbf{Accounts Payable} = \textbf{Purchases Discounts} + \textbf{Cash}$$
$$\$2,400 + \$4,600 = \$6 + \$6,994$$
$$\underline{\underline{\$7,000}} = \underline{\underline{\$7,000}}$$

> Remember: There is no discount on sales tax or freight.

Schedule of Accounts Payable

Now let's prove that the sum of the accounts payable subsidiary ledger at the end of the month is equal to the controlling account, Accounts Payable, at the end of April for Art's Wholesale Clothing Company. To do so, creditors with an ending balance in Art's accounts payable subsidiary ledger must be listed in the schedule of accounts payable (see Fig. 10-15). At the end of the month, the total owed ($7,130) in Accounts

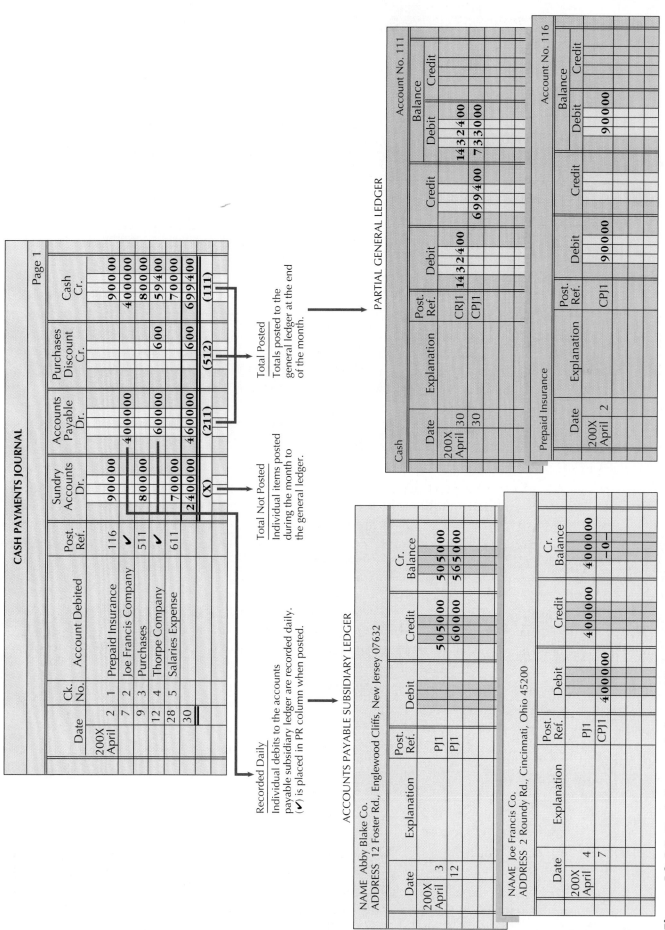

Figure 10-14 Cash Payments Journal Recording and Posting

Controlling Account →

Accounts Payable — Account No. 211

Date	Explanation	Post. Ref.	Debit	Credit	Balance Debit	Balance Credit
200X April 9		GJ1	20000		20000	
30		PJ1		1193000		1173000
30		CPJ1	460000			713000

Purchases — Account No. 511

Date	Explanation	Post. Ref.	Debit	Credit	Balance Debit	Balance Credit
200X April 9		CPJ1	80000		80000	
30		PJ1	738000		818000	

Purchases Discount — Account No. 512

Date	Explanation	Post. Ref.	Debit	Credit	Balance Debit	Balance Credit
200X April 30		CPJ1		600		600

Salaries Expense — Account No. 611

Date	Explanation	Post. Ref.	Debit	Credit	Balance Debit	Balance Credit
200X April 28		CPJ1	70000		70000	

NAME John Sullivan Co.
ADDRESS 18 Print St., Wellesley, Mass. 01980

Date	Explanation	Post. Ref.	Debit	Credit	Cr. Balance
200X April 7		PJ1		98000	98000
25		PJ1		50000	148000

NAME Thorpe Co.
ADDRESS 3 Access Rd., Chicago, Illinois 60430

Date	Explanation	Post. Ref.	Debit	Credit	Cr. Balance
200X April 6		PJ1		80000	80000
9		GJ1	20000		60000
12		CPJ1	60000		-0-

Figure 10-14 (continued)

ART'S WHOLESALE CLOTHING COMPANY SCHEDULE OF ACCOUNTS PAYABLE APRIL 30, 200X		
Abby Blake Co.		$5 6 5 0 00
John Sullivan Co.		1 4 8 0 00
Total Accounts Payable		$7 1 3 0 00

Figure 10-15
Schedule of Accounts Payable

Payable, the controlling account in the general ledger, should equal the sum owed the individual creditors that are listed on the schedule of accounts payable. If it doesn't, the journalizing, posting, and recording must be checked to ensure that they are complete. Also, the balances of each title should be checked.

Trade Discounts

Trade discounts are reductions from the purchase price. Usually, they are given to customers who buy items to resell or to use to produce other salable goods.

Amount of Trade Discount = List Price − Net Price

Different trade discounts are available to different classes of customers. Often, trade discounts are listed in catalogs that contain the list price and the amount of trade discount available. Such catalogs usually are updated by discount sheets.

Trade discounts have *no relationship* to whether a customer is paying a bill early. Trade discounts and list prices are not shown in the accounts of either the purchaser or the seller. Cash discounts are not taken on the amount of trade discount.

For example, look at the following:

- List price, $800.
- 30% trade discount.
- 5% cash discount.
- Thus: Invoice cost of $560 ($800 − $240) less the cash discount of $28 ($560 × .05) results in a final cost of $532 if the cash discount is taken.

The purchaser as well as the seller would record the invoice amount at $560.

> Trade discounts are not reflected on the books.

Learning Unit 10-3 Review

AT THIS POINT you should be able to

- Journalize, post, and record transactions utilizing a cash payments journal. (p. 398)
- Prepare a schedule of accounts payable. (p. 401)
- Compare and contrast a cash discount to a trade discount. (p. 401)

SELF-REVIEW QUIZ 10-3

(The forms you need are on pages 319–322 of the *Study Guide and Working Papers*.)

Given the following information, journalize, crossfoot, and, when appropriate, record and post the transactions of Melissa Company. Use the same headings as used for Art's Clothing. All purchases discounts are 2/12, n/30. The cash payments journal is page 2.

Accounts Payable Subsidiary Ledger

Name	Balance	Invoice No.
Bob Finkelstein	$300	488
Al Jeep	200	410

Partial General Ledger

Account No.	Balance
Cash 110	$700
Accounts Payable 210	500
Purchases Discount 511	—
Advertising Expense 610	—

200X

June 1 Issued check no. 15 to Al Jeep in payment of its May 25 invoice no. 410 less purchases discount.

8 Issued check no. 16 to Moss Advertising Co. to pay advertising bill due, $75, no discount.

9 Issued check no. 17 to Bob Finkelstein in payment of its May 28 invoice no. 488 less purchases discount.

SOLUTION TO SELF-REVIEW QUIZ 10-3

MELISSA COMPANY
CASH PAYMENTS JOURNAL

Page 2

Date	Ck. No.	Account Debited	Post. Ref.	Sundry Accounts Dr.	Accounts Payable Dr.	Purchases Discount Cr.	Cash Cr.
200X June 1	15	Al Jeep	✔		200 00	4 00	196 00
8	16	Advertising Expense	610	75 00			75 00
9	17	Bob Finkelstein	✔		300 00	6 00	294 00
30				75 00	500 00	10 00	565 00
				(X)	(210)	(511)	(110)

$75 + $500 = $10 + $565
$575 = $575

Figure 10-16 Cash Payments Journal

ACCOUNTS PAYABLE SUBSIDIARY LEDGER

NAME Bob Finkelstein
ADDRESS 112 Flying Highway, Trenton, New Jersey 08611

Date		Explanation	Post. Ref.	Debit	Credit	Cr. Balance
200X June	1	Balance	✔			3 0 0 00
	9		CPJ2	3 0 0 00		–0–

NAME Al Jeep
ADDRESS 118 Wang Rd., Saugus, Mass. 01432

Date		Explanation	Post. Ref.	Debit	Credit	Cr. Balance
200X June	1	Balance	✔			2 0 0 00
	1		CPJ2	2 0 0 00		–0–

Figure 10-17
Accounts Payable
Subsidiary Ledger

Quiz Tip:
The normal balance of
the accounts payable
subsidiary ledger is
a credit.

PARTIAL GENERAL LEDGER

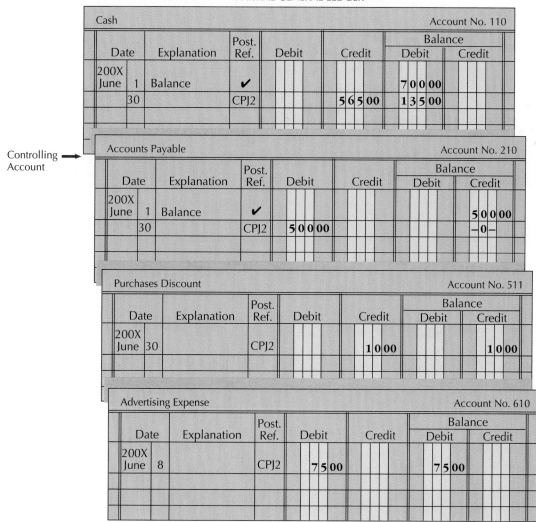

Cash — Account No. 110

Date		Explanation	Post. Ref.	Debit	Credit	Balance Debit	Balance Credit
200X June	1	Balance	✔			7 0 0 00	
	30		CPJ2		5 6 5 00	1 3 5 00	

Controlling Account →

Accounts Payable — Account No. 210

Date		Explanation	Post. Ref.	Debit	Credit	Balance Debit	Balance Credit
200X June	1	Balance	✔				5 0 0 00
	30		CPJ2	5 0 0 00			–0–

Purchases Discount — Account No. 511

Date		Explanation	Post. Ref.	Debit	Credit	Balance Debit	Balance Credit
200X June	30		CPJ2		1 0 00		1 0 00

Advertising Expense — Account No. 610

Date		Explanation	Post. Ref.	Debit	Credit	Balance Debit	Balance Credit
200X June	8		CPJ2	7 5 00		7 5 00	

Figure 10-18 Partial General Ledger

SOLUTION & TIPS TO COMPREHENSIVE PROBLEM: PUTTING THE PIECES TOGETHER

(The forms you need are on pages 322–324 of the *Study Guide and Working Papers.*)

Record the following transactions into special or general journals. Record and post as appropriate.

Note: All credit sales are 2/10, n/30. All merchandise purchased on account has 3/10, n/30 credit terms.

Solution Tips to Journalizing

200X

Mar.	1	J. Ling invested $2,000 into the business.	CRJ
	1	Sold merchandise on account to Balder Co., $500, invoice no. 1.	SJ
	2	Purchased merchandise on account from Case Co., $500.	PJ
	4	Sold $2,000 of merchandise for cash.	CRJ
	6	Paid Case Co. from previous purchases on account, check no. 1.	CPJ
	8	Sold merchandise on account to Lewis Co., $1,000, invoice no. 2.	SJ
	10	Received payment from Balder for invoice no. 1.	CRJ
	12	Issued a credit memorandum to Lewis Co. for $200 for faulty merchandise.	GJ
	14	Received payment from Lewis Co.	CRJ
	16	Purchased merchandise on account from Noone Co., $1,000.	PJ
	17	Purchased equipment on account from Case Co., $300.	PJ
	18	Issued a debit memorandum to Noone Co. for $500 for defective merchandise.	GJ
	20	Paid salaries, $300, check no. 2.	CPJ
	24	Paid Noone balance owed, check no. 3.	CPJ

Figure 10-19
Sales Journal

Record accounts receivable subsidiary ledger immediately.

J. LING, CO.
SALES JOURNAL

Page 1

Date		Account Debited	Terms	Invoice No.	PR	Dr. Acc. Rec Cr. Sales
200X Mar.	1	Balder Co.	2/10, N/30	1	✔	500 00
	8	Lewis Co.	2/10, N/30	2	✔	1000 00
	31					1500 00
						(112) (410)

Total posted at end of month to these accounts.

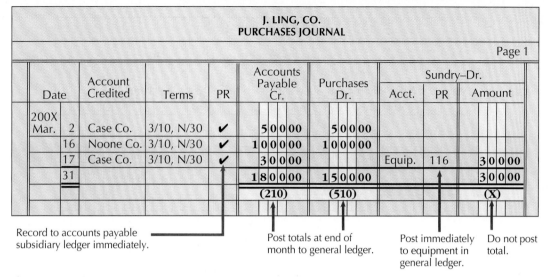

Figure 10-20 Purchases Journal

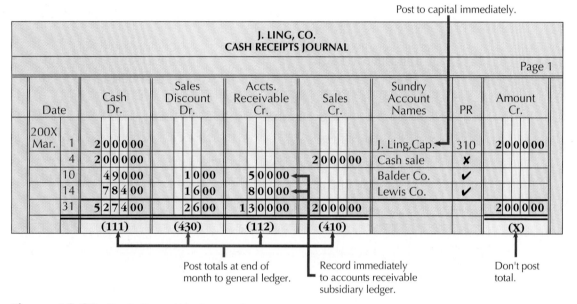

Figure 10-21 Cash Receipts Journal

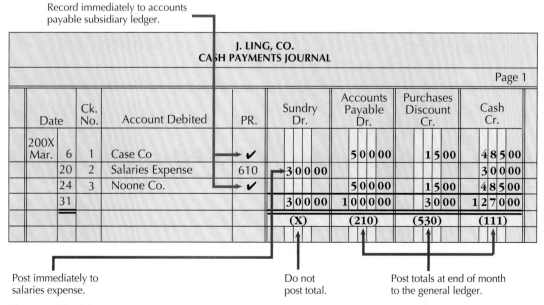

Figure 10-22 Cash Payments Journal

Figure 10-23
General Journal

	Date		Account Titles and Description	PR	Dr.	Cr.
200X Mar.	12		Sales Returns and Allowances	420	2 0 0 00	
			Accounts Receivable, Lewis Co.	112 ✓		2 0 0 00
			Issued Credit Memo			
	18		Accounts Payable, Noone Co.	210 ✓	5 0 0 00	
			Purchases Returns and Allowances	520		5 0 0 00
			Issued Debit Memo			

GENERAL JOURNAL   Page 1

Record and post immediately to subsidiary and general ledgers.

Figure 10-24
Subsidiary and General Ledgers

ACCOUNTS RECEIVABLE SUBSIDIARY LEDGER

Balder Company

Date	PR	Dr.	Cr.	Dr. Bal.
200X 3/1	SJ1	500		500
3/10	CRJ1		500	——

Lewis Company

Date	PR	Dr.	Cr.	Dr. Bal.
200X 3/8	SJ1	1,000		1,000
3/12	GJ1		200	800
3/14	CPJ1		800	——

ACCOUNTS PAYABLE SUBSIDIARY LEDGER

Case Company

Date	PR	Dr.	Cr.	Cr. Bal.
200X 3/2	PJ1		500	500
3/6	CPJ1	500		——
3/17	PJ1		300	300

Noone Company

Date	PR	Dr.	Cr.	Cr. Bal.
200X 3/16	PJ1		1,000	1,000
3/18	GJ1	500		500
3/24	CPJ1	500		——

GENERAL LEDGER

Cash 111

3/31 CRJ1 5,274	1,270 3/31 CPJ1
Balance 4,004	

Sales 410

	1,500 3/31 SJ1
	2,000 3/31 CRJ1
	3,500 Balance

Accounts Receivable 112

3/31 SJ1 1,500	200 3/12 GJ1
Balance 0	1,300 3/31 CRJ1

Sales Returns + Allowances 420

3/12 GJ1 200	

Equipment 116

3/17 PJ1 300	

Sales Discount 430

3/31 CRJ1 26	

Accounts Payable 210			
3/18 GJ1	500	1,800	3/31 PJ1
3/31 CPJ1	1,000	300	Balance

Purchases 510		
3/31 PJ1	1,500	

J. Ling, Capital 310		
	2,000	3/1 CRJ1

Purchase Ret. + Allow. 520		
	500	3/18 GJ1

Purchase Discount 530		
	30	3/31 CPJ1

Salaries Expense 610		
3/20 CPJ1	300	

Summary of Solution Tips

Chapter 9: Seller

Sales journal
Cash receipts journal
Accounts receivable subsidiary ledger
Sales (Cr.)
Sales Returns + Allowances (Dr.)
Sales Discounts (Dr.)
Accounts Receivable (Dr.)
Issue a credit memo
   or
Receive a debit memo
Schedule of accounts receivable

Chapter 10: Buyer

Purchases journal
Cash payments journal
Accounts payable subsidiary ledger
Purchases (Dr.)
Purchase Returns + Allowances (Cr.)
Purchase Discounts (Cr.)
Accounts Payable (Cr.)
Receive a credit memo
   or
Issue a debit memo
Schedule of accounts payable

When Do I Do What? A Step-by-Step Walk-Through of This Comprehensive Problem

Transaction What to Do Step-by-Step

200X

Mar. 1 *Money Received:* Record in cash receipts journal. Post immediately to J. Ling, Capital, because it is in Sundry.

    1 *Sale on Account:* Record in sales journal. Record immediately to Balder Co. in accounts receivable subsidiary ledger. Place a ✓ in PR column of sales journal when subsidiary is updated.

    2 *Buy Merchandise on Account:* Record in purchases journal. Record to Case Co. immediately in the accounts payable subsidiary ledger.

    4 *Money In:* Record in cash receipts journal. No posting needed (put an ✕ in PR column).

    6 *Money Out:* Record in cash payments journal. Save $15, which is a Purchases Discount. Record immediately to Case Co. in accounts payable subsidiary ledger (the full amount of $500).

    8 *Sales on Account:* Record in sales journal. Update immediately to Lewis in accounts receivable subsidiary ledger.

   10 *Money In:* Record in cash receipts journal. Because Balder pays within 10 days, it gets a $10 discount. Record the full amount immediately to Balder in the accounts receivable subsidiary ledger.

Transaction	What to Do Step-by-Step
12	*Returns:* Record in general journal. Seller issues credit memo resulting in higher sales returns and customers owing less. All postings and recordings are done immediately.
14	*Money In:* Record in cash receipts journal:

$$\$1,000 - \$200 \text{ returns} = \$800$$
$$\underline{\times .02}$$
$$\$\ 16 \text{ discount}$$

Record immediately the $800 to Lewis in the accounts receivable subsidiary ledger.

16	*Buy Now, Pay Later:* Record in purchases journal. Record immediately to Noone Co. in the accounts payable subsidiary ledger.
17	*Buy Now, Pay Later:* Record in purchases journal in Sundry. This item is not merchandise for resale. Record and post immediately.
18	*Returns:* Record in general ledger. Buyer issues a debit memo reducing the Accounts Payable due to Purchases Return and Allowances. Post and record immediately.
20	*Salaries:* Record in cash payments journal, sundry column. Post immediately to Salaries Expense.
24	*Money Out:* Record in cash payments journal. Save 3% ($15), a Purchases Discount. Record immediately to accounts payable subsidiary ledger that you reduce Noone by $500.

End of Month:

Post totals (except Sundry) of special journal to the general ledger.

Note: In this problem at the end of the month, (1) Accounts Receivable in the general ledger, the controlling account, has a zero balance, as does each title in the accounts receivable subsidiary ledger; and (2) the balance in Accounts Payable (the controlling account) is $300. In the accounts payable subsidiary ledger, we owe Case $300. The sum of the accounts payable subsidiary ledger does equal the balance in the controlling account at the end of the month.

Summary of Key Points

Learning Unit 10-1

1. Purchases are merchandise for resale. It is a cost.
2. Purchases Returns and Allowances and Purchases Discount are contra-costs.
3. *F.O.B. shipping point* means that the purchaser of the goods is responsible for covering the shipping costs. If the terms were *F.O.B. destination,* the seller would be responsible for covering the shipping costs until the goods reached their destination.
4. Purchases discounts are not taken on freight.

Learning Unit 10-2

1. The steps for buying merchandise from a company may include the following:
   a. The requesting department prepares a purchase requisition.
   b. The purchasing department prepares a purchase order.
   c. Seller receives the order and prepares a sales invoice (a purchase invoice for the buyer).

    d. Buyer receives the goods and prepares a receiving report.

    e. Accounting department verifies and approves the invoice for payment.

2. The purchases journal records the buying of merchandise or other items on account.

3. The accounts payable subsidiary ledger, organized in alphabetical order, is not in the same book as Accounts Payable, the controlling account in the general ledger.

4. At the end of the month the total of all creditors' ending balances in the accounts payable subsidiary ledger should equal the ending balance in Accounts Payable, the controlling account in the general ledger.

5. A debit memorandum (issued by the buyer) indicates that the amount owed from a previous purchase is being reduced because some goods were defective or not up to a specific standard and thus were returned or an allowance requested. On receiving the debit memorandum, the seller will issue a credit memorandum.

Learning Unit 10-3

1. All payments of cash (check) are recorded in the cash payments journal.

2. At the end of the month, the schedule of accounts payable, a list of ending amounts owed individual creditors, should equal the ending balance in Accounts Payable, the controlling account in the general ledger.

3. Trade discounts are deductions off the list price that have nothing to do with early payments (cash discounts). Invoice amounts are recorded *after* the trade discount is deducted. Cash discounts are not taken on trade discounts.

Key Terms

Accounts payable subsidiary ledger A book or file that contains in alphabetical order the name of the creditor and amount owed from purchases on account.

Cash payments journal (cash disbursements journal) A special journal that records all transactions involving the payment of cash.

Controlling account The account in the general ledger that summarizes or controls a subsidiary ledger. Example: The Accounts Payable account in the general ledger is the controlling account for the accounts payable subsidiary ledger. After postings are complete, it shows the total amount owed from purchases made on account.

Debit memorandum A memo issued by a purchaser to a seller, indicating that some Purchases Returns and Allowances have occurred and therefore the purchaser now owes less money on account.

F.O.B. Free on board, which means without shipping charge either to the buyer or seller up to or from a specified location. In the view of one or the other, the shipment is *free* on board the carrier.

F.O.B. destination *Seller* pays or is responsible for the cost of freight to purchaser's location or destination.

F.O.B. shipping point *Purchaser* pays or is responsible for the shipping costs from seller's shipping point to purchaser's location.

Invoice approval form Used by the accounting department in checking the invoice and finally approving it for recording and payment.

Purchase invoice The seller's sales invoice, which is sent to the purchaser.

Purchase order A form used in business to place an order for the buying of goods from a seller.

Purchase requisition A form used within a business by the requesting department asking the purchasing department of the business to buy specific goods.

Purchases Merchandise for resale. It is a cost.

Purchases Discount A contra-cost account in the general ledger that records discounts offered by suppliers of merchandise for prompt payment of purchases by buyers.

Purchases journal A multicolumn special journal that records the buying of merchandise or other items on account.

Purchases Returns and Allowances A contra-cost account in the ledger that records the amount of defective or unacceptable merchandise returned to suppliers and/or price reductions given for defective items.

Receiving report A business form used to notify the appropriate people of the ordered goods received along with the quantities and specific condition of the goods.

Questions, Mini Exercises, Exercises, and Problems

Discussion Questions

1. Explain how net purchases is calculated.
2. What is the normal balance of Purchases Discount?
3. What is a contra-cost?
4. Explain the difference between F.O.B. shipping point and F.O.B. destination.
5. F.O.B. destination means that title to the goods will switch to the buyer when goods are shipped. Agree or disagree. Why?
6. What is the normal balance of each creditor in the accounts payable subsidiary ledger?
7. Why doesn't the balance of the controlling account, Accounts Payable, equal the sum of the accounts payable subsidiary ledger during the month?
8. What is the relationship between a purchase requisition and a purchase order?
9. What purpose could a typical invoice approval form serve?
10. Explain the difference between merchandise and equipment.
11. Why would the purchaser issue a debit memorandum?
12. Explain the relationship between a purchases journal and a cash payments journal.
13. Explain why a trade discount is not a cash discount.

Mini Exercises

(The forms you need are on page 326 of the *Study Guide and Working Papers.*)

Overview

1. Complete the following table:

To the Seller		To the Buyer
Sales	↔	a. _____
Sales Returns and Allowances	↔	b. _____
Sales discount	↔	c. _____
Sales journal	↔	d. _____
Cash receipts journal	↔	e. _____
Credit memorandum	↔	f. _____
Schedule of accounts receivable	↔	g. _____
Accounts receivable subsidiary ledger	↔	h. _____

Blueprint: Purchases and Cash Payments Journals

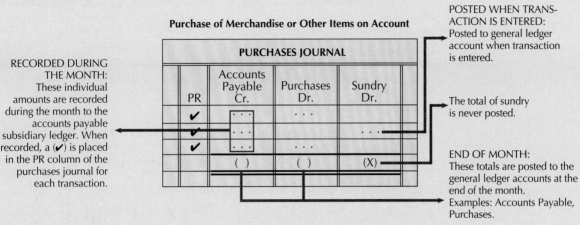

Purchase of Merchandise or Other Items on Account

RECORDED DURING THE MONTH: These individual amounts are recorded during the month to the accounts payable subsidiary ledger. When recorded, a (✔) is placed in the PR column of the purchases journal for each transaction.

POSTED WHEN TRANSACTION IS ENTERED: Posted to general ledger account when transaction is entered.

The total of sundry is never posted.

END OF MONTH: These totals are posted to the general ledger accounts at the end of the month. Examples: Accounts Payable, Purchases.

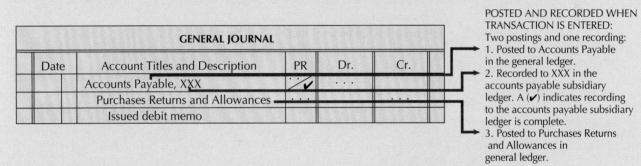

Issuing a Debit Memo (or Receiving a Credit Memo)

POSTED AND RECORDED WHEN TRANSACTION IS ENTERED: Two postings and one recording:
1. Posted to Accounts Payable in the general ledger.
2. Recorded to XXX in the accounts payable subsidiary ledger. A (✔) indicates recording to the accounts payable subsidiary ledger is complete.
3. Posted to Purchases Returns and Allowances in general ledger.

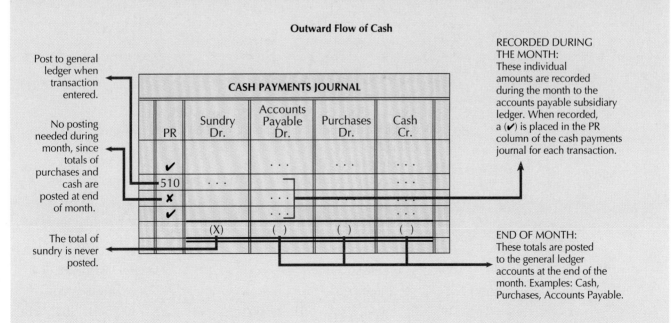

Outward Flow of Cash

Post to general ledger when transaction entered.

No posting needed during month, since totals of purchases and cash are posted at end of month.

The total of sundry is never posted.

RECORDED DURING THE MONTH: These individual amounts are recorded during the month to the accounts payable subsidiary ledger. When recorded, a (✔) is placed in the PR column of the cash payments journal for each transaction.

END OF MONTH: These totals are posted to the general ledger accounts at the end of the month. Examples: Cash, Purchases, Accounts Payable.

2. Complete the following table:

	Category	↑	↓	Temporary or Permanent
Purchases				
Purchases Returns and Allowances				
Purchases Discount				

Calculating Net Purchases

3. Calculate Net Purchases from the following: Purchases, $8; Purchases Returns and Allowances, $3; Purchases Discounts, $1.

Purchases Journal, General Journal, Recording, and Posting

4. Match the following to the three journal entries (more than one number can be used).

   1. Journalized into purchases journal.
   2. Record immediately to subsidiary ledger.
   3. Post totals from purchases journal (except sundry total) at end of month to general ledger.
   4. Journalized in general journal.
   5. Record and post immediately to subsidiary and general ledgers.

      a. Bought merchandise on account from Ryan.com, invoice no. 12, $40.
      b. Bought equipment on account from Jone Co., invoice no. 13, $75.
      c. Issued debit memo no. 1 to Ryan.com for merchandise returned, $7, from invoice no. 12.

Recording Transactions in Special Journals

5. Indicate in which journal each transaction will be journalized:

   1. SJ   **4.** CPJ
   2. PJ   **5.** GJ
   3. CRJ

_____ **a.** Issued credit memo no. 2, $29.
_____ **b.** Cash sales, $180.
_____ **c.** Received check from Blue Co., $50 less 3% discount.
_____ **d.** Bought merchandise on account from Mel Co., $35, invoice no. 20, terms 1/10, n/30.
_____ **e.** Cash purchase, $15.
_____ **f.** Issued debit memo to Mel Co., $15, for merchandise returned from invoice no. 20.

6. From the following prepare a schedule of Accounts Payable for Web.com for May 31, 200X:

Accounts Payable Subsidiary Ledger

Rowe Co.

			5/7	PJ1	60

Bloss Co

5/25	CPJ1	10	5/20	PJ1	50

General Ledger

Accounts Payable

5/31	CPJ	10	5/31	PJ1	110

Exercises

(The forms you need are on pages 327–329 of the *Study Guide and Working Papers*.)

10-1. From the purchases journal in Figure 10-25, record to the accounts payable subsidiary ledger and post to general ledger accounts as appropriate.

Recording to the accounts payable subsidiary ledger and posting to the general ledger from a purchases journal.

			Date of Invoice	Terms	Post Ref.	Accounts Payable Credit	Purchases Debit	Sundry-Dr.		
Date		Account Credited						Account	PR	Amount
200X June	3	Rey.com	May 3	1/10, n/30		8 0 0 00	8 0 0 00			
	4	Lane.com	May 4	n/10, EOM		9 0 0 00	9 0 0 00			
	8	Sail.com	May 8			4 0 0 00		Equipment		4 0 0 00

PURCHASES JOURNAL — Page 1

Figure 10-25 Purchases Journal

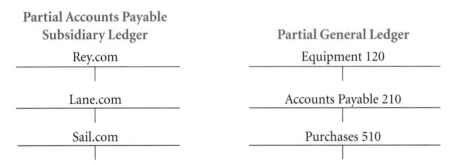

Partial Accounts Payable Subsidiary Ledger

Rey.com

Lane.com

Sail.com

Partial General Ledger

Equipment 120

Accounts Payable 210

Purchases 510

10-2. On July 10, 200X, Aster Co. issued debit memorandum no. 1 for $400 to Reel Co. for merchandise returned from invoice no. 312. Your task is to journalize, record, and post this transaction as appropriate. Use the same account numbers as found in the text for Art's Wholesale Clothing Company. The general journal is page 1.

Journalizing, recording, and posting a debit memorandum.

10-3. Journalize, record, and post when appropriate the following transactions into the cash payments journal (p. 2) for Morgan's Clothing. Use the same headings as found in the text (p. 398). All purchases discounts are 2/10, n/30.

Journalizing, recording, and posting a cash payments journal.

Accounts Payable Subsidiary Ledger

Name	Balance	Invoice No.
A. James	$1,000	522
B. Foss	400	488
J. Ranch	900	562
B. Swanson	100	821

Partial General Ledger

Account	Balance
Cash 110	$3,000
Accounts Payable 210	2,400
Purchases Discount 511	
Advertising Expense 610	

200X

Apr. 1 Issued check no. 20 to A. James Company in payment of its March 28 invoice no. 522.

8 Issued check no. 21 to Flott Advertising in payment of its advertising bill, $100, no discount.

15 Issued check no. 22 to B. Foss in payment of its March 25 invoice no. 488.

Schedule of accounts payable.

10-4. From Exercise 10-3, prepare a schedule of accounts payable and verify that the total of the schedule equals the amount in the controlling account.

F.O.B. destination.

10-5. Record the following transaction in a transaction analysis chart for the buyer: Bought merchandise for $9,000 on account. Shipping terms were F.O.B. destination. The cost of shipping was $500.

Trade and cash discounts.

10-6. Angie Rase bought merchandise with a list price of $4,000. Angie was entitled to a 30% trade discount as well as a 3% cash discount. What was Angie's actual cost of buying this merchandise after the cash discount?

Group A Problems

(The forms you need are on pages 330–351 of the *Study Guide and Working Papers*.)

Journalizing, recording, and posting a purchases journal.

10A-1. Abby Kim recently opened Skates.com. As the bookkeeper of her company, please journalize, record, and post when appropriate the following transactions (account numbers are Store Supplies, 115; Store Equipment, 121; Accounts Payable, 210; Purchases, 510):

200X

June 4 Bought $700 of merchandise on account from Mail.com, invoice no. 442, dated June 5, terms 2/10, n/30.

5 Bought $4,000 of store equipment from Norton Co., invoice no. 502, dated June 6.

8 Bought $1,400 of merchandise on account from Rolo Co., invoice no. 401, dated June 9, terms 2/10, n/30.

14 Bought $900 of store supplies on account from Mail.com, invoice no. 419, dated June 14.

Check Figure:
Total of purchases column
$2,100

10A-2. Mabel's Natural Food Store uses a purchases journal (p. 10) and a general journal (p. 2) to record the following transactions (continued from April):

200X

May 8 Purchased $600 of merchandise on account from Aton Co., invoice no. 400, dated May 9, terms 2/10, n/60.

10 Purchased $1,200 of merchandise on account from Broward Co., invoice no. 420, dated May 11, terms 2/10, n/60.

12 Purchased $500 of store supplies on account from Midden Co., invoice no. 510, dated May 13.

14 Issued debit memo no. 8 to Aton Co. for merchandise returned, $400, from invoice no. 400.

17 Purchased $560 of office equipment on account from Relar Co., invoice no. 810, dated May 18.

24 Purchased $650 of additional store supplies on account from Midden Co., invoice no. 516, dated May 25, terms 2/10, n/30.

Journalizing, recording, and posting a purchases journal as well as recording debit memorandum and preparing a schedule of accounts payable.

Check Figure:
Total schedule of accounts payable $5,810

The food store has decided to keep a separate column for the purchases of supplies in the purchases journal. Your tasks are to

1. Journalize the transactions.
2. Post and record as appropriate.
3. Prepare a schedule of accounts payable.

Accounts Payable
Subsidiary Ledger

Name	Balance
Aton Co.	$400
Broward Co.	600
Midden Co.	1,200
Relar Co.	500

Partial General Ledger

Account	Number	Balance
Store Supplies	110	$ —
Office Equipment	120	—
Accounts Payable	210	2,700
Purchases	510	16,000
Purchases Returns and Allowances	512	—

10A-3. Wendy Jones operates a wholesale computer center. All transactions requiring the payment of cash are recorded in the cash payments journal (p. 5). The account balances as of May 1, 200X, are as follows:

Journalizing, recording, and posting a cash payments journal. Preparing a schedule of accounts payable.

Accounts Payable
Subsidiary Ledger

Name	Balance
Alvin Co.	$1,200
Henry Co.	600
Soy Co.	800
Xon Co.	1,400

Check Figure:
Total of Schedule of Accounts Payable $1,900

Partial General Ledger

Account	Number	Balance
Cash	110	$17,000
Delivery Truck	150	—
Accounts Payable	210	4,000
Computer Purchases	510	—
Computer Purchases Discount	511	—
Rent Expense	610	—
Utilities Expense	620	—

Your tasks are to

1. Journalize the following transactions.
2. Record to the accounts payable subsidiary ledger and post to the general ledger as appropriate.
3. Prepare a schedule of accounts payable.

200X

May 1   Paid half the amount owed Henry Co. from previous purchases of appliances on account, less a 2% purchases discount, check no. 21.

3   Bought a delivery truck for $8,000 cash, check no. 22, payable to Bill Ring Co.

    6   Bought computer merchandise from Lectro Co.,
check no. 23, $2,900.

   18   Bought additional computer merchandise from Pulse Co.,
check no. 24, $800.

   24   Paid Xon Co. the amount owed less a 2% purchases discount,
check no. 25.

   28   Paid rent expense to King's Realty Trust, check no. 26, $2,000.

   29   Paid utilities expense to Stone Utility Co., check no. 27, $300.

   30   Paid half the amount owed Soy Co., no discount, check no. 28.

10A-4. Abby Ellen opened Abby's Toy House. As her newly hired accountant, your
tasks are to

1. Journalize the transactions for the month of March.
2. Record to subsidiary ledgers and post to the general ledger as appropriate.
3. Total and rule the journals.
4. Prepare a schedule of accounts receivable and a schedule of accounts payable.

The following is the partial chart of accounts for Abby's Toy House:

> *Comprehensive Problem: All special journals and the general journal. Schedule of accounts payable and accounts receivable.*

> *Check Figures:*
> Total of Schedule of accounts receivable $7,600
> Total of schedule of accounts payable $9,000

Abby's Toy House Chart of Accounts

Assets		Revenue	
110	Cash	410	Toy Sales
112	Accounts Receivable	412	Sales Returns and Allowances
114	Prepaid Rent	414	Sales Discounts
121	Delivery Truck	**Cost of Goods**	
Liabilities		510	Toy Purchases
210	Accounts Payable	512	Purchases Returns and Allowances
Owner's Equity		514	Purchases Discount
310	A. Ellen, Capital	**Expenses**	
		610	Salaries Expense
		612	Cleaning Expense

200X

Mar.   1   Abby Ellen invested $8,000 in the toy store.

    1   Paid three months' rent in advance, check no. 1, $3,000.

    1   Purchased merchandise from Earl Miller Company on account, $4,000,
invoice no. 410, dated March 2, terms 2/10, n/30.

    3   Sold merchandise to Bill Burton on account, $1,000, invoice no. 1, terms
2/10, n/30.

    6   Sold merchandise to Jim Rex on account, $700, invoice no. 2, terms 2/10, n/30.

    8   Purchased merchandise from Earl Miller Co. on account, $1,200, invoice no.
415, dated March 9, terms 2/10, n/30.

    9   Sold merchandise to Bill Burton on account, $600, invoice no. 3, terms
2/10, n/30.

    9   Paid cleaning service, check no. 2, $300.

   10   Jim Rex returned merchandise that cost $300 to Abby's Toy House. Abby
issued credit memorandum no. 1 to Jim Rex for $300.

   10   Purchased merchandise from Minnie Katz on account, $4,000, invoice no.
311, dated March 11, terms 1/15, n/60.

   12   Paid Earl Miller Co. invoice no. 410, dated March 2, check no. 3.

   13   Sold $1,300 of toy merchandise for cash.

   13   Paid salaries, $600, check no. 4.

   14   Returned merchandise to Minnie Katz in the amount of $1,000. Abby's Toy
House issued debit memorandum no. 1 to Minnie Katz.

   15   Sold merchandise for $4,000 cash.

16   Received payment from Jim Rex, invoice no. 2 (less returned merchandise) less discount.

16   Bill Burton paid invoice no. 1.

16   Sold toy merchandise to Amy Rose on account, $4,000, invoice no. 4, terms 2/10, n/30.

20   Purchased delivery truck on account from Sam Katz Garage, $3,000, invoice no. 111, dated March 21 (no discount).

22   Sold to Bill Burton merchandise on account, $900, invoice no. 5, terms 2/10, n/30.

23   Paid Minnie Katz balance owed, check no. 5.

24   Sold toy merchandise on account to Amy Rose, $1,100, invoice no. 6, terms 2/10, n/30.

25   Purchased toy merchandise, $600, check no. 6.

26   Purchased toy merchandise from Woody Smith on account, $4,800, invoice no. 211, dated March 27, terms 2/10, n/30.

28   Bill Burton paid invoice no. 5, dated March 22.

28   Amy Rose paid invoice no. 6, dated March 24.

28   Abby invested an additional $5,000 in the business.

28   Purchased merchandise from Earl Miller Co., $1,400, invoice no. 436, dated March 29, terms 2/10, n/30.

30   Paid Earl Miller Co. invoice no. 436, check no. 7.

30   Sold merchandise to Bonnie Flow Company on account, $3,000, invoice no. 7, terms 2/10, n/30.

Group B Problems

(The forms you need are on pages 330–351 of the *Study Guide and Working Papers.*)

10B-1. From the following transactions of Abby Kim's Skate.com, journalize in the purchases journal and record and post as appropriate:

Journalizing, recording, and posting a purchases journal.

200X

June 4   Bought merchandise on account from Rolo Co., invoice no. 400, dated June 5, $1,800, terms 2/10, n/30.

5   Bought store equipment from Norton Co., invoice no. 518, dated June 6, $6,000.

8   Bought merchandise on account from Mail.com, invoice no. 411, dated June 5, $400, terms 2/10, n/30.

14   Bought store supplies on account from Mail.com, invoice no. 415, dated June 13, $1,200.

Check Figure:
Total of purchases column $2,200

10B-2. As the accountant of Mabel's Natural Food Store (1) journalize the following transactions into the purchases (p. 10) or general journal (p. 2), (2) record and post as appropriate, and (3) prepare a schedule of accounts payable. Beginning balances are in the *Study Guide and Working Papers.*

Journalizing, recording, and posting a purchases journal as well as recording the issuing of a debit memorandum and preparing a schedule of accounts payable.

200X

May 8   Purchased merchandise on account from Broward Co., invoice no. 420, dated May 9, $500, terms 2/10, n/60.

10   Purchased merchandise on account from Aton Co., invoice no. 400, dated May 11, $900, terms 2/10, n/60.

12   Purchased store supplies on account from Midden Co., invoice no. 510, dated May 13, $700.

14   Issued debit memo no. 7 to Aton Co. for merchandise returned, $400, from invoice no. 400.

Check Figure:
Total of schedule of accounts payable $6,000

17 Purchased office equipment on account from Relar Co., invoice no. 810, dated May 18, $750.

24 Purchased additional store supplies on account from Midden Co., invoice no. 516, dated May 25, $850.

Journalizing, recording, and posting a cash payments journal. Preparing a schedule of accounts payable.

10B-3. Wendy Jones has hired you as her bookkeeper to record the following transactions in the cash payments journal. She would like you to record and post as appropriate and supply her with a schedule of accounts payable. (Beginning balances are in your workbook or Problem 10A-3, p. 415 in the text.)

200X

May

1 Bought a delivery truck for $8,000 cash, check no. 21, payable to Randy Rosse Co.

3 Paid half the amount owed Henry Co. from previous purchases of computer merchandise on account, less a 5% purchases discount, check no. 22.

6 Bought computer merchandise from Jane Co. for $900 cash, check no. 23.

18 Bought additional computer merchandise from Jane Co., check no. 24, $1,000.

24 Paid Xon Co. the amount owed less a 5% purchases discount, check no. 25.

28 Paid rent expense to Regan Realty Trust, check no. 26, $3,000.

29 Paid half the amount owed Soy Co., no discount, check no. 27.

30 Paid utilities expense to French Utility, check no. 28, $425.

Check Figure:
Total of schedule of accounts payable $1,900

10B-4. As the new accountant for Abby's Toy House, your tasks are to
1. Journalize the transactions for the month of March.
2. Record to subsidiary ledgers and post to the general ledger as appropriate.
3. Total and rule the journals.
4. Prepare a schedule of accounts receivable and a schedule of accounts payable.

(Use the same chart of accounts as in Problem 10A-4, p. 416. Your *Study Guide and Working Papers* has all the forms you need to complete this problem.)

Check Figures:
Total of schedule of accounts receivable $9,900
Total of schedule of accounts payable $9,200

200X

Mar.

1 Abby invested $4,000 in the new toy store.

1 Paid two months' rent in advance, check no. 1, $1,000.

1 Purchased merchandise from Earl Miller Company, invoice no. 410, dated March 2, $6,000, terms 2/10, n/30.

3 Sold merchandise to Bill Burton on account, $1,600, invoice no. 1, terms 2/10, n/30.

6 Sold merchandise to Jim Rex on account, $800, invoice no. 2, terms 2/10, n/30.

8 Purchased merchandise from Earl Miller Company, $800, invoice no. 415, dated March 9, terms 2/10, n/30.

9 Sold merchandise to Bill Burton on account, $700, invoice no. 3, terms 2/10, n/30.

9 Paid cleaning service, $400, check no. 2.

10 Jim Rex returned merchandise that cost $200 to Abby. Abby issued credit memorandum no. 1 to Jim Rex for $200.

10 Purchased merchandise from Minnie Katz, $7,000, invoice no. 311, dated March 11, terms 1/15, n/60.

12 Paid Earl Miller Co. invoice no. 410, dated March 2, check no. 3.

13 Sold $1,500 of toy merchandise for cash.

13 Paid salaries, $700, check no. 4.

14 Returned merchandise to Minnie Katz in the amount of $500. Abby issued debit memorandum no. 1 to Minnie Katz.

15 Sold merchandise for cash, $4,800.

16 Received payment from Jim Rex for invoice no. 2 (less returned merchandise) less discount.

16   Bill Burton paid invoice no. 1.

16   Sold toy merchandise to Amy Rose on account, $6,000, invoice no. 4, terms 2/10, n/30.

20   Purchased delivery truck on account from Sam Katz Garage, $2,500, invoice no. 111, dated March 21 (no discount).

22   Sold to Bill Burton merchandise on account, $2,000, invoice no. 5, terms 2/10, n/30.

23   Paid Minnie Katz balance owed, check no. 5.

24   Sold toy merchandise on account to Amy Rose, $2,000, invoice no. 6, terms 2/10, n/30.

25   Purchased toy merchandise, $800, check no. 6.

26   Purchased toy merchandise from Woody Smith on account, $5,900, invoice no. 211, dated March 27, terms 2/10, n/30.

28   Bill Burton paid invoice no. 5, dated March 22.

28   Amy Rose paid invoice no. 6, dated March 24.

28   Abby invested an additional $3,000 in the business.

28   Purchased merchandise from Earl Miller Co., $4,200, invoice no. 436, dated March 29, terms 2/10, n/30.

30   Paid Earl Miller Co. invoice no. 436, check no. 7.

30   Sold merchandise to Bonnie Flow Company on account, $3,200, invoice no. 7, terms 2/10, n/30.

Real-World Applications

10R-1. Angie Co. bought merchandise for $1,000 with credit terms of 2/10, n/30. Owing to the bookkeeper's incompetence, the 2% cash discount was missed. The bookkeeper told Pete Angie, the owner, not to get excited. After all, it was a $20 discount that was missed, not hundreds of dollars. Could you please act as Mr. Angie's assistant and show the bookkeeper that his $20 represents a sizable equivalent interest cost? In your calculation assume a 360-day year. Make some written recommendations so that this situation will not happen again.

10R-2. Jeff Ryan completed an Accounting I course and was recently hired as the bookkeeper of Spring Co. The special journals have not been posted, nor are Dr. and Cr. used on the column headings. Please assist Jeff by marking, in Figure 10-26, the Dr. and Cr. headings as well as setting up and posting to the general ledger and recording to the subsidiary ledger. (Only post or record the amounts, because no chart of accounts is provided.) Make some written recommendations on how a new computer system may lessen the need for posting.

Hint: $R = \dfrac{I}{PT}$

YOU make the call

Critical Thinking/Ethical Case

10R-3. Spring Co. bought merchandise from All Co. with terms 2/10, n/30. Joanne Ring, the bookkeeper, forgot to pay the bill within the first 10 days. She went to Mel Ryan, head accountant, who told her to backdate the check so that it looked like the bill was paid within the discount period. Joanne told Mel that she thought they could get away with it. Should Joanne and Mel backdate the check to take advantage of the discount? You make the call. Write down your specific recommendations to Joanne.

Figure 10-26
Special and General
Journals

SALES JOURNAL		
Account	PR	
Blue Co.		4 8 0 0 00
Jon Co.		5 6 0 0 00
Roff Co.		6 4 0 0 00
Totals		16 8 0 0 00

PURCHASES JOURNAL		
Account	PR	
Ralph Co.		4 0 0 0 00
Sos Co.		6 0 0 0 00
Jingle Co.		8 0 0 0 00
Totals		18 0 0 0 00

GENERAL JOURNAL			
Sales Returns and Allowances		1 6 0 0 00	
Accounts Receivable, Jon Co.			1 6 0 0 00
Customer returned merchandise			
Accounts Payable, Jingle Co.		8 0 0 00	
Purchases, Returns, and Allowances			8 0 0 00
Returned defective merchandise			

CASH RECEIPTS JOURNAL*						
Cash Dr.	Sales Discount Dr.	Accounts Receivable Cr.	Sales Cr.	Sundry-Dr.		
				Account Name	PR	Amount Cr.
4 7 0 4 00	9 6 00	4 8 0 0 00		Blue Co.		
1 9 6 0 00	4 0 00	2 0 0 0 00		Jon Co.		
5 0 0 0 00			5 0 0 0 00	Sales		
20 0 0 0 00				Notes Payable		20 0 0 0 00
3 1 3 6 00	6 4 00	3 2 0 0 00		Roff Co.		
4 6 0 0 00			4 6 0 0 00	Sales		
39 4 0 0 00	2 0 0 00	10 0 0 0 00	9 6 0 0 00	Totals		20 0 0 0 00

* *Note:* This company's set of columns differs from that shown in the chapter.

CASH PAYMENTS JOURNAL					
Account	PR	Sundry	Accounts Payable	Purchases Discount	Cash
Sos Co.			3 0 0 0 00	6 0 00	2 9 4 0 00
Salaries Expense		2 6 0 0 00			2 6 0 0 00
Jingle Co.			4 0 0 0 00	8 0 00	3 9 2 0 00
Salaries Expense		2 6 0 0 00			2 6 0 0 00
Totals		5 2 0 0 00	7 0 0 0 00	1 4 0 00	12 0 6 0 00

Internet Exercises: L. L. Bean; Amazon.com

EX-1. [www.llbean.com] Each holiday season an extraordinary amount of merchandise is moved from online retailers like L. L. Bean from their warehouses to their customers. In the previous chapter you learned about the handling of sales and cash receipts transactions. In this chapter you learned about the other side of those transactions, Purchases and Cash Payments, using the related special journals.

Retailers wish to know their profits by product line or by department. From your examination of this Web site, suggest several columns that might appear in a purchases journal. For each suggestion state whether it would be a "debit" or "credit" column.

EX-2. [**www.amazon.com**] When merchandise for resale is paid for by the seller, the transaction is recorded in the cash payments journal. At the same time, an entry is made on the subsidiary ledger of the vendor. When all of the transactions are journalized and posted a schedule of accounts payable may be prepared. In a manual accounting system, individual ledger cards for vendors can become misplaced. If your coworker were to find a subsidiary ledger card but did not know whether to return it to Accounts Payable or the Accounts Receivable Department, how could you assist in getting it to the right place? Which columns of the ledger card could you examine to answer this dilemma?

Continuing Problem

Eldorado Computer Center

Tony was very happy to see the progress made by using the specialized journals. For the month of February he will add two more journals (purchases journal and cash payments journal). To assist you in recording the transactions, the following is an updated schedule of accounts payable as of January 31, 200X.

Schedule of Accounts Payable

Office Depot	$ 50
System Design Furniture	1,400
Pac Bell	150
Multi Systems, Inc.	450
Total Accounts Payable	$2,050

Assignment

(See pages 356–361 in the *Study Guide and Working Papers.*)

1. Journalize the transactions in the appropriate journals (cash payments, purchases journal, or general journal).
2. Record in the accounts payable subsidiary ledger and post to the general ledger as appropriate. A partial general ledger is included in the *Study Guide and Working Papers.*
3. Prepare a schedule of accounts payable as of February 28, 200X.

The transactions for the month of February are as follows:

200X

Feb.

1   Prepaid the rent for the months of February, March, and April, $1,200, check no. 2585.

4   Bought merchandise on account from Multi Systems, Inc., purchase order no. 4010, $450; terms are 3/10, n/30.

8   Bought office supplies on account from Office Depot, purchase order no. 4011, $250; terms are n/30.

9   Purchased merchandise on account from Computer Connection, purchase order no. 4012, $500; terms are 1/30, n/60.

15   Paid purchase order no. 4010 in full to Multi Systems, Inc.; check no. 2586.

21   Issued debit memorandum no. 10 to Computer Connection for merchandise returned from purchase order no. 4012, $100.

27   Paid for office supplies, $50, check no. 2587.

APPENDIX

WHAT SPECIAL JOURNALS WOULD LOOK LIKE IN A PERPETUAL ACCOUNTING SYSTEM

Figure A-1
A Sales Journal under a Perpetual System

ART'S WHOLESALE CLOTHING COMPANY
SALES JOURNAL
Page 1

Date		Account Debited	Terms	Invoice No.	Post Ref.	Dr. Acc. Rec Cr. Sales	Cost of Goods Sold Dr. Merchandise Inventory Cr.
200X Apr.	3	Hal's Clothing	2/10, n/30	1	✔	800 00	560 00
	6	Bevans Company	2/10, n/30	2	✔	1600 00	1120 00
	18	Roe Company	2/10, n/30	3	✔	2000 00	1400 00
	24	Roe Company	2/10, n/30	4	✔	500 00	350 00
	28	Mel's Dept. Store	2/10, n/30	5	✔	900 00	630 00
	29	Mel's Dept. Store	2/10, n/30	6	✔	700 00	490 00
	30						
						6500 00	4550 00
						(113) (411)	(510) (114)

What's new:

In journal: New columns for Cost of Goods Sold (Dr.) and Inventory (Cr.). Each time a charge sale is earned, the Cost of Goods Sold increases and the amount of Inventory at cost is reduced.

In general ledger: New ledger accounts for Inventory and Cost of Goods Sold.

Example: On April 3, Art's Wholesale sold Hal's Clothing $800 of merchandise on account. This sale cost Art $560 to bring this merchandise into the store.

ART'S WHOLESALE CLOTHING COMPANY
CASH RECEIPTS JOURNAL
Page 1

Date		Cash Dr.	Sales Discount Dr.	Accounts Receivable Cr.	Sales Cr.	Sundry — Account Name	Post Ref.	Amount Cr.	Costs of Goods Sold Dr. Merchandise Inventory Cr.
200X Apr.	1	800 00				Art Newner, Capital	311	800 00	
	4	784 00	16 00	800 00		Hal's Clothing	✔		
	15	900 00			900 00	Cash Sales	x		630 00
	16	980 00	20 00	1000 00		Bevans Company	✔		
	22	1960 00	40 00	2000 00		Roe Company	✔		
	27	500 00				Store Equipment	121	500 00	
	30	1200 00			1200 00	Cash Sales	x		840 00
		14324 00	76 00	3800 00	2100 00			850 00	1470 00
		(111)	(413)	(113)	(411)			(X)	(510) (114)

Figure A-2 A Cash Receipts Journal under a Perpetual System

What's new:

In journal: New columns for Cost of Goods Sold (Dr.) and Inventory (Cr.). Each time a cash sale is earned, the Cost of Goods Sold increases and the amount of Inventory at cost is reduced.

In general ledger: New ledger accounts for Inventory and Cost of Goods Sold.

Example: On April 15, Art's Wholesale made cash sales for $900. These sales cost Art $630 to bring them into the store.

ART'S WHOLESALE CLOTHING COMPANY
PURCHASES JOURNAL

Date		Account Credited	Date of Invoice	Inv. No.	Terms	Post Ref.	Accounts Payable Credits	Merchandise Inventory Debit	Sundry–Dr. Account	Post Ref.	Amount
200X Apr.	3	Abby Blake Company	April 3	228	2/10, n/60	✔	5 0 5 0 00	5 0 0 0 00	Freight-In	514	5 0 00
	4	Joe Francis Company	April 5	388		✔	4 0 0 0 00		Equip.	121	4 0 0 0 00
	6	Thorpe Company	April 6	415	1/10, n/30	✔	8 0 0 00	8 0 0 00			
	7	John Sullivan Company	April 6	516	n/10, EOM*	✔	9 8 0 00	9 8 0 00			
	12	Abby Blake Company	April 13	242	1/10, n/30	✔	6 0 0 00	6 0 0 00			
	25	John Sullivan Company	April 26	612		✔	5 0 0 00		Supplies	115	5 0 0 00
	30										
							11 9 3 0 00	7 3 8 0 00			4 5 5 0 00
							(211)	(114)			(X)

Figure A-3 A Purchases Journal under a Perpetual System

What's new:

In journal: The column for Purchases is replaced with a column for Inventory. The cost of all merchandise bought on account for resale is debited to Inventory.

In ledger: New ledger account for Inventory.

Example: On April 7, Art's Wholesale bought $980 of merchandise for resale to customers from John Sullivan Company.

ART'S WHOLESALE CLOTHING COMPANY
CASH PAYMENTS JOURNAL

Page 1

Date		Ck. No.	Account Debited	Post Ref.	Sundry Accounts Dr.	Accounts Payable Dr.	Merchandise Inventory Cr.	Cash Cr.
200X Apr.	2	1	Prepaid Insurance	116	9 0 0 00			9 0 0 00
	7	2	Joe Francis Company	✔		4 0 0 0 00		4 0 0 0 00
	9	3	Merchandise Inventory	114	8 0 0 00			8 0 0 00
	12	4	Thorpe Company	✔		6 0 0 00	6 00	5 9 4 00
	28	5	Salaries Expense	611	7 0 0 00			7 0 0 00
	30							
					2 4 0 0 00	4 6 0 0 00	6 00	6 9 9 4 00
					(X)	(211)	(114)	(111)

Figure A-4 A Cash Payments Journal under a Perpetual System

What's new:

In journal: New column for Merchandise Inventory replaces the Purchase Discount column. In the perpetual system, a purchase discount reduces the cost of merchandise inventory.

In general ledger: New ledger account for Merchandise Inventory.

Example: On April 12, Art's wholesale paid Thorpe Company the amount owed less a 1% discount.

COMPUTERIZED ACCOUNTING APPLICATION FOR CHAPTER 10

PART A: Recording Transactions in the Sales, Receipts, Purchases, and Payments Journals

PART B: Computerized Accounting Instructions for Abby's Toy House (Problem 10A-4)

Before starting on this assignment, read and complete the tasks discussed in Parts A, B, and F of the Computerized Accounting appendix at the back of this book and complete the Computerized Accounting Application assignments for Chapter 3, Chapter 4, the Valdez Realty Mini Practice Set (Chapter 5), and the Pete's Market Mini Practice Set (Chapter 8).

PART A: RECORDING TRANSACTIONS IN THE SALES, RECEIPTS, PURCHASES, AND PAYMENTS JOURNALS

Where to Record Sales and Cash Receipts

The Sales/Invoicing and Receipts features in Peachtree Complete Accounting were designed to work with the accounts receivables and general ledger modules in an integrated fashion. When transactions are recorded in the Sales/Invoicing and Receipts windows, the program automatically posts the customer's account in the accounts receivable subsidiary ledger, records the journal entry, and posts all accounts affected in the general ledger. However, the type of transactions recorded in the Sales/Invoicing and Receipts windows in Peachtree Complete Accounting differ from the types of transactions recorded in these journals in a manual accounting system. An explanation of the differences appears in the following chart:

Name of Computerized Entry Window	Types of Transactions Recorded in Computerized Journal
Sales/Invoicing	Sales of merchandise on account Sales returns and allowances
Receipts	Cash sales and payments from credit customers on account

Computerized Aged Receivables

An Aged Receivables report (the computerized version of a schedule of accounts receivable) for The Mars Company appears below (terms of 2/10, n/30 are offered to all credit customers of The Mars Company):

The Mars Company: Customer Aged Detail as at 3/1/04

	Total	Current	31 to 60	61 to 90	91+
John Dunbar					
910 2/25/04 Invoice	500.00	500.00	—	—	—
Kevin Tucker					
912 2/26/04 Invoice	550.00	550.00	—	—	—
	1,050.00	1,050.00			

Where to Record Purchases and Cash Payments

The Purchases and Payments windows in Peachtree Complete Accounting are designed to work with the accounts payable and general ledger modules in an integrated fashion.

When transactions are recorded in the Purchases and Payments windows, the program automatically posts the vendor's account in the accounts payable subsidiary ledger, records the journal entry, and posts all accounts affected in the general ledger. However, the type of transactions recorded in the Purchases and Payments windows in

Peachtree Complete Accounting differ from the types of transactions recorded in these journals in a manual accounting system. An explanation of the differences appears in the following chart:

Name of Computerized Journal	Types of Transactions Recorded in Computerized Journal
Purchases Window	Purchases of merchandise and other items on account
	Purchase returns and allowances
Payments Journal	Cash payments to credit and cash vendors

An Aged Payables report (the computerized version of a schedule of accounts payable) for The Mars Company appears below:

Aged Payables

The Mars Company: Vendor Aged Detail as at 3/1/04

	Total	Current	31 to 60	61 to 90	91+
Laurie Snyder					
569 2/27/04 Invoice	435.00	435.00	—	—	—
Young's Space Simulations					
790 2/25/04 Invoice	112.00	112.00	—	—	—
	547.00	547.00			

1. Click on the Start button. Point to Programs; point to the Peachtree folder and select Peachtree Complete Accounting. Your desktop may have the Peachtree icon allowing for a quicker entrance into the program.

   Open the Company Data Files

2. Follow the "Open a File" instructions in Part A of the Computerized Accounting appendix at the back of this book to open **Mars Company.**

3. Click on the **Maintain** menu option. Then select **Company Information.** The program will respond by bringing up a dialogue box allowing the user to edit/add information about the company. In the **Company Name** entry field at the end of **Mars Company,** add a dash and your name "**-Student Name**" to the end of the company name. Click on the OK button to return to the Menu Window.

   Add Your Name to the Company Name

4. On March 1, 2004 sold merchandise to Kevin Tucker on account, $800, invoice #913, terms 2/10, n/30 consisting of the following:

   How to Record a Sale on Account

Stock #	Description	Quantity
001	Space Age Lamp	2
002	Solar Clock	5
005	Space Shuttle Model	1

5. Select **Sales/Invoicing** from the **Tasks** menu. Using the magnifying glass next to the **Customer ID** field, select Kevin Tucker by double clicking on his name. You are then moved to the **Invoice #** field. Type in "913". Press the TAB key that then moves you to the **Date** field. It should already reflect Mar 1, 2004 but if not, type in the date or use the calendar to the right of the field to select this date. TAB until you reach the **Quantity** field. Type in "2" and click TAB. This will move you to the **Item** field. Using the pull down menu, select the first item 001 Space Age Lamp by double clicking on it. This moves you to the **Description** field that will automatically fill in with information stored in the Inventory module. In fact, Peachtree will fill in all of the remaining fields as you tab through them until you are back to the **Quantity**

field. Enter the remaining items from the above table in the same manner as the Lamp. Your screen should look like this:

How to Preview a Sales Journal

6. Before printing this transaction, you may wish to see how Peachtree will record the transaction. Click on the **Journal** icon on the tool bar. This activates a feature of Peachtree called "Accounting Behind the Screens" and allows the user a look at the workings of the program. It will bring up a Sales Journal showing exactly how it will post this invoice. That is to say, it will show you what accounts will be debited and which accounts credited. Note that Peachtree uses a perpetual inventory system and has created the entries to move the goods sold out of the Inventory account and into the Cost of Sales (COGS) account.

7. Close the Sales Journal window. If you have made an error anywhere on the invoice, simply click in the field containing the error and correct it.

How to Edit a Sale or Purchase Entry Prior to Posting

8. After verifying that the journal entry is correct, click on the **Print** icon to print this invoice. You will be asked to select a form. As with the payroll checks, Peachtree supports a variety of blank invoice formats. It will also print its own format on plain paper. Select **Invoice Plain** (default) for your printing. Peachtree will both print and post the transaction in one step. A blank invoice is displayed, ready for additional transactions to be recorded. If you wish to batch print later, you can simply hit the **Save** icon which will store the invoice for printing using the **Select a Report** option under the **Accounts Receivable** reports. We will print all our invoices as we create them.

How to Print/Post a Sales Entry

9. On March 5, 2004 issued credit memorandum #CM14 to Kevin Tucker for the return of one of the lamps he purchased. Peachtree uses the same entry window, **Sales/Invoicing,** to record credits issued to customers. There are two primary differences. One is that quantities will be entered as negative amounts and the second is that the printing will be accomplished with a Credit form rather than an Invoice form.

How to Record a Credit Memo

10. Select **Sales/Invoicing** from the **Tasks** menu. Using the magnifying glass next to the **Customer ID** field, select Kevin Tucker by double clicking on his name. You are then moved to the **Invoice #** field. Type in "CM14". Press the TAB key that then moves you to the **Date** field. Type in the date "Mar 5, 2004" or use the calendar to the right

of the field to select this date. TAB until you reach the **Quantity** field. Type in "−1" (negative one) and click TAB. This will move you to the **Item** field. Using the pull down menu, select the first item 001 Space Age Lamp by double clicking on it. This moves you to the **Description** field that will automatically fill in with information stored in the Inventory module. In fact, Peachtree will fill in all of the remaining fields as you tab through them until you are back to the **Quantity** field. Your screen should look like this:

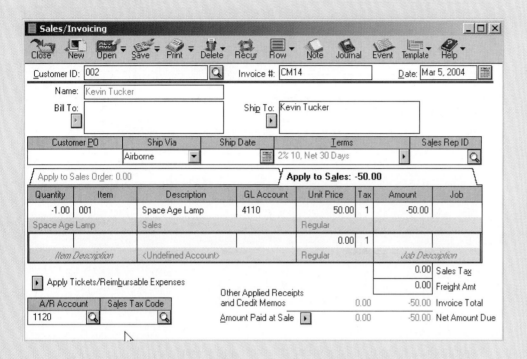

11. You may again use the **Journal** icon to see what this entry will look like in the Sales Journal.

Preview the Entry

12. Close the Sales Journal window; then make any editing corrections that may be required.

13. After verifying that the journal entry is correct, click on the Print icon to print this transaction. Select **Credit Plain** as the form on which to print the credit memo. When you are finished, close the **Sales/Invoicing** box.

Print the Credit Memo

14. On March 7, 2004 received check #1634 from Kevin Tucker in the amount of $735 in payment of invoice #913 ($800), dated March 1, less credit memorandum #CM14 ($50), less 2 percent discount ($16 − 1 = $15 net sales discount). Select **Receipts** from the **Tasks** menu. Peachtree will place the current date in the **Deposit ticket ID** field. You can accept this or change it to the date of the transaction. We will use the date of the transaction throughout the book. Using the magnifying glass, select customer Kevin Tucker. This will bring up a listing of the invoices and credits currently open in his account. The cursor will automatically move to the **Reference** field. We can enter Kevin's check number, 1634, in this field. The **Receipt Number** is similar to an invoice number and we will start with #105. We can now select the invoices and/or credits that are included in Kevin's payment. In the column marked **Pay** are small boxes that can be checked by clicking on them with the mouse. This marks the invoices selected for payment with the check received. We will check the boxes at the end of the lines containing invoice #913 and credit memo #CM14 which is associated with this invoice. Note that the field for **Receipt Amount** automatically reflects the amount of his payment. Please note that if we were receiving cash as the result of a cash sale or for any other reason rather than a payment on account, we would use the **Apply to Revenues** tab instead of the **Apply to Invoices** tab. In that screen, we can use any GL account we like to offset the

How to Record a Cash Receipt from a Credit Customer

receipt of the cash. If you recorded this payment on account correctly, your screen should look like this:

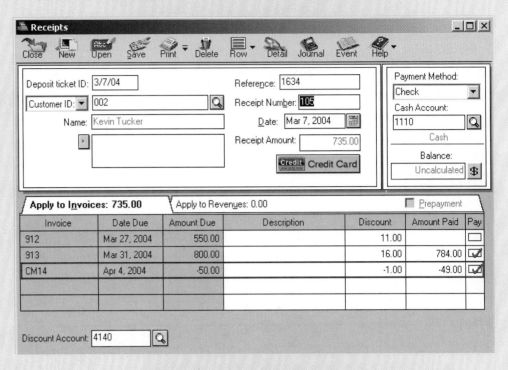

How to Preview the Receipts Journal

15. As before, we can preview how Peachtree will handle this transaction behind the screens by clicking on the **Journal** icon. This will bring up a Receipts Journal reflecting the accounts that will be affected by this entry.

16. Close the Sales Journal window. If you have made an error anywhere on the invoice, simply click in the field containing the error and correct it.

How to Post a Receipts Entry

17. After verifying that the journal entry is correct, click on the **Print** icon to post this transaction. You could also click on **Save** to post but not print the receipt. A blank Receipts Journal dialog box is displayed, ready for additional Receipts transactions to be recorded. Close the Receipts dialog box when you are finished.

18. On March 15, 2004 purchased merchandise from Young's Space Simulations on account, $278, invoice #796, terms 2/10, n/30 consisting of the following:

How to Record a Purchase on Account

Stock #	Description	Quantity
001	Space Age Lamp	5
003	Martian Landscape Lithograph	5
004	Simulated Moon Rock	9

19. Select **Purchases/Receive Inventory** from the **Tasks** menu. Using the magnifying glass next to the **Customer ID** field, select 002 Young's Space Simulations by double clicking on his name. You are then moved to the **Invoice #** field. Type in "796". Press the TAB key that then moves you to the **Date** field. Type in the date "Mar 15, 2004" or use the calendar to the right of the field to select this date. TAB until you reach the **Quantity** field. Type in "5" and click TAB. This will move you to the **Item** field. Using the pull down menu, select the first item 001 Space Age Lamp by double clicking on it. This moves you to the **Description** field that will automatically fill in with information stored in the Inventory module. In fact, Peachtree will fill in all of the remaining fields as you tab through them until you are back to the **Quantity** field. Should your Unit Price be different than that brought up by Peachtree, you can easily change the amount rather than tabbing through that field. If we were purchasing something besides merchandise inventory, we would skip over the Quantity and Item fields and fill in the Description, GL Account, and Amount fields based on

what we purchased and its cost. If you entered our inventory purchase correctly, your screen should look like this:

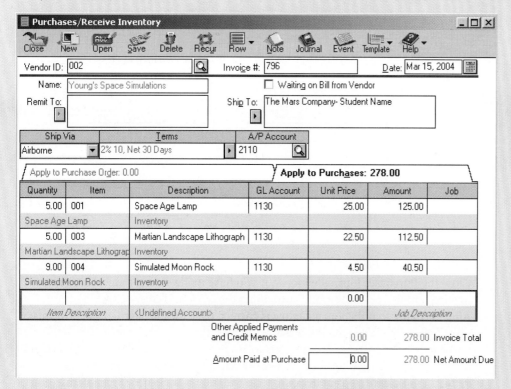

20. Before posting this transaction, you may wish to see how Peachtree will record the transaction. Click on the **Journal** icon on the tool bar. This activates a feature of Peachtree called "Accounting Behind the Screens" and allows the user a look at the workings of the program. It will bring up a Purchases Journal showing exactly how it will post this invoice. That is to say, it will show you what accounts will be debited and which accounts credited.

21. Close the Purchases Journal window. If you have made an error anywhere on the invoice, simply click in the field containing the error and correct it.

22. After verifying that the journal entry is correct, click on the **Save** icon to post this transaction. A blank Purchases screen is displayed, ready for additional Purchase transactions to be recorded.

23. On March 17, 2004 returned two of the Space Age Lamps to Young's Space Simulations with a value of $50. Issued debit memo #DM27. Select **Purchases/Receive Inventory** from the **Tasks** menu. Using the magnifying glass next to the **Customer ID** field, select 002 Young's Space Simulations by double clicking on his name. You are then moved to the **Invoice #** field. Type in "DM27". Press the TAB key that then moves you to the **Date** field. Type in the date "Mar 17, 2004" or use the calendar to the right of the field to select this date. TAB until you reach the **Quantity** field. Type in "−2" (negative two) and click TAB. This will move you to the **Item** field. Using the pull down menu, select the first item 001 Space Age Lamp by double clicking on it. This moves you to the **Description** field that will automatically fill in with information stored in the Inventory module. In fact, Peachtree will fill in all of the remaining fields as you tab through them until you are back to the **Quantity** field. Your screen should look like the screen on page 430.

24. Before posting this transaction, you may wish to see how Peachtree will record the transaction. Click on the **Journal** icon on the tool bar. This activates a feature of Peachtree called "Accounting Behind the Screens" and allows the user a look at the workings of the program. It will bring up a Purchases Journal showing exactly how it will post this invoice. That is to say, it will show you what accounts will be debited and which accounts credited.

How to Preview a Purchases Journal Entry

How to Post a Purchases Journal Entry

How to Record a Debit Memo

How to Preview a Purchases Journal Entry

25. Close the Purchases Journal window. If you have made an error anywhere on the invoice, simply click in the field containing the error and correct it.

26. After verifying that the journal entry is correct, click on the **Save** icon to post this transaction; then close the Purchases window.

27. On March 25, 2004 issued check #1007 to Young's Space Simulations in the amount of $223.44 in payment of invoice #796 ($278), dated March 15, less debit memorandum #DM27 ($50), less 2 percent discount ($5.56 − 1.00 = $4.56 net purchases discount). Select **Payments** from the **Tasks** menu. Using the magnifying glass, select vendor Young's Space Simulations. This will bring up a listing of the invoices and credits currently open in this account. TAB to the **Date** field and type in "March 25, 2004" or use the calendar to select this date. In the column marked **Pay** are small boxes that can be checked by clicking on them with the mouse. This marks the invoices selected for payment with the check you are creating. We will check the boxes at the end of the lines containing invoice #796 and debit memo #DM27 which is associated with this invoice. If we need to make a payment for something that is not already recorded in our accounts payable, we can use the **Apply to Expenses** tab instead of the **Apply to Invoices** tab that we are using. We can write a check for any purpose, including pre-paid expenses, using this feature. With our payment, note that the field for the amount of the check automatically reflects the amount of this payment. Also note that the **Check Number** field is left blank. This field is used only to enter a check that has already been written or printed. We will enter the check number when we print the check. Your screen should look like the Payments screen on page 431.

28. Before printing this check, you may wish to see how Peachtree will record the transaction. Click on the **Journal** icon on the tool bar. It will bring up a Disbursements Journal showing exactly how it will post this payment. That is to say, it will show you what accounts will be debited and which accounts credited.

29. Close the Disbursements Journal window. If you have made an error anywhere on the check, simply click in the field containing the error and correct it. If you need to change which invoice to pay, click on the red check for the incorrect invoice to deselect it and reselect the correct invoice.

30. After verifying that the check is correct, click on the **Print** icon to print this check. You will be presented with a Print Forms: Disbursement Checks selection box. As before, Peachtree has the ability to print on a variety of different blank check forms. Since we will be printing on plain white paper, it does not matter which form we choose. Accept the default. Start with check #1007. Click on **Print** to continue. The check will now print. You may need to tell your printer to continue since it may want you to insert the blank check forms. A blank Payment window

Post the Entry

How to Record a Cash Payment to a Credit Vendor

How to Preview a Disbursements Journal Entry

How to Print a Check

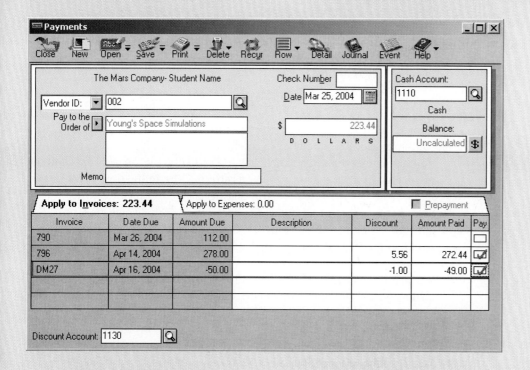

is displayed, ready for additional Payments transactions to be recorded. Close the Payments dialog box.

31. From the **Reports** menu, select **Accounts Receivable.** This will bring up a Select a Report dialogue box containing a list of several receivables related reports available to us. Select **Aged Receivables** to bring up the schedule of receivables still owed to Mars Company. Click on the **Print** icon to print the report.

32. Close the Aged Receivables window. From the Select A Report dialogue box, select Accounts Payable from the **Report Area** portion of the window. This will bring up a selection of payables related reports. Select **Aged Payables** to bring up the schedule of payables still owed by the Mars Company. Click on the **Print** icon to print the report.

33. Close the Aged Payables window. From the Select A Report dialogue box, select General Ledger from the **Report Area** portion of the window then print the following reports:

    a. General Ledger Trial Balance (Totals = 16,201.00)
    b. General Ledger Report (Cash = $10,511.56)

34. You may wish to experiment with some of the other reports that are available in the various areas of Peachtree's report area. Some examples you might want to see are a Sales Journal, Purchases Journal, Cash Receipts Journal, etc. Exit the program when you are finished.

PART B: COMPUTERIZED ACCOUNTING INSTRUCTIONS FOR ABBY'S TOY HOUSE (PROBLEM 10A-4)

1. Click on the Start button. Point to Programs; point to the Peachtree folder and select Peachtree Complete Accounting. Your desktop may have the Peachtree icon allowing for a quicker entrance into the program.

2. Follow the "Open a File" instructions in Part A of the Computerized Accounting appendix at the back of this book to open **Abby's Toy House.**

3. Click on the **Maintain** menu option. Then select **Company Information.** The program will respond by bringing up a dialogue box allowing the user to edit/add information about the company. In the **Company Name** entry field at the end of **Abby's Toy House,** add a dash and your name "**-Student Name**" to the end of the company name. Click on the OK button to return to the Menu Window.

How to Display and Print a Customer Aged Receivables Report

How to Display and Print a Vendor Aged Payables Report

Print Reports

Open the Company Data Files

Add Your Name to the Company Name

Record Transactions

4. Record the following transactions for March using the appropriate General(G), Sales/Invoicing(S), Receipts(R), Purchases(PU), and Payments(PA) windows. Use the same forms when printing invoices, credits, and checks as in Part A, changing the starting numbers as needed.

2004

Mar.

1   Abby Ellen invested $8,000 in the toy store. (G)

1   Paid three month's rent in advance, check #1, $3,000. (G)

1   Purchased merchandise from Earl Miller Company on account, $4,000, invoice #410, terms 2/10, n/30 consisting of the following: 6- Mountain Bikes, 12- Bike Carriers, 8- Deluxe Bike Seats. (PU)

3   Sold merchandise to Bill Burton on account, $1,000, invoice #1, terms 2/10, n/30 consisting of the following: 1- Mountain Bike, 1- Bike Carrier. (S)

6   Sold merchandise to Jim Rex on account, $700, invoice #2, terms 2/10, n/30 consisting of the following: 3- Bike Carriers, 1- Deluxe Bike Seat. (S)

8   Purchased merchandise from Earl Miller Co. on account $1,200, invoice #415, terms 2/10, n/30 consisting of the following: 2- Mountain Bikes, 4- Bike Carriers. (PU)

9   Sold merchandise to Bill Burton on account, $600, invoice #3, terms 2/10, n/30 consisting of the following: 3- Bike Carriers. (S)

9   Paid cleaning service $300, check #2. (G)

10 Jim Rex returned merchandise that cost $300 to Abby's Toy House consisting of the following: 1- Bike Carrier, 1- Deluxe Bike Seat. Abby issued credit memorandum #1 to Jim Rex for $300. Remember to use negative quantities. (S)

10 Purchased merchandise from Minnie Katz on account, $4,000, invoice #311, terms 1/15, n/60 consisting of the following: 2- Doll Houses w/ Furniture, 4- Porcelain Face Dolls, 10- Yo Yo's, Designer, 10- Magic Kits. (PU)

12 Issued check #3 to Earl Miller Co. in the amount of $3,920 in payment of invoice #410 ($4,000), dated March 2, less 2 percent discount ($80). (PA)

13 Sold $1,300 of toy merchandise for cash consisting of the following: 1- Doll House w/ Furniture, 1- Magic Kit. (Use the Receipts window with Customer Name and Reference fields reflecting "Cash". Receipt #101. Change Payment Method to Cash. Use the Apply to Revenues tab and list the items sold accepting all other defaults.) (R)

13 Paid salaries, $600, check #4. (G)

14 Returned merchandise to Minnie Katz in the amount of $1,000 consisting of the following: 1- Doll House w/ Furniture, 2 Porcelain Face Dolls. Debit memorandum #DM1. (PU)

15 Sold merchandise for $4,000 cash consisting of the following: 3- Mountain Bikes, 3- Bike Carriers, 2- Magic Kits, 4- Yo Yo's, Designer. See 13th for cash sale. Receipt #102. (R)

16 Received check #9823 from Jim Rex in the amount of $392 (receipt #103) in payment of invoice #2 ($700), dated March 6, less credit memorandum #CM1 ($300), less 2 percent discount ($14 − 6 = $8 net sales discount). Change payment method to Check. (R)

16 Received check # 4589 from Bill Burton in the amount of $1,000 (receipt #104) in payment of invoice #1, dated March 2. Notice how Peachtree does not factor in the discount since it is past the discount date. (R)

16 Sold merchandise to Amy Rose on account, $4,000, invoice #4, terms 2/10, n/30 consisting of the following: 1- Porcelain Face Doll, 3- Mountain Bikes, 4- Bike Carriers, 3- Deluxe Bike Seats. (S)

20 Purchased delivery truck on account from Sam Katz Garage, $3,000, invoice #111 (no discount). (PU) Since this is not an inventory item, you do not need to fill in the **Quantity** or **Item** fields. You must type in the

Description. Peachtree will default the GL code to a truck since this vendor was set up to do so. You will need to type in the purchase price in the **Amount** field. (PU)

22 Sold to Bill Burton merchandise on account, $900, invoice #5, terms 2/10, n/30 consisting of the following: 3- Magic Kits. (S)

23 Issued check #5 to Minnie Katz in the amount of $2,970 in payment of invoice #311 ($4,000), dated March 10, less debit memorandum #DM1 ($1,000), less 1 percent discount ($40 − 10 = $30 net purchases discount). (PA)

24 Sold toy merchandise on account to Amy Rose, $1,100, invoice #6, terms 2/10, n/30 consisting of the following: 1- Porcelain Face Doll, 1- Magic Kit, 3- Yo Yo's, Designer. We will allow the customer to exceed her credit limit. (S)

25 Purchased toy merchandise for cash from Woody Smith while waiting for an account to be approved, $600, check #6 consisting of the following: 2- Marionettes, Hand Carved. (Use the Payments window, Apply to Expenses tab and list the items purchased) (PA)

26 Purchased toy merchandise from Woody Smith on account, $4,800 (receipt #105), invoice #211, terms 2/10, n/30 consisting of the following: 16- Marionettes, Hand Carved. (PU)

28 Received check #4598 from Bill Burton in the amount of $882 (receipt #106) in payment of invoice #5 ($900), dated March 22, less 2 percent discount ($18). (R)

28 Received check #3217 from Amy Rose in the amount of $1,078 in payment of invoice #6, dated March 24, less 2 percent discounts ($22). (R)

28 Abby invested an additional $5,000 in the business. (G)

28 Purchased merchandise from Earl Miller Co. $1,400, invoice #436, terms 2/10, n/30 consisting of the following: 3- Mountain Bikes, 2- Bike Carriers. (PU)

30 Issued check #7 to Earl Miller Co. in the amount of $1,372 in payment of invoice #436 ($1,400), dated March 28, less 2 percent discount ($28). (PA)

30 Sold merchandise to Bonnie Flow Company on account, $3,000, invoice #7, terms 2/10, n/30 consisting of the following: 5- Marionettes, Hand Carved. (S)

5. Print the following reports accepting all defaults:

a. Aged Receivables
b. Aged Payables
c. General Journal
d. General Ledger Report

Print Reports

CHAPTER 11

Preparing a Worksheet for a Merchandise Company

With Special Appendix on What Worksheets Look Like in a Perpetual Inventory System

Jessica is a classmate of yours who recently got a part-time job at Hansen's Pharmacy. She told you the other day that she and the other employees of Hansen's recently completed a physical inventory of the store. As Jessica said, "You wouldn't believe it, but everything in the store had to be counted last Saturday night after we closed. We kept track of the quantity of each item and its price. It was a lot of work and I'm glad it's over."

You begin to realize that good accounting not only depends on following accounting rules and practices but also relies on activities such as an accurate physical count of inventory. Whether Jessica knew it or not, she played an important role in the accounting cycle for her employer by helping to take inventory on that Saturday night.

Hansen's Pharmacy is no different than thousands of other businesses which maintain an inventory. A physical inventory must be periodically taken to adjust the accounting records for inventory amounts. Other accounting adjustments must also be made by most businesses for rent, supplies, insurance, depreciation, and wages.

In Chapter 11, we will learn how to make various adjustments to the accounts of a merchandising business such as Hansen's Pharmacy. We also will discover in this chapter that the ideal way to properly track the adjustments made to the accounts of a merchandising business is to use a device called a *worksheet*. After completing this chapter, you will have a much richer understanding of the role of the worksheet in accounting and the adjustment process for a business.

Learning Objectives

- Figuring adjustments for merchandise inventory, unearned rent, supplies used, insurance expired, depreciation expense, and salaries accrued. (p. 436)

- Preparing a worksheet for a merchandise company. (p. 439)

In Chapters 9 and 10 we discussed the special journals and subsidiary ledgers of a merchandise company. Appendix material provided an introduction to perpetual inventory. Now we shift our attention to recording adjustments and completing a worksheet for a merchandise company. Note that the appendix at the end of the chapter shows worksheets for a perpetual system.

Learning Unit 11-1 — Adjustments for Merchandise Inventory and Unearned Rent

Gross sales
− Sales Ret. + Allow.
− Sales Discount
= Net sales

Net sales
− Cost of goods sold
= Gross profit
− Operating expenses
= Net income

Cost of goods sold
  Beginning inventory
+ Net purchases
+ Freight-in
− Ending inventory
= Cost of goods sold

First adjustment transfers the amount in beginning inventory from Merchandise inventory to Income Summary.

Note that Income Summary has no normal balance of debit or credit.

The Merchandise Inventory account shows the goods that a merchandise company has available to sell to customers. There are several ways of keeping track of the cost of goods sold (the total cost of the goods sold to customers) and the quantity of inventory that a company has on hand. In this chapter we discuss the periodic inventory system, in which the balance in inventory is updated only at the end of the accounting period.* This system is used by companies like Art's Wholesale Clothing Company, which sell a variety of merchandise with low unit prices.

Assume Art's Wholesale Clothing Company started the year with $19,000 worth of merchandise. This merchandise is called beginning merchandise inventory or simply beginning inventory. The balance of beginning inventory never changes. Instead, all purchases of merchandise are recorded in the Purchases account. During the accounting period $52,000 worth of such purchases were made and recorded in the Purchases account.

At the end of the period, the company takes a physical count of the merchandise in stock; this amount is called ending merchandise inventory or simply ending inventory. It is calculated on an inventory sheet as shown in Figure 11-1. This $4,000, which is the ending inventory for this period, will be the beginning inventory for the next period.

When the income statement is prepared, the cost of goods sold section requires two distinct numbers for inventory. The beginning inventory adds to the cost of goods sold, and the ending inventory is subtracted from the cost of goods sold (see margin aids at right). Remember that the two figures for beginning and ending inventory were calculated months apart. Thus, combining these amounts to come up with one inventory figure would not be accurate.

Note that in the calculation (in the margin) of cost of goods sold a new title called Freight-In is shown. Freight-in is a cost of goods sold account that records the shipping cost to the buyer. Note that net sales less cost of goods sold equals gross profit. Subtracting operating expenses from gross profits equals net income.

ADJUSTMENT FOR MERCHANDISE INVENTORY

Adjusting the Merchandise Inventory account is a two-step process because we must record the beginning inventory and ending inventory amounts separately. The first step deals with beginning merchandise inventory.

Given: Beginning Inventory, $19,000

Our first adjustment removes beginning inventory from the asset account (Merchandise Inventory) and transfers it to Income Summary. We do so by crediting Merchandise Inventory for $19,000 and debiting Income Summary for the same amount. This adjustment is shown on page 437 in T account form and on a transaction analysis chart:

*For a discussion of the perpetual inventory system, see the appendix at the end of Chapter 9, page 380.

Figure 11-1
Ending Inventory Sheet

ART'S WHOLESALE CLOTHING COMPANY ENDING INVENTORY SHEET AS OF DECEMBER 31, 20X2			
Amount	Explanation	Unit Cost	Total
20	Ladies' Jackets code 14-0	$50	$1,000
10	Men's Hats code 327	10	100
90	Men's Shirts code 423	10	900
100	Ladies' Blouses code 481	20	2,000
			$4,000
Counted by _____ Checked and priced by _____			

Merchandise Inventory 114	Income Summary 313
Bal. 19,000 | Adj. 19,000	Adj. 9,000 |

(A)

Accounts Affected	Category	↑ ↓	Rules
Income Summary	—	—	Dr.
Merchandise Inventory	Asset	↓	Cr.

(The adjusting entries would be recorded first on the worksheet and then in the general journal.)

The second step is entering the amount of ending inventory ($4,000) in the Merchandise Inventory account. This step is done to record the amount of goods on hand at the end of the period as an asset and to subtract this amount from the cost of goods sold (because we have not sold this inventory yet). To do so, we debit Merchandise Inventory for $4,000 and credit Income Summary for the same amount. This adjustment is shown below in T account form and on a transaction analysis chart:

> **Second adjustment** updates inventory account with a figure for ending inventory.

Merchandise Inventory 114	Income Summary 313
Bal. 19,000 | Adj. 19,000	Adj. 19,000 | Adj. 4,000
Adj. 4,000 |	

(B)

Let's look at how this process or method of recording merchandise inventory is reflected in the balance sheet and income statement (see Figure 11-2). Note that the $19,000 of beginning inventory is assumed sold and is shown on the income statement as part of the cost of goods sold. The ending inventory of $4,000 is assumed not to be sold and is subtracted from the cost of goods sold on the income statement. The ending inventory becomes next month's beginning inventory on the balance sheet. When the income statement is prepared, we will need a figure for beginning inventory as well as a figure for ending inventory.

> Beginning inventory $19,000
> + Net cost of* purchases   50,910
> = Cost of goods available for sale $69,910
> − Ending inventory   4,000
> = Cost of goods sold $65,910
> * Purchases − PD − PRA

ADJUSTMENT FOR UNEARNED RENT

A second new account we have not seen before is a liability called Unearned Rent or Rent Received in Advance. This account records the amount collected for rent before the service (renting the space) has been provided.

Suppose Art's Wholesale Clothing Company is subletting a portion of its space to Jesse Company for $200 per month. Jesse Company sends Art a check for $600 for three

> Note:
> If Freight-In was involved, it would have been added to net cost of purchases.

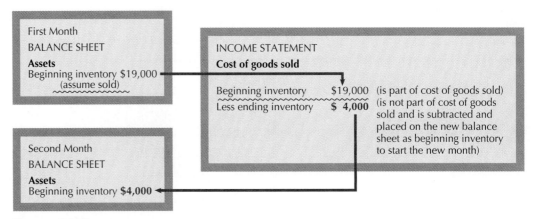

Figure 11-2
Recording Inventory on a Partial Balance Sheet and Income Statement

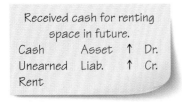

Received cash for renting space in future.

| Cash | Asset | ↑ | Dr. |
| Unearned Rent | Liab. | ↑ | Cr. |

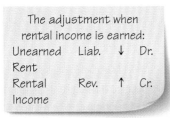

The adjustment when rental income is earned:

| Unearned Rent | Liab. | ↓ | Dr. |
| Rental Income | Rev. | ↑ | Cr. |

months' rent paid in advance. This unearned rent ($600) is a liability on the balance sheet because Art's Wholesale owes Jesse Company three months' worth of occupancy.

When Art's Wholesale fulfills a portion of the rental agreement—when Jesse Company has been in the space for a period of time—this liability account will be reduced and the Rental Income account will be increased. Rental Income is another type of revenue for Art's Wholesale.

Remember that under accrual accounting, revenue is recognized when it is earned, whether payment is received then or not. Here, Art's Wholesale collected cash in advance for a service that it has not performed as yet. A liability called Unearned Rent is the result. Art's Wholesale may have the cash, but the Rental Income is not recorded until it is earned. There are other types of unearned revenue besides unearned rent. Examples are subscriptions for magazines, legal fees collected before the work is performed, and insurance.

Learning Unit 11-1 Review

AT THIS POINT you should be able to

- Define the periodic method of inventory accounting. (p. 436)
- Explain why beginning and ending inventory are two separate figures in the cost of goods sold section on the income statement. (p. 436)
- Calculate net sales, cost of goods sold, gross profit, and net income. (p. 437)
- Show how to calculate a figure for ending inventory. (p. 437)
- Explain why Unearned Rent is a *liability* account. (p. 438)

SELF-REVIEW QUIZ 11-1

(The forms you need are on page 362 of the *Study Guide and Working Papers*.)

Given the following, prepare the two *adjusting* entries for Merchandise Inventory on 12/31/0X.

Merchandise Inventory, 1/1/0X	$ 8,000
Purchases	9,000
Merchandise Inventory, 12/31/0X	4,000
Cost of Goods Sold	10,000
Unearned Magazine Subscriptions	8,000

SOLUTION TO SELF-REVIEW QUIZ 11-1

Dec.	31	Income Summary	8 0 0 0 00		
		Merchandise Inventory		8 0 0 0 00	
	31	Merchandise Inventory	4 0 0 0 00		
		Income Summary		4 0 0 0 00	

Figure 11-3 Merchandise Inventory Adjustments

Accounting in the Reel World

Even Accountants Wear Tevas . . .

Invented in the 1980s for hardcore water sports enthusiasts, Tevas sandals are now so ubiquitous that everyone from kayakers to couch potatoes (and yes, even accountants) wear them. Chances are, you probably have some Tevas (from Hebrew for "nature") in your closet. Where did you buy them? In the local shoe store or online? How many styles did you get to choose between?

As you'll see in the Tevas on-location video on your DVD, the company sells its sandals through retailers and online. Pay attention to the challenges presented by selling Tevas online,

particularly as they relate to managing inventory. And then, after you have watched this short video, answer the questions below:

1. How are the needs for forecasting Tevas inventory different for retailers and for the company's e-commerce Web site?
2. What inventory system—periodic or perpetual—do you think would work best for the online Tevas store and why?
3. What are the main challenges in keeping Tevas' e-commerce Web site humming and how do these challenges translate into expenses for the company?

Learning Unit 11-2   Completing the Worksheet

In this unit we prepare a worksheet for Art's Wholesale Clothing Company. For convenience, we reproduce the company's chart of accounts in Figure 11-4.

Figure 11-5 (p. 441) shows the trial balance that was prepared on December 1, 200X, from the special journals of Art's Wholesale. (Note that it is placed directly in the first two columns of the worksheet.)

In looking at the trial balance, we see many new titles that have appeared since we completed a trial balance for a service company in Chapter 5. Let's look specifically at these new titles in the summary in Table 11-1, p. 442.

Note the following:

- **Mortgage Payable** is a liability account that records the increases and decreases in the amount of debt owed on a mortgage. We discuss this account more in the next chapter, when financial reports are prepared.
- **Interest Expense** represents a nonoperating expense for Art's Wholesale and thus is categorized as Other Expense. The interest would be a regular expense if it were incurred for business purposes. We look at this expense in the next chapter.
- **Unearned Revenue** is a liability account that records receipt of payment for goods and services in advance of delivery. Unearned Rent is a particular example of this general type of account.

Figure 11-4
Art's Wholesale Clothing Company Chart of Accounts

CHART OF ACCOUNTS

Assets 100–199
111   Cash
112   Petty Cash
113   Accounts Receivable
114   Merchandise Inventory
115   Supplies
116   Prepaid Insurance
121   Store Equipment
122   Accum. Depreciation, Store Equipment

Liabilities 200–299
211   Accounts Payable
212   Salaries Payable
213   Federal Income Tax Payable
214   FICA—Social Security Payable
215   FICA—Medicare Payable
216   State Income Tax Payable
217   SUTA Tax Payable
218   FUTA Tax Payable
219   Unearned Rent*
220   Mortgage Payable

Owner's Equity 300–399
311   Art Newner, Capital
312   Art Newner, Withdrawals
313   Income Summary

Revenue 400–499
411   Sales
412   Sales Returns and Allowances
413   Sales Discount
414   Rental Income

Cost of Goods Sold 500–599
511   Purchases
512   Purchases Discount
513   Purchases Returns and Allowances
514   Freight-In

Expenses 600–699
611   Salaries Expense
612   Payroll Tax Expense
613   Depreciation Expense, Store Equipment
614   Supplies Expense
615   Insurance Expense
616   Postage Expense
617   Miscellaneous Expense
618   Interest Expense
619   Cleaning Expense
620   Delivery Expense

*Although Unearned Rent is the only term under Liabilities not using payable, it is a liability.

We have already discussed adjustments (p. 437), which make up the two-step process involved in adjusting Merchandise Inventory at the end of the accounting period. Now we show T accounts and transaction analysis charts for some more adjustments that need to be made at this point for a merchandise firm, just as they must for a service company.

Adjustment C: Rental Income Earned by Art's Wholesale, $200

A month ago, Cash was increased by $600, as was a liability, Unearned Rent. Art's Wholesale received payment in advance but had not earned the rental income. Now, because $200 has been earned, the liability is reduced and Rental Income can be recorded for the $200. This step is shown as follows:

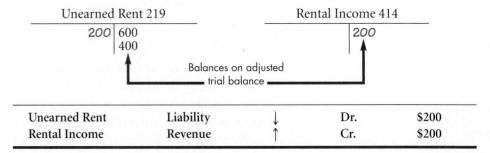

| Unearned Rent | Liability | ↓ | Dr. | $200 |
| Rental Income | Revenue | ↑ | Cr. | $200 |

Adjustment D: Supplies on Hand, $300

$500 worth of supplies has been used up; thus there is a need to increase Supplies Expense and decrease the asset Supplies.

Figure 11-5
Trial Balance Section of the Worksheet

		Trial Balance	
		Dr.	Cr.
Cash		1292000	
Petty Cash		10000	
Accounts Receivable		1450000	
Merchandise Inventory		1900000	
Supplies		80000	
Prepaid Insurance		90000	
Store Equipment		400000	
Acc. Dep., Store Equipment			40000
Accounts Payable			1790000
Federal Income Tax Payable			80000
FICA-Soc. Sec. Payable			45400
FICA-Medicare Payable			10600
State Income Tax Payable			20000
SUTA Tax Payable			10800
FUTA Tax Payable			3200
Unearned Rent			60000
Mortgage Payable			232000
Art Newner, Capital			790500
Art Newner, Withdrawals		860000	
Income Summary			
Sales			9500000
Sales Returns and Allowances		95000	
Sales Discount		67000	
Purchases		5200000	
Purchases Discount			86000
Purchases Returns and Allowances			68000
Freight-In		45000	
Salaries Expense		1170000	
Payroll Tax Expense		42000	
Postage Expense		2500	
Miscellaneous Expense		3000	
Interest Expense		30000	
		12736500	12736500

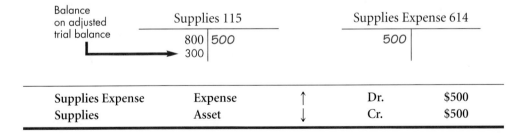

	Balance on adjusted trial balance	Supplies 115		Supplies Expense 614	
		800	500	500	
	→	300			

Supplies Expense	Expense	↑	Dr.	$500
Supplies	Asset	↓	Cr.	$500

Adjustment E: Insurance Expired, $300

Because insurance has expired by $300, Insurance Expense is increased by $300 and the asset Prepaid Insurance is decreased by $300.

Balance on adjusted trial balance	Prepaid Insurance 116		Insurance Expense 615	
	900	300	300	
→	600			

TABLE 11-1 Summary of New Account Titles

Title	Category	Report(s) Found on	Normal Balance	Temporary or Permanent
Petty Cash	Asset	Balance Sheet	Dr.	Permanent
Merchandise Inventory* (Beginning)	Asset	Balance Sheet from prior period	Dr.	Permanent
	Cost of Goods Sold	Income Statement of current period		
Federal Income Tax Payable	Liability	Balance Sheet	Cr.	Permanent
FICA—Social Security Payable	Liability	Balance Sheet	Cr.	Permanent
FICA—Medicare Payable	Liability	Balance Sheet	Cr.	Permanent
State Income Tax Payable	Liability	Balance Sheet	Cr.	Permanent
SUTA Tax Payable	Liability	Balance Sheet	Cr.	Permanent
FUTA Tax Payable	Liability	Balance Sheet	Cr.	Permanent
Unearned Rent†	Liability	Balance Sheet	Cr.	Permanent
Mortgage Payable	Liability	Balance Sheet	Cr.	Permanent
Sales	Revenue	Income Statement	Cr.	Temporary
Sales Returns and Allowances	Contra Revenue	Income Statement	Dr.	Temporary
Sales Discount	Contra Revenue	Income Statement	Dr.	Temporary
Purchases§	Cost of Goods Sold	Income Statement	Dr.	Temporary
Purchases Discount	Contra-Cost of Goods Sold	Income Statement	Cr.	Temporary
Purchases Returns and Allowances	Contra-Cost of Goods Sold	Income Statement	Cr.	Temporary
Freight-In	Cost of Goods Sold	Income Statement	Dr.	Temporary
Payroll Tax Expense	Expense	Income Statement	Dr.	Temporary
Postage Expense	Expense	Income Statement	Dr.	Temporary
Interest Expense	Other Expense	Income Statement	Dr.	Temporary

*The ending inventory of current period is a contra-cost of goods sold on the income statement and will be an asset on the balance sheet for next period.

†Referred to as Unearned Revenue.

§Note that the category for Purchases and Freight-In are Cost of Goods Sold, whereas Purchases Discounts and Purchases Returns and Allowances are Contra-Cost of Goods Sold.

Insurance Expense	Expense	↑	Dr.	$300
Prepaid Insurance	Asset	↓	Cr.	$300

Adjustment F: Depreciation Expense, $50

When depreciation is taken, Depreciation Expense and Accumulated Depreciation are both increased by $50. Note that the cost of the store equipment remains the same.

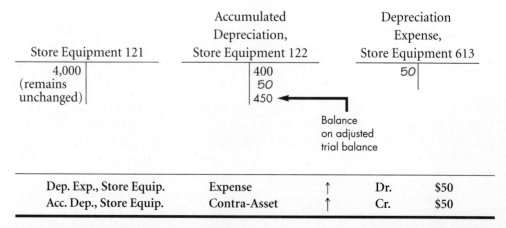

Dep. Exp., Store Equip.	Expense	↑	Dr.	$50
Acc. Dep., Store Equip.	Contra-Asset	↑	Cr.	$50

Adjustment G: Salaries Accrued, $600

The $600 in Salaries Accrued causes an increase in Salaries Expense and Salaries Payable.

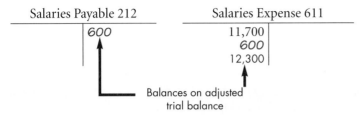

(Cont. on page 445)

	Trial Balance Dr.	Trial Balance Cr.	Adjustments Dr.	Adjustments Cr.	Adjusted Trial Balance Dr.	Adjusted Trial Balance Cr.
Cash	1292000				1292000	
Petty Cash	10000				10000	
Accounts Receivable	1450000		(B)	(A)	1450000	
Merchandise Inventory	1900000		400000	1900000	400000	
Supplies	80000			(D)50000	30000	
Prepaid Insurance	90000			(E)30000	60000	
Store Equipment	400000				400000	
Acc. Dep., Store Equipment		40000		(F) 5000		45000
Accounts Payable		1790000				1790000
Federal Income Tax Payable		80000				80000
FICA-Soc. Sec. Payable		45400				45400
FICA-Medicare Payable		10600				10600
State Income Tax Payable		20000				20000
SUTA Tax Payable		10800				10800
FUTA Tax Payable		3200				3200
Unearned Rent		60000	(C)20000			40000
Mortgage Payable		232000				232000
Art Newner, Capital		790500				790500
Art Newner, Withdrawals	860000		(A)	(B)	860000	
Income Summary			1900000	400000	1900000	400000
Sales		9500000				9500000
Sales Returns and Allowances	95000				95000	
Sales Discount	67000				67000	
Purchases	5200000				5200000	
Purchases Discount		86000				86000
Purchases Returns and Allowances		68000				68000
Freight-In	45000				45000	
Salaries Expense	1170000		(G)60000		1230000	
Payroll Tax Expense	42000				42000	
Postage Expense	2500				2500	
Miscellaneous Expense	3000				3000	
Interest Expense	30000				30000	
	12736500	12736500				
Rental Income				(C)20000		20000
Supplies Expense			(D)50000		50000	
Insurance Expense			(E)30000		30000	
Depreciation Expense, Store Equip.			(F) 5000		5000	
Salaries Payable				(G)60000		60000
			2465000	2465000	13201500	13201500

Figure 11-6 Worksheet with Three Columns Filled Out

$19,000 of beginning inventory is assumed sold during the period and thus is part of the cost of goods sold. By placing it in the debit column of Income Summary we increase the cost of goods sold.

$4,000 is the cost of ending inventory at the end of the period. It is assumed to be unsold and therefore is not part of the cost of goods sold. By placing it in the credit column of Income Summary we reduce the cost of goods sold.

$95,000 is the credit balance of Sales. The Sales Returns and Allowances, $950, and Sales Discount, $670, are placed on the debit side, which represents a reduction to total sales:
(Cr.) Sales
(Dr.) Less: Sales Returns and Allowances
(Dr.) Less: Sales Discount

The Purchases account, $52,000, is on the debit side, reflecting an increase in costs due to purchasing additional merchandise. The Purchases Discount, $860, and Purchases Returns and Allowances, $680, are on the credit side, which reduces cost of purchases:
(Dr.) Purchases
(Cr.) Less: Purchases Returns and Allowances
(Cr.) Less: Purchases Discount

Freight-in adds to the cost of goods sold.

Rental Income, which falls under the category "other income" for Art's Wholesale, is increased by $200, because the first month's rental agreement has been fulfilled.

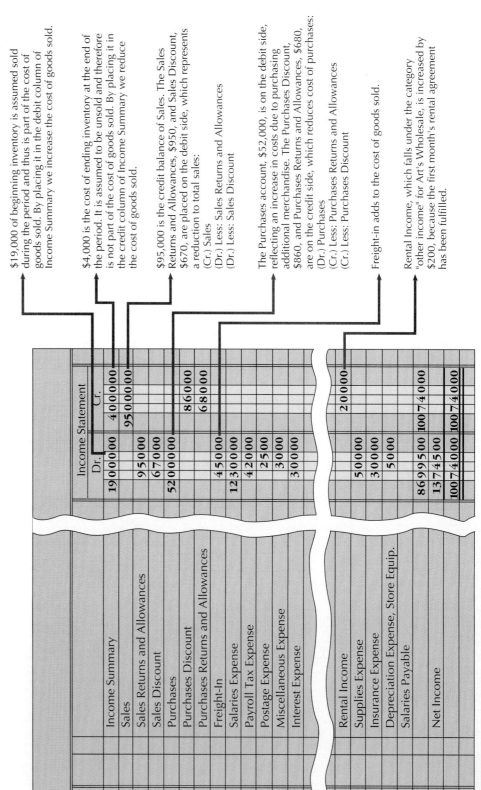

	Income Statement	
	Dr.	Cr.
Income Summary	19 0 0 0 00	4 0 0 0 00
Sales		95 0 0 0 00
Sales Returns and Allowances	9 5 0 00	
Sales Discount	6 7 0 00	
Purchases	52 0 0 0 00	
Purchases Discount		8 6 0 00
Purchases Returns and Allowances		6 8 0 00
Freight-In	4 5 0 00	
Salaries Expense	12 3 0 0 00	
Payroll Tax Expense	4 2 0 00	
Postage Expense	2 5 00	
Miscellaneous Expense	3 0 00	
Interest Expense	3 0 00	
Rental Income		2 0 0 00
Supplies Expense	5 0 00	
Insurance Expense	3 0 0 00	
Depreciation Expense, Store Equip.	5 0 00	
Salaries Payable		
	86 9 9 5 00	100 7 4 0 00
Net Income	13 7 4 5 00	
	100 7 4 0 00	100 7 4 0 00

Figure 11-7 Income Statement Section of the Worksheet

Salaries Expense	Expense	↑	Dr.	$600
Salaries Payable	Liability	↑	Cr.	$600

Figure 11-6, p. 443, shows the worksheet with the adjustments and adjusted trial balance column filled out. Note that the adjustment numbers in Income Summary from beginning and ending inventory are also carried over to the adjusted trial balance and are not combined.

The next step in completing the worksheet is to fill out the income statement columns from the adjusted trial balance, as shown in Figure 11-7, p. 444.

The next step in completing the worksheet is to fill out the balance sheet columns (Fig. 11-8). Note how ending inventory is carried over to the balance sheet from the adjusted trial balance column. Take time also to look at the placement of the payroll tax liabilities as well as Unearned Rent on the worksheet.

Figure 11-9, on pages 446–447, is the completed worksheet.

> **Remember:**
> We do not combine the $19,000 and $4,000 in Income Summary. When we prepare the cost of goods sold section for the formal financial statement, we will need both a beginning and an ending figure for inventory.

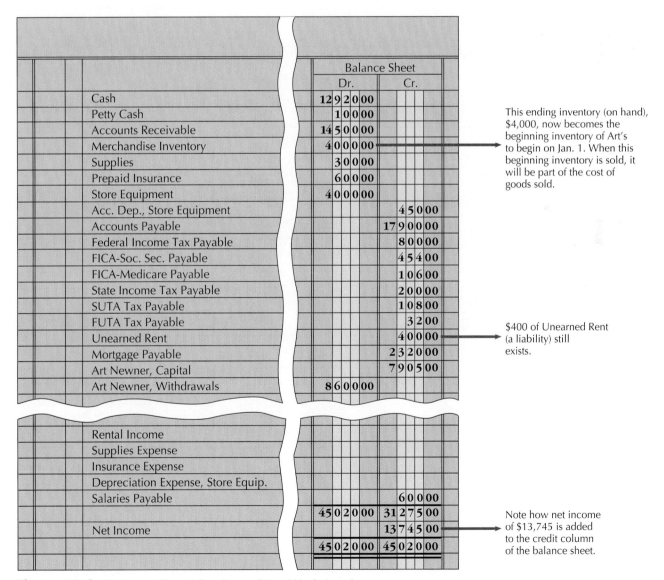

This ending inventory (on hand), $4,000, now becomes the beginning inventory of Art's to begin on Jan. 1. When this beginning inventory is sold, it will be part of the cost of goods sold.

$400 of Unearned Rent (a liability) still exists.

Note how net income of $13,745 is added to the credit column of the balance sheet.

Figure 11-8 Balance Sheet Section of the Worksheet

WORKSHEET
FOR YEAR ENDED DECEMBER 31, 200X

	Trial Balance Dr.	Trial Balance Cr.	Adjustments Dr.	Adjustments Cr.
Cash	12920 00			
Petty Cash	100 00			
Accounts Receivable	1450 00			
Merchandise Inventory	19000 00		(B)4000 00	(A)19000 00
Supplies	800 00			(D)500 00
Prepaid Insurance	900 00			(E)300 00
Store Equipment	4000 00			
Acc. Dep., Store Equipment		400 00		(F) 50 00
Accounts Payable		17900 00		
Federal Income Tax Payable		800 00		
FICA—Social Security Payable		454 00		
FICA—Medicare Payable		106 00		
State Income Tax Payable		200 00		
SUTA Tax Payable		108 00		
FUTA Tax Payable		32 00		
Unearned Rent		600 00	(C)200 00	
Mortgage Payable		2320 00		
Art Newner, Capital		7905 00		
Art Newner, Withdrawals	8600 00			
Income Summary			(A)19000 00	(B)4000 00
Sales		95000 00		
Sales Returns and Allowances	950 00			
Sales Discount	670 00			
Purchases	52000 00			
Purchases Discount		860 00		
Purchases Returns and Allowances		680 00		
Freight-In	450 00			
Salaries Expense	11700 00		(G)600 00	
Payroll Tax Expense	420 00			
Postage Expense	25 00			
Miscellaneous Expense	30 00			
Interest Expense	300 00			
	127365 00	127365 00		
Rental Income				(C)200 00
Supplies Expense			(D)500 00	
Insurance Expense			(E)300 00	
Depreciation Expense, Store Equip.			(F) 50 00	
Salaries Payable				(G)600 00
			2465 00	2465 00
Net Income				

Figure 11-9 Completed Worksheet

LEARNING UNIT 11-2 447

Adjusted Trial Bal. Dr.	Adjusted Trial Bal. Cr.	Income Statement Dr.	Income Statement Cr.	Balance Sheet Dr.	Balance Sheet Cr.
12 9 2 0 00				12 9 2 0 00	
1 0 0 00				1 0 0 00	
14 5 0 0 00				14 5 0 0 00	
4 0 0 0 00				4 0 0 0 00	
3 0 0 00				3 0 0 00	
6 0 0 00				6 0 0 00	
4 0 0 0 00				4 0 0 0 00	
	4 5 0 00				4 5 0 00
	17 9 0 0 00				17 9 0 0 00
	8 0 0 00				8 0 0 00
	4 5 4 00				4 5 4 00
	1 0 6 00				1 0 6 00
	2 0 0 00				2 0 0 00
	1 0 8 00				1 0 8 00
	3 2 00				3 2 00
	4 0 0 00				4 0 0 00
	2 3 2 00				2 3 2 00
	7 9 0 5 00				7 9 0 5 00
8 6 0 0 00				8 6 0 0 00	
19 0 0 0 00	4 0 0 0 00	19 0 0 0 00	4 0 0 0 00		
	95 0 0 0 00		95 0 0 0 00		
9 5 0 00		9 5 0 00			
6 7 0 00		6 7 0 00			
52 0 0 0 00		52 0 0 0 00			
	8 6 0 00		8 6 0 00		
	6 8 0 00		6 8 0 00		
4 5 0 00		4 5 0 00			
12 3 0 0 00		12 3 0 0 00			
4 2 0 00		4 2 0 00			
2 5 00		2 5 00			
3 0 00		3 0 00			
3 0 0 00		3 0 0 00			
	2 0 0 00		2 0 0 00		
5 0 0 00		5 0 0 00			
3 0 0 00		3 0 0 00			
5 0 00		5 0 00			
	6 0 0 00				6 0 0 00
132 0 1 5 00	132 0 1 5 00	86 9 9 5 00	100 7 4 0 00	45 0 2 0 00	31 2 7 5 00
		13 7 4 5 00			13 7 4 5 00
		100 7 4 0 00	100 7 4 0 00	45 0 2 0 00	45 0 2 0 00

Figure 11-9 (continued)

Learning Unit 11-2 Review

AT THIS POINT you should be able to

- Complete adjustments for a merchandise company. (p. 440)
- Complete a worksheet. (pp. 446–447)

SELF-REVIEW QUIZ 11-2

(Use the foldout worksheet at the end of the *Study Guide and Working Papers*.)

From the trial balance shown on Figure 11-10, complete a worksheet for Ray Company. Additional data include the following: (A and B) On December 31, 200X, ending inventory was calculated as $200; (C) Storage Fees Earned, $516; (D) Rent Expired, $100; (E) Depreciation Expense, Office Equipment, $60; (F) Salaries Accrued, $200.

Figure 11-10
Trial Balance of Ray Company

Account Title	Trial Balance Dr.	Trial Balance Cr.
Cash	2 4 8 6 00	
Merchandise Inventory	8 2 4 00	
Prepaid Rent	1 1 5 2 00	
Prepaid Insurance	6 0 00	
Office Equipment	2 1 6 0 00	
Accumulated Depreciation, Office Equipment		5 6 0 00
Unearned Storage Fees		2 5 1 6 00
Accounts Payable		1 0 0 00
B. Ray, Capital		1 9 3 2 00
Income Summary	—	—
Sales		11 0 4 0 00
Sales Returns and Allowances	5 4 6 00	
Sales Discount	2 1 6 00	
Purchases	5 2 5 6 00	
Purchases Returns and Allowances		1 6 8 00
Purchases Discount		1 0 2 00
Salaries Expense	2 0 1 6 00	
Insurance Expense	1 3 9 2 00	
Utilities Expense	9 6 00	
Plumbing Expense	2 1 4 00	
	16 4 1 8 00	16 4 1 8 00

SOLUTION TO SELF-REVIEW QUIZ 11-2

The solution is shown on page 449 in Figure 11-11.

Quiz Tip:
The ending inventory of $200 becomes next month's beginning inventory.

RAY COMPANY
WORKSHEET
FOR YEAR ENDED DECEMBER 31, 200X

	Trial Balance Dr.	Trial Balance Cr.	Adjustments Dr.	Adjustments Cr.	Adjusted Trial Balance Dr.	Adjusted Trial Balance Cr.	Income Statement Dr.	Income Statement Cr.	Balance Sheet Dr.	Balance Sheet Cr.
Cash	248600				248600				248600	
Merchandise Inventory	82400		(B) 20000	(A) 82400	20000				20000	
Prepaid Rent	115200			(D) 10000	105200				105200	
Prepaid Insurance	6000				6000				6000	
Office Equipment	216000				216000				216000	
Acc. Dep., Store Equipment		56000		(E) 6000		62000				62000
Unearned Storage Fees		251600	(C) 51600			200000				200000
Accounts Payable		10000				10000				10000
B. Ray, Capital		193200				193200				193200
Income Summary			(A) 82400	(B) 20000	82400	20000	82400	20000		
Sales		1104000				1104000		1104000		
Sales Returns and Allowances	54600				54600		54600			
Sales Discount	21600				21600		21600			
Purchases	525600				525600		525600			
Purchases Returns and Allowances		16800				16800		16800		
Purchases Discount		10200				10200		10200		
Salaries Expense	201600		(F) 20000		221600		221600			
Insurance Expense	139200				139200		139200			
Utilities Expense	9600				9600		9600			
Plumbing Expense	21400				21400		21400			
	1641800	1641800								
Storage Fees Earned				(C) 51600		51600		51600		
Rent Expense			(D) 10000		10000		10000			
Depreciation Expense, Equipment			(E) 6000		6000		6000			
Salaries Payable				(F) 20000		20000				20000
			190000	190000	1687800	1687800	1092000	1202600	595800	485200
Net Income							110600			110600
							1202600	1202600	595800	595800

Figure 11-11 Worksheet for Ray Company

Chapter Review

Learning Unit 11-1

1. The periodic inventory system updates the record of goods on hand only at the *end* of the accounting period. This system is used for companies with a variety of merchandise with low unit prices.
2. In the periodic inventory system, additional purchases of merchandise during the accounting period will be recorded in the Purchases account. The amount in beginning inventory will remain unchanged during the accounting period. At the end of the period, a new figure for ending inventory will be calculated.
3. Beginning inventory at the end of the accounting period is part of the cost of goods sold, whereas ending inventory is a reduction to cost of goods sold.
4. The perpetual inventory system keeps a continuous record of inventory. It is used by companies with high amounts of inventory.
5. Net sales less cost of goods sold equals gross profit. Gross profit less operating expenses equals net income.
6. Unearned Revenue is a liability account that accumulates revenue that has *not* been earned yet, although the cash has been received. It represents a liability to the seller until the service or product is performed or delivered.

Learning Unit 11-2

1. Two important adjustments in the accounting for a merchandise company deal with the Merchandise Inventory account and with the Unearned Revenue account (unearned rent).
2. When a company delivers goods or services for which it has been paid in advance, an adjustment is made to reduce the liability account Unearned Revenue and to increase an earned revenue account.

Key Terms

Beginning merchandise inventory (beginning inventory) The cost of goods on hand in a company to *begin* an accounting period.

Cost of goods sold Total cost of goods sold to customers.

Ending merchandise inventory (ending inventory) The cost of goods that remain unsold at the *end* of the accounting period. It is an asset on the new balance sheet.

Freight-in A cost of goods sold account that records shipping cost to buyer.

Gross profit Net sales less cost of goods sold.

Interest Expense The cost of borrowing money.

Mortgage Payable A liability account showing amount owed on a mortgage.

Periodic inventory system An inventory system that, at the *end* of each accounting period, calculates the cost of the unsold goods on hand by taking the cost of each unit times the number of units of each product on hand.

Perpetual inventory system An inventory system that keeps *continual track* of each type of inventory by recording units on hand at the beginning, units sold, and the current balance after each sale or purchase.

Unearned Revenue A liability account that records receipt of payment for goods or services in advance of delivery.

Blueprint: A Worksheet for a Merchandise Company

Account Titles	Adjustments Dr.	Adjustments Cr.	Adjusted Trial Balance Dr.	Adjusted Trial Balance Cr.	Income Statement Dr.	Income Statement Cr.	Balance Sheet Dr.	Balance Sheet Cr.
Cash			X				X	
Petty Cash			X				X	
Accounts Receivable			X				X	
Merchandise Inventory	X-E	X-B	X-E				X-E	
Supplies			X				X	
Equipment			X				X	
Acc. Dep., Store Equipment				X				X
Accounts Payable				X				X
Federal Income Tax Payable				X				X
FICA-Social Security Payable				X				X
FICA-Medicare Payable				X				X
State Income Tax Payable				X				X
SUTA Tax Payable				X				X
FUTA Tax Payable				X				X
Unearned Sales				X				X
Mortgage Payable				X				X
A. Flynn, Capital				X				X
A. Flynn, Withdrawals			X				X	
Income Summary*	X-B	X-E	X-B	X-E	X-B	X-E		
Sales				X		X		
Sales Returns and Allow.			X		X			
Sales Discount			X		X			
Purchases			X		X			
Purchases Ret. and Allow.				X		X		
Purchases Discount				X		X		
Freight-In			X		X			
Salaries Expense			X		X			
Payroll Tax Expense			X		X			
Insurance Expense			X		X			
Depreciation Expense			X		X			
Salaries Payable				X				X
Rental Income				X		X		

* Note that the figures for beginning (X-B) and ending inventory (X-E) are never combined on the Income Summary line of the worksheet. When the formal income statement is prepared, two distinct figures for inventory will be used to explain and calculate cost of goods sold. Beginning inventory adds to cost of goods sold; ending inventory reduces cost of goods sold.

Questions, Mini Exercises, Exercises, and Problems

Discussion Questions

1. What is the function of the Purchases account?
2. Explain why Unearned Revenue is a liability account.
3. In a periodic system of inventory, the balance of beginning inventory will remain unchanged during the period. True or false?

4. What is the purpose of an inventory sheet?

5. Why do many Unearned Revenue accounts have to be adjusted?

6. Explain why figures for beginning and ending inventory are not combined on the Income Summary line of the worksheet.

Mini Exercises

(The forms you need are on page 364 of the *Study Guide and Working Papers*.)

Adjustment for Merchandise Inventory

1. Given the following, journalize the adjusting entries for merchandise inventory. Note that ending inventory has a balance of $14,000.

Merchandise Inventory 114		Income Summary 313	
30,000			

Adjustment for Unearned Fees

2.

   a. Given the following, journalize the adjusting entry. By December 31, $300 of the unearned dog walking fees were earned.

Unearned Dog Walking Fees 225		Earned Dog Walking Fees 441	
	650 12/1/XX		4,000 12/1/XX

   b. What is the category of unearned dog walking fees?

Worksheet

3. Match the following:

   1. Located on the Income Statement debit column of the worksheet.
   2. Located on the Income Statement credit column of the worksheet.
   3. Located on the Balance Sheet debit column of the worksheet.
   4. Located on the Balance Sheet credit column of the worksheet.

   _____ a. Ending Merchandise Inventory
   _____ b. Unearned Rent
   _____ c. Sales Discount
   _____ d. Purchases
   _____ e. Rental Income
   _____ f. Petty Cash

Merchandise Inventory Adjustment on Worksheet

4. Adjustment column of a worksheet:

   Merchandise Inventory   Ⓐ   Ⓑ
   Income Summary   Ⓑ   Ⓐ

   Explain what the letters A and B represent. Why are they never combined?

Income Summary on the Worksheet

5.

	Adj.		ATB		Income Statement	
	Dr.	**Cr.**	**Dr.**	**Cr.**	**Dr.**	**Cr.**
Income Summary	A	B	C	D	E	F

Given a figure of beginning inventory of $500 and a $700 figure for ending inventory, place these numbers on the Income Summary line of this partial worksheet.

Exercises

(The forms you need are on page 365 of the *Study Guide and Working Papers*.)

11-1. Indicate the normal balance and category of each of the following accounts.

> a. Unearned Revenue
> b. Merchandise Inventory (beginning of period)
> c. Freight-in
> d. Payroll Tax Expense
> e. Purchases Discount
> f. Sales Discount
> g. FICA — Social Security Payable
> h. Purchases Returns and Allowances

Categorizing account titles.

11-2. From the following, calculate (a) net sales, (b) cost of goods sold, (c) gross profit, and (d) net income: Sales, $22,000; Sales Discount, $500; Sales Returns and Allowances, $250; Beginning Inventory, $650; Net Purchases, $13,200; Ending Inventory, $510; Operating Expenses, $3,600.

Calculating net sales, cost of goods sold, gross profit, and net income.

11-3. Allan Co. had the following balances on December 31, 200X:

Unearned revenue.

Cash		Unearned Janitorial Service
2,100			600

Janitorial Service
	7,200

The accountant for Allan has asked you to make an adjustment, because $400 of janitorial services has just been performed for customers who had paid two months. Construct a transaction analysis chart.

11-4. Lesan Co. purchased merchandise costing $400,000. Calculate the cost of goods sold under the following different situations:

Calculating cost of goods sold.

> a. Beginning inventory $40,000 and no ending inventory.
> b. Beginning inventory $50,000 and a $60,000 ending inventory.
> c. No beginning inventory and a $30,000 ending inventory.

11-5. Prepare a worksheet from the following information using Figure 11-12, p. 454:

Preparing a worksheet.

a/b.	Merchandise Inventory, ending	13
c.	Store Supplies on hand	4
d.	Depreciation on Store Equipment	4
e.	Accrued Salaries	2

Group A Problems

(The forms you need are on page 366 of the *Study Guide and Working Papers*. You can also use the foldout worksheets at the end of the *Study Guide and Working Papers*.)

Calculating net sales, cost of goods sold, gross profit, and net income.

11A-1. Based on the following accounts, calculate:

> a. Net sales.
> b. Cost of goods sold.
> c. Gross profit.
> d. Net income.

Check Figure:
Net income. $1,958

Figure 11-12
Trial Balance for
Moore Co.

MOORE CO. TRIAL BALANCE DECEMBER 31, 200X		
	Dr.	Cr.
Cash	8 00	
Accounts Receivable	5 00	
Merchandise Inventory	11 00	
Store Supplies	10 00	
Store Equipment	20 00	
Accumulated Depreciation, Store Equipment		6 00
Accounts Payable		5 00
J. Moore, Capital		34 00
Income Summary	—	—
Sales		64 00
Sales Returns and Allowances	9 00	
Purchases	23 00	
Purchases Discount		3 00
Freight-In	3 00	
Salaries Expense	10 00	
Advertising Expense	13 00	
Totals	112 00	112 00

Accounts Payable	$ 4,800
Operating Expenses	1,500
Lang.com, Capital	18,200
Purchases	1,300
Freight-In	70
Ending Merchandise Inventory, Dec. 31, 200X	55
Sales	5,000
Accounts Receivable	400
Cash	700
Purchases Discount	40
Sales Returns and Allowances	210
Beg. Merchandise Inventory, Jan. 1, 200X	75
Purchases Returns and Allowances	66
Sales Discount	48

Comprehensive Problem: Completing a worksheet for a merchandise company.

11A-2. From the trial balance in Figure 11-13, p. 455, complete a worksheet for Jim's Hardware. Assume the following:

a/b. Ending inventory on December 31 is calculated at $310.
  c. Insurance expired, $150.
  d. Depreciation on store equipment, $60.
  e. Accrued wages, $90.

Comprehensive Problem: Completing a worksheet.

11A-3. The owner of Waltz Company has asked you to prepare a worksheet from the trial balance in Figure 11-14, p. 455.
Additional data:

a/b. Ending merchandise inventory on December 31, $1,805.
  c. Office supplies used up, $210.
  d. Rent expired, $195.
  e. Depreciation expense on office equipment, $550.
  f. Office salaries earned but not paid, $310.

JIM'S HARDWARE
TRIAL BALANCE
DECEMBER 31, 200X

	Dr.	Cr.
Cash	7 8 6 00	
Accounts Receivable	1 1 5 2 00	
Merchandise Inventory	6 0 0 00	
Prepaid Insurance	6 8 4 00	
Store Equipment	2 1 6 0 00	
Accumulated Depreciation, Store Equipment		6 6 0 00
Accounts Payable		5 1 6 00
Jim Spool, Capital		1 6 3 2 00
Income Summary	—	—
Hardware Sales		1 1 0 4 0 00
Hardware Sales Returns and Allowances	5 4 6 00	
Hardware Sales Discount	2 1 6 00	
Purchases	5 2 5 6 00	
Purchases Discount		1 6 8 00
Purchases Returns and Allowances		1 0 2 00
Wages Expense	1 7 1 6 00	
Rent Expense	7 9 2 00	
Telephone Expense	1 1 4 00	
Miscellaneous Expense	9 6 00	
	1 4 1 1 8 00	1 4 1 1 8 00

Figure 11-13
Trial Balance for Jim's Hardware

Check Figure:
Net income $1,984

WALTZ COMPANY
TRIAL BALANCE
DECEMBER 31, 200X

	Dr.	Cr.
Cash	5 4 0 8 00	
Petty Cash	2 4 0 00	
Accounts Receivable	2 5 1 2 00	
Beginning Merchandise Inventory, Jan. 1	5 0 9 2 00	
Prepaid Rent	6 1 6 00	
Office Supplies	9 4 4 00	
Office Equipment	9 2 8 0 00	
Accumulated Depreciation, Office Equipment		7 6 0 0 00
Accounts Payable		5 9 6 4 00
K. Waltz, Capital		5 4 7 6 00
K. Waltz, Withdrawals	4 8 0 0 00	
Income Summary	—	—
Sales		5 2 4 8 4 00
Sales Returns and Allowances	9 6 00	
Sales Discount	2 4 0 0 00	
Purchases	2 9 3 1 6 00	
Purchases Discount		1 6 00
Purchases Returns and Allowances		3 4 8 00
Office Salaries Expense	7 4 0 8 00	
Insurance Expense	2 4 0 0 00	
Advertising Expense	8 0 0 00	
Utilities Expense	5 7 6 00	
	7 1 8 8 8 00	7 1 8 8 8 00

Figure 11-14
Trial Balance for Waltz Company

Check Figure:
Net income $5,300

Figure 11-15
Trial Balance for Ron's
Wholesale Clothing
Company

RON'S WHOLESALE CLOTHING COMPANY TRIAL BALANCE DECEMBER 31, 200X		
	Dr.	Cr.
Cash	4 4 6 0 00	
Petty Cash	3 0 0 00	
Accounts Receivable	7 5 0 0 00	
Merchandise Inventory	9 0 0 0 00	
Supplies	1 0 0 0 00	
Prepaid Insurance	8 5 0 00	
Store Equipment	2 5 0 0 00	
Acc. Dep., Store Equipment		1 5 0 0 00
Accounts Payable		10 6 3 5 00
Federal Income Tax Payable		5 0 0 00
FICA—Social Security Payable		4 5 4 00
FICA—Medicare Payable		1 0 6 00
State Income Tax Payable		1 5 0 00
SUTA Tax Payable		1 0 8 00
FUTA Tax Payable		3 2 00
Unearned Storage Fees		3 2 5 00
Ron Win, Capital		12 5 0 0 00
Ron Win, Withdrawals	4 3 0 0 00	
Income Summary	—	—
Sales		45 0 0 0 00
Sales Returns and Allowances	1 4 7 5 00	
Sales Discount	1 3 3 5 00	
Purchases	26 0 0 0 00	
Purchases Discount		5 5 0 00
Purchases Returns and Allowances		4 0 0 00
Freight-In	2 2 5 00	
Salaries Expense	12 0 0 0 00	
Payroll Tax Expense	4 2 0 00	
Interest Expense	8 9 5 00	
	72 2 6 0 00	72 2 6 0 00

Comprehensive Problem:
Completing a worksheet
with payroll and unearned
revenue.

11A-4. From the trial balance in Figure 11-15 and additional data, complete the worksheet for Ron's Wholesale Clothing Company.
Additional data:

Check Figure:
Net loss $824

a/b. Ending merchandise inventory on December 31, $6,000.
   c. Supplies on hand, $400.
   d. Insurance expired, $600.
   e. Depreciation on store equipment, $400.
   f. Storage fees earned, $176.

Group B Problems

(The forms you need are on page 366 of the *Study Guide and Working Papers*.)

Calculating net sales, cost
of goods sold, gross profit,
and net income.

11B-1. From the following accounts, calculate (a) net sales, (b) cost of goods sold, (c) gross profit, and (d) net income.

Sales Discount	$ 452
Purchases Returns and Allowances	64
Beginning Merchandise Inventory, Jan 1, 200X	79
Sales Returns and Allowances	191

Purchases Discounts	42
Cash	3,895
Accounts Receivable	441
Sales	3,950
Ending Merchandise Inventory, Dec. 31, 200X	75
Freight-In	41
Purchases	1,152
R. Roland, Capital	1,950
Operating Expenses	895
Accounts Payable	129

Check Figure:
Net income $1,321

11B-2. As the accountant for Jim's Hardware, you have been asked to complete a worksheet from the trial balance in Figure 11-16 as well as additional data. Additional data:

Comprehensive Problem: Completing a worksheet for a merchandise company.

a/b. Cost of ending inventory on December 31, $480.
  c. Insurance expired, $112.
  d. Depreciation on store equipment, $90.
  e. Accrued wages, $150.

11B-3. From Figure 11-17, p. 458, complete a worksheet for Waltz Company. Additional data:

Comprehensive Problem: Completing a worksheet.

a/b. Ending merchandise inventory on December 31, $1,600.
  c. Office supplies on hand, $90.
  d. Rent expired, $110.
  e. Depreciation expense on office equipment, $250.
  f. Salaries accrued, $180.

11B-4. From the trial balance in Figure 11-18, p. 459, and additional data, complete the worksheet for Ron's Wholesale Clothing Company.

Comprehensive Problem: Completing a worksheet with payroll and unearned revenue.

Figure 11-16
Trial Balance for Jim's Hardware

Check Figure:
Net income $8,686

JIM'S HARDWARE TRIAL BALANCE DECEMBER 31, 200X	Dr.	Cr.
Cash	9 6 0 0 00	
Accounts Receivable	1 6 0 0 00	
Merchandise Inventory	7 3 6 00	
Prepaid Insurance	1 1 1 2 00	
Store Equipment	3 2 0 0 00	
Accumulated Depreciation, Store Equipment		1 6 8 0 00
Accounts Payable		1 4 0 8 00
J. Spool, Capital		2 5 7 6 00
Income Summary		
Hardware Sales		14 8 0 0 00
Hardware Sales Returns and Allowances	7 2 8 00	
Hardware Sales Discount	6 8 8 00	
Purchases	7 0 8 8 00	
Purchases Discounts		2 4 0 00
Purchases Returns and Allowances		2 4 8 00
Wages Expense	2 3 0 4 00	
Rent Expense	1 8 4 0 00	
Telephone Expense	5 5 2 00	
Miscellaneous Expense	1 4 4 00	
	20 9 5 2 00	20 9 5 2 00

Figure 11-17
Trial Balance for Waltz
Company

WALTZ COMPANY TRIAL BALANCE DECEMBER 31, 200X	Dr.	Cr.
Cash	3 8 0 0 00	
Petty Cash	1 0 0 00	
Accounts Receivable	3 4 0 0 00	
Merchandise Inventory	5 2 0 4 00	
Prepaid Rent	1 2 0 0 00	
Office Supplies	1 3 6 0 00	
Office Equipment	9 6 8 0 00	
Accumulated Depreciation, Office Equipment		4 0 4 0 00
Accounts Payable		7 9 6 4 00
K. Waltz, Capital		5 4 7 6 00
K. Waltz, Withdrawals	5 0 0 0 00	
Income Summary	—	—
Sales		52 4 6 2 00
Sales Returns and Allowances	1 1 6 00	
Sales Discount	2 2 0 0 00	
Purchases	29 2 9 6 00	
Purchases Discounts		1 2 0 8 00
Purchases Returns and Allowances		1 3 5 0 00
Office Salaries Expense	7 4 0 8 00	
Insurance Expense	2 2 0 0 00	
Advertising Expense	8 0 0 00	
Utilities Expense	7 3 6 00	
	72 5 0 0 00	72 5 0 0 00

Check Figure:
Net income $6,850

Additional data:

a/b. Ending merchandise inventory on December 31, $9,000.
   c. Supplies on hand, $50.
   d. Insurance expired, $55.
   e. Depreciation on store equipment, $100.
   f. Storage fees earned, $115.

Real-World Applications

11R-1. Kim Andrews prepared the income statement in Figure 11-19 (p. 459) on a
cash basis for Ed Sloan, M.D.

Dr. Sloan has requested written information from Kim as to what his professional fees earned would be under the accrual-basis system of accounting. Kim
has asked you to provide Dr. Sloan with this information, based on the following
facts that Kim ignored in the original preparation of the financial report:

	20X1	20X2
Accrued Professional Fees	$4,200	$5,300
Unearned Professional Fees	6,200	4,250

Make a written recommendation about the advantages of an accrual system to
Dr. Sloan.

RON'S WHOLESALE CLOTHING COMPANY TRIAL BALANCE DECEMBER 31, 200X		
	Dr.	Cr.
Cash	2 6 0 0 00	
Petty Cash	3 0 00	
Accounts Receivable	3 0 0 0 00	
Merchandise Inventory	3 6 0 0 00	
Supplies	2 7 0 00	
Prepaid Insurance	1 8 0 00	
Store Equipment	1 0 0 0 00	
Accumulated Depreciation, Store Equipment		4 9 6 00
Accounts Payable		4 5 9 0 00
FIT Payable		3 5 0 00
FICA—Social Security Payable		1 9 4 00
FICA—Medicare Payable		4 6 00
SIT Payable		1 0 0 00
SUTA Tax Payable		6 0 00
FUTA Tax Payable		1 4 00
Unearned Storage Fees		3 5 0 00
Ron Win, Capital		2 7 3 4 00
Ron Win, Withdrawals	1 8 0 0 00	
Income Summary	—	—
Sales		1 9 4 0 0 00
Sales Returns and Allowances	5 6 0 00	
Sales Discount	4 8 0 00	
Purchases	8 6 0 0 00	
Purchases Discount		2 4 0 00
Purchases Returns and Allowances		1 6 0 00
Freight-In	1 0 0 00	
Salaries Expense	6 0 0 0 00	
Payroll Tax Expense	1 9 4 00	
Interest Expense	3 2 0 00	
	2 8 7 3 4 00	2 8 7 3 4 00

Figure 11-18 Trial Balance for Ran's Wholesale Clothing Company

Check Figure:
Net loss $8,686

ED SLOAN, M.D. INCOME STATEMENT FOR YEAR ENDED DECEMBER 31, 20X2	
Professional Fees Earned	5 0 0 0 0 00
Expenses	1 8 0 0 0 00
Net Income	3 2 0 0 0 00

Figure 11-19 Income Statement for Ed Sloan, M. D.

11R-2. Abby Jay is having a difficult time understanding the relationship of sales, cost of goods sold, gross profit, and net income for a merchandise company. As the accounting lab tutor, you have been asked to sit down with Abby and explain how to calculate the missing amounts in each situation listed here. Keep in mind that each situation is a distinct and separate business problem.

	Sales	Beg. Inv.	Purchases	End Inv.	Cost of Goods Sold	Gross Profit	Expense	Net Income or Loss
Sit. 1	320,000	200,000	160,000	?	260,000	?	80,000	?
Sit. 2	380,000	140,000	?	180,000	200,000	?	100,000	80,000
Sit. 3	480,000	200,000	?	160,000	?	220,000	140,000	80,000
Sit. 4	?	160,000	280,000	140,000	?	160,000	140,000	?
Sit. 5	440,000	160,000	260,000	?	240,000	?	100,000	?
Sit. 6	280,000	120,000	?	140,000	160,000	?	?	40,000
Sit. 7	?	160,000	200,000	120,000	?	160,000	?	−20,000
Sit. 8	320,000	?	200,000	140,000	?	120,000	?	40,000

Explain in writing why gross profit does not always mean cash.

YOU make the call

Critical Thinking/Ethical Case

11R-3. Jim Heary is the custodian of petty cash. Jim, who is short of personal cash, decided to pay his home electrical and phone bill from petty cash. He plans to pay it back next month. Do you feel Jim should do so? You make the call. Write down your specific recommendations to Jim.

Internet Exercises: Saturn

EX-1. [www.saturn.com] An automobile dealer with a large inventory has a huge amount of cash invested in his product. The investment requires careful accounting to safeguard the asset both from a physically safe viewpoint and from a safe accounting standpoint. Because each of the individual units in an automobile inventory is identifiable, automobile inventories lend themselves as excellent candidates for perpetual inventory accounting.

At the end of an accounting period, what procedures would a car dealer like Saturn take to determine if all of the units in its perpetual inventory are accounted for? How would you adjust the inventory for an extra unit found on the sales lot, if the unit was not in the perpetual inventory records?

EX-2. [www.saturn.com] In the previous example you determined what entries to make for inventory that was not on the accounting records or for inventory that was in the accounting records but not on the location.

In this exercise, state how each of the following independent cases would affect gross profit. State whether gross profit is UNDERSTATED or OVER-STATED and give a reason for the answer you choose in each case.

a. One unit of inventory in the accounting records is not on the location.
b. One unit of inventory on the location is not in the accounting records.
c. One unit shown as a sale in the accounting records is on the location.

Continuing Problem

Eldorado Computer Center

The first six months of the year have concluded for Eldorado Computer Center, and Tony wants to make the necessary adjustments to his accounts to prepare accurate financial statements.

Assignment

(The worksheet is in the envelope at the end of the *Study Guide and Working Papers.*)

To prepare these adjustments, use the trial balance in Figure 11-20, p. 462, and the following inventory that Tony took at the end of March:

10 dozen $\frac{1}{4}$" screws at a cost of $10 a dozen.

5 dozen $\frac{1}{2}$" screws at a cost of $7 a dozen.

2 feet of coaxial cable at a cost of $5 per foot.

There was $300 worth of merchandise left in stock.

Depreciation of computer equipment:

Computer depreciates at $33 a month; purchased July 5.

Computer workstations depreciate at $20 per month; purchased September 17.

Shop benches depreciate at $25 per month; purchased November 5.

Depreciation of office equipment:

Office equipment depreciates at $10 per month; purchased July 17.

Fax machine depreciates at $10 per month; purchased November 20.

Six months' worth of rent at a rental rate of $400 per month has expired.

Remember: If any long-term asset is purchased in the first 15 days of the month, Tony will charge depreciation for the full month. If an asset is purchased later than the 16th, he will not charge depreciation in the month it was purchased.

Complete the 10-column worksheet for the six months ended March 31, 200X.

| Account Titles | Trial Balance | |
	Dr.	Cr.
Cash	1251665	
Petty Cash	10000	
Accounts Receivable	119000	
Prepaid Rent	280000	
Supplies	43200	
Merchandise Inventory		
Computer Shop Equipment	380000	
Accumulated Depr. CS Equip.		9900
Office Equipment	105000	
Accum. Depr. Office Equip.		2000
Accounts Payable		284000
T. Freedman, Capital		740600
T. Freedman, Withdrawals	201500	
Income Summary		
Service Revenue		1980000
Sales		970000
Sales Return and Allowances	40000	
Sales Discounts	22000	
Advertising Exp.	80000	
Rent Exp.		
Utilities Exp.	29000	
Phone Exp.	15000	
Supplies Exp.		
Insurance Exp.	10000	
Postage Exp.	17500	
Depreciation Exp. C.S. Equip.		
Depreciation Exp. Office Equip.		
Miscellaneous Exp.	1000	
Wage Expense	203000	
Payroll Tax Expense	22635	
Purchases	95000	
Purch. Ret. & Allow.		10000
Totals	3996500	3996500

Figure 11-20
Trial Balance for Eldorado Computer March 31, 200X

APPENDIX

A WORKSHEET FOR ART'S WHOLESALE CLOTHING CO. USING A PERPETUAL INVENTORY SYSTEM

What's New: The Merchandise Inventory account does not need to be adjusted. The $4,000 figure for merchandise is the up-to-date balance in the account. The difference between beginning inventory and ending inventory will be part of a new account called *Cost of Goods Sold* on the worksheet.

How the $65,910 of Cost of Goods Sold was calculated from a periodic setup:

	Purchases	$52,000	←	**Assumed sold; part of cost**
+	Merchandise Inventory	$15,000	←	**Beg. Inv. − Ending Inv.**
				$19,000 − $4,000
−	Purchases Discount	860	→	**Reduces costs**
−	Purchases Returns and Allowances	680	↗	
+	Freight-in	450	→	**Adds to cost**
		$65,910		**Cost of Goods Sold**

What's Deleted from the Periodic Worksheet: Account titles for Purchases, Purchases Discounts, Purchases Returns and Allowances, and Freight-in.

Note: Net income is the same on the periodic and the perpetual worksheets.

PROBLEM FOR APPENDIX

Using the solution to Self-Review Quiz 11-2 (p. 448), convert this worksheet to a perpetual inventory system worksheet. (The worksheet is in the envelope at the end of the *Study Guide and Working Papers*.)

ART'S WHOLESALE CLOTHING CO.
WORKSHEET
FOR YEAR ENDED DECEMBER 31, 200X

Account Titles	Trial Balance Dr.	Trial Balance Cr.	Adjustments Dr.	Adjustments Cr.	Adjusted Trial Balance Dr.	Adjusted Trial Balance Cr.	Income Statement Dr.	Income Statement Cr.	Balance Sheet Dr.	Balance Sheet Cr.
Cash	12920.00				12920.00				12920.00	
Petty Cash	100.00				100.00				100.00	
Accounts Receivable	14500.00				14500.00				14500.00	
Merchandise Inventory	4000.00				4000.00				4000.00	
Supplies	800.00			(B) 500.00	300.00				300.00	
Prepaid Insurance	900.00			(C) 300.00	600.00				600.00	
Store Equipment	4000.00				4000.00				4000.00	
Acc. Dep., Store Equip.		400.00		(D) 50.00		450.00				450.00
Accounts Payable		17900.00				17900.00				17900.00
Federal Income Tax		800.00				800.00				800.00
FICA—Social Security		454.00				454.00				454.00
FICA—Medicare		106.00				106.00				106.00
State Income Tax		200.00				200.00				200.00
SUTA Tax		108.00				108.00				108.00
FUTA Tax Payable		32.00				32.00				32.00
Unearned Rent		600.00	(A) 200.00			400.00				400.00
Mortgage Payable		23200.00				23200.00				23200.00
Art Newner, Capital		79050.00				79050.00				79050.00
Art Newner, Withdrawal	8600.00				8600.00				8600.00	
Sales		95000.00				95000.00		95000.00		
Sales Returns and Allow.	950.00				950.00		950.00			
Sales Discount	670.00				670.00		670.00			
Cost of Goods Sold	65910.00				65910.00		65910.00			
Salaries Expense	11700.00		(E) 600.00		12300.00		12300.00			
Payroll Tax Expense	420.00				420.00		420.00			
Postage Expense	25.00				25.00		25.00			
Miscellaneous Expense	30.00				30.00		30.00			
Interest Expense	300.00				300.00		300.00			
	125825.00	125825.00								
Rental Income				(A) 200.00		200.00		200.00		
Supplies Expense			(B) 500.00		500.00		500.00			
Insurance Expense			(C) 300.00		300.00		300.00			
Dep. Exp., Store Equip.			(D) 50.00		50.00		50.00			
Salaries Payable				(E) 600.00		600.00				600.00
			1650.00	1650.00	126475.00	126475.00	81455.00	95200.00	45020.00	31275.00
Net Income							13745.00			13745.00
							95200.00	95200.00	45020.00	45020.00

Figure A-1   Worksheet for Art's Wholesale Clothing Co.

RAY COMPANY
WORKSHEET
FOR YEAR ENDED DECEMBER 31, 200X

Account Titles	Trial Balance Dr.	Trial Balance Cr.	Adjustments Dr.	Adjustments Cr.	Adjusted Trial Balance Dr.	Adjusted Trial Balance Cr.	Income Statement Dr.	Income Statement Cr.	Balance Sheet Dr.	Balance Sheet Cr.
Cash	2,486 00				2,486 00				2,486 00	
Merchandise Inventory	2,000 00				2,000 00				2,000 00	
Prepaid Rent	1,152 00			(B) 100 00	1,052 00				1,052 00	
Prepaid Insurance	60 00				60 00				60 00	
Office Equipment	2,160 00				2,160 00				2,160 00	
Accumulated Dep., Off. Equip.		560 00		(C) 60 00		620 00				620 00
Unearned Storage Fees		2,516 00	(A) 516 00			2,000 00				2,000 00
Accounts Payable		100 00				100 00				100 00
B. Ray, Capital		1,932 00				1,932 00				1,932 00
Sales		11,040 00				11,040 00		11,040 00		
Sales Returns and Allowances	546 00				546 00		546 00			
Sales Discounts	216 00				216 00		216 00			
Cogs*	5,610 00				5,610 00		5,610 00			
Salaries Expense	2,016 00		(D) 200 00		2,216 00		2,216 00			
Insurance Expense	1,392 00				1,392 00		1,392 00			
Utilities Expense	96 00				96 00		96 00			
Plumbing Expense	214 00				214 00		214 00			
	16,148 00	16,148 00								
Storage Fees Earned				(A) 516 00		516 00		516 00		
Rent Expense			(B) 100 00		100 00		100 00			
Dep. Expense, Equip.			(C) 60 00		60 00		60 00			
Salaries Payable				(D) 200 00		200 00				200 00
			876 00	876 00	16,408 00	16,408 00	10,450 00	11,556 00	595,8 00	4,852 00
Net Income							1,106 00			1,106 00
							11,556 00	11,556 00	5,958 00	5,958 00

*$624 ($824 − $200) + $5,256 − $168 − $102.

Figure A-2 Worksheet for Ray Company

CHAPTER 12

Completion of the Accounting Cycle for a Merchandise Company

One thing about school that you like and at the same time dislike are tests. Tests are good because they provide you with feedback on your progress, which may make you feel that you've learned something. At the same time, you know that tests are not the most enjoyable thing about going to school, and studying for tests becomes a lot of hard work.

The same thing happens in accounting for a business. Generally, the "test" of whether a business is doing well or poorly depends on if it is earning a profit. Accounting provides feedback about this critical "test." And accounting can also help a business to evaluate how much cash it has in the bank, how much it has invested, its amount of property, plant, and equipment, and what it owes to others on a regular basis. Accounting does this through the use of financial statements.

Whether a business is small like James Hardware and Lumber Company or Hansen's Pharmacy, or gigantic like Microsoft or General Motors, a business will prepare financial statements on a regular basis. The income statement provides results about whether a business is earning or losing money, while the balance sheet is used to evaluate the financial position of a business at a particular point in time.

In Chapter 12 we will learn how to use the worksheet to prepare the financial statements for a business. We will also discuss preparing adjusting and closing entries, the post-closing trial balance, and reversing entries.

After you complete this chapter, you will better understand how accounting reports the results of the test of profit or loss from operating a business and be able to evaluate its financial position. And now you know that tests don't end when you graduate; they exist for all companies in business today.

Learning Objectives

- Preparing financial statements for a merchandise company. (p. 468)
- Recording adjusting and closing entries. (p. 477)
- Preparing post-closing trial balance. (p. 482)
- Completing reversing entries. (p. 483)

In this chapter we discuss the steps involved in completing the accounting cycle for a merchandise company. The steps involved include preparing financial reports, journalizing and posting adjusting and closing entries, preparing a post-closing trial balance, and reversing entries.

Learning Unit 12-1   Preparing Financial Statements

As we discussed in Chapter 5, when we were dealing with a service company rather than a merchandise company, the three financial statements can be prepared from the worksheet. Let's begin by looking at how Art's Wholesale Clothing Company prepares the income statement.

THE INCOME STATEMENT

Art is interested in knowing how well his shop performed for the year ended December 31, 200X. What were its net sales? Were there many returns of goods from dissatisfied customers? What was the cost of the goods brought into the store versus the selling price received? How many goods were returned to suppliers? What is the cost of the goods that have not been sold? What was the cost of the Freight-in account? The income statement in Figure 12-1 (p. 469) is prepared from the income statement columns of the worksheet. Note that there are no debit or credit columns on the formal income statement; the inside columns in financial reports are used for subtotaling, not for debit and credit.

The income statement is broken down into several sections. Remembering the sections can help you set it up correctly on your own. The income statement shows

$$
\begin{array}{l}
\text{Net Sales} \\
\underline{- \text{ Cost of Goods Sold}} \\
= \text{Gross Profit} \\
\underline{- \text{ Operating Expenses}} \\
= \text{Net Income from Operations} \\
+ \text{ Other Income} \\
\underline{- \text{ Other Expenses}} \\
= \text{Net Income}
\end{array}
$$

Let's take these sections one at a time and see where the figures come from on the worksheet.

Revenue Section

Sales
− Sales Ret. & Allow.
− Sales Discount
= Net Sales

Net Sales   The first major category of the income statement shows net sales. The figure here—$93,380—is not on the worksheet. Instead, the accountant must combine the amounts for gross sales, sales returns and allowances, and sales discount found on the worksheet to arrive at a figure for net sales. Thus these individual amounts are not summarized in a single figure for net sales until the formal income statement is prepared.

ART'S WHOLESALE CLOTHING COMPANY
INCOME STATEMENT
FOR YEAR ENDED DECEMBER 31, 200X

Revenue:			
Gross Sales			$95 000 00
Less: Sales Ret. and Allow.	$ 95000		
Sales Discount	67000		1 62000
Net Sales			$93 380 00
Cost of Goods Sold:			
Merchandise Inventory, 1/1/0X		$19 000 00	
Purchases		$52 000 00	
Less: Purch. Discount	$ 86000		
Purch. Ret. and Allow.	68000	1 54000	
Net Purchases		$50 460 00	
Add: Freight-In		45000	
Net Cost of Purchases		50 910 00	
Cost of Goods Available for Sale		$69 910 00	
Less: Merch. Inv., 12/31/0X		4 000 00	
Cost of Goods Sold			65 910 00
Gross Profit			$27 470 00
Operating Expenses:			
Salaries Expense		$12 300 00	
Payroll Tax Expense		42000	
Dep. Exp., Store Equip.		5000	
Supplies Expense		50000	
Insurance Expense		30000	
Postage Expense		2500	
Miscellaneous Expense		3000	
Total Operating Expenses			13 625 00
Net Income from Operations			$13 845 00
Other Income:			
Rental Income		$ 20000	
Other Expenses:			
Interest Expense		30000	10000
Net Income			$13 745 00

ART'S WHOLESALE CLOTHING COMPANY
PARTIAL WORKSHEET
FOR YEAR ENDED DECEMBER 31, 200X

	Income Statement	
	Dr	Cr
Income Summary	19 00 00 00	4 00 00 00
Sales		95 000 00
Sales Returns and Allowances	95000	
Sales Discount	67000	
Purchases	52 000 00	
Purchases Discount		86000
Purchases Returns and Allowances		68000
Freight-In	45000	
Salaries Expense	12 300 00	
Payroll Tax Expense	42000	
Postage Expense	2500	
Miscellaneous Expense	3000	
Interest Expense	30000	
Rental Income		20000
Supplies Expense	50000	
Insurance Expense	30000	
Depreciation Expense, Store Equip.	5000	
Salaries Payable		
	86 995 00	100 074 00
Net Income	13 745 00	
	100 074 00	100 074 00

Figure 12-1 Partial Worksheet and Income Statement

Cost of Goods Sold Section

> Beg. Inventory
> \+ Net Cost of Puchases
> − Ending Inventory
> = Cost of Goods Sold

The figures for Merchandise Inventory are shown separately on the worksheet. The $19,000 represents the beginning inventory of the period, and the $4,000, calculated from an inventory sheet is the ending inventory. Note on the financial report that the cost of goods sold section uses two separate figures for inventory.

Note that the following numbers are not found on the worksheet but are shown on the formal income statement (they are combined by the accountant in preparing the income statement):

> **Remember:**
> In the periodic inventory system, goods brought in during the accounting period are added to the Purchases account, not to the Merchandise Inventory account.

- Net Purchases: $50,460 (Purchases − Purchases Discount − Purchases Returns and Allowances)
- Net Cost of Purchases: $50,910 (Net Purchases + Freight-in)
- Cost of Goods Available for Sale: $69,910 (Beginning Inventory + Net Cost of Purchases)
- Cost of Goods Sold: $65,910 (Cost of Goods Available for Sale − Ending Inventory)

Gross Profit

> Net Sales
> − Cost of Goods Sold
> = Gross Profit

Gross profit ($27,470) is calculated by subtracting the cost of goods sold from net sales ($93,380 − $65,910). The amount is not found on the worksheet.

Operating Expenses Section

Like the other figures we have discussed, the business's operating expenses do not appear on the worksheet. To get this figure ($13,625), the accountant adds up all the expenses on the worksheet.

Many operating companies break expenses down into those directly related to the selling activity of the company (selling expenses) and those related to administrative or office activity (administrative expenses or general expenses). Here's a sample list broken down into these two categories:

Operating Expenses

- Selling Expenses:
    - Sales Salaries Expense
    - Delivery Expense
    - Advertising Expense
    - Depreciation Expense, Store Equipment
    - Insurance Expense
        - Total Selling Expenses
- Administrative Expenses:
    - Rent Expense
    - Office Salaries Expense
    - Utilities Expense
    - Supplies Expense
    - Depreciation Expense, Office Equipment
        - Total Administrative Expenses
            - Total Operating Expenses

Other Income (or Other Revenue) Section

The Other Income or Other Revenue section is used to record any revenue other than revenue from sales. For example, Art's Wholesale makes a profit from subletting a portion of a building. The $200 of rental income the company earns from this is recorded in the Other Income section.

Other Expenses Section

The Other Expenses section is used to record nonoperating expenses, that is, expenses that are not related to the main operating activities of the business. For example, Art's Wholesale owes $300 interest on money it has borrowed. That expense is shown in the Other Expenses section.

STATEMENT OF OWNER'S EQUITY

The information used to prepare the statement of owner's equity comes from the balance sheet columns of the worksheet. Keep in mind that the capital account in the ledger should be checked to see whether any additional investments have occurred during the period. Figure 12-2 below shows how the worksheet aids in this step. The

> The statement of owner's equity is the same for a merchandise business as for a service firm.

Figure 12-2
Preparing Statement of Owner's Equity from the Worksheet

> Any additional investment by the owner would be added to his or her beginning capital amount.

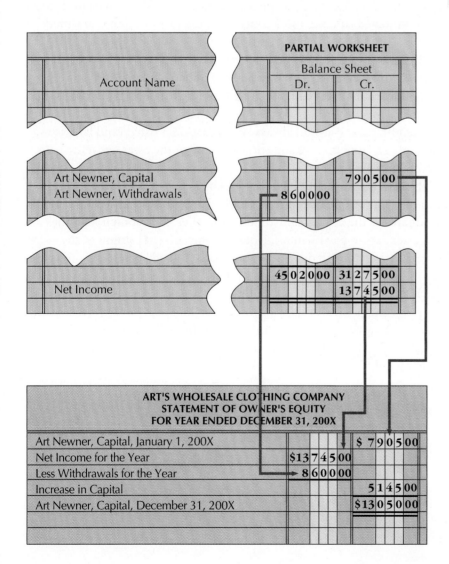

ending figure of $13,050 for Art Newner, Capital, is carried over to the balance sheet, which is the final report we look at in this chapter.

THE BALANCE SHEET

Figure 12-3 on p. 473 shows how a worksheet is used to aid in the preparation of a classified balance sheet. A classified balance sheet breaks down the assets and liabilities into more detail. Classified balance sheets provide management, owners, creditors, and suppliers with more information about the company's ability to pay current and long-term debts. They also provide a more complete financial picture of the firm.

The categories on the classified balance sheet are as follows:

- Current assets are defined as cash and assets that will be converted into cash or used up during the normal operating cycle of the company or one year, whichever is longer. (Think of the operating cycle as the time period it takes a company to buy and sell merchandise and then collect accounts receivable.)

    Accountants list current assets in order of how easily they can be converted into cash (called *liquidity*). In some cases, Accounts Receivable can be turned into cash more quickly than Merchandise Inventory. For example, it can be quite difficult to sell an outdated computer in a computer store or to sell last year's model car this year.

- Plant and Equipment are long-lived assets that are used in the production or sale of goods or services. Art's Wholesale has only one plant asset, store equipment; other plant assets could include buildings and land. The assets are usually listed in order according to how long they will last; the shortest-lived assets are listed first. Land would always be the last asset listed (and land is never depreciated). Note that we still show the cost of the asset less its accumulated depreciation.

- Current liabilities are the debts or obligations of Art's Wholesale that must be paid within one year or one operating cycle. The order of listing accounts in this section is not always the same; many times companies will list their liabilities in the order they expect to pay them off. Note that the current portion of the mortgage, $320 (that portion due within one year), is listed before Accounts Payable.

- Long-term liabilities are debts or obligations that are not due and payable for a comparatively long period, usually for more than one year. For Art's Wholesale there is only one long-term liability, Mortgage Payable. The long-term portion of the mortgage is listed here; the current portion, due within one year, is listed under current liabilities.

Mortgage Payable:
$2,320
− 320 current portion
$2,000 long-term liability

ART'S WHOLESALE CLOTHING COMPANY
WORKSHEET
FOR YEAR ENDED DECEMBER 31, 200X

	Balance Sheet	
	Dr.	Cr.
Cash	1292000	
Petty Cash	10000	
Accounts Receivable	1450000	
Merchandise Inventory	400000	
Supplies	30000	
Prepaid Insurance	60000	
Store Equipment	400000	
Acc. Dep., Store Equipment		45000
Accounts Payable		1790000
Federal Income Tax Payable		80000
FICA-Social Security Payable		45400
FICA-Medicare Payable		10600
State Income Tax Payable		20000
SUTA Tax Payable		10800
FUTA Tax Payable		3200
Unearned Rent		40000
Mortgage Payable		232000
Art Newner, Capital		790500
Salaries Payable		60000
	4502000	3127500
Net Income		1374500
	4502000	4502000

ART'S WHOLESALE CLOTHING COMPANY
CLASSIFIED BALANCE SHEET
FOR YEAR ENDED DECEMBER 31, 200X

Assets

Current Assets:			
Cash	$1292000		
Petty Cash	10000		
Accounts Receivable	1450000		
Merchandise Inventory	400000		
Supplies	30000		
Prepaid Insurance	60000		
Total Current Assets		$3242000	
Plant and Equipment:			
Store Equipment	$400000		
Less: Accum. Depreciation	45000	355000	
Total Assets		$3597000	

Liabilities

Current Liabilities:			
Mortgage Payable (current portion)	$ 32000		
Accounts Payable	1790000		
Federal Income Tax Payable	80000		
FICA–Social Security Payable	45400		
FICA–Medicare Payable	10600		
State Income Tax Payable	20000		
SUTA Tax Payable	10800		
FUTA Tax Payable	3200		
Salaries Payable	60000		
Unearned Rent	40000		
Total Current Liabilities		$2092000	
Long-Term Liabilities:			
Mortgage Payable		200000	
Total Liabilities		$2292000	

Owner's Equity

Art Newner, Capital, December 31, 200X		1305000
Total Liabilities and Owner's Equity		$3597000

Figure 12-3 Partial Worksheet and Classified Balance Sheet

Learning Unit 12-1 Review

AT THIS POINT you should be able to

- Prepare a detailed income statement from the worksheet. (p. 469)
- Explain the difference between selling and administrative expenses. (p. 470)
- Explain which columns of the worksheet are used in preparing a statement of owner's equity. (p. 471)
- Explain as well as compare current assets with plant and equipment. (p. 472)
- Using Mortgage Payable as an example, explain the difference between current and long-term liabilities. (p. 472)
- Prepare a classified balance sheet from a worksheet. (p. 473)

SELF-REVIEW QUIZ 12-1

(The forms you need are on pages 372–374 of the *Study Guide and Working Papers*.)

Using the worksheet on page 449 from Self-Review Quiz 11-2, prepare in proper form (1) an income statement, (2) a statement of owner's equity, (3) a classified balance sheet for Ray Company.

SOLUTIONS TO SELF-REVIEW QUIZ 12-1

1.

RAY COMPANY INCOME STATEMENT FOR YEAR ENDED DECEMBER 31, 200X					
Revenue:					
Sales					$11 040 00
Less: Sales Ret. and Allow.				$ 546 00	
Sales Discount				216 00	762 00
Net Sales					$10 278 00
Cost of Goods Sold:					
Merchandise Inventory, 1/1/0X				$ 824 00	
Purchases			$5 256 00		
Less: Pur. Ret. and Allow.	$ 168 00				
Purchases Discount	102 00		270 00		
Net Purchases				4 986 00	
Cost of Goods Available for Sale				$ 5 810 00	
Less: Merchandise Inv., 12/31/0X				200 00	
Cost of Goods Sold					5 610 00
Gross Profit					$4 668 00
Operating Expenses:					
Salaries Expense			$ 2 216 00		
Insurance Expense			1 392 00		
Utilities Expense			96 00		
Plumbing Expense			214 00		
Rent Expense			100 00		
Depreciation Exp., Equip.			60 00		
Total Operating Expenses					4 078 00
Net Income from Operations					$ 590 00
Other Income:					
Storage Fees					516 00
Net Income					$ 1 106 00

Figure 12-4 Income Statement for Ray Company

Quiz Tip:
Note that Cost of Goods Sold has a separate figure for beginning inventory and ending inventory.

2.

Figure 12-5
Statement of Owner's
Equity for Ray Company

RAY COMPANY STATEMENT OF OWNER'S EQUITY FOR YEAR ENDED DECEMBER 31, 200X	
B. Ray, Capital, 1/1/0X	$ 1 9 3 2 00
Net Income for the Year	1 1 0 6 00
B. Ray, Capital, 12/31/0X	$ 3 0 3 8 00

3.

RAY COMPANY BALANCE SHEET DECEMBER 31, 200X			
Assets			
Current Assets:			
Cash	$ 2 4 8 6 00		
Merchandise Inventory	2 0 0 00		
Prepaid Rent	1 0 5 2 00		
Prepaid Insurance	6 0 00		
Total Current Assets		$ 3 7 9 8 00	
Plant and Equipment:			
Office Equipment	$ 2 1 6 0 00		
Less: Accumulated Depreciation	6 2 0 00	1 5 4 0 00	
Total Assets		$ 5 3 3 8 00	
Liabilities			
Current Liabilities			
Accounts Payable	$ 1 0 0 00		
Salaries Payable	2 0 0 00		
Unearned Storage Fees	2 0 0 0 00		
Total Liabilities		$ 2 3 0 0 00	
Owner's Equity			
B. Ray, Capital, December 31, 200X		3 0 3 8 00	
Total Liabilities and Owner's Equity		$ 5 3 3 8 00	

Figure 12-6   Balance Sheet for Ray Company

Learning Unit 12-2
Journalizing and Posting Adjusting and Closing Entries; Preparing the Post-Closing Trial Balance

JOURNALIZING AND POSTING ADJUSTING ENTRIES

From the worksheet of Art's Wholesale (repeated here in Fig. 12-7, p. 478, for your convenience), the adjusting entries can be journalized from the adjustments column and posted to the ledger. Keep in mind that the adjustments have been placed only on the worksheet, not in the journal or in the ledger. At this point, the journal does not reflect adjustments and the ledger still contains only unadjusted amounts.

Partial Ledger

Merchandise Inventory 114				Income Summary 313	
19,000	19,000			19,000	4,000
4,000					

Supplies 115				Supplies Expense 614	
800	500			500	

Prepaid Insurance 116				Insurance Expense 615	
900	300			300	

Accum. Dep., Store Equipment 122				Dep. Expense, Store Equip. 613	
	400			50	
	50				

Salary Payable 212				Salaries Exp. 611	
	600			12,000	
				600	

Unearned Rent 219				Rental Income 414	
200	600				200

The journalized and posted adjusting entries are shown in Figure 12-8. Note that the liability Unearned Rent is reduced by $200 and Rental Income has increased by $200.

ART'S WHOLESALE CLOTHING CO.
WORKSHEET
FOR YEAR ENDED DECEMBER 31, 200X

	Trial Balance Dr.	Trial Balance Cr.	Adjustments Dr.	Adjustments Cr.
Cash	12920 00			
Petty Cash	100 00			
Accounts Receivable	14500 00			
Merchandise Inventory	19000 00		(B)4000 00	(A)19000 00
Supplies	800 00			(D)500 00
Prepaid Insurance	900 00			(E)300 00
Store Equipment	4000 00			
Acc. Dep., Store Equipment		400 00		(F) 50 00
Accounts Payable		17900 00		
Federal Income Tax Payable		800 00		
FICA—Social Security Payable		454 00		
FICA—Medicare Payable		106 00		
State Income Tax Payable		200 00		
SUTA Tax Payable		108 00		
FUTA Tax Payable		32 00		
Unearned Rent		600 00	(C)200 00	
Mortgage Payable		2320 00		
Art Newner, Capital		7905 00		
Art Newner, Withdrawals	8600 00			
Income Summary			(A)19000 00	(B)4000 00
Sales		95000 00		
Sales Returns and Allowances	950 00			
Sales Discount	670 00			
Purchases	52000 00			
Purchases Discount		860 00		
Purchases Returns and Allowances		680 00		
Freight-In	450 00			
Salaries Expense	11700 00		(G)600 00	
Payroll Tax Expense	420 00			
Postage Expense	25 00			
Miscellaneous Expense	30 00			
Interest Expense	300 00			
	127365 00	127365 00		
Rental Income				(C)200 00
Supplies Expense			(D)500 00	
Insurance Expense			(E)300 00	
Depreciation Expense, Store Equip.			(F) 50 00	
Salaries Payable				(G)600 00
			24650 00	24650 00
Net Income				

Figure 12-7 Completed Worksheet

Adjusted Trial Bal.		Income Statement		Balance Sheet	
Dr.	Cr.	Dr.	Cr.	Dr.	Cr.
1292000				1292000	
10000				10000	
1450000				1450000	
40000				40000	
3000				3000	
6000				6000	
40000				40000	
	45000				45000
	1790000				1790000
	80000				80000
	45400				45400
	10600				10600
	20000				20000
	10800				10800
	3200				3200
	40000				40000
	232000				232000
	790500				790500
860000				860000	
1900000	400000	1900000	400000		
	9500000		9500000		
95000		95000			
67000		67000			
5200000		5200000			
	86000		86000		
	68000		68000		
45000		45000			
1230000		1230000			
42000		42000			
2500		2500			
3000		3000			
30000		30000			
	20000		20000		
50000		50000			
30000		30000			
5000		5000			
	60000				60000
13201500	13201500	8699500	10074000	4502000	3127500
		1374500			1374500
		10074000	10074000	4502000	4502000

Figure 12-7 (continued)

Figure 12-8
Journalized and Posted
Adjusting Entries

		ART'S WHOLESALE CLOTHING CO. GENERAL JOURNAL							
									Page 2
Date		Account Titles and Description	PR		Dr.			Cr.	
		Adjusting Entries							
	31	Income Summary	313		19 00 0 00				
		Merchandise Inventory	114					19 0 0 0 00	
		Transferred beginning inventory							
		to Income Summary							
	31	Merchandise Inventory	114		4 00 0 00				
		Income Summary	313					4 0 0 0 00	
		Records cost of ending inventory							
	31	Unearned Rent	219		2 0 0 00				
		Rental Income	414					2 0 0 00	
		Rental Income earned							
	31	Supplies Expense	614		5 0 0 00				
		Supplies	115					5 0 0 00	
		Supplies consumed							
	31	Insurance Expense	615		3 0 0 00				
		Prepaid Insurance	116					3 0 0 00	
		Insurance expired							
	31	Dep. Exp., Store Equipment	613		5 0 00				
		Acc. Dep., Store Equipment	122					5 0 00	
		Depreciation on equipment							
	31	Salaries Expense	611		6 0 0 00				
		Salaries Payable	212					6 0 0 00	
		Accrued salaries							

JOURNALIZING AND POSTING CLOSING ENTRIES

In Chapter 5, we discussed the closing process for a service company. The goals of closing are the same for a merchandise company. These goals are (1) to clear all temporary accounts in the ledger to zero and (2) to update capital in the ledger to its latest balance. The company must use the worksheet and the steps listed here to complete the closing process.

Step 1: Close all balances on the income statement credit column of the worksheet, except Income Summary, by debits.
Then credit the total to the Income Summary account.

Step 2: Close all balances on the income statement debit column of the worksheet, except Income Summary, by credits.
Then debit the total to the Income Summary account.

Step 3: Transfer the balance of the Income Summary account to the Capital account.

Step 4: Transfer the balance of the owner's Withdrawal account to the Capital account.

Figure 12-9
General Journal Closing
Entries

	Date	Account Titles and Description	PR	Dr.	Cr.
		ART'S WHOLESALE CLOTHING CO. GENERAL JOURNAL			Page 2
		Closing Entries			
	31	Sales	411	9500000	
		Rental Income	414	20000	
		Purchases Discount	512	86000	
		Purchases Ret. and Allow.	513	68000	
		Income Summary	313		9674000
		Transfers credit account balances			
		on income statement column of			
		worksheet to Income Summary			
	31	Income Summary	313	6799500	
		Sales Returns and Allowances	412		95000
		Sales Discount	413		67000
		Purchases	511		5200000
		Freight-In	514		45000
		Salaries Expense	611		1230000
		Payroll Tax Expense	612		42000
		Postage Expense	616		2500
		Miscellaneous Expense	617		3000
		Interest Expense	618		3000
		Supplies Expense	614		5000
		Insurance Expense	615		3000
		Depreciation Expense, Store Equip.	613		5000
		Transfers all expenses, and			
		deductions to Sales are			
		closed to Income Summary			
	31	Income Summary	313	1374500	
		A. Newner, Capital	311		1374500
		Transfer of net income to			
		Capital from Income Summary			
	31	A. Newner, Capital	311	860000	
		A. Newner, Withdrawals	312		860000
		Closes withdrawals to			
		Capital Account			

Let's look now at the journalized closing entries in Figure 12-9. When these entries are posted, all the temporary accounts will have zero balances in the ledger, and the Capital account will be updated with a new balance.

Let's take a moment to look at the Income Summary account in T account form:

```
               Income Summary 313
       Adj.    19,000 |  4,000   Adj.
       Clos.   67,995 | 96,740   Clos.
               86,995 | 100,740

   Net Income → Clos.  13,745 |
```

Note that Income Summary before the closing process contains the adjustments for Merchandise Inventory. The end result is that the net income of $13,745 is closed to the Capital account.

THE POST-CLOSING TRIAL BALANCE

The post-closing trial balance shown in Figure 12-10 is prepared from the general ledger. Note first that all temporary accounts have been closed and thus are not shown on this post-closing trial balance. Note also that the ending inventory figure of the last accounting period, $4,000, becomes the beginning inventory figure on January 1, 20X3.

Figure 12-10
Post-Closing Trial Balance for Art's Wholesale Clothing Company

ART'S WHOLESALE CLOTHING COMPANY POSTCLOSING TRIAL BALANCE DECEMBER 31, 200X	Dr.	Cr.
Cash	12 9 2 0 00	
Petty Cash	1 0 0 00	
Accounts Receivable	14 5 0 0 00	
Merchandise Inventory	4 0 0 0 00	
Supplies	3 0 0 00	
Prepaid Insurance	6 0 0 00	
Store Equipment	4 0 0 0 00	
Accum. Depreciation, Store Equipment		4 5 0 00
Accounts Payable		17 9 0 0 00
Federal Income Tax Payable		8 0 0 00
FICA—Social Security Payable		4 5 4 00
FICA—Medicare Payable		1 0 6 00
State Income Tax Payable		2 0 0 00
SUTA Tax Payable		1 0 8 00
FUTA Tax Payable		3 2 00
Salary Payable		6 0 0 00
Unearned Rent		4 0 0 00
Mortgage Payable		2 3 2 0 00
Art Newner, Capital		13 0 5 0 00
	36 4 2 0 00	36 4 2 0 00

Learning Unit 12-2 Review

AT THIS POINT you should be able to

- Journalize and post adjusting entries for a merchandise company. (p. 477)
- Explain the relationship of the worksheet to the adjusting and closing process. (p. 480)
- Complete the closing process for a merchandise company. (p. 481)
- Prepare a post-closing trial balance and explain why ending merchandise inventory is not a temporary account. (p. 482)

SELF-REVIEW QUIZ 12-2

(The forms you need are on page 375 of the *Study Guide and Working Papers*.)

Using the worksheet on page 449 from Self-Review Quiz 11-2, journalize the closing entries.

SOLUTION TO SELF-REVIEW QUIZ 12-2

Figure 12-11
Closing Entries Journalized

Date		Account Titles and Description	PR	Dr.	Cr.
					Page 2
		Closing			
Dec.	31	Sales		11 04 0 00	
		Storage Fees Earned		5 1 6 00	
		Purchases Returns and Allowances		1 6 8 00	
		Purchases Discount		1 0 2 00	
		Income Summary			11 82 6 00
	31	Income Summary		10 09 6 00	
		Sales Returns and Allowances			5 4 6 00
		Sales Discount			2 1 6 00
		Purchases			52 5 6 00
		Salaries Expense			22 1 6 00
		Insurance Expense			1 3 9 2 00
		Utilities Expense			9 6 00
		Plumbing Expense			2 1 4 00
		Rent Expense			1 0 0 00
		Depreciation Exp., Equipment			6 0 00
	31	Income Summary		1 1 0 6 00	
		B. Ray, Capital			1 1 0 6 00

Quiz Tip:
Note in the first closing entry that the four account titles (now listed as debits) were found on the worksheet as credits in the income statement column.

Learning Unit 12-3 — Reversing Entries (Optional Section)

The accounting cycle for Art's Wholesale Clothing Company is completed. Now let's look at **reversing entries,** an optional way of handling some adjusting entries. Reversing entries are general journal entries that are the opposite of adjusting entries. Reversing entries help reduce potential errors and simplify the recordkeeping process. If Art's accountant does reversing entries, routine transactions can be done in the usual steps.

Reversing entries are an option; they are not mandatory.

To help explain the concept of reversing entries, let's look at these two adjustments that could be reversed:

1. When there is an increase in an asset account (no previous balance).
   Example: Interest Receivable
          Interest Income
   (Interest earned but not collected is covered in later chapters.)

2. When there is an increase in a liability account (no previous balance).
   Example: Wages Expense
          Wages Payable

With the exception of businesses in their first year of operation, accounts such as Accumulated Depreciation or Inventory cannot be reduced because they have previous balances.

Art's bookkeeper handles an entry without reversing for salaries at the end of the year (see Fig. 12-12). Note that the permanent account, Salaries Payable, carries over to the new accounting period a $600 balance. Remember that the $600 was an expense of the prior year.

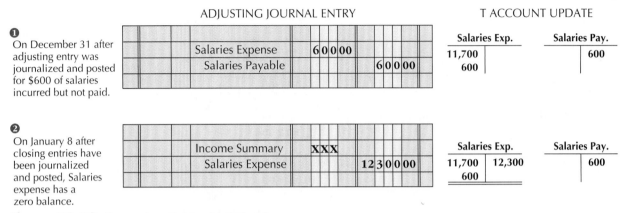

❶ On December 31 after adjusting entry was journalized and posted for $600 of salaries incurred but not paid.

❷ On January 8 after closing entries have been journalized and posted, Salaries expense has a zero balance.

Figure 12-12 Reversing Entries Not Used

	Salaries Payable	600 00	
	Salaries Expense	1400 00	
	Cash		2000 00

Salaries Exp. | 1,400
Salaries Pay. | 600 | 600
Cash | | 2,000

Figure 12-13 Entry When Optional Reversing Entry Is Not Used

❶ On December 31 adjustment for salary was recorded.

Salaries Exp. 11,700 / 600
Salaries Pay. | 600

❷ Closing entry on December 31.

Salaries Exp. 11,700 / 12,300 ; 600
Salaries Pay. | 600

❸ On January 1 (first day of the following fiscal period) reverse adjusting entry was made for salary on December 31(a "flipping" adjustment).

| Jan. | 1 | Salaries Payable | 600 00 | |
| | | Salaries Expense | | 600 00 |

Salaries Exp. | 600
Salaries Pay. 600 | 600

This way, the liability is reduced to 0. We know it will be paid in this new period, but the Salaries Expense has a credit balance of $600 until the payroll is paid. When the payroll of $2,000 is paid, the following results:

❹ Paid Payroll $2,000.

| Jan. | 1 | Salaries Expense | 2000 00 | |
| | | Cash | | 2000 00 |

Salaries Exp. 2,000 | 600
Cash | 2,000

Figure 12-14 Reversing Entries Used

On January 8 of the new year, the payroll to be paid is $2,000. If the optional reversing entry is *not* used, the bookkeeper must make the journal entry in Figure 12-13.

To do so, the bookkeeper has to refer back to the adjustment on December 31 to determine how much of the salary of $2,000 is indeed a new salary expense and what portion was shown in the old year although not paid. It is easy to see how potential errors can result if the bookkeeper pays the payroll but forgets about the adjustment in the previous year. In this way, reversing entries can help avoid potential errors.

Figure 12-14 shows the four steps the bookkeeper would take if reversing entries were used. Note that Steps 1 and 2 are the same whether the accountant uses reversing entries or not.

Note that the balance of Salaries Expense is indeed only $1,400, the *true* expense in the new year. Reversing results in switching the adjustment the first day of the new period. Also note that each of the accounts ends up with the same balance no matter which method is chosen. Using a reversing entry for salaries, however, allows the accountant to make the normal entry when it is time to pay salaries.

Learning Unit 12-3 Review

AT THIS POINT you should be able to

- Explain the purpose of reversing entries. (p. 484)
- Complete a reversing entry. (p. 484)
- Explain when reversing entries can be used. (p. 484)

SELF-REVIEW QUIZ 12-3

Explain which of the following situations could be reversed:

1.
Supplies Exp.		Supplies	
200		800	200

2.
Wages Exp.		Wages Payable	
3,200			200
200			

3.
Sales		Unearned Sales	
	4,000	50	200
	50		

SOLUTIONS TO SELF-REVIEW QUIZ 12-3

(The forms you need are on page 376 of the *Study Guide and Working Papers*.)

1. Not reversed: asset Supplies is decreasing, not increasing.
2. Reversed: liability is increasing and no previous balance exists.
3. Not reversed: liability is decreasing and a previous balance exists.

Chapter Review

Summary of Key Points

Learning Unit 12-1

1. The formal income statement can be prepared from the income statement columns of the worksheet.
2. There are no debit or credit columns on the formal income statement.
3. The cost of goods sold section has a figure for beginning inventory and a separate figure for ending inventory.
4. Operating expenses could be broken down into selling and administrative expenses.
5. The ending figure for Capital is not found on the worksheet. It comes from the statement of owner's equity.
6. A classified balance sheet breaks assets into current and plant and equipment. Liabilities are broken down into current and long-term.

Learning Unit 12-2

1. The information for journalizing, adjusting, and closing entries can be obtained from the worksheet.
2. In the closing process all temporary accounts will be zero and the Capital account is brought up to its new balance.
3. Inventory is not a temporary account. The ending inventory, along with other permanent accounts, will be listed in the post-closing trial balance.

Learning Unit 12-3

1. Reversing entries are optional. They could aid in reducing potential errors and can simplify the recordkeeping process.
2. The reversing entry "flips" the adjustment on the first day of a new fiscal period. Thus, the bookkeeper need *not* look back at what happened in the old year when recording the current year's transactions.
3. Reversing entries are only used if (a) assets are increasing and have no previous balance or (b) liabilities are increasing and have no previous balance.

Key Terms

Administrative expenses (general expenses)   Expenses such as general office expenses that are incurred indirectly in the selling of goods.

Classified balance sheet   A balance sheet that categorizes assets as current or plant and equipment and groups liabilities as current or long-term.

Current assets   Assets that can be converted into cash or used within one year or the normal operating cycle of the business, whichever is longer.

Current liabilities   Obligations that will come due within one year or within the operating cycle, whichever is longer.

Long-term liabilities   Obligations that are not due or payable for a long time, usually for more than a year.

Operating cycle   Average time it takes to buy and sell merchandise and then collect accounts receivable.

Other expenses   Nonoperating expenses that do not relate to the main operating activities of the business; they appear in a separate section on the income statement. One example given in the text is Interest Expense, interest owed on money borrowed by the company.

Other income   Any revenue other than revenue from sales. It appears in a separate section on the income statement. Examples: Rental Income and Storage Fees.

Plant and equipment   Long-lived assets such as buildings or land that are used in the production or sale of goods or services.

Reversing entries   Optional bookkeeping technique in which certain adjusting entries are reversed or switched on the first day of the new accounting period so that transactions in the new period can be recorded without referring back to prior adjusting entries.

Selling expenses   Expenses directly related to the sale of goods.

Questions, Mini Exercises, Exercises, and Problems

Discussion Questions

1. Which columns of the worksheet aid in the preparation of the income statement?
2. Explain the components of cost of goods sold.
3. Explain how operating expenses can be broken down into different categories.
4. What is the difference between current assets and plant and equipment?
5. What is an operating cycle?
6. Why journalize adjusting entries *after* the formal reports in a manual system have been prepared?
7. Explain the steps of closing for a merchandise company.
8. Temporary accounts could appear on a post-closing trial balance. Agree or disagree.
9. What is the purpose of using reversing entries? Are they mandatory? When should they be used?

Mini Exercises

(The forms you need are on page 378 of the *Study Guide and Working Papers.*)

Calculate Net Sales

1. From the following, calculate net sales:

Purchases	$ 80	Sales Discount	$ 5
Gross Sales	140	Operating Expenses	25
Sales Returns and Allowances	10		

Calculate Cost of Goods Sold

2. Calculate Cost of Goods Sold:

Freight-in	$ 5	Ending Inventory	$15
Beginning Inventory	20	Net Purchases	50

Calculate Gross Profit and Net Income

3. Using Mini Exercises 1 and 2, calculate

   a. Gross Profit.
   b. Net Income or Net Loss.

Blueprint: Financial Statements

(1) INCOME STATEMENT					
Revenue:					
Sales				$ XXX	
Less: Sales Ret. and Allow.			$ XXX		
Sales Discount			XXX	XXX	
Net Sales				$ XXXX	
Cost of Goods Sold:					
Merchandise Inventory, 1/1/0X			$ XXX		
Purchases		$XXX			
Less: Purchases Discount	$XXX				
Purch. Ret. and Allow.	XXX	XXX			
Net Purchases		XXX			
Add: Freight-In		XXX			
Net Cost of Purchases			XXX		
Cost of Goods Avail. for Sale			$XXXX		
Less: Merch. Inv., 12/31/0X			XXX		
Cost of Goods Sold				XXXX	
Gross Profit				$XXXX	
Operating Expenses:					
~~			$XXX		
~~			XXX		
~~			XXX		
Total Operating Expenses				XXX	
Net Income from Operations				$ XXX	
Other Income:					
Rental Income			$ XXX		
Storage Fees Income			XXX		
Total Other Income			$ XXX		
Other Expenses:					
Interest Expenses			XXX	XXX	
Net Income:				$ XXX	

(2) STATEMENT OF OWNER'S EQUITY			
Beginning Capital		$XXX	
Additional Investments		XXX	
Total Investment		$XXX	
Net Income	$XXX		
Less: Withdrawals	XXX		
Increase in Capital		XXX	
Ending Capital		$XXX	

(3) BALANCE SHEET				
Assets				
Current Assets:				
Cash		$ XXXX		
Acccounts Receivable		XXXX		
Merchandise Inventory		XXXX		
Prepaid Insurance		XXX		
Total Current Assets			$ XXXX	
Plant and Equipment:				
Store Equipment	$XXXX			
Less Accumulated Depreciation	XXXX	$XXXX		
Office Equipment	$XXXX			
Less Accumulated Depreciation	XXX	XXX		
Total Plant and Equipment			XXXX	
Total Assets			$XXXX	
Liabilities				
Current Liabilities:				
Unearned Revenue		$XXX		
Mortgage Payable (current portion)		XXX		
Accounts Payable		XXX		
Salaries Payable		XX		
FICA—Social Security Payable		XX		
FICA—Medicare Payable		XX		
Income Taxes Payable		XX		
Total Current Liabilities			$XXX	
Long-Term Liabilities				
Mortgage Payable			$XXX	
Total Liabilities			$XXXX	
Owner's Equity				
Capital*			XXXX	
Total Liabilities and Owner's Equity			$XXXX	

* From statement of owner's equity

Classification of Accounts

4. Match the following categories to each account listed below:
   1. Current Asset.
   2. Plant and Equipment.
   3. Current Liabilities.
   4. Long-Term Liabilities.

   _____ **a.** Merchandise Inventory   _____ **f.** Mortgage Payable (Not Current)
   _____ **b.** Unearned Rent   _____ **g.** FUTA Payable
   _____ **c.** Prepaid Insurance   _____ **h.** Accumulated Depreciation
   _____ **d.** SUTA Payable   _____ **i.** FICA-Social Security Payable
   _____ **e.** Store Equipment   _____ **j.** Petty Cash

Reversing Entries

5. **a.** On January 1, prepare a reversing entry. On January 8, journalize the entry to record the paying of salary expense, $900.
   b. What will be the balance in Salaries Expense on January 8 (after posting)?

December 31:

Salaries Expense		Salaries Payable
900 | 1,200 closing		| 300 Adj.
Adj. 300 |		

Exercises

(The forms you need are on pages 378–380 of the *Study Guide and Working Papers.*)

Preparing cost of goods sold section.

12-1. From the following accounts, prepare a cost of goods sold section in proper form: Merchandise Inventory, 12/31/X1, $6,000; Purchases Discount, $900; Merchandise Inventory, 12/1/X1, $4,000; Purchases, $58,000; Purchases Returns and Allowances, $1,000; Freight-in, $300.

Categorizing and classifying account titles.

12-2. Give the category, the classification, and the report(s) on which each of the following appears (for example: Cash — asset, current asset, balance sheet):

   a. Salaries Payable.   **e.** SIT Payable.
   b. Accounts Payable.   **f.** Office Equipment.
   c. Mortgage Payable.   **g.** Land.
   d. Unearned Legal Fees.

Journalizing closing entries.

12-3. From the partial worksheet in Fig. 12-15, on p. 491, journalize the closing entries of December 31 for A. Slow Co.

Preparing partially completed balance sheet.

12-4. From the worksheet in Exercise 12-3, prepare the assets section of a classified balance sheet.

Reversing entry.

12-5. On December 31, 20X1, $300 of salaries has been accrued. (Salaries before the accrued amount totaled $26,000.) The next payroll to be paid will be on February 3, 20X2, for $6,000. Please do the following:

   a. Journalize and post the adjusting entry (use T accounts).
   b. Journalize and post the reversing entry on January 1.
   c. Journalize and post the payment of the payroll. Cash has a balance of $15,000 before the payment of payroll on February 3.

A. SLOW CO.
WORKSHEET
FOR YEAR ENDED DECEMBER 31, 200X

Account Titles	Income Statement Dr.	Income Statement Cr.	Balance Sheet Dr.	Balance Sheet Cr.
Cash			19300	
Merch. Inventory			45000	
Prepaid Advertising			56100	
Prepaid Insurance			3000	
Office Equipment			108000	
Accum. Depr., Office Equip.				21000
Accounts Payable				25800
A. Slow, Capital				96600
Income Summary	36200	45000		
Sales		552000		
Sales Returns and Allowances	22300			
Sales Discount	10800			
Purchases	262800			
Purchases Returns and Allow.		3400		
Purchases Discount		5100		
Salaries Expense	108300			
Insurance Expense	69600			
Utilities Expense	4800			
Plumbing Expense	5700			
Advertising Expense	1500			
Depr. Expenses, Office Equip.	3000			
Salaries Payable				7500
	525000	605500	231400	150900
Net Income	80500			80500
	605500	605500	231400	231400

Figure 12-15 Worksheet for A. Slow Co.

Group A Problems

(The forms you need are on pages 381–391 of the *Study Guide and Working Papers.*)

12A-1. Prepare a formal income statement from the partial worksheet for Ring.com in Figure 12-16 on p. 492.

Check Figure:
Net Income from operations $761

12A-2. Prepare a statement of owner's equity and a classified balance sheet from the worksheet for James Company in Figure 12-17 on p. 492. *Note:* Of the Mortgage Payable, $200 is due within one year.

12A-3. a. Complete the worksheet for Jay's Supplies in Figure 12-18 on p. 493.
   b. Prepare an income statement, a statement of owner's equity, and a classified balance sheet. (*Note:* The amount of the mortgage due the first year is $800.)
   c. Journalize the adjusting and closing entries.

Check Figure:
Total Assets $33,340

12A-4. Using the ledger balances and additional data shown on page 493, do the following for Callahan Lumber for the year ended December 31, 200X:

   1. Prepare the worksheet.
   2. Prepare the income statement, statement of owner's equity, and balance sheet.
   3. Journalize and post adjusting and closing entries. (Be sure to put beginning balances in the ledger first.)

Check Figure:
Net Income $4,340

Figure 12-16
Partial Worksheet for
Ring.Com

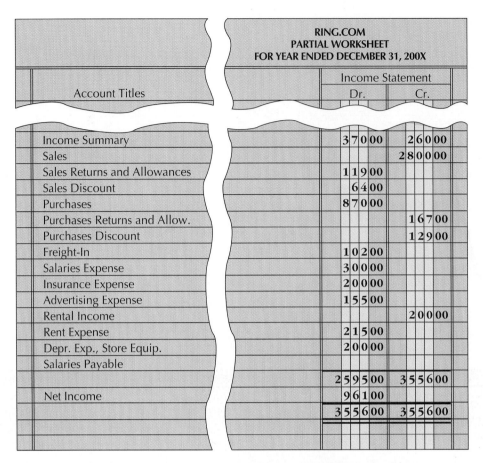

RING.COM
PARTIAL WORKSHEET
FOR YEAR ENDED DECEMBER 31, 200X

Account Titles	Income Statement Dr.	Income Statement Cr.
Income Summary	3 7 0 00	2 6 0 00
Sales		2 8 0 0 00
Sales Returns and Allowances	1 1 9 00	
Sales Discount	6 4 00	
Purchases	8 7 0 00	
Purchases Returns and Allow.		1 6 7 00
Purchases Discount		1 2 9 00
Freight-In	1 0 2 00	
Salaries Expense	3 0 0 00	
Insurance Expense	2 0 0 00	
Advertising Expense	1 5 5 00	
Rental Income		2 0 0 00
Rent Expense	2 1 5 00	
Depr. Exp., Store Equip.	2 0 0 00	
Salaries Payable		
	2 5 9 5 00	3 5 5 6 00
Net Income	9 6 1 00	
	3 5 5 6 00	3 5 5 6 00

Figure 12-17
Partial Worksheet for
James Company

> Preparing a statement of owner's equity and a classified balance sheet from a worksheet.

JAMES COMPANY
WORKSHEET
FOR YEAR ENDED DECEMBER 31, 200X

Account Titles	Balance Sheet Dr.	Balance Sheet Cr.
Cash	2 3 5 0 00	
Petty Cash	9 0 00	
Accounts Receivable	1 3 5 0 00	
Merchandise Inv.	4 0 0 0 00	
Supplies	3 2 5 00	
Prepaid Insurance	5 0 0 00	
Store Equipment	2 8 0 0 00	
Acc. Dep., Store Eq.		7 0 0 00
Automobile	1 7 0 0 00	
Acc. Dep., Auto.		2 2 5 00
Accounts Payable		2 8 0 0 00
Taxes Payable		2 4 0 0 00
Unearned Rent		1 8 5 0 0 00
Mortgage Payable		4 5 0 00
H. James, Capital		1 2 4 0 0 00
H. James, With.	1 0 0 00	
Salaries Payable		6 0 0 00
	3 4 3 6 5 00	3 8 0 7 5 00
Net Loss	3 7 1 0 00	
	3 8 0 7 5 00	3 8 0 7 5 00

JAY'S SUPPLIES
WORKSHEET
FOR YEAR ENDED DECEMBER 31, 200X

Account Titles	Trial Balance Dr.	Trial Balance Cr.	Adjustments Dr.	Adjustments Cr.
Cash	2000 00			
Accounts Receivable	3000 00			
Merch. Inv., 1/1/XX	11000 00	(B)	10400 00	11000 00 (A)
Prepaid Insurance	1880 00			500 00 (E)
Equipment	3400 00			
Accum. Dep., Equipment		1080 00		400 00 (D)
Accounts Payable		5080 00		
Unearned Training Fees		2120 00	(C) 320 00	
Mortgage Payable		1200 00		
P. Jay, Capital		10560 00		
P. Jay, Withdrawals	4280 00			
Income Summary		(A)	11000 00	10400 00 (B)
Sales		9580 00		
Sales Returns and Allowances	3200 00			
Sales Discount	2600 00			
Purchases	6360 00			
Purchases Returns and Allow.		1360 00		
Purchases Discount		320 00		
Freight-In	2680 00			
Advertising Expense	11400 00			
Rent Expense	1000 00			
Salaries Expense	1360 00			
	132640 00	132640 00		
Training Fees Earned				320 00 (C)
Dep. Exp., Equipment			(D) 400 00	
Insurance Expense			(E) 500 00	
			22620 00	22620 00

Figure 12-18 Worksheet for Jay's Supplies

4. Prepare a post-closing trial balance.
5. Journalize the reversing entry for wages.

Acct. No.

110	Cash	$ 1,340
111	Accounts Receivable	1,300
112	Merchandise Inventory	4,550
113	Lumber Supplies	269
114	Prepaid Insurance	218
121	Lumber Equipment	3,000
122	Accum. Depr., Lumber Equipment	490
220	Accounts Payable	1,160
221	Wages Payable	—
330	J. Callahan, Capital	7,352
331	J. Callahan, Withdrawals	3,000
332	Income Summary	—
440	Sales	22,800
441	Sales Returns and Allowances	200
550	Purchases	14,800

Comprehensive Problem.
Worksheet preparation: preparing financial reports, journalizing and posting adjusting and closing entries, preparing a post-closing trial balance, and journalizing reversing entry.

Check Figure:
Net Income $4,336

551	Purchases Discount	285
552	Purchases Returns and Allowances	300
660	Wages Expense	2,480
661	Advertising Expense	400
662	Rent Expense	830
663	Dep. Expense, Lumber Equipment	—
664	Lumber Supplies Expense	—
665	Insurance Expense	—

Additional Data

a./b.	Merchandise inventory, December 31	$ 4,900
c.	Lumber supplies on hand, December 31	75
d.	Insurance expired	150
e.	Depreciation for the year	250
f.	Accrued wages on December 31	95

Group B Problems

(The forms you need are on pages 381–391 of the *Study Guide and Working Papers*.)

12B-1. From the partial worksheet shown in Figure 12-19, prepare a formal income statement.

12B-2. From the worksheet shown in Figure 12-20 on p. 494, complete

a. Statement of owner's equity.
b. Classified balance sheet.

Note: Of the Mortgage Payable, $3,000 is due within one year.

> Preparing an income statement from a worksheet.

> Preparing a statement of owner's equity and a classified balance sheet from a worksheet.

Figure 12-19
Partial Worksheet of Ring.Com

> Check Figure:
> Net income from operations $845

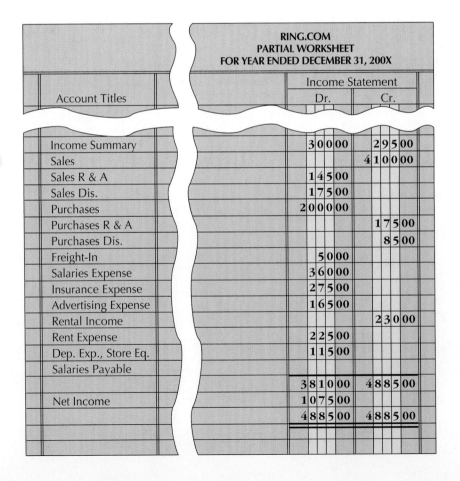

RING.COM
PARTIAL WORKSHEET
FOR YEAR ENDED DECEMBER 31, 200X

Account Titles	Income Statement Dr.	Income Statement Cr.
Income Summary	3 0 0 00	2 9 5 00
Sales		4 1 0 0 00
Sales R & A	1 4 5 00	
Sales Dis.	1 7 5 00	
Purchases	2 0 0 0 00	
Purchases R & A		1 7 5 00
Purchases Dis.		8 5 00
Freight-In	5 0 00	
Salaries Expense	3 6 0 00	
Insurance Expense	2 7 5 00	
Advertising Expense	1 6 5 00	
Rental Income		2 3 0 00
Rent Expense	2 2 5 00	
Dep. Exp., Store Eq.	1 1 5 00	
Salaries Payable		
	3 8 1 0 00	4 8 8 5 00
Net Income	1 0 7 5 00	
	4 8 8 5 00	4 8 8 5 00

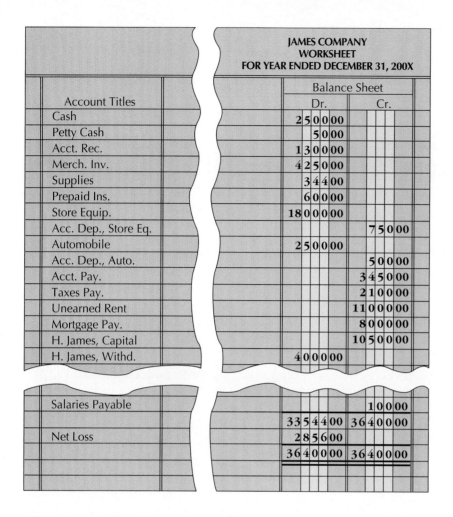

Figure 12-20
Worksheet for James Company

JAMES COMPANY
WORKSHEET
FOR YEAR ENDED DECEMBER 31, 200X

Account Titles	Balance Sheet Dr.	Balance Sheet Cr.
Cash	2 5 0 0 00	
Petty Cash	5 0 00	
Acct. Rec.	1 3 0 0 00	
Merch. Inv.	4 2 5 0 00	
Supplies	3 4 4 00	
Prepaid Ins.	6 0 0 00	
Store Equip.	1 8 0 0 0 00	
Acc. Dep., Store Eq.		7 5 0 00
Automobile	2 5 0 0 00	
Acc. Dep., Auto.		5 0 0 00
Acct. Pay.		3 4 5 0 00
Taxes Pay.		2 1 0 0 00
Unearned Rent		1 1 0 0 0 00
Mortgage Pay.		8 0 0 0 00
H. James, Capital		1 0 5 0 0 00
H. James, Withd.	4 0 0 0 00	
Salaries Payable		1 0 0 00
	3 3 5 4 4 00	3 6 4 0 0 00
Net Loss	2 8 5 6 00	
	3 6 4 0 0 00	3 6 4 0 0 00

Check Figure:
Total Assets $28,294

Completing the worksheet; preparing financial reports; and journalizing adjusting and closing entries.

Check Figure:
Net Loss $12,050

Comprehensive Problem: Worksheet preparation, preparing financial reports, journalizing and posting adjusting and closing entries, preparing a post-closing trial balance, and journalizing reversing entry.

Check Figure:
Net Income $2,730

12B-3. From the partial worksheet in Figure 12-21 on p. 495, your tasks are to

1. Complete the worksheet.
2. Prepare the income statement, statement of owner's equity, and classified balance sheet. The amount of the mortgage due the first year is $800.
3. Journalize the adjusting and closing entries.

12B-4. From the following ledger balances and additional data on pages 494–495, do the following:

1. Prepare the worksheet.
2. Prepare the income statement, statement of owner's equity, and balance sheet.
3. Journalize and post adjusting and closing entries. (Be sure to put beginning balances in the ledger first.)
4. Prepare a post-closing trial balance.
5. Journalize the reversing entry for wages.

Acct. No.

110	Cash	$ 940
111	Accounts Receivable	1,470
112	Merchandise Inventory	5,600
113	Lumber Supplies	260
114	Prepaid Insurance	117
121	Lumber Equipment	2,600
122	Acc. Dep., Lumber Equipment	340
220	Accounts Payable	1,330

JAY'S SUPPLIES
WORKSHEET
FOR YEAR ENDED DECEMBER 31, 200X

Account Titles	Trial Balance Dr.	Cr.	Adjustments Dr.	Cr.
Cash	3000 00			
Accounts Receivable	3000 00			
Merch. Inventory, 1/1/XX	11700 00		(B)8000 00	11700 00 (A)
Prepaid Insurance	1000 00			350 00 (E)
Equipment	5000 00			
Accum. Dep., Equipment		1900 00		500 00 (D)
Accounts Payable		2100 00		
Unearned Training Fees		1450 00	(C)400 00	
Mortgage Payable		2400 00		
P. Jay, Capital		27750 00		
P. Jay, Withdrawals	4000 00			
Income Summary			(A)11700 00	8000 00 (B)
Sales		100800 00		
Sales Returns and Allowances	4100 00			
Sales Discount	2800 00			
Purchases	70000 00			
Purchases Returns and Allow.		2000 00		
Purchases Discounts		1400 00		
Freight-In	2700 00			
Advertising Expense	8000 00			
Rent Expense	8500 00			
Salaries Expense	16000 00			
	139800 00	139800 00		
Training Fees Earned				400 00 (C)
Dep. Exp., Equipment			(D)500 00	
Insurance Expense			(E)350 00	
			20950 00	20950 00

Figure 12-21 Worksheet for Jay's Supplies

221	Wages Payable	
330	J. Callahan, Capital	7,562
331	J. Callahan, Withdrawals	3,500
332	Income Summary	—
440	Sales	23,000
441	Sales Returns and Allowances	400
550	Purchases	14,700
551	Purchases Discount	440
552	Purchases Returns and Allowances	545
660	Wages Expense	2,390
661	Advertising Expense	400
662	Rent Expense	840
663	Dep. Exp., Lumber Equipment	—
664	Lumber Supplies Expense	—
665	Insurance Expense	—

Additional Data

a./b. Merchandise inventory, December 31 $ 3,900
            c. Lumber supplies on hand, December 31   60

d. Insurance expired   50
e. Depreciation for the year   400
f. Accrued wages on December 31   175

Real-World Applications

12R-1. Chan Company recently had most of its records destroyed in a fire. The information for 20X1 (Fig. 12-22) was discovered by the bookkeeper. Please assist the bookkeeper in reconstructing an income statement for 20X1.

12R-2. Hope Lang, a junior accountant, has the December 31, 200X trial balance of Gregot Company sitting on her desk. Attached is a memo from her supervisor requesting that a classified balance sheet be prepared. Hope gathers the following data:

1. A physical inventory at December 31 showed $80,000 on hand.
2. Office supplies on hand was $600.
3. Insurance unexpired was $750.
4. Depreciation (straight-line) is based on a 25-year life.

Using the trial balance of Gregot Co. in Figure 12-23 on p. 497, please assist Hope with this project. *Hint:* Ending figure for capital is $115,850.

CHAN COMPANY
GENERAL JOURNAL

Page 2

Date		Description	PR	Dr.	Cr.
Dec.	31	Income Summary	312	3 6 3 0 00	
		Sales Returns and Allowances	420		1 4 0 00
		Sales Discount	430		3 0 00
		Purchases	500		2 4 0 0 00
		Delivery Expense	600		9 0 00
		Salaries Expense	610		8 4 0 00
		Rent Expense	620		3 0 00
		Office Supplies Expense	630		5 0 00
		Advertising Expense	640		1 0 00
		Dep. Exp., Store Equipment	650		4 0 00
	31	Sales	410	5 5 4 2 00	
		Purchases Discount	510	1 2 0 00	
		Purchases Returns and Allowances	520	1 0 0 00	
		Income Summary	312		5 7 6 2 00
	31	Income Summary	312	3 7 3 2 00	
		J. Chan, Capital	310		3 7 3 2 00

Beg. Inv. $1,400
End. Inv. 3,000

Figure 12-22 General Journal for Chan Company

GREGOT COMPANY TRIAL BALANCE DECEMBER 31, 200X	Dr.	Cr.
Cash	11 0 0 0 00	
Accounts Receivable	38 0 0 0 00	
Inventory, Jan. 1	80 0 0 0 00	
Prepaid Insurance	2 0 0 0 00	
Office Supplies	1 0 0 0 00	
Land	17 5 0 0 00	
Building	50 0 0 0 00	
Accumulated Depreciation, Building		10 0 0 0 00
Notes Payable		40 0 0 0 00
Accounts Payable		30 0 0 0 00
G. Gregot, Capital		98 4 0 0 00
G. Gregot, Withdrawals	13 0 0 0 00	
Income Summary	—	—
Retail Sales		329 0 0 0 00
Sales Returns and Allowances	21 0 0 0 00	
Sales Discount	8 0 0 0 00	
Purchases	215 5 0 0 00	
Purchases Returns and Allowances		11 6 0 0 00
Purchases Discount		4 0 0 0 00
Transportation-In	5 0 0 0 00	
Advertising Expense	2 5 0 0 00	
Wage Expense	55 0 0 0 00	
Utilities Expense	3 5 0 0 00	
	523 0 0 0 00	523 0 0 0 00

Figure 12-23 Trial Balance for Gregot Company

YOU make the call

Critical Thinking/Ethical Case

12R-3. Janet Flynn, owner of Reel Company, plans to apply for a bank loan at Petro National Bank. Because the company has a lot of debt on its balance sheet, Janet does not plan to show the loan officer the balance sheet. She plans only to bring the income statement. Do you feel that this move is a sound financial move by Janet? You make the call. Write down your specific recommendations to Janet.

Internet Exercises: Aware; ExxonMobil

EX-1. [www.aware.com]   Aware is an electronics firm that claims to be positioning itself for rapid growth in the DSL technology market. The financial statements it presents are straightforward. Look over the 2001 balance sheet and comment on its classifications, using those presented in this chapter as a guide.

EX-2. [www.exxonmobil.com.financials.html] This is another exercise in looking at the classifications in classified balance sheets. ExxonMobil is a vastly different company from Aware in Exercise 1. Observe, however, the classifications in the balance sheet of ExxonMobil. How does it compare to that of Aware? How is it different? Notice how they are basically the same as presented in this chapter.

Continuing Problem

Eldorado Computer Center

Using the worksheet in Chapter 11 for Eldorado Computer Center, journalize and post the adjusting entries and prepare the financial statements. (See page 402 in the *Study Guide and Working Papers*.)

THE CORNER DRESS SHOP

Reviewing the Accounting Cycle for a Merchandise Company

(The forms you need are on pages 415–437 of the *Study Guide and Working Papers*. This practice set will help you review all the key concepts of a merchandise company, along with the integration of payroll, including the preparation of Form 941.)

    Because you are the bookkeeper of The Corner Dress Shop, we have gathered the following information for you. It will be your task to complete the accounting cycle for March.

Betty Loeb's dress shop is located at 1 Milgate Rd., Marblehead, MA 01945. Its identification number is 33-4158215.

THE CORNER DRESS SHOP POSTCLOSING TRIAL BALANCE FEBRUARY 28, 200X	1	2
Cash	2 3 3 4 90	
Accounts Receivable	2 2 0 0 00	
Petty Cash	3 5 00	
Merchandise Inventory	5 6 0 0 00	
Prepaid Rent	1 8 0 0 00	
Delivery Truck	6 0 0 0 00	
Accumulated Depreciation, Truck		1 5 0 0 00
Accounts Payable		1 9 0 0 00
FIT Payable		1 1 1 6 00
FICA—Social Security Payable		1 3 3 9 20
FICA—Medicare Payable		3 1 3 20
SIT Payable		7 5 6 00
SUTA Payable		9 7 9 20
FUTA Payable		1 6 3 20
Unearned Rent		8 0 0 00
B. Loeb, Capital		9 1 0 3 10
	17 9 6 9 90	17 9 6 9 90

Balances in subsidiary ledgers as of March 1 are as follows:

Accounts Receivable		Accounts Payable	
Bing Co.	$ 2,200	Blew Co.	$ 1,900
Blew Co.	—	Jones Co.	—
Ronald Co.	—	Moe's Garage	—
		Morris Co.	—

Payroll is paid monthly:

FICA rate	Social Security 6.2% on $87,000
	Medicare 1.45% on all earnings
SUTA rate	4.8% on $7,000
FUTA rate	.8% on $7,000
SIT rate	7%
FIT	Use table provided on page 503.

The payroll register for January and February is provided. In March, salaries are as follows:

Mel Case	$3,325
Jane Holl	4,120
Jackie Moore	4,760

Your tasks are to

1. Set up a general ledger, accounts receivable subsidiary ledger and accounts payable subsidiary ledger, auxiliary petty cash record, and payroll register. (Be sure to update ledger accounts based on information given in the post-closing trial balance for February 28 before beginning.)
2. Journalize the transactions and prepare the payroll register.
3. Update the accounts payable and accounts receivable subsidiary ledgers.
4. Post to the general ledger.
5. Prepare a trial balance on a worksheet and complete the worksheet.
6. Prepare an income statement, statement of owner's equity, and classified balance sheet.
7. Journalize the adjusting and closing entries.
8. Post the adjusting and closing entries to the ledger.
9. Prepare a post-closing trial balance.
10. Complete Form 941 and sign it as of the last day in April.

CHART OF ACCOUNTS
FOR THE CORNER DRESS SHOP

Assets

110	Cash
111	Accounts Receivable
112	Petty Cash
114	Merchandise Inventory
116	Prepaid Rent
120	Delivery Truck
121	Accumulated Depreciation, Truck

Liabilities

210	Accounts Payable
212	Salaries Payable
214	Federal Income Tax Payable
216	FICA — Soc. Sec. Payable
218	FICA — Medicare Payable
220	State Income Tax Payable
222	SUTA Tax Payable
224	FUTA Tax Payable
226	Unearned Rent

Owner's Equity

310	B. Loeb, Capital
320	B. Loeb, Withdrawals
330	Income Summary

Revenue

410	Sales
412	Sales Returns and Allowances
414	Sales Discount
416	Rental Income

Cost of Goods Sold

510	Purchases
512	Purchases Returns and Allowances
514	Purchase Discount

Expenses

610	Sales Salaries Expense
611	Office Salaries Expense
612	Payroll Tax Expense
614	Cleaning Expense
616	Depreciation Expense, Truck
618	Rent Expense
620	Postage Expense
622	Delivery Expense
624	Miscellaneous Expense

THE CORNER DRESS SHOP
PAYROLL REGISTER
JANUARY AND FEBRUARY 200X

Employees	Allow. and Marital Status	Cum. Earnings	Salary	Earnings Reg.	O/T	Gross	Cum. Earnings
Mel Case	M – 2		3 3 0 0 00	3 3 0 0 00		3 3 0 0 00	3 3 0 0 00
Jane Holl	M – 1		3 4 0 0 00	3 4 0 0 00		3 4 0 0 00	3 4 0 0 00
Jackie Moore	M – 0		4 1 0 0 00	4 1 0 0 00		4 1 0 0 00	4 1 0 0 00
Totals for Jan.			10 8 0 0 00	10 8 0 0 00		10 8 0 0 00	10 8 0 0 00
Mel Case	M – 2	3 3 0 0 00	3 3 0 0 00	3 3 0 0 00		3 3 0 0 00	6 6 0 0 00
Jane Holl	M – 1	3 4 0 0 00	3 4 0 0 00	3 4 0 0 00		3 4 0 0 00	6 8 0 0 00
Jackie Moore	M – 0	4 1 0 0 00	4 1 0 0 00	4 1 0 0 00		4 1 0 0 00	8 2 0 0 00
Totals for Feb.		10 8 0 0 00	10 8 0 0 00	10 8 0 0 00		10 8 0 0 00	21 6 0 0 00

PAYROLL REGISTER

Taxable Earnings			Deductions					Ck.	Distribution	
	FICA		FICA						Office Salary	Sales Salary
Unemp.	Soc. Sec.	Medicare	Soc. Sec.	Medicare	FIT	SIT	Net Pay	No.	Expense	Expense
3 3 0 0 00	3 3 0 0 00	3 3 0 0 00	2 0 4 60	4 7 85	2 8 8 00	2 3 1 00	2 5 2 8 55		3 3 0 0 00	
3 4 0 0 00	3 4 0 0 00	3 4 0 0 00	2 1 0 80	4 9 30	3 4 4 00	2 3 8 00	2 5 5 7 90			3 4 0 0 00
4 1 0 0 00	4 1 0 0 00	4 1 0 0 00	2 5 4 20	5 9 45	4 8 4 00	2 8 7 00	3 0 1 5 35			4 1 0 0 00
10 8 0 0 00	10 8 0 0 00	10 8 0 0 00	6 6 9 60	1 5 6 60	1 1 1 6 00	7 5 6 00	8 1 0 1 80		3 3 0 0 00	7 5 0 0 00
3 3 0 0 00	3 3 0 0 00	3 3 0 0 00	2 0 4 60	4 7 85	2 8 8 00	2 3 1 00	2 5 2 8 55		3 3 0 0 00	
3 4 0 0 00	3 4 0 0 00	3 4 0 0 00	2 1 0 80	4 9 30	3 4 4 00	2 3 8 00	2 5 5 7 90			3 4 0 0 00
4 1 0 0 00	4 1 0 0 00	4 1 0 0 00	2 5 4 20	5 9 45	4 8 4 00	2 8 7 00	3 0 1 5 35			4 1 0 0 00
10 8 0 0 00	10 8 0 0 00	10 8 0 0 00	6 6 9 60	1 5 6 60	1 1 1 6 00	7 5 6 00	8 1 0 1 80		3 3 0 0 00	7 5 0 0 00

200X

Mar. 1   Bing paid balance owed, no discount.

     2   Purchased merchandise from Morris Company on account, $10,000, terms 2/10, n/30.

     2   Paid $6 from the petty cash fund for cleaning package, voucher no. 18 (consider it a cleaning expense).

     3   Sold merchandise to Ronald Company on account, $7,000, invoice no. 51, terms 2/10, n/30.

     5   Paid $3 from the petty cash fund for postage, voucher no. 19.

     6   Sold merchandise to Ronald Company on account, $5,000, invoice no. 52, terms 2/10, n/30.

MARRIED Persons—MONTHLY Payroll Period
(For Wages Paid in 200X)

If the wages are— At least	But less than	0	1	2	3	4	5	6	7	8	9	10
		\multicolumn{11}{c}{And the number of withholding allowances claimed is—}										

The amount of income tax to be withheld is—

At least	But less than	0	1	2	3	4	5	6	7	8	9	10
$3,240	$3,280	$358	$320	$282	$244	$206	$168	$130	$94	$69	$44	$18
3,280	3,320	364	326	288	250	212	174	136	98	73	48	22
3,320	3,360	370	332	294	256	218	180	142	104	77	52	26
3,360	3,400	376	338	300	262	224	186	148	110	81	56	30
3,400	3,440	382	344	306	268	230	192	154	116	85	60	34
3,440	3,480	388	350	312	274	236	198	160	122	89	64	38
3,480	3,520	394	356	318	280	242	204	166	128	93	68	42
3,520	3,560	400	362	324	286	248	210	172	134	97	72	46
3,560	3,600	406	368	330	292	254	216	178	140	101	76	50
3,600	3,640	412	374	336	298	260	222	184	146	107	80	54
3,640	3,680	418	380	342	304	266	228	190	152	113	84	58
3,680	3,720	424	386	348	310	272	234	196	158	119	88	62
3,720	3,760	430	392	354	316	278	240	202	164	125	92	66
3,760	3,800	436	398	360	322	284	246	208	170	131	96	70
3,800	3,840	442	404	366	328	290	252	214	176	137	100	74
3,840	3,880	448	410	372	334	296	258	220	182	143	105	78
3,880	3,920	454	416	378	340	302	264	226	188	149	111	82
3,920	3,960	460	422	384	346	308	270	232	194	155	117	86
3,960	4,000	466	428	390	352	314	276	238	200	161	123	90
4,000	4,040	472	434	396	358	320	282	244	206	167	129	94
4,040	4,080	478	440	402	364	326	288	250	212	173	135	98
4,080	4,120	484	446	408	370	332	294	256	218	179	141	103
4,120	4,160	490	452	414	376	338	300	262	224	185	147	109
4,160	4,200	496	458	420	382	344	306	268	230	191	153	115
4,200	4,240	502	464	426	388	350	312	274	236	197	159	121
4,240	4,280	508	470	432	394	356	318	280	242	203	165	127
4,280	4,320	514	476	438	400	362	324	286	248	209	171	133
4,320	4,360	520	482	444	406	368	330	292	254	215	177	139
4,360	4,400	528	488	450	412	374	336	298	260	221	183	145
4,400	4,440	539	494	456	418	380	342	304	266	227	189	151
4,440	4,480	550	500	462	424	386	348	310	272	233	195	157
4,480	4,520	561	506	468	430	392	354	316	278	239	201	163
4,520	4,560	572	512	474	436	398	360	322	284	245	207	169
4,560	4,600	582	518	480	442	404	366	328	290	251	213	175
4,600	4,640	593	525	486	448	410	372	334	296	257	219	181
4,640	4,680	604	535	492	454	416	378	340	302	263	225	187
4,680	4,720	615	546	498	460	422	384	346	308	269	231	193
4,720	4,760	626	557	504	466	428	390	352	314	275	237	199
4,760	4,800	636	568	510	472	434	396	358	320	281	243	205
4,800	4,840	647	579	516	478	440	402	364	326	287	249	211
4,840	4,880	658	589	522	484	446	408	370	332	293	255	217
4,880	4,920	669	600	532	490	452	414	376	338	299	261	223
4,920	4,960	680	611	542	496	458	420	382	344	305	267	229
4,960	5,000	690	622	553	502	464	426	388	350	311	273	235
5,000	5,040	701	633	564	508	470	432	394	356	317	279	241
5,040	5,080	712	643	575	514	476	438	400	362	323	285	247
5,080	5,120	723	654	586	520	482	444	406	368	329	291	253
5,120	5,160	734	665	596	528	488	450	412	374	335	297	259
5,160	5,200	744	676	607	539	494	456	418	380	341	303	265
5,200	5,240	755	687	618	549	500	462	424	386	347	309	271
5,240	5,280	766	697	629	560	506	468	430	392	353	315	277
5,280	5,320	777	708	640	571	512	474	436	398	359	321	283
5,320	5,360	788	719	650	582	518	480	442	404	365	327	289
5,360	5,400	798	730	661	593	524	486	448	410	371	333	295
5,400	5,440	809	741	672	603	535	492	454	416	377	339	301
5,440	5,480	820	751	683	614	546	498	460	422	383	345	307
5,480	5,520	831	762	694	625	556	504	466	428	389	351	313
5,520	5,560	842	773	704	636	567	510	472	434	395	357	319
5,560	5,600	852	784	715	647	578	516	478	440	401	363	325
5,600	5,640	863	795	726	657	589	522	484	446	407	369	331
5,640	5,680	874	805	737	668	600	531	490	452	413	375	337
5,680	5,720	885	816	748	679	610	542	496	458	419	381	343
5,720	5,760	896	827	758	690	621	553	502	464	425	387	349
5,760	5,800	906	838	769	701	632	563	508	470	431	393	355
5,800	5,840	917	849	780	711	643	574	514	476	437	399	361

$5,840 and over   Use Table 4(b) for a **MARRIED person** on page 34. Also see the instructions on page 32.

8　Paid $10 from the petty cash fund for first aid emergency, voucher no. 20.

9　Purchased merchandise from Morris Company on account, $5,000, terms 2/10, n/30.

9　Paid $5 for delivery expense from petty cash fund, voucher no. 21.

9　Sold more merchandise to Ronald Company on account, $3,000, invoice no. 53, terms 2/10, n/30.

9　Paid cleaning service, $300, check no. 110.

10　Ronald Company returned merchandise costing $1,000 from invoice no. 52; The Corner Dress shop issued credit memo no. 10 Ronald Company for $1,000.

11　Purchased merchandise from Jones Company on account, $10,000, terms 1/15, n/60.

12　Paid Morris Company invoice dated March 2, check no. 111.

13　Sold $7,000 of merchandise for cash.

14　Returned merchandise to Jones Company in amount of $2,000; The Corner Dress Shop issued debit memo no. 4 to Jones Company.

14　Paid $5 from the petty cash fund for delivery expense, voucher no. 22.

15　Paid taxes due for FICA (Social Security and Medicare) and FIT for February payroll, check no. 112.

15　Sold Merchandise for $29,000 cash.

15　Betty withdrew $100 for her own personal expenses, check no. 113.

15　Paid state income tax for February payroll, check no. 114.

16　Received payment from Ronald Company for invoice no. 52, less discount.

16　Ronald Company paid invoice no. 51, $7,000.

16　Sold merchandise to Bing Company on account, $3,200, invoice no. 54, terms 2/10, n/30.

21　Purchased delivery truck on account from Moe's Garage, $17,200.

22　Sold merchandise to Ronald Company, on Account, $4,000, Invoice no. 55, terms 2/10, n/30.

23　Paid Jones Company the balance owed, check no. 115.

24　Sold merchandise to Ronald Company on Account, $4,000, Invoice no. 55, terms 2/10, n/30.

25　Purchased merchandise for $1,000 check no. 116.

27　Purchased merchandise from Blew Company on account, $6,000, terms 2/10, n/30.

27　Paid $2 postage from the petty cash fund, voucher no. 23.

28　Ronald Company paid invoice no. 55 dated March 22, less discount.

28　Bing Company paid invoice no. 54 dated March 16.

29　Purchased merchandise from Morris Company on onacnt, $9,000, terms 2/10, n/30.

30　Sold merchandise to Blew Company on account, $10,000, invoice no. 57, terms 2/10, n/30.

30　Issued check no. 117 to replenish to the same level the petty cash fund.

30　Recorded payroll in payroll register.

30　Journalized payroll entry (to be paid on 31st).

30   Journalized employer's payroll tax expense.

31   Paid payroll checks no. 118, no. 119, and no. 120.

Additional Data

a./b. Ending merchandise inventory, $13,515.

c. During March, rent expired, $600.

d. Truck depreciated, $150.

e. Rental income earned, $200 (one month's rent from subletting).

COMPUTERIZED ACCOUNTING APPLICATION FOR THE CORNER DRESS SHOP MINI PRACTICE SET (CHAPTER 12)

ACCOUNTING CYCLE FOR A MERCHANDISE COMPANY

Before starting on this assignment, read and complete the tasks discussed in Parts A, B, and F of the Computerized Accounting appendix at the back of this book and complete the Computerized Accounting Application assignments for Chapter 3, Chapter 4, Valdez Realty Mini Practice Set (Chapter 5), Pete's Market Mini Practice Set (Chapter 8), and Chapter 10.

This practice set will help you review all the key concepts of a merchandise company along with the integration of payroll, including the preparation of Form 941.

Since you are the bookkeeper for The Corner Dress Shop, we have gathered the following information for you. It will be your task to complete the accounting cycle for March.

The Corner Dress Shop: Trial Balance As at 3/1/04

		Debits	Credits
1110	Cash	$ 2,502.90	$ —
1115	Petty Cash	35.00	—
1120	Accounts Receivable	2,200.00	—
1130	Inventory	5,600.00	—
1140	Prepaid Rent	1,800.00	—
1250	Delivery Truck	6,000.00	—
1251	Accum. Dep — Delivery Truck	—	1,500.00
2110	Accounts Payable	—	1,900.00
2310	Federal Income Tax Payable	—	1,284.00
2320	State Income Tax Payable	—	756.00
2330	FICA — Soc. Sec. Payable	—	1,339.20
2335	FICA — Medicare Payable	—	313.20
2340	FUTA Payable	—	163.20
2350	SUTA Payable	—	979.20
2400	Unearned Rent	—	800.00
3110	Betty Loeb, Capital	$ —	$ 9,103.10
		$ 18,137.90	$18,137.90

The Corner Dress Shop: Customer Aged Detail As at 3/1/04

			Total	Current	31 to 60	61 to 90
Bing Co.						
12	1/1/04	Invoice	2,200.00	—	2,200.00	—

The Corner Dress Shop: Vendor Aged Detail As at 3/1/04

			Total	Current	31 to 60	61 to 90
Blew Co.						
422	2/16/04	Invoice	1,900.00	1,900.00	—	—

The Corner Dress Shop, owned by Betty Loeb, is located at 1 Milgate Road, Marblehead, Massachusetts, 01945. Her employer identification number is 33-4158215. Federal Income Tax (FIT), State Income Tax (SIT), Social Security, Medicare, FUTA, and SUTA are all calculated automatically by the program based on the following assumptions and built-in tax rates:

- FICA: Social Security, 6.2 percent on $84,900; Medicare, 1.45 percent on all earnings.
- SUTA: 4.8 percent on the first $7,000 in earnings.
- FUTA: .8 percent on the first $7,000 in earnings.
- Employees are paid monthly. The payroll is recorded and paid on the last day of each month.
- FIT is calculated automatically by the program based on the marital status and number of exemptions claimed by each employee.
- SIT for Massachusetts is calculated automatically by the program based on the marital status and number of exemptions claimed by each employee. Note that since Peachtree uses a different method for calculating FIT and SIT, your answers may not match the manual practice set causing slight differences in the payroll checks.

1. Click on the Start button. Point to Programs; point to the Peachtree folder and select Peachtree Complete Accounting. Your desktop may have the Peachtree icon allowing for a quicker entrance into the program.

2. Follow the "Open a File" instructions in Part A of the Computerized Accounting appendix at the back of this book to open **The Corner Dress Shop**.

3. Click on the **Maintain** menu option. Then select **Company Information**. The program will respond by bringing up a dialogue box allowing the user to edit/add information about the company. In the **Company Name** entry field at the end of **The Corner Dress Shop**, add a dash and your name "-**Student Name**" to the end of the company name. Click on the OK button to return to the Menu Window.

4. To see what inventory items The Corner Dress Shop has available, let's print a listing. Select **Inventory** from the **Reports** menu. Select **Inventory Valuation Report** from the **Reports** List. Accept all defaults and print the resulting report. You will see that we have 6 items in our inventory. In addition, we can see our current cost on each item. Save this report to compare with a similar report you will print at the end of this practice set.

5. Peachtree's Inventory module allows the user to easily add new items or make changes to existing items such as recording price changes. Since you will be asked to change prices later in the practice set, let's take a look at how that works now. Do not actually change any of the fields for the item we will be looking at.

   - Select **Inventory Items** from the **Maintain** menu.
   - In the **Item ID** field, select "6000" using the Look Up feature.
   - In the **Description** field, you will see the current description of this inventory item. Should a change be needed, we would simply place the cursor where the change needs to be made and edit as needed.
   - Under the **General** Tab is a field where we can select and then enter a longer description of this item that will appear on sales and/or purchase invoices when we include this item on sales or purchase invoices.
   - The current selling price for this item is kept in the **Sales Price #1** field. Peachtree has the capability of storing multiple prices for an item. This feature can be activated by clicking on the arrow to the right of the **Sales Price #1** field. Go ahead and click on this arrow. A table is presented which allows us to enter up to 5 different selling prices. Different customers can be assigned to different price levels in this manner. Since we have only one price, we can **Cancel** the Multiple Pricing Level box to return to the Maintain Inventory Items window. When you are

Open the Company Data Files

Add Your Name to the Company Name

Printing an Inventory Valuation Report

Maintain Inventory Items

prompted to change prices later in the practice set, you will simply change the price in the **Sales Price #1** field rather than add multiple prices.

- Unit/Measure, Item Type, and Location are sorting and information fields that can be used as needed and have no restrictions as to content except length.

- The **Cost Method** field is where we can select the cost assumption to use with this item. Using the pull down menu, you can see our selection consists of FIFO, LIFO, or Average. We will leave the setting at "Average". These cost assumptions will be discussed in greater detail in Chapter 16.

- Peachtree has used default information to select the GL accounts needed for an inventory transaction. If there is some need to change these, we can decline the defaults and select any account we may need. Since there is no need to change these accounts, we will leave them at their default settings.

- We could also establish a minimum stock level and have Peachtree warn us when we fall below this level. We can also establish a reorder point that Peachtree can use to generate an inventory reorder listing.

- We can also select the vendor from whom we would normally order this item. Peachtree uses this and all the information we can see in this window to work interactively with Peachtree's other modules and report features.

- Your screen should look like this:

Record March
Transactions

6. Record the following transactions for March using the appropriate General (G), Sales/Invoicing (S), Receipts (R), Purchases (PU), and Payments (PA) windows. Use the same forms when printing invoices, credits and checks as in Chapter 10 changing the starting numbers as needed. Accept defaults for any field for which you are not given data. Use the date of the transaction for the Deposit Ticket ID field.

2004

Mar. 1 Received check #7634 from the Bing Co. in the amount of $2,200 in payment of invoice #12 ($2,200), dated January 1. If prompted, accept Cash as the cash account. Receipt #101. (R)

2 Purchased merchandise from the Morris Co. on account, $10,000, invoice #1210, terms 2/10, n/30 consisting of 184- Style 1000 and 180- Style 2000 dresses. (P)

3 Sold merchandise to the Ronold Co. on account, $7,000, invoice no. 51, terms 2/10, n/30 consisting of 48- Style 1000, 30- Style 2000, 8- Style 3000, 9- Style 4000, 8- Style 5000, and 8- Style 6000 dresses. (S)

6 Sold merchandise to the Ronold Co. on account, $5,000, invoice #52, terms 2/10, n/30 consisting of 48- Style 1000, 24- Style 2000, 5- Style 3000, 3- Style 4000, 3- Style 5000, and 3- Style 6000 dresses. (S)

9 Purchased merchandise from the Morris Co. on account, $5,000, invoice #1286, terms 2/10, n/30 consisting of 92- Style 1000 and 90- Style 2000 dresses. (P)

9 Sold merchandise to the Ronold Co. on account $3,000, invoice #53, terms 2/10, n/30 consisting of 20- Style 1000, 20- Style 2000, 4- Style 3000, 2- Style 4000, and 4- Style 5000 dresses. (S)

9 Paid cleaning service $300, check #110 to Ronda's Cleaning Service. In the Payments window selecting Cash as the cash account:

- Enter Ronda's name in the Pay To field
- Enter a description of the payment in the Description column
- Select the correct GL account for this line (Cleaning Expense)
- Enter the amount in the Amount column.
- Print the check as you did in Chapter 10. (PA)

10 Ronold Co. returned merchandise that cost $1,000 from invoice #52 consisting of 4- Style 1000, 5- Style 2000, 2- Style 3000, 1- Style 4000, 2- Style 5000, and 1- Style 6000 dresses. The Corner Dress Shop issued credit memorandum #CM 10 to the Ronald Co. for $1,000. Remember to use negative quantities for returns. (S)

11 Purchased merchandise from the Jones Co. on account $10,000, invoice #4639, terms 1/15, n/60 consisting of 144- Style 3000 and 124- Style 4000 dresses. (P)

12 Issued check #111 to the Morris Co. in the amount of $9,800 in payment of invoice #1210 ($10,000), dated March 2, less 2 percent discount ($200). (PA)

13 Sold $7,000 of merchandise for cash consisting of 24- Style 1000, 30- Style 2000, 24- Style 3000, and 29- Style 4000 dresses. Be sure to use CASH for the customer name and for the Reference fields. Use Receipt #102. (R)

14 Returned merchandise to the Jones Co. in the amount of $2,000 consisting of 32- Style 3000 and 22- Style 4000 dresses. Remember to use negative quantities for returns. Assign DM4 as the invoice number. (P)

15 Paid FIT, Social Security, and Medicare taxes due for February payroll, check #112 in the amount of $2,936.40. Make the check payable to the IRS. You may wish to print a General Trial Balance first to determine how much to pay for each account. Use the procedure established with your payment on the 9th adding as many lines as you need to pay all the liability accounts needed. (PA)

15 Due to increased operating costs, The Corner Dress Shop must raise its selling prices as follows:

Style 1000	$ 60.00
Style 2000	$ 70.00
Style 3000	$ 80.00
Style 4000	$ 90.00
Style 5000	$110.00
Style 6000	$120.00

Make these changes using the procedures discussed at the start of this practice set before continuing.

15   Sold merchandise for $29,000 cash consisting of 124- Style 1000, 144- Style 2000, 72- Style 3000, 61- Style 4000, 1- Style 5000, and 1- Style 6000 dresses. Use CASH for the Name and Reference fields. If you do not end up with $29,000 as your total, check to make sure you accomplished the price changes correctly. Receipt #103. (R)

15   B. Loeb withdrew $100 for her own personal expenses, check #113. (PA)

15   Paid SIT tax for February payroll, check #114. Make the check payable to the State of Massachusetts. (PA)

16   Received check #5432 from the Ronold Co. in the amount of $3,920 in payment of invoice no. 52 ($5,000), dated March 6, less credit memo CM 10 ($1,000), less 2 percent discount ($100 − 20 = $80, net sales discount). Receipt #104. (R)

16   Received check #5447 from the Ronold Co. in the amount of $7,000 in payment of invoice no. 51, dated March 3. Receipt #105. (R)

16   Sold merchandise to the Bing Co. on account, $3,200, invoice #54, terms 2/10, n/30 consisting of 12- Style 1000, 10- Style 2000, 11- Style 3000, and 10- Style 4000 dresses. Be sure to use the correct invoice number when printing. (S)

21   Purchased delivery truck on account from Moe's Garage, invoice #7113, $17,200.

- Select Moe's Garage in the Vendor ID field
- Enter the invoice number and date
- Ship via Customer Pickup
- Enter a description of the payment in the Description column
- Verify the correct GL account for this line (Delivery Truck)
- Enter the amount in the Amount column. (PU)

22   Sold merchandise to the Ronold Co. on account $4,000, invoice #55, terms 2/10, n/30 consisting of 24- Style 1000, 24- Style 2000, 3- Style 3000, 2- Style 4000, 2- Style 5000, and 2- Style 6000 dresses. (S)

23   Issued check #115 to the Jones Co. in the amount of $7,920 in payment of invoice #4639 ($10,000), dated March 11, less debit memo #DM4 ($2,000), less 1 percent discount ($100 − 20 = $80 net purchases discount). (PA)

24   Sold merchandise to the Bing Co. on account, $2,000, invoice #56, terms 2/10 n/30 consisting of 1- Style 2000, 10- Style 3000, 10- Style 4000, 1- Style 5000, and 1- Style 6000 dresses. (S).

25   Purchased merchandise for $1,000 cash from the Jones Company, check #116, consisting of 16- Style 3000 and 11- Style 4000 dresses. Use the Quantity and Item fields in the Payments window just as you would in the Purchases window. (PA)

27   Purchased merchandise from the Blew Co. on account, $6,000, invoice #437, terms 2/10, n/30 consisting of 60- Style 5000 and 66- Style 6000 dresses. (P)

28   Received check no. 5562 from the Ronold Co. in the amount of $3,920 in payment of invoice 55 ($4,000), dated March 22, less 2 percent discount ($80). Receipt #106. (R)

28   Received check #8127 from the Bing Co. in the amount of $3,200 in payment of invoice #54, dated March 16. (R)

29   Purchased merchandise from the Morris Co. on account, $9,000, invoice #1347, terms 2/10, n/30 consisting of 150- Style 1000 and 150- Style 2000

dresses. The vendor has changed his prices on these items so instead of accepting Peachtree's default for the unit prices, enter $28.00 and $32.00 for the Style 1000 and Style 2000, respectively. (P)

30 Sold merchandise to the Blew Co. on account, $10,000, invoice #57, terms 2/10, n/30 consisting of 6- Style 3000, 5- Style 4000, 41- Style 5000, and 38- Style 6000 dresses. (S).

30 The Auxiliary Petty Cash Record for March listed the following: Postage Expense, $5; Delivery Expense, $10; Cleaning Expense, $6; Miscellaneous Expense, $10. Issued check #117 to replenish the petty cash fund. The check should be made out to CASH. (PA)

31 Issued payroll checks for March wages as follows:

Employee	March Wages	Check no.
Case, Mel	$3,325	118
Holl, Jane	$4,120	119
Moore, Jackie	$4,760	120

Use **Select for Payroll Entry** under the **Tasks** menu. Use 31 March as the Pay End date as well as for the check date.

7. Print the following reports:

a. General Ledger Trial Balance
b. Aged Receivables
c. Aged Payables
d. Payroll Register
e. 941 (FedForm 941 2002). Print this report on plain paper unless you have the blank forms available.

Print Reports

8. Open the General Journal; then record adjusting journal entries based on the following adjustment data:

a. During March, rent expired, $600.
b. Truck depreciated $150.
c. Rental income earned, $200 (one month's rent from subletting). This is an unearned income adjustment.

Record March Adjusting Entries

9. After you have posted the adjusting journal entries, close the General Journal, then print the following reports:

a. General Journal
b. General Ledger Trial Balance
c. General Ledger Report
d. Income Statement
e. Balance Sheet
f. Inventory Valuation Report

Print Reports

10. Compare the Inventory Valuation Report with the one created at the start of this practice set. Note that the first two items, the ones whose cost price changed when we last purchased them, have neither the original prices of $25.00 and $30.00 nor the new prices of $28.00 and $32.00, respectively. Peachtree has created a weighted-average for these items. You will study the mechanics behind this calculation in Chapter 16.

11. Peachtree contains dozens of reports that you could examine at this time. Feel free to experiment with looking at the various report options available to you in the Reports menu.

Other Reports

12. In order to close the accounting period we must now advance the period.

Advance Dates

👆 Using your mouse, click on **System** from the **Tasks** menu. Select **Change Accounting Periods**.

- Using the pull down menu, select period 4 - Apr 1, 2004 to Apr 30, 2004 and click on **OK**.
- You will be asked whether you wish to print reports before continuing. Since we have already printed our reports, we can answer "No".
- Note that the status bar at the bottom of the screen now reflects that you are in period 4. You would be ready to start recording the April transactions.

CHAPTER 13

Accounting for Bad Debts

A restaurant that you like to dine at is called The Skillet. The food is good, the prices are reasonable, and it offers a good alternative to the student cafeteria. You ate there last week, and so you decide to stop by today for a quick meal.

When you walk into the restaurant, you notice a handwritten sign taped to the front door that reads, "No checks — No exceptions." Last week you paid for your meal with a check. As you look at a menu you notice that the grilled chicken sandwich deluxe, one of your favorites, has gone up 50 cents in price. A cup of coffee now costs 10 cents more as well.

You ask the waitress about the new check policy as you place your order. "The owner received too many bouncing checks, so he can no longer afford to take checks. He also had to raise prices to cover the losses from the bad checks." You think about how the problem of bad checks has caused prices to go up and made it less convenient to eat at The Skillet.

When a customer does not or cannot pay part or all of what it owes to a business, the business incurs a bad debt. Unfortunately, bad debts are a reality of doing business today. Increasing prices is only one way of responding to the problem of bad debts.

Understanding the accounting for bad debts is important to operating a business. In this chapter we will learn about the Allowance for Doubtful Accounts and Bad Debts Expense accounts. We also discuss the two major approaches to estimating bad debts and how to prepare an aging of Accounts Receivable to determine the amount of accounts that may become uncollectible.

Learning Objectives

- Describing how the Bad Debts Expense account and the Allowance for Doubtful Accounts account are used to record bad debts. (p. 516)

- Using the income statement approach and the balance sheet approach to estimate the amount of Bad Debts Expense. (p. 519)

- Preparing an Aging of Accounts Receivable. (p. 521)

- Writing off an account using the Allowance for Doubtful Accounts account. (p. 523)

- Using the direct write-off method. (p. 524)

Eventually, all companies (Internet-based or not) that sell goods or services on account will come upon customers that do not pay their bills. The question of these *bad debts* affects the company's credit policy. If a company extends credit too easily, it may end up with too many uncollectible accounts. On the other hand, if the credit policy is too strict, the company will end up losing customers to other firms with easier credit policies, which could also mean lost profit.

This chapter looks at how bad debts are recorded in the accrual system of accounting. It also discusses when accounts receivable turn into bad debts (or uncollectible accounts), how and what to charge them to, and how to write them off.

Learning Unit 13-1　　Accrual Accounting and Recording Bad Debts

As discussed in Chapter 2, the accrual system of accounting matches earned revenue with expenses that have been incurred in producing revenue during an accounting period. One expense incurred as a result of sales on credit or on account is a bad debts expense. The problem is that it may take as long as a year for the seller to realize that the debt is uncollectible. What happens in the meantime? How can the books be kept up-to-date?

One way is to estimate at the end of the year what percentage of sales made during that year will turn out to be bad debts. There are several ways of arriving at the percentage. At the moment, let's say Abby Ellen Company estimates that 1.6% of its sales of $100,000 for the year 20X1 will not be collectible; thus, the company expects not to collect $1,600 of the $100,000 owed it from sales. (Other ways to estimate the amount are discussed in Learning Unit 13-2.)

Two accounts that we haven't discussed before, Bad Debts Expense and Allowance for Doubtful Accounts, are needed. **Bad Debts Expense** is an expense account whose normal balance is a debit; it is a temporary account that is closed to Income Summary at year's end. **Allowance for Doubtful Accounts** is a contra-asset account that accumulates the expected amount of bad debts as of a given date; its normal balance is a credit. It is a permanent account that is *not* closed to Income Summary at the end of the year.

In the case of Abby Ellen Company, which expects to be unable to collect $1,600 of the $100,000 owed it from sales, at the end of the year (20X1) an adjustment is made debiting Bad Debts Expense and crediting Allowance for Doubtful Accounts for $1,600. This transaction (Fig. 13-1) is shown with a transaction analysis chart.

> Will go on income statement as an operating expense and eventually be closed to Income Summary.

1 Accounts Affected	2 Category	3 ↑ ↓	4 Rules
Bad Debts Expense	Expense	↑	Dr.
Allowance for Doubtful Accounts	Contra-Asset	↑	Cr.

Figure 13-1
Estimating Bad Debts

	20X1					
	Dec.	31	Bad Debt Expense	1 6 0 0 00		
			Allowance for Doubtful Accounts		1 6 0 0 00	
			Record estimate of bad debts.			

ABBY ELLEN COMPANY PARTIAL BALANCE SHEET DECEMBER 31, 20X1			
Assets			
Current Assets:			
Cash			$ 51 4 0 0 00
Accounts Receivable	$100 0 0 0 00		
Less: Allowance for Doubtful Accounts	1 6 0 0 00	98 4 0 0 00	
Merchandise Inventory		200 0 0 0 00	
Total Current Assets		$349 8 0 0 00	

Figure 13-2
Partial Balance Sheet

> Writing off an account. *Note:* Bad Debts Expense is not involved.

The allowance account is subtracted from Accounts Receivable, leaving a net realizable value of $98,400. Net realizable value is the amount Abby Ellen Company expects to collect. When an account is written off, the net realizable value doesn't change, because both the Accounts Receivable and the Allowance for Doubtful Accounts are reduced (see Fig. 13-2).

> Will go on balance sheet as a reduction to Accounts Receivable. The normal balance of the allowance account is a credit. It will not be closed at the end of the period.

Think of the Allowance for Doubtful Accounts as a reservoir that is filled before bad debts occur. The reservoir is drained when a customer's bill is declared uncollectible. Abby Ellen Company estimates that out of its $100,000 of credit sales, $1,600 will prove to be uncollectible, but it does not know which accounts those will be.

> Accounts Receivable – Allowance for Doubtful Accounts = Net Realizable Value

WRITING OFF AN ACCOUNT DEEMED UNCOLLECTIBLE

At some point a customer's bill must be written off as uncollectible. Let's look at how Abby Ellen Company would write off the account of Jones Moore on June 5, 20X2. (The $200 sale was made in 20X1.)

Remember, at the end of 20X1, Abby made an adjusting entry increasing Bad Debts Expense (debit) and filling the Allowance for Doubtful Accounts (credit) with the estimate of accounts receivable that will not be collectible. The journal entry shown in Figure 13-3 is recorded to write off this account.

Note that we did *not* debit the account Bad Debts Expense, because the estimate for this account was made on December 31, 20X1 (and applies to that year, not to 20X2). When that estimate was made, we did not know which bills would turn out to be uncollectible. Once the debt is identified as uncollectible, we reduce both the Allowance account and the controlling account Accounts Receivable and update the accounts receivable subsidiary ledger. The subsidiary ledger will be credited just as the controlling account is.

The Bad Debts Expense was recorded in the old year when credit sales were earned.

20X2 June	5	Allowance For Doubtful Accounts	2 0 0 00	
		Accounts Receivable, J. Moore		2 0 0 00
		Writing off J. Moore account.		

Figure 13-3
Bad Debt Written Off

Learning Unit 13-1 Review

AT THIS POINT you should be able to

- Define and explain the purpose of Bad Debts Expense and Allowance for Doubtful Accounts. (p. 516)
- Explain why the subsidiary ledger account cannot be updated at the time the Bad Debts Expense is estimated. (p. 516)
- Prepare an adjusting entry for Bad Debts Expense. (p. 516)
- Prepare a partial balance sheet showing the relationship between the Allowance for Doubtful Accounts and Accounts Receivable. (p. 517)
- Explain net realizable value. (p. 517)
- Prepare a journal entry to write off a customer's debt in a year following the sale. (p. 517)

SELF-REVIEW QUIZ 13-1

(The forms you need are on page 1 of the *Study Guide and Working Papers*.) Respond true or false to the following:

1. The Bad Debts Expense account should be updated only when the customer's debt is declared to be uncollectible.
2. The Allowance for Doubtful Accounts is a contra-asset account on the balance sheet.
3. Bad Debts Expense is part of cost of goods sold.
4. Net realizable value equals Accounts Receivable less Allowance for Doubtful Accounts.
5. When a customer's debt is written off as uncollectible, the account Allowance for Doubtful Accounts is credited.

> *Quiz Tip:*
> The Allowance account fills with a credit and drains with a debit.

SOLUTIONS TO SELF-REVIEW QUIZ 13-1

1. False   2. True   3. False   4. True   5. False

 Accounting in the Reel World

Giving Credit Where Credit is Due

How much do you typically deposit into your bank account?

On a typical day, Oracle, the nation's second largest software company, deposits $30 million into its East and West Coast bank lock boxes.

With this amount of money flowing into the company, it's easy to see why improving the automated accounts receivables process is absolutely crucial to the health of Oracle's credit policy and, ultimately, its business. Oracle has refined the system so much that the accounts receivable department only needs to look at 130 of every 1,000 invoices generated.

Watch the Oracle on-location video segment on your DVD to see what happens behind the scenes when a customer makes a purchase, and then answer the questions below.

1. What is the main reason that Oracle needs accuracy in recording accounts receivables?
2. Suppose you are one of the Oracle managers charged with developing e-commerce business solutions. Is data from accounts receivable at all relevant to how you perform your job? Explain your answer.
3. How do you think Oracle's improved accounts receivable system helps the company decrease bad debts?

Learning Unit 13-2   The Allowance Method: Two Approaches to Estimating the Amount of Bad Debts Expense

As mentioned earlier, at the end of each year companies must estimate what percentage of their sales for that year will turn out to be uncollectible accounts or bad debts. How is this estimate arrived at? In this unit we look at two of the most common ways of arriving at this amount: the income statement approach and the balance sheet approach. The diagram in Figure 13-4 outlines these methods.

THE INCOME STATEMENT APPROACH

Abby Ellen Company uses the income statement approach to calculate how much Bad Debts Expense will be associated with this year's sales. Based on the past several years, the company has averaged Bad Debts Expense of 1% of *net* credit sales. From

Bad Debts Expense can be based on a percentage of the dollar volume of net credit sales on the Income statement.

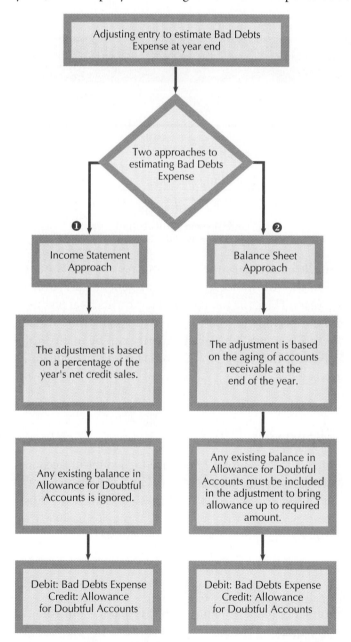

Figure 13-4
Two Approaches to Estimating Amount of Bad Debts Expense

Figure 13-5
Estimating Bad Debts
Based on Percentage
of Sales

	20X4							
	Dec.	31	Bad Debts Expense		80000			
			Allowance for Doubtful Accounts				80000	
			Record estimate of bad debts					
			(.01 × $80,000)					

the following facts, let's prepare an adjusting entry to record the Bad Debts Expense that is based on a percentage of net credit sales (see Fig. 13-5).

20X4	Dr.	Cr.
Sales (all credit)		$95,000
Sales Returns and Allowances	$10,000	
Sales Discount	5,000	
Accounts Receivable	7,000	
Allowance for Doubtful Accounts		100

Analysis:
—Sales	$95,000
—SRA	10,000
—Sales Discount	5,000
Net Credit Sales	$80,000

1 Accounts Affected	2 Category	3 ↑ ↓	4 Rules
Bad Debts Expense	Expense	↑	Dr.
Allowance for Doubtful Accounts	Contra-Asset	↑	Cr.

When it is posted, the Allowance account looks like the following:

Allowance for Doubtful Accounts

Dr.	
	100 → Balance *before* adjustment
	800 → Adjustment
	900 → New Balance

Beginning balance in Allowance account represents potential bad debts from previous periods.

The income statement approach emphasizes the matching requirements of the income statement. The $100 in the Allowance account represents a carryover of potential bad debts from *prior* years. Thus, the total of $900 represents total potential uncollectible accounts of several periods of sales. If, over the years, the estimate for Bad Debts Expense has been inaccurate, an adjusting entry can be made in the current year's Bad Debts Expense. If that happens, the company may reevaluate its percentage and use $1\frac{1}{2}$% instead of 1%.

THE BALANCE SHEET APPROACH

The balance sheet approach bases the new total Allowance for Doubtful Accounts on the current Accounts Receivable on the balance sheet. Thus, the adjustment is reduced by the old balance in Allowance for Doubtful Accounts. When the adjustment is credited, the new balance will reflect the state of Accounts Receivable. (See Fig. 13-4.) This approach focuses on the aging of Accounts Receivable.

Aging classifies uncollected amounts of individual customers according to days past due.

Aging of Accounts Receivable

The longer a bill has been due and not paid, the more likely it is that it is not going to be paid. Therefore, one way of estimating the amount of bad debts for the year just

TABLE 13-1 Aging of Accounts Receivable

| Name of Customer | Total Balance | Not Yet Due | Days Past Due | | | |
			1–30	31–60	61–90	Over 90
Jane Elliot	$ 100	$ 100				
Joshua Harras	30			$ 30		
Alan Kedbury	160	160				
John Sullivan	180				$160	$ 20
Sheri Lissan	80	80				
Others	6,450	3,260	$2,000	840	40	310
Totals	$7,000	$3,600	$2,000	$870	$200	$330
Percent of total (rounded to nearest whole percent)	100%	51% $\left(\dfrac{\$3,600}{\$7,000}\right)$	29% $\left(\dfrac{\$2,000}{\$7,000}\right)$	12% $\left(\dfrac{\$870}{\$7,000}\right)$	3% $\left(\dfrac{\$200}{\$7,000}\right)$	5% $\left(\dfrac{\$330}{\$7,000}\right)$

past is to look at Accounts Receivable and analyze it according to how many days past due the accounts are. This process is called aging of Accounts Receivable.

Table 13-1 shows an analysis that the Abby Ellen Company did on December 31, 20X0. Note that 29% of the total receivables for Abby Ellen are past due from 1 to 30 days. (This analysis will also provide feedback to the credit department about how well the current credit policy is working.) Now let's look at how the company will estimate what balance in the Allowance for Doubtful Accounts is required to meet probable bad debts.

> Today, with a computer, an analysis of Accounts Receivable can be completed quickly.

The schedule shown in Table 13-2 below is prepared to assist the company in calculating the needed balance. In this schedule, Abby Ellen Company has applied a sliding scale of percents (3, 4, 10, 20, 50), based on previous experience, to the total amount of receivables due in each time period. For example, of the $3,600 not yet

TABLE 13-2 Balance Required to Meet Probable Bad Debts

	Amount	Estimated Percent Considered to Be Bad Debts Expense	Amount Needed in Allowance for Doubtful Accounts to Cover Estimated Bad Debts Expense
Not Yet Due	$3,600	3	$108 ($3,600 × .03)
Days Past Due			
1–30	2,000	4	80
31–60	870	10	87
61–90	200	20	40
Over 90	330	50	165
Total Accounts Receivable	$7,000	Total Balance Required in Allowance for Doubtful Accounts	$480
Less current balance			−100
Adjusting entry			$380

due, 3% or $108, will probably never be paid. Looking at this schedule reveals that Abby Ellen Company needs $480 to cover estimated bad debts. *Currently,* the balance in the Allowance account is $100. Thus, to reach a balance of $480, we must adjust the balance of the account by the adjusting journal entry shown in Figure 13-6.

Bad Debts Expense			Allowance for Doubtful Accounts		
Dr.		Cr.	Dr.		Cr.
380				100	Beg. Balance
				380	Adj.
				480	New balance in Allowance

The desired balance of $480 is now reached. If the Allowance had a *debit* balance of $100 before the adjustment, the amount of the adjusting entry would be $580 credit to the Allowance to arrive at the $480 balance. Once again, the adjustment *must* consider the existing balance in the Allowance account before the adjusting entry is prepared.

<table>
<tr><td>20X4
Dec.</td><td>31</td><td>Bad Debts Expense</td><td>3 8 0 00</td><td></td></tr>
<tr><td></td><td></td><td>   Allowance for Doubtful Accounts</td><td></td><td>3 8 0 00</td></tr>
<tr><td></td><td></td><td>   Estimate of bad debts</td><td></td><td></td></tr>
</table>

Figure 13-6
Estimating Bad Debts Based on Aging of Receivables

> Some companies that feel aging is too time-consuming may estimate bad debts based on a percentage of total Accounts Receivable.

> The balance in the Allowance for Doubtful Accounts is not ignored.

Learning Unit 13-2 Review

AT THIS POINT you should be able to

- Explain the two approaches to estimating Bad Debts Expense. (p. 519)
- Explain why the balance in the Allowance for Doubtful Accounts is ignored when an adjusting entry for bad debts is prepared in the income statement approach. (p. 520)
- Show how to prepare an aging of Accounts Receivable. (p. 521)
- Explain how the aging of Accounts Receivable is used to arrive at the balance required in the Allowance for Doubtful Accounts. (p. 521)

SELF-REVIEW QUIZ 13-2

(The forms you need are on page 1 of the *Study Guide and Working Papers.*)

From the following, prepare an adjusting journal entry for Bad Debts Expense for (1) the income statement approach and (2) the balance sheet approach.

Allowance for Doubtful Accounts			**Income Statement Approach**	
Dr.		Cr.	Net Sales	$160,000
	400		1% of Net Sales	

Balance Sheet Approach		**Percent Considered Bad Debts**
Not yet due:	$4,000	4
Days past due:		
1–30	3,000	5
31–60	400	10
Over 60	5,000	30

SOLUTION TO SELF-REVIEW QUIZ 13-2

(1)	Dec.	31	Bad Debts Expense	1 6 0 0 00		
			Allowance for Doubtful Accounts		1 6 0 0 00	
			(.01 × $160,000)			
(2)		31	Bad Debts Expense	1 4 5 0 00		
			Allowance for Doubtful Accounts		1 4 5 0 00	
			$4,000 × .04 = $ 160			
			3,000 × .05 = 150			
			400 × .10 = 40			
			5,000 × .30 = 1,500			
			$1,850			

Figure 13-7
Estimating Bad Debts

$1,850 is amount required.

Quiz Tip:
Note allowance adjusted:
$1,850 − $400 = $1,450

Learning Unit 13-3   Writing off and Recovering Uncollectible Accounts

WRITING OFF AN ACCOUNT USING THE ALLOWANCE FOR DOUBTFUL ACCOUNTS

Let's assume that on March 18, 20X7, the Abby Ellen Company determines that the account of Jill Sullivan for $900 is uncollectible. (The sale to Jill Sullivan was back in 20X6.) Thus, this Accounts Receivable amount should no longer be considered an asset and should be written off. The journal entry in Figure 13-8 reduces the Allowance for Doubtful Accounts and reduces the Accounts Receivable controlling account as well as the accounts receivable subsidiary ledger.

Key Points:

- This journal entry does *not* affect any expenses. Remember that Bad Debts Expense is not affected when an account is finally written off. The estimate for Bad Debts Expense was recorded in the previous year before the bad debt actually occurred.
- If more than one customer is written off, a compound entry can be used, debiting Allowance for the total and crediting each individual account.
- The net realizable value of Accounts Receivable is unchanged. Let's prove it:

	Balances Before the Write-Off		**Balances After the Write-Off**
Accounts Receivable	$12,000	$900 write-off	$11,100
Less: Allowance for Doubtful Accounts	2,000	$900 drain	1,100
Estimated realizable value	$10,000	No change	$10,000
	(what to expect to collect)		

Recording Recovered Debts Using Allowance for Doubtful Accounts What would happen if Jill Sullivan paid all or part of the debt after Abby Ellen Company wrote it off? Consider this situation: Assume that Jill Sullivan is able to pay off half of

20X7						
Mar.	18	Allowance for Doubtful Accounts		9 0 0 00		
		Accounts Receivable, Jill Sullivan			9 0 0 00	
		Wrote off Sullivan account				

Figure 13-8
Jill Sullivan Account
Written Off

her debt and send a check to Abby Ellen Company on February 1, 20X8. (Keep in mind that her account was written off on March 18, 20X7, and the original sale was made in 20X6.) To record this payment, Abby Ellen Company reverses in part the entry that was made to write off the account in the amount expected to be recovered and records the amount received from Jill. Figure 13-9 shows the journal entries to record the recovery of $450 out of the original amount of $900:

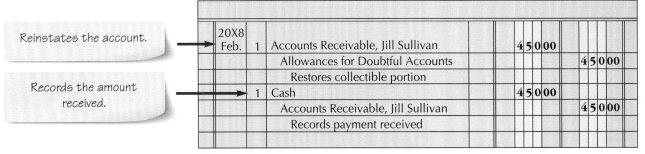

Reinstates the account.

Records the amount received.

20X8							
Feb.	1		Accounts Receivable, Jill Sullivan		4 5 0 00		
			Allowances for Doubtful Accounts				4 5 0 00
			Restores collectible portion				
	1		Cash		4 5 0 00		
			Accounts Receivable, Jill Sullivan				4 5 0 00
			Records payment received				

Figure 13-9 Reinstatement of a Bad Debt

The reason we record both a debit and a credit to Accounts Receivable is that it provides a clear picture of the transactions involving Jill Sullivan. If the company is considering giving credit again to Jill Sullivan, these previous records could be of assistance in determining how much if any credit could be extended. Note how the first entry reinstates the account and the second entry records the cash received.

THE DIRECT WRITE-OFF METHOD

The direct write-off method does not fulfill the matching principle but is acceptable for federal income tax reporting.

When a company cannot reasonably estimate its Bad Debts Expense, it may use the **direct write-off method**. Using this method, an account that is determined to be uncollectible would be directly written off to this year's Bad Debts Expense account without regard to when the original sale was made. In this method, the Allowance for Doubtful Accounts is not used, because no adjustment is needed at the end of the year to estimate Bad Debts Expense. The journal entry would be a debit to Bad Debts Expense and a credit to Accounts Receivable.

Recording Recovered Debts Using the Direct Method   Let's suppose that Jill Sullivan repays half of her outstanding debt after Abby Ellen Company has written it off. The recovered debt would be accounted for using the direct write-off method as shown in Figure 13-10.

Figure 13-10
Direct Write-off Method to Record Bad Debt

Writing off Jill Sullivan on March 18, 20X7. Note that the Allowance account is not used. See p. 522.

20X7							
Mar.	18		Bad Debts Expense		9 0 0 00		
			Accounts Receivable, Jill Sullivan				9 0 0 00
			Wrote off account				

A new account title, **Bad Debts Recovered,** must be created (Fig. 13-11). Think of this account as a revenue account found in the Other Income section of an income statement.

In the direct write-off method, when the amount is written off, no Allowance for Doubtful Accounts is used. Instead, the debit is to Bad Debts Expense. If the debt is recovered later, the direct method credits Bad Debts Recovered (an account in the Other Revenue category). In effect, this method increases the revenue and puts the Accounts Receivable back on the books. If recovery is made the same year (let's say on May 1) as the debt is written off, the entry made to write off the account is reversed (Fig. 13-12).

Bad Debts Recov.	Other Revenue	↑	Cr.

		20X8										
		Feb.	1	Acct. Rec., Jill Sullivan			4 5 0 00					
				Bad Debts Recovered						4 5 0 00		
				Restores collectible portion								
			1	Cash			4 5 0 00					
				Acct. Rec., Jill Sullivan						4 5 0 00		
				Records payment received								

Figure 13-11
Direct Write-Off Method to Record Recovery

Recovery of half the amount owed by Jill Sullivan on February 1, 20X8. Note that Bad Debts Recovered is used instead of Allowance for Doubtful Accounts.

		20X7										
		May	1	Accounts Receivable, Jill Sullivan			4 5 0 00					
				Bad Debts Expense						4 5 0 00		

Figure 13-12 Recovery Made in Same Year

On the balance sheet, Accounts Receivable is recorded at gross. No Allowance account or realizable amount is used.

Learning Unit 13-3 Review

AT THIS POINT you should be able to

- Write off an account using the Allowance for Doubtful Accounts method. (p. 523)
- Explain why net realizable value is unchanged after a write-off is complete. (p. 523)
- Prepare journal entries to recover entire or partial amounts that were once declared uncollectible. (p. 524)
- Explain the direct write-off method and prepare appropriate journal entries for write-off and recovery. (p. 525)

SELF-REVIEW QUIZ 13-3

(The forms you need are on page 2 of the *Study Guide and Working Papers.*)
   Respond true or false to the following:

1. When an account using the Allowance for Doubtful Accounts method is written off in a period following the sale, the result is a debit to Bad Debts Expense and a credit to Accounts Receivable.
2. The direct write-off method will sometimes use the Allowance for Doubtful Accounts.
3. When an account is written off (using the Allowance for Doubtful Accounts method), net realizable value is unchanged.
4. Bad Debts Recovered is an asset.
5. A debit balance in the Allowance for Doubtful Accounts indicates that the estimate for Bad Debts Expense was too low.

SOLUTIONS TO SELF-REVIEW QUIZ 13-3

1. False   **2.** False   **3.** True   **4.** False   **5.** True

Chapter Review

Summary of Key Points

Learning Unit 13-1

1. If accrual accounting is used, Bad Debts Expense should be recognized in the year the sale was earned, even though the actual write-off may not yet have taken place.
2. Bad Debts Expense is an expense found on the income statement.
3. The Allowance for Doubtful Accounts is a contra-asset account found on the balance sheet that accumulates the amount of estimated uncollectibles before they are actually written off.
4. Net realizable value equals Accounts Receivable minus Allowance for Doubtful Accounts.
5. When an account is written off, the Allowance for Doubtful Accounts is debited and Accounts Receivable is credited (along with the subsidiary ledger account).

Learning Unit 13-2

1. The two approaches to estimating Bad Debts Expense are the income statement approach and the balance sheet approach.
2. The income statement approach estimates Bad Debts Expense based on a percent of net sales. (Some companies use credit sales, some use total sales.) The balance is ignored in the Allowance for Doubtful Accounts when the Bad Debts Expense is estimated from sales of the period.
3. The balance sheet approach estimates the balance required in the Allowance for Doubtful Accounts by aging the Accounts Receivable. The balance in the Allowance account will have to be adjusted based on the aging of the receivables.

Learning Unit 13-3

> After the write-off, net realizable value is unchanged.

1. When an account is written off (using the Allowance account) in years following the sale, the result is to debit the Allowance for Doubtful Accounts and credit Accounts Receivable. Do not debit Bad Debts Expense, because it has already been recorded in the year the sale was earned.
2. When an uncollectible account has been written off and is now recovered, the entry reverses the original write-off by debiting Accounts Receivable and crediting the Allowance for Doubtful Accounts. Then the cash received is debited and the Accounts Receivable is credited.
3. The direct write-off method will recognize the Bad Debts Expense when the customer account is declared uncollectible. The direct method does *not* use the Allowance for Doubtful Accounts, because no estimate is made for bad debts. This method does not follow the matching principle in the accrual basis of accounting.
4. Bad Debts Recovered is classified as Other Revenue when a customer account is reinstated after being written off in the direct method.

Key Terms

Aging of Accounts Receivable The procedure of classifying accounts of individual customers by age group, where age is the number of days elapsed from due date.

Allowance for Doubtful Accounts A contra-asset account that is subtracted from Accounts Receivable. This account accumulates the *expected* amount of uncollectibles as of a given date.

Bad Debts Expense The operating expense account that estimates the amount of credit sales that will probably not be collectible in a given accounting period when the Allowance method is used. For the direct write-off method, this account would be the actual amount written off.

Bad Debts Recovered   When an account receivable has been written off and is recovered, this account, which is in the Other Revenue category, is credited in the direct write-off method if the recovery is in a year *following* the write-off.

Balance sheet approach   A method used to calculate the amount *required* in the Allowance for Doubtful Accounts to cover expected uncollectibles. This method is based on the Accounts Receivable amount and the aging process. The adjustment to the Allowance for Doubtful Accounts will bring the new balance of that account to the new required level.

Direct write-off method   The method of writing off uncollectibles when they occur and thus *not* using the Allowance for Doubtful Accounts. This method does not fulfill the matching principle of accrual accounting.

Income statement approach   A method that estimates the amount of Bad Debts Expense that will result based on a percent of net credit sales for the period. The amount of the expected bad debt is added to the existing balance of Allowance for Doubtful Accounts.

Net realizable value   The amount (Accounts Receivable–Allowance for Doubtful Accounts) that is expected to be collected.

Questions, Mini Exercises, Exercises, and Problems

Discussion Questions

1. Explain the matching principle in relationship to recording Bad Debts Expense.

2. What is the purpose of the Allowance for Doubtful Accounts?

3. What is net realizable value?

4. When an account receivable is written off, Bad Debts Expense must be debited. True or false? Please discuss.

5. Explain why the Allowance for Doubtful Accounts is a contra-asset account.

6. Recording Bad Debts Expense is a closing entry. True or false? Defend your position.

7. The income statement approach used to estimate bad debts is based on Accounts Receivable on the balance sheet. Accept or reject. Why?

8. In which approach is the balance of the Allowance for Doubtful Accounts considered when the estimate of Bad Debts Expense is made? Please explain.

9. Why would a company age its Accounts Receivable?

10. Using the Allowance for Doubtful Accounts method, what journal entries would be made to write off an account as well as later record the recovery of the accounts receivable?

11. Why doesn't net realizable value change when an account is written off in the use of the Allowance account?

12. What is the purpose of using a direct write-off method?

13. Explain the purpose of the Bad Debts Recovered account.

Mini Exercises

(The forms you need are on page 4 of the *Study Guide and Working Papers*.)

Blueprint: Summary of Recording Bad Debts Expense, Write-Offs, and Recovery

Situation	Allowance for Doubtful Accounts Method		Direct Write-Off Method
	A. Income Statement Approach	B. Balance Sheet Approach	

Adjusting entry to record estimated uncollectible accounts	Bad Debts Expense XX
	  Allowance for Doubtful Accounts XX
	
	Based on percent of net sales. Balance in Allowance account is ignored.
		Bad Debts Expense XX
		  Allowance for Doubtful Accounts XX
		
		Aging of Accounts Receivable determines amount needed in Allowance account. Balance in Allowance account is adjusted.
			None

Account receivable is determined to be uncollectible	Allowance for Doubtful Accounts XX
	  Accounts Receivable, XX
		Allowance for Doubtful Accounts XX
		  Accounts Receivable, XX
			Bad Debts Expense XX
			  Accounts Receivable, XX

Bad debts are recovered	Accounts Receivable, XX
	  Allowance for Doubtful Accounts XX
	Cash XX
	  Accounts Receivable, XX
		Accounts Receivable, XX
		  Allowance for Doubtful Accounts XX
		Cash XX
		  Accounts Receivable, XX
			Accounts Receivable, XX
			  Bad Debts Recovered* XX
			Cash XX
			  Accounts Receivable, XX

Balance sheet update	**Shows net realizable value**	**Shows net realizable value**	**Does not show net realizable value**

*Used if recovery is not in the same year as the sale.

Categorizing Accounts

1. a. Complete the following transactional analysis chart:

	Category	↑ ↓	Rules
Bad Debts Expense			
Allowance for Doubtful Accounts			

b. On which financial statement will each title be recorded?
c. Which account is temporary? Which account is permanent?

Allowance Method

2. Complete Figure 13-13:

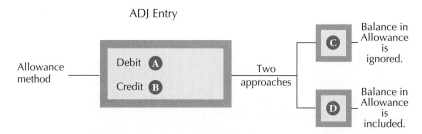

Figure 13-13
Two Approaches to Estimating Bad Debts Using Allowance Method

Journalize Adjusting Entries for Income Statement and Balance Sheet Approach

3. Given the balance in the Allowance for Doubtful Accounts of $200 credit, prepare adjusting entries for Bad Debts based on the following assumptions:

a. Bad Debts to be 5% of Net Credit Sales or $600.
b. Based on Aging of Accounts Receivable, Bad Debts should be $500.

Writing Off Uncollectible Accounts and Reinstatement: Allowance Method

4. Journalize entries for the following situations (assume allowance method):

Situation 1: Wrote off Bill Allen as a bad debt two years after the sale for $50.
Situation 2: Reinstated Bill Allen, who sent in his past due amount.

Writing Off Uncollectible Account and Reinstatement: Direct Write-Off Method

5. Journalize entries for the following situation (assume direct write-off method):

Situation 1: Wrote off Bill Allen as a bad debt two years after the sale of $50.
Situation 2: Reinstated Bill Allen, who sent in his past due amount two years after it had been written off.

Exercises

(The forms you need are on pages 5–6 of the *Study Guide and Working Papers.*)

13-1. Bob.com has requested that you prepare a partial balance sheet on December 31, 20XX, from the following: Cash, $110,000; Petty Cash, $70; Accounts Receivable, $70,000; Bad Debts Expense, $50,000; Allowance for Doubtful Accounts, $14,000; Merchandise Inventory, $19,000.

Preparing a partial balance sheet with Allowance for Doubtful Accounts.

13-2. The following information is given:

Accounts Receivable	Sales	Sales Returns and Allowances
30,000		110,000		500	

	Sales Discount	Allowance for Doubtful Accounts
	9,500			5,000

Calculating Bad Debts Expense by income statement approach.

Calculating Bad Debts
Expense by balance sheet
approach.

Journalize the adjusting entry on December 31, 20XX, for Bad Debts Expense, which is estimated to be 4% of net sales. The income statement approach is used.

13-3. Assuming that in Exercise 13-2 the balance sheet approach is used, prepare a journalized adjusting entry for Bad Debts Expense. Based on an aging of Accounts Receivable, an $8,000 balance in the Allowance account will be needed to cover bad debts.

Journalizing adjustment
for Bad Debts as well as
reinstatement by
Allowance method; comparison with direct write-off method.

13-4. Austin Co., which uses an Allowance for Doubtful Accounts, had the following transactions in 20X5 and 20X6. (Use the income statement approach.)

20X5

Dec.   31   Recorded Bad Debts Expense of $12,000.

20X6

Apr.   3   Wrote off Angie Ring account of $4,000 as uncollectible.
June   4   Wrote off Mike Catuc account of $3,000 as uncollectible.

20X7

Aug.   5   Recovered $500 from Mike Catuc.

     a. Journalize the transactions. (The company uses the income statement approach in estimating bad debts.)
     b. Journalize how Austin Co. would record the Mike Catuc bad debt situation if the direct write-off method were used.

Journalizing adjustments
for Bad Debts Expense (1)
based on percent of sales
and (2) based on aging of
Accounts Receivable with
balance of Allowance for
Doubtful Accounts, a
debit balance.

13-5. Rowe Company had credit sales of $200,000 during 20X7. The balance in the Allowance for Doubtful Accounts is a $1,000 debit balance. Journalize the Bad Debts Expense for December 31 using each of the following methods:

     a. Bad Debts Expense is estimated at 1.5% of credit sales.
     b. The aging of Accounts Receivable indicates that $2,200 will be required in the Allowance account to cover Bad Debts Expense.

Group A Problems

(The forms you need are on pages 7–13 of the *Study Guide and Working Papers*.)

13A-1. Angel.com has requested that you prepare journal entries from the following (this company uses the Allowance for Doubtful Accounts method based on the income statement approach):

The income statement
approach: journalizing Bad
Debts Expense and writing
accounts off.

20X7

Dec.   31   Recorded Bad Debts Expense of $12,000.

20X8

Jan.   7   Wrote off Gene Smore's account of $800 as uncollectible.
Mar.   5   Wrote off Paul Jane's account of $600 as uncollectible.
July   8   Recovered $300 from Paul Jane.
Aug.   19   Wrote off Bob Seager's account of $1,300 as uncollectible.
Aug.   24   Wrote off Jill Neuman's account of $750 as uncollectible.
Nov.   19   Recovered $400 from Bob Seager.

Check Figure:
August 24:
Dr.: Allowance for Doubtful
Accounts
Cr.: Accounts Receivable,
Jill Neuman

13A-2. Given the information presented in Figure 13-14 on p. 531:

     a. Prepare on December 31, 20X8, the adjusting journal entry for Bad Debts Expense.
     b. Prepare a partial balance sheet on December 31, 20X8, showing how net realizable value is calculated.
     c. If the balance in the Allowance for Doubtful Accounts was a $300 debit balance, journalize the adjusting entry for Bad Debts Expense on December 31, 20X8.

The balance sheet
approach: aging analysis
and journalizing of Bad
Debts Expense.

ALVIE CO. DECEMBER 31, 20X8			
	Amount	Estimated Percent Considered to Be Bad Debts Expense	Estimated Amount Needed in Allowance for Doubtful Accounts
Not yet due	$130,000	.01	
0–60	9,000	.05	
61–180	8,000	.20	
Over six months	5,000	.40	
	$152,000		

Figure 13-14 Aging of Accounts Receivable

Check Figure:
Net realizable value
$146,650

Balances: Cash, $30,000; Accounts Receivable, $152,000; Allowance for Doubtful Accounts, $300; Inventory, $12,000.

13A-3. T. J. Rack Company uses the direct write-off method for recording Bad Debts Expense. At the beginning of 20X8, Accounts Receivable has a $119,000 balance. Journalize the following transactions for T. J. Rack:

The direct write-off method.

20X8

Mar.	13	Wrote off S. Rose's account for $1,800.
Apr.	14	Wrote off P. Soy's account for $750.

20X9

Nov.	8	P. Soy paid bad debt of $750 that was written off April 14, 20X8.
Dec.	7	Wrote off J. Miller's account as uncollectible, $285.
Dec.	12	Wrote off D. Lovejoy's account for $375 due from sales made on account in 20X7.

Check Figure:
Dec. 7:
Dr.: Bad Debt Expense
Cr.: Acc. Rec., J. Miller

13A-4. Simon Company completed the following transactions:

20X8

Jan.	9	Sold merchandise on account to Ray's Supply, $1,500.
Jan.	15	Wrote off the account of Pete Runnels as uncollectible because of his death, $600.
Mar.	17	Received $400 from Roland Co., whose account had been written off in 20X7. The account was reinstated and the collection recorded.
Apr.	9	Received 10% of the $4,000 owed by Lane Drug. The remainder was written off as uncollectible.
June	15	The account of Mel's Garage was reinstated for $1,200. The account was written off three years ago and collected in full today.
Oct.	18	Prepared a compound entry to write the following accounts off as uncollectible: Jane's Diner, $200; Keen Auto, $400; Ralph's Hardware, $600.
Nov.	12	Sold merchandise on account to J. B. Rug, $1,900.
Dec.	31	Based on an aging of Accounts Receivable, it was estimated that $7,000 will be uncollectible out of a total of $160,000 in Accounts Receivable.
Dec.	31	Closed Bad Debts Expense to Income Summary.

Journalizing and posting adjustments for Bad Debts Expense and write-offs and recovery based on balance sheet approach. Preparation of partial balance sheet.

From the preceding as well as the following additional data:

	Acct. No.	Balance
Allowance for Doubtful Accounts	114	$4,100
Income Summary	312	—
Bad Debts Expense	612	—

Check Figure:
Total current assets
$272,360

a. Journalize the transactions.

b. Post to Allowance for Doubtful Accounts, Income Summary, and Bad Debts Expense accounts as needed. (Be sure to record the beginning balance in the Allowance account in your *Study Guide and Working Papers*.)

c. Prepare a current assets section of the balance sheet. Ending balances needed: Cash, $13,000; Accounts Receivable, $160,000; Office Supplies, $2,110; Merchandise Inventory, $103,000; Prepaid Rent, $1,250.

Group B Problems

(The forms you need are on pages 7–13 of the *Study Guide and Working Papers*.)

13B-1. Angel.com has requested that you prepare journal entries from the following (this company uses the Allowance for Doubtful Accounts method based on the income statement approach).

20X7

Dec. 31 Recorded Bad Debts Expense of $14,800.

20X8

Jan. 7 Wrote off Woody Tree's Account of $1,200 as uncollectible.
Mar. 5 Wrote off Jim Lantz's account of $600 as uncollectible.
July 8 Recovered $600 from Jim Lantz.
Aug. 19 Wrote off Mabel Hest's account of $750 as uncollectible.
Aug. 24 Wrote off Jim O'Reilly's account of $950 as uncollectible.
Nov. 19 Recovered $500 from Mabel Hest.

13B-2. Given the following information and the information in Figure 13-15: Cash, $42,000; Accounts Receivable, $173,000; Allowance for Doubtful Accounts, $400; Merchandise Inventory, $12,000:

a. Prepare on December 31, 20X8, the adjusting journal entry for Bad Debts Expense.

b. Prepare a partial balance sheet on December 31, 20X8, showing how net realizable value is calculated.

c. If the balance in the Allowance for Doubtful Accounts was a $400 debit balance, journalize the adjusting entry for Bad Debts Expense on December 31, 20X8.

13B-3. T. J. Rack Company uses the direct write-off method for recording Bad Debts Expense. At the beginning of 20X8, Accounts Receivable has an $88,000 balance. Journalize the following transactions for T. J. Rack:

The income statement approach: journalizing Bad Debts Expense and writing accounts off.

Check Figure:
Aug. 24:
Dr.: Allow for D.A.
Cr.: Acc. Rec., Jim O'Reilly

The balance sheet approach: aging analysis and journalizing of Bad Debts Expense.

Check Figure:
Net realizable value
$166,000

The direct write-off method.

Figure 13-15
Aging of Accounts Receivable

		Amount	Estimated Percent Considered to Be Bad Debts Expense	Estimated Amount Needed in Allowance for Doubtful Accounts	
		ALVIE CO. DECEMBER 31, 20X8			
Not yet due		$150,000	.02		
0–60		10,000	.06		
61–180		9,000	.20		
Over six months		4,000	.40		
		$173,000			

20X8

Mar. 13 Wrote off Jill Diamond's account for $1,950.

Apr. 14 Wrote off Buffy Hall's account for $900.

20X9

Nov. 8 Buffy Hall paid debt of $900 that was written off April 14, 20X8.

Dec. 7 Wrote off Joe Francis's account as uncollectible, $880.

Dec. 12 Wrote off Joe Martin's account for $410 from sales made on account in 20X7.

> Check Figure:
> Dec. 7:
> Dr.: Bad Debt Expense
> Cr.: Acc. Rec., Joe Francis

13B-4. Simon Company completed the following transactions:

> Journalizing and posting adjustments for Bad Debts Expense and write-offs and recovery based on balance sheet approach. Partial balance sheet prepared.

20X8

Jan. 9 Sold merchandise on account to Lowe's Supply, $1,900.

Jan. 15 Wrote off the account of Kevin Reese as uncollectible because of his death, $700.

Mar. 17 Received $300 from J. James whose account had been written off in 20X7. The account was reinstated and the collection recorded.

Apr. 9 Received 20% of the $5,000 owed by Long Drug. The remainder was written off as uncollectible.

June 15 The account of Morse's Garage was reinstated for $3,100. The account was written off three years ago and collected in full today.

Oct. 18 Prepared a compound entry to write the following accounts off as uncollectible: Sal's Diner, $800; Ring Auto, $1,300; Neel's Hardware, $800.

Nov. 12 Sold merchandise on account to Able Roy, $1,950.

Dec. 31 Based on an aging of Accounts Receivable, it was estimated that $8,000 will be uncollectible out of a total of $170,000 in Accounts Receivable.

Dec. 31 Closed Bad Debts Expense to Income Summary.

> Check Figure:
> Total current assets
> $284,200

From the above as well as the following additional data:

	Acct. No.	Balance
Allowance for Doubtful Accounts	114	$3,300
Income Summary	312	—
Bad Debts Expense	612	—

a. Journalize the transactions.

b. Post to Allowance for Doubtful Accounts, Income Summary, and Bad Debts Expense Account as needed.

c. Prepare a current assests section of the balance sheet. Ending balances needed: Cash, $24,000; Accounts Receivable, $170,000; Office Supplies, $3,000; Merchandise Inventory, $94,000; Prepaid Rent, $1,200.

Real-World Applications

13R-1. Joan Rivers, the newly hired bookkeeper of Lyon Company, has until 5:00 P.M. today to prepare an analysis of Accounts Receivable by age on December 31 as well as record the entry for Bad Debts Expense. Please assist Joan, who has found the following invoices and balances scattered on her desk (see Fig.13-16). Terms of all sales are n/30. Explain in writing why the allowance method is used.

13R-2.

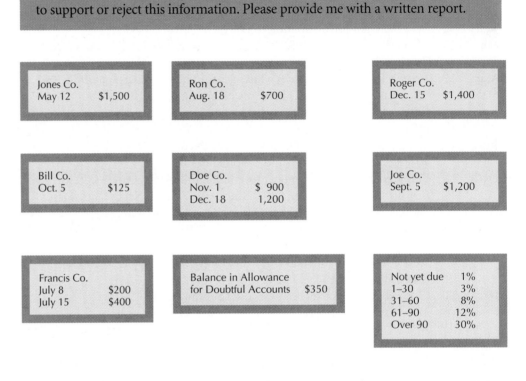

> ## MEMO
>
> To: Al Jones
>
> From: Peter Flynn, Pres.
>
> Re: Bad Debts
>
> At a party last night a friend of mine told me that we should not be using the direct write off method. He told me that it doesn't fulful the matching principle of accounting. Check the Tax Reform Act of 1986 in your Research Department to support or reject this information. Please provide me with a written report.

Figure 13-16
Invoices and Balances

Jones Co.	
May 12	$1,500

Ron Co.	
Aug. 18	$700

Roger Co.	
Dec. 15	$1,400

Bill Co.	
Oct. 5	$125

Doe Co.	
Nov. 1	$ 900
Dec. 18	1,200

Joe Co.	
Sept. 5	$1,200

Francis Co.	
July 8	$200
July 15	$400

Balance in Allowance for Doubtful Accounts	$350

Not yet due	1%
1–30	3%
31–60	8%
61–90	12%
Over 90	30%

YOU make the call

Critical Thinking/Ethical Case

13R-3. Pete Sazich, the accountant for Moore Company, feels that all bad debts will be eliminated if credit transactions are done by credit card. He also feels that the cost of the credit cards should be added to the price of the goods. Pete feels that in the future the Allowance method will be totally eliminated. You make the call. Write a letter stating your opinion regarding this matter to Pete's boss.

Internet Exercises: Dun and Bradstreet

EX-1. [www.dnb.com/english/aboutdnb/index.htm]   Dun and Bradstreet is one of the world's best-known names in reporting and analyzing business credit. D and B prides itself in providing credit and financial management services to businesses. From this site, look into some of the areas in which Dun and Bradstreet can help businesses.

1. Briefly state what these functions are and how a new or existing business could be served in this manner.
2. What is D and B doing in the "new economy" based upon Web businesses?

EX-2. [**http://www.cccsintl.org/**]   The Consumer Credit Counseling Service assists individuals who have gotten into credit problems. This not-for-profit organization helps by working out problems between creditors and individuals with the hope of keeping debtors out of bankruptcy. When you arrive at this site, click on "debt counseling services" and investigate the types of help available from this organization. What is the advantage to creditors in working with this agency?

Continuing Problem

Eldorado Computer Center

The Eldorado Computer Center currently has an $11,900 balance in Accounts Receivable. Here is a current schedule of Accounts Receivable:

Eldorado Computer Center
Schedule of Accounts Receivable
March 31, 20XX

Taylor Golf	$ 2,900
Vita Needle	8,100
Accu Pac	900
Total	$11,900

Assignment

(See p. 17 in your *Study Guide and Working Papers.*)

    Although Accu Pac's account is not 90 days past due, Freedman has determined that it is necessary to write off the entire balance because the business has been foreclosed. Make the necessary journal entry using the direct write-off method.

CHAPTER 14

Notes Receivable and Notes Payable

You stop by the bank to deposit your paycheck. You notice several bright orange signs in the lobby that read, "Get a no-hassle loan for just about anything. Our interest rates are great! Ask our bankers about applying today!" After making your deposit, you think about how competitive the banking industry is today and the fact that your bank will loan people money for any number of purposes. Do banks like to loan money to businesses as well?

Banks do loan money to businesses as well as to individuals. But in today's competitive business environment, many companies are also eager to finance their sales directly with customers. For example, one way a customer may finance a large purchase directly with the seller is by signing a promissory note. Or, a customer may be given more time to pay an outstanding account balance by signing a note. Promissory notes are known as notes receivable to the seller, and notes payable to the buyer of goods or services.

In this chapter we will learn about notes receivable and notes payable. We will discuss how to calculate interest on promissory notes and when a note should be paid. We will also find out how to journalize note transactions, handle dishonored notes, discount a note at a bank, and make adjustments for interest expense and interest income at the end of an accounting period.

After completing this chapter, you will understand how businesses use notes to buy and sell goods or services. Then you will know that when it comes to one business selling its goods or services to another, the bank is not the only place where a company can finance its purchases.

Learning Objectives

- Determining interest calculations and maturity dates on notes. (p. 538)
- Journalizing entries to record renewal of a note, dishonoring of a note, eventual receipt of payment, and note given in exchange for equipment purchased. (p. 542)
- Discounting an interest-bearing note receivable and recording a discounted note that has been dishonored. (p. 547)
- Handling adjustments for interest expense and interest income. (p. 551)

Notes receivable: asset.
Notes payable: liability.

So far the accounts receivable and accounts payable transactions we have been discussing have involved informal promises: Purchase orders and sales receipts are not formal written promises. In this chapter we turn to transactions by buyers and sellers that require promissory notes (or notes), which are *formal written promises.* Notes receivable record amounts owed to a company by others. Notes payable record amounts the company itself owes.

Companies use notes instead of informal promises for many reasons, such as (1) recording sales of high-cost items like farm machinery or construction equipment that have long-term credit periods (usually over 60 days), (2) giving additional time to settle past due accounts, or (3) borrowing money from a bank for a fee. The fee that is charged for the use of one's money over a period of time is called **interest.** In addition, a note gives the seller or lender a stronger legal claim for collecting a past due account because the note acts as formal proof of the transaction.

Learning Unit 14-1 Promissory Notes, Interest Calculations, and Determining Maturity Dates

Before looking at recording notes receivable and notes payable, let's discuss the structure of a note and how to determine interest calculations and *maturity dates* (when the note comes due).

A **promissory note** (often called simply a *note*) is a written promise by a borrower to pay a certain sum of money to the lender at a fixed future date. Figure 14-1 is a promissory note that Able Company issued to Green Company. Take a moment to look at the structure of this note. The following explanation is keyed to the figure:

Figure 14-1
A Promissory Note

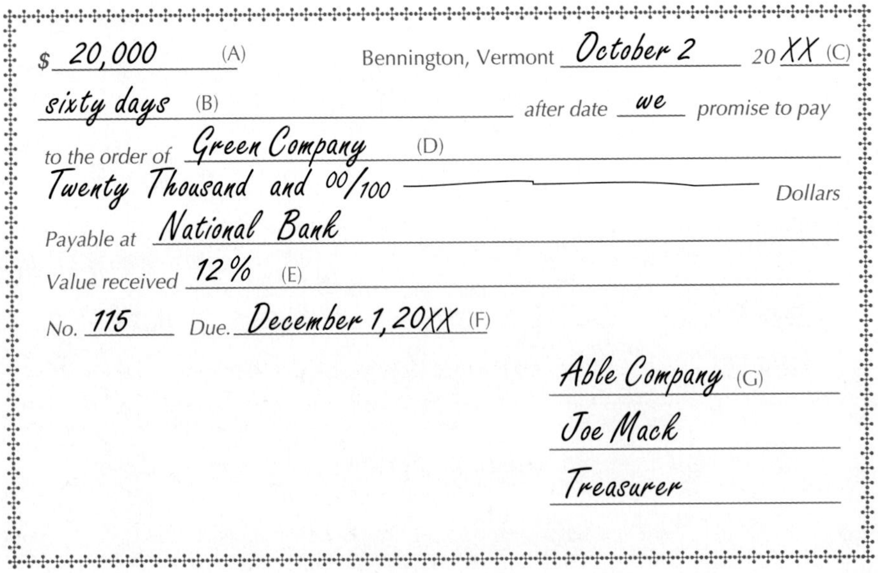
$ 20,000 (A) Bennington, Vermont October 2 20XX (C)

sixty days (B) after date we promise to pay

to the order of Green Company (D)

Twenty Thousand and 00/100 Dollars

Payable at National Bank

Value received 12 % (E)

No. 115 Due. December 1, 20XX (F)

Able Company (G)

Joe Mack

Treasurer

a. Able Company is borrowing $20,000; this amount is called the **principal.**

b. Money is being borrowed for 60 days.

c. The note is issued on October 2, 20XX.

d. The Green Company is the payee to whom the note is payable.

e. The note carries a 12% annual interest rate. (Even though the note is for 60 days, interest is stated as a yearly rate.)

f. The date the note will come due, December 1, 20XX, is called the maturity date.

g. Able Company is the maker, or the one promising to pay the note plus interest when it comes due.

The maker (Able Company) is the borrower. The borrower calls this obligation a note payable. The payee (Green Company) views this note as an asset called a note receivable. Able Company's interest expense is interest income for Green Company. Remember that interest expense is classified on the income statement as Other Expenses and interest income is Other Income.

> Think of the payee as the lender.

> The maker is often also called the payor or debtor.

> Most interest on notes will be paid on the maturity date. We will cover exceptions later in the chapter.

HOW TO CALCULATE INTEREST

The formula for calculating the interest on a note is

Interest = **Principal** × **Rate** × **Time**

↑ The face value or amount stated on note indicating amount borrowed

↑ Percent per year

↑ Years or fraction of year

Let's look at some illustrative situations to show specific interest calculations.

Interest calculated for one year on a $6,000 12% note:

$$I = P \times R \times T$$
$$12\% = .12 \text{ or } \tfrac{12}{100} = \$6,000 \times .12 \times 1$$
$$= \$720$$

Interest calculated for five months on an $8,000 10% note: Time is expressed in twelfths of a year; thus five months is

$$I = P \times R \times T$$
$$= \$8,000 \times .10 \times \tfrac{5}{12}$$
$$= \$333.33$$

Interest calculated for exact number of days based on a 360-day year, 60 days at 6% on a $4,000 note: When the note is given in days, the fraction for time is

$$\frac{\textbf{Exact Number of Days}}{\textbf{360}}$$

> Some federal agencies use 365 days, but common business practice is to use 360.

So we have

$$I = P \times R \times T$$
$$= \$4,000 \times .06 \times \tfrac{60}{360}$$
$$= \$40$$

HOW TO DETERMINE MATURITY DATE

Maturity Date Determined by Exact Days

30 days have September, April, June, and November; all the rest have 31, except February, which has 28 (29 during a leap year).

To determine the maturity date of a 90-day note dated June 21, the following could be set up (or you could count on a calendar):

Number of days remaining in June (30 − 21)	9
Days in July	31
Days in August	31
Number of days at end of August	71
Days in September to reach 90	19
Term of note	90

Thus, the maturity date of the note is September 19. Another way to calculate the maturity date is to use a table of days in a year (see Table 14-1 below).

The original note is dated June 21. Look at the top of the table for June and down the left column to day 21. The point of intersection reveals that June 21 is day 172 of

TABLE 14-1 Days in a Year

Day of Month	Jan.	Feb.*	Mar.	Apr.	May	June	July	Aug.	Sept.	Oct.	Nov.	Dec.	Day of Month
1	1	32	60	91	121	152	182	213	244	274	305	335	1
2	2	33	61	92	122	153	183	214	245	275	306	336	2
3	3	34	62	93	123	154	184	215	246	276	307	337	3
4	4	35	63	94	124	155	185	216	247	277	308	338	4
5	5	36	64	95	125	156	186	217	248	278	309	339	5
6	6	37	65	96	126	157	187	218	249	279	310	340	6
7	7	38	66	97	127	158	188	219	250	280	311	341	7
8	8	39	67	98	128	159	189	220	251	281	312	342	8
9	9	40	68	99	129	160	190	221	252	282	313	343	9
10	10	41	69	100	130	161	191	222	253	283	314	344	10
11	11	42	70	101	131	162	192	223	254	284	315	345	11
12	12	43	71	102	132	163	193	224	255	285	316	346	12
13	13	44	72	103	133	164	194	225	256	286	317	347	13
14	14	45	73	104	134	165	195	226	257	287	318	348	14
15	15	46	74	105	135	166	196	227	258	288	319	349	15
16	16	47	75	106	136	167	197	228	259	289	320	350	16
17	17	48	76	107	137	168	198	229	260	290	321	351	17
18	18	49	77	108	138	169	199	230	261	291	322	352	18
19	19	50	78	109	139	170	200	231	(262)	292	323	353	19
20	20	51	79	110	140	171	201	232	263	293	324	354	20
21	21	52	80	111	141	(172)	202	233	264	294	325	355	21
22	22	53	81	112	142	173	203	234	265	295	326	356	22
23	23	54	82	113	143	174	204	235	266	296	327	357	23
24	24	55	83	114	144	175	205	236	267	297	328	358	24
25	25	56	84	115	145	176	206	237	268	298	329	359	25
26	26	57	85	116	146	177	207	238	269	299	330	360	26
27	27	58	86	117	147	178	208	239	270	300	331	361	27
28	28	59	87	118	148	179	209	240	271	301	332	362	28
29	29		88	119	149	180	210	241	272	302	333	363	29
30	30		89	120	150	181	211	242	273	303	334	364	30
31	31		90		151		212	243		304		365	31

*For leap years, February has 29 days, and the number of each day after February 28 is one greater than the number given in the table.

the year. If we add 172 and 90 (length of note) we get 262. By searching in the table for 262, we see the date of maturity is September 19.

Maturity Date Determined by Number of Months

If the note were expressed in months rather than days, the table or calendar would not be needed. The maturity date could be found by counting the months from the date the note was issued, regardless of number of days in each month. Here are some examples:

Date of Note	Length of Note	Maturity Date	
March 31	Two months	May 31	
April 30	Three months	July 31	(last day of
July 31	Two months	September 30	month)

Learning Unit 14-1 Review

AT THIS POINT you should be able to

- Explain the advantages of using notes instead of informal promises. (p. 538)
- Define and explain the structure of a promissory note. (p. 538)
- Calculate interest on notes in days, monthly, or yearly. (p. 538)
- Calculate maturity date by days in the month, by special chart, or by months. (p. 540)

SELF-REVIEW QUIZ 14-1

(The forms you need are on page 14 of the *Study Guide and Working Papers.*)
1. Calculate the interest for the following:

   a. $10,000   12%   1 year
   b. 9,000   13%   7 months
   c. 7,000   10%   80 days

2. Find the maturity date of an 80-day note dated March 3 by (a) days in each month and (b) using a days-in-a-year chart.

3. Find the maturity date of a note dated March 31, due in five months.

SOLUTIONS TO SELF-REVIEW QUIZ 14-1

1.   a. $10,000 × .12 × 1 = $1,200.

   b. $9,000 × .13 × $\frac{7}{12}$ = $682.50.

   c. $7,000 × .10 × $\frac{80}{360}$ = $155.56.

2.   a.
Number of days remaining in March (31 − 3)	28
Days in April	30
Number of days at end of April	58
Days in May to reach 80	22
Maturity date—May 22	80

b. March 3   62   days
                  + 80
                  142   May 22

3. March 31, April, May, June, July, August 31 .

Learning Unit 14-2   Recording Notes

> We use general journal entries to keep things simple instead of using special journals.

To understand how notes can be used to extend credit periods and to see how a note is paid off, let's look at some illustrative transactions involving Mace Company and Jane Company.

Sale of Merchandise on Account   On August 1, 20XX, Mace Company sold $6,000 of merchandise on account to Jane Company (Fig. 14-2).

TIME EXTENSION WITH A NOTE

On September 1, the end of the credit period, Jane Company gave a $6,000, 60-day, 13% note to Mace Company to gain additional time to settle the past due account. The entries in Figure 14-3 would be made on the books of the buyer and seller.

When this transaction is journalized, both Accounts Receivable and Accounts Payable are reduced. With *notes* a subsidiary ledger is usually *not* needed, because the file of the notes provides all the information.

Mace might accept this note as an extension because (1) if Jane Company doesn't pay, a formal written promise is in hand, and (2) interest is accumulating on the note.

Seller →

The end result of this transaction is a shifting of assets of Mace Company from Accounts Receivable to Notes Receivable.

Buyer →

For Jane Company, the result is a shift in liabilities from Accounts Payable to Notes Payable.

Figure 14-2
Sale of Merchandise on Books of Seller and Buyer

ON BOOKS OF SELLER—MACE COMPANY

Aug.	1	Accounts Receivable, Jane Co.	6 0 0 0 00		
		Sales		6 0 0 0 00	
		Sold merchandise on account			

ON BOOKS OF BUYER—JANE COMPANY

Aug.	1	Purchases	6 0 0 0 00		
		Accounts Payable, Mace Co.		6 0 0 0 00	
		Purchased merchandise on account			

Figure 14-3
Time Extension of a Note

			SELLER—MACE COMPANY										
Sept.	1	Notes Receivable		6 0 0 0 00							
		Accounts Receivable, Jane Co.				6 0 0 0 00			
		Received 60-day, 13% note for							
		extension of past due account							

> Notes Receivable is a current asset on the balance sheet.

			BUYER—JANE COMPANY										
Sept.	1	Accounts Payable, Mace Co.		6 0 0 0 00						
		Notes Payable				6 0 0 0 00			
		Issued 60-day, 13% note for							
		extension of past due account							

> Notes Payable is a current liability on the balance sheet.

NOTE DUE AND PAID AT MATURITY

Now let's look at the journal entries that will be made if Jane Company pays off the note on October 31 (Fig. 14-4). It is important to emphasize that the interest is calculated on the maturity date of the note.

Figure 14-4
Note Paid at Maturity

			SELLER—MACE COMPANY										
Oct.	31	Cash		6 1 3 0 00						
		Notes Receivable				6 0 0 0 00			
		Interest Income				1 3 0 00			
		Collected Jane Company note							

$$[\$6,000 \times .13 \times \frac{60}{360} = \$130 \text{ Interest Income}]$$

			BUYER—JANE COMPANY										
Oct.	31	Notes Payable		6 0 0 0 00						
		Interest Expense		1 3 0 00						
		Cash				6 1 3 0 00			
		Paid note to Mace Company							

$$[\$6,000 \times .13 \times \frac{60}{360} = \$130 \text{ Interest Expense}]$$

NOTE RENEWED AT MATURITY

If Jane Company is unable to pay the $6,130 at maturity, it is possible for the company to renew all or part of the note. Let's assume that the company can pay the interest of $130 and give another note for 90 days at 13%. The transaction could be recorded as shown in Figure 14-5 on the books of the buyer and seller.

Note on the seller's books how the interest is received, the old note is canceled, and the new note is put on the books.

DISHONORED NOTE

Mace Company does not have to renew the note if Jane Company fails to pay it at maturity. In this situation the note is said to be a **dishonored note.** Another way to describe this situation is to say that Jane Company has **defaulted** on its note.

Figure 14-5
Note Renewed at Maturity

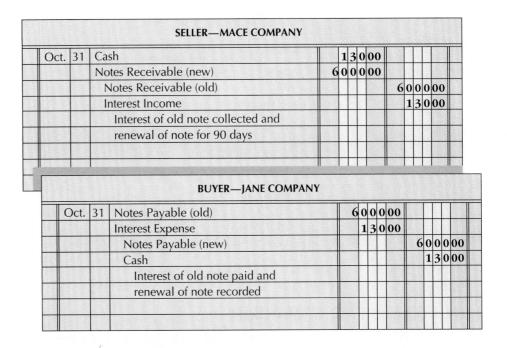

SELLER—MACE COMPANY

Oct.	31	Cash	1 3 0 00		
		Notes Receivable (new)	6 0 0 0 00		
		Notes Receivable (old)		6 0 0 0 00	
		Interest Income		1 3 0 00	
		Interest of old note collected and			
		renewal of note for 90 days			

BUYER—JANE COMPANY

Oct.	31	Notes Payable (old)	6 0 0 0 00		
		Interest Expense	1 3 0 00		
		Notes Payable (new)		6 0 0 0 00	
		Cash		1 3 0 00	
		Interest of old note paid and			
		renewal of note recorded			

> Only unmatured notes are in the Notes Receivable account.

SELLER—MACE COMPANY

(A) Oct.	31	Accounts Receivable, Jane Co.	6 1 3 0 00		
		Interest Income		1 3 0 00	
		Notes Receivable		6 0 0 0 00	
		Recorded note receivable dishonored			

BUYER—JANE COMPANY

(A) Oct.	31	Notes Payable	6 0 0 0 00		
		Interest Expense	1 3 0 00		
		Accounts Payable, Mace Co.		6 1 3 0 00	
		Recorded note payable dishonored			

SELLER—MACE COMPANY

(B) Dec.	1	Cash	6 1 3 0 00		
		Accounts Receivable, Jane Co.		6 1 3 0 00	
		Recorded payment of note			
		receivable dishonored			

BUYER—JANE COMPANY

(B) Dec.	1	Accounts Payable, Mace Co.	6 1 3 0 00		
		Cash		6 1 3 0 00	
		Payment of note payable dishonored			

Figure 14-6 Note Dishonored and Repaid on Books of Seller and Buyer

On Jane's and Mace's books the amounts in Notes Receivable and Notes Payable will then be removed and transferred back to Accounts Receivable and Accounts Payable, because the note has reached the maturity date. At the same time, whether the note is paid or not, the interest expense is due and payable and should be recorded (for Mace Company this is Interest Income, and for Jane Company it is Interest Expense).

Let's see what entries would look like if Jane Company first defaults and then finally pays the amount owed on December 1 (see Fig. 14-6). To keep it simple, no additional charges will be calculated for the extra month Jane Company has taken to pay off the amount owed to Mace Company.

NOTE GIVEN IN EXCHANGE FOR EQUIPMENT PURCHASED

A note may be given in exchange for an asset that is purchased. For instance, suppose Jane Company decided to buy from Ronald Company some display racks for $7,000. Because the price was high, Jane Company gave a note instead of buying the racks on account. The note issued by Jane Company was a 60-day, 9% interest-bearing note for $7,000. This transaction is recorded on the books of the buyer and seller as shown in Figure 14-7.

When the note is paid at maturity, the same transactions discussed earlier would result.

SELLER—RONALD COMPANY				
May	9	Notes Receivable	7 0 0 0 00	
		Sales		7 0 0 0 00
		Sold display racks with a		
		60-day, 9% note		

BUYER—JANE COMPANY				
May	9	Store Equipment	7 0 0 0 00	
		Notes Payable		7 0 0 0 00
		Purchased display racks with a		
		60-day, 9% note		

Figure 14-7
Note Exchanged for an Asset

Learning Unit 14-2 Review

AT THIS POINT you should be able to

- Journalize entries for buyer and seller to record the extension of a past due account by issuing a note. (p. 542)
- Explain why a subsidiary ledger may not be needed with Notes Payable and Notes Receivable. (p. 543)

💭 Journalize entries for the buyer and seller to record renewal of a note, dishonoring of a note, eventual receipt of payment, and a note given in exchange for equipment purchased. (p. 544)

SELF-REVIEW QUIZ 14-2

(The forms you need are on page 19 of the *Study Guide and Working Papers*.)
Journalize the following transactions for Action Company:

A. Action Company sold $8,000 of merchandise on account to Brian Company.

B. Action Company received a 60-day, $8,000, 12% note for a time extension of a past due account of Brian Company.

C. Collected the Brian Company note on the maturity date.

D. Brian Company renewed the note for 90 days and paid interest on the old note. (Alternative to Step C.)

E. Assuming that Brian Company defaulted in Step C, record the note receivable dishonored.

F. Brian Company paid the note receivable dishonored.

SOLUTION TO SELF-REVIEW QUIZ 14-2

Figure 14-8
Journalized Transactions of Action Company

			Debit	Credit
(A)		Accounts Receivable, Brian Co.	8 0 0 0 00	
		Sales		8 0 0 0 00
		Sold merchandise on account		
(B)		Notes Receivable	8 0 0 0 00	
		Accounts Receivable, Brian Co.		8 0 0 0 00
		Started note at 12% for 60 days		
(C)		Cash	8 1 6 0 00	
		Interest Income		1 6 0 00
		Notes Receivable		8 0 0 0 00
		Collected Brian Co. note		
		($8,000 × .12 × $\frac{60}{360}$ = $160)		
(D)		Cash	1 6 0 00	
		Notes Receivable	8 0 0 0 00	
		Notes Receivable		8 0 0 0 00
		Interest Income		1 6 0 00
		Collected interest and renewed note		
(E)		Accounts Receivable, Brian Company	8 1 6 0 00	
		Notes Receivable		8 0 0 0 00
		Interest Income		1 6 0 00
		Brian Co. defaulted on note		
(F)		Cash	8 1 6 0 00	
		Accounts Receivable, Brian Company		8 1 6 0 00
		Brian Co. paid dishonored note		

Learning Unit 14-3   How to Discount Customers' Notes

Many times a company that accepts notes from customers will not (or cannot) wait to receive its cash until the maturity date. Instead, it goes to a bank and exchanges the note for cash. This process is called discounting a note. The company will endorse the note and receive the maturity value of the note (principal plus interest) less what the bank charges for holding the note from the date of discounting until the maturity date. The time period during which the bank holds the note (until maturity) is called the discount period.

> Think of the bank discount as the cost of cashing in a note before maturity.

The amount that the bank charges the company is called the bank discount. It is the difference between what the company receives from the bank and the maturity value of the note. The actual amount of money the company receives when a note is discounted is called the proceeds (maturity value less the bank discount).

Let's see how Marvin Company discounts an interest-bearing note receivable. The best way to understand the process is to take it step-by-step.

HOW TO DISCOUNT AN INTEREST-BEARING NOTE RECEIVABLE

Marvin Company received an $8,000, 90-day, 12% note from Jee Company dated October 1. On October 31 Marvin Company needed cash to finance its inventory, so it discounted the note to Blue Bank, which charges a bank discount rate of 14%. An overview of the process is shown in Figure 14-9.

> What Marvin Company will receive from bank is called the proceeds.

Step 1:   Find the *maturity* value of the note:

> Find maturity value.

    (a) $\$8,000 \times .12 \times \dfrac{90}{360} = \$240$ **Interest**

    (b)   **Maturity Value = Principal + Interest**
                        = \$8,000 + \$240
                        = \$8,240

Step 2:   Calculate the *discount* period (number of days from the date of discounting until the maturity date):

> Calculate discount period.

    90 Days   **Note**
   − 30 Days   **Expired before discounting (Oct. 31 − Oct. 1)**
   = 60 Days   **That bank holds note until it comes due**

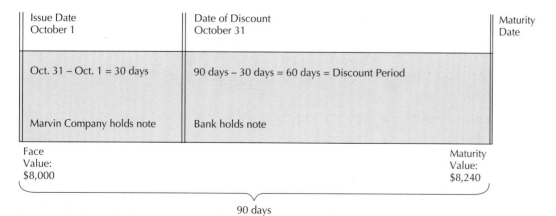

Figure 14-9 Discounting a Note Receivable, $8,000 at 12% for 90 Days

Calculate bank discount.

Step 3: Calculate the bank discount (what the bank charges Marvin Company for holding the note until maturity: To do so, we use the following formula:

$$\text{Bank Discount} = \text{Maturity Value} \times \text{Bank Discount Rate} \times \frac{\text{No. of Days Bank Holds Note until Maturity}}{360 \text{ Days}}$$

$$= \$8,240 \times .14 \times \frac{60}{360}$$
$$= \$192.27$$

Note that the bank discount is based on the maturity value, because we are borrowing the maturity value for the number of days in the discount period.

Calculate proceeds.

Step 4: Calculate the proceeds (what Marvin Company receives from the bank in the discounting process):

$$\text{Proceeds} = \text{Maturity Value} - \text{Bank Discount}$$
$$= \$8,240 - \$192.27$$
$$= \$8,047.73$$

If Marvin Company could have waited until the maturity date, it would have received $8,240. By discounting the note the company lost interest of $192.27, or the cost charged by the bank to hold the note until maturity. Let's look at how Marvin Company would record this item on its books (Fig. 14-10; again, for simplicity, we use general journal entries rather than special journals).

Journalizing the discounted note receivable:

$8,047.73
−8,000.00
$ 47.73
(Interest Income)

Figure 14-10
Discounting a Note with Interest Income

Oct.	31	Cash	8047 73		
		Notes Receivable		8000 00	
		Interest Income		47 73	
		Discounted Jee Company's			
		90-day, 12% note at 14%			

There is Interest Income because the proceeds Marvin Company received were more than the face value of the note ($8,000). In actuality, if the proceeds had been *less* than the $8,000, Marvin Company would have incurred an interest expense. That could have happened, for example, if Marvin Company held the note for only a short period of time and Blue Bank had a bank discount rate much higher than the original note. Suppose the note was discounted after being held only 2 days, and the bank's discount rate was 18%. The bank discount, or amount the bank charges, would be calculated as follows:

maturity value   discount period

$$\text{Bank Discount} = \$8,240 \times .18 \times \frac{88}{360}$$
$$= \$362.56$$

Thus, the proceeds to Marvin Company would be

$$\text{Proceeds} = \$8,240 - \$362.56$$
$$= \$7,877.44$$

Note that here Marvin Company is receiving less than the $8,000 face value of the note. The general journal entry of Marvin Company would thus look as shown in Figure 14-11.

Oct.	31	Cash		7 8 7 7 44			
		Interest Expense		1 2 2 56			
		Notes Receivable			8 0 0 0 00	
		To record discount of note				

Figure 14-11
Discounting a Note
with Interest Expense

PROCEDURE WHEN A DISCOUNTED NOTE IS DISHONORED

Who is liable for the note if Jee Company fails to pay the note at maturity? The answer is Marvin Company.

When Marvin Company endorsed the note to Blue Bank, it agreed to pay the note at maturity if Jee Company failed to. The potential liability is called a contingent liability. Until the note is paid, Marvin Company will state this contingent liability as a footnote on its balance sheet.

At some point before maturity, Jee Company is notified that Blue Bank is holding the note. Let's assume that the maturity date is reached and Jee Company defaults. Blue Bank notifies Marvin Company and charges Marvin Company the full amount of the note, including interest and a $5 protest fee, which is the charge made by Blue Bank for notifying Marvin Company that the note was presented to the maker for payment and was not received. Thus, the bank charges Marvin Company (and Marvin will in turn charge Jee Company) the following:

> *Note:*
> If Marvin Company endorsed the note without recourse, it would not have any liability. Instead, the bank would have liability if Jee Company did not pay.

Note	$8,000
Interest	240
Protest Fee	5
	$8,245

The entry is recorded on Marvin Company's book as shown in Figure 14-12.

Dec.	30	Accounts Receivable, Jee Co.		8 2 4 5 00		
		Cash			8 2 4 5 00
		To record default			

Figure 14-12
Default of Note

You can be sure that Marvin Company will try to collect this $8,245 from Jee Company. Marvin Company may charge additional interest for this delay in paying the $8,245. For simplicity, we have left this step out. If the $8,245 becomes uncollectible, the account could be written off as a bad debt using the Allowance for Doubtful Accounts method discussed in Chapter 13.

Learning Unit 14-3 Review

AT THIS POINT you should be able to

- Define and explain discounting, maturity value, discount period, bank discount, and proceeds. (p. 547)
- Explain the four steps required in discounting an interest-bearing note receivable. (p. 547)
- Prepare a journal entry to record the proceeds of a note. (p. 548)

- Define contingent liability and compare it with an endorsement without recourse. (p. 549)
- Journalize the entry to record a discounted note that has been dishonored. (p. 549)

SELF-REVIEW QUIZ 14-3

(The forms you need are on pages 20–21 of the *Study Guide and Working Papers*.)

Al Gene Company received a $10,000, 60-day, 12% note from Broom Company dated July 5, 20XX. On August 3, Al Gene Company discounted the note to Ryan Bank, which charged a bank discount rate of 15%.

a. Complete the four steps to discount the note.

b. Journalize the entry to record the proceeds.

c. Journalize the entry if a default occurs, assuming a $5 protest fee.

SOLUTION TO SELF-REVIEW QUIZ 14-3

a. Step 1: Maturity value (principal + interest)

$$I = \$10,000 \times .12 \times \frac{60}{360}$$
$$= \$200$$
$$MV = \$10,000 + \$200$$
$$= \$10,200$$

Step 2: Discount period:

July 31	
− 5	
26	Days Al Gene Held Note in July
3	Days Al Gene Held Note in August
29	Days Al Gene Held Note
60	Days
− 29	Days
31	Days Bank Holds Note

Step 3: Bank discount:

$$\text{Bank Discount} = \text{Maturity Value} \times \text{Bank Discount Rate} \times \frac{\text{No. of Days Bank Holds Note Until Maturity}}{360}$$

$$= \$10,200 \times .15 \times \frac{31}{360}$$
$$\quad \text{(Step 1) (Given in facts)}$$
$$= \$131.75$$

Step 4: Proceeds:

$$\text{Proceeds} = \text{Maturity Value} - \text{Bank Discount}$$
$$= \$10,200 - \$131.75$$
$$= \$10,068.25$$

Figure 14-13
Default of Note

b.	Aug.	3	Cash		10	0	6	8	25				
			Notes Receivable							10	0	0	0	0	0
			Interest Income									6	8	25
			Discounted Broom Company											
			12% note at 15%											
c.	Sept.	3	Accounts Receivable, Broom Company		10	2	0	5	00				
			Cash							10	2	0	5	00
			To record default											

Learning Unit 14-4 — Discounting One's Own Note: Handling Adjustments for Interest Expense and Interest Income

DISCOUNTING ONE'S OWN NOTE

In the last unit we looked at how a note of a customer was discounted. Now our attention shifts to Jones Company, which is borrowing $10,000 by giving Alvin Bank its own 12%, 60-day note on December 16, 20XX. In this case, Alvin Bank deducts the interest in advance. The following is the formula to calculate the bank discount (cost of borrowing) and the proceeds (what Jones Company gets):

$$\textbf{Bank Discount} = (\textbf{Maturity Value}) \times (\textbf{Interest Rate}) \times \frac{\textbf{Discount Period}}{360}$$

$$= \$10,000 \quad \times \quad .12 \quad \times \quad \frac{60}{360}$$

$$= \$200$$

$$\textbf{Proceeds} = \textbf{Maturity Value} - \textbf{Discount}$$

$$= \$10,000 - \$200$$

$$= \$9,800$$

> Note that maturity value here is the same as the original principal, because interest is deducted in advance.

Thus, Jones Company receives $9,800 and at the time of maturity will pay back $10,000. The $200 of interest is recorded in a new account called **Discount on Notes Payable.** This account is a contra-liability account that is subtracted from Notes Payable on the balance sheet, where it looks like the following:

> Discount on Notes Payable is a contra-liability.

Current Liabilities

Notes Payable	$10,000	
Less: Discount on		
Notes Payable	200	
		$9,800

Later in this unit, when we talk about adjustments, we see that as the note matures, the discount will be reduced and then charged to Interest Expense. For now, however, let's record the journal entry for Jones Company as it discounts its own note with interest deducted in advance (Fig. 14-14).

Figure 14-14
Discounted Note with
Interest Deducted in
Advance

Dec.	16	Cash	9 80 0 00			
		Discount on Notes Payable	2 0 0 00			
		Notes Payable			10 0 0 0 00	
		Discounted own note at 12%				

Accounts Affected	Category	↑↓	Rules	
Cash	Asset	↑	Dr.	$9,800
Discount on Notes Payable	Contra-Liability	↑	Dr.	$200
Notes Payable	Liability	↑	Cr.	$10,000

When the note is paid, the accountant will debit Notes Payable for $10,000 and credit Cash for $10,000.

Note: Although the bank interest rate is stated at 12%, the truth is that Jones Company really has the use of only $9,800. To calculate the true interest rate, which is called the effective interest rate, the following formula applies:

$$\text{Effective Interest Rate} = \frac{(\text{Maturity Value of Note}) \times (\text{Bank Interest Rate})}{\text{Amount of Cash Proceeds Received from Note}}$$

$$= \frac{\$10,000 \times .12}{\$9,800}$$

$$= 12.24\%$$

Now let's look at how adjustments will be handled for some of the transactions presented in this chapter.

Effective interest rate: The cost of borrowing the $10,000 is not 12% but really almost 12 1/4%.

INTEREST: THE NEED FOR ADJUSTMENTS

Because interest-bearing notes are often taken out and then paid off in different accounting periods, it is necessary to adjust or bring up-to-date Interest Income and Interest Expense. The following diagram shows why we need to adjust as well as who does the adjusting:

Accrued Interest Income	Accrued Interest Expense
Must adjust for income that has been earned during the period but has not been received or recorded because payment is not yet due.	Must adjust for interest that has been incurred during the period but has not been paid or recorded because payment is not yet due.
↓	↓
Notes Receivable (payee)	(A) Note Payable (maker) (B) Company's own discounted note

The payee is the seller and the maker is the buyer.

Let's look at how to record adjustments for Interest Income and Interest Expense from the following: Bog Company receives a $24,000, 60-day, 10% note on December 16, 200X, from Jan Company.

Figure 14-15
Adjusting for Interest
Accrued

Step 1: Calculate interest on the note:

$$\textbf{Interest} = \textbf{\$24,000} \times \textbf{.10} \times \frac{\textbf{60}}{\textbf{360}}$$
$$= \textbf{\$400}$$

Step 2: Calculate the number of days the note has already run before the end of the current period (see Table 14-1 on p. 540):

Dec. 31	(end of period)
−Dec. 16	(starting date of note)
15	Days

Step 3: Calculate interest incurred for this period:

$$\text{Length of note} \rightarrow \frac{\textbf{15 Days}}{\textbf{60 Days}} = \frac{1}{4} \times \textbf{\$400}$$
$$= \textbf{\$100}$$

Another way to calculate the interest is

$$\textbf{\$24,000} \times \textbf{.10} \times \frac{\textbf{15}}{\textbf{360}} = \textbf{\$100}$$

Step 4: Prepare the adjusting journal entries (Fig. 14-16):

On Books of *Seller* (Holder of Note)

Dec.	31	Interest Receivable	1 0 0 00		
		Interest Income		1 0 0 00	
		Adj. for int.			

On Books of *Buyer* (Debtor)

Dec.	31	Interest Expense	1 0 0 00		
		Interest Payable		1 0 0 00	
		Adj. for int.			

Figure 14-16 Adjustment for Interest on Note

Interest Receivable	
100 Current Asset on balance sheet	

Interest Expense	
100 Other Expense on income statement	

Interest Income	
	100 Other Income on income statement

Interest Payable	
	100 Current Liability on balance sheet

Figure 14-17
No Reversing Entry

SELLER

Feb.	14	Cash		2440000			
		Interest Receivable				10000	
		Notes Receivable				2400000	
		Interest Income				30000	
		Received payment of note					

BUYER

Feb.	14	Notes Payable		2400000			
		Interest Expense		30000			
		Interest Payable		10000			
		Cash				2440000	
		Paid off note					

When the note is paid off on February 14, the first two entries are made, assuming that no reversing entry is used, as shown in Figure 14-17.

Note that by not using reversing entries, the bookkeepers of the buyer and seller had to look up the amount of accrued interest that was recorded in the *old* year so that this year's interest expense or income would not be overstated.

If a reversing entry (which is optional) is used, the entries shown in Figure 14-18 are made.

The last adjustment deals with a firm discounting its own note. Back on page 551, at the beginning of this unit, we saw Jones Company discounting its own note on December 16 for $10,000 for 60 days at 12% interest. Jones Company actually received $9,800 and recorded the $200 interest deducted in advance by the bank in a contra-liability account called *Discount on Notes Payable*.

Discount on Notes Payable		Interest Expense	
200			

Figure 14-18
Reversing Entry Made

SELLER

Feb.	14	Cash		2440000			
		Notes Receivable				2400000	
		Interest Income				40000	
		Received payment of note					

BUYER

Feb.	14	Notes Payable		2400000			
		Interest Expense		40000			
		Cash				2440000	
		Paid off note					

Dec.	31	Interest Expense		5 0 00				
		Discount on Notes Payable				5 0 00		
		Recognition of expense incurred						

Figure 14-19
Recording Interest and
Reducing Balance of
Discount on Notes Payable

At the end of December, 15 out of the 60 days have passed. Thus, one-fourth of the interest on this note should be recorded in the old year. To record this interest, we reduce the amount in the Discount on Notes Payable by $50 $(\frac{1}{4} \times \$200)$. The journal entry shown in Figure 14-19 is made.

Accounts Affected	Category	↑↓	Rules	
Interest Expense	Other Expense	↑	Dr.	$50
Discount on Notes Payable	Contra-Liability	↓	Dr.	$50

The current liability on the balance sheet will look as follows:

Current Liabilities

Notes Payable	$10,000	
Less: Discount on Notes Payable	150	
		$9,850

When the note is paid the journal entry shown in Figure 14-20 will result.

$$\frac{45\,days}{60\,days} \times \$200$$

Feb.	14	Notes Payable		10 0 0 00				
		Interest Expense		1 5 0 00				
		Discount on Notes Payable				1 5 0 00		
		Cash				10 0 0 00		
		Note paid						

Figure 14-20
Note Paid Off

Learning Unit 14-4 Review

AT THIS POINT you should be able to

- Explain the purpose of the Discount on Notes Payable account. (p. 551)
- Calculate the effective interest rate. (p. 552)
- Make adjustments for interest income and interest expense at the end of the period. (p. 552)
- Adjust the Discount on Notes Payable account. (p. 554)

SELF-REVIEW QUIZ 14-4

(The forms you need are on page 21 of the *Study Guide and Working Papers*.)

Respond true or false to the following:

1. No bank deducts interest in advance.

2. Discount on Notes Payable is a contra-liability account.

3. When Discount on Notes Payable is reduced, Interest Expense results.

4. The effective rate of interest is lower than the stated rate.

5. Reversing entries are never used to adjust interest at the end of a period of time.

SOLUTIONS TO SELF-REVIEW QUIZ 14-4

1. False   **2.** True   **3.** True   **4.** False   **5.** False

Chapter Review

Learning Unit 14-1

1. A promissory note is a written promise bys a borrower to pay a certain sum of money to a lender at a fixed future date. The note may be interest-bearing or non-interest-bearing.
2. The payee is the party to whom the note is payable.
3. The maker is the one who will pay the promissory note.
4. Maturity date is the time when the note comes due.
5. $$\text{Interest} = \text{Principal} \times \text{Rate} \times \frac{\text{Number of Days}}{360}$$.

Learning Unit 14-2

1. Notes Payable is a current liability on the balance sheet.
2. Notes do not need subsidiary ledgers.
3. Interest Income for the payee is Interest Expense for the maker.
4. A note that is not paid at maturity is said to be dishonored.
5. Notes may be renewed as well as issued to buy assets.

Learning Unit 14-3

1. Maturity Value = Principal + Interest.
2. Discount period = Number of Days from Date of Discounting until Maturity Date.
3. The bank discount is what the bank charges for holding a note until the maturity date, as shown in the formula:

$$\text{Bank Discount} = \text{Maturity Value} \times \text{Bank Discount Rate} \times \frac{\text{No. of Days Bank Holds Note until Maturity}}{360 \text{ Days}}$$

4. Proceeds is what one receives from bank in the discounting process (the maturity value minus the bank discount).
5. If a discounted note is dishonored, the original holder of the note may be liable for payment unless the note was endorsed without recourse. This liability is called *contingent liability*.

Learning Unit 14-4

1. In discounting one's own note, the interest is usually deducted in advance.
2. The interest that is deducted in advance is recorded in a contra-liability account called Discount on Notes Payable.
3. The effective interest rate is higher than the stated rate.
4. At the end of the period, adjustments are made for Interest Income and Interest Expense that have accrued or built up. These entries can be reversed on the first day starting the next period to simplify recording when interest is paid or received in the new period.
5. The interest in the Discount on Notes Payable account is adjusted by reducing the Discount on Notes Payable and recording it as Interest Expense.

Key Terms

Bank discount   What the bank charges to hold a note until maturity (maturity value − proceeds).

Contingent liability   Liability on the part of one who discounts a note to pay if the maker of the note defaults at maturity date.

Default   Failure of maker to pay the maturity value of a note when due.

Discounting a note   The process or act of transferring the note to a bank before the maturity date.

Discount on Notes Payable   The amount of interest deducted in advance by the lender. This account reduces Notes Payable to actual cash value.

Discount period   The amount of time the bank holds a note that was discounted until the maturity date.

Dishonored note   A note that was not paid at maturity by the maker.

Effective interest rate   The true rate of simple interest.

Interest   The cost of using money for a period of time.

Maker   One promising to pay a note.

Maturity date   Due date of the promissory note.

Maturity value   The value of the note that is due on the date of maturity (principal + interest).

Note payable   A promissory note from the maker's point of view.

Note receivable   A promissory note from the payee's point of view.

Payee   One to whom a note is payable.

Principal   The face amount of the note.

Proceeds   Maturity value less bank discount.

Promissory note   A formal written promise by a borrower to pay a certain sum at a fixed future date.

Questions, Mini Exercises, Exercises, and Problems

Discussion Questions

1. List three reasons why a company may use Notes Payable instead of Accounts Payable.
2. Explain the parts of a promissory note.
3. What is the difference between finding a maturity date by (a) days or (b) months?
4. Notes Receivable is a current liability on the balance sheet. Accept or reject. Why?
5. Why is a subsidiary ledger not needed for notes?
6. Only matured notes are listed in the Notes Receivable account. Please discuss.
7. Explain what will happen if a maker defaults on a note. (Assume the note has not been discounted.)
8. List the four steps to arrive at proceeds in the process of discounting a note.
9. What is meant by a contingent liability?
10. When could interest be deducted in advance by a lender?
11. What is the normal balance of the Discount on Notes Payable account?
12. How is the effective interest rate calculated?
13. How could Discount on Notes Payable be adjusted?

Mini Exercises

(The forms you need are on pages 23−24 of the *Study Guide and Working Papers.*)

Determining Maturity Date

1. Find the maturity date of the following:

   a. 120-day note dated July 8.
   b. 90-day note dated October 8.

Blueprint: Notes Payable and Notes Receivable

SELLER (Payee) **BUYER (Maker)**

Sales of merchandise on account

SELLER (Payee)		BUYER (Maker)	
Accounts Receivable, XXX		Purchases	
Sales		Accounts Payable, XXX	
Sold on account		Bought on account	

Time extension with a note

SELLER (Payee)		BUYER (Maker)	
Notes Receivable		Accounts Payable, XXX	
Accounts Receivable, XXX		Notes Payable	
Transferred to note rec.		Transferred to note pay.	

Note due and paid

SELLER (Payee)		BUYER (Maker)	
Cash		Notes Payable	
Interest Income		Interest Expense	
Notes Receivable		Cash	
Received payment		Paid off note	

Note renewed at maturity

SELLER (Payee)		BUYER (Maker)	
Cash		Notes Payable	
Notes Receivable (new)		Interest Expense	
Notes Receivable (old)		Notes Payable (new)	
Interest Income		Cash	
Renewed note		Renewed note	

Note given in exchange for equipment purchased

SELLER (Payee)		BUYER (Maker)	
Notes Receivable		Store Equipment	
Sales		Notes Payable	
Sold on note rec.		Bought equip. for note	

(Continued)

Blueprint: Notes Payable and Notes Receivable (cont.)

SITUATIONS AFFECTING SELLER ONLY

Discounting a note—receiving more than face value

Cash		
Interest Income		
Notes Receivable		
Loaned discounted note		

Discounting a note—receiving less than face value

Cash		
Interest Expense		
Notes Receivable		
Loaned discounted note		

SITUATION BORROWING FROM BANK

Discounted note dishonored

Accounts Receivable, XXX		
Cash		
Discounted customer note		

Discounting one's own note

Cash		
Discount on Notes Payable		
Notes Payable		
Borrowed with a discount		

(continued)

Blueprint: Notes Payable and Notes Receivable (cont.)

ADJUSTMENTS	SELLER	BUYER
Adjust interest	**20X1** Dec. 31 — Interest Receivable / Interest Income / Interest adj.	**20X1** Dec. 31 — Interest Expense / Interest Payable / Interest adj.
Note paid (no reversing entry was made)	**20X2** Feb. 1 — Cash / Interest Receivable / Interest Income / Notes Receivable / Received cash from note	**20X2** Feb. 1 — Interest Expense / Interest Payable / Notes Payable / Cash / Paid cash for note
Note paid (reversing entry was made)	Feb. 1 — Cash / Interest Income / Notes Receivable / Received cash from note	Feb. 1 — Interest Expense / Notes Payable / Cash / Paid cash for note
Recognizing interest from discount on Notes Payable	Dec. 31 — Interest Expense / Discount on Notes Payable / Adjustment for interest	

Calculate Maturity Value

2. Find the maturity value of the following:
   a. $6,000   6%   9 months
   b. $8,000   7%   70 days

Recording Notes for Buyer and Seller

3. For each of the following transactions for Frank Co. (the seller), journalize what the entry would be for the buyer.

   a. Accounts Receivable, Bore Co.   7,000
          Sales   7,000
              Sold on account
   b. Notes Receivable   7,000
          Accounts Receivable, Bore Co.   7,000
              Transferred to note rec.
   c. Cash   7,140
          Notes Receivable   7,000
          Interest Income   140

Discounting a Note

4. Pete Jones discounted a $9,000, 8%, 90-day note at Friend Bank. He recorded the following entry:

   Cash   9,100
       Notes Receivable   9,000
       Interest Income   100

   How much interest did Pete Jones lose by discounting the note?

Four Steps in the Discounting Process

5. Blue Co. received a $1,000, 6%, 60-day note from Aluin Co. dated August 10. On August 30 Blue discounted the note at Reel Bank, which charged a discount rate of 8%. Calculate the following:

   a. Maturity value.
   b. Discount period.
   c. Bank discount.
   d. Proceeds.

Journal Entry for Discounting

6. Journalize the discounted note for Blue from Mini Exercise 5.

Defaulting

7. If Aluin defaults on the note from Mini Exercise 5, what would be the journal entry for Blue Co., assuming a $5 protest fee?

Discounting One's Own Note

8. Aster Co. discounts its own note at a bank. This $5,000 note results in the bank deducting $300 interest in advance. Draw a transactional analysis box for this situation.

Adjusting the Discount

9. If in Mini Exercise 8 the discount of $100 needs to be adjusted at year end, what would be the journalized adjusting entry?

Exercises

(The forms you need are on pages 25–26 of the *Study Guide and Working Papers*.)

14-1. Calculate the interest for the following:

    a. $17,000   7%   1 year

    b. $20,000   10%   7 months

    c. $ 9,000   12%   80 days

Calculating interest.

14-2. Determine the maturity date for each of the following without the use of tables:

NOTE ISSUED	LENGTH OF TIME
a. January 17, 20X4	30 days
b. July 14, 20X4	90 days
c. May 31, 20X4	4 months
d. June 25, 20X4	75 days

Determining maturity date without tables.

14-3. Use the table in the text (p. 540) to prove your answers for Exercise 14-2.

Determining maturity date by tables.

14-4. On May 15, 20X4, Ralph Co. gave Blue Co. a 180-day, $9,000, 8% note. On July 21, Blue Co. discounted the note at 9%.

    a. Journalize the entry for Blue to record the proceeds.

    b. Record the entry for Blue if Ralph fails to pay at maturity.

Discounting a note and journalizing entry for proceeds.

14-5. Jamie Slater negotiated a bank loan for $30,000 for 120 days at a bank rate of 10%. Assuming the interest is deducted in advance, prepare the entry for Jamie to record the bank loan.

Discount on Notes Payable.

Group A Problems

(The forms you need are on pages 27–32 of the *Study Guide and Working Papers*.)

14A-1. Journalize the following entries for (1) the buyer and (2) the seller. Record all entries for the buyer first.

Journalizing Notes Receivable and Notes Payable along with note dishonored.

20X9

June	11	Lee Company sold $7,000 of merchandise on account to Rover Company.
July	11	Lee Company received a 90-day, $5,000, 8% note for a time extension of a past due account of Rover Company.
Oct.	9	Collected the Rover Company note on the maturity date.
Oct.	9	Assume Rover Company defaulted on its July 11 note and record the dishonored note.
Oct.	15	Rover Company paid the note receivable that was dishonored on October 9 (no additional interest is charged).

Check Figure:
Oct. 9   Interest Income and Interest Expense $100

14A-2. On May 1, 20X4, Apples Company received a $30,000, 90-day, 9% note from Fletcher Company dated May 1. On June 20, 20X4, Apples discounted the note at Run Bank at a discount rate of 10%.

Identifying steps in discounting a note along with journal entry.

    1. Calculate the following:

        a. Maturity value of the note.

        b. Number of days the bank will hold the note until maturity date.

        c. Bank discount.

        d. Proceeds.

Check Figure:
Proceeds $30,334.17

    2. Journalize the entry to record the proceeds.

14A-3. Journalize the following transactions for Joye Company:

20X1

June	18	Joye discounted its own $40,000, 90-day note at National Bank at 10%.
Sept.	16	Paid the amount due on the note of June 18. (Be sure to record interest expense from Discount on Notes Payable.)
Nov.	2	Joye discounted its own $20,000, 120-day note at National Bank at 11%.
Dec.	31	Record the adjusting entry for interest expense.

14A-4. Journalize the following transactions for Rochester Company:

20XX

Apr.	18	Received $15,000, 80-day, 11% note from Mark Castle in payment of account past due.
May	9	Wrote off the Hal Balmer account as uncollectible for $600. (Rochester uses the Allowance method to record bad debts.)
July	7	Mark Castle paid Rochester the note in full.
Nov.	11	Gave Reech Company a $9,000, 30-day, 12% note as a time extension of account now past due.
Nov.	15	Hal Balmer paid Rochester amount previously written off on May 9.
Dec.	3	Discounted its own $5,000, 90-day note at Tree Bank at 10%.
Dec.	5	Received a $10,000, 60-day, 12% note dated December 5 from Beverly Fields in payment of account past due.
Dec.	11	Paid principal and interest due on note issued to Reech Company from November 11 note.
Dec.	16	Received a $20,000, 60-day, 11% note from Larry Company in payment of account past due.
Dec.	28	Discounted the Beverly Fields note to Realty Bank at 13%.
Dec.	31	Recorded adjusting entries as appropriate.

Group B Problems

(The forms you need are on pages 27–32 of the *Study Guide and Working Papers.*)

14B-1. Journalize the following entries for (1) the buyer and (2) the seller.

20X9

July	10	Lee Company sold $8,000 of merchandise on account to Connors Company.
Aug.	10	Lee Company received a 90-day, $6,000, 9% note for a time extension of past due account of Rover Company.
Nov.	8	Collected the Rover Company note on the maturity date.
Nov.	8	Assuming Rover Company defaulted on November 8, record the dishonored note.
Nov.	16	Rover Company paid the note receivable that was dishonored on November 8 (no additional interest is charged).

14B-2. On June 2, 20X4, Apples Company received a $40,000, 90-day, 11% note from Fletcher Company dated June 2. On July 16, 20X4, Apples discounted the note at Run Bank at a discount rate of 12%.

1. Calculate the following:

   a. Maturity value of the note.
   b. Number of days the bank will hold the note until maturity date.
   c. Bank discount.
   d. Proceeds.

2. Journalize the entry to record the proceeds.

Sidebar notes:

Discounting of one's own note.

Check Figure:
Nov. 2 Discount on Notes Payable $733.33

Comprehensive Problem Integration of Notes Receivable and Notes Payable with Allowance for Doubtful Accounts and discounting.

Check Figure:
Dec. 31 Interest Expense $38.89

Journalizing Notes Receivable and Notes Payable along with note dishonored.

Check Figure:
Nov. 8 Interest Expense and Interest Income $135

Identifying steps in discounting a note along with journal entry.

Check Figure:
Proceeds $40,469.80

14B-3. As the bookkeeper of Joye Company, record in the general journal the following transactions:

Discounting one's own note.

Check Figure:
Dec. 31   Interest Expense
$467.50

20X2

May	9	Joye discounted its own $25,000, 90-day note at National Bank at 10%.
Aug.	7	Paid the amount due on the note of May 9. (Be sure to record Interest Expense from Discount on Note Payable.)
Oct.	7	Joye discounted its own $18,000, 120-day note at National Bank at 11%.
Dec.	31	Record the adjusting entry for Interest Expense.

14B-4. Record the following entries into the general journal of Rochester Company:

Comprehensive Problem.
Integration of Notes
Receivable and Notes
Payable with Allowance for
Doubtful Accounts and
discounting.

Check Figure:
Dec. 31   Interest Income
$9.17

20XX

May	12	Received $13,000, 90-day, 9% note from Mark Castle in payment of account past due.
June	15	Wrote off the Hal Balmer account as uncollectible for $900 using the Allowance method.
Aug.	10	Mark Castle paid Rochester the note in full.
Nov.	2	Gave Reech Company a $20,000, 30-day, 8% note as a time extension of account now past due.
Nov.	18	Hal Balmer paid Rochester amount previously written off on June 15.
Dec.	2	Discounted its own $10,000, 90-day note at Tree Bank at 9%.
Dec.	2	Received a $6,000, 60-day, 11% note dated December 3 from Beverly Fields in payment of account past due.
Dec.	2	Paid principal and interest due on note issued to Reech Company from November 2 note.
Dec.	16	Received a $2,000, 60-day, 11% note from Larry Company in payment of account past due.
Dec.	28	Discounted the Beverly Fields note to Realty Bank at 12%.
Dec.	31	Recorded adjusting entries as appropriate.

Real-World Applications

14R-1. Abby Scale, the bookkeeper of Roland Company, is having difficulty calculating the amount that is due Agent Company on March 19. Based on the following information, prepare a detailed calculation of the amount due Agent.

Roland issued Agent a $2,000, 60-day, 12% note dated December 19, 20X1. Roland was notified by Alvin Bank that the note had been discounted by Agent and that the note would be payable to Alvin Bank. On February 18, the bookkeeper of Roland became ill and the note wasn't paid. Alvin Bank notified Agent and charged them an additional $9 protest fee. On March 19, Abby decided to pay Agent the amount owed. Agent indicated they were charging the maturity value of the note, the protest fee, and interest on *both* for 30 days beyond maturity at 14%. Do you think these charges are fair? Make your recommendation in writing.

14R-2. Moe Ring has left the following notes on your desk. As the new bookkeeper of Ryan Company, you realize that no adjusting entries were made in 20X1.

Notes Receivable		Notes Payable	
11/25/X1	$20,000	12/16/X1	$33,600
12%	150 days	15%	30 days

   a. Please prepare the appropriate adjusting entries.

   b. Moe would like to know whether reversing entries are needed. Prepare a set of T accounts to show what would result on the books in the year 20X2 when the notes are paid (1) if there are no reversing entries and (2) if reversing entries are made. Provide Moe with a written justification for the use of reversing entries.

YOU make the call

Critical Thinking/Ethical Case

14R-3. Kevin Hoffaman works as a teller in Victory Bank. Yesterday, he looked up confidential information concerning several friends. Kevin told his girlfriend all about the confidential information. Do you think Kevin acted appropriately? You make the call. Write down your recommendations to Kevin.

Internet Exercises: U.S. Escrow; GMAC Commercial Finance

EX-1. [**www.factors.net**]   Businesses who buy accounts receivable (thus, practicing discounting as presented in the chapter) are known as *factors*. At some time in your spending history you have probably been involved with a factor, either knowingly or unknowingly. For example, when you joined the health club and signed a note agreeing to pay monthly for the right to be a member, the health club probably sold your note to a factor. From this Web site, determine why it is that some companies wish to sell their accounts receivable.

EX-2. [**www.gmacbc.com**]   When you approach this Web site, click on "About Us" and read about how GMAC works with businesses to provide them funding via discounting and purchasing "paper" from them. This site explains some of the considerations that a business should look at when attempting to obtain financing in this market. Apply what this chapter taught you about discounting. Navigate through the site and summarize how GMAC assists businesses with financing.

Continuing Problem

Several banks have offered loans to the Eldorado Computer Center for their expansion. However, Freedman wants to weigh each option to determine the best financial situation for the company. Currently, the Eldorado Computer Center is trying to collect from its customers to strengthen the cash flow of the business.

Assignment

(See p. 37 in your *Study Guide and Working Papers*.)

   Using the information provided by each bank, determine the due date and interest amount for each.

Bank of America	A 90-day note dated April 15 for $20,000 at a 6% interest rate
Bank One	A 120-day note dated April 10 for $40,000 at a 5% interest rate
Capital One Bank	A 75-day note dated April 5 for $30,000 at a 4% interest rate

SUBWAY Case

SIGNS OF THE TIMES

"Perfecto!" Stan shouted up to his friends Javier and Miguel. The two men had just launched their own handyman service, and Stan had given them their first job: installing his new Subway "face" sign—the sign with the Subway logo that goes on the front of the restaurant.

Six months ago, Subway had notified all franchisees that they would be required to install signs with the new logo.

"To tell you the truth Stan," said Rashid, "I can't see that there's much difference between the old sign and the new one."

"Well, it's a rather subtle change—the Subway lettering is closer together, less curvy, and slants to the right rather than straight up and down," said Stan. "But there's nothing subtle about the cost," he laughed. "Five grand!"

"Whew," Rashid's jaw dropped, "All that for a new slant?"

"As it happens," said Stan, "Subway did mounds of marketing research and found that customers perceive the slanting letters to mean speedier service. Anyway, now that there's new logo, any stores that have the old one immediately look out-of-date."

The $5,000, Stan mused later, was nothing compared to what he would have to spend to remodel his entire restaurant in the next year or two. Subway Restaurants had recently announced the first complete interior and exterior revamp in the company's history. Called "Tuscany Décor," the new design includes earth tones, wood finishing, brass rails, tiled flooring, and brick textured walls. Stan was impressed when it was unveiled at the last franchisee convention; not only would the new décor be a better match for the chain's commitment to healthy, fresh food but it would also attract the more upscale customers moving into the area. Still, how to pay for it?

Stan was in a position not uncommon for businesses of all sizes: the need to spend money to make more money. After spending $3,000 on his new bake oven, Stan didn't have the capital to spend $5,000 on a new sign—not to mention the thousands that he would have to spend to redo the interior with the new Tuscany décor. He checked the interest rates at his bank and calculated what it would cost him to repay a note with a principal of $5,000, an interest rate of 9%, and a time of 120 days.

$$\$5,000 \times .09 \times \frac{120}{360} = \$150$$

"150 bucks," thought Stan. "That's steep. I wonder if I could do better at another bank?" Stan then checked with Country Bank. They offered him $5,000, an interest rate of 8-3/4%, and a time of 90 days.

$$\$5,000 \times .0875 \times \frac{90}{360} = \$109.37$$

"Just a little over $100 is more like it," thought Stan, "But how can I pay it back in only three months? That really puts the pressure on. Is it worth the $41 difference to pay back the loan so fast? It's 30 days more or $41 more. In either case I can deduct the interest from my taxes as a business expense. So it's really a $41 difference. But, what about when I take out a loan for the remodel? The difference will be in hundreds of dollars. Hmmm. Time to call Lila!"

Discussion Questions

1. Which loan would you take if you were in Stan's place? Why?
2. Assume Stan wanted the loan on October 1. What is the maturity date for the 90-day loan? The 120-day loan?
3. Why do some loans use 360 days and other loans 365? Which would be better for Stan?

CHAPTER 15

Accounting for Merchandise Inventory

You find that you could use a new shirt or two and a pair of jeans. You drive over to University Clothiers. The clothing store has been in business for years, and it specializes in serving students from your campus.

As you shop, you find that there aren't any shirts you like in light blue. The only color of jeans in your size and style you like is khaki. Kathy Nguyen, the store manager, asks if she can help you. "Well, I would be happy if you could just change the color of these shirts and this pair of jeans," you reply. "I wish I could!" Kathy says. "It's an ongoing challenge to keep the right sizes and colors in inventory. Unfortunately, there are items we can't keep in stock, and others we can't sell at all," Kathy tells you.

As you leave the store, you think about what Kathy Nguyen said. Some items are almost always out of stock while the store is overstocked with others. Accurately managing an inventory is a challenge for any merchandising business. For example, one of the goals of accounting for inventory is to reconcile what is in the store with what is found in the books of the store.

Knowing how to apply good accounting practices to a company's inventory helps it to efficiently manage one of its most valuable assets. In this chapter we will learn about journalizing transactions using the perpetual inventory system and the differences between the two types of inventory systems, perpetual and periodic. We will discuss how to use a subsidiary ledger for inventory and how to determine the ending value of inventory. And we will find out how to estimate the ending value of an inventory using either the retail or gross profits method.

Learning Objectives

- Understanding and journalizing transactions using the perpetual inventory system and explaining the difference between perpetual and periodic inventory systems. (p. 570)

- Maintaining a subsidiary ledger for inventory. (p. 575)

- Understanding periodic methods of determining the value of the ending inventory. (p. 579)

- Estimating ending inventory using the retail method and gross profit method and understanding how the ending inventory amount affects financial reports. (p. 585)

Have you ever thought of the perfect present for someone at Christmas time only to find that everyone else in the world had the same idea, and the stores were out of stock? In recent years such gifts have included Elmo, Barney, Pokemon, Beanie Babies, home computers, and various video games. Having the right quantities of inventory is crucial to a retail business. It's bad to run out of stock and miss out on sales revenue, especially during the holidays, but it's also harmful to have too much of an item. A store must consider the cost of carrying inventory, and it must also worry about product obsolescence or the possibility of a fad running its course before all the products are sold. A good example is your local computer store. Models change so quickly that an inventory of old models could mean losing sales to competitors.

In Chapter 11 we discussed the periodic inventory system. A major weakness of the periodic system is that inventory is checked and counted only at the beginning and end of the accounting period and therefore managers do not know the actual amount of inventory on hand nor the actual cost of goods sold until the end of the accounting period. Today, with computers in so many businesses, the trend is toward perpetual inventory. Managers need to have *current* information about how much of their capital is tied up in inventory, and they need to have *current* information about the profitability of their sales of merchandise. The *perpetual* system of accounting for merchandise inventory provides this information on a transaction-by-transaction basis. Managers can know the balance of inventory and the profitability of sales as soon as each sale is completed. The perpetual system requires extra time and effort to gain these benefits, but, fortunately, computers can handle much of the detail. In this chapter we look at how the perpetual inventory system can be used in a merchandising business. We also compare the perpetual system to the periodic system.

In the last part of the chapter we discuss how to assign costs to inventory using the *periodic inventory system,* because many businesses with small inventories still use this system.

Learning Unit 15-1   Perpetual Inventory System

In the **perpetual inventory system*** we have two key accounts: Merchandise Inventory and Cost of Goods Sold.

The Merchandise Inventory account is an asset account that will reveal the current balance of inventory at all times (perpetually). This account is the same that was used in the previous discussion of the periodic inventory system, but in the periodic system the balance of the Merchandise Inventory was correct *only* at the end of each accounting period. In the perpetual system entries will be recorded to the Merchandise Inventory account each time the store purchases new merchandise and each time the store sells merchandise to a customer.

The other key account is the Cost of Goods Sold account. As merchandise is sold to customers, an entry will be recorded that will remove the cost of the merchandise from the Merchandise Inventory account and transfer that cost to the Cost of Goods Sold account. Thus, the Merchandise Inventory account will show the correct cost

---

* An Appendix on Perpetual Inventory was included in Chapter 9.

for the inventory on hand, and the Cost of Goods Sold account will show the cumulative total cost of all merchandise that has been sold to customers during the accounting period.

With the perpetual inventory system the key accounts, Merchandise Inventory and Cost of Goods Sold, will always provide current information to managers about their investment in inventory and the cost of the merchandise sold to customers.

Accounts Affected	Category	↑ ↓	Rules
Merchandise Inventory	Asset	↑	Dr.
Cost of Goods Sold	Cost of Goods Sold	↑	Cr.

You have been hired to work for a software retail business called Painless Bytes. A best seller for Painless Bytes is an accounting software package called A-I-B, (Always In Balance). Let's record some transactions relating to buying and selling A-I-B software. Because most businesses buy their merchandise inventory on account, we use Accounts Payable in the transactions.

20XX

June 2 Purchased 10 packages of A-I-B software at a cost of $25 per package for a total of $250.

June	2	Merchandise Inventory		2 5 0 00		
		Accounts Payable				2 5 0 00
		To record the purchase of inventory				

Figure 15-1
Purchase of Inventory in Perpetual System

Note that the asset account, Merchandise Inventory, has been increased by the cost of the new merchandise we have purchased (Fig. 15-1). Now let's look at a sales transaction.

20XX

June 3 Sold three software packages for cash to a customer at $50 each for a total of $150.

June	3	Cash		1 5 0 00		
		Sales Revenue				1 5 0 00
		To record sale of 3 packages of A-I-B				
June	3	Cost of Goods Sold		7 5 00		
		Merchandise Inventory				7 5 00
		To record the cost of goods sold				

Figure 15-2
Matching Sales to Cost of Goods Sold

Note that in the perpetual inventory system we record both the retail value of the sale (three units at $50) in the Sales Revenue account and the cost of the sale (three units at $25) in the Cost of Goods Sold account with two related transactions (Fig. 15-2).

What if the customer returns one of the packages? Assuming that the returned package is still in new condition, here is what we would record:

20XX
June   5   Allowed the customer to return one package for a cash refund, $50.

Figure 15-3
Sales Return to Seller

June	5	Sales Returns and Allowances		50 00		
		Cash				50 00
		To record the return of one				
		package A-I-B				

June	5	Merchandise Inventory		25 00		
		Cost of Goods Sold				25 00
		To record return of one package				
		A-I-B at cost				

In this transaction (Fig. 15-3) we must record the reduction in revenue of $50 and we must also record that we now have returned one package of software to our inventory by adding the $25 cost of that unit back to the Merchandise Inventory account.

Once in a while a business may have to return some inventory that came in damaged or for some other reason. Painless Bytes would prepare a debit memo. Let's see how this transaction is handled in a perpetual inventory system.

20XX
June   6   Returned one damaged A-I-B software package from the June 2 purchase.

Figure 15-4
Return by Buyer
of Merchandise

June	6	Accounts Payable		25 00		
		Merchandise Inventory				25 00
		To record return of damaged A-I-B				
		package to vendor				

This transaction (Fig. 15-4) reduced what is owed the vendor by $25, the cost of the package, and we reduced the Asset account—Merchandise Inventory—because we returned the item to the vendor. *Note:* We do not use a Purchases Returns and Allowances account when we are recording in a perpetual inventory system. The Asset account Merchandise Inventory is directly reduced by the amount we returned to our vendor.

Now let's look at how these transactions relate to the accounts and to the financial statements. In the T accounts in Figure 15-5 you can see that the Merchandise Inventory account shows the correct balance for the seven software packages remaining in inventory and that the Cost of Goods Sold account shows

GENERAL LEDGER ACCOUNTS

Figure 15-5
General Ledger Accounts

Sales Revenue			Sales Returns and Allowances		
Dr.	Cr.		Dr.	Cr.	
	6/3	150	6/5	50	
	Bal	150	Bal	50	

Merchandise Inventory			Cost of Goods Sold		
Dr.	Cr.		Dr.	Cr.	
6/2	250		6/3	75	
	6/3	75		6/5	25
6/5	25				
	6/6	25			
Bal	175		Bal	50	

Balance Sheet

Assets		Liabilities and Owner's Equity
Cash		$xxxxx
Inventory		$ 175

Income Statement

Revenues	
Sales	$150
Sales R&A	$ 50
Net Sales	$100
Cost of Goods Sold	$ 50
Gross Profit	$ 50

the correct amount for the cost of the two software packages actually sold. Asset accounts such as Merchandise Inventory are shown on the balance sheet, and the Sales and Cost of Goods Sold accounts appear on the income statement. Remember that we calculate Gross Profit when we subtract Cost of Goods Sold from Sales. In fact, we know the gross profit on each sale just as soon as the sale is completed.

COMPARISON OF THE PERPETUAL AND PERIODIC INVENTORY SYSTEMS

In our discussion of the perpetual inventory system, the primary benefit from this system is that the value of merchandise inventory is known after every purchase and sale. The cost of goods sold is known after every sale. The Merchandise Inventory account becomes an active account. The cost of goods sold is now an account in the general ledger rather than just an item on the income statement. The *periodic inventory system* does not give accurate or up-to-date information about merchandise inventory or cost of goods sold until after an ending inventory is taken.

The taking of a physical inventory at least once a year is not eliminated by a business that uses the perpetual inventory system. An inventory must be taken at least once a year to detect any inventory recording errors, shoplifting, or damages to the merchandise inventory.

The comparisons of recording of transactions in the two systems are revealed in Figure 15-6. The chart shows that in a perpetual inventory system, the Purchases, Purchases Returns and Allowances, and Freight accounts *do not* exist. Inventory and Cost of Goods Sold are updated immediately.

Figure 15-6 Comparison of Perpetual and Periodic Systems

Transaction	Perpetual System		Periodic System	
(A) Sold merchandise that cost $8,000 on account for $20,000	Acc. Receiv.	20 000 00	Acc. Receiv.	20 000 00
	Sales	20 000 00	Sales	20 000 00
	Cost of Goods Sold	8 000 00		
	Merch. Inventory	8 000 00		
(B) Purchased $900 of merchandise on account	Merch. Inventory	9 00 00	Purchases	9 00 00
	Acc. Payable	9 00 00	Acc. Payable	9 00 00
(C) Paid $50 freight charges.	Merch. Inventory	5 0 00	Freight-in	5 0 00
	Cash	5 0 00	Cash	5 0 00
(D) Customer returned $200 of merchandise. Cost of merchandise was $100	Sales Ret. & Allow.	2 00 00	Sales Ret. & Allow.	2 00 00
	Accounts Receiv.	2 00 00	Accts. Receiv.	2 00 00
	Merchandise Inv.	1 00 00		
	Cost of Goods Sold	1 00 00		
(E) Returned $400 of merchandise previously bought on account due to defects.	Acc. Payable	4 00 00	Acc. Payable	4 00 00
	Merch. Inv.	4 00 00	Pur. Ret. and Allow	4 00 00

Learning Unit 15-1 Review

AT THIS POINT you should be able to

- Explain the perpetual inventory system. (p. 570)
- Journalize transactions for a perpetual inventory system. (p. 571)
- Explain the difference between the perpetual and periodic inventory systems. (p. 573)

SELF-REVIEW QUIZ 15-1

(The blank forms you need are on page 39 of the *Study Guide and Working Papers*.)

Journalize the following transactions for a firm that uses a perpetual inventory system:

a. Bought $200 of merchandise on account.

b. Sold $100 of merchandise on account that cost $50.

c. Allowed a customer to return for cash $30 worth of inventory. Our cost was $15.

d. We got permission from our vendor to return $30 worth of inventory.

SOLUTIONS TO SELF-REVIEW QUIZ 15-1

a.

Merchandise Inventory	200 00	
Accounts Payable		200 00

Figure 15-7
Journalized Entries
in a Perpetual System

b.

Accounts Receivable	100 00	
Sales		100 00

Cost of Goods Sold	50 00	
Merchandise Inventory		50 00

c.

Sales Returns and Allowances	30 00	
Cash		30 00

Merchandise Inventory	15 00	
Cost of Goods Sold		15 00

d.

Accounts Payable	30 00	
Merchandise Inventory		30 00

Learning Unit 15-2   Using a Subsidiary Ledger for Inventory

Suppose the business Painless Bytes sells many different kinds of software packages. How can Painless Bytes keep track of the cost and balances of a variety of inventory items? How do stores such as Wal-Mart keep track of the thousands of items that they keep in inventory? The answer is found in the use of a subsidiary ledger for inventory and the use of computers to maintain the subsidiary ledger.

Do you recall from Chapters 9 and 10 that when we had a large number of Account Receivable or Account Payable accounts, we used subsidiary ledgers to maintain the details for each customer or vendor? This same accounting procedure can be used to keep track of inventory. Our Merchandise Inventory account becomes a control account keeping track of the total balance of inventory, while the details are kept in separate inventory records in a subsidiary ledger for inventory. Let's first show our existing inventory account with a subsidiary ledger and with the transactions from

Subsidiary Ledger Records

General Ledger Account

Merchandise Inventory

Dr.		Cr.	
6/2	250		
		6/3	75
6/5	25		
		6/6	25
Bal	175		

A-I-B Software

Date	Purchased	Sold	Balance
6/2	10 @ $25		$250
6/3		3 @ $25	$175
6/5		(1) @ $25	$200
6/6	(1) @ $25		$175

Learning Unit 15-1. On the left is our inventory account in T form, and on the right is an inventory record form for our A-I-B product.

Notice that the inventory record form on the right contains the detail about the quantity and per unit cost for the transactions posted to the general ledger account on the left. Notice too that the return of 6/5 is recorded in the inventory record as a negative sale and that the ending balances agree. The debit memo transaction of 6/6 is entered as a negative purchase and again the ending balances agree. Try using your calculator to see if you can also calculate the running balance shown in the inventory record.

In this next transaction Painless Bytes adds R&C, (Rows and Columns), a spreadsheet software package, to the line of software it sells.

June   6   Purchased 7 packages of R&C software on account at a cost of $225 per package and a total of $1,575.

Note in Figure 15-8 that the Merchandise Inventory account has again been increased by the cost of the new merchandise we have purchased. Because we now have two products in inventory, our inventory ledger will have a new inventory record form for the R&C product. Check out the way our inventory records relate to the Merchandise Inventory account.

Figure 15-8
Purchase of Inventory
in Perpetual System

June	6	Merchandise Inventory	1575 00		
		Accounts Payable		1575 00	
		To record the purchase of inventory			

General Ledger Account

Merchandise Inventory

Dr.		Cr.	
6/2	250		
		6/3	75
6/5	25		
6/6	1,575	6/6	25
Bal	1,750		

Subsidiary Ledger Records

Product #1:   A-I-B Software

Date	Purchased	Sold	Balance
6/2	10 @ $25		$ 250
6/3		3 @ $25	$ 175
6/5		(1) @ $25	$ 200
6/6	(1) @ $25		$ 175

Product #2:   R&C Software

Date	Purchased	Sold	Balance
6/6	7 @ $225		$1,575

Does the total of the balances of the two inventory records agree with the Merchandise Inventory account?

Now let's try another sales transaction.

20XX
June   9   Sold two A-I-B packages at $50 each and three R&C packages at $295 each for a total of $985.

Figure 15-9
Matching Sales and Cost
of Goods Sold

June	9	Cash	985 00		
		Sales Revenue		985 00	
		Sold 2 A-I-B and 3 R&C			
June	3	Cost of Goods Sold	725 00		
		Merchandise Inventory		725 00	
		To record the cost of goods sold			

Again, we record both the total sales price of the transaction and the cost of the merchandise sold (Fig. 15-9). Do you know how we arrived at the cost of goods sold figure of $725? A quick look at the inventory record forms will show us how we know the cost of goods sold.

General Ledger Account

Merchandise Inventory

Dr.		Cr.	
6/2	250		
		6/3	75
6/4	25		
6/6	1,575	6/6	25
		6/9	725
Bal	1,025		

Subsidiary Ledger Records

Product #1:   A-I-B Software

Date	Purchased	Sold	Balance
6/2	10 @ $25		$ 250
6/3		3 @ $25	$ 175
6/4	(1) @ $25		$ 200
6/5	(1) @ $25		$ 175
6/6		2 @ $25	$ 125

Product #2:   R&C Software

Date	Purchased	Sold	Balance
6/6	7 @ $225		$1,575
6/9		3 @ $225	$ 900

We obtained the cost of goods sold total when we posted the quantities sold to each of the inventory records. Two units of A-I-B at $25 each plus three units of R&C at $225 each equals a total cost of $725. Notice that the ending balances of the two products will total to the same amount as the balance shown in the Merchandise Inventory account.

In summary, a business with a variety of products in inventory will use an inventory subsidiary ledger with an individual record for each different product. These records will contain the details about the quantity and cost of inventory on hand and will allow calculation of the cost of goods sold on each sale.

Computerized accounting systems can handle a perpetual inventory system with ease. You have no doubt seen such systems in operation when the clerk at your local store used a laser scanner or a bar code to enter your purchases into the cash register. The transaction put into the cash register will record the sale and update the cost of goods sold and inventory. Computerized systems keep track of inventory by many different methods. When figuring the value of the inventory, they could use average cost; first in, first out (FIFO); or last in, first out (LIFO). The example in Figure 15-10 uses the FIFO method in determining the cost of the merchandise for each sale.

Inventory Control

Item VX113   Maximum 22
Description Digital Clock   Reorder Level 12
Location Storeroom 1   Reorder Quantity 10

	Received				Sold			Balance		
Date	Units	Cost per Unit	Total	Units	Cost per Unit	Total	Units	Cost per Unit	Total
20XX Jan. 1	Balance		FWD				14	50	$ 700
12				2	50	100	12	50	600
19	10	60	600				{12	50	
							{10	60	1,200
25				8	50	400	{ 4	50	
							{10	60	800

Figure 15-10
An Inventory Record

Learning Unit 15-2 Review

AT THIS POINT you should be able to

- Understand how a subsidiary ledger for inventory works with a controlling account for inventory. (p. 575)
- Journalize and post transactions that affect the general ledger Merchandise Inventory account as well as the individual inventory records in the Merchandise Inventory subsidiary ledger. (p. 576)

SELF-REVIEW QUIZ 15-2

(The forms you need are on page 40 of the *Study Guide and Working Papers*.)

Journalize and post the following transactions for a firm that uses a subsidiary ledger for Merchandise Inventory. Only post to the accounts that you have.

- **a.** Bought 3 X-Products at $3 each on account.
- **b.** Sold one of the X-Products we purchased above for cash, $6.
- **c.** Bought 4 more X-Products at $3 and 5 Z-Products at $10 on account.
- **d.** Sold for cash 2 more X-Products at $6 each and 3 Z-Products at $20 each.

SOLUTIONS TO SELF-REVIEW QUIZ 15-2

a.

Merchandise Inventory	114 ✔	9 00		
Accounts Payable			9 00	

b.

Cash		6 00		
Sales			6 00	
Cost of Goods Sold		3 00		
Merchandise Inventory	114 ✔		3 00	

c.

Merchandise Inventory	114 ✔	6 2 00		
Accounts Payable			6 2 00	

d.

Cash		7 2 00		
Sales			7 2 00	
Cost of Goods Sold		3 6 00		
Merchandise Inventory	114 ✔		3 6 00	

Figure 15-11
Inventory Account in General and Subsidiary Ledgers

General Ledger Account

Merchandise Inventory

Dr.		Cr.	
a.	9	b.	3
c.	62	d.	36
Bal.	32		

Subsidiary Ledger Records

Product #1: X Product

Date	Purchased	Sold	Balance
a.	3 @ $3		9
b.		1 @ $3	6
c.	4 @ $3		18
d.		2 @ $3	12

Product #2: Z Product

Date	Purchased	Sold	Balance
c.	5 @ $10		50
d.		3 @ $10	20

Learning Unit 15-3   Methods of Determining the Value of the Ending Inventory When Using the Periodic Inventory System

For a small business or any business using the **periodic inventory system,** the method used to assign costs to ending inventory will have a direct effect on the company's cost of goods sold and gross profit. Note in the table how the ending inventory does in fact have an effect on the gross profit.

	Situation A		Situation B		Situation C		Situation D	
Net Sales		$50,000		$50,000		$50,000		$50,000
Beginning Inventory	$ 4,000		$ 4,000		$ 4,000		$ 4,000	
Net Purchases	20,000		20,000		20,000		20,000	
Cost of Goods Available for Sale	24,000		24,000		24,000		24,000	
Ending Inventory	5,000		6,000		7,000		8,000	
Cost of Goods Sold		19,000		18,000		17,000		16,000
Gross Profit		$31,000		$32,000		$33,000		$34,000

If all inventory brought into a store had the same cost, it would be simple to calculate the ending inventory, and we would not have to have this discussion. Unfortunately, things are not that easy; often the very same products are purchased and brought into the store at different costs during the same accounting period. Over the years, four generally accepted methods have been developed to assign a cost to ending inventory. The reason these methods are needed is that often inventory is brought in at different times. The result is that the inventory is made up of many past purchases at *different* prices. Think of the inventory methods as a way of tracing costs. These methods are (1) specific invoice; (2) first in, first out; (3) last in, first out; and (4) weighted average. Each is based on an assumed flow of costs, not on the actual physical movement of goods sold in a store.

We now look at how the four inventory cost assumptions are applied within the periodic inventory system. The following situation occurred at Jones Hardware. Jones

Hardware sells rakes. The job before us is to come up with the value of the ending inventory and cost of goods sold using the four methods we have listed. The following table provides us with all the information needed to accomplish our task.

Goods Available for Sale

		Units	Cost		Total
January 1	Beginning Inventory	10	@ $10	=	$100
March 15	Purchases	9	@ 12	=	108
August 18	Purchases	20	@ 13	=	260
November 15	Purchases	5	@ 15	=	75
		44			$543

Actual inventory on December 31 revealed that 12 rakes remained in stock.

SPECIFIC INVOICE METHOD

In the specific invoice method, the cost of ending inventory is assigned by identifying each item in that inventory by a specific purchase price and invoice number, and maybe even by serial number.

For our example of this method, let's assume that Jones Hardware knew that six of the rakes not sold were from the March 15 invoice and the other six were from the August 18 purchase. Thus, $150 was assigned as the actual cost of ending inventory. If the total cost of goods available for sale is $543 and we subtract the actual cost of ending inventory ($150), this method provides a figure of $393 for cost of goods sold.

Specific Invoice Method

	Goods Available for Sale			Calculating Cost of Ending Inventory		
	Units	Cost	Total	Units	Cost	Total
January 1 Beg. Inventory	10	@ $10 =	$100			
March 15 Purchased	9	@ 12 =	108	6	@ $12	$ 72
August 18 Purchased	20	@ 13 =	260	6	@ 13	78
November 15 Purchased	5	@ 15 =	75			
	44		$543	12		$150

Cost of Goods Available for Sale $543
Less: Cost of Ending Inventory =   150
Cost of Goods Sold $393

Let's look at the pros and cons of this method.

Specific Invoice Method: A Reference Guide

Pros	Cons
1. Simple to use if company has small amount of high-cost goods, such as autos, jewels, boats, or antiques. 2. Flow of goods and flow of cost are the same. 3. Costs are matched with the sales they helped to produce.	1. Difficult to use for goods with large unit volume and small unit prices such as nails at a hardware store or packages of toothpaste at a drug store. 2. Difficult to use for decision-making purposes; ordinarily an impractical approach because companies usually deal with high-cost unique items.

FIRST IN, FIRST OUT METHOD (FIFO)

In the **FIFO method,** we assume that the oldest goods are sold first. Therefore, the items in the ending inventory will be valued at the costs shown on the most recent invoices.

FIFO Method

	Goods Available for Sale			Calculating Cost of Ending Inventory		
	Units	Cost	Total	Units	Cost	Total
January 1 Beg. Inventory	10 @	$10 =	$100			
March 15 Purchased	9 @	12 =	108			
August 18 Purchased	20 @	13 =	260	7 @	$13 =	$ 91
November 15 Purchased	5 @	15 =	75	5 @	15 =	75
	44		$543	12		$166

Cost of Goods Available for Sale $543
Less: Cost of Ending Inventory = 166
Cost of Goods Sold $377

In our Jones Hardware example the ending inventory of 12 rakes on hand is assigned a cost from the last two purchase invoices of rakes (purchases made on November 15 and part of the purchases made on August 18), totaling $166. Think of the inventory as being taken from the bottom layer first, then the next one up. If our ending inventory is valued at $166, our cost of goods sold must be $377.

Following are the pros and cons of this method.

FIFO Method: A Reference Guide

Pros	Cons
1. The cost flow tends to follow the physical flow; most businesses try to sell the old goods first (perishables such as fruit or vegetables). 2. The figure for ending inventory is made up of current costs on the balance sheet (because inventory left over is assumed to be from goods last brought into the store).	1. During periods of inflation this method will produce higher income on the income statement and thus more taxes to be paid (discussed later in the chapter). 2. Recent costs are not matched with recent sales, because we assume *old* goods are sold first.

LAST IN, FIRST OUT METHOD (LIFO)

Under the **LIFO method,** it is assumed that the goods *most recently acquired* are sold first. Therefore, the items in the ending inventory will be valued at the invoice costs shown from the top of the list down.

For Jones Hardware this assumption means that the 12 rakes not sold were assigned costs from the 10 listed in beginning inventory and 2 from the March 15 invoice. The ending inventory totals $124 and the cost of goods sold would be $419.

LIFO Method

	Goods Available for Sale			Calculating Cost of Ending Inventory		
	Units	Cost	Total	Units	Cost	Total
January 1 Beg. Inventory	10	@ $10	= $100	10	@ $10	= $100
March 15 Purchased	9	@ 12	= 108	2	@ 12	= 24
August 18 Purchased	20	@ 13	= 260			
November 15 Purchased	5	@ 15	= 75			
	44		$543	12		$124

Cost of Goods Available for Sale → $543
Less: Cost of Ending Inventory = 124
Cost of Goods Sold $419

The pros and cons of this method are as follows.

LIFO Method: A Reference Guide

Pros	Cons
1. Cost of goods sold is recorded at or near current costs, because costs of *latest* goods acquired are used. 2. Matches current costs with current selling prices. 3. During periods of inflation this method produces the lowest net income, which is a tax advantage. (The lower cost of ending inventory means a higher cost of goods sold; with a higher cost of goods sold, gross profit and ultimately net income are smaller and thus taxes are lower.)	1. Ending inventory is valued at very old prices. 2. Doesn't match physical flow of goods (but can still be used to calculate flow of costs).

WEIGHTED-AVERAGE METHOD

The weighted-average method calculates an average unit cost by dividing the *total cost* of goods available for sale by the *total units* of goods available for sale. In this example the total cost of goods available for sale was $543, and the total units available for sale were 44. Taking the $543 and dividing that number by the 44 total units for the period gives a $12.34 weighted average per unit.

Weighted-Average Method

	Goods Available for Sale		
	Units	Cost	Total
January 1 Beg. Inventory	10	@ $10	= $100
March 15 Purchased	9	@ 12	= 108
August 18 Purchased	20	@ 13	= 260
November 15 Purchased	5	@ 15	= 75
	44		$543

$$\frac{\$543}{44} = \$12.34 \text{ weighted-average cost per unit}$$

12 rakes × $12.34 = $148.08

Cost of Goods Available for Sale $543.00
Less: Cost of Ending Inventory =   148.08
Cost of Goods Sold $394.92

The pros and cons of this method are as follows:

Weighted-Average Method: A Reference Guide

Pros	Cons
1. Weighted average takes into account the number of units purchased at each amount, not a simple average cost. Good for products sold in large volume, such as grains and fuels. 2. Accountant assigns an equal unit cost to each unit of inventory; thus when the income statement is prepared, net income will not fluctuate as much as much as with other methods	1. Current prices have no more significance than prices of goods bought month earlier. 2. Compared with other methods, the most recent costs are *not* matched with current sales. This fact is important in financial reporting so as to provide an accurate picture of the company. 3. Cost of ending inventory is not as up-to-date as it could be using another method.

In this illustration Jones Hardware assumes that the 12 units left on hand are *average* units and therefore assigns an *average* cost figure of $12.34 to each of the 12 rakes left in inventory. Thus, we have a fair approximation of the cost of the ending inventory at $148.08 and of the amount of cost of goods sold, $394.92.

Remember that all four methods are acceptable accounting procedures. Management needs to select the method best suited to its business and be consistent in the application of that method.

WHEN CAN AN INVENTORY METHOD BE CHANGED?

In accounting there is a principle of consistency, which means that once a business selects a particular accounting method, it should follow it consistently from one year to the next without switching to another method. In the previous part of this chapter, we saw four methods of inventory valuations causing four different results for a business in terms of cost of goods sold and, ultimately, net income. Therefore, if a company kept switching from LIFO to FIFO each year, significant changes would result in the profit it reported. The financial reports would become undependable. Keeping with the same method allows readers of the financial reports to make meaningful comparisons of the cost of ending inventory, cost of goods sold, and so forth from year to year.

The principle of consistency doesn't mean that a company can *never* change from one method of inventory valuation to another. If a change is decided upon, however, the company should fully disclose the change, the effects of the change on profit and inventory valuation, and the justification for change in a footnote on the financial report. This principle is called the full disclosure principle in accounting.

ITEMS THAT SHOULD BE INCLUDED IN THE COST OF INVENTORY

Goods in Transit

On the date inventory is taken, goods in transit should be added to inventory if the ownership of the inventory has been transferred to the buyer. For example, if the merchandise was purchased *F.O.B. shipping point,* the buyer becomes the owner of the merchandise when the merchandise is placed on the carrier at the shipping point. On the other hand, if the buyer purchases the merchandise *F.O.B. destination,* the seller has ownership of the merchandise until the merchandise reaches the destination, and it should not be included in the cost of the buyer's inventory.

Merchandise on Consignment

Consignment means that a business (the consignor) is selling its merchandise through an agent (the consignee) who doesn't own the merchandise but who has possession of it. Consigned merchandise belongs to the consignor and should not be included in the consignee's inventory cost.

Damaged or Obsolete Merchandise

If the merchandise is not saleable, it should *not* be added to the cost of the inventory. For merchandise that is saleable but at a lower cost, the value of that inventory should be estimated at a conservative figure and added to the cost of the inventory.

Learning Unit 15-3 Review

AT THIS POINT you should be able to

- Calculate cost of ending inventory and cost of goods sold by specific invoice; first in, first out; last in, first out; and weighted-average method. (p. 580)
- Explain the pros and cons of each method used to calculate cost of ending inventory and cost of goods sold. (p. 580)
- Explain the principles of consistency and full disclosure. (p. 583)
- Explain how merchandise in transit, merchandise on consignment, and damaged or obsolete merchandise are counted in calculating inventory. (p. 583)

SELF-REVIEW QUIZ 15-3

(The forms you need are on page 41 of the *Study Guide and Working Papers*.)

1. From the information given here, calculate the cost of inventory as well as the cost of goods sold using the (a) specific invoice, (b) weighted-average, (c) first in, first out, and (d) last in, first out methods.

	Goods Available for Sale			Additional Fact: Inventory Not Sold
	Units	Cost	Total	
January 1 Beg. Inventory	40	@ $ 8	= $ 320	40 from January 1
April 1 Purchased	20	@ 9	= 180	
May 1 Purchased	20	@ 10	= 200	4 from May 1
October 1 Purchased	20	@ 12	= 240	4 from October 1
December 1 Purchased	20	@ 13	= 260	
	120		$1,200	

2. Respond true or false to the following:

   a. It is possible for a company to change from LIFO to FIFO if the company follows specific guidelines.

b. Goods in transit (shipped F.O.B. shipping point) will not be included as part of the inventory for the purchaser.

c. Damaged goods are always added to the cost of inventory.

SOLUTIONS TO SELF-REVIEW QUIZ 15-3

1. a. Total cost of goods available for sale $1,200
Less ending inventory based on specific invoices:

40 units from Jan. 1 purchased at $8	$320	
4 units from May 1 purchased at $10	40	
4 units from Oct. 1 purchased at $12	48	
48 units in ending inventory		408
Cost of goods sold		$ 792

b. $1,200 ÷ 120 units = $10 weighted-average cost per unit.

Total cost of goods available for sale		$1,200
Less ending inventory priced at weighted-average basis: 48 units at $10.00	480	
Cost of goods sold		$ 720

c.
Total cost of goods available for sale		$1,200
Less ending inventory priced on FIFO:		
20 units from Dec. 1 at $13	$260	
20 units from Oct. 1 at $12	240	
8 units from May 1 at $10	80	
48 units in ending inventory		580
Cost of goods sold		$ 620

d.
Total cost of goods available for sale		$1,200
Less ending inventory priced on LIFO:		
40 units from Jan. 1 at $8	$320	
8 units from April 1 purchased at $9	72	
48 units in ending inventory		392
Cost of goods sold		$ 808

2. a. True   **b.** False   **c.** False

Learning Unit 15-4   Estimating Ending Inventory

The actual taking of a physical inventory is time-consuming and expensive. Because of the time and expense involved, most businesses take a physical inventory only once a year. For the business using the periodic inventory system, the need to have an inventory cost figure more often may become necessary. That is especially true when a business makes interim financial reports. This business may find that estimating the inventory rather than taking a physical inventory is accurate enough. Another reason to estimate the ending inventory is in case of a fire when the inventory may be destroyed. The business would need an inventory cost figure when it submits a claim of loss to the insurance company.

Two common and recognized ways to estimate ending inventory are the **retail method** and the **gross profit method.**

RETAIL METHOD

To use the retail method, a business must have the following information available:

1. Beginning inventory at cost and at retail (selling price).
2. Cost of net purchases at both cost and at retail.
3. The net sales at retail.

Let's look at the diagram below to see how French Company estimates ending inventory at cost by the retail method.

French completed the following steps to arrive at an ending inventory cost of $3,600.

Step 1:   Calculate cost of merchandise available for sale at cost and retail.

Step 2:   Calculate the cost ratio (cost of goods available for sale at cost divided by cost of goods available for sale at retail). It cost French Company .60, or 60 cents for each $1 of sales for the merchandise.

Step 3:   Deduct net sales from retail value of merchandise available for sale to arrive at an estimated ending inventory at retail.

Step 4:   Multiply cost ratio (.60 in this case) times ending inventory at retail to arrive at ending inventory at cost of $3,600.

Keep in mind that at year end French will take a physical inventory.

The Retail Inventory Method

		Cost	Retail
	Goods Available for Sale:		
	Beginning Inventory	$ 4,100	$ 6,900
	Net Purchases	7,900	13,100
Step 1 →	Cost of Goods Available for Sale	$12,000	$20,000
Step 2 →	Cost Ratio (relationship between cost and retail) $\frac{\$12,000}{\$20,000} = 60\%$		
Step 3 →	Net Sales at Retail		14,000
↳	Inventory at Retail		$ 6,000
Step 4 →	Ending Inventory at Cost, $ 6,000 × .60	$ 3,600	

GROSS PROFIT METHOD

Another method of estimating ending inventory without taking a physical count is the gross profit method. The method develops a relationship among sales, cost of goods sold, and gross profit in estimating the cost of ending inventory.

To use this method a company would have to keep track of the following:

1. Average gross profit rate.
2. Net sales, beginning inventory, and net purchases.

> Freight, if any, would be added to cost of net purchases.

The steps Moose Company takes to estimate its ending inventory are shown in the accompanying diagram. We assume a normal gross profit rate of 30% of net sales. If 30 cents on a dollar is profit, 70 cents on a dollar is cost.

The Gross Profit Method

	Goods Available for Sale:		
	Inventory, January 1, 20XX		$10,000
	Net Purchases		4,000
Step 1 →	Cost of Goods Available for Sale		$14,000
	Less: Estimated Cost of Goods Sold:		
	Net Sales at Retail	$6,000	
Step 2 →	Cost percentage (100% − 30%)	.70	
	Estimated Cost of Goods Sold		4,200
Step 3 →	Estimated Inventory, January 31, 20XX		$ 9,800

Step 1: Moose determines cost of goods available for sale (beginning inventory plus net purchases).

Step 2: Moose estimates cost of goods sold by multiplying cost percentage (70%) times net sales.

Step 3: Moose subtracts cost of goods sold from cost of goods available for sale to arrive at an estimated inventory of $9,800.

This method, besides helping prepare financial statements, can help determine the amount of inventory on hand at the time of a fire or can verify at year's end the accuracy of the physical inventory.

Before concluding this unit, let's look at how an error made in calculating ending inventory will affect financial statements.

How Incorrect Calculation of Ending Inventory Affects Financial Statements

As we have stated before, assigning costs to ending inventory can have an effect on cost of goods sold, gross profit, net income, and current assets as well as owner's capital. Let's look at a diagram to see—if a mistake is in fact made—what items on the income statement will be affected and what the mistake's impact will be over time.

	Correct		Incorrect	
	20X1	20X2	20X1	20X2
Sales	$200	$300	$200	$300
Cost of Goods Sold:				
Beginning Inventory	$ 30	$ 70	$ 30	$ 60
Purchases	95	85	95	85
Goods Available for Sale	125	155	125	145
Ending Inventory	−70 55	−100 55	−60 65	−100 45
Gross Profit	$145	$245	$135	$255

Summary:

	Correct	Incorrect	Difference
Year X1, Gross Profit	$145	$135	− $10
Year X2, Gross Profit	245	255	+ 10
Total effect of mistake after two periods			0

Note that when the incorrect figure of $60 is used for ending inventory in 20X1, it causes cost of goods sold to be $65 instead of $55 and profit to be $135 instead of $145. In other words, when ending inventory is understated ($60 instead of $70), cost of goods sold is overstated and profit is understated.

As we look next at 20X2, we see that the ending incorrect inventory of 20X1 is carried as the beginning inventory of 20X2. The understatement of beginning inventory in 20X2 of $60 (instead of $70) causes cost of goods sold to be understated and gross profit to be overstated. Thus, at the end of 20X2, the error will be self-correcting.

To review, look at the following diagram and prove it to yourself by going back over the previous explanation.

> Ending inventory works in same direction as profit, Beginning inventory is inversely related.

If the Item Is	Overstated	Understated
Beginning Inventory	Profit is understated	Profit is overstated
Ending Inventory	Profit is overstated	Profit is understated

Keep in mind that since ending inventory is recorded as a current asset on the balance sheet, any mistake will cause the assets to be under- or overstated. The statement of owner's equity will also be affected, since we have seen that the net income will be over- and understated.

Learning Unit 15-4 Review

AT THIS POINT you should be able to

- Calculate ending inventory by the retail method. (p. 586)
- Calculate ending inventory by the gross profit method. (p. 587)
- Explain how understating or overstating ending inventory will affect financial reports. (p. 587)

SELF-REVIEW QUIZ 15-4

(The forms you need are on page 42 of the *Study Guide and Working Papers.*)

1. Alon Company needs to estimate its month-end inventory. From the following, estimate the cost of ending inventory on September 30 by the retail method.

	Cost	Retail
Beginning Inventory	$ 8,000	$10,000
Net Purchases	40,000	60,000
Net Sales		30,000

(Carry out the cost ratio to the nearest hundredth percent.)

2. Respond true or false to the following:

   a. The retail inventory method is an estimate.

   b. The cost ratio in the gross profit method represents only sales, not costs.

   c. The first step in the gross profit method is to determine cost of goods available for sale.

   d. If ending inventory is overstated, net income will be overstated.

   e. If beginning inventory is overstated, net income will be overstated.

SOLUTIONS TO SELF-REVIEW QUIZ 15-4

		Cost	Retail
1.	Beginning Inventory	$8,000	$10,000
	Net Purchases	40,000	60,000
	Cost of Goods Available for Sale	$48,000	70,000
	Cost Ratio, $48,000/$70,000 = 68.57%		
	Net Sales at Retail		30,000
	Inventory at Retail		$40,000
	Ending Inventory at Cost,		
	$40,000 × .6857	$27,428	

2. **a.** True   **b.** False   **c.** True   **d.** True   **e.** False

Chapter Review

Learning Unit 15-1

1. In the perpetual inventory method we have two key accounts that are kept up-to-date at all times. These accounts are Merchandise Inventory and Cost of Goods Sold.
2. Each purchase of merchandise is recorded by a debit to the Merchandise Inventory account.
3. Each sale requires two entries. One entry records the revenue or selling price of the merchandise, and the other entry transfers the cost of the items sold from the Merchandise Inventory account to the Cost of Goods Sold account.
4. Sales returns also require two entries. One entry is to record the reduction in revenue in a Sales Returns and Allowance account, and the other entry is to move the cost of the items returned back to the Merchandise Inventory account from the Cost of Goods Sold account.
5. When the business returns merchandise to the vendor because of damage or some other reason, the Merchandise Inventory account is credited because the merchandise is no longer available to sell.
6. The comparison of the perpetual inventory system and the periodic inventory system reveals the Purchases, Purchases Returns and Allowances, and Freight accounts do not exist in the perpetual inventory system. The accounts Merchandise Inventory and Cost of Goods Sold become active accounts in the perpetual inventory system.

Learning Unit 15-2

1. If there are many items in inventory, a subsidiary inventory ledger will be used to keep track of the details of quantities and cost for each item in inventory.
2. An inventory record form will be used for each item in the inventory. This form has columns for recording the quantities and cost of units purchased and units sold, and it provides a running balance of inventory on hand.
3. When selling an item, the inventory record form provides the cost information for the debit to Cost of Goods sold and the credit to Merchandise Inventory.
4. The total cost represented by all the inventory record forms will equal the balance of the Merchandise Inventory account in the general ledger.

Learning Unit 15-3

1. In assigning a cost to ending inventory, the flow of goods may *not* follow the actual flow of costs.
2. The specific invoice method identifies each item in inventory with a specific invoice in assigning a cost of ending inventory. It matches costs exactly with revenues.
3. FIFO assumes the old goods are sold first. Because ending inventory is valued at most recent costs, FIFO provides the most realistic figure for ending merchandise inventory.
4. LIFO assumes the newest goods are sold first. It provides the most realistic figure for cost of goods sold. LIFO may also reduce income taxes.
5. The weighted-average method provides an average unit cost of all inventory. Weighted-average inventory value generally falls somewhere between LIFO and FIFO.
6. Accounting principles requires consistency in the use of the inventory method that is adopted.

7. Goods in transit should be added to the value of the inventory. Merchandise on consignment and damaged or obsolete merchandise should not be included in the value of the inventory.

Learning Unit 15-4

1. Taking a physical inventory is costly and time-consuming.
2. If a business needs to take an inventory more often than once a year, the retail method or gross profit method is used to prepare interim financial statements or to submit a claim for insurance purposes.
3. The ending inventory amount has an effect on the financial reports, and a mistake will cause the assets to be understated or overstated. Net income will also be understated or overstated by this mistake.

Key Terms

Consignee A company or person to whom merchandise is consigned but who doesn't have ownership.

Consignment Sales of goods through an agent who has possession but not ownership.

Consignor The one who consigns merchandise to the consignee.

Consistency The accounting principle that requires companies to follow the same accounting methods or procedures from period to period.

FIFO (First in, First out) method Valuing of inventory assuming that the company sells the first goods received in the store.

Full disclosure principle The accounting principle that requires companies to fully disclose on their financial reports changes in accounting procedures and methods along with effects of the change as well as justification for change.

Gross profit method A method used to determine the value of the ending inventory using a predetermined gross profit rate. This method can be used to determine value of ending inventory if a loss from fire occurs.

LIFO (Last in, Last out) method Valuing of inventory with the assumption the last goods received in the store are the first to be sold.

Periodic inventory system An inventory system that does not keep continuous inventory of merchandise on hand.

Perpetual inventory system The inventory system of a company that keeps a continuous (perpetual) record of inventory on hand and of the cost of goods sold.

Retail method A method used to determine the value of the ending inventory using a cost to retail ratio. Often used for interim financial reports.

Specific invoice method Valuing of inventory where each item is identified with a specific invoice.

Weighted-average method Valuing of inventory where each item is assigned the same unit cost. This unit cost is found by dividing cost of goods available for sale by the total number of units for sale.

Questions, Mini Exercises, Exercises, and Problems

Discussion Questions

1. Why would a manager prefer the perpetual inventory system over the periodic system of inventory?

2. What are the two key accounts in the perpetual inventory system?

3. In the perpetual system, what account is debited to record the cost of merchandise purchased?

4. Why are there two entries required to record each sale in the perpetual inventory system?

5. Explain the relationship between the Merchandise Inventory account and the subsidiary inventory ledger.

6. Must the flow of cost in inventory match the physical movement of merchandise? Please explain.

Blueprint: Methods of Estimating Inventory

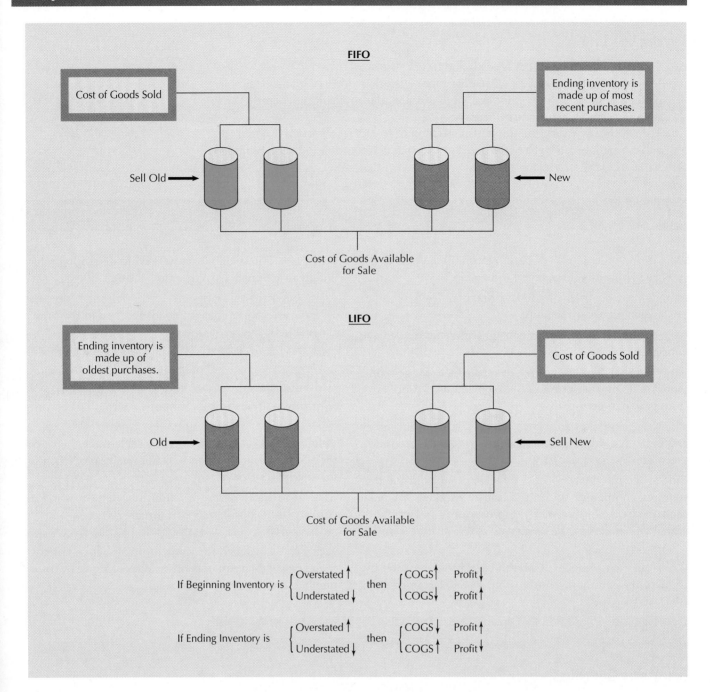

7. What are the four methods of inventory valuation? Explain each.

8. During inflation, which inventory method will provide the lowest income on the income statement?

9. Which inventory method provides the most current valuation of inventory on the balance sheet? Please explain.

10. Explain why goods in transit (F.O.B. shipping point) to buyer and goods issued on consignment are added to inventory valuations.

11. When ending inventory is understated, what effect will it have on cost of goods sold and net income?

12. Why would a company use the retail method to determine the value of the ending inventory? Why would it use the gross profit method?

Blueprint: Methods of Estimating Inventory (cont.)

Summary of Pros and Cons of Inventory and Valuation Methods

Pros	Cons	
1. Simple to use if company has small amount of high-cost goods, such as autos, jewels, boats, or antiques. 2. Flow of goods and flow of cost are the same. 3. Costs are matched with the sales they helped to produce.	1. Difficult to use for goods with large unit volume and small unit prices, such as nails at a hardware store or packages of toothpaste at a drug store. 2. Difficult to use for decision-making purposes; ordinarily an impractical approach.	**Specific Invoice**
Pros	**Cons**	
1. The cost flow tends to follow the physical flow; most businesses try to sell the old goods first (perishables such as fruit or vegetables). 2. The figure for ending inventory is made up of current costs on the balance sheet (because inventory left over is assumed to be from goods last brought into the store).	1. During inflation, this method will produce higher income on the income statement and thus more taxes to be paid. 2. Recent costs are not matched with recent sales, because it assumes *old* goods are sold first.	**FIFO**
Pros	**Cons**	
1. Cost of goods sold is stated at or near current costs, because costs of *latest* goods acquired are used. 2. Matches current costs with current selling prices. 3. During inflation, this method produces the lowest net income, which is a tax advantage. (The lower cost of ending inventory means a higher cost of goods sold; with a higher cost of goods sold, gross profit and ultimately net income are smaller and thus taxes are lower.)	1. Ending inventory is valued at very old prices. 2. Doesn't match physical flow of goods (but can still be used to calculate flow of costs).	**LIFO**
Pros	**Cons**	
1. Weighted-average takes into account the number of units purchased at each amount, not a simple average cost. Good for products sold in large volume, such as grains and fuels. 2. Accountant assigns an equal unit cost to each unit of inventory; thus when the income statement is prepared, net income will not fluctuate as much as with other methods.	1. Current prices have no more significance than prices of goods bought months earlier. 2. Compared with other methods, the most recent costs are *not* matched with current sales. 3. Cost of ending inventory is not as up-to-date as it could be using another method.	**Weighted-Average Method**

Mini Exercises

(The blank forms you need are on pages 43–44 of the *Study Guide and Working Papers*.)

Transaction Analysis

1. Complete the following transaction analysis:

Accounts Affected	Category	↑ ↓	Rules
Merchandise Inventory		↓	
Cost of Goods Sold		↑	

Journal Entries

Use the perpetual inventory system.

2. Journalize the following transaction in correct form:

20XX
Mar. 1 Sold merchandise on account, $500. The merchandise cost $300.

3. Journalize the following transaction in correct form:

20XX
Mar. 15 A customer returned merchandise for a cash refund of $250. The item cost the seller $125.

4. Journalize the following transaction in correct form:

20XX
Mar. 20 The business returned to the vendor a damaged inventory item that cost $150.

Estimating Inventory Value

5. From the following information calculate the cost of ending inventory and cost of goods sold using the (a) FIFO, (b) LIFO, and (c) weighted-average methods.

		Units	Cost
January 1	Beginning Inventory	5	$1
March 6	Purchased	3	2
August 9	Purchased	2	3
December 10	Purchased	4	4

The ending inventory reveals six items unsold.

Retail Inventory Method

6. Complete the following using the retail inventory method. (Round cost ratio to nearest whole percent.)

	Cost	Retail
Goods Available for Sale		
Beginning Inventory	$50	$100
Net Purchases	70	90
Cost of Goods Available for Sale	A	B
Cost Ratio	C	
Net Sales at Retail		140
Inventory at Retail		D
Ending Inventory	E	

Gross Profit Method

7. Complete the following using the gross profit method. Assume a normal gross profit rate of 40% of net sales.

Goods Available for Sale

Inventory January 1, 20XX		$50
Net Purchases		10
Cost of Goods Available for Sale		A
Less: Estimated Cost of Goods Sold:		
Net Sales at Retail	$40	
Cost percentage	B	
Estimated Cost of Goods Sold		C
Estimated Inventory Jan. 31, 20XX		D

Exercises

(The blank forms you need are on pages 48–50 of the *Study Guide and Working Papers*.)

Journalizing perpetual entries.

15-1. The DMM Electric Company uses the perpetual inventory system. Record these transactions in a two-column journal.

20XX

Feb.
3 Purchased 10 model 77DX light fixtures on account from Dealer's Electric at total cost of $230, terms n/30.

5 Sold 3 model U67 light fixtures for cash for $84 total. The cost of these 3 fixtures amounted to $54.

6 Our customer returned 1 model U67 light fixture. We gave the customer a $28 cash refund.

10 We issued a debit memo for $23 to Dealer's Electric for 1 model 77DX light fixture that came in damaged in the shipment of February 3.

Perpetual inventory: subsidiary ledgers.

15-2. The RJM Company uses the perpetual inventory system with a subsidiary ledger for inventory. Enter the following information into the inventory balance for product U47. Be sure to keep the balance on hand up-to-date.

20XX

Nov.
5 Purchased 5 units at a cost of $10 each. (There were no units on hand prior to this purchase.)

6 Sold 3 units for $16 each. (*Hint:* The inventory record form only contains information about the cost of a product, not the selling price!)

7 Sold 1 unit for $15.50.

10 Purchased 12 additional units at a cost of $10 each.

Journalizing perpetual entries.

15-3. Journalize and post the preceding transactions using a two-column journal.

15-4. CVR Sales uses the FIFO method with the perpetual inventory system. Enter the following information into the inventory record form for product 44BX. Be sure to keep the balance on hand up-to-date.

FIFO: perpetual method.

20XX

Oct.
1 Balance on hand: 3 units at a cost of $21 each.

2 Purchased 5 units at a cost of $23 each.

5 Sold 2 units for $31 each. (Remember to use cost and not selling price in the inventory record.)

6 Sold 5 units for $31 each.

8 Purchased 6 units at a cost of $24 each.

Periodic method.

15-5. The Loyola Company uses the periodic inventory system. Calculate the cost of ending inventory and cost of goods sold using the (a) FIFO, (b) LIFO, and (c) weighted-average methods. Loyola sells only one product called SM57.

		Units	Cost per Unit
January 1	Beginning inventory	50	$ 9
March 18	Purchased	12	10
August 19	Purchased	40	12
November 8	Purchased	48	13

Ending inventory is 52 units.

15-6. From the following facts, calculate the correct cost of inventory for Ray Company.

Shipping goods.

- Cost of inventory on shelf, $4,000, which includes $300 of goods received on consignment.
- Goods in transit en route to Ray Company shipped F.O.B. shipping point, $22,000.
- Goods in transit en route to Ray shipped F.O.B. destination, $300. Ray Company has $600 worth of goods on consignment in Alice's Dress Shop.

Retail inventory.

15-7. Miles Company's May 1 inventory had a cost of $58,000 and a retail value of $72,000. During May, net purchases cost $255,000 with a retail value of $405,000. Net sales at retail for Miles Company during May were $225,000. Calculate the ending inventory at cost using the retail inventory method. (Round the cost ratio to the nearest hundredth percent.)

Gross profit method.

15-8. Amy Company on January 1, 20XX, had inventory costing $30,000 and during January had net purchases of $67,000. Over recent years, Amy Company's gross profit has averaged 40% on sales. Given that the company has net sales of $106,000, calculate an estimated cost of ending inventory using the gross profit method.

Group A Problems

(The blank forms you need are on pages 51–60 of the *Study Guide and Working Papers*.)

Journalizing perpetual inventory.

15A-1. The Wren Company uses the perpetual inventory system. Record these transactions in a two-column journal. All credit sales are n/30.

20XX

Mar.	5	Purchased merchandise on account totaling $1,750. Terms n/30.

Check Figure:
Mar. 13
Dr. Cost of Goods Sold $290
Cr. Merch. Inventory $290

Mar.
- 5 Purchased merchandise on account totaling $1,750. Terms n/30.
- 6 Sold merchandise on account to Tommy Dorsey for $85. This merchandise cost $63.
- 8 Returned $100 of defective merchandise purchased March 5.
- 9 Sold $125 of merchandise for cash. This merchandise cost $98.
- 9 Allowed a return for credit of $7 of merchandise sold on March 6. The cost of the returned merchandise was $5. (*Hint:* Don't forget to return the cost of the merchandise to the Merchandise Inventory account.)
- 10 Purchased $800 of merchandise on account from BG Supply. Terms n/30.
- 12 Received payment from Tommy Dorsey for the March 6 sale less the return.
- 13 Sold $380 of merchandise for cash. The cost was $290.

Journalizing perpetual inventory.

15A-2. Mr. E. L. Best owns an electronics supply company called Best Electronics. His company uses the perpetual inventory system with a subsidiary inventory ledger to maintain control over an inventory of thousands of electronic parts. See page 597 for the quantities and costs for three of the parts in his inventory.

Part No.	Quantity on Hand	Cost per Unit
KT88	3	$17.50
EL34	22	16.40
12AX7	5	8.70

Check Figure:
KT88 Ending balance
$192.50

Your job is to

1. Enter the preceding beginning balances in the inventory record forms; beginning inventory is $456.80.
2. Journalize and post the following transactions.

20XX

Oct. 10 Purchased the following on account:

Part No.	Quantity	Cost per Unit
KT88	24	$17.50
12AX7	36	8.70

(*Hint:* Be sure to update each inventory record.)

11 Sold 4 number KT88 units for cash at a selling price of $27.50 each. (*Hint:* Remember to record both the revenue and the cost. The cost data will be found in the inventory record form for this part number. Don't forget to update the form.)

13 Sold the following for cash:

Part No.	Quantity	Sales Price per Unit
KT88	12	$27.50
EL34	8	25.00
12AX7	14	12.90

15 A customer brought back 1 of KT88 bought two days ago because it did not work.

16 Best Electronics sent back to the vendor the faulty KT88 that the customer brought back.

15A-3. Agree Company uses a perpetual inventory system. From the following information, prepare an inventory record form (a) assuming that the FIFO method is in use and (b) assuming that the LIFO method is in use. Assume on January 1, 20XX, a beginning inventory of 800 units at a cost of $8 each.

Perpetual: LIFO, FIFO.

Check Figure:
Ending balance
(b) $11,960

RECEIVED			SOLD	
Date	Quantity	Cost per Unit	Date	Quantity
Apr. 15	220	$ 7	Mar. 8	500
Nov. 12	800	9	Oct. 5	350
Dec. 31	700	10	Nov. 30	400

15A-4. Ashley Company, using the periodic inventory system, began the year with 250 units of product B in inventory with a unit cost of $35. The following additional purchases of the product were made:

Periodic inventory.

Apr. 1	300 units @ $40 each
July 5	400 units @ 50 each
Aug. 15	500 units @ 60 each
Nov. 20	150 units @ 70 each

Check Figure:
(b) LIFO Cost of Goods
Sold $62,500

At end of year, Ashley Company had 500 units of its product unsold. Your task is to calculate cost of ending inventory as well as cost of goods sold by the (a) FIFO, (b) LIFO, and (c) weighted-average methods. (Round the weighted average to the nearest cent.)

Retail inventory method.

15A-5. Marge Company uses the retail method to estimate cost of ending inventory for its monthly interim reports. From the following facts, estimate Marge's ending inventory at cost for the end of January. (Round the cost ratio to the nearest tenth percent.)

Check Figure:
$20,196 Ending Inventory at cost

January 1 inventory at cost	$ 16,500
January 1 inventory at retail	32,000
Net purchases at cost	110,800
Net purchases at retail	195,000
Net sales at retail	191,000

Gross profit method.

15A-6. Over the past four years the gross profit rate for Hall Company was 30%. Last week a fire destroyed all Hall's inventory. Luckily, all the records for Hall were in a fireproof safe and indicated the following facts:

Check Figure:
$26,290 Estimated Inventory

Inventory (January 1, 20XX)	$ 39,000
Sales	128,500
Sales Returns	3,200
Purchases	78,000
Purchases Returns and Allowances	3,000

Please estimate the cost of inventory that was destroyed in the fire.

Group B Problems

(The blank forms you need are on pages 51–60 of the *Study Guide and Working Papers.*)

Journalizing perpetual inventory.

15B-1. The Wren Company uses the perpetual inventory system. Record these transactions in a two-column journal. All credit sales are n/30.

20XX

Mar. 15 Purchased merchandise on account totaling $1,450. Terms n/30.
16 Sold merchandise on account to Bobby Hackett for $92. This merchandise cost $71.
18 Returned $120 of defective merchandise purchased March 15.
19 Sold $230 of merchandise for cash. This merchandise cost $175.
19 Allowed a return for credit of $14 of merchandise sold on March 16. The cost of the returned merchandise was $11. (*Hint:* Don't forget to return the cost of the merchandise to the Merchandise Inventory account.)
20 Purchased $900 of merchandise on account from JT Supply. Terms n/30.
22 Received payment from Bobby Hackett for the March 16 sale less the return.
23 Sold $410 of merchandise for cash. The cost was $320.

Check Figure:
Mar. 23
Dr. Cost of Goods Sold
$320
Cr. Merch. Inventory
$320

Journalizing perpetual inventory.

15B-2. Mr. E. L. Best owns an electronics supply company called Best Electronics. His company uses the perpetual inventory system with a subsidiary inventory ledger to maintain control over an inventory of thousands of electronic parts. Here are the quantities and costs for three of the parts in his inventory:

Check Figure:
12AU7 Ending balance
$117

Part No.	Quantity on Hand	Cost per Unit
6L6	4	$12.50
EL84	18	9.40
12AU7	3	7.80

Your job is to

1. Enter the above beginning balances in the inventory record forms; beginning inventory is $242.60.

2. Journalize and post the following transactions.

20XX

Oct.   10   Purchased the following on account:

Part No.	Quantity	Cost per Unit
6L6	18	$12.50
12AU7	28	7.80

(*Hint:* Be sure to update each inventory record.)

11   Sold 4 number 12AU7 units for cash at a selling price of $18.50 each. (*Hint:* Remember to record both the revenue and the cost. The cost data will be found in the inventory record form for this part number. Don't forget to update the form.)

13   Sold the following for cash:

Part No.	Quantity	Sales Price per Unit
6L6	10	$18.50
EL84	9	14.00
12AU7	12	11.80

15   A customer brought back 1 6L6 that was bought two days ago because it did not work.

16   Best Electronics returned to the vendor the faulty part that was returned yesterday.

15B-3. Agree Company uses a perpetual inventory system. From the following information, prepare an inventory record form (a) assuming that the FIFO method is in use and (b) assuming that the LIFO method is in use. Assume on January 1, 20XX, a beginning inventory of 500 units at a cost of $7 each.

Perpetual: LIFO, FIFO.

Check Figure: $6,900

RECEIVED			SOLD	
Date	Quantity	Cost per Unit	Date	Quantity
Apr. 15	200	$ 8	Mar. 8	400
Nov. 12	300	9	Oct. 5	300
Dec. 31	600	10	Nov. 30	200

15B-4. On January 1, 20XX, Ashley Company, a company that uses the periodic inventory system, began with 150 units of product B in inventory with a unit cost of $20. The following additional purchases of the product were made:

Periodic inventory.

Apr. 1	210 units @ $30 each
Jul. 5	500 units @ 40 each
Aug. 15	450 units @ 50 each
Nov. 20	200 units @ 60 each

Check Figure:
LIFO $52,900   Cost of Goods Sold

At end of year, Ashley Company had 400 units of its product unsold. Your task is to calculate cost of ending inventory as well as cost of goods sold by the (a) FIFO, (b) LIFO, and (c) weighted-average methods. (Round the weighted average to the nearest cent.)

Retail inventory method.

Check Figure:
$28,450 Ending inventory

15B-5. Marge Company uses the retail method to estimate cost of ending inventory for its monthly interim reports. From the following facts, estimate Marge's ending inventory at cost for the end of January. (Round the cost ratio to the nearest hundredth percent.)

January 1 inventory at cost	$ 17,000
January 1 inventory at retail	35,000
Net purchases at cost	119,000
Net purchases at retail	204,000
Net sales at retail	189,000

Gross profit method.

Check Figure:
$15,762.50 Estimated
inventory

15B-6. Over the past four years the gross profit rate for Hall Company was 35%. Last week a fire destroyed all Hall's inventory. Luckily, all the records for Hall were in a fireproof safe and indicated the following facts:

Inventory (January 1, 20XX)	$ 5,400
Sales	127,000
Sales Returns	3,250
Purchases	94,900
Purchases Returns and Allowances	4,100

Using the gross profit method, estimate the cost of inventory that was destroyed in the fire.

Real-World Application

15R-1. The following inventory errors were discovered during an internal audit:

a. The beginning inventory was overstated by $200.
b. The ending inventory was understated by $300.
c. $900 of purchases were unrecorded.
d. A sales return of $1,500 was not recorded.

Indicate what effect these mistakes (treat each one separately) will have on (1) the cost of goods sold, (2) the gross profit, and (3) the owner's equity. Please provide a written explanation.

YOU make the call

Critical Thinking/Ethical Case

15R-2. Lyon Co. has used a perpetual inventory system for six months. The president of the company has issued a memo stating that the new computer system has failed to deliver acceptable standards in servicing the customers and too many goods are out of stock. Fran, Lyon's accountant, blames the Computer Department and tells the president to fire the head of that department. The president wants to return immediately to a periodic inventory system. You make the call. Write down your recommendations to the president.

Internet Exercises: Conn's Audi Exchange

EX-1. [www.conns.com] Merchandise inventory represents one of the major investments of a retailing business. Accounting for inventory is a much more diverse process than presented in the chapter you have just studied. In addition to FIFO, LIFO, perpetual, and periodic, there are many other terms associated with inventory. The computer age allows companies to maintain perpetual inventory records even if they are reporting inventory on a periodic basis.

LIFO achieved recognition in the United States when a major revision of the Internal Revenue Code was undertaken in 1954. LIFO provides a tax-saving device for businesses who use it, by deferring the payment of taxes to future periods.

Assume that Conn's has merchandise available for sale of $25,000,000. When they count their inventory and value it at $7,000,000 using FIFO and at $5,000,000 using LIFO, how does this affect their gross profit under each method? Which method provides the LOWER gross profit?

EX-2. [www.audiexchange.com/] One method of inventory accounting discussed in the chapter is that of "specific identification." Specific identification is usually employed in companies that have a large amount of inventory, both in terms of dollars and in terms of numbers of units. An automobile dealership lends itself to specific identification. The number used to track the inventory from purchase through point of sale is the car's serial number. It is unique to each car. Pay a visit to your local shopping mall. What other types of businesses do you notice that could easily employ specific identification for inventory accounting?

Continuing Problem

Eldorado Computer Center

The Eldorado Computer Center had 300 pieces of merchandise inventory as of March 31, 20XX. The inventory was purchased with prices as follows:

Lot	Price Each Piece	Number of Pieces	Total Cost
First lot	$1.00	100	$100
Second lot	$1.75	100	$175
Third lot	$2.00	80	$160
Fourth lot	$2.50	100	$250
Fifth lot	$1.65	100	$165

Lot numbers represent oldest to newest.

Assignment

(See page 64 in the *Study Guide and Working Papers*.)

Using the FIFO, LIFO, and weighted-average methods, calculate the dollar value of the Eldorado Computer Center's ending inventory.

SUBWAY Case

HOW NOT TO SAY "OOPS, WE'RE OUT OF THAT!"

- Subway uses approximately 60 acres of lettuce a day—the equivalent of more than 17 football fields of lettuce.
- If you take all the cheese that is produced for Subway restaurants in a year and place each slice end to end, they will reach halfway to the moon.
- The manufacturing of Subway cookie dough requires 14.4 million eggs a year and the service of 46,602 busy hens.

With his sales climbing higher and higher, Stan Hernandez does his part to layer football fields with lettuce, send cheese ropes to the moon, and ensure the full employment of 46,602 hens. Yet, just how do Stan and his fellow Subway franchisees manage the flow of so many perishable goods in and out of their restaurants every day? By physically counting the goods.

"Not again," Wanda moaned, when Rashid asked her to begin taking inventory of the stockroom. "We did that last week."

"You bet," countered Rashid, "and we do it every week, as you remember."

"But my sister works at Wal-Mart and they only take inventory once a year."

Stan couldn't help overhearing their conversation as he sat crunching numbers at his back office computer and came out from behind his desk.

"Wanda, as I explained to you during training," Stan said patiently, "Subway requires all of its restaurants to do a physical count of their inventory once a week. We're in a very different business than Wal-Mart. We have to make sure that we have enough cheese, lettuce, bread dough, chicken, tuna, tomatoes . . . you name it, but not too much or it will spoil. And I sure don't want to run out of our special sauce for these new sweet onion chicken teriyaki sandwiches."

"It seems like every other sandwich I make is a sweet onion chicken teriyaki," said Wanda. "It's my favorite, too, so I sure don't want us to run out of it." She got out her clipboard of inventory report forms and immediately began taking stock.

The need to keep a steady supply of goods, such as its Teriyaki sandwich sauce, on hand is just one of the reasons that Subway requires its franchisees to take a physical inventory every week. Physically counting the goods also serves as a control mechanism to prevent or spot employee theft and to prevent restaurant owners from under-reporting sales and, hence, paying fewer royalties to Subway.

In terms of physical flow, perishable inventory must be FIFO; the first inventory in is the first used, so that nothing is allowed to get stale or spoiled. If a Subway restaurant owner uses the FIFO method for accounting, the cost follows the physical flow. Although every Subway shop owner uses the FIFO method for physical flow, not every owner chooses this method of accounting. Some prefer LIFO for financial accounting, because, with this method, the cost of goods sold is matched to current selling prices. In a time of inflation, when prices rise quickly, LIFO saves taxes because it lowers net income.

Subway currently uses a periodic inventory system. Perhaps, with widespread use of the POS cash registers, Subway will create a perpetual inventory system one day. However, Wanda, Rashid, Ellen, and their fellow sandwich artists and Subway managers will still do a weekly physical count of inventory because spoilage, shrinkage, and theft are always possible.

Discussion Questions

1. Learning Unit 15-4 discusses the retail inventory method. Why does Subway insist on a physical count?

2. The different benefits LIFO and FIFO offer Stan are discussed above. Why might Stan choose a weighted-average method of accounting for inventory costs?

3. The price of tomatoes, lettuce, peppers, and onions are subject to changes, depending on growing conditions in Florida, California, Mexico, and other parts of the United States and the world. What effect might this changeability have on the method of financial accounting a Subway restaurant owner chooses?

PERPETUAL INVENTORY SYSTEM

Before starting on this assignment, read and complete the tasks discussed in Parts A, B, and F of the Computerized Accounting Appendix at the back of this book and complete the Computerized Accounting Application assignments for Chapter 3, Chapter 4, Valdez Realty Mini Practice Set (Chapter 5), Pete's Market Mini Practice Set (Chapter 8), Chapter 10, and The Corner Dress Shop Mini Practice Set (Chapter 13).

One of the most powerful features of a computerized accounting system is its ability to maintain perpetual inventory records easily and accurately. In the prior Computer Workshops this feature was demonstrated as you recorded purchases and sales of inventory. Peachtree Complete Accounting has the ability to maintain perpetual inventory records through its Inventory module. Peachtree Complete Accounting can use FIFO, LIFO, or the weighted-average method as its inventory cost flow assumption. While a default assumption can be set, one can be designated for each inventory item individually.

In this Computer Workshop you will be working with the data files for a company called The Paint Place. The Paint Place uses the Sales/Invoicing, Receipts, Purchases, Payments and Inventory modules of Peachtree Complete Accounting to maintain its accounting and perpetual inventory records. The Paint Place extends terms of 2/10, n/30 to all of its credit customers. The inventory items currently stocked by The Paint Place appear below:

Inventory List

The Paint Place Inventory Synopsis 3/1/04

No.	Description	Unit	Sell	Quantity	Cost	Value	Margin (%)
1	Latex Flat	Gallon	16.95	642	7.47	4,795.74	55.93
2	Latex Semi-gloss	Gallon	16.95	1,066	7.47	7,963.02	55.93
3	Latex High-gloss	Gallon	16.95	600	7.47	4,482.00	55.93
4	Oil High-gloss	Gallon	17.95	801	8.97	7,184.97	50.03
5	Oil Semi-gloss	Gallon	17.95	502	8.97	4,502.94	50.03
						28,928.67	

Open the Company Data Files

1. Click on the Start button. Point to Programs; point to the Peachtree folder and select Peachtree Complete Accounting. Your desktop may have the Peachtree icon allowing for a quicker entrance into the program.
2. Follow the "Open a File" instructions in Part A of the Computerized Accounting Appendix at the back of this book to open **The Paint Place.**

Add Your Name to the Company Name

3. Click on the **Maintain** menu option. Then select **Company Information.** The program will respond by bringing up a dialogue box allowing the user to edit/add information about the company. In the **Company Name** entry field at the end of **The Paint Place,** add a dash and your name "**-Student Name**" to the end of the company name. Click on the OK button to return to the Menu Window.

Adding or Editing Inventory Items

4. Peachtree Complete Accounting allows the user to quickly, and easily add new inventory items to the Inventory module. This is accomplished by selecting **Inventory Items** from the **Maintain** menu. From this window, we can also obtain and edit infor-

mation about items currently in our inventory. To illustrate how easily inventory items can be added, let's add a new product to **The Paint Place's** inventory module.

- Select **Inventory Items** from the **Maintain** menu.
- In the **Item ID** field, type "006" and hit TAB.
- In the **Description** field, type in "Oil Flat" and hit TAB.
- We are now in a field where we can change the type of inventory item this is. Since this will be a regular stocked item, we can accept the default of Stock Item by hitting TAB again.
- We are now in a field where we can select and then enter a longer description of this item that will appear on sales and/or purchase invoices when we select it. Since we do not have a longer description, we can TAB until we reach the **Sales Price #1** field.
- We will sell this item normally for $16.95 so enter this amount.
- Peachtree has the capability of storing multiple prices for an item. This feature can be activated by clicking on the arrow to the right of the **Sales Price #1** field. Go ahead and click on this arrow. A table is presented which allows us to enter up to 5 different selling prices. Different customers can be assigned to different price levels in this manner. Since we will have only one price, we can **Cancel** the Multiple Pricing Level box.
- TAB until you reach **Cost Method**. Here is where we can select the cost assumption to use with this item. Using the pull down menu, you can select FIFO, LIFO or Average. We will select "Average". TAB to Unit/Measure field.
- Since the paint is sold in 1-gallon cans, type in "Gallon" in this field.
- Peachtree has used default information to select the GL accounts needed for an inventory transaction. Unless there is some need to change these, we will accept the defaults. In fact, we will accept Peachtree's default information on the rest of the accounts in this window. We will also not use the **Custom Fields** or **History** tabs in this window. Your entry should look like this:

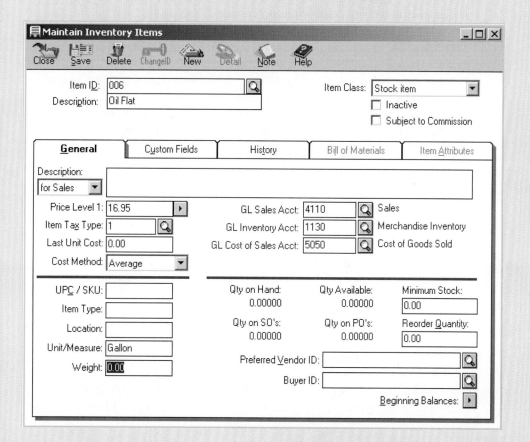

- Clicking on **Save** will place this item in our inventory module.
- We can view and edit information about items in our inventory from this window as well. We can use the magnifying glass next to the **Item ID** field to select any item from our inventory by double clicking on it. Once it is in the Maintain Inventory Items box, we can click on and change information as needed.

Record Transactions

5. Using the procedures learned in Chapter 10 (feel free to refer back to that chapter if you need to review a procedure), record the following transactions. Accept defaults for any fields for which you are not given information. Remember to use the Plain Invoice format for sales invoices and to insert the invoice number during the printing process for all print activities:

2004

Mar. 1   Sold 5 gallons of Oil High-gloss (Item #4) at $17.95 per gallon to Elaine Anderson on account, invoice #5469, $89.75, terms 2/10, n/30.

2   Received invoice #6892 from Wholesale Paints in the amount of $1,504 for the purchase of 200 gallons of Latex High-gloss (Item #3) at $7.52 per gallon (don't forget to change the **Unit Price**), terms 2/10, n/30.

3   Received invoice #CC675 from the Painter's Supply in the amount of $906 for the purchase of 100 gallons of Oil High-gloss (Item #4) at 9.06 per gallon (don't forget to change the **Unit Price**), terms 2/10, n/30.

4   Sold 5 gallons of Oil High-gloss paint (Item #4) at $17.95 per gallon to Jake Kerns on account, invoice #5470, $89.75, terms 2/10, n/30.

6   Received check #8723 from Wes Young in the amount of $3,225.13 in payment of invoice #5468 ($3,290.95), dated February 28, less 2 percent discount ($65.82). Receipt #501.

7   Issued check #2345 to Vantage Tints in the amount of $1,082.84 in payment of invoice #5658 ($1,116.33), dated February 28, less 3 percent discount ($33.49). Again, enter the discount amount in the discount field next to the invoice in the Payments window.

14   Sold 10 gallons of Latex Semi-gloss (Item #2) at $16.95 per gallon to Elaine Anderson on account, $169.50, invoice #5471, terms 2/10, n/30.

16   Received invoice #6943 from Wholesale Paints in the amount of $1,134 for the purchase of 150 gallons of Latex Semi-gloss (Item #2) at 7.56 per gallon (don't forget to change the **Unit Price**), terms 2/10, n/30.

19   Received invoice #CC691 from Painter's Supply in the amount of $1,618.75 for the purchase of 175 gallons of Oil Semi-gloss (Item #5) at 9.25 per gallon (don't forget to change the **Unit Price**), terms 2/10, n/30.

21   Sold 10 gallons of Latex Semi-gloss (Item #2) at $16.95 per gallon to Jake Kerns on account, $169.50, invoice #5472, terms 2/10, n/30.

24   Sold 25 gallons of Oil Semi-gloss paint (Item #5) at $17.95 per gallon to Elaine Anderson on account, $448.75, invoice #5473, terms 2/10, n/30.

25   Received invoice #CC787 from Painter's Supply in the amount of $465 for the purchase of 50 gallons of Oil Semi-gloss (Item #5) at 9.30 per gallon (don't forget to change the **Unit Price**), terms 2/10, n/30.

31   Sold 25 gallons of Oil Semi-gloss (Item #5) at $17.95 per gallon to Jake Kerns on account, $448.75, invoice #5474, terms 2/10, n/30.

How to Display an Inventory Activity Detail Report

6. You may wish to see how active the items in your inventory have been. Peachtree has a Unit Activity Report which will summarize the units bought for any selected period. Select **Inventory** from the **Reports** menu. Select Inventory Unit Activity Report. Accept all defaults. Your screen will look like that at top of p. 607.

Inventory Valuation

7. An important inventory report is the Inventory Valuation Report. From the same report screen, select Inventory Valuation report and accept all defaults. Your screen will look like that shown in the middle of p. 607.

The Paint Place-Student Name
Inventory Unit Activity Report
For the Period From Mar 1, 2004 to Mar 31, 2004
Filter Criteria includes: 1) Stock/Assembly. Report order is by ID. Report is printed with Truncated Long Descriptions.

Item ID Item Description Item Class	Beg Qty	Units Sold	Units Purc	Adjust Qty	Assembly Qty	Qty on Hand
001 Latex Flat Stock item	642.00					642.00
002 Latex Semi-Gloss Stock item	1066.00	20.00	150.00			1196.00
003 Latex High-Gloss Stock item	600.00		200.00			800.00
004 Oil High-Gloss Stock item	801.00	10.00	100.00			891.00
005 Oil Semi-Gloss Stock item	502.00	50.00	225.00			677.00
006 Oil Flat Stock item						
		80.00	675.00			

The Paint Place-Student Name
Inventory Valuation Report
As of Mar 31, 2004
Filter Criteria includes: 1) Stock/Assembly. Report order is by ID. Report is printed with Truncated Long Descriptions.

Item ID Item Class	Item Description	Unit	Cost Met	Qty on Hand	Item Value	Avg Cost	% of Inv Value
001 Stock item	Latex Flat	Gallon	Average	642.00	4,795.74	7.47	14.16
002 Stock item	Latex Semi-Gloss	Gallon	Average	1196.00	8,947.51	7.48	26.42
003 Stock item	Latex High-Gloss	Gallon	Average	800.00	5,986.00	7.48	17.68
004 Stock item	Oil High-Gloss	Gallon	Average	891.00	8,001.22	8.98	23.63
005 Stock item	Oil Semi-Gloss	Gallon	Average	677.00	6,134.11	9.06	18.11
006 Stock item	Oil Flat	Gallon	Average				
					33,864.58		100.00

8. As you can see from the report menu, there are numerous other reports Peachtree can utilize. These are outside the scope of this class.

9. Print the following reports accepting all defaults:

   a. General Ledger Trial Balance
   b. Aged Receivables
   c. Aged Payables
   d. Income Statement
   e. Balance Sheet

Print Reports

10. Click on the File menu; then click on Exit to end the current work session and return to your Windows desktop.

Exit from the Program

CHAPTER 16

Accounting for Property, Plant, Equipment, and Intangible Assets

You and your friend Paul were discussing the prices of new automobiles the other day after class. You learned that Paul's father travels extensively by car in his business. Paul told you that his dad wears out a car in about 18 months.

"My dad just bought a new Buick," Paul told you. "My dad needs a new car for his business, but it costs him a lot of money every time he buys one. He drives the car off the lot and it's immediately worth $3,000 less than its sticker price." You look at Paul, a little puzzled. "The new car is suddenly a used car once it's driven off the car lot. I guess you can say the loss in value is due to depreciation," Paul replies.

Cars, trucks, buildings, equipment, and other long-term assets that are used in a business for more than one year or operating cycle lose value over time. To account for the loss in the value of such assets as an expense of the business, the assets are depreciated. As we learned in Chapter 4, depreciation spreads the cost of an asset over the periods in which it is used in a business.

In this chapter we will look at how a business depreciates its property, plant, and equipment. We will learn how to calculate the cost of an asset, apply one of four depreciation methods to its cost, and how to calculate depreciation for tax purposes. We will also look at the difference between capital and revenue expenditures, the concept of amortization, and preparing journal entries for retiring, selling, or exchanging assets. After completing this chapter, you will better understand how to correctly account for and depreciate long-term assets, whether they are considered "new" or "used."

Learning Objectives

- Calculating the cost of an asset. (p. 610)

- Calculating depreciation using one of four methods: straight line, declining balance, units of production, and sum of the years' digits. (p. 612)

- Calculating depreciation for tax purposes using the Modified Accelerated Cost Recovery System. (p. 616)

- Explaining the difference between capital expenditures and revenue expenditures. (p. 620)

- Journalizing entries for discarding, selling, or exchanging plant assets. (p. 623)

- Explaining amortization and how it applies to intangible assets. (p. 628)

In Chapter 12 we classified assets as either current or plant and equipment. Current assets are those that are used up in a company's operations or converted into cash within one year or one accounting cycle, whichever is longer. Long-term assets, such as plant and equipment, provide benefits to a company for more than one year or one accounting cycle. Types of long-term assets include property (such as land), plant (such as buildings), and equipment (such as trucks and tools). Another classification of assets is called intangible assets. These assets are rights owned by a business that do not involve a *physical* object. Examples are patents or franchises. Intangible assets are also considered long-term assets.

In this chapter we look at how to calculate a long-term asset's overall cost and its depreciation (depreciation being the allocation of the cost of the asset over its lifetime). We also show how to record expenditures involved in improving or repairing an asset and how to account for the disposal of these assets.

Learning Unit 16-1　Cost of Property, Plant, and Equipment

The cost of property, plant, and equipment is not just the price one pays to buy it. One must also include the cost involved in getting it into position and in condition for use in the company. Thus, the cost of a machine includes freight, assembly, and all other costs that are needed to get the machine up and ready to run.

For example, Smith ordered a machine with a list price of $20,000 with terms of 3/10, n/30. There was a freight charge of $1,500 to cover transportation to the railroad station. Smith had to pay $250 to transport the machine from the railroad station to corporate headquarters. Total costs of assembling and installation amounted to $700. In addition, Smith purchased a special concrete foundation for $900 to keep the machine from tilting when operational. The life of the machine is expected to be 15 years.

Note that cash discount is deducted in arriving at total cost of machine. If sales tax were involved, it too would be added to the cost of the asset.

How Smith Calculates Cost of Machine

List price	$20,000
Less: Cash discount (.03 × $20,000)	600
Net purchase price	19,400
Freight	1,500
Transportation from railroad station	250
Assembly and installation	700
Special foundation	900
Total cost of machine	$22,750

Entries to record freight, assembly, installation, and so forth would be made as a debit to the Machinery account and as a credit to Cash.

Cost of machine will be matched with revenue.

The $22,750 cost of the asset will be spread over the years the machine helps Smith produce revenue. This example is one of the matching principle. Notice, however, that all these additional costs were reasonable and necessary to get the machine *ready for use.* If the buyer causes negligence, illegal acts, or gross inefficiencies to occur, these acts would be charged to an expense and not to the cost of the asset.

Let's look now at how to record the cost of land.

LAND AND LAND IMPROVEMENTS

When land (which has unlimited useful life) is purchased, there are usually many incidental costs that are considered part of the *cost* of the land. These costs include surveying, commissions to attorneys and real estate brokers, title searches, grading, draining, and clearing the property. If there is a special one-time assessment made for paving a street or installing sewers, it should be charged to cost of land, because it adds "permanent value" to the land.

> Land does not depreciate, because it has an unlimited life.

Now let's look at some items related to land that will not be added to cost of land. Land Improvements is an asset account that records improvements to land that have a *limited* useful life. Some examples are driveways, fences, shrubbery, paving of parking lots, and sprinkler systems. These improvements are subject to depreciation, and thus we need an account that is kept separate from the Land account, which does *not* depreciate.

BUILDINGS

The cost of buying a building would include the purchase price and all the cost of repairs and other expenses to get the building *ready for use*. For construction of a new building, the cost would include all reasonable and necessary payments for labor, insurance, building permits, architect's fees, legal fees, and so on to get the building ready for use.

If a building and land are purchased for one lump-sum payment, the cost must be separated (allocated) for each, because land will not depreciate, but buildings will.

Learning Unit 16-1 Review

AT THIS POINT you should be able to

- Explain how to classify property, plant, and equipment. (p. 610)
- Calculate the cost of an asset. (p. 610)
- Explain the difference between land and land improvements. (p. 611)

SELF-REVIEW QUIZ 16-1

(The forms you need are on page 65 of the *Study Guide and Working Papers*.)
Respond true or false to the following:

1. Land does not depreciate.
2. Total cost of acquiring an asset cannot include cost of freight.
3. Land improvements are not subject to depreciation.
4. A cash discount is added to list price.
5. Sales tax is added to cost of asset.

SOLUTIONS TO SELF-REVIEW QUIZ 16-1

1. True   2. False   3. False   4. False   5. True

Accounting in the Reel World

Cocooning and Accounting

In times of economic and political uncertainty, not only do people tend to invest in real estate but they also tend to spend more time "cocooning"—giving way to the impulse to stay inside when the going outside gets too tough.

Home Depot, the nation's largest home improvement chain, is a major beneficiary of this trend. With over 400 stores across the country, the company has risen to the top by offering a huge assortment of home improvement products, competitive prices, and superior customer service. Yet, when it comes to expanding the business, Home Depot can't simply open a new store every time housing starts to go up. It takes millions to build a store and stock it with products, so the decision as to where and when to build a new unit is complicated. As you watch the Home Depot on-location video segment on your DVD—or as you stroll through the wide aisles of Home Depot looking for plaster and dry wall—think about the company's physical assets. Then answer the questions below.

1. When Home Depot constructs a new store, what are some of the property, plant, and equipment costs for which they have to account?

2. Suppose that Home Depot purchases an existing building and land in one lump-sum payment. Are the costs handled separately or together? Explain your answer.

3. As the economy worsens, chains like Home Depot often cut back and close down stores. If Home Depot sells a store building as well as the physical assets within it, how do they see whether this sale results in a gain or loss? If there is a gain on the sale of one of Home Depot's plant assets, how is it categorized on the income statement?

Learning Unit 16-2   Depreciation Methods

Now that you know which long-term assets are depreciable, let's look at different methods for computing depreciation. If you want to check any of the concepts of depreciation we discussed in Chapter 4, take a moment to refer back to page 124.

When a company calculates its periodic depreciation expense, different methods will produce significantly different results. Thus, the method of depreciation chosen will affect the net income for current as well as future periods as well as the book value (cost of asset less accumulated depreciation) of the asset on the balance sheet.

Let's assume that Melvin Company purchased a truck on January 1, 20XX, for $20,000, with a residual value (salvage value) of $2,000 and an estimated life of five years. The following are the four common depreciation methods that Melvin Company could use:

> Think of residual value as trade-in value at the end of estimated life.

1. Straight-line method.
2. Units-of-production method.
3. Double declining-balance method.
4. Sum-of-the-years'-digits method (an optional section).

STRAIGHT-LINE METHOD

The straight-line method is simple to use, because it allocates the cost of the asset (less residual value) evenly over its estimated useful life. (At the time an asset is acquired, an estimate is made of its usefulness or useful life in terms of number of years it would last, amount of output expected, and so forth.) Let's look at how Melvin Company calculates its depreciation expense for each of the estimated five years of usefulness using the straight-line method. Take a moment to read the key points in the parentheses below the accompanying table.

The formula is

$$\frac{\text{Cost} - \text{Residual Value}}{\text{Service Useful Life in Years}} = \frac{\$20,000 - \$2,000}{5} = \$3,600$$

End of Year	Cost of Delivery Truck	Yearly* Depreciation Expense	Accumulated Depreciation, End of Year	Book Value, End of Year (Cost − Accum. Dep.)
1	$20,000	$3,600	$ 3,600	$16,400
2	20,000	3,600	7,200	12,800
3	20,000	3,600	10,800	9,200
4	20,000	3,600	14,400	5,600
5	20,000	3,600	18,000	2,000
	↑	↑	↑	↑
	(Cost of machine doesn't change.)	(Note that depreciation expense is the same each year.)	(Accumulated depreciation increases by $3,600 each year.)	(Book value each year is lowered by $3,600 until residual value of $2,000 is reached.)

*The depreciation rate is 100% ÷ 5 years = 20%. The 20% is then multiplied times the cost minus the residual value.

UNITS-OF-PRODUCTION METHOD

With the units-of-production method it is assumed that *passage of time* does not determine the amount of depreciation taken. Depreciation expense is based on *use*, be it total estimated miles, tons hauled, or estimated units of production (for example, the number of shoes a machine could produce in its expected useful life). The accompanying table shows the calculations that Melvin Company makes for its truck using the units-of-production method (note that for this example the truck is assumed to have an estimated life of 90,000 miles).

> Depreciation expense is directly related to use, not to passage of time.

The formula is

$$\frac{\text{Cost} - \text{Residual Value}}{\text{Estimated Units of Production}} = \frac{\$20,000 - \$2,000}{90,000 \text{ Miles}} = \$.20 \text{ per Mile}$$

$$(\$.20) \times (\text{Number of Miles Driven}) = \text{Depreciation Expense for Period}$$

End of Year	Cost of Delivery Truck	Miles Driven in Year	Yearly Depreciation, Expense	Accumulated Depreciation, End of Year	Book Value, End of Year (Cost − Accum. Dep.)
1	$20,000	30,000	$6,000	$ 6,000	$14,000
2	20,000	21,000	4,200	10,200	9,800
3	20,000	15,000	3,000	13,200	6,800
4	20,000	5,000	1,000	14,200	5,800
5	20,000	19,000	3,800	18,000	2,000
		↑	↑		↑
		(After 5 years, truck has been driven 90,000 miles.)	(Depreciation expense is directly related to number of miles driven.)		(Residual value of $2,000 is reached.)

DOUBLE DECLINING-BALANCE METHOD

The double declining-balance method is an accelerated method in which a larger depreciation expense is taken in earlier years and smaller amounts in later years. For this reason it is called an accelerated depreciation method. This method depreciates at twice the straight-line rate, which is why it is called the *double* declining-balance method.

A key point in this method is that *residual value* is *not* deducted from cost in the calculations, although the asset cannot be depreciated below its residual value. To calculate depreciation, take the following steps:

1. Calculate the straight-line rate and double it:

$$\frac{100\%}{\text{Useful Life}} \times 2$$

2. At the *end of each year* multiply the rate times the book value of the asset at the beginning of the year.

Let's look at how Melvin Company calculates the depreciation on its truck using this method. Be sure to note the $592 in year 5 of depreciation expense. We could not take more than the $592 or we would have depreciated the asset below the residual value.

Note that the rate of .40 is not changed (20% × 2.)

End of Year	Cost	Accumulated Depreciation, Beg. of Year	Book Value Beg. of Year (Cost − Acc. Dep.)	Dep. Exp. (Book Value Beg. of Year × Rate)	Accumulated Depreciation, End of Year	Book Value, End of Year (Cost − Acc. Dep.)
1	$20,000		$20,000	$8,000 ($20,000 × .40)	$ 8,000	$12,000 (20,000 − 8,000)
2	20,000	$ 8,000	12,000	4,800 (12,000 × .40)	12,800 (8,000 + 4,800)	7,200
3	20,000	12,800	7,200	2,880 (7,200 × .40)	15,680	4,320
4	20,000	15,680	4,320	1,728 (4,320 × .40)	17,408	2,592
5	20,000	17,408	2,592	592	18,000	2,000
	↑ (Original cost remains the same.)			↑ (Depreciation is limited to $592, because the asset cannot depreciate below the residual value.)		↑ (The book value now equals the residual value.)

OPTIONAL SECTION: SUM-OF-THE-YEARS'-DIGITS METHOD

The sum-of-the-years'-digits method places more depreciation expense in the early years rather than in the later years to match revenue and expenses better, because an asset's productivity may be reduced in later years. To use it, you multiply cost minus residual times a certain fraction. This fraction is made up of the following:

1. The *denominator.* The denominator is based on how many years the asset is likely to last (say five). You then add the sum of the digits of five years $(1 + 2 + 3 + 4 + 5)$, which equals 15; 15 is the denominator. [There is also a formula to use for the denominator: $N(N + 1)/2$, where N stands for number of years of useful life (in our case, five years). In our case, the formula would give $5(5 + 1)/2 = 15$.]
2. The *numerator.* The years in reverse order are the numerator (in our case, 5, 4, 3, 2, 1).

Thus, in year 1 the fraction would be $\frac{5}{15}$; in year 2, $\frac{4}{15}$; in year 3, $\frac{3}{15}$; in year 4, $\frac{2}{15}$; in year 5, $\frac{1}{15}$. In each year you would multiply this fraction times cost minus residual to find the depreciation expense. This process is shown in the following table.

End of Year	$\begin{pmatrix}\text{Cost} \\ \text{Minus} \\ \text{Residual}\end{pmatrix} \times \begin{pmatrix}\text{Fraction} \\ \text{for Year}\end{pmatrix} =$		Yearly Depreciation Expense	Accumulated Depreciation, End of Year	Book Value, End of Year (Cost − Accum. Dep.)
1	$18,000 ×	$\frac{5}{15}$	= $6,000	$ 6,000	$14,000 ($20,000 − $6,000)
	(20,000 − 2,000)				
2	18,000 ×	$\frac{4}{15}$	= 4,800	10,800	9,200
3	18,000 ×	$\frac{3}{15}$	= 3,800	14,400	5,600
4	18,000 ×	$\frac{2}{15}$	= 2,400	16,800	3,200
5	18,000 ×	$\frac{1}{15}$	= 1,200	18,000	2,000
	↑ (Fraction for year is multiplied times cost minus residual.)		↑ (Depreciation expense in first year is highest.)	↑ (Each year depreciation accumulates by a smaller amount.)	↑ (Book value goes down each year until residual is reached.)

Take a moment to make sure you see how the figures for these calculations are arrived at before moving on to the next method.

Now let's look at how Melvin Company could handle depreciation calculations for partial years (if it bought a truck on May 4).

DEPRECIATION FOR PARTIAL YEARS

When depreciating for partial years, we assume that for any asset purchased before the 15th of the month, depreciation is calculated for a full month. After the 15th of the month, the depreciation is disregarded for the month.

Straight-Line Method

For Melvin Company, if the truck was purchased on May 4, depreciation expense would be calculated as follows:

$$\frac{\$20,000 - \$2,000}{5 \text{ Years}} \times \frac{8}{12} = \$2,400$$

We use 8 because the truck was bought on May 4. Do not count the first four months of the year in the calculation of depreciation. The following year the full yearly depreciation would be taken.

Units-of-Production Method

The units-of-production method would not be affected, because depreciation is based on usage, not passage of time.

Double Declining-Balance Method

Because Melvin has the benefit of the truck for eight months, his depreciation on year 1 would be

$$\left(\$20,000 \times .40\right) \times \frac{8}{12}$$

In year 2 and in future years the annual rate of 40% is multiplied times the *current* book value.

Sum-of-the-Years'-Digits Method (Optional Section)

If the truck is bought on May 4, Melvin would receive benefits of eight months of $4,000 $\left(\$18,000 \times \frac{5}{15}\right) \times \frac{8}{12}$. In the following year, Melvin would assume benefits of the last four months of the first year and the first eight months of the second year. Let's look at the calculation for year 2:

$$\text{Year 2} = \left(\$18,000 \times \frac{5}{15}\right) \times \frac{4}{12} + \left(\$18,000 \times \frac{4}{15}\right) \times \frac{8}{12}$$

Depreciation completed from old year first

DEPRECIATION FOR TAX PURPOSES: MODIFIED ACCELERATED COST RECOVERY SYSTEM (MACRS), INCLUDING THE TAX ACT OF 1989

The 1986 tax act generally overhauled the depreciation setup of property placed in service after December 31, 1986. This Modified Accelerated Cost Recovery System is known as MACRS.* Previous methods we have discussed have been for

---

*MACRS has been renamed the General Depreciation System (GDS). The one-half year depreciation convention is not covered. See the latest IRS publication.

Original calculation is on p. 613.

Original calculation on p. 614.

Original calculation on p. 615.

financial reporting, not for tax purposes. This tax law requires a business to depreciate assets placed in service after December 31, 1986. To do so, two factors must be known:

1. Recovery classification.
2. MACRS depreciation rates.

Look for a moment at Figure 16-1 on page 618.

According to the 1986 act, classes 3, 5, 7, and 10 use 200% declining balance, switching to straight line, whereas classes 15 and 20 use 150% declining balance, switching to straight line. Both residential and nonresidential real property must use straight line. Note that the recovery period is $27\frac{1}{2}$ years for residential property and $31\frac{1}{2}$ years for nonresidential property.

Let's use Table 16-1 to calculate depreciation on the purchase of a nonluxury car for $5,000 on March 19, 1990.

When we use Table 16-1, we do not have to decide which year we should switch from the declining-balance to the straight-line method.

> Note that the auto is now a five-year class.

TABLE 16-1 Annual Recovery (Percent of Original Depreciable Basis)

Recovery Year	3-Year Class (200% Depreciable Basis)	5-Year Class (200% Depreciable Basis)	7-Year Class (200% Depreciable Basis)	10-Year Class (200% Depreciable Basis)	15-Year Class (150% Depreciable Basis)	20-Year Class (150% Depreciable Basis)
1	33.00	20.00	14.28	10.00	5.00	3.75
2	45.00	32.00	24.49	18.00	9.50	7.22
3	15.00*	19.20	17.49	14.40	8.55	6.68
4	7.00	11.52*	12.49	11.52	7.69	6.18
5		11.52	8.93*	9.22	6.93	5.71
6		5.76	8.93	7.37	6.23	5.28
7			8.93	6.55*	5.90*	4.89
8			4.46	6.55	5.90	4.52
9				6.55	5.90	4.46*
10				6.55	5.90	4.46
11				3.29	5.90	4.46
12					5.90	4.46
13					5.90	4.46
14					5.90	4.46
15					5.90	4.46
16					3.00	4.46
17						

*Identifies when switch is made to the straight-line method.

Year	Depreciation
1	$.20 \times \$5,000 = \$1,000$
2	$.32 \times \$5,000 = 1,600$
3	$.1920 \times \$5,000 = 960$
4	$.1152 \times \$5,000 = 576$
5	$.1152 \times \$5,000 = 576$
6	$.0576 \times \$5,000 = 288$

THE TAX ACT OF 1989

In 1989 the Omnibus Budget Reconciliation Act was passed. One section of the act dealt with depreciation of cellular phones and similar equipment under MACRS. Because cellular phones are subject to personal use, the tax act now treats them as listed property. Thus, unless business use is greater than 50%, the straight-line method of depreciation is required.

The following classes use a 200% declining balance, switching to straight line:

- 3 year: Race horses more than 2 years old or any horse other than a race horse that is more than 12 years old at time placed into service; special tools of certain industries
- 5 year: Automobiles (not luxury); taxis; light general-purpose trucks, semiconductor manufacturing equipment; computer-based telephone central office switching equipment; qualified technological equipment; property used in connection with research and experimentation
- 7 year: Railroad track; single-purpose agricultural (pigpens) or horticultural structure; fixtures, equipment, and furniture
- 10 year: The 1986 law doesn't add any specific property under this class.

The following classes use a 150% declining balance, switching to straight line:

- 15 year: Municipal wastewater treatment plants; telephone distribution plants and comparable equipment used for two-way exchange of voice and data communications
- 20 year: Municipal sewers

The following classes use straight line:

- 27.5 year: Only residential rental property
- 31.5 year: Only nonresidential real property

Figure 16-1 Summary of Classes for the Tax Reform Act of 1986

Learning Unit 16-2 Review

AT THIS POINT you should be able to

- Explain and calculate the four methods of depreciation. (p. 612)
- Calculate depreciation for partial years. (p. 615)
- Explain and calculate depreciation for MACRS. (p. 616)

SELF-REVIEW QUIZ 16-2

(The forms you need are on pages 65–66 of the *Study Guide and Working Papers*.)

From the following facts complete depreciation schedules for the (a) straight-line, (b) units-of-production, (c) declining-balance, and (d) sum-of-the-years'-digits methods (optional).

Cost of equipment	$40,000
Residual value	7,000
Service life	5 years

Remember: Residual value is not subtracted in the declining-balance method, although the equipment cannot be depreciated below residual value.

Estimated units of output	20,000
Units produced in year 1:	8,000
2:	2,000
3:	5,000
4:	2,800
5:	2,200

SOLUTIONS TO SELF-REVIEW QUIZ 16-2

a.

End of Year	Cost of Equipment	Yearly Depreciation Expense	Accumulated Depreciation, End of Year	Book Value, End of Year (Cost − Acc. Dep.)
1	$40,000	$6,600	$ 6,600	$33,400 ($40,000 − $6,600)
2	40,000	6,600	13,200	26,800
3	40,000	6,600	19,800	20,200
4	40,000	6,600	26,400	13,600
5	40,000	6,600	33,000	7,000 ← Book value now equals residual value.

b.

End of Year	Cost of Equipment	Units of Output in Year	Yearly Depreciation Expense	Accumulated Depreciation, End of Year	Book Value, End of Year

$$\frac{\$40,000 - \$7,000}{20,000 \text{ units}} = \$1.65$$

End of Year	Cost of Equipment	Units of Output in Year	Yearly Depreciation Expense	Accumulated Depreciation, End of Year	Book Value, End of Year
1	$40,000	8,000	$13,200 (8,000 × $1.65)	$13,200	$26,800
2	40,000	2,000	3,300	16,500	23,500
3	40,000	5,000	8,250	24,750	15,250
4	40,000	2,800	4,620	29,370	10,630
5	40,000	2,200	3,630	33,000	7,000

c.

End of Year	Cost	Accumulated Depreciation, Beg. of Year	Book Value Beg. of Year (Cost − Acc. Dep.)	Dep. Exp. (B.V. Beg. of Year × Rate)	Acc. Dep., End of Year	Book Value, End of Year (Cost − Acc. Dep.)
1	$40,000	—	$40,000	$16,000 ($40,000 × .40)	$16,000	$24,000 ($40,000 − $16,000)
2	40,000	$16,000	24,000	9,600 ($24,000 × .40)	25,600	14,400 ($40,000 − $25,600)
3	40,000	25,600	14,400	5,760	31,360	8,640
4	40,000	31,360	8,640	1,640	33,000	7,000

Only $1,640 could be taken so that book value would not go below residual value.

Rate is 40%

$$\frac{100\%}{5 \text{ Years}} = \frac{1.00}{5}$$

$$= .20 = 20\%$$

$$2 \times 20\% = 40\%$$

d. (optional)

End of Year	Cost Less Residual × Rate = Yearly Depreciation Expense	Accumulated Depreciation, End of Year	Book Value, End of Year
1	$\$33,000 \times \dfrac{5}{15} = \$11,000$	$11,000	$29,000 ($40,000 − $11,000)
2	$\$33,000 \times \dfrac{4}{15} = 8,800$	$19,800	$20,200
3	$\$33,000 \times \dfrac{3}{15} = 6,600$	$26,400	$13,600
4	$\$33,000 \times \dfrac{2}{15} = 4,400$	$30,800	$ 9,200
5	$\$33,000 \times \dfrac{1}{15} = 2,200$	$33,000	$ 7,000

Learning Unit 16-3   Capital and Revenue Expenditures and Disposal of Plant Assets

Now that we have seen depreciation calculations, let's look at capital and revenue expenditures and the disposal of plant assets.

CAPITAL EXPENDITURES

Capital expenditures include the original cost of an asset as well as payments that improve on or enlarge existing assets. Capital expenditures may be broken down into three categories: additions or enlargements, extraordinary repairs, and betterments. The differences among these three categories are based on whether or not the change will add to the value of the asset, extend the life of the asset, or only improve its efficiency. For example, adding a new wing to a school building will increase the value of the asset, so it is categorized as an addition or enlargement. Overhauling an aircraft engine definitely extends the life of the asset, so it is categorized as an extraordinary repair. Adding a CB radio to a fleet of delivery trucks improves the efficiency of the asset but does not extend its life, so it is categorized as a betterment. These three categories are shown in the chart in Figure 16-2.

It may be a little difficult at first to see the difference between betterments and extraordinary repairs. Betterments do not extend the life of the asset; the cost of a betterment is debited to the asset account. Extraordinary repairs do extend the life of the asset. The result of the extraordinary repair is to cancel some of the past depreciation.

The following is an example of how to analyze and record an extraordinary repair to a machine that has a cost of $20,000, has no residual value, and has an estimated life of 10 years.

Additions or enlargements and betterments are charged to the asset account.

Machine		Accumulated Depreciation, Machine	
20,000			16,000 (after 8 years)

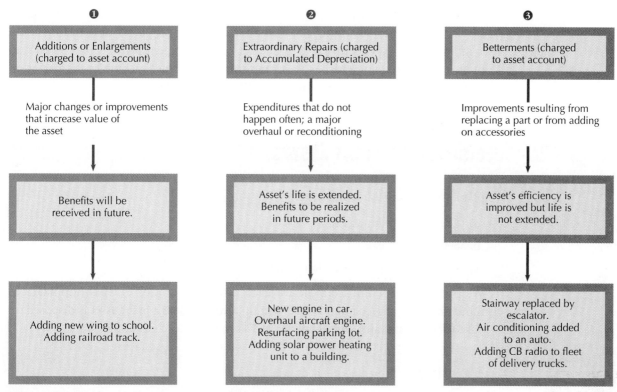

Figure 16-2 Three Categories of Capital Expenditures

Note that after eight years the book value of the machine is $4,000 ($20,000 − $16,000). On March 30, a major overhaul of the machine is completed for $3,000. It is believed that this overhaul will extend the machine's life by three years. Thus, the journal entry to record this extraordinary repair is as shown in Figure 16-3.

Mar.	30	Accumulated Depreciation, Machine	3 0 0 0 00	
		Cash		3 0 0 0 00
		To record extraordinary repair		

Figure 16-3
Overhaul Extends
Asset's Life

Because the machine's life is extended by three years, there are now five years of depreciation to be taken. The new annual depreciation of $1,400 (instead of $2,000) is calculated as follows:

Book value before extraordinary repair	**$4,000**
Extraordinary repair	3,000
New book value	**$7,000 ÷ 5 years = $1,400 per year**

If there were an estimated residual value, it would be subtracted from the new book value.

REVENUE EXPENDITURES

Another type of expenditure occurs after an asset has been acquired. *Revenue expenditures* are payments made for ordinary maintenance of an asset or unnecessary or unreasonable situations. These expenditures occur on a regular basis and are recorded as expenses. Examples include changing oil and greasing a car, replacing window panes, changing tires on a truck, repainting a car and adding a sun roof. When an expenditure is treated as a revenue expenditure, it is recorded on the income statement as an expense and thus reduces net income in the period in which it occurred. Now let's turn our attention to the disposal of certain plant assets.

DISPOSAL OF PLANT ASSETS

We now move on to the basic accounting procedures followed when disposing of plant assets in the following ways:

a. Discarding plant assets.

b. Selling plant assets.

c. Exchanging for similar plant assets.

We present a different example for each category (a, b, or c). It is important to remember that depreciation is recorded up until the date a plant asset is disposed of. Take time to compare journal entries to T accounts in each example.

A. Disposal by Discarding Plant Assets

A company discards a plant asset when it is no longer operational (for example, machinery or a truck that no longer works). That also means that no other company is willing to buy or exchange something for the asset.

Situation 1: No Gain or Loss. Boulder Company is disposing of a $7,000 truck with no residual value that has been fully depreciated (remember that it is possible to keep using a fully depreciated asset, but in this case the asset—the truck—is no longer in working order). Because the asset has been fully depreciated, there will be no need to bring any depreciation up-to-date before getting rid of it.

The journal entry shown in Figure 16-4 is made after disposing of the truck.

Figure 16-4
Disposing Fully
Depreciated Truck

Accumulated Depreciation, Truck	7 0 0 0 00	
Truck		7 0 0 0 00

Here is how the ledger for these accounts would look after posting:

Truck		Accumulated Depreciation, Truck	
7,000	7,000	7,000	7,000

Therefore, the truck and the accumulated depreciation associated with it are off the books. Note that there was no gain or loss here.

Situation 2: Loss on Disposal. Moore Company disposed of a partially depreciated truck. The truck, costing $6,000, was considered worthless (depreciation of $5,000 to date). Because nothing is received for this asset that has a book value of $1,000, the difference between the cost of the truck and the accumulated depreciation is a loss. The Loss on Disposal account is categorized as Other Expense on the income statement. Let's look at the journal entry for this loss on disposal (Fig. 16-5) and see how the ledger would look after posting.

Loss on Disposal of Plant Asset	1 0 0 0 00	
Accumulated Depreciation, Truck	5 0 0 0 00	
Truck		6 0 0 0 00

Figure 16-5
Loss on Disposal of Truck

Truck	Accumulated Depreciation, Truck	Loss on Disposal of Plant Asset
6,000	6,000	5,000	5,000	1,000	

Situation 3: Loss from Fire. Missan Company received a check for $500 from an insurance company, settling a claim on a machine costing $1,500 that was damaged by fire before the end of its useful life. There was a balance in Accumulated Depreciation of $900. Figure 16-6 shows the journal entry Missan Company records when it receives the $500 check:

Cash	5 0 0 00	
Loss from Fire	1 0 0 00	
Accumulated Depreciation, Machinery	9 0 0 00	
Machinery		1 5 0 0 00

Figure 16-6
Loss from Fire

There is a loss from the fire of $100; the book value of the machine was $600 ($1,500 − $900), and the amount received from the insurance company was $500.

Here is how the ledger would look after posting:

Machinery	Accumulated Depreciation, Machinery	Loss from Fire
1,500	1,500	900	900	100	

Now our attention turns to situations when assets could be sold rather than discarded.

B. Disposal by Selling Plant Assets

Situation 4: Gain on Sale. Mason Company sold a truck costing $7,000 for $1,500 cash. The balance in Accumulated Depreciation is $6,000.

To see whether this sale results in a gain or loss, Mason Company must calculate whether the amount of cash received is greater or less than the book value of the truck. If the amount received is greater than the book value, there is a gain. A gain on the sale of a plant asset is categorized as Other Income on the income statement. Let's look at the calculation:

Cost of truck	$7,000	Amount received	$1,500
Less accumulated depreciation	6,000	Less book value	1,000
Book value	$1,000	Gain on sale	$ 500

Because there is a gain on the sale, the journal entry in Figure 16-7 is made.

Cash	1 5 0 0 00	
Accumulated Depreciation, Truck	6 0 0 0 00	
Truck		7 0 0 0 00
Gain on Sale of Plant Asset		5 0 0 00

Figure 16-7
Gain on Sale of Truck

Here is what the ledger would look like after posting:

Truck		Accumulated Depreciation, Truck	
7,000	7,000	6,000	6,000

Gain on Sale of Plant Asset	
	500

Situation 5: Loss on Sale.   Let's assume that in the previous situation Mason Company receives only $900 cash for the truck.

Now let's look at the calculation Mason Company does to see whether there is a loss or gain:

Cost of truck	**$7,000**
Less accumulated depreciation	**− 6,000**
Book value	**1,000**
Amount received	**− 900**
Loss on sale	**$ 100**

When price is less than book value, there is a loss. Because Mason's truck has a book value of $1,000 and the cash received is $900, the end result is a loss of $100 on the sale of the plant asset. This entry is categorized as Other Expense on the income statement. Figure 16-8 shows the journal entry prepared by Mason to record this loss.

Figure 16-8
Loss on Sale of Truck

Cash		9 0 0 00	
Accumulated Depreciation, Truck		6 0 0 0 00	
Loss on Sale of Plant Asset		1 0 0 00	
Truck			7 0 0 0 00

Here is what the ledger would look like after posting:

Truck		Accumulated Depreciation, Truck		Loss on Sale of Plant Asset	
7,000	7,000	6,000	6,000	100	

The final category of disposal is exchanging a plant asset rather than discarding or selling.

C. Disposal by Exchanging for Similar Plant Assets

Situation 6: Loss on Exchange.   VTR Company trades its old machine costing $19,000 for a new one for a cash price of $22,000 less a trade-in allowance of $2,000. Accumulated Depreciation of the old machine has a balance of $16,000. A trade-in allowance is given when you are buying a new car, for example, and trade in your old one for a sum of money that is applied to the price of the new car. A loss on exchange will result if the book value of the old machine is greater than what is received for the trade-in allowance. Let's look at how VTR calculates its loss on this machine exchange.

Step 1:   Calculate the book value of the old machine:

Cost	$19,000
− Accumulated depreciation	16,000
Book value	$ 3,000

Step 2: Compare the book value of the old machine with the trade-in:

$3,000	Book value of old
2,000	Trade-in
$1,000	Loss

Because the book value of the old machine is $3,000 and VTR receives only a $2,000 trade-in, the result is a $1,000 loss. Figure 16-9 shows the journal entry prepared by VTR.

	Debit	Credit
Machinery	22 0 0 0 00	
Loss on Exchange of Machinery	1 0 0 0 00	
Accumulated Depreciation, Machinery	16 0 0 0 00	
Machinery		19 0 0 0 00
Cash		20 0 0 0 00

Figure 16-9
Loss on Exchange
of Machinery

The entry puts on the books the cost of the new machine as well as records the loss on the exchange and the removal of the old machine and the related accumulated depreciation. Note that cash is reduced by $20,000 (cash price less trade-in). Here is what the ledger would look like after posting:

Machinery (Old)		Accumulated Depreciation, Machinery	
19,000	19,000		16,000	16,000

Machinery (New)		Loss on Exchange of Machinery	
22,000		1,000	

Situation 7: Gain Is Absorbed into Cost of New Machine. The Accounting Principles Board has ruled that when a gain exists on an exchange of a similar asset it should not be recorded as a gain, but the new asset should be equal to the book value of the old asset plus cash given in the exchange. In other words, no account called Gain is used, *but the actual gain is absorbed into the cost of the new machine.* The reason behind this decision was that an exchange of similar assets is not the result of an earnings process. In this situation we assume that VTR (situation 6) will receive a $5,000 trade-in allowance (instead of the $2,000) for trading in an old machine for a new machine for a cash price of $22,000. VTR will complete the following steps to calculate the new cost of the machine (assuming a gain). Remember that a gain would be absorbed into the cost of the new machine for exchanges of similar assets.

1. Calculate the book value of the old machine.

2. Identify the cash paid (cash price less trade-in).

3. Calculate the value of the new machine as it will show up on the books. (This value is called the *cash basis* of the machine.) This step is done by adding Steps 1 and 2.

Let's now look at VTR's actual calculation of these steps.

Step 1: Calculate the book value of the old machine:

$$\begin{array}{r} \$19,000 \\ -\ 16,000 \\ \hline = \$3,000 \end{array}$$

Step 2:   Identify cash paid:

$17,000 ($22,000 − $5,000)

Step 3:   New cash basis (Step 1 + Step 2):

$20,000 ($3,000 + $17,000)

Note that the cash basis is $20,000, not $22,000 as stated as the original cost of the new equipment. Note also that the new machine shows up on the books at the value of the things that were given up for it: an old machine with a book value of $3,000 and cash of $17,000.

Now let's look at how VTR records this exchange on its books (Fig. 16-10).

Figure 16-10
Gain Absorbed into Cost
of New Machine

Machinery		20000 00	
Accumulated Depreciation, Machinery		16000 00	
Machinery			19000 00
Cash			17000 00

Note that there is no account that records the gain. The gain is absorbed into the cost of the new asset. Remember that a gain results in *less* depreciation in the future, because the cost of the machine has a value of $20,000, not $22,000. The ledger when posted would look as follows:

Machinery (Old)		Accumulated Depreciation, Machinery	
19,000	19,000	16,000	16,000

Machinery (New)	
20,000	

Income tax rules agree with accountants regarding nonrecognition of gains and absorbing them into the cost of the new asset (situation 7). The Internal Revenue Service also believes losses should not be recognized and thus should be absorbed into the cost of new assets.* Often two sets of records are kept. Situation 6 followed guidelines of the Accounting Principles Board. Situation 8 follows tax rules of the Internal Revenue Service. Compare the two.

Situation 8: Loss Is Absorbed in Cost of New Asset.   Let's assume that VTR receives only a $2,000 trade-in allowance instead of $5,000 (situation 7) when the old machine is traded in for the new machine for a cash price of $22,000. VTR calculates the cost basis of the new machine (assuming it uses the income tax method of absorbing losses into the cost of the new machine) as follows:

Cost of old machine	$19,000
− Accumulated depreciation	16,000
= Book value	3,000
+ Cash paid ($22,000 − $2,000)	20,000
= Cost basis of new machine	$23,000

---

*Accountants will do this only if the loss is considered to be immaterial.

This loss of $1,000 (VTR having received $1,000 less than the book value) is *added on* to the cost of the new machine, resulting in a cost basis of $23,000. VTR records the exchange in the journal as shown in Figure 16-11.

Machinery		23 00 0 00			
Accumulated Depreciation, Machinery		16 00 0 00			
Machinery				19 00 0 00	
Cash				20 00 0 00	

Figure 16-11
Loss Absorbed into Cost of Machine

Note that there is no Loss account. The loss has been absorbed into the cost of the equipment, the result being that more depreciation will be taken in future periods ($23,000 versus $22,000), because the cost of the new equipment is $1,000 higher.

Here is what the ledger would look like after posting:

Machinery (Old)			Accumulated Depreciation, Machinery	
19,000	19,000		16,000	16,000

Machinery (New)	
23,000	

Learning Unit 16-3 Review

AT THIS POINT you should be able to

- Compare and contrast capital and revenue expenditures. (p. 620)
- Prepare journal entries to record discarding, selling, or exchanging plant assets. (p. 622)
- Compare and contrast Internal Revenue procedures with those of the Financial Accounting Principles Board regarding gains and losses that result from exchanges of plant assets. (p. 625)

SELF-REVIEW QUIZ 16-3

(The forms you need are on page 66 of the *Study Guide and Working Papers.*)
Respond true or false to the following:

1. In selling a plant asset, a gain results if cash received is greater than the book value of the asset sold.

2. A loss on exchange of equipment can result if the book value of the old equipment is less than the trade-in allowance.

3. The Financial Accounting Principles Board does not recognize gains on exchange of similar assets.

4. Internal Revenue Service rules are consistent with the Financial Accounting Principles Board in recognizing losses when assets are exchanged.

5. When a loss is absorbed into the cost of an asset, it allows for more depreciation in future periods.

6. Revenue expenditures extend the useful life of an asset.

7. Putting an air conditioner in a truck is an example of a betterment.

SOLUTIONS TO SELF-REVIEW QUIZ 16-3

1. True　　**2.** False　　**3.** True　　**4.** False　　**5.** True　　**6.** False　　**7.** True

---

Learning Unit 16-4　　Natural Resources and Intangible Assets

There's another type of long-term asset, natural resources, that we haven't discussed yet. Natural resources consist of natural assets such as oil, coal, or timber. The acquisition of oil wells or timber is recorded at cost, and as the oil or timber or coal is extracted from the earth, the allocation of that cost occurs through a process known as depletion. Depletion is similar to the units-of-production method of depreciation, discussed earlier in the chapter, and is listed as an operating expense on the income statement.

Let's take the example of a coal deposit. If a coal deposit has 200,000 tons available and was purchased for $200,000, the depletion per ton is $1. Thus, if 91,000 tons were removed from the deposit in 20X1, the depletion charge that year would be recorded as shown in Figure 16-12.

Figure 16-12

Accumulated Depletion is a contra-asset on the balance sheet.

	20X1						
	Dec.	31	Depletion of Coal Deposit	91 0 0 0 00			
			Accumulated Depletion, Coal			91 0 0 0 00	

Coal Deposit
200,000 |
(on balance sheet)

Accumulated Depletion, Coal
| 91,000
(on balance sheet)

Depletion of Coal Deposit
91,000 |
(on income statement)

INTANGIBLE ASSETS

Intangible assets are long-lived assets that have no physical existence but do represent valuable legal rights and monetary relationships that benefit a company. (In fact, Prepaid Insurance, Notes, and Accounts Receivable are intangible, but they are classified as *current* assets.) We are looking at intangible assets classified in the *long-term* asset section. Examples include patents, copyrights, franchises, and goodwill. Intangible assets are recorded at cost on the balance sheet and usually have no contra-accounts.

The process of allocating the cost of an intangible asset over all the periods it provides benefits is called *amortization*. The expense incurred in acquiring these assets is **amortized**; that means it is written off over a fixed number of years. **Amortization expense** is an operating expense on the income statement.

Patents

A **patent** is an exclusive right to the owner to sell or produce his or her discovery or invention. Let's assume that on January 1, 20XX, a patent costing $100,000 is amortized over 10 years. The adjusting entry shown in Figure 16-13 is made.

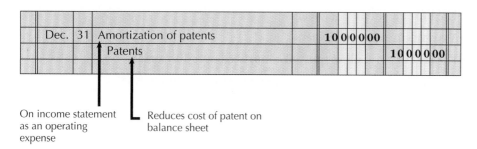

On income statement as an operating expense

Reduces cost of patent on balance sheet

> A patent is good for 20 years but is amortized for a shorter period.

Figure 16-13
Amortizing a Patent

Copyrights

Copyrights are exclusive rights granted to owners by the federal government to publish artistic, literary, or musical work. In the United States a copyright is granted for the life of the creator and for 50 years thereafter. The cost of the copyright is recorded as a cost and amortized over its expected useful life in an account called Amortization Expense, Copyrights.

Franchises

A **franchise** is the result of someone purchasing an exclusive privilege or right to sell a manufacturer's product or a service in a specifically defined geographical location. Holiday Inns, for example, are franchises. The cost of obtaining a franchise is amortized over its life or 40 years, whichever is shorter.

Goodwill

When all or part of a business is purchased, the difference between the price paid and the value of the identifiable assets is called **goodwill.** Goodwill occurs when the expected rate of future earnings is greater than the rate of earnings for the industry standard. Some considerations that may cause goodwill could include brand names, business location, and service. It is not easy to pinpoint the exact amount of goodwill in each accounting period. Thus, in the accounting profession it is agreed not to put a cost on goodwill until a company is bought or sold.

> Cost of assets purchased
> − Value of assets identified
> = Goodwill

Learning Unit 16-4 Review

AT THIS POINT you should be able to

- Define depletion and accumulated depletion and indicate their normal balances and on which financial reports they are located. (p. 628)
- Explain amortization. (p. 629)

- Discuss how a patent is amortized. (p. 629)
- Explain the life of a copyright. (p. 629)
- Define and explain how goodwill is calculated. (p. 629)

SELF-REVIEW QUIZ 16-4

(The forms you need are on page 66 of the *Study Guide and Working Papers.*)
Respond true or false to the following:

1. Intangible assets are depleted, not amortized.
2. The life of a patent is 12 years.
3. A copyright lasts for 25 years.
4. The cost of a franchise must be amortized over 40 years.
5. Goodwill represents excess earning power for a company.

SOLUTIONS TO SELF-REVIEW QUIZ 16-4

1. False   2. False   3. False   4. False   5. True

Chapter Review

Summary of Key Points

Learning Unit 16-1

1. The total cost of an asset includes all expenditures that are reasonable and necessary in acquiring it and getting it into position and in condition for use in the company.
2. Cash discounts are deducted from the cost of an asset.
3. Incidental costs related to the purchase of land and special costs that add a permanent value are added to the cost of land.
4. The Land Improvements account records improvements to land that have a limited useful life (such as driveways or fences). This account is subject to depreciation.
5. The cost of buying a building would include purchase price and all cost of repairs and other expenses to get the building ready for use. When constructing a new building, the cost would include all payments necessary to get the building ready for use.

Learning Unit 16-2

In this unit we look at four different depreciation methods.
1. Straight-line method:

   a. Depreciation expense is the same each year.
   b. Book value each year is lowered until residual value is reached.

2. Units-of-production method: Depreciation expense is directly related to output or usage of asset.
3. Double declining-balance method:

   a. Residual value is not deducted from cost.
   b. Depreciation expense is book value at beginning of year times rate.
   c. Asset cannot depreciate below book value.

4. Sum-of-the-years'-digits method (optional section):

   a. Fraction for the year is multiplied times cost less residual value.
   b. Depreciation in year 1 is highest.

5. Depreciation can be taken for partial years. If an asset is purchased in the first 15 days of the month, the whole month is considered in the depreciation calculation.
6. MACRS are for tax reporting, whereas the other four depreciation methods are used for financial reports.

Learning Unit 16-3

1. Capital expenditures include the original cost of an asset and three categories of additional payments:

   a. Additions or enlargements: major changes or improvements that increase the value of an asset.
   b. Extraordinary repairs: extend the life of the asset.
   c. Betterments: improvements that increase efficiency but do not extend the life of an asset. Additions or enlargements and betterments are charged to the asset account; extraordinary repairs are charged to Accumulated Depreciation.

2. After an asset is acquired, the expenditures for ordinary maintenance and unnecessary or unreasonable situations that do not try to extend useful life are treated as expenses of the current period and are called *revenue expenditures.*
3. A plant asset can be disposed of by discarding, selling, or exchanging it.

4. The Loss on Disposal account appears as Other Expense on the income statement.
5. A gain on sale of an asset occurs if the cash received is greater than the book value of the asset. Such a gain appears as Other Income on the income statement.
6. When a plant asset is exchanged, loss occurs when the trade-in allowance is less than the book value of the asset.
7. In an exchange of similar assets, the Financial Accounting Principles Board has ruled that gains are to be absorbed into the cost of the new asset.
8. Income tax rules require that gains *and losses* on exchange of assets be absorbed into the cost of the new asset. This requirement is inconsistent with the Financial Accounting Principles Board's ruling on losses.

Learning Unit 16-4

1. Natural resources, such as oil, coal, or timber, will deplete over a period of time as resources are extracted. Depletion expense is listed as an operating expense on the income statement.
2. Accumulated depletion is a contra-asset on the balance sheet.
3. Intangible assets, such as patents, copyrights, franchises, and goodwill, are also used up over a period of years. Amortization is the process of estimating and recording the charges as these intangible assets are used up.
4. Amortization expenses are operating expenses on the income statement.
5. A patent is good for 20 years; a copyright is granted for the life of the creator and 50 years thereafter.
6. The cost of obtaining a franchise is amortized over its life or 40 years, whichever is shorter.
7. Because it is not easy to put a price on goodwill in each accounting period, it is not until a company is bought or sold that a cost is placed on goodwill.

Key Terms

Accelerated depreciation   More depreciation taken in early years of an asset's life, decreasing amounts in later years.

Additions or enlargements   Major changes or improvements that increase the value of an asset (such as adding a new wing to a school).

Amortization expense   An operating expense on the income statement relating to intangible assets.

Amortize   To charge a portion of an expenditure over a fixed number of years.

Betterments   Improvements that increase the efficiency of an asset by adding accessories or replacing parts.

Book value   Cost of asset less accumulated depreciation.

Capital expenditures   Original cost of an asset as well as additions or enlargements, extraordinary repairs, and betterments.

Copyright   The exclusive right that is granted by the federal government to sell and reproduce literary, musical, or artistic works for a period of time.

Depletion   Amount of natural resources that has been exhausted by mining, pumping, and so forth for a period of time.

Double declining-balance method   An accelerated depreciation method that uses up to twice the straight-line rate times book value of asset to calculate depreciation expense. Residual value is not subtracted from the cost of an asset in determining depreciation.

Extraordinary repairs   Infrequent expenditures that extend an asset's life (such as a new engine in a car).

Franchise   A right granted by business or government to produce or sell goods in a specific geographic region. Examples are a Burger King or Holiday Inn.

Goodwill   When a business is purchased, the difference between the price paid and the value of the identifiable assets is goodwill. Goodwill may depend on brand names, business location, service, or other elements; it is a valuable asset that plays an important part in the expected rate of future earnings of a business.

Income tax method   When plant assets are exchanged, tax law says the gain or loss must be absorbed into the cost of the new asset.

Intangible assets   Assets having no physical substance (such as patents or franchises).

Land Improvements   An asset account that records improvements made to land; such improvements have a limited life and are subject to depreciation (an example is a driveway or fences).

Modified Accelerated Cost Recovery System (MACRS) A system for businesses to calculate depreciation for tax purposes based on the Tax Laws of 1986 and 1989. Also known as the General Depreciation System (GDS).

Patent An exclusive right to sell or produce one's discovery or invention. A patent is good for 20 years.

Residual (salvage) value The amount of the asset's cost that will be recovered when the asset is sold, traded in, or scrapped.

Straight-line method Method that allocates an equal amount of depreciation over an asset's period of usefulness.

Sum-of-the-years'-digits method An accelerated method that allocates depreciation each period of an asset's life by multiplying a fraction for that period times cost less residual value.

Trade-in allowance A value received when one asset is traded in on the purchase of another asset. For example, when you buy a new car you may trade in your old car for an amount of money that is applied toward the purchase of the new car.

Units-of-production method A depreciation method that is based on usage and not on time. An example of units of production is the numbers of shoes a machine could produce in its expected useful life.

Useful life At the time an asset is acquired an estimate is made of its usefulness in terms of years, output, and so forth.

Blueprint: Key Accounts

Review of Key Accounts

Account	Category*	↑	Normal Balance	Financial Report Found on
Equipment	Plant Asset	Dr.	Dr.	Balance Sheet
Buildings	Plant Asset	Dr.	Dr.	Balance Sheet
Land	Plant Asset	Dr.	Dr.	Balance Sheet
Loss on Disposal of Plant Asset	Other Expense	Dr.	Dr.	Income Statement
Loss from Fire	Other Expense	Dr.	Dr.	Income Statement
Gain on Sale of Plant Asset	Other Income	Cr.	Cr.	Income Statement
Loss on Exchange of Machinery	Other Expense	Dr.	Dr.	Income Statement
Depletion of Coal Deposit	Operating Expense	Dr.	Dr.	Income Statement
Accumulated Depletion	Contra-Asset	Cr.	Cr.	Balance Sheet
Coal Deposit	Natural Resource	Dr.	Dr.	Balance Sheet
Patents	Intangible Asset	Dr.	Dr.	Balance Sheet
Amortization Expense	Operating Expense	Dr.	Dr.	Income Statement
Copyrights, Franchises, or Goodwill	Intangible Assets	Dr.	Dr.	Balance Sheet

*We use Plant Assets to represent property, plant, and equipment.

Questions, Mini Exercises, Exercises, and Problems

Discussion Questions

1. What types of payment are considered "reasonable and necessary" when determining the cost of an asset?

2. What is the purpose of the Land Improvements account?

3. What is the difference between revenue and capital expenditures?

4. What are four methods of calculating depreciation? Briefly explain the key points of each.

5. What is the purpose of the Modified Accelerated Cost Recovery System?

6. A betterment is a revenue expenditure. True or false? Please explain.

7. Which method of depreciation does *not* deduct residual value in its calculation?

8. When a plant asset is sold, a loss results if the cash received is greater than book value. Defend or reject. Please explain.

9. A loss on an exchange of plant assets occurs when the book value of the old machine is more than the trade-in allowance. True or false?

10. Explain how the income tax method differs from the Accounting Principles Board ruling with regard to the recording of exchanges of plant assets that result in a loss.

11. What is the purpose of the Accumulated Depletion account?

12. List and describe three intangible assets.

Mini Exercises

(The forms you need are on pages 68–69 of the Study Guide and Working Papers.)

Cost of Property, Plant, and Equipment

1. Calculate the total cost of the machine given the following:

List price	$2,000
Cash discount	5%
Freight	$ 50
Assembly	150
Special foundation	50

Straight-Line Method

2. Mel Jones depreciates his truck by the straight-line method. Calculate the yearly depreciation expense given the following:

Cost	$6,000
Residual value	$1,000
Service of useful life	10 years

Book Value

3. If a machine had a cost of $4,000 with an accumulated depreciation of $1,000, what would be its book value?

Units-of-Production Method

4. If Mel Jones (Mini Exercise 2) depreciated his truck by the units-of-production method, calculate the first year's depreciation based on the following: cost $6,000; residual value $1,000. Estimated mileage is 100,000. The truck was driven 8,000 miles in year 1.

Double Declining-Balance Method

5. If Mel Jones (Mini Exercise 2) depreciated his truck by the double declining-balance method, calculate the depreciation expense for year 1.

Sum-of-the-Years'-Digits Method (Optional)

6. If Mel Jones (Mini Exercise 2) depreciated his truck by the sum-of-the-years'-digits method, calculate the first year's depreciation. Round the answer to the nearest dollar.

Capital and Revenue Expenditures

7. Identify each situation as a Capital or Revenue Expenditure.

Situation	Capital Expenditure		Revenue Expenditure
	Addition	Betterment/ Extraordinary Repair	
a. New tires			
b. New air conditioning for a car			
c. New car engine			
d. New addition on school			

Loss and Gains

8. Complete the following:

	Account	Category	Financial Statement Found on
a. Accumulated Depletion			
b. Loss on Disposal of Plant Assets			
c. Gain on Sale of Plant Assets			

Exchange with Loss

9. Pete Co. traded in an old machine costing $10,000 for a new machine for a cash price of $13,000 with a trade-in allowance of $3,000. Accumulated Depreciation on the old machine was $6,000.

   a. What is the book value of the old machine? What is the loss?
   b. Provide a journal entry to record the exchange.

Exchange with Gain

10. Assume in Mini Exercise 9 the trade-in value was $5,000. Prepare a journal entry to record the exchange.

Income Tax Method

11. If in Mini Exercise 9 the income tax method was used, prepare the journal entry to record the exchange.

Exercises

(The forms you need are on pages 70–72 of the *Study Guide and Working Papers.*)

16-1. Mack Company incurred the following expenditures to buy a new machine:

   - Invoice, $30,000 less 10% cash discount.
   - Freight charges, $500.
   - Assembly charges, $1,400.
   - Special base to support machine, $505.
   - Machine dropped and repaired, $350.

   What is the actual cost of the machine?

Calculating cost of equipment.

16-2. From the following, prepare depreciation schedules for the first two years for (a) straight-line, (b) units-of-production, (c) double declining-balance at twice the straight-line rate, and (d) sum-of-the-years'-digits (optional) methods.

   - Machine purchased on January 1, $1,440.
   - Residual value, $240.
   - Estimated useful life, five years.
   - Total estimated output, 600 units.
   - Output year 1, 100 units.
   - Output year 2, 200 units.

Depreciation schedules.

Depreciation schedules.

16-3. Larson Co., whose accounting period ends on December 31, purchased a machine for $6,800 on January 1 with an estimated residual value of $800 and estimated useful life of 10 years. Prepare depreciation schedules for the current as well as the following year using (a) straight-line, (b) double declining-balance at twice the straight-line rate, and (c) sum-of-the-years'-digits methods (optional).

Loss on exchange and income tax methods.

16-4. A machine that cost $9,000 with $3,900 of accumulated depreciation was traded in for a similar machine having a $5,800 cash price. An $800 trade-in was offered by the seller.

    a. Calculate the book value of the old machine.
    b. Calculate the loss on the exchange.
    c. Prepare the journal entry for the exchange.
    d. Calculate the cost basis of the new equipment if the income tax method is used and prepare a journal entry.

Patent.

16-5. On May 1, 20X1, Osgood Company bought a patent at a cost of $5,000. It is estimated that the patent will give Osgood a competitive advantage for 10 years. Record in general journal form amortization for 20X1 and 20X2. (Assume December 31 is the end of the accounting period for Osgood.)

MACRS and Tax Reform Act of 1986.

16-6. Pultzer Company bought a light general-purpose truck for $9,000 on March 8, 1991. Calculate the yearly depreciation using the MACRS method.

Group A Problems

(The forms you need are on pages 74–79 of the *Study Guide and Working Papers.*)

Property, plant, and equipment transactions.

16A-1. Record the following transactions into the general journal of Orange Company:

20XX

Feb.	5	Purchased land for $86,000. The $86,000 included attorney's fees of $5,000.
	18	Orange Company decided to pave the parking lot for $5,400.
Mar.	24	Purchased a building for $90,000, putting down 30% and mortgaging the remainder.
	29	Bought equipment for $32,000. Freight and assembly were an additional $4,000.
May	10	Added a new wing for $175,000 to building that was purchased on March 24.
June	15	Performed ordinary repair work on equipment purchased March 29, $750, to maintain its normal operations.
July	1	Bought a truck for $14,000.
Oct.	15	Added a hydraulic loader to truck, $2,200.
Nov.	30	Truck purchased in July was brought in for grease and oil, $33.
Dec.	30	Overhauled truck's motor for $900, extending its life by more than one year.
Dec.	31	Changed tires on truck, $325.

Check Figure:
Feb. 18
Dr.   Land Improvement
      $5,400
Cr.   Cash $5,400

Methods of computing depreciation.

16A-2. On January 1, 20X1, a machine was installed at Lavy Factory at a cost of $58,000. Its estimated residual value at the end of its estimated life of four years is $18,000. The machine is expected to produce 80,000 units with the following production schedule:

- 20X1: 12,000 units
- 20X2: 27,000 units
- 20X3: 15,000 units
- 20X4: 26,000 units

Complete depreciation schedules for (a) straight-line, (b) units-of-production, (c) double declining-balance at twice the straight-line rate, and (d) sum-of-the-years'-digits (optional) methods.

Check Figure:
(d) Depr. expense 20X3
$8,000

16A-3. On June 13, 20X1, Cook Company bought equipment for $4,080. Its estimated life is four years with a residual value of $240. Prepare depreciation schedules for 20X1, 20X2, and 20X3 for (a) straight-line, (b) double declining-balance at twice the straight-line rate, and (c) sum-of-the-years'-digits (optional) methods.

Check Figure:
(c) Depr. expense 20X1 $896

16A-4. Journalize the following transactions for the Robe Company and below each entry show all calculations:

20XX

Jan. 1 Sold a truck for $1,250 that cost $6,750 and had accumulated depreciation of $6,100.

Feb. 10 A machine costing $3,200 with accumulated depreciation of $2,450 was destroyed in a fire. The insurance company settled the claim for $300.

May 1 Traded in a machine costing $19,400 with $16,500 of accumulated depreciation for a new machine costing $25,100 with a trade-in allowance of $2,700. Note that depreciation is up-to-date. The loss is to be recognized.

July 8 Traded in a machine costing $40,000 with $34,000 of accumulated depreciation (which is up-to-date) for a new machine for a cash price of $45,000 and a trade-in allowance of $8,000.

Aug. 9 Journalize the May 1 transaction using the income tax method.

Sept. 12 A truck costing $7,000 and fully depreciated was disposed of.

Disposing of plant assets.

Check Figure:
May:
Loss on exchange
$200 Dr.

Group B Problems

(The forms you need are on pages 74–79 of the *Study Guide and Working Papers*.)

16B-1. Journalize the following transactions for Orange Company.

20XX

Apr. 1 Purchased a machine for $89,500 along with an additional charge for freight and assembly of $1,500.

8 Purchased land at a cost of $22,000. The $22,000 included attorney's fees of $2,500.

15 Purchased a building for $90,000, putting down 10% and mortgaging the remainder.

29 At a cost of $1,900, cleared and graded the land purchased on April 8 (the additional cost considered as part of the cost of land).

May 1 Performed regular maintenance work on machinery, $160, to maintain its normal operations.

8 Painted the building purchased on April 15, $2,900. Painting was necessary to have the building ready for proper use.

30 Purchased a second airplane for company business, $65,000.

June 30 Installed a hydraulic loader on a truck at a cost of $2,900.

July 30 First airplane's engine was overhauled for $7,900.

Sept. 30 Building is completely renovated at a cost of $30,000, which will extend its life by 10 years.

Property, plant, and equipment transactions.

Check Figure:
May 8:
Dr. Building $2,900
Cr. Cash $2,900

16B-2. On January 1, 20X1, Lavy Factory installed a new machine at a cost of $117,000. Its estimated residual value at the end of its estimated life of four years is $9,000. The machine is expected to produce 90,000 units with the following production schedule:

Methods of computing depreciation.

- 20X1: 11,000 units
- 20X2: 9,000 units
- 20X3: 11,000 units
- 20X4: 59,000 units

Check Figure:
(d) Dep. expense 20X3 $21,600

Complete depreciation schedules for (a) straight-line, (b) units-of-production, (c) double declining-balance at twice the straight-line rate, and (d) sum-of-the-years'-digits (optional) methods.

16B-3. On April 5, 20X1, Cook Company bought equipment for $6,200. Its estimated life is five years with a residual value of $200. Prepare depreciation schedules for 20X1, 20X2, and 20X3 for (a) straight-line, (b) double declining-balance at twice the straight-line rate, and (c) sum-of-the-years'-digits (optional) methods.

16B-4. Journalize the following transactions for the Robe Company and below each entry show all calculations:

20XX

Jan.	1	Sold a truck for $3,600 that cost $12,800 and had accumulated depreciation of $10,900.

Feb.	8	A machine costing $4,000 with accumulated depreciation of $3,390 was destroyed in a fire. The insurance company settled the claim for $150.
May	9	Traded in a machine costing $18,500 with $15,750 of accumulated depreciation (which is up-to-date) for a new machine costing $26,200 with a trade-in allowance of $2,600. The loss is to be recognized.
July	10	Traded in a machine costing $39,500 with $35,700 of accumulated depreciation (depreciation is up-to-date) for a new machine for a cash price of $44,000 and a trade-in allowance of $11,500.
Aug.	19	Journalize the May 9 transaction using the income tax method.
Sept.	12	A truck costing $11,000 and fully depreciated was disposed of.

Real-World Applications

16R-1. On August 1, 20X1, Hope Co. purchased a customized light truck for $96,000 cash. On August 3, special shelving was added to the truck for $6,000. The truck has a useful life of six years with a trade-in value of $12,000 and is depreciated by the straight-line method. On January 1, 20X4, Hope Co. was trying to decide whether to overhaul the truck at a cost of $15,000 or buy a new truck for $100,000 and depreciate it by MACRS. Overhauling the truck would increase its useful life by two years, and residual value would remain at $12,000.

As the accountant of Hope Co., you have been called into a meeting with Mr. Reynolds, the vice president, to further discuss this matter. Bring all your data with you, along with a written recommendation.

16R-2.

MEMO

To: Hal Owen

From: Pete Sanchez

Re: Decision on general-purpose truck

We need your assistance on which depreciation method would be best for us to use. I'm thinking that we should use MACRS instead of the straight-line method for both financial and tax purposes. We could save lots of dollars! Could you verify my decision (or not) and work up the numbers for me based on the following:

Cost:	$20,000
Life:	Five years
Residual:	$5,000

Work up a comparison of MACRS and straight-line depreciation along with a written recommendation to help Pete Sanchez make his decision.

YOU make the call

Critical Thinking/Ethical Case

16R-3. Pete went to an auto dealer to buy a new Jeep. The salesperson told Pete that cars really appreciate in value. He cited antique cars as a perfect example. The dealer went on to tell Pete that buying a car represents some great tax savings. He told Pete that leasing is getting less and less popular. Should Pete buy a new car? You make the call. Write down your recommendations to Pete.

Internet Exercises: Boeing; Lufthansa

EX-1. [**www.boeing.com**]   This site shows you about how much you would have to pay to have a Boeing jetliner for your weekend jaunts. The costs in the examples are for jets ready to fly away from the production line. Before you commit to deciding which model you want, you have some homework to do. Write down some of the costs that you, or the airline you own, would have to consider as part of the cost of this valuable asset. Consider the factors you learned in this chapter that are part of the cost of an asset and consider factors like who will pay for delivery of the jet to the runway near your desert retreat. Give some examples of "revenue expenditures" that would go into operation of your plane.

EX-2. [**www.lufthansa.com**]   Many industries have special ways of depreciating their Plant and Equipment assets. One method taught in this chapter on Plant and Equipment assets is that of "units of production." An airline is required by federal regulations to completely overhaul its engines every 2,000 flight hours. The engines are completely stripped down and rebuilt at that point. This results in a completely reconditioned engine. The cost of one of these engines is, perhaps, $5 million.

   1. Using the number of flight hours, what is the "per unit" depreciation if the "unit" is 1 hour of operation?
   2. If the engine is operated for a total of 1,500 hours this year, how much depreciation will be recorded using the units-of-production method?

CHAPTER 17

Partnerships

You went to see your doctor for your annual physical. Dr. John Stewart has been your family's doctor for years, and you've known him for most of your life. When you go to your doctor's office, you notice that there are now three doctors' names on the front door. It appears that Dr. Stewart has expanded his practice with the addition of two new doctors.

As Dr. Stewart is examining you, he tells you about Dr. Mary Silva and Dr. Dean Roberts. "They are two fine physicians who are just starting out. I'm now in partnership with them. In a few years I plan to retire and leave this practice entirely to them."

You were always used to seeing Dr. Stewart when you were sick. Now that he is in a partnership, you may be treated by one of the other doctors on your next visit. Dr. Stewart was in business as a sole proprietor. Now he has changed his practice by forming a partnership.

Many people today run their businesses using the form of organization known as a partnership. Partnerships can be a practical way to operate a business, whether it be a professional practice such as a medical or law office or a business such as a restaurant or automobile dealership.

In this chapter we will learn how to journalize the formation of a partnership and how to calculate a partner's share of net income or loss based on the partner's beginning capital investment or using a fractional ratio. We will also discuss the journal entries used to admit or withdraw a partner from a partnership and to pay bonuses to partners. We also discuss the journal entries involved in the liquidation process and how to prepare a statement of liquidation.

Learning Objectives

- Journalizing the entry for formation of a partnership. (p. 644)
- Calculating a partner's share of net income based on fractional ratio, beginning capital investment, and salary and interest allowances. (p. 645)
- Preparing a statement of partners' equity. (p. 648)
- Journalizing entries to record admitting a new partner, withdrawal of a partner, and bonuses to partners. (p. 650)
- Journalizing entries involved in the liquidation process and preparing a statement of liquidation. (p. 655)

Up to this point we have been using the sole proprietorship form of business organization in discussing the accounting process. We are now ready to look at another form of business organization, the partnership.

A partnership, as defined by the Uniform Partnership Act, is "an association of two or more persons to carry on as co-owners a business for profit." Examples of partnerships include service businesses and professional practitioners, such as physicians, dentists, attorneys, and accountants. Many small wholesale as well as retail companies are formed as partnerships. Your local convenience store may be a partnership.

The recording of business transactions involving assets, liabilities, revenue, and expenses is handled the same for both a sole proprietorship and a partnership. The major difference in recording business transactions for these two forms of organization lies in the capital account(s). A sole proprietorship has only one capital and withdrawals account, whereas in a partnership each owner has his or her own separate capital and withdrawals account. First we look at the characteristics of a partnership and how it is formed.

Learning Unit 17-1   Partnership Characteristics and Formation of Partnerships

It is quite easy to form a partnership. When two or more people agree orally or in writing to be partners, a contract results. Although the oral agreement is binding, it makes more sense to seek legal advice and have a formal written agreement prepared. Putting agreements in writing may minimize conflicts in the future. This written agreement, which formalizes the partners' relationship, is called the articles of partnership.

Some things that should be included in the written articles of partnership are the following:

> The more partners a partnership has, (1) the easier it may be to finance the business with the owners' investments and (2) the more unique abilities may result from the different backgrounds of the owners.

1. Name and address of each partner, along with the date of agreement.
2. Rights and responsibilities of each partner.
3. Amount that each partner is investing.
4. Specific manner in which partners' profits or losses will be shared.
5. Provisions for one or more partners quitting the partnership.
6. How new partners will be admitted.
7. How assets will be distributed if the business is completely terminated.
8. How accounting records will be maintained.

CHARACTERISTICS OF PARTNERSHIPS

Limited Life

A partnership has a limited life. An advantage is that it does have more flexibility than some other forms of ownership to react to the marketplace because legal restrictions are minimal. When there is a change in the membership of a partnership—when someone new joins or when someone leaves—the partnership is dissolved, however. Dissolution can occur if a partner dies, becomes incapacitated, goes bankrupt, or withdraws. Admission of a new partner or expiration of the life of the partnership as stated in the articles of partnership could also result in the partnership being dissolved. If a partnership is dissolved, a new partnership can be formed and the business can continue to operate without any interruptions.

Mutual Agency

Mutual agency means that the actions of one partner are binding on all the other partners. For example, Jill Joy, who is a partner in a merchandise business, enters into a contract with Flynn Company to lease a building. This contract is binding on all Jill's partners, because the transaction was within the scope of the business. If Jill, on the other hand, entered into a contract to provide *legal* work to another company, it would not be binding on the partners, because legal work is not in the normal scope of a merchandise company.

Mutual agency allows each partner to act for the partnership as a whole, because all the partners are agents for the business. Poor judgment on the part of one partner, however, could, through mutual agency, result in heavy losses to all partners. An advantage of a partnership is that a credit rating is usually higher because more than one partner is responsible for the company's debt. So the mutual agency characteristic of a partnership can be both an advantage and a disadvantage.

Unlimited Liability

Unlimited liability means that if a partnership is unable to pay its obligations, all general partners are individually liable to cover with their *personal* assets the obligations the partnership cannot meet. Think of a general partner as one who risks not only the personal investment in the partnership but also personal assets. If the personal assets of some of the partners are exhausted, the other partners have the responsibility for covering the debts outstanding. There are, however, a few exceptions to this rule. First, a partner just entering an existing partnership is not held liable for past obligations before joining the partnership. Second, in some states some members of a partnership have liability only up to the amount they have invested in the partnership. These people are called limited partners.

Co-ownership of Property

Co-ownership of property means that all partners share all the assets of the partnership. For example, if Bill Boyd invests cash and Joyce Regan invests a building in their partnership, the assets become the property of the partnership. Joyce no longer has a specific claim to the building. Ownership is now shared by Bill and Joyce.

Taxation

The partnership itself does not pay taxes, but the partners pay taxes on the share of net income that has been allocated to each of them. (Note that the tax is on the net income and not on the amount that a partner has withdrawn from the partnership.) Remember that in a sole proprietorship, like a partnership, owners are not paid salaries. They take withdrawals from the company.

FORMATION OF A PARTNERSHIP

Let's look now at the journal entries that are needed when a partnership is formed. The important point is that when partners invest in a business, the assets should be recorded at their current fair value. This value is established by having the assets appraised. Partners have to agree on the amounts assigned to the noncash assets.

These costs now represent the true acquisition cost to the partnership. Appraising of assets at their current fair value avoids inequities in the balances of the capital accounts of the partners.

Let's look at the following situation: On June 1, 20XX, Jane Reedy and Bill Burr enter into a partnership. Reedy invests from her old business $9,000 cash and store equipment worth $25,000 with accumulated depreciation of $5,000. The current appraised value of the equipment is $28,000. Also on the books is Accounts Receivable of $2,000 with an Allowance for Doubtful Accounts of $500. The partnership will take on the responsibility for a $6,000 note issued by Reedy. Burr invests $20,000 cash in the partnership. The journal entries in Figure 17-1 record this information.

Figure 17-1

Investing into a Partnership

These entries could be recorded in the cash receipts journal. Note that the $32,500 is the assets minus the liabilities.

20XX						
June	1	Cash	9 0 0 0 00		
		Accounts Receivable	2 0 0 0 00		
		Store Equipment	28 0 0 0 00		
		Allowances for Doubtful Accounts		5 0 0 00	
		Notes Payable		6 0 0 0 00	
		J. Reedy, Capital		32 5 0 0 00	
	1	Cash	20 0 0 0 00		
		B. Burr, Capital		20 0 0 0 00	

Note that the store equipment has no accumulated depreciation associated with it, because the appraised value is now the new book value. If the old book value was used, Reedy's capital would be understated. Reedy should not be penalized because her investment has increased. Any additional investments made by the partners will result in a journal entry that debits Cash and credits the partners' Capital accounts.

Learning Unit 17-1 Review

AT THIS POINT you should be able to

- Define a partnership and compare its equity section with that of a sole proprietorship. (p. 642)
- List the characteristics of a partnership. (p. 643)
- Journalize the formation of a partnership, recording assets at current fair value. (p. 644)

SELF-REVIEW QUIZ 17-1

(The forms you need are on page 84 of the *Study Guide and Working Papers*.)
Respond true or false to the following:

1. Articles of partnership are required in forming a partnership.
2. Limited life means that when a partnership is dissolved, the business ceases operations.
3. Unlimited liability could result from mutual agency.

4. Co-ownership of property means each asset belongs to the person who invested it.

5. Assets invested in the formation of a partnership are recorded at current fair value.

SOLUTIONS TO SELF-REVIEW QUIZ 17-1

1. False   **2.** False   **3.** True   **4.** False   **5.** True

Learning Unit 17-2   Division of Net Income and Net Loss Among Partners

Partners work so as to gain a share of the net income of their partnership; they do not earn salaries as their employees do. As a matter of fact, they cannot legally hire themselves and pay themselves a salary. There are several ways to divide up net income and net loss among partners based on partners' differing talent and abilities, time spent working for the partnership, and amount of investment in the partnership.

We need to introduce two terms to help describe how net income is divided among partners. One way is through a salary allowance. A salary allowance is not the same thing as the Salary Expense involved in paying employees, and it is not in fact a salary at all; it is just a way to divide net income. It is usually used to account for unequal service contributions among partners, such as if one partner worked full time for the business and the other put in only 20 hours a week. In such a case, the partners might agree to pay $1,000 per week to the first partner and $500 per week to the other. This money would come out of the net income earned by the partnership.

Another way to divide net income among partners is through interest allowance. This method is usually used when partners have put different amounts into the partnership as an initial investment. Let's say that one has invested $5,000 and the other has invested $10,000. At the end of the accounting period, they would each get 10% interest on their investment: The first would get $500 ($5,000 × .10) and the second would get $1,000 ($10,000 × .10). This method is used because it would be unfair to give half of net income to the first partner when that partner invested only one-third of the capital.

Now let's look at several different situations to see how a partnership might divide its net income or net loss. These situations will be based on the following facts. Dot Alexander, John Sullivan, and Sheldon Brown invested $8,000, $6,000, and $4,000, respectively, in a partnership. The partnership in the first year had a net income of $24,300.

Situation 1

Partners could not agree on how to share net income of $24,300. The law states that if an agreement is not reached on how partners share earnings, they will be divided equally.

The Calculation: $24,300 ÷ 3 = $8,100 to each partner

The journal entry at closing to allocate net income will look like the one in Figure 17-2.

Figure 17-2
Share Net Income Equally

The journal entry at closing to allocate net income looks like this one.

20XX					
Dec.	31	Income Summary	24 3 0 0 00		
		Dot Alexander, Capital		8 1 0 0 00	
		John Sullivan, Capital		8 1 0 0 00	
		Sheldon Brown, Capital		8 1 0 0 00	

Note that the closing process now divides the net income into the *three* capital accounts. In a sole proprietorship, the net income was closed to the one capital account. If this situation involved net loss instead of net income, each capital account would be debited and the credit would be to Income Summary.

Situation 2

Partners share net income of $24,300 in the ratio of their beginning capital investments.

The Calculation:

Step 1: Find the total capital invested:

Alexander	$ 8,000
Sullivan	6,000
Brown	4,000
	$18,000

Step 2: Set up a ratio (fraction) of each partner's investment to the total of capital invested ($18,000):

Alexander	*Sullivan*	*Brown*
$\dfrac{\$8,000}{\$18,000}$	$\dfrac{\$6,000}{\$18,000}$	$\dfrac{\$4,000}{\$18,000}$

Step 3: Multiply the ratio in Step 2 by the amount of income to be distributed.

Alexander: $\dfrac{\$8,000}{\$18,000} \times \$24,300 = \$10,800$

Sullivan: $\dfrac{\$6,000}{\$18,000} \times \$24,300 = \$8,100$

Brown: $\dfrac{\$4,000}{\$18,000} \times \$24,300 = \$5,400$

The journal entry at closing to allocate net income will look like the one in Figure 17-3.

Figure 17-3
Share Net Income Based on Ratio of Investments

20XX					
Dec.	31	Income Summary	24 3 0 0 00		
		Dot Alexander, Capital		10 8 0 0 00	
		John Sullivan, Capital		8 1 0 0 00	
		Sheldon Brown, Capital		5 4 0 0 00	

This ratio in Step 2 may be used if the net income of the company is related only to the amount the partners have invested. Alexander has invested the most ($8,000) and thus receives the largest portion of the earnings ($10,800).

Alternative to Ratio Based on Investment Only: Some partnerships share net income according to an agreed-upon ratio. If a ratio is 3:2:1, it means that 3/6 of net income goes to one partner, 2/6 to the next, and 1/6 to the last. Such a fractional ratio could be based on service as well as capital investment. Such ratios are called profit and loss ratios.

Situation 3

Partners' services and capital contributions are unequal, but net income does cover salary and interest allowance. The salary allowance is used to compensate for the partners' unequal service contributions, and the interest allowance is used to compensate for their unequal investments. One way to share net income in this situation is as follows:

a. Annual salary allowance of $6,000 to Alexander, $6,000 to Sullivan, and $9,000 to Brown.

b. Ten percent interest on each partner's capital investment.

c. Remaining net income or net loss shared equally.

	Alexander		Sullivan		Brown		Total
a. Salary Allowance	$6,000	+	$6,000	+	$9,000	=	$21,000
b. Interest on Capital Investments							
.10 × $8,000	800						
.10 × $6,000		+	600				
.10 × $4,000				+	400		
Total Interest Allowance						=	1,800
Total Salary and Interest Allowance	$6,800	+	$6,600	+	$9,400	=	$22,800
c. Net Income $24,300							
Less: Salary and Interest 22,800							
Income to be distributed equally $ 1,500	500		500		500		
Share of Net Income to Partners	$7,300	+	$7,100	+	$9,900	=	$24,300

The journal entry at closing to allocate net income will look like Figure 17-4.

	20XX						
	Dec.	31	Income Summary	24 30 0 00			
			D. Alexander, Capital		7 30 0 00		
			J. Sullivan, Capital		7 10 0 00		
			S. Brown, Capital		9 90 0 00		

Figure 17-4
Net Income Left After Salary and Interest Allowance

Note that in this case there was still net income remaining after salary and interest allowances. In the next situation we see that net income doesn't always cover all the salary and interest allowance.

Partners' services and capital contributions are unequal, but net income does not cover salary and interest allowance. Assume (1) net income is $20,700 and (2) salary and interest allowance are the same as in Situation 3.

Whether net income covers the salaries and interest makes *no difference* in calculating the salary or interest allowance. As shown in the accompanying calculation, the total of salaries and allowances is $22,800. Net income is only $20,700; thus the partners must all share by $700 each in a reduction of the profits allocated to them. Remember that items (a) and (b) are calculated first *before* we consider the difference between net income and the amount that is needed to cover salary and interest allowance. There is no need to think of the $700 deficit as a loss; think of it as a reduction in the share of profits, because all the interest and salary allowance was not covered.

		Alexander		Sullivan		Brown		Total
a.	**Salary Allowance**	$6,000	+	$6,000	+	$9,000	=	$21,000
b.	**Interest on Capital Investments:**							
	.10 × $8,000	800						
	.10 × $6,000		+	600				
	.10 × $4,000				+	400		
	Total Interest Allowance						=	1,800
	Total Salary and Interest Allowance	$6,800	+	$6,600	+	$9,400	=	$22,800
c.	**Net Income**	$20,700						
	Less: Salary and Interest	22,800						
	Deficit to be shared equally	<$ 2,100>	<700>		<700>		<700>		
	Share of Net Income to Partners		$6,100	+	$5,900	+	$8,700	=	$20,700

Figure 17-5
Deficit to Be Shared Equally by all Partners

	20XX									
	Dec.	31	Income Summary		20 7 0 00 0					
			D. Alexander, Capital				6 1 0 0 00		
			J. Sullivan, Capital				5 9 0 0 00		
			S. Brown, Capital				8 7 0 0 00		

On their personal tax returns, partners are taxed on their net income in the partnership, whether they withdraw it or not. For example, Alexander would pay taxes on $7,300, even though she withdrew only $4,000.

PARTNERSHIP FINANCIAL STATEMENT

Just as we had a statement of owner's equity for a sole proprietorship, we can prepare a statement of partners' equity. The statement in Figure 17-6 was prepared from Situation 3.

Figure 17-6
Statement of Partner's Equity

ALEXANDER, SULLIVAN, AND BROWN STATEMENT OF PARTNERS' EQUITY FOR YEAR ENDED DECEMBER 31, 20XX			
	Alexander	Sullivan	Brown
Capital Balances, January 1, 20XX	$ 8 0 0 0 00	$ 6 0 0 0 00	$ 4 0 0 0 00
Add: Net Income for 20XX	7 3 0 0 00	7 1 0 0 00	9 9 0 0 00
Totals	$15 3 0 0 00	$13 1 0 0 00	$13 9 0 0 00
Less: Withdrawals	4 0 0 0 00	5 0 0 0 00	8 0 0 0 00
Capital Balances, December 31, 20XX	$11 3 0 0 00	$ 8 1 0 0 00	$ 5 9 0 0 00

The ending balances for each partner would then be reported on the balance sheet. Think of the statement of partner's equity as a supporting document to arrive at a new figure for each capital account on the balance sheet.

Learning Unit 17-2 Review

AT THIS POINT you should be able to

- Explain why salary and interest allowances are not expenses when used to divide up earnings of a partnership. (p. 645)
- Calculate partners' earnings if shared (a) equally, (b) by ratio of beginning capital or fractional ratio, and (c) by salary and interest allowances. (p. 646)
- Prepare a statement of partners' equity. (p. 648)

SELF-REVIEW QUIZ 17-2

(The forms you need are on page 85 of the *Study Guide and Working Papers.*)

From the following information, calculate the partners' share of net income. J. French and J. Small receive salary allowances of $60,000 and $48,000, respectively. The interest allowance is 12% of their beginning balances of $160,000 and $120,000, respectively. The remainder of the net income will be divided evenly. Net income for the year was $150,000.

SOLUTION TO SELF-REVIEW QUIZ 17-2

	French		Small	=	Total
Salary Allowance	$60,000	+	$48,000	=	$108,000
Interest on Capital Investments:					
.12 × $160,000	19,200				
.12 × $120,000		+	14,400		
Total Interest Allowance				=	33,600
Total Salary and Interest Allowance	$79,200	+	$62,400	=	$141,600
Net Income $150,000					
Less: Salary and Interest 141,600					
Income to be					
distributed equally $8,400	→ 4,200		4,200		
Share of Net Income to Partners	$83,400	+	$66,600	=	$150,000

Learning Unit 17-3   Recording Admissions and Withdrawals of Partners

This unit looks at how the capital structure of a partnership may change due to (1) admission of a new partner or (2) withdrawal of a partner.

ADMISSION OF A NEW PARTNER

There are two ways to join a partnership:

1. **Purchase of an equity interest** from one or more of the existing partners.
2. Make an investment in the business.

No matter what approach is taken, the admission of a new partner will technically dissolve the old partnership. Let's look at how Peter Mix bought into the partnership of Jones and Ryan.

Buying an Equity Interest from an Original Partner

The partners' balance sheet of Jones and Ryan looked as shown in Figure 17-7 before Peter Mix purchased an interest in the company (there are no liabilities).

Figure 17-7
Balances Before Buying an Equity Interest

JONES AND RYAN				
Assets		**Partners' Equity**		
Cash	$ 5 0 0 0 00	Jones, Capital	$ 6 0 0 0 00	
Other Assets	7 0 0 0 00	Ryan, Capital	6 0 0 0 00	
Total Assets	$12 0 0 0 00	Total Equities	$12 0 0 0 00	

On April 3 Ryan sold Peter Mix his equity in the company for $9,000. The entry is recorded on the books of the partnership as shown in Figure 17-8.

Figure 17-8
Sale of Equity to Peter Mix

Apr.	3	Ryan, Capital	6 0 0 0 00		
		Mix, Capital		6 0 0 0 00	

The end result of this transaction is to transfer the $6,000 capital account of Ryan to Mix. Note that the difference in the selling price of $3,000 ($9,000 − $6,000) doesn't affect the books of the partnership, because the cash is paid directly to Ryan and not to the business. Think of it as a side transaction. All this transaction does is transfer the equity amounts. Any personal profit the former partner makes is of a personal nature and is not reflected in the accounts of the business.

Keep in mind also that Jones must agree to the equity exchange by Ryan if Mix is to become a partner. If Jones agrees, a new partnership contract is formed along with new profit or loss ratios. If Jones doesn't accept Mix as a partner, Mix still has the right to share in Ryan's profits and losses, but he will have no voice in the running of the company until he is admitted as a partner.

> Ryan cannot force Jones to accept Mix as a partner.

Investing in an Existing Partnership

As an alternative to buying equity from an existing partner, one may simply invest assets in the partnership on one's own. For example, assume Roger Foss wants to invest cash in a business on July 8 so that he will have a one-third interest in the partnership. Before Roger makes his investment, the partners' equity is as follows:

> Having a one-third interest doesn't mean Roger has rights to one-third of the net income. The partners must agree on how to share profit and loss.

PARTNERS' EQUITY

B. Blee, Capital	$3,000
A. Jarvis, Capital	1,000

Roger wants one-third interest, and the $4,000 ($3,000 + $1,000) represents two-thirds interest; therefore, Roger will have to contribute $2,000

$\dfrac{\$4,000}{2 \text{ parts}} = \$2,000 \text{ per part}$

OR

$\dfrac{\$4,000}{X} = \dfrac{2}{3}$

$2X = \$12,000$

$X = \$6,000$

$\underline{\$2,000}$ **Roger's Contribution**
$\underline{\$6,000}$ **Total Capital with Roger's Contribution**

to gain the one-third interest. The entry to record the admission of Roger Foss would be as shown in Figure 17-9.

July	8	Cash		2 0 0 0 00	
		R. Foss, Capital			2 0 0 0 00

Figure 17-9
Admission of a Partner

Recording a Bonus to the Old Partners When Admitting a New Partner

When the equity of a partnership in reality is worth more than the amounts recorded in its accounting records, the partners may require an incoming partner to pay an additional amount or **bonus.** This situation could result if a company had an outstanding earnings record with even higher expectations in the future compared with other companies in the industry. Let's see how it would work from the previous example of Roger Foss, assuming the partners Blee and Jarvis on July 8 require a payment of $3,500 (instead of $2,000) to give Foss a one-third interest.

> The bonus to the old partners will be shared in their profit and loss ratio.

Blee and Jarvis, Capital	$4,000	
Investment of Foss	3,500	
Capital of New Partnership	$7,500	Foss only needed to invest $2,000
$\frac{1}{3}$ interest of Foss ($\frac{1}{3} \times \$7,500$)	$2,500	to gain a one-third interest, but the old partners required $3,500.

$\dfrac{\$7,500}{3 \text{ parts}} = \$2,500 \text{ per part}$

Note that the $1,000 ($3,500 − $2,500) difference represents the bonus the old partners will share. The old partners share all losses and gains equally. Thus, the journal entry to admit Foss is as shown in Figure 17-10.

July	8	Cash		3 5 0 0 00	
		B. Blee, Capital			5 0 0 00
		A. Jarvis, Capital			5 0 0 00
		R. Foss, Capital			2 5 0 0 00

Figure 17-10
Admission of a Partner Resulting in a Bonus

Recording a Bonus to a New Partner

A firm often is anxious to bring into the company a new partner who has special skills, business contacts, or abilities. The old partners then must accept a reduction in their capital balances to make up the difference in what the new partner invests compared with the new partner's capital balance. Let's play back the previous example by looking at how "anxious" Blee and Jarvis are to obtain the managerial talents of Roger Foss. Now the old partners have required Foss on July 8 to invest only $1,400 to have a one-third interest in the business.

> Capital of new partner minus investment of new partner equals bonus by which old owners will reduce their capital balance, using their profit and loss ratio.

$$\frac{\$5,400}{3 \text{ parts}} = \$1,800 \text{ per part}$$

Blee and Jarvis, Capital	$4,000
Investment of Foss	1,400
Capital of New Partnership	$5,400
$\frac{1}{3}$ interest of Foss $\left(\frac{1}{3} \times \$5,400\right)$	$1,800

Note that Foss invested only $1,400, while in reality he needed to invest $1,800. Thus, the old partners are absorbing equally the bonus of $400 ($1,800 − $1,400) by reducing their capital balance. The journal entry to record the admitting of Foss to the partnership is as shown in Figure 17-11.

> **Remember:**
> A one-third interest in equity doesn't necessarily entitle Foss to one-third of the income. His share depends on the agreement set up by the partners.

July	8	Cash	1 4 0 0 00		
		B. Blee, Capital	2 0 0 00		
		A. Jarvis, Capital	2 0 0 00		
		R. Foss, Capital		1 8 0 0 00	

Figure 17-11 Journalizing Bonus to Partners

RECORDING PERMANENT WITHDRAWAL OF A PARTNER

> Any loss or gain in the revaluation is shared according to the partners' profit and loss ratio.

When a partnership contract is drawn up, it usually states the procedures to be followed when a partner withdraws. Often the procedures include an audit of the accounting records and the adjustment of the assets to their current fair market value. These steps are done so that the capital of the retiring partner does indeed reflect the current value of his or her equity. Let's look at (1) the balance sheet before revaluation of Ring, Rotter, and Freeze; (2) the entry made to record revaluation; (3) the new, revalued balance sheet; and (4) withdrawal of J. Freeze (assume no liabilities). Partners of Ring, Rotter, and Freeze have a profit and loss ratio of 1/2, 1/4, and 1/4, respectively.

$$\text{Ring} = \frac{1}{2} \times \$400$$
$$= \$200$$
$$\text{Rotter} = \frac{1}{4} \times \$400$$
$$= \$100$$
$$\text{Freeze} = \frac{1}{4} \times \$400$$
$$= \$100$$

1. The balance sheet before revaluation is shown in Figure 17-12.

RING, ROTTER, AND FREEZE						
Assets			**Partners' Equity**			
Cash		$ 2 2 0 0 00	A. Ring, Capital			$ 4 4 0 0 00
Merchandise Inventory		3 2 0 0 00	B. Rotter, Capital			2 0 0 0 00
Store Equipment	$ 4 0 0 0 00		J. Freeze, Capital			2 0 0 0 00
Less Acc. Dep.	1 0 0 0 00	3 0 0 0 00				
Total Assets		$ 8 4 0 0 00	Total Equities			$ 8 4 0 0 00

Figure 17-12 Balance Sheet Before Revaluation

2. When the accountant completes the audit, it is reported that inventory, owing to market conditions, is overvalued by $400. The journal entry to record the revaluation is shown in Figure 17-13.

Figure 17-13
Journal Entry to Record Revaluation

Nov.	30	A. Ring, Capital	2 0 0 00		
		B. Rotter, Capital	1 0 0 00		
		J. Freeze, Capital	1 0 0 00		
		Merchandise Inventory		4 0 0 00	

3. Here is the new, revalued balance sheet (Fig. 17-14):

RING, ROTTER, AND FREEZE					
Assets			**Partners' Equity**		
Cash		$ 2 2 0 0 00	A. Ring, Capital		$ 4 2 0 0 00
Merchandise Inventory		2 8 0 0 00	B. Rotter, Capital		1 9 0 0 00
Store Equipment	$ 4 0 0 0 00		J. Freeze, Capital		1 9 0 0 00
Less Acc. Dep.	1 0 0 0 00	3 0 0 0 00			
Total Assets		$ 8 0 0 0 00	Total Equities		$ 8 0 0 0 00

Figure 17-14 New Revalued Balance Sheet

4. The entry to record the withdrawal of Freeze from the partnership is shown in Figure 17-15.

Nov.	30	J. Freeze, Capital	1 9 0 0 00	
		Cash		1 9 0 0 00

Figure 17-15
Withdrawal of Partner

> The withdrawal means a new partnership and a new profit and loss ratio for Ring and Rotter.

> A partner who wants "out" quickly may be willing to take less than book value of the equity.

RECORDING PERMANENT WITHDRAWAL WHEN A PARTNER TAKES ASSETS OF LESS VALUE THAN BOOK EQUITY

In the last situation Freeze received the revalued amount of his capital by taking out $1,900 in cash. Often, when a partner retires, the assets may not be revalued. In this case the partners have to agree whether the assets are overvalued and whether the withdrawing partner should settle for less than the book value of his or her equity. For example, let's look at the balance sheet for Joll, Smoot, and Jangles (Fig. 17-16) to see what will happen if Smoot settles for less than his book value on July 31 (assume a profit and loss ratio of 2:2:1).

JOLL, SMOOT, AND JANGLES			
Assets		**Partners' Equity**	
Cash	$25 0 0 0 00	R. Joll, Capital	$28 0 0 0 00
Merchandise Inventory	29 0 0 0 00	A. Smoot, Capital	18 0 0 0 00
		B. Jangles, Capital	8 0 0 0 00
Total Assets	$54 0 0 0 00	Total Equities	$54 0 0 0 00

Figure 17-16
Balance Sheet Before Settlement

$$\frac{2:1}{\begin{array}{c}2/3\text{ for Joll}\\1/3\text{ for Jangles}\end{array}}$$

R. Joll $= \frac{2}{3} \times \$6,000$
$= \$4,000$

B. Jangles $= \frac{1}{3} \times \$6,000$
$= \$2,000$

Smoot is extremely anxious to withdraw from the partnership and is willing to accept a cash settlement of $12,000. Joll and Jangles will share the $6,000 ($18,000 − $12,000) of capital that Smoot does not take with him in the ratio of 2:1. The journal entry to record the withdrawal of Smoot is shown in Figure 17-17.

July	31	A. Smoot, Capital	18 0 0 0 00	
		Cash		12 0 0 0 00
		R. Joll, Capital		4 0 0 0 00
		B. Jangles, Capital		2 0 0 0 00

Figure 17-17
Withdrawal of Smoot When Assets Valued at Less Than Book Equity

Now let's look at what could happen if Smoot withdrew assets valued at *more* than his book equity.

RECORDING PERMANENT WITHDRAWAL WHEN A PARTNER TAKES ASSETS OF GREATER VALUE THAN BOOK EQUITY

Using the previous example, Smoot might withdraw assets valued at *more* than book equity if

1. Partnership assets are undervalued, and
2. Joll and Jangles are anxious to have him retire.

Assume the assets are undervalued by $12,000 and the owners want to leave them this way. Thus, Smoot's capital would be increased by $4,800 $\left(\frac{2}{5} \times \$12,000\right)$, and the other owners' equity would be reduced to cover this $4,800 increase to Smoot's capital. The entry in Figure 17-18 would be recorded when Smoot leaves the partnership.

Figure 17-18
Smoot Withdraws Assets Valued More Than Book Equity

July	31	A. Smoot, Capital	18 0 0 0 00		
		R. Joll, Capital	3 2 0 0 00		
		B. Jangles, Capital	1 6 0 0 00		
		Cash		22 8 0 0 00	

R. Joll $= \frac{2}{3} \times \$4,800$
$= \$3,200$
B. Jangles $= \frac{1}{3} \times \$4,800$
$= \$1,600$

Note that Smoot receives in cash the $18,000 value of his capital plus the $4,800 to reflect the capital of $22,800 agreed upon by the other owners. Note also how the capital of Joll and Jangles was reduced according to their profit and loss ratio.

Remember that when a partner dies, the partnership ends, and the estate is entitled to receive the proper value of the capital account of the deceased after an audit and revaluation of the assets. Journal entries for the death of a partner are similar to those for other situations when a partner leaves. To have enough cash to pay the full value of the deceased partner's capital account, partnerships often carry life insurance policies on partners.

Learning Unit 17-3 Review

AT THIS POINT you should be able to

- Explain how a new partner can be admitted in a partnership. (p. 649)
- Journalize the entry to record the admitting of a partner. (p. 650)
- Explain why a one-third interest doesn't mean that the net income is split three ways. (p. 651)
- Calculate as well as journalize a bonus to old partners when a new partner is admitted. (p. 651)
- Calculate as well as journalize a bonus to a new partner. (p. 652)
- Explain how assets might be revalued when a partner withdraws. (p. 652)
- Calculate as well as journalize entries to record withdrawal of a partner taking assets for less or more than book equity if assets are not revalued. (p. 653)

SELF-REVIEW QUIZ 17-3

(The forms you need are on page 86 of the *Study Guide and Working Papers*.)
Respond true or false to the following:

1. When new partner, Cohen, buys an equity of existing partner, Lee-Ying, the cash account is always increased in the business.

2. The profit and loss ratio must be based on the capital balances of the partners.

3. A bonus to old partners is based on their profit and loss ratio.

4. A bonus to a new partner could result if the old partners are anxious to recruit the new partner.

5. Any loss or gain when assets are revalued is shared in the partners' profit and loss ratio.

6. Assets of a partnership cannot be revalued.

7. A partner, Jaworski, can never withdraw assets that are valued at less than his book equity.

8. A partner who withdraws assets of greater value than book equity causes the capital of the remaining partners to decrease when assets are not revalued.

SOLUTIONS TO SELF-REVIEW QUIZ 17-3

1. False 2. False 3. True 4. True 5. True 6. False
7. False 8. True

Learning Unit 17-4   The Liquidation of a Partnership

Up to this point we have looked at the admission and withdrawal of partners. Each time this happens, a new partnership is formed and any losses or gains are shared in an agreed-upon ratio. The operations of the business continue, of course, even when the new partnership is formed. In this unit we look at three situations in which a partnership is **liquidated.** Liquidation occurs when the business is completely ended by converting assets into cash and paying off obligations and equity. The following steps complete a liquidation:

1. Assets are sold for cash with any loss or gain recognized.

2. Any loss or gain is divided among the partners based on their profit or loss ratio.

3. Creditors are paid off.

4. Remaining cash is distributed to the partners based on their capital balances.

We will look at three different situations based on the following information. Peters, French, and Smith are liquidating their business on May 31, 20XX. The partners have a profit and loss ratio of 3:2:1. Figure 17-19 shows the updated balance sheet at the end of May. Note that at this point we've closed out the temporary accounts.

Figure 17-19
Balance Sheet Before
Liquidation

PETERS, FRENCH, AND SMITH BALANCE SHEET MAY 31, 20XX		
Assets		
Cash	$ 7 0 0 0 00	
Other Assets	138 0 0 0 00	
Total Assets	$145 0 0 0 00	
Liabilities and Partners' Equity		
Liabilities	$ 25 0 0 0 00	
Jane Peters, Capital	30 0 0 0 00	
Joe French, Capital	70 0 0 0 00	
Alan Smith, Capital	20 0 0 0 00	
Total Liabilities and Partners' Equity	$145 0 0 0 00	

Using this information, let's look at three different situations in which liquidation occurs.

Situation 1

Selling assets at a gain (assets sold for $144,000).

The Liquidation Process

Step 1: Record sale of assets along with any loss or gain from realization* (gain = $144,000 − $138,000) on June 7 (Fig. 17-20).

Figure 17-20
Selling Assets at a Gain

June	7	Cash	144 0 0 0 00	
		Other Assets		138 0 0 0 00
		Loss or Gain from Realization		6 0 0 0 00

Step 2: Loss or gain from realization is allocated to each partner in ratio of 3:2:1 (Fig. 17-21).

Figure 17-21
Selling Assets at a Loss

Peters: $\frac{3}{6}$ × $6,000

French: $\frac{2}{6}$ × $6,000

Smith: $\frac{1}{6}$ × $6,000

June	7	Loss or Gain from Realization	6 0 0 0 00	
		Jane Peters, Capital		3 0 0 0 00
		Joe French, Capital		2 0 0 0 00
		Alan Smith, Capital		1 0 0 0 00

Step 3: Pay claims of the creditors on June 15 (Fig. 17-22).

Figure 17-22
Payment to Creditors

June	15	Liabilities	25 0 0 0 00	
		Cash		25 0 0 0 00

---

*Realization means the conversion of noncash assets into cash as part of the liquidation process. It can result in either gain or loss. The account Loss or Gain from Realization is similar to the Cash Short and Over account discussed in Chapter 6. The account will be closed separately, because closing entries take place before liquidation. In using this account think of loss as a debit and gain as a credit.

The Ledger Before Step 4

J. Peters, Capital	J. French, Capital	A. Smith, Capital	Cash
30,000	70,000	20,000	7,000	25,000
3,000	2,000	1,000	144,000	
		Bal: 126,000		

Step 4: Distribute cash that is left to partners based on their capital balance (Fig. 17-23). *No* profit and loss ratios are used in this step.

June	30	Jane Peters, Capital	33 0 0 0 00			
		Joe French, Capital	72 0 0 0 00			
		Alan Smith, Capital	21 0 0 0 00			
		Cash			126 0 0 0 00	

Figure 17-23
Cash Paid to Owners

The accompanying statement of liquidation gives a comprehensive report of the liquidation process involved in Situation 1. Keep in mind that the liquidation process takes time to complete; it isn't done overnight.

PETERS, FRENCH, AND SMITH
STATEMENT OF LIQUIDATION
FOR MONTH OF JUNE 20XX

	Cash	+	Other Assets	=	Liabilities	+	Capital Peters	+ French	+ Smith
Balances before realization	$7,000	+	$138,000	=	$25,000	+	$30,000	+ $70,000	+ $20,000
Recording gain from sales of assets	+$144,000	−	$138,000				+3,000	+2,000	+1,000
Balances updated	$151,000			=	$25,000		$33,000	+ $72,000	+ $21,000
Paying of liabilities	−$25,000				−$25,000				
Balances updated	$126,000			=			+$33,000	+ $72,000	+ $21,000
Distribution of cash to partners	−$126,000			=			−$33,000	− $72,000	− $21,000

Now let's look at what would happen if the assets were sold at a loss.

Situation 2

Selling assets at a loss (assets sold for $126,000).

The Liquidation Process

Step 1: Record sale of assets with loss or gain from realization (loss = $138,000 − $126,000) on June 7 (Fig. 17-24).

June	7	Cash	126 0 0 0 00			
		Loss or Gain from Realization	12 0 0 0 00			
		Other Assets			138 0 0 0 00	

Figure 17-24
Selling Assets at a Loss

Step 2: Loss or gain from realization is allocated to each partner in ratio of 3:2:1 (Fig. 17-25).

Figure 17-25
Loss Allocated to Owners

June	7	J. Peters, Capital	6 0 0 0 00	
		J. French, Capital	4 0 0 0 00	
		A. Smith, Capital	2 0 0 0 00	
		Loss or Gain from Realization		12 0 0 0 00

Step 3: Pay claims of creditors (Fig. 17-26).

Figure 17-26
Payment to Creditors

June	15	Liabilities	25 0 0 0 00	
		Cash		25 0 0 0 00

The Ledger Before Step 4

J. Peters, Capital	J. French, Capital	A. Smith, Capital	Cash
6,000 | 30,000	4,000 | 70,000	2,000 | 20,000	7,000 | 25,000
			126,000
			Bal: 108,000

Step 4: Distribute cash that is left to partners based on their capital balances on June 30 (Fig. 17-27).

Figure 17-27
Payment to Owners

No profit and loss ratios are used in this step.

June	30	J. Peters, Capital	24 0 0 0 00	
		J. French, Capital	66 0 0 0 00	
		A. Smith, Capital	18 0 0 0 00	
		Cash		108 0 0 0 00

The accompanying statement of liquidation provides a comprehensive report of this liquidation process.

PETERS, FRENCH, AND SMITH
STATEMENT OF LIQUIDATION
FOR MONTH OF JUNE 20XX

	Cash	+ Other Assets	= Liabilities	+ Peters	+ French	+ Smith
					Capital	
Balances before realization	$7,000 +	$138,000	= $25,000	+ $30,000 +	$70,000 +	$20,000
Recording loss from sales of assets	+$126,000 −	$138,000		−6,000	−4,000	−2,000
Balances updated	$133,000		= $25,000	$24,000 +	$66,000 +	$18,000
Paying of liabilities	−$25,000		−$25,000			
Balances updated	$108,000		=	$24,000 +	$66,000 +	$18,000
Distribution of cash to partners	−$108,000		=	−$24,000 −	$66,000 −	$18,000

In the final situation, the partners are unable to cover a deficit from the sale of assets.

Situation 3

Selling assets at a loss, with some partner's capital not being enough to cover the deficit (assets sold for $42,000).

The Liquidation Process

Step 1:   Record sale of assets along with any loss or gain from realization (loss = $138,000 − $42,000) on June 7 (Fig. 17-28).

June	7	Cash	42 00 0 00	
		Loss or Gain from Realization	96 00 0 00	
		Other Assets		138 00 0 00

Figure 17-28
Loss from Realization

Step 2:   Loss or gain from realization is allocated to each partner in ratio 3:2:1 (Fig. 17-29).

June	7	J. Peters, Capital	48 00 0 00	
		J. French, Capital	32 00 0 00	
		A. Smith, Capital	16 00 0 00	
		Loss or Gain from Realization		96 00 0 00

Figure 17-29
Loss Allocated to
Each Partner

Peters: $\frac{3}{6} \times \$96,000$

French: $\frac{2}{6} \times \$96,000$

Smith: $\frac{1}{6} \times \$96,000$

French: $\frac{2}{3} \times \$18,000$

Smith: $\frac{1}{3} \times \$18,000$

When the loss exceeds the capital balance of a partner and the partner cannot make up the deficit, the other partners have unlimited liability to make up the deficit.

Peters, Capital	French, Capital	Smith, Capital
48,000 | 30,000	32,000 | 70,000	16,000 | 20,000

Note that Peters has a deficit of $18,000 ($48,000 − $30,000). The other partners must share this deficit in their profit and loss ratio of 2:1 (Fig. 17-30).

June	7	Joe French, Capital	12 00 0 00	
		Alan Smith, Capital	6 00 0 00	
		Jane Peters, Capital		18 00 0 00

Figure 17-30
Sharing of Deficit
by Owners

Peters, Capital	French, Capital	Smith, Capital
48,000 | 30,000	32,000 | 70,000	16,000 | 20,000
_____ | 18,000	12,000 |	6,000 |

Note that now *Smith* has a $2,000 deficit. French is the only partner left with a capital balance and thus is liable for this deficit (Fig. 17-31).

June	7	Joe French, Capital	2 00 0 00	
		Alan Smith, Capital		2 00 0 00

Figure 17-31
French Only Partner
Left With a Balance

Step 3:   Pay claims of creditors on June 15 (Fig. 17-32).

Figure 17-32
Pay Creditors

June	15	Liabilities	25 00 0 00	
		Cash		25 00 0 00

Step 4:   Distribute remaining cash on June 30 (Fig. 17-33).

Figure 17-33
Pay Cash to Owner

June	30	J. French, Capital	24 00 0 00	
		Cash		24 00 0 00

French, Capital

32,000	70,000
12,000	
2,000	

The accompanying statement of liquidation provides a comprehensive report of this liquidation process.

PETERS, FRENCH, AND SMITH
STATEMENT OF LIQUIDATION
FOR MONTH OF JUNE 20XX

	Cash	+ Other Assets	= Liabilities	+	Capital Peters	+ French	+ Smith
Balances before realization	$7,000 +	$138,000	= $25,000	+	$30,000 +	$70,000	+ $20,000
Recording loss from sale of assets	+$42,000 −	$138,000	=	−	48,000 −	32,000	− 16,000
Balances updated	$49,000		$25,000	−	$18,000 +	$38,000	+ $4,000
Deficit of Peters covered by partners in ratio 2:1				+	$18,000 −	$12,000	− 6,000
Balances updated	$49,000		= $25,000		+	$26,000	− $2,000
Deficit of Smith covered by French						− $2,000	+ $2,000
Balances updated	$49,000		= $25,000		+	$24,000	
Paying of liabilities	−$25,000		$25,000				
Balances updated	$24,000		=			$24,000	
Distribution of cash to French	−$24,000				−	$24,000	

Learning Unit 17-4 Review

AT THIS POINT you should be able to

- Explain the steps of the liquidation process. (p. 655)
- Explain why the profit and loss ratio is not used to pay off the partners in the liquidation process. (p. 656)
- Prepare a liquidation statement. (p. 657)

SELF-REVIEW QUIZ 17-4

(The forms you need are on page 87 of the *Study Guide and Working Papers.*)

From the information given here, journalize the (A) sale of assets, (B) loss or gain from realization, (C) payment of liabilities, and (D) distribution of remaining cash to the partners.

1. Cash, $4,000; Other Assets, $13,000; Liabilities, $2,000; Jay, Capital, $3,000; Joger, Capital, $5,000; and Ynet, Capital, $7,000.

2. Partners share losses or gains in a 3:1:1 ratio.

3. Assets sold for $16,000.

SOLUTION TO SELF-REVIEW QUIZ 17-4

(A)	Cash	16 000 00		
	Other Assets		13 000 00	
	Loss of Gain from Realization		3 000 00	
(B)	Loss or Gain from Realization	3 000 00		
	Jay, Capital		1 800 00	
	Joger, Capital		6 00 00	
	Ynet, Capital		6 00 00	
(C)	Liabilities	2 000 00		
	Cash		2 000 00	
(D)	Jay, Capital	4 800 00		
	Joger, Capital	5 600 00		
	Ynet, Capital	7 600 00		
	Cash		18 000 00	

Figure 17-34
Sale, Distribution, and Payment to Creditors and Owners

Jay: $\frac{3}{5} \times \$3,000$

Joger: $\frac{1}{5} \times \$3,000$

Ynet: $\frac{1}{5} \times \$3,000$

Chapter Review

Learning Unit 17-1

1. Forming a partnership is quite easy and can be agreed upon in writing or orally. Having a written articles of partnership clearly spells out the "specifics" of the partnership.
2. Although the life of a partnership is limited, dissolving a partnership does not mean that the business will cease operations.
3. Mutual agency means that in most cases all partners are bound by the acts of one partner who enters into a contract as an agent of the company.
4. In the formation of a partnership, one records assets at their current fair value.

Learning Unit 17-2

1. Salary and interest allowances are not expenses but mechanisms used to divide net income or net loss among partners. Salary is based on personal service; interest is based on a percent of each partner's capital balance.
2. Whether net income covers the salary and interest allowances makes no difference in calculating them; they are allocated, and *then* one looks to see the effect on partners' equity.
3. The statement of partners' equity is a supporting document that calculates the ending capital balance found on the balance sheet for each partner.

Learning Unit 17-3

1. When a new partner buys an equity interest from an existing partner, any personal profit belongs to the existing partner and is not recorded in the partnership. All that results on the partnership's books is a change of equity.
2. One partner cannot force other partners to accept a new partner.
3. A one-quarter equity interest doesn't necessarily mean a one-quarter share of all earnings; it would depend on the profit and loss ratio agreed upon by the partners.
4. A bonus is given to old partners if a new partner contributes more than his or her equity interest. On the other hand, a bonus is given to a new partner if he or she invests less than equity interest. The bonus is shared based on the profit and loss ratio.
5. At the time a partner leaves, a partnership may be audited and assets adjusted to their current fair market value. Revaluations are shared between the partners based on the profit and loss ratio.
6. A partner may withdraw for less than or more than book equity. The difference is then shared by the other partners based on the profit and loss ratio. If assets are not revalued, partners must agree whether assets are overstated or not, and then the equity change of the partner who is leaving is shared in profit and loss ratio by the other partners.

Learning Unit 17-4

1. Liquidation is the winding-up process involved in ending a business.
2. Liquidation steps include the following:

   a. Selling assets for cash.
   b. Dividing loss or gain for realization among partners.
   c. Paying creditors.
   d. Paying remaining cash to partners based on capital balances.

Key Terms

Articles of partnership   The written contract that spells out the details of the agreement among the partners.

Bonus   When a new partner is admitted, he or she may pay more or less than equity interest. If the new partner pays more, the old partners share a bonus in the profit and loss ratio. Of course, the opposite could result, and the new partner could receive a bonus if he or she invests less than equity interest.

Co-ownership of property   Each partner owns a share of the assets.

Deficit   Amount by which net income falls short of salary and interest allowance.

General partner   A partner who has unlimited liability.

Interest allowance   A mechanism for dividing earnings of a partnership based on a percent of capital balances of the partners (not an expense).

Limited life   Partnership is dissolved by admission, withdrawal, or death of a partner. Although the partnership is dissolved, the operations of the business continue.

Limited partner   The partner's liability is limited to the amount of investment in the partnership.

Liquidation   Occurs when a business is terminated, the assets are sold, and liabilities and partners are paid off.

Mutual agency   Act of a single partner is binding on all members of the partnership.

Partnership   The association of two or more persons who act as co-owners of a business.

Profit and loss ratio   An agreed-upon ratio used to divide earnings or losses of a partnership.

Purchase of an equity interest   Transfer of ownership between an existing partner and a new partner.

Realization   The conversion of noncash assets into cash in the liquidation process.

Salary allowance   A mechanism for dividing earnings of a partnership based on personal services provided by the partners (not an expense).

Uniform Partnership Act   Laws enacted in most states that govern how a partnership is formed, operated, and liquidated.

Unlimited liability   Partners may be personally liable for debts of the partnership.

Blueprint: Advantages and Disadvantages of a Partnership

Advantages	Disadvantages
1. Ease of formation; legal status under Uniform Partnership Act.	1. Limited life expectancy; any changes in membership dissolve the partnership.
2. Ability to raise more capital than a sole proprietorship.	2. Mutual agency; action by one partner binds all other partners.
3. Pooled resource of talents.	3. Unlimited liability; each partner must cover partnership debts with personal assets.
4. Flexibility to react to the marketplace, because legal restrictions are minimal.	4. Cannot admit a new partner without agreement of all other partners; a partner cannot withdraw without agreement of all other partners.
5. Credit rating usually higher, because more than one partner is responsible for company's debts.	

Questions, Mini Exercises, Exercises, and Problems

Discussion Questions

1. How is the equity of a partnership different from that of a sole proprietorship?
2. List five characteristics of a partnership.
3. What is the function of the articles of partnership?

4. Explain how a company could operate even when being dissolved.

5. Mutual agency could create unlimited liability. Agree or disagree. Defend your position.

6. Explain why salary and interest allowances are not expenses for a partnership.

7. Give an example of a fractional ratio.

8. The statement of partners' capital is a required report. Accept or reject. Defend your position.

9. What is meant by a "side transaction" when a new partner is admitted by an existing partner's selling the new partner equity?

10. What is meant by a "bonus" when a partner is admitted?

11. When a partner withdraws, why would a partnership revalue its assets?

12. Why would a partner who is withdrawing take more or less than book equity?

13. What are the four steps of the liquidation process?

Mini Exercises

(The forms you need are on pages 89–90 of the *Study Guide and Working Papers.*)

Forming a Partnership

1. Alice Hall and Jim Brown enter into a partnership. On July 1, 200X, Alice invests $5,000 cash in the partnership. Jim invests $2,000 cash and store equipment worth $6,000 with accumulated depreciation of $2,000. The equipment has a current appraised value of $7,000. Prepare a journal entry to record this transaction.

Division of Net Income

2. James Slater, Scupper Ring, and Molly Flynn invested $2,000, $4,000, and $6,000, respectively. At the end of the first year, the company's net income was $21,000. Assuming no agreement was reached on how to share net income, prepare a journal entry at closing to allocate net income.

Division of Net Income Based on Beginning Capital Balances

3. If the partners in Mini Exercise 2 share net income based on their beginning capital investments, what would be the journal entry at closing to allocate net income?

Calculating Total Salary and Interest Allowance

4. If the partners in Mini Exercise 2 have the following agreement, please calculate the total salary and interest allowance:

   a. *Salary Allowance:* Slater, $7,000; Ring, $6,000; and Flynn, $4,000.
   b. 10% interest on capital investments.

Share of Net Income to Partners; Deficit Sharing

5. Using your answer in Mini Exercise 4, how much more income is to be distributed to the partners (assume each shares equally) after the salary and interest allowance? If net income was $17,990, how much would the partners share in the deficit?

Admission of a New Partner

6. On March 8, Alan Oll sold his equity in the partnership to B. Mills for $4,000. Alan's capital account had a $3,000 balance. Record the journal entry.

Investing into an Existing Partnership

7. Pete Raul wants to have a one-third interest in a law practice that has two partners with capital balances as follows:

R. Seel, Capital	$4,000
A. Pool, Capital	1,000

How much must Pete invest into the partnership?

Calculating Profit and Loss Ratio

8. From the following capital balances, calculate the profit and loss ratio for each account:

B. Bool, Capital	$100
A. Jones, Capital	500
T. Pool, Capital	400

Liquidation

9. From the following, journalize the (a) sale of assets and (b) loss or gain from liquidation realization. Given:

Cash	$ 3,000
Other Assets	15,000
Liabilities	3,000
Moxie, Capital	4,000
Carol, Capital	6,000
Earl, Capital	5,000

Partners agreed to share losses or gains in a 4:1:2 ratio and sold assets for $19,200.

Exercises

(The forms you need are on pages 91–92 of the *Study Guide and Working Papers.*)

17-1. Earl Munroe and Carol Rogers form a partnership on May 1, 20XX. Munroe contributes $40,000. Rogers contributes $28,000 cash and land costing $18,000 with a current fair value of $29,000. A $30,000 note payable due Rogers is assumed by the new partnership. Please prepare the journal entries to record Munroe's and Rogers's investment in the partnership.

Journal entries to record investing into a partnership.

17-2. A. Lot and B. Stall have decided their partnership earnings will be shared as follows: (a) 10% interest allowance on capital balances at beginning of year, (b) remainder to be shared equally. Capital balances of A. Lot and B. Stall at the beginning of the year are $80,000 and $30,000, respectively. Net income is $16,000 for the year. Record the journal entry to update the capital balances of A. Lot and B. Stall on December 31.

Interest allowance.

17-3. Julie Elliott, Tami DiVito, and Abby Ellen are partners who share losses and gains in a ratio of 2:2:1. Their capital balances are $5,000, $6,000, and $4,000, respectively. The partners are anxious to have Tami retire and have paid her $12,000. Give the journal entry to record the payment to Tami along with the absorption of the amount over book equity by Julie and Abby on July 31, 20XX.

Withdrawal of partner taking assets greater than book equity.

17-4. L. White, V. Slye, and E. Rothe are partners with capital balances of $90,000, $80,000, and $70,000, respectively. Rothe sells his interest in the company for $88,000 to P. Smith. White and Slye have consented to the new partner. Record the journal entry for the admission of Smith on April 8.

Admission of new partner.

17-5. Sullivan, Roe, and Hinch have capital balances before liquidation of $12,000, $24,000, and $32,000, respectively. Cash balance is $48,000, and the principals share losses and gains in a 3:2:1 ratio. All noncash assets are sold, for a gain on

Liquidation.

realization of $24,000. In your calculations assume there are no liabilities. What will each partner receive in cash in the liquidation process?

Group A Problems

(The forms you need are on pages 93–99 of the *Study Guide and Working Papers*.)

17A-1. (a) The partnership of Bell and Shell began with the partners investing $4,000 and $2,400, respectively. At the end of the first year, the partnership earned net income of $8,200. Under each of the following independent situations, calculate how much of the $8,200 each is entitled to:

Situation 1:   No agreement on how income was to be shared.
Situation 2:   Bell and Shell share income based on the beginning-of-year investment ratio.
Situation 3:   Salary allowance of $2,800 to Bell and $2,400 to Shell. Ten percent interest on beginning year's investment. Remainder split equally.

(b) In Situation 3, what would the earnings to each partner be if net income were $4,000?

17A-2. Bob Kerne and Whitney Blak are partners with capital balances of $1,600 and $800, respectively. They share all profits and losses equally. From the following independent situations, journalize the admission of the new partner, Jack Ray:

Situation 1:   Ray purchased Blak's interest for $6,000, paying it personally to Blak.
Situation 2:   Ray invested an amount exactly equal to one-third interest in the partnership.
Situation 3:   Ray invested $1,800 for a one-third interest. Kerne and Blak share the bonus.
Situation 4:   Ray invested $600 for a one-third interest. Bonus is credited to Ray's account.

17A-3. Lane, Right, and Von are partners. On July 30, 20XX, the balance sheet was as follows:

Cash	$12,000	Lane, Capital	$ 7,500
Inventory	5,000	Right, Capital	12,500
Other Assets	8,000	Von, Capital	5,000
Total Assets	$25,000	Total Liab. + Equity	$25,000

The partners agree to share all losses and gains in a 2:2:1 ratio. Von is withdrawing from the partnership. From the following independent situations, journalize the withdrawal of Von:

Situation 1:   Von sells his equity to Jones for $18,000. Partners agree to admission of Jones.
Situation 2:   On withdrawal of Von, inventory is determined to be overvalued by $1,000. (Before withdrawal, assets are revalued to current fair market value.) Be sure to record entry to revalue inventory as well as the withdrawal of Von.
Situation 3:   Von is paid $3,000 out of the assets of the partnership. Because the assets are overvalued, the partners do not want to decrease the recorded asset values.
Situation 4:   Von is paid $8,500 out of the assets of the partnership. Because the assets are undervalued, the partners do not want to increase the recorded asset values.

17A-4. The partnership of Jones, Reston, and Sullivan is being liquidated. All gains and losses are shared in a 3:2:1 ratio. Before liquidation, their balance sheet looks as follows:

Liquidation of a partnership.

Cash	$22,500	Liabilities	$ 6,300
Other Assets	14,700	A. Jones, Capital	11,100
		C. Reston, Capital	18,000
		J. Sullivan, Capital	1,800
Total Assets	$37,200	Total Liab. + Equity	$37,200

Check Figure:
Sit. 2: Loss or gain from realization $9,000 Dr.

Journalize the entries needed in the liquidation process under the following independent situations and assume a date of October 1, 20XX, for sale of assets and October 15 for paying off liabilities and distributing cash to partners:

Distributing partners' earnings.

Situation 1:   Sold other assets for $32,700.
Situation 2:   Sold other assets for $5,700.
Situation 3:   Sold other assets for $2,100. Sullivan cannot cover his deficit.

Group B Problems

(The forms you need are on pages 93–99 of the *Study Guide and Working Papers*.)

17B-1. (a) B. Bell and R. Shell began a partnership by investing $4,800 and $3,200, respectively. At the end of the first year, the partnership earned net income of $7,600. Under each of the following independent situations, calculate how much of the $7,600 each is entitled to:

Situation 1:   No agreement on how income was to be shared.
Situation 2:   Bell and Shell share income based on the beginning-of-year investment ratio.
Situation 3:   Salary allowance of $2,480 to Bell and $2,800 to Shell. Twelve percent interest on beginning year's investment. Remainder split equally.

Check Figure:
(b) Deficit to be shared equally $640

(b) In Situation 3 what would the earnings to each partner be if net income were $5,600?

17B-2. Bob Kerne and Whitney Blak are partners with capital balances of $3,000 and $1,000, respectively. They share all profits and losses equally. From the following independent situations, journalize the admission of the new partner, Jack Ray:

Admission of a new partner under various assumptions.

Situation 1:   Ray purchases Blak's interest for $6,000, paying it personally to Blak.
Situation 2:   Ray invested an amount exactly equal to one-fifth interest in the partnership.
Situation 3:   Ray invested $2,000 for a one-fifth interest. Kerne and Blak share the bonus.
Situation 4:   Ray invested $300 for a one-fifth interest. Bonus is credited to Ray's account.

Check Figure:
Sit. 3: $800 Bonus to old partners

17B-3. Lane, Right, and Von are partners of LRV Repairs Service. On July 31, 20XX, the balance sheet was as follows:

Withdrawal of a partner.

Cash	$50,000	Lane, Capital	$30,000
Inventory	20,000	Right, Capital	15,000
Other Assets	10,000	Von, Capital	35,000
Total Assets	$80,000	Total Liab. + Equity	$80,000

The partners agree to share all losses and gains in a 2:1:2 ratio. Von is withdrawing from the partnership. From the following independent situations, journalize the withdrawal of Von:

Check Figure:
Sit. 1:
Dr. Von, Capital
                $35,000
Cr. Jones, Capital
                $35,000

Situation 1:   Von sells his equity to Jones for $120,000. Partners agree to admission of Jones.

Situation 2:   On withdrawal of Von, inventory is determined to be overvalued by $6,000. (Before withdrawal, assets are revalued to current fair market value.)

Situation 3:   Von is paid $32,000 out of the assets of the partnership. Although the assets are overvalued, the partners do not want to decrease the recorded asset values.

Situation 4:   Von is paid $44,000 out of the assets of the partnership. Because the assets are undervalued, partners do not want to increase the recorded asset values.

17B-4. Jones, Reston, and Sullivan are liquidating their partnership. All losses and gains are shared in a 4:2:1 ratio (not based on investment). Before liquidation their balance sheet looked as follows:

<table>
<tr><td>Cash</td><td>$ 800</td><td>Liabilities</td><td>$ 6,000</td></tr>
<tr><td>Other Assets</td><td>19,200</td><td>A. Jones, Capital</td><td>4,000</td></tr>
<tr><td></td><td></td><td>C. Reston, Capital</td><td>8,000</td></tr>
<tr><td></td><td></td><td>J. Sullivan, Capital</td><td>2,000</td></tr>
<tr><td>Total Assets</td><td>$20,000</td><td>Total Liab. + Equity</td><td>$20,000</td></tr>
</table>

Journalize the entries needed in the liquidation process under the following independent situations (assume a date of July 1, 20XX, for sale of assets and a date of July 15 to pay off liabilities and distribute cash that is left to the partners):

Situation 1:   Sold other assets for $26,200.
Situation 2:   Sold other assets for $17,800.
Situation 3:   Sold other assets for $10,800; Jones cannot cover his deficit. (For simplicity, round any calculations to the nearest dollar.)

Real-World Applications

17R-1. Al Ring and Marvin Smoy are partners who are extremely worried about the financial condition of their company. As of December 31, 20XX, their balance sheet revealed the following:

Assets		**Liabilities and Owner's Equity**	
Cash	$ 30,000	Liabilities	$ 60,000
Noncash assets	400,000	A. Ring, Capital	200,000
		M. Smoy, Capital	170,000
Total Assets	$430,000	Total Liab. + Equity	$430,000

There is a pending lawsuit that could result in a settlement of more than $400,000 against the company for negligence. Al wants out of the partnership before the case is settled. Marvin claims they are both in this together. As the accountant, could you explain in writing to Al how the situation looks? All losses and gains are shared in a 2:1 ratio.

17R-2. On May 15 Peter Rig and Joan Fess formed a partnership in the catering business. Peter invested $30,000 in cash and $8,000 in equipment. Joan invested land worth $15,000, a building worth $24,000, and merchandise worth $8,000.

The partners decided that they would insure the building and its contents beginning June 1. On May 28 a fire broke out and destroyed half of the merchandise, the building, and the equipment. That night Rig and Fess decided to liquidate the business.

Rig told Fess that he would take his cash (which was in a fireproof safe) and Fess would take the land. Fess argued that in a partnership Rig couldn't do that. Could you settle this dispute? Make your recommendations in writing.

Liquidation of a partnership.

Check Figure:
Sit 2: Loss or gain from
realization $1,400 Dr.

YOU make the call

Critical Thinking/Ethical Case

17R-3. Jee Jones is in a partnership with Alvin Scott and Morry Flynn. Jee signed a long-term contract with a supplier without telling either partner. When Alvin heard about it, he hit the roof. He told Jee the partnership could not afford this contract and he would have nothing to do with it. Do you think Alvin should be upset? You make the call. Write down your recommendations to Alvin.

Internet Exercises: West Legal Directory; Touch N'Go Systems

EX-1. [**www.wld.com**]   You have now learned about general liability partnerships. Your text teaches you that a partnership shall have at least one general partner who is "generally" liable for the partnership's debts.

In recent years, a new partnership device has become popular in many states. This device is called a "limited liability partnership" or LLP. Begun in Texas, the LLP is now functional in at least 21 states and the District of Columbia.

Examine this site and list some of the differences between a general partnership and a limited liability partnership. Determine if your state has a limited liability partnership law.

EX-2. [**www.touchngo.com/Section350.htm**]   A general guideline for states to govern partnerships is the Uniform Partnership Act. This law was presented to the states as a "model" law. Most of the states have adopted it, and most of them have modified it from its original version.

The act states how partnerships account for transactions affecting the partners just as it specifies how to account for transactions with those outside the partnership. This Web site presents the State of Alaska's version of the act. Your text presented a method of liquidating a partnership. The Web site shows the text of the Alaska law. Read the text of the law and comment on how its provisions compare with the liquidation procedures written in the text.

Corporations

Organization and Capital Stock

You've spent your weekend completing a term paper that is due Monday. It seems other students are using every photocopy machine on campus; it's that time of the school term when everyone is working on their term papers at once. As an alternative, you decide to drop by the copy shop in town.

When you walk into The CopyCat Store, you see that the atmosphere is a little less chaotic. The shop has a dozen or more self-service copy machines and several people behind the counter working on various large copy projects. The copies cost a little more than at school, but it's worth every extra cent to make a quality photocopy of your term paper, which you need to hand in on time.

After paying for your copies, the clerk puts them in a bag. You notice that the printing on the bag reads, "The CopyCat Store Inc. now has over 500 locations nationwide to serve you. The CopyCat Store Inc. is a publicly held company listed on the American Stock Exchange." You had no idea that The CopyCat Store was incorporated and publicly held; you had thought it was only one small store located in town.

Like many large corporations today, The CopyCat Store probably started out with one location. By forming a corporation, The CopyCat Store was able to raise capital and expand its business by selling stock. This is a major reason why the corporate form of ownership is very popular today.

In this chapter we discuss the advantages and disadvantages of a corporation and how a corporation is formed. We will learn about accounting for capital stock transactions, including calculating dividends on preferred and common stock. We will also find out how to record stock transactions under a stock subscription plan. After completing this chapter you will understand how The CopyCat Store grew to be a nationwide enterprise.

Learning Objectives

- Defining a corporation; establishing a corporation; listing the advantages and disadvantages of a corporation. (p. 672)

- Journalizing entries for issuing par-value stock, no-par stock, and no-par with stated value stock. (p. 678)

- Calculating dividends on preferred and common stock. (p. 682)

- Recording capital stock transactions under a stock subscription plan. (p. 685)

So far we've learned about sole proprietorships and partnerships; now we're going to learn about corporations. A corporation like Cisco Systems is a separate legal entity. We first look at how a corporation is formed, along with its main characteristics.

Learning Unit 18-1   Forming a Corporation; Characteristics of the Corporate Structure

Four steps are involved in forming a corporation.

Step 1: The incorporators, those wishing to form the corporation, apply to a state for a charter. They do so by submitting articles of incorporation drawn up by an attorney, together with a fee. The articles of incorporation consist of the following information:

1. Name of the corporation and incorporation date.
2. Purpose of business.
3. Organizational structure.
4. Expected life (usually "forever").
5. Primary location of business.
6. Types of stock to be offered. (Stock is what owners purchase to gain ownership rights in the company. We look at stock in detail in a few moments.)

Step 2: The Office of the Secretary of State reviews the application and, if deemed in order, a charter (often called a certificate of incorporation) is issued to the incorporators. Copies of the charter and the articles of incorporation are placed on file for public record.

> When the charter is issued, the corporation's legal entity is established.

Step 3: The stock is issued by the corporation to the owners (called stockholders).

Step 4: The stockholders meet to elect a board of directors and adopt the bylaws of the corporation. Often in a new corporation the stockholders become the directors. As the company grows, people are appointed to the board who are not stockholders. Records of meetings of the board of directors and stockholders are kept in a minute book, as directed by law. The board of directors appoints the officers to run the company; it is the board's job to oversee the overall management of the corporation, whereas the officers follow the policies set up by the board.

ADVANTAGES OF THE CORPORATE FORM OF ORGANIZATION

1. Limited Liability/Separate Legal Entity

Stockholders have limited liability; they are not personally liable for the obligations of the corporation, because a corporation is a separate and distinct legal entity. The corporation enters into contracts, buys or sells property, and sues or is sued in its own name. Thus, the only amount the stockholders can lose is the amount of their investment in the business. Of course, stockholders can still be held liable for any fraudulent or negligent actions they perform in connection with the corporation.

2. Unlimited Life

A corporation's life is perpetual (goes on forever) except in the case of bankruptcy, mergers, or vote of the stockholders.

3. Ease of Transferring Ownership Interest

When an owner invests in a corporation, each share of ownership is represented by one or more formal documents called stock certificates. The stockholder can sell or transfer shares of some corporations through *brokerage firms*, companies that act as middlemen in the trading of stock. This trading occurs at various marketplaces called *stock exchanges*. On the back of the certificate is a form that the seller endorses. A key point is that when the shares of stock are sold by the stockholder, the sale has *no* effect on the company's assets and liabilities. What happens is really a *shift* in the ownership.

4. No Mutual Agency

In a corporation there is no mutual agency as there is in a partnership. For example, if John Jones is a stockholder of Passon Corporation and enters into a contract with the city of Lynn, this action by John cannot bind the corporation to complete the contract with the city of Lynn.

5. Ease of Raising Capital

With no mutual agency, with limited liability, and with the ease of transferring ownership interest, the investment in a corporation becomes attractive to many people. As a result, the corporation can raise large amounts of capital by assembling investment groups of stockholders.

DISADVANTAGES OF THE CORPORATE STRUCTURE

1. Difficulties in Forming a Corporation/Government Regulations

As we have seen, a corporation is more difficult to form than a sole proprietorship or a partnership. Incorporators must complete the articles of incorporation and pay an incorporation fee. The complexity of forming a corporation also usually means hiring a lawyer to deal with legal aspects. When granted a certificate of incorporation, corporations are required to fulfill many state and federal regulations and to file many governmental reports.

2. Corporate Taxation

Because the corporation is a separate legal entity, its income is taxed by the federal government. The corporation may also be taxed at the state and local levels. At the same time, any income that is distributed to the stockholders is taxable to the stockholders. Thus, there is double taxation of a corporation's earnings.

Learning Unit 18-1 Review

AT THIS POINT you should be able to

- Explain the steps in forming a corporation. (p. 672)
- List as well as explain the advantages and disadvantages of the corporate form of organization. (p. 673)

SELF-REVIEW QUIZ 18-1

(The forms you need are on page 103 of the *Study Guide and Working Papers*.)
Respond true or false to the following:

1. The articles of incorporation document is quite easy to fill out.
2. A corporation is a separate legal entity.
3. The officers of a corporation always elect the board of directors.
4. Stocks can be transferred by stockholders without affecting the operations of a corporation.
5. Double taxation does exist in a corporate structure.

SOLUTIONS TO SELF-REVIEW QUIZ 18-1

1. False   2. True   3. False   4. True   5. True

Learning Unit 18-2 | Stockholders' Equity: Retained Earnings and Capital Stock

The equity section of a balance sheet of a corporation differs from that of a sole proprietorship or a partnership. In the sole proprietorship, we have simply a capital account and a withdrawals account. In the partnership, there is a separate capital and withdrawals account for each partner. With the corporation, the stockholders' equity section is broken down into two major parts:

1. **Paid-in Capital** is the amount that stockholders have invested in the business. It is equal to the values of the assets (usually cash) that have been contributed to the business.
2. **Retained earnings** are accumulated profits that are retained or kept in the corporation. Retained earnings does not mean cash; cash is an *asset*, whereas retained earnings is part of stockholders' *equity*.

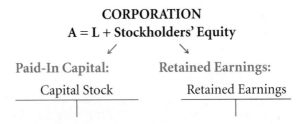

CORPORATION
A = L + Stockholders' Equity

Paid-In Capital: Retained Earnings:
   Capital Stock   Retained Earnings

Let's look more closely at the term *capital stock*.

CAPITAL STOCK

In return for their investment in the corporation, stockholders are issued shares of capital stock. Think of ownership of a corporation as being represented by shares of stock. There are two classes of capital stock, common and preferred. The charter of the corporation indicates the maximum amount of shares of each class of capital stock that a company can legally issue, but the company does not have to issue all of it. **Authorized capital stock** is the amount listed in the charter, **issued capital stock** refers to the shares sold to the stockholders, and **outstanding capital stock** means

In Chapter 19, we look at the difference between issued and outstanding stock.

shares sold and in the stockholders' possession. Let's look at the two classes of capital stock, beginning with common stock.

CHARACTERISTICS OF COMMON STOCK

The most prevalent type of capital stock is called common stock. When a corporation has only one kind of capital stock, it will be common stock. When the stock is issued, the owners receive certain rights from the corporation. These rights include the following:

1. The right to vote at stockholders' meetings.
2. The right to share in profits by receiving dividends.
3. The right to dispose of or sell their stock.
4. The right to maintain their proportionate ownership interest in the company. This right is called preemptive right. For example, if Jill Evans owns 15% of the common stock of the corporation, she would have the chance to also purchase 15% of any *additional* common stock that is issued, before it is offered to the public at large.
5. The right, when a company is liquidated, to share in assets after creditors and others with prior claims are paid off.

CHARACTERISTICS OF PREFERRED STOCK

Another type of capital stock some corporations may issue is called preferred stock. It is stock that provides stockholders with prior claim to a corporation's profits and assets over holders of common stock. Corporations watch current market conditions and try to offer preferred stock that will be attractive to investors. Holders of preferred stock often give up some of the rights that go with common stock—such as voting rights, preemptive rights, or even some earnings potential—in return for their more stable earnings that come from preferred stock. In many ways preferred stock is a less risky investment than common stock.

DIVIDENDS ON COMMON AND PREFERRED STOCK

Dividends are paid to stockholders as their share of the corporation's profits. A dividend must be voted by the board of directors, and if it has been a bad year for profits, the board may refuse to vote a dividend. Keep in mind a company may decide against a dividend in a good year, feeling it may be wise to invest money in research and development, etc.

As mentioned, preferred stock gives its stockholders a prior claim to a corporation's profits over holders of common stock. There are several ways that could happen:

We show how to calculate dividends for preferred and common stock on pp. 681–682.

1. If a preferred stock is cumulative, the holders have a right to a certain dividend every year. If in some years the board does not issue a dividend, the amount payable will accumulate until the earnings justify the payout. At this time the preferred stockholders will get dividends for all past years as well as the current year before the holders of common stock get any dividend.

For example, Moore Company has 3,000 shares of cumulative preferred stock that is entitled to a dividend of $3 per share. In 20X7, owing to financial problems, Moore Company decided to pay no dividend. Thus, the company has dividends in arrears of $9,000. No dividends can be paid to common stockholders until the preferred dividends are paid off in full: the amount in arrears plus the current year's dividend. Because financial conditions improved in 20X8, Moore paid the $9,000 of dividends in arrears (3,000 shares × $3) to holders of preferred stock plus the current year's dividend of $9,000.

2. If a preferred stock is noncumulative, holders have a right to the current year's dividend, but there are no holdovers from past years when dividends were not declared.

3. If a preferred stock is nonparticipating, each year the holders of preferred stock receive a certain percent as dividend and the remainder goes to common stock. Thus, if a company declared a dividend of $50,000, the preferred stockholders would get their usual percent and the common stockholders would get all the rest, even if it was a greater percent dividend than preferred got.

4. If a preferred stock is participating, preferred stockholders get their yearly dividend and can get a percent of what's left over, splitting it in various ways with common stockholders.

STOCK VALUE (FOR CAPITAL STOCK)

When a corporation is created, it issues a certain number of shares of stock, which are then sold to stockholders. At the time that the corporation receives its charter, the board of directors may assign a par value to the stock, something like $25 or $50 a share. This value is entirely arbitrary; no one can say that the stock is really worth that much. It is a way of dividing up ownership of the corporation into a number of units and putting a value on each unit. Many companies have par values of 5 or 10 cents per share. The key point about par value is that it is a value assigned arbitrarily. It is stated on the stock certificate. Figure 18-1 can be used as a summary as you read the rest of the chapter.

In most states the assigning of par value per share times the number of shares issued for a corporation represents the legal capital, an amount that a corporation must retain in the business for protection of creditors. Because the concept of par value can be quite misleading, some corporations will issue no-par stock, stock with no par value. Thus, the *entire* proceeds from selling this issue represents the legal capital (number of shares issued times amount investors paid for each share).

Most states permit (or some require) that the directors of a company set a stated value on the shares. This value also is arbitrary but can be changed by the board of directors. Stated value, which has the same purpose as par value, may be less confusing to investors, because it is not printed on the stock certificates.

Whether a stock is issued at par value, no par value with no stated value, or no par value with stated value, the capital stock account can be updated with entries that indicate whether investors paid more or less than par value or stated value. We look at specific examples of recording capital stock in the next unit.

Learning Unit 18-2 Review

AT THIS POINT you should be able to

- Explain the difference between authorized and issued stock. (p. 674)
- List the characteristics of common and preferred stock. (p. 675)

Stock Can Be Issued with:

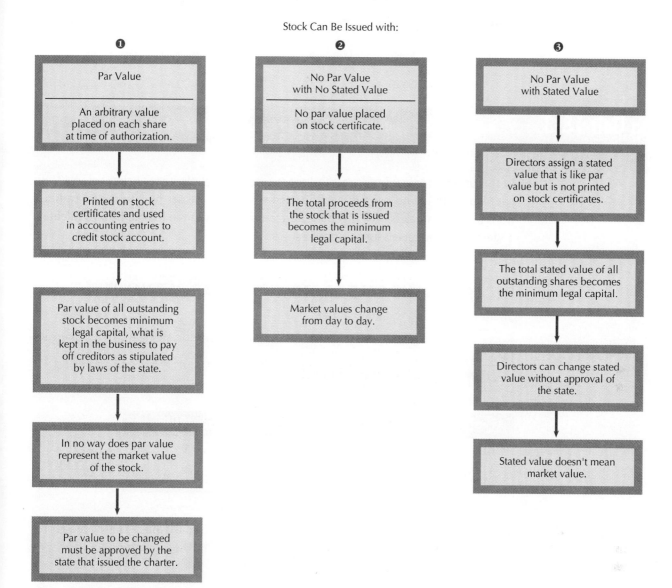

Figure 18-1 Par, No-Par, and Stated Value

- Define and explain cumulative, noncumulative, participating, and nonparticipating preferred stock. (p. 676)
- Define and explain par value, legal capital, no-par stock, and stated value. (p. 676)

SELF-REVIEW QUIZ 18-2

(The forms you need are on page 103 of the *Study Guide and Working Papers*.)
Respond true or false to the following:

1. Retained Earnings is part of Paid-in Capital.
2. Preferred stock is the most prevalent type of capital stock.
3. Preemptive right allows one to maintain one's proportionate ownership interest in a company.
4. Preferred stock that is cumulative is entitled to dividends in arrears.
5. Par value doesn't represent the market value of the stock.
6. Stock cannot be issued at par value.

SOLUTIONS TO SELF-REVIEW QUIZ 18-2

1. False   **2.** False   **3.** True   **4.** True   **5.** True   **6.** False

---

Learning Unit 18-3   Recording Capital Stock Transactions and Calculating Dividends

In this unit we look at how to record the issuing of stock that has (1) par value, (2) no par value, and (3) no par value with stated value. We also see how to record transactions in which stock is exchanged for noncash assets. We then look at how to calculate dividends for preferred and common stock.

RECORDING THE SALE OF STOCK THAT HAS PAR VALUE

Situation 1: Selling Common Stock at Par

Roger Company sells 200 shares of a $10 par-value common stock at $10 per share on February 3, 20XX.

Here is an analysis of the transaction:

Accounts Affected	Category	↑ ↓	Rules	
Cash	Asset	↑	Dr. $2,000	$10 par
				×200 shares
Common Stock	SE	↑	Cr. $2,000	= $2,000

Common Stock is recorded at number of shares times par value. That value represents the legal capital. The journal entry would be as shown in Figure 18-2.

Figure 18-2
Selling Stock at Par

20XX Feb.	3	Cash		2 0 0 0 00	
		Common Stock			2 0 0 0 00

Situation 2: Selling Preferred Stock at Par

Roger Co. sells 300 shares of $50 par-value preferred stock at $50 on March 18, 20XX.

Once again, here is an analysis of the transaction:

Accounts Affected	Category	↑ ↓	Rules	
Cash	Asset	↑	Dr. $15,000	300 shares
				× $50 par
Preferred Stock	SE	↑	Cr. $15,000	= $15,000

Preferred Stock is recorded at number of shares times par value. The journal entry would be as shown in Figure 18-3.

Figure 18-3
Selling Preferred Stock
at Par

20XX Mar.	18	Cash		15 0 0 0 00		
		Preferred Stock			15 0 0 0 00	

Situation 3: Selling Common Stock at a Premium (More than Par Value)

Roger Co. sells 50 shares of $10 par-value common stock at $15 on June 8, 20XX.

The Analysis: The common stock is recorded at par value. Because this stock is sold at a premium (more than par value), the excess of the par value will be recorded in a new account called Paid-in Capital in Excess of Par Value—Common. Note in the transactional analysis that follows that this account is part of stockholders' equity. On the balance sheet it will be listed below Common Stock in the Paid-in Capital section of stockholders' equity.

Accounts Affected	Category	↑ ↓	Rules	
Cash	Asset	↑	Dr. $750	→ 50 shares × $15
Common Stock	SE	↑	Cr. $500	→ 50 shares × $10 par
Paid-in Capital in Excess of Par Value—Common	SE	↑	Cr. $250	→ 50 shares × $5 excess per share over par

The journal entry will be as shown in Figure 18-4.

Figure 18-4
Selling Common Stock
at a Premium

20XX June	8	Cash		7 5 0 00		
		Common Stock			5 0 0 00	
		Paid-in Capital in				
		Excess of Par Value—Common			2 5 0 00	

Situation 4: Selling Common Stock at a Discount (Below Par)*

Roger Co. sells 100 shares of $10 par value common stock at $8 on July 3, 20XX.

The Analysis: When a stock is sold below par, a discount on stock results. An account called Discount on Common Stock records the discount. It is a contra-stockholders' equity account that will reduce the Common Stock account it is related to. Some states do not allow stock to be sold at a discount.

Accounts Affected	Category	↑ ↓	Rules	
Cash	Asset	↑	Dr. $800	→ 100 shares × $8
Discount on Common Stock	Contra SE	↑	Cr. $200	→ 100 shares × $2 ($10 par − $8)
Common Stock	SE	↑	Cr. $1,000	→ 100 shares × $10 par

The journal entry will be as shown in Figure 18-5.

---

*This situation does not occur very often.

Figure 18-5
Selling Common Stock at a Discount

20XX July	3	Cash	800 00	
		Discount on Common Stock	200 00	
		Common Stock		1000 00

Now let's look at how to record the sale of stock with no par value, with or without stated value.

Note: Corporations cannot legally sell stock at less than the stated value.

RECORDING SALE OF STOCK WITH NO PAR VALUE AND STATED VALUE

Situation 5: Selling No-Par Common Stock with No Stated Value

Moss Co. sells 300 shares of no-par common stock for $20 per share on July 19, 20XX.

The transaction analysis chart shows the following:

Accounts Affected	Category	↑ ↓	Rules	
Cash	Asset	↑	Dr. $6,000	} 300 shares × $20
Common Stock	SE	↑	Cr. $6,000	

The journal entry will be as shown in Figure 18-6.

Figure 18-6
Selling No-Par Common Stock with No Stated Value

20XX July	19	Cash	6000 00	
		Common Stock		6000 00

Situation 6: Selling No-Par Common Stock with a Stated Value

Reese Co. sells 200 shares of no-par common stock with a stated value of $40 for $50 per share on June 19, 20XX.

The Analysis: An excess over the stated value will be recorded in a stockholders' equity account called **Paid-in Capital in Excess of Stated Value—Common.**

Accounts Affected	Category	↑ ↓	Rules	
Cash	Asset	↑	Dr. $10,000	→ 200 shares × $50
Common Stock	SE	↑	Cr. $8,000	→ 200 shares × $40
Paid-in Capital in Excess of Stated Value—Common	SE	↑	Cr. $2,000	→ 200 shares × $10 ($50 − $40)

The journal entry will be as shown in Figure 18-7.

Figure 18-7
Selling No-Par Common
Stock with Stated Value

20XX July	19	Cash		1 0 0 0 0 0			
		Common Stock			8 0 0 0 0		
		Paid-in Capital in Excess of					
		Stated Value—Common			2 0 0 0 0		

RECORDING TRANSACTIONS IN WHICH STOCK IS EXCHANGED FOR NONCASH ASSETS

Situation 7: Exchanging Stock for Noncash Assets

On July 8, Moss Corporation exchanged 3,000 shares of $10 par-value common stock for machinery, buildings, and land. The assets had fair market values of $5,000, $10,000, and $20,000, respectively.

The Analysis: Assets are recorded at fair market value; common stock is recorded at par value. If fair market value is not available for assets, one can try to find the market (not par) value of the stock. In this chapter we assume fair market value of assets is available. The difference between fair market value and par is recorded in the account Paid-in Capital in Excess of Par. Par value is *never* used to measure the selling price of the assets.

Accounts Affected	Category	↑ ↓	Rules	
Machinery	Asset	↑	Dr. $5,000	
Buildings	Asset	↑	Dr. $10,000	} Fair market value
Land	Asset	↑	Dr. $20,000	
Common Stock	SE	↑	Cr. $30,000	→ 300 shares × $10 par
Paid-in Capital in Excess of Par—Common	SE	↑	Cr. $5,000	→ ($35,000 − $30,000)

The journal entry will be as shown in Figure 18-8.

Figure 18-8
Exchanging Stock for
Noncash Assets

20XX July	8	Machinery		5 0 0 0 00		
		Buildings		1 0 0 0 0 00		
		Land		2 0 0 0 0 00		
		Common Stock			3 0 0 0 0 00	
		Paid-in Capital in				
		Excess of Par—Common			5 0 0 0 00	

Situation 8*: Issuing Stock to Organizers of a Business for Services Performed

On June 8, Rose Corporation issued 2,000 shares of $10 par common stock to the organizers of the business for services performed.

The Analysis: Organization Cost in the formation of a corporation (legal fees, printing of stock certificates, etc.) is an intangible asset on the balance sheet. It is

---

*At the time of writing, amortization cost is now expensed rather than an asset. For our discussion, it is an asset that will be amortized.

usually amortized over 5 years (can be up to 40 years) because that life is used for income tax returns.

Accounts Affected	Category	↑ ↓	Rules
Organization Cost	Asset*	↑	Dr. $20,000
Common Stock	SE	↑	Cr. $20,000

*Now being expensed

The journal entry will be as shown in Figure 18-9.

Figure 18-9
Organization Costs

20XX June	8	Organization Cost	20 000 00	
		Common Stock		20 000 00

HOW TO CALCULATE DIVIDENDS

Table 18-1 summarizes the process of calculating dividends, which is divided into four steps. For our calculation, we use these basic facts:

TABLE 18-1 Four-Step Procedure for Calculating Dividends

The Formula	The Calculation	Preferred Stock	Common Stock	Total Dividends
Step 1: Dividend for preferred Number of shares × par value per share × rate of dividend	1,000 shares × $200 × .06 = $12,000	$12,000		$ 12,000
Step 2: Dividend for common Number of shares × par value per share × rate of dividend	6,000 shares × $100 × .06 = $36,000		$36,000	36,000
Step 3: Find total par value Number of shares × par value per share (preferred) *plus* Number of shares × par value per share (common)	1,000 shares × $200 = $200,000 6,000 shares × $100 = 600,000 Total par = $800,000			
Step 4: Allocate remainder of dividend based on par value				

$$\text{Preferred} = \frac{\text{Par Value of Preferred}}{\text{Total Par Value}} \times \text{Remainder of Dividend}$$

$\frac{\$200,000}{\$800,000} \times \$102,000^* = \$25,500$		25,500		25,500

$$\text{Common} = \frac{\text{Par Value of Common}}{\text{Total Par Value}} \times \text{Remainder of Dividend}$$

$\frac{\$600,000}{\$800,000} \times \$102,000^* = \$76,500$			76,500	76,500
		$37,500	$112,500	$150,000

*$150,000 − $48,000 = $102,000.

- $150,000 dividend declared.
- Preferred stock is 6% and fully participating.
- Preferred stock: 1,000 shares, $200 par.
- Common stock: 6,000 shares, $100 par.

Step 1: To calculate preferred dividends, you multiply the number of shares (1,000) times the par value ($200) per share times the rate of dividend (6%). The result is a $12,000 dividend to preferred.

Step 2: To calculate the common stock dividend, you multiply the number of shares (6,000) times the par value per share ($100) times the same rate of dividend (6%). The result is a dividend of $36,000.

Step 3: At this point $48,000 of the $150,000 of dividends has been apportioned. Because the preferred is participating—which means it can share in additional dividends beyond the 6% dividend—the next step is to find the total par value and allocate the remainder of the dividend based on the total par.

Note in Step 3 how the number of shares of preferred is multiplied by the $200 par and the number of common shares is multiplied by the $100 par. Thus, total par is $800,000.

Step 4: Because preferred is one-fourth of the total par, preferred is allocated $25,500 $(\frac{1}{4} \times \$102,000)$ and common is allocated three-fourths of the $102,000, or $76,500.

We can see that both were paid the same percent on par by the following calculations:

PREFERRED:

$$\frac{\textbf{Total Dividends}}{\textbf{Total Par Value of Preferred}} = \frac{\$37,500}{\$200,000} = 18.75\%$$

COMMON:

$$\frac{\textbf{Total Dividends}}{\textbf{Total Par Value of Common}} = \frac{\$112,500}{\$600,000} = 18.75\%$$

The end result is that the dividends were equally divided in terms of percentage, because preferred was fully participating.

Learning Unit 18-3 Review

AT THIS POINT you should be able to

- Record transactions that issue stock with or without par value. (p. 678)
- Explain the account called Paid-in Capital in Excess of Par Value. (p. 679)
- Tell what the normal balance is for the account Discount on Common Stock. (p. 679)
- Explain when the account Paid-in Capital in Excess of Stated Value is used. (p. 681)
- Calculate Capital in Excess of Par Value when stock is exchanged for noncash assets. (p. 681)
- Explain when one uses the account called Organization Cost. (p. 681)
- Calculate dividends on common and preferred stock. (p. 682)

SELF-REVIEW QUIZ 18-3

(The forms you need are on pages 104–105 of the *Study Guide and Working Papers*.)

1. Journalize the following transactions:

20XX

July	5	Boston Company sells 200 shares of $20 par-value common stock at $20.
Aug.	8	Jess Company sells 100 shares of $10 par-value common stock at $25.
Oct.	9	Mellisa Company sells 300 shares of no-par common stock with a stated value of $30 for $50 per share.
Nov.	12	Moss Company issued 1,000 shares of $25 par-value common stock to the organizers of the firm for services rendered costing $30,000.

2. From the following, calculate the dividends for common and preferred stock.

- Fourteen percent fully participating preferred stock.
- Board declared a $210,000 dividend.
- Preferred stock: 3,000 shares, $100 par.
- Common stock: 7,000 shares, $100 par.

SOLUTIONS TO SELF-REVIEW QUIZ 18-3

1.

20XX					
July	5	Cash	4 0 0 0 00		
		Common Stock		4 0 0 0 00	
Aug.	8	Cash	2 5 0 0 00		
		Common Stock		1 0 0 0 00	
		Paid-in Capital in Excess			
		of Par Value—Common		1 5 0 0 00	
Oct.	9	Cash	15 0 0 0 00		
		Common Stock		9 0 0 0 00	
		Paid-in Capital in Excess			
		of Stated Value—Common		6 0 0 0 00	
Nov.	12	Organization Cost	3 0 0 0 0 00		
		Common Stock		2 5 0 0 0 00	
		Paid-in Capital in Excess			
		of Par Value—Common		5 0 0 0 00	

Figure 18-10 Journalizing Issuances of Stock

2.

	Preferred	Common
Dividends for preferred:		
(3,000 shares × $100 par) × .14 =	$42,000	
Dividends for common:		
(7,000 shares × $100 par) × .14 =		$98,000
Amount to be divided based on total par value:		
($210,000 − $140,000) = <u>$70,000</u>		

Total Par:
   Preferred: 3,000 shares × $100 par = $ 300,000
   Common: 7,000 shares × $100 par = __700,000__
                           Total $1,000,000

   Preferred: $\dfrac{\$300,000}{\$1,000,000}$ × $70,000 = $21,000   21,000

   Common: $\dfrac{\$700,000}{\$1,000,000}$ × $70,000 = $49,000   __49,000__
                                       Totals $63,000 $147,000

Proof:

   Preferred: $\dfrac{\$63,000}{\$300,000}$ = 21%   Common: $\dfrac{\$147,000}{\$700,000}$ = 21%

Learning Unit 18-4   Recording Capital Stock Transactions Under a Stock Subscription Plan

In the last unit we assumed that stocks were immediately issued and full payment of cash or other assets was received. In this unit we examine stock transactions under stock subscription plans. Under such plans, buyers pledge to buy certain stocks but pay in installments or in a later lump sum. In most cases companies will not issue the actual stock certificates to these buyers until payment is complete.

Let's look at how Krump Corporation receives subscriptions for 1,000 shares of $100 par-value common stock at $160 per share on April 1, 20XX. Two equal installments will be paid on August 1 and November 1 by the buyer.

April 1: Accepted Subscription for 1,000 Shares at $160 per Share

Because the stock certificates will not be issued until paid in full, Krump Corporation records the ownership at par value in a temporary stockholders' equity account called Common Stock Subscribed. This account is shown in the Paid-in Capital section below the issue of the Common Stock. The amount due is recorded in an account called Subscriptions Receivable—Common Stock. The difference between the par value and the issue price is accumulated in a permanent account called Paid-in Capital in Excess of Par Value—Common.

Here is an analysis of the transaction:

Represents amount due on stock subscription. It is a current asset on the balance sheet.

Stock reserved but not fully paid.
(1,000 shares × $100 par)

Accounts Affected	Category	↑ ↓	Rules
Subscriptions Receivable— Common Stock	Asset	↑	Dr. $160,000
Common Stock Subscribed	SE	↑	Cr. $100,000
Paid-in Capital in Excess of Par Value—Common	SE	↑	Cr. $60,000

1,000 shares × $160
1,000 shares × $60 par

The journal entry will be as shown in Figure 18-11.

Figure 18-11
Accepted Subscriptions
in Excess of Par

	20XX Apr.	1				
			Subscriptions Receivable—			
			Common Stock	160 0 0 0 00		
			Common Stock Subscribed		100 0 0 0 00	
			Paid-in Capital in Excess of Par		60 0 0 0 00	

August 1: Received First Installment on Common Stock Subscription

Accounts Affected	Category	↑ ↓	Rules
Cash	Asset	↑	Dr. $80,000
Subscriptions Receivable—Common Stock	Asset	↓	Cr. $80,000

The journal entry will be as shown in Figure 18-12.

Figure 18-12
Received Installment
from Stock Subscription

	20XX Aug.	1	Cash	80 0 0 0 00	
			Subscriptions Receivable—		
			Common Stock		80 0 0 0 00

November 1: Received Final Installment on Common Stock Subscription

Accounts Affected	Category	↑ ↓	Rules
Cash	Asset	↑	Dr. $80,000
Subscriptions Receivable—Common Stock	Asset	↓	Cr. $80,000

The journal entry will be as shown in (Figure 18-13).

Figure 18-13
Received Final Installment
from Stock Subscription

	20XX Nov.	1	Cash	80 0 0 0 00	
			Subscriptions Receivable—		
			Common Stock		80 0 0 0 00

November 1: Issued 1,000 Shares of Fully Paid Common Stock

Accounts Affected	Category	↑ ↓	Rules
Common Stock Subscribed	SE	↓	Dr. $100,000
Common Stock	SE	↑	Cr. $100,000

The journal entry will be as shown in Figure 18-14.

	20XX						
	Nov.	1	Common Stock Subscribed	10 00 00 00		
			Common Stock			10 00 00 00	

Figure 18-14
Issued Fully Paid
Common Stock

Remember that stock is recorded at par value. At this point the Common Stock Subscribed account in the ledger (when posted) is reduced to a zero balance, and the Common Stock account records the issued stock (which has been paid for).

STOCKHOLDERS' EQUITY

Before concluding this chapter, let's take a moment to set up a simplified stockholders' equity section of a balance sheet. The numbers in Figure 18-15 are not related to the previous situations. The goal here is to show you the structure of Paid-in Capital and Retained Earnings. In the Blueprint on page 692, the complete layout of stockholders' equity is illustrated by the source-of-capital approach, which lists classes of stockholders first. An alternative way, called the legal capital approach, lists all legal capital first and is illustrated in the next chapter. Both approaches are acceptable.

> The names and addresses of each stockholder are kept in a subsidiary ledger. The Stock account is the controlling account.

Stockholders' Equity		
Paid in Capital:		
Common Stock, $100 par value; authorized		
10,000 shares, 7,000 issued and outstanding	$ 700 00 0 0 00	
Common Stock Subscribed, 2,000 shares at par	200 00 0 00	
Paid-in Capital in Excess of Par Value—Common	300 00 0 00	
Total Paid-in Capital	$1200 0 0 0 00	
Retained Earnings	400 0 0 0 00	
Total Stockholders' Equity	$1600 0 0 0 00	

Figure 18-15
Stockholder's Equity
Section of Balance Sheet

Learning Unit 18-4 Review

AT THIS POINT you should be able to

- Journalize the entries in a stock subscription plan. (p. 685)
- Explain the purpose of Common Stock Subscribed. (p. 686)
- Prepare a simplified stockholders' section. (p. 687)

SELF-REVIEW QUIZ 18-4

(The forms you need are on page 106 of the *Study Guide and Working Papers*.)

Journalize the entries to record the stock subscription plan for Moose Corp. On October 1 Moose Corp. received subscriptions for 500 shares of $50 par-value common stock at $80 per share. The buyer will pay two equal installments on December 31 and March 31.

SOLUTIONS TO SELF-REVIEW QUIZ 18-4

Figure 18-16
Stock Subscriptions and Installments Received

Oct.	1	Subscriptions Receivable—			
		Common Stock	4 0 0 0 00		
		Common Stock Subscribed			2 5 0 0 00
		Paid-in Capital in Excess of Par			
		Value—Common			1 5 0 0 00
Dec.	31	Cash	2 0 0 0 00		
		Subscriptions Receivable—			
		Common Stock			2 0 0 0 00
Mar.	31	Cash	2 0 0 0 00		
		Subscriptions Receivable—			
		Common Stock			2 0 0 0 00
	31	Common Stock Subscribed	2 5 0 0 00		
		Common Stock			2 5 0 0 00

Chapter Review

Learning Unit 18-1

1. The articles of incorporation are submitted to the state when one wants to form a corporation. It contains all the specifics of the proposed corporation. If approved, a charter (certificate of incorporation) is issued to incorporators.
2. Advantages of a corporation include limited liability, a separate legal entity, unlimited life, ease of transferring ownership interest, no mutual agency, and ease in raising capital. Disadvantages include difficulties in forming a corporation, government regulations, and double taxation.

Learning Unit 18-2

1. Stockholders' equity is broken down in Paid-in Capital and Retained Earnings.
2. Retained Earnings records the accumulated profits that are retained or kept in the corporation.
3. Authorized stock represents the total amount of stock that can be legally issued. Outstanding stock represents the amount of stock issued.
4. Common stockholders have the right to vote, share in profits, sell their ownership, and receive assets at liquidation, if available; they also have preemptive rights (the right to maintain their proportionate ownership interest in the company).
5. Buyers of preferred stock, to gain stability of earnings, may give up voting rights, preemptive rights, and so forth. Preferred stock can be cumulative, noncumulative, participating, nonparticipating, or a combination.
6. Par value is an arbitrary value. It doesn't mean market value. Stocks may have a par value, no par, or no par with a stated value.
7. Legal capital is the amount that a corporation must retain in the business for the protection of the creditors. It may be based on par value, no par value, or stated value.

Learning Unit 18-3

1. Common stock or preferred stock with par value is recorded by number of shares times par value. If stock is sold for more than par, the difference is recorded in a stockholders' equity account called Paid-in Capital in Excess of Par Value. If a stock is sold below par, the difference is recorded in a contra-stockholders' equity account called Discount on Common Stock.
2. If no-par stock with a stated value is sold at a price higher than stated value, the difference is recorded in a stockholders' equity account called Paid-in Capital in Excess of Stated Value.
3. Assets are recorded at fair market value when exchanged for stock. Any difference between par value of stock and fair market value is recorded in a stockholders' equity account called Capital in Excess of Par.
4. Organization Cost is an intangible asset on the balance sheet. Today, it is being expensed.
5. The calculation for a dividend to common or preferred with par value is (number of shares × par) × rate. If preferred is fully participating, the allocation of the remainder is based on par value of each class of stock over the total par value. This fraction is multiplied times remainder of dividend.

Learning Unit 18-4

1. The source-of-capital approach will present the paid-in capital component of stockholders' equity by classes of stockholders. There is no attempt to list legal capital first.

2. Subscriptions Receivable is an asset representing amounts due on stock that has been subscribed to. It is a current asset on the balance sheet.
3. Common Stock Subscribed is a stockholders' equity account that acts as a temporary account until a subscription is paid for. When paid, the Common Stock Subscribed account is reduced and the Common Stock account is increased.

Key Terms

Articles of incorporation   Document submitted by incorporators when applying for a charter.

Authorized capital stock   As stated in its charter, the number of shares of capital stock (common and preferred) that a corporation can sell.

Capital stock   Classes of stock that represent the fractional elements of ownership of a corporation.

Certificate of incorporation   Document granted by the state authorizing the creation of a corporation.

Charter   Document issued to a corporation by the state that includes certificate of incorporation along with articles of incorporation.

Common stock   Part of paid-in capital representing the basic ownership equity of the corporation. If the corporation has only one class of stock, it will be common stock.

Common Stock Subscribed   Temporary stockholders' equity account that records at par value stock that has been subscribed to but not fully paid for.

Corporation   Business organization that is both a legal and accounting entity.

Cumulative preferred stock   Stock that entitles its holders to any undeclared dividends that have accumulated before common stockholders receive their dividends.

Directors   Officers elected by stockholders to represent the company and establish policies for the company.

Discount on stock   The difference between the par value of the stock and an amount less than the par value that the stockholders have contributed. Discounts do not happen very often.

Dividend   Cash, other assets, or shares of stock that a corporation issues to the stockholders.

Dividends in arrears   Dividends owed to preferred stockholders that must be paid before common stockholders can receive their dividends.

Incorporators   Persons responsible for getting the corporation formed.

Issued capital stock   Stock that the corporation issues for assets or services contributed by the stockholders.

Legal capital   Minimum amount of capital that a corporation must leave in the company (cannot be withdrawn by stockholders) for protection of the creditors.

Legal capital approach   Method of preparing Paid-in Capital by listing the legal section first. (See Blueprint at end of Chapter 19.)

Limited liability   Freedom of stockholders from *personal* liability for the debts of the corporation.

Minute book   Book that records meetings of the board of directors or stockholders.

Noncumulative preferred stock   Preferred stock that does not entitle its holders to a dividend for any year in which a dividend is not declared.

Nonparticipating preferred stock   Preferred stock that entitles its holders only to a certain percent dividend, the remainder going to holders of common stock.

No-par stock   Stock with no par value. A stated value could be placed on it.

Organization Cost   An intangible asset that records the initial cost of forming the corporation, such as legal and incorporating fees. Today, it is now being expensed.

Outstanding capital stock   Stock that is held and owned by stockholders.

Paid-in Capital   Section of stockholders' equity representing what stockholders have invested into the corporation.

Paid-in Capital in Excess of Par Value — Common   Difference between what stockholders invest and par value. This amount is not credited to the Stock account.

Paid-in Capital in Excess of Stated Value — Common   Difference between what stockholders invest and the stated value placed on stock by the board of directors. This amount is not credited to the Stock account.

Participating preferred stock   Stock that entitles its holders not only to a fixed dividend but also to an opportunity to share in additional dividends with common stockholders.

Par value   An arbitrary value that is placed on each share of stock. Par value represents legal capital and not market value.

Preemptive right   The right of the stockholder to purchase additional shares of stock to maintain a proportionate interest when the corporation issues additional stock.

Preferred stock   Class of capital stock that has preference to a corporation's profits and assets.

Premium   A term that records the sale of stock at more than par value. In this book we use the account Paid-in Capital in Excess of Par to record the premium received.

Retained earnings   Accumulated profits of a corporation that have been kept in the business and not paid out as dividends. Retained Earnings is part of stockholders' equity.

Source-of-capital approach   Method of preparing Paid-in Capital by listing classes of stockholder sources of capital (see p. 692 for example).

Stated value   Arbitrary value placed by the board of directors on each share of no-par stock to fulfill legal capital requirements.

Stock certificate   Formal document issued to investors in a corporation that shows the number of shares purchased.

Stockholders   Owners of the stock of the corporation.

Stock subscription   A contractual agreement to buy a certain number of shares of stock from a corporation at a specific price.

Subscriptions Receivable—Common Stock   Current asset on balance sheet that represents amount due on stock subscriptions.

Questions, Mini Exercises, Exercises, and Problems

Discussion Questions

1. What is the difference between the articles of incorporation and a charter?
2. Who elects the board of directors?
3. List the advantages of the corporate form of organization.
4. Explain the difference between paid-in capital and retained earnings.
5. Why can't a company issue more stock than is authorized?
6. What does *preemptive right* mean?
7. Distinguish among legal capital, par value, no par value, and no par value with a stated value.
8. Preferred stock can never be cumulative *and* nonparticipating. True or false? Support your answer.
9. What is the normal balance and the category of the account Discount on Common Stock?
10. How does one calculate Paid-in Capital in Excess of Par Value or Stated Value?
11. Explain the account Paid-in Capital in Excess of Par Value as it relates to exchange of stock for noncash assets.
12. What is the purpose of the account Organization Costs?
13. In stock subscriptions, why does one credit Common Stock Subscribed?

Mini Exercises

(The forms you need are on pages 108–109 of the *Study Guide and Working Papers*.)

Stockholders' Equity

1. Marci Corporation has capital stock of $5,000. Its Retained Earnings account has a $12,000 balance. Cash has a balance of $10,000. What is the total of stockholders' equity for Marci Corporation?

Cumulative Preferred

2. Moore Co. owed $10,000 each year for three years to holders of cumulative preferred stock. This year Moore pays out $100,000 in dividends to preferred and common. How much did each class of stock receive?

Journalizing Sales of Stock

3. Journalize the following (p. 693):

Blueprint: Source-of-Capital Approach

VALLEY CO. PARTIAL BALANCE SHEET			
Assets			
Current Assets:			
Subscriptions Receivable, Common 8% Stock	XXX		
Intangible Assets:			
Organization Cost		XXX	
Total Assets			XXX
Liabilities			

(balance sheet continues, break indicated)

Stockholders' Equity			
Paid-in Capital:			
Preferred 12% stock, $10 par value, authorized 20,000 shares, 8,000 shares issued	XXX		
Paid-in Capital in Excess of Par Value—preferred	XXX		
Total Paid-in Capital by preferred stockholders		XXX	
Common Stock, no par value, stated value $10 per share, authorized 100,000 shares, 30,000 issued and outstanding	XXX		
Common Stock Subscribed, 1,000 shares at par	XXX		
Paid-in Capital in Excess of Stated Value—Common	XXX		
Total Paid-in Capital by common stockholders		XXX	
Total Paid-in Capital		XXX	
Retained Earnings		XXX	
Total Stockholders' Equity			XXX

Note that preferred stock is listed before common stock.

20XX

July	8	Pete Co. sells 300 shares of $10 par-value common stock at $10.
Oct.	15	Jon Co. sells 200 shares of $10 par-value common stock at $15.
Nov.	28	Angel Co. sells 200 shares of no-par common stock with a stated value of $20 for $30 per share.
Dec.	30	Lowe Co. issues 500 shares of $10 par-value common stock to organizers of the firm for services rendered costing $7,500.

Cumulative and Participating Preferred

4. From the following calculate the dividends for common and preferred stock:

- 7% fully participating preferred stock.
- The board declared a $150,000 dividend.
- Preferred stock 2,000 shares, $100 par value; common stock 8,000 shares, $100 par.

Stock Subscriptions

5. Journalize the entries to record the stock subscription plan for Blue Co. On October 1, Blue received subscriptions for 200 shares of $25 par-value common stock at $40 per share. The buyer will pay two equal installments on December 31 and March 31.

Exercises

(The forms you need are on pages 110–111 of the *Study Guide and Working Papers*.)

18-1. Val Corporation was authorized to issue 30,000 shares of common stock. Record the journal entry for each of the following independent situations, assuming Val issues 6,000 shares at $11 on July 20, 20XX:

- **a.** Common stock has a $10 par value.
- **b.** Common stock has no par and no stated value.
- **c.** Common stock is no-par stock with a stated value of $8.

Journalizing transactions for sale of stock.

18-2. On July 10, 20XX, Zeron Corporation issued 3,000 shares of common stock with a par value of $100 in exchange for equipment with a fair market value of $320,000. Journalize the appropriate entry.

Exchange of stock for non-cash assets.

18-3. Vetco Corporation in its first three years of operation paid out the following dividends:

- Year 1: 0
- Year 2: $30,000
- Year 3: $90,000

Calculating dividends to preferred and common.

Given that Vetco has 3,000 shares of $100 par 9% cumulative, nonparticipating preferred stock and 15,000 shares of $25 par value common stock, what would be the total dividends paid each year to holders of common and preferred?

18-4. On January 1, 20XX, Lavrel Corporation issued on a subscription basis 1,000 shares of $50 par-value common stock at $90 per share. Two equal installments were to be made on July 1 and December 31. Prepare the appropriate journal entries on January 1, July 1, and December 31 to record this stock subscription for Lavrel Corporation.

Stock subscription.

18-5. Scupper Corporation began its business on January 1, 20XX. It sold at $30 per share 6,000 shares of no-par common stock with a stated value of $20 per share. The charter of Scupper indicated 40,000 shares were authorized. Retained earnings were $60,000 on December 31. Prepare the stockholders' equity section for Scupper on December 31, 20XX, using page 692 as a guide.

Stockholders' equity.

Group A Problems

(The forms you need are on pages 112–120 of the *Study Guide and Working Papers*.)

18A-1. The following is the Paid-in Capital section of stockholders' equity for the Larson Corporation on June 1, 20XX:

Recording capital stock transactions; preparing Paid-in Capital section of stockholders' equity.

Paid-in Capital:

Preferred Stock, $100 par, authorized 20,000 shares, 4,000 shares issued	$ 400,000
Paid-in Capital in Excess of Par Value—Preferred Stock	120,000
Common Stock, $25 par, authorized 50,000 shares, 20,000 shares issued	500,000
Paid-in Capital in Excess of Par Value—Common Stock	160,000
Total Paid-in Capital	$1,180,000

Check Figure:
(2) Paid-in capital
$2,732,000

The following transactions occurred in the months of June and July:

20XX

June
1 Issued 3,000 shares of preferred stock at $102 per share.
2 Issued 7,000 shares of common stock at $40 per share.
15 Issued 8,000 shares of common stock at $42 per share.

July
2 Issued 5,000 shares of preferred stock at $104 per share.
18 Issued 2,000 shares of common stock in exchange for building and land with a fair market value of $60,000 and $50,000, respectively.

1. Journalize the preceding entries and update the stockholders' equity ledger. Accounts are provided in the workbook.
2. Prepare a new Paid-in Capital section of stockholders' equity as of July 31, 20XX.

Calculating dividends for preferred and common stock.

18A-2. Katie Corporation has 20,000 shares outstanding of $10 par-value 8% preferred stock and 40,000 shares outstanding of $10 par-value common stock. In its first five years of operation, the company paid the following dividends: 20X1, 0; 20X2, $16,000; 20X3, $48,000; 20X4, 0; 20X5, $82,000. Calculate the dividends paid to preferred and common stockholders under the following three independent situations:

Check Figure:
(b) Pref: $16,000   20X2
        32,000   20X3
        32,000   20X5

a. Preferred stock is noncumulative and nonparticipating.
b. Preferred stock is cumulative and nonparticipating.
c. Preferred stock is cumulative and fully participating.

Preparing a stockholders' equity section of a balance sheet.

18A-3. From the following partial mixed list, select the appropriate titles and prepare a stockholders' equity section using the source-of-capital approach as shown on the Blueprint on page 692 for Xenon Corporation on July 31, 20XX:

Check Figure:
Stockholders' equity
$1,445,000

Office Equipment	$100,000
Land	200,000
Paid-in Capital in Excess of Par Value—Preferred Stock	100,000
Building	80,000
Accounts Receivable	120,000
Notes Receivable	40,000
Organization Costs	10,000
Common Stock, $10 par value (60,000 shares issued and outstanding; 80,000 shares authorized)	600,000
Retained Earnings	200,000
Subscriptions Receivable—Common Stock	80,000
Patents	10,000
Preferred 14% Stock, $50 Par (6,000 shares issued; 7,000 shares authorized)	300,000

Common Stock Subscribed at Par	225,000
Paid-in Capital in Excess of Par Value—Common Stock	20,000

18A-4. Joilet Corporation has just been issued a charter by the state of New York. This charter gives Joilet the authority to issue 400,000 shares of $10 par-value common stock. From the following transactions,

1. Prepare journal entries to record the transactions of Joilet Corp. for the month of August.
2. Prepare the Paid-in Capital section of Joilet's balance sheet at the end of the month.

20XX

Aug. 11 Issued 1,800 shares of stock for land and building with a fair market value of $13,000 and $17,500, respectively.

16 Accepted subscriptions to 20,000 shares of stock for $250,000 to be paid in two equal installments.

22 Collected first installment on 10,000 shares of the common stock subscribed on August 16.

28 Sold 7,000 shares of stock for $88,000.

30 Collected last installment on 10,000 shares of the common stock subscribed on August 16 and issued the shares.

> Stock subscriptions and exchange of stock for non-cash assets.

> Check Figure:
> Total Paid-in Capital
> $368,500

Group B Problems

(The forms you need are on pages 112–120 of the *Study Guide and Working Papers.*)

18B-1. The following is the Paid-in Capital section of stockholders' equity for the Larson Corporation on June 1, 20XX:

> Recording capital stock transactions; preparing Paid-in Capital section of stockholders' equity.

Paid-in Capital:

Preferred Stock, $25, par, authorized 20,000 shares, 5,000 shares issued	$125,000
Paid-in Capital in Excess of Par Value—Preferred Stock	37,500
Common Stock, $10 par, authorized 100,000 shares, 20,000 shares issued	200,000
Paid-in Capital in Excess of Par Value—Common Stock	45,000
Total Paid-in Capital	$407,500

> Check Figure:
> Total paid-in capital
> $678,500

The following transactions occurred in the months of June and July:

20XX

June 1 Issued 2,000 shares of preferred stock at $28 per share.

4 Issued 4,000 shares of common stock at $13 per share.

15 Issued 5,000 shares of common stock at $16 per share.

July 2 Issued 1,000 shares of preferred stock at $29 per share.

18 Issued 2,000 shares of common stock in exchange for building and land with a fair market value of $25,000 and $29,000, respectively.

1. Journalize and post the preceding entries and update the stockholders' equity ledger accounts provided in the workbook.
2. Prepare a new Paid-in Capital section of stockholders' equity as of July 31, 20XX.

18B-2. Katie Corporation has 10,000 shares outstanding of $20 par-value 10% preferred stock and 120,000 shares outstanding of $5 par-value common stock. In its first five years of operation, the company paid the following dividends: 20X1, 0; 20X2, $16,000; 20X3, $80,000; 20X4, $84,000; 20X5, $120,000. Calculate the dividends

> Calculating dividends for preferred and common stock.

paid to preferred and common stockholders under the following three independent situations:

a. Preferred stock is noncumulative and nonparticipating.
b. Preferred stock is cumulative and nonparticipating.
c. Preferred stock is cumulative and fully participating.

18B-3. From the following partial mixed list, select the appropriate titles and prepare a stockholders' equity section using the source-of-capital approach as shown in the blueprint on page 692 for Xenon Corporation on July 31, 20XX.

Paid-in Capital in Excess of Par Value—Common Stock	$ 1,400
Common Stock Subscribed at Par	8,800
Paid-in Capital in Excess of Par Value—Preferred Stock	12,000
Land	15,000
Office Equipment	7,600
Preferred 14% Stock, $50 Par (400 shares issued; 8,000 shares authorized)	20,000
Patents	1,600
Subscriptions Receivable—Common Stock	12,000
Retained Earnings	28,000
Common Stock $10 par value (8,000 shares issued; and outstanding; 50,000 shares authorized)	80,000
Organization Costs	1,200
Notes Receivable	5,000
Accounts Receivable	18,000
Building	5,000

18B-4. The state of New York has issued a charter to Joilet Corporation with the authorization to issue 10,000 shares of $100 par-value common stock. From the following transactions,

1. Journalize the transactions for Joilet for the month of September.
2. Prepare the Paid-in Capital section of Joilet Corporation's balance sheet at the end of the month.

20XX
Sept.   8   Issued 500 shares of stock for land and building with a fair market value of $29,000 and $24,000, respectively.
         14   Accepted subscriptions to 300 shares of its stock for $39,000 to be paid in two equal installments.
         22   Collected first installment on 150 shares of the common stock subscribed on September 14.
         24   Sold 500 shares of stock for $59,000.
         30   Collected last installment on 150 shares of the common stock subscribed on September 14 and issued the shares.

Real-World Applications

18R-1. The partial balance sheet of Freedom Corporation had as of July 31, 20XX, the following balances:

Preferred Stock, $10 Par	$ 95,000
Paid-in Capital in Excess of Par—Preferred	65,000
Common Stock, $100 par	180,000

Paid-in Capital in Excess of Par—Common	220,000
Common Stock Subscribed	10,000
Retained Earnings	520,000
Subscriptions Receivable	60,000
Bonds Payable	$300,000

The bookkeeper, Alice Fall, is quite concerned that the company has not kept enough legal capital in the business. She wants the board of directors to immediately change the par value, because the market value of the stock has increased. She believes it is only fair to protect the rights of the creditors. Support or rebut Alice Fall's position in writing.

18R-2. Bill Murray and Jim Smith, full-time high school teachers, had worked together in overnight camping for years. They both felt it was time to start their own overnight camp. Bill estimated he would be able to invest $30,000 and Jim could invest $2,000. Both agreed that they would need at least $200,000 to finance the purchase of land as well as the building of bunks and administrative offices.

Jim felt that forming a corporation was too involved and wanted to form a partnership. Bill, on the other hand, who trusted no one, felt that the corporate structure was best.

Jim and Bill have come to you to recommend what form of organization is best for them and how they can or should raise the money. Please write them a recommendation.

YOU make the call

Critical Thinking/Ethical Case

18R-3. Avan Corporation just published its financial statements. The president of Avan told the accountants not to include in the annual report any information about a pending lawsuit. The president thought it would only worry the stockholders. Do you think the president is correct in not including any information about the pending lawsuit in the annual report? You make the call. Write down your recommendations to the president.

Internet Exercises: Secretary of State, Missouri; New York Stock Exchange

EX-1. [http://www.sos.star.mo.us]   Before a company can offer its stock to the public it must publish a prospectus. The prospectus contains a myriad of information about the company, about its officers, about who its accountants are, along with much more statistical information. Most states offer online information about the requirements for a stock to be offered in that state. This site, presented by the State of Missouri, provides information on how to read a prospectus. The state you are in probably offers a similar site or a document similar to this one.

Within this document, find the answers to these questions:

1. What is the "legal status" of a prospectus?
2. When will you receive a prospectus of a company in which you may invest?
3. Why is it important for you to read the "use of proceeds" section?
4. What can you learn about the investment policy of the company from the dividend section?

EX-2. [www.nyse.com/members/members.html]   The world's best-known stock exchange is the New York Stock Exchange (NYSE). Many people look at the NYSE as a huge auction, which is an accurate portrayal of what occurs on the floor of the exchange. Stockbrokers around the world are connected with NYSE, offering a way for buyers and sellers of stock to come together to transact their exchange.

1. Read "the role of the specialist" and briefly state what that role is.
2. Read "the role of the floor broker" and briefly state what that role is.
3. How do these two positions interact at the NYSE?

SUBWAY Case

INGOOD COMPANY

The waitress set down a plate of nachos and two pints of beer in front of Stan and his old college buddy, Ron Ebbers. Ever since they'd run into each other at Stan's Subway restaurant, the two have rekindled their friendship over beer and nachos at a local restaurant.

"Sales still on the up and up?" Ron asked Stan.

"Yep. It just doesn't seem to matter how weak the economy is," said Stan, "People will always want a sandwich that's healthy, great tasting, and good value. And now," Stan lifted a glass, "*salud*— a toast—because as of today I'm a corporation!"

"Cheers, Stan the Man!" exclaimed Ron and clinked Stan's beer mug, "but doesn't incorporating cost you more money, in legal fees and taxes?"

"Well, that may be true, but if I don't incorporate and anything goes wrong or some wacko sues me, that could cost me my shirt! Now I have limited liability, but I still pay wages to my employees, send in my royalty fees to Subway, and *muchos* profits still go to me."

"Maybe *I* should buy stock in Subway," Ron interrupted. "I've been dabbling in the market lately and Subway seems like a good bet!"

"Unfortunately, you can't buy stock in Subway," said Stan. "Doctor's Associates, the corporation that owns the Subway brand, is privately owned by the founders Fred DeLuca and Dr. Peter Buck."

"Doctor's Associates?!" Stan exclaimed, "That's strange. I know the food has helped people lose weight and eat healthy, but is Subway run by a health care outfit?"

"No, it's actually kind of interesting. In 1965 Fred DeLuca was just a teenager who wanted to go to college and become a doctor, but he didn't have enough money. Then his family friend Peter Buck loaned him the money to start a submarine sandwich joint. DeLuca, of course, never did become a doctor, but Peter Buck holds a Ph.D. in nuclear physics, so they called themselves Doctor's Associates—they're the 'doctors' and we franchisees are the 'associates'. "

"I guess we all have dreams that we don't carry out," Ron mused.

"Hey, don't look so *triste*, amigo. I know you're stuck in a dead-end job now, but maybe now is the time to think about new opportunities."

"Whaddaya mean?" Ron asked.

"There's a great space on Alameda Avenue on the other side of Los Palmos— near that fancy new apartment complex. I've been thinking of eventually opening up another store, but I don't want to go it alone. However, I might consider going into a partnership with you to own Subway #2."

"Well, given the liability risks you just mentioned—which I assume apply to partnerships as well as sole proprietorships, what about a corporation?" said Ron eagerly. "You could be the majority shareholder and I could have a smaller interest in the restaurant until I learn the ropes and eventually buy you out."

"Whoa there. Let's not talk about buying anyone out just yet," laughed Stan. "Before you do anything—if you're serious about being a Subway owner—you'll need to go to Subway University."

Ron raised his glass, "Salute."

"No man, *salud*," corrected Stan. "A toast. To *opportunidades del futuro y amistad.* To future opportunities and friendship."

Discussion Questions

1. What are all the advantages and disadvantages of forming a corporation?
2. What do you think is the best way for Stan and Ron to own a Subway restaurant jointly? Partnership or corporation? Why?

CHAPTER 19

Corporations

Stock Values, Dividends, Treasury Stock, and Retained Earnings

Your accounting instructor asked a stockbroker to speak to your class recently. The broker discussed the process of stock trading and how various events influence the marketplace. The class discussion became very interesting when a fellow student asked, "How can anyone really know what a company's stock is worth after the recent scandals with companies like Enron and Worldcom?" The broker replied, "Your question is an excellent one. Much of a stock's value is based on what is reported on its financial statements. Accurate and truthful accounting practices are crucial for any publicly held company. That's why it's important for you as students to learn good accounting practices — then you will know what's right when it comes to number crunching."

The market price of stock is made up of many factors both inside and outside of a company. One factor affecting the market price of stock is the payment of dividends by a company. Another factor is the accurate reporting of earnings, assets, and liabilities as shown on a company's income statement and balance sheet. Ethical accounting practices and the accurate reporting of amounts help a company to present a truthful and honest picture of its worth to its employees, investors, and even its competitors.

In this chapter we will learn how to calculate the book value of preferred and common stock. We will look at journalizing the payment of a cash and stock dividend and the purchase and sale of treasury stock. We will also discuss the preparation of a company's statement of retained earnings. After studying this chapter you will have a much better idea about items connected with stock value, and you'll know the right way to report such amounts when accounting for a company's stock.

Learning Objectives

- Calculating the book value of preferred and common stock. (p. 702)

- Journalizing entries to record issuance of a cash dividend and a stock dividend. (p. 705)

- Journalizing the purchase and sale of treasury stock. (p. 711)

- Preparing a statement of retained earnings. (p. 714)

In this chapter we continue the study of aspects of corporate equity that we began in the last chapter. We discuss a number of topics, including stock values, how and why dividends are declared and paid, why a corporation buys back its own stock, and the restrictions on retained earnings.

In Chapter 18 we discussed two types of stock value: par value and stated value. In Learning Unit 19-1 we turn our attention to other stock values.

Learning Unit 19-1   Understanding Stock Values: Redemption, Market, and Book Value

REDEMPTION VALUE

When a corporation issues preferred stock, it often reserves the right to retire or redeem that stock for a specific price. At the time the stock is issued, this price per share, called redemption value, is determined, and people buy the stock knowing that the corporation can redeem it at this price.

MARKET VALUE

> Stock prices are traded in decimals today. They used to be traded in fractional amounts.

The price at which shares of capital stock are bought and sold in the open market is called the market value. Economic conditions, a company's earnings, and investors' expectations all play a factor in determining the market price.

BOOK VALUE PER SHARE

Book value per share is, in general, the total of stockholders' equity (assets minus liabilities) divided by the number of shares issued. Why is book value used? For several reasons:

1. When a company seeks a loan, banks may specify a minimum book value for a loan to be approved.
2. If a merger is being negotiated, book value may be used as a factor in setting an exchange ratio of stock. For example, based on book value, 1 share of Octon Co. stock could fairly be issued for 3 shares of Xeron Co. stock, if the book value of Octon stock is $30 and the book value of Xeron stock is $10.
3. Book value may be used when contracts are made. For example, an individual may receive in the future an option to buy or sell stock based on future book value. (That value is *not* market value, which is based on current prices.)

It is important to emphasize that book value doesn't represent what an owner might receive if the assets of a company were *liquidated*. At the time of liquidation the assets may be sold at prices quite different from the values on the books, which are based on cost and not current market prices.

CALCULATING BOOK VALUE WITH ONLY ONE CLASS OF STOCK

When a corporation has only common stock, book value is calculated using the following equation:

$$\text{Book Value per Share} = \frac{\text{Total Stockholders' Equity}}{\text{Total Shares Outstanding}}$$

As an example, we use the stockholders' equity shown in Figure 19-1 for Jones Corporation and calculate book value per share of common stock.

The book value is $45 per share ($450,000/10,000 shares). Thus, for each share of stock owned, $45 would be received *if* the corporation were liquidated without any losses from disposing of assets. By the time assets are disposed of, the owner might get much less than book value.

JONES CORPORATION STOCKHOLDERS' EQUITY		
Paid-in Capital:		
Common Stock, $25 par value; 10,000 shares		
authorized, issued, and outstanding	$250 00 0 00	
Paid-in Capital in Excess of Par Value—Common	110 00 0 00	
Total Paid-in Capital	$360 00 0 00	
Retained Earnings	90 00 0 00	
Total Stockholders' Equity	$450 00 0 00	

Figure 19-1
Stockholder's Equity

CALCULATING BOOK VALUE WITH BOTH PREFERRED AND COMMON STOCK

When there are two classes of stock, before book value can be calculated the stockholders' equity must be allocated (divided up) for each class of stock. First, for preferred stock, a corporation assigns the redemption value (or par value if there is no redemption value) of the stock along with any dividends in arrears (any dividends that are owed to holders of preferred stock but have not yet been paid out). This total of redemption value plus dividends in arrears is divided by the number of preferred shares outstanding. The *remainder* of stockholders' equity is assigned to the common stockholders, and the book value of the common stock is calculated by that amount divided by the number of common stock shares outstanding. Book value can be shown in the following formulas:

$$\text{Book Value Preferred} = \frac{\text{Redemption Value + Dividends in Arrears}}{\text{Number of Shares of Preferred Stock Outstanding}}$$

$$\text{Book Value Common} = \frac{\text{Stockholders' Equity − Amount Assigned to Preferred}}{\text{Number of Shares of Common Stock Outstanding}}$$

Let's illustrate this situation by looking at the stockholders' equity of Ryan Corporation (Fig. 19-2) and performing the necessary calculations.

Given: Redemption value of preferred is $103; there are $14,000 worth of dividends in arrears.

Thus,

$$\text{Book Value Preferred} = \frac{\$206,000 + \$14,000}{2,000 \text{ Shares}}$$

$$= \frac{\$220,000}{2,000 \text{ Shares}} = \$110 \text{ per Share}$$

and

$$\text{Book Value Common} = \frac{\$894,000 - \$220,000}{10,000 \text{ Shares}}$$

$$= \frac{\$674,000}{10,000 \text{ Shares}} = \$67.40 \text{ per Share}$$

Figure 19-2
Calculating Book Value
from Stockholder's Equity

RYAN CORPORATION STOCKHOLDERS' EQUITY			
Paid-in Capital:			
Preferred 7% Stock, $100 per value, authorized			
3,000 shares cumulative and nonparticipating,			
2,000 shares issued and outstanding	$200 00 0 00		
Paid-in Capital in Excess of Par Value—Preferred	10 0 0 00		
Total Paid-in Capital by Preferred Stockholders		$210 00 0 00	
Common Stock, $50 par value, authorized 12,000			
shares, 10,000 shares issued and outstanding	500 00 0 00		
Paid-in Capital in Excess of Par Value—Common	20 0 0 00		
Total Paid-in Capital by Common Stockholders		520 00 0 00	
Total Paid-in Capital		$730 00 0 00	
Retained Earnings		164 00 0 00	
Total Stockholders' Equity		$894 00 0 00	

Redemption value
$103 × 2,000 shares

Total Stockholders' Equity		$894 00 0 00	
Less: Equity Applicable to Preferred Stock:			
Redemption Value	$206 00 0 00		
Dividends in Arrears	14 0 0 00	(220 00 0 00)	
Equity Allocated to Common Stock			$674 00 0 00

Note: When preferred stock is redeemed, the paid-in capital in excess of par is *not* returned and thus is *not* included as part of the preferred equity in the book-value calculation.

Learning Unit 19-1 Review

AT THIS POINT you should be able to

- List and define other stock values besides par value. (p. 702)
- Explain the purpose of book value. (p. 702)
- Calculate the book value of preferred and common stock. (p. 703)

SELF-REVIEW QUIZ 19-1

(The forms you need are on page 126 of the *Study Guide and Working Papers.*)

From the following information calculate the book value for preferred and common stock:

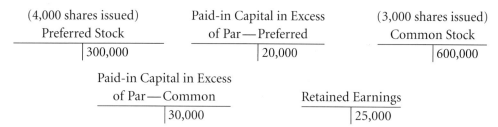

(4,000 shares issued) Preferred Stock	Paid-in Capital in Excess of Par—Preferred	(3,000 shares issued) Common Stock
300,000	20,000	600,000

Paid-in Capital in Excess of Par—Common	Retained Earnings
30,000	25,000

Dividends in arrears amount to $15,000. Assume a redemption value on preferred stock of $90 per share.

SOLUTION TO SELF-REVIEW QUIZ 19-1

$90 per share × 4,000 shares redemption value

Figure 19-3

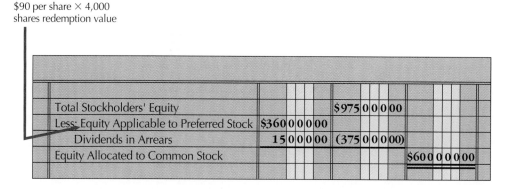

Total Stockholders' Equity		$975 00 00	
Less: Equity Applicable to Preferred Stock	$360 00 00		
Dividends in Arrears	15 00 00	(375 00 00)	
Equity Allocated to Common Stock			$600 00 00

PREFERRED STOCK Book Value per Share	COMMON STOCK Book Value per Share
$\dfrac{\$375{,}000}{4{,}000 \text{ shares}} = \$93.75$	$\dfrac{\$600{,}000}{3{,}000 \text{ shares}} = \$200$

Learning Unit 19-2   Dividends

In this unit we discuss the distribution of cash, stock, or other assets that the board of directors declares as dividends. Dividends, as we have seen, are the distribution of earnings of the corporation. It is important to realize that only the board of directors of a corporation has the authority to determine whether a dividend is to be paid, how much it will be, who receives it, and when and how it will be paid.

Three important dates are associated with the dividend process.

1. **Date of declaration:** The day the board of directors announces its decision to pay a dividend. This date creates a liability to the company called **Dividend Payable.**

2. **Date of record:** The date established by the board of directors that determines which stockholders will receive the dividend. These stockholders can be identified in the corporation's subsidiary stockholders' ledger at this date of record.

3. **Date of payment:** The date that the dividend is actually paid to stockholders of record.

> The board of directors declares the dividend.

> Date of record is usually two to four weeks after date of declaration.

CASH DIVIDENDS

The distribution of earnings of a corporation in the form of cash to its stockholders is called a cash dividend. For example, on March 8, 20XX, the board of directors of Tell Corporation declares a $2 cash dividend per share on the 5,000 shares issued and outstanding. The dividend will be paid on April 16, 20XX, to stockholders of record on March 25, 20XX. Let's look at how to analyze as well as record this cash dividend.

> There must be a sufficient balance in retained earnings and cash to pay the dividend.

Date of Declaration: March 8, 20XX: The following chart analyzes this transaction.

Declaration of dividends reduces Retained Earnings. A legally declared dividend is a current liability on the balance sheet.

Accounts Affected	Category	↑ ↓	Rules
Retained Earnings	SE	↓	Dr. $10,000
Dividends Payable	Liability	↑	Cr. $10,000

The journal entry will look like Figure 19-4.

Figure 19-4
Declaring A Cash Dividend

> Note that no entry is made at the date of record.

Mar.	8	Retained Earnings	1 0 0 0 0 00		
		Dividends Payable		1 0 0 0 0 00	
		Dividends declared of $2 to stockholders			
		of record Mar. 25, 20XX: payable on			
		Apr. 16, 20XX, as declared by board			
		of directors.			

Date of Payment: April 16, 20XX: Here is an analysis of the dividend payment.

Accounts Affected	Category	↑ ↓	Rules
Dividends Payable	Liability	↓	Dr. $10,000
Cash	Asset	↓	Cr. $10,000

The journal entry will look like Figure 19-5.

Figure 19-5
Payment of Cash Dividend

Apr.	16	Dividends Payable	1 0 0 0 0 00		
		Cash		1 0 0 0 0 00	
		Payment of dividend to stockholders of			
		record on Mar. 25, 20XX.			

The end result of these transactions is to reduce Cash and Retained Earnings. (*Remember: Retained Earnings doesn't mean Cash. Cash is an asset, whereas Retained*

Earnings is part of stockholders' equity.) In effect, the company is distributing part of its accumulated income to stockholders.

THE STOCK DIVIDEND

A stock dividend occurs when a corporation issues its own stock instead of a distribution of assets to its stockholders. There are a number of reasons why a stock dividend is declared instead of a cash dividend:

> A stock dividend doesn't reduce cash or the total of stockholders' equity.

1. To satisfy stockholders' expectations. The corporation doesn't have enough cash to pay a cash dividend and offers the stock dividend instead. The stockholders make no new investment to receive this type of dividend.
2. To increase permanent capital in the business (because more stock is issued).
3. To reduce the market value of the stock, because the price may be too high in the trading on the open market. When more stock is supplied with no demand for it, stock prices go down.
4. Because income tax is avoided until the stock received is sold.

RECORDING A STOCK DIVIDEND

A stock dividend will *not* reduce total stockholders' equity the way a cash dividend does. The end result of a stock dividend is to transfer an amount based on market value from Retained Earnings to Paid-in Capital.* After a stock dividend a stockholder will own a larger number of shares, but the *total* ownership equity stays the same. Let's look at Jesse Corporation to illustrate recording a stock dividend.

On December 27, 20XX, Jesse Corporation declared a 10% stock dividend distributable January 27 to stockholders of record on January 13. Figure 19-6 shows the stockholders' equity of Jesse Corporation before the dividend was declared. The current fair market value of the stock is $30 per share.

Figure 19-6
Stockholder's Equity

Stockholders' Equity		
Paid-in Capital:		
Common Stock, $20 par value,		
15,000 shares authorized, 10,000 shares issued		
and outstanding	$200 000 00	
Paid-in Capital in Excess of Par, Common	24 000 00	
Total Paid-in Capital by Common Stockholders	224 000 00	
Retained Earnings	62 000 00	
Total Stockholders' Equity		$286 000 00

*For larger stock dividends (over 25% of the outstanding stock) the amount is based on par.

Recording the Declaration of the Dividend: The following chart is an analysis of this transaction.

Accounts Affected	Category	↑ ↓	Rules
Retained Earnings	SE	↓	Dr. $30,000
Common Stock Dividend Distributable	SE	↑	Cr. $20,000
Paid-in Capital in Excess of Par Value—Stock Dividend	SE	↑	Cr. $10,000

Retained Earnings is decreased by $30,000. To arrive at that figure we multiply the market value of the stock ($30) times the number of shares issued in the dividend (1,000). The number of shares issued in the dividend is the number of shares issued and outstanding (10,000) times the percent of dividend declared (10%). The Common Stock Dividend Distributable is 1,000 shares times the par value of the common stock ($20).

The journal entry will look like Figure 19-7.

Figure 19-7
Declaration of Stock
Dividend

	20XX					
	Dec.	27	Retained Earnings	30 00 00		
			Common Stock Dividend Distributable		20 00 00	
			Paid-in Capital in Excess of Par			
			Value—Stock Dividend		10 00 00	
			Records declaration of a 10% stock			
			dividend to stockholders of record			
			as of Jan. 13; payable Jan. 27 as			
			declared by the board of directors.			

Note that the Common Stock Dividend Distributable account, which records the par value of the stock, is *not* a liability; it is not payable with assets. It is part of stockholders' equity. When the stock is issued, this account will be reduced and transferred into Common Stock.

Let's first see what the stockholders' equity would look like if it were prepared between the declaration and the payment date. Note in Figure 19-8 that the stocks are listed first, followed by all the additional paid-in capital. This type of layout is called the *legal approach;* earlier we showed the *source-of-capital* approach. Both ways are acceptable.

Recording the Issuance of the Stock Dividend: Let us first analyze.

Accounts Affected	Category	↑ ↓	Rules
Common Stock Dividend Distributable	SE	↓	Dr. $20,000
Common Stock	SE	↑	Cr. $20,000

Figure 19-8
Legal Approach

Stockholders' Equity				
Paid-in Capital:				
Common Stock, $20 par value,				
15,000 shares authorized, 10,000 shares issued				
and outstanding	$200 000 00			
Common Stock Dividend Distributable,				
1,000 shares	20 000 00			
Total Common Stock issued and				
to be issued		$220 000 00		
Additional Paid-in Capital:				
Paid-in Capital in Excess of Par				
Value—Common	24 000 00			
Paid-in Capital in Excess of Par				
Value—Stock Dividend	10 000 00			
Total Additional Paid-in Capital		34 000 00		
Total Paid-in Capital		$254 000 00		
Retained Earnings		32 000 00		
Total Stockholders' Equity		$286 000 00		

Then the journal entry would look like Figure 19-9.

Figure 19-9
Issuance of Stock Dividend

Jan.	27	Common Stock Dividend Distributable	20 000 00	
		Common Stock		20 000 00
		Issuance of stock dividend declared		
		on Dec. 27 to stockholders of record		
		as of Jan. 13.		

The Stock Split

A **stock split** is the issuance by a corporation of additional stock to cause a large drop in the market price of the outstanding stock; no assets are received in return. The corporation reduces the par value or stated value of the authorized stock with an increase in the number of shares authorized, issued, and outstanding. The stock split, however, doesn't change the Retained Earnings account as a stock dividend did. To repeat, the stock split will

1. Increase the number of shares outstanding.
2. Reduce the par or stated value in proportion.

For example, a two-for-one split on 10,000 shares of $20 par would result in 20,000 shares with a $10 par value. The total equity remains the same. Because the stock split doesn't change the balance of any ledger account, only a *memorandum notation** in the journal, as well as in the Stock account, would be needed to update the accounting

---

*An example of such a notation is, "Called in the outstanding $20 par value 10,000 shares of common stock and issued 20,000 shares of $10 par-value common stock for old shares previously outstanding."

record. The number of shares in this transaction has doubled, but the corporation total equity has not changed; thus the market price of $80 per share would drop to approximately $40. If Jay Owen owned 100 shares before the split, he would own 200 now, but his market value would be the same.

BEFORE	AFTER
100 shares × $80 = $8,000	200 shares × $40 = $8,000

Jay will benefit from the stock split if

1. The stock price rises on the market.
2. Dividends per share are increased.

Learning Unit 19-2 Review

AT THIS POINT you should be able to

- List as well as explain the three important dates associated with the dividend process. (p. 705)
- Journalize the appropriate entries for a cash dividend. (p. 706)
- List possible reasons for a stock dividend. (p. 707)
- Journalize appropriate entries for a stock dividend. (p. 708)
- Compare and contrast a stock split to a stock dividend. (p. 709)

SELF-REVIEW QUIZ 19-2

(The forms you need are on page 127 of the *Study Guide and Working Papers*.)

Journalize the appropriate entries from the following facts. On September 24, 20XX, the Directors of Movy Co. declared a 5% stock dividend to be issued on November 8 to stockholders of record on October 10. There are 20,000 shares outstanding. The stock has a par value of $10 and a current market value of $15 per share.

SOLUTION TO SELF-REVIEW QUIZ 19-2

Figure 19-10
Stock Dividend Declared

($15 × 1,000 shares)
($10 par × 1,000 shares)

20XX							
Sept.	24	Retained Earnings	15 0 0 0 00				
		Common Stock Dividend Distributable			10 0 0 0 00		
		Paid-in Capital in Excess of Par					
		Value—Stock Dividend			5 0 0 0 00		
Nov.	8	Common Stock Dividend Distributable	10 0 0 0 00				
		Common Stock			10 0 0 0 00		

Learning Unit 19-3   Treasury Stock

Previously issued preferred or common stock that has been reacquired by the corporation (or given as a gift to the corporation) is known as **treasury stock.** Why would a corporation reacquire previously issued stock? Some reasons include the following:

1. A need to issue more stock for stock option plans or for use in acquiring other corporations.

2. A desire to reduce the number of shares of stock outstanding, which might be done to create a favorable market for the sale of the stock.

3. Anticipation of an opportunity at a later date to reissue stock at a higher price.

The following are some of the characteristics of treasury stock:

1. The purchase of treasury stock does not change the amount of issued stock.

2. The purchase of treasury stock does reduce outstanding stock. Remember that stock can be issued but not outstanding.

3. Treasury stock does not have rights to dividends or voting situations (because it is not outstanding).

4. Treasury stock is a contra-stockholders' equity account.

5. When treasury stock is bought, it is recorded at the purchase price. This purchase of treasury stock does not reduce the balance in the Retained Earnings account.

6. Many state laws will restrict the amount of retained earnings available for dividends if treasury stock exists, because the purchase of treasury stock reduces assets and stockholders' equity (like a cash dividend). This restriction is commonly shown in a footnote on the balance sheet.

Let's look now at how to record the purchase of treasury stock.

PURCHASE OF TREASURY STOCK

On June 1, 20XX, Ashly Corporation has 5,000 shares of $10 par-value common stock and 2,000 shares of preferred stock outstanding. The corporation on June 1 purchases 1,000 shares of its own common stock at a price of $12 per share. The following is the analysis as well as journal entry to record the purchase:

	Accounts Affected	Category	↑ ↓	Rules
(1,000 shares × $12) ➝	Treasury Stock—Common	Contra SE	↑	Dr. $12,000
	Cash	Asset	↓	Cr. $12,000

Record treasury stock at the purchase price of $12 (Fig. 19-11). Note that the par value of common is not affected. Think of an *increase* in treasury stock as a reduction to stockholders' equity.

Figure 19-11
Purchase of Treasury Stock

	June	1	Treasury Stock—Common	1 2 0 0 0 0	
			Cash		1 2 0 0 0 0
			Purchase at $12 per share of		
			1,000 shares of previously		
			issued stock.		

SALE OF TREASURY STOCK

Treasury stock can be reissued at a price above or below the cost of reacquiring the stock. Let's look at how Ashly Company could on July 8 sell 100 shares of the treasury stock at $15 per share that was reacquired on June 1 for $12 per share.

This chart analyzes the transaction:

	Accounts Affected	Category	↑ ↓	Rules
(100 shares × $15) ⟶	Cash	Asset	↑	Dr. $1,500
(100 shares × $12) ⟶	Treasury Stock—Common	Contra SE	↓	Cr. $1,200
(100 shares × $3) ⟶	Paid-in Capital from Treasury Stock	SE	↑	Cr. $300

Think of a *decrease* in treasury stock resulting in an increase to stockholders' equity.

The journal entry looks like Figure 19-12.

Figure 19-12
Sale of Treasury Stock

	July	8	Cash	1 5 0 0 00	
			Treasury Stock—Common		1 2 0 0 00
			Paid-in Capital from Treasury Stock		3 0 0 00
			Sold 100 shares of Treasury stock		
			purchased at $12.		

The Treasury Stock account is decreased by the number of shares reissued times the *cost* when the stock was reacquired by the company. The credit to **Paid-in Capital from Treasury Stock** represents the amount over what was paid for acquiring the treasury stock.

If a corporation sells treasury stock for less than cost, the result is a decrease in stockholders' equity that is recorded in Paid-in Capital from Treasury Stock until the balance of the account is 0. Any further decrease in this account will directly reduce Retained Earnings, because Paid-in Capital from Treasury Stock will not be a negative balance.

EXAMPLE OF STOCKHOLDERS' EQUITY WITH TREASURY STOCK

Now let's see what stockholders' equity will look like with the accounts Treasury Stock and Paid-in Capital from Treasury Stock (Fig. 19-13).

Figure 19-13
Stockholder's Equity

Paid-in Capital:		
Preferred Stock, 14/%, $100 par value,		
authorized 6,000 shares, 2,000 shares		
issued and outstanding		$200 000 00
Common Stock $10 par, authorized 9,000		
shares, 5,000 shares issued and 4,100		
outstanding, 900 shares in treasury		50 000 00*
Additional Paid-in Capital:		
Paid-in Capital in Excess of Par		
Value—Preferred	10 000 00	
Paid-in Capital in Excess of Par		
Value—Common	30 000 00	
Paid-in Capital from Treasury Stock	3 000 00	
Total Additional Paid-in Capital		40 300 00
Total Paid-in Capital		$290 300 00
Retained Earnings		60 000 00
		$350 300 00
Deduct: Treasury Stock—Common		
(900 shares at cost)		10 800 00
Total Stockholders' Equity		$339 500 00

* $50,000 = shares issued (5,000) x par ($10)

The 900 shares of treasury stock don't reduce the number of shares issued; they reduce the number of shares outstanding.

Learning Unit 19-3 Review

AT THIS POINT you should be able to

- Define and explain the characteristics of treasury stock (p. 711)
- Journalize the purchase as well as sale of treasury stock. (p. 712)
- Explain why treasury stock is a contra-stockholders' equity account. (p. 712)

SELF-REVIEW QUIZ 19-3

(The forms you need are on page 127 of the *Study Guide and Working Papers.*)

Record the following transactions in general journal form (no explanation needed):

1. Also Company acquired 100 shares of its own $10 par common stock at $15 per share.

2. Fifty of the treasury shares are reissued at $18 per share.

3. Forty of the treasury shares are reissued at $6 per share.

SOLUTION TO SELF-REVIEW QUIZ 19-3

Figure 19-14
Purchase and Sale
of Treasury Stock

❶	Treasury Stock (100 × $15)	1 5 0 0 00	
	Cash		1 5 0 0 00
❷	Cash ($18 × 50)	9 0 0 00	
	Treasury Stock (50 × $15)		7 5 0 00
❸	Paid-in Capital from Treasury		
	Stock (50 × $3)		1 5 0 00
	Cash ($6 × 40)	2 4 0 00	
	Paid-in Capital from Treasury Stock	1 5 0 00	
	Retained Earnings	2 1 0 00	
	Treasury Stock (40 × $15)		6 0 0 00

Note that Retained Earnings is reduced by $210, because Paid-in Capital is down to a zero balance:

$$
\begin{array}{ll}
\$150 & (50 \times \$3) \\
-\ 360 & (40 \times \$9) \\
\hline
\$<210>
\end{array}
$$

Learning Unit 19-4   Appropriation of Retained Earnings and the Statement of Retained Earnings

In the first three units of this chapter we saw that cash dividends as well as stock dividends reduce the amount of Retained Earnings. Now we look at how companies indicate to those reading their financial reports that some of the Retained Earnings are not available for declaration of dividends; they are **Appropriated (Restricted) Retained Earnings.**

> *Restrictions on Retained Earnings limit the amount that is available to declare dividends.*

This *appropriating* of retained earnings could be either voluntary or contractual. For example, the board of directors could voluntarily decide that a portion of earnings should be used for plant expansion instead of for dividends. If a company enters into a loan with a bank, the bank may require the company to keep a minimum balance in Retained Earnings to protect its rights until the loan is repaid. Companies in many states are required to keep a minimum in the Retained Earnings account at the level of legal capital. We saw in the last unit that treasury stock could result in Retained Earnings being restricted to the cost of the treasury stock.

> *No actual cash is involved in the appropriation of Retained Earnings.*

In years past these special appropriations were recorded by transferring portions of the Retained Earnings account to accounts such as Retained Earnings Appropriated for Plant Expansion or Retained Earnings Appropriated for Contra Obligations. In reality, these appropriations didn't reduce total Retained Earnings; they just *shifted* a portion into an account that revealed its special purpose. For example, an entry to restrict $20,000 for plant expansion would be as shown in Figure 19-15.

Retained Earnings				20	0	0	0	00									
Appropriation for Plant Expansion									20	0	0	0	00				

Figure 19-15
Plant Expansion Restriction

After the appropriation or restriction has passed (for example, the loan has been paid off), the balance is transferred back to the Retained Earnings account. No cash is involved in the appropriation.

Today, to make things clear to investors, most companies report restrictions by using a footnote to the Retained Earnings account. Restrictions on Retained Earnings do not have to be updated in the ledger; thus the use of a footnote is a common practice. (It is good practice to write a memo in the Retained Earnings account to identify each appropriation.) A footnote to announce such restrictions would look like the following:

> The loan agreement with Jones Bank contains a restriction on the payment of cash dividends. Approximately $600,000 of retained earnings was free of such a restriction as of June 30, 20XX.

PREPARING THE STATEMENT OF RETAINED EARNINGS

In past chapters we discussed the income statement, balance sheet, statement of owner's equity, and statement of partners' equity. We now turn our attention to a statement of retained earnings that will reveal the changes in retained earnings over a period of time. The changes in retained earnings result from the following:

1. Net income or loss.

2. Dividends declared.

3. Effects of prior period adjustments.

Often an error in a financial report of a company from a prior period may not be discovered until a later period. If the error is considered *material*, a prior period adjustment should be made to the beginning balance of Retained Earnings. Let's look at a specific example.

Eight months after the close of its books Ralston Company discovered that depreciation was understated by $12,000, which meant in the old period that Depreciation Expense was understated by $12,000 and Net Income was overstated by $12,000. If Net Income was overstated, Retained Earnings also was overstated, because Net Income is closed into Retained Earnings. Thus, the entry shown in Figure 19-16 is recorded in the *new* year to adjust the prior period error (we ignore tax effect here).

Retained Earnings				12	0	0	0	00									
Accumulated Depreciation, Equipment									12	0	0	0	00				

Figure 19-16
Adjustment of Prior Period Error

A statement of retained earnings for the Ralston Company would look like Figure 19-17.

Figure 19-17
Statement of Retained
Earnings

The statement of retained
earnings is a formal report.

RALSTON COMPANY STATEMENT OF RETAINED EARNINGS YEAR ENDED DECEMBER 31, 20X2		
Retained Earnings, Jan. 1, 20X2	$350 0 0 0 00	
Less: Prior Period Adjustment:		
Correction of 20X1 error	12 0 0 0 00	
Retained Earnings, Jan. 20X2, corrected	$338 0 0 0 00	
Add: Net Income for 20X2	40 0 0 0 00	
Total	$378 0 0 0 00	
Deduct: Dividends declared in 20X2	28 0 0 0 00	
Retained Earnings, Dec. 31, 20X2	$350 0 0 0 00	

This ending figure of $350,000 will appear in the stockholders' equity section of the balance sheet.

ACCOUNTING CYCLE FOR A CORPORATION

Before we conclude our discussion of corporations, Figure 19-18 provides a simplified sample of a worksheet for a corporation. This worksheet will give you a better idea of what titles such as Subscriptions Receivable, Common Stock, Paid-in Capital, and Retained Earnings look like when all are combined on one worksheet.

The cycle is then to prepare financial reports as well as journalize and post the adjusting and closing entries. We use Retained Earnings instead of Capital in the closing process. Also in the adjusting process we adjust the income tax owed. The Income Tax account is closed to Income Summary. The steps are quite similar to those discussed for a merchandise company.

A key point is that the net income shown on the income statement could be substantially different from that reported for tax purposes; certain deductions on the tax return will differ from the expenses on the corporation's books.

JANE CORPORATION
WORKSHEET
FOR YEAR ENDED DECEMBER 31, 20X3

Account Name	Trial Balance Dr.	Trial Balance Cr.	Adjustments Dr.	Adjustments Cr.	Adjusted Trial Balance Dr.	Adjusted Trial Balance Cr.	Income Statement Dr.	Income Statement Cr.	Balance Sheet Dr.	Balance Sheet Cr.
Cash	X				X				X	
Notes Receivable	X				X				X	
Accounts Receivable	X				X				X	
Subscriptions Rec., Com. Stock	X				X				X	
Merch. Inventory	X		O	X	O				O	
Prepaid Rent	X			X	X				X	
Office Equipment	X				X				X	
Acc. Dep., Office Equip.		X		X		X				X
Organization Costs	X				X				X	
Notes Payable		X				X				X
Accounts Payable		X				X				X
Dividends Payable, Com.		X				X				X
Common Stock		X				X				X
Common Stock Div. Dist.		X				X				X
Paid-in Capital in Excess of Par—Common Stock		X				X				X
Common Stock Subscribed		X				X				X
Paid-in Capital from Treasury Stock		X				X				X
Retained Earnings		X				X				X
Income Summary			X	O	X	O	X	O		
Sales (totals)		X				X		X		
Purchases	X				X		X			
Purch. Ret. and Allow.		X				X		X		
Expenses (totals)	X				X		X			
Expenses (Adj.)	X		X		X		X			
Income Tax	X		X		X		X			
Income Tax Payable				X		X				X

0 = Ending inventory

Figure 19-18 Worksheet for Jane Corporation

Learning Unit 19-4 Review

AT THIS POINT you should be able to

- Explain what could lead to appropriations of Retained Earnings. (p. 714)
- Explain why footnotes are used on financial reports instead of appropriation accounts to report restrictions to Retained Earnings. (p. 715)
- Prepare a statement of retained earnings. (p. 716)

SELF-REVIEW QUIZ 19-4

(The forms you need are on page 128 of the *Study Guide and Working Papers.*)

From the following data prepare a statement of retained earnings for Janet Corporation for the year ended December 31, 20X3:

- Retained Earnings, January 1, 20X3, $650,000.
- Dividends, 20X3, $50,000.
- Correction of error from 20X1, $50,000 for Net Income that was discovered to be understated.
- Net Income, 20X3, $80,000

SOLUTION TO SELF-REVIEW QUIZ 19-4

Figure 19-19
Statement of Retained Earnings

JANET CORPORATION STATEMENT OF RETAINED EARNINGS YEAR ENDED DECEMBER 31, 20X3	
Retained Earnings, Jan. 1, 20X3	$650 0 0 0 00
Add: Prior Period Adjustment,	
Correction of 20X1 error	50 0 0 0 00
Retained Earnings, Jan. 20X3, corrected	$700 0 0 0 00
Add: Net Income for 20X3	80 0 0 0 00
Total	$780 0 0 0 00
Deduct: Dividends declared in 20X3	50 0 0 0 00
Retained Earnings, Dec. 31, 20X3	$730 0 0 0 00

Chapter Review

Summary of Key Points

Learning Unit 19-1

1. Redemption value is the price per share a corporation pays to holders of preferred stock when the stock is retired or redeemed.
2. Market value represents the open-market price of stock bought and sold. Market value doesn't mean the same thing as book value.
3. Book value per share is the amount or value of net assets on a company's books for each share of stockholders' stock in the equity of the corporation. Book value is calculated for preferred and common separately.

Learning Unit 19-2

1. Dividends represent cash, stock, or other assets distributed to stockholders. The board of directors has the authority to declare dividends.
2. Three important dates associated with the dividend process are date of declaration, date of record, and date of payment.
3. A cash dividend results in a reduction of Retained Earnings and an eventual reduction in Cash.
4. Retained earnings doesn't mean cash.
5. A stock dividend will not reduce stockholders' equity like a cash dividend will. The end result is a transfer of retained earnings to Paid-in Capital.
6. Common Stock Dividend Distributable is a stockholders' equity account that is recorded at par value. It is not a liability account.
7. A stock split has no effect on Retained Earnings or any other ledger account. It increases the number of shares outstanding as well as reduces par or stated value.

Learning Unit 19-3

1. Treasury Stock is a contra-stockholders' equity account that is recorded at cost. It represents stock that was previously issued and is now reacquired or received as a gift by a corporation.
2. Treasury stock is recognized as issued but not outstanding for dividends or voting situations.
3. Paid-in Capital from Treasury Stock can never have a negative balance. Any additional "loss" is reduced in Retained Earnings.

Learning Unit 19-4

1. Appropriations of Retained Earnings can be contractual or voluntary.
2. Appropriations restrict the amount of Retained Earnings available for dividends.
3. Common practice today is to use footnotes on the balance sheet to reveal any appropriations of Retained Earnings.
4. The statement of retained earnings is made up of (1) beginning balance, (2) corrections of prior periods, (3) net income, and (4) dividends.

Key Terms

Appropriated (Restricted) Retained Earnings That portion of Retained Earnings that is not available for dividends.

Book value per share Amount of net assets that a stockholder would receive on a per-share basis, assuming no gain or loss on the sale of the assets.

Cash dividend Dividend that is paid in cash.

Common Stock Dividend Distributable Stockholders' equity account that accumulates a stock dividend that has been declared but not yet issued and distributed.

Date of declaration   The date upon which the board of directors of a corporation formally declares a dividend.

Date of payment   The date the dividend is paid.

Date of record   The date of ownership that determines which stockholders will receive the dividend.

Dividend   Cash or other assets that a corporation distributes as earnings to stockholders.

Dividend Payable   Liability showing amount of cash dividend owed.

Market value   The price that a buyer pays to purchase shares of capital stock in the open market. Of course, for every buyer there is a seller.

Paid-in Capital from Treasury Stock   Stockholders' equity account that records amounts more or less than par value of treasury stock sold. The balance of this account can never be negative.

Prior period adjustment   Correction made in the current year of a mistake made in previous years. The adjustment is updated on the statement of retained earnings.

Redemption value   The price per share a corporation pays to redeem or retire capital stock.

Statement of retained earnings   A financial report that reveals the changes in retained earnings for a particular period of time.

Stock dividend   Stock that is distributed to stockholders instead of cash or other assets.

Stock split   Issuing of additional shares of stock to stockholders; total par or stated value remains the same.

Treasury stock   Stock that has been issued but has been bought back by the corporation or received as a gift.

Questions, Mini Exercises, Exercises, and Problems

Discussion Questions

1. What is the difference between market value and book value?
2. List the three important dates that are associated with the dividend process.
3. Why is no journal entry needed at the date of record?
4. Explain some possible reasons a company may declare a stock dividend instead of a cash dividend.
5. Explain why stock dividends will not reduce total stockholders' equity.
6. Common Stock Dividend Distributable is a liability. Accept or reject. Defend your position.
7. Explain the difference between a stock dividend and a stock split.
8. Treasury stock is really an asset. Defend or reject. Support your argument.
9. All treasury stock is recognized as issued and outstanding for dividends. True or false? Please explain.
10. Explain the purpose of the account Paid-in Capital from Treasury Stock.
11. Appropriation of retained earnings is always done for a contractual reason. Accept or reject. Defend your position.
12. Restrictions on retained earnings have to be updated in the ledger. Agree or disagree. Why?
13. What elements make up the statement of retained earnings?

Mini Exercises

(The forms you need are on page 130 of the *Study Guide and Working Papers.*)

Book Value per Share for Preferred and Common

1. Given the following prepare the book value per share for preferred and common stock:

   - Preferred Stock $80,000; 1,000 shares issued.
   - Common Stock $150,000; 800 shares issued.

Blueprint: Legal Capital Approach

MOOSE COMPANY PARTIAL BALANCE SHEET			
Stockholders' Equity			
Paid-in Capital:			
Preferred Stock 12%, $10 par value, authorized 30,000 shares, 9,000 shares issued and outstanding		XX	
Common Stock, $10 par value, authorized 100,000 shares, 40,000 shares issued and 29,000 shares outstanding, 11,000 shares in treasury	XX		
Common Stock Dividend Distributable	XX	XX	
Additional Paid-in Capital:			
Paid-in Capital in Excess of Par Value—Preferred	XX		
Paid-in Capital in Excess of Par Value—Common	XX		
Paid-in Capital in Excess of Par Value—Stock Dividend	XX		
Paid-in Capital from Treasury Stock	XX		
Total Additional Paid-in Capital		XX	
Total Paid-in Capital		XX	
Retained Earnings		XX	
Deduct: Treasury Stock		XX	
Total Stockholders' Equity			XX

Note that legal capital is listed first. See page 692 for Blueprint example of the source-of-capital approach. Both approaches are acceptable, and in the real world both are used.

- Retained Earnings, $8,500.
- Dividend in Arrears, $4,000.
- Paid-in capital in excess of par: preferred, $5,000.
- Paid-in capital in excess of par: common, $6,000.
- Redemption value on preferred stock, $16.

Cash Dividend

2. On March 15, 20XX, the board of directors of Vision Corporation declared $3 cash dividend per share on the 6,000 shares issued and outstanding. The dividend will be paid on April 18, 20XX, to stockholders of record on March 19, 20XX. Record journal entries for date of declaration and date of payment.

Stock Dividend

3. On December 24, 20XX, Fress Corporation declared a 5% stock dividend distributable January 18 to stockholders of record on January 8. Currently Fress has 5,000 shares of common stock issued and outstanding. The stock has a par value of $20. The current fair market value of the stock is $35. Journalize (a) the declaration of the dividend and (b) the issuance of the stock dividend.

Treasury Stock

4. Journalize the following transactions:

  a. Janson Co. acquired 50 shares of its own $5 par-value common stock at $10 per share.

  b. Twenty-five of the Treasury shares are reissued at $13 per share.

  c. Twenty of the Treasury shares are reissued at $4 per share.

Prior Period Adjustment

5. Seven months after its closing, Brooks Co. discovered that depreciation was understated by $8,000. Provide the journal entry to adjust the prior period error (ignore any tax effects).

Exercises

(The forms you need are on pages 131–132 of the *Study Guide and Working Papers*.)

19-1. From the following information determine the book value for preferred and common stocks assuming $15,000 of dividends are in arrears on the preferred stock.

Calculating book value of preferred and common.

STOCKHOLDERS' EQUITY

Preferred Stock 12% cumulative and nonparticipating, $20 par value, $19 redemption value, 10,000 shares issued and outstanding	$200,000
Common Stock, $10 par value, 40,000 shares issued and outstanding	400,000
Retained Earnings	80,000
Total Stockholders' Equity	$680,000

19-2. Poole Corporation has 300,000 shares of common stock issued and outstanding. On June 9, 20X6, the board of directors declared a $.50 per share dividend, payable on July 16, 20X6, to stockholders of record on June 29, 20X6. Record the appropriate journal entries on June 9 and July 16.

Cash dividend.

19-3. On July 31, 20X1, Harvey Corporation had the following stockholders' equity:

Stock dividend.

Common Stock, $10 par value, authorized 90,000 shares, 60,000 shares issued and outstanding	$600,000
Retained Earnings	200,000
Total Stockholders' Equity	$800,000

On August 5, 20X1, the board of directors declared a 10% stock dividend to be issued on September 6, 20X1, to the stockholders of record on August 19, 20X1. At time of declaration the market price was $17 per share. Prepare the appropriate journal entries for this stock dividend.

19-4. Given the following stockholders' equity:

Common Stock, $7 par value, authorized 100,000 shares, 80,000 shares issued and outstanding	$ 560,000
Retained Earnings	500,000
Total Stockholders' Equity	$1,060,000

Journalize the following entries:

Treasury stock.

20XX

Apr.	3	Issued 5,000 shares at $12 per share.
	9	Reacquired 200 shares at $8 per share.
	15	Reissued 100 shares of treasury stock at $10 per share.
	17	Reissued 50 shares of treasury stock at $7 per share.

19-5. From the following, prepare in proper form a statement of retained earnings for Williams Company for the year ended December 31, 20X4.

Statement of retained earnings.

		Prior period adjustment increase in recording expense for Land in	
Retained Earnings, January 20X4	$40,000	20X2 (disregard taxes)	$14,000
Net Income, 20X4	$60,000	Dividends Paid, 20X4	$20,000

Group A Problems

(The forms you need are on pages 133–143 of the *Study Guide and Working Papers.*)

19A-1. The stockholders' equity of Oscar Company is as follows:

STOCKHOLDERS' EQUITY

Paid-in Capital:

Preferred 10% Stock, $100 par value, authorized 5,000 shares, cumulative and nonparticipating, 4,000 shares issued and outstanding	$400,000		
Paid-in Capital in Excess of Par Value—Preferred	50,000		
Total Preferred Paid-in Capital by Preferred Stockholders		$450,000	
Common Stock, $50 par value, authorized 15,000 shares, 6,000 shares issued and outstanding	$300,000		
Paid-in Capital in Excess of Par Value—Common	60,000		
Total Paid-in Capital by Common Stockholders		360,000	
Total Paid-in Capital		$810,000	
Retained Earnings		160,000	
Total Stockholders' Equity		$970,000	

Calculating book value with and without dividends in arrears.

Check Figure: Book value preferred $108

Given a redemption value of $108, calculate the book value of preferred and common stock, assuming

  a. No dividends in arrears.
  b. Two years' dividends in arrears.

19A-2. Lance Corporation has 400,000 shares of $7 par-value common stock issued and outstanding. Record the following entries into the general journal for Lance:

Cash and stock dividends.

Check Figure: Aug. 4 Paid-in Capital in Excess of Par Value—Stock Dividend $80,000 Cr.

20XX		
July	2	Declared a cash dividend of $.60 per share.
Aug.	1	Paid the $.60 cash dividend to the stockholders.
Aug.	4	Declared a 4% stock dividend. The current market price is $12 per share.
Sept.	12	Issued the stock dividend declared on August 4.
Oct.	1	Declared an 8% stock dividend. The current market price is $17 per share.
Nov.	2	Issued the stock dividend on October 1.

19A-3. At the beginning of January 20XX, the stockholders' equity of Long View Corporation consisted of the following:

Paid-in Capital:

Common Stock, $25 par value, authorized 50,000 shares, 13,000 shares issued and outstanding	$325,000	
Paid-in Capital in Excess of Par Value— Common	70,000	
Total Paid-in Capital by Common Stockholders	$395,000	
Retained Earnings	160,000	
Total Stockholders' Equity		$555,000

1. Record the following transactions in general journal form.
2. Prepare the stockholders' equity section at year-end using the Blueprint on page 721 as a guide.
3. Prepare a statement of retained earnings at December 31, 20XX.

Accounts are provided in the *Study Guide and Working Papers.* Be sure to put in the beginning balances.

20XX

June 4 Long View Corporation purchased 1,000 shares of treasury stock at $28.

20 The board of directors voted a $.20 per share cash dividend payable on July 15 to stockholders of record on July 2.

July 15 Cash dividend declared on June 20 is paid.

Sept. 5 Sold 300 shares of the treasury stock at $36 per share.

29 Sold 700 shares of the treasury stock at $27 per share.

Oct. 10 The board of directors declared a 6% stock dividend distributable on January 2 to stockholders of record on November 2. The market value of the stock is currently $38 per share.

Dec. 31 Closed the net income of $60,000 in the Income Summary account to Retained Earnings.

19A-4. The following is the stockholders' equity of Piersal Corporation on October 1, 20XX:

Paid-in Capital:

Preferred 14% Stock, $10 par value, authorized 6,000 shares, 3,000 shares issued and outstanding		$ 30,000	
Common Stock, $10 par value, authorized 20,000 shares, 10,000 shares issued and outstanding		100,000	
Additional Paid-in Capital:			
Paid-in Capital in Excess of Par Value—Preferred	$10,000		
Paid-in Capital in Excess of Par Value—Common	5,000		
Paid-in Capital in Excess of Par Value—Stock Dividend	4,000		
Total Additional Paid-in Capital		19,000	
Total Paid-in Capital		$149,000	
Retained Earnings		200,000	
Total Stockholders' Equity			$349,000

1. Journalize the following transactions in general journal form.
2. Prepare the stockholders' equity section of the balance sheet using the legal capital approach as of December 31, 20XX.

Your *Study Guide and Working Papers* has accounts to update ledger balances. Be sure to put in the beginning balances. Use the Blueprint on page 721 as a guide to the setup of stockholders' equity.

20XX

Oct. 3 Declared a $.40 per share dividend on the common stock and a $1.20 per share dividend on the preferred. (The Dividends Payable account will record amounts for both common and preferred, although companies could set up Common Dividend Payable and Preferred Dividend Payable accounts.)

Nov. 15 Dividends were paid that were declared on October 3.

18 Purchased 300 shares of its own common stock at $13 per share.

25 Reissued 50 shares at $16 per share.

26 Declared a 20% stock dividend on common. Market value of stock is $40 per share.

Dec. 29 Distributed stock dividend declared on November 26.

30 Reissued 100 shares of treasury stock at $12 per share.

31 Closed the Income Summary account, which had net income of $80,000, to Retained Earnings.

Group B Problems

(The forms you need are on pages 133–143 of the *Study Guide and Working Papers.*)

19B-1. Given a redemption value of $105, calculate the book value of preferred and common stock, assuming (1) no dividends in arrears and (2) two years' dividends in arrears from the following stockholders' equity of Oscar Company:

Calculating book value with and without dividends in arrears.

STOCKHOLDERS' EQUITY

Paid-in Capital:		
Preferred 12% Stock, $100 par value, authorized 3,000 shares, cumulative and nonparticipating, 1,000 shares issued and outstanding	$100,000	
Paid-in Capital in Excess of Par Value— Preferred	80,000	
Total Paid-in Capital by Preferred Stockholders		$ 180,000
Common Stock, $75 par value, authorized 12,000 shares, 8,000 shares issued and outstanding	$600,000	
Paid-in Capital in Excess of Par Value— Common	70,000	
Total Paid-in Capital by Common Stockholders		670,000
Total Paid-in Capital		$ 850,000
Retained Earnings		300,000
Total Stockholders' Equity		$1,150,000

Check Figure:
(a) Book value preferred $105

Cash and stock dividends.

Check Figure:
Sept. 6   Paid-in Capital in
Excess of Par Value—Stock
Dividend $40,000 Cr.

19B-2. Lance Corporation has 200,000 shares of $10 par value common stock issued and outstanding. Record the following entries into the general journal for Lance:

20XX

Aug.	3	Declared a cash dividend of $.30 per share.
Sept.	4	Paid the $.30 cash dividend to the stockholders.
	6	Declared a 5% stock dividend. The current market price is $14 per share.
	29	Issued the stock dividend declared on September 6.
Nov.	1	Declared a 10% stock dividend. The current market price is $17 per share.
	29	Issued the stock dividend declared on November 1.

Cash and stock dividend;
treasury stock; prepara-
tion of stockholders'
equity and statement of
retained earnings.

19B-3. At the beginning of January 20XX, the stockholders' equity of Long View Corporation consisted of the following:

Paid-in Capital:

Common Stock, $30 par value, authorized 70,000 shares, 15,000 shares issued and outstanding	$450,000
Paid-in Capital in Excess of Par Value—Common	60,000
Total Paid-in Capital by Common Stockholders	510,000
Retained Earnings	300,000
Total Stockholders' Equity	$810,000

Check Figure:
Total Stockholders' Equity
$817,300

1. Record the following transactions in general journal form.
2. Prepare a stockholders' equity section, using the Blueprint on page 721.
3. Prepare a statement of retained earnings at December 31, 20XX.

Accounts are provided in the *Study Guide and Working Papers.* Be sure to put in the beginning balances.

20XX

May	3	Long View Corporation purchased 2,000 shares of treasury stock at $40.
	15	The board of directors voted a $.70 per share cash dividend payable on July 9 to stockholders of record on June 13.
July	9	Cash dividend declared on May 15 is paid.
Sept.	15	Sold 200 shares of treasury stock at $50 per share.
Oct.	10	Sold 300 shares of treasury stock at $38 per share.
Nov.	1	The board of directors declared a 20% stock dividend distributable on January 2 to stockholders of record on November 17. The market value of the stock is $60 per share.
Dec.	31	Closed the net income of $75,000 in the Income Summary account to Retained Earnings.

Journalizing and posting
various stockholders'
equity situations and
preparing stockholders'
equity section by a legal
capital approach.

19B-4. The following is the stockholders' equity of Piersal Corporation on November 1, 20XX:

Paid-in Capital:

Preferred 12% Stock, $10 par value, authorized 8,000 shares, 2,000 shares issued and outstanding		$ 20,000
Common Stock, $10 par value, authorized 15,000 shares, 10,000 shares issued and outstanding		100,000
Additional Paid-in Capital:		
Paid-in Capital in Excess of Par Value—Preferred	$30,000	
Paid-in Capital in Excess of Par Value—Common	10,000	

Check Figure:
Total Stockholders' Equity
$273,600

Paid-in Capital in Excess of Par Value— Stock Dividend	7,000	
Total Additional Paid-in Capital		47,000
Total Paid-in Capital		$167,000
Retained Earnings		86,000
Total Stockholders' Equity		$253,000

1. Journalize the following transactions in general journal form.
2. Prepare the stockholders' equity section of the balance sheet using the legal capital approach (see the Blueprint on p. 721) as of December 31, 20XX.

Your *Study Guide and Working Papers* has accounts to update ledger balances. Be sure to put in beginning balances.

20XX

Nov. 3 Due to increased sales, the board of directors of Piersal declared a $3 per share dividend on the common stock and a $1.50 per share dividend on the preferred. (The Dividends Payable account records both common and preferred.)

8 Purchased 500 shares of its own common stock at $16 per share.

15 Reissued 200 shares at $18 per share.

16 Declared a 10% stock dividend on common. Market value is $25 per share.

Dec. 15 Dividends were paid that were declared on November 3.

28 Distributed stock dividend declared on November 16.

30 Reissued 200 shares at $15 per share.

31 Closed the Income Summary account, which had net income of $55,000, to Retained Earnings.

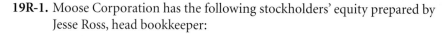

Real-World Applications

19R-1. Moose Corporation has the following stockholders' equity prepared by Jesse Ross, head bookkeeper:

Paid-in Capital:	
Common Stock, $5 par, 3000 shares authorized, 1,600 shares issued, of which 900 shares are in the treasury	$ 4,500
Paid-in Capital in Excess of Par Value—Common	2,000
Total Paid-in Capital	5,500
Retained Earnings	2,000
Total	7,500
Add: Cost of Treasury Stock	7,000
Total Stockholders' Equity	$14,500

Explain what error(s) Jesse has made in the preparation of stockholders' equity. Also, Moose Corporation wants to declare a cash dividend of $3 per share. Is it feasible? Show your calculations along with a written explanation.

19R-2. Margaret Jones owns 100 shares of Johnson Corporation. She receives in the mail a notice that a two-for-one stock split is being declared. Currently, the stock is trading on the open market at $120 per share. After the split 600,000 shares will be outstanding. Margaret is very worried that this split will reduce her book value, resulting in a loss of market value. She feels her preemptive right has been ignored. She believes that a stock dividend is the best way for the corporation to go. Respond in writing specifically to Margaret's concerns.

YOU make the call

Critical Thinking/Ethical Case

19R-3. Alan Homes serves on the board of directors of Flynn Company. The president of Flynn told him that in three weeks the corporation would announce a 25% increase in dividends. Alan called his neighbor to tell him to buy some stock. The neighbor told his friend about the stock and the friend told him that Alan was acting unethically. The neighbor called Alan back and Alan told him that no one will know the difference, that in business this happens all the time, and that he shouldn't be left out. Do you think Alan's behavior is appropriate? You make the call. Write down your recommendation to Alan's neighbor.

Internet Exercises: Dow Jones; Hillenbrand Industries

EX-1. [**www.averages.dowjones.com**]   Daily one hears news of the Dow Jones Industrial Averages (DJIA). Additionally, Dow Jones tracks selected utility stocks and transportation stocks. These stocks make up the equally important but less publicized Dow Jones Utilities Averages and the Dow Jones Transportation Averages.

The DJIA consists of 30 industrial stocks. The list is not a static one and does periodically add and delete component stocks from its listing. Glancing down the list at this site you can see the names of companies you probably recognize, but you might not have realized that those companies were components of the DJIA.

Select a stock from the list and do some stock research on that company by finding its Web site. Determine the following information about the stock:

1. What is the 52 week high/low price range of the stock?
2. What is the dividend paying history of the stock?
3. What is the company's earnings per share?
4. What was the closing price of that stock in yesterday's trading?
5. Look under "news" on the company's Web site. Summarize one of the news stories.

EX-2. [**www.hillenbrand.com**]   Go to the corporate fact sheet for Hillenbrand Industries and find its net revenues and net income.

SUBWAY Case

BUCKING TRADITION

"A convenience store?" asked Stan, incredulous.

"Yep, a convenience store," replied Carrie Zabrinsky, "or, as they say in the business, a c-store."

Stan had arranged a meeting with his Subway development agent, Carrie, to discuss expansion of his Subway franchise to another location. His future partner, Ron, was almost through with his training program at "Subway University," and Stan had just promoted his

Sandwich Artist, Rashid, to manager. By leaving a lot of the day-to-day operations in Rashid's hands, Stan planned to help Ron open the new Subway. Everything seemed to be going according to plan, yet he hadn't bargained on the new location being in a Pitt's Stop convenience store!

"Stan, just hear me out," Carrie insisted, "That site you have your eye on is extremely expensive. Also, with nothing around it but that new luxury apartment complex and some very upscale shops, it won't generate the foot traffic you need. This c-store, however, is in a prime high-traffic location."

"But the square footage is so small," Stan protested, pointing to the floor plan in front of him.

"Listen, Stan, in the fast food industry Subway leads the pack in opening nontraditional units. There are now over 3,700 Subway restaurants in c-stores, airports, gas stations, schools, grocery stores and even in hospitals. Headquarters wouldn't encourage these arrangements if they weren't highly lucrative. Sure, these smaller units typically generate less revenue than a full size restaurant, but they're also cheaper to build and maintain. Look at the figures: opening in a c-store typically costs as little as $30,000 to develop, while the traditional venue is more like $66,000."

"And you've got a captive audience, I guess," admitted Stan, "particularly in hospitals and schools. What I would've given to eat a sweet onion chicken teriyaki sandwich instead of that stuff that passed for food in high school!"

"Now you're getting the picture," Carrie smiled. "Just imagine. You go into the c-store at 10:00 P.M. to buy a quart of milk or some batteries and then you smell fresh baked gourmet bread. Your stomach growls and you buy a Subway 6-inch."

"Okay, okay," Stan said, "Once I get some figures for the lease and find out more about this Pitt's Stop's business and its management, I'll run this by Ron. I'm not sure this is what he had in mind when he quit his job to own a Subway."

"Well, he had profits in mind, didn't he?" asked Carrie.

Discussion Questions

1. How might opening a Subway in a convenience store reduce expenses?
2. How might this arrangement increase sales? Suppose you're Stan's development agent and you want him to open a Subway in a gas station. How would you sell him on this arrangement?
3. Like all corporations, Doctor's Associates Inc.'s goal is to increase earnings per share. How does expansion into nontraditional sites help achieve this goal?

Corporations and Bonds Payable

Being a student, you are probably on a tight budget. You find you're in need of some extra cash. How will you get the money? You might ask your boss if you could work extra hours on your job, which may make your school schedule a real headache. You might sell your stereo, computer, or your car. You could ask friends and relatives for a loan. Or you may even consider applying for a loan from a bank.

Corporations of all sizes ask the same question every day. Your accounting instructor told you about Smith's Auto Parts. The company has just expanded its business operations from one store in town to six additional stores in two other states. Smith's had several financing options from which to choose. It could have raised capital by selling stock. It could have gone to a bank and obtained a loan. Or Smith's could have obtained financing by selling bonds.

How did Smith's Auto Parts raise the necessary capital for its store expansion? Your instructor said the owners of Smith's Auto Parts decided the company could best manage its debt through issuing bonds to various investors. Bonds provide a way for a corporation to raise large amounts of capital and manage its own debt without using banks or other lending institutions.

In this chapter we will explore how to account for bonds. We will learn about recording bond transactions and interest payments. We will discuss amortizing bond premiums and discounts using either the straight-line or interest methods. We will also look at journalizing adjusting entries at year end and entries for the retirement of bonds and bond sinking funds. After completing this chapter you will understand the importance of bond financing for a corporation when it needs "extra cash."

Learning Objectives

- Journalizing the recording of bonds as well as interest payments. (p. 732)
- Amortizing bond discounts and bond premiums by the straight-line method and by the interest method. (p. 736)
- Journalizing year-end adjusting entries for bonds. (p. 744)
- Journalizing entries related to retirement of bonds and to sinking funds. (p. 746)

A corporation can raise funds by issuing stock or long-term notes payable. Notes or stock are good sources of funds when a company borrows from only one bank or other type of lending institution, but they may not provide the total amount of funds needed. In the last two chapters we saw how companies issue stock. Now our attention shifts to notes. After all, businesses like Dell Computer and General Motors may need to borrow millions of dollars. This chapter looks at how corporations can raise large amounts of money from groups of lenders by issuing a type of long-term interest-bearing note payable called a **bond.**

Learning Unit 20-1   Structure and Characteristics of a Bond

Each **bond certificate,** usually issued in denominations of $1,000, contains the following:

1. **Face value** (principal): the amount that the corporation must repay to the lender at maturity date.
2. **Contract rate** (stated interest rate): the annual interest rate, which is based on face value. Usually this interest is paid *semi*annually. The dates of interest payment are also printed on the certificate.

For example, if Joe Rosse owns a $1,000, 12%, 20-year bond that is issued by Von Corporation, it means the following:

1. At the end of 20 years Joe will receive the $1,000.
2. Every six months Joe will receive an interest check for $60 $\left(\$1,000 \times .12 \times \frac{6}{12}\right)$

There is also another way to calculate semiannual interest:

$$\frac{12\%}{2} = \textbf{Semiannual Rate of 6\%}$$
$$.06 \times \$1,000 = \$60$$

The information on the bond certificate is written by the corporation into a more formal agreement called the **bond indenture.** This agreement is usually monitored by a **trustee** (often a bank), who represents the group of bondholders.

> Trustee (usually a bank) monitors bondholders' interest as stipulated in the bond indenture.

If, before the 20 years have passed, Joe wants to cash in the bond, he can sell it on the securities exchange (like the stock exchange, but dealing in the buying and selling of bonds rather than stock). Bonds are negotiable and generally transferable. Let's assume Joe calls his broker, who indicates that the current market price of the bond is quoted at 94, a percentage (94%) of the bond's face value. This price can be higher or lower than the face amount (100, or 100%), depending on current rates of interest as well as other market factors. If market interest rates are high compared with the current bond's interest rate, the percentage would be lower. Why? The reason is that the bond's interest is not as attractive as current rates. The 94 means that a buyer is willing to pay $940 (.94 × $1,000) for the bond. If the quote were 104, then Joe could receive $1,040 (1.04 × $1,000) for the bond.

> A bond quote of 70 would mean that a bond with a face value of $1,000 is selling for $700 (.70 × $1,000).

The following is a list of different types of bonds. Keep in mind that each bond issue may have special arrangements besides the customary repayment plans. Don't memorize this list; use it as a reference.

TYPES OF BONDS

Corporations can offer many types of bonds. The following are some examples.

Secured Bonds: The corporation issuing the bonds pledges specific assets such as equipment or property as security for meeting the terms of the bond agreement.

> Assets are pledged as security for debt.

Debenture Bonds: The issuing corporation pledges no specific assets as collateral; thus the bonds are unsecured. Risk is higher than with secured bonds; these bonds will generally require a higher rate of interest to make them attractive to the investor.

> General credit rating of company is the only security the lender receives.

Serial Bonds: These bonds are made up of a series, each having its own maturity date. For example, a bond issue of $2,000,000 could be made up of a series of twenty $100,000 bonds, one series maturing at the end of each year for a period of 20 years.

> Different maturity dates of serial bonds give flexibility to investors.

Registered Bonds: Owners of bonds are registered with the issuing company, and interest is mailed to the owners of record.

> Only the registered owner can sell a registered bond.

Callable Bonds: These bonds have a provision stating that they can be called in by a corporation after a certain date. When a bond issue is called in, the corporation has to pay a price above the face value of the bond.

> Callability gives more flexibility to the corporation as interest rates change.

Convertible Bonds: The bondholder may be allowed to convert bonds into shares of stock. For this right, bondholders give up fixed interest payments for what they hope will be higher stock prices.

> Convertibility gives the bond buyer the option of becoming a stockholder.

STOCKS VERSUS BONDS

Why would a corporation prefer to raise money by selling bonds rather than by issuing and selling stock? Let's look at an example. Should Rojer Corporation obtain long-term funds by selling $500,000 worth of 12% bonds, or issue 12% preferred stock for $500,000? Rojer Corporation wants to make the most of its tax savings as well as earnings per share (EPS) of common stock:

$$\text{EPS} = \frac{\text{After-Tax Earnings} - \text{Dividends for Preferred}}{\text{Number of Shares of Common Stock Outstanding}}$$

> EPS = earnings per share of stock.

We are assuming Rojer Corporation has earnings of $700,000 and we assumed a tax rate of 40%. The table on p. 734 is a worked-out solution to this problem by the corporation's accountant.

Looking just at the numbers, Rojer Corporation would be better off issuing *bonds*, because the $60,000 of bond interest that the corporation would pay to bondholders would serve to reduce earnings on which the corporation would have to pay tax. On the other hand, *dividends* paid to stockholders would not reduce earnings on which the corporation would pay taxes (the dividend for preferred stock is not an expense, as bond interest is, but a distribution of net income *after* tax). With bonds, the common stockholders have an earnings per share of $4.80 versus $4.50.

> Note bond interest of $60,000 lowers earnings subject to tax. Bond interest is deductible for federal income tax purposes.

Other factors, however, should be considered when deciding whether to issue stocks or bonds to raise money, such as how interest rates are moving in the economy or whether the corporation can meet the bond interest payments each period for 10 years. If interest rates are high, it may be that the bond issue should be delayed to get more favorable interest rates.

> A dividend is a distribution of net income after tax. It is not deductible for federal income tax purposes.

Stocks Versus Bonds (Stock Dividends Versus Bond Interest)

	$500,000 12% Preferred Stock Issued	$500,000 12% Bond (10-Year) Issued
Earnings before Taxes or Finance Costs	$700,000	$700,000
Less: Bond Interest	—0—	60,000 (.12 × $500,000)
Earnings Subject to Income Tax	$700,000	$640,000
Less: Income Tax (40%)	280,000	256,000
Net Income	420,000	384,000
Less: Preferred Dividend	60,000 (.12 × $500,000)	—0—
Earnings Available to Common Stockholders	360,000	384,000
Number of Common Stock Shares Outstanding	80,000	80,000
Earnings per Share	$4.50 $\left(\dfrac{\$360,000}{80,000}\right)$	$4.80 $\left(\dfrac{\$384,000}{80,000}\right)$

For a comparison of stocks and bonds, see the Blueprint on page 750.

Before concluding this unit, let's see how Rojer Corporation would record the sale and pay interest on the 12%, $500,000 bonds.

On January 1, Rojer Corporation issued its bonds (Fig. 20-1).

Figure 20-1
Issuance of Bonds

> Bonds Payable is a long-term liability on the balance sheet.

Jan.	1	Cash	500 00 0 00	
		Bonds Payable		500 00 0 00
		Records issuance of bonds		

It then made semiannual interest payments to its bondholders (Fig. 20-2).

Figure 20-2
Semiannual Interest Paid

> $500,000 × .12 × $\frac{6}{12}$ = $30,000, or 12% / 2 = .06 × $500,000 = $30,000.

June	30	Bond Interest Expense	30 00 0 00	
		Cash		30 00 0 00
		Paid semiannual interest expense		

This entry will be recorded twice a year for 10 years. At the end of 10 years, Rojer will record the bond maturity.

On the year of retirement, the journal entry would look like Figure 20-3.

Figure 20-3
Bonds Retired

Dec.	31	Bonds Payable	500 00 0 00	
		Cash		500 00 0 00
		Retired bonds		

The face value of the bond, $500,000 has been repaid on maturity date.

BONDS SOLD BETWEEN INTEREST DATES

What would happen if Rojer Corporation issued the bonds on January 1 but did not actually sell them until March 1? Interest would have to be paid for January and February. How is that handled? And what happens if a person buys a bond that was issued in August, but the person buys it in November? As stated earlier, bond issuers only pay interest every six months. So, when a buyer purchases a bond between the six-month interest dates, the buyer pays the purchase price of the bond *plus* the interest that has built up since the last interest payment date. Keep in mind interest is being paid only twice a year. Think of it as an adjustment as the interest accrues. On the next payment, the buyer will receive the full interest payment for the six-month period. Let's show this by seeing how Rojer Corporation records the sale of bonds on March 1 that were issued on January 1 (Fig. 20-4).

Accrued Interest

$$(\$500{,}000 \times .12 \times \tfrac{2}{12} = \$10{,}000)\ \text{or}\ \$500{,}000 \times$$

$$.06 \times \left(\frac{2\ \text{months}}{6\ \text{months}}\right)$$

↑ semiannual rate

Mar.	1	Cash	510 0 0 0 00		
		Bonds Payable		500 0 0 0 00	
		Bond Interest Payable		10 0 0 0 00	
		Bond issue plus 2 months' accrued interest			

Figure 20-4
Bonds Issued with Accrued Interest

Note the buyer pays $510,000 instead of $500,000, because $10,000 of the accrued interest has been accumulated. On June 30, the $10,000 is repaid along with interest earned for four months (Fig. 20-5).

Accrued interest originally collected is returned to investor.

June	30	Bond Interest Payable	10 0 0 0 00		
		Bond Interest Expense	20 0 0 0 00		
		Cash		30 0 0 0 00	
		Record semiannual interest payment			

Figure 20-5
Semiannual Interest Paid

$$(\$500{,}000 \times .12 \times \tfrac{4}{12} = \$20{,}000)\ \text{or}\ \$500{,}000 \times$$

$$.06 \times \left(\frac{4\ \text{months}}{6\ \text{months}}\right)$$

↑ semiannual rate

In the next unit we look at how to record bond issues when the selling price is less or more than the face value.

Learning Unit 20-1 Review

AT THIS POINT you should be able to

- Explain face value and contract interest rate. (p. 732)
- Calculate the cost of a bond from a bond quote. (p. 732)
- Explain the different classifications of bonds. (p. 733)
- Explain the pros and cons of financing with preferred stock versus bonds. (p. 733)
- Record accounting entries to record issuing of bonds at par as well as the semiannual interest payment. (p. 734)
- Explain and record an accounting entry for accrued bond interest. (p. 735)

SELF-REVIEW QUIZ 20-1

(The forms you need are on page 148 of the *Study Guide and Working Papers*.)

Prepare general journal entries to record the following (treat items 4 and 5 as a separate situation from items 1 through 3):

1. Issued 20 $10,000 12% bonds that mature in 10 years at face value on January 1.
2. Paid semiannual interest on June 30.
3. Bonds retired at end of 10th year.
4. Bonds sold on May 1 instead of January 1 due to poor market conditions.
5. Paid semiannual interest on June 30 from bonds issued on May 1.

SOLUTION TO SELF-REVIEW QUIZ 20-1

Figure 20-6
Bond Transactions

❶	Cash	200 0 0 0 00	
	Bonds Payable		200 0 0 0 00
❷	Bond Interest Expense	12 0 0 0 00	
	Cash		12 0 0 0 00
	(I = $200,000 × .12 × $\frac{6}{12}$		
	or $200,000 × .06 semiannual rate)		
❸	Bonds Payable	200 0 0 0 00	
	Cash		200 0 0 0 00
❹	Cash	208 0 0 0 00	
	Bonds Payable		200 0 0 0 00
	Bond Interest Payable		8 0 0 0 00
	(Accrued interest = $200,000 × .12 × $\frac{4}{12}$		
	or $200,000 × .06 × $\frac{4}{6}$ = $8,000)		
❺	Bond Interest Payable	8 0 0 0 00	
	Bond Interest Expense	4 0 0 0 00	
	Cash		12 0 0 0 00
	(Bond Interest Expense = $200,000 × .12 × $\frac{2}{12}$		
	or $200,000 × .06 × $\frac{2}{6}$ = $4,000)		

Learning Unit 20-2   Bonds Issued at a Discount or Premium; Amortization by the Straight-Line Method

> On a given day the market rate for bond interest will vary from corporation to corporation: "supply versus demand."

When a corporation issues bonds, it must

1. Receive approval from the board of directors of the corporation as well as from a governmental regulatory agency, the Securities and Exchange Commission.
2. Print the bonds.
3. Advertise the bond issue.

The problem is that by the time these steps have been done, the rate of interest stated on the bond, the *contract* rate, may be lower or higher than the current *market* rate of interest. Investors may require higher rates of interest if the bond issue appears to be different than others offered by companies that may have had fewer financial difficulties.

For example, let's assume that Jossy Corporation is attempting to sell its 12% bond issue. The current market rate is 13%. To make its bonds more attractive (investors are looking for the best return on their investment), Jossy decides to sell the bonds for less than face value (91, or 91% of the face value of $1,000). The bondholder will still receive yearly interest of $120 per bond (.12 × $1,000) but will only pay $910 (.91 × $1,000) per bond. Thus, investors' annual or effective rate of interest is 13.2% ($120/$910). The difference between the *issue price* ($910) and the face value ($1,000) is called the *discount*.

Conversely, if Jossy Corporation sells the bond for *more* than the face value (if its contract rate is higher than the market rate), the difference between issue price and face value is called a *premium*.

RECORDING AND AMORTIZING BONDS ISSUED AT A DISCOUNT

To illustrate how to record a bond discount, let's look at the Ronson Corporation, which on January 1, 20XX, issued 200, 12%, $1,000, 10-year bonds at 97 (97% of face value). The discount is used because the current market rate is 12.4%, and Ronson has to be competitive to make its bond attractive to investors. Bondholders will receive a yearly dividend of $120, with an effective rate of 12.4% ($120/$970). The accounts that will make up the journal entry include the following:

Cash	Asset	↑	Dr. $194,000	.97 × $200,000
Discount on Bonds Payable	Contra-Liability	↑	Dr. $6,000	($200,000 − $194,000)
Bonds Payable	Liability	↑	Cr. $200,000	Face value

The journal entry will look like Figure 20-7.

Jan.	1	Cash		194 00 0 00	
		Discount on Bonds Payable		6 00 0 00	
		Bonds Payable			200 0 0 0 00
		Record Bond Issue			

Figure 20-7
Bond Issued at a Discount

Let's look at how the Discount on Bonds Payable would look on the balance sheet.

Long-Term Liabilities:

12 percent Bonds Payable	$200,000	
Less: Discount on Bonds Payable	6,000	$194,000

For bonds sold at a discount, the carrying value (also called book value) of $194,000 is the face value of $200,000 minus the discount on bonds payable of $6,000. At maturity (after 10 years), the carrying value will be the same as face value ($200,000).

When each interest payment is made, a portion of the Discount on Bonds Payable is transferred to increase Interest Expense. This portion is called Amortization of Discount on Bonds Payable. Bond discount causes the total interest expense to increase, because the bond is sold for less than face value, resulting in higher costs of borrowing.

Before looking at how to amortize the discount, let's prove that the interest expense will be more than the contract amount of interest of $240,000 (.12 × $200,000 × 10 years) for 10 years.

Total amount to be paid to bondholder	$440,000 ($200,000 bonds + $240,000 interest)
Total amount to be received from sale of bond	−$194,000
Interest to be paid over life of bond	$246,000
Average interest expense per year	$ 24,600 ($246,000 ÷ 10 years)
Semiannual interest expense	$ 12,300

If no discount has been made, the semiannual payment will be $12,000 ($200,000 × .12 × $\frac{6}{12}$ or $200,000 × .06). Now the discount results in an additional $300 of interest expense *each* semiannual payment ($6,000 ÷ 20 periods).

The journal entry for each semiannual payment and amortization of discount will be as shown in Figure 20-8.

Figure 20-8
Semiannual Payment and Amortization of Discount by Straight-Line Method

June	30	Bond Interest Expense	12 3 0 0 00		
		Discount on Bonds Payable			3 0 0 00
		Cash			12 0 0 0 00
		Semiannual interest and amortization of			
		discount			

After posting, the ledger would look as follows:

Discount on Bonds Payable

6,000 | 300
5,700 |

Bond Interest Expense

12,300 |

> If there were no discount or premium, the semiannual interest payment would be $12,000.

> $200,000   Face value of bond
> 5,700   Bond discount
> $194,300   New carrying value
> After 10 years, the balance on Discount on Bonds Payable will be zero.

After this amortization the carrying value (book value) of the bond has increased from $194,000 to $194,300. By the end of 10 years the carrying value will be back to $200,000, or the amount due at maturity.

In this unit we calculate amortization of the bond's discount by the straight-line method; in the next unit we use the *interest* method. The straight-line method transfers an equal amount of bond discount to interest expense over equal periods of time.

Table 20-1 shows the straight-line method of amortizing a bond discount over the life of the bond for each semiannual period. At the end of the life of the bond, the

TABLE 20-1 Amortization Schedule for Bond Discount Using the Straight-Line Method for Each Semiannual Period

Period	Carrying Value, Beg. of Period	Total Interest Expense	Interest to Be Paid Bondholders (.06 × Face Value)*	Amortized Discount Transferred to Increase Interest Expense	Carrying Value, End of Period
1	$194,000 (200,000 − 6,000)	$12,300	$12,000 (200,000 × .06)	$300 (6,000 ÷ 20 periods)	$194,300 (194,000 + 300)
2	194,300	12,300	12,000	300	194,600
3	194,600	12,300	12,000	300	194,900
4	194,900	12,300	12,000	300	195,200
19	199,400	12,300	12,000	300	199,700
20	199,700	12,300	12,000	300	200,000

The balance in the Discount on Bonds Payable account should be equal to zero at the end of the 20 periods.

*Half of annual rate of 12% = 6% semiannual rate.

Discount on Bonds Payable has a zero balance, and the original $6,000 has been transferred to Interest Expense. At this point, the book value or carrying value of a bond ($200,000) is what is paid at maturity.

Year-End Adjusting Entry: Accrued Interest and Amortization of Discount on Bonds Payable.   Let's consider what would happen if the semiannual interest payment were on April 1 and October 1. On December 31, $6,000, three months' interest would be accrued $\left(\$12,000 \times \frac{3}{6}\right)$. The amount of discount to be amortized would be $150 $\left(\$300 \times \frac{3}{6}\right)$. The journal entry would be recorded as shown in Figure 20-9.

Dec.	31	Bond Interest Expense	6 1 5 0 00	
		Discount on Bonds Payable		1 5 0 00
		Bond Interest Payable		6 0 0 0 00
		Accrued interest and amortization		

Straight-line allocates an equal amount of discount to Interest Expense each period.

Note: 10 years with interest semiannually means 20 periods (10 years × 2).

Figure 20-9
Discount to Be Amortized by Straight-Line Method

Bond Interest Expense:
$\$12,300 \times \frac{3}{6} = \$6,150$

Bond Interest Payable:
$\$12,000 \times \frac{3}{6} = \$6,000$

Note that the Discount on Bonds Payable does indeed increase total bond interest expense from $6,000 to $6,150. This adjusting entry would then be reversed on January 1, as shown in Figure 20-10.

Jan.	1	Bond Interest Payable	6 0 0 0 00	
		Discount on Bonds Payable	1 5 0 00	
		Bond Interest Expense		6 1 5 0 00
		Reversing entry		

Figure 20-10
Adjusting Entry Reversed

Bond Discount Adjustment:
$\$300 \times \frac{3}{6} = \$150$

The regular payment made on April 1 would look like Figure 20-11.

Apr.	1	Bond Interest Expense	12 3 0 0 00	
		Discount on Bonds Payable		3 0 0 00
		Cash		12 0 0 0 00
		Semiannual interest and amortizaton of discount		

Figure 20-11
Paid Semiannual Interest and Amortized Discount

RECORDING AND AMORTIZING BONDS ISSUED AT A PREMIUM

To illustrate bonds issued at a premium, let's look at Ronson Corporation again, but assume on January 1 it issued its 200, 12% bonds at 102 (102% of face value). This premium occurred because the current market rate was 11.8% and Ronson's bonds were thus very attractive to investors. The bondholders would receive per bond the yearly interest payment of $120 (.12 × $1,000 bond) with an effective rate of 11.8% ($120/$1,020). The accounts that will make up the journal entry include the following:

Bonds are issued at a premium if the contract rate is greater than the market rate.

The Premium on Bonds Payable is added to the face value of the bond.

1.02 × $200,000

Cash	Asset	↑	Dr. $204,000
Premium on Bonds Payable	Liability	↑	Cr. $4,000
Bonds Payable	Liability	↑	Cr. $200,000

$\begin{pmatrix} \$204,000 \\ -\$200,000 \end{pmatrix}$
Face value

The journal entry will look like Figure 20-12.

Jan.	1	Cash	204 0 0 0 00			
		Premium on Bonds Payable			4 0 0 0 00	
		Bonds Payable			200 0 0 0 00	
		Issued bond at premium				

Figure 20-12 Bond Issued at a Premium

> Note that the Premium on Bonds Payable is *added* to Bonds Payable to arrive at the carrying value of $204,000.

Let's see how the Premium on Bonds Payable would look on the balance sheet:

Long-Term Liabilities:

12 percent Bonds Payable	$200,000	
Add: Premium on Bonds Payable	4,000	$204,000

When each interest payment is made, a portion of the Premium on Bonds Payable is transferred to *reduce* Interest Expense. This portion is called Amortization of Premium on Bonds Payable. Let's prove that the interest expense will be less than the contractual amount of $240,000 for 10 years.

> If there were no discount or premium, the semi-annual interest would be $12,000.

Total amount to be paid to bondholders	$440,000	($200,000 bonds + $240,000 interest)
Total amount to be received from sale of bonds	−204,000	
Interest to be paid over life of bond	$236,000	
Average interest expense per year	$ 23,600	($236,000 ÷ 10 years)
Semiannual interest expense	$ 11,800	

If no premium were made, the semiannual interest expense would be $12,000 ($200,000 × .12 × $\frac{6}{12}$ or $200,000 × .06). Now the premium results in *reducing* the interest expense for each semiannual payment by $200 ($4,000 premium ÷ 20 periods).

The journal entry for semiannual payment will look like Figure 20-13.

June	30	Bond Interest Expense	11 8 0 0 00			
		Premium on Bonds Payable	2 0 0 00			
		Cash			12 0 0 0 00	
		Semiannual payment and premium				
		amortization				

Figure 20-13 Paid Semiannual Payment and Amortized Premium

After posting, the ledger will look like the following:

Premium on Bonds Payable			Bond Interest Expense	
	200	4,000	11,800	
		3,800		

TABLE 20-2 Amortization Schedule for Bond Premium Using the Straight-Line Method for Each Semiannual Period

Period	Carrying Value, Beg. of Period	Total Interest Expense	Interest to Be Paid to Bondholder (.06 × Face Value)	Amortized Premium to Decrease Interest Expense	Carrying Value, End of Period
1	$204,000	$11,800	$12,000	$200	$203,800
	(200,000 + 4,000)		(.06 × 200,000)		(204,000 − 200)
2	203,800	11,800	12,000	200	203,600
3	203,600	11,800	12,000	200	203,400
4	203,400	11,800	12,000	200	203,200
19	200,400	11,800	12,000	200	200,200
20	200,200	11,800	12,000	200	200,000

The balance in the Premium on Bonds Payable account should be equal to zero at the end of the 20 periods.

We're using the straight-line method of amortizing the bond premium over the life of the bond for each semiannual period. This method is shown in Table 20-2. Note that at the end of the schedule, the carrying value is reduced to $200,000 and the balance in the Premium account is zero.

Learning Unit 20-2 Review

AT THIS POINT you should be able to

- Calculate the effective rate. (p. 732)
- Explain why a bond will sell at a discount or premium. (p. 737)
- Define and explain Discount on Bonds Payable. (p. 737)
- Explain why a discount will increase interest expense when semiannual interest is paid. (p. 737)
- Journalize the recording of bonds issued at a discount. (p. 738)
- Journalize year-end adjusting entries. (p. 739)
- Prepare an amortization schedule of a bond discount by the straight-line method. (p. 738)
- Define and explain Premium on Bonds Payable. (p. 739)
- Explain why a premium on bonds payable will decrease interest expense when semiannual interest is paid. (p. 740)
- Journalize the recording of bonds issued at a premium. (p. 740)
- Prepare an amortization schedule of a bond premium by the straight-line method. (p. 741)

SELF-REVIEW QUIZ 20-2

(The forms you need are on page 148 in the *Study Guide and Working Papers*.)

Prepare a partial amortization schedule as on page 738 using the straight-line method for the first three semiannual periods based on the following facts: 100, 14%, 10-year bonds issued at 98. Each bond has a $1,000 face value.

SOLUTION TO SELF-REVIEW QUIZ 20-2

Period	Carrying Value, Beg. of Period	Total Interest Expense	Interest Paid to Bondholders (.07 × Face Value)	Amortized Discount Transferred to Increase Interest Expense	Carrying Value, End of Period
1	$98,000	$7,100	$7,000	$100 (2,000 ÷ 20 periods)	$98,100 (98,000 + 100)
2	98,100	7,100	7,000	100	98,200
3	98,200	7,100	7,000	100	98,300

Learning Unit 20-3   Amortization of Bond Discounts and Premiums by the Interest Method

In the last unit we amortized the discount or premium by the straight-line method. The problem with this method is that it recognizes an equal amount of interest expense each period, even though the bond's carrying value changes. Accountants think that it is inconsistent for interest expense to stay the same while the amount owed changes. They think interest should be a *constant percentage of the carrying value.* For this reason, another method, called the *interest method,* is used in amortizing bond discounts and premiums. The Accounting Principles Board has ruled that the straight-line method may be used only if the results do not materially differ from those of the interest method.

AMORTIZING THE BOND DISCOUNT BY THE INTEREST METHOD

The **interest method of amortization** makes interest expense a constant percentage of the bond carrying value.

The goal of the interest method is to calculate the interest expense to be recorded each year as a constant percentage of the carrying value of the bonds. The interest amount will thus not be the same each period. There are two formulas to use to reach this goal:

1. Carrying value of bonds at beginning of period × market interest rate = interest expense of carrying value to be recorded.

2. Face value × contract rate = interest expense to bondholders. The discount to be amortized is the difference between (1) and (2).

> Discount on bond:
> $200,000 − $178,808 = $21,192

To illustrate this method, let's assume Yang Corporation is issuing $200,000 of 12%, 10-year bonds on April 1. Interest is to be paid on October 1 and April 1. The selling price of the bonds is $178,808. The market rate is 14%.

Look at the amortization schedule shown in Table 20-3. Note that the discount amount to be amortized is not constant, as it is in the straight-line method. As a matter of fact, to prove that the interest expense is a constant percentage of the carrying value, let's look at semiannual periods 2 and 19.

$$\text{Period 2: } \frac{\$12,553}{\$179,325} = .07 \qquad \text{Period 19: } \frac{\$13,746}{\$196,373} = .07$$

TABLE 20-3 Amortization Schedule for Bond Discount for Each Semiannual Period Using the Interest Method

Period	(1) Carrying Value, Beginning of Period	(2) Interest Paid to Bondholders (.06 × Face Value)*	(3) Interest Expense to Be Recorded (.07 × Carrying Value)	(4) Discount to Be Amortized	(5) Carrying Value, End of Period
1	$178,808 (200,000 − 21,192)	$12,000	$12,517 (.07 × 178,808)	$517	$179,325 (178,808 + 517)
2	179,325	12,000	12,553	553	179,878
3	179,878	12,000	12,591	591	180,469
19	196,373	12,000	13,746	1,746	198,119
20	198,119	12,000	13,881	1,881	200,000

Adjusted for rounding

*Use 6%, because 12% is for the whole year and the calculations are made semiannually.

Note: Column 4 is the difference between columns 2 and 3.

On October 1, the date of the first semiannual interest payment, the entry in Figure 20-14 would occur.

Oct.	1	Bond Interest Expense	12 5 1 7 00	
		Discount on Bonds Payable		5 1 7 00
		Cash		12 0 0 0 00
		Semiannual payment and amortization		

Figure 20-14
Paid Semiannual Payment and Amortized Discount by Interest Method

Bond Interest Expense:
$12,553 × \frac{3}{6} = $6,276.50

Bond Interest Payable:
$12,000 × \frac{3}{6} = $6,000

YEAR-END ADJUSTMENT

On December 31, three months' interest of $6,000 ($\frac{3}{6}$ × $12,000) has accrued, as well as $276.50 ($\frac{3}{6}$ of $553), the second-period discount shown on the amortization schedule. The adjusting year-end entry in Figure 20-15 is prepared.

Dec.	31	Bond Interest Expense	6 2 7 6 50	
		Discount on Bonds Payable		2 7 6 50
		Bond Interest Payable		6 0 0 0 00
		Year-end adjustment		

Figure 20-15
Year-End Adjustment

The reversing entry on January 1 and the entry to record payment of interest on April 1 would look like Figure 20-16.

AMORTIZING THE BOND PREMIUM BY THE INTEREST METHOD

Yang Corporation issues on April 1 $200,000 of 12% bonds with interest paid on October 1 and April 1. The selling price of the bonds is $224,926. The market interest

Figure 20-16
Reversing Entry and
Payment of Interest

Jan.	1	Bond Interest Payable		6 0 0 0 00			
		Discount on Bonds Payable		2 7 6 50			
		Bond Interest Expense				6 2 7 6 50	
		Reversing entry					
Apr.	1	Bond Interest Expense		12 5 1 7 00			
		Discount on Bonds Payable				5 1 7 00	
		Cash				12 0 0 0 00	
		Semiannual interest and amortization of					
		discount					

TABLE 20-4 Amortization Schedule for Bond Premium for Each Semiannual Period Using the Interest Method

Period	(1) Carrying Value, Beg. of Period	(2) Interest Paid to Bondholder (.06 × Face Value)	(3) Interest Expense to Be Recorded, (.05 × Carrying Value)	(4) Premium to Be Amortized	(5) Carrying Value, End of Period
1	$224,926	$12,000	$11,246	$754	$224,172 ($224,926 − $754)
2	224,172	12,000	11,209	791	223,381
19	203,726	12,000	10,186	1,814	201,912
20	201,912	12,000	10,088	1,912	200,000

Note: Column 4 is the difference between columns 2 and 3. Column 5 is column 1 minus column 4.

rate is 10%. The amortization schedule is shown in Table 20-4. On Oct. 1 the entry in Figure 20-17 records the semiannual payment.

Figure 20-17
Paid Interest and
Amortized Premium by
Interest Method

Oct.	1	Bond Interest Expense		11 2 4 6 00			
		Premium on Bonds Payable		7 5 4 00			
		Cash				12 0 0 0 00	
		Semiannual interest and premium					
		amortization					

YEAR-END ADJUSTMENT

It should be noted that on December 31, three months' interest has accrued as well as the need to amortize half the premium (for the second period). The journal entry in Figure 20-18 records this year-end adjustment.

Bond Interest Expense:
$\frac{3}{6} \times \$11,209 = \$5,604.50$

Premium on Bonds Payable:
$\frac{3}{6} \times \$791 = \$395.50$

Bond Interest Payable:
$\frac{3}{6} \times \$12,000 = \$6,000$

Dec.	31	Bond Interest Expense		5 6 0 4 50			
		Premium on Bonds Payable		3 9 5 50			
		Bond Interest Payable				6 0 0 0 00	
		Year-end adjustment					

Figure 20-18 Year-End Adjustment

The reversing entry on January 1 and the payment of interest in April would look like Figure 20-19.

Jan.	1	Bond Interest Payable	6 0 0 0 00		
		Premium on Bonds Payable		3 9 5 50	
		Bond Interest Expense		5 6 0 4 50	
		Reversing entry			
Apr.	1	Bond Interest Expense	11 2 0 9 00		
		Premium on Bonds Payable	7 9 1 00		
		Cash		12 0 0 0 00	
		Semiannual interest and amortization of premium			

Figure 20-19
Reversing Entry and
Payment of Interest

Learning Unit 20-3 Review

AT THIS POINT you should be able to

- Prepare an amortization schedule for bond discounts using the interest method. (p. 743)
- Prepare an amortization schedule for bond premiums using the interest method. (p. 744)
- Journalize year-end adjustments. (p. 744)

SELF-REVIEW QUIZ 20-3

(The forms you need are on page 148 of the *Study Guide and Working Papers*.)

Prepare a partial amortization schedule like the preceding one using the interest method for the first three periods based on the following facts: 100, 12%, 10-year bonds issued at a selling price of $89,404. Assume a market rate of 14%.

SOLUTION TO SELF-REVIEW QUIZ 20-3

Period	(1) Carrying Amount, Beg. of Period	(2) Interest Paid to Bondholders (.06 × Face Value)	(3) Interest Expense to Be Recorded, (.07 × Carrying Value)	(4) Discount to Be Amortized	(5) Carrying Amount, End of Period
1	$89,404	$6,000	$6,258	$258	$89,662
2	89,662	6,000	6,276	276	89,938
3	89,938	6,000	6,296	296	90,234

Learning Unit 20-4   Retirement of Bonds and Bond Sinking Funds

In the first unit of this chapter we mentioned callable bonds, which permit the corporation to reacquire bonds at a price based on a percentage of face value. Some corporations retire them and issue new bonds (called *bond refunding*) to take their place, paying a lower rate of interest. If this call provision doesn't exist, a company can repurchase its bonds in the open market and then retire them. By retiring bonds, companies can decrease the amount of debt they owe. If interest rates are high, the retirement of bonds could result in substantial cash savings, even if new bonds are issued at lower rates.

When the bonds are retired before they reach maturity, the following points have to be recognized:

1. Any amortization of discount or premium must be brought up-to-date at the time of retirement.
2. The premium or discount as well as the bond liability account must be removed.
3. Any gain or loss is recognized on the retirement of the bonds as an extraordinary item that will be shown on the income statement.

Let's use Roberts Corporation as an example. On June 30 the corporation retired a $500,000, 10% bond issue that had an unamortized premium of $19,000. The bonds were called in at 105 (105% of face value). All journal entries relating to interest payments and premium amortization were completed before the bonds' retirement. The entry to record the retirement of the bonds by Roberts Corporation would look like Figure 20-20.

Figure 20-20
Retirement of Bond

Bonds Payable	500 00 0 00	
Premium on Bonds Payable	19 0 0 0 00	
Loss on Bond Retirement	6 0 0 0 00	
Cash		525 0 0 0 00
Retirement of bond		

Note that the difference between the bond carrying value of $519,000 ($500,000 + $19,000) and actual cash paid results in the loss of $6,000. Of course, if the carrying value were greater than the cash paid, a gain would be realized.

THE BOND SINKING FUND

$500,000 × 1.05 = $525,000
Sinking fund table, 8%

15 → .0368295

Often a corporation will agree to establish a fund that will accumulate assets over the life of the bond so as to pay off the bondholders at maturity. In fact, such a fund is often a requirement stated in the bond indentures. This fund is called a **sinking fund.**

For example, Morrel Corporation issued 8%, 15-year bonds for $80,000, agreeing to deposit $2,946.40 at the end of the year so that by the end of the fifteenth year the fund would contain $80,000 to pay off bondholders. Sinking fund tables are available that make these periodic deposits easy to calculate. For example, Morrel's accountant would go to a sinking fund table and look up 8% for 15 periods and find a table factor of .0368295. By multiplying the $80,000 × .0368295, one comes up with a yearly deposit of $2,946.40, which, at this rate of interest compounded annually, will at the end of 15 years bring a total of $80,000.

The following would be the journal entries for Morrel Corporation for establishing the sinking fund (Fig. 20-21):

The Analysis:

Long-term investment	→	Sinking Fund	Asset	↑	Dr.
		Cash	Asset	↓	Cr.

The Journal Entry:

Sinking Fund	2 9 4 6 40		
Cash		2 9 4 6 40	
Establishing sinking fund			

Figure 20-21
Sinking Fund Established

When interest is earned on the balance in the sinking fund, the following entry results (Fig. 20-22):

The Analysis:

Sinking Fund	Asset	↑	Dr.
Sinking Fund Earned	Other Revenue	↑	Cr.

The Journal Entry:

Sinking Fund	2 3 5 00	
Sinking Fund Earned ($2,946 x .08)		2 3 5 00
Interest earned		

Figure 20-22
Interest Earned on Sinking Fund

When the bonds are paid off, there may be a little more or less cash than is needed in the sinking fund. The entry to record the payment of the bonds by Morrel is shown in Figure 20-23 (assume $50 extra in the sinking fund).

Keep in mind that the money in the sinking fund cannot be used to meet other current expenses or liabilities. Thus, the sinking fund is recorded in the long-term investment section of the balance sheet. Any cash left over is returned to the Cash account.

Cash	5 0 00	
Bonds Payable	80 0 0 00	
Bond Sinking Fund		80 0 5 0 00
Payment of bonds		

Figure 20-23
Payoff of Bonds

Learning Unit 20-4 Review

AT THIS POINT you should be able to

- Journalize the gain or loss on the retirement of bonds. (p. 746)
- Explain as well as journalize entries relating to sinking funds. (p. 747)

SELF-REVIEW QUIZ 20-4

(The forms you need are on page 149 of the *Study Guide and Working Papers.*)
Journalize the following transactions:

A. Retired $300,000 of bonds that had a $20,000 premium for 106.

B. Set up a sinking fund account with an initial deposit of $3,000.

C. Earned $325 interest on the sinking fund balance.

D. Sinking fund of $90,000 was used to retire bondholders' amount to $89,900.

SOLUTION TO SELF-REVIEW QUIZ 20-4

Figure 20-24
Bond Transactions

		Debit	Credit
(A)	Bonds Payable	300 000 00	
	Premium on Bonds	20 000 00	
	Cash		318 000 00
	Gain on Retirement		2 000 00
(B)	Sinking Fund	3 000 00	
	Cash		3 000 00
(C)	Sinking Fund	325 00	
	Sinking Fund Earned		325 00
(D)	Bonds Payable	90 000 00	
	Sinking Fund		90 000 00

Chapter Review

Learning Unit 20-1

1. Bond certificates state face value and contract rate of interest.
2. A bond indenture is a formal agreement that spells out specifics of the bond issue. The trustee, usually a bank, makes sure the bond indenture is fulfilled.
3. Bonds are negotiable and are quoted in the market as a percentage of the face value. For example, 95 means 95% a $1,000 bond, or $950.
4. There are many types of bonds. In this chapter we discuss secured, debenture, serial, registered, callable, and convertible bonds.
5. To a corporation trying to decide whether to issue stocks or bonds to raise money, an important difference between stocks and bonds is that stock dividends are a distribution of net income *after* tax, whereas bond interest expense is deductible from earnings *before* tax.
6. If bonds are sold between interest dates, the buyer pays the price of the bond plus accrued interest. This accrued interest is paid back when the semiannual interest payment is made.

Learning Unit 20-2

1. By the time a bond is actually issued, the contract rate of interest may be lower or higher than the effective or actual market rate.
2. A bond discount means that the issue price of bonds is less than the face value.
3. A bond premium means that the issue price of bonds is greater than the face value.
4. Discount on Notes Payable is a contra-liability found on the balance sheet. It is not an immediate expense. It will be amortized at the time of the interest payment and thus will increase the total interest expense.
5. The straight-line method of amortizing bond discounts transfers an equal amount of bond discount to interest expense over equal periods of time.
6. Premium on Bonds Payable is a liability found on the balance sheet. It will be amortized at each semiannual payment to decrease interest expense over the life of the bond.

Learning Unit 20-3

1. In the interest method of amortizing a bond discount or premium, interest expense is a constant *percentage* of the carrying value of the bonds. Thus, interest amount will *not* be constant each period.
2. The amortization of the period is the difference between interest expense to be recorded and interest expense paid to bondholders.

Learning Unit 20-4

1. When bonds are retired before their maturity date:

   a. Amortization of the bond discount must be up-to-date.
   b. The bond liability and either the discount or the premium must be removed.
   c. A gain or loss is recognized as an extraordinary item on the income statement.

2. A bond sinking fund is set up by a corporation to pay bondholders at maturity.
3. The sinking fund is an asset on the balance sheet under long-term investments.

Key Terms

Amortization of Discount on Bonds Payable, Amortization of Premium on Bonds Payable Writing off the bond premium or discount as a decrease or increase to interest expense for each interest period.

Bond An interest-bearing note payable usually in $1,000 denominations issued by a corporation to a large group of lenders.

Bond certificate A piece of paper held by bondholder showing evidence of a bond(s) issued by a corporation to be payable on a specified date for a specific sum to the order of the person named in the bond certificate or to the bearer.

Bond indenture A contract that spells out the provisions of the contract between the corporation and bondholder.

Callable bond Bond with a provision that it can be called in by a corporation after a certain date.

Carrying value (book value) Face value of bond less bond discount or plus bond premium.

Contract rate Rate of interest (based on face value) stated on bond certificate and bond indenture.

Convertible bond Bondholders have the option of converting bonds into stock at a specified exchange rate.

Debenture bonds Bonds that are unsecured and are issued only on the general credit of a corporation.

Discount on Bonds Payable Account used when bonds are issued below face value; indicates market rate of interest is higher than contract rate. This account is a contra-liability account.

Effective rate The real or actual rate of interest to the borrowing corporation, which affects interest payment and the bond premium or discount to be amortized.

Face value The amount the corporation must repay to the bondholder at the maturity date.

Interest method of amortization This method amortizes the premium or discount to *record* interest expense, being equal to the carrying value of the bond times the market rate. The interest expense is a constant percentage of the carrying value. The discount or premium to be amortized is the difference between the interest to be recorded and the interest paid to bondholders.

Premium on Bonds Payable Account used when bonds are issued above face value; indicates market rate is below contract rate. This account is a liability account.

Registered bond Bondholders of record are registered with the corporation, and interest checks are sent directly to them.

Secured bond Bond issued by a corporation that pledges specific assets as security to meet the terms of the bond agreement.

Serial bonds Bonds issued in a series, each one of which has a different maturity date and thus comes due at a different time.

Sinking fund A fund that accumulates cash to pay off bonds when they are retired.

Sinking Fund Earned Other revenue account used to record earnings on sinking fund balance.

Straight-line method A method recognizing equal amounts of interest expense for each period when amortizing a bond discount or premium.

Trustee Organization (usually a bank) or person who monitors a bond indenture for the protection of bondholders.

Blueprint: Stocks vs. Bonds

Stocks	Bonds
1. Stockholders are the owners of the corporation.	1. Bondholders are creditors to a corporation.
2. Stockholders are paid off in liquidation only after claims of creditors are satisfied.	2. Bondholders, in liquidation, have claims on assets (along with other creditors) before stockholders.
3. Dividends are paid only if earnings are sufficient; there is no fixed charge as there is with bond interest. Dividends are not an expense; they are a distribution of income.	3. Interest expense is a fixed charge. Failure to pay could result in creditors bringing bankruptcy proceedings against the corporation.
4. Stockholders have voting rights except with preferred stock.	4. Bondholders have no voting rights.
5. Dividends are deducted *after* tax on earnings.	5. Interest is deductible from earnings *before* tax.
6. Stockholders continue to receive dividends; they are not "paid off."	6. Bondholders are eventually repaid the principal.

Questions, Mini Exercises, Exercises, and Problems

Discussion Questions

1. Explain the selling price of a bond quoted at 88.
2. What is the difference between a secured bond and a debenture bond?
3. Dividends reduce earnings before taxes. True or false? Explain.
4. Accrued interest results in the seller paying extra for bonds. True or false? Explain.
5. Explain why a bond may sell at a premium.
6. Why isn't Discount on Bonds Payable an immediate expense?
7. Premium on Bonds Payable will cause total interest expense to be reduced. True or false?
8. The straight-line method of amortizing a bond discount or premium will result in an uneven amount of discount or premium that increases or decreases expense each period. Accept or reject. Why?
9. What is the carrying value of a bond?
10. Why does the interest method of amortizing a discount or premium use the market rate in calculating interest expense to be recorded?
11. Explain how a gain or loss on retirement of bonds before the maturity date is recorded.
12. What is the purpose of a bond sinking fund?

Mini Exercises

(The forms you need are on pages 151–152 of the *Study Guide and Working Papers*.)

Bond Journal Entries

1. Journalize the following transactions:

    a. Issued five $10,000, 6% bonds that mature in 20 years at face value on January 1.
    b. Paid semiannual interest on June 30.
    c. Bonds retired at end of 20 years.

Bond Issued at a Discount

2. On January 1, Borg Co. issued ten $1,000, 6%, 10-year bonds at 96. Record the journal entry.

Interest and Amortization of Discount

3. From Mini Exercise 2, record on June 30 the semiannual payment and amortization of the discount.

Bond Issued at Premium

4. Redo Mini Exercise 2 with straight-line assuming the bond sells for 105.

Interest and Amortization of Premium with Straight-Line Method

5. From Mini Exercise 4, record on June 30 the semiannual payment and amortization of premium on bonds payable.

Amortization of Bond Discount by Interest Method

6. *Facts:* Bond issue: $100,000, 6%, 10-year bonds; selling price of bonds $78,000. Market rate 8%. Calculate the following:

    a. Carrying value beginning of period.
    b. Interest paid to bondholders every six months.
    c. Interest expense each six-month period to be recorded.
    d. Discount to be amortized.
    e. Carrying value end of period.

Journalizing the Semiannual Payment of Amortization of Discount

7. For Mini Exercise 6, record a journal entry for the first semiannual interest payment on October 1.

Amortization of Bond Premium by Interest Method

8. *Facts:* Bond issue: $100,000, 6%, 10-year bonds; selling price of bonds, $120,000; market rate, 4%. Calculate the following:

    a. Carrying value beginning of period.
    b. Interest paid to bondholders each six months.
    c. Interest expense each six-month period.
    d. Premium to be amortized.
    e. Carrying value at end of period.

Journalizing the Semiannual Payment and Amortization of Bond Premium

9. For Mini Exercise 8, record the journal entry for the first semiannual interest payment on October 1.

Sinking Fund

10. Journalize the following transactions:

    a. Set up a sinking fund with an initial deposit of $5,000.
    b. Earned $110 interest on sinking fund balance.
    c. Sinking fund of $15,000 was used to pay off bondholders in the amount of $15,000.

Exercises

(The forms you need are on pages 153–155 in the *Study Guide and Working Papers.*)

20-1. Heller Corporation and Langle Corporation have both earned $100,000 before bond interest and taxes. The companies have the same number of outstanding shares but different capital structures. Calculate the earnings per share of common stock for both companies from the following:

	HELLER	LANGLE
10% bond payable	200,000	—0—
10% preferred stock	—0—	200,000
Common stock $10 par, 30,000 shares outstanding	300,000	300,000
Operating income before interest and income taxes (assume a 30% tax rate)	100,000	100,000

20-2. On January 1, 20XX, Alpha Corporation issued $800,000 of 10%, 30-year bonds to lenders at par (100). Interest is to be paid semiannually on July 1 and January 1. Journalize the following entries:

Calculating earnings per share.

Recording sale of bonds at par, paying interest, and retirement of issue.

a. Issued the bonds.

b. Paid semiannual interest payment.

c. Retirement of bonds, assuming interest expense is up-to-date.

20-3. Quick Corporation issued $300,000 of 10%, 10-year bonds at 98 on May 1, 20XX, with semiannual interest payable on May 1 and November 1. Amortization of discount is by the straight-line method. Record the journal entries for the following:

Bond sold at discount; straight-line method to amortize discount.

a. Issuance of bonds.

b. Semiannual interest payment on November 1 and amortization of discount.

c. Retirement of bonds at maturity.

20-4. Redo the journal entries for Exercise 20-3 assuming bonds sold at 102.

20-5. On July 1 Jonald Corporation issued 10%, 10-year bonds with a face value of $100,000 for $90,000, because the current market rate is 12%. Record the following entries, assuming the *interest method* is used to amortize the discount on bonds. Round discount to nearest dollar.

Bonds sold at discount; straight-line method to amortize discount.

a. Issuance of bonds.

b. Semiannual interest payment on December 31 and amortization of discount.

c. Semiannual interest payment on June 30 and amortization of discount.

Bonds sold at discount; interest method to amortize discount.

20-6. On January 1 Last Corporation sold $350,000 of 10-year sinking fund bonds. The corporation expects to earn 10% on the sinking fund balance and is required to deposit $23,609 at the end of each year with the trustee. Record the following entries:

Sinking funds.

a. The first deposit.

b. Earnings of $2,361 at end of first period.

c. Payment of bondholders with sinking fund having a balance of $350,500.

20-7. From the following prepare the long-term liabilities section of a balance sheet:

Preparing a long-term liabilities section on the balance sheet.

Sinking fund	$300,000
Premium on 10% bonds	3,000
Discount on 12% bonds	5,000
10% Bonds Payable	500,000
12% Bonds Payable	200,000

Group A Problems

(The forms you need are on pages 156–160 of the *Study Guide and Working Papers*.)

20A-1. On January 1, 20X5, Angel Corporation sold $400,000 of 8%, 10-year bonds at 97. Interest is to be paid on June 30 and December 31. The straight-line method of amortizing the discount is used. Prepare (1) an amortization schedule for the first three semiannual periods and (2) journal entries to record the following:

Amortization schedule; bond issue; straight-line amortization of discount.

a. Bond issue on January 1.

b. Semiannual interest payments on June 30 and December 31 for interest and amortization of discount.

c. If the bonds were issued on March 1 and interest was paid on September 1 and March 1, what would be the year-end adjusting entry on December 31 to record accrued interest and amortization of discount?

Check Figure: Amortized discount each period $600

Amortization schedule;
bond issue; accrued
interest, straight-line
amortization of premium;
year-end adjusting entry.

20A-2. On May 1, 20X5, Deever Corporation issued $500,000 of 10%, 20-year bonds at 102. The interest is payable on November 1 and May 1. The premium is amortized by the straight-line method. Prepare an amortization schedule for the first three semiannual periods and journalize the following transactions:

20X5
May	1	Bonds issued.
Nov.	1	Paid semiannual interest and amortized premium.
Dec.	31	Accrued bond interest and amortized premium.

Check Figure:
Amortized premium
$250

20A-3. On January 1, 20X7, Vex Corporation issued $300,000 of 10%, 10-year bonds for $257,616, yielding a market rate of 12%. Interest is paid on July 1 and December 31. Vex uses the interest method to amortize the discount.

1. Prepare an amortization schedule for the first three semiannual periods.
2. Prepare journal entries to record:

   a. Bond issuance on January 1.
   b. Semiannual interest payments on July 1 and December 31 as well as amortization of discount.

Amortization schedule;
interest method of amortization of discount; year-end
adjusting entry.

3. If the bond were issued on March 1 and interest was paid on September 1 and March 1, what would be the year-end adjusting entry on December 31, 20X7, to record accrued interest and amortization of discount?

Check Figure:
Discount to be amortized
period 1 $456.96

20A-4. On April 1, 20X6, Potter Corporation issued $200,000 of 10%, 5-year bonds for $204,100, yielding a market rate of 9%. Interest is paid on October 1 and April 1. Potter Corporation uses the interest method to amortize the premium.

Amortization schedule;
interest method of amortization of premium; year-end
adjusting entry.

1. Prepare an amortization schedule for the first three semiannual periods.
2. Prepare journal entries to record the following:

   a. Bond issuance on April 1.
   b. Semiannual interest payment and amortization of premium on October 1.
   c. The year-end adjusting entry to record expense and premium amortization.

Check Figure:
Premium to be amortized
period 1 $815.50

Group B Problems

(The forms you need are on pages 156–160 in the *Study Guide and Working Papers.*)

Amortization schedule;
bond issue; straight-line
amortization of discount.

20B-1. On January 1, 20X6, Angel Corporation sold $300,000 of 12%, 10-year bonds at 92. Interest is to be paid on June 30 and December 31. The straight-line method of amortizing the discount is used. Prepare (1) an amortization schedule for the first three semiannual periods and (2) journal entries to record (a) the bond issue on January 1 and (b) semiannual interest payments on June 30 and December 31 for interest and amortization of discount. (c) If the bonds were issued on March 1 and interest was paid on September 1 and March 1, what would be the year-end adjusting entry on December 31 to record interest payment and amortization of discount?

Check Figure:
Amortized discount
$1,200

Amortizaton schedule; bond
issue; accrued interest;
straight-line amortization
of premium; year-end
adjusting entry.

20B-2. On April 1, 20X6, Deever Corporation issued $600,000 of 6%, 10-year bonds at 104. The interest is payable on October 1 and April 1. The premium is amortized by the straight-line method. Prepare an amortization schedule for the first three semiannual periods and journalize the following transactions:

20X6

Apr. 1 Bonds issued

Oct. 1 Paid semiannual interest and amortization of premium.

Dec. 31 Accrued bond interest and amortization premium.

Check Figure:
Amortized premium
$1,200

20B-3. On January 1, 20X8, Vex Corporation issued $400,000 of 12%, 10-year bonds for $350,937, yielding a market rate of 14%. Interest is paid on July 1 and December 31. Vex uses the interest method to amortize the discount. Prepare an amortization schedule for the first three semiannual periods and prepare journal entries to record the following:

Amortization schedule; interest method of amortization of premium; year-end adjusting entry.

   a. Bond issuance on January 1.
   b. Semiannual interest payment on July 1 and December 31 as well as amortization of discount.

If the bonds were issued on March 1 and interest was paid on September 1 and March 1, what would be the year-end adjusting entry on December 31, 20X8, to record accrued interest and amortization of discount?

Check Figure:
Discount to be amortized
$565.59

20B-4. On March 1, 20X8, Potter Corporation issued $100,000 of 12%, 10-year bonds for $104,408, yielding a market rate of 10%. Interest is paid on September 1 and March 1. Potter Corporation uses the interest method to amortize the premium.

Amortization schedule; interest method of amortization of discount; year-end adjusting entry.

   1. Prepare an amortization schedule for the first three semiannual periods.
   2. Prepare journal entries to record the following:

   a. Bond issuance on March 1.
   b. Semiannual interest payment and amortization of premium on September 1.
   c. The year-end adjusting entry to record interest expense and premium amortization.

Check Figure:
Premium to be amortized
period 1 $779.60

Real-World Applications

20R-1. Ryan Small, president of Janis Corporation, has hired you as a financial consultant to analyze three proposals made by the board of directors to raise additional funds of $3,000,000.

The Plans

   1. Issued 12% preferred stock.
   2. Issued additional common stock at $10 par.
   3. Issue 14%, 20-year bonds.

Given

   - Tax rate, 48%.
   - Estimated corporation earnings, $1,800,000 annually before bond interest.

Assume

   - Before plan, 300,000 shares of $10 par outstanding. All new stock would be issued at par.

Please submit a written recommendation with supporting data to Mr. Small as soon as possible.

20R-2. The board of directors of French Corporation is planning to announce a new 10-year bond issue of $300,000. The contract rate of the bonds is 12%. Owing to several delays, the bonds in the marketplace are now 14%.

The directors think this bond issue has to raise at least $280,000 in cash to meet its financial needs. As the company's financial consultant, calculate the actual selling price of the bonds and make appropriate written recommendations to the board of directors of French regarding the pros and cons of the bond issue.

Given

1. Present value of $1.00 at compound interest for 20 periods at 7% equals .2584.
2. Present value of $1.00 received periodically for 20 periods at 7% equals 10.5940.

YOU make the call

Critical Thinking/Ethical Case

20R-3. Alice wants to buy bonds, but her husband, Pete, thinks stocks would be a better deal. Pete was watching a finance show on TV that said stocks would be going up and that now is the time to buy stock. He called Alice over and said, "I told you so." Alice told her husband that it was no time to take a risk with their money. Do you think Pete is correct in his thinking? You make the call. Write down your recommendations to Alice and her husband.

Internet Exercises: Moody's; Dow Jones

EX-1. [www.moodys.com/moodys.com]   Bonds represent indebtedness of a corporation and are reported on the balance sheet as liabilities. Bonds are usually issued in minimum amounts of $5,000 and may range much higher than that. A bond gets a "rating," similar to a credit rating. This "bond rating" is done by commercial companies like Moody's. You are able to borrow money more easily when you have an excellent credit rating. Companies who rely on bonds as a source of capital are able to borrow more and at more favorable rates when their credit standing is high.

Here you can view the rating codes by which bond issues are assessed. The codes go from Aaa down to C, with Aaa being the highest grade available to the most creditworthy companies. Just as an individual's credit rating may go up or down, corporate credit ratings may also fluctuate. Bond ratings change subject to changes in markets and changing circumstances within a company. After reviewing these categories:

1. Where in the Moody's rating system do bonds begin to become speculative?
2. What are some reasons for the transition to speculative status?
3. What effect does a decreasing rating have on the interest of new issues of bonds from that company?

EX-2. [**www.averages.dowjones.com**] In Chapter 19 you became familiar with the companies that comprise the Dow Jones Industrial Averages. Now revisit that site and select a company different from the one you selected before. Go to that company's home page and determine what its bond rating is. Most of the companies will have been rated by Moody's. Some will have been rated by other rating services. Compare the ratings of the different services when this occurs.

CHAPTER 21

Statement of Cash Flows

You take your car over to Lindsay's Garage for an oil change. You notice a bumper sticker prominently displayed on the wall behind the front counter in the waiting area of the garage. It reads, "Happiness is Positive Cash Flow." You ask George Lindsay, the owner of the garage, about the sticker as you pay your bill. "I'm a mechanic, not an accountant," George says to you while smiling, because he knows you're taking an accounting class. "The sticker is kind of my motto. Cash is what makes the most sense to me, and I feel good when I've got more money coming in here than going out the door."

Cash flow is an interesting and important part of operating any business. There are companies that have had respectable net income, a healthy balance sheet, and then have gone into bankruptcy. The reason: poor cash flow. The accounting profession requires companies to prepare income statements, balance sheets, and statements of retained earnings. The profession also requires companies to prepare a special statement that discloses the sources and uses of cash. This statement is known as the statement of cash flows. This fourth financial statement provides invaluable information about the cash flow of a company that is not available from the other statements.

In this chapter we will first learn the purposes behind the statement of cash flows. We discuss how to prepare the operating activities section of the statement using either the direct or indirect method. We will then look at how to prepare a statement of cash flows for a business. After completing this chapter you should be able to explain from an accounting and business standpoint why "happiness is positive cash flow."

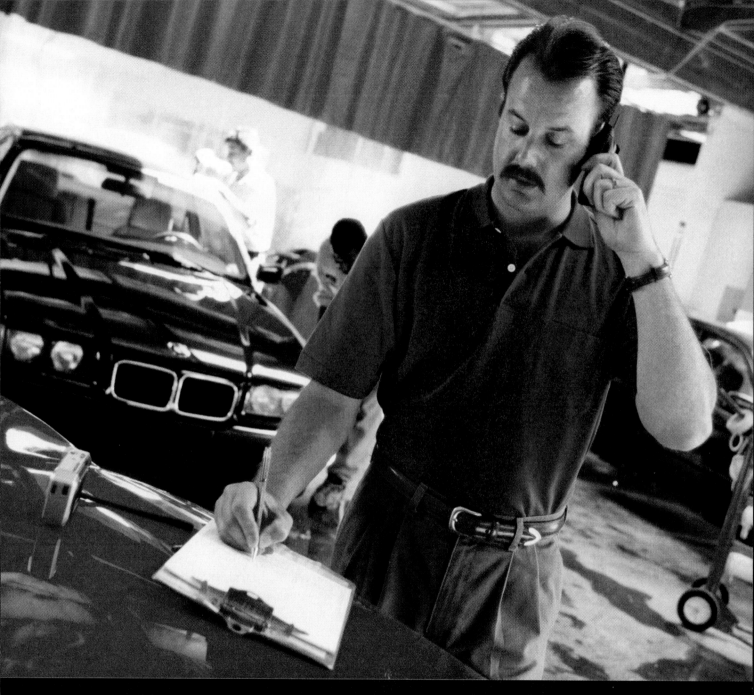

Learning Objectives

- Understanding the purpose of a statement of cash flows. (p. 760)

- Preparing the operating activities section of the statement of cash flows using the indirect method. (p. 760)

- Preparing the operating activities section of the statement of cash flows using the direct method. (p. 767)

- Preparing a statement of cash flows. (p. 769)

In preceding chapters we analyzed as well as prepared three financial statements. Let's quickly review the purposes of each statement.

- Income statement: For a given period shows the results of the company's operations. The net income or loss results in an increase or decrease to retained earnings.
- Statement of retained earnings: Summarizes the changes in retained earnings of a company during a period of time.
- Balance sheet: Shows the end-of-period financial position of a company at a particular date.

In this chapter we turn our attention to a fourth major financial statement that is used to better understand the operating, investing, and financing activities of a company. It is called the statement of cash flows, and it summarizes the sources and uses of cash by a company during an accounting period. It is easy to compute the change in cash balance by looking at the comparative balance sheet, but just the change in total cash tells us nothing about specific cash transactions. The statement of cash flows not only shows in detail the sources and uses of cash; it also gives readers of the financial statements a good basis for judging the possible future cash flows. Internal users of the financial statements (such as management) can also benefit by understanding how to read the statement of cash flows.

Learning Unit 21-1   Statement of Cash Flows: Indirect Method

We use as our example in this chapter the Zabel Company, which sells soccer equipment and supplies. To prepare a statement of cash flows, we need to obtain information from the other financial statements prepared for the company: the income statement, the statement of retained earnings, and the balance sheet. These statements are shown in Figures 21-1 below, 21-2 (p. 761), and 21-3 (p. 761). Note that the balance sheet shown in Figure 21-3 is slightly different from the ones we have shown in the past. This one is a comparative balance sheet, which shows figures from two separate years side by side. We discuss this type of statement in more detail in Chapter 22.

Figure 21-1
Financial Statement of Zabel

ZABEL COMPANY INCOME STATEMENT FOR YEAR ENDED DECEMBER 31, 2004		
Sales		$190 000 00
Cost of Goods Sold		106 000 00
Gross Profit		$ 84 000 00
Operating Expenses:		
Salaries Expense	$ 51 040 00	
Insurance Expense	7 200 00	
Rent Expense	3 600 00	
Depreciation Expense	11 000 00	
Miscellaneous Expense	1 200 00	
Total Operating Expenses		74 040 00
Net Income		$ 9 960 00

ZABEL COMPANY STATEMENT OF RETAINED EARNINGS FOR YEAR ENDED DECEMBER 31, 2004		
Retained Earnings, January 1, 2004		$ 38 14 00 00
Net Income for the Year	$ 9 96 00 00	
Less: Cash Dividends	8 00 00 00	
Increase in Retained Earnings		1 96 00 00
Retained Earnings, December 31, 2004		$ 40 10 00 00

Figure 21-2
Financial Statement of Zabel

ZABEL COMPANY COMPARATIVE BALANCE SHEET AS OF DECEMBER 31, 2003, AND DECEMBER 31, 2004			
Assets	2004	2003	Increase (Decrease)
Current Assets:			
Cash	$ 2 90 00 00	$ 2 48 00 00	$ 42 00 00
Accounts Receivable	19 56 00 00	14 72 00 00	4 84 00 00
Merchandise Inventory	30 00 00 00	32 00 00 00	(2 00 00 00)
Prepaid Insurance	60 00 00	40 00 00	20 00 00
Total Current Assets	$ 53 06 00 00	$ 49 60 00 00	$ 3 46 00 00
Plant and Equipment:			
Office Equipment	$ 96 00 00 00	$ 66 00 00 00	$ 30 00 00 00
Accum. Dep., Office Equipment	(37 20 00 00)	(26 20 00 00)	(11 00 00 00)
Total Plant and Equipment	$ 58 80 00 00	$ 39 80 00 00	$ 19 00 00 00
Total Assets	$111 86 00 00	$ 89 40 00 00	$ 22 46 00 00
Liabilities			
Current Liabilities:			
Notes Payable—Short Term (used to purchase inventory)	$ 17 40 00 00	$ 14 80 00 00	$ 2 60 00 00
Accounts Payable	36 00 00	46 00 00	(10 00 00)
Total Current Liabilities	$ 17 76 00 00	$ 15 26 00 00	$ 2 50 00 00
Long-Term Liabilities:			
Long-Term Note Payable	$ 28 00 00 00	$ 20 00 00 00	$ 8 00 00 00
Total Liabilities	$ 45 76 00 00	$ 35 26 00 00	$ 10 50 00 00
Stockholders' Equity			
Common Stock, $10 par	$ 11 00 00 00	$ 10 00 00 00	$ 1 00 00 00
Paid-in Capital in Excess of Par	15 00 00 00	6 00 00 00	9 00 00 00
Retained Earnings	40 10 00 00	38 14 00 00	1 96 00 00
Total Stockholders' Equity	$ 66 10 00 00	54 14 00 00	$ 11 96 00 00
Total Liabilities and Stockholders' Equity	$111 86 00 00	$ 89 40 00 00	$ 22 46 00 00

Figure 21-3
Comparative Balance Sheet for Zabel

A short way to remember the activity classifications

Transactions with customers, vendors, and employees are operating activities.

Transactions involving the purchase or sale of plant assets are investing activities.

Transactions involving the creditors or stockholders are financing activities.

The statement of cash flows consists of three main sections: (1) net cash flows from operating activities, (2) cash flows from investing activities, and (3) cash flows from financing activities. Some of the complexities of this statement are beyond the scope of this text, but the following paragraphs contain a few examples of transactions reported in each of the three sections mentioned above.

Operating activities include selling products or services to customers. Cash inflows from operating activities include cash collected from customers. Cash outflows from operating activities include paying for merchandise inventory, salaries, rent, and other such expenses.

Investing activities include such things as purchase or sale of plant and equipment, buying stocks and bonds (of other companies), and making loans to other businesses or individuals.

Financing activities include raising money by issuing stocks and bonds, repurchasing of the company's stock, and paying cash dividends to the stockholders.

A fourth classification reported on the statement of cash flows is called noncash investing and financing activities, which includes such transactions as issuing shares of stock in exchange for assets such as land and buildings. Although cash is not involved, the event is reported because no other financial statement specifically discloses the transaction. If the stock in the above example was issued for cash (financing activity, a cash increase) and if we used the cash proceeds to purchase land and a building (investing activity, a cash decrease), the event would be disclosed on the statement of cash flows in two separate sections. Because our example is a noncash transaction, it can be reported on the statement of cash flow as a footnote or on a separate schedule listing such transactions.

CASH FLOWS FROM OPERATING ACTIVITIES: INDIRECT METHOD

A business needs a positive cash flow to survive. A company's ability to raise money from financing activities (issuing stocks, bonds, or long-term notes) is often tied to its success in generating cash flow from its operations. The operating activities section of the statement of cash flows is therefore of great importance to potential investors and creditors.

This section introduces a procedure known as the indirect method of reporting cash flows from operating activities. Note that the distinction between the indirect method and the direct method (discussed in the next learning unit) only applies to the operating activities section of the statement of cash flows.

In the indirect method we are converting the net income on the income statement from the accrual basis to the cash basis. As we have been learning throughout this text, businesses normally usually report their net income on the accrual basis, which places the primary emphasis on *when* the revenues are earned and *when* the expenses are incurred.

The indirect method's name comes from the way we view the income statement. We begin with the bottom line of the income statement and work backwards until we have computed net cash flow from operating activities. We begin the operating activities section with the net income as reported on the income statement (see Figure 21-4) and convert it from the accrual basis to the cash basis. Figure 21-4 shows how the net cash flows from operating activities are computed for the Zabel Company using the indirect method.

In this example, the first item to be added to the net income is Depreciation Expense. The depreciation is *added back* to net income because it was subtracted

ZABEL COMPANY
STATEMENT OF CASH FLOW (INDIRECT METHOD)
FOR YEAR ENDED DECEMBER 31, 2004

Cash Flows from Operating Activities:		
Net Income from Operations	$ 9 9 6 0 00	
Add (deduct) items to Convert Net Income from		
Accrual Basis to Cash Basis:		
Depreciation Expense	11 0 0 0 00	
Increase in Accounts Receivable	(4 8 4 0 00)	
Decrease in Merchandise Inventory	2 0 0 0 00	
Increase in Prepaid Insurance	(2 0 0 00)	
Increase in Notes Payable (Short Term)	2 6 0 0 00	
Decrease in Accounts Payable	(1 0 0 00)	
Net Cash Provided by Operating Activities		$ 20 4 2 0 00

Figure 21-4
Statement of Cash Flow—
Indirect Method

out as an expense on the income statement to derive the $9,960 net income. You will recall that when depreciation is recorded, the entry involves a debit to Depreciation Expense and a credit to Accumulated Depreciation. Neither of these accounts involves cash. Because depreciation is therefore a "noncash" expense, it is added back to net income when using the indirect method. Next, each of the current assets and current liabilities are examined to determine their effect on cash flow.

The aid sheet shown in Figure 21-5 is useful for remembering whether to add or subtract a given item on the statement of cash flow. Alternatively, some instructors prefer the simple opposite effect/same effect approach. For current assets, cash flow has the *opposite effect,* whereas for current liabilities, the cash flow has the *same effect.* For example, the increase in Accounts Receivable (a current asset) must be subtracted, whereas the increase in Short-Term Notes Payable (a current liability) would be added.

After each of the above items is listed with its proper sign, the entire list is combined with net income to compute the net cash provided by operating activities of $20,420. The term *net cash provided* by operating activities is commonly used if the result is positive, whereas *net cash used* in operating activities indicates that the result is negative. As you might imagine, the goal is to have a strong positive cash flow from operating activities. A negative operating cash flow cannot be tolerated for very long. Investors and creditors would hesitate to provide funds to a firm that cannot generate a positive cash flow from its operating activities.

CASH FLOWS FROM INVESTING ACTIVITIES

The cash flows from investing activities section of the statement of cash flows includes (1) the purchase and sale of other companies' stocks and bonds, (2) the buying and

	Add to Net Income If This Account Has:	Deduct from Net Income If This Account Has:
Current Assets	DECREASED	INCREASED
Current Liabilities	INCREASED	DECREASED

Figure 21-5
Aid Sheet for Converting from Accrual Basis to Cash Basis

disposal of plant assets, and (3) making loans to other parties. We analyze the noncurrent accounts to find these activities. For example, the following transactions would be recorded in this section:

1. Sale or purchase of equipment.
2. Sale or purchase of land.
3. Cash spent to invest in other companies' stocks and bonds.
4. Cash received from sales of stock or bond investments.
5. Loaning cash to borrowers.

On the balance sheet for Zabel Company, we see an increase in plant and equipment from 2000 to 2001 of $30,000. Thus, the cash outflow for equipment would be reported as shown in Figure 21-6.

Figure 21-6
Cash Outflow for Equipment

Cash Flows from Investing Activities		
Purchase of Plant Asset	$(30 000 00)	
Net Cash Flows Used in Investing Activities		$(30 000 00)

CASH FLOWS FROM FINANCING ACTIVITIES

The cash flows from financing activities section of the statement of cash flows records transactions such as the following:

1. Issuance of long-term notes and bonds.
2. Issuance of common stock.
3. Purchasing and reissuing treasury stock.
4. Payment of cash dividends.
5. Retirement of bonds.

From the comparative balance sheet for Zabel Company, we see that the Long-Term Notes Payable account increased by $8,000. This increase is shown as a source (increase) of cash, because an increase in Long-Term Notes Payable means that more cash has been borrowed and therefore has been received by the business. Also, note that the issuance of $10,000 of common stock has *increased* the cash flows, whereas the payment of $8,000 in dividends results in a *decrease* in cash flows. The end result is that net cash provided by financing activities has increased by $10,000, as shown in Figure 21-7.

Figure 21-7
Net Cash Flows Provided by Financing Activities

Cash Flows from Financing Activities		
Issuance of Long-Term Note	$ 8 000 00	
Issuance of Common Stock	10 000 00	
Payment of Dividends	(8 000 00)	
Net Cash Flows Provided by Financing Activities		$ 10 000 00

To arrive at net change in cash for the overall statement, we perform the following calculation:

Net Cash Provided by Operating Activities	$ 20,420
− Cash Flow Used by Investing Activities	(30,000)
+ Net Cash Provided by Financing Activities	10,000
= Net Increase in Cash	$ 420

Figure 21-8 shows all three sections together in the statement of cash flows.

Note that at the bottom of the statement of cash flows the cash has increased by $420 (just as is shown for cash on the comparative balance sheet), but this report gives us a complete breakdown of just what caused the cash to increase by $420.

The statement of cash flows is helpful in evaluating, comparing, and predicting future cash flows. By dividing this report into three sections, creditors as well as investors can judge how cash flows from operations compared with those from investing or financing activities. For example, in the case of Zabel Company, an investor or a creditor can see that there has been a substantial reduction in cash in one area (investing), only to be offset by an increase in cash from the other areas (operating and financing).

A second approach, known as the direct method, gives a more useful presentation of cash flows from operating activities. Although this method gives more understandable data, many firms think it much easier to use the indirect method to prepare the reports. Regardless of method used, the cash flows from operating activities will be the same. The direct method is illustrated in Learning Unit 21-2.

ZABEL COMPANY
STATEMENT OF CASH FLOWS—INDIRECT METHOD
FOR YEAR ENDED DECEMBER 31, 2004

Net Cash Flows from Operating Activities			
Net Income	$ 9 960 00		
Add (Deduct) Items to Convert Net Income			
from Accrual Basis to Cash Basis:			
Depreciation Expense	11 000 00		
Increase in Accounts Receivable	(4 840 00)		
Decrease in Merchandise Inventory	2 000 00		
Increase in Prepaid Insurance	(2 00 00)		
Increase in Short-Term Notes Payable	2 600 00		
Decrease in Accounts Payable	(1 000 00)		
Net Cash Flows from Operating Activities		$ 20 420 00	
Cash Flows from Investing Activities			
Purchase of Plant Asset	$(30 000 00)		
Net Cash Flows Used by Investing Activities		(30 000 00)	
Cash Flows from Financing Activities			
Issuance of Long-Term Note	$ 8 000 00		
Issuance of Common Stock	10 000 00		
Payment of Dividends	(8 000 00)		
Net Cash Provided by Financing Activities		10 000 00	
Net Increase in Cash		$ 420 00	
Beginning Balance of Cash		2 480 00	
Ending Balance of Cash		$ 2 900 00	

Figure 21-8
Statement of Cash Flows—
Indirect Method

Learning Unit 21-1 Review

AT THIS POINT you should be able to

- Explain the components of a statement of cash flows. (p. 763)
- Calculate net cash flows from operating activities using the indirect method. (p. 763)
- Calculate net cash flows from investing activities. (p. 763)
- Calculate net cash flows from financing activities. (p. 763)
- Prepare a complete statement of cash flows using the indirect method. (p. 763)

SELF REVIEW QUIZ 21-1

(The forms you need are on page 166 of the *Study Guide and Working Papers.*)
    From Figure 21-9, calculate net cash flows from operating activities.

Figure 21-9
Income Statement for
Johnson Company

JOHNSON COMPANY INCOME STATEMENT FOR YEAR ENDED DECEMBER 31, 2004		
Sales		$150 000 00
Cost of Goods Sold		90 000 00
Gross Profit		$ 60 000 00
Operating Expenses:		
Salaries Expense	$40 000 00	
Depreciation Expense	3 000 00	
Advertising Expense	8 000 00	
Total Operating Expenses:		51 000 00
Net Income		$ 9 000 00

Additional Data	2001	2000
Accounts Receivable	$ 10 600 00	$ 4 000 00
Merchandise Inventory	10 000 00	12 000 00
Prepaid Advertising	1 400 00	3 000 00
Accounts Payable	18 000 00	15 000 00
Salaries Payable	1 800 00	1 900 00

SOLUTION TO SELF-REVIEW QUIZ 21-1

Figure 21-10
Net Cash Flow from
Operating Activities

Net Cash Flow from Operating Activities:	
Net Income	
Add (deduct) Items to Convert Net Income to Cash	$ 9 000 00
Basis from the Accrual Basis:	
Depreciation Expense	3 000 00
Increase in Accounts Receivable	(6 600 00)
Decrease in Merchandise Inventory	2 000 00
Decrease in Prepaid Advertising	$ 1 600 00
Increase in Accounts Payable	3 000 00
Decrease in Salaries Payable	(1 000 00)
Net Cash Flow from Operating Activities:	$ 11 900 00

Learning Unit 21-2   Statement of Cash Flows: Direct Method

As indicated in Learning Unit 21-1, cash flows from operating activities include the cash effects of transactions such as selling goods or services to customers and paying for merchandise inventory and operating expenses. Many accountants prefer the direct method of reporting the cash flows from operating activities. This approach provides useful information and is easily understood by the users of the financial statements.

The direct method requires listing major groups of operating cash receipts and cash payments. We first compute cash receipts from customers. Because most firms sell products or services on account as well as for cash, the sales figure on the income statement is not the same as total cash received. We analyze Accounts Receivable and combine its change (increase or decrease) with the sales figure from the income statement. If Accounts Receivable has *increased*, there is a negative impact on cash, so the amount of the increase is *subtracted* from sales. If Accounts Receivable has *decreased*, there is a positive effect on cash, so the amount of the decrease is *added* to sales. Thus, for computing cash received from customers, we can treat Accounts Receivable as we did in the indirect method by using the *opposite effect*.

The same reasoning applies to cash payments, except that because these are outflows of cash, any change with a *positive* cash effect is *subtracted* (because a positive effect means less cash to pay out). Any change with a *negative* cash effect is *added* (because a negative effect means more cash to pay out).

Our first example of an operating cash outflow is cash paid for merchandise inventory. We begin the computation with Cost of Goods Sold and then adjust by the change in the Merchandise Inventory account. A further adjustment is necessary to account for changes in Accounts Payable and Short-Term Notes Payable (if notes were used to pay for inventory, as in our example). Specifically, if the balance of Merchandise Inventory has increased, there would be a *negative* cash effect that would be *added* in the computation of cash paid for merchandise. If Merchandise Inventory has decreased, it is a *positive* cash effect that is *subtracted* to compute cash paid for merchandise. After adjusting for inventory changes, if Accounts Payable has increased, the cash effect is positive and thus would be subtracted from the computation. If Accounts Payable has decreased, the cash effect is negative and thus would be added to the calculation. The changes in Short-Term Notes Payable (assuming notes were used to pay for inventory) would be analyzed in the same way as Accounts Payable.

Cash paid for operating expenses is handled in much the same way as cash paid for merchandise inventory. Cash paid for salaries, for instance, is computed by combining the change in Salaries Payable with the amount of Salary Expense from the income statement. If Salaries Payable has increased (positive cash effect), the amount of increase is subtracted from Salary Expense. If this account has decreased (negative cash effect), the amount of the decrease would be added to the Salary Expense.

For expenses involving a prepayment (such as Prepaid Insurance), the insurance expense balance would be combined with the change in Prepaid Insurance. If Prepaid Insurance had increased (negative cash effect), the amount of the change would be added to insurance expense to compute cash paid for insurance. If Prepaid Insurance

---

A simple way to identify whether a particular change has a positive or negative cash effect.

Current Asset Increase: Negative effect on cash because more of our cash has been spent on that asset compared with the previous balance sheet date. Example: Inventory increasing means that more of our dollars are tied up in the inventory.

Current Asset Decrease: Positive effect on cash because less of our cash has been spent on that asset compared with the previous balance sheet date. Example: Inventory decreasing means that fewer of our dollars are tied up in the inventory.

Current Liability Increase: Positive effect on cash because compared with a year ago, less of the liability has been paid off (leaving more cash in our pockets).

Current Liability Decrease: Negative effect on cash because although we do not owe as much as we did a year ago, we have paid more of it off (and have less cash still in our pockets).

had decreased (positive cash effect), the amount of the change would be subtracted from insurance expense.

We now look at an example of the computation of net cash flow from operating activities. The Zabel Company computes cash received from customers by combining the sales figure from the income statement with the change in Accounts Receivable from the comparative balance sheet (see Figures 21-1 and 21-3). Sales is $190,000, and Accounts Receivable has *increased* by $4,840. Because the increase in Accounts Receivable means a negative cash effect (more of our money is currently in the pockets of our customers!), it is *subtracted* from sales to arrive at the cash collected from customers figure of $185,160. This computation is illustrated in Figure 21-11.

A second computation in Figure 21-11 shows cash paid for inventory. The Cost of Goods Sold figure is adjusted for changes in Merchandise Inventory, Accounts Payable, and Short-Term Notes Payable (if such notes are used to finance inventory). In our example, Cost of Goods Sold of $106,000 is adjusted by subtracting the decrease in Inventory, subtracting the increase in Short-Term Notes Payable, and adding the decrease in Accounts Payable to arrive at the Cash Paid for Inventory figure of $101,500.

Cash Paid for Insurance is also illustrated in Figure 21-11 by adding the decrease in Prepaid Insurance to the Insurance Expense to yield $7,400 for Cash Paid for Insurance.

Figure 21-12 (p. 769) shows the complete statement of cash flows for the Zabel Company using the direct method. Note that the investing activities and financing activities sections are the same as in Figure 21-8, because the distinction between the indirect and direct methods only applies to the cash flows from operating activities section.

> To summarize, we can still use the "same effect/opposite effect" reasoning mentioned in the previous learning unit. Current asset cash effects are always the opposite effect, whereas current liability cash effects are always the same effect.

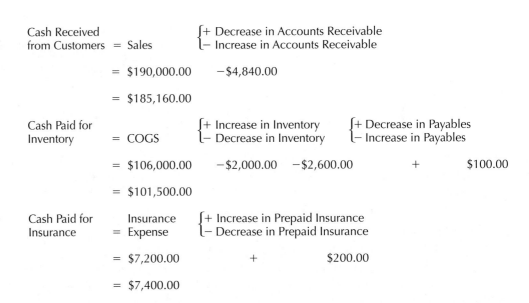

Note: The other items on Zabel's net cash flows from operating activities section do not require any adjustment, because there were no current asset or current liability changes from the income statement figures for such items as salaries, rent, and miscellaneous expenses.

Figure 21-11 Computations for Zabel Company's Net Cash Flows from Operating Activities

ZABEL COMPANY
STATEMENT OF CASH FLOWS—DIRECT METHOD
FOR YEAR ENDED DECEMBER 31, 2004

Net Cash Flows from Operating Activities			
Cash Received from Customers		$185 1 6 0 00	
Cash Paid for Merchandise Inventory	$(101 5 0 0 00)		
Cash Paid for Salaries	51 0 4 0 00		
Cash Paid for Insurance	(7 4 0 0 00)		
Cash Paid for Rent	(3 6 0 0 00)		
Cash Paid for Miscellaneous Expenses	(1 2 0 0 00)		
Total Cash Paid for Operating Activities		(164 7 4 0 00)	
Net Cash Flows from Operating Activities		$ 20 4 2 0 00	
Cash Flows from Investing Activities			
Purchase of Plant Asset	$(30 0 0 0 00)		
Net Cash Used by Investing Activities		(30 0 0 0 00)	
Cash Flows from Financing Activities			
Issuance of Long-Term Note	$ 8 0 0 0 00		
Issuance of Common Stock	10 0 0 0 00		
Payment of Dividends	(8 0 0 0 00)		
Net Cash Provided by Financing Activities		10 0 0 0 00	
Net Increase in Cash		$ 4 2 0 00	
Beginning Balance of Cash		2 4 8 0 00	
Ending Balance of Cash		$ 2 9 0 0 00	

Figure 21-12 Statement of Cash Flows—Direct Method

Learning Unit 21-2 Review

AT THIS POINT you should be able to

- Explain the difference between the direct method and the indirect method. (p. 767)
- Compute the net cash flows from operating activities section of the statement of cash flows. (p. 769)

SELF-REVIEW QUIZ 21-2

(The forms you need are on page 167 of the *Study Guide and Working Papers.*)

Using the data from Self-Review Quiz 21-1 on page 766, show in good form the cash flows from the operating activities section of the statement of cash flows for the Johnson Company using the direct method.

SOLUTION TO SELF-REVIEW QUIZ 21-2

Figure 21-13
Net Cash Flows from
Operating Activities

Net Cash Flow from Operating Activities:		
Cash Received from Customers		$143 400 00
Cash Paid for Merchandise Inventory	$ 85 000 00	
Cash Paid for Salaries	40 100 00	
Cash Paid for Advertising	6 400 00	
Total Cash Paid for Operating Activities		131 500 00
Net Cash Flows from Operating Activities:		$ 11 900 00

Explanations of above computations:

Cash from Customer = Sales − Increase in Accounts Receivable
Cash Paid for Inventory = CGS − Decrease in Inventory − Increase in Accounts Payable
Cash Paid for Salaries = Salary Expense + Decrease in Salaries Payable
Cash Paid for Advertising = Advertising Expense − Decrease in Prepaid Advertising

Chapter Review

Summary of Key Points

Learning Unit 21-1

1. In the statement of cash flows, net change in cash equals net cash from operating activities plus or minus cash from investing activities plus or minus cash from financing activities.
2. In figuring the net cash from operating activities section of the statement, it is necessary to convert the net income from the income statement from the accrual basis to the cash basis. This change affects the following accounts: Depreciation Expense, Accounts Receivable, Inventory, Prepaid Expenses, Accounts Payable, and Short-Term Notes Payable. Note that we are analyzing current assets and current liabilities to see their effect on net income. This approach to computing cash flows from operating activities is known as the indirect method.
3. Cash flows from investing activities include such things as purchase and sale of stocks and bonds (of other companies), buying and selling plant assets, and lending money to other parties.
4. Cash flows from financing activities include such things as issuing and repaying long-term notes and bonds, issuing common stock, buying back common stock (treasury stock), and paying dividends.

Learning Unit 21-2

1. An alternative way of preparing the net cash from operating activities section of the statement is called the direct method.
2. The direct method requires listing separately the major categories of cash inflows and outflows. The major cash inflow for most firms is the cash received from customers, which is computed by adjusting the sales figure by the change in Accounts Receivable.
3. Cash outflows under the operating activities section include cash paid for inventory, cash paid for salaries, and cash paid for other operating expenses. In each case, the appropriate income statement figure is adjusted by the changes in one or more current asset or current liability accounts.
4. Regardless of the method selected, the net cash from operating activities will be the same. Also, the distinction between the direct and indirect methods only applies to net cash from operating activities. The investing and financing sections remain the same.

Key Terms

Cash inflow   Any increase in cash is called a cash inflow or a source of cash. When listing the total for a major section of the statement of cash flows, if cash is increased, the figure is often described as "cash provided" by operating activities (or by investing activities or financing activities).

Cash outflow   A decrease in cash is called a cash outflow or a use of cash. When listing a total for a major section of the statement of cash flows, if cash has decreased, the figure is often described as "cash used" in operating activities (or in investing activities or financing activities).

Comparative balance sheet   A balance sheet listing financial condition for two or more years in a side-by-side manner. This format allows the reader to make quick comparisons between the two balance sheet dates.

Direct method   One of two methods of preparing the net cash flow from operating activities section of the statement of cash flows. Each of the major areas of sources and uses of cash for operations is detailed separately.

Financing activities   Activities relating to raising money from investors and creditors such as the issuance of stocks and bonds and long-term notes; also, repurchase of outstanding stock and retiring bonds and notes as well as paying dividends.

Indirect method   One of two methods of preparing the net cash flow from the operating activities section of the statement of cash flows. Involves converting the accrual basis net income figure from the income statement to the cash basis net income.

Investing activities   Activities such as purchase and sale of plant and equipment and placing excess cash in stocks, bonds, and notes of other companies.

Noncash investing and financing activities   Transactions such as the issuance of stock in exchange for land would be listed in a footnote or a separate schedule to the statement of cash flows, because such transactions would not be separately reported on any other financial statement.

Operating activities   Those activities most closely related to conducting the business for which the enterprise was established. Activities such as selling merchandise and services to customers and paying salaries and other expenses needed to continue earning the operating revenue are classified as operating activities.

Statement of cash flows   A financial report that provides a detailed breakdown of the specific increases and decreases in cash during an accounting period. It helps readers of the statement evaluate past performance as well as predict future cash flows of the business.

Blueprint: Statement of Cash Flows

Indirect Method

Net Cash Flows from Operating Activities		
Net Income		XXX
Add (Deduct) Items to Convert Net		
Income to Cash Basis:		
Depreciation Expense		XX
Increase in Accounts Receivable		(XX)
Decrease in Inventory		XX
Increase in Prepaid Expenses		(XX)
Increase in Accounts Payable		XX
Decrease in Salaries Payable		(XX)
Net Cash Flows from Operating Activities		XXX
Cash Flows from Investing Activities		
Purchase of Investment Securities	(XXX)	
Purchase of Equipment	(XXX)	
Sale of Land	XXX	
Cash Used by Investing Activities		(XXX)
Cash Flows from Financing Activities		
Issuance of Common Stock	XX	
Payment of Dividends	(X)	
Cash Provided by Financing Activities		XX
Net Increase in Cash		XXX
Beginning Balance of Cash		XXX
Ending Balance of Cash		XXX

Direct Method

Net Cash Flows from Operating Activities		
Cash Received from Customers		XXX
Cash Paid for Inventory	XXX	
Cash Paid for Salaries	XX	
Cash Paid for Insurance	X	
Cash Paid for Rent	X	
Cash Paid for Other Expenses	XX	
Total Cash Paid for Operations		XX
Net Cash Flows from Operating Activities		XXX

Questions, Mini Exercises, Exercises, and Problems

Discussion Questions

1. List the three main sections of the statement of cash flows.
2. Explain how net cash flows from operating activities is calculated using the indirect method.
3. Explain how net cash flows from operating activities is calculated using the direct method.
4. The issuance of stock is an investing activity. Agree or disagree. Why?
5. Explain how a creditor might analyze a statement of cash flows.
6. Explain what is meant by financing activities.
7. Explain why depreciation is *added* to net income when using the indirect method.

Mini Exercises

(The forms you need are on page 168 of the *Study Guide and Working Papers.*)

Calculating Net Cash Flows from Operating Activities: Indirect Method

1. The following accounts showed an increase or a decrease from the comparative balance sheet. Explain which account will be added to net income and which will be subtracted in calculating net cash flows for operating activities.

    a. Accounts Receivable: increase.
    b. Inventory: decrease.
    c. Short-Term Notes Payable: increase.
    d. Accounts Payable: decrease.

2. From the following, calculate the net cash flow from operating activities:

	2003	2004
Merchandise Inventory	$2,000	$2,500
Accounts Receivable	500	700
Prepaid Insurance	400	300
Accounts Payable	1,000	600
Salaries Payable	500	700

For the year ended 2004:

Net Income	$1,900
Depreciation Expense	500

Calculating Net Cash Flows from Operating Activities: Direct Method

3. Using the data from Mini Exercise 2 plus the additional information in Figure 21-14, compute net cash flows from operating activities using the direct method.

Figure 21-14
Income Statement

Sales		$ 800 00
Cost of Goods Sold		240 00
Gross Profit		$ 560 00
Expenses:		
Depreciation Expense	$ 50 00	
Salary Expense	220 00	
Insurance Expense	70 00	
Miscellaneous Expense	30 00	
Total Expenses		370 00
Net Income		$ 190 00

Calculating Cash Flows from Financing Activities

4. From the following, calculate net cash flows from financing activities:

Payments of Dividends	$ 6,000
Issuance of Common Stock	2,000
Issuance of Long-Term Note	14,000

Calculating Change in Cash

5. Given the following, calculate net change in cash:

Net Cash Flows from Operating Activities	$3,000
Net Cash Used by Investing Activities	(1,000)
Net Cash Provided by Financing Activities	600

Exercises

(The forms you need are on page 169 of the *Study Guide and Working Papers*.)

Converting to cash basis: indirect method.

21-1. Complete the following chart regarding the indirect method.

	Add to Net Income	Subtract from Net Income
?	Decrease	Increase
?	Increase	Decrease

Net cash flow from operating activities: indirect method.

21-2. From the following, calculate the net cash flow from operating activities (use the indirect method):

	2003	2004
Accounts Receivable	$5,900	$7,900
Prepaid Insurance	900	850
Accounts Payable	4,000	4,600
Salaries Payable	1,200	2,200

For the year ended 2004:

Net Income $17,000

Depreciation Exp: 4,000

21-3. From the following, calculate the net cash flow from operating activities (use the direct method):

Net cash flow from operating activities: direct method.

Sales	$9,000
Cost of Goods Sold	4,400
Salary Expense	1,600
Insurance Expense	800
Other Expenses (all cash)	1,000

Changes in current assets and liabilities:

Accounts Receivable increased by $600.
Inventory increased by $500.
Accounts Payable increased by $100.
Salaries Payable decreased by $200.
Prepaid Insurance decreased by $150.

21-4. For each of the following transactions, identify the appropriate section of the statement of cash flows (OA = Operating, IA = Investing, FA = Financing, and NC = Noncash).

Identification of cash flow activity area.

_____ **a.** Sold merchandise to customers.
_____ **b.** Purchase of equipment.
_____ **c.** Buy stocks of another corporation.
_____ **d.** Pay dividends to stockholders.
_____ **e.** Paid salaries to employees.
_____ **f.** Issue stock in exchange for equipment.

Group A Problems

(The forms you need are on pages 170–171 of the *Study Guide and Working Papers*.)

21A-1. From the following income statement (Fig. 21-15), balance sheet (Fig. 21-16), and additional data for Dent Company, prepare a statement of cash flows using the indirect method.

Statement of cash flows: indirect method.

Figure 21-15
Income Statement for Dent

DENT COMPANY INCOME STATEMENT FOR THE YEAR ENDED DECEMBER 31, 2004		
Sales		$ 95 5 0 0 00
Cost of Goods Sold		69 1 0 0 00
Gross Profit		$ 27 4 0 0 00
Operating Expenses:		
Rent Expense	$ 7 5 0 0 00	
Depreciation Expense	7 0 0 0 00	
Salaries Expense	6 6 0 0 00	
Miscellaneous Expense	3 2 0 0 00	
Total Operating Expenses		24 3 0 0 00
Net Income		$ 3 1 0 0 00

Figure 21-16
Balance Sheet for Dent

DENT COMPANY BALANCE SHEET DECEMBER 31, 2004		
Assets	2004	2003
Current Assets:		
Cash	$ 3 4 0 0 00	$ 2 6 0 0 00
Accounts Receivable, Net	5 6 0 0 00	4 5 0 0 00
Merchandise Inventory	2 2 0 0 00	2 0 0 0 00
Prepaid Rent	1 0 0 0 00	1 2 0 0 00
Total Current Assets	$ 12 2 0 0 00	$ 10 3 0 0 00
Plant and Equipment:		
Store Equipment	$ 58 0 0 0 00	$ 50 0 0 0 00
Accum. Dep., Store Equipment	(12 0 0 0 00)	(5 0 0 0 00)
Total Plant and Equipment	$ 46 0 0 0 00	$ 45 0 0 0 00
Total Assets	$ 58 2 0 0 00	$ 55 3 0 0 00
Liabilities		
Current Liabilities:		
Notes Payable—Short Term	$ 6 8 0 0 00	$ 5 2 0 0 00
Accounts Payable	4 4 0 0 00	4 8 0 0 00
Total Current Liabilities	$ 11 2 0 0 00	$ 10 0 0 0 00
Long-Term Liabilities:		
Bonds Payable	$ 12 5 0 0 00	$ 15 0 0 0 00
Total Liabilities	$ 23 7 0 0 00	$ 25 0 0 0 00
Stockholders' Equity		
Common Stock, $1 par	$ 22 5 0 0 00	$ 20 0 0 0 00
Retained Earnings	12 0 0 0 00	10 3 0 0 00
Total Stockholders' Equity	$ 34 5 0 0 00	$ 30 3 0 0 00
Total Liabilities and Stockholders' Equity	$ 58 2 0 0 00	$ 55 3 0 0 00

Additional Data:

1. All Plant and Equipment was purchased in cash.
2. Sold additional 2,500 shares of stock for cash at par.
3. A $1,400 dividend was declared and paid.
4. Short-term notes used to finance inventory.

Statement of cash flows: direct method.

21A-2. From the financial statements and additional information provided in Problem 21A-1 for the Dent Company, prepare a statement of cash flows using the direct method.

Group B Problems

(The forms you need are on pages 170–171 of the *Study Guide and Working Papers.*)

Statement of cash flows: indirect method.

21B-1. From the following income statement (Fig. 21-17), balance sheet (Fig. 21-18), and additional data for Blumer Company (p. 778), prepare a statement of cash flows using the indirect method.

BLUMER COMPANY
INCOME STATEMENT
FOR THE YEAR ENDED DECEMBER 31, 2004

Sales		$ 36 000 00
Cost of Goods Sold		25 000 00
Gross Profit		$ 11 000 00
Operating Expenses:		
Depreciation Expense—Equipment	$ 80 000	
Depreciation Expense—Machinery	50 000	
Advertising Expense	66 000	
Salaries Expense	1 80 000	
Miscellaneous Expense	3 60 000	
Total Operating Expenses		7 36 000
Net Income		$ 3 64 000

Figure 21-17
Income Statement for Blumer

BLUMER COMPANY
BALANCE SHEET
DECEMBER 31, 2004

Assets	2004	2003
Current Assets:		
Cash	$ 2 04 000	$ 54 000
Accounts Receivable, Net	2 68 000	2 91 000
Merchandise Inventory	3 20 000	2 43 000
Total Current Assets	$ 7 92 000	$ 5 88 000
Plant and Equipment:		
Office Equipment, Net	$ 6 03 000	$ 4 53 000
Machinery, Net	4 83 000	3 03 000
Land	1 18 000	48 000
Total Plant and Equipment	$ 12 04 000	$ 8 04 000
Total Assets	$ 19 96 000	$ 13 92 000
Liabilities		
Current Liabilities:		
Notes Payable—Short Term	$ 2 08 000	$ 1 98 000
Accounts Payable	10 000	15 000
Total Current Liabilities	$ 2 18 000	$ 2 13 000
Long-Term Liabilities:		
Mortgage Payable	$ 2 12 000	$ 1 77 000
Total Liabilities	$ 4 30 000	$ 3 90 000
Stockholders' Equity		
Common Stock, $1 par	$ 9 53 000	$ 7 53 000
Retained Earnings	6 13 000	2 49 000
Total Stockholders' Equity	$ 15 66 000	$ 10 02 000
Total Liabilities and Stockholders' Equity	$ 19 96 000	$ 13 92 000

Figure 21-18
Balance Sheet for Blumer

Additional Data:

1. All increases in Plant and Equipment were paid for in cash.
2. No dividend was declared in 2004.
3. Sold 2,000 shares of stock for cash at par value.

Hint: Office Equipment and Machinery are recorded at *net* on the balance sheet. Be sure to add back depreciation expense to the cost of the assets in 2004 to compute the actual cost of the additional assets purchased.

21B-2. From the financial statements and additional information provided in Problem 21B-1 for the Blumer Company, prepare a statement of cash flows using the direct method.

> Statement of cash flows: direct method.

Real-World Applications

21R-1. Diane Clubb is trying to convert income statement items from an accrual basis to a cash basis. Accounts Receivable at the beginning of the year totaled $205,000. At the end of the year Accounts Receivable amounted to $240,000. On the income statement using accrual accounting, sales were $360,000. Depreciation Expense is $18,000 on the accrual income statement.

    Diane calculates her cash received from customers to be $305,000. Do you accept her calculation? What written recommendations could you suggest to Diane? How would she calculate the amount of cash paid for advertising if Advertising Expense was listed as $6,000 and the Prepaid Advertising account showed a decrease of $400?

21R-2. Pat Kinne is trying to calculate how much cash is being paid to suppliers of her firm's inventory during 2004. Cost of Goods Sold was reported at $190,500. Pat thinks she needs more data than are provided. From the following facts, could you show Pat how to calculate cash paid to suppliers as well as explain whether this method of computation is a part of the direct method or the indirect method?

	12/31/2004	12/31/2003
Accounts Receivable	$39,000	$37,000
Merchandise Inventory	50,400	53,000
Accounts Payable	28,500	30,700
Notes Payable (used to buy		
Merchandise Inventory)	17,000	15,000
Salaries Payable	11,000	11,200

YOU make the call

Critical Thinking/Ethics Case

21R-3. Risch Company each year prepares an income statement and balance sheet. Tom Martin, the controller, issued a memo to Debbie Kreiger, vice president, that the company should prepare a statement of cash flows. Debbie called the controller and told him that there is no way she will let a cash flows statement be published, that this type of information is for internal purposes only, and that the public has no right to these data. She said that the competition would kill them if they got this information. Do you agree with Debbie's position or with Tom's? Write your recommendation to Dave Risch, the chief executive officer.

Internet Exercises: HP

EX-1. [**www.hp.com/hpinfo/investor/financials/annual/200/financialstatements/ ccscf/htm**].   It is important in the study of accounting and in the preparation of financial statements to understand the uniformity that goes into them. This makes the reading and analysis by knowledgeable users much easier. Imagine how confusing it would be if HP had one way to prepare the statement, Microsoft had another, and Apple had yet another way.

   This uniformity of format and content also is a good indicator that textbooks do approach the "real world" of accounting! The only difference is the complexity of the statements that are published in the "real world."

   Check out their financial reports and look at their statement of cash flows.

EX-2. [**www.hp.com/hpinfo/investor/99financials/annual/20/**]   In a statement of cash flows, the amounts invested in equity securities (stocks) are shown as investing activities. The amounts received from the investments of others into a company's stock is a financing activity.

   In the operating section of the HP statement of cash flows is a category entitled "Other, Net." Do you think the earnings on investments are lumped into operating cash?

CHAPTER 22

Analyzing Financial Statements

You're busy studying for midterms and you have managed to catch a cold all at the same time. You remember the cough syrup your parents always gave you when you were sick; it tasted terrible, but it really helped your symptoms. You decide that some of that cough syrup will help you now. You call McPherson's Pharmacy to see if they sell it. They have the medicine, and you to go to the shop to buy a bottle.

As you approach the front counter of the shop you see Bill McPherson, the owner of the pharmacy, going over what appears to be financial statements at his desk. He is using a calculator and is busy writing down numbers on a scratch pad. You cough uncontrollably as Mr. McPherson is lost in his world of numbers. "Sorry to take you away from your work," you tell Mr. McPherson as you cough again. "No, no, I apologize for not seeing you standing there sooner. I was busy analyzing the numbers my accountant gives me. I've got to think about the numbers before I can relate them to our business. Take care of that cough, okay?" Mr. McPherson replies as he hands you a white bag containing your cough syrup.

Analyzing financial statements is an important aspect to managing any business. It is not merely enough to have financial statements prepared; the statement amounts and their relationship to each other tell owners and investors a great deal about the financial health of a business.

In this chapter we will learn about analyzing financial statements by preparing comparative balance sheets. We will also discuss how to use vertical and horizontal analysis techniques and learn how to calculate four types of ratios commonly used in financial statement analysis.

Learning Objectives

- Preparing comparative balance sheets. (p. 782)
- Using horizontal and vertical analysis techniques. (p. 786)
- Calculating the four different types of ratios: liquidity ratios, asset management ratios, debt management ratios, and profitability ratios. (p. 789)

Financial reports are used by investors, creditors, and management to assist in making business decisions. Typical business decisions might involve such questions as the following:

- *For investors:* How profitable is the company when compared with competing companies? Will dividends be paid? Can the company expand with adequate financing?
- *For creditors:* Does the company have enough cash to pay back periodic interest payments as well as the balance on maturity?
- *For management:* Is the company operating as efficiently as possible? How can we do better?

The four financial statements that we have discussed in earlier chapters—the balance sheet, the income statement, the statement of retained earnings, and the statement of cash flows—help provide the answers to these questions. In this chapter we discuss how to analyze the numbers that appear on these statements.

Numbers on a financial statement may not have meaning in and of themselves; they must be placed in a context. This context may be a comparison with last year's figures, a comparison with other companies in the same industry, or even a comparison with other figures on the same report.

In the following units we look at what the numbers mean as well as how to apply that meaning toward making useful business decisions.

Learning Unit 22-1   Horizontal and Vertical Analysis of Balance Sheets

In the comparative balance sheet, a statement showing data from two or more periods side by side, shown in Figure 22-1, the accountant has placed the current year's balance sheet figures next to figures from the preceding year's balance sheet. The third column shows the amount of increase or decrease in the 20X8 figures over the 20X7 figures, and the last column shows the percentage of decrease or increase of 20X8 over 20X7. This type of analysis, in which each item on the report is compared with the same item in other periods, is called horizontal analysis.

HORIZONTAL ANALYSIS OF THE BALANCE SHEET

Let's perform a sample horizontal analysis on one of the items on Scrupper Supply Company's comparative balance sheet. Look at the entry for Cash in Figure 22-1. In 20X8 it is $3,040 and in 20X7 it was $4,080, for a decrease of $1,040. This decrease is placed in parentheses on the report to show that it is a decrease and not an increase. To figure the percentage that this decrease represents, you use the equation

$$\text{Percent} = \frac{\text{Amount of Change}}{\text{Base (Old Year)}}$$

In this case it would be

$$\frac{\$1,040}{\$4,080} = 25.5\%$$

This type of analysis is called horizontal analysis because in each case you are comparing two figures across columns, from one period to another, rather than comparing figures

Figure 22-1
Comparative
Balance Sheet

SCRUPPER SUPPLY COMPANY COMPARATIVE BALANCE SHEET AS OF DECEMBER 31, 20X8, AND DECEMBER 31, 20X7				
Note: Most recent year is shown first. → Assets	December 31		Amount of Increase or Decrease During 20X8	Percent Increase or Decrease During 20X8
	20X8	20X7		
Current Assets:				
Cash	$ 3 040 00	$ 4 080 00	$ (1 040 00)	(25.5)
Accounts Receivable, Net	20 000 00	16 000 00	4 000 00	25
Merchandise Inventory	24 160 00	26 120 00	(1 960 00)	(7.5)
Prepaid Expenses	800 00	600 00	200 00	33.3
Total Current Assets	$ 48 000 00	$ 46 800 00	$ 1 200 00	2.6
Plant and Equipment:				
Office Equipment, Net	$125 200 00	$116 800 00	$ 8 400 00	7.2
Total Assets	$173 200 00	$163 600 00	$ 9 600 00	5.9
Liabilities				
Current Liabilities:				
Notes Payable	$ 20 960 00	$ 17 320 00	$ 3 640 00	21
Accounts Payable	240 00	280 00	(40 00)	(14.3)
Total Current Liabilities	$ 21 200 00	$ 17 600 00	$ 3 600 00	20.5
Long-Term Liabilities:				
Mortgage Payable	60 000 00	60 000 00	–0–	–0–
Total Liabilities	$ 81 200 00	$ 77 600 00	$ 3 600 00	4.6
Stockholders' Equity				
Common Stock, $10 par value	$ 60 000 00	$ 60 000 00	–0–	–0–
Retained Earnings	32 000 00	26 000 00	6 000 00	23.1
Total Stockholders' Equity	$ 92 000 00	$ 86 000 00	$ 6 000 00	7.0
Total Liabilities and Stockholders' Equity	$173 200 00	$163 600 00	$ 9 600 00	5.9

within a column. Although cash decreased by 25.5%, Scrupper's retained earnings increased by 23.1%. You can see that the percentages in the last column in Figure 22-1 cannot be added down the column to total 100%; each figure relates only to the figures for the same item across the other columns. These percentages provide us with a quick way of monitoring specific accounts.

VERTICAL ANALYSIS OF THE BALANCE SHEET

In vertical analysis, each item on a report is shown as a percent of a total base. The base will be either total assets or total liabilities and stockholders' equity on a balance sheet, and it can be total sales on an income statement. Look at the comparative balance sheet in Figure 22-2. Each item is listed for 20X8, and next to it is a percentage, which is that item's percentage of total assets or total liabilities and stockholders'

Figure 22-2

Vertical Analysis of a Comparative Balance Sheet

SCRUPPER SUPPLY COMPANY COMPARATIVE BALANCE SHEET DECEMBER 31, 20X8, AND DECEMBER 31, 20X7				
Assets	20X8		20X7	
Current Assets:				
Cash	$ 3 0 4 0 00	1.8%	$ 4 0 8 0 00	2.5%
Accounts Receivable, Net	20 0 0 0 00	11.5	16 0 0 0 00	9.8
Merchandise Inventory	24 1 6 0 00	13.9	26 1 2 0 00	16.0
Prepaid Expenses	8 0 0 00	.5	6 0 0 00	.4
Total Current Assets	$ 48 0 0 0 00	27.7%	$46 8 0 0 00	28.7%
Plant and Equipment:				
Office Equipment, Net	125 2 0 0 00	72.3%	116 8 0 0 00	71.4%
Total Assets	$173 2 0 0 00	100.0%	$163 6 0 0 00	100.0%
Liabilities				
Current Liabilities:				
Notes Payable	$ 20 9 6 0 00	12.1%	$ 17 3 2 0 00	10.6%
Accounts Payable	2 4 0 00	.1	2 8 0 00	.2
Total Current Liabilities	$ 21 2 0 0 00	12.2%	$ 17 6 0 0 00	10.8%
Long-Term Liabilities:				
Mortgage Payable	60 0 0 0 00	34.6%	60 0 0 0 00	36.7%
Total Liabilities	$ 81 2 0 0 00	46.9%	$ 77 6 0 0 00	47.5%
Stockholders' Equity				
Common Stock, $10 par value	$ 60 0 0 0 00	34.6%	$ 60 0 0 0 00	36.7%
Retained Earnings	32 0 0 0 00	18.5	26 0 0 0 00	15.9
Total Stockholders' Equity	$ 92 0 0 0 00	53.1%	$ 86 0 0 0 00	52.6%
Total Liabilities and Stockholders' Equity	$173 2 0 0 00	100.0%	$163 6 0 0 00	100.0%*

* Total equals 100% due to rounding.

equity. In the next column each item is listed for the preceding year, 20X7, and then the item is listed as a percentage of total assets or total liabilities and stockholders' equity.

Take the item Cash as an example again. In 20X8, Cash is $3,040 and total assets $173,200; thus Cash represents 1.8% of total assets for this year. In 20X7, Cash was $4,080 and total assets $163,600; thus Cash was 2.5% of total assets in that year.

Note how in this type of analysis you do add down the columns to total 100%, unlike horizontal analysis. Keep in mind that vertical analysis provides us with *another* way of analyzing financial reports that contain data for two or more successive accounting periods.

A shorter version of this report can be seen in Figure 22-3, in which are listed just the percentages of two columns that have been analyzed. Such a report in general is called a common-size statement; this particular one is a common-size comparative balance sheet.

Figure 22-3
Common-Size Comparative
Balance Sheet

SCRUPPER SUPPLY COMPANY
COMMON-SIZE COMPARATIVE BALANCE SHEET
DECEMBER 31, 20X8, AND DECEMBER 31, 20X7

	December 31	
Assets	20X8	20X7
Current Assets:		
Cash	1.8%	2.5%
Accounts Receivable, Net	11.5	9.8
Merchandise Inventory	13.9	16.0
Prepaid Expenses	.5	.4
Total Current Assets	27.7%	28.7%*
Plant and Equipment:		
Office Equipment, Net	72.3%	71.4%
Total Assets	100.0%	100.0%
Liabilities		
Current Liabilities:		
Notes Payable	12.1%	10.6%
Accounts Payable	.1	.2
Total Current Liabilities	12.2%	10.8%
Long-Term Liabilities:		
Mortgage Payable	34.6%	36.7%
Total Liabilities	46.9%	47.5%
Stockholders' Equity		
Common Stock, $10 par value	34.6%	36.7%
Retained Earnings	18.5	15.9
Total Stockholders' Equity	53.1%	52.6%
Total Liabilities and Stockholders' Equity	100.0%	100.0%*

* Total equals 100% due to rounding.

The common-size statement makes it easy to see, for example, that from 20X7 to 20X8 there was a drop in inventory (it went from 16% to 13.9% as a percent of total assets) and an increase in accounts receivable (from 9.8% to 11.5%). The common-size statement is often used to compare companies of different sizes; that way the dollar amounts do not get in the way and it is easier to see each item as a percent of the base in each company.

Learning Unit 22-1 Review

AT THIS POINT you should be able to

- Explain the items making up a comparative balance sheet. (p. 782)
- Compare and contrast vertical and horizontal analysis. (p. 783)
- Explain the advantage of a common-size statement. (p. 784)

SELF-REVIEW QUIZ 22-1

(The blank forms you need are on page 174 of the *Study Guide and Working Papers*.) Complete the comparative balance sheet in Figure 22-4.

Figure 22-4
Comparative Balance Sheet

Assets	December 31		Amount of Increase or Decrease during 20X5	Percent Increase or Decrease during 20X5
	20X5	20X4		
Current Assets:				
Cash	$ 5 0 0 0 00	$ 4 0 0 0 00		
Accounts Receivable, Net	4 0 0 0 00	2 5 0 0 00		
Merchandise Inventory	6 0 0 0 00	5 6 0 0 00		
Prepaid Expenses	2 0 0 0 00	4 0 0 00		
Total Current Assets				
Plant and Equipment:				
Store Equipment, Net	146 0 0 0 00	125 0 0 0 00		
Total Assets				

SOLUTION TO SELF-REVIEW QUIZ 23-1

Figure 22-5
Completed Comparative Balance Sheet

Assets	December 31		Amount of Increase or Decrease during 20X5	Percent Increase or Decrease during 20X5
	20X5	20X4		
Current Assets:				
Cash	$ 5 0 0 0 00	$ 4 0 0 0 00	$ 1 0 0 0 00	25 ($1,000/$4,000)
Accounts Receivable, Net	4 0 0 0 00	2 5 0 0 00	1 5 0 0 00	60
Merchandise Inventory	6 0 0 0 00	5 6 0 0 00	4 0 0 00	7.1
Prepaid Expenses	2 0 0 0 00	4 0 0 00	1 6 0 0 00	400
Total Current Assets	$ 17 0 0 0 00	$ 12 5 0 0 00	$ 4 5 0 0 00	36
Plant and Equipment:				
Store Equipment, Net	146 0 0 0 00	125 0 0 0 00	21 0 0 0 00	16.8
Total Assets	$163 0 0 0 00	$137 5 0 0 00	$ 25 5 0 0 00	18.5

Learning Unit 22-2   Horizontal and Vertical Analysis of Income Statements; Trend Analysis

In the last unit we showed how to perform a horizontal and a vertical analysis of the balance sheet for Scrupper Supply Company. We now show how to perform the same two types of analysis on the income statement for Scrupper Supply Company.

HORIZONTAL ANALYSIS OF THE INCOME STATEMENT

Figure 22-6 shows a comparative income statement for Scrupper Supply Company using horizontal analysis. As in horizontal analysis for the balance sheet, each item on the income statement is compared with the same item for the preceding year; the amount of increase or decrease is recorded and then shown as a percent. For net sales, the amount was $302,000 in 20X7 compared with $317,600 in 20X8; that is an increase of $15,600, which comes out to a 5.2% increase ($15,600/$302,000). The percent increase or decrease is the amount of increase or decrease divided by the figure for the base year of 20X7.

VERTICAL ANALYSIS OF THE INCOME STATEMENT

Figure 22-7 shows the vertical analysis of a comparative income statement for Scrupper Supply Company. In the case of an income statement, the base used is net sales. (On a balance sheet, it is assets or total liabilities and stockholders' equity.) Thus, on the vertical analysis of an income statement, each item is calculated as a percentage of net sales.

From such an analysis of a comparative income statement we can easily see that cost of goods sold decreased (from 64.2 to 62.3%) from 20X7 to 20X8, selling expenses increased (from 18.2 to 20.0%), and profit before tax was up (7.5 to 10.0%). If we had listed just the percentages (each item as percentage of net sales) and left out the dollar amounts, we would have produced a common-size comparative income statement.

TREND ANALYSIS

A special type of horizontal analysis, called trend analysis, deals with the percentage of changes in a certain item over several years. For example, if we want to understand why sales in 20X8 are 118% of 20X5 of Scrupper Supply Company, we have to look at

SCRUPPER SUPPLY COMPANY COMPARATIVE INCOME STATEMENT FOR YEARS ENDED DECEMBER 31, 20X8, AND 20X7				
	December 31		Amount of Increase or Decrease During 20X8	Percent of Increase or Decrease During 20X8
	20X8	20X7		
Net Sales	$317 600 00	$302 000 00	$ 15 600 00	5.2
Cost of Goods Sold	198 000 00	194 000 00	4 000 00	2.1
Gross Profit from Sales	$119 600 00	108 000 00	11 600 00	10.7
Operating Expenses:				
Selling	$ 63 600 00	$ 55 000 00	8 600 00	15.6
General and Administrative	20 000 00	26 000 00	(6 000 00)	(23.1)
Total Operating Expenses	$ 83 600 00	$ 81 000 00	$ 2 600 00	3.2
Operating Income	$ 36 000 00	$ 27 000 00	9 000 00	33.3
Less Interest Expense	4 200 00	4 300 00	(1 00 00)	(2.3)
Income before Taxes	$ 31 800 00	$ 22 700 00	$ 9 100 00	40.1
Income Taxes	15 900 00	11 350 00	4 550 00	40.1
Net Income	$ 15 900 00	$ 11 350 00	$ 4 550 00	40.1

Figure 22-6
Horizontal Analysis of a Comparative Income Statement

Figure 22-7
Vertical Analysis of a
Comparative Income
Statement

	SCRUPPER SUPPLY COMPANY COMPARATIVE INCOME STATEMENT FOR YEARS ENDED DECEMBER 31, 20X8, AND DECEMBER 31, 20X7			
Assets	20X8		20X7	
Net Sales	$317 600 00	100 %	$302 000 00	100 %
Cost of Goods Sold	198 000 00	62.3	194 000 00	64.2
Gross Profit from Sales	$119 600 00	37.7%	108 000 00	35.8%
Operating Expenses:				
Selling	$ 63 600 00	20.0%	$ 55 000 00	18.2 %
General and Administrative	20 000 00	6.3	26 000 00	8.6
Total Operating Expenses	$ 83 600 00	26.3%	$ 81 000 00	26.8 %
Operating Income	$ 36 000 00	11.3%	27 000 00	8.9
Less Interest Expense	4 200 00	1.3	4 300 00	1.4
Income before Taxes	$ 31 800 00	10.0%	$ 22 700 00	7.5 %
Income Taxes	15 900 00	5.0%	11 350 00	3.75
Net Income	$ 15 900 00	5.0%	$ 11 350 00	3.75%

figures for several years. Following are listed figures for sales, cost of goods sold, and gross profit for 20X5 to 20X8:

	20X8	20X7	20X6	20X5
Sales	$317,600	$302,000	$290,000	$270,000
Cost of Goods Sold	198,000	194,000	184,000	142,000
Gross Profit	$119,600	$108,000	$106,000	$128,000

When the trend analysis is developed, a base year is chosen. We will choose 20X5 (the base year is usually the earliest year listed). For each of the following years, each item is stated as a percentage of the amount of the base year. For example, sales in 20X8 as a percentage of the base year equal 118%. The calculation is as follows:

$$\text{Base} \longrightarrow \frac{\$317,600}{\$270,000} = 118\%$$

Thus sales in 20X8 have increased by 18% since 20X5. Over a period of years these percentages are analyzed in relation to a company's history as well as to industry averages that are supplied by companies like Robert Morse Associates and Dun & Bradstreet.

The following is the trend analysis for Scrupper Supply Company for sales, cost of goods sold, and gross profit.

	20X8	20X7	20X6	20X5
Sales	118%	112%	107%	100%
Cost of Goods Sold	139	137	130	100
Gross Profit	93	84	83	100

Note that in 20X6 sales increased 7% from 20X5, but cost of goods sold was up 30%, resulting in gross profit being down 17%. Such analysis can reveal internal problems in Scrupper Supply Company or industrywide problems in a certain year. For example, Scrupper might want to investigate why cost of goods sold has risen 39% in the last three years.

Learning Unit 22-2 Review

AT THIS POINT you should be able to

- Analyze income statement items by vertical and horizontal analysis. (p. 787)
- Prepare a trend analysis. (p. 788)

SELF-REVIEW QUIZ 22-2

(The blank forms you need are on page 174 of the *Study Guide and Working Papers*.)

From the following prepare a trend analysis (round to nearest whole percent using 20X3 as the base year).

	20X6	20X5	20X4	20X3
Sales	$189,000	$165,000	$142,000	$130,000
Cost of Goods Sold	85,000	124,000	99,000	88,000
Gross Profit	$104,000	$ 41,000	$ 43,000	$ 42,000

SOLUTION TO SELF-REVIEW QUIZ 22-2

	20X6	20X5	20X4	20X3
Sales	145%	127%	109%*	100%
Cost of Goods Sold	97	141	113	100
Gross Profit	248	98	102	100

Learning Unit 22-3   Ratio Analysis

Another method for understanding the numbers on the financial statement is the use of ratio analysis. A **ratio** is the relationship of two quantities or numbers, one divided by the other. **Ratio analysis** looks at the relationship of figures on the financial statement. For example, if Broome Company's net income is $10,000 and sales are $100,000, the ratio of sales to net income may be expressed as follows:

a. Net income is $\frac{1}{10}$ or 10% of sales ($10,000 / $100,000 = .1 = $\frac{1}{10}$ = 10%) .

b. Ratio of sales to net income is 10 to 1 or 10 times net income (10:1).

c. For every $10 of sales, Broome Company earns $1.00 of net income.

In this unit we look at a number of different ratios that are used to analyze different aspects of a business. To be meaningful, ratios are often compared with other standards, such as past company ratios or industrywide ratios. The ratios we discuss fall into four general categories:

- **Liquidity ratios** measure a company's ability to meet short-term obligations.
- **Asset management ratios** measure how effectively a company is using its assets.

---

*$142,000/$130,000.

- **Debt management ratios** measure how well a company is using debt versus its equity position.
- **Profitability ratios** measure a company's ability to earn profits.

Let's now do the calculations as well as provide an explanation of each ratio. All calculations for the ratios come from the financial reports of Scrupper Supply Company presented in the last two units.

LIQUIDITY RATIOS

Current Ratio

The **current ratio** expresses the relationship of Scrupper's current assets to its current liabilities, as follows:

20X8

- Total current assets, $48,000.
- Total current liabilities, $21,200.

$$\text{Current Ratio} = \frac{\text{Current Assets}}{\text{Current Liabilities}} = \frac{\$48,000}{\$21,200} = 2.26:1$$

Thus, for each $1 of debt, Scrupper has $2.26 of current assets to meet its short-term debt obligations.

It is important to note that this ratio should be evaluated in terms of (1) the type of business Scrupper is in, (2) the composition of current assets, and (3) the type of credit terms Scrupper extends. Ratios can also be compared from year to year to spot trends in a company or in an industry. For example, in 20X7 the current ratio for Scrupper Supply Company (p. 795) was 2.66 ($46,800/$17,600). This year's current ratio is 2.26, which means that Scrupper's ability to pay off short-term debts has decreased from last year to this year. The ratio is something creditors and investors, as well as the management of Scrupper Corporation, will be interested in.

Depending on the inventory or prepaid expenses, the current assets might not be worth what is shown on the balance sheet. For example, if Scrupper Supply Company has overstocked amounts of inventory, a high current ratio could occur. If Scrupper has a large amount of prepaid insurance or rent, it will not be possible to convert these assets into cash, because they have already been paid for. Thus current ratio is not a very rigorous test of Scrupper's ability to pay its short-term debts. The next ratio we discuss shows that more clearly.

Acid Test Ratio (Quick Ratio)

The **acid test ratio** divides those assets that are most easily converted into cash (called **quick assets**) by the current liabilities. To determine quick assets, we subtract Merchandise Inventory and Prepaid Expenses from current assets (which usually leaves Cash, Notes Receivable, and Accounts Receivable). Thus, the acid test ratio would look like this equation:

$$\text{Acid Test Ratio} = \frac{\text{Current Assets} - \text{Merchandise Inventory} - \text{Prepaid Expenses}}{\text{Current Liabilities}}$$

$$= \frac{\$23,040}{\$21,200} = 1.09:1$$

Thus, for each $1 of short-term debt there is $1.09 of current or quick assets to meet them. This ratio should be at least 1:1 to pass the acid test or be acceptable. If you compare this 1.09:1 ratio with the current ratio figure of 2.26:1, you will see what a difference the inclusion of Merchandise Inventory and Prepaid Expenses makes.

ASSET MANAGEMENT RATIOS

Accounts Receivable Turnover

The accounts receivable turnover ratio shows how many times in a year Scrupper is able to convert its accounts receivables into cash. Usually, the higher the turnover, the better, because a company does not want its money tied up in something that is not yielding any revenue. The turnover rate depends on the length of the credit period Scrupper gives its customers (for Scrupper, all sales are on credit). Scrupper's income statement is on page 788.

$$\text{Accounts Receivable Turnover} = \frac{\text{Net Credit Sales}}{\text{Average Accounts Receivable}}$$

At the end of 20X7 Accounts Receivable was $16,000; at the end of 20X8 it was $20,000. We thus take $18,000 as a figure for *average* accounts receivable.

$$\text{Accounts Receivable Turnover} = \frac{\$317,600}{\$18,000} = 17.6$$

Thus Scrupper is able to turn over its accounts receivable 17.6 times a year. Of course, this turnover rate has to be compared with industry standards and must be seen in the context of how aggressive Scrupper is in its attempts to collect the accounts receivable. The next ratio breaks these steps into the number of days per collection period for accounts receivable.

Average Collection Period

In 20X8, Scrupper Supply Company turns its accounts receivable into cash every 20.7 days:

$$\text{Average Collection Period} = \frac{365 \text{ days}}{\text{Accounts Receivable Turnover}} = \frac{365}{17.6}$$
$$= 20.7$$

If Scrupper's average collection period increases, although its credit terms have not changed, it may necessitate a greater emphasis on collecting outstanding accounts receivable.

Inventory Turnover

The inventory turnover ratio calculates the number of times the *inventory* turns over in one period. Usually, a high inventory turnover means that the company has tied up less cash in inventory. Scrupper calculates its inventory turnover for 20X8 as follows:

$$\text{Inventory Turnover} = \frac{\text{Cost of Goods Sold}}{\text{Average Inventory}}$$
$$= \frac{\$198,000}{\$25,140} = 7.9$$

$$\left(\frac{\$24,160 + \$26,120}{2} \right)$$

A high inventory turnover means that there is less inventory obsolescence. If inventory turnover is slow, it could mean that Scrupper's sales are not keeping pace with the purchasing department.

Asset Turnover

The asset turnover ratio shows whether Scrupper Supply Company is using its assets effectively to generate sales. Scrupper calculates this ratio as follows for 20X8:

$$\text{Asset Turnover} = \frac{\text{Net Sales}}{\text{Total Assets}} = \frac{\$317,600}{\$173,200} = 1.8 \text{ Times}$$

(*Note:* Assets that are not used in producing sales, such as investments, are subtracted from total assets.) In general, the higher the asset turnover rate, the better. A low asset turnover rate compared with industry standards could mean that the company is not generating enough sales for its investment in its assets.

DEBT MANAGEMENT RATIOS

Debt to Total Assets

The debt to total assets ratio indicates the amount of assets that are financed by creditors. A low ratio would be favorable to creditors, because in liquidation they would be more likely to be paid. On the other hand, stockholders like to see a higher ratio so as to attempt to maximize their return. The following is Scrupper's debt to total assets ratio for 20X8:

$$\text{Debt to Total Assets} = \frac{\text{Total Liabilities}}{\text{Total Assets}} = \frac{\$81,200}{\$173,200} = 46.9\%$$

A low percentage (if that were the case for Scrupper) could possibly mean that more financing by bonds and so forth may be in order.

Debt to Stockholders' Equity

The debt to stockholders' equity ratio attempts to measure the risk of the creditors in relation to the risk taken by the stockholders. For example, for 20X8 the ratio of debt to stockholders' equity for Scrupper Supply Company is as follows:

$$\text{Debt to Stockholders' Equity} = \frac{\text{Total Liabilities}}{\text{Stockholders' Equity}}$$

$$= \frac{\$81,200}{\$92,000} = 88.3\%$$

If the industry norm is 60%, Scrupper's ratio could mean that the company has too much debt financing. In general, there is no guideline as to what the ratio of debt to stockholders' equity should be.

Times Interest Earned (Interest Coverage Ratio)

The times interest earned ratio is of interest to creditors because it indicates the degree of risk to creditors from a company defaulting on interest payments. For example, for 20X8 Scrupper Supply Company calculates its times interest earned ratio as follows:

$$\text{Times Interest Earned} = \frac{\text{Income Before Taxes and Interest Expense}}{\text{Interest Expense}}$$

$$= \frac{\$36,000}{\$4,200} = 8.6 \text{ Times}$$

The 8.6 means that the income of Scrupper could be reduced to approximately $\frac{1}{9}$ its current amount (before taxes and interest) and Scrupper would still have income that is equivalent to its interest charges. Thus, the higher the times interest earned ratio is, the more likely it is that the interest payment will be made, even if earnings start to decline.

Now let's turn our attention to calculating ratios involving the profitability of the company.

> Remember: Debt is not bad. It provides a company with flexible financing plans.

PROFITABILITY RATIOS

Gross Profit Rate

The **gross profit rate** reveals how much profit from each sales dollar is generated to cover administrative and selling expenses. For example, for Scrupper Supply Company in 20X8, $.38 of each $1 resulted in profit *before* selling and general administrative expenses. This ratio was calculated as follows:

> If this rate goes down, it could mean price cutting between competitors.

$$\text{Gross Profit Rate} = \frac{\text{Gross Profit}}{\text{Net Sales}} = \frac{\$119,600}{\$317,600} = 37.7\%$$

Return on Sales

In 20X8 Scrupper Supply Company earned 10 cents for each sales dollar. This **return on sales ratio** is calculated as follows:

$$\text{Return on Sales} = \frac{\text{Net Income before Taxes}}{\text{Net Sales}} = \frac{\$31,800}{\$317,600} = 10\%$$

> Some firms use after-tax figures in calculation. When making comparisons, be sure to check which method is used. They are both acceptable.

Stores that have a low inventory turnover (furniture, autos) will have a high return on sales because the goods are priced high. On the other hand, a store that has a high inventory turnover (like a grocery store) will price its goods lower, resulting in a lower return per dollar of sales. If the 10 cents is low compared with its competitors, Scrupper should try to lower its cost and expenses as a percentage of its total sales.

> As with other ratios, an individual company's performance should be compared with industry standards.

Rate of Return on Total Assets

Scrupper Supply Company wishes to measure the amount of profitability it has earned in 20X8 on each dollar it has invested in assets. This figure can be calculated by the rate of **return on total assets ratio,** as follows:

> This ratio shows the earnings power of Scrupper Supply.

$$\text{Rate of Return on Total Assets} = \frac{\text{Net Income before Interest and Taxes}}{\text{Total Assets}}$$

$$= \frac{\$36,000}{\$173,200} = 20.8\%$$

If the 20.8% rate is lower than that of Scrupper's competitors, it could be the result of decreases in return on sales or asset turnover (or a combination of both), which can be seen from the following alternative calculation:

$$\left(\begin{array}{c}\textbf{Return on}\\\textbf{Sales}\end{array}\right) \times \left(\begin{array}{c}\textbf{Total Asset}\\\textbf{Turnover}\end{array}\right) = \left(\begin{array}{c}\textbf{Rate of Return on}\\\textbf{Total Assets}\end{array}\right)$$

$$\frac{\$36,000^*}{\$317,600} \times \frac{\$317,600}{\$173,200} = 20.8\%$$

Rate of Return on Common Stockholders' Equity

The return on common stockholders' equity ratio aids Scrupper in evaluating how well it is earning profit for its common stockholders. The rate of return on common stockholders' equity is calculated as follows:

$$\left(\begin{array}{c}\textbf{Rate of Return}\\\textbf{on Common}\\\textbf{Stockholders'}\\\textbf{Equity}\end{array}\right) = \frac{(\textbf{Net Income Before Taxes}) - (\textbf{Preferred Dividends})}{(\textbf{Common Stockholders' Equity})}$$

$$= \frac{\$31,800 - 0}{\$92,000} = 34.6\%$$

This return has to be compared with that of Scrupper's competitors. If the rate is higher than the industry standards, Scrupper is using debt financing wisely.

Learning Unit 22-3 Review

AT THIS POINT you should be able to

- Define, compare, and contrast the following four types of ratios: liquidity ratios, asset management ratios, debt management ratios, and profitability ratios. (p. 789)
- Explain and show the calculations for the following: current ratio, acid test ratio, accounts receivable turnover, average collection period, inventory turnover, asset turnover, debt to total assets, debt to stockholders' equity, times interest earned, gross profit rate, return on sales, rate of return on total assets, and rate of return on common stockholders' equity. (p. 790)

SELF-REVIEW QUIZ 22-3

(The blank forms you need are on page 176 of the *Study Guide and Working Papers*.)

From Scrupper's balance sheet and income statement, calculate the 13 ratios presented in this unit for 20X7. Assume the following: Accounts Receivable at the end of 20X6 was $18,000; Merchandise Inventory at the end of 20X6 was $26,000.

---

*The $36,000 is before interest and taxes.

SOLUTION TO SELF-REVIEW QUIZ 22-3

1. Current ratio:

$$\frac{\text{Current Assets}}{\text{Current Liabilities}} = \frac{\$46,800}{\$17,600} = 2.66$$

2. Acid test:

$$\frac{\text{Current Assets } - \text{ Merchandise Inv. } - \text{ Prepaid Expenses}}{\text{Current Liabilities}}$$
$$= \frac{\$20,080}{\$17,600} = 1.14$$

3. Accounts receivable turnover:

$$\frac{\text{Net Credit Sales}}{\text{Average Accounts Receivable}} = \frac{\$302,000}{\$17,000} = 17.8$$

4. Average collection period:

$$\frac{365 \text{ Days}}{\text{Accounts Receivable Turnover}} = \frac{365}{17.8} = 20.5 \text{ Days}$$

5. Inventory turnover:

$$\frac{\text{Cost of Goods Sold}}{\text{Average Inventory}} = \frac{\$194,000}{\$26,060} = 7.4$$

6. Asset turnover:

$$\frac{\text{Net Sales}}{\text{Total Assets}} = \frac{\$302,000}{\$163,600} = 1.8 \text{ Times}$$

7. Debt to total assets:

$$\frac{\text{Total Liabilities}}{\text{Total Assets}} = \frac{\$77,600}{\$163,600} = 47.4\%$$

8. Debt to stockholders' equity:

$$\frac{\text{Total Liabilities}}{\text{Stockholders' Equity}} = \frac{\$77,600}{\$86,000} = 90.2\%$$

9. Times interest earned:

$$\frac{\text{Income Before Taxes and Interest Expense}}{\text{Interest Expense}} = \frac{\$27,000}{\$4,300} = 6.3 \text{ Times}$$

10. Gross profit rate:

$$\frac{\text{Gross Profit}}{\text{Net Sales}} = \frac{\$108,000}{\$302,000} = 36\%$$

11. Return on sales:

$$\frac{\text{Net Income Before Taxes}}{\text{Net Sales}} = \frac{\$22,700}{\$302,000} = 7.5\%$$

12. Rate of return on total assets:

$$\frac{\text{Net Income Before Interest and Taxes}}{\text{Total Assets}} = \frac{\$27,000}{\$163,600} = 16.5\%$$

13. Rate of return on common stockholders' equity:

$$\frac{\text{Net Income Before Taxes} - \text{Preferred Dividends}}{\text{Common Stockholders' Equity}} = \frac{\$22,700 - 0}{\$86,000}$$
$$= 26.4\%$$

Chapter Review

Summary of Key Points

Learning Unit 22-1

1. Investors, creditors, and management need to analyze financial statements.
2. Horizontal analysis compares each item in a financial statement with the same item from another period.
3. Vertical analysis compares each item in a financial statement as a percentage of a certain base (usually net sales on an income statement and total assets or total liabilities and stockholders' equity on the balance sheet).
4. A common-size statement shows two or more vertically analyzed columns, usually with the dollar figures deleted and replaced by percentages.

Learning Unit 22-2

1. Vertical and horizontal analysis can be used to analyze income statements as well as balance sheets.
2. In a vertical analysis of an income statement, items are given as a percentage of net sales (as the base).
3. Trend analysis provides a financial picture of how accounts change over the years.

Learning Unit 22-3

1. Ratio analysis shows relationships between two figures, such as ratio of sales to net income or of current assets to current liabilities. These ratios can then be compared with ratios from other years, other companies, or industry standards as a means of analysis.
2. Liquidity ratios measure the ability of a company to meet its short-term obligations.
3. Asset management ratios measure how effectively a company is using its assets.
4. Debt management ratios measure if there is an appropriate mix of debt versus equity financing.
5. Profitability ratios measure the company's ability to earn profits.
6. All ratios should be analyzed in relation to industry standards as well as economic conditions prevailing in the marketplace.

Key Terms

Accounts receivable turnover ratio A ratio that indicates the number of times accounts receivables are converted to cash within a given period and the effectiveness of a company's credit policy.

Acid test ratio A liquidity ratio; those assets that are most easily converted to cash are divided by current liabilities to indicate ability to pay off short-term debt. Also called *quick ratio*.

Asset management ratios Those ratios—accounts receivable turnover, average collection period, inventory turnover, and asset turnover—that measure how effectively a company uses its assets.

Asset turnover ratio A ratio that indicates how efficiently a company uses its assets to generate sales and thus helps measure the overall efficiency of the company.

Average collection period A ratio that shows how quickly moneys owed are received from customers and thereby measures how effectively a company collects its accounts receivables.

Common-size statements Comparative reports in which each item is expressed as a percentage of a base amount without dollar amounts.

Comparative balance sheets Current and past financial reports covering two or more successive periods that place data in single columns side by side.

Current ratio A liquidity ratio; current assets are divided by current liabilities to indicate a company's ability to pay its short-term debt. This ratio does not provide as much certainty as the acid test ratio.

Debt management ratios Those ratios—debt to total assets, debt to stockholders' equity, and times interest earned—that measure a company's mix of debt and equity financing.

Debt to stockholders' equity ratio A ratio in which total liabilities are divided by the amount of stock that is owned to measure the risk creditors run in comparison with stockholders.

Debt to total assets ratio A ratio that shows how much of a company's assets are financed by creditors.

Gross profit rate A profitability ratio that indicates how well net sales cover administrative and selling expenses.

Horizontal analysis Amounts of items compared on the same line of comparative financial reports. Horizontal analysis can also be in the form of a trend analysis.

Inventory turnover ratio An asset management ratio that indicates how quickly inventory moves off the shelf and therefore how well a company sells its product.

Liquidity ratios The two ratios—current ratio and acid test ratio—that measure a company's ability to pay off short-term debts.

Profitability ratios Those ratios—gross profit rate, return on sales, return on total assets, and return on common stockholders' equity—that measure a company's ability to earn a profit.

Quick assets Those assets—mainly cash, accounts receivable, and notes receivable—that can be easily turned into money.

Ratio A relationship of two quantities or numbers, one divided by the other. See the Blueprint on pages 799–800.

Ratio analysis An examination of the relationship between two numbers or sets of numbers on financial reports. Analyses of ratios, especially over time, can give a fairly clear picture of how well a company conducts its business.

Return on common stockholders' equity ratio A profitability ratio that indicates how well a company is managing debt financing to earn a profit for holders of common stock.

Return on sales ratio A profitability ratio that shows the relationship of net income before taxes to net sales and thereby the effectiveness of a company's pricing policy.

Return on total assets ratio A profitability ratio that measures how wisely a company has invested in and managed its assets. This ratio can be arrived at in two ways: (1) net income before interest and taxes divided by total assets and (2) return on sales multiplied by asset turnover.

Times interest earned ratio A debt management ratio indicating the degree of risk to lenders that a company will default on its interest payments. Also called *interest coverage ratio*.

Trend analysis A type of horizontal analysis that deals with percentage changes in items on the financial reports for several years. This analysis uses a base year to calculate the percentage change of each item.

Vertical analysis Comparing items in a financial report by expressing each item as a percentage of a certain base total.

Questions, Mini Exercises, Exercises, and Problems

Discussion Questions

1. Compare and contrast the needs of investors, creditors, and management as they relate to financial statement analysis.

2. Horizontal analysis cannot be presented on comparative financial statements. True or false? Please explain.

3. What is meant by vertical analysis?

4. Common-size statements use horizontal analysis. True or false? Please explain.

5. Why is a base year chosen in trend analysis?

6. How can ratios be expressed?

7. Explain the following types of ratios:

   a. Liquidity.
   b. Asset management.
   c. Debt management.
   d. Profitability.

8. What current asset accounts are deleted in the calculation of the acid test ratio? Why?

9. What could a low accounts receivable turnover rate indicate?

10. Stockouts could easily result if inventory is higher than it should be. True or false? Please explain.

11. What does possible liquidation have to do with the ratio of debt to total assets?

12. Rate of return on assets is affected by return on sales and asset turnover. Agree or disagree.

Mini Exercises

(The blank forms you need are on page 177 of the *Study Guide and Working Papers*.)

Horizontal Analysis Balance Sheet

1. Calculate the amount of increase or decrease as well as the percentage of increase or decrease. (Round to the nearest tenth of a percent.)

	20X8	20X7	AMOUNT	%
a. Accounts Receivable	$600	$500		
b. Accounts Payable	400	600		

Vertical Analysis Balance Sheet

2. Complete a vertical analysis of the assets. (Round to the nearest tenth of a percent as needed.)

a. Cash	$ 500
b. Accounts Receivable	600
c. Merchandise Inventory	900
d. Office Equipment	1,000
Total Assets	$3,000

Blueprint: Ratios

Ratio	Formula	What Calculation Says	Key Points
1. Current ratio	$\dfrac{\text{Current Assets}}{\text{Current Liabilities}}$	For each $1 of current liabilities, how many dollars of current assets are available to meet the current debt.	The ratio should be evaluated based on the type of business credit terms, along with the composition of the current assets.
2. Acid test ratio	$\dfrac{\text{Current Assets} - \text{Merchandise Inventory} - \text{Prepaid Expenses}}{\text{Current Liabilities}}$	For each $1 of current liabilities, how many dollars of cash and near-cash assets are available to meet the current debt.	Because inventory and prepaid expenses may not be easily converted into cash, they are not used in the calculation.
3. Accounts receivable turnover	$\dfrac{\text{Net Credit Sales}}{\text{Average Accounts Receivable}}$	How many times accounts receivable is collected and turned into cash.	Cash sales are not included in the calculation. High turnover is often the best unless the credit terms cause a reduction in sales.

Continued

Blueprint: Ratios (Cont.)

Ratio	Formula	What Calculation Says	Key Points
4. Average collection period	$$\frac{365\ Days}{Accounts\ Receivable\ Turnover}$$	The number of days that it takes a business to collect its accounts receivable.	If the average collection period goes up and the credit terms remain the same, increased collection attempts should be emphasized.
5. Inventory turnover	$$\frac{Cost\ of\ Goods\ Sold}{Average\ Inventory}$$	The time period it takes from the purchase of inventory until its sale.	High turnover indicates low amounts of inventory. Care must be taken if frequent stockouts occur.
6. Asset turnover	$$\frac{Net\ Sales}{Total\ Assets}$$	How effectively the company is using its assets to generate sales.	A low turnover could mean excessive investment in assets or that the sales volume is too low.
7. Debt to total assets	$$\frac{Total\ Liabilities}{Total\ Assets}$$	Amount of assets financed by the creditors.	A low percent reduces creditors' risk if liquidation occurs. The higher the percentage, the more coverage a company is using.
8. Debt to stockholders' equity	$$\frac{Total\ Liabilities}{Stockholders'\ Equity}$$	Amount of debt in relation to total stockholders' equity.	The higher the percentage, the more interest cost results for stockholders.
9. Times interest earned	$$\frac{Income\ Before\ Taxes\ and\ Interest\ Expense}{Interest\ Expense}$$	Degree of risk to creditors if a company defaults on interest payments.	A high times interest earned means a company can have declines in earnings but have the ability to meet its annual interest obligations.
10. Gross profit rate	$$\frac{Gross\ Profit}{Net\ Sales}$$	Profit from a sales dollar that will be used to cover expenses (general, selling, etc)	This rate could drop if stiff competition results in price cuts.
11. Return on sales	$$\frac{Net\ Income\ Before\ Taxes}{Net\ Sales}$$	How much a company earns on each sales dollar.	A company with a low inventory turnover rate usually prices goods for a high return on sales.
12. Rate of return on total assets	$$\frac{Net\ Income\ Before\ Interest\ and\ Taxes}{Total\ Assets}$$	Without looking at how assets are financed, this ratio measures how productively total assets have been used	The rate of return can be increased by controlling costs and expenses as well as increasing asset turnover
13. Rate of return on common stockholders' equity	$$\frac{Net\ Income\ Before\ Taxes - Preferred\ Dividends}{Common\ Stockholders'\ Equity}$$	Measures a company's ability to earn profits for the common stockholder.	If this rate is higher than a return on total assets, the company is using financial leverage to its benefit.

Common-Size Income Statement

3. Prepare a common-size income statement from the following (use net sales as 100%):

Net Sales	$500
Cost of Goods Sold	300
Gross Profit from Sales	200
Operating Expenses	60
Net Income	$140

Trend Analysis

4. Complete a trend analysis from the following data of Blue Corporation using 20X5 as the base year. (Round to nearest percent.)

	20X8	20X7	20X6	20X5
Sales	$800	$700	$600	$500
Gross Profit	600	200	500	300
Net Income	100	60	25	50

Ratios

5. From the data given calculate the following. (Round to the nearest hundredth or hundredth of a percent as needed.)

    a. Current ratio.   **c.** Asset turnover ratio.
    b. Acid test ratio.   **d.** Gross profit rate.

Net Sales	$300,000
Current Assets	42,000
Gross Profit	104,000
Current Liabilities	17,000
Total Assets	149,000
Merchandise Inventory	5,000
Prepaid Expenses	3,000

Exercises

(The blank forms you need are on pages 178–179 of the *Study Guide and Working Papers.*)

22-1. From the following, complete a comparative income statement for Auster Co. for December 31, 20X8, and December 31, 20X9. (Round to the nearest hundredth of a percent as needed.)

Comparative income statement.

	20X9	20X8
Net Sales	$70,000	$40,000
Cost of Goods Sold	30,000	20,000
Operating Expenses	17,000	12,000
Interest Expense	5,000	4,000
Net Income (loss)	18,000	4,000

22-2. From the following, prepare a common-size income statement for Ted Co. by converting the dollar amounts into percentages. (Round to the nearest tenth of a percent.) Use net sales as 100%.

Common-size income statement.

	20X9	20X8
Net Sales	$500,000	$400,000
Cost of Goods Sold	400,000	355,000
Gross Profit from Sales	100,000	45,000
Operating Expenses	60,000	30,000
Net Income	$ 40,000	$ 15,000

Common-size comparative
balance sheet.

22-3. From the following comparative balance sheet of Hoster Co., prepare a common-size comparative balance sheet. (Round all percentages to the nearest tenth of a percent.)

DECEMBER

	20X9	20X8
Current Assets	$ 90,000	$ 50,000
Plant and Equipment	450,000	310,000
Total Assets	$540,000	$360,000
Current Liabilities	$ 10,000	$ 30,000
Long-Term Liabilities	30,000	100,000
Common Stock	300,000	200,000
Retained Earnings	200,000	30,000
Total Liabilities and Stockholders' Equity	$540,000	$360,000

22-4. Complete a trend analysis from the following data of Band Corporation using 20X5 as the base year. (Round to the nearest percent.)

Trend analysis.

	20X8	20X7	20X6	20X5
Sales	$600,000	$500,000	$400,000	$300,000
Gross Profit	166,000	141,000	112,000	124,000
Net Income	48,000	41,000	22,000	38,000

22-5. From the given income statement of Canry Co. as well as from the additional data, compute the following:

Asset turnover, inventory
turnover, accounts receivable turnover.

    a. Asset turnover for 20X7.
    b. Inventory turnover for 20X7.
    c. Accounts receivable turnover for 20X7.

	20X7	20X6
Net Sales	$800,000	$700,000
Cost of Goods Sold	710,000	490,000
Gross Profit	$ 90,000	$210,000
Operating Expenses (includes taxes)	70,000	160,000
Net Income	$ 20,000	$ 50,000

Additional Data

	20X7	20X6
Year-End Accounts Receivable	$ 60,000	$ 50,000
Year-End Inventory	90,000	70,000
All sales were on credit		
Total Assets	230,000	160,000

Group A Problems

(The blank forms you need are on pages 180–189 of the *Study Guide and Working Papers*.)

22A-1. From the comparative balance sheet of Hesler Corporation in Figure 22-8, p. 803 (a) prepare a horizontal analysis of each item for the amount of increase or decrease as well as the percent increase or decrease (to the nearest tenth of a percent); (b) vertically analyze the 20X8 column of the balance sheet (to the nearest tenth of a percent).

Horizontal and vertical
analysis of a balance
sheet.

22A-2. From the comparative income statement of Oper Company in Figure 22-9, (p. 803):

Horizontal, vertical, and
common-size preparation
of an income statement.

    a. Prepare a horizontal analysis with the amount of increase or decrease during 20X8 along with the percent increase or decrease during 20X7 (to the nearest tenth of a percent).

Figure 22-8

Comparative Balance Sheet of Hesler Co.

HESLER CORPORATION COMPARATIVE BALANCE SHEET DECEMBER 31, 20X8, AND DECEMBER 31, 20X7	December 31	
Assets	20X8	20X7
Current Assets:		
Cash	$ 390 00 00	$ 370 00 00
Accounts Receivable, Net	280 00 00	161 00 00
Merchandise Inventory	470 00 00	150 00 00
Prepaid Expenses	160 00 00	130 00 00
Total Current Assets	$ 805 00 00	$ 361 00 00
Plant and Equipment:		
Office Equipment, Net	$115 00 00 00	$110 00 00 00
Total Assets	$195 50 00 00	$146 10 00 00
Liabilities		
Current Liabilities:		
Notes Payable	$ 200 00 00	$ 260 00 00
Accounts Payable	212 00 00	240 00 00
Total Current Liabilities	$ 412 00 00	$ 500 00 00
Long-Term Liabilities:		
Mortgage Payable	$ 500 00 00	$ 400 00 00
Total Liabilities	912 00 00	900 00 00
Stockholders' Equity		
Common Stock, $10 par value	$ 500 00 00	$ 300 00 00
Retained Earnings	543 00 00	261 00 00
Total Stockholders' Equity	$104 30 00 00	$ 561 00 00
Total Liabilities and Stockholders' Equity	$195 50 00 00	$146 10 00 00

Check Figure:
Cash increase 5.4%

Figure 22-9

Comparative Income Statement for Oper Co.

OPER COMPANY COMPARATIVE INCOME STATEMENT FOR YEARS ENDED DECEMBER 31, 20X8, AND DECEMBER 31, 20X7	Years Ended December 31	
	20X8	20X7
Net Sales	$288 00 00 0	$275 00 00 0
Cost of Goods Sold	197 00 00 0	170 00 00 0
Gross Profit from Sales	$ 91 00 00 0	$105 00 00 0
Operating Expenses:		
Selling	$ 50 00 00 0	$ 51 00 00 0
General and Administrative	21 00 00 0	23 00 00 0
Total Operating Expenses	$ 71 00 00 0	$ 74 00 00 0
Operating Income	$ 20 00 00 0	$ 31 00 00 0
Less Interest Expense	6 00 00 0	8 00 00 0
Income before Taxes	14 00 00 0	23 00 00 0
Income Taxes	5 60 00 0	9 20 00 0
Net Income	$ 8 40 00 0	$ 13 80 00 0

AUSTIN COMPANY COMPARATIVE INCOME STATEMENT FOR YEARS ENDED DECEMBER 31, 20X8, AND 20X7		
	Years Ended December 31	
	20X8	20X7
Net Sales	$430 0 0 0 00	$376 0 0 0 00
Cost of Goods Sold	238 0 0 0 00	221 0 0 0 00
Gross Profit from Sales	$192 0 0 0 00	$155 0 0 0 00
Operating Expenses:		
Selling	$ 1204 0 0 00	$110 0 0 0 00
General and Administrative	21 6 0 0 00	22 4 0 0 00
Total Operating Expenses	$ 142 0 0 0 00	$132 4 0 0 00
Operating Income	$ 50 0 0 0 00	$ 226 0 0 00
Less Interest Expense	8 2 0 00	8 6 0 0 00
Income before Taxes	$ 418 0 0 00	$ 14 0 0 0 00
Income Taxes	12 5 4 0 00	5 6 0 0 00
Net Income	$ 29 2 6 0 00	$ 8 4 0 0 00

Figure 22-10 Comparative Income Statement for Austin Co.

Check Figure:
Cost of goods sold
increase 15.9%

Calculating ratios from
financial reports.

Check Figure:
Current ratio   2.22

Ratio calculations, common-size percentages, and
trend analysis.

Check Figure:
20X8   Current assets 72%

Horizontal analysis, vertical
analysis, and common-size
preparation of a balance
sheet.

Check Figure:
Cash   3.3%

Horizontal analysis, vertical analysis, and common
size preparation of an
income statement.

b. Vertically analyze the 20X8 column of the income statement (to the nearest tenth of a percent).

c. Prepare a common-size comparative income statement (to the nearest tenth of a percent).

22A-3. From the income statement and balance sheet of Austin Company (Figs. 22-10 and 22-11, p. 805), compute for 20X8: (a) current ratio, (b) acid test ratio, (c) accounts receivable turnover, (d) average collection period, (e) inventory turnover, (f) asset turnover, (g) debt to total assets, (h) debt to stockholders' equity, (i) times interest earned, (j) gross profit rate, (k) return on sales, (l) return on total assets, and (m) return on common stockholders' equity.

22A-4. From the information about Vargo Corporation in Figures 22-12 (p. 805) and 22-13 (p. 806):

a. For each year calculate its current ratio and acid test ratio.

b. For each year prepare the income statement in common-size percentages. (Round to the nearest tenth of a percent.)

c. Prepare a trend analysis of the balance sheet using 20X6 as the base year (Round to the nearest percent.)

Group B Problems

(The blank forms you need are on pages 180–189 of the *Study Guide and Working Papers.*)

22B-1. From the comparative balance sheet of Hesler Corporation in Figure 22-14 (p. 806):

a. Prepare a horizontal analysis of each item for the amount of increase or decrease as well as the percent increase or decrease (to the nearest tenth of a percent).

b. Vertically analyze the 20X8 column of the balance sheet (to the nearest tenth of a percent).

22B-2. From the comparative income statement of Oper Company in Figure 22-15 (p. 807):

a. Prepare a horizontal analysis with the amount of increase or decrease during 20X8 along with the percent increase or decrease during 20X7 (to the nearest tenth of a percent).

Figure 22-11

Comparative Balance Sheet for Austin Co.

AUSTIN COMPANY
COMPARATIVE BALANCE SHEET
DECEMBER 31, 20X8, AND DECEMBER 31, 20X7

	December 31	
Assets	20X8	20X7
Current Assets:		
Cash	$ 11 000 00	$ 24 440 00
Accounts Receivable, Net	416 00 00	362 00 00
Merchandise Inventory	612 00 00	624 00 00
Prepaid Expenses	5 600 00	3 200 00
Total Current Assets	$119 40 0 00	$126 20 0 00
Plant and Equipment:		
Office Equipment, Net	$ 656 00 00	$63 00 0 00
Total Assets	$185 00 0 00	$189 20 0 00
Liabilities		
Current Liabilities:		
Notes Payable	$ 368 00 00	$ 352 00 00
Accounts Payable	170 00 00	158 00 00
Total Current Liabilities	$ 538 00 00	$ 510 00 00
Long-Term Liabilities:		
Mortgage Payable	$ 396 00 00	$ 300 00 00
Total Liabilities	$ 934 00 00	$ 810 00 00
Stockholders' Equity		
Common Stock, $10 par value	$ 560 00 00	$510 00 00
Retained Earnings	356 00 00	572 00 00
Total Stockholders' Equity	$ 916 00 00	$108 20 0 00
Total Liabilities and Stockholders' Equity	$185 00 0 00	$189 20 0 00

Figure 22-12

Comparative Income Statement for Vargo Corp.

VARGO CORPORATION
COMPARATIVE INCOME STATEMENT
FOR YEARS ENDED DECEMBER 31, 20X8, 20X7, 20X6

	20X8	20X7	20X6
Net Sales	$ 32 000 00	$ 28 000 00	$ 24 400 00
Cost of Goods Sold	23 450 00	196 000	172 000
Gross Profit from Sales	$ 855 000	$ 840 000	$ 720 000
Operating Expenses:			
Selling	$ 460 000	$ 482 000	$ 345 600
General and Administrative	240 000	228 000	248 200
Total Operating Expenses	$ 700 000	$ 710 000	$ 593 800
Operating Income before Taxes	$ 155 000	$ 130 000	$ 126 200
Income Taxes	62 000	52 000	50 400
Net Income	$ 93 000	78 000	$ 75 800

VARGO CORPORATION COMPARATIVE BALANCE SHEET FOR YEARS ENDED DECEMBER 31, 20X8, 20X7, 20X6			
Assets	20X8	20X7	20X6
Current Assets*	$ 2046 00	$ 1782 00	$ 2842 00
Plant and Equipment	10000 00	9000 00	8400 00
Total Assets	$ 12046 00	$ 10782 00	$ 11242 00
Liabilities and Stockholders' Equity			
Current Liabilities	$ 1000 00	$ 960 00	$ 920 00
Common Stock	7000 00	6200 00	6400 00
Retained Earnings	4046 00	3622 00	3922 00
Total Liabilities and Stockholders' Equity	$ 12046 00	$ 10782 00	$ 11242 00

* 20X8 Inventory, $484; 20X7, $310; 20X6, $600.

Figure 22-13 Comparative Balance Sheet for Vargo Corp.

HESLER CORPORATION COMPARATIVE BALANCE SHEET DECEMBER 31, 20X8, AND DECEMBER 31, 20X7	December 31	
Assets	20X8	20X7
Current Assets:		
Cash	$ 16500 00	$ 12300 00
Accounts Receivable, Net	5250 00	4470 00
Merchandise Inventory	6600 00	7800 00
Prepaid Expenses	930 00	570 00
Total Current Assets	$14430 00	$14070 00
Plant and Equipment:		
Office Equipment, Net	$35160 00	$33000 00
Total Assets	$49590 00	$47070 00
Liabilities		
Current Liabilities:		
Notes Payable	$ 7200 00	$ 5400 00
Accounts Payable	4500 00	2850 00
Total Current Liabilities	$11700 00	$ 8250 00
Stockholders' Equity		
Common Stock, $10 par value	$30000 00	$30000 00
Retained Earnings	7890 00	8820 00
Total Stockholders' Equity	$37890 00	$38820 00
Total Liabilities and Stockholders' Equity	$49590 00	$47070 00

Figure 22-14 Comparative Balance Sheet for Hesler Corp.

OPER COMPANY
COMPARATIVE INCOME STATEMENT
FOR YEARS ENDED DECEMBER 31, 20X8, AND DECEMBER 31, 20X7

	Year Ended December 31	
	20X8	20X7
Net Sales	$ 12 2 5 0 00	$ 8 8 8 0 00
Cost of Goods Sold	6 0 5 0 00	4 2 4 0 00
Gross Profit from Sales	6 2 0 0 00	4 6 4 0 00
Operating Expenses:		
Selling	2 7 0 0 00	1 9 2 0 00
General and Administrative	1 0 5 0 00	9 6 0 00
Total Operating Expenses	3 7 5 0 00	2 8 8 0 00
Operating Income	2 4 5 0 00	1 7 6 0 00
Less Interest Expense	2 2 5 00	2 2 0 00
Income before Taxes	2 2 2 5 00	1 5 4 0 00
Income Taxes	8 9 0 00	6 1 6 00
Net Income	$ 1 3 3 5 00	$ 9 2 4 00

Figure 22-15
Comparative Income Statement for Oper Co.

Check Figure:
20X8 Net sales increase 38%

b. Vertically analyze the 20X8 column of the income statement (to the nearest tenth of a percent).

c. Prepare a common-size comparative income statement (to the nearest tenth of a percent).

22B-3. From the income statement and balance sheet of Austin Company (Figs. 22-16 and 22-17, p. 808), compute for 20X8: (a) current ratio, (b) acid test ratio, (c) accounts receivable turnover, (d) average collection period, (e) inventory turnover, (f) asset turnover, (g) debt to total assets, (h) debt to stockholders' equity, (i) times interest earned, (j) gross profit rate, (k) return on sales, (l) return on total assets, and (m) return on stockholders' equity.

Calculating ratios from financial reports.

Check Figure:
Current ratio 2.12

AUSTIN COMPANY
COMPARATIVE INCOME STATEMENT
FOR YEARS ENDED DECEMBER 31, 20X8 AND DECEMBER 31, 20X7

	Years Ended December 31	
	20X8	20X7
Net Sales	$ 99 0 0 0 00	$ 89 2 5 0 00
Cost of Goods Sold	50 5 0 0 00	55 0 0 0 00
Gross Profit from Sales	48 5 0 0 00	34 2 5 0 00
Operating Expenses:		
Selling	27 0 5 0 00	25 9 0 0 00
General and Administrative	3 5 5 0 00	4 0 0 0 00
Total Operating Expenses	30 6 0 0 00	29 9 0 0 00
Operating Income	17 9 0 0 00	4 3 5 0 00
Less Interest Expense	4 5 5 0 00	2 2 5 0 00
Income before Taxes	13 3 5 0 00	2 1 0 0 00
Income Taxes	5 3 4 0 00	8 4 0 00
Net Income	$ 8 0 1 0 00	$ 1 2 6 0 00

Figure 22-16 Comparative Income Statement for Austin Co.

Figure 22-17
Comparative Balance
Sheet for Austin Co.

AUSTIN COMPANY COMPARATIVE BALANCE SHEET DECEMBER 31, 20X8, AND DECEMBER 31, 20X7		
	December 31	
Assets	20X8	20X7
Current Assets:		
Cash	$ 3 4 0 0 00	$ 5 4 0 0 00
Accounts Receivable, Net	9 7 5 0 00	8 7 0 0 00
Merchandise Inventory	14 5 0 0 00	14 9 0 0 00
Prepaid Expenses	1 2 0 0 00	8 5 0 00
Total Current Assets	$ 28 8 5 0 00	$29 8 5 0 00
Plant and Equipment:		
Office Equipment, Net	$ 14 9 0 0 00	$ 11 0 0 0 00
Total Assets	$ 43 7 5 0 00	$40 8 5 0 00
Liabilities		
Current Liabilities:		
Notes Payable	$ 9 7 5 0 00	$ 9 0 5 0 00
Accounts Payable	3 8 5 0 00	3 4 0 0 00
Total Current Liabilities	$ 13 6 0 0 00	$ 12 4 5 0 00
Long-Term Liabilities:		
Mortgage Payable	$ 10 0 0 0 00	$ 7 5 0 0 00
Total Liabilities	$ 23 6 0 0 00	$19 9 5 0 00
Stockholders' Equity		
Common Stock, $10 par value	$ 14 0 5 0 00	$12 0 0 0 00
Retained Earnings	6 1 0 0 00	8 9 0 0 00
Total Stockholders' Equity	$ 20 1 5 0 00	$20 9 0 0 00
Total Liabilities and Stockholders' Equity	$ 43 7 5 0 00	$40 8 5 0 00

> Ratio calculations, common-size percentages, trend analysis.

22B-4. From the information about Vargo Corporation in Figures 22-18 and 22-19 (p. 809):

    a. For each year calculate its current and acid test ratios.

    b. For each year prepare the income statement in common-size percentages. (Round to the nearest tenth of a percent.)

    c. Prepare a trend analysis of the balance sheet using 20X6 as the base year. (Round to the nearest percent.)

> Check Figure:
> 20X8   Current assets
> 136%

Real-World Applications

22R-1. You have been hired as a consultant to determine which of the two following companies is in overall better shape. From the accompanying information, prepare a schedule of ratio calculations that can be derived from the facts along with your recommendations. Both companies are in the same industry.

VARGO CORPORATION
COMPARATIVE INCOME STATEMENT
FOR YEARS ENDED DECEMBER 31, 20X8, 20X7, 20X6,

	20X8	20X7	20X6
Net Sales	$55,500.00	$50,400.00	$38,700.00
Cost of Goods Sold	40,200.00	37,200.00	23,700.00
Gross Profit from Sales	$15,300.00	$13,200.00	$15,000.00
Operating Expenses:			
Selling	$7,200.00	$4,800.00	$5,400.00
General and Administrative	5,700.00	2,730.00	3,750.00
Total Operating Expenses	$12,900.00	$7,530.00	$9,150.00
Operating Income before Taxes	2,400.00	5,670.00	5,850.00
Income Taxes	960.00	2,268.00	2,340.00
Net Income	$1,440.00	$3,402.00	$3,510.00

Figure 22-18
Comparative Income Statement for Vargo Corp.

VARGO CORPORATION
COMPARATIVE BALANCE SHEET
DECEMBER 31, 20X8, 20X7, 20X6

Assets	20X8	20X7	20X6
Current Assets*	$6,720.00	$5,550.00	$4,950.00
Plant and Equipment	18,000.00	12,000.00	10,500.00
Total Assets	$24,720.00	$17,550.00	$15,450.00
Liabilities and Stockholders' Equity			
Current Liabilities	$2,400.00	$1,800.00	$1,560.00
Common Stock	11,700.00	10,800.00	7,500.00
Retained Earnings	10,620.00	4,950.00	6,390.00
Total Liabilities and Stockholders' Equity	$24,720.00	$17,550.00	$15,450.00

* Inventory: 20X8, $1,350; 20X7, $1,800; 20X6, $1,200.

Figure 22-19
Comparative Balance Sheet for Vargo Corp.

	Joyne Co.	Smokey Co.
Cash	$ 17,000	$ 28,000
Accounts Receivable, Net	18,000	55,000
Inventory	80,000	96,000
Plant and Equipment, Net	90,000	170,000
	$205,000	$349,000
Current Liabilities	$ 58,000	$ 89,000
Mortgage Payable	40,000	60,000
Common Stock	79,000	175,000
Retained Earnings	28,000	25,000
	$205,000	$349,000
Sales (all credit)	$230,000	$380,000
Cost of Goods Sold	160,000	275,000
Interest Expense	8,000	12,000
Income Taxes	10,000	16,000
Net Income	24,000	40,000

22R-2. The bookkeeper of Blue Co. is trying to determine (a) the amount of average inventory, (b) the accounts receivable average balance, and (c) the balance of cash from the following information:

Prepaid Rent	$16,000
Accounts Receivable Turnover	9 times
Cost of Goods Sold	$270,000
Inventory Turnover	27
Current Liabilities	$90,000
Credit Sales	$270,000

The bookkeeper's assistant thinks there is not enough information available to complete the calculations. Accept or reject the assistant's remarks. Please provide a written response.

YOU make the call

Critical Thinking/Ethical Case

22R-3. Jill Land, president of Loon Co., is happy to report to the company's stockholders that the company has increased its cash position by 20% from last year. Its average collection period has decreased by 12 days. Jill knows some customers are unhappy about the new credit terms but believes that you cannot please everyone; that's part of business. Do you think Loon Co. is on the right track? One shareholder is quite upset to learn that the company is holding so much cash. Do you agree with the company's belief that increasing the cash position by 20% is sound? You make the call. Write down your recommendation to Jill.

Internet Exercises: Delta

EX-1. [www.delta.com/inside/investors/annual_reports/2000_annual/ar_frameset.html] Welcome back to Delta Airlines' Web site for another look at its financial statements. For this exercise make a "common-size" balance sheet using the numbers in the "2000" column. If not available, use 2001. The key to this is knowing that in a common-size balance the "100%" figure is Total Assets.

EX-2. [www.delta.com/inside/investors/annual_reports/2000_annual/ar_frameset.html] Calculate the following ratios using the 2000 financial statements:

1. Current Ratio.
2. Accounts Receivable Turnover.
3. Asset Turnover.
4. Debt to Total Assets.
5. Debt to Stockholders' Equity.

SUBWAY Case

"AND THE WINNER IS . . ."

"And the Number 1 for sales this month is . . ." Carrie Zabrinsky smiled broadly and paused to add a little suspense to the announcement. As a Development Agent for Subway, she had decided to give the franchisees in her region a little push by spurring some healthy rivalry among them. Every month for the next year she was holding a contest to see which franchisee had the highest sales.

". . . Stan Hernandez for his Subway of Los Palmos!" announced Carrie. "Stan, come up here and get your award." Stan bounded up to the stage, still in a state of shock. Carrie handed him a handsome framed certificate as well as a travel voucher for two nights—all expenses paid—in the Sunset Sands resort.

"Wow!" was all Stan could say at first, but he quickly gained his composure and even delivered a short speech. Stan thanked Subway for providing a wonderful business concept and product. He thanked his wonderful, hardworking employees, his junior partner Ron and also his accountant Lila. "While it's true that we rang up the sales, Lila Hernandez crunched those numbers," Stan told Carrie, "and gave me a crash course in accounting!"

Carrie's new contest required the franchisees in her region to send her a lot of accounting information—information that not only enabled her to see which restaurant had the highest sales, but also allowed her to do some troubleshooting. Stan emails a monthly management report to Carrie, consisting of an Income Statement. He does the balance sheet quarterly, and Carrie then does a horizontal analysis of Stan's balance sheet, comparing each line to its budget and to last year. That tells her if Stan is on target and points up any weak areas in the business. Then she does a vertical analysis of Stan's Balance Sheet to arrive at percents of the totals.

Carrie compares Stan's results (in percentages) with each of the other restaurants in his region, using a common-size statement. This exercise is useful because, although each shop is different in size, a common-size statement deals only in percentages. This comparison quickly points up exceptions, which may be good or bad. In either case, Carrie Zabrinsky then has the clues she needs to discover a strength other shops can copy or a weakness Stan can fix.

"So, Stan the man," says Ron Ebbers after the award ceremony, "Are you going to take me to the Sunset Sands to celebrate? As your junior partner, I feel I should share in your success."

"We'll just wait until our c-store is number 1 in sales!" said Stan. "In the meantime, I think it's the perfect time for Ana and I to take our first trip together." Stan Hernandez had a lot to celebrate—a budding love relationship, a thriving business, and a renewed friendship with Ron that had turned into a promising partnership. "In fact," said Stan, getting out his cell phone, "I'm going to call Ana right now to tell her the good news!"

Discussion Questions

1. Why does the Development Agent use a common-size statement to compare restaurants in her region?
2. Why does she use both horizontal and vertical analyses of the Balance Sheets for the restaurants in her region?

CHAPTER 23

The Voucher System

You received a rebate in the mail yesterday. After purchasing 25 floppy disks, you mailed in your sales receipt and a form to receive a five-dollar rebate. On the computer-printed check was printed "Voucher # 00385452." You thought a check number would have been printed on the check. Why did the company use a voucher number rather than a check number? What is a voucher anyway?

Companies may use a voucher system to keep tighter control over cash payments. A voucher system is one way to help ensure that cash payments are properly authorized and validated before checks are issued. When a company uses a voucher system, no check can be written unless an authorized person within the company has approved a written form known as a voucher.

In this chapter we will discuss the voucher system. We will learn how to prepare vouchers, record them in a voucher register, and record the payment of vouchers in a check register. We will also look at handling nonroutine transactions using a voucher system. And we will learn how to record invoices using the net amount method. After completing this chapter you will know how voucher systems work and understand why a company may use such a system when issuing rebate checks to its customers.

Learning Objectives

- Preparing vouchers, recording them in a voucher register, and recording payment of vouchers in a check register. (p. 815)

- Recording revised vouchers to handle nonroutine transactions in a voucher system. (p. 821)

- Using the net amount method to record invoices and payment. (p. 822)

In small companies owners may be able to do or look at every step of their business themselves. As such companies grow larger and as the sheer number of business transactions multiplies, however, that becomes impossible. How, then, do owners or managers keep control over the activities of a company? If they don't sign every check themselves or approve every purchase themselves, how do they know if money is being spent in approved ways, or even where it's going? Some rules have to be formulated for employees to impose order; such rules and procedures are referred to as *internal control*. One type of system used to implement this internal control is called a *voucher system*.

In Chapter 10 we discussed the steps taken when a company purchases goods. You might take a moment to look back at those pages (pp. 391–392), because we use these steps in this chapter to explain how a voucher system works. The steps include the following:

1. Preparing a purchase requisition and getting it authorized.
2. Preparing a purchase order, which specifies details such as company, number of items, and so forth, and getting it authorized.
3. The company receiving the purchase order preparing a sales invoice specifying number and type of goods and price.
4. The company receiving the goods inspecting the shipment, checking it against the purchase order and the sales invoice, and completing a receiving report.
5. Someone in the accounting department verifying the numbers (checks the purchase order, the invoice, and the receiving report to make sure the numbers are in agreement and no steps are left out). This person then issues a voucher for payment, which is authorized.
6. Issuing payment in the form of a check.

These steps show internal control, in the form of a voucher system, at work. Other procedures discussed in other chapters of this text also are part of internal control, including banking procedures and petty cash and change funds.

What is a voucher? A **voucher** (see the sample shown later) is a written authorization form that is used for every cash payment the company makes. It contains all the details of the transaction in question along with the signatures of appropriate employees as authorization. A **voucher system,** then, is a system in which no payment is made without an approved voucher.

CHARACTERISTICS OF A VOUCHER SYSTEM

A number of principles of internal control are embedded in the voucher system. Perhaps the most important is the separation of duties. In a voucher system no one person in a company is in control of all transactions or of everything to do with one transaction. The person who approves purchase and payment is different from the person who makes the accounting entries related to these functions, and that person is different from the person who signs and mails the checks. In this way no one can do anything without other people supplying approval.

A second important principle, perhaps the backbone of a voucher system, is the rule that no purchases are made without an approved voucher backed up by documentation. There are several layers of documentation and authorization here, beginning with a purchase requisition, moving on to a purchase order, and ending up with actual payment by a check. At every layer and step the appropriate documents are presented, checked, and approved before going further.

There is a lot of cross-referencing and cross-checking in a voucher system. Every document is numbered; transactions are recorded in different places by different people and backed up by reference to numbers of other documents. In this way it is always possible to trace one transaction all the way through the system. After a purchase is made and paid for, the documents and forms are kept on file for a certain period of time to allow such checks to be made.

In the next two learning units we show how a voucher system works in a specific company and then how certain transactions are handled that don't fit into the voucher system. The specific company we use is Jones Company.

Learning Unit 23-1   Handling Transactions in a Voucher System

Jones Company is a medium-sized merchandise business that believes in strong internal control practices and procedures. It uses the voucher system to control all cash payments except payments out of the petty cash fund. Company rules state that all invoices must be compared with purchase requisitions, purchase orders, and receiving reports before payment and that all payments must, of course, be supported by appropriate documents and authorizations.

Jones Company's voucher system is made up of the following elements:

1. Vouchers.
2. Voucher register.
3. Unpaid voucher file.
4. Check register.
5. Paid voucher file.

To see this system in action, let's follow one transaction all the way through. To begin with, Jones Company decides to buy $4,500 worth of merchandise from Beam Enterprise. The purchase order is shown in Fig. 23-1. When the merchandise is received,

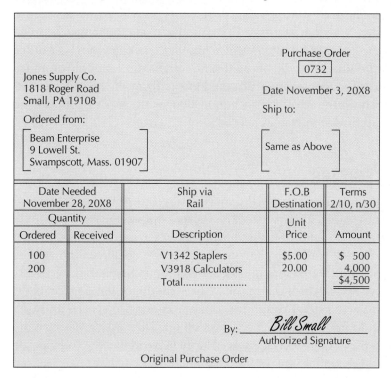

Figure 23-1
Purchase Order

Figure 23-2
Invoice

Invoice
Invoice Number: B20
Date: November 28, 20X8

Beam Enterprise
9 Lowell St.
Swampscott, Mass. 01907

Sold to: Jones Supply Co.
1818 Roger Road
Small, PA 19108

Ship to: Same

Your Purchase Order Number 0732	Invoice Number B20	Salesman Munroe	Terms 2/10, n/30	Shipped via: Rail (PPD) F.O.B. Destination

Quantity		Description	Unit Price	Amount
Ordered	Received			
100	100	V1342 Staplers	$5.00	$ 500
200	200	V3918 Calculators	20.00	4,000
		Total......................		$4,500

Original Invoice

along with an invoice (Fig. 23-2), a special serially numbered form called a *voucher* is prepared (Fig. 23-3).

THE VOUCHER

In preparing the voucher the invoice from Beam Enterprise is compared with the purchase requisition, purchase order, and receiving report to be sure that it matches the specific requirements and prices of the order. For example, the information in Figure 23-1, the purchase order, does indeed match the information on the invoice shown in Figure 23-2. The original supporting documents (purchase orders, etc.) are attached to the voucher. Note that there is a front and back side to the voucher. The front side indicates the voucher number, invoice number and date, purchase order number, to whom the amount will be paid, and verification steps. For Jones Company, all supporting documents are attached to the front of the voucher and folded. The back side shows the account distribution along with space to complete the payment summary and final approvals as needed.

THE VOUCHER REGISTER

Using the approved account distributions, the voucher is recorded in a special journal called the voucher register (Fig. 23-4, p. 818). This journal replaces the purchases journal. Note that the vouchers are entered in the voucher register in numerical order at the time the liability is *incurred*. For Jones, the Vouchers Payable credit column records the amount due on each voucher (before any discounts) for purchases of merchandise, services, or other assets. Special debit columns have been set up for Jones's accountant based on how often they're used. The sundry column, as in other special journals, records amounts that do not have special columns set up. The posting rules are the same as we covered in the past for special journals. Keep in mind that the columns for date of payment and check number are *not* filled in until *time of payment*.

Figure 23-3
Voucher, front

```
                        VOUCHER

Jones Supply Co.              Voucher No. 23
1818 Roger Road
Small, PA 19108              Date check needed:
                             December 5, 20X8
Invoice
Number and Date:            Payable to:   Beam Enterprise
B20 November 28, 20X8                     9 Lowell Street
                                          Swampscott, MA 01907
Purchase
Order Number: 0732           Invoice Amount       $4,500
                             Less: Discount            90
                             Net Amount Due       $4,410

Verification Steps:          Approved by:       Date

(1) Invoice compared with purchase
    requisition and purchase order      JS         12/1/X8
(2) Invoice compared with receiving
    report                              BM         12/1/X8
(3) Extensions and footings done        BJ         12/1/X8
(4) Approved for payment                PS         12/3/X8
```

```
   Account Distributory       Voucher No. 23

Debit          Amount        Date check needed: 12/5/X8

Purchases      $4,500        Payable to:
Supplies
Salaries Expense             Beam Enterprise
Repair Expense               9 Lowell Street
Sundry                       Swampscot, MA 01907

                             Summary of Voucher

                             Invoice Amount     $4,500
                             Less: Discount          90
                             Net Amount Due     $4,410

                             Payment Summary of Voucher

                             Date: 12/5/X8
                             Amount: $4,410
                             Check No.: 55

                             Recorded in Voucher
Credit Vouchers              Register by: ___PM___
Payable for Total  $4,500

Distribution approved by: ___JS___
(Accounting Department)
```

When a balance sheet is prepared, the term *Accounts Payable* is used instead of *Vouchers Payable*, because users of financial reports are more used to that wording.

UNPAID FILE VOUCHER

Each voucher, once it has been recorded in the voucher register, is filed in an **unpaid voucher file** according to due date. This file is often referred to as a **tickler file.** Although the amount owed Beam is $4,500, there is a $90 cash discount available if

> The voucher remains in the unpaid file until paid.

VOUCHER REGISTER

Date		Voucher Number	Payable to	Date of Payment	Check Number	Voucher Payable Cr.	Purchases Dr.	Supplies Dr.	Repair Expense Dr.	Sundry Accounts Account	Sundry Accounts PR	Sundry Accounts Dr.	Sundry Accounts Cr.
20X8 Dec.	2	22	Petty Cash	12/4	53	50 00				Petty Cash	114	50 00	
	3	23	Beam Enterprise	12/5	55	4500 00	4500 00						
	3	24	Ron Co.	12/4	54	425 00		425 00					
	7	25	Rose Co.	12/9	56	28 00			28 00				
	9	26	Blew Co.	12/30	67	1000 00				Equip.	121	1000 00	
	15	27	Security Bank	12/27	58	5150 00				Note Payable	211	5000 00	
										Int. Exp.	531	150 00	
	28	42	Internal Revenue Service	12/28	65	900 00				FICA Tax* Payable	212	250 00	
										FIT Tax Payable	216	650 00	
	9	43	Payroll	12/29	66	4000 00				Salary and Wages Payable	210	4000 00	
						20665 00	7950 00	600 00	1015 00			11100 00	
						(212)	(513)	(116)	(562)			(X)	

* Includes Medicare and Social Security.

Figure 23-4 Voucher Register

Beam receives payment by December 8, 20X8. Thus the voucher is filed on a *December 5 due date,* anticipating that it will take three days in the mail for Beam to receive it.

In the voucher system, the accounts payable ledger is not used; for Jones, the unpaid file is its subsidiary ledger for the controlling account Vouchers Payable in the general ledger. At the end of the month, Jones Company will prepare a schedule of vouchers payable, just as we discussed in Chapter 7 for the schedule of accounts payable, with the total of all unpaid vouchers being equal to the ending balance in Vouchers Payable in the general ledger.

> Payment requires notation in three places:
> 1. Check register.
> 2. Voucher register payment column.
> 3. Back of voucher.

CHECK REGISTER

On December 5, Jones Company records the payment to Beam in a special journal called a **check register.** The check register replaces the cash payments journal in recording the payment of vouchers payable. Note in Figure 23-5 that the Vouchers Payable account is debited for $4,500, whereas Purchases Discount is credited for $90 and Cash in Bank for $4,410. The date of payment, along with check number, is updated in the voucher register. Posting of the check register follows the same rules as other special journals. (*Note:* Once the voucher has been paid, it should be marked "Paid" so as to avoid duplication of payments.)

PAID VOUCHER FILE

After Beam's voucher is paid, it is filed by Jones in a **paid voucher file.** The voucher is filed in sequential order according to the voucher numbers. Some companies will file the voucher alphabetically based on the creditor's name. Jones keeps all paid vouchers for six years. This amount of time will vary from company to company.

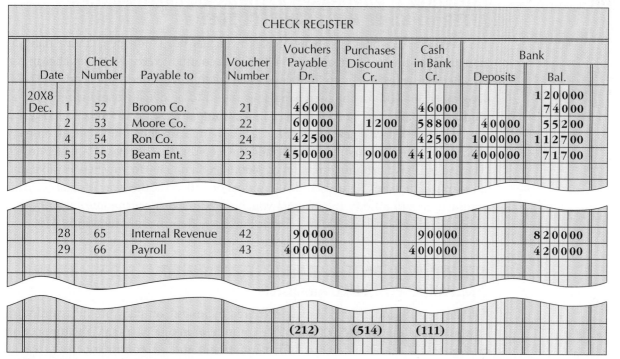

CHECK REGISTER									
Date	Check Number	Payable to	Voucher Number	Vouchers Payable Dr.	Purchases Discount Cr.	Cash in Bank Cr.	Bank		
							Deposits	Bal.	
20X8 Dec. 1	52	Broom Co.	21	4 6 0 00		4 6 0 00		1 2 0 0 00 7 4 0 00	
2	53	Moore Co.	22	6 0 0 00	1 2 00	5 8 8 00	4 0 0 00	5 5 2 00	
4	54	Ron Co.	24	4 2 5 00		4 2 5 00	1 0 0 0 00	1 1 2 7 00	
5	55	Beam Ent.	23	4 5 0 0 00	9 0 00	4 4 1 0 00	4 0 0 0 00	7 1 7 00	
28	65	Internal Revenue	42	9 0 0 00		9 0 0 00		8 2 0 0 00	
29	66	Payroll	43	4 0 0 0 00		4 0 0 0 00		4 2 0 0 00	
				(212)	(514)	(111)			

Figure 23-5 Check Register

Learning Unit 23-1 Review

AT THIS POINT you should be able to

- List and define the components of a voucher system. (p. 814)
- Explain the steps to record and pay a voucher. (p. 815)
- Discuss why the unpaid file voucher is recorded by due dates. (p. 817)

SELF-REVIEW QUIZ 23-1

(The blank forms you need are on page 194 of the *Study Guide and Working Papers.*)
Respond true or false to the following:

1. All companies use the same voucher system.
2. Supporting documents are attached to a voucher.
3. The account distribution is used to record the voucher in the voucher register.
4. Vouchers are recorded in the voucher register in alphabetical order.
5. A schedule of vouchers payable can be prepared from the unpaid voucher file at the end of the month.

SOLUTIONS TO SELF-REVIEW QUIZ 23-1

1. False   2. True   3. True   4. False   5. True

Learning Unit 23-2   Recording Additional Transactions in Jones's Voucher System

SITUATION 1: PURCHASES RETURNS AND ALLOWANCES AFTER VOUCHER HAS BEEN RECORDED

On December 26, Jones Company prepared voucher no. 32 for merchandise that was bought from Booth Company for $400. The accountant records the voucher in the voucher register as a debit to Purchases and a credit to Vouchers Payable for $400. On December 28, $100 of the merchandise is found to be defective and is returned to Booth Company. The procedure that Jones Company uses is to cancel the original voucher and prepare a new voucher for $300. Figure 23-6 shows how Jones Company records the cancellation of voucher 32 and the recording of the revised voucher no. 39. The end result is a debit to Purchases of $400, a credit of $300 to Vouchers Payable, and a credit to Purchases Returns and Allowances of $100. Another way of handling this transaction is to modify the original voucher and make a *general journal* entry that debits Vouchers Payable $100 and credits Purchases Returns and Allowances $100.

SITUATION 2: PARTIAL PAYMENTS PLANNED AFTER VOUCHER PREPARED FOR FULL AMOUNT

On January 18, voucher no. 64 was prepared by Jones Company on the assumption it would pay Ron Co. $15,000 for office equipment in one payment. The top section of Figure 23-7 shows a debit to Office Equipment and a credit to Vouchers Payable for $15,000.

VOUCHER REGISTER

Date	Voucher Number	Payable to	Date of Payment	Check Number	Voucher Payable Cr.	Purchases Dr.	Account	PR	Sundry Accounts Dr.	Cr.
Dec. 18	32	Booth Co.	Canceled Voucher	See No. 39	40000	40000				
28	39	Booth Co.			30000		Voucher Payable	212	40000	
							Purchases Returns and Allowances	515		10000

Figure 23-6 Voucher Register with Purchases, Returns, and Allowances

VOUCHER REGISTER

Date	Voucher Number	Payable to	Date of Payment	Check Number	Vouchers Payable Cr.	Account	PR	Sundry Accounts Dr.	Cr.
Jan. 18	64	Ron Co.	Canceled 1/29	V69-71	15000000	Office Equip.	121	15000000	
29	69	Ron Co.			5000000	Vouchers Payable	212	5000000	
29	70	Ron Co.			5000000	Vouchers Payable	212	5000000	
29	71	Ron Co.			5000000	Vouchers Payable	212	5000000	

Figure 23-7 Voucher Register with Partial Payments

Owing to a cash shortage, on January 29 it was decided by Jones Company to pay Ron Company in three equal installments on February 8, 19, and 21. Thus, the original voucher on January 18 is canceled and a *new* voucher is prepared for each installment. Note in Figure 23-7 how the old voucher is canceled and the new vouchers are prepared. In the date of payment column, the January 18 line shows the cancellation along with the new date recording the new voucher (1/29). The check number column indicates which new vouchers are replacing the canceled voucher. Note in the sundry column how Vouchers Payable is debited three times to cancel the original voucher.

RECORDING PURCHASES AT NET AMOUNT

> The net approach means that a Purchases Discount account is not needed.

In this chapter Jones Company recorded all invoices at the gross amount, although the check register did show a Purchases Discount column. Many companies, on the other hand, record purchases at net. When a discount is missed using the net approach, a title called Discount Lost is shown in the payment column of the voucher register. Let's look at journal entries showing the same purchase recorded at gross and at net.

(A) Mill Company buys merchandise on account from Ryan Company for $8,000. Terms are 2/10, n/30. Mill Company issues voucher no. 299.

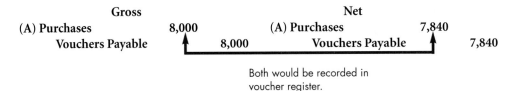

Gross			Net		
(A) Purchases	8,000		(A) Purchases	7,840	
Vouchers Payable		8,000	Vouchers Payable		7,840

Both would be recorded in voucher register.

If Discount Is Taken on Time

(B) Mill Company issues check no. 531 in payment of voucher no. 299 less the cash discount.

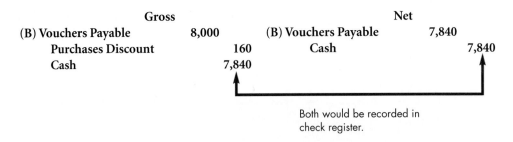

Gross			Net		
(B) Vouchers Payable	8,000		(B) Vouchers Payable	7,840	
Purchases Discount		160	Cash		7,840
Cash		7,840			

Both would be recorded in check register.

If Discount Is Missed

(C) Mill Company issues check no. 531 in payment of voucher no. 299. The discount date has passed.

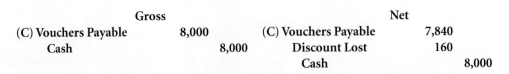

Gross			Net		
(C) Vouchers Payable	8,000		(C) Vouchers Payable	7,840	
Cash		8,000	Discount Lost	160	
			Cash		8,000

Note that when the discount is missed in the net method, the Purchases Discount Lost account is used. (The end-of-chapter problems and exercises record all vouchers at gross unless otherwise stated.)

Learning Unit 23-2 Review

AT THIS POINT you should be able to

- Record transactions in a voucher system involving purchases returns and allowances and/or partial payments. (p. 820)
- Explain how the Discount Lost account could be used in a voucher system. (p. 822)

SELF-REVIEW QUIZ 23-2

(The blank forms you need are on page 195 of the *Study Guide and Working Papers.*)
Record the following entries in the voucher register for Joe Corporation:

20X8

Oct.   10   Prepared voucher no. 82 for purchase of merchandise for $3,000 from Rose Co.

Oct.   15   Returned $400 of the merchandise purchased from Rose Co. on October 10 due to poor workmanship. Joe Corp. canceled voucher no. 82 and replaced it with voucher no. 95.

SOLUTION TO SELF-REVIEW QUIZ 23-2

VOUCHER REGISTER

Date	Voucher Number	Payable to	Date of Payment	Check Number	Voucher Payable Cr.	Purchases Dr.	Account	Sundry Accounts		
								PR	Dr.	Cr.
20X8 Oct. 10	82	Rose Co.	Canceled Voucher	See No. 95	3 00 0 00	3 00 0 00				
15	95	Rose Co.			2 60 0 00		Vouchers Payable		3 00 0 00	
							Purchases Returns and Allowances			4 00 00

Figure 23-8 Voucher Register

Chapter Review

Summary of Key Points

Learning Unit 23-1

1. In a voucher system, no payment is made without an approved form called a *voucher*. The voucher system consists of these elements: vouchers, voucher register, unpaid voucher file, check register, and paid voucher file.
2. Supporting documents are attached to a voucher.
3. When approved, the distribution of accounts is the basis for the entry into the voucher register.
4. The voucher register, a special journal, replaces the purchases journal.
5. Cash discounts can be taken advantage of by filing vouchers in an unpaid voucher file (tickler file) by due dates.
6. A schedule of vouchers payable can be prepared at the end of the month. The accounts payable subsidiary ledger in a voucher system is eliminated.
7. The check register is a special journal that replaces the cash payments journal.

Learning Unit 23-2

1. After a voucher is recorded, a purchases return can be recorded by canceling the original voucher and debiting Vouchers Payable and crediting Vouchers Payable and Purchases Returns and Allowances.
2. For partial payments after a voucher has been prepared, the old voucher is canceled and a new voucher is prepared for each installment.
3. Companies recording invoices at the net amount would record any discounts missed in the Discount Lost account.

Key Terms

Check register A special journal that replaces the cash payments journal in recording payments of vouchers.

Paid voucher file Holds paid vouchers filed either in sequential order by voucher number or alphabetically by creditor's name.

Unpaid voucher file (tickler file) The file containing unpaid vouchers; arranged by due dates to take advantage of cash discounts.

Voucher A written authorization form containing data about a transaction along with proper authorizations for payment, account distributions, and so forth.

Voucher register A special journal replacing the purchases journal; records prenumbered vouchers at the time the liabilities are incurred.

Voucher system An internal control system designed to control a company's cash payments.

Vouchers Payable A liability account in the general ledger that represents the controlling account for the sum of individual vouchers.

Questions, Mini Exercises, Exercises, and Problems

Discussion Questions

1. What is the structure of a voucher?
2. List the five components of a voucher system.
3. What source documents are attached to a voucher?
4. Compare a voucher register to a purchases journal.

Blueprint: Steps to Record and Pay a Liability Using the Voucher System

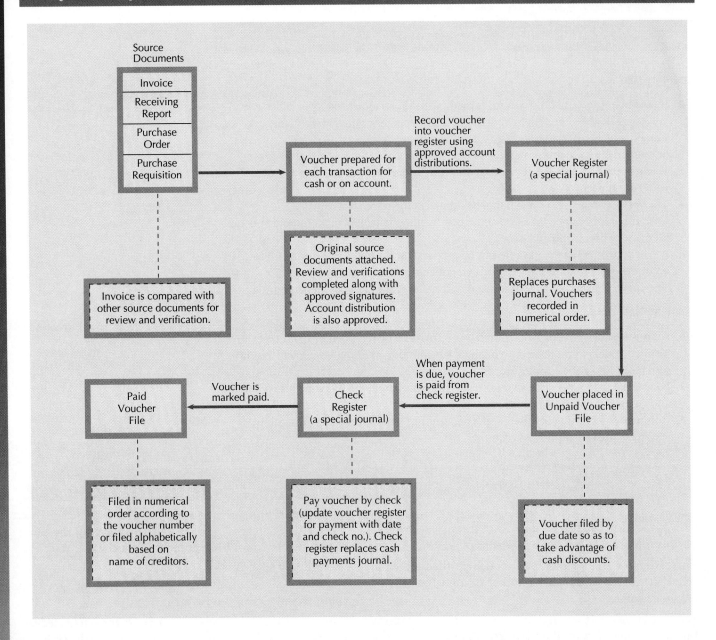

5. Why are vouchers filed by due dates?

6. Posting to a voucher register is quite different from posting to other special journals. Agree or disagree. Why?

7. Why is an accounts payable ledger eliminated in the voucher system?

8. Once a voucher is recorded, it cannot be canceled. True or false? Why?

9. Explain how partial payments would be recorded in the voucher register.

Mini Exercises

(The blank forms you need are on page 197 of the *Study Guide and Working Papers*.)

Journal Entries to Record and Pay Vouchers

1. Record the following transactions into the general journal:

20XX

June   9   Voucher no. 8 was prepared for the purchase of $500 of merchandise from Reel Co.; terms 2/10, n/30.

12   Voucher no. 9 was prepared for $1,000 of equipment; terms 2/10, n/30.

16   Check no. 15 was issued in payment of voucher no. 8.

Petty Cash

2. Record the following transactions into the general journal. The company uses a voucher system along with a petty cash fund.

20XX

Sept.   9   Voucher no. 18 was prepared to establish petty cash for $90.

28   Voucher no. 42 was prepared to replenish the petty cash fund from the following receipts: supplies $15; delivery $18.

Purchases Returns and Allowances

3. On November 15, Pete Co. prepared a voucher for $500 for merchandise purchased from Pool Co. on November 19. Pete Co. decided to return the merchandise due to poor workmanship for $200. Record the general journal entries.

Equal Installments

4. On April 8, Pete Co. prepared voucher no. 18 to record purchases of equipment for $1,200. On April 16, Pete Co. decided to pay $1,200 in two equal installments (voucher nos. 21 and 22). Record the general journal entries.

Gross Versus Net

5. Record the following transactions at (a) gross and (b) net:

20XX

Dec.   8   Bought merchandise on account from Pill Co.; terms 2/10, n/30, $6,000. Voucher no. 31 was prepared.

20   Issued check no. 480 in payment of voucher no. 31.

Exercises

(The blank forms you need are on pages 198–199 of the *Study Guide and Working Papers*.)

23-1. Agnes Company, which is a medium-sized firm, uses a voucher system. Record each of the following entries in general journal form (explanations can be omitted).

General journal entries to record and pay vouchers.

20X9

July   6   Voucher no. 50 was prepared for the purchase of $7,000 of merchandise from Loop Company; terms 2/10, n/30.

9   Voucher no. 51 was prepared for the purchase of $4,000 of equipment; terms 2/10, n/30.

15   Check no. 55 was issued in payment of voucher no. 51.

16   Check no. 56 was issued in payment of voucher no. 50.

23-2. Dan Company uses a voucher system along with a petty cash fund. Record each of the following entries in general journal form (explanations can be omitted):

General journal entries to record and pay vouchers; includes establishment and replenishment of petty cash.

20X9

Aug.   10   Purchased $500 of merchandise from Glow Company; voucher no. 150 was prepared; terms 2/10, n/30.

14   Voucher no. 151 was prepared to establish petty cash for $70.

16   Issued check no. 60 in payment of voucher no. 150.

17   Check was issued to pay voucher no. 151.

28   Voucher no. 152 was prepared to replenish the petty cash fund from the following receipts: supplies, $17; delivery, $19.

Recording purchases returns and allowances.

23-3. On November 10, 20X9, a voucher for $1,000 for merchandise purchased from Gurn Company was prepared by Doll Corporation. On November 14, Doll decided to return the merchandise due to poor workmanship. The price of the merchandise was $600. Record the entries in general journal form for November 10 and 14 (explanations can be omitted).

Recording partial payments.

23-4. On March 15, 20X9, Lori Company prepared voucher no. 89 to record the purchase of equipment for $900. On March 18, Lori Company decided to pay $900 in two equal installments. (Voucher nos. 90 and 91 were prepared.) Prepare the appropriate journal entries in general journal form for March 15 and 18.

Gross versus net in recording invoices.

23-5. Marvin Company records invoices at gross in its voucher system. From the following transactions, (a) record in general journal form the appropriate entries at gross and (b) record the entries as if Marvin Company recorded invoices at net.

20X9

Dec. 15 Bought merchandise on account from Levron Corporation; terms 2/10, n/30; $9,000 voucher no. 300 was prepared.

29 Issued check no. 600 in payment of voucher no. 300.

Group A Problems

(The forms you need are on pages 200–206 of the *Study Guide and Working Papers.*)

23A-1. Rowley Corporation uses a voucher system. Record the following transactions into the voucher register:

Recording entries in the voucher register.

20X9

June 8 Purchased office equipment from Tam Corporation, $900; voucher no. 300 was prepared.

12 Established a petty cash fund of $70; voucher no. 301 was prepared.

14 Purchased merchandise from Screen Corporation, $800; voucher no. 302 was prepared.

15 Purchased office supplies from Longview Corp., $900; voucher no. 303 was prepared.

29 Voucher no. 304 was prepared to replenish the petty cash fund based on the following receipts: supplies, $34; postage, $16.

Check Figure:
June 12
Dr. Petty cash (sundry)
$70
Cr. Voucher payable $70

23A-2. Skippy Corporation uses a voucher system. Record the following transactions into the voucher register and/or check register as appropriate:

Voucher and check register: routine transactions.

20X9

July 5 Purchased merchandise for $2,000 from Dork Company; terms 2/10, n/30; voucher no. 280 was prepared authorizing payment on July 15.

8 Purchased merchandise for $6,000 from Hornet Company; terms 2/10, n/30; voucher no. 281 was prepared authorizing payment on July 18.

15 Paid amount due Dork from voucher no. 280; check no. 91.

18 Paid amount due Hornet from voucher no. 281; check no. 92.

29 Voucher no. 282 was prepared for July rent to be paid to Loy Realty, $2,500.

30 Purchased office equipment for $2,900 from Lyle Company; voucher no. 283 was prepared.

30 Paid amount due Loy Realty from voucher no. 282; check no. 93.

Check Figure:
July 18
Dr. Voucher payable
$6,000
Cr. Purchases discount
$120
Cr. Cash $5,880

23A-3. Jona Corporation has been using a voucher system for several years. Prepare entries in the voucher register and check register for the following transactions:

Voucher and check register with cancellation due to purchases returns and allowances.

20X8

Sept. 1 Purchased merchandise inventory from Ricardo Corporation for $6,000; terms 2/10, n/30; voucher no. 68 was prepared.

5 Purchased merchandise inventory from Ree Corporation for $7,000; terms 2/10, n/30; voucher no. 69 was prepared.

8 Issued check no. 75 to pay for voucher no. 69.

10 Issued check no. 76 to pay for voucher no. 68.

14 Purchased merchandise inventory from Langle Corporation for $9,000; terms 2/10, n/30; voucher no. 70 was prepared.

17 Returned $3,000 of the merchandise to Langle Corporation due to poor workmanship; voucher no. 71 was prepared to replace voucher no. 70.

20 Issued check no. 77 to pay for voucher 71.

23A-4. The Swellon Company uses a voucher system. Record the following transactions:

20X9
Mar.

1 Voucher no. 200 was prepared for the purchase of $4,000 worth of merchandise inventory from Rolo Company; terms 2/10, n/30.

2 Voucher no. 201 was prepared for freight-in that was to be paid to Lance Company, $300.

3 Office supplies were purchased from Marge Company for $400; terms 2/10, n/30; voucher no. 202 was prepared.

8 Check no. 150 was issued in payment of voucher no. 200.

10 Purchased office equipment from Hal's Company for $10,000; payment is to be in two equal installments. Voucher nos. 203 and 204 were prepared to cover these payments.

12 Check no. 151 was issued to pay voucher no. 203.

12 Check no. 152 was issued to pay voucher no. 201.

18 Purchased $6,000 of merchandise from Lowe Corporation; terms 2/10, n/30; voucher no. 205 was prepared.

20 Purchased $3,000 of merchandise from Ken Company; terms 2/10, n/30; voucher no. 206 was prepared.

25 Check no. 153 was issued to pay voucher no. 205.

27 Returned $1,000 of merchandise bought from Ken Company; voucher no. 206 was canceled and voucher no. 207 was prepared.

29 Issued check no. 154 to pay voucher no. 207.

Group B Problems

(The blank forms you need are on pages 200–206 of the *Study Guide and Working Papers*.)

23B-1. Daper Company uses a voucher system. Record the following transactions into the voucher register:

20X8
July

10 Purchased office equipment from Smooth Company, $1,600; voucher no. 400 was prepared.

13 Established a petty cash fund of $60; voucher no. 401 was prepared.

14 Purchased merchandise from Roy Corporation, $650; voucher no. 402 was prepared.

15 Purchased office supplies from Kendall Corporation, $600; voucher no. 403 was prepared.

29 Voucher no. 404 was prepared to replenish the petty cash fund based on the following receipts: supplies, $28; postage, $14.

23B-2. Caven Company uses a voucher system. Record the following transactions into the voucher register and/or check register as appropriate:

20X9
May

6 Purchased merchandise for $2,000 from Hall Company; terms 2/10, n/30; voucher no. 600 was prepared authorizing payment on May 14.

8 Purchased merchandise for $8,000 from Ryan Company; terms 2/10, n/30; voucher no. 601 was prepared authorizing payment on May 17.

14 Paid amount due Hall Company from voucher no. 600; check no. 300.

Check Figure:
Sept 8
Dr. Voucher payable $7,000
Cr. Purchases discount $140
Cr. Cash $6,860

Voucher and check register with cancellation and partial payments.

Check Figure:
Mar. 25
Dr. Voucher payable $6,000
Cr. Purchases discount $120
Cr. Cash $5,880

Recording entries in the voucher register.

Check Figure:
July 13
Dr. Petty cash (sundry) $60
Cr. Voucher payable $60

Voucher and check register: routine transactions.

17   Paid amount due Ryan Company from voucher no. 601; check no. 301.

25   Voucher no. 602 was prepared for June rent to be paid to Paul Realty, $800.

30   June rent was paid by check no. 302.

30   Purchased office equipment for $3,000 from Kline Company; voucher no. 603 was prepared.

23B-3. Lava Company has been using a voucher system for several years. Prepare entries in the voucher register and check register for the following transactions:

20X8

Nov.

1   Purchased merchandise inventory from Lester Corporation for $9,000; terms 2/10, n/30; voucher no. 52 was prepared.

6   Purchased merchandise inventory from Jungle Corporation for $7,000; terms 2/10, n/30; voucher no. 53 was prepared.

8   Issued check no. 50 to pay for voucher no. 53.

10   Issued check no. 51 to pay for voucher no. 52.

14   Purchased merchandise inventory from Horv Corporation for $11,000; terms 2/10, n/30; voucher no. 54 was prepared.

17   Returned $2,000 of the merchandise to Horv Corporation due to poor workmanship; voucher no. 55 was prepared to replace voucher no. 54.

19   Issued check no. 52 to pay for voucher no. 55.

23B-4. Krown Corporation uses a voucher system. Record the following transactions:

20X9

June

1   Voucher no. 100 was prepared for the purchase of $6,000 worth of merchandise inventory from Langley Corporation; terms 2/10, n/30.

2   Voucher no. 101 was prepared for freight-in that was to be paid to J. Kane Company, $400.

3   Office supplies were purchased from Harold Company for $600; terms 2/10, n/30; voucher no. 102 was prepared.

8   Check no. 150 was issued in payment of voucher no. 100.

10   Purchased office equipment from Lyon Company for $7,000; payment is to be in two equal installments. Vouchers nos. 103 and 104 were prepared to cover these payments.

12   Check no. 151 was issued to pay voucher no. 103.

12   Check no. 152 was issued to pay voucher no. 101.

18   Purchased $5,000 of merchandise from Von Company; terms 2/10, n/30; voucher no. 105 was prepared.

20   Purchased $5,000 of merchandise from Lallan Company; terms 2/10, n/30; voucher no. 106 was prepared.

25   Check no. 153 was issued to pay voucher 105.

26   Returned $200 of merchandise bought from Lallan Company; voucher no. 106 was canceled and voucher no. 107 was prepared.

27   Issued check no. 154 to pay voucher no. 107.

Real-World Applications

23R-1. Mel Ring has recently opened a pizza shop. Over lunch, a salesman told Mel that to control his operation he should set up a voucher system so that all bills would be paid on time and properly approved. Mel thinks that in 10 years he will probably franchise his pizza operation. As his accountant, do you think the voucher system is the best way to go? Why? Please respond in writing.

23R-2. Morris Company uses a voucher system. For the past two years the bookkeeper has recorded installment purchases as a lump-sum payment in the voucher register. The bookkeeper thinks an unpaid voucher file is not needed because cash discounts are minimal compared with total dollar sales. When his supervisor is out to dinner, the bookkeeper will sign her name to the distribution accounts authorization. His supervisor has told him not to worry, because she can adjust "any mistakes" later on.

After two weeks from the date a voucher is paid, the bookkeeper destroys all pertinent data about the transaction. May Weston, an accounting intern, is quite upset about what's going on at Morris Company. Her textbook theory is not being followed, but her supervisor has told her that textbook principles are not always followed in the real world. Are May's concerns justified? State in writing your reasons.

YOU make the call

Critical Thinking/Ethical Case

23R-3. Most Companies uses the voucher system. Due to poor profitability, several employees in the accounting office were let go. Joe Rose, who handled the verification of the vouchers in the voucher register, was now given the responsibility of writing the checks from the check register. The head of accounting thought Joe was the most honest person in the company and that all would be fine. Do you agree with this move? What would you recommend? You make the call. Write down your recommendation to Jay Flynn, head of accounting.

Internet Exercises: General Dynamics; General Electric

EX-1. [**www.generaldynamics.com/**]   Voucher systems provide high degrees of internal control in acquiring inventory and in controlling cash payments. Your text has also emphasized the assistance a voucher system provides in assuring that all purchases discounts earned are taken. Missing a purchase discount is a costly event. The person responsible for ascertaining that all of them are taken will quickly fall from grace if discounts are not taken. Here is an example of how important discounts are. For this exercise you are the person who is responsible for this important step.

You have an invoice due for $100,000. You also have the authority to borrow money on a 30-day basis if it is necessary. The interest rate you would borrow the money at is 12%. This invoice has a discount of 3% if paid within the next 10 days. Today, you don't have the cash but you know you will in 30 days. What you must determine is whether you should borrow the money to pay the invoice. These are the decisions money managers at companies like General Dynamics face routinely.

What is your recommendation in this case?

EX-2. [**www.ge.com/**]   This is an excellent Web site for many reasons. Pay attention while here to the tabs on personal finance. You will find them both helpful and enlightening in working with your own cash and investments.

A large business protects its assets with good internal controls. One internal control measure that large companies employ is that of using vouchers. As this chapter explained, vouchers are in place for every payment of cash, from the highest expenditure to the lowest petty cash reimbursement.

General Electric uses vouchers to control its cash and to centralize its payment system. Not every GE branch operation maintains its own accounting records. Purchases and payments are centralized as an additional method of internal control.

Discuss how you believe this helps or hinders GE's day-to-day cash operation.

CHAPTER 24

Departmental Accounting

You went to shop for a gift for your mom's birthday. You stopped at Benton's, a regional department store located in town. You figured you would be able to find just the right gift at the store, since it has a number of various departments, which carry everything from clothing to cookware.

While shopping, you noticed that one corner of the second floor was being remodeled. A bright orange poster read, "A new shopping experience coming soon." As you are making your purchase you ask a sales associate about the new department. "There was a photo studio and frame gallery there, but it wasn't very successful, so the store decided to use the space for a new line of sportswear," the sales associate tells you. You thought about the change. The department approach to running a business makes good business sense, because the store can drop a department with poor sales and replace it with something it hopes will do better.

Departmental accounting can be used when a company's operations are divided into departments, whether the company is a retail business or a manufacturer. Many companies use departmental accounting to track profit and expenses for their various activities because it is an effective means to evaluate how specific departments contribute to the overall financial success of a company.

In this chapter we will explore departmental accounting. We will learn how to prepare income statements focusing on gross income, departmental income, and departmental contribution margin. After completing this chapter you will understand how departmental accounting works and why it is so popular in business today.

Learning Objectives

- Preparing income statements focusing on gross profit by department. (p. 834)

- Preparing income statements focusing on departmental net income. (p. 837)

- Preparing income statements focusing on departmental contribution margin. (p. 840)

Many large companies find it necessary to keep separate accounting records for their various departments so that management can see how efficient each department is and how each contributes to overall performance. This chapter focuses on various accounting and reporting aids that allow management to do so.

We use as our example Catlin's Department Store, which sells mainly clothing. The manager of the Adult Clothes Department at the store is quite concerned about the department's performance; there has been talk by upper management of the possibility of reducing the space of the Adult Department in favor of expanding the Children's Department.

Learning Unit 24-1   The Income Statement: Focus on Gross Profit by Department

Each department of Catlin's Department Store is a unit in which the manager has the responsibility for controlling and incurring certain costs as well as generating revenue. Each unit, or department, is known as a **profit center.** If a manager had the responsibility for controlling costs, but not for directly generating revenue, the unit would be called a **cost center** (an example is the office maintenance department at Catlin's).

Figure 24-1 shows the income statement for Catlin's Department Store. As you can see from this figure, the total gross profit of the company is $373,800 ($841,300 − $467,500), and the operating expenses are $170,000.

To break down the gross profit figure by department, a company must gather information about each department. It does so by setting up separate accounting records for each department, with separate accounts for Sales, Sales Returns and

Figure 24-1
Income Statement for
Catlin's Department Store

CATLIN'S DEPARTMENT STORE INCOME STATEMENT FOR YEAR ENDED DECEMBER 31, 20X8			
Revenue from Sales:			
Sales		$870 000 00	
Less: Sales Returns and Allowances	$14 700 00		
Sales Discount	14 000 00	28 700 00	
Net Sales			$841 300 00
Cost of Goods Sold:			
Merchandise Inventory, Jan. 1, 20X8		$143 000 00	
Purchases	$499 000 00		
Less: Purchases Returns and			
Allowances	15 400 00		
Purchases Discount	16 100 00	467 500 00	
Cost of Goods Available for Sale		610 500 00	
Less: Merchandise Inventory,			
Dec. 31, 20X8		143 000 00	
Cost of Goods Sold			$467 500 00
Gross Profit on Sales			373 800 00
Operating Expenses			170 000 00
Income before Taxes			203 800 00
Income Tax Expense			89 520 00
Net Income			$114 280 00

Allowances, Sales Discount, Merchandise Inventory, Purchases, Purchases Returns and Allowances, and Purchases Discount. Once this information has been separated by department, we can calculate the gross profit of each department. The use of a computer makes it possible to record and gather information for many departments easily and quickly.

Let's look at an example. Figure 24-2 shows how in the sales journal of Catlin's Department Store there is a Sales account for the Children's Department and one for the Adult Department.

CATLIN'S DEPARTMENT STORE SALES JOURNAL							
Date	Account Debited	Invoice Number	Post. Ref.	Accounts Receivable Dr.	Children's Sales Cr.	Adult Sales Cr.	
Nov. 3	Marsie Rose	325	✔	1 9 0 00	1 0 0 00	9 0 00	
8	Bill Stone	326	✔	1 8 5 00	1 7 5 00	1 0 00	
				(115)	(411)	(412)	

Figure 24-2 Sales Journal of Catlin's Department Store

Figure 24-3 (p. 836) is an income statement showing the gross profit for each department and the combined totals. You would not see a balance sheet prepared in this way, broken down by department; only an income statement is done this way. Keep in mind that an income statement indicates how well a business or department is performing.

> Income statements can be broken down by departments; balance sheets are not.

Learning Unit 24-1 Review

AT THIS POINT you should be able to

- Explain the difference between a cost center and a profit center. (p. 834)
- Prepare an income statement focusing on gross profit by department. (p. 834)

SELF-REVIEW QUIZ 24-1

(The blank forms you need are on page 210 of the *Study Guide and Working Papers*.)
Respond true or false to the following:

1. In a cost center a manager directly generates revenue.
2. Each department can have its own separate accounts for Sales, Sales Returns and Allowances, and so forth, to record information for the income statement.
3. A balance sheet is always separated by departments.

SOLUTIONS TO SELF-REVIEW QUIZ 24-1

1. False   2. True   3. False

CATLIN'S DEPARTMENT STORE
INCOME STATEMENT SHOWING DEPARTMENTAL GROSS PROFIT
FOR YEAR ENDED DECEMBER 31, 20X8

Account	Children's	Adult	Total
Revenue from Sales:			
Sales	$580 000 00	$290 000 00	$870 000 00
Less: Sales Returns and Allowances	$6 500 00	$8 200 00	$14 700 00
Sales Discounts	8 000 00 14 500 00	6 000 00 14 200 00	14 000 00 28 700 00
Net Sales	$565 500 00	$275 800 00	$841 300 00
Cost of Goods Sold:			
Merchandise Inventory, Jan. 1, 20X8	75 000 00	$68 000 00	$143 000 00
Purchases	$289 000 00	$210 000 00	$499 000 00
Less: Purchases Returns and Allowances	6 900 00	8 500 00	15 400 00
Purchases Discounts	8 200 00 273 900 00	7 900 00 193 600 00	16 100 00 467 500 00
Cost of Goods Available for Sale	348 900 00	$261 600 00	610 500 00
Less: Merchandise Inventory, Dec. 31, 20X8	79 000 00	64 000 00	143 000 00
Cost of Goods Sold	$269 900 00	$197 600 00	467 500 00
Gross Profit on Sales	$295 600 00	$78 200 00	$373 800 00
Operating Expenses			170 000 00
Income before Taxes			203 800 00
Income Tax Expense			89 520 00
Net Income			$114 280 00

Figure 24-3 Income Statement with Gross Profit Broken Down by Department

Learning Unit 24-2   The Income Statement: Focus on Departmental Net Income

DEPARTMENTAL INCOME FROM OPERATIONS

So far we have shown how gross profit has been accumulated by department. In this unit we look at how the $170,000 of operating expenses can be allocated by department if we want to extend departmental reporting beyond gross profit.

The operating expenses of Catlin's Department Store that can be traced and identified directly to separate departments are called direct expenses. An example is the salaries of the salespeople who work only for the Children's Department at Catlin's. The operating expenses that cannot be identified with a specific department but are incurred on behalf of the company are called indirect expenses. An example is the expense incurred in the upkeep of the building in which Catlin's is located.

In Figure 24-4 below we can see a sample of operating expenses that can now be apportioned to the Children's and Adult departments. Note that the total is still $170,000. Now let's see how these calculations for operating expenses were arrived at. Figure 24-5 (p. 838) is a summary of how the expenses were apportioned. Following that is a detailed explanation. Use Figure 24-5 as a reference sheet as you read the explanation that follows.

Figure 24-4
Operating Expenses Apportioned by Department

CATLIN'S DEPARTMENT STORE INCOME STATEMENT SHOWING DEPARTMENTAL INCOME BEFORE TAX FOR YEAR ENDED DECEMBER 31, 20X8	Children's	Adult	Totals
Net Sales	$565 500 00	$275 800 00	$841 300 00
Cost of Goods Sold	269 900 00	197 600 00	467 500 00
Gross Profit on Sales	$295 600 00	$ 78 200 00	$373 800 00
Operating Expenses:			
Sales Salaries	$ 25 000 00	$ 15 000 00	$ 40 000 00
Building Expense	12 000 00	4 000 00	16 000 00
Delivery Expense	6 000 00	4 000 00	10 000 00
Advertising Expense	9 000 00	5 000 00	14 000 00
Depreciation Expense	22 500 00	7 500 00	30 000 00
Administrative Expense	40 000 00	20 000 00	60 000 00
Total Operating Expenses	$ 114 500 00	$ 55 500 00	$170 000 00
Income before Taxes	$181 100 00	$ 22 700 00	$203 800 00
Income Tax Expense			89 520 00
Net Income			$ 114 280 00

1. Sales Salaries

The payroll records of Catlin's show that salespeople in the Children's Department were paid $25,000 and salespeople in the Adult Department were paid $15,000. These expenses can be identified with specific departments, so they are considered direct expenses.

2. Building Expense

The costs relating to the occupancy of Catlin's building are lumped into an account called Building Expense. Building Expense is an indirect expense, apportioned on the

	Children's		Adult		Total Operating Expense	
	Direct	Indirect	Direct	Indirect	Direct	Indirect
(1) Sales Salaries	$25,000.00		$15,000.00		$40,000.00	
(2) Building Expense		$12,000.00		$4,000.00		$16,000.00
(3) Delivery Expense	6,000.00		4,000.00		10,000.00	
(4) Advertising Expense	7,000.00	2,000.00	4,000.00	1,000.00	11,000.00	3,000.00
(5) Depreciation Expense		22,500.00		7,500.00		30,000.00
(6) Administrative Expense		40,000.00		20,000.00		60,000.00
	$38,000.00	$76,500.00	$23,000.00	$32,500.00	$61,000.00	$109,000.00
					$170,000	

Figure 24-5 Direct and Indirect Operating Expenses by Department

basis of square footage. Catlin's allocates the total cost of Building Expense of $16,000 on the basis of the number of square feet that each department occupies. Catlin's total space is 40,000 square feet, with the Children's Department occupying 30,000 square feet and the Adult Department 10,000 square feet. Building Expense is allocated to each department as follows:

Children's

$$\frac{30,000 \text{ ft}^2}{40,000 \text{ ft}^2} = .75 = 75\%$$

$$.75 \times \$16,000 = \$12,000$$

Adult

$$\frac{10,000 \text{ ft}^2}{40,000 \text{ ft}^2} = .25 = 25\%$$

$$.25 \times \$16,000 = \$4,000$$

Thus, of the $16,000 in Building Expense, the Children's Department is allocated $12,000 and the Adult Department $4,000.

3. Delivery Expense

The Children's Department shipped 60% of all merchandise, and the Adult Department shipped 40% of the merchandise. The total cost of Delivery Expense is $10,000. Because the exact amount of Delivery Expense is traceable to each department, it is considered a direct expense. If the cost of delivery is *not* specifically traceable to each department, it is considered an indirect expense and can be charged to departments based on past delivery records. Delivery Expense is calculated as follows:

Children's

$$.60 \times \$10,000 = \$6,000$$

Adult

$$.40 \times \$10,000 = \$4,000$$

4. Advertising Expense

Advertising Expense for Catlin's totaled $14,000. Of that total, $4,000 was spent on advertising adult clothes and $7,000 on advertising children's clothes. The remaining $3,000 ($14,000 − $11,000) was spent on advertising the store's image in general. Thus, this $3,000 is an indirect expense. How would you divide this expense by department? One common way is to apportion it based on gross sales of each department, as follows:

Gross Sales: $580,000 Children's
290,000 Adult
$870,000 Total Gross Sales

Children's	Adult
$\dfrac{\$580,000}{\$870,000} \times \$3,000$	$\dfrac{\$290,000}{\$870,000} \times \$3,000$
$= \dfrac{2}{3} \times \$3,000 = \$2,000$	$= \dfrac{1}{3} \times \$3,000 = \$1,000$

Thus, of the $3,000 of indirect expenses, $2,000 is charged to the Children's Department and $1,000 to the Adult Department.

5. Depreciation Expense

Catlin's Department Store apportions depreciation on its building based on the square footage each department occupies. (Some companies apportion depreciation based on the average cost of the equipment in each department.) Catlin's has 40,000 square feet, of which the Children's Department takes up 30,000 (3/4) and the Adult Department takes up 10,000 (1/4). The amount of Depreciation Expense charged to each department is calculated as follows:

> Depreciation Expense is an indirect expense.

Children's	Adult
$\dfrac{3}{4} \times \$30,000 = \$22,500$	$\dfrac{1}{4} \times \$30,000 = \$7,500$

6. Administrative Expense

Administrative expenses are incurred for the company as a whole and are not broken down by department; they are thus indirect expenses. In the case of Catlin's, it was decided that the Administrative Expense of $60,000 would be divided on the basis of each department's gross sales. We saw this method of allocation used in Advertising Expense. The calculation for indirect expenses charged to each department is as follows:

$$
\begin{array}{rl}
\$580,000 & \text{Children's} \\
\underline{290,000} & \text{Adult} \\
\$870,000 & \text{Total Gross Sales}
\end{array}
$$

Children's	Adult
$\dfrac{\$580,000}{\$870,000} = \dfrac{2}{3}$	$\dfrac{\$290,000}{\$870,000} = \dfrac{1}{3}$
$\dfrac{2}{3} \times \$60,000 = \$40,000$	$\dfrac{1}{3} \times \$60,000 = \$20,000$

Now take a moment to review Figure 24-4 to make sure you understand how we arrived at the total operating expenses of $170,000.

Learning Unit 24-2 Review

AT THIS POINT you should be able to

- Explain the difference between direct and indirect expenses. (p. 837)
- Explain how operating expenses are allocated to specific departments. (p. 837)
- Prepare, in proper form, an income statement showing departmental income before tax. (p. 837)

SELF-REVIEW QUIZ 24-2

(The blank forms you need are on page 211 of the *Study Guide and Working Papers*.)
Given the following, apportion the Rent Expense on the basis of floor space:

	Dept. A	Dept. B	Total
Floor space	208,000	112,000	320,000
Rent expense			$ 30,800

SOLUTION TO SELF-REVIEW QUIZ 24-2

Apportionment of Rent Expense:

Dept. A	Dept. B
$\dfrac{208,000}{320,000} \times \$30,800 = \$20,020$	$\dfrac{112,000}{320,000} \times \$30,800 = \$10,780$

Learning Unit 24-3   The Income Statement Showing Departmental Contribution Margin

> In this approach, indirect expenses are separated from direct expenses.

Referring back to Figure 24-4 (p. 837), income before taxes for the Children's Department equaled $181,100 and the Adult Department showed $22,700. Some accountants think these figures are misleading, because the indirect expenses in Figure 24-5 were apportioned to the total operating expenses of each department. An alternative to this approach to indirect expense allocation is shown in Figure 24-6, which lists direct departmental expenses and the contribution each department makes to cover indirect expenses. This breakdown is called the contribution margin, which can also be defined as the gross profit of a department minus its direct expenses. This approach charges to a department only those expenses that are directly traceable to it. Note in Figure 24-6 that the Children's Department contributes $257,600 to cover indirect expenses and net income. This figure is quite different from the $181,100 listed in Figure 24-4.

Supporters of this approach think indirect expenses are not controlled by the department manager and thus should not be used in evaluating departmental performance. Some accountants contend that even if a department is eliminated, the indirect expenses would not be decreased. For example, Catlin spends $3,000 in advertising that is basically aimed at advertising the store's overall image, and that expense would still remain if the Adult Department or the Children's Department were eliminated.

Determining whether certain departments at Catlin's should be expanded or reduced would involve investigation of the financial reports presented in the chapter along with topics such as the following:

1. The effect that dropping a department would have in terms of loss of its contribution margin. For example, would closing a jewelry department in a clothing store reduce the store's total administrative expenses?

2. The effect one department has in drawing customers to other departments. Do customers who come into the store to look at jewelry go on to look at dresses in another department?

CATLIN'S DEPARTMENT STORE INCOME STATEMENT SHOWING DEPARTMENTAL CONTRIBUTION MARGIN FOR YEAR ENDED DECEMBER 31, 20X8			
	Children's	Adult	Totals
Net Sales	$565 500 00	$275 800 00	$841 300 00
Cost of Goods Sold	269 900 00	197 600 00	467 500 00
Gross Profit on Sales	$295 600 00	$ 78 200 00	373 800 00
Direct Departmental Expenses			
Sales Salaries	$ 25 000 00	$ 15 000 00	$ 40 000 00
Advertising Expense	7 000 00	4 000 00	11 000 00
Delivery Expense	6 000 00	4 000 00	10 000 00
Total Direct Departmental Expenses	$ 38 000 00	$ 23 000 00	$ 61 000 00
Contribution Margin	$ 257 600 00	$ 55 200 00	$312 800 00
Indirect Departmental Expenses			
Building Expense			$ 16 000 00
Advertising Expense			3 000 00
Depreciation Expense			30 000 00
Administrative Expense			60 000 00
Total Indirect Expenses			$109 000 00
Income before Taxes			$203 800 00
Income Tax Expense			89 520 00
Net Income			$114 280 00

Figure 24-6
Income Statement Showing Department Contribution Margin

3. Trends in the industry. Even though a certain department is not doing well, all the competing stores have such a department; the answer may be to cut down the size of the department rather than eliminate it.

4. Ability of suppliers to meet increasing demand for items. For example, it would not be a good idea to open a pastry shop in Catlin's until one had lined up a number of good, reliable suppliers.

We conclude this unit with an example that shows how eliminating a department that has a net loss may in fact cause an even greater loss in the overall net income for the company. The situation is as follows:

	Depts. A, B, C,	Dept. D Only	Totals for Depts. A–D	Totals if Dept. D Is Eliminated
Sales	$1,469,000	$130,000	$1,599,000	$1,469,000
Cost of Goods Sold	869,000	82,000	951,000	869,000
Gross Profit	600,000	48,000	648,000	600,000
Direct Expenses	340,000	31,000	371,000	340,000
Contribution Margin	260,000	17,000	277,000	260,000
Indirect Expenses	130,000	26,000	156,000	156,000
Net Income (Loss)	$ 130,000	$ (9,000)	$ 121,000	$ 104,000

Note that if Department D is eliminated, net income of the other departments is reduced by $17,000, from $121,000 to $104,000. This change is the result of losing the contribution margin of $17,000 from Department D.

Learning Unit 24-3 Review

AT THIS POINT you should be able to

- Explain why an income statement might report departmental contribution margin rather than listing all direct and indirect expenses under total operating expenses. (p. 840)
- Prepare an income statement showing the contribution margin. (p. 841)

SELF-REVIEW QUIZ 24-3

(The blank forms you need are on page 211 of the *Study Guide and Working Papers.*) Respond true or false to the following:

1. Allocating indirect expenses will never be subjective.
2. A direct expense is traceable to a respective department.
3. Direct expenses of a department in the contribution margin approach are combined with indirect expenses.
4. Eliminating one department could reduce sales of another department.
5. Contribution margin equals gross profit on sales plus direct department expenses.

SOLUTIONS TO SELF-REVIEW QUIZ 24-3

1. False   2. True   3. False   4. True   5. False

Chapter Review

Learning Unit 24-1

1. A profit center means that a manager is responsible for controlling certain costs as well as generating revenues.
2. Separate accounts for Sales, Purchases, and so forth can be set up for each department so as to calculate departmental gross profit.
3. Income statements can be broken down by department; balance sheets are not.

Learning Unit 24-2

1. Direct expenses can be directly identified with a specific department.
2. The method used to apportion indirect expenses to departments may vary from company to company; there is no one absolute method.
3. One department's direct expense may be another department's indirect expense.
4. One way to apportion indirect expenses such as Advertising Expense or Administrative Expense by department is on the basis of each department's gross sales.

Learning Unit 24-3

1. Indirect expenses are *not* combined with direct expenses when preparing an income statement showing departmental contribution margin.
2. Gross profit on sales minus direct departmental expenses equals contribution margin.

Key Terms

Contribution margin A department's net profit, used to cover indirect expenses.

Cost center A unit or department that incurs costs but does not generate revenues.

Direct expenses Expenses that can be traced directly to a specific department.

Indirect expenses Expenses that cannot be traced directly to one department.

Profit center A unit or department that incurs costs and generates revenues.

Questions, Mini Exercises, Exercises, and Problems

Discussion Questions

1. What is the difference between a cost center and a profit center?
2. Explain how gross profit is calculated.
3. Special journals are not used in departmental accounting. True or false? Please explain.
4. Compare and contrast indirect expenses and direct expenses.
5. Explain how advertising expense could be both a direct cost and an indirect cost for a company.
6. Square footage is often used to allocate indirect costs to various departments within a company. True or false?
7. An income statement showing departmental income before tax does not list individual operating expenses for each department. True or false? Please explain.
8. Explain why a company might prepare an income statement showing each department's contribution margin.

Blueprint: Departmental Accounting

Situation 1:
Income statement showing departmental gross profit

	DEPT. A	DEPT. B	TOTAL
Net Sales	1	2	3 (1 + 2)
− Cost of Goods Sold	4	5	6 (4 + 5)
= Gross Profit on Sales	7 (1 − 4)	8 (2 − 5)	9 (3 − 6)
− Operating Expenses			10
= Income before Taxes			11 (9 − 10)
− Income Tax Expense			−12
= Net Income			13

Situation 2:
Income statement showing departmental income before tax

Direct and indirect expenses allocated →

	DEPT. A	DEPT. B	TOTAL
Net Sales	1	2	3 (1 + 2)
Cost of Goods Sold	4	5	6 (4 + 5)
Gross Profit on Sales	7 (1 − 4)	8 (2 − 5)	9 (3 − 6)
Operating Expenses			
Salaries Expense	10	11	12 (10 + 11)
Delivery Expense	13	14	15 (13 + 14)
Depreciation Expense	16	17	18 (16 + 17)
Administrative Expense	19	20	21 (19 + 20)
Total Operating Expenses	22 (10 + 13 + 16 + 19)	23 (11 + 14 + 17 + 20)	24 (12 + 15 + 18 + 21)
Income before Taxes	25 (7 − 22)	26 (8 − 23)	27 (9 − 24)
Income Tax Expense			28
Net Income			29 (27 − 28)

Situation 3:
Income statement showing departmental contributions to indirect expenses

	DEPT. A	DEPT. B	TOTAL
Net Sales	1	2	3 (1 + 2)
Cost of Goods Sold	4	5	6 (4 + 5)
Gross Profit on Sales	7 (1 − 4)	8 (2 − 5)	9 (3 − 6)
Direct Departmental Expenses			
Sales Salaries	10	11	12 (10 + 11)
Advertising Expenses	13	14	15 (13 + 14)
Delivery Expenses	16	17	18 (16 + 17)
Total Direct Expenses	19 (10 + 13 + 16)	20 (11 + 14 + 17)	21 (12 + 15 + 18)
Contribution to Indirect Expenses	22 (7 − 19)	23 (8 − 20)	24 (9 − 21)
Indirect Departmental Expenses			
Building Expense			25
Advertising Expenses			26
Depreciation Expenses			27
Total Indirect Expenses			28 (25 + 26 + 27)
Income before Taxes			29 (24 − 28)
Income Tax Expense			30
Net Income			31 (29 − 30)

PROBLEM 7A-4 OR PROBLEM 7B-4 (CONCLUDED)

UNION DUES PAYABLE

ACCOUNT NO. 218

Date	Explanation	Post Ref.	Debit	Credit	Balance Debit	Balance Credit

WAGES AND SALARIES PAYABLE

ACCOUNT NO. 220

Date	Explanation	Post Ref.	Debit	Credit	Balance Debit	Balance Credit

FACTORY SALARIES EXPENSE

ACCOUNT NO. 610

Date	Explanation

CHAPTER 7
SUMMARY PRACTICE TEST:
PAYROLL CONCEPTS AND PROCEDURES—EMPLOYEE TAXES

Part I Instructions

Fill in the blank (s) to complete the statement.

1. The ___Fair___ ___Labor___ ___Standards___
   ___Act___ states the maximum hours a worker will work at regular rate of pay.

2. Form ___W-4___ aids the employer in knowing how much to deduct for federal income tax.

3. The base for FICA-Medicare will ___Not___ ___Change___ from year to year.

4. ___Circular___ ___E___ of the employer's tax guide has tables available for deductions for FIT and FICA (Social Security and Medicare).

5. ___Workers___ ___Compensation___ ___Insurance___ protects employees against losses due to injury or death incurred while on the job.

6. Data from the ___Payroll___ ___Register___ will provide the needed information to record the payroll entry in the general journal.

charged to specific accounts.

8. The credit to Wages and Salaries Payable in recording the payroll entry in the general journal represents _A NET_ _Earnings_ .

9. FICA-Social Security Payable is a _Liability_ found on the balance sheet.

10. Each quarter has _13_ weeks.

Part II Instructions

Answer true or false to the following.

F **1.** The individual earnings record is updated from the general journal.

T **2.** The account distribution columns of the payroll register provide data to record which accounts will be debited to record the total payroll when a journal entry is prepared.

F **3.** FICA-Medicare Payable is an asset for the employer.

F **4.** Gross pay plus deductions equals net pay.

F **5.** Form W-4 aids in calculating FICA-Social Security.

T **6.** The employer will match the employee's contribution for FICA (Social Security and Medicare).

T **7.** Each quarter has 13 weeks.

T **8.** The normal balance of FIT Payable is a credit.

OFFICE SALARIES EXPENSE ACCOUNT NO. 612

Date	Explanation	Post Ref.	Debit	Credit	Balance Debit	Balance Credit

Mini Exercises

(The blank forms you need are on pages 213–214 of the *Study Guide and Working Papers.*)

Appropriating Rent to Departments Based on Sales

1. The cost of rent of $6,000 for Moore Co. is appropriated to each department based on sales. Given the following, assign the cost of rent to each department:

Rent	Toys	Clothing
$6,000	$20,000	$40,000

Appropriating Fire Insurance Based on Square Footage

2. Calculate the assignment of fire insurance of $16,000 to each department:

INDIRECT EXPENSE	BASIS OF ASSIGNMENT	BAKERY	GROCERY
Fire Insurance	4,000 ft² total	1,000 ft²	3,000 ft²

Calculating Net Income from Total Operating Expenses

3. Given the following, calculate net income:

	Dept. 1	Dept. 2
Net Sales	$4,000	$6,000
Cost of Goods Sold	1,000	2,000
Operating Expenses		$2,500
Income Tax Expense, 40% rate		

Calculating Departmental Net Income

4. From the following, calculate departmental income before tax. Assume a tax rate of 40%.

	Dept. A	Dept. B
Net Sales	$3,000	$4,000
Cost of Goods Sold	1,000	1,200
Delivery Expense	500	700
Advertising Expense	400	500
Depreciation Expense	200	300

Calculating Contribution Margin

5. Calculate the contribution margin for each department and income before taxes, based on the following:

	Dept. A 1,000 Ft²	Dept. B 2,000 Ft²
Net Sales	$5,000	$10,000
Cost of Goods Sold	2,000	6,000
Sales Salaries	$800 (30% directly related to Dept. A and 70% related to Dept. B)	
Rent Expense	$400	
Advertising Expense	$900 ($400 directly related to Dept. A and $200 related to Dept. B)	

> Appropriating rent to departments based on sales.

Exercises

(The blank forms you need are on pages 215–216 of the *Study Guide and Working Papers.*)

24-1. The cost of rent of $8,000 for Poller Company is appropriated to each department based on its sales. Given the following, assign the cost of rent to each department:

	Jewelry	**Hardware**	**Automotive**
Sales	$30,000	$50,000	$20,000

> Appropriating fire insurance based on square footage.

24-2. Complete the assignment of fire insurance to each department.

Indirect Expense	Amount	Basis of Assignment	Candy Sales		Ice Cream Sales		Pizza Sales	
Fire Insurance	$90,000	30,000 ft^2 total	18,000 ft^2	A	7,500 ft^2	B	4,500 ft^2	C

24-3. Given the following, calculate net income:

> Calculating net income from total operating expenses.

	Dept. 1	**Dept. 2**
Net Sales	$30,000	$40,000
Cost of Goods Sold	14,000	26,000
Operating Expenses		$16,000
Income Tax Expense, 30% rate		

24-4. From the following, calculate departmental income before tax. Assume a tax rate of 30%.

> Calculating departmental income.

	Dept. A	**Dept. B**
Net Sales	$200,000	$250,000
Cost of Goods Sold	100,000	125,000
Delivery Expense	24,000	28,000
Advertising Expense	23,000	22,000
Depreciation Expense	25,000	24,000

24-5. Calculate the contribution margin for each department and income before taxes, based on the following:

> Calculating contribution margin.

	Dept. A **10,000 Ft^2**	**Dept. B** **20,000 Ft^2**
Net Sales	$60,000	$90,000
Cost of Goods Sold	25,000	50,000
Sales Salaries	8,000 (40% directly related to Dept. A and 60% to Dept. B)	
Rent Expense	5,000	
Advertising Expense	18,000 ($3,000 directly related to Dept. A and $9,000 to Dept. B)	

> Preparing an income statement showing departmental gross profit.

Group A Problems

(The blank forms you need are on pages 217–222 of the *Study Guide and Working Papers.*)

24A-1. From the following data, prepare in proper form an income statement showing departmental gross profit (assume a 25% tax rate) for Bill's Variety for the year ended December 31, 20X9.

Cash	$12,000
Accounts Receivable	6,000
Allowance for Doubtful Accounts	1,500
Merchandise Inventory, January 1, 20X9, Grocery	7,000
Merchandise Inventory, January 1, 20X9, Pizza	5,000
Merchandise Inventory, December 31, 20X9, Grocery	19,000
Merchandise Inventory, December 31, 20X9, Pizza	7,000
Equipment	15,000
Acc. Depreciation, Equipment	9,100
Accounts Payable	10,200
B. Smith, Capital	10,500
B. Smith, Withdrawals	3,100
Sales, Grocery	20,000
Sales, Pizza	18,000
Sales Returns and Allowances, Grocery	2,000
Sales Returns and Allowances, Pizza	3,000
Purchases, Grocery	22,400
Purchases, Pizza	14,500
Purchases Returns and Allowances, Grocery	800
Purchases Returns and Allowances, Pizza	400
Total Operating Expenses	4,700

Check Figure:
Total net income $4,950

24A-2. Given the following information about the clothing and hardware departments of Sally Company, prepare a departmental expense allocation sheet showing expenses by department.

Constructing a departmental expense sheet.

ACCOUNT	INDIRECT	DIRECT	
		Clothing	Hardware
1. Rent Expense	$14,000		
2. Insurance Expense	7,000	$1,400	$2,600
3. Depreciation Expense		300	700
4. Advertising Expense	2,000		
5. Supplies Expense	3,000		
6. Salaries Expense	6,400		

Check Figure:
Total indirect expenses
$32,400

Additional Facts

	Clothing	Hardware
Net sales	$70,000	$30,000
Cost of goods sold	50,000	18,000
Floor space	200 ft^2	500 ft^2

Allocation Basis

Rent and Insurance:	Floor space
Advertising and Supplies:	Net sales
Salaries:	Gross profit of clothing and hardware departments

24A-3. From the following partial data, prepare an income statement showing departmental income before tax along with net income for Pete's Corporation for the year ended December 31, 20X9:

Assigning direct expenses and preparing an income statement showing departmental income before tax.

Net Sales, TVs	$60,000
Net Sales, Washers	30,000

Cost of Goods Sold, TVs	39,000
Cost of Goods Sold, Washers	18,000

Income tax rate 30%
TV Dept., 5,000 sq. ft.
Washers, 3,000 sq. ft.

		Basis of Allocation
Sales Salary Expense	$4,500	Net sales
Building Expense	4,800	Square footage
Delivery Expense	2,700	Net sales
Depreciation Expense	800	Square footage

24A-4. Educator Company has requested that you (1) assign indirect expenses to its jewelry and fur departments as appropriate and (2) prepare an income statement for November 20X9 showing departmental contribution margins along with net income. Assume a 30% tax rate.

	Jewelry: 30,000 Ft^2	Fur: 10,000 Ft^2	Indirect Cost
Net Sales	$280,000	$220,000	
Merchandise Inventory (Nov. 1)	50,000	70,000	
Merchandise Inventory (Nov. 30)	35,000	30,000	
Purchases	200,000	100,000	
Purchases Discount	10,000	20,000	
Salaries	2,900	2,100	$10,000
Depreciation	25,000	21,300	
Advertising	1,000	2,000	20,000
Administrative			32,000
Rent Expense			12,000

Allocation of Indirect Expenses

Salaries are based on net sales. All other indirect expenses are based on square footage.

Group B Problems

(The blank forms you need are on pages 217–222 of the *Study Guide and Working Papers*.)

24B-1. From the following data, prepare in proper form an income statement showing departmental gross profit (assume a 25% tax rate) for Randy Company for the year ended December 31, 20X9:

Cash	$13,100
Accounts Receivable	6,200
Allowance for Doubtful Accounts	2,400
Merchandise Inventory, January 1, 20X9, Cosmetics	8,000
Merchandise Inventory, January 1, 20X9, Jewelry	6,000
Merchandise Inventory, December 31, 20X9, Cosmetics	19,000
Merchandise Inventory, December 31, 20X9, Jewelry	8,000
Equipment	19,000
Acc. Depreciation, Equipment	9,200
Accounts Payable	13,500
R. Glade, Capital	14,000
R. Glade, Withdrawals	5,000
Sales, Cosmetics	20,000

Sales, Jewelry	18,000
Sales Returns and Allowances, Cosmetics	2,000
Sales Returns and Allowances, Jewelry	1,500
Purchases, Cosmetics	24,800
Purchases, Jewelry	15,100
Purchases Returns and Allowances, Cosmetics	900
Purchases Returns and Allowances, Jewelry	500
Total Operating Expenses	5,500

24B-2. Given the following information about the Toys and Clothing departments of Avery Company, prepare a departmental expense allocation sheet showing expenses by department:

ACCOUNT	INDIRECT	DIRECT Toys	Clothing
1. Rent Expense	$15,000		
2. Insurance Expense	21,000	$1,900	$1,700
3. Depreciation Expense		1,000	700
4. Advertising Expense	3,000		
5. Supplies Expense	10,000		
6. Salaries Expense	30,000		

Constructing a departmental expense sheet.

Check Figure:
Total indirect expenses
$79,000

Additional Facts

	Toys	Clothing
Net sales	$20,000	$30,000
Cost of goods sold	10,000	20,000
Floor space	1,000 ft^2	2,000 ft^2

Allocation Basis

Rent and Insurance:	Floor space
Advertising and Supplies:	Net sales
Salaries:	Gross profit of toys and clothing departments

24B-3. From the following partial data, prepare an income statement showing departmental income before tax along with net income for Logan Corporation for the year ended December 31, 20X9:

Net Sales, Rugs (10,000 ft^2)	$180,000
Net Sales, Furniture (30,000 ft^2)	220,000
Cost of Goods Sold, Rugs	55,000
Cost of Goods Sold, Furniture	69,000
Income tax rate, 30%	

Assigning direct expenses and preparing an income statement showing departmental income before tax.

Check Figure:
Net income $70,000

Basis of Allocation

Sales Salary Expense	$60,000	Net Sales
Building Expense	20,000	Square footage
Delivery Expense	80,000	Net sales
Depreciation Expense	16,000	Square footage

24B-4. Lonestar Company has requested that you (1) assign indirect expenses to its Candy and Grocery departments as appropriate and (2) prepare an income statement for November 20X9 showing departmental contribution margins along with net income. Assume a 30% tax rate.

Assigning indirect expenses and preparing an income statement showing departmental contributions to indirect expenses.

	Candy: 20,000 Ft^2	Grocery: 30,000 Ft^2	Indirect Cost
Net Sales	$18,000	$22,000	
Merchandise Inventory (November 1)	1,000	1,500	
Merchandise Inventory (November 30)	2,000	2,500	
Purchases	9,250	8,450	
Purchases Discount	250	450	
Salaries	750	1,500	$2,500
Depreciation	1,250	250	
Advertising	250	1,500	
Administrative			7,500
Rent Expense			2,000

Allocation of Indirect Expenses

Salaries are based on net sales. All other indirect expenses are based on square footage.

Real-World Applications

24R-1. Dot Jensen received the following memorandum:

MEMO

To: Dot Jensen, Manager of Children's Clothing

From: Bill Barnes

Re: Annual evaluation

Based on the following data (attached), I am sorry to inform you that you will not be rehired at the end of your current contract. Your department's performance was far below the budgeted level we had projected for this period.

Dot is quite upset and thinks her evaluation is not justified. Analyze the data to see whether Dot's evaluation is indeed not justifiable. What additional factors might be considered? Please respond in writing.

ATTACHMENT: ANNUAL EVALUATION DATA		
Clothing Sales		$320,000
Cost of Goods Sold		170,000
Gross Profit		$150,000
Operating Expenses:		
Hourly Wages	$75,000	
Manager's Salary	40,000	
Depreciation of Building	15,000	
Interest on Long-Term Bonds	12,000	
Payroll Taxes	16,000	
Total Operating Expenses		158,000
Departmental Loss		(8,000)

24R-2. Moore Markets is considering the elimination of the Bakery Shop. Based on the following data, make your written recommendations to Jim Moore, president of Moore Markets:

	Produce	Dairy	Bakery
Sales	$60,000	$90,000	$82,000
Cost of Goods Sold	19,000	58,000	67,000
Gross Profit	$41,000	$32,000	$15,000
Direct Expenses	12,000	6,000	8,000
Indirect Expenses	6,000	12,000	4,000
Total Operating Expenses	18,000	18,000	12,000
Net Income before Tax	$23,000	$14,000	$ 3,000

YOU make the call

Critical Thinking/Ethical Case

24R-3. Hernando Favor had been working in the bakery department of Long Company for four years when he was promoted to the accounting department. Since his promotion, sales in the bakery department have slipped and management is considering cutting the department in half. Hal Moore, who works in the bakery, will be laid off. Hernando has thought about shifting some of his sales figures in his accounting records to the bakery department from other departments so as to save his friend Hal from losing his job. Hernando thinks no one will find out in the long run, because he knows the bakery can increase sales. Do you feel Hernando has clear justification for his actions? You make the call. Write down your recommendation to Hernando.

Internet Exercises: Caesar's Palace; K2Sports

EX-1. [**www.caesars.com**]   From the Web site you can visualize that Caesar's World has several profit centers. The obvious profit centers are the casino and gaming operations, Caesar's Palace Hotels in Nevada, New Jersey, and Indiana, and an online shopping mall.

If you have ever visited Caesar's Palace, you know that it has an extensive shopping mall within the hotel and casino operation. It is also among the "showiest" of the showplace hotels in Las Vegas.

1. Can you name at least two additional departments not mentioned on the Web site? Think of what is available in a hotel but is not specifically mentioned in the Web site.

2. How do you believe that Caesar's evaluates its overall operation with "departmental" accounting? In your answer to this question mention profit centers and cost centers and connect them to Caesar's operations.

EX-2. [**http://www.k2sports.com**]   This site is an excellent example of a departmentalized operation. The main page shows operations in four areas: ski, snowboards, skates, and bikes. After you browse through the Web site, answer these questions based upon your impressions of the company:

1. Are these four areas "profit centers" or "cost centers"?

2. Does each of these generate "gross profit"?

3. From the chapter's discussion of "contribution margin," what kind of costs would go into a "contribution margin" income statement?

4. What kind of fixed costs or common costs do you believe K2 would have, and how would you incorporate them into a departmental statement?

Manufacturing Accounting

You need extra light in your room. After finishing your studies one evening, you go to the large discount retail store a few miles from campus. There you find a floor lamp that is on sale. You discover that it comes disassembled in a box. No problem, you can put it together at school.

Back in your room, you find that the assembly is more work than you had thought. The lamp came with instructions, a parts list, several metal tubes, three shades, and a few nuts and bolts in various sizes. After spreading all of the parts out on the floor, you begin the assembly. After 45 minutes, the lamp looks like the one in the instructions, and you are ready to plug it in.

You think about all the parts in the lamp. They were all produced from an engineer's plans, and after you followed the instructions, the parts turned into a lamp. How does a business keep track of the parts inventories and the cost of the parts? How does the accountant arrive at a final retail price for the lamp?

The accounting process for a manufacturer is different from that for a retailer or a service business. A manufacturer must account for many costs—raw materials, the labor used to produce a product, and various items of overhead. Manufacturing accounting is used to track and record the costs of making a product during the production process.

In this chapter we discuss manufacturing accounting. We will learn to prepare a cost of goods manufactured schedule, to record transactions found in the manufacturing process, and to prepare a worksheet for a manufacturing company. After completing this chapter you will better understand the process of accounting for the various parts that became your floor lamp.

Learning Objectives

● Preparing a cost of goods manufacturing schedule. (p. 854)

● Journalizing transactions recording the manufacturing process. (p. 862)

● Preparing a worksheet for a manufacturing company. (p. 865)

Manufacturing accounting refers to the specialized accounting concepts and techniques that are required to record, report, and control the operations of a manufacturing company properly. The financial accounting procedures discussed in the previous merchandising chapters are all still valid in a manufacturing firm, but they are supplemented by the manufacturing accounting to be presented in this chapter, including some new terms and techniques that were not considered or required in the accounting for merchandising operations.

Learning Unit 25-1   Cost of Goods Manufactured and the Income Statement

In a manufacturing company it is necessary to separate the manufacturing costs from all other selling and administrative expenses, because product costs, inventory costs, and even gross profit come from the manufacturing process. One way of thinking about it is to imagine manufacturing costs being incurred in one building and the other costs in another building as shown in Figure 25-1.

Figure 25-1

All the costs incurred in the manufacturing building are manufacturing costs, including the managers' salaries, maintenance, all the labor, all materials, supplies, electricity, rent, and the depreciation of manufacturing property and machinery. In addition, it is necessary to allocate a portion of the accounting, personnel, purchasing, and data processing departments each month based on their contribution to manufacturing.

The administrative building would house top management, sales personnel, and other administrative personnel and their supplies and expenses.

ELEMENTS OF MANUFACTURING COST

Once we have determined which are administrative and which are manufacturing costs, we can break the manufacturing costs into three elements: raw material, direct labor, and manufacturing overhead.

Raw material (or direct material) consists of all the items of material that will become a part of the product or will change the quality or characteristics of the product. For example, for a furniture manufacturer, the raw material includes lumber, metal parts, fabric, epoxy, finishing material, and even nuts and bolts. In a company that manufactures aluminum products, raw material includes the pure aluminum and the additives that are inserted to make the aluminum shiny or dull or rigid or flexible.

Direct labor includes the wages of those *personnel* whose efforts directly change the quality or characteristics of the products. In a furniture manufacturing company, the direct labor includes the person who saws the table top, the person who paints the furniture, the person who attaches the handles to the drawers, and so on. In that same company, however, the supervisor, the maintenance person, and the forklift driver are *not* direct labor.

Manufacturing overhead consists of all other manufacturing costs not included in raw material or direct labor. Manufacturing overhead includes many diverse items such as indirect labor, maintenance, engineering, manufacturing supervision, and supplies. Some of the most common items of manufacturing overhead are as follows:

- Maintenance wages and supplies.
- Production supervision and expenses.
- Depreciation expense of manufacturing assets.
- Rent expense for buildings or machinery.
- Electricity for manufacturing.
- Insurance expense for manufacturing.
- Indirect labor: material handlers.
- Manufacturing clerical wages.

MANUFACTURING INVENTORIES

In a merchandise firm there is one inventory made up of goods for sale. In a manufacturing firm there are *three* major inventories: raw material, work-in-process, and finished goods. (In addition, there are other minor inventories for such things as maintenance supplies and operating supplies.)

The *raw material inventory* consists only of the cost of the items of raw material being held for production plus the freight cost to bring the material in. The acquisition of raw material is recorded as Purchases, the account reserved for the purchase of raw material.

The *work-in-process inventory* represents the cost of the products being processed (the step before becoming finished goods) and includes the raw material, direct labor, and the manufacturing overhead costs incurred at the time of the inventory.

The *finished goods inventory* consists of the manufacturing cost of the products that have been completed and are awaiting shipment to customers.

COST OF GOODS SOLD

To prepare an income statement for a manufacturing company, we first must figure the cost of goods sold. This section of the income statement for a manufacturing company is somewhat different from that of a merchandise company. The following diagram shows how cost of goods sold is calculated for a merchandise firm and for a manufacturing company.

LAYOUT TO CALCULATE COST OF GOODS SOLD

Merchandising Company	Manufacturing Company
Beginning Merchandise Inventory	Beginning Finished Goods Inventory
+ Net Purchases	+ Cost of Goods Manufactured
= Cost of Merchandise Available for Sale	= Cost of Goods Available for Sale
− Ending Merchandise Inventory	− Ending Finished Goods Inventory
= Cost of Goods Sold	= Cost of Goods Sold

As you can see in the diagram, the cost of goods manufactured replaces the purchases of the merchandise company statement. The purpose of the cost of goods sold section is to properly match the manufacturing costs with the sales, and for this reason it is necessary to include the beginning and ending finished goods inventories so as to calculate the cost. For example, the sales may have been for 500 units of product, whereas the company manufactured only 400 units this month. In this case there would be a 100-unit reduction in inventory. Thus, by adding the cost of goods manufactured to the beginning inventory and subtracting the ending inventory, the result will be the cost of 500 units of product. Similar reasoning is applied if the units manufactured for the month exceed the units sold.

The cost of goods manufactured is figured on a separate form or schedule. This statement is shown in Figure 25-2. There are a few key points to be remembered when preparing this figure:

Figure 25-2
Statement of Cost of
Goods Manufactured

DUKE MANUFACTURING COMPANY STATEMENT OF COST OF GOODS MANUFACTURED FOR MONTH ENDED 6/30/X8				
Direct Materials:				
Raw Material Inventory, 6/1/X8			$ 5000 00	
Plus: Net Purchases	5500 0 00			
Less: Raw Material Inventory, 6/30/X8	800 0 00	4700 0 00		
Raw Material Cost				$ 5200 0 00
Direct Labor				9000 0 00
Overhead:				
Factory Supervision	$ 3700 0 00			
Maintenance Labor	1500 0 00			
Electricity	600 0 00			
Maintenance Supplies	500 0 00			
Operating Supplies	300 0 00			
Depreciation of Machinery	400 0 00			
Total Overhead				7000 0 00
Total Manufacturing Costs				21200 0 00
+ Work-in-Process Inventory, 6/1/X8				700 0 00
− Work-in-Process Inventory, 6/30/X8				900 0 00
Total Cost of Goods Manufactured				$21000 0 00

1. Cost of raw materials equals beginning raw materials inventory plus purchases less ending inventory of raw materials.

2. Total manufacturing costs incurred equals the following:

> Cost of Raw Material Used
> + Direct Labor
> + Factory Overhead

3. Cost of goods manufactured equals the following:

> Total Manufacturing Costs
> + Beginning Work-in-Process
> − Ending Work-in-Process

The first step in preparing the cost of goods manufactured is the calculation of the raw material cost for the month. If the accounting department has its records on a computer, the raw material cost may be readily available. If it is not, the cost must be calculated as shown by adding purchases to the beginning raw material inventory and then subtracting the ending inventory. The direct labor cost is usually a single figure found on the payroll or the labor distribution report. The overhead costs are then totaled and added to the raw material and direct labor to arrive at the total costs for the month. *The final step is to add the beginning work-in-process inventory and subtract the ending inventory.* Keep in mind that we subtract ending inventory, because it is not part of the cost of goods manufactured (yet).

Let's see how this figure is then used in preparing the income statement, shown in Figure 25-3.

DUKE MANUFACTURING COMPANY INCOME STATEMENT FOR MONTH ENDED 6/30/X8			
Sales			$400 0 0 0 00
Cost of Goods Sold:			
Finished Goods Inventory 6/1/X8	$ 25 0 0 0 00		
Plus: Cost of Goods Manufactured	210 0 0 0 00		
Cost of Goods Available for Sale	235 0 0 0 00		
Less: Finished Goods Inventory 6/30/X8	15 0 0 0 00		
Cost of Goods Sold		220 0 0 0 00	
Gross Profit		180 0 0 0 00	
Operating Expenses:			
Selling Expenses	$ 55 0 0 0 00		
Administrative Expense	65 0 0 0 00	120 0 0 0 00	
Net Income (before taxes)		$ 60 0 0 0 00	

Figure 25-3
Income Statement for a Manufacturing Firm

Learning Unit 25-1 Review

AT THIS POINT you should be able to

- Define and explain the three elements of manufacturing costs: raw material, direct labor, and manufacturing overhead. (p. 854)
- Define and explain the three major inventories in a manufacturing company: raw material, work-in-process, and finished goods. (p. 855)
- Compare the cost of goods sold section on an income statement for a merchandising company with the cost of goods manufactured section for a manufacturing company. (p. 855)
- Prepare a cost of goods manufactured schedule. (p. 856)

SELF-REVIEW QUIZ 25-1

(The blank forms you need are on page 228 of the *Study Guide and Working Papers*.)

Using the following accounts and amounts, prepare a separate statement of cost of goods manufactured and a cost of goods sold section of the income statement:

Finished Goods Inventory, June 1	$ 45,000
Depreciation of Machinery	15,000
Purchases (Net)	250,000
Maintenance Labor	15,000
Raw Material Inventory, June 1	15,000
Direct Labor	320,000
Work-in-Process Inventory, June 1	30,000
Factory Supervision Salaries	45,000
Finished Goods Inventory, June 30	60,000
Raw Material Inventory, June 30	20,000
Indirect Factory Labor	120,000
Work-in-Process Inventory, June 30	40,000
Factory Electricity Expense	15,000

SOLUTION TO SELF-REVIEW QUIZ 25-1

Statement of Cost of Goods Manufactured

Raw Material Inventory, June 1	$ 15,000	
Plus: Net Purchases	250,000	
Less: Raw Material Inventory, June 30	20,000	
Raw Material Cost		$245,000
Direct Labor		320,000
Overhead:		
Depreciation	$ 15,000	
Maintenance Labor	15,000	
Factory Supervision Salaries	45,000	
Indirect Labor	120,000	
Electricity Expense	15,000	210,000
Total Manufacturing Costs		$775,000
Plus: Work-in-Process Inventory, June 1		30,000
Less: Work-in-Process Inventory, June 30		40,000
Total Cost of Goods Manufactured		$765,000

Cost of Goods Sold

Finished Goods Inventory, June 1	$ 45,000
Plus: Cost of Goods Manufactured	765,000
Cost of Goods Available for Sale	810,000
Less: Finished Goods Inventory, June 30	60,000
Cost of Goods Sold	$750,000

Learning Unit 25-2 — The Flow of Manufacturing Costs

THE ACCUMULATION OF MANUFACTURING COSTS

As the raw material, direct labor, and overhead are charged into the manufacturing process, they must be recorded. The issuance of material from the warehouse, the assignment of labor to departments, and the movement of the products through the process must be provided to the cost accountants as the basis for journal entries.

Source Documents: The required data are submitted to the cost accountants through various source documents. The timely receipt of legible documents is often a problem in some companies, and employees must be made aware of their importance.

Receiving reports are prepared by the receiving department to acknowledge receipt of all material and supplies from vendors. A typical receiving report is shown in Figure 25-4. The accounting copy becomes a part of the vendor payment voucher, along with the purchase order and the vendor invoice.

Material requisitions are the documents initiated by the manufacturing personnel, or other users, to request material from the inventory warehouse. The requisition (Fig. 25-5) is presented to the storekeeper as the materials are issued. Copies of the requisitions are kept in accounting as a basis for charging material into production.

A clock card is a card used by each hourly employee to clock in and out of the factory each day. A typical clock card is shown in Figure 25-6. The cards are collected each week by the payroll department and become a basis for the payroll check and for charging labor into production.

```
┌─────────────────────────────────────────────────┐
│               RECEIVING REPORT                   │
├─────────────────────────────────────────────────┤
│ Received from:          Receiving Report No. 1031│
│ Adams Company           Date: 6/20/X8            │
├──────────┬───────────────┬──────────┬────────────┤
│          │               │  Unit    │  Total     │
│ Quantity │  Description   │  Price   │  Price     │
├──────────┼───────────────┼──────────┼────────────┤
│ 50 Gals. │    Paint       │$6.50/Gal.│  $325.00   │
├──────────┴───────────────┴──────────┴────────────┤
│            Revilo Manufacturing Co.              │
│            Inspected By  MS                       │
│            Received By   BJ                       │
└─────────────────────────────────────────────────┘
```

Figure 25-4
Receiving Report

```
┌─────────────────────────────────────────────────┐
│             MATERIAL REQUISITION                 │
├─────────────────────────────────────────────────┤
│ Department             Requisition No. 3648      │
│ Finishing              Date: 6/20/X8             │
├──────────┬───────────────┬──────────┬────────────┤
│          │               │  Unit    │  Total     │
│ Quantity │  Description   │  Price   │  Price     │
├──────────┼───────────────┼──────────┼────────────┤
│ 8 Gals.  │  White Paint   │  $6.50   │  $52.00    │
├──────────┴───────────────┴──────────┴────────────┤
│            Revilo Manufacturing Co.              │
│            Inspected By  CY                       │
│            Received By   FU                       │
└─────────────────────────────────────────────────┘
```

Figure 25-5
Material Requisition

```
┌─────────────────────────────────────────────────┐
│                 CLOCK CARD                       │
│                                                  │
│          Name:  David Ross                       │
│          Social Sec. No.  420-80-5178            │
│          Department:  Cutting                    │
│          Clock No.  1432                         │
├──────┬──────┬──────┬──────┬──────┬──────────────┤
│ Day  │  In  │ Out  │  In  │ Out  │   Hours      │
├──────┼──────┼──────┼──────┼──────┼──────────────┤
│ Mon  │ 7:58 │      │      │ 4:03 │    8         │
│ Tue  │ 7:57 │      │      │ 4:01 │    8         │
│ Wed  │ 8:00 │      │      │ 4:02 │    8         │
│ Thu  │ 7:59 │      │      │ 5:02 │    9         │
│ Fri  │ 7:57 │      │      │ 4:03 │    8         │
│ Sat  │      │      │      │      │              │
│ Sun  │      │      │      │      │              │
├──────┴──────┴──────┴──────┼──────┼──────────────┤
│       Total Hours         │      │    41        │
└───────────────────────────┴──────┴──────────────┘
```

Figure 25-6
Clock Card

Lot tickets, or move tickets, are documents that are written by departmental managers to reflect the movement of products, or parts of products, from one department to another. The department receiving the products must verify the quantity and quality of the products. These tickets become the basis for transferring costs between departments and to finished goods inventory. An example of a lot ticket is shown in Figure 25-7.

A labor distribution report is a byproduct of the payroll that has been reassembled into the categories of direct labor, maintenance labor, and so forth. Based on this report, the cost accountants charge labor into departments. An example of a typical labor distribution report is shown in Figure 25-8.

Figure 25-7
Lot Ticket

LOT TICKET	
Date Transferred from: Assembling	Transferred To: Finishing
Quantity	Description
20 Tables 20 Tables	36" Oak 36" Pine
	Received By __MB__

Figure 25-8
Labor Distribution Report

LABOR DISTRIBUTION REPORT WEEK ENDING 9/10/X8				
Employee	Department	Hours	Rate	Total
Direct Labor: James Amos Andrew Brown —	Cutting Cutting	42 39	$6.20 6.00	$260.40 234.00
Indirect Labor: Don Able Carl Baker —	Cutting Cutting	40 40	7.20 7.50	280.00 300.00

Figure 25-9
Bill of Lading

BILL OF LADING			
Shipper's No.			7/15/X8
Name of Customer __A.R. Owens__ Consigned To __Same__ Destination __Chicago__ State __Ill__ Route _____			
No. of Packages	Description	Weight	Class
60	Tables	3600	2
B.P. Smith Co. Atlanta, Georgia			__A.R.__ Agent

Bills of lading are documents that are used to show the shipment of products to customers. The cost accounting copies of the bills become the basis for recording the transfer of the cost of the products from the finished goods inventory to the cost of goods sold. A typical bill of lading is shown in Figure 25-9.

THE FLOW OF MANUFACTURING COSTS

To record and control manufacturing costs as the products move through the manufacturing process properly, it is necessary to establish the pattern of the flow of the costs. To do so, we use a flowchart.

The Flowchart: Figure 25-10 illustrates the movement of the material, labor, and overhead through the operation. Each step of the flow, from A to H, is illustrated and is followed by an example of the journal entries and the source documents for each step. *It should be noted that the journal entries reflect a debit to the destination and a credit to the source.*

> More explanations, along with an extra demonstration problem, follow the journal entries.

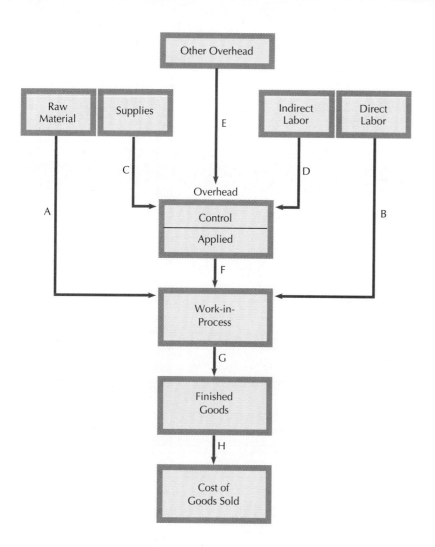

Figure 25-10
Flow of Costs

This process may seem overwhelming, so take the time to match each step in Figure 25-10 with its corresponding journal entry in Figure 25-11. Remember that the debit is to the destination and the credit is to the source. See the Blueprint on page 871 for samples involving T accounts.

Overhead Application: As shown in the flow of cost journal entries C, D, and E, the debit is to an account called Overhead—Control and in F the credit is to the account Overhead—Applied. It is desirable to maintain both these overhead accounts to avoid errors and confusion. Overhead—Control is used for the accumulation of all actual overhead costs as debits, and the Overhead—Applied is credited for the application of overhead to production.

It is necessary to apply overhead each week to determine the total costs for that week. Some overhead accounts, however, such as electricity, supervision, and depreciation, are not known until the end of the month. For this reason, an overhead rate must be established as a basis for applying the overhead. There are several methods of determining a rate, depending on the type of operation of the company.

The most common and practical methods are based on direct labor or machine hours. A rate can be developed from the annual budget of the overhead costs and the *direct labor dollars* (wages of those persons whose efforts *directly* affect the characteristics of the products manufactured) as follows:

Annual Overhead ÷ Annual Direct Labor Dollars
$500,000   ÷ $1,000,000   = 50%

SOURCE DOUMENTS

			Debit	Credit
Material requisitions	(A)	Work-in-Process Inventory	2 0 0 0 0 0	
		Raw Material Inventory		2 0 0 0 0 0
Labor distribution report	(B)	Work-in-Process Inventory	1 8 0 0 0 0	
		Payroll		1 8 0 0 0 0
Material requisitions	(C)	Overhead—Control	4 0 0 0 0	
		Supplies Inventory		4 0 0 0 0
Labor distribution report	(D)	Overhead—Control	1 0 0 0 0 0	
		Payroll		1 0 0 0 0 0
Various	(E)	Overhead—Control	1 0 0 0 0 0	
		Supervision Salaries		6 0 0 0 0
		Rent Expense		1 0 0 0 0
		Depreciation Expense		2 0 0 0 0
		Electricity Expense		1 0 0 0 0
None	(F)	Work-in-Process Inventory	25 0 0 0 0	
		Overhead—Applied		25 0 0 0 0
Lot tickets	(G)	Finished Goods Inventory	22 0 0 0 0	
		Work-in-Process Inventory		22 0 0 0 0
Bills of lading	(H)	Cost of Goods Sold	24 0 0 0 0	
		Finished Goods Inventory		24 0 0 0 0

Figure 25-11   Journal Entries

Based on this calculation, overhead can be applied to production each week or month at a rate of 50% of the direct labor cost charged to production. For example, if the direct labor this month is $20,000, overhead would be applied at $10,000, as shown in Figure 25-12.

Figure 25-12
Applying Overhead

	Debit	Credit
Work-in-Process Inventory	1 0 0 0 0 0	
Overhead—Applied		1 0 0 0 0 0

Another much-used rate is based on *direct labor hours:*

Annual Overhead ÷ Annual Direct Labor Hours
$500,000   ÷   200,000 Hours   = $2.50/Hour

In this case, the rate of $2.50 per direct labor hour would be applied as overhead. If direct labor hours this month were 2,000 hours, the applied overhead would be $5,000, as shown in Figure 25-13.

Figure 25-13
Apply Overhead by Direct Labor Hours

	Debit	Credit
Work-in-Process Inventory	5 0 0 0 0	
Overhead—Applied		5 0 0 0 0

Still another method that is convenient in some companies is based on *machine hours,* as follows:

Annual Overhead ÷ Annual Machine Hours
$500,000   ÷ 100,000 Machine Hours = $5.00/Hour

Using the $5.00 per machine hour rate, if the machine ran 3,000 hours, the overhead applied would be $15,000.

DEMONSTRATION PROBLEM

To further illustrate the journal entries and overhead application, consider the following transactions and the resulting journal entries (Fig. 25-14) for the month of August:

A. Issued raw material from the storeroom costing $69,000.

B. Charged direct labor into production, $60,000.

C. Issued supplies from the storeroom costing $6,000.

D. Incurred indirect labor costs of $15,000.

E. Charged the following expenses to overhead: rent, $3,000; supervision, $12,000; depreciation, $4,000; electricity, $6,000.

F. Applied overhead at 85% of direct labor dollars.

G. Transferred completed products costing $200,000 to finished goods.

H. Sold products costing $208,000.

Journal Entries

			Debit	Credit
(A)	Work-in-Process Inventory		69 000 00	
	Raw Material Inventory			69 000 00
(B)	Work-in-Process Inventory		60 000 00	
	Payroll			60 000 00
(C)	Overhead—Control		6 000 00	
	Supplies Inventory			6 000 00
(D)	Overhead—Control		15 000 00	
	Payroll			15 000 00
(E)	Overhead—Control		25 000 00	
	Rent Expense			3 000 00
	Supervision Expense			12 000 00
	Depreciation Expense			4 000 00
	Electricity Expense			6 000 00
(F)	Work-in-Process Inventory		51 000 00	
	Overhead—Applied			51 000 00
(G)	Finished Goods Inventory		200 000 00	
	Work-in-Process Inventory			200 000 00
(H)	Cost of Goods Sold		208 000 00	
	Finished Goods Inventory			208 000 00

Figure 25-14
Manufacturing
Transactions

Learning Unit 25-2 Review

AT THIS POINT you should be able to

- List the six source documents covered in this unit and explain the function of each in the accounting process. (p. 859)
- List the steps of the flowchart showing the movement of raw materials through the manufacturing process. (p. 861)
- Explain the difference between Overhead — Control and Overhead — Applied. (p. 861)

SELF-REVIEW QUIZ 25-2

(The blank forms you need are on page 229 of the *Study Guide and Working Papers.*)

Prepare the general journal entries required to record the following transactions (omit explanations):

A. Charged raw material into production, $6,000.

B. Charged direct labor into production, $8,000.

C. Issued operating supplies, $2,000.

D. Charged indirect labor into production, $5,000.

E. Incurred the following overhead: supervision, $4,500; rent, $1,000; depreciation, $500; electricity, $1,500; maintenance, $2,500.

F. Applied overhead to production at 180% of direct labor dollars.

G. Transferred products to finished goods, $9,000.

H. Sold products costing $10,000.

SOLUTION TO SELF-REVIEW QUIZ 25-2

			Debit	Credit
(A)	Work-in-Process		6 0 0 0 00	
	Raw Material			6 0 0 0 00
(B)	Work-in-Process		8 0 0 0 00	
	Payroll			8 0 0 0 00
(C)	Overhead—Control		2 0 0 0 00	
	Supplies Inventory			2 0 0 0 00
(D)	Overhead—Control		5 0 0 0 00	
	Payroll			5 0 0 0 00
(E)	Overhead—Control		10 0 0 0 00	
	Supervision			4 5 0 0 00
	Rent			1 0 0 0 00
	Depreciation			5 0 0 00
	Electricity			1 5 0 0 00
	Maintenance			2 5 0 0 00
(F)	Work-in-Process		14 4 0 0 00	
	Overhead—Applied			14 4 0 0 00
(G)	Finished Goods Inventory		9 0 0 0 00	
	Work-in-Process			9 0 0 0 00
(H)	Cost of Goods Sold		10 0 0 0 00	
	Finished Goods			10 0 0 0 00

Figure 25-15
Journalized Manufacturing Transactions

Learning Unit 25-3   Worksheet for a Manufacturing Company

In past chapters we viewed worksheets for a service company as well as a merchandise company. We now examine and explain the preparation of a worksheet for a manufacturing company. Figure 25-16 shows a worksheet for Roe Corporation. We have changed companies to provide you with more insight into other account titles used by different companies. The theory is the same. We then see how reports are prepared from the worksheet. Let's first look at some key points to remember when a worksheet is prepared. Keep in mind that the steps of the accounting cycle for a manufacturing company are the same as those used for a merchandise company.

KEY POINTS TO LOOK AT ON THE WORKSHEET

Key points on the worksheet include the following:

1. New set of columns for statement of cost of goods manufactured.
2. Beginning balances of raw materials inventory, $570, and work-in-process, $1,230, are listed in the debit column of statement of cost of goods

See number of key points circled on the worksheet (Fig. 25-16).

Account Titles	Trial Balance Dr.	Trial Balance Cr.	Adjustments Dr.	Adjustments Cr.	① Statement of Cost of Goods Manufactured Dr.	Cr.	Income Statement Dr.	Cr.	Balance Sheet Dr.	Cr.
Cash	135000								135000	
Accounts Receivable	153000								153000	
Allowance for Doubtful Accounts		48000		(B)66000						114000
Raw Materials Inventory	57000				②57000	②96000			②96000	
Work-in-Process Inventory	123000				②123000	②159000			②159000	
Finished Goods Inventory	75000						③75000	54000	54000	
Factory Supplies	99000			(A)78000					21000	
Prepaid Factory Insurance	105000			(D)75000					30000	
Factory Machinery	648000								648000	
Acc. Dep., Factory Mach.		120000		(C)84000						204000
Note Payable (due within 30 days)		225000								225000
Common Stock $10		225000								225000
Retained Earnings		180000								180000
Sales (Net)		2430000						2430000		
Raw Material Purchases (Net)	540000				540000					
Direct Labor	330000		(E)132000		462000					
Indirect Labor	102000		(E)48000		150000					
Heat, Light, and Power	174000				174000					
Machinery Repairs	45000				45000					
Rent Expense—Factory	180000				180000					
Selling Expense—Control	261000					④	261000			
Administrative Expenses (Control)	201000		(E)33000				234000			
	3228000	3228000								
Factory Supplies Expense			(A)78000		78000					
Bad Debts Expense			(B)66000				66000			
Dep. Expense—Factory Mach.			(C)84000		84000					
Factory Insurance Expense			(D)75000		75000					
Accrued Payroll Payable				(E)213000						213000
			516000	516000	1968000	255000	2349000	2484000	1296000	1161000
Cost of Goods Manufactured						1713000	1713000			
					1968000	1968000	2349000	2484000	1296000	1161000
Net Income							135000			135000
							2484000	2484000	1296000	1296000

Figure 25-16 Worksheet for a Manufacturing Company

manufactured. Ending balances of $960 and $1,590 are entered in the credit column.

3. Finished goods inventory is not listed on the statement of cost of goods manufactured. The beginning figure of finished goods, $750, is listed in the debit column of the income statement, whereas the ending balance of finished goods, $540, is listed in the credit column of the income statement and debit column of the balance sheet.

4. These are expenses that are not part of the cost of manufacturing and thus are not listed on the statement of cost of goods manufactured.

REPORTS PREPARED FROM THE WORKSHEET

The following reports can be prepared from the worksheet.

Cost of Goods Manufactured (Fig. 25-17)

ROE CORPORATION STATEMENT OF COST OF GOODS MANUFACTURED FOR YEAR ENDED DECEMBER 31, 20XX		
Direct Materials:		
Raw Materials Inventory (Beg.)	$ 5 7 0 00	
Raw Materials Purchased (Net)	5 4 0 0 00	
Cost of Available Raw Materials	5 9 7 0 00	
Less: Raw Materials Inventory (End.)	9 6 0 00	
Cost of Raw Materials Used		$ 5 0 1 0 00
Direct Labor		4 6 2 0 00
Factory Overhead:		
Indirect Labor	$ 1 5 0 0 00	
Heat, Light, and Power	1 7 4 0 00	
Rent Expense	1 8 0 0 00	
Machinery Repairs	4 5 0 00	
Factory Supplies Expense	7 8 0 00	
Dep. Exp., Factory Machinery	8 4 0 00	
Factory Insurance Expense	7 5 0 00	
Total Factory Overhead		$ 7 8 6 0 00
Total Manufacturing Cost Incurred		1 7 4 9 0 00
Plus: Work-in-Process (Beg.)		1 2 3 0 00
Less: Work-in-Process (End.)		1 5 9 0 00
Cost of Goods Manufactured*		$ 1 7 1 3 0 00

* This amount will go on the cost of goods sold section of the income statement, as shown on page 868.

Figure 25-17
Statement of Cost of Goods Manufactured

The Income Statement

Figure 25-18 is the income statement for Roe Corporation. Note how the $17,130 from the statement of cost of goods manufactured is listed below the beginning finished goods inventory. Note that the operating expenses, which were not part of the cost of the goods sold, are listed below gross profit. For example, Bad Debts Expense, a selling expense, had no part in the production of bean bag chairs for Roe. Remember that the cost of goods manufactured is not the same as the cost of goods sold.

The Balance Sheet

Figure 25-19 is the completed balance sheet of Roe Corporation. The net income of $1,350 in Figure 25-18 helps update retained earnings in Figure 25-19. Note how under current assets the manufacturing company lists its raw materials and work-in-process as well as finished goods.

Figure 25-18
Income Statement

ROE CORPORATION INCOME STATEMENT FOR YEAR ENDED DECEMBER 31, 20XX			
Net Sales			$ 24 3 0 0 00
Cost of Goods Sold:			
Finished Goods Inventory (Beg.)	$ 7 5 0 00		
Cost of Goods Manufactured	17 1 3 0 00		
Cost of Goods Available for Sale	$17 8 8 0 00		
Less: Finished Goods Inventory (End.)	5 4 0 00		
Cost of Goods Sold:			$17 3 4 0 00
Gross Profit on Sales			$ 6 9 6 0 00
Operating Expenses:			
Selling Expense*	$ 3 2 7 0 00		
Administrative Expense	2 3 4 0 00		
Total Operating Expenses			$ 5 6 1 0 00
Net Income (before taxes)			$ 1 3 5 0 00

* Includes the $660 of bad debt expense.

Figure 25-19
Balance Sheet

ROE CORPORATION BALANCE SHEET DECEMBER 31, 20XX			
Assets			
Current Assets:			
Cash			$ 1 3 5 0 00
Accounts Receivable	$ 1 5 3 0 00		
Less: Allowance for Doubtful Accounts	1 1 4 0 00	$ 3 9 0 00	
Inventories			
Raw Materials	$ 9 6 0 00		
Work-in-Process	1 5 9 0 00		
Finished Goods	5 4 0 00	$ 3 0 9 0 00	
Prepaid Expenses:			
Factory Supplies	$ 2 1 0 00		
Prepaid Factory Insurance	3 0 0 00	$ 5 1 0 00	
Total Current Assets		$ 5 3 4 0 00	
Plant and Equipment			
Factory Machinery	$ 6 4 8 0 00		
Less: Accum. Depreciation, Factory Machinery	2 0 4 0 00	$ 4 4 4 0 00	
Total Assets		$ 9 7 8 0 00	

Figure 25-19
(*continued*)

Liabilities and Stockholders' Equity			
Current Liabilities:			
Notes Payable	$ 2 2 5 0 00		
Accrued Payroll Payable	2 1 3 0 00	$ 4 3 8 0 00	
Stockholders' Equity			
Common Stock, $10 par 225 shares	$ 2 2 5 0 00		
Retained Earnings*	3 1 5 0 00	$ 5 4 0 0 00	
Total Liabilities and Stockholders' Equity		$ 9 7 8 0 00	

* Beginning Retained Earnings + Net Income.

Learning Unit 25-3 Review

AT THIS POINT you should be able to

- Explain the key points to consider in a worksheet for a manufacturing company. (p. 865)
- From the worksheet, prepare a statement of cost of goods manufactured along with the income statement and balance sheet. (p. 868)

SELF-REVIEW QUIZ 25-3

(The blank forms you need are on page 229 of the *Study Guide and Working Papers*.)
Respond true or false to the following:

1. The figure for cost of goods manufactured is always placed in the credit column of the income statement on the worksheet.

2. Finished goods are not listed in the statement of cost of goods manufactured.

3. All expenses are listed in the cost of goods manufactured.

4. The ending balances of raw materials inventory and work-in-process are entered in the debit columns of cost of goods manufactured.

SOLUTIONS TO SELF-REVIEW QUIZ 25-3

1. False   2. True   3. False   4. False

Chapter Review

Summary of Key Points

Learning Unit 25-1

1. Manufacturing costs are broken into raw materials, direct labor, and manufacturing overhead.
2. A manufacturing firm has three major inventories: raw materials, work-in-process, and finished goods.
3. Cost of goods manufactured is prepared first, before the income statement is completed.

Learning Unit 25-2

1. When journal entries are prepared to record the movement of material, labor, and overhead through the operation of a company, each debit is the destination and each credit is the source.
2. Overhead may be applied based on direct labor hours, direct labor dollars, or machine hours.

Learning Unit 25-3

1. The steps of the accounting cycle for a manufacturing company are the same as those used for a merchandise company.
2. The worksheet for a manufacturing company has columns for items used to calculate the statement of cost of goods manufactured. This figure is then updated on the income statement debit column of the worksheet.

Key Terms

Bill of lading A formal document issued to the carrier of the finished product. It is the basis for charging the cost of goods sold.

Clock card A card used by employees when clocking in and out of the factory; it becomes the basis for the payroll.

Direct labor The wages of those persons whose efforts directly affect the quality or other characteristics of the products manufactured.

Labor distribution report A report issued by the payroll department to categorize all the types of labor incurred during the week.

Lot ticket A document prepared to show the movement of materials or products between departments. Also called *move ticket*.

Manufacturing overhead All the manufacturing costs except raw material and direct labor.

Material requisition A document used to order material or supplies from the storeroom that is the basis for charging material into production.

Raw material Material that is to be processed into a finished product or that changes the quality or characteristics of the product.

Receiving report A document prepared by the receiving department to evidence the receipt of material or supplies that were ordered.

Blueprint: Manufacturing Elements

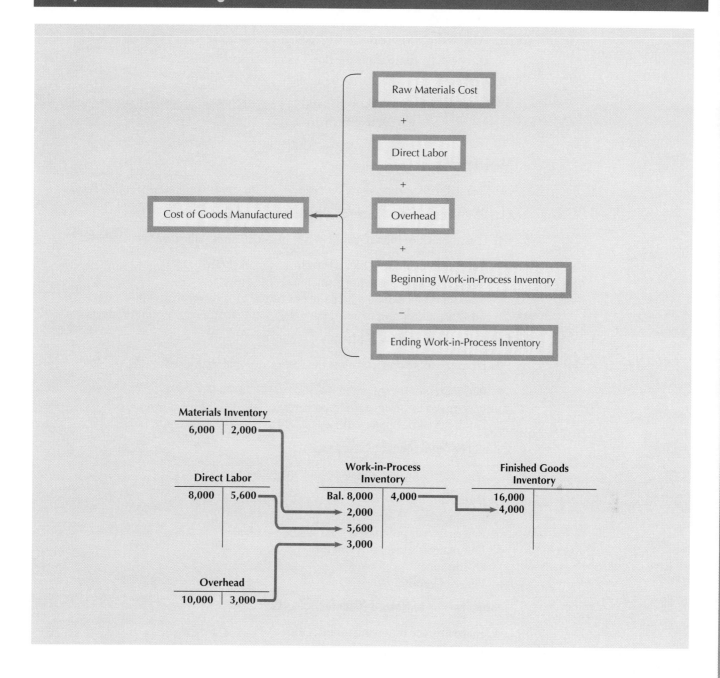

Questions, Mini Exercises, Exercises, and Problems

Discussion Questions

1. Into what three elements can manufacturing costs be broken?

2. Direct labor includes the wages of those personnel whose efforts indirectly change the quality or characteristics of the product. True or false? Please explain.

3. What are the three major inventories of a manufacturing firm?

4. Explain how to calculate the total cost of goods manufactured.

5. Explain the purpose of receiving reports as well as materials requisitions.

6. What tickets become the basis for transferring costs between departments to finished goods inventory?

7. What is the purpose of a bill of lading?

8. Draw a diagram to show the flow of manufacturing costs.

9. Explain how overhead may be applied.

10. Compare and contrast the structure of a worksheet for a merchandise company and a manufacturing company.

Mini Exercises

(The blank forms you need are on page 231 of the *Study Guide and Working Papers*.)

Classifications of Raw Material, Direct Labor, and Overhead

1. Classify each of the following as raw material, direct labor, or overhead:

    a. Finishing material for a furniture manufacturer.
    b. Depreciation expense of manufacturing assets.
    c. Labor of a person who paints furniture for a furniture manufacturer.
    d. Pure aluminum in a company that manufactures aluminum products.

Calculating Cost of Raw Materials

2. From the following, calculate the cost of raw materials used:

Raw materials Inventory, January 1	$ 5,000
Raw materials Inventory, December 31	12,000
Purchases of raw materials	70,000

Calculating Total Manufacturing Costs

3. From the following, calculate total manufacturing costs:

Direct labor	$ 7,000
Raw materials inventory, June 30	4,500
Raw materials purchases	15,000
Raw materials inventory, June 1	3,000
Overhead	4,000
Finished goods	8,000

Journal Entries to Record Manufacturing Costs

4. Journalize the following transactions:

    a. Storeroom issued raw materials costing $5,000.
    b. Direct labor of $3,000 was charged into production.
    c. Supplies costing $2,000 were issued by the storeroom.
    d. Indirect labor cost of $4,000 was incurred.
    e. Rent of $1,000 and Depreciation of $400 were charged to overhead.

5. Identify where each title is placed on the worksheet.

    1. Cost of goods manufactured column.
    2. Income statement column.
    3. Balance sheet.

        _____ **a.** Raw materials purchases.
        _____ **b.** Ending finished goods inventory.
        _____ **c.** Ending raw materials inventory.
        _____ **d.** Sales.

Exercises

(The blank forms you need are on page 232 of the *Study Guide and Working Papers*.)

25-1. Classify each of the following as raw material, direct labor, or overhead:

    a. The lumber in making furniture.
    b. The insurance for a factory.
    c. The wages of a forklift driver.
    d. A manufacturing foreman's salary.

Classifications of raw material, direct labor, and overhead.

25-2. From the following balances, calculate the cost of raw material used:

Raw materials inventory, January 1	$ 60,000
Raw materials inventory, December 31	90,000
Purchases of raw materials	800,000

Calculating raw materials costs.

25-3. From the following, calculate total manufacturing costs:

Direct labor	$ 80,000
Raw materials inventory, May 30	9,600
Raw materials purchases	70,000
Raw materials inventory, May 1	9,000
Overhead	75,000
Finished goods	120,000

Calculating total manufacturing costs.

25-4. From the following transactions, prepare the appropriate general journal entries for the month of May:

    a. Raw materials costing $75,000 were issued from the storeroom.
    b. Direct labor of $65,000 was charged into production.
    c. Supplies costing $7,000 were issued from the storeroom.
    d. Indirect labor costs of $18,000 were incurred.
    e. Rent of $3,000 and depreciation of $500 were charged to overhead.
    f. Eighty percent of the direct labor dollars used were applied to overhead.
    g. Completed products costing $70,000 were transferred to finished goods.
    h. Products costing $39,000 were sold.

Journal entries to record flow of manufacturing costs and the application of overhead.

25-5. a. In which columns on the worksheet would the following additional data be placed?

	Year-End Figures	Column
Raw materials	$34,000	
Goods-in-process	19,500	
Finished goods	30,000	

    b. In which columns would the beginning-of-year figures be placed?

Placement of data on a worksheet for a manufacturing company.

Group A Problems

(The blank forms you need are on pages 233–234 of the Study Guide and Working Papers.)

25A-1. An analysis of the accounts of Harwood Manufacturing reveals the following data for the month ended July 31, 20XX:

Inventories	Beginning	Ending
Raw materials	$18,000	$ 19,000
Work-in-process	13,000	17,000
Finished goods	15,000	14,000

Preparing a cost of goods manufactured schedule.

Check Figure:
Total cost of goods manufactured $307,000

Costs Incurred

Raw materials purchased, $130,000; direct labor, $130,000; manufacturing overhead, $52,000. These specific overheads included indirect labor, $20,000; factory insurance, $9,000; depreciation on machinery, $10,000; machinery repairs, $4,000; factory utilities, $6,000; and miscellaneous factory costs, $3,000.

Instructions

Prepare a cost of goods manufactured statement.

25A-2. As the bookkeeper of Ace Manufacturing, you are to record the following transactions in the general journal for the month of November:

> **a.** Raw materials of $80,000 were issued from the storeroom.
> **b.** Charged $60,000 of direct labor to production.
> **c.** Supplies costing $7,000 were issued from the storeroom.
> **d.** Incurred indirect labor costs of $15,000.
> **e.** The following expenses were charged to overhead: rent, $3,000; supervision, $8,000; depreciation, $4,000; electricity, $6,500.
> **f.** Overhead was applied at 90% of direct labor dollars.
> **g.** Transferred completed products costing $160,000 to finished goods.
> **h.** Sold products costing $198,000.

25A-3. From the information in Figure 25-20, prepare a worksheet for Keep Corporation (assume no adjustments).

	TRIAL BALANCE	
	Cr.	Dr.
Cash	6 2 4 0 00	
Raw Materials Inventory	8 8 8 0 00	
Goods-in-Process Inventory	7 4 4 0 00	
Finished Goods Inventory	10 3 2 0 00	
Factory Supplies	3 2 4 0 00	
Prepaid Factory Supplies	3 6 0 00	
Desks	9 6 0 00	
Machinery	57 2 4 0 00	
Acc. Depreciation, Machinery		8 2 8 0 00
Accounts Payable		3 1 2 0 00
Common Stock $10 Par		60 0 0 0 00
Retained Earnings		8 0 4 0 00
Sales		115 6 8 0 00
Raw Materials Purchases	38 4 0 0 00	
Direct Labor	22 3 2 0 00	
Indirect Labor	9 9 6 0 00	
Machinery Repairs	7 2 0 00	
Selling Expenses	14 7 6 0 00	
Administrative Expense	10 0 8 0 00	
Factory Supplies Expense	1 3 2 0 00	
Depreciation of Machinery	2 8 8 0 00	
	195 1 2 0 00	195 1 2 0 00

Figure 25-20 Trial Balance of Keep Corporation

Additional Data

Year-End Figures

Raw materials	$11,400
Goods-in-process	8,280
Finished goods	10,200

Check Figure:
Net income $18,480

Group B Problems

(The blank forms you need are on pages 233–234 of the *Study Guide and Working Papers.*)

25B-1. An analysis of the accounts of Harwood Manufacturing reveals the following data for the month ended July 31, 20XX:

Preparing a cost of goods manufactured schedule.

Inventories	Beginning	Ending
Raw materials	$16,000	$22,000
Work-in-process	12,000	16,000
Finished goods	16,000	14,000

Check Figure:
Total cost of goods manu-
factured $249,000

Costs Incurred

Raw materials purchased, $130,000; direct labor, $90,000; manufacturing overhead, $39,000. These specific overheads included indirect labor, $9,600; factory insurance, $8,000; depreciation on machinery, $7,600; machinery repairs, $6,000; factory utilities, $6,300; and miscellaneous factory costs, $1,500.

Instructions

Prepare a cost of goods manufactured statement.

25B-2. From the following transactions in May for Ace Manufacturing, record the appropriate general journal entries:

Journalizing entries to record manufacturing costs and application of overhead.

  a. Raw materials of $70,000 were issued from Ace's storeroom.
  b. Charged $75,000 of direct labor to production.
  c. Supplies of $4,000 were issued from the storeroom.
  d. Indirect labor costs were incurred for $20,000.
  e. The following expenses were charged to overhead: rent, $5,000; supervision, $9,000; depreciation, $6,200; electricity, $9,000.
  f. Overhead was applied at 80% of direct labor dollars.
  g. Completed products costing $180,000 were transferred to finished goods.
  h. Sold products costing $208,000.

Check Figure:
d. Dr. Overhead control
$20,000
Cr. Payroll $20,000

25B-3. From the information in Figure 25-21, prepare a worksheet for Keep Corporation (assume no adjustments).

Preparing a worksheet for a manufacturing company.

Additional Data

Year-End Figures

Raw materials	$ 285
Goods-in-process	2,070
Finished goods	2,550

Check Figure:
Net income $2,055

	TRIAL BALANCE	
	Cr.	Dr.
Cash	1310 00	
Raw Materials Inventory	2220 00	
Goods-in-Process Inventory	1860 00	
Finished Goods Inventory	2580 00	
Factory Supplies	560 00	
Prepaid Factory Insurance	590 00	
Desks	240 00	
Machinery	14310 00	
Acc. Depreciation, Machinery		2070 00
Accounts Payable		780 00
Common Stock $10 Par		15000 00
Retained Earnings		2010 00
Sales		28920 00
Raw Materials Purchases	9600 00	
Direct Labor	5580 00	
Indirect Labor	2490 00	
Machinery Repairs	180 00	
Selling Expenses	3690 00	
Administrative Expense	2520 00	
Factory Supplies Expense	330 00	
Depreciation of Machinery	720 00	
	48780 00	48780 00

Figure 25-21 Trial Balance of Keep Corporation

Real-World Applications

25R-1. Peter Roel had to leave the office on urgent business and has asked you to close the costs into the manufacturing summary account. Please do so. Why do you think Peter forgot to close the accounts? Provide a written response.

MEMO

To: Peter Roel, Bookkeeper

From: M. V. Rooy, Vice President

Re: Closing Entries

I notice that you forgot to close the costs that appeared in the statement of cost of goods manufactured into the manufacturing summary account. Here is a blueprint of the form. Please provide them to me as soon as possible.

Manufacturing Summary	XXX	
Raw Materials Inventory		XXX
Raw Materials Inventory	XXX	
Manufacturing Summary		XXX
Manufacturing Summary	XXX	
Work-in-Process Inventory		XXX
Work-in-Process Inventory	XXX	
Manufacturing Summary		XXX

YOU make the call

Critical Thinking/Ethical Case

25R-2. Dot Lovet works in the receiving department of a leading publishing company. She has become good friends with many of the suppliers. At 4 P.M., Joe Andrews delivered a truckload of art supplies. Joe was in a hurry and asked Dot to accept the order. He promised that everything was there. Dot signed the receiving report without verifying the specifics of the order. Two weeks later the art department called complaining that their department was being charged for items they never received. The accounting department has already processed the payment to this vendor. If you were Dot's supervisor, what would you do in this situation? You make the call. Write down your recommendation to Dot.

Internet Exercises: Papa Johns; Ford Motors

EX-1. [**www.papajohns.com/**]   Papa Johns is the third largest pizza retailer in the United States. Believe it or not, we can consider them as "manufacturers" of pizza! The "direct" costs of the pizza include the dough, the sauces, the toppings (raw materials), and the labor of those who work in the kitchen baking the pizzas (direct labor).

Let's take a look at the "factory overhead" or "indirect costs" that go into a pizza. What are five examples of "indirect costs" that go into creation of a pizza?

EX-2. [**www.ford.com**]   In manufacturing accounting three major categories of costs are considered—Raw or Direct Materials, Direct Labor, and Factory Overhead. In a manufacturing process the "direct" costs are usually easily identified. The area of Factory Overhead is the most difficult area of costs to identify.

In a large manufacturing environment such as Ford has, there are literally hundreds of indirect costs to account for in the production process. List five of the indirect assembly personnel costs that would go into Factory Overhead.

How Companies Record Credit Card Sales in Their Special Journals

RECORDING BANK CREDIT CARDS

Example: Credit Card Sale of $100, MasterCard: It is interesting to note that for bank credit cards (MasterCard, Visa), the sales are recorded in the seller's Cash Receipts Journal, because the slips are converted into cash immediately. Bank credit cards are not treated as accounts receivable. The fee the bank charges, $2\frac{1}{2}$ to 6 percent, is usually deducted, and the bank credits the depositor's account immediately for the net. The end result for the seller is as follows:

Accounts Affected	Category	↑ ↓	Rules
Cash	Asset	↑	Dr. $94.
Credit Card Expense	Expense	↑	Dr. 6
Sales	Revenue	↑	Cr. 100

									CASH RECEIPTS JOURNAL					
Date	Cash Dr.	Credit Card Expense Dr.	Accounts Receivable Cr.	Sales Credited	Sales Tax Payable Cr.	Sundry — Account Name	Amount Cr.
	94 00	6 00		100 00			

It is the responsibility of the credit card company to sustain any losses (bad debts) from customers' nonpayment. If the bank waits to take the discount until the end of the month, the seller makes a nonpayment entry in the cash payment journal to record the credit card expense; the end result would be credit card expense up and cash balance down. Usually, the bank sends the charge on the monthly statement. *Remember: Bank credit cards are not treated as accounts receivable.*

RECORDING PRIVATE COMPANY CREDIT CARDS

Private companies such as American Express are considered by sellers as accounts receivable. The seller periodically summarizes the sales slips and submits them to the private credit card company for payment (which the company will pay quickly). Let's look at two situations to show how a company would handle its accounting procedures for these credit sales transactions.

Situation 1:   On May 4, Morris Company sold merchandise on account of $53 to Bill Blank. Bill used American Express. Assume Morris Company has a low dollar volume and few transactions.

Note in Figure A-1 how the sale of $53 is recorded in the sales journal. Keep in mind that Morris is treating American Express, not Bill Blank, as the accounts receivable. In Figure A-2 we see on June 8 payment is received from American Express and results in the following:

1. Cash increasing by $50.35.
2. Credit card expense rising by $2.65.
3. Accounts receivable being reduced by the $53 originally owed by American Express.

Situation 2:   On March 31, Blue Company summarized its credit card sales for American Express. Payment was received on April 13 from American Express. Assume Blue Company has a high dollar volume and many transactions.

Note in Figure A-3 how each credit company has its own column set up. In the ledger there is an account set up for each as well; the posting to the ledger would be done at the end of the month. With high volume and the need to record many transactions, the use of these additional columns (versus Figure A-1) will result in increased efficiency. Figure A-4 shows the receipt of money from American Express less the credit card expense charge.

Figure A-1
Morris Co. Sales Journal

	Date	Invoice	Description of Accounts Receivable	PR	Accounts Receivable Dr.	Sales Tax* Payable Cr.	Sales Cr.	
			MORRIS COMPANY SALES JOURNAL					
	May 4	692	American Express		53 00	3 00	50 00	
			(Bill Blank)					

* Assume a 6% sales tax.

	Date	Cash Dr.	Sales Discount Dr.	Credit Card Expense Dr.	Accounts Receivable Cr.	Sales Tax Payable Cr.	Account Name	PR	Amount Cr.	
				MORRIS COMPANY CASH RECEIPTS JOURNAL			Sundry			
	June 8	50 35		2 65*	53 00		American Express			
							(Bill Blank)			

* Assume credit card expense of 5%. Note that the $2.56 is 5% × $53.

Figure A-2 Morris Co. Cash Receipts Journal

BLUE COMPANY SALES JOURNAL

Date	Invoice Number	Description of Accounts Receivable	PR	Accounts Receivable Dr.	Credit Cards American Express Dr.	Credit Cards Diners Club Dr.	Sales Tax Payable Cr.	Credit Card Sales Cr.	Sales Cr.
Mar. 31		Summary of American Express			1197000		57000	1140000	
					(112)			(401)	

Figure A-3 Blue Co. Sales Journal

BLUE COMPANY CASH RECEIPTS JOURNAL

Date	Cash Dr.	Sales Discount Dr.	Credit Card Expense Dr.	Accounts Receivable Cr.	Credit Card Accounts Rec. American Express Cr.	Credit Card Accounts Rec. Diners Club Cr.	Sales Cr.	Sales Tax Payable Cr.	Sundry Account Name	PR	Amount Cr.
Apr. 13	1125180		71820		1197000				Summary of American Express payments		

Figure A-4 Blue Co. Cash Receipts Journal

Computerized Accounting

Part A AN INTRODUCTION

Accounting procedures are essentially the same whether they are performed manually or on a computer. The following is a list of the account cycle steps in a manual accounting system as compared to the steps in a computerized accounting system.

STEPS OF THE ACCOUNTING CYCLE

Manual Accounting System

1. Business transactions occur and generate source documents.
2. Analyze and record business transactions in a manual journal.
3. Post or transfer information from journal to ledger.
4. Prepare a trial balance.
5. Prepare a worksheet.
6. Prepare financial statements.
7. Journalize and post adjusting entries.
8. Journalize and post closing entries.
9. Prepare a post-closing trial balance.

Computerized Accounting System

1. Business transactions occur and generate source documents.
2. Analyze and record business transactions in a computerized journal.
3. Computer automatically posts information from journal to ledger.
4. Trial balance is prepared automatically.
5. Enter necessary adjustments directly.
6. Financial statements are prepared automatically.
7. Completed prior to preparation of financial statements.
8. Closing procedures are completed automatically.
9. Trial balance is automatically prepared as needed.

The accounting cycle comparison shows that the accountant's task of initially analyzing business transactions in terms of debits and credits (both routine business transactions and adjusting entries) is required in both manual and computerized accounting systems. However, in a computerized accounting system, the "drudge" work of posting transactions, creating and completing worksheets and financial statements, and performing the closing procedures is all handled automatically by the computerized accounting system.

In addition, computerized accounting systems can perform accounting procedures at greater speeds and with greater accuracy than can be achieved in a manual accounting system. It is important to recognize, however, that the computer is only a tool that can accept and process information supplied by the accountant. Each business transaction and adjusting entry must first be analyzed and recorded in a computerized journal correctly; otherwise, the financial statements generated by the computerized accounting system will contain errors and will not be useful to the business.

Before a business can begin to use a computerized accounting system, and specifically the Peachtree Complete Accounting system, it must have the following items in place:

1. A computer system
2. Computer software
    a. Operating system software
    b. Peachtree Complete Accounting (any version)

COMPUTER SYSTEM

A computer system consists of several electronic components that together have the ability to accept user-supplied data; input, store, and execute programmed instructions; and output results according to user specifications. The physical computer and its related devices are the hardware, while the stored program that supplies the instructions is called the software.

To understand how a computer system works, we must first look at a conceptual computer that demonstrates the major components and functions of a computer system. The conceptual computer shown in Figure B-1 has four major elements—input devices, processing/internal memory unit, secondary storage devices, and output devices. The illustration also shows the flow of data into the computer and of processed information out of the computer.

Input devices are used to feed data and instructions into the computer. Once the data and instructions are entered, the computer must be able to store them internally and then process the data based on the instructions. Storage and processing occur in the processing/internal memory unit.

There are two types of internal computer memory: random-access memory (RAM) and read-only memory (ROM). RAM is the largest portion of the memory but still has limited capacity; consequently, secondary storage devices are needed. In addition, RAM is temporary—anything stored in RAM is erased when power to the computer is interrupted. Therefore, data stored in RAM must be saved to a secondary storage medium through the use of a secondary storage device before the power is turned off. ROM is permanent memory and consists of those instruction sets necessary to start the computer and receive initial messages from input devices. ROM takes up only a small portion of the total internal memory capacity of a computer system.

Figure B-1
Conceptual Computer

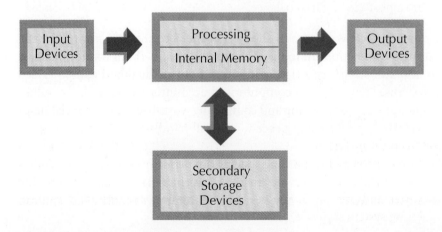

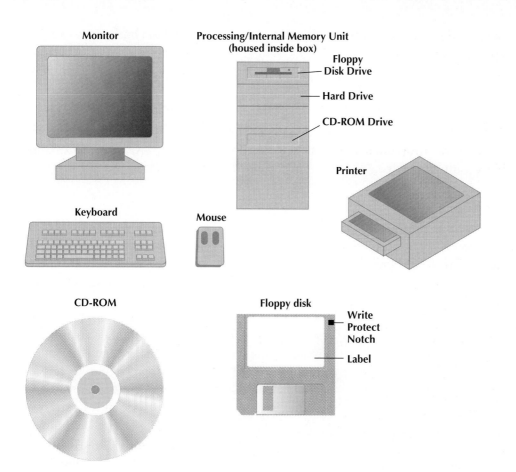

Figure B-2
Typical Configuration of
a Microcomputer System

Figure B-3
Storage Media

Finally, the results of processing must be made available to computer users through output devices. These components form a collection of devices referred to as computer hardware because they have physical substance. In a typical microcomputer system (see Figure B-2) a keyboard and mouse are used for input and a printer and monitor are used for output. The processing/internal memory unit is housed inside a box along with secondary storage devices consisting of a hard drive unit, one or more floppy disk drives, and a CD-ROM drive.

Computer hardware can do nothing without a computer program. Computer programs are supplied on floppy disks or CD-ROMs, which are secondary storage media used in floppy disk or CD-ROM drives. Figure B-3 shows an example of a floppy disk and a CD-ROM.

To operate a particular computer program you must first load the program into the system's internal memory (RAM) through the use of a floppy disk or CD-ROM drive or by accessing the program that has been installed and stored on the system's hard drive. Once RAM accesses a program, the computer can execute the program instructions and process data as directed by the user through the keyboard or mouse. At the end of a processing session, the results may be viewed on the monitor, printed on the printer, and/or stored permanently on a floppy disk or hard drive.

COMPUTER SOFTWARE

The computer can do nothing without a computer program. Computer programs control the input, processing, storage, and output operations of a computer. Computer programmers write the instructions that tell the computer to execute certain procedures and process data. There are two broad categories of computer software; operating system software and applications software.

Operating System Software

Operating system software provides the link between the computer hardware, applications software, and the computer user. It consists of programs that start up the computer, retrieve applications programs, and allow the computer operator to store and retrieve data. Operating system software controls access to input and output devices and access to applications programs. There are several popular operating systems for microcomputers. They include Windows 95/98/2000/XP, DOS, DOS combined with Windows 3.XX, OS/2, the Macintosh operating system, and UNIX.

Applications Software

Applications software refers to programs designed for a specific use. The five most common types of business applications software are database management, spreadsheet, work processing, communications, and graphics. Spreadsheet software allows the manipulation of data and has the ability to project answers to "what if" questions. For example, a spreadsheet program could project a company's profit next year if sales increased by 10 percent and expenses increased by 6 percent. Word processing software enables the user to write and print letters, memos, and other documents. Graphic software displays data visually in the form of graphic images, and communications software allows your computer to "talk" to other computers. But to accomplish communications you need additional hardware: a modem to transmit and receive data over telephone lines. Database management software stores, retrieves, sorts, and updates an organized body of information. Most computerized accounting systems are designed as database management software. Accounting information is data that must be organized and stored in a common base of data. This allows the entry of data and the retrieval of information in an organized and systematic way.

Applications software is frequently linked with a particular operating system. Database management, spreadsheet, word processing, graphics, communication, accounting, and other software applications are available in versions that work with most of the popular operating systems. For example, if your computer system is using Windows XP you would purchase the Windows XP version of a word processing program. If you were using a Macintosh computer and operating system you would purchase the Macintosh version of a spreadsheet program.

Accounting Applications Software   Most computerized accounting software is organized into modules. Each module is designed to process a particular type of accounting data such as accounts receivable, accounts payable, or payroll. Each module is also designed to work in conjunction with the other modules. When modules are designed to work together in this manner, they are referred to as integrated software. In an integrated accounting system each module handles a different function but also communicates with the other modules. For example, to record a sale on account, you would make an entry into the accounts receivable module. The integration feature automatically records this entry in the sales journal, updates the customer's account in the accounts receivable subsidiary ledger, and posts all accounts affected in the general ledger. Thus in an integrated accounting system, transaction data are only entered once. All of the other accounting procedures required to bring the accounting records up-to-date are performed automatically through the integration function.

Peachtree Complete Accounting   The most current version of Peachtree Complete Accounting has been selected for use in this text to demonstrate and help you learn how to use a computerized accounting system. It is easy to use, fully integrated, and available in versions that work with several different operating systems. The program can be used to maintain the accounting data for a sole proprietorship, a partnership or a corporation. It will accommodate service, merchandising, and manufacturing businesses. The payroll functions in this version are based on the federal and state tax laws in effect in 2003 and contain educational version tax tables for working in those chapters that require them. They are not intended to be accurate but rather are intended to demonstrate the process used by Peachtree. The workshops contained in this text are designed to illustrate how manual accounting concepts will be handled by a computerized accounting system. They are not intended to provide a comprehensive course of study for a computerized accounting system.

WORKING WITH PEACHTREE COMPLETE ACCOUNTING

Before you begin to work with Peachtree Complete Accounting you need to be familiar with your computer hardware and the Windows operating system. When you are running Windows, your work takes place on the desktop. Think of this area as resembling the surface of a desk. There are physical objects on your real desk and there are windows and icons on the Windows desktop. There are minor differences between the various versions of Windows. The figures will reflect a typical Windows 2000 Desktop. Other Windows versions will have small differences but will be essentially the same.

A mouse is an essential input device for all Windows applications. A mouse is a pointing device that assumes different shapes on your monitor as you move the mouse on your desk. According to the nature of the current action, the mouse pointer may appear as a small arrowhead, an hourglass, or a hand. There are five basic mouse techniques:

- Click — To quickly press and release the left mouse button.
- Double-click — To click the left mouse button twice in rapid succession.
- Drag — To hold down the left mouse button while you move the mouse.
- Point — To position the mouse pointer over an object without clicking a button.
- Right-click — To quickly press and release the right mouse button.

The Windows 2000 Desktop

Figure B-4 shows a typical opening Windows 2000 screen. Your desktop may be different, just as your real desk is arranged differently from those of your colleagues.

- **Desktop icons:** Graphic representations of drives, files, and other resources. The desktop icons that display will vary depending on your computer setup.
- **Start button:** Clicking on the Start button displays the start menu and lets you start applications.
- **Taskbar:** Contains the Start button and other buttons representing open applications.

Applications Window

As you work with Peachtree Complete Accounting two kinds of windows will appear on your desktop. The Main Menu window is where all activities in Peachtree will begin. An application window contains a running application. The name of the application and the application's menu bar will appear at the top of the application

Figure B-4
Windows 2000 Desktop
(Partial)

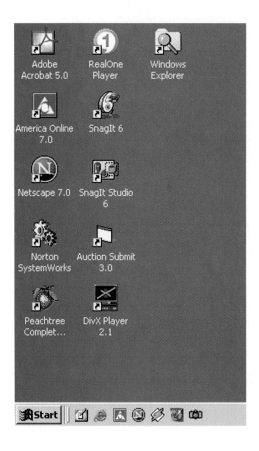

Figure B-5
Peachtree Main Menu
Application Window

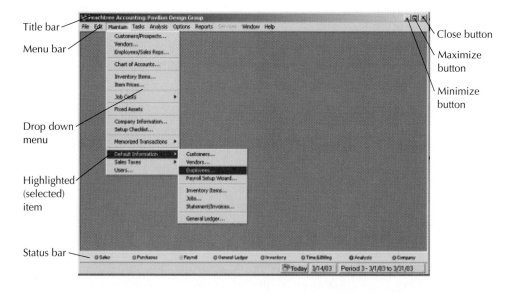

window. Regardless of the windows that are open on your desktop, most windows have certain elements in common. See Figure B-5 above.

- **Minimize button:** Clicking on this button minimizes a window and displays it as a task button on the taskbar.
- **Maximize button:** Clicking on this button enlarges the window so that it fills the entire desktop. After you enlarge a window, the Maximize button is

replaced by a Restore button (a double box, not shown) that returns the window to the size it was before it was maximized.

- **Close button:** Clicking on this button will close the window.
- **Title bar:** Displays the name of the application.
- **Menu bar:** This window element lists the available menus for the window.
- **Drop down menu:** Shows the options available under each menu option.
- **Highlighted (selected) item:** The active selection in a Drop down menu.
- **Status bar:** A line of text at the bottom of many windows that gives more information about a field. If you are unsure of what to enter in a field, select it with your mouse and read the status bar.

Dialog Boxes

A dialog box appears when additional information is needed to execute a command. There are different ways to supply that information; consequently, there are different types of dialog boxes. Most dialog boxes (see Fig. B-6) are for specific functions and tasks and require you to supply the data for that task. After you supply the needed information, you can choose a command button to carry out a command such as to Post or Print.

- **Folder tabs:** Some dialog boxes have multiple pages of entry fields available to them. These tabs allow you to switch between available screens.
- **Arrow button:** A button with an arrow will generally bring up a pull down menu of options for that field.
- **Text box:** When you move to an empty text box, an insertion point appears in the far left-hand side of the box. The text you type starts at the insertion point. If the box you move to already contains text, this text is selected

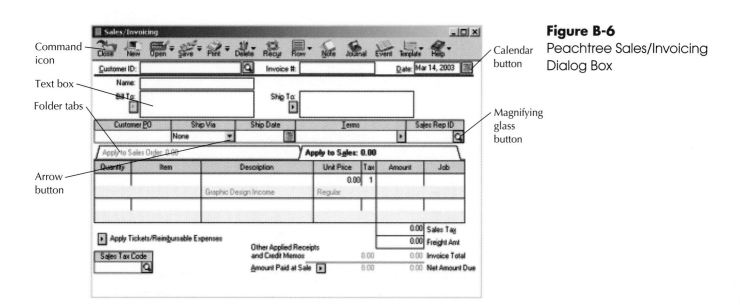

Figure B-6
Peachtree Sales/Invoicing Dialog Box

(highlighted), and any text you type replaces it. You can also delete the selected text by pressing the DELETE or BACKSPACE key.

- **Command icons:** Choose (click) on a command icon to initiate an immediate action such as carrying out or canceling a command. The Close, Print and Post buttons are common command buttons.

- **Magnifying glass button:** Click on this button to pull down a list of choices. Some fields will not show the magnifying glass until the field has been selected.

- **Calendar button:** Click on this button to bring up a calendar in order to select the date to be inserted in the field next to the button.

Other dialog boxes (see Fig. B-7) may require that choices be made, request additional information, provide warnings, or give messages indicating why a requested task cannot be accomplished.

- **Highlighted (selected) item:** To highlight and/or select an item in a displayed list, click on the item. Some may require a double-click to select. In Figure B-7, highlighting an item in the Report Area will bring up a list associated with that item in the Report List box. Highlighting an item in the Report List box will bring up a description in the Report Description box.

- **Scroll bar:** A bar that may appear at the bottom and/or right side of a window or dialog box if there is more text than can be displayed at one time within the window.

- **Scroll arrow:** A small arrow at the end of a scroll bar that you click on to move to the next item in the list. The top and left arrow scroll to the previous item; the bottom and right arrows scroll to the next item.

- **Scroll box:** A small box in a scroll bar. You can use the mouse to drag the scroll box left or right, or up or down. The scroll box indicates the relative position in the list.

Figure B-7
Peachtree Select a Report
Dialog Box

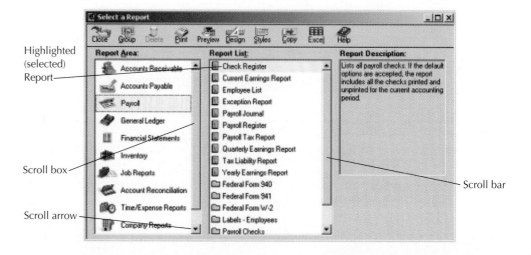

Open Company...	Ctrl+O
New Company...	Ctrl+N
Print...	Ctrl+P
Print Preview	Ctrl+W
Page Setup...	
Back Up...	Ctrl+B
Restore...	Ctrl+R
Online Backup...	
Select Import/Export...	
Data Verification...	
Payroll Tax Tables	▶
Exit	

Figure B-8
Peachtree **File** Menu

Using Menus

Commands are listed on menus, as shown in Figure B-8. Each item on the **Main Menu bar** has its own menus, which are listed by selecting the menu. When a menu is displayed, choose a command by clicking on it or by typing the **Underlined letter** to execute the command. You can also bypass the menu entirely if you know the **Keyboard equivalent** shown to the right of the command when the menu is displayed.

A **Dimmed command** indicates that a command is not currently executable; some additional action has to be taken for the command to become available. Some commands are followed by **Ellipses** (. . .) to indicate that more information is required to execute the command. The additional information can be entered into a dialog box, which will appear immediately after the command has been selected.

Although Peachtree has 10 menu options available on the **Main Menu bar,** most of your activities will involve the **Maintain, Tasks,** or **Reports** menus. The **Tasks** menu contains all of our routine, day to day activities such as invoicing customers, paying vendors, generating payroll, et al. The **Maintain** menu allows us to add, delete and edit customers, vendors, employees and default options, et al. The **Reports** menu allows us to generate the information contained in Peachtree in a variety of formats including custom designed ones.

Working in the Windows 2000 Environment

You can use a combination of mouse and keyboard techniques to navigate within the Windows 2000 environment. For example, you can click on an item to select it, and then press the ENTER key to choose it, or you can just double-click on the item. Peachtree Complete Accounting is designed for a mouse, but it also provides keyboard equivalents for almost every command. It may seem confusing at first that there are several different ways to do the same thing. You will find this flexibility useful. For example, if your hands are already on the keyboard, it may be faster to use the keyboard equivalent of a mouse command. Alternatively, if your hand is already on the mouse, it may be faster to use the mouse technique to carry out a command. When a procedure in an assignment says to select or choose an item, generally use whichever method you prefer. Alternative procedures are often provided as well. It is not necessary to memorize any particular technique, just be flexible and willing to experiment. As you gain experience with the program, you will develop personal preferences, and the various techniques will become second nature.

Opening a File in Peachtree Complete

As with any other Windows program, files in Peachtree are opened by using the **Open Company** option from the **File** menu. Peachtree will then open up an Open Company dialog box where you can tell Peachtree where to find the files you need. The files that have been supplied with this text for the sample companies should reside in the same directory as the Peachtree program files, generally "Peachw". Each company will have its own folder that can be read by the Open Company dialog box. If you do not see these files when you first open the box, you may need to change the directory or drive to one your instructor will specify.

Before starting any assignment, it is suggested that you create a backup of the files for that sample company in the event you need to restore back to the beginning of the assignment.

Backing Up a File in Peachtree Complete

Peachtree has the capability to quickly and easily back up your data to protect against accidental loss.

1. You must have already opened the files of the company you wish to back up. Let's say we wish to backup Bellwether Garden Supply. We would open that company using the **Open** feature from the **File** menu option.

2. While in the Menu Window, select **Back Up** from the **File** menu option. This will bring up the Back Up Company dialogue box as follows:

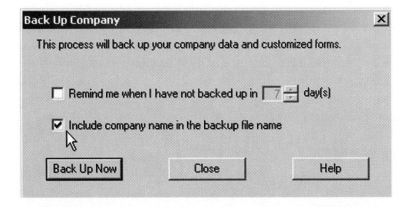

3. Click in the box next to **Include company name in the backup file name.** This will make Peachtree use the company name in the filename it selects for the backup. You could also use this dialogue box to have Peachtree provide a reminder at periodic intervals but we will leave this option alone for now. Press **Back Up Now** to continue.

4. You are now presented with a Save Back Up for Bellwether Garden Supply as: dialog box:

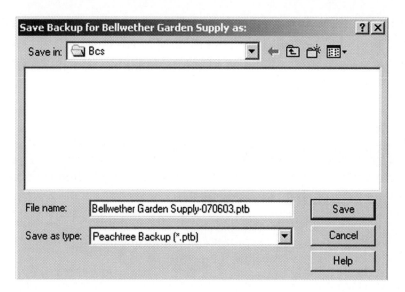

5. Click **Save.**

6. Peachtree will save your data files into one compressed .ptb file to any drive or path you specify including a floppy drive. It defaults to the location where the program files are stored and specifically to the folder where the company files are kept. It will also default to the company name followed by the date. You can change the name if desired. Use the **Save in** pull down menu to save the files to a location specified by your instructor. This could be a network drive, a student floppy disk, or even the local hard drive. Click **Save** and then **Ok** to complete the process. You now have a back up of your data. You should consider saving each and every day to protect yourself against possible loss. Peachtree will use the date as part of the backup's name so you could have a separate backup for each day. You do not have to accept the name Peachtree assigns and you can use a name with more meaning to you.

See Parts C and D of this appendix for information on using these backups.

Part B   INSTALLING PEACHTREE COMPLETE ACCOUNTING/STUDENT DATA FILES

This section of the appendix discusses several basic operations that you need to complete to install the Peachtree Complete Accounting program and the student data files disk for use in completing the computer Workshop assignments in this text.

SYSTEM REQUIREMENTS

The recommended minimum software and hardware requirements your computer system needs to run both Windows and Peachtree Complete Accounting successfully are:

- Microsoft Windows XP, 2000, 98, 95, or Windows NT 4.0 with Service Pack 5 or 6.

- A personal computer with a Pentium 233 MHz or higher processor is required but 350 MHz or better is recommended.

- A hard disk with 80–110 MB of free disk space.

- One 3.5 inch high-density floppy disk drive (if student floppy backups are desired).

- A CD-ROM drive (optional if installed on a network).
- 48 MB RAM required but 128 MB RAM is recommended.
- A 256 color SVGA or similar high-resolution monitor that is supported by Windows with a resolution of at least 800 × 600.
- Internet Explorer 5.x or higher installed.
- A printer that is supported by Windows.
- A mouse that is supported by Windows.

CD-ROM CONTENTS

The Peachtree Complete Accounting installation and program files (in condensed form) and the Student Data Files for use in completing the Computer Workshops are on the CD-ROM that accompanies this text.

Installation Procedures

To install Peachtree Complete Accounting on your hard disk, follow these instructions:

1. Start Windows.
2. Make sure that no other programs are running on your system.
3. Insert the CD-ROM in your CD-ROM drive.
4. Click on the Start button; then click on Run.
5. Type d:setup and press the ENTER key. For d, substitute the letter of your CD-ROM drive.
6. Select the items you wish to install and install them.
7. Put your CD-ROM away for safekeeping.

Installing Peachtree Complete Accounting on a Network

Peachtree Complete Accounting can be used in a network environment as long as each student uses a separate Student Data Files source to store his or her data files. Students should consult with their instructor and/or network administrator for specific procedures regarding program installation and any special printing procedures required for proper network operation.

Student Data File Integrity

Peachtree will run most efficiently if the student data files are installed on a hard drive. This can occur on the local hard drive or in a student folder on a network drive. Since it is possible that student files may be tampered with between class sessions, it is recommended that students back up and restore their files with a floppy disk each class day. Each student can also have a separate, password protected storage area on the network for the company files. Peachtree's back up and restore functions are quick and easy. The specific procedures will be discussed in Part A and E of this appendix.

Installation Default Settings

In the 2003 version of Peachtree Complete Accounting, you may encounter some differences in your screens to the screen captures contained in this book. This is due in part to the fact that Peachtree will install to one set of settings on a machine that has contained a previous version of Peachtree and to a second set of setting on a machine to which you are installing Peachtree for the first time. In order to ensure that your screens will be the same as those in this book, make or confirm the following selections from the Options menu item:

Open any company within Peachtree Complete Accounting 2003. Select Global from the Options menu.

1. Select the Accounting tab.

2. In the section entitled Hide General Ledger Accounts, remove any checkmarks from the three boxes in that section by left clicking on the checkmark.

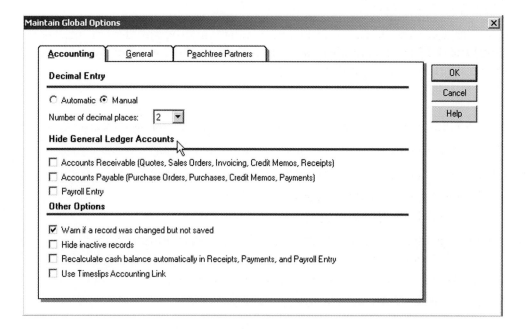

3. Click on the General tab of this same screen.

4. In the Color Scheme section, click on the radio button next to Classic.

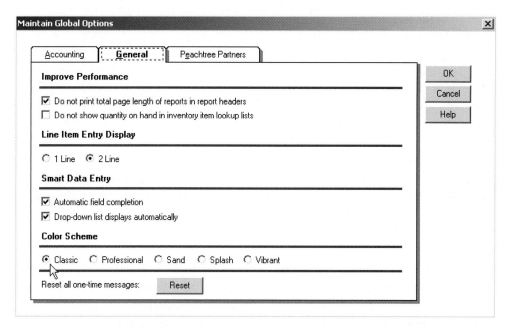

5. Click OK and exit Peachtree to make the changes permanent.

You can see the differences in the following illustrations that show both configurations.

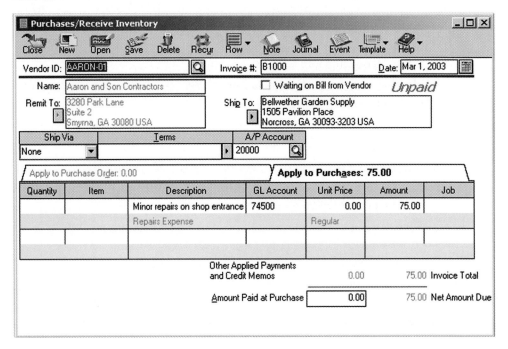

Sand with GL accounts hidden.

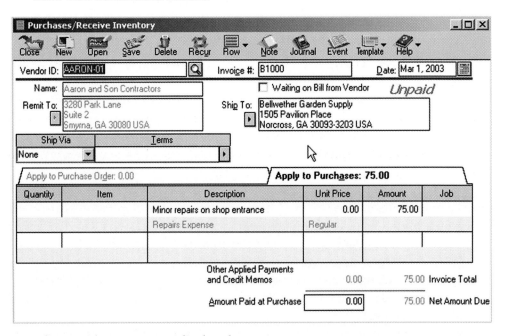

Classic with GL accounts displayed.

Part C   CORRECTING TRANSACTIONS

Once a transaction is posted in Peachtree Complete Accounting, the journal entry will be reflected in the accounting records. You will, however, be allowed to freely edit transactions due to the way the program has been configured for you. Peachtree does have an audit feature that would not allow you to make corrections without creating an audit trail of all such changes. This feature of Peachtree Complete Accounting is designed to ensure that a good audit trail of all transactions is constantly maintained within the program. This feature is turned on and off in the **Company Information** of the **Maintain** menu option. In a real world working situation, this feature would be turned on. Unless your instructor has you turn this feature on, you will be able to correct errors quickly and easily without creating a record of those corrections.

If you should detect an error while in any of Peachtree's input screens prior to posting or printing, you can quickly and easily correct the error prior to continuing with the transaction.

Correcting Unposted Errors.

1. Using your mouse, click in the field that contains the error. This will highlight the selected text box information so that you can change it.

2. Type the correct information; then press the TAB key to enter it. You may then either TAB to other fields needing corrections or again use the mouse to click in the proper field.

3. If you have selected an incorrect account or any other type of look-up information, use the pull down menu to select the correct account or information. This will replace the incorrect account with the correct account.

4. To discard an entry and start over, click on the Delete icon. You will not be given the opportunity to verify this step so be sure you want to delete the transaction before selecting this option. This option may not be available on every input screen.

5. Review the entry for accuracy after any editing corrections.

6. Complete the transaction by posting or printing.

Should you detect an error after you have posted the transaction, it can still be quickly and easily corrected. The only additional step needed to correct a posted transaction is to find it and bring it up on your screen.

Correcting Posted Errors.

Generate an on-screen report which will contain the document needing correction. As an example, a sales invoice can be found in an Aged Receivables Report, an Invoice Register, or a Sales Journal. A General Journal entry can be found in a General Journal or a General Ledger report. While other ways to locate a document exist, this is the easiest to use.

Select the line of the report containing the item needing correction by single clicking the mouse cursor. This will place a blue box around the line and the cursor will turn into a magnifying glass with a Z in the center. Peachtree Complete 2003 comes packaged with a sample company called Bellwether Garden Supply. Looking at a General Journal report under the Reports menu, your screen will look like Figure B-9.

By double clicking on any selected line, you can bring up that particular transaction. If, for example, we double click the selection from Figure B-9, we are presented with the screen on Figure B-10.

We could now edit any field of this entry and **Save** it again. The procedures that were presented for correcting an unposted transaction can now be applied. You can experiment with this feature in the sample company if your program has Bellwether installed.

Part D   HOW TO REPEAT OR RESTART AN ASSIGNMENT

You always have the option to repeat an assignment for additional practice or start over on an assignment. You simply restore the sample company files back to their

Figure B-9
General Journal

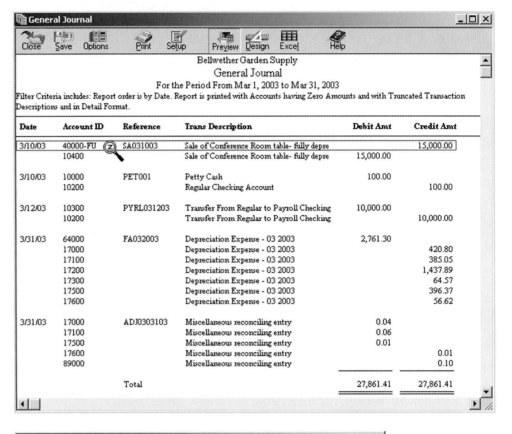

Figure B-10
General Journal Entry

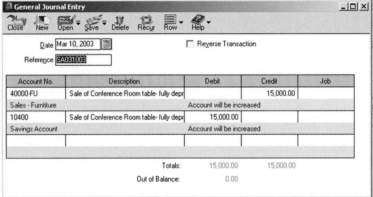

original state using the Backup created at the start of the assignment (see Part A). The procedure for restoring a file is very similar:

1. Open the company whose files you wish to restore. Let's say we wish to restore Bellwether Garden Supply. We would open that company using the **Open** feature from the **File** menu option.

2. While in the Menu Window, select **Restore** from the **File** menu option. This will bring up the Open Backup File dialogue box as shown at the top of page B-17.

3. Peachtree will default to the folder where the regular company files are kept. If you are keeping your backups on a floppy or on a drive/path other than the one Peachtree is defaulting to, you must use the **Look in** option to change the drive and select the correct path from the options given. You may have several backups made at different points in time so be sure to select the correct one. In the example above, there is only one backup so we would select Bellwether Garden Supply-070603.ptb (or the name you used in Part A). This was a backup made on July 6, 2003. After you have selected the correct filename, click on **Open**.

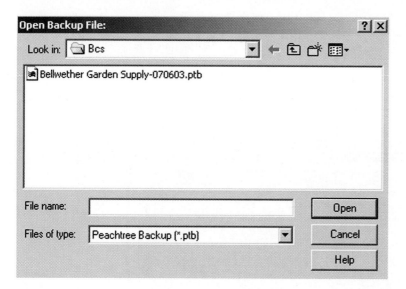

Part E	HOW AND WHEN TO USE THE BACKUP COPY OF A COMPANY'S DATA FILES

At certain times in the assignments you are asked to make a backup copy of a company's data files. There are several reasons why you might wish to access the backup copy of a company's data files. For example, you may not have printed a required report in an assignment before advancing the period to a new month or before adding additional transactions. You may have several errors and simply want to start an assignment over or to a point prior to the errors rather than correct the many mistakes.

If you backup your data using a different filename each day, you will have the option of restoring from any of these files. It would be wise to indicate in your text the point at which you created each backup so you will know what transactions have been completed at each of the backup's dates.

Part F	PRINT AND DISPLAY SETTING IN PEACHTREE COMPLETE

When you install Peachtree Accounting, the program automatically installs the printer established as the default Windows printer as the default printer for Peachtree Accounting. If you have not yet installed a default printer in Windows, you will need to do so prior to attempting to print any reports from the Peachtree Accounting program. Refer to your Windows manual for information on installing a printer.

The installation process for the Windows default printer does not ensure that the default printer and display settings within Peachtree Accounting will work to your satisfaction; consequently, you should test and if necessary adopt a different set of print settings. Changing the settings as detailed below does not result in a permanent change to the report and this process must be repeated each time you use a standard report. Custom reports can be created with permanent fonts.

If you need to change the font sizes or typefaces on your reports, you can do that from within Peachtree. Each report that you select will have an **Options** button as illustrated in Figure B-11.

Figure B-11
Options Button

Figure B-12
Fonts Tab

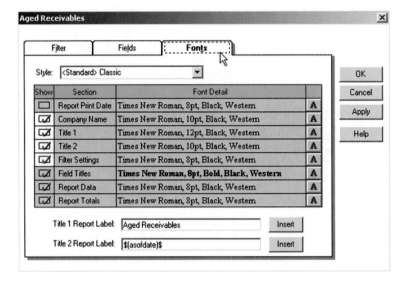

Selecting **Options** will bring up a dialog box with multiple tabs containing various parameters that can be changed for the report. One of these tabs is **Fonts** from which you can change the typeface and font for each item on the report. See Figure B-12.

Index

Photo Credits